ASHE Reader Series

ASHE Reader on Planning and Institutional Research

Marvin W. Peterson, Editor

Lisa A. Mets, Andrea Trice,
and David D. Dill, Associate Editors

Bruce Anthony Jones, Series Editor

PEARSON CUSTOM PUBLISHING

Cover photo: "Excavation Series," by Brian Stevens.

Printed in the United States of America

10 9 8 7 6 5 4 3 2 1

Please visit our website at www.pearsoncustom.com

ISBN 0–536–02368–9

BA 990099

PEARSON CUSTOM PUBLISHING
160 Gould Street/Needham Heights, MA 02494
A Pearson Education Company

CONTENTS

Acknowledgments

Preparing the initial volume of any new ASHE Reader is an intriguing and challenging opportunity. The editors were fortunate in having the assistance of several groups. An Advisory Board of 23 nationally recognized scholars and professionals from ASHE, AIR and SCUP provided invaluable advice on the content and format of this volume. A Higher Education Resource Faculty group of 24 individuals who were offering courses on institutional research and planning shared their syllabi, references lists and ideas for resource materials which added immeasurably to the contents of this volume. Both of these groups, supplemented by members of the AIR and SCUP Publications Committees, assisted in rating an extensive list of potential references for inclusion. We are grateful for their support, insight and judgment in shaping both the form and content of the volume.

We also acknowledge the wisdom of the ASHE Reader Committee in recognizing the expanding interest in this area of higher education instruction, their willingness to approve this initiative, and their support of the editors. Our thanks go to Jeffrey Rohrlick, graduate student at the University of Michigan Center for the Study of Higher and Postsecondary Education, for providing assistance in the early stages of this Reader. We are most indebted to Margaret Plawchan who assisted in the preparation of this Reader.

THE EDITORS

Marvin W. Peterson is Professor of Higher Education at the University of Michigan Center for the Study of Higher and Postsecondary Education and Research Program Director of the National Center for Postsecondary Improvement. He is a past president of ASHE, AIR and SCUP and former editor of New Directions for Institutional Research.

Lisa A. Mets, formerly Associate Director of the Center for Research on Learning and Teaching at the University of Michigan, is Executive Assistant to the President at Eckerd College. She is a former member of the SCUP Publications Committee and editor of the SCUP newsletter.

Andrea Trice is a Research Associate at Northwestern University.

David D. Dill is Professor of Public Policy at the University of North Carolina—Chapel Hill. He is a past president of SCUP and former editor of *Planning for Higher Education*.

Advisory Board Members

Higher Education Faculty Resource Group

The following were identified through ASHE, AIR, and SCUP sources as individuals teaching courses in institutional research and/or planning. They each provided syllabi, suggested readings, and also served as raters of potential articles.

John Andes
Professor
Educational Leadership Studies
West Virginia University
Course Title: Institutional Research and
    Planning

Lesley Andres
Assistant Professor
Department of Educational Studies
University of British Columbia
Course Title: Institutional Research and
    Planning

Robert Barak
Deputy Executive Director
Iowa Board of Regents
Course Title: Higher Education Program
    Planning and Evaluation

William Brazziel
Director of Higher Education Programs
University of Connecticut
Course Title: Area and Regional Planning in
    Higher Education

John Chase
Director of Budget and Planning
The University of British Columbia
Course Title: Research and Planning

Antonia D'Onofrio
Associate Professor
Widener University
Course Title: Planning and Evaluation

Robert Fenske
Professor of Higher Education
Division of Educational Leadership and Policy
    Studies
Arizona State University
Course Title: Institutional Research/Strategic
    Planning in Higher Education

E. Raymond Hackett
Associate Professor and Director
Higher Education Program
Auburn University
Course Titles:Educational Forecasting
Educational Planning

Oliver Hensley
Professor
Higher Education Program
Texas Tech University
Course Title: Institutional Planning in Higher
    Education

Martha Hesse
Senior Presidential Advisor and
Assistant Provost
Michigan State University
Course Title: Planning, Evaluation, and
    Decision Making in Post-Secondary
    Education

Edward Hines
Department of Educational Administration
Illinois State University
Course Title: Educational Administration and
    Foundations

James Honan
Lecturer on Education
Harvard University
Course Title: Planning and Strategy
    Development in Colleges and Universities

Rick Kroc
Director of Student Research
University of Arizona

William Lasher
Associate Professor
Department of Educational Administration
The University of Texas at Austin
Course Title: Institutional Research and
    Planning

G. Gregory Lozier
Managing Associate
Coopers & Lybrand LLP
Course Title: Planning and Institutional
    Research

Larry Mayes
Coordinator of Institutional Research
University of Kentucky Community College
    System
Course Title: Research in Higher Education

Frank Schmidtlein
Associate Professor of Higher Education
University of Maryland College Park
Course Title: Higher Education Planning

Daryl Smith
Professor, Education and Psychology
Center for Educational Studies
The Claremont Graduate School
Course Title: Institutional Planning in
    Educational Settings

Tom Sork
Associate Professor of Educational Studies
University of British Columbia
Course Title: Strategic Planning in Higher
    Education

Elizabeth Stanley
Director, Institutional Research
Iowa State University
Course Title: Institutional Research in Higher
    Education

Ward Sybouts
Professor
Department of Educational Administration
University of Nebraska, Lincoln
Course Title: Systems Planning

David Tan
Associate Professor of Higher Education
Department of Educational Leadership and
    Policy Studies
University of Oklahoma
Course Title: Institutional Research in Higher
    Education

Alton Taylor
Professor
University of Virginia
Course Title: Management Planning in Higher
    Education

Patrick Terenzini
Professor and Senior Scientist
Center for the Study of Higher Education
Pennsylvania State University
Course Title: Planning and Institutional
    Research

Purpose and Development of the Reader

This volume of the ASHE Reader is intended for both an academic and a professional audience. Its primary audience is higher education faculty and students studying institutional research and planning. However, it is also useful for training and development workshops and seminars offered by professional associations such as AIR and SCUP and for professional development activities sponsored by campus-based institutional research and planning offices. Both of these areas regularly attract large members of new staff and emphasize staff development.

Creating this initial ASHE Reader on Planning and Institutional Research involved an extended gestation with a sizable number of scholars and practitioners in the institutional research and planning communities. In the initial stage, after obtaining the ASHE Reader Committee's approval of our prospectus, the following steps were taken. An Advisory Board was appointed and responded to a series of questions on the structure, format and content areas for the Reader. Simultaneously, a survey of all Higher Education Program chairs provided by ASHE was needed to identify faculty currently teaching institutional research and/or planning. All agreed to serve on our Higher Education Resource Faculty Group. They shared their syllabi with us and provided suggestions regarding the format and content of the Reader.

In the second stage, we took several steps to identify potential articles for inclusion in the Reader and books to include in a list of recommended reference texts. We conducted a thorough literature search and review of published literature sources over the past 10 years; this yielded a list of many potential publications. We reviewed syllabi received from the Resource Faculty Group to identify the readings they included in their courses. We also invited a larger group of over 100 individuals to suggest articles, book chapters, and other resources that might be included in the Reader. This group consisted of the Reader's Advisory Board and Faculty Resource Group members supplemented by AIR Publications Committee members, SCUP Publications Advisory Board members, and consulting editors of *Research in Higher Education*, *Planning in Higher Education*, and the *New Directions for Institutional Research* series.

Once a potential list of articles was compiled, it was sent in survey form to our Advisory Board Members and the Higher Education Faculty Resource Group. They rated each item for its relevance to the Reader and its overall quality. Their responses were tallied and used as a guide for making the final selections for the Reader. Due to space limitations, many scholarly and professional works of high quality and importance could not be included.

In selecting articles, we used the following guidelines. Selections:

a) were drawn primarily from the higher education literature. The syllabi provided by the Resource Faculty identified numerous non-higher education references, but there were few that were commonly used.

b) did not include articles on very specific institutional research techniques and methods or ones focused on highly specific planning topics, issues or analytic approaches. These were far too numerous.

c) favored research based, conceptual, or synthesis articles and avoided case studies describing or advocating particular techniques and methods or "how-to" articles.

d) attempted to provide coverage which reflects the broad current models and approaches to planning and nature and role of institutional research.

Finally, we developed the extensive Part V, Other Resources. Part V-A includes "Related Higher Education Reference Books." Those were identified from the syllabi and suggestions made by the Higher Education Resource Faculty. Part V-B includes related publications, specifically *New Directions for Institutional Research*, the *AIR Professional File* series, and *Planning for Higher Education*. The descriptions of relevant Data Base Resources (Part V-C), Periodic Data Reports (Part V-D) and Related Professional Associations (Part V-E) were prepared by the editors using the most recent information provided by the appropriate publication or source organization. A special section on "Using the Internet" was prepared by John Milam (Part V-F).

Although the development of this volume has been an intensive effort and involved an extensive array of faculty and professionals, it represents an initial effort. Planning and institutional research are rapidly changing processes on our campuses, very dynamic professional fields, and the subject of an ever expanding amount of research and literature. Readers are invited to share with the editors their reactions, insights and suggestions for improving future editions of this initial volume.

Introduction and Overview

To paraphrase the late Aaron Wildavsky, a noted political scientist from the University of California at Berkeley, "If planning (and institutional research) is everything, perhaps it is (they are) nothing." Those involved in planning and institutional research may often identify with this sentiment as they deal with an ever expanding array of institutional units, functions, processes, dynamics, and issues. Both areas have been the subject of varied definitions and descriptions. It is beyond the scope of this brief overview to this Reader to expound on the vast purview of institutional research and of planning or their myriad definitions. Suffice it to say that higher education scholars, administrators, and professional practitioners of this arena now all understand the central nature of these two crucial, interrelated management processes or functions. They understand that both are critical processes that permeate or cut across an institution's structures and functions, contribute to its governance and decision making processes, and utilize its information technology.

Institutional research is understood to be a process of gathering, analyzing and interpreting information which leads to "improved understanding, planning and operation of institutions of higher education" (AIR Statement, 1998). Planning is understood to be a process or set of activities related to governance and management that "provide future oriented guidance for an institution attempting to chart a course between its complex and changing external environment and its internal capacities." Clearly, institutional research informs managerial and operational functions as well as planning decisions and activities. However, planning depends on sound information and analysis about the managerial and operational performance of an institution and its units as well. Both depend on internal data about an institution and its functioning and about key elements in the institution's external environment. Such was not always the case. A brief historical picture of the evolution of these two processes and their growing interrelationship and a brief summary of the current status and some speculation about future challenges may provide a helpful context for the users of this Reader.

An Evolutionary Perspective

While institutional research and planning processes today are related activities that permeate an institution and are intertwined, that was not always the case. As formally recognized institutional processes, both are post-World War II phenomena. Each developed separately and only recently have become interrelated; and this has lead to their integration or coordination. Prior to World War II, neither planning nor institutional research offices nor formalized activities in either were prevalent.

No doubt, planning had always existed but primarily as an institutional mission, plan or leader's vision (Peterson, 1986). Harvard had a mission and strategy to train "learned clergy and lettered people" to be schoolmasters and religious and political leaders and designed a residential setting with a lay board to accomplish that mission. Thomas Jefferson, on a more grandiose scale, designed an educational plan for the entire state of Virginia and threw in the academic mission and structure, the campus plan and even designed buildings for the University of Virginia. Others like

Charles Eliot at Harvard and William Rainey Harper at the University of Chicago guided the evolution of the modern, complex graduate and research university during their presidencies. But vision, missions, and plans were not embodied in on-going planning processes or offices.

Similarly, pre-World War II studies of institutional problems and issues were well documented by Cowley (1959) in his lecture on "Two-and-a-Half Centuries of Institutional Research." But these too were mostly one-time, ad hoc or special purpose studies and not the work of an on-going institutional office or management process. The development of both institutional research and planning as formally organized offices or functions in colleges and universities begins in the 1950's.

Three eras reflect the development of institutional research and planning—initially as separate but later as coordinated or integrated institutional processes. They reflect a response to major challenges institutions were facing in each era. They are linked in a common resource, the institution's information infrastructure, which is also central to understanding their development and interrelationship. These, developments were reflected in their respective professional associations (See Table 1).

Table 1 Evolution of Planning and Institutional Research

Era of Planning and Institutional Research	Emerging Patterns: 1950–1970	Expansion and Formalization: 1970–1985	Proliferation, and Coordination: 1985–Present	A Postsecondary Knowledge Industry: 2000 and Beyond
Institutional Pressures	Growth and Expansion	Management, Access and Accountability	Retrenchment, Academic Quality and Effectiveness	Institutional Redesign
Primary Developments	Descriptive and Developmental Efforts	Analytic and Comparative Approaches	Evaluation; Qualitative Focus and Policy Analysis	Postsecondary Knowledge Industry Analysis
Institutional Research Planning	Plans: Campus, Facility, Financial and Academic	Forecasting and Long Range Planning Process	Strategic Planning	Contextual Planning
Information Infrastructure	Basic Internal Data and Record Keeping	MIS Design, Forecasting and Simulation Models	Decision Support Systems, Distributed	Computing Data Warehouses, Work Stations,and the Internet

Emergent Patterns: 1950–1970

Institutional Challenges

The 1950's and 1960's witnessed extraordinary growth in U.S. higher education (See Table 1). This growth occurred primarily in the public sector as both the number and size of institutions increased. During this period, institution leaders were challenged to provide policy makers with a sense of direction for their institutions; to justify their need for new campuses, facilities and funds; and to account for the financial resources they were absorbing to assure continued confidence and support. The climate and need for planning and for data collection and analysis was ripe.

Institutional Research

Executive officers, struggling with expanding campuses, enrollment growth and curricular offerings, expressed concern for data. Initiatives sponsored by the American Council on Education and regional coordinating boards like WICHE, SREB and NEBHE all offered workshops and seminars to assist institutions in establishing institutional studies and research offices. Early institutional research offices usually were established as small offices headed by a former faculty member and reporting to the President or Chief Executive Officer. The focus was on rather basic descriptive reports and analyses, such as: institutional self studies, student and enrollment analyses, space inventories and needs, and budget and financial analysis. Data base building efforts were minimal and limited to improving internal record keeping and data collection procedures.

Planning

During this same time span similar forces and concerns led to the formation of planning offices with formal planning responsibilities. Not surprisingly the initial offices were focused on campus and facilities planning and were usually headed by individuals with architectural or campus planning expertise. The offices were added to the campus administrative structure for business affairs. By the mid- to late 1960's concerns about the effects of campus size, the growth and proliferation of new disciplines and specializations, and some early studies of students that were critical of campus life led to an emerging interest in academic planning. Campus plans, once the realm of architects and facilities planners, began to give way to new academic plans for innovative institutions with differing academic structures and patterns. Self studies, prompted by internal concerns and the growing interest in accreditation, also led to plans with an academic and educational focus. Similarly, early financial studies and foundation-sponsored initiatives encouraged institutions—particularly private ones—to take an interest in financial plans or forecasts. But planning during this era was clearly separate from institutional research and focused on a campus, facility, academic master, or financial plan. It did not include the establishment of a continuous process of planning. Planning offices created "plans."

Information

Neither planning nor institutional researchers in this era were actively focused on the information infrastructure of their institutions. However, both had an active interest in accurate internal records of enrollments, faculty, facilities, and finances, and they encouraged their improvement.

Professional

Not surprisingly, professional associations representing the interests of these two new administrative groups were established at this time. The Society for College and University Planning (SCUP) was founded in 1966. While initially dominated by campus and facilities planners, its membership was open and would later expand to include a broader array of planners. A bit earlier an institutional research forum, convened by invitation only in 1961, was opened to broader participation due to demand the following year. The Association for Institutional Research (AIR), an outgrowth of these annual forums, was founded in 1965. By the end of the 1960's, both associations had over 500 members, sponsored an annual conference and began sponsoring newsletters and embryonic publications. Both included extensive debates about the nature and role of their function in the institution along with concerns for professional development of their members. A national study, *The Managerial Revolution* (Rourke & Brooks, 1966), summarized the rapid expansion of this early phase of institutional research as a critical management function on college and university campuses. Although a similar study does not exist for planning, it would probably reflect the same.

Expansion and Formalization: 1970–1985

Institutional Challenges

A wave of campus activism in the late 1960's and early 1970's was spurred by the civil rights movement, the Vietnam War and negative student reaction to their increasingly large, impersonal institution (See Table 1). This would be followed in the mid 1970's by an economic recession and the pressure to do "more with less" as enrollment demand slowed and financial resources became more constrained. The pressures on institutions were for more effective management (both controlling campus disruption and campus costs), for better marketing and access, and for greater access and accountability from public officials. Pressures for both institutional research and for planning would continue to grow, and both areas would expand and become more formalized.

Institutional Research

The impact on institutional research reflects both the disruption and the economic issues. In an attempt to assuage public officials' concern about disruptions and to address the growing internal concerns about campus and educational life, analyzing quality became a focus for institutional research. Formal, centralized offices with several professionals (at least in larger institutions) became commonplace and took on an array of analytic activities. Interestingly, the American Council on Education's emphasis on reputational studies (Roose and Anderson, 1970) expanded the quality focus and prompted an interest in comparative research. While institutional researchers were giving more emphasis to internal studies of campus climate, student attitudes and behavior, and program quality, the national surveys provided them with a basis for more externally-oriented comparative studies across institutions and for examining correlates of quality in addition to just focusing on their own campus. As resources tightened, the external press for greater accountability brought increased attention to program review, financial cost studies using more complex quantitative indices of efficiency, and concerns about education and campus life. Constrained enrollment growth and civil rights activity would also increase attention on both marketing studies and the improvement of access. These attempts to examine both quality and efficiency, to use inter-institutional comparative data, and to examine external markets and conditions engaged institutional researchers more deeply in issues of building institutional data bases.

Planning

Across campus planners were also responding to the new institutional challenges. Both academic and resource planning activities began to expand on many campuses albeit in a rather fragmented way. The issues of unplanned growth of campuses in the sixties, combined with the disruptions, were beginning to raise serious educational and academic planning issues. The emphasis on academic and campus quality and the economic pressures to do more with less were heightened by the realization that the rise in enrollments was also beginning to abate. Issues of enrollment forecasting, faculty supply and demand, and program need/demand led to a substantial increase in academically-oriented planning activity and began to overlap with institutional research interests.

Resource planning—both human and fiscal—also expanded. The economic constraints led to numerous experiments attempting to link budgets with institutional plans (zero based, program, and formula budgets linked to planning). Forecasting and simulation models designed to project enrollments and analyze costs attracted the interests of planners. Planners now rejected static plans and began to emphasize forecasting and the use of simulation models. They also began establishing long range planning processes to engage participants throughout the institution and attempted to link current institutional performance and future projections in a process that continuously revised plans. Barriers between academic, resource (especially financial) and campus/facility planning began to fall. Centralized planning offices that combined various areas of planning and managed or guided the long range planning process became a familiar fixture. More importantly, institutional researchers and planning activities were beginning to overlap. They were beginning to share common needs for data and measures to use for analysis, simulation models, and forecasting.

Information

During the 1970's, the National Center for Higher Education Management Systems (NCHEMS), formed with federal funding, was spearheading national efforts to clarify and refine data element definitions, to gain some agreement on various indices of performance, to create analytic models to measure quality and productivity (both quantitatively), and to communicate more clearly to external constituents (Lawrence & Service, 1977). They also were concerned with forecasting models to predict enrollment and faculty and financial supply and demand. Institutional researchers and planners participated actively in these national efforts. On campus, with the advent of mainframe computers, they began to become very involved with the development of management data bases and information systems.

Professional

Despite the increasing commonality of interest in these new management issues, the development of data bases and indicators, and the various analytic and forecasting models, the two professional associations continued to grow and develop as separate organizations. AIR began to aggressively build a publications program, establishing its *New Directions for Institutional Research* monograph series in 1974 and *Professional File* series in 1978. AIR's focus would be primarily on improving the methods and techniques of institutional research and the research capabilities of its members. SCUP meanwhile concentrated on expanding its focus beyond campus and facility planning to include the emerging interests in academic planning, resource planning, and the development of comprehensive or integrative planning. They too established a journal, *Planning for Higher Education*. Both began to add professional development workshops and seminars to the repertoire of services to their members. SCUP's focus would be more on broad institutional problems and issues and how to bring planning to bear on them. AIR would focus more on improving the methods and techniques of institutional research and to expand analytic activity to new areas of institutional activity. These differences in emphasis continue to the current time.

Proliferation and Coordination: 1985-Present

Institutional Challenges

Two new realities confronted higher education institutions in the late 1980's and early 1990's, and they shaped both institutional research and planning (See Table 1). First, by the early 1980's it became apparent that, even as the economic recession of the 1970's receded, longer-term constraints were emerging. Demographics and increased college attendance rates suggested long-term enrollment constraints. Competition for students was increasing in a postsecondary market that now clearly included proprietary institutions. Other demands for public funds were increasing and public priorities for spending on higher education were shifting as policy makers' demands for financial accountability and responsibility continued to grow. Second, in the mid 1980's the national reports on education and on higher education (National Commission on Excellence In Education, 1983; Study Group on Excellence in Higher Education, 1984) brought the issue of educational quality to a new level of public consciousness. In higher education, this was reflected in new demands for educational quality and effectiveness and for assessments of students, faculty and programs. Institutions were now faced with improving their effectiveness—demonstrating improved educational quality—while facing the 1980's prospect of "Reduction, Reallocation and Retrenchment" (Mortimer, 1979). Once again planning and institutional research are affected.

Planning

During the decade of the 1980's and extending into the 90's, planning reflected two major changes. Since many of the institutional constraints were external and changing and reflected demands for quality in a highly competitive environment, the primary emphasis shifted from designing long range planning processes and continuously updating and modifying institutional plans to strategic planning (Keller, 1983). The focus of strategic planning is on understanding an institution's environment, its competition, and its strengths and weaknesses. The intent is to establish one's market niche to refine the institution's primary mission, define its market, and develop a strategy or set of strategies that give the institution a comparative advantage to succeed in that market. The nature and popularity of strategic planning has greatly expanded and proliferated planning-related activity on most campuses. However, it has also fragmented it. Formerly long range or comprehensive planning tended to be viewed as a single institutional process or activity. However, strategic planning has recognized that institutions of higher education are often collections of academic units functioning in quite different markets that are loosely coupled. As such strategic planning is often dispersed or decentralized to different units or functions within an institution. Further, strategic planning often recognizes the need for sub-strategies under the central mission. But academic, educational, recruitment and enrollment, faculty human resource, financial, facilities, information technology, development or issue focused sub-strategies are often guided by different administrators or require differing expertise. This added to the pattern of fragmentation.

The inclusion of a focus on educational quality or effectiveness in planning requires broad participation. So the proliferation of planning activity is often accompanied by more fragmented activity as well. The response of professionals in the planning community has been to focus on planning as an institutional process or function not as a single office or administrative unit. Rather planning is increasingly viewed as an array of planning activities to be coordinated and linked where necessary. Planning provides guidance on how to plan effectively and allows units to pursue their own plans when appropriate. In effect, planners seek to balance proliferation with coordination.

Institutional Research

The quality demands of this era and adoption of a strategic planning approach has had a similar effect on institutional research. The new focus on educational quality has increased demand for student, faculty, program, curricular and instructional assessment and evaluation, increasing the array of institutional data collected and analyzed. It has also shifted the focus to more qualitative modes of assessment and evaluation and to studying soft phenomena like culture as well as concrete elements. While some of these activities are run out of traditional institutional research offices, they are also found in separate student assessment, program review, or evaluation offices; and this increases its fragmentation.

The advent of strategic planning also has increased the number and type of analytic studies on most campuses. It has fostered increased attention to screening or environmental assessment, internal review, evaluation of academic and administrative functions, and comparative analysis of competing institutions. It has also increased institutional researchers' awareness of the need for studies assessing strategic alternatives and policy analysis. In a sense, it has proliferated the demand for institutional research activities at the same time that it has made institutional research and planning more compatible. By and large institutional researchers have recognized the proliferation in I.R. studies and the varying places where they are done. Now they often see their role as keeping track of the myriad studies and reports completed across campus and coordinating them to assure access to them and to limit duplication.

Information

The linkage between planning and institutional research activity also was fostered during the 1980's by the changing nature of campus information technology. For instance, the focus on strategic planning increased the need for access to external data bases by both planning and institutional research. The availability of management information systems, developed in the 1970's and early 1980's, made this more feasible. Further the information technology focus shifted from designing data bases and management information systems to decision support systems designed to provide direct, easily accessible, relevant information related to planners' and decision makers' needs. The advent of microcomputers and flexible software and distributed networks linked to extensive data bases has made it easier for individual administrators outside of formal institutional research and planning offices to conduct institutional studies and/or to conduct planning related analytic studies.

Professional

The professional arena has reflected these developments as well. After a brief leveling of membership in both AIR and SCUP in the early to mid 1980's when institutional administrative staff and travel budgets were limited, each has continued their membership rise to over 4,000 in each. Their emphasis on the development of active regional organizations reflects the growth of each and concern for involving the large number of new members. Their expansion of specially tailored workshops and publications reflects the new topics and trends. More importantly, both now recognize institutional research and planning as institutional processes in which many individuals and offices in institutions may be engaged. The focus is on understanding the breadth of those activities, how to improve them, and to address ways to monitor, coordinate and guide them in the best interests of the institution and of the units represented by those activities.

Balancing Fragmentation and Integration: The Current Context

This evolutionary picture provides some useful insights into the current state of development of institutional research and planning. *First*, the process of proliferation and fragmentation and the struggle for coordination and integration is ongoing. Both institutional research and planning are, and continue to be, expanding areas of activity engaged in by more units and individuals. As such there is a tendency toward proliferation and fragmentation in each and a need to integrate the various activities of each. Clearly, both planning and institutional research have evolved in structure and function from limited and concentrated activities which were usually directed by an individual (emergent era), to a broader array of activities housed in a larger somewhat centralized office which directs most of the activity (formalized era), to a well understood institutional process which encompasses an extensive array of activities carried out in many different offices and which need to be coordinated and guided at present. *Second*, the nature of each has been shaped in large part by the pressures or challenges facing higher educational institutions at various times. They are institutional processes or functions which have aided the institution in adapting to new pressures and challenges and have themselves been changed. *Third*, while initially both institutional research and planning focused on managerial issues and were rationally and quantitatively focused, they have both come to have an educational and academic focus as well and to include both quantitative and qualitative approaches to analysis in institutional studies and to use interpretive or judgmental as well as rational approaches to planning decisions. Similarly both have shifted from a primarily internal institutional focus to one which combines internal and external foci, data and issues. *Fourth*, while the approaches to planning and the methods and techniques of institutional research are not immutable, neither do new ones supersede older ones. Plans and forecasting are still elements in a strategic planning process. Descriptive profiles, analytic studies and evaluation research still are useful in institutional studies. *Fifth*, while planning and institutional research are differentiated and have developed separately, they also are increasingly integrated. They share a common interest in responding to new institutional challenges and to improving institutional performance. Increasingly, planning raises new issues or topics for analysis and institutional research develops new methods and techniques to inform the former. Or, alternately, institutional research studies highlight problems and issues that need to be addressed in institutional planning. And *finally*, they both have a mutual interest in developing and using the institution's information infrastructure. These patterns of integration are now seen in many institutions where institutional research and planning are now either merged activities in a single office, have separate offices under a common executive office, or have a formal relationship and coordinate their activities.

2000 and Beyond: New Challenges and New Roles

Speculating about the future of institutions of higher education is highly risk prone and uncertain at best. However, few would disagree that the environment of higher education is changing rapidly and that our institutions are being challenged to respond. Both planning and institutional research, as noted, are institutional processes or functions that are key players in how institution's respond to new challenges from that changing environment (See Table 1). As such, it is the editors' assumption that students, as prospective professionals in this arena, need to consider the emerging challenges faced by their institutions, how it affects planning and institutional research and, in turn, their own preparation and career plans. The significance of this suggestion is reflected in the diverse forecasts of the future ranging from Peter Drucker's (1992) speculation about the demise of the research university in the next twenty years to James Duderstadt's (1998) very different two visions of a "massive restructuring of the higher education industry" or a "culture of learning." Therefore, it is the editors' intent to stimulate those using this Reader to spend some part of their own learning effort in speculating on the future of their institutions, this evolving professional arena, and their own future careers and learning needs.

A Societal and Industry Perspective

It is not easy to spot an emerging environmental trend, consider its implications for one's institution, develop a way to analyze it, and design a response strategy. But the intent of several selections in this Reader is to examine more broadly what may be happening in our societal context that may portend changes to our postsecondary industry as we enter the 21st Century and what that implies for our institutions and their planning and institutional research processes. The industry perspective is an uncomfortable one for many in higher education who reject it as inappropriate metaphor. But by industry, we refer to a set of organizations (in this case postsecondary institutions) who produce similar products or services, use similar resources, and compete for both (Porter, 1980). The argument is simple. Current societal changes are reshaping our industry in extensive ways that could drastically challenge or alter our institutions.

Changing Conditions in Postsecondary Education

While three readings in Part I address the changing societal conditions and their impact on our postsecondary industry or institutions, Duderstadt's (1998) article on "The 21st Century University: A Table of Two Futures" offers the broadest perspective. He examines driving forces at the intersection of financial imperatives for our postsecondary institutions, changing societal needs, and technological changes. Clearly, he sees the latter as the strongest and most pervasive. This broad analysis leads to speculation on his two scenarios. The first is a massive restructuring in the higher education industry marked by unbundling of our educational delivery and research functions, an emerging commodity market for educational services, and a propensity towards mergers and acquisitions including the prospect for hostile take over. The second and perhaps less threatening is a scenario of a learning culture. This envisions a postsecondary world that is learner centered and affordable, emphasizes lifelong learning, adopts interactive and collaborative educational processes, and accommodates a diversity of learners, learning styles and delivery systems. He concludes with a set of questions that need to be addressed and an action agenda for institutional leaders.

The Peterson and Dill (1997) chapter on "Understanding the Competitive Environment of the Postsecondary Knowledge Industry" provides a more systematic and focused analysis of the interaction of societal challenges to the postsecondary industry using an analytic model that focuses on six forces affecting the nature of an industry. The societal challenges include pressures on the postsecondary industry for increased diversity, expanded use of technology, improvements in academic quality, greater contribution to economic productivity of society, demands for postsecondary relearning or continued learning, and globalization of postsecondary learning systems and institutions. The impact of these challenges on the postsecondary industry are examined in terms of the effects on its core technology, the entry of new provider organizations including non-educational ones, the expanding markets for and power of customers or learners, the increasing demands and changing role of suppliers of resources, and the threat of substitute services to delivery learning. They postulate the emergence of a postsecondary knowledge industry no longer limited to postsecondary institutions. This new industry, they suggest, raises a set of institutional planning questions that consider: redefinition of the emerging industry and an institution's role in it, the redirection of an institution's mission and pattern of external relationships, the reorganization and restructuring of academic and management functions, and an effort to recreate the nature of academic work and an academic culture—a challenge for institutional redesign.

The third reading on the changing conditions, Gumport and Sporn's (1999) "Institutional Adaptation: Demands for Management Reform and University Administration," is the most theoretical and focuses more directly on the societal and institutional interface rather than on the industry. They examine societal changes in the economy, political arena and technology and the institutional environment which faces issues of costs, effectiveness and access. These societal changes are placed in the context of seven theories of environment-organization interaction: open systems, contingency, population ecology, institutional isomorphism, strategic choice, resource dependence, and network organizations. Those theories suggest patterns or strategies of institutional response or adaptation to the changing environment. The authors then argue that the interaction of these environmental forces and institutional demands or constraints form a management imperative to develop a response strategy which expands the role of administration and requires greater attention to establishing resource relationships, sustaining institutional legitimacy, and changing the nature of administrative authority and governance patterns.

Impacts on Planning and Institutional Research

While these three readings address the future from slightly different levels and perspectives of analysis and suggest overlapping but different environmental changes and institutional challenges, all raise important questions for institutional leaders and critical challenges for planners and institutional researchers. The literature on the changing role of planning and on institutional research is less well developed although discussions of this topic are pervasive at their professional meetings. Two readings in this Reader specifically address this arena.

Planning

Peterson's (1997) chapter on "Using Contextual Planning to Transform Institutions" expands on the Peterson and Dill discussion of the institutional challenges of the emerging postsecondary knowledge industry and develops a new notion of planning that is broader than strategic planning. Whereas strategic planning includes an external focus, it usually examines changes impacting institutions within a well-defined postsecondary industry and strives to identify viable market niches that reflect institutional strengths and comparative advantage. However, contextual planning begins with the assumption of an industry in flux and raises the potential of institutional redesign which may require macro-organizational or transformational change. In addition to addressing redesign issues of redefining the industry and institutional role in it, the redirection of mission and external relationships, the reorganization of academic and management structures, and the reform or recreation of academic work and culture, it adopts a differing set of planning activities than those included in strategic planning. Contrasting the two, contextual planning includes emphasis on insight and using intuitive judgment as much as rational environmental analysis; focusing on institutional initiatives or broad directions rather than specific mission modifications or revised purposes; investing in infrastructure to support change rather than designing specific strategies and programs; providing incentives for change rather than goals, objectives and formal rewards; creating the possibility for wide involvement in the institutional direction and initiatives; using information internally to communicate the direction of change, the opportunities for involvement, and examples of interesting and successful initiatives, and externally to publicize the institution's efforts and changing nature; and building integrative managerial, evaluative and coordinating patterns as the institution changes rather than attempting to prescribe them carefully in advance. Such an approach suggests a more entrepreneurial style but one which fosters change in institutional role and mission, structural patterns, cultural norms, and work roles.

Institutional Research

Institutional researchers have long been prone to reexamine their professional role and function. Early debates over its role as "management servant" (Brumbaugh, 1960) vs. "autonomous institutional critic" (Dressel, 1971) have given way progressively to "organizational intelligence" office (Tetlow, 1979), "change agent and action researchers" (Lindquist, 1980), "telematics technologist" (Sheehan, 1982), "political partisan" (Firnberg and Lasher, 1983), "decision intermediary" (Peterson, 1985), and "policy analyst" (Saunders, 1992). However, the management decision support role has become predominant (Saupe, 1990). However, the emergence of a postsecondary knowledge industry and the new challenge of institutional redesign presents a new challenge to institutional research.

An article by Peterson (1999), "The Role of Institutional Research: From Improvement to Redesign," examines the changing role of the institutional researcher in an emerging postsecondary knowledge industry and an institution addressing issues of institutional redesign or transformation. Institutional research could add the role of "postsecondary knowledge analyst." In this role, it would place greater emphasis on activities associated with monitoring the changing societal and industry conditions (a new focus for scanning), reviewing strategic institutional options as it faces macro-change choices, monitoring the peripheral changes in the institution where most nontraditional activity and change occur, develop new approaches of assessment in program review for new learners and new types of delivery systems, and analyze the institutional capacity for and readiness to change. In effect, institutional research could become a proactive management guide for the institution addressing issues of institutional redesign.

Information

Clearly, the information technology that informs and provides a common link between planning and information technology is and will continue to evolve rapidly. Data bases are being replaced by the notion of data warehouses; comprehensive integrated software is being developed at many institutions; more sophisticated, powerful and faster work stations are available to many campus administrators not just planners and institutional researchers; and the growth of telecommunications and use of the Internet expands the access to external data, sharing of data across the industry, and doing comparative analyses. The literature capturing the application and uses of information technology in institutional research and planning is only emerging. Like the technology itself, it is changing rapidly and is often out of date before it is adopted.

A Challenge to the User

Students of planning and institutional research should go beyond the readings suggested here. New concepts and practices; new articles, books and papers; and ideas from diverse sources will enrich a discussion of the future of our postsecondary institutions, our industry, and planning and institutional research. Those entering this arena as a scholar, a professional or a university administrator seeking to understand the changing nature or potential of planning and institutional research should find 2000 and beyond a fascinating, if uncertain, opportunity.

References

Brumbaugh, A. J. *Research Designed to Improve Institutions of Higher Education*. Washington, D.C.: American Council on Education, 1960.

Cowley, W. H. Two and a Half Centuries of Institutional Research. In Axt, R.G. and Springer, H.E. (Eds.). *College Self-Study: Lectures on Institutional Research*. Boulder, Colo.: WICHE, 1959.

Dressel, P. and Associates (Ed.). *Institutional Research In the University*. San Francisco: Jossey-Bass, 1971.

Drucker, P. *Managing for the Future: The 1990s and Beyond*. New York: Dutton, 1992.

Duderstadt, J. The 21st Century University: A Tale of Futures. Paper presented at North American and Western European Colloquium on the Challenges Facing Higher Education. Glion, Switzerland, May, 1998.

Firnberg, J. and Lasher, W. *The Politics and Pragmatics of Institutional Research*. NDIR, Vol. 38. San Francisco: Jossey-Bass, 1983.

Keller, G. *Academic Strategy: The Management Revolution In American Higher Education*. Baltimore, Md.: Johns Hopkins University Press, 1983.

Lawrence, G. and Service, A. (Eds). *Quantitative Approaches to Higher Education Management: Potential, Limits and Challenges*. ASHE-ERIC Research Report, Vol. 4. Washington, D.C.: American Association for Higher Education, 1977.

Lindquist, J. *Increasing the Use of Institutional Research*. NDIR, Vol. 32. San Francisco: Jossey-Bass, 1981.

Mortimer, K. P. and Tierney, M.L. *The Three R's of the Eighties: Reduction, Retrenchment and Reallocation*. AAHE-ERIC Report No. 4. Washington, D.C.: AAHE, 1979.

National Commission on Excellence. *A Nation at Risk*. Washington, D.C.: U.S. Department of Education, 1983.

Peterson, M. and Corcoran, M. Proliferation or Professional Integration: Transition or Transformation. In Corcoran, M. and Peterson, M. (Eds.). *Institutional Research in Transition*. NDIR, Vol. 46. San Francisco: Jossey-Bass, 1985.

Peterson, M. and Dill, D. Understanding the Competetive Environment of the Postsecondary Knowledge Industry. In Peterson, M.; Dill, D. and Mets, L. (Eds.). *Planning and Management for a Changing Environment*. San Francisco: Jossey-Bass, 1997.

Peterson, M. W. In Peterson, M.; Dill, D. and Mets, L. (Eds.). *Planning and Management for a Changing Environment*. San Francisco: Jossey-Bass, 1997.

Peterson, M.W. Continuity Challenge and Change: An Organizational Perspective on Planning Past and Future. *Planning for Higher Education*. Vol. 14, No. 3, 1986.

Peterson, M. W. Institutional Research: An Evolutionary Perspective. In Corcoran, M. and Peterson, M.W. (Eds.). *Institutional Research In Transition*. NDIR, Vol. 46. San Francisco: Jossey-Bass, 1985.

Peterson, M. W. The Role of Institutional Research: From Improvement to Redesign. In Volkwein, J. F., (Ed.). *Studying Institutional Research: The Best of What We Know*. NDIR, Vol. 102. San Francisco: Jossey-Bass, 1999.

Porter, M. *Competitive Strategy*. New York: Free Press, 1980.

Roose, K. D. and Anderson, C. J. *A Rating of Graduate Programs*. Washington, D.C.: American Council on Education, 1970.

Rourke, F. E. and Brooks, G. E. *The Managerial Revolution in Higher Education*. Baltimore, Md.: Johns Hopkins University Press, 1966.

Saunders, L. Policy Analysis: Neither Institutional Research Nor Planning. In Gill, J. and Saunders, L. (Eds.). *Developing Effective Policy Analysis in Higher Education*. NDIR, Vol. 76. San Francisco: Jossey-Bass, 1992.

Saupe, J. *The Functions of Institutional Research*. Tallahassee, Fla.: Association for Institutional Research, 1990.

Sheehan, B. *Information Technology*. NDIR, Vol. 35. San Francisco: Jossey-Bass, 1982.

Study Group on the Condition of Excellence in American Higher Education. *Involvement in Learning*. Washington, D.C.: NIE, 1984.

Tetlow, W. *Using Microcomputers for Planning and Management Support*. NDIR, Vol. 44. San Francisco: Jossey-Bass, 1984.

Organization of the Reader

Because of the breadth of topics potentially covered by a *Reader on Planning and Institutional Research*, this Reader has not attempted to cover the extensive array of specific approaches, analytic methods, techniques and topics, and issues. The Reader also does not include the extensive practitioner-oriented articles that provide guidance on how to conduct institutional research and planning activities nor case studies of institutions' experiences. The emphasis is on articles about institutional research and planning that enhance conceptual understanding, report research findings, synthesize conceptual or broad practice topics or issues, provide important perspectives on the field, and address current emerging topics and issues.

The first four sections of the Reader are organized to provide a comprehensive coverage of planning and institutional research. Those sections are: I. Planning Theories, Models and Approaches; II. Role and Nature of Institutional Research; III. Planning Domains, Elements and Issues; IV. Institutional Research Approaches, Topics and Issues. A final section, V. Other Resources, is designed to assist individuals using this Reader to easily access other publications, organizations, and data sources that are part of institutional research and planning. A brief description of these sections and the references that follow is presented at the start of each section.

PART I

PLANNING MODELS AND APPROACHES

CHAPTER I
PLANNING MODELS AND APPROACHES

Planning, as a primary institutional process, is generally conceived of as those future-oriented institutional activities concerned with the establishment of institutional direction and mission, the formulation of strategies, and the development of institutional capacity to achieve it. The planning process is a major contributor to the adaptive function of an institution. The literature in this section examines the array of models of or approaches to the planning process. Since the Reader is focused on institutional-level planning, it does not include references related to state-level planning. Those wishing to add materials focused at that level should consult the *ASHE Reader on Public Policy* (Goodchild, Lovell, Hines, & Gill, 1997).

Four selections provide an overview of theories and models of planning. In the first article, "Planning, Decisions and Human Nature," Keller discusses planning in the context of theories of human nature. Peterson, in "Alternative Approaches to Planning," discusses the nature of the planning process, interprets it in the context of differing organizational theories and models, and examines strategic planning and the issues in fitting it to other organizational dynamics. In "Conceptual Distinctions in University Planning," Neufeld identifies and discusses five models of planning: rational, strategic, incremental, advocacy, and organizational development. The chapter on "Using Conceptual Planning to Transform Institutions" by Peterson suggests a new model of planning that addresses the emergence of a postsecondary knowledge industry and the need to plan for institutional redesign or transformation.

Four articles offer an opportunity to examine planning and the planning process in more detail. The concept of strategy, the basis for strategic planning, is the focus of a recent examination. Presley and Leslie provide a comprehensive review of the historical development, the many notions, and the different higher education levels of strategy and an analysis of what those imply. In a research-based article, "College and University Planning: Perspectives from a Nation-Wide Study," Schmidtlein and Milton identify the planning activities and dynamics reported by campus executive officers. Bean and Kuh provide a focused look at problems encountered in planning in "A Typology of Planning Problems." And at the individual level, Hurst and Peterson report on "The Impact of a Chief Planning Officer on the Administrative Environment for Planning" in a research-based article.

The final three selections examine the changing external environment and speculate on its implications for postsecondary education in the years ahead. In the broadest terms, Duderstadt examines societal needs, financial imperatives and technology and suggests two scenarios in "The 21st Century University: A Tale of Two Futures." Peterson and Dill, in "Understanding the Competitive Environment of the Postsecondary Knowledge Industry," take an industry perspective and analyze external challenges that are affecting our postsecondary industry and present institutions with a new planning agenda. In the most theoretical of these four works, Gumport and Sporn's "Institutional Adaptation: Demands for Management Reform and University Administration" contrasts the changing societal and institutional environments and places it in the context of organization-environment theories. The resulting analysis examines the need for institutional reform.

Planning, Decisions, and Human Nature

GEORGE KELLER

Should planning concentrate more on people and less on process?

George Keller is book review editor of this journal and an award-winning education writer, editor, and planner. He took his undergraduate and graduate degrees at Columbia University and is the former chair of higher education studies at the University of Pennsylvania's Graduate School of Education. This article was presented at the SCUP 32nd Annual Conference in Chicago.

Few demands have been made more insistently in recent years than the one that U.S. higher education must change. Yet most higher education planners—and many education critics themselves—believe that colleges and universities are extremely reticent to make any but the most cosmetic changes.

Therefore, one of the central issues in higher education planning and implementation today is how to get people in academic life to accept change. Put another way, how can planners and campus executives get professors, staff people, and alumni to make the hard decisions that will bring their institutions more in line with radically new, contemporary conditions?

In my 15 years of consulting with more than 200 institutions, no question has been asked more often than, "How can I get the people at this campus to consent to changes?" Even scholars who understand the urgency of some kind of reforms on their campus balk when the difficult decisions must be made.

The standard answer given by American scholars of management, leadership, and planning about how to effect change is to get the *process* right. Then people will accept change easily. For example, it is fashionable for advocates to suggest that presidents and their planners involve nearly everyone in designing the changes to get maximum "buy-in." Out of this broad, democratic involvement some sort of "consensus" for change is said to emerge magically. The consensus then allows the college to move toward new strategic initiatives harmoniously and with wide backing.

That no such process has ever resulted in a major change at any university, or is ever likely to do so, does not prevent the proponents of this theory from continuing to advocate it often and with astonishing confidence.

These theories about the importance of process derive from a culture that is addicted to technique. They are also the theories of an increasingly bookish and quantitative social science cohort that has gradually withdrawn from close observations of the way people actually behave and from trying to fathom why people do what they do. Real people figure less and less in the current planning literature.

Of course, good processes can help. So can shrewd, persistent, courageous leadership, and powerful outside pressures. But the "black hole" in education planning, I think, is our neglect of human nature. If we planners want to help our colleges and universities adjust to the new environment, we need to concentrate less on process and more on what makes human beings tick.

The struggle to understand the chief determinants of human nature is as old as Homer and Confucius. An assumption of what people are really like underlies every body of thought and proposal for action, although some proponents do not realize their assumptions. Fat books have been written on the subject.[1] In this

"Planning, Decisions, and Human Nature," by George Keller, reprinted from *Planning for Higher Education*, Vol. 26, Winter 1997–98. Society for College and University Planning.

short paper, I want only to remind education planners in a concise, necessarily superficial way about a few of the prevalent views of what propels people in our society today. I think that only if we recognize that there are major subterranean forces at work in people's psyches during a planning process can we find out what will work better in preparing those on campus for change and in encouraging them to make bold decisions for their college.

There are, of course, hundreds of views of human nature—from Jean-Jacques Rousseau's belief that people are naturally good but are corrupted by the deformed institutions that civilization has created to Joseph De Maistre's view that people are naturally cruel, selfish animals kept in check only by religious prescriptions and autocratic governments with strong police forces. I will describe briefly only five views, in no ranking or order.

All will be familiar to you. But to find out why educational change is so difficult, why tough decisions are rarely made, and why rational plans often fail to get implemented, I think we need to understand people's motivations. I hope this small paper will help refine your powers of understanding.

What Makes People Act As They Do?

1. *Freud and the libido hurdle.* In the past decade, Sigmund Freud's reputation has been severely battered, but his view of human behavior is still widely accepted.[2] To Freud, each person has an inextinguishable, biological, pleasure-seeking drive that he called the "id." The id is especially dominant when we are infants, sucking breast milk, craving hugs, and crawling about naked as we please. But to avoid chaos and the wild, destructive clash of pleasure-seeking people, adults have developed rules, taboos, and punishments, what Freud called the "reality principle" or "superego." Parents early on introduce these societal constraints to their infants and young children, and depending on how these are introduced our "character" is shaped, usually by age six or so, and mostly by puberty. As Freud said, "The child is father to the man."

From the contest between an individual's id and society's superego, each of us develops a tense, tentative balance called our "ego." Some egos are "up tight"; others are uninhibited, sexually ambitious, and pleasure-seeking. Our lives—our egos—are balancing acts between our inner drives (which become increasingly "unconscious") and doing what society, our jobs, and our institutions demand.

The id is powerful and persistent, Freudians contend. It frequently steers our supposedly conscious behavior. It fashions our myths, such as the Garden of Eden, or a place called heaven, or Karl Marx's classless, stateless, communist utopia—all notions of total pleasure and freedom, devoid of superego obligations and work.

Freud's view is sometimes seen as a tragic one because happiness and a reasoned life depend on constraints, repression, and renunciation of much of our libidinous drives and acceptance of larger realities than our personal satisfaction.[3] It may also be a tragic view for planners because proposals for change, new structures, and new duties at work tend to upset many people's delicate balance between their inner drives and desires and the outer demands of improved academic life. As a result, calls for educational change usually arouse considerable anxiety and often elicit defensive stratagems to protect the relatively soothing status quo. To some people, calls for change can even induce behavior that is neurotic, that is, erratic and highly emotional speech and actions caused by excessive anxiety, insecurity, or emotional upset. Planning is a superego discipline that in the short term causes upset and reduction of pleasure.

2. *Marx and the exploitation gambit.* The Marxian view of human nature and behavior was immensely popular during the 1930s, '40s, and '50s. Many U.S. student radicals also employed it in the late 1960s and early 1970s, and it is still the armature of many American deconstructionists and so-called critical theorists, who are surprisingly abundant at present-day colleges and universities.

Karl Marx argued that all humans have some basic needs such as food, drink, shelter, and sex but that all other desires are "relative" to the prevailing modes of production in the society or historical period. The way that any population produces its food, material goods, and other economic artifacts enormously influences how people think and what they desire as well as what they fear.

Moreover, whether people own or control the means of production—a factory owner, a banker, an agricultural landowner, or a university board of trustees and their president—or whether they are merely workers, borrowers of money, farmhands, or graduate-student teaching assistants also shapes their interests, outlooks, and behavior. Thus, the structure of the economy and our position in the economy (or class) profoundly influence our human nature and our position on issues. All other cultural activities such as art, religion, morality, and philosophy are in Marx's view only a "superstructure," a body of rationalizations that reinforces the economy's and our own needs.

In a modern, competitive, capitalist society, Marx alleges, the dominant motive necessary to keep the economy strong is profit, the famous "bottom line." Owners tend to exploit workers to make a profit, and workers tend to unionize, agitate for profit sharing, and strike or rebel to get their fair share of the profits. Class warfare is constant and indigenous for any society—except, Marx dreamed, in a future communal society where no one owned anything.

To many Marxists on college campuses, higher education is perennially in danger of being used by capitalists and their political allies for their own economic benefit. Hence, calls for change are suspect as "selling out" to potential donors and wealthy producers, or as attempts to turn higher education into a business instead of being an outside critic of bourgeois, capitalist society.

At the research universities and elite colleges, a strange new reason for resistance to change has appeared, alert Marxists might say. At these institutions many professors have become capitalists,[4] preferring to conduct research and consult instead of teaching undergraduates because their incomes will be greater, and exploiting their secretaries, graduate student assistants, parents and their tuition payments, cafeteria workers, and support staff to keep their own salaries high and privileges numerous. They can't help it; they are infected with the capitalist values of their society.

In effect, the knowledge-creating professors, once regarded as being no more productive than poets and priests, have become capitalist entrepreneurs, and universities have become "factories of knowledge," producing new products and ideas—from genetically altered plants and new software for computers to medical cures and better procedures for managing organizations. Ownership, production, and exploitation are assuming new forms in the postindustrial society.[5] So, at the knowledge-generating institutions numerous affluent professors, pressed to reform their practices, will act much as factory owners might when faced with calls for higher taxes, more help for the needy, and proletarian demands for better treatment of the workers.

3. *Darwin and the survival instinct.* Though Charles Darwin published his famous book, *The Origin of Species*, in 1859, most people have been reluctant until recently to accept the idea that humans are animals and a constituent part of nature and its evolution. But entomologist Edwin O. Wilson's 1975 book *Sociobiology* kicked off a resurgent interest in humans as biological animals with considerable genetic components and with an imperative to adapt to their changing environments in ways similar to that of other creatures in nature. So in the past 20 years there has been an explosion of interest in human biology, from finding genes for schizophrenia, obesity, and Alzheimer's disease to postulating the genetic components of people's IQ. Most scientists now agree that the human brain has evolved to form our species over the past several million years. A new psychology based on a Darwinian view of human nature is emerging.[6]

The essence of Darwin's view is that all animals, including humans, have a biological pull toward survival and perpetuation of the species. To survive, we must develop a fitness for our environment. Nature selects the most fit. The young aborigines of Australia and the schoolboys and schoolgirls in New England prep schools all study and develop skills to respond to what they believe will enable them to survive and prosper in their different climates, cultures, and surroundings. Even moral acts, altruism, and love are said to be useful to selfish survivalists.[7]

Two modern variations of the Darwinian view of human nature are worth noting. One is the series of fascinating experiments by Amos Tversky of Stanford and Daniel Kahneman, now of Princeton.[8] Their award-winning research has shown repeatedly that people will make statistical errors, predictions, and choices in favor of protecting what they have against choosing something new. People worry about losses and only under great pressure adapt to new conditions.

The other is the well-known utility function or rational-choice theory popularized by economists who need a fixed view of human nature on which to base their theories. The theory of *homo economicus* is now used by many other social scientists too for quantification purposes. This view assumes that people will always make choices in their self-interest, usually for monetary or material gain but sometimes for more leisure, fame, or love of country.[9] That is, people are consistently selfish and interested in gains—as they perceive what will most maximize their welfare. They choose what they feel is best for their survival and security.

The Darwinian view of human nature assumes that during planning sessions and policy deliberations most people (if not all) will be influenced heavily by considerations of: How will this affect me? The good of the college or of the students will usually take a back seat to concerns about personal or family survival, security, or gain. But clever planners can persuade by emphasizing the urgency of adapting to the new environment.

4. *Herder and the herd instinct.* Not many Americans know about Johann von Herder (1744–1803), the German theologian, literary critic, and social philosopher. His work and ideas have been excavated, however, by Isaiah Berlin, the brilliant intellectual historian at Oxford, and Herder's core ideas are suddenly much in vogue these days.[10]

In response to the French Enlightenment, which believed that people are basically the same everywhere with only minor cultural differences, Herder argued that differences of language, culture, belief systems, and historical traditions are absolutely central, not just minor factors. To Herder the need to belong to a community is a basic human need, like the need for food or sleep. He wrote, "Men, if they are to exercise their faculties fully . . . need to belong to identifiable groups, each with its own outlook, style, traditions, historical memories, and language." Herder invented the word "nationalism" and was fascinated by the Jews, who have kept alive a quasitribal culture for many centuries.

Herder wrote that while there are human necessities to stay alive, there is no one human nature, but a plurality of human natures on this earth. Each civilization, each ethnic group, each religious sect, and each language group has its own special spirit, forms of literature and art, and values—its *Volksgeist*—from which most things flow. Portuguese citizens are uncomfortable in Finland, and the Chinese are uncomfortable in Nigeria or Saudi Arabia. Tribes, cults, and small nations are the natural communities of the world, and large nation-states like the former Soviet Union, Canada, China, or the United States—or Mexico, the former Zaire, and the former Yugoslavia—must acknowledge the distinctive subcultures in their midst.

To understand these distinctive communities, Herder thought you needed to get inside them and learn to know their peculiar way of thinking and acting. He called this *Einfuhlung*, or feeling into, or empathy. Quantitative social science can never understand such communities.

The modern American college or university is a remarkable example of Herder's social views. African Americans, gays, radical feminists, Baptists, Mexican Americans, elitist intellectuals, athletes, secular egalitarians, raspberry-haired art students, ROTC militarists, devotees of fraternities and sororities, and hard-core quantitative scientists all fight to be recognized as special communities with different values and attributes. During any campus attempt at broad-scale planning and strategic change, planners must walk through a thicket of people with such special interests and distinctive aims and values, many of whom feel victimized by the other groups and assert their own "rights" to full recognition.

Modern Herderites might say that renovating U.S. higher education, which is so inclusive and diverse, requires a deep understanding of the plurality of human natures at an institution and statesmanlike adjudication of their special interests and concerns, along with a powerful educational vision to unite them somehow. Most people though are extremely reluctant to consider changes that would unite everyone in a visionary new strategy and impinge on the life of their special association.

5. *Madison, sin, and salvation.* James Madison, probably the most intellectual and wisest of this republic's founding fathers, was a short, slender, frail, soft-spoken man who hated all sports and never wore anything but black. A graduate of what is now Princeton, Madison was educated in the Calvinist view of human nature, which, following St. Augustine, believed deeply in original sin but also in the possibility of generous, beautiful acts if one listens for the voice of God and follows the teaching of his divine son, Jesus of Nazareth. As Madison wrote in his *Federalist Paper No. 55:*

> As there is a degree of depravity in mankind which requires a certain degree of circumspection and distrust, so there are other qualities in human nature which justify a certain portion of esteem and confidence.

All people have the capacity for both good and evil, with the latter predominating. The trick in society is therefore to arrange a government and other institutions that inhibit the nasty, sinful side of people and develop and encourage their finer and more public-spirited sensibilities.

The dark side of human nature, to Madison, most commonly took the form of "factions," which he wrote in the famous *Federalist No. 10* are "sown in the nature of man." Factions are selfish interest groups, passionate mobs, or clandestine cabals that attack the rights of others and the general good of a locality or nation. These factions need "checks and balances," which Madison tenaciously advocated. "Ambition must be made to counteract ambition," he said. He also authored the Bill of Rights to protect citizens from factions inside or outside government.

Colleges and universities too might be said to have their factions or special interest groups, from fierce faculty advocates of tenure and noisy alumni who love football and other sports to proponents of higher education as a form of job training and devotees of special curriculums such as black studies, Chicano studies, Jewish studies, women's studies, or Great Books studies. So higher education planners must deal with people, Madisonians would point out, who have both a selfish, sinful, vicious side and a reasonable, charitable, and imaginative side.

While the leading disciple of Madison in the past half century has been the social and religious philosopher Reinhold Niebuhr,[11] others of a Madisonian bent such as the Canadian philosopher Charles Taylor or the sociologist Robert Bellah have recently called attention to the prevailing quest among Americans to "find one's self," to achieve personal happiness, and to express their individual natures, often to the neglect of the needs of institutions. Taylor especially worries that the twin nature of our being—toward both self-aggrandizement and the outside values of religious love, patriotism, social justice, and the like—is breaking down. He writes:

> In earlier views, being in touch with some source—God, say, or the Idea of the Good—was considered essential to full being; now the source we have to connect with is deep within us. This is part of the massive subjective turn of modern culture, a new form of inwardness. . . .
>
> It is the idea that I am free when I decide for myself what concerns me, rather than being shaped by outside influences. . . . It accords crucial moral importance to a kind of contact with myself, with my own inner nature.[12]

Madison would not be surprised. He would try, I suspect, to invent ways to encourage the other, more large-hearted, magnanimous, civic side to be expressed. Planners may need to consider the invention of forms that blunt the excessive concern for self, recognizing the nature and preoccupations of many contemporary people.[13] Planners also need to stress that good universities are necessary for self-expression.

Dealing with People

Clearly, I have no easy answer to the question, What will work in altering most people's reluctance to make changes in our colleges and universities? But I strongly believe that our chances of effecting change will increase if we keep in mind the internal components and fears of those people who must live with the changed academic circumstances brought about by the midwifery of strategic initiatives.

One of my favorites among the most recent colloquialisms is the expression, "You know where I'm coming from?" I think we planners will have greater success if we take time to find out where the principals in any incipient college or university set of changes are "coming from."

Whether a person is a closet Freudian, Marxist, Darwinian, Herderite, or Madisonian (or some other basic nature), he or she can recognize that life will be poorer without the superego, a more communal view, better adaptive behavior, a more diverse institution that tolerates subcultures, or adherence to some entity beyond the self or one's faction.

So education planners can use the knowledge about human nature to make changes seem beneficial instead of threatening by appealing to people's egos, or to their economic self-interest, or to their need to survive in the new social climate, or to protect their special community, or to permit their self-expression to flourish.

Above all, we need to acknowledge that strategic change is closer to theater than to science, closer to tragedy than to carving soap. Making wise, farsighted decisions about our campuses, perhaps the most central of all institutions in our knowledge-based society, is as difficult, intricate, and important as any work in the world today.[14] Even that pessimistic scholar of organizations, James March, admits: "The idea of decision making gives meaning to purpose, to self, to the complexities of social life. It ennobles as it frustrates."[15]

Notes

1. See, for example, Merle Curti, *Human Nature in American Thought: A History* (Madison: University of Wisconsin Press, 1980).
2. Malcolm Macmillan, *Freud Evaluated: The Completed Arc* (New York: North-Holland, 1991); Frank Sulloway, *Freud, Biologist of the Mind: Beyond the Psychoanalytic Legend*, rev. ed. (Boston: Harvard University Press, 1992); Frederick Crews, ed., et al., *The Memory Wars: Freud's Legacy in Dispute* (New York: New York Review of Books, 1995); Richard Webster, *Why Freud Was Wrong: Sin, Science, and Psychoanalysis* (New York: Basic Books, 1995).
3. See, for example, the essays by Paul Roazen, Jerome Bruner, Erich Fromm, and David Ries-

man in *Sigmund Freud*, ed. Paul Roazen (Englewood Cliffs: Prentice-Hall, 1973). Also see Peter Gay, *Freud for Historians* (New York: Oxford University Press, 1985).
4. Sheila Slaughter and Larry Leslie, *Academic Capitalism: Politics, Policies, and the Entrepreneurial University* (Baltimore: Johns Hopkins University Press, 1997).
5. Daniel Bell, *The Coming of Post-Industrial Society: A Venture in Social Forecasting* (New York: Basic Books, 1973).
6. See Robert Wright, *The Moral Animal: Why We Are the Way We Are: The New Science of Evolutionary Psychology* (New York: Pantheon, 1994); Jerome Barkow, Leda Cosmides, and John Tooby, *The Adapted Mind: Evolutionary Psychology and the Generation of Culture* (New York: Oxford University Press, 1992).
7. George Keller, "Neuroscience, Moral Psychology, and the New Foundations of Transformational Planning" (paper presented at the annual conference of the Society for College and University Planning, San Francisco, July 26, 1994).
8. Amos Tversky and Daniel Kahneman, "Judgement Under Uncertainty: Heuristics and Biases," *Science* 185 (1974): 1124–31.
9. Gary Becker, "Nobel Lecture: The Economic Way of Looking at Behavior," *Journal of Political Economy* 101 (June 1993): 385–409.
10. See Isaiah Berlin, *Vico and Herder: Two Studies in the History of Ideas* (New York: Viking Press, 1976); Isaiah Berlin and Ramin Jahanbegloo, *Conversations with Isaiah Berlin* (New York: Charles Scribner's Sons, 1991).
11. See, for example, Reinhold Niebuhr, *The Nature and Destiny of Man: A Christian Interpretation* (New York: Charles Scribner's Sons, 1953).
12. Charles Taylor, *The Ethics of Authenticity* (Boston: Harvard University Press, 1992), pp. 26, 29.
13. The "communitarian" movement advocates greater concern for organizations, institutions, communities. See Amitai Etzioni, *The New Golden Rule: Community and Morality in a Democratic Society* (New York: Basic Books, 1996).
14. George Keller, "Examining What Works in Strategic Planning," in *Planning and Management for a Changing Environment: A Handbook on Redesigning Postsecondary Institutions*, eds. Marvin Peterson, David Dill and Lisa Mets (San Francisco: Jossey-Bass, 1997).
15. James March, *A Primer on Decision Making: How Decisions Happen* (New York: The Free Press, 1994), pp. 271–72.

Analyzing Alternative Approaches to Planning

Marvin W. Peterson

Note: This chapter was prepared under a grant from the Carnegie Corporation of New York to the University of Michigan.

Because conceptual and pragmatic confusion often inhibits successful institutional planning, this chapter offers a conceptual framework for viewing institutional planning and research, identifies the major organizational issues in designing an integrated planning function, and provides a context for the remaining chapters in this book. Five basic questions guide its organization:

1. What is planning and what are the major concepts that describe it?

2. What are the major theoretical models of or approaches to planning and how do they differ?

3. What is strategic planning and what are its major elements? How do environmental factors and external relationships affect planning?

4. What is tactical planning and its major elements? How are they related to strategic planning and to each other?

5. What are the major institutional issues in developing an institutional planning function?

The authors of other chapters of this book deal implicitly and explicitly with the first two questions, but I present a broad institutional definition and array of theoretical models of planning that encompass the varied perspectives of all the authors of this book. My discussion of strategic planning relating the institution to its environment grows from the chapters in Part One dealing with the implications of major environmental changes and external organizations for institutional planning and research and sets the stage for the other chapters in Part Two, which detail the major elements of strategic planning. My analysis of tactical or intrainstitutional planning serves as a preface to the chapters in Part Three on academic planning and institutional research, in Part Four on allocating resources, and in Part Five on evaluation and assessment. And my description of major organizational issues lays the groundwork for those Part Six and Seven chapters that examine patterns of institutional planning and research in different types of institutions, the process of developing planning and research, and their linkage to governance, leadership, and information systems.

Definition of Planning

Planning can be viewed as emanating from different levels of social behavior: individual (Michael, 1973), organizational (Drucker, 1969), or societal (Etzioni, 1968). At the organizational level, it can be viewed as a separate, analytically oriented institutional function (Ackoff, 1970), as an integral part of the decision-making and control function (Anthony, 1965), or as a more politically oriented policymaking function (Bauer and Gergen, 1968). To analyze and improve college and university planning, a broad institutional perspective is useful. From

"Analyzing Alternative Approaches to Planning," by Marvin W. Peterson, reprinted from *Improving Academic Management: A Handbook of Planning and Institutional Research*, edited by P. Jedamus and M. W. Peterson, 1989. Jossey-Bass Publishers, Inc.

this perspective, planning can be defined as a conscious process by which an institution assesses its current state and the likely future condition of its environment, identifies possible future states for itself, and then develops organizational strategies, policies and procedures for selecting and getting to one or more of them. This definition views planning as a key organizational process that may or may not be developed as part of the larger institutional management function; and it assumes (1) that the institution and its members are concerned about future as well as current states of the institution and the means for getting them, (2) that they choose to develop a conscious planning process to reach these states rather than rely on the whims of key individuals or sporadic responses to unpredictable external events, and (3) that some attempt to assess institutional strengths and weaknesses and to examine the environment for constraints and opportunities can lead to changes that are beneficial to the institution's vitality. This definition says little about how this planning process is conceived, how it can be organized, what subprocess it includes, and how planning relates to other institutional processes, functions, and structures. However, its focus on planning as *process* emphasizes a dynamic view of planning in contrast to a static view.

Static and Dynamic Views of Planning. A static view of planning is illustrated by the development of a "plan" rather than a "planning process." New institutions that begin with a master plan and other institutions that develop a master plan or complete a self-study by adopting specific recommendations for future directions are engaged in static planning: creating a plan or a sense of future direction. Such occasional or periodic plans may be useful during uneventful times, but recent experience suggests their inadequacy as demands on conditions affecting institutions change rapidly. The failure of a master plan predicated on false assumptions about clientele is reflected in the Riesman, Gusfield and Gamson (1970) study of Oakland University; and Ladd's 1970 report on self-studies for the Carnegie Commission describes the weaknesses of periodic self-study in major universities when such study is not linked to ongoing institutional planning or governance processes. Examples of institutional master plans produced for varied rea-

sons and then left to repose on library shelves are numerous. If reassessed and updated regularly, such plans could be an integral part of their institution's planning process. But most experts now agree that development of an effective continuing planning process through a dynamic view of planning is as crucial as creating a master plan.

The development of a planning process does not, of course, preclude varying regularity or continuity of planning. Ad hoc, intermittent, or continuous planning may all be part of the process. Ad hoc and often short-term planning is frequently necessary when unanticipated events occur, such as an unforeseen drop in resources or the opportunity to acquire or merge with a nearby campus. And some planning activities, such as updating master plans, can often be done most realistically on a periodic basis rather than by expecting the possibility of continuous planning. The balance of ad hoc, intermittent, and continuous planning for different planning activities is a crucial issue in the development of a planning process and needs to be anticipated by those charged with responsibility for it.

Planning as Process, Structure, and Technology. Defining planning as an organizational process does not imply that the formal structure or technology of that process is unimportant; but colleges and universities often introduce formal structures for planning, such as a new office or a prestigious committee, or adopt new techniques, such as resource simulations, Delphi surveys, forecasting, and needs assessments, on the assumption that these themselves are planning. As with the adoption of a static plan, however, formal structures and techniques do not assure that institutional purposes are reviewed or changed or that means of achieving them are adopted. A focus on planning as process reflects the fact that colleges and universities, as human service organizations with labor intensive functions, need to place their primary emphasis on the pattern of activities and relationships among individuals involved in planning. Structures and techniques do make important contributions to planning, but they need to be recognized as parts of the process rather than preeminent or independent of the process. It is useful to think of institutional planning as consisting of three interrelated parts, as depicted in Figure 1.

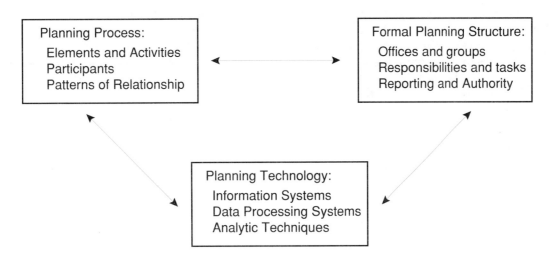

Figure 1. Parts of the Planning Process

An institution's *planning process* may be viewed as made up of several elements arrayed in two broad categories: (1) strategic elements, such as environmental scanning, institutional assessment, values assessment, and master planning, which focus on the broadest issues of institutional policy and direction; and (2) tactical elements, such as program planning, priority setting, resource allocation, and program review, which focus on policy implementation—each of the seven elements of course, include a wide array of activities which are described by the participants in the planning process and the patterns of relationship among and between these participants and their activities. The *formal planning structure* involves the organizationally defined offices and positions and groups, their responsibilities and tasks, and their reporting and authority patterns as they participate in the process. And *planning technology* refers to the information systems (institutional and noninstitutional data bases), and data-processing systems (manual and semiautomated as well as computer hardware and software), and the analysis and research techniques that serve the planning function. In practice, the distinction between process, structure, and technique often becomes blurred, yet emphasizing each can lead to very different conceptions of planning. (For example, a formal structure may exist with an unclear process or inadequate techniques.)

Merely defining planning as a dynamic institutional process which includes formal planning structures and techniques that are easily described does not provide an adequate basis for analyzing or designing one. Additional concepts or variables which can be used to understand the planning process can be organized into three broad categories: those that describe the domain, some process characteristics, and the organizational pattern of planning. The domain and process concepts also serve as a basis for comparing six models of planning to be discussed later. These concepts capture, in large part, the institution's rationale for its planning process. Failure to recognize the distinctions these concepts imply often leads to conflicts among and between planners, administrators, and faculty who do not agree on how to approach the planning process or what it should accomplish.

Domain Concepts of Planning Process

The Content of Planning. Conceptually, there are three dimensions which provide an overview of the content domain of planning. One describes the "planning elements" or subprocesses of planning which may be part of the institutional planning process. These generally include: environmental assessment, institutional assessment, values assessment, master planning (including the establishment of mission, role, and scope; setting goals and objectives; and designing institutional strategies), program planning, priority setting and resource allocation, and the program review. Each of these elements often incorporates a variety of more focused planning activities and each is discussed later in the chapter.

Content may also focus on different organizational units or types of resources included in an institution's planning process. Organizationally, planning may occur around structural units, such as colleges, departments, centers, bureaus, and the like, or around various functions, such as the National Center for Higher Education Management System (NCHEMS) typology of academic, research, service, and other support functions with its related program and output classification structure. Resource elements on which planning may focus often include physical facilities, fiscal resources (operating and capital), human resources (students, faculty, and staff), and information resources.

Historically, planning in most higher education institutions has included only some of these planning elements, organizational units, and types of resources or has treated them somewhat separately. The current challenge is to integrate them all in the planning process.

Basic Institutional Unit for Planning. Perhaps the most crucial decision in designing the planning process is the planner's perception of the basic units from which the institution is formed, which are the primary focus for planning. To a large degree, this decision shapes the remaining concepts and serves as the basis for the theoretical models of planning discussed later. Planning can emanate from six sets of perceptions about the institutional units, which are the primary building blocks for planning:

1. a set of formally devised responsibilities and offices and well-defined processes and structures for relating to them

2. a collection of individuals and groups with their own needs, abilities, and natural but related activity patterns and interests

3. an array of members' attitudes, opinions, and values, which reflect a set of belief systems

4. a well-defined quantifiable set of clients, members, and resources organized around tasks, functions, and product or output services

5. a set of interest groups organized around issues that may conflict and/or change

6. a collection of individuals or groups that are autonomous and self-directed.

Planning cannot always make such a clear distinction, yet there is often a tendency for planners to stress one of these six different basic sets without examining the appropriateness. Stressing different basic units suggests six different theories or models (Table 2) of the planning process. Is the stress on the formal-rational, natural-human groups, belief systems, tasks and techniques, interest groups, or autonomous professional units?

Institutional Purpose and Motive of Planning. The institution's purpose or motive for engaging in planning in the first place may be the most overlooked dimension in designing a planning process. Aside from the fashionable imperative that institutions should plan, a growing body of literature suggests planning has some positive impacts if done well. It is a legitimate response to external group pressures, fosters an increased awareness of or more clearly defines critical problems facing the institution, increases external perceptions of being well managed, and improves communication and understanding of how interdependent the parts of the institution really are. The question of why any institution engages in planning is rarely answered. Answers may be found by examining the objectives of and expectations for planning: the role of the planning office and the institutional function that planning serves.

The answer is seldom found in a formal institutional document defining planning objectives and only occasionally in a governing or coordinating board's decree or a presidential mandate. Even when they exist, such formal directives are only a part of the picture. Institutions may commence planning because of critical events (a major budget crisis or a sudden enrollment decline or shift) or pressure from external groups (a critical accrediting report or a legislative or state agency) or a key personality (the president, a faculty leader, an influential consultant, or a second-echelon administrator). The concern, however, is to identify the formal directives, events, and personalities involved in initiating planning and to recognize that many sources or events shape their initial expectations of results. These expectations will change over time and must be reassessed periodically to assure that the formal objectives and informal expectations are not in opposition or that widely conflicting and/or unrealistic expectations for planning are not emerging.

Is the role or function of the planning process or of the planners to *identify critical issues* and problems confronting or likely to confront the institution for examination and review by the broader membership or its governance machinery? Is it to *assist others* (deans or department chairs) in incorporating planning activities in their own realms of responsibility? Is it to *coordinate* planning activities that are the responsibility of other administrative and academic units? Is it to *develop plans* and critically to *examine alternatives?* Or is it to prepare for and assist in *implementing action plans* and major institutional changes? In effect, the distinction is the continuum between staff and line planning and objective but neutral planning and advocacy planning. In reality, institutional planning will often adopt different roles or purposes at different times and on different issues. Yet failure to distinguish or recognize this difference or to confront conflicting expectations may subvert a planning process.

A frequently unexamined purpose for planning is the role or function it plays in meeting the needs of the entire institution. Planning can contribute to at least four functional needs of a college or university—the first two more externally oriented and the second two more internally oriented. Planning whose primary function is institutional *adaptation* is concerned with adapting the institution to external changes. As such, its primary concern is with selection and modification of the institutional mission (functions, clientele, and major organizational and resource strategies) to ensure long-term viability. Planning that seeks to accomplish this function is ambitious, threatening, and difficult to manage. A less-ambitious externally oriented function of planning focuses on *problems in boundary relations.* Its primary concern is with improving or maintaining the flow of resources to and from the institutions and with the groups that affect it (for example, identifying new student clienteles or improving the institution's image with legislature). Such planning activities, which are more fragmented, may eventually affect insti-

tutional mission; but they are not as difficult to manage and are not seen as threatening to its entire fabric. A more internally oriented function for planning is one that focuses on the *improvement of institutional management*: making programs more effective or efficient through changing resource allocation, improving their operation, or evaluating them. Planning focused around improving or resolving problems in resource allocation, program functioning, or institutional processes is less likely to change radically an institution's mission but may aid in achieving it. The other internal function for planning is improving or dealing with problems in the *human maintenance* dimension. This focus attempts to maximize institutional procedures and processes that improve faculty and staff morale, commitment, and performance and opportunities for individual (or group) growth and development in ways that serve the institutions. All four of these institutional functions can be addressed by a planning process, and in practice it is difficult to maintain distinctions between them.

The conditions initiating planning will foster some formal purposes and expectations. More rational assessment of institutional needs or environmental pressures may suggest different purposes or desired outcomes for planning. The evolving role of the planning process or office may identify still others. However, the major institutional problems that must be addressed will likely vary over time—sometimes requiring major changes of institutional mission and at other times dealing with more focused problems. These differing purposes for, expectations of, and desired outcomes of planning need to be examined to ensure that the planning effort is focused on the most pressing institutional needs and that the right planning activities and expertise are being utilized (revision of the master plan will not revitalize an outdated faculty and a planner skilled in economic forecasting may not be good at planning an improved faculty incentive system).

Internal or External Orientation. Because planning at any level involves some attempt to balance institutional strengths and weaknesses with environmental limitations and opportunities, a critical planning concept is its external or internal orientation. A major dimension to consider is the institution's *relative control* over environmental trends and groups in determining its resource flow. To the extent external factors dominate, planning must stress outside trends and forces. To the extent the institution feels it can control its key resources and influence or afford to ignore its major external groups, planning can focus on internal institutional concerns. For example, state colleges located in nonpopulous areas have much less control over their future than do larger prestigious universities located near key population areas. In most institutions, planning needs to be sensitive to both internal and external factors.

Future Orientation. Planning is future oriented, so an important concept in the planning process is how the institution of its planners choose to view it. Two dimensions are helpful in clarifying this concept. First, the time perspective on the future can vary: *Short* (two to three years), *middle* (four to five years), and *long* (ten years) seems to be the current institutional time line. It is usually somewhat longer for state agencies. The choice of time frame depends on the predictability of the events being planned for and the feasibility of making the requisite changes. The more certainty with which an event can be predicted far into the future, the more reasonable is a longer-time perspective. The current trend seems to be toward shorter time frames on institutional master plans. As uncertainties about college attendance rates for various groups, competitive factors, and economic conditions increase, master plans seem to become shorter term and require more regular updating. But they are probably more flexible and realistic.

The nature of an institutional future planners choose to focus on is a second dimension that largely reflects their view of the untapped potential of their institution and its control over the environment. Are they choosing to take an *ideal or utopian* view of the future of their institution, reflecting the belief that their institution has the potential to shape its own future and to ignore its environment; a *realistic but feasible* view of their institutional future, which reflects an assessment of how their institution can accommodate to the most likely and dominant environmental trends; or a *potential capability* view, which suggests the institution can develop its own human capacities further and overcome the external trends? A less future-oriented perspective is one that concentrates on improvement in efficiency and/or

management effectiveness but will be basically unchanged by either environmental focus or major internal changes.

Concern for the future is even reflected in the debate over the nature of planning decisions. Is planning making decisions about future states, about future implications of current decisions, or about the implications of foreseeable events or conditions (contingency planning)?

Planning Typologies: Organizational Level, Substance, and Decision Type. Planning typologies are closely related to the level or content of the organizational issues and the type of decisions being dealt with and have implications for the type of evidence (information) considered, the analytical techniques used, and the decision process employed.

A major planning typology distinguishes substantive (ends) and expedient or procedural (means) planning (Patola, Lehmann, and Blischke, 1970). Substantive planning assumes a central role, for planning is developing, assessing, and/or modifying the desired ends of planning: broad statements of institutional mission, goals, and objectives, and major functional or programmatic strategies or directions. The key assumption is that clarity of substantive ends will provide direction and improve the probability of attaining these ends. Procedural planning focuses more attention on the institutional means for achieving a plan or objective. It assumes substantive ends are given (by a higher governing body or state agency, for example) or are widely understood. Planning then concentrates on designing processes of resource allocation, operating decision guidelines, evaluating, and other institutional procedures likely either to accomplish the substantive plans or to improve organizational effectiveness and efficiency.

A similar but more concrete typology related to a hierarchical view of the institution is between strategic, tactical, and operational planning (Anthony, 1965); Glenny, and others, 1971). The terminology has the unfortunate connotation of military planning, where the terms were widely used. Strategic planning has a broad focus and deals with substantive issues of purpose and direction; it usually has an external orientation and is primarily concerned with defining an institution's relationship to its larger environment. It addresses the questions of *what business we are in, where we are going.*

Tactical planning, like procedural planning, is more limited and intrainstitutional in its orientation. It deals with manipulating resources, programs, and other means of achieving strategic plans or goals. It addresses the question *how do we get there?* Operational planning is concerned with the design of institutional procedures to carry out tactical or strategic plans (such as Program Evaluation and Review Techniques [PERT] or CPM techniques). It develops control mechanisms to assure the institution and its resource flows function as planned. The tripartite distinction becomes increasingly useful as higher educational institutions and their leaders become aware of the need to consider external groups, forces, and trends in establishing directions, to understand their institution's capacity to respond, and to assure they use resources efficiently.

Policy planning and contingency planning are quite different typologies. They have as their principal focus major environmental changes or internal problems that suggest a critical future condition, choice, or decision for the institution. Both seek to analyze the factors affecting that condition or choice, to define it and its probability of occurrence more clearly, and to assess the likely impact of alternative policies or decision choices. Clearly, policy and contingency planning, which begins with specific situations rather than broader planning concerns, may deal with strategic or substantive, tactical or procedural, or operational planning issues and may cut across them. Advocates of policy analysis (Weathersby and Balderston, 1973) argue that dealing rationally and analytically with issues as they emerge is more realistic than trying to deal with broad issues of mission, goals, and strategies and leads to a pattern of preferences and precedents that constitutes institutional plans. Contingency advocates stress its realism in facing uncertain situations and say it can be part of any planning approach. These three content focuses of planning may be practiced separately or integrated into a more comprehensive planning process.

The process of planning and these typologies all imply decision making. Two useful decision typologies in planning are those of Anthony (1965) and Simon (1957). Anthony suggests a hierarchy of policy decisions that focus on institutional missions, goals, and strategies; management decisions that are concerned with program selection, resource allocation, and effective goal accomplishment; and operational decisions concerned with routine and day-to-day decisions. This reflects the distinction of substantive or strategic, procedural or tactical, and operational planning. Simon elaborates by distinguishing between value and factual decisions, which has extensive implications for planning and highlights a major problem. Value decisions are ones for which judgments have to be rendered on the goodness or badness, desirability or undesirability, of a decision and where the criteria for it are not easily measurable. Factual decisions can be formulated in terms of a choice based on more quantifiable and measurable criteria. The distinction, though not always operationally clear, is helpful to planners. Value decisions are more difficult. Yet substantive or strategic planning often confronts planners and college and university decision makers with value-laden policy choices: To what extent should we shift our emphasis from liberal to career education? Is it more desirable to reduce costs by eliminating programs or releasing personnel on a seniority basis? Should the college invest in a high-cost marketing program in hopes of attracting students or concentrate funds on program improvement and faculty development to attract them? Such decisions involve substantial value dimensions as well as factual ones. Tactical or operational planning tends to deal with more tangible and factual decision issues: Are programs accomplishing their goals? Are resources being used for purposes allocated and efficiently?

Analytically, the planner hopes to reduce value choices to more factual dimensions, but the fact-value distinction has other implications. Value-loaded policy decisions suggest the collection of more "soft data," such as perceptual measures (opinions, attitudes, and such) of changes in societal values or program quality that may not be as "hard" or objective as that useful to measure the managerial decisions about program goal accomplishment or operational decisions. Hard or objective data, useful in analyzing factual decisions, are more amenable to inclusion in a retrievable management information system than those for value-based decisions. Further, value decisions probably require the participation of more affected parties in exploring the nature of the issue, the implications of alternatives, and the opinions of disparate parties. Thus, the type of decision is related to the type of planning and has implications for the type of data collected for inclusion in an information system, for analyses that can be done and even for the decision process utilized (Peterson, 1972).

Process Concepts or Characteristics of Planning

Two planning process dynamics (goal centeredness and decision-making and analytical style) and two bases for participation (expertise and representation) are four basic concepts that describe most planning processes.

Planning Process Dynamics. Although our most common views of planning are shaped by rational notions of goals, planning can vary in terms of the goal centeredness of the process. Table 1 contrasts the degree to which an institution addresses single or multiple goals and the formality of their adoption. A *goal-centered* planning process stresses a single goal or highest priority. This type of emphasis is unrealistic in larger, complex institutions, and difficult to gain support for even in a small one. Yet, particularly in times of crisis, highly visible goals may serve as a catalyst. In most institutional planning, a multiple set of goals is identified. Because they are often contradictory, they are not useful guides to action unless *prioritized*. *Consensus-centered* planning with the informally derived single goal or priority is often desired in smaller institutions. However, it is difficult to achieve or may exist and not be realized. There is substantial evidence that consensus goals are strong motivators and may lead to later formal endorsement. Finally, many institutions have multiple goals and have neither formalized them nor established a set of priorities. Such a *pluralistic* set of goals, if identified and accepted, may serve to limit unrelated activities and make the transition to a more formal set of priorities easier to negotiate if resources are constraining.

Table 1. Institutional Goal Centeredness

Mode of Adoption	Number of Goals Emphasized	
	Single	*Multiple*
Formalized Prioritized	Goal Centered	Priority Centered
Informal	Consensus Centered	Pluralistic

The second concept combines two interrelated process dimensions: the decision-making and analysis style planners emphasize. Five dynamics describe this concept. The most widely discussed is *neutral, rational analysis* of planning issues typically approached in a criterion-referenced, problem-solving mode (seeking the best comparative solution, for example, accomplishment of goals and objectives). This is appropriate where planning issues and alternatives are clear and where goals are agreed upon. Second, when planning issues, alternatives, and goals are unclear or decisions value laden, analysis and decision making can be approached through *reasoned discussion*, in which varied perspectives, points of view, and modes of analysis are shared in debate format. The emphasis is on the logic of the analysis and the positions stated. In such a situation, a third alternative approach might involve *collaborative learning*, about both the problem and the mode of analysis. This is often appropriate if planning is being introduced to a staff for the first time or in a small institution with limited formal planning and analysis experience. Unfortunately, planning often occurs in situations where there are sharply contrasting and competing perspectives. Here a fourth approach is to encourage *advocacy analysis* (different analysts may discover different data, differing approaches suggest different choices, and differing groups will interpret results differently). Such analysis usually leads to bargaining and negotiations, compromise, or coalition building to resolve planning differences. This may be likely in large institutions with units competing for declining resources or in institution-state agency dealings on planning issues where each has a different perspective. Finally, in highly decentralized or autonomous units, planning efforts may require highly *varied modes* of analysis and decision making that can only be *loosely coordinated*. This is probably most appropriate in the large institution whose units have independent resources and limited dependence on one another—an increasingly uncommon occurrence.

Bases of Participation. Although essentially characteristics describing the dynamics of the planning process, the two dimensions of participation in planning, the nature of the expertise required and the pattern of representation, are too central not to be treated separately. Different planning tasks require different kinds of expertise. The *planning process* expert has a conception of how to organize, marshal resources for, involve participants in, understand the nuances of, and obtain action as a result of planning. The *planning analyst* expert may share expertise with the process expert but is more proficient in technical research and analysis skills and in the use of information systems, research methods, and computer technology. The *organizational design and development* skill suggests another planning expertise. Because much planning involves organizational design or revision, understanding the human needs and interactions, organizational processes, and structural implications of trends, alternatives, and motivational schemes in implementing changes is an appropriate expertise. *Political skills* or knowledge of situations involving conflicting interests may be needed. *Academic* or *administrative* expertise about academic or functional units provides other expert bases for planners.

Planning representation can be limited to an *expert planning staff* if there is enough trust and respect for the planners and those who selected them and if the planning issues are somewhat objective. More often, representation is broadened to include other individuals with technical (information system, simulation modeling, or economic forecasting) and administrative responsibilities. Planning representation then becomes a rationally selected oligarchy of *planners and administrative specialists*. Another pattern of representation is often the self-selected *political oligarchy*, where representation reflects key interest groups (minorities or alumni). An elected or selected *intellectual or leadership elite* (the faculty blue ribbon committee) constitutes another pattern. On occasion in smaller institutions, planning may include a more *egalitarian democracy* involving all interested parties. The expertise stressed in planning and the bases for representation may vary; but the critical issue is for each institution to reflect on its own traditions, approach to planning, and planning problems; balance the expertise that can carry out the planning process; and include respected representatives to ensure legitimacy.

Organization of the Planning Process

The identification of several domain and process concepts that can be used to describe planning suggests seven related organizing concepts for the planning process itself.

Comprehensiveness. The discussion of the content of planning (a domain concept) suggests it might vary in its comprehensiveness. Two dimensions, "comprehensiveness of planning elements" and "of organizational scope," capture this concept.

A planning process is more comprehensive as it includes more of the elements of planning: master planning (including environmental, institutional, and values assessment), program planning, priority setting and resource allocation, and program review. Virtually all institutions have a resource allocation process, which may or may not have a priority setting and a planning perspective; many have some form of organized program review process, which again may not be planning related. The least prevalent major planning elements, but ones that are increasingly being instituted, are master planning or program planning. An institution that has all four and takes a longer-term perspective has a more comprehensive institutional planning process. The literature suggests the desirability of comprehensive planning; but comprehensive planning requires a major commitment of institutional resources and there is, to date, little objective evidence about the greater effectiveness of a fully comprehensive planning process.

Not only can a planning process be more or less comprehensive but so can the scope of organizational functions and programs (academic, research, service, and support), organizational units (colleges and departments), and types of resources (fiscal, human, physical, and information) considered in each of the major planning elements. Earlier planning efforts tended to be very limited in scope, for example, campus and physical facilities planning. More recent master planning attempts, planning-related resource allocation efforts, and some planning simulations, which reflect more constrained resources, have tended to be more comprehensive. Although this may be inevitable, it makes management of the planning process much more complex and difficult.

Planning Element Emphasis. An institution's planning may be comprehensive but choose to emphasize different elements in the planning process. State mandates for planning may argue for master planning. Severe budgetary constraints or work load issues may require greater priority in resource allocation. Concern about quality in outmoded programs may suggest emphasis on evaluation. However, whether one element is more or less superior for institutional redirection or redistribution is unresolved and probably depends on which process has the most trust in a particular institution.

Similarly, planning can emphasize different organizational functions, units, or resources. Academic planning gets greater attention as enrollments shift. Planning in research areas becomes more active in periods of uncertainty about soft funding. Human resource planning becomes more crucial under the countervailing pressures of projected stable and older staff and stress on affirmative action. Comprehensive planning may anticipate some of these and moderate the need for special emphasis, yet planning needs to vary its attention to different planning pressures or needs in the institution.

Integrated-Fragmented Nature of Planning. Although planning may be comprehensive, the major planning elements or the organizational units on which they focus may operate in a highly integrated or very fragmented manner. Rational arguments call for close integration of master planning, program planning, resource allocation, and program review; yet these elements occur on different time cycles (such as ten-year state-mandated master plans, annual budget cycles, and five-year program review cycles) or may be the responsibility of widely separated administrative units. The degree of integration, coordination, or fragmentation of the planning elements required in any institution is one that needs to be carefully examined.

Similarly, planning for the organizational elements (academic programs, physical facilities, human resources, or financial affairs) has often emerged as separate planning activities. Planning for academic programs is often divorced from research planning, yet the interplay of soft and hard funds makes them inseparable. Review of graduate programs is often coordinated

under the aegis of the graduate dean while undergraduate programs are reviewed at the college or academic vice-presidential level, yet the two depend on the same staff and common resources at the department level. The degree to which programs and resources need to be integrated at the institutional level in the master plan, in priority setting that guides resource allocation, or in program planning and review or remain fragmented is a perplexing problem.

Fragmented planning is easier to accomplish and may meet some planning needs. As the pressure for a higher degree of integration of planning elements and among these different organizational units and resource segments increases, planning becomes more complex and needs careful consideration to assure that the varied planning activities are not counterproductive. The problems suggested by the degree of comprehensiveness and integration among the major planning elements and the differing organizational units and resources are the best argument for a carefully designed planning process and a major administrative assignment to coordinate them—particularly in a large institution.

Flexibility. The discussion of comprehensiveness, emphasis, and integration of planning suggests a concern for flexibility in the planning process or in its major elements. Most planning models suggest a highly *regularized* planning process that in practice often becomes rigid. Yet the need for flexibility has already been noted because many planning demands and issues are either unpredictable and/or beyond the institution's control (for example, the first Arab oil crisis with its energy costs, facilities and scheduling implications). Planning cycles should also allow some flexibility for delays, unforeseen problems, and changing planning emphases. However, it is also important to note the value of deadlines and the need to have planning lead to progress and not just activity. Finally, the desirability of flexibility probably varies among planning elements— clearly, it is less feasible and the negative consequences of too much flexibility may be greater in the resource allocation process than in program evaluation or master planning.

Organizational Penetration. Because there is a tendency to think of planning at an institutional level, it is important to think of it in terms of its level of organizational penetration.

Is planning merely an activity engaged in by executive officers, or does it permeate the school and college or even the department? Are the impacts of planning decisions communicated and felt only at the highest level or does it lead to changes further down the organizational chart? If planning is to make a difference, it should be accepted beyond the upper administrative echelons and major planning priorities and policies should be consistently implemented wherever they reasonably apply.

Analytical Sophistication. The initial definition of planning assumed analysis of planning issues and problems was a part of the process. With increased pressures for accountability and effective use of scarce resources, all institutional planning decisions need justification. To some extent, the planning process and its elements are viewed as more sophisticated if they are based on a reliable and comprehensive data base, use modern research and analysis techniques, and can produce complex planning studies. This conception leads to the overdrawn implication that computer-based, retrievable information systems and on-line analytical models are synonymous with analytical sophistication. However, information can be overused; computers can be leased; and analytical models can be inappropriate or misinterpreted. Although analytical sophistication is desirable, it should be judged on *adequacy* of information provided, *appropriateness* of the analyses, and *efficient and timely* preparation—not the systems, models, and machines from which it emanated. Unfortunately, analytical sophistication still implies a good institutional data base, persons skilled in research and analysis, and knowledge of relevant extrainstitutional data and techniques used elsewhere—all expensive technical adjuncts to planning. Fortunately, services and models to increase analytical sophistication are becoming more readily available and less expensive for smaller institutions and are no longer just the province of large or wealthy ones.

Structure of a Planning Group. Probably no concept receives greater attention than this one. Four dimensions always seem to emerge as significant: *selection* (How were they selected and by whom? Was the selection process legitimate in light of institutional traditions?), *composition* (What was the basis of expertise and representation for the members? Is there a good mix of

planning and administrative expertise and of functional, affected, or interested parties, as institutional representation patterns would suggest, or a reason for deviating?), *permanence* (Is the planning group intended to have continuity? If so, is that provided for in the selection process?), and *responsibility* (Is it clear that this planning group knows its function as planners and its specific institutional charge?). Clearly, the appropriate structure will vary by institution and may also vary by the major planning element involved. The crucial variables are competence for the task and legitimacy in the wider institution.

Theoretical Models and Approaches to Planning

To be successful, planning must accommodate to the traditions, governance and administrative style, and problems facing the particular institution. If the planning process fits these broader institutional patterns, it is more likely to be legitimately accepted and integrated into the institution. If it contrasts significantly, resistance to or an isolated or ineffectual planning process is likely to result. It is also possible to design a planning process that differs from traditional modes of governance as a mechanism for changing them. However, that introduces two challenges: changing governance *and* the development of an effective planning process. Although there is neither a proven best model of planning nor a pure model, following are six quasi models or approaches to planning that have been identified in the literature. Each is described briefly using the concepts describing the domain and process characteristics identified in the previous section and includes a commentary on the most appropriate institutional settings or conditions (see Table 2).

Formal-Rational Model. A rational view of the planning process is the most complete and widely recognized model of planning in higher education and in other types of organizations. It overlaps considerably with the organizational development and technocratic/empirical models and is the easiest to describe. The basic paradigm, developed in the 1950s (Taylor, 1976), assume a rational, comprehensive sequence of planning elements and includes formulation of institutional mission based on a

Table 2. Theoretical Planning Models and Primary Dimensions: Institutional Rationale for Planning Models

Model	Planning Domain					Planning Process	
	Basic Institutional Planning Unit	Planning Orientation	Future Orientation	Institutional Purpose/Function	Planning Typologies	Planning Dynamics	Bases for Participation
Formal—Rational	Formal offices, processes and structures	Internal, external, or both	Most likely; probable	Adaptation—goal and mission definition and change; managerial—goal achievement	Substantive and procedural; strategic and tactical	Goal-centered; problem solving; rational analysis	Planning process expertise; functional or rational representation
Organizational Development	Natural groups; needs, abilities, attitudes, and activity patterns	Internal	Achieve members' capability	Maintenance—growth and development	Procedural and tactical	Consensus centered; collaborative interaction; learning and problem solving	O.D. expertise; egalitarian community or natural democracy
Technocratic/Empirical	Quantifiable; clients, members and resources; tasks, functions and outcomes	Internal	Improve current condition	Managerial—improved efficiency and effectiveness	Procedural and tactical	Goal centered; problem solving; rational analysis	Planning technology expertise; technical or administrative oligarchy
Philosophical Synthesis	Member attitudes, opinions, and values; belief systems	Internal	Ideal state	Maintenance—strengthen resolve	Substantive	Consensus oriented; reasoned discussion, debate and persuasion; logic	Intellectual expertise; elite community or oligarchy
Political Advocacy	Interest groups and issues	Internal, external, or both	Feasible state	Boundary—deal with conflicts; Adaptive—accommocate new pressures	Policy and contingency	Priority oriented or pluralistic; bargaining, negotiation, coalition formation; advocacy and analysis	Interest group leadership or political organizing expertise; interest-group representation
Coordinated Anarchy	Autonomous units, groups or individuals	Internal	Achieve autonomous capability	Can vary by unit	Varies by unit	Pluralistic; loosely coordinated; varied analysis	Expertise in units' activity minimal representation by unit

situational appraisal, development of goals and objectives, establishment of broad program and resource strategies, selection and design of action programs, implementation, and review. The intent is a completed cycle of activities that then acts to become self-assessing and self-correcting. The process is based on a rational assumption that mission and objectives can be clearly formulated and will guide the other cyclic activities. In effect, because subsequent cycle iterations do not begin in the same initial state, the process is a spiral rather than a repetitive cycle.

Figures 2 and 3 suggest two alternative views of the rational planning process in higher education today. Both highlight the major planning process elements an institution may engage in and in which major planning decisions are made: strategic or master planning (including institutional values, and environmental assessment), priority setting and resource allocation, program planning, implementation, and program evaluation. Both suggest the influence of the larger institution's values, governance patterns, and administrative style. However, Figure 2 views planning as a closed cycle (or spiral) of activities. Strategic planning activities are differentiated from but seen as linked to tactical planning and implementation. The cycle of elements is comprehensive, but it highlights the fact that planning may occur for differing types of institutional programs or functions (academic, research, service and support) or organizational units and may include various types of resources (fiscal—both operating and capital—human, physical, and information processing).

Figure 3 views the planning process from a different perspective (Dror, 1963; Poulton, 1979). Initiating conditions are seen as key forces in establishing expectations for planning. The major planning elements are seen as ongoing but parallel rather than linked in a regular cycle. Each planning element may have its own planning organization of roles, functions, and participants, which may be similar or different and may change over time. The outcomes of planning are seen as changes in four broad areas: decision making and organizational processes; organizational purposes, structure, or programs; expectations for the planning effort; and the institution's administrative style. Figure 3 views planning as an

emergent phenomenon and reflects the reality that planning may not be comprehensive, that is, the major planning elements may not be fully developed, closely integrated, or even equally emphasized to have effective institutional planning.

In applying either view of this rational paradigm, administrators and planners often attempt to prescribe the detailed activities within each element, assign responsibilities for them and formally adopt the process. Not only is the planning process formal and rational, but there is a tendency to view the college or university as that set of formally defined offices, processes, and structures for which or to which the planning process is applied (that is, a college has a formal mission and goal statement developed, has resources allocated and programs implemented in accordance with the plan, and is reviewed and evaluated on the basis of the performance compared to the plan). This process can be applied at the unit level (a department), to an office (the dean), or to an institutional process (admissions). The similarity to program, planning, and budgeting (PPB) and formal management by objectives (MBO) systems, which are central to many institutional planning efforts, is obvious.

The planning orientation can be either internal to the institution's needs and problems or external to the changes or pressures of the environment. The primary purpose of planning can vary, depending on its orientation—an external orientation may lead to an adaptive role by revising or redefining institutional mission and goals or an internal focus will likely lead to a managerial role by seeking to improve goal achievement (efficiency or effectiveness) or programs and processes. This planning model relies on both substantive or strategic and procedural or tactical planning typologies. Because of its rational orientation, the planning focus will probably tend to be on a most likely or probable institutional future state.

The dynamics of formal-rational planning tend to be goal centered—seeking a formal goal or clear set of priorities that will guide other behavior. Decision-making reflects a problem-solving mode because each planning element has its own problem focus (define mission, set goals, and so forth), and rational, analytical techniques (including behavioral and soft data) can be utilized. Because of the

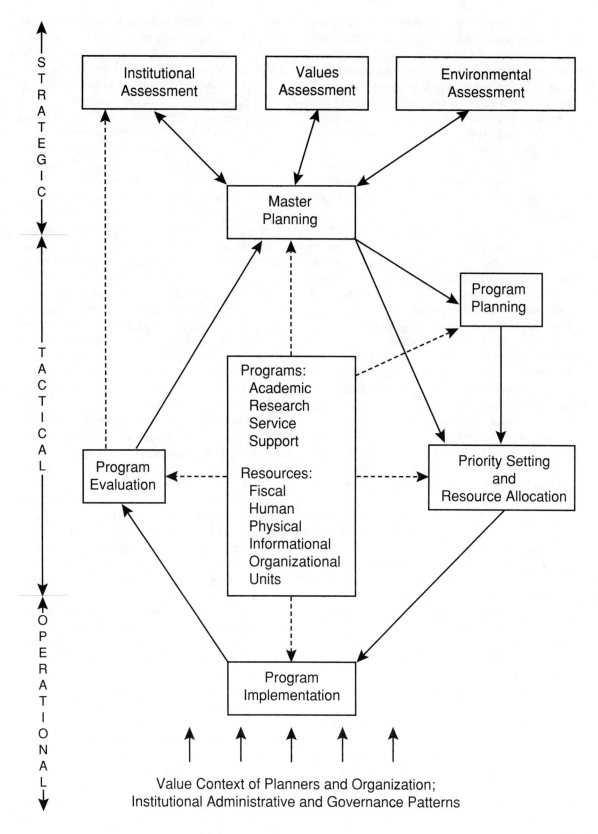

Figure 2. The Rational Planning Cycle

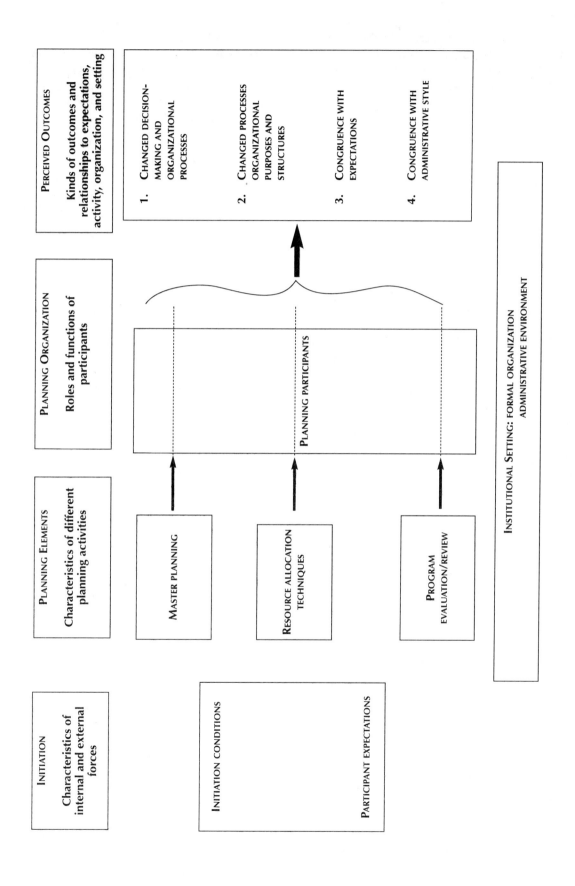

degree of formalization of the planning process, a high degree of expertise in the process and in analysis is typically valued. The process is applied to formal units of the institution, so functional or administrative representation is likely to be the most valued.

The advantage of this formal-rational model is the high visibility, clarity, and continuity it gives to the planning process. Because it is formalized and focused on formal units, it should not be as subject to whims of personality or internal political squabbles. Its comprehensive set of activities suggests it should be linked to implementation. On the assumption it includes a formal planning staff, there should be expertise for analytical and process skills required for effective planning.

The disadvantages flow from the fact that the processes and governance mechanisms in most colleges and universities are often not as rational as the model presumes. Because each element in the rational cycle can be extensive, the fiscal and human resources required for the planning process are often high—particularly in smaller colleges that lack the resources. The planning elements themselves have different life cycles (budget-annual, reviews-five years, and so forth) and are difficult to coordinate. The added complexity of trying to operate this cycle at several institutional levels at once can become unmanageable. Because of the formalization and rationality, there may be a danger of developing a staff of planners isolated from the real activities of the institution. Finally, there is substantial concern that this highly rational model fosters only incremental, and seldom fundamental, changes and that it may not be responsive enough to meet immediate pressures or entrepreneurial opportunities.

Organizational Development (O.D.) Model. The O.D. model of planning or planned change has its roots in the human relations tradition. It begins with a rational paradigm of the planning process similar to the formal-rational model (that is, the stages or activities are diagnosis, action planning, implementation, and evaluation). However, this model is far less concerned about the formality of the planning process itself and begins with a very different basic assumption about the makeup of the institution for which planning is done. It begins with a focus on the organization as composed of individuals or natural human groups whose needs,

abilities, attitudes, and activities make up the social, cultural, and activity patterns of the institution rather than on formal structures and processes. In this model, planning is concerned with innovation and change conducted in an experimental (trial and evaluation) mode. Targets for change are the organization's culture, management style, work structure, decision-making patterns, communication, interaction, and influence. The major planning issue is to understand the institution or group as a human system and to develop its capacity to plan as a means of improving individual, collective, and organizational well-being. Planning (as well as other human organization dynamics) is viewed as a process of learning for all members of the institution (Bennis and others, 1976; Michael, 1973).

Although some organizational development experts have emphasized the role of the extrainstitutional environment (Lawrence and Lorsch, 1969), the primary emphasis of this approach to planning is internal—focusing on the members themselves. There is a strong emphasis on internal institutional change in this approach to planning, but the primary emphasis is on the human maintenance function—improving the performance of and growth and development opportunities for individuals and groups in the organization. The offshoot may be adaptive changes in institutional mission or managerial improvement of the institution or its programs. Because of the nature of the basic unit and internal planning orientation, this type of planning tends to be more procedural and tactical (changing organization culture, processes, and so forth) than substantive or strategic; and the nature of the institutional future planned for is one that seeks to maximize member capabilities.

The dynamics emphasized in an O.D. approach are usually consensus centered—seeking change goals most members will endorse. Decision-making emphasizes collaboration, frequent and open interaction around issues and problems, and learning about the issues, the alternatives, and means of analysis. Analysis usually emphasizes rational, problem-solving approaches to achieving consensus, assessing alternatives, and evaluating performance.

The significant advantage of the O.D. approach to planning is the emphasis on change and the strong motivating force it may unleash in individuals if done effectively. Like the rational approach, it is visible, may include a comprehensive set of planning elements, and attempts to link planning to implementation.

The disadvantages of this approach are the tendency to rely on outside, respected change agents to initiate the process, a difficult role for a planning officer to perform. The often-internal orientation is also a significant weakness today, although an external perspective can be built in. Critics point out that in large institutions, those where planning requires autonomous or even antagonistic groups to deal with each other or where resources are shrinking, such collaborative, consensus-oriented planning is idealistic or naive. Another concern is the time-consuming nature of the O.D. approach and the uncertainty about whether realistic goals (given external pressures) will emerge.

Technocratic/Empirical Model. Unlike the first two models, the technocratic/empirical model emphasizes planning techniques and is not in a pure sense a process model. However, because of the recent emphasis on planning techniques, it is a useful pseudomodel to consider. It tends to rely on rational process notions (usually systems analysis), but the techniques generally deal with only limited segments of the planning process (for example, Delphi techniques for goal setting or forecasting for resource flows). However, there are planning techniques that attempt to serve all the elements in a comprehensive planning process. One example is the NCHEMS attempt to develop a comprehensive, consistently defined, and integrated management information system that can be aggregated at various levels, arrayed around differing program and outcome structures, and used for analytical techniques and models on specific planning problems. Implicit in the rational PPB process (Schick, 1968) is a set of systems analysis techniques that deal with overall planning, alternative program assessment (and evaluations of selected ones), and budgeting or resource algorithms.

What is important about this quasi model, however, is not its coherence or its comprehensive or segmented character but the fact that it reflects a planning approach that began in the late 1960s, continues today, and emphasizes empirical techniques. Implicit in this approach is the assumption that the basic units of a college or university are quantifiable, measurable

resources (the number of important characteristics of fiscal, physical, and human resources) that can be traced through a clearly defined, functionally linked set of tasks, activities, programs, functions, and outcomes. These constitute the basic structure on which empirical techniques can be rationally applied at various stages in the planning process.

Such planning techniques can be either internally or externally oriented. Environmental scanning, trend analysis, forecasting, simulation modeling, market research, consumer or institutional needs assessment, scenario development, Delphi, budget analysis, cost-benefit techniques, evaluation models, and myriad data collection, analysis, and statistical techniques are but a few of the arsenal of techniques. The 1960s focus was on techniques that dealt with internal planning and served a managerial purpose—planning activities aimed at improving efficiency and effectiveness. The type of planning emphasized was more procedural or tactical than strategic, and the future concern was with improving the current condition of the institution. However, more recent large-scale, state-level data bases, awareness of data on environmental trends, market assessment techniques, and such have focused more externally and potentially play an adaptive function—assessing the appropriateness of mission and goals, a strategic planning concern.

Because the technocratic/empirical approach tends to adopt a rational process model of planning and a formal hierarchical view of an institution (for example, the NCHEMS program structure), it adopts rational dynamics and tends to be goal centered or concerned with more formalized priorities. The approach to decision making reflects a problem-solving mode that emphasizes rational analysis of the problems and alternatives. The planner in this approach is assumed to have expertise in the underlying techniques of computer and information systems and research skills. Participation is more likely to be limited to technical planning staff, heads of analytical units (budget, information systems, institutional research, and so forth), and administrative staff with analytical skills.

The advantages of this approach are its greater emphasis on precision and analysis, on the preparation of more quantifiable and rational justifications for plans, and on conveying an image of sophisticated planning and greater accountability. The development of complex analytical techniques (such as resource simulation models) has also provided administrators and planners with greater understanding of the institution.

The disadvantages are often the inability of planners with this emphasis to deal with the many nonrational dimensions of planning (the value-laden choices or the unresolvable conflicts, for instance) and such staff planners' isolation from administrative and governance channels, which renders their work less useful. The fragmented nature of many planning techniques and the tendency to expect too much from an empirical technique often deters the development of a more comprehensive planning process (for example, resource simulations do not set the priorities or make the decisions about where to reduce resources). Finally, the expense of sophisticated information systems, computer facilities, and analytical staff often may not be justified in smaller colleges or in larger institutions where less-sophisticated techniques might suffice.

Philosophical Synthesis. Like the technocratic/empirical model, this is not a well-developed process model of planning. This approach is grand in scope and draws on many disciplines and fields of endeavor. As a planning process, this mode asks fundamental questions about the current and future nature of society, humankind, teaching and learning, and knowledge. The planning concern is to probe beneath these fundamental questions to more basic trends or assumptions about where our political, social, ethical, economic, and educational environments are going and to develop a rationale (a mission) for the institution that guides our institutional decisions and programs. In the 1960s, new institutions founded on the ecology movement (University of Wisconsin-Green Bay and Evergreen State College), with a new educational rationale (University of California-Santa Cruz or Hampshire College), with a new delivery system (Empire State College), and others reflect such a philosophical synthesis in their planning. Existing institutions engage in such planning in debates over general education (Harvard University) or the role of career and occupational versus liberal education. Despite its presence, this process is often not conceived of as planning be-

cause these discussions do not occur regularly and their linkage to tactical planning, implementation, or review is unclear at best. However, because this approach is useful in thinking through some of our most complex academic and educational mission issues, it needs to be better understood and refined as an approach to planning.

This approach begins with the members of the institution as its basic planning units. However, unlike the O.D. approach, which focuses on their behavioral and psychological nature, this approach focuses on their intellectual and human traditions—seeking members' common values and belief systems on which to build. The planning debate may range over external and internal institutional patterns, but the common tendency is to seek an internal synthesis and rationale the faculty can support and believe reflects external realities. This approach to planning primarily serves a maintenance function; that is, it gives the faculty a more tangible sense of the rationale for their institution, their approach to the curriculum, their students, or their educational process. In a sense, it serves to focus superordinate goals that may motivate individual performances or collective action. Any adaptive, change-oriented, or managerial-oriented function of this approach is secondary. Despite the internal basis for its rationale, this approach deals with some of the most complex substantive and implicitly strategic planning issues. Because of the heavy emphasis on internal development of a rationale, the concern for the institution's future may often seem to be seeking a utopian or ideal state rather than a feasible or realistic one.

The dynamics of planning are consensus oriented in seeking a common mission and rationale; however, intellectual debates can be heated and divisive if norms of professional behavior do not prevail. The decision dynamics tend to reasoned discussion, debate, and persuasion. Although the complex issues and varied backgrounds of participants allow for varied types of analysis, the stress is on logical argumentation first and analysis second (indeed, formalized analysis of issues that could be part of such debates is often missing). The planner's expertise in this mode is his or her own intellectual expertise—a respected reputation in a field or discipline and ability to deal logically with philosophical debate. The basis for participation is at once broad or narrow, depending on the restrictive or inclusive norms of the institution. It could vary from an oligarchy of respected faculty (and administrators), to an elite community of faculty, to a community of learners.

The advantages of this approach are unclear. The process is often observed in visible and occasionally prestigious institutions with a strong central mission. When it works, it often engenders wide involvement in basic questions of institutional mission. The disadvantages are that it is an intensive, time-consuming (critics would even say inefficient) process that seldom yields fundamental change and is not a comprehensive and well-integrated process. Yet, given our concerns about the need for a strong sense of purpose in many of our institutions, we might learn more about how to utilize this process more efficiently, to integrate appropriate analytical techniques, and to link it to more tactical planning concerns.

Political Advocacy. Like a technical/empirical and philosophical synthesis, this approach is not a well-developed planning model, but it seems to have a somewhat clearer process notion of how major issues are determined in colleges and universities. The notion of process suggests five stages (Baldridge, 1971): (1) social context analysis, in which the problem or issue emerges and the various interest groups concerned with it are identified; (2) interest articulation, in which interest groups develop their positions on the issue and attempt to influence others; (3) policy formulation, in which policy positions are developed, analyzed, and reacted to by the interest groups; (4) legislative transformation, in which a policy is formally enacted or endorsed by a legitimate planning or governance group; and (5) enactment, in which the regulations and guidelines for administrators who enforce and operating units who follow the policy are prepared. Unlike the rational and O.D. models, this one downplays mission and goals and accentuates policy issues as the focal point for planning. Many have suggested institutional master plans are often a compromise set of policy positions developed by such a process rather than a rationally conceived set of missions and goal statements. The major difference is that this approach assumes the basic organizing units of colleges and universities are interest groups and issues the institution

must confront and that, whether desirable or not, all planning and decision making needs to begin with this assumption.

Given the basic assumption, planning can be either internally or externally oriented. It will vary by the issue, the internal or external position of the interest group (for example, legislative fiscal agency and institutional groups), and the internal or external concerns of on-campus interest groups. To a greater extent than the other approaches, this model is capable of dealing with boundary conflicts between the institution and its external pressure groups. It can also serve an adaptive role in redirecting the institution as new policies lead to an accommodation with internal and external issues or pressures. This type of planning implicitly focuses on policy issues—these may be either strategic and substantive or tactical and procedural and are not necessarily related. Indeed, the major concern of a planner utilizing this approach is to forge policies that are not mutually inconsistent and that represent a viable picture of the institution's mission and direction. Because the approach is pragmatic, the concern is to develop an institutional future that is a feasible state amidst the varying issues and pressure groups.

Because the political approach focuses on policy, the strategic direction is more likely to be pluralistic, attempting to accommodate diverse missions and goals. At best in a carefully controlled legislative transformation or policy enactment process, one would expect a priority-centered planning process. The decision dynamics in the planning process accentuate bargaining, negotiation, compromise, coalition formation, and the like—rationally oriented problem solving or consensus occurs only when it occurs naturally. This mode encourages advocacy analysis; either analyzing the issue from the perspectives of the interest groups or letting them do their own. This does not mean rational, empirical techniques will not be used but recognizes that even those may lead to the defense of different positions, depending on the nature of the data, the technique used, and the criteria of choice applied.

Planning expertise in interest-group dynamics, political organizing, and policy analysis is more important than in the other models. The basis for representation stressed most often reflects either all the interest groups or at least those with power to influence the policy decision or block its implementation.

The advantages of this process are the practical reality that many institutions seem to operate this way and that, in a period of declining resources, attempts to redirect or reduce them will be focused around explicit and difficult policy choices on which intense interest groups will emerge and need to be dealt with. Given the more stabilizing tendency and function often encountered by the other approaches, the encouragement of conflict and the focus on real issues around which policy choices need to be made may induce more change than the others. The critics, of course, point out that the sense of direction may be lost if issues and policies are dealt with piecemeal. Other disadvantages are potential dominance of large or powerful interest groups, who may advocate policies not in the long-term best interest of the institution. The lack of a clear link to implementation and evaluation processes to assure that plans become reality is a concern. Perhaps the greatest disadvantage is the complex problem the planner or chief administrator has in coalescing a sense of direction while designing a policy-legislating process that is legitimate and prevents abuses, being aware of the differing interests and dynamics on different issues, and knowing which issues are ready for policy formulation.

The political advocacy model, like the philosophical synthesis, offers a pragmatic view of some of our most difficult planning issues. Many planners suggest an understanding of political dynamics is useful within a rational process model.

Coordinated Anarchy. This final planning model is probably the least discussed and hardest to describe. It is not based on a rational process, as were the first three; it lacks the consensus orientation of philosophical synthesis; and it does not have the basic sense of process and policy analysis represented in the political model. This model begins with the view that the basis for organizing a college or university is and should be productive but highly autonomous units (separate colleges and professional schools, departments, specialized research centers or institutes, administrative units, and such). This view of a university was emphasized by Kerr (1963), and its dynamics

were described as a process of organized anarchy by Cohen and March (1974). The underlying assumption is that professionals in these autonomous units are best able to foster progress in their area, that spontaneity should be encouraged, and that constraints should be limited. In such a setting, planning is only a loosely coordinated process. The sense of direction is both prospective and retrospective: Areas making great strides, in a burst of spontaneity (biomedicine), or likely to be in great demand (energy-related research or career-oriented fields) will shape priorities for development and receive increased resources; areas that have outlived their usefulness will be reduced; and areas that are valued or unique but currently out of vogue (humanities or Chinese studies five years ago) will be protected. Institutional planning is a continuous attempt to assess where each autonomous unit and its environmental forces are tending, to reformulate that sense of movement or goals within some broader philosophical synthesis of the institutional mission, and to reflect it in the allocation priorities. Planning could be encouraged and facilitated in each unit.

Clearly, the institutional planning orientation in this model depends on the autonomous units. Each unit may vary in its own orientation but is presumed to be both internal and external. The function of planning is an adaptive, change-oriented mode. Yet because the coordination of planning and any centralized sense of direction is limited, the actual function will vary widely, depending on each unit's planning success. Institutional-level planning will generally be limited to substantive issues or strategic planning with less procedural or tactical emphasis. However, it can vary widely in each unit. The nature of the institutional future is conceived as a flexible one as the autonomous units are encouraged to achieve their maximum capability.

Clearly, this planning model is pluralistic, attempting to accommodate and foster diverse goals. Planning decisions among and between units are closely coordinated only where there are strong interdependent relationships or shared resources among units. A varied array of analytical planning techniques could be used by each unit; but at the central institutional level, they would focus most on assessing external trends and monitoring unit progress and resource needs. This mode suggests the need for planners who are knowledgeable about each unit's field or discipline. Representation on planning may vary, depending on each unit's approach, but, at the central level, suggests representation from the units by the key unit administrator or planner and by highly respected academics.

The advantages of this model are the strong emphasis on spontaneity (often criticized in the other models), the incentive for each unit to do its own planning and development, and the argument that units that relate to different, rapidly changing environments (such as law and medicine) are in the best position to respond to them. Some suggest this model is only applicable in large, complex universities or those segments of a university that are nearly self-supporting.

The disadvantages include the suggestion that this model presumes slack or fluid resources, that many units are not in fact autonomous but merely seemed to be during an era of expansion, and that reduced resources increase the interdependence among units. Because this model suggests a pluralistic and loosely coordinated institutional planning process that depends on each unit, there is concern the institution may respond too slowly to declining units, which then drain resources from other stronger and more viable ones, or it may not have developed the capacity to deal with major resource and enrollment reductions.

Radical and Anti-Planning: A Commentary. Colleges and universities have always harbored severe critics of rational planning. President Enarson (1975) of Ohio State defends "intuitive" planning, and Lindblom (1959) suggests we really just "muddle through." However, three of the models described (philosophical synthesis, political advocacy, and coordinated anarchy) incorporate some of the concerns of radical planners who have difficulty accepting the more objective, mission- and goal-directed, and formalized process notions reflected in the first three models (formal-rational, organizational development, and technocratic/empirical). The three more radical planning models also reflect, in different ways, the failure of the rationalists to deal with the intellectual nature of higher education (philosophical synthesis), the reality of interest groups and conflict (political advocacy), and

the lack of spontaneity and freedom (coordinated anarchy). The concerns of the antiplanners, those who reject all notions of planning, are not dealt with.

It is important to recognize that in any institutional planning process, a dominant model or approach will probably emerge. It will, no doubt, not be a pure model but rather some combination. This dominant model stands a better chance of success if it takes as its basic planning focus an organizing assumption that reflects the basic tradition of the institution; if the planning orientation, purpose, and content reflect the real planning issues facing the institution; and if the dynamics of planning and participation reflect the governance process and administrative style of the institution. Within the planning process and its elements, variations in approach will occur. Such variation is natural if the planning process is to accommodate to different planning issues and contexts and will likely be tolerated if that rationale is understood and communicated.

Two observations are helpful in organizing the remainder of this chapter. First, despite this discussion and identification of six models or approaches to planning, it is apparent that a rational process notion pervades three of them (the formal-rational, organizational development, and technocratic/empirical approaches). Several recent widely publicized models of comprehensive planning for higher education are compatible with this rational process paradigm (see Casasco, 1970; Fuller, 1976; Parekh, 1975; Sturner, 1974; and those developed by Academy for Educational Development (AED), NCHEMS, American Association of State Colleges and Universities (AASCU), Council for Advancement of Small Colleges (CASC), and other professional associations and consulting or development organizations). The PPB, MBO, Management Information Systems (MIS), and other decision-making and analytical approaches tend to assume the paradigm. Second, the distinction of strategic planning that focuses on an institution's relationship with its large environment and tactical planning that focuses on more internal planning issues is conceptually useful in thinking about two levels of planning.

Therefore, the next two sections of this chapter and Parts Two through Five of the book are organized around the planning elements identified at the strategic and tactical level in the formal-rational model (Figure 2). This organization is to enable a logical order of examination of the different levels and elements of planning, their purposes or functions, and some of the issues in trying to relate them to each other. The intent is not to suggest the formal-rational process is either the most effective or even the best picture of reality. Indeed, as will be suggested later, the overall planning process and that within each element probably will and should depend upon institutional traditions and governance patterns and the nature of the planning problems being dealt with.

Strategic Planning

Although planning serves many functions, the primary purpose of strategic planning is to foster institutional adaptation by assuring congruence between an institution and its relevant and often changing environment, by developing a viable design for the future of the institution, by modifying it as needed, and by devising strategies that facilitate its accomplishment. Strategic and master planning are often considered synonymous; however, they usually encompass four broad elements:

1. environment assessment or scanning (to identify trends or potential changes in the environment and their implications for the institution)

2. institutional assessment (to clarify strengths, weaknesses, problems, and capabilities of the institution)

3. values assessment (to consider values, aspirations, and ideals of various constituencies and responsibilities of the institution to them and the larger public)

4. master plan creation (to devise a strategic pattern, design, or direction for the institution on the basis of the first three elements)

Strategic planning then seeks to establish the fundamental assumptions about the environment, the institution, and the future form of the institution. It involves policy decisions, which are the broadest and most encompassing decisions concerned with a college's or a university's long-term future. Those generally include major assumptions about the environ-

ment, its trends, and impacts on the institution; assumptions or conclusions about the institution's current strengths, weaknesses, and problems that need to be considered or addressed in the future; the philosophy and rationale for the institution; the proposed mission, role, and scope of the institution and its objectives and goals; the organizational, administrative, and governance structure for the institution; the major program (academic, research, service, and support) and resource (fiscal, physical, human, and information) strategies or policies to guide the fulfillment of the plan; and a tentative set of priorities. These decisions may or may not reside in a single master-planning document. Strategic planning then deals with the organization-environment interface and is intended to provide a framework within which tactical planning occurs. Before examining the elements of strategic planning, a brief discussion of that interface focus is in order.

The Organization/Environment Interface: Concepts and Alternative Approaches. Although strategic planning can be pursued without reference to the environment, one of its major contributions is to provide a framework within which the organization-environment interface can be examined. It assumes an institution's long-term viability depends on a planning process that produces and revises its strategic or master plan either in response to external pressures or to enhance its resources from and position in that environment. This assumption suggests some key concepts that define an institution's environment and help identify an institution's strategy for relating to it.

Because environments are complex, one usually attempts to "segment" them. One general approach (Cope, 1978) begins with a framework for segmenting the environment into four broad sectors or subenvironments, each with its own forecasting methodology. Those are social (including demography), political, economic, and technological environments. Cope proposes ways of incorporating these various forecasts into a force-field analysis and into master planning. A more institutionally specific approach (Peterson, 1977) to segmenting the environment is presented in Figure 4. It begins with the assumption that resource flows or linkages (financial, human, enrollments, program need/demand, policy or issue pressures, and external-governance

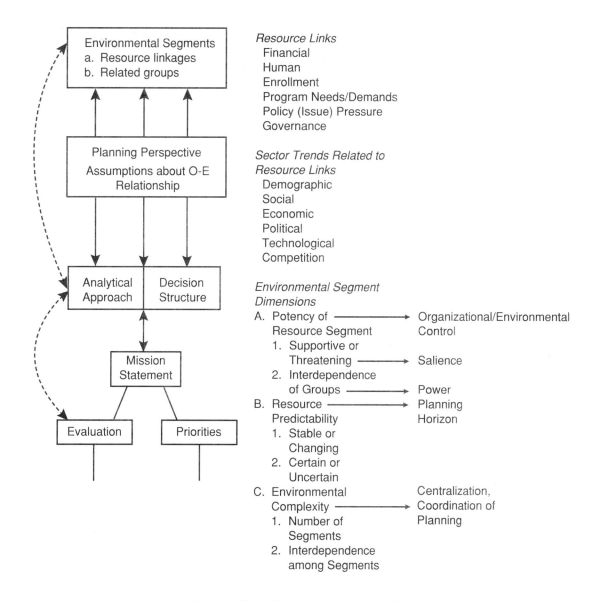

Figure 4. The College Environment Interface

groups) are the basis for segmenting the environment. Key groups related to or potentially affecting each resource link or sublink (for example, various types of operating revenue) are identified as a resource segment. Analysis of the groups forming each resource segment and of basic trends in environmental sectors (for instance, Cope's social, economic, political, technological, plus demographic and competition trends) that might affect resource flows is the focus of this approach. The resource segment view suggests some important concepts on which they can be examined. These concepts further suggest seven strategies or approaches for relating to the environment.

Each resource segment can be distinguished by the *independence* or *interdependence* of the groups that are part of it. Similarly, the groups in the segment can be viewed as basically *supportive* of or *threatening* to the institution. Figure 5 suggests the importance of these two dimensions. As the groups in a segment become increasingly interdependent, they are likely to have more *power* or *potency*. As they become more antagonistic or threatening, they are likely to use that power to *control* the flow of resources. When the external segment's power is low and the institution controls the resource flow, planning can probably focus on the internal or tactical planning issues; how-

Environmental Segment Is

	Supportive	Threatening
Independent	*Low Potency:* Organization controls resource flow	
Interdependent		*High Potency:* Environmental segment controls resource flow

Groups in Environmental Segment Are (Independent / Interdependent)

Figure 5. Potency of Environmental Resource Segment

ever, under reverse conditions, greater attention has to be given to externally oriented or strategic planning. This dimension of *potency* of the segment and organizational or environmental *focus of control* of the resource flow is helpful in defining an environmental strategy.

Each resource segment can also be characterized by the *degree of change* and *certainty* of its resource flow (or in the underlying sector trends that affect it). Figure 6 suggests that as the segment's resource flow is more changing and uncertain, its *predictability* decreases. This makes long-term planning more difficult. The assessment of the predictability of resource flows also affects the appropriate planning strategy.

Figure 7 identifies seven strategies or approaches an institution may adopt in relating to an environmental segment and suggests how these are related to the degree of resource *predictability* and organization versus environmental *locus of control* over the resource flow. Each approach reflects different assumptions about the resource segment's predictability and its locus of control of the resource flow. In turn, each approach suggests different patterns in the institution's primary *decision motive and process,* the *analytical technique* most closely associated with the approach, and the *benefits* of this approach. Table 3 summarizes each of the approaches. (For a detailed discussion, see Peterson, 1977.)

Amount of Resource Flow Is

	Stable	Changing
Certain	*Highly Predictable:* Long-term planning feasible	
Uncertain		*Highly Unpredictable:* Short-term planning feasible

Direction of Resource Flow Is (Certain / Uncertain)

Figure 6. The Predictability of the Environmental Resource Flow

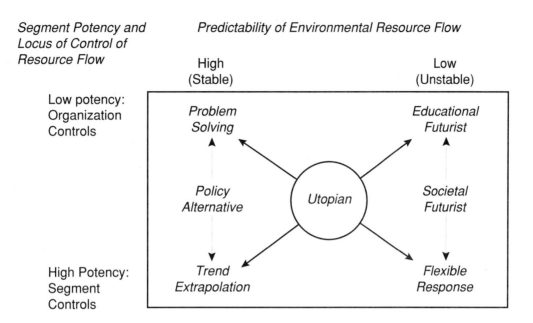

Figure 7. Organizational Planning Approaches for Different Environments

These approaches to organization-environment relations are of necessity oversimplified and seldom exist in pure form. The environments of higher educational institutions are often extremely complex and suggest conflicts. For example, as resource-related segments increase in number and flow in varying patterns to different units, decentralized planning by units in the institution who understand the resource flow is appropriate. Yet as those resource segments become more interdependent (when one increases, another decreases or one is competed for by several units), more centralized or coordinated planning becomes necessary and extremely complex. Further, there is the political reality that plans to deal with an environmental segment or group often create external reactions or changes in the environment. For example, planned staff reductions to offset enrollment declines may encourage union organizers to intervene, or plans by a public institution to raise private capital funds may deter approvals from the state.

These alternative approaches do, however, imply several things. First, higher education planners need to examine their most important resource links. This could result in a clearer definition of the relevant environment and their service region, in a better understanding of those resource flows in the future and their own assumptions about them, and in foresee-

ing critical resource issues and identifying alternatives for dealing with them. Second, the need for different approaches for different resource segments and the likelihood that several may be used simultaneously suggest the need for planning groups that can utilize a variety of decision processes, analytical approaches, and external as well as internal data sources. Third, because different organizational units may have somewhat different resource environments, there is a need to design the strategic planning function carefully—the process needs to look at the degree of centralization and/or coordination of planning decisions and the integration of analytical support for those decisions. Fourth, because externally oriented planning is complex and involves decisions based on external dynamics that many college and university personnel may not be aware of, there is a crucial need both to educate those in planning bodies about this external world and to communicate the nature of this planning activity to those whose resources, programs, and jobs may be affected by them.

Environment Assessment or Scanning. This element of strategic planning (see Chapters Nine through Twelve), often developed to a highly sophisticated degree in private industry, is one of the least developed in institutional-level planning, but it is receiving increased emphasis. To date, the emphasis has been primar-

Table 3.   Alternative Organization/Environment Planning Approaches

Planning Perspective	Environmental Assumption[a]	Locus of Organizational/ Environmental Control	Major Decision Issue (Motive)	Primary Decision Process[b]	Primary Analytical Approach[c]	Major Benefit or Value
1. Trend extrapolation	Predictable	Environmental	Prepare for impact of the trend (demand usually)	Rational	Forecasting	Consider long-term changes
2. Policy alternatives (organizational or environmental)	Predictable and clear choices	Organizational or environmental	Make or respond to choice (demand/ need)	Rational, value, or political	Forecasting and simulation	Forced to face likely choices
3. Societal futurists	Limited predictability; substantial differences likely	Environmental	Select likely future; decide educational meaning (role in society)	Inspired, rational, and value	Scenarios, Delphi	Consider new and radical possibilities
4. Educational futurists	Limited predictability; substantial differences likely	Either or technological	Decide likely future (prepare for radical change)	Inspired, rational, and value	Scenarios, Delphi	Consider new and radical possibilities
5. Utopian	Predictable (at least a segment)	Organizational	Commitment to ideal (perpetuate traditional, achieve ideal)	Value	—	Provides a vision to believe in
6. Problem-solving	Stable or very predictable	Organizational	Resolve internal weaknesses (improvement)	Rational	Organizational analysis	Forces internal assessment
7. Flexible, responsive	Very unpredictable	Environmental	Respond to shifts in demand (marketing or political survival)	Political	Market analysis, flexibility	Creates flexible and responsive organization

[a]Planning time perspective depends on time span over which environment is predictable and risk planner is willing to take in going beyond that time span.

[b]*Rational*—information-based decisions; expert or administrative judgment.
Value—value preference decisions; democratic or participatory process.
Political—influence-based decisions; partisan representative process.
Inspired—creative decisions; open solicitation of original or knowledgeable thinkers.

[c]Many techniques in these broad approaches.

ily on assessing demographic conditions and enrollment potentials, but it is expanding to other resource segments.

The primary purpose of environmental scanning and assessment for strategic planning is to identify opportunities in a college or university's environment that planners may choose to exploit or constraints they may choose to avoid or attempt to circumvent. They attempt to identify underlying sector trends or key characteristics in an institution's environmental segments, to forecast resource flows where possible, and to suggest their institutional implications.

Environmental scanning in higher education today is usually structured in one of three ways: an analytical activity of a staff or an institutionwide planning body of staff; an analytical assignment to a separate institutional research or other administrative group; or a planning group that adopts a less research-oriented focus but includes members knowledgeable about external environments. The strategies or approaches are essentially those discussed in the previous section. The focus is on trends in environmental sectors, on resource segments and flows, on market analysis of needs or demand, and on competitive conditions. The techniques are largely rational: trend analysis, forecasting, simulation modeling of institutional environments, marketing surveys, environmental needs assessment, Delphi and scenario building, and analysis of competitive conditions and even legal-political or governmental controls and constraints or mandates. The range of resources and environmental segments suggests an extensive array of external data sources (census, economic condition, public opinion surveys, or governmental regulations) and a wide array of techniques.

The intent of environmental assessment, however, is not to make plans or set goals but to provide a realistic picture of the external environment within which strategic planning takes place. At a minimum it allows one to question the underlying resource segment and environmental sector assumptions implicit in an institution's current direction or plan; it can suggest opportunities for and constraints to planning; and it might identify likely impacts of alternative future courses of action. The limits are the difficulties in clearly defining the environment and its segments, the lack of institu-

tional staff knowledgeable in this methodology (or who are too sophisticated), and an array of studies and analyses that are expensive or of little use if not clearly focused by good planning questions.

Institutional Assessment. The purpose of institutional assessment (see Chapter Twenty-One) in strategic planning is to obtain a rational picture of an institution's current functioning: What are the strengths and weaknesses of its various academic, research, service, and support functions; of its staff and other resources; of its programs; and of its patterns and processes of governance and administration? This picture is intended to ensure planning addresses major internal problems that need to be resolved, identifies priority areas for development (either to accentuate strengths or to strengthen weaknesses), and assesses the institution's capacity to move in new directions and/or to understand the institutional implications of their planning choices.

Most institutions practice institutional assessment, although it may not be comprehensive or related to planning. Institutional self-assessments have been popular for three decades in different forms. Accreditation constitutes a part of this picture. So do state higher education agencies, executive staff, and legislative groups through planning, budgetary, and review activity, which is extensive and increasing in many states (Folger, 1977). The accumulation of ongoing program reviews supplemented by ad hoc studies and evaluations and the review of institutional operating reports provides another form of institutional self-assessment. These diverse activities may provide a legitimate basis for ongoing institutional assessment but are often piecemeal or require extensive revision to get a useful self-assessment for planning. Most institutionwide strategic planning accepts and incorporates self-assessment, often to the detriment of externally oriented environmental assessment. It may be a carefully structured part of the strategic or master planning activity, a separate function of an institutional research or special study group, or an attempt to provide a broad array of data and reports to a widely representative planning group.

Perhaps more important than the purpose, patterns, and structure of this activity is the need to relate the design, strategy, and analytical techniques of institutional assessment to the needs of planning. First, good institutional evaluation needs to provide a picture of the major resources supplied to (inputs), the activity of (processes), and results (outcomes or impacts) of all major units or programs in an institution (Dressel, 1976). Increasingly sophisticated information and reporting systems make such data readily available (for example, NCHEMS data elements, program and outcomes structures, and reporting formats), which is useful for longitudinal examination of institutional conditions to see if they are improving or worsening and to make comparisons among and between similar units. The stress on common analytical techniques and recent work on information exchange procedures at NCHEMS (Peterson, 1976) make it feasible to have institutional assessment for internal and intrainstitutional comparisons. Second, the assessment of organizational processes, practiced for some time in government and industry, is getting increased emphasis in higher education as planners recognize the need to improve these dimensions of their institution. (Examples include the Educational Testing Service's *Institutional Functioning Inventory* and American Council on Education's recently acquired Higher Education Management Inventory survey.) There is also extensive emphasis on measuring qualitative as well as quantitative performance in assessing results (outcomes and impacts), productivity, or cost-benefit ratios compared to goals or performance standards. These require more sophisticated analyses and/or special studies but are particularly relevant to ongoing planning based on rational notions of goals and objectives. A third notion of institutional assessment is the extensive array of partial (student flow, faculty flow, and so on) or more comprehensive (RRPM, CAMPUS, TOTAL, and so on) resource models used to understand the functioning of the institution, to forecast the impacts of resource changes, or to assess the consequences of substantive (program) or procedural (administrative parameters) plans or changes. Finally, a more complex notion of institutional assessment is to examine its overall functional performance (*productive:* measure of performance of academic, research, and service functions; *human maintenance:* staff quality, morale, and such; *managerial:* efficient and effective use of processes and resources; *boundary:* effective resource acquisition and

product or institution image measure; and *adaptives:* capacity to change according to plan or appropriate circumstance).

Strong institutional assessment clearly serves to strengthen the institution's focus on real internal problems, capacities for responding to external conditions, and ability to make changes. It also serves as a basis for later evaluation and assessment of performance. However, the need for a large and/or expensive staff for and the time-consuming nature of elaborate institutional assessment studies must be balanced with the need for useful planning information.

Values Assessment. This element of strategic planning (see Chapters Seven through Nine) is frequently discussed, yet it is perhaps the least understood dimension. Educational institutions in their mission, purposes, and strategies either reflect implicitly or have made explicitly decisions about certain value choices. These constitute a rationale for the institution: a set of decisions about clientele, about institutional functions and responsibilities, and about commitments to society, to the clientele, to the educational process, and to institutional working relationships. Neither the nature of these commitments nor the process by which they were arrived at is clear in most institutional planning. The intent of values assessment, then, is to identify the basic value choices and their implications and to assist in developing a rationale for the institutional plan or planning process.

If it exists, value assessment is likely to be the result of a series of discussions by an institutionwide planning or governance body or an epilogue to the planning process. Some value assessment techniques are beginning to emerge. At the broadest level, societal values can be ascertained by reviewing studies of various sectors or writings of futurists and by using Delphi techniques with either the institutional planning group or a broader array of respondents (Wilson, 1974). On a more focused basis, interviews of key internal and external constituents can be useful in identifying members' perceptions of institutional roles and responsibilities. Analyses of charters, mission statements from higher governing boards, and governmental mandates are another source of these value insights. Another important approach involves surveying constituent groups. The key is to identify potential, as well as current, constituent groups and to develop a values instrument that reflects a particular institution's important value choice. (ETS' *Institutional Goals Inventory* has been used this way and a new scheme developed by the Resource Center for Planned Change at AASCU is another example.)

Raising value questions and obtaining some consensus or agreement that divergent values will be accommodated is acknowledged as important. Failure to do so may lead to future planning conflicts or to lower commitment to the process. Yet this activity is still embryonic and will probably continue to be dealt with through broad representation in planning, by planners' sensitivity to seeing that basic issues surface, and by extensive discussion and debate.

Master Plan Creation. "Master plan" (see Chapter Eight), a term often synonymous with institutionwide or strategic planning, may incorporate the three previous elements (environmental, institutional, and values assessment), draw on them from related administrative units, or utilize them more implicitly. Here it refers to the process that decides how the institutional planning process will function; incorporates environmental, institutional, and values assessment information into a set of planning choices (the seven strategic policy decisions) or plan for the institution; and gets that process and plan accepted and implemented.

How the institutional planning process will be designed is the subject of this entire chapter. However, the decision about how it will function is also crucial. If an ongoing and comprehensive institutionwide strategic or master planning process is selected, that decision will have crucial consequences for the direction of the institution, may affect the regular governance processes, and requires a substantial resource commitment. Decisions to launch strategic or master planning may be made by state or institutional governing boards or by institutional leaders. However, on the basis of institutional experience, it is clear that the design of the process (and its elements) needs careful consideration, review, and approval by internal as well as external governance bodies if it is to function effectively.

Institutional master planning will vary, depending on whether a more rational (or O.D. or technocratic/empirical) or less rational (philo-sophical synthesis, political advocacy, or controlled anarchy) process model is assumed. The more rational will tend to make greater use of top down, centralized, or highly coordinated and analytically oriented processes with more organized participation. Structures for master planning seem to fit the following modes:

1. the elected "blue ribbon" committee of highly respected institutional leaders (Princeton University initiated this pattern during a budget crisis and has continued it as an effective and legitimate group that revises priorities annually.)

2. the institutional "team leadership" approach with selected leaders of various major constituencies: (faculty senate, student government, executive officers, deans, and board members) (Wichita State University has launched such an approach with a grant from the Kellogg Foundation.)

3. the "administrative team" approach, in which the executive officers, perhaps with board members and an analytical support staff, take on the function as a part of their role (This is consistent with the MBO tradition and, its proponents claim, improves the integration of planning and implementation and clarifies responsibilities. Furman University and Colorado State University, among others, have adopted such an approach.)

4. the "line executive officer-planner" approach, in which a chief executive officer, perhaps with an advisory group of any of the previous types, assumes responsibility for strategic and tactical planning and may oversee the related analytical offices (These plans are usually presented to the key governing board for review and approval.)

5. the "subcommittee" approach, in which a subcommittee, usually with diverse membership of the board or an institutionwide governing body, is assigned the institutional planning task

6. the "combination" approach

Each of these patterns may reflect differences in institutional decision-making style and/or administrative style. They will vary in their reliance on analytical staff for institutional, environmental, and value assessment and for reviewing the implications of alternative goals and strategies. Their mode of selection, composition, permanence, and responsibility can also differ.

For an ongoing strategic master planning group to influence implementation, key responsibilities are to update the environmental trends and assumptions to keep the plan viable, to revise priorities and see that resource allocation decisions reflect them, to review institutional reports and program reviews to assess progress, and to see that the master plan is updated when needed and that the planning process functions in the best interests of the institution. Obtaining acceptance for the master plan suggests the need for a master planning group that is consistent with the tradition and governance structure of the institution, has some continuity of membership, has board representation, and is coordinated with the major institutional governance body.

The advantages associated with master planning are the insight gained from carefully examining the institutional, environmental, and values contexts of the institution; the sense of wholeness and completeness from a well-documented and organized master plan; and the sense of purpose from one that is legitimately endorsed and enforced. The disadvantages include the extremely difficult and complex nature of the task: conflicting trends; the difficulty of reaching agreement on goals, strategies, and priorities; and the often large numbers of individuals and groups involved. The process can be time-consuming, expensive, and lead to little specific action or change. Streamlining this process once it is in place and incorporating the concept of continuous updating and reranking are essential if it is to become a framework for tactical planning.

Tactical Planning

Tactical planning serves two primary functions: preserve the vitality of institutional units and assure the implementation and achievement of the master plan or some set of institutional priorities. The three planning elements I shall discuss, program planning, priority setting and resource allocation, and program review, have been treated extensively in the literature. As we become more concerned about faculty and administrative redirection and training, staff development is increasingly being considered a subelement of tactical planning, although I shall not discuss it here.

Program Planning. Program planning (academic, research, service, support, or administrative programs) is an element that can be independent of institutional planning and may be a separate process at the program level (see Chapters Thirteen through Sixteen; Heydinger, forthcoming). Our interest in program planning is primarily as an activity that links master planning and resource allocation. Its purpose is twofold: to develop programs that contribute to the accomplishment of institutional goals and that are themselves effective. The distinction between new and existing programs is useful.

The development of new programs when resources are limited and student and/or client demands are changing is a critical activity. The past practice of allowing programs to evolve from other ones, to depend on the interests of faculty entrepreneurs, or to utilize outside funds for development was often inadequate and unresponsive. In times of constraint, existing programs are conservative, individual faculty members find their normal work loads heavier and their access to funds more difficult, and external funds are limited. Consequently, some institutions are developing a more conscious new program development process that may occur at the central administrative, school, or department level. The general steps they encourage are clear: set institutional priorities for program development, provide incentive or developmental funds to underwrite developmental activity, establish a review process to identify the resource needs and other institutional impacts of the new program, select programs for further development, and provide assistance in clearing extrainstitutional program review and approval processes. The latter step can be especially critical for public institutions in states with new program approval procedures. This element should reflect institutional priorities, suggests the need for a clear process and analytical support, and involves the resource allocation process.

Planning for continuing programs is usually tied more closely to the actual budgetary process. However, attempts are made to develop program plans that go beyond the normal budget cycle and identify program goals and priorities for expansion or reduction with their resource implications. Program planning can adopt a more or less rational process, depending on the approach to planning, and can be done from the bottom up (programs prepare and submit their own goals and plans) or from the top down (they conform to prescribed priorities and guidelines). The former can inundate the planning process with inordinate and irreconcilable paperwork, and the latter is likely to produce resistance or stability rather than change. A major concern is to provide a framework of priorities for continuing program planning, to allow for and reward incentives aimed at new efforts, and to prepare enough background information on program operating data and performance efficiently to accomplish the data-generating aspect of program planning.

In planning for new and continuing programs, needs assessment techniques for current and potential clientele, market studies of supply and demand, and the increasing array of program planning and resource models are important analytical tools. Depending on one's approach to planning, the process may emphasize more or less rational processes and the structure to govern it may be dominated by administrators, faculty, or analytical staff. The key is to relate program planning, to the extent feasible, to institutional goals and program development priorities and to assure that the resource allocation process reflects them.

Priority Setting and Resource Allocation. These interrelated activities (see Chapters Seventeen through Twenty) are well developed in the literature, particularly resource allocation and budgeting (Caruthers and Orwig, 1979). In the past, they were often not integrated into the institutional planning process, leaving the actual resource allocation process unaffected by planning and reducing the chances of planning redirecting resources or having desired effects. The purpose of these two activities from a planning perspective is to translate plans into shorter-term (two- to three-year) program and resource priorities and to reflect those in the allocation process—providing, along with program planning, the primary linkage of strategic institutional planning to implementation.

The priority-setting activity in most institutions is either not present or very unclear (perhaps deliberately) and is probably the most controversial. Whether done explicitly as a master planning activity, separately, or implicitly in the budget process, priorities affect or reflect real resource distribution. Its importance is highlighted by the fact that experts disagree on the extent to which planning and budgeting can and should be integrated. Some argue the specific budget pressures and time constraints are incompatible with planning (Schmidtlein and Glenny, 1977), and others contend their separation is a major difficulty (Schick, 1966). Priorities are in the middle.

Priority setting, both for program development and planning and for other resources, is the key interface between planning and resource allocation. It also coincides with the primary interface between longer-term institutional goals and objectives and the current short-term resource constraints, opportunities, and ongoing commitments. Even when it is an explicit activity with rational intent, the process is going to involve nonrational and political dynamics. Priority setting can be the responsibility of an institutionwide planning group (Princeton has made this the primary focus of their planning group annually), a separate budget priorities body (the University of Michigan utilizes this approach), or a responsibility of the budgetary group. The exact locus and structure will probably reflect institutional traditions of planning and budgeting and of administrative or faculty involvement. If priority setting is to have a legitimate impact on budgeting and program development, the group responsible for it needs to be clearly identified and the process by which it occurs needs to be understood. The selection and composition of the group will depend on institutional governance patterns and on the planning model adopted. The authority of this group in relation to program development and budgeting also needs to be understood. Analytical support for assessing the short-term implications of external (for example, economic decline or inflation) and internal (for example, bargaining agreements) impacts on the institutional resource mix and the implications of differing priority choices is required. However, only if priority choices are made prior to specific annual program and resource distribution decisions is there certain to be movement toward institutional goals.

Budgeting, the most common form of resource allocation, is not inherently a planning process. Its primary function is to improve the efficient allocation of resources, often an implicit function of planning. Caruthers and Orwig (1979) discuss the varied purposes and I have already noted its linkage to priority setting and program development. However, it is important to recognize the increasingly wide array of budgeting approaches and their relation to planning (see Chapters Seventeen and Eighteen).

Program Review. Program review (academic, research, service, or administrative programs) has not been widely viewed as a planning element (see Chapters Twenty-Two through Twenty-Four). In the past, it has been associated with specialized accreditation and maintaining minimum quality or standards. More recent concerns that program demand/need is shifting, that across-the-board and other forms of non-program-based resource reductions have reached their limit, that program efficiency or effectiveness may be suffering under these shifts and declines, and that institutions cannot afford all their programs have led to a more visible, planning-oriented role for this activity. State-level program review is now extensive and may even mandate institutional program review activities (Barak and Berdahl, 1978). In a planning setting, program review has four purposes: to determine if program purposes and goals are appropriate in light of institutional objectives (or can be justified as unique); to assess the need and/or demand for a program and its resource requirements; to assess if the program is performing or accomplishing those purposes and goals and how it might improve; and to determine, in light of the program review and situation's program and resource priorities, whether the program should be expanded, continued, reduced, reorganized, or discontinued. Program review that reflects institutional priorities can become a mechanism for program redirection and resource reallocation (either by revising program resource needs or freeing resources through program closure). These planning purposes suggest a far more rigorous notion of program review. It can lead to summative judgments as well as review for minimum standards or formative recommendations for improvement.

Designing a program review system that is responsive to planning needs provides a means for program change, and supports resource reallocation faces several problems. Structurally, program review may be the province of an institutionwide group, of separate but coordinated review groups (graduate education, undergraduate, extension, or administrative area), of a specialized staff working for an institutionwide planning or governance body, or even of an externally mandated group (state higher education agency or legislative review group). Patterns of selection, composition, permanence, and responsibility vary and need to be clearly defined and understood. The problem in initial design of such groups is the threatening nature of planning-oriented reviews. Prior review practices by different groups and the special interests of various internal (faculty, deans, vice-presidents, or a specialized review staff) and external (accrediting or state board) groups have led to well-staked-out turfs, positions on program review, or fears of this new mode. Thus, it is crucial that program review be designed to build on existing practices where reasonable, develop a structure and a process that is carefully reviewed and approved, and have strong support for its purposes by governance bodies, administrative officers, and the institutionwide planning body.

Approaches to program review, like budgeting, are well documented elsewhere (Dressel, 1976; see also the Jossey-Bass New Directions for Program Evaluation Series). Approaches include input or efficiency models, objective versus goal attainment models, goal-free models, process-oriented models, comprehensive models, and adversarial models (see Craven, 1980). All generally assume a similar set of stages in conducting an evaluation that usually includes a definitional phase for determining issues, participants, purposes, and processes; a data collection and information analysis phase; an interpretation and reporting phase; and a judgment and evaluation phase. These variations suggest the need for a program review group that is not only aware of its planning role but sensitive to issues in designing an evaluation process.

Other major issues in designing a program review process often occur around the following: Are program reviews cyclical or reserved for atypical (or marginal) programs? Does the program conduct an initial review or is it done externally? Are all programs subjected to the same review approach or model—the same process? Because program review is often an extensive and time-consuming process, several institutions (Michigan State University, for example) have devised extensive program- or department-based information and reporting systems for monitoring or auditing the program performance. This requires an extensive database; but once it is in place, it provides a database for program planning and budgeting as well as review and a means of identifying problem programs between review cycles.

Although institutions are reluctant to close programs, several have found it useful to establish a second phase in the review—by either an external or internal group. This is especially critical if program closure includes the release of tenured staff. Such decisions are becoming more common and may be a primary reallocation source for future program development. Yet it highlights the need to design review processes that anticipate such circumstances and to devise procedures for resource reallocation and staff release.

Strategic and Tactical Planning—A Comment. For the sake of clarity, this discussion of the elements of strategic and tactical planning has assumed a comprehensive formal-rational approach or model. However, it should be recalled that the institutional planning process (or the major elements) may be more similar to the other five models. Or it may be a combination of the conceptual dimensions of a planning process (see Table 2): institutional planning unit focus; internal/external orientation; purpose for planning; future orientation; planning typologies; and dynamics of goal centeredness, style of decision making and analysis, and bases for participation. The overall planning process may also vary in its organizing dimensions: comprehensiveness, planning element emphasis, integration, process flexibility, organizational penetration, analytical sophistication, or planning group structures. To the extent that the planning elements do exist, the notion of future-oriented priority setting based on internal and external realities and the willingness to reallocate resources is essential to any or all these elements if there is to be an institutional planning process or function that guides or changes the institution.

Contextual and Organizational Fit Issues

Planning is not an isolated process or function. The discussion of the planning process, its concepts and theories, and the major strategic and tactical elements has touched on the relationship of the planning process to the basic concept of organization, to its role or purpose in the institution, and to the larger environment. However, designing a planning process must also entail adapting it more specifically to the institution. The following are some institutional fit issues that will influence the planning process design. They reflect planning's critical interface with the governance, administrative or leadership patterns, and analytical and information-processing segments of the institution.

Linking Planning and Governance. Because planning is designed to influence some of the broadest and most critical decisions an institution can make, it needs to be closely integrated into the governance or decision-making system (see Chapter Twenty-Five), which can be examined along three dimensions.

First, if planning and those participants it attracts reflect the decision-making style of the governance bodies it seeks to influence, it is more likely to be a process they understand and view as *legitimate*. In large part, this will be a reflection of the culture of the institution, which includes patterns of analysis, participation, communication, and influence. The six theoretical models of a planning process are closely analogous to institutional decision-making styles. It is also feasible to adopt one style for master planning (for example, the more bureaucratic formal-rational model to fit a state mandate or reflect executive decision patterns), another for academic program review (a more collegial developmental or philosophical approach to reflect faculty patterns), and another for resource allocation (a representative, political approach reflecting competitive behavior). In reality, these approaches are not simple or easy to gauge. Current governance patterns may be unproductive (for example, highly political budgeting competition), and it may be desirable to approach them differently in the planning process.

Second, the *authority* and *responsibility* relationships of the planning group to the governance bodies or administrators need to be considered. Do institutional goals need approval by the university senate, the board of trustees, or both? Do recommendations on program planning or review decisions go to deans, school executive committees, the academic vice-president, an institutionwide curriculum committee, or the faculty senate? Failure to define these relationships often leads to jurisdictional squabbles or delays and can even undermine the entire planning process. Of course, this does not resolve the situation when groups with different views claim final jurisdiction. The question of who can initiate ideas or alternatives for a planning group's consideration and who is responsible for implementing a recommendation are just as important as who acts on it.

Third, the structural *representation* or participation links with related governance groups and administrative levels have already been discussed but deserve mention. They are especially important when new planning processes that may affect existing patterns are being designed (such as when an institutionwide program planning or review process affects the dean's role or when a group that will have to act on or implement recommendations desires more effective communication).

Leadership and Administrative Style. To the extent that administrators dominate the governance process, allocate resources, or implement planning decisions, it is essential that a planning process and/or a major element have the support and commitment of the president and associated executive officers. This truism from the industrial planning literature is reflected in most higher education experience with planning. It may not be sufficient, but it usually is a necessary condition for effective planning. Support for planning should include staff, resources, and the commitment to utilize its results, as well as encouragement.

A crucial dimension within the planning process is the leadership and administrative style of a planning officer. The purpose of planning differentiates coordinating, supportive, analytical, and advocacy styles or planning leadership. The level of a planner's appointment, expertise, and credentials reflects status that adds or detracts from his or her leadership role. However, the planning officer's external leadership that relates effectively to institutional governance and administration and internal style of administering a planning staff may not necessarily be the same.

Planning Centralization or Decentralization. This issue is partly one of institutional authority and responsibility for planning as it relates to governance and administration. However, it is also an issue in the structure of the planning process. In public institutions, the issue is initially one at the state-institution boundary. To what extent is institutional planning, resource allocation, and program review prescribed by statewide plans for the respective institutions and by the processes of these major planning elements? Within an institution, it is a question of whether the primary responsibility for master planning, priority setting, resource allocation, and program review activities will occur at an institutionwide level, at the school and college level, or at some lower level (and whether it will vary by element). As institutions become larger, have more autonomy, have less-threatening external circumstances, and have more diverse and resource independent units, decentralized planning elements are more feasible and possibly more suitable to the needs of their particular unit. However, many institutions face the reverse or mixed characteristics. There is no easy answer. To the extent that planning elements are more decentralized, the problems of coordinating planning efforts increase.

Coordinating Planning with Analytical and Information Systems. Throughout this chapter, the relationship of planning or its major elements to information resources and analytical techniques has been emphasized (see Chapter Twenty-Six). Information systems development, computing resources, and analytical techniques for use in higher education have grown rapidly in the past decade, have been widely discussed (Lawrence and Service, 1977; Staman, 1979), and will continue to change. The problem for planners is threefold. First, keeping up with changes in these areas as they relate to planning is a professional development task for persons with primary planning responsibility. The second aspect is how to assure that the institution's information, computing, and analytical resources serve the planning function. Solutions are *structural*, giving a high-level planning officer direct responsibility for computer and information systems development and related analytical studies; lie in *staff expertise* provided directly or on an as-

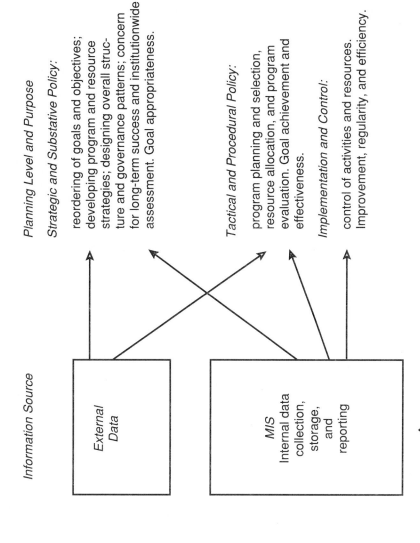

Type of Research

Policy Research:

Long-range studies of organizational goal achievement and resource utilization
Comparative research of other higher education institution
Studies of overall structure and functioning of the institution
Research on environmental conditions affecting the institution
Forecasting alternative futures and their impact on the institution

Operations Research:

Devising forecasting and simulation models of institutional and environmental dynamics
Evaluating alternative program and resource strategies and specific decisions

Evaluation Research:

Assessment of program input, process, and output; variables over time
Measures of goal achievement and unintended effects of programs
Cost and productivity measurement

Descriptive Research:

Analysis and reports of current operations
Developing formulas
Comparing actual to allocated or projected data

Planning Level and Purpose

Strategic and Substative Policy:

reordering of goals and objectives; developing program and resource strategies; designing overall structure and governance patterns; concern for long-term success and institutionwide assessment. Goal appropriateness.

Tactical and Procedural Policy:

program planning and selection, resource allocation, and program evaluation. Goal achievement and effectiveness.

Implementation and Control:

control of activities and resources. Improvement, regularity, and efficiency.

Information Source

External Data

MIS
Internal data collection, storage, and reporting

Systems Design and Analysis

signed basis to the planning office; or are an *acquired* service from other university offices or external purveyors of such services. These alternatives need to be reviewed in relation to the status and responsibility of the chief planning officer, the centrality of the planning function in the institution, and the demands for information and analytical services by other units.

Figure 8 summarizes the third aspect: the nature of the relationship between type of planning and some broad research and information categories. As one moves from implementation through tactical to strategic planning, the decision issues and the nature of the research design and analytical techniques become more complex, require more nonstandard and external data sources (other institutions, environmental data, and so forth), and use more complicated data collection strategies. However, the value-laden nature of strategic policy issues is also less likely to lead to clear decisions, and the costs of analysis are likely to increase. I have already discussed the nature of this dilemma and the emphasis an institution should give to information and analytical system development.

Administrative Structure of Planning. The structure of the planning group (selection, composition, permanence, and responsibility) and the bases for participation (expertise and representation) were discussed earlier (also see Chapters Twenty-Five through Twenty-Seven). The design of an administrative staff structure for planning (who is responsible and what constitutes the staff) is interwoven with the desired comprehensiveness, emphasis, and intended integration of the planning process and with planning's relation to institutional governance, its pattern of centralization, its coordination with information and analytical systems, and the size of the institution. The issue here is the administrative one. Should planning be part of the line responsibility of all administrators from the president down (an MBO alternative), the part-time assignment of an assistant to an executive officer or president, the responsibility of an expanded institutional research office, a full-time staff director, or the primary responsibility of an executive officer? Clearly, all patterns currently exist and there is little evidence on which to base a choice from among them.

As planning, particularly in larger institutions, becomes more comprehensive (more planning elements and organizational units and resources) and mandated by external governance groups, includes more decentralized patterns among the elements, and is more analytically oriented, the number of planning groups, direct participants, units affected, meetings, and studies to coordinate increases rapidly. Under these circumstances, the argument for a high-level staff or line planning office becomes more convincing. The staffing of such an office is beyond the scope of this discussion but clearly requires some staff with broad planning and organizational expertise (presumably the director), staff with varied research design and evaluation expertise, and staff with programming and information system design expertise.

Planning as Organizational Change. The adaptive or change-oriented function of planning was identified at the start of this chapter, yet much of the criticism of planning is the tendency to rationalize stability. Planning to effect institutional change needs to produce short-range (one- or two-year) results in order to maintain the commitment of executive officers and the involvement of participants and to know that it is working, that is, it needs to have some short-term, viable purposes and expectations, as with any other institutional activity.

Perhaps as critically, the planning process or its director needs to examine strategies of change that might guide the activity. Is it to exert pressure for *incremental* but consistent change, to foster *planned change* (organizational development) efforts, to stress *decisive* and occasionally extensive changes, or to let change *emerge* from the various dynamics of planning? Is change to emphasize directive or *authority-based* methods, *participatory* processes, *rational* solutions, or *conflict* modes? The role of the planning office as initiator, neutral analyst, process coordinator, or advocate was discussed. The concept of a change strategy can shape the work of a planning staff, its relation to others, and its own effectiveness and needs to be examined carefully.

Planning as Education and Communication. Comprehensive planning involves many participants and affects numerous groups. Planning and its elements are processes that may not be fully understood, involve analysis of problems and issues about which most institutional members have little information, and influence decisions that can have wide consequences. Planning—or a planning officer—needs as a primary objective the development of regular and informative means of communication with constituents, participants, and governance links, explaining planning processes, emergent issues and alternatives, and rationales for recommendations.

Similarly, because planning will be a new activity and responsibility for many administrators and has a continuous turnover of participants on planning bodies and planning staff members, education about planning is also a useful objective. In designing an institution-wide planning process, Wichita State University established a professional development center with training in the various planning activities as part of its program for faculty and administrators.

Planning Evaluation. Information on the outcomes, impacts, and benefits of planning is only beginning to emerge in case studies and a few comparative works (for example, Chapters Twenty-Eight through Thirty-One). Therefore, except to provide examples, it is unlikely such studies will directly help an institution revise and improve its planning process. Designing a planning process is an evolutionary activity. As such, it might benefit from a well-devised evaluation plan that examines how the design issues raised in this chapter have been resolved, the degree to which the purpose or expectations of planning (or its elements) are being met, the reasons for its successes and failures, and the costs and resources utilized.

Conclusion

Implicit in this chapter has been the notion of critical questions an institution can or should ask itself in designing a planning process. I have summarized these.

The Rationale for Planning. What general model or approach to planning (Table 2) is appropriate to our institution—formal-rational, organizational development, technocratic/empirical, philosophical synthesis, political advocacy, or controlled anarchy—or a modification or combination of them? • What is to be included in the content of planning—elements, organi-

zational units, resources? • What assumption about the basic institutional unit for planning best reflects our tradition and self-image? • What primary purpose or institutional function (need) do we want planning to serve—adaptive (major redefinition or changes), managerial (improved effectiveness and efficiency), maintenance (improved capacity for known growth, development, and performance) or boundary (dealing with major problems of external relations)? What is the priority on these functions? And what are the specific planning expectations, desired outcomes, or formal goals under each? • What role is the planning process expected to play in achieving this purpose—1. identify critical issues, 2. assist others in doing studies, 3. coordinate assessments, 4. develop and examine alternatives, or 5. advocate action? • Are the major problems confronting the long-term viability of our institution internal, external, both, or uncertain? • What is the nature of the institutional future that planning should emphasize—most likely or probable, feasible, improvement of current, ideal, or allow members or units to achieve their capability? • What is the planning typology emphasized—substantive (ends) or procedural (means); strategic (master planning), tactical (and implementation); or policy and/or contingency issues? • What are the dynamics of this planning process? Is it goal-centered, consensus-oriented, priority-oriented, or pluralistic? Are planning decision processes likely to be oriented to problem solving; organized learning; reasoned debate and discussion; bargaining, negotiation, compromise, and coalitional; or loosely coordinated? Is analysis likely to emphasize quantitative rationality, qualitative rationality, reasoned logic, collaboration, or advocacy? • What is the basis for participation in planning? Does the planner role emphasize planning process, organizational development, intellectual, rational analysis, or political expertise? Is participation based on representation of administrative units, technical units, functional groups, affected units, interest groups, or elite or egalitarian democratic principles?

Planning Process Overall Design. • The institutional planning process (and its major elements) can be organized along the following dimension: Is the planning process (or element) intended to be comprehensive or limited in planning elements or subelements; comprehensive or limited in organizational scope—programs (academic, research, service, support) or resources (human, financial, physical, and information)? What is emphasis on process elements and organizational programs and resources; integrated or fragmented view of elements and organizational programs and resources; integrated or fragmented view of elements, programs, and resources; flexibility, regularity, rigidity or planning processes; degree of organizational penetration; degree of analytical sophistication; or structure of the planning group (selection, composition, permanence, and responsibility)? • How is the institutional environment to be viewed? How is the environment delineated—by sectors (political, social, economic, technological, competitive, or other) or segments (resource flows)? How can environmental segments be typified on interdependence, supportiveness, potency or control of resource flow, and predictability? What are the boundaries of the service or resource region for each segment? • What approach to organization-environment interface is appropriate for each segment; trend, policy alternatives, problem solving, societal futurist, educational futurist, flexible responsive, utopian, or a combination? • How do the organization-environment approaches vary on decision motive, decision process, analytical approach, and benefits and limits?

Strategic Planning Elements. Which strategic planning elements are to be developed—environmental assessment, institutional assessment, values assessment, or master planning? • How is each to be organized? • How is each structured in terms of purpose, structure or model, analytical approach, and issues?

Tactical Planning Elements. Which tactical planning elements are to be developed—program planning, priority setting, resource allocation, or program review? • How is each to be organized? • How can each be organized or described in terms of purpose, structure of model, analytical approach, and issues?

Overall Organization. How can the overall planning process be organized in relation to the larger institutional context? • How is it linked to governance in terms of decision-making style (six models), patterns of authority and responsibility, and membership linkages? • What is the institutional leadership's support for, commitment to, and utilization of planning? • What is the leadership style of the planning di-

rector—externally and internally? • How centralized or decentralized is each of the major planning elements? • How is planning coordinated with analytical and information systems services in the institution in terms of planning staff updating and development and organizational linkages (authority for, planning staff expertise, or acquired services)? • Where does administrative responsibility for planning rest? • What is the size and expertise of the planning staff, if any? • What is the change strategy employed by planners—incremental, planned, abrupt, emergent or directive, participatory, political? • How does the planning staff develop methods to meet its needs for communication about planning and education about planning? • How does the institution intend to evaluate its planning process and elements? Who is responsible?

References

Ackoff, R. A. *Concept of Corporate Planning.* New York: Wiley, 1970.

Anthony, R. *Planning and Control Systems.* Cambridge, Mass.: Harvard Graduate School of Business, 1965.

Baldridge, V. *Power and Conflict in the University.* New York: Wiley, 1971.

Barak, R., and Berdahl, R. *State Level Program Review.* Denver, Colo.: Education Commission of the States, 1978.

Bauer, R., and Gergen, K. (Eds.). *The Study of Policy Formulation.* New York: Free Press, 1968.

Bennis, W., and others. *The Planning of Change.* New York: Holt, Rinehart and Winston, 1976.

Caruthers, J., and Orwig, M. *Budgeting in Higher Education.* ERIC/AAHE Report No. 3, Washington, D.C.: American Association for Higher Education, 1979.

Casasco, J. *Planning Techniques for University Management.* Washington, D.C.: American Council on Education, 1970.

Cohen, M., and March, J. *Leadership and Ambiguity.* New York: McGraw-Hill, 1974.

Cope, R. *Strategic Policy Planning.* Littleton, Colo.: Ireland Educational Corporation, 1978.

Craven, E. *New Directions for Institutional Research: Alternative Models of Academic Program Evaluation,* no. 27. San Francisco: Jossey-Bass, 1980.

Dressel, P. L. *Handbook of Academic Evaluation: Assessing Institutional Effectiveness, Student Progress, and Professional Performance of Decision Making in Higher Education.* San Francisco: Jossey-Bass, 1976.

Dror, Y. "The Planning Process: A Facet Design." *International Review of Administrative Sciences*, 1963, 29, 44–58.

Drucker, P. *The Age of Discontinuity*. New York: Harper & Row, 1969.

Enarson, H. "The Art of Planning." *Educational Record*, 1975, 56, 170–174.

Etzioni, A. *The Active Society*. New York: Free Press, 1968.

Folger, J. (Ed.). *New Directions for Institutional Research: Increasing the Public Accountability for Higher Education*, no. 16. San Francisco: Jossey-Bass, 1977.

Fuller, B. "A Framework for Academic Planning." *Journal of Higher Education*, 1976, 48, 65–77.

Glenny, L., and others. *Coordinating Higher Education for the 1970's*. Berkeley, Calif.: Center for Research and Development in Higher Education, University of California, 1971.

Heydinger, R. (Ed.). *New Directions for Institutional Research: Emerging Approaches to Academic Program Planning*. San Francisco: Jossey-Bass, forthcoming.

Kerr, C. *Uses of the University*. Cambridge, Mass.: Harvard University Press, 1963.

Ladd, D. *Changes in Educational Policy*. New York: McGraw-Hill, 1970.

Lawrence, G. B., and Service, A. *Quantitative Approaches to Higher Education Management*. Washington, D.C.: ERIC/AAHE, 1977.

Lawrence, P., and Lorsch, J. *Developing Organizations*. Reading, Mass.: Addison-Wesley, 1969.

Lindblom, C. "The Science of Muddling Through." *Public Administration Review*, 1959, 19, 79–88.

Michael, D. *On Learning to Plan—and Planning to Learn: The Social Psychology of Changing Toward Future-Responsive Societal Learning*. San Francisco: Jossey-Bass, 1973.

Palola, E., Lehmann, T., and Blischke, W. *Higher Education By Design*. Berkeley: Center for Research and Development in Higher Education, University of California, 1970.

Parekh, S. *Long Range Planning: An Institution Wide Approach to Increasing Academic Vitality*. Washington, D.C.: Change Magazine Press, 1975.

Peterson, M. "Decision Type, Structure, and Process Evaluation." *Higher Education: International Journal of Education and Planning*, 1972, 1.

Peterson, M. *New Directions for Institutional Research: Benefiting from Interinstitutional Research*, no. 12. San Francisco: Jossey-Bass, 1976.

Peterson, M. "Alternative Strategies of Planning the Institution-Environment Interface." In C. Adams (Ed.), *Improving the Process of Administration in Higher Education*. Washington, D.C.: Association of Instrumental and Decision Sciences, 1977.

Poulton, N. "Impacts of Planning Activities in Research Universities: A Comparative Analysis of Five Institutional Experiences." Unpublished doctoral dissertation, University of Michigan, 1979.

Riesman, D., Gusfield, J., and Gamson, Z. *Academic Values and Mass Education*. New York: Doubleday, 1970.

Schick, A. "The Road to PPB: The Stages of Budget Reform." *Public Administration Review*, 1966, 26, 243–258.

Schick, A. *Planning, Programming, and Budgeting: A Systems Approach to Management*. Chicago: University of Chicago Press, 1968.

Schmidtlein, F., and Glenny, L. *State Budgeting for Higher Education*. Berkeley: Center for Research and Development in Higher Education, University of California, 1977.

Simon, H. *Administrative Behavior*. New York: Free Press, 1957.

Staman, M. (Ed.). *New Directions for Institutional Research: Examining New Trends in Administrative Computing*, no. 22. San Francisco: Jossey-Bass, 1979.

Sturner, W. *Action Planning on Campus*. Washington, D.C.: American Association of State Colleges and Universities, 1974.

Taylor, B. "New Dimensions in Corporate Planning." *Long Range Planning*, 1976, 9, 80–106.

Weathersby, G., and Balderston, F. "PPBS in Higher Education Planning and Management." Parts I, II, and III in *Higher Education*. 1972, 2, 191–205; 1973, 1, 229–318; 1973, 2, 33–67.

Wilson, I. "Socio-Political Forecasting." *Management Business Review*. July 1974, 15–25.

Conceptual Distinctions In University Planning

BARBARA NEUFELD

Purpose and Background

This article is intended to further an understanding of university planning and to facilitate improvements in university planning practice. This task is addressed by drawing some important conceptual distinctions derived from planning literature and by highlighting the results of a comparative case study which employed those conceptual distinctions.

Planning as a field of study is not well developed. In many respects it could be characterized as a confusing array of amorphous, overlapping, and rarely applied concepts, models and frameworks. The gulf between the loose abstractions of planning theory literature and the largely anecdotal reflections of planning practice literature is especially wide. This article presents an exploration of that ill-defined middle ground between planning theory and practice.

Planning and Decision-Making

Broadly defined, planning is any form of anticipatory decision-making. More specifically university planning encompasses the determination of immediate university needs or goals, the formulation of a preferred course of action to achieve those goals or satisfy those needs, and the means by which the selected course of action is to be implemented. In short, planning should assist in deciding what to do and how to do it (Pounds & Strickland, 1980).

Although planning facilitates decision-making, it does encompass all aspects of decision-making. It does not, for example, include (but might preclude) decision-making which is *ad hoc*, or capricious. Thus planning does, to varying degrees, formalize decision-making by implying actions or interventions which must be deliberate and intentional. It also implies a conscious attempt to view activities as a set rather than as isolated phenomena. The desired end condition or product is not an unintended outcome of a number of unrelated activities or events and, should, therefore precede implementation. Planning also, tends to involve a great variety of tasks, integrated within a complex process, which are collectively directed towards a conscious purpose and should eventually lead to a specified end state.

For a university, planning is an organizational function within an administrative structure. It should be undertaken on an on going basis by the institutional membership. Again to be relevant, the planning function must be linked to the institution's decision-making process which itself reflects the power structure of the institution. Implementation is inherent planning. Thus planning is action-oriented by serving as an instrument of administrative accountability, and by assisting in resource allocation and decision-making. The link between planning and resource allocation is determined by planning priorities.

"Conceptual Distinctions in University Planning," by Barbara Neufeld, reprinted from *Educational Planning*, Vol. 9, No. 1, 1993. Memphis State University.

Framework for Analysis

Given the somewhat confused state of planning thought, yet recognizing the potentially pivotal role of planning in facilitating decision-making, it is essential that case study analysis of planning be systematic in its linkages to planning theory and in the methods employed. To do otherwise would simply contribute to the confusion.

The use of planning models in planning practice provides a conceptual framework to facilitate data organization analysis, theory building and structured practice. However, such models generally lack specific strategies for action because of the limited extent to which models have been applied, tested, and evaluated in practice.

The point of departure for this analysis is five planning models—models which embrace a diversity of planning orientations, methods and related organizational structures. In employing these models it is appreciated that planning practice is unlikely to mirror any single model and that much planning is less the conscious application of a theoretical model and more the *ad hoc* design of a planning approach to suit a particular set of planning problems—generally without the conscious consideration of alternative planning models. Nevertheless the institution's plans and planning process may contain elements of more than one planning model—their inclusion being an outcome of a specific strategy to meet a specific problem. Moreover, whether intentional or unintentional, the extent to which a planning initiative mirrors model characteristics still provides an opportunity for testing and refining that model.

In presenting and applying the models, it also needs to be acknowledged that the models characterized are not consistently defined or applied. This problem has been compounded by the loose use of terminology with the same terms being applied to different phenomena and different terms being applied to the same phenomena. However, recognizing the need for consistent model characteristics, by drawing upon a range of planning literature, it was possible to identify a series of general tendencies rather than absolute properties of each model.

The planning models also represent the mainstream planning theories—ideal types, frequently referenced in the planning literature. Other potential theories tend to be subsets, variations or hybrids of the five major planning models described in this article.

Appreciating the qualifications noted above, university planning was analyzed against the characterizations of the following five major planning models: rational, strategic, incremental, organizational development, and advocacy. The planning models were described according to four major aspects: ends of planning, nature of planning, organization for planning, planning environment.

Ends of planning refers to the university's goals, its mission and the values, implicit or explicit, inherent in the planning approach. *Nature of planning* pertains to how the university goes about planning. It includes the information or knowledge employed, the procedures used to review and amend, discard or adapt decisions, the outcomes of planning activities (products), the level of detail, and the time-frame. *Organization for planning* describes the organizational structure types, the media of communications, the explicitness of rules, the direction of control, the roles/skills possessed by actors, and the resources available for planning. *Planning environment* addresses the inter-relationships between planning and the university (internal environment), societal (external environment), and political environments.

The Planning Models

Rational Planning

Under the rational planning model an attempt is made, at considerable expense in time, effort and money, to prepare and implement a comprehensive long-range plan. According to Cope (1985), the rational planning model assumes a long-range planning horizon since change is only slowly achieved and provides a blueprint for the future:

Long-range plans usually result in a plan for ten years, a blueprint, often prepared in a planning office. The long-range plan is usually a lengthy document containing details about the institution's mission and degree programs, numbers of faculty and students by degree programs, numbers of graduates by degree programs, as well as a list of goals and objectives for teaching, research and service. The long-range plans have been dominated by an internal perspective and generally assume relatively closed boundaries. Long-range planning is usually characterized as inside-out planning. The elements of science dominate this form of planning. (Cope, 1985, p. 14).

The major steps in the rational decision-making process are as follows:

1. Decisionmakers are assumed to agree on the goals that govern a given decision;

2. Decisionmakers identify all alternative courses of action that are relevant to their goals;

3. Decisionmakers identify all relevant consequences of each alternative; and

4. Using some appropriate calculus, decisionmakers compare the sets of consequences and decide upon the optimum alternative. (Culhane, Friesema, & Beecher, 1987, p. 2).

The task, for a comprehensive long-range plan, would entail: a careful definition of the university's short, medium, and long term goals (e.g. annual, three to five years, and five to ten years, respectively); data collection, beyond the statistics provided by its usual management information system; the analysis of these statistics relative to the planning goals; the formulation of a range of alternative ways by which the institution might achieve its goals; the systematic analysis and evaluation of the alternatives; the selection and refinement of the preferred alternative; the development of an implementation plan including monitoring and updating procedures; and, the formulation of contingency plans in case changes in the comprehensive plans are required. These, or similar steps, are all advocated in descriptions of the rational planning model. They appear in the work of several authors including, for example, R. Boxx and J. W. Johnson (1980); R. G. Cope (1981); G. Keller (1987); A Faludi (1978, 1983); G. J. Allison (1971); J. M. Bryson (1988); H. A. Simon (1976); J. Rosenhead (1980); D. Lelong and R. Shirley (1984); and D. W. Lang (1983).

The rational planning model offers a university administration systematic procedures for defining the institution's planning ends and means. Under this planning model, the planner is seen as politically neutral and objective and the planning work is viewed as isolated from and immune to political pressures. With reliance upon expert guidance for senior decision-makers, planning is essentially undemocratic. Widespread political participation is regarded as inconsistent with the efficient control of the planning process by the planning experts. Its products are ostensibly objective in the sense that they are based on technical expertise and detailed data. However, the model ignores the internal distribution of political power and the value conflicts which must be taken into account for the successful adoption and implementation of planning change. It assumes that it is possible to separate ends and means and to consider them independently. It further assumes that consensus can be reached among the major stakeholders, by means of a rational planning process, on the values which underlie the planning intention. It also is of questionable practicality given the limited resources available to university planning, the turbulent nature of the internal and external planning environment, and the inherent resistance of the university membership to centralized top-down planning.

The rational planning model assumes highly technical short-term planning and quantitative analysis to address such matters as annual budgeting and enrollment in the context of a master plan of a long-term image. However, Simon (1976) and Lindblom (1973) contend that comprehensive analysis tends to be thwarted by the general disagreements on goals by planning participants in a bureaucratic structure and by the difficulty of meeting data needs.

Strategic Planning

Strategic planning begins with the assumption that some aspects of a university's operation are functioning well and require little or no intervention. Therefore, attention can be focused on a small number of problem and opportunity areas. This approach assumes that the planning environment is difficult to predict or control, that planning is difficult and divisive, and that the resources available for planning are modest and must be concentrated where they have the greatest effect.

Strategic planning concentrates on key operating decisions facing the institution in the intermediate future (three years). Goals are broadly defined such that the institution can flexibly respond to changing conditions and demands. Options are also defined with an appreciation of internal and external environmental constraints and opportunities.

This model generally employs a participatory planning approach—an approach which accords well with the traditional university committee style of decision-making. Both personal and processed knowledge are employed. As such, it fits easily into administrative procedural modes of institutions of higher education by facilitating the tapping of the broad-ranging experience and technical knowledge of university faculty and staff.

Strategic planning balances the planning process and the planning products with a careful attention to the procedures by which decisions are made and commitments implemented. Planning products tend to be short and focused, interim working papers rather than the grand master plan characteristic of rational planning. Strategic planning assumes an open hierarchical organizational structure with extensive vertical and horizontal communications and participation. Management skills are stressed. This planning model is described *inter alia* in the work of G. Keller (1987); R. G. Cope (1981); S. Young (1981); and J. L. Miller, Jr. (1983).

Strategic planning shares many of the same tasks as rational planning but emphasizes creativity, flexibility and participation by the university membership generally through its normal committee decision-making system. Strategic planning is motivated by the desire for selectively rational and focused institutional decision-making. This model employs long and medium range plans which are reformulated periodically.

The short term objectives reflect a realistic knowledge of likely resources and probabilities of successful implementation. Strategic choices, in turn, lead to long-run goals. In successive years as opportunities are identified, objectives can be redefined, resources reappraised, data updated, and projections re-calculated. In good strategic planning, therefore, future risk is minimized as the proposed goals and the means are directly linked to problems and implementation. Strategic planning employs a long-run perspective but focuses on specific tactics and issues. However, at the heart of strategic planning, is a fundamental contradiction between its espoused participation and openness and the needs of an apolitical process which assumes expert knowledge and value consensus. This model may reflect changing environments and use available resources but it lacks mechanisms for resolving conflicts and overcoming institution inertia.

Incremental Planning

Incremental planning treats the planning process as the marginal annual adjustment toward some vaguely defined preferred condition (Keller, 1987, p. 114). It involves preparing successive approximations to change the decision-making process. Lindblom (1965) describes the process as "partisan mutual adjustment." As interest groups may vary in their opinion over an issue or policy decision, planning participants may, at best, arrive at consensus only to the extent that current decisions move incrementally from past decisions (Culhane, Friesema, & Beecher, 1987). This planning model may also be defined as *disjointed incrementalism* (Braybrooke and Lindblom, 1970, pp. 81–110). Budget allocations generally follow the institution's historical patterns with only minor upward or downward adjustments in response to the internal political process of debating longer term priorities against various manifest immediate needs. This approach has been termed the incremental planning model. Discussion of its advantages and disadvantages are found *inter alia* in the writings of E. Bell (1978); D. Braybrooke and C. E. Lindblom (1970); C. E. Lindblom (1965); and G. Keller (1987).

Incremental planning has limited intentions, is realistic and takes full account of the conflicts inherent in the institution's decision-making process. Because it is modest in interaction it is equally modest in results. It tends to be seen as spasmodic and, sometimes, inconsistent. The key to success with incremental planning is to achieve piece-meal changes consistent with some long term goals. In this way, long-term planned change can be demonstrated.

Advocacy Planning

Advocacy planning describes an openly competitive mode of planning. Institutional stakeholders present their "cases" and "bargain" to advance their specific interests in annual or longer term planning and resource allocation decision-making. This planning model has the inherent instability of a political process. Some stakeholders are more effective representatives for their "cause" than others. Not all stakeholders have equal representation. Some, for example, are relegated to minor committees in which at best they might mitigate the effect of a decision they would oppose. Alliances among groups of stakeholders also shift as the decision under discussion changes.

This political contest rewards the politically astute, numerically strong, dynamic and articulate as well as those whose "case" is most consistent with current priorities. For a university the outcome of the planning represented by annual resource allocations depends upon both the power positions of groups within the institution and upon the competitive position of the university itself in the higher education system. Recognizing the likely imbalance in the competitive positions of various stakeholders planning, resources need to be distributed such that each stakeholder can compete equally within the planning process. This model is described *inter alia* by E. Bell (1978); J. M. Bryson (1988); and H. L. Thompson (1979).

Advocacy planning recognizes that neither the planning activity nor the planners are politically neutral. It acknowledges that underrepresented interest groups should be heard and may need assistance to participate effectively in institutional decision-making. Yet the model provides only limited guidance as to how planning decisions can be made without creating "winners" and "losers." Thus, frequently it fails to assist in the achievement of compromises which integrate the concerns of affected groups.

Organizational Development Planning

The organizational development planning model assumes the need for an open/participatory planning process as a pre-condition to the achievement of planned change. As such the planning process is both educative and instrumental. Philosophically, it is a direct contrast to autocratically imposed change. It assumes that unless organizational members have experiences whereby they learn about the need for proposed change, the activities which will foster the changes, and how to lessen (or avoid) the adverse effects of the changes, most members will favor the *status quo* and will resist the proposed planned changes.

Under an organization learning/consensus formation, the various interested and affected parties work together in a non-hierarchical system of small groups to define the new goals, discuss alternative implementation strategies, re-allocate resources and evaluate the implemented change. Consensus is achieved through dialogue and mutual socialization into the prejudices, satisfactions, wants and needs of other institutional members. This model is discussed *inter alia* by B. S. Uebling (1981); P. Shrivastava (1983); and D. Michael (1973).

Organizational development planning is attractive because of its humanistic experimentation and flexibility. However, it is also utopian in its failure to come to terms with the discord between personal and organizational needs and desires. It assumes (often erroneously) that deeply ceded value and organizational differences can be harmoniously resolved by dialogue among persons who, generally, do not have the technical expertise to outline, explicitly, the alternative available to solve the problems under discussion. In times of restraints, organizations must make hard choices. It cannot be assumed that any agreement on planned change, in conditions of restraint, will be freely accepted by the adversely affected groups. The willing and complacent victim is not a common figure in universities.

Case Studies—Methodology

Inasmuch as no planning model has been judged best practice, the planning characteristics of each of three institutions were compared with the characteristics of five planning models. The case studies were intended not only to analyze and interpret planning practice but also to refine and adapt planning theory in university settings. The universities selected all had sufficient planning experience to permit a retrospective analysis. Although they share a bicameral system of governance there were important differences pertaining to enrollment levels, planning approaches, and geographic settings.

Interviews were conducted with various "key" planning participants at the universities. These participants included: academic administrators for their role in shaping academic policies and planning; executive level staff because of their pivotal roles in budgeting and its linkages to planning, and senior planning officials as a result of their direct, substantive and ongoing involvement in planning. The analysis addressed documentary evidence and then interview evidence, in three progressively more detailed iterations.

In describing and analyzing the decisions and processes of the universities, an initial set of documents are analyzed and exploratory interviews were conducted. Concomitantly, the five major planning models from the planning literature were analyzed to provide a framework within which to couch information derived from the second and third rounds of interviews and all documents and materials. The same format was followed in all three case studies. Planning characteristics of each university were analyzed and compared.

In analyzing and describing planning characteristics of each university, planning participants interviewed were differentiated according to senior and lower levels to represent a grouping method in the executive/staff hierarchy. The interview format was formulated, and the interview form was pretested and modified based on results. The second and third round of interviews were then conducted. The interview format questions were classified according to the following four aspects: ends of planning; nature of planning; organization for planning; and planning environment. Interviewees were asked to look at each question according to the aspects and elaborate on their planning activity(ies) and approach to planning. Each interviewee looked at a list of structured answers (model answers were not always in same sequence) according to the four aspects as described in the planning literature of the five major planning models. Respondents were also asked to check the appropriate box(es) which most closely resembled planning at their institution.

Responses from planning participants were then compiled. The analysis served to dis-

tinguish between primary responses (i.e. answer most frequently selected) and secondary responses (i.e. less frequently chosen), and according to senior level (e.g. Chair of Senate/Board, President, Vice-Presidents) and according to lower level (e.g. Directors, Associate Vice-Presidents, Deans, Chairs of Department, and Secretary of Senate/Board). The qualitative analysis served to identify specific substantive reasons and examples. The elaborations were taped. In order to quantify the results, each response per planning model aspect (or answer set) was assigned a value of one point. If the respondent selected more than one response per answer set, the responses were weighted (e.g. if respondent checked off two replies, each was assigned a value of 0.5; if two responses were checked off, but one ranked higher than the other, the replies were weighted accordingly, (e.g. 0.66, 0.33). This procedure ensured that responses did not receive undue weight while ensuring the distinctions made were reflected in analysis.

The data were then analyzed. The analysis drew upon the documentary evidence, the exploratory interviews, the elaborations of structured interviews, and the supplementary interviews. The distribution of responses was analyzed using a series of histograms. The histograms were used to assess whether there was general unanimity as to the planning characteristics or whether the informants, to a lesser or greater extent, disagreed. Common responses overall, and within and between senior and lower respondents, were intended to reflect value or opinion consensus, good communications, and good implementation potential.

The data were then interpreted by comparing planning experience against the planning models. The intention was to determine whether the blend of planning models evident at each university contained inherently incompatible elements. If the elements of the planning approach were consistent and mutually supportive, then the planning approach was considered more likely to be effective. However, if various elements of the planning worked at cross purposes, then the effectiveness of the effort could be seriously constrained.

The evaluation also included addressing the issue of the extent to which the ends for planning as documented and espoused were actually achieved. It also addressed the extent to which the planning process as documented and espoused corresponded with the planning process which occurred. In undertaking this evaluation it was recognized that there were serious limitations concerning the degree of precision possible. The documentation of which planning ends were achieved and whether they were a consequence of planning was, at best, extremely limited. Records of the planning processes as they actually occurred were even more fragmentary. The statements of ends tended to be very broad (e.g. excellence in education). Thus, the analysis of the extent to which ends were achieved is highly problematic. The institutions tended to produce long lists of objectives for planning but rarely produced more than extremely general overviews of the planning process envisioned. Consequently, the comparison of intended or espoused with actual planning process characteristics was constrained. This lack of documentation of either the planning process or its consequences is, of course, suggestive of a flawed planning process. However, the general implications and conclusions drawn provided useful, broad insights into the nature of university planning.

Data were then synthesized according to general observations and lessons about university planning and in terms of applications and extensions to the planning models.

Case Studies— Observations and Lessons

Although the complete case study analysis cannot be presented in this article it is possible to derive several general observations and lessons. The case study universities, for example, had a reasonably well-defined sense of mission and frequently, lengthy lists of ambitious goals and objectives. Goals and objectives, however, tended to be too broadly defined to permit a systematic monitoring of the extent to which they were being attained. Priorities, moreover, were rarely defined nor was a timetable established for the realization of short or medium term objectives. A further general failing was the lack of a full appreciation of resources requirements, value divisions with the university community, and administrative inertia.

The planning process at the case study universities tended to be outlined in very broad terms. Consequently, it was often poorly understood by planning participants. In addition, planning process, as it occurred (i.e. paper trail), was very poorly documented. Without a clear record of the planning process it is difficult to identify and ameliorate weaknesses or to enhance strengths.

Planning of the case study universities was generally characterized by an almost naive belief in collegiality and the voluntary commitment of resources. Although a considerable effort was made to provide a diversity of formal and informal structures and procedures to foster planning participation and to facilitate consensus-building, much less effort was devoted to the establishment of mechanisms to address highly divisive voices or to provide the communicative and creative skills for planning participants to function effectively in the planning process. These limitations were compounded by weakly developed systems for monitoring the relative effectiveness of the planning structures and procedures employed.

An especially problematic area tended to be interconnections among planning levels (e.g. university-wide vs. local unit), time horizons (e.g. short term vs. long term) and forms (e.g. academic vs. administrative planning). Although much was written about the need for such interconnections the evidence of measures to facilitate such interconnections was much less in evidence. In a similar fashion, although the need for flexibility and innovation was stressed, this acknowledgement was not extended to a systematic characterization of the internal and external planning environments such that the planning processes and structures could be designed and adapted to anticipate and respond to changing environmental conditions. As a consequence, the changes which were introduced tended to be less a reaction to environmental condition changes and more a shift in the preferences of those in pivotal planning positions.

Conclusions

The three case study universities are diverse and complex organizations. They are characterized by a wide array of values, interests, and expertise, a multiplicity of decision-making levels with short, medium and long-range implications, a collegial decision-making tradition, only moderate resources available for planning, and a turbulent planning environment.

The analysis confirmed that neither a single planning model nor a combination of models was selected and applied directly by university planning. Instead, what tended to occur in practice was that planning approaches were designed (or more frequently evolved) in response to the particular issues and circumstances at an institution. When planning approaches are formulated in this manner, they tend to exhibit characteristics of more than one planning model. Perceptions of planning characteristics also vary among planning participants. These non-deliberate blended planning models represent a realistic response to the planning environment. However, because they evolved and were largely developed without reference to the characteristics, strengths and limitations of the various planning models, as detailed in the higher education planning literature, there is a danger that they will contain contradictions and inconsistencies that may inhibit the planning effort.

The case study analysis, against the framework of the five major planning models, has assisted in theory building. However, further extensions beyond the ideal types represented by the models are still possible. For example, the rational planning model assumes that all aspects of the university's operation should be planned, and the incremental planning model assumes that very few aspects of the university's operations would be subject to planning. Similarly, the organizational development planning model stresses consensus building as the heart of planning, and both the advocacy and the incremental planning models see conflict as inherent to planning. It is important not to assume that each university should strive for middle ground between such extremes. Instead, for example, conflict accommodating and consensus building mechanisms and strategies are likely to be both necessary for different aspects of the university's operations

and at different stages in the evolution of planning at the institution. Indeed, they may be considered complementary strategies within the same planning unit or activity. Similarly, some elements of the university's operation may require a more comprehensive planning treatment at particular junctures in time than others. However, the choice of the appropriate mix of structures and process can only be realized by a thorough understanding of the internal and external planning environments, systematic monitoring procedures, a commitment to substantive rather than cosmetic planning efforts with direct connections to university decision-making, and lastly, but most importantly, a commitment to build upon the knowledge base represented by planning theory and reflective planning practice.

In terms of initiating a planning effort within a university, the strategic planning model is a reasonable point of departure, inasmuch as university planning practice has tended to mirror many of the characteristics of this planning model. However, university planning also needs to draw upon the other planning models. These models offer many important lessons for university planning, as exemplified by the incremental planning model, which points to the need for an improved understanding of the administrative/bureaucratic system of the university. The conscious blending of planning model aspects, while appreciating the need to guard against contradictory elements, can facilitate the design of planning to suit particular decision-making situations (e.g. the use of the rational planning model for technical planning situations).

The planning models in their present form are too conceptual for direct application in planning practice. These theory-practice gaps can be further narrowed through additional case studies; deliberately experimental planning initiatives which consciously blend and apply model-based approaches to specific planning problem types; a further effort to draw upon insights provided through social science, public policy, business management and educational planning research; and a particular effort to derive planning environment typologies (e.g. types of administrative structures) such that planning approaches could be more readily designed to fit particular classes of environmental characteristics.

ASHE Reader on Planning and Institutional Research

As progress is made in the design and adaptation of basic planning approaches, the university can move to the next step of determining appropriate methods, strategies and tactics. It could also refine the concepts, models and frameworks to be used, determine the procedures and formal and informal structures to be established, and prepare guidelines and establish skills development programs. Interconnections among various elements of the planning programs could then be more readily identified and considered. Through the course of formulating and progressively refining the planning approach, adaptations will be necessary to suit institutional types (e.g. small liberal arts universities) as well as the unique characteristics of each institution. Plan formulation, refinement and application process must be highly iterative as it is extended towards and applied in practice. A systematic approach to monitoring and feedback through plan formulation and application is also critical to ensuring that the plan is both appropriate to the setting within which it is applied and that it evolves jointly with its internal and external environments.

In conclusion, the gulf between planning theory and practice remains wide. However, we need not be condemned to esoteric conceptual musings and loosely structured, anecdotal descriptions of practice. By combining and extending the available planning models through experimental planning initiative and by deriving and testing current and new models and frameworks through case studies, the promise exists to progressively formulate classes of planning approaches which are both theoretically rigorous and empirically relevant. What remains to be determined is whether the will exists to realize that potential.

References

Allison, G. T. (1971), *Essence of decision: Explaining the Cuban missile crisis.* Boston: Little Brown and Company.

Bell, E. (1978). Administrative planning: Science or art? *Planning for Higher Education, 7* (3), 12–15.

Boxx, R., & Johnson, J. W. (1980). An examination of formalized planning as currently used in institutions of higher learning. *Planning for Higher Education 8* (4), 25–39.

Braybrooke, D., & Lindblom, C. E. (1970). *A strategy of decision.* New York: The Free Press.

Bryson, J. M. (1988). *Strategic planning for public and nonprofit organizations. A guide to strengthening and sustaining organizational achievement.* San Francisco: Jossey-Bass Publishers.

Cope, R. G. (1981). Strategic planning, management and decision-making. *AAHE-ERIC/Higher Education Research, 9.* Washington, D.C.: American Association for Higher Education.

Cope. R. G. (1985). A contextual model to encompass the strategic planning concept: Introducing a newer paradigm. *Planning for Higher Education, 13* (3), 13–20.

Culhane, P. J., Friesema, H. P., & Beecher, J. A. (1987). Forecasts and environmental decisionmaking. *The Content and Predictive Accuracy of Environmental Impact Statements.* Social Impact Assessment Series No. 14. Boulder and London: Westview Press, Inc.

Faludi, A. (1978). *Essays on planning theory and education.* New York: Pergamon Press.

Faludi, A. (1983). Critical rationalism and planning methodology. *Urban Studies,* 265–278.

Faludi, A. (ed.). (1973). The Science of Muddling Through. *A Reader in Planning Theory.* Oxford: Pergamon Press.

Keller, G. (1987). *Academic strategy: The management revolution in American higher education.* Baltimore: The Johns Hopkins University Press.

Lang, D. W. (1983, May). *Planning and decision-making in universities.* University of Toronto: Office of the Vice-President (Research and Planning) and Registrar.

Lelong, D., & Shirley, R. (1984). Planning: Identifying the focus points for action. *Planning for Higher Education, 12* (4), 1–7.

March, J. & Simon, H. (1958). *Organizations.* New York: John Wiley.

Michael, D. (1973). *On learning to plan . . . and planning to learn: The social psychology of changing toward future responsive societal learning.* San Francisco: Jossey-Bass.

Miller, J. L. Jr. (1983). Strategic planning as pragmatic adaption. *Planning for Higher Education, 12* (1), 41–47.

Pounds, H. R., & Strickland, D. C. (1980). Developing a planning unit at the state level to meet the needs of the public. *Planning for Higher Education, 9* (1), 12–17.

Rosenhead, J. (1980). Planning under uncertainty: The inflexibility of methodologies. *Journal of the Operational Research Society, 31*(3), 209–216.

Shrivastava, P. (1983). A typology of organizational learning systems. *Journal of Management Studies, 20*(1), 7–28.

Simon, H. A. (1976). *Administrative behavior* (3rd ed.). New York: Macmillan.

Thompson, H. L. (1979). A case study of a different approach to planning. *Planning for Higher Education, 8*(2).

Uehling, B. S. (1981). Planning as if people mattered. Goals for quality higher education. *Planning for Higher Education, 93*, 33–37.

Young, S. (1981). Some dimensions of strategic planning for higher education. *Planning for Higher Education, 9*(4), 1–7.

Using Contextual Planning To Transform Institutions

Marvin W. Peterson

This chapter examines contextual planning, a new strategy for or approach to planning that may be more appropriate for a turbulent environment in which the character of the postsecondary system or industry is also in a state of flux. Chapter One discussed such an environment, in which the emergence of a postsecondary knowledge industry suggests the need to consider broad planning questions dealing with redefining that industry and the institution's role in it, redirecting institutional mission and external relationships, redesigning or reorganizing institutional structures and processes, and reforming or recreating a new academic culture.

Planning in an environment that addresses these questions needs to be *proactive*, attempting to shape as well as to understand the newly emerging postsecondary knowledge industry. Planning needs to have the potential to *transform* the institution in extensive and significant ways. Planning, therefore, needs to anticipate *macro change* approaches that are multilevel and designed to alter external relationships, change internal structures, and incorporate concern for reshaping individual roles and the institution's culture. Such a strategy, designed to guide our institutions into the twenty-first century, needs to be a *comprehensive* one, requiring *leadership* that is multidimensional, willing to take risks, and able to provide a consistent and committed effort.

Contextual planning is not seen as unrelated to or inconsistent with effective long-range or strategic planning approaches. Rather, it is seen as an extension of our understanding of planning necessitated by and related to the changing nature of our institutional environment and our system or industry. In presenting a contextual approach, this chapter first addresses the evolutionary nature of planning to suggest the relationship of long-range, strategic, and conceptual planning. These three approaches are then contrasted to clarify the nature of contextual planning and its relationship to the other two. A process view, identifying the elements of contextual planning, further provides insight into its nature and applicability. A brief case study shows how the approach is useful in understanding one institution's efforts to redirect its mission for the twenty-first century. Finally, a set of conditions for implementing contextual planning is discussed.

The Historical Evolution of Planning Approaches: A Contingency Model

As noted in Chapter One, planning for and by postsecondary institutions is largely a post-1950 phenomenon. As with many management functions in colleges and universities, the development of both the content focus of planning and approaches to planning have been sporadic, uneven, and highly varied. Regarding content, campus and facilities planning emerged earliest as a formal activity on many campuses in the 1950s, when enrollment demand exploded and the need for new and expanded campuses was pressing. Financial and

"Using Contextual Planning to Transform Institutions," by Marvin W. Peterson, reprinted from *Planning and Management for a Changing Environment*, edited by M. W. Peterson, D. D. Dill and L. A. Mets, 1997. Jossey-Bass Publishers, Inc.

resource planning became a visible concern in the late 1960s and early 1970s, when enrollment demand leveled and economic factors required a realistic assessment of the future. In the mid-1970s and early 1980s the emphasis shifted to enrollment forecasting and academic program planning, as both enrollment demand and financial resources remained constrained and institutional competition for scarce resources increased. Comprehensive or integrated planning, like academic planning, was occasionally implemented from the mid-1970s on, when continuing constraints required broader institutional attempts to become more efficient and effective. One analysis, using a contingency model, has suggested that these fragmented and varied patterns in the development of planning have largely been responses to the changing management pressures on institutions induced by changing environmental conditions (Peterson, 1986).

A similar contingency view of approaches to planning—the notion that the content and nature of planning are dependent on or responses to changes in the environment—provides a useful model for understanding the more general development of long-range, strategic, and contextual planning approaches. A brief history of the changing, post-World War II external conditions for higher and postsecondary education provides some perspective on their institutional impact on the evolution of organizational models, notions of institutional performance, and approaches to planning that have emerged. Of particular note is how the approach to planning reflects the changing character of the resource environment (availability of finances, demand for services, and degree of public support) and the changing definition of the higher or postsecondary industry, which reflects the primary focus of an institution's competitive milieu. Table 1 portrays a model suggesting how these approaches to planning are related to the condition of the institution's resource environment and its industry perspective.

1950–1975: Plans, Forecasting, and Long-Range Planning

Following World War II and extending through the 1960s, U.S. higher education experienced an unprecedented period of growth and expansion marked by strong government financial support, expanding enrollment demands, and very positive public support. Institutions defined other traditional higher educational institutions as their industry (see Chapter One). Competition for expanding student enrollments and financial resources was limited and usually focused within one's own institutional-type sector. During this period, the pressure on institutional management was to provide a sense of direction for their growing institution and to account for the expanding human, financial, and physical resources they were absorbing in order to maintain public support. Two internally oriented models of organization emerged in the literature; they emphasized the purposive nature of the institutions and helped us understand and manage these growing institutions. The first, the formal rational or bureaucratic organization (Stroup, 1966), focused on building rational structures to administer and develop mechanisms to account for growing resource flows and needs. The second, the collegial model, was also stressed; it reflected our notions of colleges and universities as self-contained communities of learners (Goodman, 1964), professionals (Clark, 1963), or constituents with a common community of interests (Millett, 1962). The focus of performance during this era was primarily on resources: the quantitative characteristics of students, faculty, programs, and facilities needed to justify financial resources. Planning emphasized developing formal institutional or campus master plans to justify resources and guide development; it began to rely on self-studies to document strengths and weaknesses for accreditation and to guide further development.

In the late 1960s, disruptions reflected student dissatisfaction with increasingly large, impersonal, professionalized, and formally structured institutions; the U.S. role in the Vietnam War; and the civil rights movement. In order to continue favorable environmental support, the pressure on institutional management was to maintain control on campus and to ensure greater access for minority students. Colleges and universities began to be viewed both as open systems (Katz and Kahn, 1978) and as political organizations (Baldridge, 1971) made up of competing constituencies. In part to reassure public support and to strengthen higher education's image, an emphasis on performance that was based on peer judgment of reputational quality of graduate and professional education emerged in the form of American Council on Education (ACE)-sponsored studies (Cartter, 1966; Roose and Anderson, 1970). Planning became short-term and responsive. Contingency planning designed to deal with the underlying sources of discontent was common.

By the early 1970s, an economic recession and the end of the postwar baby boom demand forced an assessment of that reality on many campuses. Meanwhile state, federal, and other external agencies were demanding greater institutional accountability and becoming more sophisticated in collecting and analyzing data and asking tough management questions. Concurrently, the 1972 Higher Education Amendments shifted federal student aid distribution from institutions directly to the student. These changes focused institutional management on improving internal efficiency, seeking new student markets, and taking planning more seriously.

New organizational thinking emphasized comprehensive, information-based managerial models to inform decisions (Lawrence and Service, 1977) or else market-oriented models designed to identify and attract new students. Performance concerns began to shift to an emphasis on results—but primarily quantitative measures of productivity (outputs) or efficiency (indices of cost per unit, workload, etc.). Planning now emphasized forecasting and the development of a long-range, continuous planning process in which assumptions, projections, and plans were constantly revised; planning began to emerge as a formal administrative position or task force on many campuses.

1975–1990: Strategic Planning

In the late 1970s and throughout the 1980s, continued economic constraints; new alternative demands for public funds; real decline in the number of traditional college-age students; and forecasts of significant changes in the economic, ethnic, and educational background of future college-age students painted a new picture of the industry and environment. Resources and enrollments would be a constraint on growth, demand was changing, and the public was clearly not as supportive. Following the 1972 Higher Education Amendments, proprietary institutions began competing with more traditional higher education institutions for students and funds in a new postsecondary industry. The management press was both to reduce, reallocate, and retrench (Mortimer and Tierney, 1979) and to become more effective. New organizational models stressed flexible, decentralized, organized anarchies (Cohen and March, 1974) or matrix models (Alpert, 1986). Colleges and universities were viewed not just as responsive institutions but as strategic organizations that could revise their priorities, change clientele and program mixes, and seek a strategic market niche within the postsecondary education industry. Performance based on results such as effectiveness or goal achievement began to be examined. By the late 1980s, criticism of both K–12 education (National Commission on Excellence in Education, 1983) and higher education (Study Group on the Condition of Excellence in American Higher Education, 1984) led some academic leaders and many public policy officials to ask for performance results reflecting student learning outcomes and to encourage the use of student

Table 1. A Contingency Model: Environmental Condition, Competitive Perspective, and Planning Approach.

Condition of Environment	Primary Competitive or Collaborative Perspective		
Resource Availability, Enrollment Demand, Public Support	Higher Education Industry	Postsecondary Education Industry	Postsecondary Knowledge Industry
1950–1975: munificent, growing, supportive	Plans, forecasting, and long-range planning		
1975–1995: constrained, changing, neutral		Strategic planning	
1995 and beyond: limited, reordering, critical			Contextual planning

and academic assessment. Strategic planning eclipsed long-range planning and became the primary focus of the 1980s (Keller, 1983).

As we entered the 1990s, two things were clear. First, our organizational and governance models, our performance criteria, and our approaches to planning are heavily influenced by external challenges. Second, the new models, criteria, and approaches do not supersede the earlier ones. Rather, they become part of a more complex picture of how we understand the organizational patterns and the governance, performance, and planning patterns in our institutions.

The 1990s and Beyond: Contextual Planning

In looking to the coming century and millennium, Chapter One portrays both our environment and our industry quite differently from those of previous decades. Changing societal conditions (new patterns of diversity, the telematics revolution, quality as learning and improvement, contribution to economic productivity, new postsecondary relearning markets, and globalization) all are seen to have extensive implications for both our postsecondary industry and our institutional environments. A postsecondary knowledge network or industry that includes many new types of organizations, focuses on the use of knowledge for learning, offers a potentially far more flexible technology for learning, and redefines our traditional working relationships from service provider to collaborator or competitor with these new types of organizations is likely to be highly competitive. The resource environment for traditional postsecondary institutions suggests that (1) financial resources will be increasingly limited as government's capacity to support—and student and parental ability to pay—continues to decline, (2) the demand for postsecondary learning services is being seriously reordered by new clientele, (3) new modes of delivery are emerging, and (4) the public perception of postsecondary education is becoming increasingly critical.

Reflecting these contextual changes in the industry and environment, new organizational models not surprisingly are already emerging. Notions of colleges and universities as conglomerate (Clark, 1995) and network (Dill and Sporn, 1995) organizations suggest institutions that are more complex combinations of units and embedded in new webs of interorganizational relationships. The notion of organizations as cultural entities (while not new) is also growing in popularity as the need to change traditional academic settings and the nature of academic work are being discussed. The challenges also suggest new performance criteria for our institutions: how they will redesign their external relationships, redefine their missions, deal with internal reorganization, and recreate or renew their institutional culture.

Amid efforts to deal with this more complex and competitive postsecondary knowledge industry and its highly turbulent environment, a new mode of planning has emerged: contextual planning. This approach is broader and more flexible than strategic planning and may be more useful in the face of a changing industry and turbulent resource environment. It is more holistic than strategic planning and deals with redesigning the *context*, both in the external environment and within the organization.

Contingency Revisited

This discussion has suggested that the approaches to planning are contingent on and reflect the changing complexity and competitiveness of the industry and the increasing turbulence in our institutional environment (Table 1). Clearly, the three approaches described in the next section are not mutually exclusive and do not replace one another. Indeed, forecasting and long-range planning processes are and will continue to be useful in a clearly defined sector of higher or postsecondary institutions with limited competition and in more favorable resource environments. Strategic planning, it is suggested, is appropriate for a clearly understood but more competitive postsecondary sector in which resources are more constrained but somewhat predictable. More importantly, the three approaches to planning may reinforce one another; forecasting and long-range planning can inform strategic planning, which in turn informs contextual planning. Or vice versa: contextual planning may lead to identifying parts of the institution whose subenvironments are more stable and offer the institution strategic advantage. We now turn to a discussion of the three approaches and an elaboration of contextual planning.

Three Planning Approaches: Elaborating Contextual Planning

Contextual planning may best be understood by contrasting it with long-range and strategic planning. Each planning approach is discussed here through definition and the primary planning question it addresses. The three are contrasted in terms of their *external and internal perspectives* (Tables 2 and 3). The external perspective examines dimensions related to their primary environmental assumption, the principal organization-environment dynamics, the institution's external strategy, and the nature of the planning process. The internal perspective examines dimensions related to the internal organizational planning focus, the assumed primary motivation mechanism emphasized, and assumptions about how to control member behavior.

Long-Range Planning

Long-range planning focuses on forecasting future resource flows and environmental trends or conditions, establishing institutional plans for that new reality, devising ways to get there and continually reassessing them (Kirschling and Huckfeldt, 1980; Wing, 1980). Long-range planning asks "What can we achieve in this en-

vironment?" and "How can we get there?" It is planning that is *responsive* to a predictably changing environment.

Long-range planning assumes the external environment controls what it is possible for the institution to achieve; that enrollment demands and resource flows are somewhat stable or changing in a manner that can be reasonably predicted; that there is limited competition from other institutions; and that institutional mission is largely defined in order that plans can be adjusted to external realities. Institutional planning relies on a rational or quasi-rational process to predict trends, develop plans, and devise a strategy for moving the institution ahead. Forecasts, environmental assumptions, and plans are the major focus.

Internally, long-range planning tends to view the institution as a formal organization. Attention is focused largely on clarifying institutional purpose, goals, policies, and procedures, on designing institutional process and programs to achieve them; and on allocating resources and monitoring performance according to them. Planning, even if participatory in style, is primarily designed to direct and control institutional behavior; it is focused on preaudits assessing the need for resources; and it assumes member behavior is constrained and can be directed to support the planned purposes.

Table 2. External Perspectives of Three Planning Approaches

Planning Approach	Environmental Assumption	Organization-Environment Dynamic	Institutional Strategy	Planning Process
Long-range planning; "responsive"	Predictable sectors and resource flows	Responsive, rational	Limited competition, adjust plans to reality	Assumptions, forecasts, and plans
Strategic planning "adaptive"	Conflicting sectors and resource flows	Adaptive, judgmental	Postsecondary education competition, comparative advantage, "fit" or "niche"	Institutional mission, image, and resource strategies
Contextual planning; "proactive"	Complex but malleable	Proactive, intuitive	Cross-industry cooperation, coalition, or competition	Redefine institutional role, mission, and external relationships

Table 3. Internal Perspectives of Three Planning Approaches

Planning Approach	Organizational Planning Focus	Motivation Mechanism	Mode of Control	Member Behavior
Long-Range planning	Purpose/policies, goals/objectives (formal organization)	Direction and control	Inputs, preaudit	Constrained behavior
Strategic planning	Program and resource allocation strategies (resources)	Guidance, review, and improvement	Outcomes assessment, postaudit	Flexible behavior
Contextual planning	Direction, values, process, and meaning (organizational culture)	Themes and visions	Sense of direction, involvement, and ownership	Empowered behavior

Strategic Planning

Strategic planning may use forecasting, but it relies more on "assessing the current and future environmental opportunities and threats, by examining the changing character of the environment and the patterns of competition within the industry, and on assessing the strengths and weaknesses of the institution in order to identify its comparative advantage, a strategic niche and appropriate strategies for competition effectively" (Peterson, 1980). Its focus is on asking "How can we modify the institution to be a more effective competitor within our environment and our industry?" It is *adaptive* planning in a clearly defined but competitive industry (Keller, 1983; Peterson, 1980; Mintzberg, 1994; Baldridge and Okimi, 1982; Schmidtlein and Milton, 1990).

While the assumption is that most of the environment is beyond the institution's capacity to control (or that some important elements of the environment are not predictable or may be in conflict), strategic planning does present both possible opportunities as well as threats; it suggests that adapting the institution's mission, purpose, and functions to the environment is desirable. It focuses on competing in a less predictable and more complex environment by understanding needs and demands, how other institutions are meeting or failing to meet them, and the strengths and weaknesses of your own institution in that competitive environment. The intent of planning is to identify your institution's comparative advantage and the market niche it will attempt to fill. Developing an adaptive strategy places greater reliance on judgment about the appropriate strat-

egy than does long-range planning. Planning focuses on modifying the institution's mission and purposes, developing a favorable "image," and designing a strategy to attract resources that ensures the institution can effectively compete in its market niche.

Internally, strategic planning acknowledges formal structure but tends to focus on the organization as a more loosely coupled pattern of structures, programs, and resources. Emphasis is placed on designing a strategy for allocating programs and resources in order to maintain the institution's comparative and competitive advantage. Implementation involves establishing goals to guide behavior and designing review processes to ensure goal achievement. Control shifts to a greater focus on results: assessments of outcomes, goal achievement, and other forms of postaudit review. Flexible member or unit behavior consistent with the strategy is encouraged so as to help the institution adapt to changing environmental and competitive forces.

Contextual Planning

Contextual planning is not a new concept to higher education (Cope, 1985; Chaffee, 1985). It may incorporate elements of long-range and strategic planning, but it is different in one basic way. It does not assume that environments are uncontrollable, that industries are permanent, or that institutions cannot change their basic mission, structure, and patterns of interorganizational relationship. Contextual planning is concerned with examining the changing nature of the institution's industry,

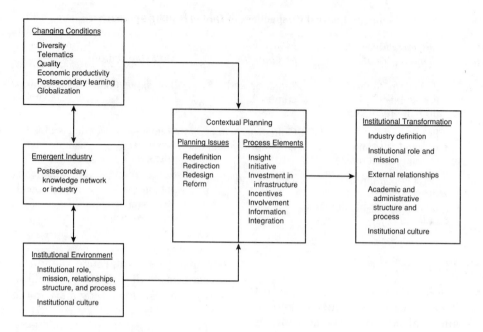

Figure 1. Framework for Contextual Planning

identifying feasible new institutional roles and external relationships, and then attempting to shape both environmental conditions and institutional arrangements to become an effective competitor in a new industry. Contextual planning is a process that focuses on creating or shaping external contexts most favorable to our institution's mission, and on designing internal institutional contexts that allow members to contribute to the new institutional roles. It asks about the changing nature of our industry and how can we shape it, as well as our institution, to ensure viability. Contextual planning is *proactive*, seeking to both shape the industry and reshape the institution.

Contextual planning, then, begins with the assumption that the environment and the industry may be changing but they can be influenced. Relationships among existing industries beyond higher and postsecondary education are seen as interactive, complex, and changing—perhaps in unpredictable ways, but malleably. In order to compete in such an environment, contextual planning must be proactive. Contextual planning examines the nature of an industry and the forces that shape it in order to understand how the industry is being redefined and what new cross-industry organizational patterns or relationships are emerging. Consideration of new patterns of competition,

coalition, or cooperation are a key part of the external strategy. Such planning involves intuitive choices as well as rational decisions or strategic judgments. The potential of contextual planning is not only in redefining an institution's industry and its own role in the industry but also in redesigning its mission and relationship to other organizations (including those in previously unrelated industries).

Internally, contextual planning may require redesigning or reorganizing an institution's primary academic functions, processes, and structures to meet a changed institutional role or mission. Since many faculty and staff chose to work in higher education because they value their work and what the institution stands for, contextual planning needs to focus on the academic and administrative culture of the institution and processes for changing that culture as well. Implementing an understanding of the redefined institutional external relationships, role and mission, and structural changes relies on providing visions and themes of what the institution will be like—what it will stand for and what it will mean to its members—to motivate them. Member control involves reforming behavior and values. It may rely on conveying the sense of direction of new institutional initiatives or a sense of urgency or importance, on using incentives or providing resources that members can use, and on creating opportunities for being involved and having a sense of ownership. Short of catastrophic changes such as threats to the institution's existence, value changes usually occur when members are empowered: fully involved in critical choices, provided incentives to participate, and assisted in learning to make the needed changes.

Thus contextual planning is an approach that does not fully replace long-range or strategic planning. But it is more holistic. It forces institutions to take a broader view of a postsecondary knowledge or learning industry and of an external environment for higher education that may include organizations from other previously unrelated industries. It seeks to examine how the larger environment and industry is changing and can be reshaped or influenced by the institution. It considers new role-and-mission options and new types of interinstitutional linkages. Then it tries to redesign or reorganize internal structures and processes appropriately and to establish or recreate an institutional culture that motivates and supports its members in responding to this new direction.

A Process View of Contextual Planning

Contextual planning is thus an approach to planning designed to respond to situations in which the nature of one's industry is in flux, significant questions about the role and mission of an institution may be raised, and extensive transformation in the institution is required. Figure 1 presents a framework for understanding contextual planning and seven process elements that seem to be reflected in this planning approach.

Contextual planning begins with an assessment of the changing conditions or challenges in the external environment, the changing nature of the postsecondary knowledge network or industry, and an assessment of the institution itself. In Chapter One, seven major challenges to the postsecondary industry and to our institutions are suggested. The changing nature of the postsecondary knowledge industry or network is also explored, as are the internal and external impacts on an institution. Nine characteristics of the emerging postsec-

ondary knowledge industry are identified. The discussion in that chapter poses four critical planning issues for institutions that choose to adopt a contextual planning approach:

> *Redefinition:* what is the nature of an emerging postsecondary knowledge industry, and what is our institution's role in it?
> *Redirection:* how should our institution's mission change to reflect these new realities, and what external relationships with other organizations should we develop?
> *Redesign:* how should we redesign or reorganize our academic functions, processes, or structures?
> *Renewal:* How do we renew or recreate our academic workplace and institutional culture to accommodate these changes? Our preparation of future faculty?

Clearly, addressing these questions raises the potential of institutional transformation: significant changes in how institutions define the industry in which they compete, new or modified notions of institutional role and mission, potential competitive or collaborative relationships with new types of organizations, substantial redesign or revision of academic and administrative structures, functions and processes, and modifications of institutional culture. These are at least potential outcomes for a contextual planning process.

While contextual planning is only an emerging approach, the experience of several institutions that have attempted to plan for a changing industry suggests at least seven elements in the planning process to guide contextual planning.

Insight

In an industry in flux, it is critical to develop understanding, an informed insight into the dynamics of a shift from an industry of postsecondary institutions to a postsecondary knowledge industry. Unlike strategic planning, which seeks to find a strategic niche in an existing industry, the focus in contextual planning is on understanding the dynamics of a moving target: a rapidly changing industry whose form is still being shaped. Planners and executive officers need to become students of their own postsecondary industry as well as of related industries. In a sense, the focus shifts to trying to understand the changing nature of a vast network of information and knowledge, of postsecondary learners, and of the organizational players in this rapidly changing area within which formal postsecondary teaching and learning occur. The attempt is to gain a perspective on where the emerging knowledge industry is heading.

While traditional planning techniques such as forecasting, trend analysis, and scenario building may be useful, they need to be focused on the intersections of the postsecondary information, computing, telecommunications, and training and development industries. In doing so, it is useful to examine not only the challenges to our current postsecondary system or industry (diversity, telematics, quality, economic productivity, postsecondary relearning and globalization) but also how those become forces reshaping the postsecondary industry identified in Chapter One:

- Who are the changing or emerging *consumers* (clientele) for postsecondary education? What are their learning needs and preferences?

- Who are our *suppliers* (sources of funds and employers of graduates), and how are they changing?

- Who are the *new competitors* entering our postsecondary educational service marketplace?

- Are *substitute services* increasingly available, and from where?

- How are *innovations* in the development and transmission of knowledge and learning changing our industry?

- Where and how is our *pattern* of *competition* changing, for both students and graduates?

If we focus both on the challenges to our existing postsecondary industry and on the emerging postsecondary knowledge industry, new and informed insights should emerge. They form the basis for defining this emerging industry and for determining the role the institution might take in attempting to shape the emerging industry or reshape the institution.

Initiatives

Beyond insight into the emerging postsecondary knowledge network or industry and

the role an institution might play, it is important for the institution to examine its own strengths and weaknesses and to establish one or more initiatives. An *initiative* is a broad thrust or sense of direction that the institution intends to take that reflects its new role and may suggest a new mission or reinforce a current one. In a rapidly changing or emerging industry, it is important to identify such an initiative to prevent being left behind. Initiatives may be a "marketing niche," as in strategic planning, but usually they focus on a broader direction: confirming a new role or mission for the institution such as serving a very different clientele, developing a new capacity, preparing for a new set of competitive conditions, etc. It implies potentially substantial institutional change but lacks highly defined objectives or specific program and resource strategies. These may emerge later, designed to establish direction but not constrain efforts or activities directed to fulfilling the initiative.

Such an initiative serves in part as a "vision," a sense of direction for the institution and its constituents. In that sense, it is both a symbolic attempt to establish a cultural meaning and direction for the institution and a signal that efforts supporting the initiative will be encouraged and supported. As with all institutional planning, attempts to stimulate broad understanding of the insights about the changing industry and to gain support for the initiative are important practical planning concerns needing to be considered. However, the key element is that the initiative be perceived as viable and that a significant opportunity for members to participate in achieving it be available.

Investment in Infrastructure

One of the key differences between strategic planning and contextual planning is how programs are identified and resources are channeled to support planning efforts. Strategic planning usually relies on defining clear priorities, identifying specific programs, and developing supportive resource strategies to compete in a strategic niche. Contextual planning, however, assumes that in an industry in flux, many programmatic efforts are desirable. Some will be modifications of existing programs, but others will be new experimental or risk-taking ventures. It also assumes that in a postsecondary institution with a well-educated professional faculty and staff there will be numerous ideas of what works best in support of a given initiative—and that those will often be different in differing parts of the institution.

Under these assumptions, a critical feature of contextual planning is to invest resources in building an infrastructure that will serve and support groups in their development of ideas, efforts, and programs consistent with an initiative. These investments can include changes in academic or administrative structures or processes to support such initiatives or to remove barriers, development of new facilities, purchase of new equipment, addition of new technological capacity, development of new external ties and relationships, initiation of changes in hiring and staffing support, and so on.

The intent is to make critical, visible investments that support movement in the direction of the initiative. It is an investment in that it is some form of comprehensive, relatively long-term support, but it is also a symbol of institutional commitment. Making such investments requires prudent resource management to redeploy resources, or creative fundraising.

Incentives

Academic professionals are often far more likely to respond to incentives than to planned priorities and predefined programs. A key element in contextual planning is to provide incentives for various units and faculty and staff to engage in program development or redesign and in changes of their personal roles or behavior to support an initiative. Incentives for involvement can be targeted for institutionwide, unit, or individual support. They may be in the form of financial support, released time from other duties, or other forms of special developmental assistance.

Incentive can come in the often overlooked form of special recognition or rewards for outstanding proposals or successful efforts. Recognizing efforts in promotion reviews is another visible way to remove barriers and garner support. The key is to provide both substantive incentives and professional or psychological rewards. Increasing participation is the key to increasing the diversity of ideas, ensuring the success of the initiative, and gaining long-term support for it.

Involvement

While investing in appropriate infrastructure and providing incentives and rewards stimulates good ideas and potential participants in supporting an initiative, there is the danger that the initiative becomes the province of a few. In most instances contextual planning involves initiatives directed at the whole institution or large segments of it. To ensure a rich array of ideas and broad participation, it is important that the opportunities for involvement be widely available (Dill and Helm, 1988; Lawler, 1992). Investments should provide resources that are readily available, and incentives should be ample to support several worthwhile efforts. Similarly barriers to involvement, such as workload, institutional policies and procedures, or other things that restrict involvement, may need to be addressed.

Equally important is that those who wish to be involved—whether supported directly or on a voluntary basis—need to have the opportunity for improvement. This involves recognition for trying something new, special training where necessary, and an opportunity to learn new skills and ways of doing things.

Information

An initiative even with wide-scale involvement can suffer if internal and external constituents lack information about or awareness of an initiative. Institutional support for major initiatives should include widely disseminated information about the reasons for and nature of the initiative, its significant investments and what they make available to faculty and staff, and the incentives for and patterns of involvement. Public recognition of success stories, new approaches, and new efforts is often gratifying to those involved.

While internal reports, newsletters, seminars, and other modes of institutional dissemination are useful in informing participants and other institutional members, external efforts should not be overlooked. Quite often, initiatives that reflect a new institutional role, mission, or mode of doing business are not readily perceived externally. Enhancing the institution's new initiative may involve changing its "image," which suggests emphasizing external coverage of the initiative via newspaper, TV, reports in professional journals, etc., as well.

Integration

A successful initiative will spawn many new ideas and efforts, a number of innovative projects, and some high-risk ventures. The intent is to better position the institution as the emergent or changing industry takes shape. Unlike strategic planning, there is less initial focus on clear program definition, tightly controlled resource guidelines, and intensive evaluation and review. Contextual planning, however, is not intended to support unending proliferation and fragmentation. Periodically, the array of activities supporting an initiative needs to be assessed. Successful efforts need to be reinforced. Similar ones may be merged to provide better focus. Some may be promising but need redirection or support. Others must be closed or folded back into ongoing activities.

The key is that contextual planning, which is designed to create new initiatives in an uncertain and rapidly changing environment, places a greater emphasis on stimulating movement than on carefully directing planning; the latter is only possible in a well-understood industry and environment. However, once the initiative is well under way, it has to be assessed and focused. The new structures, programs, and activities need to be integrated into the organization and managed as part of its ongoing efforts.

Once the initiative is successful, the institution will have substantially redirected key elements of its role and mission and established new external relationships; different internal patterns of structure and process will be emerging, and a new culture or change in academic workplace values will be in place to support this effort. At that time, as the shape of the industry and the pattern of competition becomes more settled, the new initiatives will at least partially transform the institution and its programs will become subject to a more strategic mode of planning. As the initiatives are evaluated and mature, they will need to be merged into the institutional pattern for managing its ongoing operations.

A Case Study: Technological Innovation

There are numerous examples of contextual planning, that is, redirecting an institution in the midst of industry change and environmental uncertainty. University medical schools are redesigned as hospital systems or HMOs as the health care industry is redefined. Small liberal arts colleges for traditional students become professionally oriented to serve older, part-time students in the growing training and development sector. Single-purpose colleges merge to become more comprehensive institutions serving a broader postsecondary market. However, a brief case study of a major research university's attempt to position itself in the emerging postsecondary knowledge industry may provide a useful explication of contextual planning.

Institutional Context

Throughout the 1980s, Major University, despite its national reputation and relative success, had struggled with constantly declining resources. Attempts at strategic planning and priority setting designed to facilitate institutional resource reduction and reallocation had failed to create an environment that supported cost-effectiveness. In the mid- to late 1980s, Academic Vice President Wellgood had introduced an institutionwide planning process to shift the university from a reactive to a more proactive stance and to view the external environment as challenging rather than threatening. The effort, which focused in part on reviewing essential themes and components of the university's mission, was successful in getting the strategic planning team (executive officers and faculty leaders) to focus on changes in the external environment. But no substantive plans or actions were forthcoming. A priority fund to support innovation, obtained by taxing existing unit allocations, was needed to cover other budget shortfalls. More draconian program reviews led to some downsizing of units but generated significant negative publicity, loss of morale in the affected units, resistance to program review in other areas facing similar action, and minimal savings.

Insight

In 1988, Wellgood, a nationally renowned scientist and successful academic administrator, was named president of the institution. However, before assuming office he was given a six-month sabbatical. During that time he traveled widely, visiting other university presidents, association heads, and foundation executives to gain perspective on what was happening in postsecondary education. He also engaged various groups around the university, exploring themes raised in the previous planning discussions and in his travels. These would provide the grist for his presidential inaugural address.

In that address, Wellgood stressed the need for a new paradigm in which Major University would interact with a constantly changing environment as it approached the twenty-first century. He described a university culture that relished, stimulated, and managed continuous change. He also stressed continuous renewal of the institution's role and mission and identified three distinct themes for the university. One of these emphasized establishing the university as a world leader in the use of information technology in the knowledge age. The address reflected a contextual perspective: the need to establish a planning capacity capable of both adapting to and modifying its environment, and to create an internal culture supporting change and a managerial capacity to manage it.

Initiative

The initiative focusing on information technology in an age of knowledge had been a topic of discussion during his term as academic vice president but was never clearly articulated until his inaugural address. The address was followed by intensive discussions with the faculty governing body, with the board of trustees in their annual retreat, and among executive officers and administrative groups; the discussions elicited general support for the implied direction and appropriate concern about its lack of specifics. Shortly thereafter, the president further clarified the initiative in a vision statement distributed widely on campus. This document reflected a summation of the earlier planning efforts, refinements during his pre-presidential sabbatical, and the early discussions.

Because Major University had a significant history in the development of mainframe com-

puting, several professional schools were already embarking on efforts to stimulate computer use themselves. Since Wellgood's ideas had been discussed with various planning, executive, and faculty groups, the initiative was viewed as an appropriate one. Exactly what it meant and how the institution would change was not spelled out. However, earlier discussions about strategic priorities had always engendered disagreements and even conflict among the deans.

Investment in Infrastructure

At least three critical investment decisions provided support for this initiative. One involved a structural change. An executive officer was hired to spearhead the university's effort in information technology, and a universitywide Division of Information Technology (DIT) was initiated in 1990 to coordinate varied but fragmented academic and administrative computing efforts, the libraries' use of information technology, the transition from a mainframe to a microcomputing environment, and the university's nascent internal networking and external telecommunications linkages.

A second set of internal technological investments between 1990 and 1993 led to the development of one of the country's largest privately owned phone systems; the installation of a fiber optic cable system linking all offices, classrooms, and residence halls on campus; and the development of a campuswide set of computing sites completely equipped with fully networked computers. This network provided both phone and computer jacks in all offices and was capable of handling integrated data, sound, and video transmission. The phone system allowed access to all university information resources from any location.

A third set of externally directed technological investments during the same period linked the campus to a host of local, state, national, and international computer and information networks using the latest in information and telecommunications networks. These new relationships involved contracts, partnerships, and joint ventures with numerous computing, information technology, and telecommunications firms and government agencies.

In essence, the university invested heavily in new organizational structure, technology, and external relationships to provide support for this initiative. This occurred without a clearly defined strategic niche, clear purposes to be achieved, or an internal set of priorities or programs designed to succeed. Rather, it had invested in infrastructure designed to support faculty, academic, and administrative activities consistent with the initiative.

Incentives

Several incentive programs have been an integral part of the information technology initiative. An internal Presidential Initiative fund was established to provide over $1 million to stimulate innovative, interdisciplinary, and venturesome research in this area. The Division of Information Technology established special arrangements with computer firms to provide lower educational prices and discounts to faculty, students, and staff or to academic departments and administrative units to purchase computers and software. Other incentives included on-campus repair, maintenance, and upgrade services on equipment and a comprehensive program of regularly scheduled workshops, for free or at a nominal price. Deans were encouraged to seek development funds to support or to initiate joint efforts with computer, information, and telecommunications firms to obtain equipment to add to the network or new funding for educational and research efforts related to information technology.

Involvement

In addition to the various incentives that encouraged the purchase of computers and software and provided training to large numbers of faculty, students, and staff, several other internal and externally oriented activities have promoted involvement. For example, DIT staff assist units wanting to exchange information, computer services, and telecommuter courses using the institution's internal computing network or through its links to the external networks. Customized instructional services to assist faculty and entire units in designing and implementing new computer and telecommunications courses and programs have supported a variety of specialized applications. A program to train trainers and provide workshop materials assists units in becoming more self-sufficient.

The patterns of involvement are not only internally directed. One university program on information technology integration promotes research and development efforts that use technology to build partnerships between external sponsors and university researchers. DIT also works jointly with corporate and government partners to develop new applications of information technology. The university has also taken leadership in founding or participating in consortia with other universities to expand their educational and research capacity.

This pattern of fostering widespread opportunity for involvement by faculty, staff, and students in units throughout the university both internally and in expanded relationships with external groups has greatly enhanced the involvement in this initiative and broadened the base of understanding of what can be done in a technology-driven educational and research environment.

Information

Conscious efforts to disseminate information about information technology are ubiquitous. DIT produces a bimonthly publication available in hard copy and electronically, focusing only on major university activities and participants. A variety of large-scale workshops sponsored by DIT have provided participants with information for both beginners and advanced users. In cosponsorship with other schools and colleges, a variety of symposia have explored the future of computing, information, and telecommunications technology and the changing role of universities in the age of information. On a more informal basis, the university has supported the development of specialized user-groups on e-mail who are constantly exchanging information.

Externally, DIT has supported staff presentations at various professional postsecondary associations. The university's information technology initiative has also been the focus of articles in several national professional publications. This widespread use of information has made the information initiative common knowledge throughout the university, enhanced people's understanding of its potential in many areas, and provided visible recognition for interesting new activities and their developers. Information as well as incentives and opportunities for involvement are increasing support for the initiative.

Integration

The success and rapid expansion of the information technology initiative has necessitated better understanding of its size, nature, and cost; more focused strategic planning for the effort; and more effective management of an expensive and expanding infrastructure. Recently DIT has done a series of planning reports to begin examining the various services it provides and to track the patterns of use of the university's information network. A number of reports have attempted to examine the emerging organizational structure of the information technology initiative and its relationship with and use by various academic and administrative units. These reports have led to a reorganization of DIT, its staffing, and its support service relationship to various academic and administrative units. Studies of the costs of the information technology infrastructure and various DIT services have been undertaken. Procedures for budgetary allocations for them are being designed. Preliminary efforts to charge for services are being discussed. Deans now regularly review their units' educational technology initiatives and developments in their annual budget meetings with the academic vice president. The shape of a broad initiative reflecting an industry change and with the potential to transform the institution could not be clearly seen in advance; but with maturity the initiative has required attention to the elements of good organizational design to ensure it is well managed in the future.

Institutionalizing Information Technology Initiatives

To date, the information technology initiative has spawned a wide array of activities, approved substantial investments, encouraged a variety of incentives, supported numerous modes of involvement, publicized the effort widely, and begun the process of management integration. Clearly, careful organization design, strategic planning, and more concern for managing for DIT is beginning to emerge. However, the success in an initiative designed to transform the institution using a contextual

planning approach is whether or not it stimulates new initiatives that ensure a dynamic future in pursuing information technology in the age of knowledge. As this is written, three new initiatives using information and telecommunications technology are being launched. The first is an initial $40 million investment in a new Media Union, which will combine a digitized library with links to other worldwide information sources and a facility that will provide opportunities for interdisciplinary groups of students and faculty to experiment with new modes of knowledge transmission using interactive computing, video, and telecommunications technology for learning without limits of time or location. The intent is to foster interdisciplinary efforts in which representatives from more than one school or college will create new teaching-learning modalities that can be transmitted anywhere.

A second initiative involves transforming a small school of library sciences into a school of information sciences. A new dean with a background in information and computer sciences, an infusion of new faculty, and an investment in advanced classroom technology are designing a school that will train information experts of the future and will become the core faculty in the university using modern telematics technology for teaching and learning.

Yet a third initiative involves creating a position of associate vice president for academic outreach to stimulate new external delivery modes for the university's intellectual resources, using the internal and external infrastructure that is now in place. Stay tuned!

Implementing Contextual Planning

Limited experience with contextual planning and a review of the process itself suggests several factors or conditions that are essential to implementing it successfully.

A Paradigm Shift: Perspective, Change, and Thinking

To successfully implement and guide a contextual planning process requires a paradigm shift for institutional leaders and planning participants in at least three dimensions: cross-industry knowledge perspective, change orientation, and contextual thinking. First, contextual planning focuses not on the dynamics of the postsecondary industry or a segment of it, but on the emergence of a developing yet ill-defined postsecondary knowledge industry. This focus involves examining and understanding the changes occurring in the current postsecondary industry. It also involves taking a cross-industry perspective to attempt to understand the dynamics of several related industries (computing, information resources, telecommunications, postsecondary training and development, and perhaps, entertainment) as they interact or overlap in creating this emerging postsecondary knowledge network or industry. The focus is on knowledge development, dissemination, and applications for a broad and diverse array of postsecondary learners in varied settings and by varied means.

Second, because contextual planning focuses on significant changes in the external environment and industry, suggests a proactive stance in shaping that industry, may involve redefining an institution's role and mission, and may result in major institutional redesign or reorganization, the dynamics of macro change at the industrywide and institutionwide levels take on a far more central focus. Traditionally, managing change in an existing institution is focused at the individual, program, or process level—a micro change focus. Even strategic planning or the current attention given to restructuring and reengineering tends to focus only on internal institutional changes that are limited in scope. The potential for and dynamics of significant macro change strategies need to be embraced and understood by institutional leaders and planners.

Finally, contextual planning requires contextual thinking: understanding one's external and internal environment and the dynamics between them more holistically. It means focusing on broad themes of environmental and industry change, on reexamining external relationships, on redefining an institution's role, on redesigning institutional structure, and on recreating or building culture. It requires identifying and articulating new directions and initiatives, understanding the infrastructure implications of a new initiative, and knowing how to use incentives to involve people and to provide information about the initiatives and the responses it engenders. In essence, it involves an emphasis on reshaping the external environment of one's institution and the internal design and function of the institution—reshaping internal and external contexts.

These shifts toward embracing a new industry perspective, focusing on change, and thinking contextually underscore the primary governance and planning challenge: getting the institution to focus externally on questions such as "How is the postsecondary industry being transformed by the emergence of a postsecondary knowledge industry?" "What role should our institution play in that shift?" and "How should it redefine its external relationships?" Internally, it involves addressing another question: "How to redesign or reorganize our basic educational and research processes and academic structures?" This requires understanding the institution's culture and traditions, its dominant patterns, its primary constituents and how to engage them in macro change strategies, and understanding how to recreate or reform the institution's academic culture.

New Models of Organization and Performance

Implicit in the discussion of contextual planning in an emerging industry is the need to think about new models of organization and new criteria for successful institutional performance. Our previous notions of colleges and universities as formal organizations (bureaucracies), collegial communities, political entities, or organized anarchies, while useful, may be replaced by some newer models. The institution as a "network" or "interorganizational network" is one such model. In the past, we have conceived of postsecondary institutions as part of state or multicampus systems or consortia. However, the notion of a postsecondary knowledge network or industry consisting of unbounded research linkages, postsecondary relearning enterprises, learning networks, economic development combines, or global institutions suggests a fluid network or interorganizational model, one allowing us to focus on boundary relationships, interorganizational structures, and the patterns of collaborative arrangements with other postsecondary and noneducational institutions.

Another model, a variant on the organized anarchy model, is the institution as "conglomerate" (Clark, 1995), a holding company of a variety of related postsecondary enterprises. While some large universities may already function in this way, pressures from environmental challenges to support new interdisciplinary research agendas, participate in economic development, extend postsecondary educational opportunity, and utilize new information technology all affect departments or schools differentially and suggest such a model. In a conglomerate model, the organizational intent is to develop a core identity for the institution; to design effective patterns of autonomy, coordination, and decentralization for autonomous units; and to balance the tendency to fragment the institution.

A final organizational model is not a new one but has reemerged in our discussions of contextual planning: the "organization as culture" (Clark, 1963; Tierney, 1990; Peterson and others, 1995). Contextual planning's focus on redefining the nature of our industry, on redirecting institutional roles, missions, and external relationships, and on redesigning or restructuring academic processes affects the basic pattern of academic work in teaching, learning, and research. Organizational culture, especially the beliefs faculty and staff hold about the institution, their work, and its meaning for them, is critical—both as a resistance to change and as a focus for cultural reform. Sensitivity to and management of organizational culture is an important concept in this new era.

New notions of institutional performance criteria also emerge in discussing contextual planning. While our past and current focus on resource acquisition, reputation, and results still deserves attention (noted in the introduction of this chapter), contextual planning suggests new, broader, and less clearly defined concepts related to successful redefinition of institutional role and mission, redirection of external relationships, redesign or restructuring of academic and administrative structures, and reform or re-creation of the academic workplace culture. Clearly, these are difficult performance concepts to operationalize and measure, but they reflect the success of a contextual planning process that results in extensive institutional change and transformation.

Macro Change

Colleges and universities have typically engaged in incremental or micro change strategies: changing individual faculty or administrative patterns, modifying programs or processes, changing policies and procedures, merging and separating units or occasionally closing them. One of the implications of contextual planning with its proactive focus on major challenges to an institution is the need to think in terms of engaging in more macro change efforts. Attempts to redefine institutional role and mission, redirect external relationships, redesign or reorganize academic structures, and reform culture all involve extensive and sometimes long-term change strategies. Indeed, one of the assumptions of a contextual planning process is that changes at these varying levels of the institution will be linked or integrated. While it is beyond the scope of this chapter to discuss macro change strategies, successful contextual planning involves developing such strategies to implement major institutional changes. The seven process elements of contextual planning reflect a change strategy that is extensive and longer-term, involves widespread participation, and seeks to promote structural, cultural, and behavioral change.

Contextual planning has an implicit multi-level, comprehensive strategy of change. The direction of change is broadly focused and offers most institutional units or members an opportunity to participate. The emphasis on changing infrastructure—developing the platform for or a capacity to move in a given direction—is a less-directive change strategy. The use of incentives, opportunity for involvement, and information is directed toward building support for the initiative and changing the institutional culture through people's participation. The deferral of management integration—more rational program designing, planning, resource allocation, and evaluation—is aimed at reducing barriers to change in an uncertain environment but does not obviate the need for such concerns once initiatives begin to stimulate change. Such a strategy, while comprehensive, is not always a comfortable one in limited resource environments or institutions with a history of formal planning and management approaches.

Assessment

The assessment of student learning, faculty and staff performance, academic programs, or administrative units—and even institutions—is now widely understood and practiced in postsecondary education. However, contextual planning suggests the need for several broader forms of assessment that are not currently done in most institutions. Externally, attempts to redefine one's industry require assessing the changes in the postsecondary industry and other industries related to the emerging postsecondary knowledge industry. Redirecting external relationships could involve a careful assessment of each potential interorganizational linkage and the implications of various organizational arrangements for that linkage. Redefining an institution's role and mission may involve assessing the competitive and/or collaborative implications of such a change. Internally, attempts at redesigning and restructuring should be the focus of both a predecision review of different alternatives as well as postdecision reviews of the changes adopted. A complex but equally important assessment related to institutional redesign involves attempts to assess both the institutional members' capacity and readiness for change and to monitor or assess changes in institutional culture. This broader focus on assessment of industry, institutional, and cultural patterns and changes could inform planners prior to action, support attempts at formative evaluation as changes are implemented, and ultimately serve to document the success of a contextual planning initiative over time.

Paradox: Change and Consistency, Conflict and Commitment

Contextual planning, with its emphasis on significant planning issues and potential for macro change, exaggerates a curious paradox. Major changes in postsecondary institutions are likely to lead to differing views, unclear choices, and conflict among constituents and with traditional institutional values or patterns of operation. Yet the changes engendered by contextual planning may affect large segments of the institution, require substantial resources, impact organizational culture, and be difficult to reverse. Such changes are only likely to suc-

ceed with long-term commitments and consistent efforts by institutional leaders over a long period of time. The reality is that avoiding conflicts may be less difficult in the short run but can invariably lead to the institution's failing either to introduce a major change or to implement it successfully. Although forcing constituents to address issues and choices can lead to intensive conflict, it can also lead to creative alternatives or new strategies. Such conflicts and uncertainties usually cannot be avoided, require leadership with the courage to address them, and may strengthen commitment in the long run.

Resources and Risk

Given the emphasis on macro change, investing in infrastructure to support broad initiatives, and providing incentives, contextual planning often requires the commitment of substantial resources—finances, personnel, facilities, and management credibility—to achieve the desired change. Such commitments assume the capacity to generate flexible resources and a willingness to risk their investment in implementing a planned initiative. Both creating flexible resources (often at the expense of supporting ongoing activities) and committing substantial resources to invest in infrastructure changes are risk decisions. Contextual planning requires a willingness to assess and face risks, view changes as investments, and make the changes with as much informed judgment as possible. But risk is a necessary concomitant of contextual planning that guides significant change in the institution.

Leadership: A Complex Process

Contextual planning suggests the need for multidimensional leadership. It requires leadership that has a broad and future-oriented perspective, understands complexity, is proactive, addresses conflicts, takes risks, and provides consistency and commitment in identifying and implementing changes. It requires leadership at many levels: developing external strategies, guiding internal redesign and restructuring, supporting cultural and individual change, and coordinating change strategies at these varying levels. Such leadership is likely to be the result of a team effort or of participation at differing levels, rather than the capacity of a single individual. Four forms or styles of leadership are appropriate for contextual planning (Bensimon, Neumann, and Birnbaum, 1989). "Transformational" leadership is useful in providing a vision and in identifying one or more initiatives that address the complexity of the changing environment and industry and provide a symbolic sense of direction that faculty and staff can understand and support. "Strategic" leadership clarifies new interinstitutional relationships and internal reorganizations and provides a rationale for or strategy for implementing those changes. "Managerial" leadership to realign programs, processes, policies, and resources during the period of change is particularly crucial. Finally, "interpretive" leadership that links major changes to what faculty and administrators do in their own roles and to what it means to them is important in reforming culture and ensuring the committed efforts of individuals. Providing and integrating such multiple levels and styles of leadership is the glue that holds a contextual planning process together, from initial discussion through implementation of new organizational patterns.

Summary

Contextual planning is an emerging approach to planning that supplements our earlier long-range and strategic approaches. Contextual planning differs in the breadth of its focus and its approach to guiding or steering significant institutional change. It is suggested that the three approaches to planning are contingent on the degree of turbulence in the environment and the changing nature of our industry. Only contextual planning takes into account the turbulence and complexity of the major challenges currently reshaping our institutions and our industry. The process elements of contextual planning have an implicit macro change strategy that links change at varying levels. Most importantly, contextual planning forces or assists institutions in addressing critical issues related to redefining the nature of our industry and an institution's role in it, redirecting our external relationships, redesigning academic processes and structures, and reforming or recreating our institutional culture. In an era of rapid change and complex challenges to our

postsecondary institutions and industry, it is an important new approach to planning for the twenty-first century.

Further Reading

While the literature on planning in higher education is extensive, Peterson's early chapter "Analyzing Alternative Approaches to Planning" (1981) provides a broad overview and Norris and Poulton's *A Guide for New Planners* (1991) offers a more recent perspective for those new to the field. George Keller's *Academic Strategy* (1983) remains a classic on strategic planning, while a recent critical perspective is provided by Schmidtlein and Milton's report "College and University Planning: Perspectives from a Nation-Wide Study" (1989) and their edited volume on *Adapting Strategic Planning to Campus Realities* (1990). These and other recent critiques highlight the shortcomings of strategic planning and the need to place it in its institutional context. Dolence and Norris's volume on *Transforming Higher Education* (1995) highlights the need for planning to respond to a rapidly changing environment and use planning for introducing more radical institutional changes or transformations. Contextual planning as related in this chapter is an emergent model not widely discussed. Chaffee's early work on "The Concept of Strategy" (1985) and Cope's article on "A Contextual Model to Encompass the Strategic Planning Concept" (also 1985) both approached this broader perspective institutionally, while Cameron's chapter on "Organizational Adaptation and Higher Education" (1989) provides a more extended or environmental perspective on adapting institutions to extensive environmental change.

References

Alpert, D. "Performance and Paralysis: The Organizational Context of the American Research University." *Journal of Higher Education*, 1986, *56*(3).

Baldridge, J. V. *Power and Conflict in the University.* New York: Wiley, 1971.

Baldridge, J. V., and Okimi, P. H. "Strategic Planning in Higher Education: New Tool—or New Gimmick?" *AAHE Bulletin*, 1982, *35*(2), 15–18.

Bensimon, E. M., Neumann, A., and Birnbaum, R. *Making Sense of Administrative Leadership: The "L" Word in Higher Education.* ASHE-ERIC Higher Education Report, no. 1. Washington, D.C.:

School of Education and Human Development, George Washington University, 1989.

Cameron, K. S. "Organizational Adaptation and Higher Education." *Journal of Higher Education*, 1989, *59*(3).

Cartter, A. M. *An Assessment of Quality in Graduate Education.* Washington, D.C.: American Council on Education, 1966.

Chaffee, E. E. "The Concept of Strategy: From Business to Higher Education." In J. C. Smart (ed.), *Higher Education: Handbook of Theory and Research.* Vol. 1. New York: Agathon Press, 1985.

Clark, B. R. "Faculty Culture." In T.F. Lunsford (ed.), *The Study of Campus Cultures.* Boulder: Western Interstate Commission on Higher Education, 1963.

Clark, B. R. "Complexity and Differentiation: The Deepening Problem of University Integration." In D. D. Dill and B. Sporn (eds.), *Emerging Patterns of Social Demand and University Reform: Through a Glass Darkly.* New York: Pergamon Press, 1995.

Cohen, M. D., and March, J. G. *Leadership and Ambiguity: The American College President.* New York: McGraw-Hill, 1974.

Cope, R. G. "A Contextual Model to Encompass the Strategic Planning Concept: Introducing a Newer Paradigm." *Planning for Higher Education*, 1985, *13*(3), 13–20.

Dill, D. D., and Helm, K. P. "Faculty Participation in Strategic Policy Making." In J. C. Smart (ed.), *Higher Education: Handbook of Theory and Research.* Vol. 4. New York: Agathon Press, 1988.

Dill, D. D., and Sporn, B. "University 2001: What Will the University of the Twenty-First Century Look Like?" In D .D. Dill and B. Sporn (Eds.), *Emerging Patterns of Social Demand and University Reform: Through a Glass Darkly.* New York: Pergamon Press, 1995.

Dolence, M. G., and Norris, D. M. *Transforming Higher Education.* Ann Arbor, Mich.: Society for College and University Planning, 1995.

Goodman, P. *Community of Scholars.* New York: Random House, 1964.

Katz, D., and Kahn, R. L. *The Social Psychology of Organizing.* (2nd ed.) New York: Wiley, 1978.

Keller, G. *Academic Strategy: The Management Revolution in American Higher Education.* Baltimore, Md.: Johns Hopkins University Press, 1983.

Kirschling, W. R., and Huckfeldt, V. E. "Projecting Alternative Futures." In P. Jedamus and M. Peterson (eds.), *Improving Academic Management.* San Francisco: Jossey-Bass, 1980.

Lawler, III, E. E. *The Ultimate Advantage: Creating the High Involvement Organization.* San Francisco: Jossey-Bass, 1992.

Lawrence, G. B., and Service, A. L. (Eds.) *Quantitative Approaches to Higher Education Management: Potential, Limits, and Challenge.* AAHE-Eric Research Report, no. 4. Washington, D.C.: American Association of Higher Education, 1977.

Millett, J. D. *The Academic Community.* New York: McGraw-Hill, 1962.

Mintzberg, H. *The Rise and Fall of Strategic Planning: Reconceiving Roles for Planning, Plans, Planners.* New York: Free Press, 1994.

Mortimer, K. P., and Tierney, M. L. *The Three Rs of the Eighties: Reduction, Reallocation, and Retrenchment.* AAHE-ERIC Research Report, no. 4. Washington, D.C.: American Association for Higher Education, 1979.

National Commission on Excellence in Education. *A Nation at Risk.* Washington, D.C.: U.S. Department of Education, 1983.

Norris, D. M., and Poulton, N. L. *A Guide for New Planners.* Ann Arbor, Mich.: Society for College and University Planning, 1991.

Peterson, M. W. "Analyzing Alternative Approaches to Planning." In P. Jedamus, M. W. Peterson, and Associates (eds.), *Improving Academic Management: Handbook of Planning and Institutional Research.* San Francisco: Jossey Bass, 1980.

Peterson, M. W., and others. *Total Quality Management in Higher Education: From Assessment to Improvement. An Annotated Bibliography.* Ann Arbor: University of Michigan, Center for the Study of Higher and Postsecondary Education, 1995.

Roose, K. D., and Anderson, C. J. *A Rating of Graduate Programs.* Washington, D.C.: American Council on Education, 1970.

Schmidtlein, F. A., and Milton, T. H. "College and University Planning: Perspectives from a Nation-Wide Study." *Planning for Higher Education*, 1988–89, *14*(2), 26–29.

Schmidtlein, F. A., and Milton, T. H. (eds.) *Adapting Strategic Planning to Campus Realities.* New Directions for Institutional Research, no. 67. San Francisco: Jossey-Bass, 1990.

Stroup, H. *Bureaucracy in Higher Education.* New York: Free Press, 1966.

Study Group on the Condition of Excellence in American Higher Education. *Involvement in Learning.* Washington, D.C.: National Institute of Education, 1984.

Tierney, W. G. *Assessing Academic Culture and Climate.* New Directions for Institutional Research, no. 70. San Francisco: Jossey-Bass, 1990.

Wing, P. "Forecasting Economic and Demographic Conditions." In P. Jedamus and M. Peterson (eds.), *Improving Academic Management.* San Francisco: Jossey-Bass, 1980.

Understanding Strategy: An Assessment of Theory and Practice

Jennifer B. Presley and David W. Leslie

The authors wish to acknowledge helpful comments on drafts of this paper by Frank Schmidtlein, Ellen Chaffee, and Anthony Foster. While they have helped us present our ideas more clearly, the responsibility for any remaining errors is entirely the authors'.

Introduction

Is the U.S. love affair with strategic planning over? Are we coming out of an extended period of dominance by a particular management fad? Or have we learned, adapted, and gained the wisdom to select what works and what does not? This chapter explores the continuing evolution of strategic planning theory and practice in business and in higher education, draws lessons from today's college and university practitioners, and suggests future areas of study.

1. Definitions

Business research on strategy and strategic planning began with an early emphasis on strategic planning but evolved into strategic management, and strategic thinking, with an emphasis on the content of strategy at three organizational levels: corporate, business unit and functional/operational. Higher education, on the other hand, has by and large retained a predominant interest in the process of strategy formation—that is—strategic planning, with less attention to the content of strategy. Perhaps this is because of the enduring importance of consultation and shared governance and the long-recognized significance of processes that gain the commitment of faculty who are largely responsible for implementation of change. Researchers, however, are often fuzzy about whether they are studying the *process* of strategy formation or the *effectiveness* of various strategies themselves. We will attempt to accomplish such clarification in this chapter and so provide here some definitions to guide the reader.

Defining Strategy

Definitions of strategy appear on closer examination to be statements of the *uses* of strategy, not strategy itself. We therefore begin with a working definition of strategy as *the content of decisions about how to move the organization in a particular direction*. This will help us to distinguish between the "what" of strategy, and the process of its development, generally referred to as *strategizing*, or more narrowly as *strategic planning*. What sorts of decisions would qualify for inclusion as strategy? Hax (1990) identifies six uses of strategy which are not necessarily all operative simultaneously. *Strategy* is i) a coherent unifying and integrative pattern of decisions; ii) a means of establishing an organization's purpose in terms of its long-term objectives, action programs, and resource allocation priorities; iii) a definition of a firm's competitive domain; iv) a response to external opportunities and threats and to internal strengths and weaknesses as means of achieving competitive advantage; v) a logical system for differentiating managerial tasks at corporate, business and functional levels; vi) a definition of the economic and non-economic contribution the firm intends to make to its stakeholders.

A more specific definition of purpose that captures the intended characteristics of strategy making in many higher education situations is given by Pearson (1990) as i) setting of direction; ii) concentrating effort; iii) providing consistency (i.e. concentration of effort over time); iv) ensuring flexibility. He adds that planned strategy provides management a means of understanding their business, while unplanned strategy evolves from established patterns of behavior. The latter, he argues, is more robust because it is grounded in the organization itself. We will explore these concepts in more depth later in this chapter.

Processes of Strategy Formation

Hax (1990) identifies three different processes contributing to strategy formation: i) cognitions of individuals on which understandings of the environment of strategy are based; ii) social and organizational processes by which perceptions are channeled and commitments developed; and iii) political processes by which the power to influence purpose and resources is shifted. He adds that the chief executive officer develops a broad vision of what to achieve, and manages a network of organizational forces that lead to the discovery, evolution and enrichment of that vision. *Strategic planning,* then, is a *particular process of strategy formation* aimed to accomplish Hax's second category of strategy development. It is grounded in the rational model of decision making, and also goes by the name of *formal* planning. Chaffee (1985a) placed strategic planning within the linear model of strategy formation. To the extent that strategic planning incorporates an adaptive aspect to its external environment, it could also be placed in Chaffee's adaptive model. When we use the term "strategic planning" in this chapter, we refer to the formal processes of rational decision making that influence organizational and/or resource priorities. It is significant to recognize that strategy or strategies can form without a planning process.

Types of Strategy

Pennings (1985) identified three types of strategy: a statement of intent that constrains or di-

rects subsequent activities (explicit strategy); an action of major impact that constrains or directs subsequent activities (implicit strategy); or a *rationalization* of social construction that gives meaning to prior activities. Hax (1990) elaborates on this typology by contrasting explicit with implicit strategy formation, and formal analytical processes with power-behavioral theories of organizational behavior. He adds that. ". . . it is my belief that neither the formal-analytical nor the power-behavioral paradigms adequately explain the way successful strategy-formation processes operate. While both these viewpoints have been useful in focusing academic research work, neither serves as a normative or descriptive model. To get the best out of strategy making, formal analytic thinking should also be combined with the behavioral aspects of management" (p. 38). Mintzberg adds the notion of *emergent strategy* as a pattern in a stream of individual actions, some of which may be small and emanate from well within the organization (for example, from individual faculty) (Mintzberg, 1978, 1994; Mintzberg and McHugh, 1985).

Levels of Analysis

Within both the higher education and business literature, authors often fail to distinguish whether they are examining *corporate* strategy, *business (academic) unit* strategy, or *functional/ operational* strategy—what we call the level-of-analysis. A clue can sometimes be gained from whether strategy is used as a singular or plural noun. Strategy as a singular noun may refer to corporate strategy, while strategies may refer to ways of achieving corporate vision (or strategy). The interpretation of what works, and implications of how to proceed, are profoundly different depending upon the level of the organization that is under discussion.

Corporate-level strategy. This level of strategy concerns itself with the basic mission, clientele, and goals and objectives of the organization as a whole (Shirley, 1983). Most authors recognize the need for corporate-level strategy—usually as a precursor of further strategy development or planning, although some use alternative labels when their own focus is on a different level of strategy development. Porter defines corporate strategy as the business the corporation should be in, and how the corporate office should manage the array of business units; it is "what makes the corporate whole add up to more than the sum of its business unit parts" (1987, p. 43). Chaffee's interpretive strategy will usually be operationalized at the corporate level (1985 a, b), as will Peterson's contextual strategy (1997).

Business (academic) unit strategy. This level of strategy focuses on the major strategic units within an organization. There is little consensus about the role of corporate strategy as a precursor or result of business unit strategy development. Authors who examine business/ academic unit strategy may use alternate labels for *corporate* strategy, such as the organization's vision (Mintzberg, 1994), objectives (Hax, 1990), or *umbrella strategies* (Mintzberg, 1985). Dill examines processes of strategy development at this level of analysis, but argues that institutional priority setting should focus unit strategy development (1993–94). Porter (1987) notes that his *competitive strategy* is developed at the business unit level, where knowledge about specific markets, competitors, and unit strengths is greatest. His position on the necessity of antecedent corporate strategy is ambiguous when he says that "diversified companies do not compete; only their business units do. Unless a corporate strategy places primary attention on nurturing the success of each unit, the strategy will fail, no matter how elegantly constructed. Successful corporate strategy must grow out of and reinforce competitive strategy" (p. 46). Rowley, Lujan, and Dolence (1997) focus on organizational subunit planning and argue that the organization's vision is a derivative of planning.

Functional/operational strategy(ies). Discussion of strategy at the functional level can include methods to solve problems, or development of operating activities to implement higher-order strategies. The business strategy literature largely avoids this level of analysis, but discussion does occur in fields such as Total Quality Management and Business Re-Engineering. Mintzberg and McHugh, (1985), however, might argue that this is where *corporate* strategy begins in the professional organization or adhocracy, thus highlighting the difficulty in articulating a clear distinction by level of strategic analysis.

2. The Early Years of Strategic Planning

The rational model of planning was embraced by corporate America in the expanding post World War II economic environment. Popularized by Secretary of Defense McNamara's adoption of General Motors' Planning, Programming, and Budgeting System (PPBS) in 1961 (Shapiro, 1986), extensive planning departments were established at the corporate level. These departments were commonly charged to examine internal strengths and weaknesses in light of external opportunities and threats (SWOT), and to develop and test alternative strategic options with the goal of responding to forecast change in ways that enhanced organizational position and profits. Management consultants strived to codify best practices, and groups like the Boston Consulting Group and the Design School of faculty at Harvard Business School disseminated the gospel far and wide throughout the U.S. corporate world (Mintzberg, 1990, Ansoff, 1991).

Higher education in the 1960s and 1970s also was embracing planning, with a long-range, internal orientation. Peterson (1986, 1997) explains that phases of planning in higher education were responsive to changing external conditions, and suggests that prior to the mid-1970s, characterized by enrollment growth and a supportive fiscal environment, higher education was in a period of *long-range planning*, with an emphasis on forecasting and growth. By the late 1970s, the higher education enterprise was beginning to adapt to a changing external environment of projected enrollment decline (as the baby boom ended) and tightening fiscal conditions. It moved to a strategic or *adaptive* planning mode as it tried to adapt to a quite different external environment.

3. Changing Notions of Strategic Planning in the 1980s

By the early 1980s the bloom was beginning to fade from the proverbial rose as corporate strategy researchers sought to understand the relationship between strategic planning processes and organizational outcomes. Popular authors (Ouchi, 1981; Deal and Kennedy, 1982; Peters and Waterman, 1982; Schein, 1985) advised of the importance of organizational culture to corporate success. Managers focused more on improving operational effectiveness than strategic planning in order to match the production and quality performance of Japanese industry (Porter, 1996). Welch, in one of his first acts as the new CEO of General Electric in 1983, disbanded the corporate planning division that he had inherited (Byrne, 1996). Even the most ardent proponents of formal corporate planning processes moderated their prescriptive, rational concepts to recognize the complex nature of organizations, and the importance of organizational culture in decision making and strategy implementation (Ansoff, 1991; Wilson, 1994).

Other new lines of thinking were also emerging. Mintzberg's challenge to the premise that strategy development required rational planning processes began to take hold (Mintzberg, 1978). He postulated instead a model of *emergent* strategy where, he argued, strategy could be developed implicitly through the observation of patterns in streams of individual actions. Some European consulting firms were trying to break out of the rational planning approach, recognizing that "[s]trategic change [was] accomplished by modifying the configurations of organizational values and symbols because it is through such alterations that people in organizations will acquire new cognitive schemata, which in turn will alter their behavioral dispositions to their work" (Pennings, 1985, p. 25). By the mid 1980s, then, the importance of organizational culture, symbolism, and a cognitive, interpretive view of strategy was beginning to be recognized. But many of those studying strategy in the corporate sector were not yet integrating these newer organizational concepts into their work. Mintzberg and McHugh noted that, ". . . strategy making [in almost all of the literature] *still* (emphasis ours) tended to be equated with planning—with the systematic formulation and articulation of deliberate premeditated strategies which are then implemented. . . . This view of strategy making, however, is unnecessarily restrictive; it is inconsistent with more contemporary forms of structure and sometimes with the conventional forms as well" (Mintzberg and McHugh, 1985, p.160).

Unlike corporate America in the 1980s, U.S. higher education was still moving through its *acquisition* phase—adopting strategic planning

processes as the mantra to cope with a changing external environment and increasing demands for accountability (Keller, 1983). However, in 1985, Chaffee published her groundbreaking analysis of business strategy and its relationship to higher education (Chaffee, 1985 (a), (b)), observing that strategy formation was composed of three aspects: the linear, adaptive, and interpretive. She placed the strategic planning process within the basic linear model of strategy formation, and went on to argue that effective strategic management required not only the use of rational analysis of internal and external conditions, but also adaptation to a changing external environment, and most important, the development of an *interpretive* strategy that would communicate inside and outside the organization an easily understood explanation of the aspirations and strategies of the organization. Chaffee's propositions were supported by her study of successful turnaround strategies in a set of small liberal arts colleges (Chaffee, 1984). Despite the growing evidence of the importance of context to successful strategy formation and planning, institutions were being encouraged by internal and external pressures to engage in formal planning processes, and to develop *strategic plans*. Mintzberg and McHugh's (1985) observation of the corporate world applied also to the higher education environment, not only in its research literature, but also in practice.

We noted earlier that during the 1980s, business and industry began to pay attention to production and quality processes of the Japanese, and adopted components of Total Quality Management (Porter, 1996; Hackman and Wagerman, 1995). Total Quality Management also became of interest to the higher education community (Seymour, 1993, 1995, 1996; Politi, 1995; Bogue and Saunders, 1992; Hoffman and Julius, 1995; Chaffee and Sherr, 1992; Teeter and Lozier, 1993), but was slow to take substantive hold because of the difficulty in translating its precepts to academic processes. We have not found evidence that Total Quality Management has been linked in practice to strategy development or implementation in higher education, despite their common connections to the mission, culture, and beliefs of the organization. (The potential refunding of the Education Baldrige Award in the FY 99 federal budget, whose criteria include linking quality systems to planning systems, may stimulate additional organizational progress in this area.)

4. Strategic Planning in the 1990s

Interest in strategy, if not strategic planning, has returned with a vengeance to corporate America. The August 1996 edition of *Business Week* announced on its cover that "Strategic Planning is Back" (Byrne, 1996), although close reading reveals that what is back is a focus on strategy—where the company is going and how it gets there—in contrast to the 1980s emphasis on efficiency and downsizing, or the 1970s focus on rational, quantitatively-driven planning. Those touted as the new planning gurus include Porter, a Harvard Business School professor, and Prahalad and Hamel. Porter espouses the importance of each company's *competitive strategy*: ". . . the essence of strategy is . . . choosing to perform activities differently or to perform different activities than rivals" (Porter, 1996, p. 64). He emphasizes that "positioning is not about carving out a niche. A position . . . can be broad or narrow" (1996, p. 67). Hamel and Prahalad (1989) refine the notion of strategy as "strategic intent." Recognizing that [business] strategic plans "reveal more about today's problems than tomorrow's opportunities" the goal of strategic intent is "to fold the future back into the present" (p. 66). Another popular concept is their idea of *core competence* where ". . . the real sources of advantage are to be found in management's ability to consolidate corporate-wide technologies and production skills into competencies that empower individual businesses to adapt quickly to changing opportunities" (Prahalad and Hamel, 1990, p. 81). Core competencies cross organizational boundaries and involve many levels of people and all functions. Examples they provide include Sony's capacity to miniaturize, Philip's optical-media expertise, or Citicorp's competence in systems that allowed it access to world markets 24 hours a day. It is these core competencies that differentiate the company and provide it with its competitive advantage. Another popular source, the (British) *Financial Times*, ran an article on how leading world business figures use intuition in everyday decision making, as well as in planning their companies's long-term strate-

gies. The article asserts that intuitive decision making contrasts with the use of rational management techniques promoted over the years by management experts (Lorenz, 1994). It does concede, however, that reliance on intuition must be linked with, ". . . a full understanding of markets, with new technologies and with competitive behaviour" (Lorenz, p. 20).

A recent study of 50 corporations confirmed significant shifts in corporate approaches to strategic planning since its inception (Wilson, 1994). Wilson found a marked shift of planning responsibility from staff to line managers; decentralization of strategic planning, but not all other corporate responsibilities, to business units; paying much more attention to changing markets, competitive, and technological environments; use of more sophisticated planning systems; and a growing emphasis on organization and culture as critical ingredients in execution of strategy. In summary, the lingering notion of an emphasis on rational, formalistic planning outlives the reality both of the academic and popular business literature, and of actual corporate practice. The bureaucratic model of organization, long associated with rational (strategic) planning processes (Mintzberg, 1994), may no longer explain, if it ever did, how major corporations function in the post-industrial age. Instead, they face the realities of global competition and the rapid pace of change by relying more on professional expertise and an emphasis on team work to develop the knowledge and understandings from which their strategies grow.

In contrast, the continuing interest in formal strategic plans and processes in higher education is reinforced by stakeholders beyond the institution, including public system governing and coordinating boards, and sometimes legislatures that continue to call for institutional strategic plans. Such calls operationalize the attempts of system boards and other governmental agencies to gain more control of colleges and universities in a time of scarcity and distrust through the use of planning processes that are more appropriate to the bureaucratic structure of government than the professional organizations and/or "adhocracies" of colleges and universities (Pennings, 1985; Stone and Brush, 1996; Mintzberg, 1994). Some higher education strategic planning researchers are exploring more complex approaches to understanding the conditions of effectiveness of planning processes and strategic decision making (Leslie and Fretwell, 1996; Peterson, Dill, Mets and Associates, 1997; Schmidtlein and Milton, 1990). Peterson (1997), for example, explores a new *contextual* approach to planning that seeks to accomplish organizational redefinition in response to a dramatically different future environment. Peterson argues that contextual planning is an extension of long-range (1950–1975) or strategic planning (1975–1990) approaches for organizations with the will and need to change their missions for the 21st century. Like some other strategy researchers, Peterson acknowledges the continuing role of earlier modes of planning (see, for example, Chaffee, 1985 (a), (b); Ansoff, 1991), and notes that approaches to planning are contingent on particular institutional environments. He suggests that, ". . . forecasting and long-range planning processes continue to be useful in a clearly defined sector of higher or post-secondary institutions with limited competition and in more favorable resource environments. . . ." while ". . . strategic planning is appropriate for a clearly understood but more competitive postsecondary sector in which resources are more constrained but somewhat predictable" (p. 133). Acknowledging that his contextual planning concept builds on the work of Cope (1985) and Chaffee (1985 (b)), Peterson emphasizes significant planning issues and potential for major redirection, and seeks to identify practices that influence external contexts in favor of the institution's mission. His model responds to situations where institutions ask significant questions about their role and mission, and want to accomplish extensive transformation. According to Peterson, ". . . strategic planning usually relies on defining clear priorities, identifying specific programs, and developing supportive resource strategies to compete in a strategic niche. Contextual planning, however, assumes that in an industry in flux, broad initiatives will be selected, and that many programmatic efforts to achieve those initiatives are desirable . . . [Organizations] will build an infrastructure that will serve and support groups in their development of ideas, efforts, and programs consistent with an initiative" (p. 141). This concept is quite similar to Mintzberg's *emergent* strategies, where management may set broad *umbrella* strategies or organizational boundaries, while action strategies develop in a

bottom-up process from the organization's professional experts (Mintzberg and McHugh, 1985). Leslie and Fretwell (1996), after studying a number of institutions' planning processes, conclude that strategizing has wasted time, and that planning should be conceived as a process of continuous experimentation, with many decisions emerging simultaneously on many fronts. Leslie (1996) notes, however, that such efforts need to be bounded by ". . . strong internal value systems that serve as compasses and filter information through that value system" (p. 109). This need for boundaries echoes earlier strategy research, where the importance of maintaining an appropriate distinctive organizational character grounded in the history and development of the institution was recognized as a criterion for successful turnaround management in small colleges (Chaffee, 1984).

We noted earlier the current importance of two concepts in corporate strategy: Porter's competitive strategy—the need to find a unique activity mix in order to be number one—and Prahalad and Hamel's notion of core competencies of the corporation—the need to identify organizational strengths that span individual business units in order to enhance organizations' capacities to adapt quickly to changing opportunities (Porter, 1996; Prahalad and Hamel, 1990). For higher education, these two notions reinforce the importance of developing and maintaining an interpretive strategy that incorporates an understanding of the core competencies of the institution. As institutions seek to identify their strengths during planning processes, they are in fact seeking to understand the "core competencies" that make each institution special, that explain its particular place in the grand panoply of higher education institutions. Prahalad and Hamel (1990) comment that most organizations have just a handful of core competencies, and the same is likely true for institutions of higher education. The challenging notion behind core competencies as applied to higher education is its relation to multi-disciplinarity. Bringing faculty from a variety of perspectives together to provide curricula that equip the next generation of students to prosper in the complex world of the 21st century, or encouraging faculty to work in teams to address, for example, societal problems that plague inner cities, may help to regain the social legitimacy that the enterprise so much needs. Porter's (1996) focus on competitive strategy, on the other hand, is harder to transport to higher education, and indeed raises significant questions in our minds with regard to the appropriate role of competition among higher education institutions. Is the country best served with an education enterprise driven by institutional desires to be number one? An answer to that question is beyond the scope of the current chapter, but alerts us to potential dangers when we (and our external resource providers) do not apply wisdom to a careful understanding of the similarities and differences between for profit and service organizations.

5. The Purposes of Strategic Planning

Just as strategic planning waned in popularity in the corporate world during the 1980s, being replaced first by a focus on operational effectiveness and later by a focus on strategic management, so is strategic planning in higher education now under attack. Some argue for a need to augment the rational, formalistic approach (Chaffee, 1985 (a), (b); Peterson, Dill, Mets and Associates, 1997), while others conclude that strategic planning has failed—leading one of the current authors to comment that "... [s]trategy, in the classical sense, may just be a dead issue, and ... none too soon for colleges and universities" (Leslie, 1996, p. 111).

Before finalizing the funeral arrangements, however, it is instructive to consider what might be the *purposes* of strategy and planning. As early as 1981, a taxonomy was emerging that recognized a variety of uses of strategy: (i) as corporate reports that provided a vehicle for communicating broad direction to shareholders, (ii) as a more comprehensive plan aimed at Boards of Directors and middle management that provided more illumination but avoided discussion of organizational weaknesses; (iii) as a tool for top management's consideration of competitor strength, organizational competencies, and particular issues; and finally (iv) as the CEO's private corporate strategy disclosed to no one (Edward Wrapp quoted in Andrews, 1981, p. 176). More recently, Stone and Brush (1996) explored the uses of strategic planning in entrepreneurial and non-profit organizations. Their framework begins with the formulation of a managerial dilemma: "... the need

to use informality and vagueness to gain commitment from diverse interests, and the need to demonstrate formalization of managerial practices to acquire legitimacy from critical resource suppliers. [The] framework recognizes planning as a strategy for resource acquisition rather than a strategy for resource allocation" (p. 633). Stone and Brush define commitment as, "... behavior that binds an individual to others," and legitimacy as "... external validation, a property defined by a set of social norms as appropriate" (p. 634). They examined empirically-based articles on planning in nonprofit and entrepreneurial firms and developed a matrix to relate a variety of forms of planning to different internal and external pressures (Figure 1).

Stone and Brush found that adoption and consistent use of formal planning were not widespread and provide three major reasons: i) formal planning clarifies goals and trade-offs, and is likely to increase conflict among diverse constituencies; ii) without direct control over resource flows or external events, planning efforts are easily sidetracked by exogenous shocks and planning documents become rapidly obsolete; iii) survival in both types of organization depends on variation and improvisation, and the accuracy and order of a formal process can restrict the range of possibilities. Many stated purposes of formal planning, therefore, are difficult to achieve under conditions of ambiguity. However, they found that formal planning was useful and necessary to the attainment of external validation or legitimacy and essential to resource acquisition. Nonprofits and entrepreneurial firms planned when they had to plan, that is when outside investors or funders required a formal plan before dispensing resources. These organizations used a formal planning process because they perceived it to be necessary for external validation or legitimacy and for resource acquisition rather than resource allocation. Stone and Brush found modified uses of formal (strategic) planning in use under other conditions: i) Interpretive planning was a good approach when the key purpose was to mobilize commitments of people from both within and outside the organization. The language of plans was imprecise but value-laden, allowing individuals to feel that their interests matched those stated for the organization; ii) When organizations

		Internal pressures	
		Commitment	*Legitimacy*
External	*Commitment*	Interpretive Strategy	Abbreviated Planning
Pressures	Legitimacy	Decoupled Planning	Formal Planning

Figure 1. Stone and Brush's Planning Configuration Network

From Stone and Brush (1996), p. 646

needed to gain commitment from external participants while gaining legitimacy internally (i.e. demonstrating managerial competence), an abbreviated process of formal planning was used, meeting the demands of board members for a planning process but vague enough to leave the top executive free to maneuver; iii) reverse conditions—the need to obtain internal commitment and external legitimacy—led to a planning process decoupled from core activities, similar to Cohen and March's (1974) planning as advertisement or Nutt's (1984) gesture planning. The purpose of this process is to meet external demands for planning without interfering with internal, core activities of the organization. The final category—(iv) the use of full-blown formal (strategic) planning processes—was used when the organization needed to gain legitimacy both internally and externally.

We suggest taking this framework one step further—to include the need of organizations to engage in accurate reality testing. While strategic planning may gain the support of constituents, it may or may not produce accurate assessments of the environment and of the institution's performance. We suggest, drawing an analogy to Glaser's (1991) admonition about validating performance measures, that this third dimension, the internal *validity* of strategies is crucial to their effectiveness. (A college or university that projects enrollment increases in the face of a population decline in its state or region, for example, would be basing its strategy on suspect assumptions—its plan would be of questionable *validity*.)

We have detailed this framework because of its usefulness in thinking about the varying environments faced by institutions of higher education. Do institutional plans developed in response to external system requirements differ systematically from those developed as a result of internal initiative? How should the success of a plan be evaluated? Stone and Brush's work suggests the importance of understanding the motivations for planning in research that examines the relationship of strategy, planning and outcomes in higher education.

Evidence of conditions leading to successful strategic planning

The rational process of strategic planning is most effective when well-aligned with a stable external environment which is conducive to prediction, and Frederickson (1984) found strategic planning to be most successful under these conditions in the corporate sector. He reported, on the other hand, that turbulent times are less conducive to the use of strategic planning for strategy formation. Higher education finds itself, at the least, in a turbulent environment, and perhaps in the transformational environment of the post-industrial society described by Peterson and Dill (1997). In higher education, authors have found that institutions in crisis (especially fiscal crisis) use strategic planning with mixed results (Chaffee, 1984; Schmidtlein and Milton, 1990; Leslie and Fretwell, 1996). Chaffee found that institutions that combined strategic planning efforts with adaptive and interpretive strategic management approaches were more likely to recover from their organizational difficulties (1985 (a), (b)). Leslie and Fretwell (1996) add that strategic planning is more successful when a clear vision and institutional culture already are in place.

6. The CEO and Strategic Planning

What remains largely unaddressed in both the business and higher education planning literature is how the *big picture* choices are best made at the corporate level—how to develop an interpretive strategy, how to choose transforming initiatives, how to establish a clear sense of identity that allows individual behavior and decisions to track simultaneously towards a greater whole. And which choices are most likely to work? In short, how does an organization make the whole greater than the sum of its parts? Can it emanate from a planning process, or does it emerge from the head of the CEO? This challenge is especially apparent for higher education leaders who are simultaneously faced with the need to demonstrate visionary leadership and a highly decentralized and participative faculty culture (Keller, 1995, Munitz, 1995).

Much of the work on strategy in the nonprofit sector, including higher education, has focused on processes rather than the content of strategy. In contrast, work on strategy in the corporate sector has tended to focus on content of decisions (Pennings, 1985). Furthermore, little has been said about the role of the CEO in strategy development in higher education. The literature on corporate decision making, on the other hand, firmly establishes a leadership role for the CEO in the formation of corporate strategy—setting the institutional vision, defining the boundaries of what business(es) the corporation is in, and developing a corporate culture conducive to accomplishing corporate strategy. What the literature also is clear about is that the development of ways to fulfill the corporation's goals are most appropriately lodged at the business unit level. The chairman of Hewlett-Packard describes his role in strategy development as, ". . . to encourage discussion of the white spaces, the overlap and gaps among business strategies, the important areas that are not addressed by the strategies of individual Hewlett-Packard businesses" (Byrne, 1996).

In higher education, however, reference to the CEO (President) in studies of planning is usually oblique. Stafford is outspoken on the issue (1993). Drawing upon her own presidential experience, she says that higher education confuses consultation with creation. She argues that while consultation with numerous constituencies in the college or university is vital, ". . . creation of strategy—like most acts of creation—ought to be accomplished by a small, special group—or even one or two persons, and then submitted for criticism" (p. 56). Donald Kennedy, writing of his experience as president of Stanford University asks the question, "How can big nonprogram changes in the institution be installed—changes, for example, like altering the relative rewards for undergraduate teaching and research, or changing the institution's role with respect to important external constituencies or activities?" (1994, p. 101). Stanford did not respond to such challenges through formal planning, but through executive leadership. Kennedy explains that *he himself* decided the time had come to reemphasize undergraduate teaching, and that he devoted two annual reports to the subject because the "level of consternation (and misunderstanding) was so high." (p. 103). Other authors also confer major and significant responsibilities to organizational leaders. Dill (1993–1994), for example, remarks that, ". . . planning success depends on the institution's leaders articulating the norms, or the values, standards, and criteria of the planning process verbally, and manifesting them visibly in the planning process. . . . Priorities seldom emerge from meetings and discussions, but are often suggested by leaders and then criticized and modified or reshaped through reciprocal communication and negotiation processes" (p. 10–11). In her 1985 articles, Chaffee ascribes to the CEO the responsibility for developing an *interpretive* strategy (Chaffee, 1985 (a), (b)). Twelve years later, and currently serving as president to two institutions simultaneously, Chaffee clarifies her notion of the development of interpretive strategy and the role of the CEO in her 1997 state-of-the-university address:

> In past years, I've often heard requests for more focus, a clearer sense of direction. This year, I will offer one. That's partly because it's becoming clear, and partly because a big part of my job is to tell the institutional story, past and future. . . . I hesitate to call it a vision, but that's what it is. We have a vision statement [Valley City State University: A nationally recognized learner-centered caring community committed to continuous improvement: Mayville State

University: To be known for continuing academic excellence in a cooperative, enjoyable learning environment that anticipates and responds to individual needs] for the university, so I'll call this a vision story. The story I will tell you is consistent with our vision statement, but it has more detail. Still, the story has many open spaces that have yet to be defined. You may find that disconcerting, and it is. But the open spaces represent opportunities to participate in writing the story. . . . Why and how did I choose this one? How do [presidents] know what the right vision story is? There are several criteria:

- it must be challenging and big enough to require at least several years to achieve;
- it must be feasible;
- it must be rooted firmly in the university's history and tradition;
- it must use those as the foundation on which to project a new future;
- the new future must inspire faculty and staff;
- the new future must give them enough information so that they see how they can contribute to achieving it; and
- the new future must contain the right elements to ensure that the university will be better able to attract students, dollars, and public support.

As I tried to understand just how presidents developed such a vision story, I could only resort to an image from statistics—the president does a mental factor analysis. That is to say, the president picks up zillions of bits of information and somehow they come together in the president's mind as a sensible picture. Usually, the result is not the president's idea—it is the president's sense of the best idea out there, wherever it came from. This process doesn't always work, but there's an acid test that can prevent the president from heading too far down the wrong road. That is, to share the vision story with the people of the institution to see what they think of it and how they respond to it. That is my primary purpose today (Chaffee, 1997).

The need for presidential leadership in strategy identification and articulation is not unanimously held. Chait (1993) admonishes higher education institutions for expecting CEOs to provide institutional vision, while others argue that institutional strategy and vision is the result of strategic planning— an outcome and not an input to the process (Rowley, Lujan, and Dolence, 1997). This ambiguity leads to some confusion about what is appropriately expected from higher education CEO's and deserves further exploration in future research.

7. The State Policy Context for Strategy Formation in Higher Education

We will now look at the ways in which state policy formation poses problems for strategy. The higher education "industry" as a whole is faced with profound challenges to its mission and wide skepticism about its performance. How colleges and universities navigate among the resulting threats and opportunities, and the ways in which they form strategies to position themselves to meet these challenges, however, needs to be better understood.

State Policy as Constraint

Higher education operates in a highly complex environment that mixes market forces and public policy in ways that may be only partially predictable—and that may also be capricious in effect. Colleges and universities are deeply engaged in state and national communities—giving federal and state governments, in particular, powerful roles in determining how much funding is available, who attends, and what programs will benefit from particular targeted support. While the marketplace is a powerful force affecting private institutions' strategies, state and federal governments are particularly important influences in both sectors because they control funding and the conditions on which funding is provided. State governments, in particular, have tried repeatedly to rationalize their higher education systems by using some kind of formal planning (variably and inconsistently called "master-," "comprehensive-," "long-range," or "strategic" planning). But in one case, that of California, the hazards of such a central state government role in planning have become clear.

California: A Special Case. The 1960 California Master Plan for Higher Education is often cited as the progenitor and conceptual masterpiece of subsequent state plans. It had two principal objectives: 1) to provide essentially free access to higher education for all who could benefit, and 2) to do so by carefully framing distinct missions for the community colleges, the regional state university campuses, and the University of California system. As Smelser (1974) has pointed out, the plan became a way of resolving the conflict between values of egalitarianism and competitive excellence—that is, providing mass higher education while preserving the elite meritocracy and research-oriented mission of the University. However, no matter how successfully the original California plan met the needs of a diverse and rapidly growing state, it eventually collided with other political imperatives: a powerful tax limitation movement that resulted in passage of "Proposition 13," and the competition for increasingly scarce public funds from fields like corrections. Not only has this collision (long since) effectively eliminated the principle of free access to public higher education, but it has prevented the state's public colleges and universities from adapting to a new population boom and the concomitant explosion of demand for higher education (California Postsecondary Education Commission, 1994). Reports from both Rand Corporation and the California Higher Education Policy Center (CHEPC) confirm the enormous gap between aspirations of the original Master Plan and the realities that so constrain the state's public colleges and universities (Shires, 1996; Callan, 1994). One economist was even led to recommend that the governor declare a state of emergency in California higher education (Breneman, 1995).

The case of the California Master Plan is particularly important because it shows how the political and social consensus of one era may be renegotiated by those who hold power in another era. It also shows how the power of popular movements to affect policy may overshadow even the most rational analyses of conditions and needs. Waves of such movements in California have dictated tuition charges, tax limits, stricter prison sentences, abolition of affirmative action, and so on. Taken together, these independent movements have dramatically changed the ability of public higher education in California to perform its traditional mission. More to the point, they have radically

limited (perhaps well beyond public awareness) the capacity of the system to meet foreseeable demand.

Incrementalism in Public Policy: Constraints on Higher Education Strategy

This case illustrates the problem of pluralistic control of public policy. When many actors have the power to influence decisions and commitments, and when their operating consensus is fluid, no one person or group—or any given rationale—can stabilize policy or freeze the assumptions and values that give direction to a plan. The profoundly incremental nature of most state budgeting means that most higher education funding is also incremental (Albright and Gilleland, 1994). And that, in turn, means that change is likely to be less responsive to external realities, to ideas, or to long-term projections than it is to the short-term compromises and quick-fixes that are common in legislative decision making. (See generally Wildavsky, 1997, for a description of the process.) At present, legislative decisions in the states seem to be leading to more constrained budgets (Council for Aid to Education, 1997) and increased regulation (Sabloff, 1997), with only limited room for institutions to construct their own strategies.

The ambient level of external threat to the higher education "industry" is difficult to measure, but the Council for Aid to Education's (1997) report, *Breaking the Social Contract*, analogizes it to the threats faced by the health care industry in recent years. Its main conclusion is that higher education faces an enormous strategic challenge and that colleges and universities will have to form new strategies and demonstrate performance to justify the support they have traditionally received from the marketplace and government subsidy. The essential problem lies in the mismatch between incrementalism in the evolution of public policy and rapid change in the environment to which colleges and universities need to respond—illustrated well by the California case. Understanding the external environment is an important part of any strategic effort—formal or informal. How institutions perceive their environments, what information they gather, how they interpret it, and what they do in response is an arena in which further study needs to be undertaken. Leslie and Fretwell (1996), for example, found the availability and use of information varies widely from campus to campus. However, even where information is available and used well, the constraints of public policy may limit how effectively institutions respond. Whether and how they can respond is both a matter of policy constraints and of their own internal capacity for purposeful change.

8. The Internal Decision Environment

Persistent throughout the literature on higher education management—and especially on its use of formal strategic planning—has been a sense of misalignment between the need to make timely, valid, and binding decisions and the realities of an institution that seems to operate in a somewhat anarchic fashion. The Rand report, for example, notes that, ". . . institutions are a maze of hierarchical structures operating independently of one another." It goes on to say that, "The current governance structure actually prevents institutions and institutional systems from asking . . . questions [that businesses ask when they engage in formal strategic planning]" (Council for Aid to Education, 1997, unpaginated). The Rand report implies an approach to formal strategic planning in businesses that may not be fully accurate. We have shown earlier that corporations have a blend of leadership-driven corporate strategy formation and participative emergent and implementation planning. Perhaps higher education's governance processes are in fact well structured to manage some aspects of planning, and less well positioned to handle other aspects. Those aspects of planning that involve academic program management (i.e. new programs, elimination of programs, and program quality) may be especially appropriate for the governance structure, while initiatives relating to "corporate strategy" may in fact most effectively be handled "off-line" from formal participatory processes. We presented evidence in this paper of the importance of presidential leadership to institutional strategy formation (Chaffee, 1997; Kennedy, 1994; Stafford, 1993). We acknowledge, however, the prevalent assumption that strategy formation in higher education occurs through its formal organizational processes. We explore in this section, therefore, several recent studies of organiza-

tional decision making that suggest these assumptions may be at the root of tensions about how strategy *ought* to be formed.

Schuster and colleagues (1994) describe in detail how colleges and universities have attempted to construct an internal decision environment that meets the multiple and conflicting demands of strategic planning. Their book, *Strategic Governance*, examined the problems institutions have faced as they have tried to plan more purposefully in an era of tighter resources. Most commonly, suggest the authors, institutions have met with only mixed success in planning and strategizing. One reason, suggest Schuster and colleagues, is that the participatory decision making culture in colleges and universities requires "legitimacy," or broad acceptance by those who are affected. This culture has been characterized as "political" (Baldridge, 1971), "anarchic" (Cohen and March, 1974), and "loosely coupled" (Weick, 1976). While broad participation and an egalitarian decision making process may satisfy constituents' interests in being heard, external conditions in the 1980s began to impose serious constraints on the amount of time and latitude institutions could afford in making strategic decisions.

In *Strategic Governance*, Schuster, et al. analyzed this connection between governance and planning as it emerged in something Keller (1983) had recommended, the "Joint Big Decision Committee." The "JBDC" in Keller's view would give impetus and legitimacy to the urgent planning and strategizing Keller thought was needed in hard economic times. It would bring diverse campus constituents together in a small, high-level working group where they could cooperatively make hard decisions.

But, analyzing the experience of institutions that had implemented the JBDC, Schuster and colleagues concluded that planning and governance are "asynchronous," or work at achieving different ends by different means—thus the conflict between making valid decisions and making "legitimate" decisions. Indeed, it appears that the process of deciding and the outcomes a process reaches may be independent of one another and that no "one good way" would guarantee the right decisions in a complex environment nor widely acceptable decisions in a complex organization.

Two recent studies examined how institutions behaved under pressure to strategize. Taylor and Schmidtlein (1996) and Leslie and Fretwell (1996) observed a variety of institutions facing harder choices and greater need for change as funding became more problematic, "markets" became more competitive, and public policy increased expectations for performance. Most of the institutions in both studies had recognized serious pressures and engaged in some effort to develop strategic responses to those pressures. In neither study, however, did formal strategic planning emerge as the most viable way to adapt to the contingencies facing institutions. Instead, two characteristics of the process seemed to emerge repeatedly: It is "pluralistic" and "incremental" (Taylor and Schmidtlein, 1996, p. 75). In whatever structural way the institution approached planning, it tended to be inclusive and consultative. In some cases, formal committees were appointed; in others, particularly the smallest institutions, more communal involvement was attempted. Inclusiveness generated more information, perspectives, and input to the process. It also generated more sense of ownership and legitimacy among the constituents who would be affected by the plan.

Taylor and Schmidtlein also found that the preferred mode of decision-making was a mix of the incremental and comprehensive—that is, choosing a balance of small adjustments to current activities and programs and larger, more general realignments of those activities. Both Taylor and Schmidtlein and Leslie and Fretwell concluded that, in the words of the former, "Neither unbridled entrepreneurship and competition nor encompassing planning processes were deemed satisfactory. . . ." (p. 76). Leslie and Fretwell (1996) observed that some institutions preferred a loosely coordinated, but simultaneous, effort by semi-independent subunits to deal with needed changes. Although these institutions had achieved a general consensus on the nature of the problems they faced and on an overall direction, they had not developed a formal strategic plan. By coordinating the work of subunits with good lateral communication and by tolerating the differences in their capacity to achieve change, these institutions appeared to be moving in the middle ground between unplanned incremental opportunism and rational planning, a pattern the authors labeled "simultaneous tracking." (Leslie and Fretwell, 1996, p. 234)

The findings of both studies are consistent with the findings that internal decision cultures of colleges and universities favor participation—perhaps even over reaching valid outcomes in the decision process. They further suggest that a process that favors participation may at least indirectly impede reaching closure on valid decisions. For example, the act of deciding if and how to change appears to have precisely the opposite effect in cases where it involves wide participation. Leslie and Fretwell (1996), Hearn, Clugston, and Heydinger (1993), and Schmidtlein and Milton (1990) all found that strategic planning diverted attention and action into unfamiliar channels. Leslie and Fretwell noted:

> . . . strategizing [that is strategic planning] . . . requires that [people in the organization] put aside their normal work to organize and conduct a new and unfamiliar task. That usually involves generating data and managing some kind of consensus-building process. All of this takes time and energy. Strategizing [strategic planning] in the midst of a crisis loads the organization with more work at just the time it is becoming more stressed. It also forces decisions . . . into an artificial envelope of time that is usually too short to allow serious analysis, careful thought, or realistic assessment of risks and opportunities. People feel compelled to make decisions for the sake of making decisions, which is a good way to produce bad decisions (p. 240).

Planning can put institutions on hold for an extended period because the process increases the uncertainty of those not involved directly in planning and who may be reluctant to make decisions or initiate change until they know what they are "supposed" to do. It also focuses attention on the process of constructing a new reality, new interpretations of that reality, and planning adaptations. Diverting attention from the known and understood realities may be healthy if those known and understood realities are in fact erroneous. But they may be reasonably accurate and valid, and trying to construct some different understanding that may prove to be less accurate and less valid could turn out to be an enormously expensive and discouraging effort. The opportunity cost of doing this must be weighed against the chances that an institution already knows well its strengths, weaknesses, and environmental challenges.

Obviously, we are referring here to broadly inclusive strategic planning exercises. Institutional strategizing, of course, may occur more informally and less disruptively as presidents and others in central administrative positions perceive the need to change and act to bring those changes about without elaborate process. So our point is not that strategizing, per se, is wasteful or disruptive; it is rather that we have little empirical understanding of whether "normal" and routine organizational decision making can produce good strategy, or whether some alternative (e.g. the JBDC) operating in parallel with the normal structure might in some way produce better decisions. Can a separate entity also produce decisions—no matter how valid—that will also be as legitimate as those produced by the traditional formal means of strategic planning?

A final issue related to internal decision environments involves the complexity of university decision structures. Can an organization as complex as a university develop useful corporate strategies that override the perhaps sound plans of its loosely coupled subunits? In at least one institution, we have found mention of conflict between university and subunit planning processes: "In the second year of the planning cycle, the [university's new strategic planning] process intervened. Difficult though that was, [it] required us to make immediate choices, providing an even more rigorous discipline to the process of moving the College toward its goals" (Pennsylvania State University, 1997). In this case, it appears that the university plan superseded the college plan, and that the two were not entirely consistent in focus, timing, or content. These inconsistencies raise the questions: Should the individual units develop their own plans and feed them upward—so that the university shapes and molds them into an emergent whole? Or should there be a corporate strategy to which individual units respond? What kind of role does the president (or board) play in either approach, or do presidents (or boards) sometimes act independently in generating strategy? Obviously, there has been a mix of approaches in practice and the consequences are not well-observed or understood.

9. Types of Strategy "Statements"

Despite contingencies of the external environment and the vagaries of internal decision structures, colleges and universities do engage in strategy formation of varied kinds—from the highly formal and rational to the more emergent and implicit. We have found a wide range of *published* strategic "statements" in an unsystematic, but far-reaching electronic search that likely reflects outcomes of the more formalized processes. We will briefly categorize these statements into types—acknowledging that there is no clear demarcation among these very tentative groupings. Our purpose here is not to invent or even to test a typology, but rather to highlight the problem of definition: What is the content of strategies (at least as they appear in formal plans), and do they accomplish the most fundamental purpose of strategy, which is to move the organization in a particular direction.

In this section, we will simply use examples (while not identifying institutions) of language that characterizes the varied nominal plans we have found and suggest categories into which they might fit. We do not judge their validity, their contribution to legitimacy, nor their effectiveness.

Image-polishing Statements

Some statements of strategy contain language that is clearly meant to create an image and foster greater recognition. These statements seem principally aimed at building morale and cohesion among faculty, staff, and students and—perhaps secondarily—to convey a positive impression to external constituents. While these may fulfill perfectly valid needs of the institution, especially one that suffers from a weak or fragmented internal culture, they may or may not serve to animate actual operating decisions.

Image-oriented statements give a central place to "values" and "visions" and seem to rely on vague and inclusive terminology. One such statement, for example, includes the following: "We believe in an educational and intellectual environment that fosters growth and development, social justice, understanding among people and enrichment for all who study and work [at this institution]. . . ." Another characterized its goals this way: "To be competitive as [an institution] in a constantly changing world, to prepare our graduates for the challenges of a diverse and ever changing marketplace, . . . to create a culture of mutual respect with all [our] stakeholders, . . . to identify the distinctive capabilities that would enable [this institution] to distinguish itself as an educational leader in the 21st century, . . . [and] to be a leader [in] engaging participants in both active learning and scholarly exploration in a community guided by Christian values." While these broad, value-oriented statements have obvious utility in building a more cohesive institution, and in presenting a particular face to the public, they may not be specific enough to help an institution to decide which programs to cut or what new programs to start, presuming that such specificity might be among the criteria defining a strategy.

Incremental Statement

Some statements concentrate essentially on existing realities and constraints, proposing simply to improve or further develop "life as we know it" without unrealistic ambitions or fantasy. Prosaic though incremental statements may be, they have the virtue of realism. One such statement by a public university begins with a preamble enumerating the external constraints that have hampered the institution—constraints of budget and policy. It goes on to promise pursuit of goals that largely leave its existing programs intact. It begins with a promise to ". . . gauge our performance anually within vice presidential divisions," which it does not propose to change. It continues with the following major premises:

- Ensure that the allocation of resources supports our complex mission and that different contributions made by individuals, units, and divisions in achieving the University's collective obligation for excellence in teaching, research, and service are recognized.

- Strengthen the recognition and reward structure to encourage and reinforce the highest achievement throughout the University.

- Become more internationally focused in our educational programs, topics and methods of inquiry, outreach, and operations.

- Improve the quality of University life, promote a positive University identity, enhance a sense of community, and encourage loyalty to and pride in the University.

- Promote a campus atmosphere of inclusiveness and respect that fosters full opportunities for growth and advancement to all people.

- Provide state-of-the-art technological support for instruction, student learning, research, and administration, including the development of information delivery and management systems, computing and library facilities, advanced scientific instrumentation, and computing equipment and software appropriate to the needs of individual faculty and staff. Assist faculty, staff, and students to adopt and use the changing technology as it becomes available.

Incremental statements essentially confirm and affirm the existing institutional realities and promise to hold harmless its existing programs and policies. One of the obvious functions of an incremental statement is to provide a blanket of reassurance and security in a time of threat. This particular institution had seen the state's share in its overall budget shrink from 47 percent to 27 percent—clearly not a time to be thinking expansively, or even about major changes, but also a time in which constituencies may need to be reassured that their jobs and lives do not face imminent change for the worse.

Another public institution's statement—also situated in a state that had reduced funding for higher education—concentrated heavily on efficient operation of existent programs without referring to either a need for change or possible directions for change:

> [This university] will seek ways to decrease student time to degree, increase student learning, enhance institutional productivity and productivity in teaching and learning, promote the more effective use of fixed resources, and implement comprehensive assessment and accountability procedures.

The statement included suggestions to consider a year-round calendar and "other scheduling efficiencies," better use of existing space, reengineered support services, helping students achieve their degrees more quickly and improving the learning environment, and reallocating savings to support a small increase in enroll-ment. This statement clearly anticipated no fun-damental change in the institution's mission or in its programs. Instead, it focused narrowly on how to achieve its given mission with increas-ingly constrained resources.

Incrementalism of this kind is anything but glamorous but it is obviously the preferred form of "strategy" when the environments—both internal and external—encourage stability and continuity. It is also very likely to be the model result of planning in an academic cul-ture that values consultation and democratic decision-making. Strategy, then, does not nec-essarily mean massive change or extraordinary imagination of a new future. In its most mature and calibrated form, it can be cold-eyed, realis-tic, and simply reaffirming of the essential in-stitution. Such approaches, however, reject the exhortations of the business literature (Porter, 1996) to continually seek out the unique mix of activities and deliver systems in order to have an ultimate competitive advantage. It may also lull institutions of higher education into com-placency in a rapidly changing world by seek-ing to maximize stability and minimize change.

Process-saturated Statements

Choosing to err in the direction of participation and on the side of legitimation, some state-ments appear to be satisfied with a strong show of elaborate process. In one case, the pref-ace to the document described its 31-member task force and the schedule of its meetings with external consultants and groups of internal constituents that amounted to "the largest total involvement in a schoolwide project in [this in-stitution's] history." The task force originally formed six committees that eventually de-volved themselves into five "process groups." Each process group was charged with monitor-ing and further developing between 10 and 16 discrete items.

Leslie and Fretwell (1996) reported on one institution that involved roughly 150 individu-als in an accrediting process that was conducted simultaneously with strategic planning. One re-sult of such massive involvement is the oppor-tunity to compare perspectives and exchange information—and obviously to improve the likelihood of convergence. Clearly, process has its values. On the other hand, a participatory

planning process at another institution resulted in increased uncertainty: "We probably got into the process too soon. Don't turn a five-year pro-cess into a one-year blitz and try to do 33 things all at once. There is no guarantee that [all the] initiatives will make this a better place. We'll modify as we go along, but not all of [our] 33 initiatives are going to work." (Quoted in Leslie and Fretwell, 1996, p. 233.)

Process obviously can overwhelm and ob-scure questions of validity. While broad partici-pation may improve the flow of information and satisfy the participants, it may not result in a more clearly framed and reality-tested strat-egy. In other words, participation may be a nec-essary element of strategizing, but it is clearly not sufficient to satisfy other criteria.

Substantive Statements

Some statements are substantively rich. They take account of the institution's strengths and weaknesses, and they provide a searching and realistic examination of the environment in which the institution exists. Substantive state-ments consider both continuity and change in carefully framed terms. Most importantly, they are based on good, comprehensive information.

The Governor of Kentucky developed his own strategy for higher education in that state in 1997, a document that is exceptionally candid about the current state of Kentucky's higher ed-ucation system. According to the Governor's plan, Kentucky had a "low level of population with college degrees, high cost . . . relative to number of degrees produced, low persistence rates, low production of degrees, inadequate workforce preparation, and lack of a nationally-recognized research capability" (Patton, 1997). This plan starts with a candid and honest analy-sis of the performance of the existing system, relates it to the needs and expectations of the state, and proposes specific changes and re-forms—and benchmarks for measuring progress—to achieve the governor's goals.

While this system-level plan concentrates on re-framing the missions and organization of institutions, substantive statements at the institution-level concentrate on recognizing and maximizing an institution's distinctive strengths and capabilities. For example, one small public university makes its special competence central to all of the elements of its strategy: "We have a strong foundation of commitment to learner-centered education and personal service and universal access to notebook computers." It goes on to array a set of very operational initiatives around one central theme: "To establish a customized approach to learning that enables each person or organization to have effective, convenient, and efficient access to an educational process that supports independent progress toward their goals." (For example, the plan proposes to: "Identify major changes needed for customized learning and develop a six-year schedule for achieving them.") This approach to individualized learning readily distinguishes this institution from others, and provides operational steps to meet its overall objectives.

Principle-driven Statements

Illinois's "PQP" plan may have been less specific in the beginning than Kentucky's plan, but has been no less powerful in its impact. The acronym refers to "Priorities, Quality, and Productivity"—three principles that the Illinois Board of Higher Education imposed on its public universities and by which program evaluations and approvals, budget recommendations, and policy initiatives can be judged. The process was intended to drive out weak programs and inefficiencies in the system, and enhance productivity and quality.

According to a study of the PQP plan by the California Higher Education Policy Center, "Most of the senior institutions have reduced administrative costs and have eliminated many marginal academic programs. According to the Illinois Board of Higher Education, which coordinates higher education planning for the state, more than 245 academic programs have been eliminated, consolidated or reduced in size in the four-year institutions since 1992. These actions have saved about $120 million, [and] . . . the money has been reallocated by the campuses for high priority needs, such as improvements in undergraduate education" (Trombley, 1996, p. 1). This process has also resulted in significant reaffirmation or realignment of institutional mission and the distribution of graduate programs, although different interpretations of the impact of PQP have been offered.

PQP proceeded in an open-ended fashion, driven largely by continued budget stringency that had seen higher education's share of Illinois's appropriations shrink from 13 percent to just over 11 percent during a decade, and by enrollment projections that suggested stability or only very minimal increases. The aim of this plan was to maximize the three principles of working within a set of priorities for the system as a whole, enhancing the quality of strong programs, and increasing the productivity of scarce resources invested in higher education. This approach left the substance of decisions about which programs would be cut, which programs would benefit from new investments, and which institutions would change largely open to incremental judgments that would emerge from the process.

Blunderbuss Statements

Some strategic statements seem to have been formed in an indiscriminate attempt to overwhelm an institution's problem with a wide array of initiatives. One small, selective liberal arts college with about 1,800 students published a strategy with over 70 initiatives among its proposed directions. Some of the 70 were highly specific with clear numerical goals: "Increase by [xx] percent the number of graduates who achieve post-baccalaureate national and international fellowships, internships, service and leadership opportunities." Others were far more vague and general: "Foster campus-wide intellectual community."

Although such statements appear to be the product of a cooperative effort and to offer the promise of energizing and engaging many different segments of the campus community, they nevertheless seem to encourage divergent behavior (and further dissipation of organizational coherence) rather than convergent behavior (and increased efficiency and coherence). The indiscriminate laundry-listing of potentially helpful things people might do might be more successful in further atomizing the campus and legitimizing individualization of effort—insofar as people can pick and choose the way they behave while feeling that they are legitimately supporting the accepted 'strategy.'

10. Common Elements of Statements

While form and content may differ from statement to statement, certain common elements recur. Essentially, these elements include an assessment of the institution's (or system's) environment, a recapitulation of the process that brought the statement to closure, an analysis of the institution's strengths and weaknesses, and a set of recommended actions or directions.

The statements we have reviewed—a convenience sample, to be sure, and not necessarily representative of all institutions—do show the difficulty of composing a formal plan that provides meaningful direction to a college or university, that commits it to a course of action, while it also solves the problems of "legitimacy and commitment," or acceptance by a critical mass of constituents.

But among the most striking conclusions we have reached as we examine diverse statements is the extent to which they parallel each other in actual content. This suggests that institutions are seeking a safe and acceptable middle ground of common goals and similar programs instead of courageously differentiating themselves from other institutions and seeking out new markets and new ways to compete—at least in their formal plans. The following table contains a sample of abstracted "major premises" from several strategic planning documents to illustrate how similar they are.

Abstracted Major Premises from Selected Strategic Statements

- To be competitive in a constantly changing world, to prepare our graduates for the challenges of a diverse and changing marketplace, and to create a culture of mutual respect.
- Create meaningful standards of excellence: ensure that the allocation of resources supports our complex mission; strengthen the recognition and reward structure; become more internationally focused; improve the quality of University life; promote a positive University [and] sense of community; provide state-of-the art technological support.
- Intensify the academic experience; intensify commitment to community and diversity; control costs and use assets wisely.
- Continue to improve the quality of campus life by offering students the best possible academic experience and in-

vesting in capital improvements; enhance the sense of community and positive atmosphere that exists among our students, faculty, and staff.
- Promote quality, effectiveness, efficiency, and access.
- Increase levels of accountability to students and to taxpayers, improve preparation for careers, embrace technology; strengthen K-12 partnerships; contribute significantly to economic competitiveness and the quality of life.
- Strengthen the human and physical infrastructure, make effective and innovative use of information technology, create a quality educational environment and experience, enhance diversity, build bridges to the community, increase national visibility and stature.
- Assure student access and the quality of services, enhance information technology, maintain adequate equipment, enhance campus safety and security, enhance programs on diversity, expand research initiatives, strengthen relations with business and industry and enhance workforce development, and address capital construction needs.
- Improve student access and increase graduation rates; improve the effectiveness of learning experiences; focus research to achieve optimal benefits; enhance economic development and quality of life; improve productivity.

These "premises" have been abstracted from a random selection of electronically published strategic statements. While they are partially quoted, space required that we abstract them in condensed fashion. They are intended to be illustrative, rather than direct quotation or even fully representative of all available strategic statements.

In effect, they are almost entirely incremental in tone and conventional in their scope. Almost without exception, they propose to continue the institution's major functions and programs, but to do so by using resources more efficiently while improving the human aspects of campus life and upgrading the infrastructure through which the institution operates. Almost every one pays lip service to "excellence" or "quality" in relation to undergraduate education—without elaborating on what that means or how one campus's "excellence" might differ from another's.

It is not our intent to be critical of the statements we have reviewed; undoubtedly, they are the product of good faith efforts and of hard work by committed individuals and groups, and they may well be entirely appropriate for the institutions to which they apply. On the other hand, one cannot readily find among them very many of the indicia that underlie even our non-competitive definition of strategy. We are left with three important residual problems; i) what leads diverse institutions to rhetorically isomorphic strategy statements? ii) how might institutions sharpen and differentiate their strategies more affirmatively? and iii) where does leadership and responsibility for planning lie and what role do CEOs play?

"Rhetorical isomorphism" in strategic statements

The striking uniformity among the strategic statements we reviewed—notwithstanding that they apply to diverse institutions and systems—and the generality of their rhetoric begs for further study and explanation.

Perhaps institutions operating with a reasonable amount of slack resources and an absence of urgent pressure to change do not actually plan strategically, notwithstanding that this might be the best time to do so. They may have achieved a satisfying equilibrium in the marketplace that—while subject to perturbations from year to year—is a far safer position to maintain than to change. Although institutions do engage in a process called "strategic planning" as a way to meet both internal and external expectations for rational behavior and accountability, many institutions may actually be engaged in "strategic maintenance." That is, they seek out and articulate a common understanding and shared validation of the status quo and affirm its value to their common good.

The common values of the academic community—which may have more universal than local content, institutions being more similar than different in what they try to achieve—rise to the surface easily in any sort of consensus-building process. These values, once articulated, serve as a basis for solidarity and communal

identification, so there may be a natural tendency to affirm the collective affinity for them.

This tendency satisfies one criterion for strategic decision making—commitment—but it does not satisfy another—validity. Institutions facing an objective crisis of some kind may well need solidarity to survive, but they will not survive unless they make valid decisions—decisions that are based on accurate information and realistic assessment of the institution's performance, market viability, and capacity to meet the demands of change. That requires a far more penetrating form of analysis and reality testing than does achievement of a placid and satisfying consensus. Mid-crisis is not an optimal time to begin either process, so perhaps the hard analytical work would have more powerful effects if it were done—and if consensus were built—during periods of relative "normalcy." As someone recently remarked, "Map-making skills are worth little in the epicenter of an earthquake" (Hamel and Prahalad, 1989, p. 73). On the other hand, higher education has arguably maintained a valid market position because, in the aggregate, demand has remained high and the prices colleges charge in the marketplace have been sustainable. As long as that holds true, one can expect colleges and universities to work at maintaining their position and not at changing it. That means they will not work too hard at serious strategy formation—and certainly not at substantive strategic planning.

It does suggest, however, that marginal change is a more predictable path for most institutions. Formal strategic statements then may principally serve to present to internal and external constituents the appearance of responsible and rational stewardship ("legitimacy" as defined by Stone and Brush, 1996), but they may not override the fundamental commitments of people to the *status quo*. Notwithstanding the appearance of a formal strategy, institutions may actually change more by adapting slowly and conservatively to new realities, and constructing a social consensus on the basis of their successes and failures. They may also change informally through the exercise of presidential leadership, annual budgeting exercises, and entrepreneurial initiatives. Should such informal routes to institutional transformation be acknowledged as a "strategy"? Perhaps they should if they meet threshold criteria, but those criteria have yet to be clearly defined.

Here, we confront again the question of the difference between "emergent" and "formal" strategic planning. The empirically-based research literature provides too thin a basis to help us understand under what conditions and in what ways colleges and universities change and reconstitute themselves—and particularly how they do so under varying conditions of resource abundance or constraint. The language of public strategy statements—by itself—provides only a starting point in understanding how institutions imagine their futures and what they do to realize their visions. At the very least, we recognize the need for far more understanding of the processes, especially the more informal ones, by which institutions purposefully adapt and change.

11. Institutional Change—A Role for Strategic Planning?

It is easy enough to find and analyze formal strategic statements. It is not as easy to identify and classify their impact on institutions. There is no doubt that formal strategy has resulted in change. New programs have been started, old programs closed; capital has been raised, budgets have been reformed; technology has been introduced, campuses reconstructed; off-campus centers have been initiated, new clienteles served. The studies we have reviewed, and our own experience, have provided convincing evidence that formal strategizing is—in some circumstances—one of several important and effective ways to respond to threats and opportunities. Perhaps it should be considered one tool in a broader mix of ways to change—a tool that can add information to the process, but that cannot by itself produce new understandings of institutional competencies, or community engagement in implementing new futures.

There are few contemporary case studies on which to rely. An early study by Chaffee (1984) looked at small liberal arts colleges that had experienced fiscal challenges. She found that a combination of linear, adaptive and interpretive strategies were a requisite of successful turn-around management. Leslie and Fretwell (1996) examined several institutions that changed in profound ways as a result of

imminent or foreseeable financial crises—institutions such as Tusculum College, Trenton State College (now the College of New Jersey), and Bloomfield College. While each (as well as others in their study) changed noticeably, none engaged in what one might recognize as a standardized textbook formal strategic planning exercise. They certainly strategized, but they did so in very intuitive and informal ways. All had to struggle with the disbelief of important constituents in the existence of an objective crisis, and they all had to cope with resistance to change among those constituents. Thus, the threshold issue seems to be in defining and interpreting the nature of an institution's condition and in reaching a consensus about its operating strengths and weaknesses. This may be as much a cultural and psychological process—an interpretive process—as it is a rational/analytical one. How and under what circumstances do faculty, staff, students, parents, alumni, friends, and trustees come to "know" that their institution faces threats and perhaps faces them without the resources and competencies it needs to cope with those threats? How and under what circumstances do key constituents mobilize to initiate change?

Returning to the conceptual basis we explored in the earlier part of this paper, we can now see the importance of differentiating among the sources and forms of institutional change. Formal strategic planning is perhaps the most structured and purposeful among a range of possibilities. At the other end of the continuum, "emergent" patterns of individual choices and preferences may accumulate to the point that they represent a shift in values, priorities, and practices—and result in observable, if not very explicit, change. We have not found in the literature a useful paradigm to help explain how and when change occurs in one form or another. For example, might external circumstances such as budget stringency or policy shifts require institutions to engage in nominal or substantive strategic planning? Or might the press of subtle shifts in the market or internal culture begin the process of emergent change and the evolution of implicit strategy? And what effects do the different processes of change have? These arenas for further study are as yet not well understood.

12. From Theory to Practice: Conclusions and Future Research Directions

The ultimate goal of strategy research in higher education is to improve practice. And yet there is a continuing gap between the research on strategy and the capacity of the work to speak normatively to practitioners who are seeking to find better ways of managing the enterprise. In this section we draw from our prior discussion what seem to us to be the key findings, and make suggestions for research directions that could serve to place research in greater service to practice.

Developing a multiparadigmatic approach to the study of strategy formation

Understanding how and why institutions change themselves, what contextual and environmental conditions add up to thresholds for action, and what processes create the kinds of social and psychological realities that alter behavior all need further study. We have seen that formal strategic planning is one conditionally useful tool—among other ways of bringing about change—but we need to know more about the conditions under which its use is more and less appropriate.

Both theory and practice of *strategizing and planning* have proved to be moving targets, as popular trends in management have more or less continuously substituted one form of corporate change for another. In summarizing what is known about strategy and its formation, we have become frustrated by the lack of systematic analysis of experience as well as by the shifting conceptual frames of reference over time. In short, we find it difficult to locate a convincing consensus about how to develop strategy and what kinds of results to expect from any given approach.

We do know that formal strategic planning can produce fundamental changes in certain circumstances and when it is used in conjunction with adaptive and interpretive approaches. Certainly, though, institutions may plan formally without making substantive changes in their functions or their operations. And institutions obviously make substantive changes without engaging in any explicit process of planning or strategizing. The connections between statements and outcomes are unclear at best, because there are statements without outcomes and outcomes without statements.

Studying how institutions plan and change might appropriately begin with a relatively blank conceptual slate about how institutions of higher education respond to threats and opportunities in their environments. Mintzberg and McHugh (1985) say of the emergent model of strategy formation that it is false, but,

> . . . no more false than the widely accepted conventional model—the "deliberate" (or "hothouse") view of strategy formation—which no one has bothered to test. A viable theory of strategy making must encompass both models. No organization can function with strategies that are always and purely emergent; that would amount to a complete abdication of will and leadership, not to mention conscious thought. But none can likewise function with strategies that are always and purely deliberate; that would amount to an unwillingness to learn, a blindness to whatever is unexpected (p. 196).

Undoubtedly, many institutions adapt as emergent and loosely coupled organizations, and do so without "planning." Many others just as obviously engage in purposeful and effective formal strategic planning. But most, probably, engage in all simultaneously, although with different emphases at different times. We suggest, therefore, that studies of strategy adopt a broad paradigmatic starting point.

Chaffee (1985a, b) has found that more robust forms of strategy formation integrate perceptions and understandings that result from three different perspectives, or paradigms: A firm grounding in rational, linear analysis; an understanding of how to adapt to changing environmental conditions; and an ability to articulate an intuitive, constructivist organizational metaphor that provides a future-oriented vision of the institution, or interpretive strategy. But the literature—and existing practice— seems as yet unfocused by self-conscious awareness of perspective and its consequences for the way in which planning or strategy formation go forward. We note with particular interest and concern the continuing appearance of popular and quasi-professional literature on strategic planning that does not make clear the consequences of paradigmatic perspective, nor the logic of taking different approaches to strategizing under different conditions—formal strategic planning, or the linear approach, being only one of the options.

Studying strategizing behavior *in situ* and longitudinally may help to achieve a more precise and sophisticated understanding of the combination of situations, events, and actions that shape individuals' and organizations' ways to cope with various opportunities and threats in their environments. There may or may not be regularities in coping; there may or may not be a constellation of behaviors and perceptions that could be recognized as "strategizing"; and there may or may not be systematically recognizable outcomes from different strategizing patterns. These basic empirical facts remain to be established.

Perhaps even more important, we have little understanding of the interpretive aspects of strategy. It is fairly clear that organizations weave their experience into stories or "sagas" (Clark, 1972) about themselves, and that a few use "interpretive strategy" to meet opportunities and threats to the status quo or to chart a new future (Chaffee, 1985a). These constructions of collective reality undoubtedly serve important functions in managing change. How they emerge, how they are altered, how they affect people's understandings, attitudes, and behaviors, and what impact they have on major choices institutions make have received virtually no systematic attention.

Hax's (1990) recommendation that studies of strategy begin with an examination of cognitions and of the social and organizational processes by which perceptions are channeled and commitments developed leads us to suggest framing an understanding of strategy with concepts of "organizational learning." Senge (1990) and Stacey (1992), as well as a review of research on change in schools by Louis (1993), converge on the concept of organizational learning as a way to understand change. Taken collectively, they suggest an artificial conceptual duality between, as Stacey puts it, "order and chaos in organizations." The choice is not between either of the extremes, but rather in elaborating the alternatives along a continuum from less to more structured response. Among other things, experience with "continuous" change—as with the recent move to "continuous quality improvement"—has suggested that organizations might engage in cumulative experiential learning, and that such learning may become more or less formalized in strategy.

Ethnographies of institutional change—if integrated across a substantial sample of cases—might tell us a great deal more about strategy. How people come to share understandings of crises, what range of acceptable solutions they construct, how much risk to take, what values guide choices, and how deeply change is allowed to cut are all likely to become clearer through the personal and collective stories people tell about their experiences.

Contingent Strategic Management

Although the literature on organization theory and change processes is extensive, surprisingly little hard evidence is available to help us understand—in concrete ways—what works best under which circumstances.

Different ways to understand the environment and to adapt may be relatively more useful under some circumstances than under others. Intuitively, this contextual thinking makes sense, but the empirical research is too thin to help understand how different ways to strategize may work better in some circumstances than in others. For example, we cannot really help an institution faced with an extremely turbulent and unpredictable environment select from among a variety of different approaches—say, centralized linear strategic planning vs. a decentralized interpretive approach. We know far too little about the *outcomes* of different ways to strategize: what might an institution gain by strategizing in one way versus what might it gain by doing it differently? And under what circumstances?

Unintended Consequences

One theme that emerges consistently in the literature we have reviewed is that of unintended consequences of strategy. Among other issues, the role of strategizing in generating conflict among constituents is particularly vexing. We note findings (Schuster et al, 1994; Leslie and Fretwell, 1996) that suggest strategizing—in and of itself—has the potential to create political and emotional backlash. Instead of opening individuals and organizational subunits to new directions and ideas, it may have the unintended consequence of hardening existing commitments and in increasing the energy devoted to defending those commitments. This is a serious enough issue to warrant extensive exploration—as Hax suggests when he recommends the study of politics in decision making—both for how backlash arises among both internal and external constituencies and for how it may affect the ability of the institution to engage in change. We suspect that the role presidents play in developing interpretive strategy may determine to some extent how constituents react. Unless these constituents understand clearly why new directions may be needed and how their own work and lives will be affected, they may very well see advantages to resisting change. (Certainly, conflict is to be expected when major institutional changes are anticipated, and managing that conflict must be considered a normal phase of strategy formation.)

Another unintended consequence appears to lie in the arena of "errors." That is, institutions may simply choose wrongly. Given what we know about the need to use multiple approaches, we might ask if institutions that use only one approach (the linear, for example) make more errors than institutions that combine linear, adaptive, and interpretive approaches. Does the mix work "better" (produce fewer errors) when tailored to some recognizable environmental conditions (stability vs. turbulence)?

Strategy Formation in Public System Environments

Strategies and strategic plans, particularly of public colleges and universities, connect with one another—whether systematically or unsystematically. Institutions of higher education are motivated to produce strategic plans for a variety of reasons. Their leaders may perceive an internal need to refocus academic programming, or a need to adapt pro-actively to a changing external environment. Or institutions may be required to produce plans within the context of a systemwide effort. Stone and Brush (1996) proposed a framework that suggests that plans will take on a different tenor, and that institutions will invoke different internal processes, depending upon the purpose of planning. Are institutions using different processes to formulate plans for external audi-

ences? If not, should they? To what extent do internally initiated plans account for system-imposed constraints? Do systemwide plans act as "umbrella" strategies, to use Mintzberg and McHugh's (1985) term, in guiding institutional strategy formation? Are some systemwide approaches to planning more successful at shepherding institutional ambitions than others? Are some systemwide processes of "supra-corporate" strategy formation more successful than others? Under what conditions? Obviously, one part of forming an institution's strategy involves understanding the political implications of any changes it might consider.

The Need to Study the Content of Strategy

A contributing factor to the continuing gap between theory and practice in the study of strategy in higher education is that the available research focuses on the process of strategy formation, with a particular emphasis on the study of strategic planning processes, to the almost complete exclusion of the study of effectiveness of particular strategies. We note, for example, that several of the studies we have reviewed (Leslie and Fretwell, 1996; Taylor and Schmidtlein, 1996; Schuster et al, 1994) suggest that connections do exist, but that the relationship between strategy and observable change is far from regular. Porter (1996) discusses the origins of strategic positions, and his framework has promise for examining strategy effectiveness in higher education. He identifies *variety-based positioning* where the organization focuses on producing a subset of an industry's products or services. A variety-based provider serves a wide array of customers, but will meet only a subset of their needs. An example of this in higher education would be web-based courses. His second category is *needs-based positioning*, whereby the organization provides a tailored set of activities to meet all of the needs of a particular subset of customers, based on customer preferences. Choosing which subset of customers to serve closely resembles the traditional notion of positioning. Elite private institutions, for example, provide a unique combination of activities that are price sensitive and serve all the needs of a small group of students. A third category of position is *access-based positioning*, meeting the needs of customers who are accessible in different ways. Examples include rural versus urban-based customers, and can be a function of geography or customer scale. Differentiation by type of institution might fall into this category, as would institutional size. Using a framework like this to analyze institutional strategies might lead to a better understanding of which approaches to positioning work best under particular conditions.

Leadership and Strategy

The role of presidential leadership as a component of strategy formation deserves closer attention. The similarity among strategic statements may reflect an underlying drive toward conformity in the higher education enterprise. But it may also be that at some institutions, in particular contexts, institutional strategy—big changes above the level of program reforms—emanates directly from presidential direction. How do their leadership activities complement or compete with institutions' planning processes? Do presidents tend to provide "interpretation" of emerging institutional strategies, or do they tend to respond to external pressures that are simply too uncoupled from the ongoing institutional culture to appear through evolution or a formal planning process? How do presidents use "state of the institution" addresses, and is strategy that is introduced through this channel equally well implemented as strategy that emanates from an elaborate planning process? Are there predictable consequences of particular behaviors with regard to strategy formation? Are there patterns of success that would lead to normative conclusions about different approaches under different conditions? Or is the institutional context so unique from institution to institution that no generalization can be drawn?

A second area deserving further exploration concerns how presidents might most effectively engage their institutions' strategy formation processes. Should they establish the corporate strategy (i.e. planning parameters) prior to a call for unit strategic plans or should they nurture a bottom-up, goal-free process with the expectation that emergent strategies will be identified that can constitute an institutional strategy? What kinds of risk are involved in the choice of one route or another?

Finally, are there characteristics about institutions' internal and external environments that are more likely to result in statements being utilized by institutional leaders, or does utilization depend on leadership styles and preferences? Presidents may well be judged on how they develop strategy that strengthens their institutions, but there is little good advice one could offer presidents on the basis of what is now known about their role in strategizing.

13. Summary

We have attempted a complex analysis of the state of strategy formation in institutions of higher education. Our discussions ranged from current business concepts of strategy to what we know about successful approaches to uses of formal planning as a tool for managing institutional change in higher education. Most importantly, we have tried to point out areas in which further theory development and research are needed. While the state of knowledge and practice are far from complete, we can generalize to a certain extent:

- Corporate America ceased practicing strategic planning as its mantra for success at least ten years ago.

- There is complementarity among approaches to strategy formation, and researchers should not expect to find a single "silver bullet" explanation of how organizations successfully strategize.

- Strategic planning is one tool in a kit of approaches to strategy formation. Institutions should resist the temptation to expect it to capture the totality of institutional strategizing.

- Strategy is sometimes formed through existing governance processes and sometimes through special adjuncts like "Joint Big Decision Committees." There is unlikely to be one best way, or one single way to form strategy. How effectively different approaches are combined will be contingent on institutions' cultures, histories, and circumstances. We do know that strategy emanates to some extent from institutional leaders, but we need greater understanding of the conditions under which those strategies gain acceptance and support for their implementation.

- We need better metrics for assessing the capacity of institutional governance processes to strategize. It is clear that some institutions do so readily while the effort to strategize in others produces dysfunctions. Why?

- The appropriate role of leaders in strategy formation, and strategic planning, is not well understood. There is little empirical evidence to address the success or failure of goal-free, bottom-up planning processes, versus those that are bounded by announced institutional goals or vision statements.

- Institutional strategic plans bear remarkable similarity one to the other, which suggests that existing efforts may be more focused on maintenance than on change. We do not understand very clearly why there is so much convergence among strategies or why institutions may so consistently choose parallel strategies.

- Higher education research has focused almost exclusively on the process of strategy formation, rather than the content of strategic choices or on the consequences of those choices. Researchers studying corporate strategy, in contrast, focus intensively on the content and consequences of strategy.

- More attention needs to be given to the appropriate organizational level of strategizing (corporate, unit, or functional/operational). How are unit plans best integrated across the institution?

- Strategic planning is often invoked during crisis, despite its better fit to periods of relative institutional stability.

- Alternative concepts like "organizational learning" have yet to provide widely accepted working metaphors for the way higher education adapts to changes in its environment.

Our review has left us with a sense that "strategic planning" is widely promoted in the literature on higher education as a valid response to environmental challenges. Yet the experience of the corporate world suggests that it is at best a necessary, but not sufficient, tool with which to achieve timely and appropriate

responses to those challenges. Colleges and universities do need to understand the markets and public policy arenas in which they operate. They need to act purposefully and accountably in order to satisfy their patrons in and out of government. They are corporate enterprises with constituencies both internal and external who expect to be treated as stakeholders whenever change is introduced. To satisfy all of these conditions, colleges and universities have to do more than publish a formal plan. To respond to conditions that demand response, they have to generate good ideas for programs, position themselves against potential competitors, find the resources to do old things better or new things entirely, and move people who have vested interests in the status quo to accept new ways of living and working. In many cases, they will have to remake themselves substantially in order to survive.

We have not been able to achieve a thoroughly satisfying practical or conceptual basis for helping institutions through this particular maze. But we know from experience that some have threaded it successfully. We therefore recommend that the research agenda begin, not so much by studying strategic planning or strategy formation *per se*, but by studying the experience of institutions that adapt successfully (and unsuccessfully) to their changing internal and external realities. In systematically analyzing these experiences, we may find an appropriate paradigm for understanding the ingredients of change and the hurdles institutions must overcome to bring it about. We think that paradigm will include much of what is already known about strategy formation, but we hold open minds about what else may emerge as keys to bringing about change in higher education.

References

Albright, B. N., and Gilleland, B. S. (1994). A clean slate: principles for moving to a value-driven higher education funding model. [On-line]. Available: http://www.bor.ohio/hefc/albright94.html. 1994.

Andrews, K. R. (1981). Corporate strategy as a vital function of the board. *Harvard Business Review* 59 (6); 174–184.

Ansoff, I. H. (1991). A critique of Henry Mintzberg's "The Design School: Reconsidering the Basic Premises of Strategic Management." *Strategic Management Journal* 12: 449–461.

Baldridge, J. V. (1971). *Power and Conflict in the University: Research in the Sociology of Complex Organizations.* New York: John Wiley and Sons.

Bogue, E. G., and Saunders, R. L. (1992). *The Evidence for Quality: Strengthening the Tests of Academic and Administrative Effectiveness.* San Francisco: Jossey-Bass.

Breneman, D. W. (1995). *A State of Emergency? Higher Education in California.* San Jose: California Higher Education Policy Center.

Byrne, J. A. (1996). The new strategic planning. After a decade of gritty downsizing, big thinkers are back in vogue. *Business Week* August 26: 46–52.

California Higher Education Policy Center. (1994). *Time for Decision: California's Legacy and the Future of Higher Education. A Report with Recommendations.* San Jose, CA: California Higher Education Policy Center.

California Postsecondary Education Commission. (1996). *The Challenge of the Century.* Sacramento: California Postsecondary Education Commission.

Callan, P. (1994). Public purposes and public responsibilities. Presented at the annual meeting of the California Association for Institutional Research, San Diego, CA.

Chaffee, E. E. (1984). Successful strategic management in small private colleges. *Journal of Higher Education* 55: 212–241.

Chaffee, E. E. (1985(a)). Three models of strategy. *Academy of Management Review* 10: 89–98.

Chaffee, E. E. (1985 (b)) The concept of strategy: from business to higher education. In J. Smart (ed). *Higher Education: Handbook of Theory and Research,* Vol. I. New York: Agathon Press.

Chaffee, E. E. (1997). Future Focus: The path to success. Opening address to Mayville State University and Valley City State University. Valley City, ND: Valley City State University.

Chaffee, E. E., and Sherr, L. A. (1992). *Transforming Postsecondary Education.* ASHE-ERIC Higher Education Report, No. 3, Washington, DC: George Washington University.

Chait, R. Colleges should not be blinded by vision. (1993, September 22) *Chronicle of Higher Education,* p. B1.

Clark, B. R. The organizational saga in higher education. (1972). *Administrative Science Quarterly* 17: 178–184.

Cohen, M. D., and March, J. D. (1974). *Leadership and Ambiguity.* New York: McGraw-Hill.

Cope, R. G. (1985). A contextual model to encompass the strategic planning concept: introducing a newer paradigm. *Planning for Higher Education* 13: 13–20.

Council for Aid to Education. (1997). *Breaking the Social Contract: The Fiscal Crisis in Higher Education.* Santa Barbara: Rand Corporation. [On-line] Available: http://www.rand.org

Deal T., and Kennedy, A. (1982). *Corporate Cultures: The Rites and Rituals of Corporate Life.* Reading, MA: Addison-Wesley.

Dill, D. (1993–94). Rethinking the planning process. *Planning for Higher Education* 22: 8–13.

Frederickson, J. W. (1984). The comprehensiveness of strategic decision processes: extension, observations, future directions. *Academy of Management Journal* 27: 445–466.

Glaser, M. (1991) Tailoring performance measurement to fit the organization: from generic to germane. *Public Productivity and Management Review* 14: 303–319.

Hackman, R. J., and Wagerman, R. (1995). Total quality management: empirical, conceptual and practical issues. *Administrative Science Quarterly* 40: 309–342.

Hamel, G., and Prahalad, C. K. (1989). Strategic intent. *Harvard Business Review* May–June: 63–76.

Hax, A. C. (1990). Redefining the concept of strategy and the strategy formation process. *Planning Review* May/June: 34–40.

Hearn, J. C., Clugston, R. M., and Heydinger, R. B. (1993). Five years of strategic environmental assessment efforts at a research university: a case study of an organizational innovation. *Innovative Higher Education* 18: 7–36.

Hoffman, A. M., and Julius, D. J. (eds.). (1995). *Total Quality Management: Implications for Higher Education.* Maryville, Missouri: Prescott Publishing Company.

Keller, G. (1983). *Academic Strategy: The Management Revolution in American Higher Education.* Baltimore: The Johns Hopkins University Press.

Keller, G. (1995). The vision thing in higher education. *Planning for Higher Education,* Vol. 23, Summer 1995: 8–14.

Kennedy, D. (1994). Making choices in the research university. In J. R. Cokle, E. G. Barber, and S. R. Graubard (eds.), *The Research University in a Time of Discontent.* Baltimore: The Johns Hopkins Press.

Leslie, D. W. (1996). Strategic governance: the wrong questions? a review essay of J. H. Schuster, D. G. Smith, K. A. Corak, and M. M. Yamada. *Strategic Governance: How to Make Big Decisions Better.* Phoenix, AZ: ACE/Oryx Press, 1994. *The Review of Higher Education* 20: 101–112.

Leslie, D. W., and Fretwell, E. K., Jr. (1996). *Wise Moves in Hard Times: Creating and Managing Resilient Colleges and Universities.* San Francisco: Jossey-Bass.

Lorenz, C. (1994). Use your intuition. (Leading business figures use intuition in decision-making). *The Financial Times,* June 8, p. 20.

Louis, K. S. (1993). Beyond bureaucracy: rethinking how schools change. ERIC Document 359654.

Mintzberg, H. (1978). Patterns in strategy formation. *Management Science* 24: 934–948.

Mintzberg, H. (1990). The design school: reconsidering the basic premises of strategic management. *Strategic Management Journal* 11: 171–195.

Mintzberg, H. (1994). *The Rise and Fall of Strategic Planning*. Toronto: Maxwell MacMillan.

Mintzberg, H., and McHugh, A. (1985). Strategy formation in an adhocracy. *Administrative Science Quarterly* 30: 160–197.

Munitz, B. (1995). Wanted: new leadership for higher education. *Planning for Higher Education* 24 (Fall 1995): 9–16.

Nutt, P. C. (1984). A strategic planning network for nonprofit organizations. *Strategic Management Journal* 5: 57–75.

Ouchi, W. (1981). *Theory Z*. Reading, MA: Addison-Wesley.

Patton, P. E. (1997). *A Plan for Postsecondary Education: An Agenda for the 21st Century*. Frankfurt, KY: Office of the Governor.

Pearson, G. J. (1990). An introduction to strategy. In G. J. Pearson, *Strategic Thinking*. Englewood Cliffs, NJ: Prentice Hall.

Pennings, J. M. (1985). Introduction. In J. M. Pennings and Associates. *Organizational Strategy and Change*. San Francisco: Jossey-Bass.

Pennsylvania State University. (1997). *Achieving Excellence: Strategic Plan 1997–2002*. University Park, PA: College of Liberal Arts, The Pennsylvania State University.

Peters T., and Waterman, R. (1982). *In Search of Excellence*. New York: Harper and Row.

Peterson, M. W. (1986). Continuity, challenge, and change: an organizational perspective on planning past and future. *Planning for Higher Education* 14: 7–15.

Peterson, M. W. (1997). Using contextual planning to transform institutions. In M. W. Peterson, D. D. Dill, L. A. Mets, and Associates. *Planning and Management for a Changing Environment*. San Francisco: Jossey-Bass.

Peterson, M. W., Dill, D. D., Mets, L. A., and Associates. (1997). *Planning and Management for a Changing Environment*. San Francisco: Jossey-Bass.

Peterson, M. W., and Dill, D. D. (1997). Understanding the competitive environment of the postsecondary knowledge industry. In M. W. Peterson, D. D. Dill, L. A. Mets, and Associates. *Planning and Management for a Changing Environment*. San Francisco: Jossey-Bass.

Politi, J. J. (ed.) (1995). *Applying Quality to Education*. Maryville, MO: Prescott Publishing Co.

Porter, M. E. (1987, May–June). From competitive advantage to corporate strategy. *Harvard Business Review* 65: 43–59.

Porter, M. E. (1996, November/December). What is Strategy? *Harvard Business Review* 74: 61–77.

Prahalad, C. K. and Hamel, G. (1990, May–June). The Core Competence of the Corporation. *Harvard Business Review* 68: 77–91.

Rowley, D. J., Lujan, H. D., and Dolence, M. G. (1997). *Strategic Change in Colleges and Universities*. San Francisco: Jossey Bass.

Sabloff, P. (1997). Another Reason Why State Legislatures Will Continue To Restrict Public University Autonomy. *Review of Higher Education* 20 : 141–162.

Schein, E. (1985). *Organizational Culture and Leadership*. San Francisco: Jossey-Bass.

Schmidtlein, F. A. and Milton, T. (eds.). (1990). Adapting Strategic Planning to Campus Realities. New Directions for Institutional Research, no. 67, San Francisco: Jossey-Bass.

Schuster, J. H., Smith, D. G., Corak, K. A., and Yamada, M. M. (1994). *Strategic Governance: How to Make Big Decisions Better*. Phoenix, AZ: ACE/Oryx Press.

Senge, P. M. (1990). The Fifth Discipline: The Art and Practice of the Learning Organization. New York: Doubleday/Currency.

Seymour, D. (1993). *On Quality: Causing Quality in Higher Education*. Phoenix, AZ: Oryx Press.

Seymour, D. (1995). Once Upon a Campus: Lessons for Improving Quality and Productivity in Higher Education. Phoenix, AZ: Oryx Press.

Seymour, D. (ed.). (1996). High Performing Colleges: The Malcolm Baldrige National Quality Award as a Framework for Improving Higher Education. Maryville, Missouri: Prescott Publishing Co.

Shapiro, J. Z. (1986). Evaluation Research and Educational Decision-Making: A Review of the Literature. In John Smart (ed). *Higher Education: Handbook of Theory and Research*, Vol. 2. New York: Agathon Press.

Shires, M. A. (1996). The Future of Public Undergraduate Education in California. Santa Barbara: Rand Corporation.

Shirley, R. C. (1983). Identifying the Levels of Strategy for a College or University. *Long Range Planning* 16: 92–98.

Smelser, N. J. (1974). Growth, Structural Change, and Conflict in California Public Higher Education, 1950–1970. In Neil J. Smelser and Gabriel Almond (Eds.), *Public Higher Education in California*. Berkeley: University of California Press.

Stacey, R. D. (1992). Managing the Unknowable: Strategic Boundaries Between Order and Chaos in Organizations. San Francisco: Jossey-Bass.

Stafford, R. (1993). Sheep in Wolves' Clothing, or How Not To Do Strategic Planning. *Planning for Higher Education* 22: 55–59.

Stone, M. M., and Brush, C. G. (1996). Planning in Ambiguous Contexts: The Dilemma of Meeting Needs for Commitment and Demands for Legitimacy. *Strategic Management Journal* 17: 633–652.

Taylor, A. L., and Schmidtlein, F. A. (1996). *Issues Posed by Graduate-Research Universities' Changing Environment and Their Planning Responses*. Final technical report submitted to the National Science Foundation.

Teeter, D. J. and Lozier, G. G. (Eds.). (1993). *Pursuit of Quality in Higher Education: Case Studies in Total Quality Management.* New Directions for Institutional Research, No. 78. San Francisco: Jossey-Bass.

Trombley, W. (1996). "Priorities, Quality, Productivity:" Ambitious Illinois Program Surpasses Expectations. *Crosstalk. 4*, 1. California Higher Education Policy Center.

Weick, K. E. (1977). Re-Punctuating the Problem. In *New Perspectives on Organizational Effectiveness*, by Paul S. Goodman, Johannes M. Pennings, and Associates. San Francisco, Calif.: Jossey-Bass.

Wildavsky, A. B. (1997). *The New Politics of the Budgetary Process.* (3rd ed.) New York: Longman.

Wilson, I. (1994). Strategic Planning Isn't Dead—It's Changed. *Long Range Planning* 27: 12–24.

College and University Planning: Perspectives from a Nation-Wide Study

FRANK A. SCHMIDTLEIN AND TOBY H. MILTON

An earlier version of this paper was presented at the Tenth European Association of Institutional Research Forum in August, 1988.

Introduction

In the United States, higher education administrators and scholars began to devote considerable attention to formal planning in the late 1960s. At that time, it was becoming increasingly apparent that for American colleges and universities the final decades of the twentieth century were likely to be characterized by a declining population of traditional college-age students, by increasing competition for fiscal resources, and by wavering public confidence in higher education (Mortimer and Tierney, 1979). Concerned that these changing demographic and fiscal trends could adversely effect the size and quality of a broad spectrum of American higher education institutions, many higher education professionals began to advocate using the formal planning and management approaches developed in government and corporate settings. By 1977, Shuck commented that planning is the new "religion" of higher education. Similarly Mayhew (1980) suggested that planning had become "perhaps the most widely urged activity for collegiate administrators to undertake."

Unfortunately, while many campuses across the country have devoted substantial time and money to planning, their attempts to use recommended formal planning methods frequently have been frustrating and disappointing. According to Delong and Shirley (1984), "to date, higher education planning is better known for its weaknesses and lack of impact than for its strengths and positive contributions." The literature suggests that the difficulties American higher education institutions have experienced with planning result from incongruities and inconsistencies between the assumptions underlying recommended planning approaches and the operational realities of academic institutions. Although there is considerable agreement that colleges and universities should use planning approaches that reflect their unique organizational characteristics (Peterson, 1980; Cope, 1981; Schmidtlein, 1983; Copa, 1983; Strohm, 1983; Haas, 1980), in actuality, many campuses have tried to use planning processes derived from corporate and government models with little consideration of conditions that may affect their applicability to academe.

In November, 1985, a three-year study of campus-wide planning was initiated by the National Center for Postsecondary Governance and Finance (a federally funded research consortium with headquarters at the University of Maryland, College Park). The purpose of the institutional planning project is to develop a coherent set of planning guidelines and recommendations based on information about actual conditions and constraints affecting the conduct of planning in U.S. higher education institutions. The project included three major research activities: a review of planning literature, a survey of administrators at 256 campuses, and site visits to 16 campuses for interviews with fifteen to twenty key leaders. This paper briefly summarizes U.S. higher education efforts over the past two decades. It then presents initial findings from the site visit phase of the institutional planning project, highlighting major factors and orientations that influence planning activities and behaviors across a broad range of different types of campuses in the United States. Finally, the paper discusses implications of these findings for administrators and scholars concerned with assessing and improving approaches to higher education planning.

U.S. Higher Education Planning Efforts

Until relatively recently, higher education professionals in the United States generally were somewhat skeptical about the use of formal planning and management approaches in academe. Many faculty and administrators believed such approaches were basically inconsistent with traditional academic values and behaviors (Eble, 1979; Allen and Chaffee, 1981). However, as the U.S. higher education community began in the late 1960s to recognize that changing demographic trends and emerging financial constraints might threaten the vitality of many campuses, it began to reconsider the merits of formal planning and management and to adopt the practices of government and industry as possible ways to minimize the impact of emerging conditions (Lahti, 1973; Klapstein, 1978).

During the late 1960s and 1970s, higher education developed and tried a number of different planning approaches (Baldridge and Okimini, 1982). Initially, these efforts focused on computer-assisted models emphasizing quantitative analyses, projections, and simulations. For example, with the support of the federal government, the National Center for Higher Education Management Systems (NCHEMS) developed tools and techniques to encourage and assist higher education institutions to implement more quantitatively based approaches to planning and management (Lawrence and Service, 1977). Major private U.S. foundations, including the Exxon Education Foundation (Resource Allocation Manage-

ment Program) and the Ford Foundation (Ford Foundation Program for Research in University Administration) also provided funding for large projects designed to facilitate more extensive use of management information systems and formal planning models (Poulton, 1980). Additionally, various highly structured planning and management processes were recommended (i.e., planning, programming, budgeting systems [PPBS], management by objectives [MBO], and zero-based budgeting [ZBB] in books, journals, and workshops oriented towards presidents and other senior campus administrators.

When they tried to apply the recommended planning models, many colleges and universities found they did not have sufficient time and resources (Wiseman, 1979; Tack and Resau, 1982) and/or encountered skepticism and resistance from various campus constituencies. For example, since many of the quantitatively based models were relatively complex, they could only be used on campuses with extensive computer resources and expertise. Furthermore, the degree of goal consensus and hierarchical authority needed to effectively use structured approaches such as management by objectives was lacking on many campuses. Frequently, even when planning documents were completed and apparently accepted by key campus constituencies, they became "shelf" documents that were used mainly for presentations to external agencies rather than as guides for campus decisions and actions (Ringle and Savickes, 1983).

The planning approaches that many institutions used in the late 1960s and 1970s were generally based on bureaucratic notions about organizational functioning, including the following assumptions: (1) organizational goals exist and can be specified; (2) alternative courses of action can be identified and evaluated with respect to their potential for furthering goal achievement; (3) decisions as to which courses of action to follow can be reached using logic and analytic procedures; and (4) implementation of decisions made through planning activities is feasible and likely to occur (Peterson, 1980; Hudson, 1983; Mahoney, 1983; Schmidtlein, 1983).

Now, however, organizational behavior within academic institutions is widely viewed as reflecting a varying mixture of political, structural, environmental, and psychological dynamics that is far more complex than the bureaucratic model implies (Cohen and March, 1974; Baldridge, et al., 1978). Contemporary higher education literature describes American colleges and universities as loosely coupled, open systems with multiple and poorly defined goals, unclear links between means and ends, political decision-making processes and relatively autonomous, professionally staffed subunits that often cannot or will not carry out activities suggested, or even mandated, by institutional-level administrators (Etzioni, 1964; Cohen and March, 1974; Weick, 1976; Baldridge, et al., 1978).

Possible alternatives to higher education planning based on bureaucratic, "rational" notions of organizational behavior include approaches that reflect political, incremental, and pluralistic conceptions of organizational functioning (Lindblom, 1959; Baldridge, 1971; Zemsky, Porter, and Odell, 1977). Planning approaches based on the political and incremental views of organizational behavior emphasize issues relevant to institutional interest groups, rely on bargaining and negotiation to reach decisions, and favor marginal adaptation rather than major change. Essentially, they reflect questions about the validity of the organizational goals concept (Georgiou, 1973) and about assumptions that systematic and technical analysis is, or should be, the primary basis for decision making. However, while these approaches appear to fit more closely current notions about the behavior of higher education institutions, it has been suggested that they may result in a lack of an overall "sense of direction and in inadequate attention to overall institutional health and vitality" (Peterson, 1980).

By the late 1970s, the problems with trying to use rational planning models in colleges and universities were becoming increasingly well recognized. A new approach, strategic planning, then became the most widely advocated planning approach for U.S. higher education institutions. According to Keller, strategic planning was a "third way" which blends quantitative information with the political realities of campuses (Keller, 1983).

Strategic planning's primary focus is on enhancing institutional adaptation to the external environment. This focus is considered critical to institutional survival and vitality in changing or difficult environmental conditions. Additionally, proponents of strategic planning assert that its emphasis on the integration of planning and operational decision making will help avoid the implementation problems so common with earlier higher education planning approaches. Basically, strategic planning involves (1) scanning the external environment for possible threats and opportunities, (2) assessing internal strengths and weaknesses, (3) analyzing the external and internal information, and (4) identifying major directions that will promote institutional health and viability. These directions are intended to serve as guidelines for key organizational actors and subunits to use in decision making and program development (Cope, 1981; Baldridge and Okimini, 1982; Keller, 1983).

Despite its popularity, potential difficulties in applying strategic planning in academic institutions have been identified by a number of higher education scholars and administrators. Horner (1979) contends that its emphasis on economic opportunities—critical in business-oriented strategic planning models—is not realistic in academic institutions and suggests that political considerations may be more crucial. Allen and Chaffee (1981) also suggest that strategic planning includes concepts that are not clearly related to the higher education setting and note that—like many planning models unsuccessfully tried in academe—it assumes that "unitary decisions can be made centrally" (p. 24). Furthermore, Kotler and Murphy (1981) have noted that often in higher education "growth opportunities are limited because of the need to satisfy internal constituents" (p. 486) and that the values of the "academic culture" generally are inconsistent with strategic planning's emphasis on "sensing, serving and satisfying markets" (p. 486–487). They suggest that faculty may resist presidential attempts to implement activities designed to improve organizational responsiveness to consumer needs and demands. Even Cope (1978), one of the major advocates of strategic planning, has noted the complexities and inexactness of environmental forecasting for higher education institutions, particularly in times of rapid change, and the "inevitable conflicts between institutional and departmental goals" (p. 14).

A 1984 study of strategic planning's effectiveness in the corporate world, where it was developed initially, raises some additional questions about its potential usefulness in higher education institutions (*Business Week*, 1984). This study examined thirty-three company strategies described in *Business Week* in 1979 and 1980 and found that only fourteen could be considered successful by fall, 1984. The study also suggests that, despite original intentions, in these companies, strategic planning often became a quantitative and rigid process which was resisted strongly by operating managers.

In sum, there is a considerable gap between higher education's current belief in the merits of formal institutional planning processes and the availability of planning approaches or guidelines that have demonstrated their usefulness. Much of what has been written is basically prescriptive advocacy for a particular approach based on little or no systematic analysis of actual campus-planning environments and experiences. To develop and implement more effective planning guidelines and recommendations, it is necessary to better understand planning-context purposes and constraints in diverse academic settings. The study to be described in the remaining sections of this paper sought to address this need by examining major factors and orientations that influence planning activities and behaviors at different types of campuses.

Project Methodology

The site visit phase of the institutional planning project sought to obtain indepth information on the planning perspectives of diverse campus constituencies and on the planning processes and structures at a broad range of higher education institutions across the United States. It was designed to extend information obtained from two other project research efforts (a literature review and a survey of the administrators' planning perspectives) by gathering a more complete understanding of actual campus-planning activities.

The survey of administrators' planning perspectives was sent to administrators in a stratified random sample of 256 campuses. Subsequently, 16 of these campuses were selected for site visits, including four research universities (two public and two private), four independent colleges (two religious and two

nonsectarian), four state colleges, and four public community colleges. Given limitations of time and resources, the site visit institutions were not intended to form a statistically representative sample of U.S. higher education institutions. However, a systematic effort was made to include a broad spectrum of campuses with respect to such basic characteristics as location, size, mission, and governance structure. Thus, within each major type of institution noted above, one campus was selected from each of four major geographic regions (Northeast, South, Midwest and West). The site visit sample was also designed to include two historically black institutions (one public state college and one private all-male liberal arts institution), four institutions with faculty unions, and six campuses that were part of multi-campus systems. Additionally, the institutions selected for a site visit enrolled from approximately 1,000 to over 30,000 students and were located in a diverse mix of inner-city, suburban, and rural settings. The character of the governance and planning processes at each campus was not known prior to its selection. Consequently, the extent to which the site visit institutions cover a full range of planning processes, from exemplary to ineffective, is unclear.

Permission to visit the campuses, collect relevant documents and conduct interviews with approximately fifteen to twenty campus staff members was obtained from each campus president. Campus staff exhibited a high degree of interest in the study. Thirteen of the sixteen campuses initially selected for a site visit agreed to participate, and the first three back-up campuses each agreed to cooperate.

Each site visit was conducted over a three-day period between December 1987 and early June 1988. Arrangements for conducting interviews were made in cooperation with a campus liaison identified by the president. Project staff provided each liaison with a standard list of the fifteen to twenty position titles and roles they hoped to interview. This list included the chief executive officer; senior academic, planning, business, development, and student services officers; institutional research directors; academic unit heads; faculty leaders; "typical" faculty members; and a trustee. The liaison was asked to identify appropriate individuals on his/her campus and then develop an interview schedule. In addition, campus liaisons were asked to provide relevant institutional documents, including campus planning materials, catalogues, accreditation self-studies, organization charts, and campus fact books.

A total of 255 individuals were identified for interviews at the sixteen site visit campuses. Of these, 248 (over 97 percent) were successfully completed, ranging from thirteen to nineteen persons per campus. Approximately sixty interviews were conducted at each major type of institution (research universities, sixty; state colleges, sixty-seven; liberal arts colleges, sixty; and community colleges, sixty-four). Table 1 summarizes the distribution of completed interviews by position type.

Interviews generally were conducted by two members of the project staff. A protocol, containing largely open-ended questions, was used to guide interview sessions to ensure that essential topics were covered as consistently as possible. However, the sessions were structured to provide sufficient opportunity for interviewees to express their own opinions, insights, and judgments. The interview guide included a series of questions related to each of the following major topics: (1) the interviewee's academic and professional background and current responsibilities; (2) general campus conditions and issues; (3) campus governance and decision-making structures and processes; (4) means employed to determine future campus directions; (5) characteristics of campus planning processes; and (6) perceived outcomes of planning activities. Additionally, interviewees were asked for their views on the reasons for any problems encountered in planning and for suggestions on how the campus could better determine its directions. All the in-

terviewees were extremely cooperative, responded to the questions thoughtfully and frankly, and provided many valuable and provocative insights and practical ideas about planning in the academic environment.

Campus Planning Activities

The site visits indicated that the current widespread advocacy of institutional planning in higher education has influenced a broad spectrum of colleges and universities. However, the findings also confirmed the doubts and concerns about higher education planning expressed both in the literature and in informal comments of many practicing administrators. While almost all site visit campuses had tried one or more formal campus-wide planning processes, none had been able to sustain a particular approach for more than two or three years. More significantly, few interviewees could enumerate specific outcomes or substantive benefits of the processes conducted at their campuses. In fact, they were far more articulate when discussing problems encountered in trying to plan and their frustrations with burdens imposed by externally mandated processes.

Interest in Planning

An intense interest in planning across a broad spectrum of campuses was suggested by several specific findings. During the past ten to fifteen years, fifteen of the sixteen site visit institutions had conducted or initiated at least one formal activity designed to clarify their mission and goals and/or to develop a clearer vision of their future. Furthermore, despite the limited

Table 1. Positions Held by Interviewees

Position	No.	Percent of Interviewees
Trustee	9	3.6
President/chancellor	16	6.5
Student services administrator	25	10.1
Academic administrator	66	26.6
Development officer	16	6.5
Institutional research/planning officer	13	5.2
Business/administrative affairs officer	20	8.0
Faculty member	70	28.2
Other	13	5.2
Totals	248	99.9

success with most of these efforts, currently all but three of the campuses were attempting some type of planning activity. Second, five of the campuses currently have an administrative position that includes "planning" in its title, and several additional campuses have designated planning as a specific responsibility of a particular administrative officer. Finally, the enthusiastic reaction to the study—as indicated by the willingness of campuses to participate, the unusually high percentage of successfully completed interviews, and the comments of interviewees—also appeared to demonstrate a high degree of concern about planning approaches and models. Many of the interviewees were seeking answers to dilemmas and problems they had encountered in trying to plan. They were hopeful that the project staff and the findings of the study would provide advice and guidance for their future planning efforts.

The Impetus to Plan

Since the late 1960s, planning generally has been advocated as essential for maintaining institutional health and vitality during times of changing demographic and fiscal conditions. However, the reasons many site visit campuses were concerned about and involved in planning appeared to be considerably more varied and complex. In fact, several of the campuses, which were seriously threatened by changing trends and conditions, had devoted only minimal attention to planning. On the other hand, two very different types of campuses, one a research university and one a community college, both of which appeared vital and well-positioned for the future, were trying to avoid, as one president stated, "complacency," and recently had instituted new planning efforts.

Frequently, the extent of campus planning activities mirrored the president's personal interest in formal planning. Current planning efforts at nine campuses could be traced specifically to presidential initiatives. In particular, new presidents tended to begin their tenure by devoting considerable attention to formal planning activities, and each of the four campuses with relatively new presidents were starting or revising their planning efforts. The presidents often were not very specific about their reasons for initiating or revising formal planning on

their campuses. For example, one new president, when asked why he had started a massive planning effort despite considerable faculty resistance, noted several reasons, but then frankly admitted that he had not consciously considered all of those reasons at the time—he just thought he should plan.

External agencies created other major impetuses for planning, including state or district mandates, requirements of Title III and other externally funded grant programs, and pressures from accrediting associations. The influence of state or district agencies may partially account for the slightly greater incidence of formal planning at the public two-year institutions and at the state colleges and universities. All eight of the site visit campuses in these two categories were presently involved in conducting or initiating formal planning activities, including at least five campuses which, at least in part, were responding specifically to state or district initiatives. In comparison, only three of the four private liberal arts colleges and two of the four research universities (one public and one private) were actively trying to implement formal planning at the time of the visits. Title III requirements were a past or present impetus for highly formalized planning on four campuses, and current accrediting association demands for planning, as well as specific assessment and outcomes measures, currently were impelling three campuses to focus more attention on planning.

Types of Planning Processes

The planning activities employed by site visit campuses were highly varied both in scope and process. They ranged from a presidential effort to develop a "strategic vision" for the year 2010, to comprehensive processes designed to produce detailed annual operational plans to guide budget allocations. The extent of constituency involvement also varied considerably. While some campuses had established broadly representative committees involving members recommended by campus constituencies, others relied heavily on the president's staff to coordinate planning efforts and to make major planning decisions using information forwarded through existing administrative structures. Additionally, particularly when planning appeared to be basically geared to meeting Title III or state agency demands, institutional research officers or other administrators independently developed planning documents that typically appeared to be largely ignored in decision making.

In general, interviewees judged planning approaches that were integrated with normal campus decision processes to be more satisfactory than those using broadly based committees and operating apart from traditional decision makers and governance bodies. Several campuses which had experimented with assigning primary responsibilities to a representative committee were now trying to integrate planning into normal campus structures and processes. For example, one campus, upon the advice of a consultant, had established a planning council whose members and chairperson were selected on the basis of constituency representation and "popularity." This committee worked for two years to produce a mission statement which was described by both faculty and administrators as "motherhood and apple pie," avoiding the major issues it was intended to address. The president, in view of this failure, dissolved the committee and now is trying to create a high-level policy board composed of senior faculty and administrators, which he will chair. On another campus, in an apparently more successful effort, the president hand picked a group of "bright and talented" individuals to help him develop his vision of the future and then presented and refined this vision at a retreat with the board and senior faculty and administrators. He is now planning to circulate this relatively brief document to campus constituencies to obtain further advice and insights.

Use of Data in Planning

Most recommended approaches to formal planning emphasize the importance of using good data on external trends and internal conditions. However, there was a serious lack of such data—and only minimal capability to develop it—at many site visit institutions. Only five of the sixteen campuses appeared to have good data on their external environment and internal operations. Each of these five campuses had reasonably well-established data collection and analysis units, including two particularly well-staffed and respected institutional research of-

fices (one at a community college and one at a research university) and one well-staffed office with a somewhat broader range of responsibilities. Among the eleven campuses which had less than adequate data for planning, six had, or were developing, at least some institutional research capabilities, including four campuses with new or minimally staffed institutional research offices and two which specifically assigned some data collection and analysis responsibilities to other administrators. The other five site visit institutions had minimal data that could be used to inform planning and no staff clearly assigned to the institutional research function. However, senior administrators at three campuses in this category indicated concern about the lack of data and reported that they were hoping to hire an institutional research officer in the near future.

In sum, despite the extensive efforts site visit campuses had devoted to various formal planning processes at various times during the past five to ten years, the majority of those interviewed in all types of positions were quite dissatisfied with their outcomes. Many campuses had tried various processes for one to three years, then dropped them because of perceptions that they were not worth their costs or revised them when a new president arrived. Process benefits of planning were mentioned far more frequently than substantive benefits. For example, many interviewees said that, for the first time, they learned what other areas on their campus were doing. Furthermore, in institutions initiating new processes at the time of the site visit, interviewees typically expressed considerable skepticism about the durability and outcomes of these processes. As one institutional research director suggested, campuses "periodically do formal planning under different guises." Nevertheless, the interviewees generally were not ready to abandon efforts to plan deliberately and were seeking solutions to the problems and dilemmas frustrating planning efforts. During the visits, there were many sincere requests for copies of the study's findings to help resolve frustrations encountered in determining future directions and guiding future campus planning efforts.

Planning Realities

During the preliminary review of information obtained during site visits, an initial list of important factors affecting campus planning practices was developed. While these factors, discussed in the following section, are still tentative and not complete, they illustrate some realities confronting campuses in their planning efforts.

Sources of Ideas for Contents of Plans

Earlier, organizations and persons instrumental in creating interest and pressure for campuses to undertake formal planning processes were described. Of equal interest was discovering where ideas for the contents of plans originated. The comments of those interviewed suggested that different types of ideas came from different levels within campuses.

The primary source of ideas in areas such as research and instruction came, as one might suspect, from faculty, who possess the primary expertise in their domains and typically are most aware of national developments within their fields. There are, however, potential new research and instructional initiatives that are not represented by current faculty expertise and that do not easily fit the mission or role of any one unit in a campus's organizational and programmatic structure. Often, these initiatives involve establishing a new program or department or cut across disciplines; therefore, they do not necessarily have constituencies and advocates among faculty in any one department. Consequently, such initiatives frequently are generated by deans, provosts, presidents, or other administrators whose purview encompasses clusters of units. These officials, of course, may utilize faculty committees to help identify and define such initiatives.

Other types of initiatives involve major decisions about consequences of external trends and pressures that affect the mission and structure of an entire campus as well as its individual programs. These decisions often are controversial, and frequently there is no clear consensus within the campus on desired directions. Furthermore, they typically affect important interests of existing departments, divisions, or colleges. Generally, efforts to deal with such issues appeared to originate with the

president, sometimes with support or encouragement from the governing board or other external agencies.

Recognition that different campus locations are involved in promoting different types of undertakings (depending upon the character of the effort, campus structure, and interests of campus constituencies) has implications for choices between "top down" or "bottom up" approaches to planning. A blend of both approaches appears necessary, the mix depending on the kinds of initiatives under consideration. A related question, how a particular initiative comes to be identified for consideration, is an interesting one that was not addressed in this study. Cohen and March (1974) suggest this process is a rather random one.

Achieving Legitimacy and Trust Among Participants

An issue faced by all campuses was maintaining the legitimacy of the planning process and the credibility of its leadership with various constituencies. Faculty frequently voiced concerns about their lack of effective involvement in planning and sometimes complained that even when they devoted substantial time to planning efforts, their recommendations went unheeded. However, senior campus administrators expressed concern about the faculty's inability to come to grips with sensitive problems involving program and staff reductions or with competing interests of various campus constituencies; they often commented that faculty typically focused on protecting their own "turfs" rather than on campus-wide perspectives.

Presidents wrestled with the fear of losing control of planning processes. Nevertheless, they often preferred to let others lead campus planning efforts so they could maintain a more neutral role in resolving disputes. Thus, they could avoid becoming so identified with a position that their room for maneuver and compromise was limited.

The degree to which faculty, administrators, trustees, and external agencies had trust and confidence in one another varied considerably among the sixteen campuses. However, there was a considerable degree of distrust between administrators and faculty at all campuses. Improper motives frequently were ascribed to both administrative and faculty initiatives, and rumors about these motives flourished. Establishing trust and confidence appeared to be a slow process, and sometimes they could be destroyed rapidly by a single negative incident. Frequently, communication to faculty about circumstances confronting the campus, as well as communication among faculty, was weak, contributing to low levels of trust, which, in turn, negatively affected campus planning efforts. One interviewee commented that "if it weren't for lack of faith in people, strategic planning would work." Suspicion appeared to generate problems in reaching consensus, restricted the ability of campus leaders to act on various issues, and caused excessive paperwork as attempts were made to justify actions and create records for defensive purposes.

System and state-level planning requirements placed on campuses frequently appeared to stem from distrust of campus motives and actions. Such requirements sometimes might have been intended to encourage campuses to examine their policies and directions and then reveal them to central policy makers. However, the requirements seemed to be largely "make work" efforts from the campus perspective and generally had little effect on campus actions and decisions; their primary usefulness seemed to be in assuring the external agency that the campus knew what it was doing and was well managed, i.e., it had plans. The costs to campuses of such a lack of trust and confidence among the parties involved, including system-level and state-level officials, appear very high and a topic warranting further investigation.

The Political Character of Planning

Some of those interviewed regarded planning as a "rational" means to eliminate or lessen "political" influences on campus decisions. Planning was seen as a way to overcome the effects of individuals and units pursuing their narrow self-interests and excessively protecting their own "turfs." Decisions presumably were made on the basis of objective data and the "merits" of issues, with decision making occurring primarily through traditional hierarchical structures.

These views seem to ignore the realities of campus governance. Decision power on a cam-

pus is quite dispersed. Faculty have the major role in decisions on academic matters. The primary source of power for administrators is their control over budget allocations. Various units on campuses have considerable autonomy, based on norms for organizations composed of professionals. Consequently, decisions typically involve reconciling many values and interests in a democratic fashion. This diffusion of power on a campus does not lend itself to the imposition, without compromise and accommodation, of the views of any one party. Planning is one of the ingredients in this political process, not a means to eliminate or lessen significantly its effects. One interviewee noted, "Issue avoidance and lack of follow-up cannot be fixed by planning."

Virtually all faculty and department chairs viewed planning as a means to obtain more resources for their units. They related the success or failure of planning efforts to increases in the resources received. Since most unit budgets at the site visit campuses generally increased only incrementally each year, often to compensate for inflation, department members generally believed formal campus-wide planning—as they had experienced it—was largely ineffective and costly. They rarely got additional funds to support their plans and commonly never learned why their requests were not funded. In their calculus, the considerable resources expended in meetings and in preparing planning documents were not equal to the marginal benefits they received from thinking through their priorities and learning about plans and priorities of others on their campus. In contrast, many departmental and college faculty believed their own internal planning efforts performed well.

Administrators, on the other hand, were upset with unit plans that were "wish lists," requests not constrained by realistic expectations of available resources. Administrators at several campuses were wrestling with how to encourage unit creativity without creating unrealistic expectations that could result in disillusionment with the planning process.

The Character of Planning Documents

Campus mission and role statements were essentially political documents that primarily sought to avoid restricting potential roles and interests of campuses; they were not attempts to narrowly define the character of campuses and their programs in order to provide clear guidance for operational decisions. Comprehensive campus planning documents most commonly were said to have ended up "on the shelf." Such documents possibly provided some general context within which campus decisions were made, but appeared to provide limited operational guidance. On the other hand, some documents were relatively short range and operational, tied closely to near-term budget decisions and, typically, not dealing with major strategic choices.

The comment of Dean Rusk (*Washington Post*, 1988) regarding the role of party platforms in guiding foreign policy is equally applicable to campus planning documents:

> "I've attended hundreds of meetings at which decisions had to be made, . . . and I have never, never heard anyone ask: 'Well, gee, let's get out the party platform and look at what it has to say.' Not once." (p. C2)

Planning documents developed for external agencies (i.e., grantees, accrediting agencies, or system or state higher education boards) were even more widely ignored than other types of plans. Such externally oriented documents frequently did not go through the same extensive, participatory formulation process as did internally initiated plans. Further, they frequently addressed issues of interest to the external agency rather than concerns of campus staff.

The Uncertainty of Future Events

When first queried, those interviewed expressed considerable support for formal planning efforts; however, as they reflected further they began to note the great difficulties involved in predicting future conditions affecting the campus. The uncertainties confronting campuses, they suggested, made planning difficult. Typical comments were these:

> "What comes up is as important as what is planned. That's life."

> "We react to future developments; that is the norm."

> "We engage in crisis management."

> "The provost is a problem solver, not a planner."

Given these interpretations of their circumstances, interviewees placed considerable importance on reacting promptly to emerging conditions. They wanted to maintain the ability to implement new ideas without lengthy delays for amendments to plans or for justifying departures from earlier directions. Generally, the interviewees seemed to be seeking a balance between formally examining future directions and maintaining the flexibility to react quickly to new opportunities or problems. Plans were sometimes seen as an impediment to the opportunism needed for effective entrepreneurship. Interviewees reflected sentiments of the Bahwagon Shri Rasneesh, who, upon being asked for his plans after leaving the United States, responded, "Planning is bondage."

Stability of Planning Processes

As noted earlier, at most site visit campuses, planning processes survived for only one to three cycles before being abandoned or largely revamped. Since comprehensive campus planning efforts were so costly in time, effort, and political capital, many interviewees suggested that they should take place no more frequently than every three or more years. Most of those who had recently been through a major planning cycle did not expect to repeat it in the near future. Frequently, those most enthusiastic about planning were persons who had not been through a process or were new to the campus. Persons who had experienced two or more planning cycles tended to be cynical about the results. One president spoke at some length about the considerable benefits of a major planning effort the campus recently completed. However, when asked if he were planning to repeat the exercise, he responded, "never during the remainder of my tenure as president!"

Implications of Preliminary Findings for Practitioners

The organizational, operational, political, and psychological realities affecting campus planning efforts that have been described have important implications for administrators and faculty seeking to clarify future campus directions. Some of these implications are summarized as follows.

Identifying the Focus of Planning Efforts

Central leadership is needed to identify and address changing external trends, opportunities, and campus-wide problems and issues. Departments and faculty often are not well positioned to understand the campus-wide implications of changing external conditions; even if they are aware of the circumstances, they are not likely to ignore their own self-interests in developing and implementing responses. Similarly, central leadership is required to initiate changes that cut across campus units, such as interdisciplinary programs or programs in new areas that are not within the mission of an existing unit. Additionally, decisions to reduce or eliminate the scope and size of current programs require central initiation. Operational units and faculty bodies generally will not volunteer to reduce the scope of their own activities and are reluctant to recommend reductions in the operations of their colleagues' departments.

In contrast, innovations in program areas typically depend on faculty initiative since faculty are most knowledgeable about developments in their own fields. However, central leadership can be important in encouraging faculty innovation. Innovation seemed to flourish more at campuses where administrators were perceived to be supportive of new ideas, unlikely to penalize failures, and helpful in finding ways to get good ideas implemented. Bureaucratic impediments to implementing new ideas—including paperwork and long timelines associated with presenting ideas through traditional planning processes—hampered innovation. Additionally, funds specifically designated for supporting faculty initiatives promoted faculty innovation as well as generated more positive overall faculty attitudes.

Achieving Legitimacy, Trust, and Confidence Among Participants

A reasonable level of trust and confidence among the parties involved was an important factor in the success of efforts to determine campus directions and programs. The practice of placing faculty periodically in positions where they had to deal with campus-wide issues seemed to contribute to a higher level of trust. One campus had a policy of generally selecting its high-level administrators from among its faculty. Additionally, frequent communications about a small number of issues and informal discussions among key campus leaders may be far more useful than formal planning meetings and documents.

Dealing with the Politics of Planning

Campus leaders who dislike dealing with conflicting campus self-interests will not find relief through rational planning. Clearly, planning is not a means to overcome the political character of campus decision making. One person's rational decision is quite irrational to another. Such conflicts are a part of planning, not something that planning can overcome. Plans are the outcomes of a political process on a campus rather than schemes that are mandated by central policy makers based on "objective" facts and analysis. Sophisticated analysis improves the quality of planning but does so as an ingredient in the politics of choice, not as an unambiguous blueprint for rational action. Thus, to avoid frustration and disappointment in planning efforts, campus leaders should remember what planning can and cannot accomplish. Campus leaders must use planning processes based on an understanding of the political realities of their institution and the complexities of resolving competing interests.

The Use of Planning Documents

Producing lengthy planning documents often may not be useful or appropriate. The preparation of planning documents takes a great deal of time and resources; yet these documents appear to have a rather short "shelf life." Many persons involved in planning observed that its main value resulted from the insights participants gained during the process, not from the documents produced. A careful weighing is needed of the benefits of documentation against its costs.

Planning documents must address the needs of their intended audiences. Plans that focus on overall mission and broad campus direction and those that deal with short-term operational choices have some utility. However, devoting a great deal of attention to detailed operational plans much in advance of budget formulation processes does not appear to be particularly useful. The politics of the budgetary process, so ably described by Wildavsky (1964), preclude following a clearly defined recipe worked out in advance. New circumstances emerge continuously, and important considerations often reveal themselves only in the course of reacting to particular recommendations for resource allocations. Considerable flexibility is needed to adjust budgets to unforeseen circumstances.

The Frequency of Planning Exercises

Major campus planning exercises that examine the fundamental character and directions of a campus are time consuming and costly, both financially and politically. The study findings suggest that major planning processes should not be undertaken annually. Some interviewees recommended that they take place no more often than every five years. In contrast, a process for setting budget priorities appears to be needed each year, prior to actual budget formulation. The objective of such a process should be to define campus-wide assumptions, to identify possible new initiatives for all constituencies, and to set budget parameters. This could promote coordination between units, help avoid wish lists, and permit fuller consideration of issues before final budget decisions must be made. Lengthy, formal documentation does not appear to be essential to link plans and budgets. Shared understandings and common expectations among the participants are the important consideration.

Conclusions

The preliminary observations in this paper will be tested as further analysis of findings takes place. However, as previously noted, these preliminary insights suggest that many prescriptions in current planning literature are not consistent with the realities of campus decision processes. The costs of planning need to be carefully weighed against its presumed benefits. Although the desirability of reducing uncertainty through formal planning appears compelling, future events are highly unpredictable, and plans must therefore be constantly altered to fit new circumstances. Plans are only as accurate a predictor of what is de-

sirable as the foresight of the human prophets who construct them. Rigid adherence to outdated prophecies can be dangerous. While planning can help to inform and expand one's understanding of possible futures, it cannot provide a detailed blueprint for future actions, nor can it avoid the need for skillful improvisation and careful judgment.

Frank A. Schmidtlein is *associate director of research and director of the institutional planning project;* Toby H. Milton is *associate director of the institutional planning project at the National Center for Postsecondary Governance and Finance, University of Maryland, College Park, Maryland.*

References

Allen, Richard and Chaffee, Ellen. "Management Fads in Higher Education." Mimeographed paper, NCHEMS, 1981.

Baldridge, J. Victor. *Models of University Governance: Bureaucratic, Collegial and Political.* Stanford, California: Stanford Center for Research and Development in Teaching, September, 1971.

Baldridge, J. Victor and Okimini, Patricia H., "Strategic Planning in Higher Education: New Tool— Or New Gimmick?" *AAHE Bulletin*, Vol. 35, No. 2, 1982, 6, 15–18.

Baldridge, J. Victor; Curtis, David V.; Ecker, George; and Riley, Gary L. *Policy Making and Effective Leadership.* San Francisco: Jossey-Bass, 1978.

Business Week Cover Story, "The New Breed of Strategic Planner." *Business Week*, September, 1984, 62–68.

Cohen, Michael D. and March, James G. *Leadership and Ambiguity: The American College President,* New York: McGraw-Hill Book Company, 1974.

Copa, George H. "Introduction," *Planning and Vocational Education.* Edited by George H. Copa and Jerome Moss, Jr. New York: Gregg Division, McGraw-Hill Book Company, 1983, 2–6.

Cope, Robert G. *Strategic Policy Planning: A Guide for College and University Administrators.* Littleton, Colorado: The Ireland Book Corporation, 1978.

_____, "Strategic Planning, Management, and Decision-Making." *ASHE-ERIC Higher Education Research Report No. 9.* Washington, D.C.: AAHE, 1981.

Eble, Kenneth E. *The Art of Administration.* San Francisco: Jossey-Bass, 1979.

Etzioni, Amitai. *Modern Organizations.* Englewood Cliffs, New Jersey: Prentice-Hall, Inc., 1964.

Georgiou, Petro. "The Goal Paradigm and Notes Towards a Counter Paradigm." *Administrative Science Quarterly*, Vol. 13, No. 3, 1973, 291–310.

Haas, Raymond M. "Winning Acceptance for Institutional Research and Planning." In Paul Jedamus, Marvin W. Peterson and Associates, *Improving Academic Management*. San Francisco: Jossey-Bass, 1980, 539–554.

Horner, David G. "Strategic Planning for Higher Education." *Management Focus*. San Francisco: Peat, Marwick, Mitchell & Co., 1979.

Hudson, Barclay, M. "Planning: Typologies, Applications, Issues and Contexts." *Planning and Vocational Education*. Edited by George H. Copa and Jerome Moss, Jr. New York: Gregg Division, McGraw-Hill Book Company, 1983, 18–46.

Keller, George. *Academic Strategy: The Management Revolution in American Higher Education*. Baltimore: The Johns Hopkins University Press, 1983.

Klapstein, Earl L. "New Management Thrust at Los Rios." *Community and Junior College Journal*, Vol. 50, No. 8, 1978.

Kotler, Philip and Murphy, Patrick E. "Strategic Planning for Higher Education." *Journal of Higher Education*, Vol. 52, No. 5, 1981, 470–489.

Lahti, Robert. *Innovative College Management*. San Francisco: Jossey-Bass, 1973.

Lawrence, G. Ben and Service, Allan L., eds. "Quantitative Approaches to Higher Education Management: Potential, Limits, and Challenge." *ERIC/Higher Education Research Report No. 4*, Washington, D.C.: AAHE, 1977.

Lelong, Donald and Shirley, Robert. "Planning: Identifying the Focal Points for Action." *Planning for Higher Education*, Vol. 12, No. 4, 1984, 1–7.

Lindblom, Charles. "The Science of Muddling Through." *Public Administration Review*, Vol. 19, No. 21, 1959, 79–88.

Mayhew, Lewis B. *Surviving the Eighties*. San Francisco: Jossey-Bass, 1980.

Mahoney, Thomas A. "Perspectives on Organizational Structures for Planning." *Planning and Vocational Education*. Edited by George H. Copa and Jerome Moss, Jr. New York: Gregg Division, McGraw-Hill Book Company, 1983, 81–101.

Mortimer, Kenneth P. and Tierney, Michael L. "The Three R's of the Eighties: Reduction, Reallocation and Retrenchment." *AAHE-ERIC Research Report No. 4*. Washington, D.C.: AAHE, 1979.

Peterson, Marvin W. "Alternative Approaches to Planning." In Paul Jedamus, Marvin W. Peterson and Associates, *Improving Academic Management*. San Francisco: Jossey-Bass, 1980, 113–163.

Poulton, Nick L. "Strategies of Large Universities." In Paul Jedamus, Marvin W. Peterson and Associates, *Improving Academic Management*. San Francisco: Jossey-Bass, 1980, 626–651.

Ringle, Philip M. and Savickes, Mark L. "Administrative Leadership: Planning and Time Perspective." *Journal of Higher Education*, Vol. 54, No. 6, 1983, 649–661.

Schmidtlein, Frank A. "Comprehensive and Incremental Decision Paradigms and Implications for Educational Planning." *Planning and Vocational Education*. Edited by George H. Copa and Jerome Moss, Jr. New York: Gregg Division, McGraw-Hill Book Company, 1983, 48–80.

Schuck, Emerson. "The New Planning and An Old Pragmatism." *Journal of Higher Education*, Vol. 46, No. 5, 1977, 594–601.

Strohm, Paul. "Faculty Roles Today and Tomorrow." *Academe*, January–February, 1983, 10–16.

Tack, Martha W. and Resau, Bruce A. "Linking Academic and Financial Planning at the College Level." *Planning for Higher Education*, Vol. 11, No. 1, 1982, 1–4.

Weick, Earl E. "Education Organizations as Loosely Coupled Systems." *Administrative Science Quarterly*, Vol. 21, No. 1, 1976, 1–19.

Wildavsky, Aaron. *The Politics of the Budgetary Process*. Boston: Little, Brown 1964.

Wiseman, Charles. "New Foundations for Planning Models." *Journal of Higher Education*, Vol. 50, No. 6, 1979, 726–744.

Zemsky, Robert; Porter, Randall; and Odell, Laura P. "Decentralized Planning: To Share Responsibility." *Educational Record*, Vol. 59, No. 3, 1977.

A Typology of Planning Problems

John P. Bean and George D. Kuh

Colleges and universities are profoundly affected by the vicissitudes of the external environment, including rapidly shifting levels of public support, enrollment fluctuations, quixotic revisions in federal regulations, and precipitous changes in sponsored research priorities. Inside institutions of higher education, decision-making processes have been described as "organized anarchy" [8] and have been characterized by ill-defined goals and preferences, floating coalitions taking unpredictable collective action, and a poorly understood technology that cannot reliably achieve desired ends. The number of problems facing those responsible for institutional redesign is staggering.

In this article, we develop a descriptive typology of the problems that may be encountered during planning. The typology identifies areas of potential difficulty that face both procedural planners, concerned with the processes through which problem solving will be addressed, and substantive planners, whose plans result in a new performance program [36]. The typology takes the form of a matrix in which four planning phases are represented as columns and five institutional constructs appear as rows. The matrix cells represent categories of activity that require choices by planners, choices that, if inappropriate, will likely result in problems [13].

This typology should be useful for several reasons. First, the typology helps to reduce many seemingly disparate issues and concerns into a relatively small number of categories. Second, a typology encourages richer descriptions and more exact distinctions between the different types of problems encountered in planning. Third, general categories of problems can be used across institutional settings, thereby reducing the amount of time individual planners must devote to identifying issues likely to disrupt their own planning process.

Three assumptions guided the development of the typology. First, reference to "the plan" is a matter of convenience. We subscribe to the fundamental premise of adaptive planning [1], that is, the process of planning is probably more important than any document or plan produced. Therefore, "the plan" refers not only to a document developed to guide the institution into the future (the substantive plan) but also to activities that enable members of the institution to create a "picture" of an organization's future and to develop an organizational design more useful in creating this future [32, 44). The *ideas* generated in a planning process may be more directly linked to the future of the organization than changes in the structure or personnel roles in the organization [56]. Ideas seem to have a direct bearing on organizational activities whereas structure is often only indirectly related, especially in a college or university setting.

Second, "naturalistic planning" occurs on a continuing basis regardless of formal planning exercises. Faculty, administrators, and staff are constantly involved in making decisions, anticipating problems, and acting in ways that shape the future of the organization [6, 27]. In contrast, the typology described here relates to problems in formal, conscious planning processes, initiated as a managerial function [23,

"A Typology of Planning Problems," by John P. Bean and George D. Kuh, reprinted from *The Journal of Higher Education*, Vol. 55, No. 1, 1984. Ohio State University Press.

52], and requiring a major commitment of resources by the institution [28].

Third, successful planning requires cognizance of the limits of rationality. Planning has traditionally been viewed as the intervention of reason [19] or logical analysis [30] to bring about a desired end state that would not otherwise occur. The limits of rationality in planning have been identified by numerous observers [1, 5, 50, 69, 60]. For example, no one person can know all the information about an organization [49]. What information a person does have may not be recalled or interpreted properly. Such limitations coupled with an unstable external environment result in a quasi rationality circumscribed by an inability to anticipate all the consequences of actions taken [41, 49]. Perrow [43] advocated intendedly rational behavior (i.e., logical consistency in terms of what is actually known about an issue) but cautioned against constructing planning systems that exceed human limits.

Elements of the Typology

The first phase in the planning cycle depicted in Table 1 is an assessment of the static condition of the institution's fiscal, staffing, and intellectual resources available for planning—that is, the capacity to plan. Like the front-end analysis of organizations whose members are interested in planned change activities, determining an institution's capacity to plan requires valid information concerning what work will be required, from whom, for how long, at what cost, to attain what result [12, 32, 33].

The planning process itself is comprised of three phases. The first phase is "initiation" which involves identifying the general parameters of the planning process and organizational problems to be addressed and organizing personnel and resources for planning once the decision to plan has been made ("planning to plan" [32, 49, 54]). The second phase is "development" which involves identifying the procedures and activities required to develop the plan and design implementation strategies [55]. The final phase is "implementation"—those processes and activities required to institutionalize the plan; that is, using the plan to guide the institution into the future. Although described as conceptually distinct processes, the transition from one phase to another is gradual.

The same members of the decision-making elite may be involved throughout the planning cycle, and parts of a later stage may be initiated before completion of an earlier stage [56].

Each of the five rows in the typology represents an organizational construct that has been repeatedly associated with planning problems in the planning literature and in discussions with planners. These constructs are "goals," "participation," "information and communication," "interdependence," and "resources."

"Goals" represent desired end states [16]. Goals include both the goals of the planning process as well as the institutional goals that emerge during the development and implementation of the plan.

"Participation" refers to the extent of participation in decision making and is inversely related to centralization, the degree to which power is concentrated in the organization [47]. Therefore, participation includes the degree and kind of involvement that organizational members have for initiating, developing, and implementing the plan [3].

"Information and communication" are distinct but related constructs and are combined in the typology to avoid redundancy. "Information" represents (1) knowledge about the institution and the environment useful to planners and (2) expertise in planning. "Communication" is the degree to which information is transmitted among the members of a social system [51]. Of primary interest is the manner in which information about planning, and subsequently the plan itself, is shared with members of the institution and others with a stake in the institution's prosperity.

Similar to the notion of "coupling" [22], "interdependence" is the extent to which the success of one unit of an institution is dependent on another unit of the institution or the extent to which the institution is dependent on some part of the external environment [59]. Consequently, interdependence may refer to either internal or external linkages [52]. Internal interdependence represents the degree of coupling (loose or tight) in linkages between various levels and subunits of the institution (e.g., colleges, departments, and programs). External interdependence represents the degree to which the institution is independent of the external environment (cf. "autonomy" [46]). For example, most institutions have a highly inter-

Table 1 A Typology of the Sources of Potential Problems Encountered in Planning

Organizational Constructs	Assessment of the Capacity to Plan	Initiation of Planning Activities	Development of the Plan	Implementation of the Plan
Goals	Level of institutional consensus	Purposes of planning are unclear; Goals may change during the process; Goals differ at different organizational levels; Hidden agendas	Unclear expectations for planner behavior; Conflicts with vested interests	Goal displacement; Limitations of rational processes; "Rational means to irrational ends"; Adaptability
Participation	Psychological preparedness of participants	Too many or too few people; Representative levels; Experts; Use of new or existing structures	Inadequate representation; Anarchistic behavior; Technical staff/faculty relationships; Authority not commensurate with responsibility for planning	Rewarding participation; Understanding change; Expecting conflict; Incremental adaptation
Information and communication	Access, types available; Current patterns of communication	Technical aspects of planning; Accuracy and relevance of information; Limitations of planning	Clear understanding of planning process; Periodic status reports; Balanced treatment of unit data	Communicating the plan; Appropriate level of specificity; Feedback, evaluation, and revision; Degree of flexibility of the plan
Interdependence (internal, external)	Relationships between units	Appropriate scope of planning; Degree of coupling among subunits; Timing relative to external requirements; Length of planning cycle	Involvement of units that must carry out plans; Relationship to line administrators and faculty	Environmental changes; Plan designed for external and not internal audiences
Resources	Time (staff); Expertise; Organizational slack	Adequacy for planning process	Commensurate with unit needs; Adequacy for implementation	Realistic process expectations; Conflict and turf protection; Continuation costs

dependent relationship with the external environment, relying upon state, federal, and private revenues for operational support and providing human capital resources for society [16].

"Resources" refers to fiscal, technical, and human resources, including social assets such as status and authority, available to the institution for planning [49]. The adequacy of the resources to support the planning process and the resources required to implement the plan are of particular importance.

A Typology of Planning Problems

Discussing planning problems in temporal sequence as suggested in the typology (Table 1) has intuitive appeal. Less redundancy occurs when discussing the potential problems associated with each organizational construct throughout the planning process, and therefore the discussion is organized around these constructs. The propositions implicit in the discussion of these problems are normative in character, based primarily on an extensive review of the literature but also on the writers' planning experience and common sense. That is, once a problem has been identified, its solution may be obvious.

Goals

The extent to which a consensus among goals [46] characterizes the institution should be estimated during the evaluation of the organization's capacity to plan. If a high level of consensus exists about the institution's purposes and how to achieve them, the planning process can be "closed"—that is, a logical progression of interventions can be designed to move from where the organization is at present toward these goals [32]. If consensus does not exist, developing a plan to guide the institution will have little value. A lack of consensus, or goal incongruence, is not unusual in many complex organizations, especially educational institutions [8, 20, 39, 59]. The lack of shared objectives across departments and colleges in the institution does not necessarily pose insoluble problems for planners but nevertheless must be considered as a potential saboteur throughout the planning process [48]. Therefore, some

level of agreement about institutional purposes must be developed before proceeding with other planning activities.

After the decision to plan has been made, perhaps the most serious problem planners face during the initiation phase is the inability of the members of a complex institution to identify clearly the *purposes* of planning. The original reasons for deciding to plan may be obvious to those involved in the initiation phase. For example, planning may be mandated by external agencies such as a board of trustees or an accrediting agency. Planning may also be motivated by an authentic desire to improve the quality of the institution or by the necessity to change institutional practices brought about by a decline in resources [40]. Impetus for planning, however, does not necessarily clarify the purposes of planning. If an institution begins to plan to "improve institutional quality," a great deal of confusion may result among the participants because the purpose is vague. One dean may interpret the goal to be dismissal of "low quality" faculty members, but another dean may see it as an opportunity to hire "high quality" faculty members. Ambiguous goals for planning are usually counterproductive and waste, rather than conserve, resources.

Another way of conceptualizing this step in the planning process is the conscious avoidance of what Kilmann refers to as a "Type III" error [32]. Efforts must be made to determine whether the planning process is actually addressing issues and constraints critical to the vitality of the institution as opposed to the myriad of problems that institutions face on a daily basis. As decision makers, planners in institutions of higher education can use "garbage can" decision rules [9] that increase the possibility that errors will be made in differentiating between superfluous and critical organizational problems. Therefore, a potential pitfall is related to the selection of appropriate planning goals to address the "right" problems [49].

Regardless of what the initiators perceived to be the original purposes for planning, these purposes may change over time. New members of the planning team and new opportunities or constraints presented by the institution's environment almost guarantee some shift away from the original purposes of planning [17, 26, 32, 45] and may accelerate, decelerate, or stabilize the momentum to change the organization [41]. Those who remain steadfastly attached to the original purposes fail to learn from experience and are certain to be in conflict with those whose vision of the planning process changes over time [49].

A lack of clarity about what planning is intended to accomplish and what the planning process entails also may vary by administrative level [1, 11, 44, 53]. To further complicate matters, the stated goals for planning may not be the real goals of organizational members [16]. The terms "planning goals" and "organizational goals" are often used in cavalier fashion; an organization does not have goals, only the organization's members have goals [10]. Referring to an "institution's goals" obscures the fact that an organization is comprised of its members' idiographic goals, including hidden agendas and personal, in conflict with stated, goals. For example, the reason a president endorses planning may have little to do with "improving institutional quality" or some other stated goal but may have a lot to do with appeasing the trustees. A vice–president for academic affairs may use the planning process as an opportunity to reallocate money from one college to another; a dean, to "trim the dead wood from department X"; a department chair, to revise the curriculum; and the institutional planning office, to "look good in the president's eyes and increase the number of professional staff in the office." Hidden agendas and suspicion about the planning process increase in direct proportion to the extent that the real purposes of planning remain ambiguous and the multiple goals for the process go unexamined [14, 32, 57].

In the plan development stage, a major problem related to goals concerns the degree to which behavior is congruent with the goals of the planning process. For example, if the provost appoints the members of the planning team and states the goals of the process but asserts that the process is to be open and flexible, a means/ends disjunction results. Kilmann [32] described this as a conflict between the terminal values of the organization (i.e., desirable end states of the institution) and the instrumental value of participants in the planning process (i.e., desirable modes of behavior presumably directed toward attainment of institutional end states).

Related problems stem from a vague role definition of what planners are to do. Just as the goals for the planning process are often unclear or inappropriate, role definitions for planners may vary, At one extreme, planners may consider their role to be participatory and developmental; and at the other extreme, they may see their function as being highly deterministic—"we will tell you what to do next." Administrators may view planners as a means of improving the institution, and faculty may view them as "axmen" for the administration. Unless the roles of planners can be clarified both for planners and for other members of the institution, conflict over the appropriate role for planners can undermine the planning process [55]. This problem is exacerbated when planning efforts require that staff and faculty engage in unfamiliar activities for which information and support are inadequate [52].

Another major problem occurs during the development of the plan when planning staff, administrators, and faculty begin to increase the level of specificity concerning planning goals [55]. The amount of time devoted to protecting vested interests increases as the number of participants involved in identifying and specifying the goals increases. Planning in the abstract is often casually endorsed. However, when more specific goals are endorsed, potentially negative consequences for an administrator's unit may be perceived, and the administrator is likely to attempt to block acceptance of those goals. As more people become involved, more specific objectives are blocked, thereby reducing the specificity of those goal statements considered acceptable [55].

Goal displacement [16] may occur when a planning office substitutes the means (planning or following a plan) for the ends (institutional improvement). Goal displacement is most likely to become obvious during the implementation period when planners begin to believe that carrying out the plan as described in a document is more important than improving organizational effectiveness. It is also during this phase that the limitations of intendedly rational processes become apparent [43].

During the implementation of the plan, people are likely to reinterpret the goals of the planning process to make these more congruent with their own needs and interests [59]. A planning process that mandates strict adherence to the formal, written goals from last year's version of the plan will be difficult to implement. Either managers will ignore the plan or adhering to certain elements in the plan may result in the institution losing a position of competitive advantage relative to the organizational environment [2, 20, 42]. For example, a community college might plan to phase out a business writing course only to find out six months later that a large business firm has begun to require its employees to take such a course. If the institution failed to modify the planned reduction in business writing staff, it would lose the resources it would otherwise gain to another educational institution or program. Planners must remain adaptable (Ackoff's "adaptivizing" [1]) and recognize that the dynamic nature of organizational interactions with an external environment that cannot be influenced by the institution requires the modification of past goals [49, 55].

Participation

Implicit in capacity estimation is sensing the psychological commitment of organizational members to the planning activity. Nystrom, Hedberg, and Starbuck found that most organizations go through three stages before personnel can design responses to cope with the constraints of the external environment [41]. Institutions first endure a "stagnation" period during which organizational problems are ignored or denied. Then faculty and staff experience a period of low morale during which old behavior patterns are recognized as dysfunctional or inappropriate and must be "unlearned." Finally, key staff psychologically prepare themselves to engage in redesigning aspects of the organization (planning) to respond to the environmental challenges. If this elite is not ready for planning, then formal planning activities should be delayed [56].

Active involvement by a representative group of persons likely to be affected by the plan is not usually troublesome in the capacity estimation phase of planning unless those with expertise are, for whatever reasons, unwilling to participate later. The success of a planning process, however, rests to a significant extent on who becomes involved in the initial discussions about the planning process [11, 27, 35, 57]. Involving too many people initially may

slow the process as each person defends his or her "turf" against real or imagined threats, and "too much participation during problem exploration can lead to complex and unmanageable planning" [55, p. 729]. Including too few may result in subsequent resistance to later participation or a general distrust of the planning process and of those involved. It is essential to involve representatives from the major constituencies with a legitimate stake in the process [23, 55]. Someone with planning expertise and experience, either from inside or outside of the institution, may be required to provide information about what has been learned about effective planning, to respond quickly to technical questions about timing, costs, and information needs, to estimate trade-offs concerning different procedures, and to avoid reinventing the "planning wheel" [14, 57].

With a clear purpose for planning, the structure for participation of representatives begins to emerge [27, 32]. For a planning intervention "to be successful, the participants must enjoy 'free choice' of various alternatives" [32, p. 67]. "Free choice" implies that the members are able to explore as many alternatives as they consider significant and select those that are central to their needs [3]. Equally important, members of the organization must have a sense of "ownership and a feeling of responsibility about their decisions and the consequences of those decisions. . . . Members equipped with valid information and exercising free choice can maintain their commitment over longer periods of time and can be open to change" ([32, p. 68]; see also [3]). Options for structuring participation include creation of an ad hoc administrative committee for planning, an ad hoc committee composed of both faculty and administrators, an existing faculty committee for planning, a consultant, a planning office or officer, or some combination of the above. The resource capacity of the system will likely dictate the most realistic option.

Openness and trust in the interaction among planning team members is essential for an effective planning process [3, 38]. Plans may be suspect if various constituent groups and units feel they have not been adequately represented either on the planning team or through the provision of information about the respective unit that is subsequently shared with planners. The planning process itself can be threatened by anarchistic behavior on the part of some team members [56]. For example, a department chairperson may refuse to accept the authority of the planning team, refuse to provide planners with information, and attempt to discredit the planning process. If such a person is successful in delegitimizing planning efforts, attempts to resuscitate the planning process may be useless.

Planning team members should take part regularly in those activities related to the development of the plan to ensure input from those constituent parties they represent. If planning is to be taken seriously and anarchistic behavior avoided [8], the authority of the planning team must be commensurate with the responsibility for developing and subsequently implementing the plan [23, 49]. Communication problems between technical staff (long-range planners) and academic administrators should be anticipated. The perspectives and vested interests of these groups differ appreciably: the latter tend to focus on and respond to daily crises; the former tend to overemphasize the long-range future of the institution. Routine meetings between these groups must be established early and maintained throughout the planning process [55].

Two sets of challenges surface with regard to encouraging participation during the implementation phase: (1) fostering a climate conducive to change and (2) resolving conflict. Members of the organization must be rewarded for making a plan work and sanctioned for blocking the implementation of the plan [28]. Rewards and sanctions require the availability and control of resources—either allocations of money, or implementations of policies as "side payments" [10] that benefit the employee, or through the consumptive exercise of power. In the latter case, employees may be motivated by threats of negative sanctions (demotion, loss of salary, dismissal), an alternative likely to erode staff morale. For example, if reductions in force are occurring, much energy will probably be directed toward maintaining one's position or searching for new jobs rather than serving the needs of the institution.

Various internal and external constituencies will derive differential benefits from the implementation of a plan should the interventions associated with the plan alter the status quo [45]. In times of adequate resources, fac-

ulty apathy and decision making is predictable [15]. When an institution actually implements a plan, the winners and losers of policy battles and resource allocation decisions become known. Planners must anticipate how to deal constructively with the resulting conflicts [53].

Information and Communication

Unless relevant, valid information from the units to be involved in planning is available in an acceptable form or can be generated at a reasonable cost, the institution's capacity to engage in planning is severely limited [49, 57]. For example, if accurate records do not exist concerning the number of majors in and graduates from a department over the past decade and those numbers have varied widely, projections of the level of resources necessary to serve student needs will largely be guesswork. If effective communication channels are not available and in place, the resources necessary to develop such a system with a suitable level of redundancy [25] must be taken into account in the overall planning costs.

During the initiation phase, two types of information are critical. First, information related to the technical aspects of planning, including the types of planning processes available and the kinds of data and time lines required to produce them, is essential before a wise selection of a planning process can be made [11]. Second, information can also be used to raise participants' expectations about what they can gain from the planning process. For instance, a department chairperson may interpret the phrase "to improve program quality" to mean an increase in the size of the department's staff; the dean may perceive this phrase to mean cutting out "deadwood." The use of ambiguous statements of purpose, the communication of part of the plan to one group and part to another, and creating the belief that the planning process will somehow "produce" new resources can all lead to inappropriate expectations and deep-seated conflict when such expectations are not met. Even though some participants' expectations for planning may not be in conflict, they may be inappropriate nonetheless. Planning cannot solve insoluble problems or magically create resources.

The most potentially troublesome information issues in the plan development phase are related to (1) misunderstandings about the process, (2) failure to periodically apprise relevant constituent groups of the progress of the planning team, and (3) unfair expectations for or treatment of information requested from various units and considered by the planning team. To maintain credibility and self-esteem while engaged in a most difficult task, planners must feel confident about how the process will unfold and have an accurate, realistic picture of what is required to bring about the intended consequences of planning. Planning team members must be able to converse readily with colleagues as well as with external audiences [45]. Reports of the planning teams' progress should be periodically presented to people who have a substantial interest in the organization's planning activities to maintain their commitment to planning.

Completed sections of a plan, or the "master plan," must be communicated in a timely fashion to those it will affect. "Knowing something" is a source of satisfaction and power and also increases identification with the plan [26]. How this information is communicated is crucial to the success of the planning effort. Probably the most important ingredient is whether the plan is presented as "flexible"—that is, described as guidelines as opposed to a blueprint of tasks to be accomplished by specified dates by specified people at a specified cost [32]. Although the plan must be written, a symbolic oral event—perhaps an "unveiling" of the plan, conducted by the highest appropriate official (chairperson of the board, president, chief academic officer) with representatives of those affected by the plan in attendance—should engender enthusiasm for and commitment to its implementation. This presentation should serve not only to highlight the important elements in the plan (for those who might not read it) but also to verify its level of endorsement. Plans that lack this endorsement may be taken less seriously [24, 29, 32].

Another implementation problem is the failure to accurately describe exactly what the plan entails to those responsible for implementation [22]. Simply distributing copies of the plan will not result in participants reading or understanding it and knowing what is expected of them. A reasonable amount of redundancy in communicating the plan may be necessary if the actors responsible for

implementing it are to understand what is to be done [25]. Printed copies, oral presentations, and discussions may be necessary even though each is expensive in terms of time and energy. Associated with this problem is the necessity for ensuring flexibility in the implementation of a plan. For successful implementation, most plans must be adapted incrementally at the department or program level to accommodate the demands and realities of limited resources [4, 56, 58]. If a plan appears to be inflexible, those who must implement it are likely to be alienated [47]. The description of a plan, if flexible, will permit those implementing it to feel a part of the decision-making process and to take ownership of the plan's implementation [3, 23, 26, 32].

The plan's content also affects the message received. If a plan is vague as a result of incompetence, intent, or compromises between competing factions, successful implementation cannot easily be achieved. If a plan provides only ambiguous direction, participants can implement any practices they choose and rationalize these in terms of the general plan. On the other hand, the plan may be so detailed as to suggest an intractable, deterministic bureaucracy [32]. Most faculty members have been socialized into autonomous behavior and will reject plans that threaten to routinize professional activities. A middle ground between extreme vagueness and specificity is necessary for a plan's successful implementation [41, 49].

Monitoring the plan's effects during its implementation is essential to successful planning [26]. An institution implementing a plan is usually in a state of flux, and the environment in which the organization exists also constantly changes [2, 45, 53]. Failure to evaluate how the plan is working in a fluid environment represents a serious deficiency in actively improving an institution's chances for survival and prosperity. Plans must be revised in light of new information; the "feedback loop" from the implementation phase back to the development phase is vital [2, 42, 53].

Interdependence

An institution's capacity to plan is influenced by the degree to which subunits in the organization are "specialized"—that is, the degree to which one unit is dependent upon another for success

[46] or "tightly coupled" [59]. When the units are highly interrelated, a plan must be developed for the entire organization or the activities of the different subunits will not mesh. When units are largely independent or loosely coupled, it may be a better use of resources to emphasize tactical (unit-level) planning rather than strategic or institutional planning [55]. Distinguishing between perceived versus actual interdependence is important in estimating planning capacity. English department faculty may perceive the department to be a highly independent unit, only to find that when the business school faculty begins to teach its own technical writing courses, the English department's credit hours are reduced by 25 percent. Similarly, medical school faculty may perceive a high degree of interdependence with graduate science programs. Due to separate funding sources and the fact that medical students register for almost all of their credits in medical school courses, the actual degree of interdependence may be rather low. Determining the appropriate scope for planning and accurately interpreting the relationships between units are critical elements to consider when estimating the institution's planning capacity [7, 29, 56].

The timing of planning is an interdependence problem in the initiation phase. Planners must be cognizant of personnel and departments that have recently been involved in planning activities such as self-studies or accreditation reviews that required substantial expenditures of energy and resources [49]. Requesting a department or college to participate in another planning process after recently completing a similar activity is counterproductive [26].

The length of the planning cycle is another important timing issue [29]. For departments stable in terms of clientele, resources, and philosophy, infrequent (about every ten years) planning updates may be satisfactory. For new units in a highly dynamic environment, an annual review and update of plans—making planning a continuous process—may be essential [21, 32, 53].

In the plan development phase, engendering commitment to the plan on the part of those responsible for making the plan work is too often overlooked. One strategy for increasing commitment at this point is directly involving those persons considered key implementors in some facet of the development of the plan [3, 32, 45]—for example, by assigning deans and department chairpersons to various planning subcommittees. If the planning process seems to favor one unit over others (e.g., making arbitrary exemptions from providing important data), the much-needed cooperation from other units across campus may be jeopardized.

During the implementation phase, special attention must be given to changes in the environment that create new or modify existing relationships between units [32, 45]. For example, a new federal agency might be created to distribute resources to emerging fields (e.g., space biology) that could influence relationships between biologists and engineers on the campus. Internally, new interdependencies may be formed by the combination of existing academic and administrative units or by the creation of new units to address what are perceived to be emerging opportunities or difficulties.

A more complex set of problems emerges when the plans created by an administrative unit are primarily constructed as symbols to appease an external constituency [18]. If these plans are taken literally by internal audiences as inflexible regulations that must be followed, major conflicts may result. To be effective as symbols, plans must present a clear endorsement of a particular policy or position. If such activities are not valued by the administration and not wanted by all the faculty, the price for such appeasement may be quite high. For example, the president under pressure from the board may include in the long–range plans the development of a college of veterinary medicine. Although pleasing to the board and outside agribusiness interests, it may unsettle deans and department chairpersons who fear that the operating expenses for such a college will be subtracted from their budgets. The value of plans as advertisements of a change in direction [6] to mollify external audiences must be weighed carefully against the value of plans as road maps to guide internal constituencies into the future. If planners try to accomplish everything with the same document, more may be lost than gained.

Resources

The most critical question in the capacity estimation phase of planning is whether the level of resources and commitment to planning are such that the planning process can be supported and the plan implemented [42, 53]. During this phase, institutional members must estimate the staff time necessary to develop the plan and the other activities staff and faculty must forego in order to engage in planning activities. If sufficient "organizational slack" [10] exists, additional resources for planning may not be necessary. A new "structure," such as the creation of a planning office or a blue-ribbon planning committee, may be desirable to give momentum to the planning process [55]. Next, an estimation of the total *direct* costs of the planning process must be made, including consulting fees, costs associated with the development of planning documents, and the plan itself. Finally, an estimate of the likely costs of implementation of a plan must be made. This estimate may take the form of a constraint [49]; for example, the "plan" to be developed must be based on the current level of resources plus or minus a specified percentage. Contingency planning might require the development of three plans—one for a steady level of resources, one for an increased level, and one for a decreased level [44].

Two resource problems first encountered during the initiation phase reoccur throughout the planning process: (1) the inadequate allocation of resources for planning and (2) an inaccurate assessment of the implementation costs of the proposed plan [42, 53]. Resource estimates must address both direct and indirect costs in the form of released time of staff who initiate, organize, and implement the planning process and the resulting plan. Failure to adequately allocate resources in the initiation phase may indicate to some participants a lack of commitment on the part of the administration to the planning process [21]. Exceeding budget allocations not only embarrasses planners and administrators but can also demoralize faculty. If a program faculty were asked to plan a new facility when resources cannot be provided to construct such a facility, the credibility of the administration and others involved in the planning process may be irreparably damaged.

Insufficient resources readily become apparent during the implementation phase [21]. Reallocation of resources is a common outcome of planning. As faculty realize that additional resources are unlikely to be forthcoming for their respective units, anger with the planning process may precipitate a decline in unit morale [57]. If the plan calls for reducing the student/faculty ratio but funds are not available to hire new staff, the credibility of the plan and the planning process begins to dissipate. During the implementation phase, the full extent of reallocation may be felt, creating resistance to accepting other elements of the plan. Extremely destructive interunit rivalries ("civil war") may develop, and turf protection may drain off much of the organization's resources and encourage behaviors directly counter to the purposes of the plan.

Some resources should be reserved for dealing with the psychic costs of the change implicit in implementing a plan. People will resist change, especially social change [34, 49]. When new alliances are encouraged by the plan, resources may be required to soothe bruised egos. When two departments must be combined, at least one of the department chairpersons will need a new position. Some may return happily to a faculty position, whereas others may need a change in title to enable the new department to function properly.

The final question related to resources in the implementation phase is whether the planning activities should be continued at the current level, increase in scope, or be terminated [41, 45]. An organization may not need a new plan; instead, administrators may need to focus attention on improving management practices and on motivating staff or faculty.

Planning is expensive. Rather than devote increasingly scarce resources to planning, it may be advisable for an institution to pursue long-standing goals in more efficient ways. If the results of the planning process do not seem worth the costs, efforts to move forward with formal planning activities should be delayed.

Summary

Planning "represents the working of reason in history" [19, p. 233]. People may not be rational enough nor the environment stable enough to make extensive strategic planning exercises practical. Addressing problems on a circumscribed scale increases the potential for rational action and organizational redesign [32]. Therefore, choosing an appropriate level and scope for planning may be the most important decision planners make. Planners must be cognizant of and not exceed their limitations.

In this article, we have presented the types of problems that occur throughout a planning process, from the assessment of the capacity of the system to plan to the implementation phase of planning. We focused on the types of problems associated with five organizational constructs: goals, participation, information and communication, internal and external interdependence, and resources. The underlying premise is that if potential problems in the planning process can be identified, planners may be able to avoid or ameliorate their debilitating influence. The planning problems summarized in Table 1 are not exhaustive—unanticipated problems will arise. By using a typology of planning problems, college and university officials can venture into the mayhem of "rational" planning processes better able to recognize the pitfalls that lie ahead.

References

1. Ackoff, R. L. *A Concept of Corporate Planning*. New York: Wiley, 1970.

2. _____. *Redesigning the Future: A Systems Approach to Societal Problems*. New York: Wiley, 1974.

3. Argyris, C. *Intervention Theory and Method*. Reading, Mass.: Addison-Wesley, 1979.

4. Berman, P. "A New Perspective on Implementation Design: Adaptive Implementation." In *New Perspectives on Planning, Management, and Evaluation in School Improvement*, edited by P. Hood, pp. 31–45. San Francisco: Far West Laboratory for Educational Research and Development, 1979.

5. *Carnegie Council on Policy Studies in Higher Education: A Summary of Reports and Recommendations*. San Francisco: Jossey-Bass, 1980.

6. Clark, D. L., S. McKibbin, and M. Malkas (eds.). *New Perspectives on Planning in Educational Organizations*. San Francisco: Far West Laboratory, 1980.

7. Clark, P. "Some Analytic Requirements of an Applied Organization Science." In *The Management of Organization Design*, edited by R. H. Kilmann, L. R. Pondy, and D. P. Slevin, pp. 231–49. New York: North-Holland, 1976,

8. Cohen, M. D., and J. G. March. *Leadership and Ambiguity: The American College President*. New York: McGraw-Hill, 1974.

9. Cohen, M. D., J. G. March, and J. P. Olsen. "A Garbage Can Model of Organizational Choice." *Administrative Science Quarterly*, 17 (March 1972), 1–25.

10. Cyert, R. M., and J. G. March. *A Behavioral Theory of the Firm*. Englewood Cliffs, N.J.: Prentice-Hall, 1963.

11. Dalton, G. W., P. R. Lawrence, and L. E. Greiner. *Organizational Change and Development*. Homewood, Ill.: Irwin-Dorsey, 1970.

12. Datta, L. "Front End Analysis: Pegasus or Shank's Mare?" In *Exploring Purposes and Dimensions, New Directions for Program Evaluation*, No. 1, edited by S. Anderson and C. Coles, pp. 13–30. San Francisco: Jossey-Bass, 1978.

13. Davidoff, P., and T. A. Reiner. "A Choice Theory of Planning." In *A Reader in Planning Theory*, edited by A. Faludi, pp. 11–39. New York: Pergamon, 1973.

14. Delbecq, A. L., and A. H. Van de Ven. "A Group Process Model for Problem Identification and Program Planning." *Journal of Applied Behavioral Science*, 7 (July/August 1971), 466–92.

15. Dykes, A. R. *Faculty Participation in Decision Making: Report of a Study*. American Council on Education Monograph. Washington, D.C.: American Council on Education, 1968.

16. Etzioni, A. *Modern Organizations*. Englewood Cliffs, N.J.: Prentice-Hall, 1964.

17. Freeman, T. M., and W. A. Simpson. "Using Institutional Data to Plan Academic Programs—A Case History." In *Academic Planning for the 1980s: New Directions for Institutional Research*, No. 28, edited by R. Heydinger, pp. 27-55. San Francisco: Jossey-Bass, 1980.

18. Friedmann, J. "Introduction, Part I 'The Study and Practice of Planning.'" *International Social Science Journal*, UNESCO, 11 (July 1959), 327–29.

19. _____. "A Conceptual Model for the Analysis of Planning Behavior." *Administrative Science Quarterly*, 12 (September 1967), 225–52.

20. _____. *Retracking America: A Theory of Transactive Planning*. Garden City, N.Y.: Doubleday, 1973.

21. Fuller, B. "A Framework for Academic Planning." *Journal of Higher Education*, 47 (January/February 1976), 65–77.

22. Glassman, R. B. "Persistence and Loose Coupling in Living Systems." *Behavioral Science*, 18 (March 1973), 83–98.

23. Haas, R. M. "Winning Acceptance for Institutional Research and Planning." In *Improving Academic Management*, edited by P. Jedamus and M. Peterson and Associates, pp. 539–54. San Francisco: Jossey-Bass, 1980.

24. Hage, J., and M. Aiken. *Social Change in Complex Organizations*. New York: Random House, 1970.

25. Havelock, R., et al. *Planning for Innovation through the Dissemination and Utilization of Scientific Knowledge*. Ann Arbor: Institute for Social Research, 1971.

26. Heydinger, R. B. "Academic Program Planning Reconsidered." In *Academic Planning for the 1980s: New Directions for Institutional Research*, No. 28, edited by R. B. Heydinger, pp. 97–109. San Francisco: Jossey-Bass, 1980.

27. ____, "Planning Academic Programs. " In *Improving Academic Management*, edited by P. Jedamus and M. Peterson and Associates, pp. 304–26. San Francisco: Jossey-Bass, 1980.

28. Hoenack, S. A., and D. J. Berg. "The Roles of Incentives in Academic Planning." In *Academic Planning for the 1980s: New Directions for Institutional Research*, No. 28, edited by R. B. Heydinger, pp. 73–93. San Francisco: Jossey-Bass, 1980.

29. Johnson, M. D., and H. G. Richard. "A Framework for Evaluating Institutional Planning." In *Research in Planning for Higher Education*, edited by R. Fenske, pp. 161–64. Tallahassee, Fla.: Association for Institutional Research Press, 1977.

30. Kaplan, A. "On the Strategy of Social Planning." *Policy Sciences*, 4 (March 1973), 41–61.

31. Kast, R. E., and R. E. Rosenzweig. *Organization and Management: A Systems Approach*. Second edition. New York: McGraw-Hill, 1974.

32. Kilmann, R. H. *Social Systems Design*. New York: North-Holland, 1977.

33. Kiresuk, R. J., S. H. Lund, S. Schultz, and N. E. Larsen. "Translating Theory into Practice: Change Research at the Program Evaluation Research Center." *Evaluation and Change*, 4 (Fall 1977), 89–95.

34. Lawrence, P. R. "How to Deal with Resistance to Change." *Harvard Business Review*, 32 (May/June 1954), 49–57.

35. Locke, E. A., and D. M. Schweiger. "Participation in Decision-Making: One More Look." In *Research in Organizational Behavior*, Vol. 1, edited by B. M. Staw, pp. 265–339. Greenwich, Conn.: JAI Press, 1979.

36. March, J. G., and M. A. Simon. *Organizations*. New York: Wiley, 1958.

37. Michael, D. *On Learning to Plan—And Planning to Learn: The Social Psychology of Changing Toward Future-Responsive Societal Learning*. San Francisco: Jossey-Bass, 1973.

38. Mims, R. S. "Resource Reallocation: Stopgap or Support for Academic Planning?" In *Academic Planning for the 1980s: New Directions for Institutional Research*, No. 28, edited by R. B. Heydinger, pp. 57–72. San Francisco: Jossey-Bass, 1980.

39. Mintzberg, H., D. Raisinghani, and A. Theoret. "The Structure of 'Unstructured' Decision Processes." *Administrative Science Quarterly*, 21 (June 1976), 246–75.

40. Moos, M. "The Future of the Land Grant University." *Change* (May/June 1982), 30–35.

41. Nystrom, P. C., B.L.T. Hedberg, and W. H. Starbuck. "Interacting Processes as Organization Designs." In *The Management of Organization Design*, edited by R. H. Kilmann, L. R. Pondy, and D. P. Slevin, pp. 209–30. New York: North-Holland, 1976.

42. Ozbekhan, H. "Planning and Human Action." In *Hierarchically Organized Systems in Theory and Practice*, edited by P. A. Weiss, pp. 152–81. New York: Hafner, 1971.

43. Perrow, C. "Disintegrating Social Sciences." *New York University Education Quarterly*, 12 (Winter 1981), 2–9.

44. Peterson, M. W. "Analyzing Alternative Approaches to Planning." In *Improving Academic Management*, edited by P. Jedamus and M. Peterson and Associates, pp. 113–63. San Francisco: Jossey-Bass, 1980.

45. Poulton, N. L. "Strategies of Large Universities." In *Improving Academic Management*, edited by P. Jedamus and M. Peterson and Associates, pp. 626–50. San Francisco: Jossey-Bass, 1980.

46. Price, J. L. *Handbook of Organizational Measurement*. Lexington, Mass.: D. C. Heath, 1972.

47. ____, *The Study of Turnover*. Ames, Iowa: Iowa State University Press, 1977.

48. Riesman, D., J. Gusfield, and Z. Gamson. *Academic Values and Mass Education*. New York: Doubleday, 1970.

49. Schmidtlein, F. A. "Decision Process Paradigms in Education." *Educational Researcher*, 3 (May 1974), 4–11.

50. Simon, H. A. *Administrative Behavior*. Second edition. New York: Macmillan, 1957.

51. Tannenbaum, A. S. (ed.). *Control in Organizations*. New York: McGraw-Hill, 1968.

52. Toll, J. S. "Strategic Planning: An Increasing Priority for Colleges and Universities." *Change* (May/June 1982), 36–37.

53. Trist, E. L. "Action Research and Adaptive Planning." In *Experimenting with Organizational Life*, edited by A. W. Clark, pp. 94–110. New York: Plenum, 1976.

54. Trotter, B. *Planning for Planning*. Ottawa, Canada; Association of Universities and Colleges of Canada, 1974.

55. Van de Ven, A. H. "Problem Solving, Planning, and Innovation. Part I. Test of the Program Planning Model." *Human Relations*, 33 (October 1980), 711–40.

56. ____. "Problem Solving, Planning, and Innovation. Part II. Speculations for Theory and Practice." *Human Relations*, 33 (November 1980), 757–79.

57. Van de Ven, A. H., and R.A. Koenig. "Process Model for Program Planning and Evaluation." *Journal of Economics and Business*, 28 (Spring/Summer 1976), 161–70.

58. Weatherly, R., and M. Lipsky. "Street-Level Bureaucrats and Institutional Innovation:

Implementing Special Education Reform." *Harvard Educational Review*, 47 (May 1977), 171–97.

59. Weick, K. E. *The Social Psychology of Organizing.* Second edition. Reading, Mass.: Addison-Wesley, 1979.

60. Wildavsky, A. *The Politics of the Budgetary Process.* Second edition. Boston, Mass.: Little, Brown, 1974.

John P. Bean is assistant professor and George D. Kuh is associate professor, Department of Educational Leadership and Policy Studies, Indiana University.

Journal of Higher Education, Vol. 55, No. 1 (January/February 1984)

The Impact of a Chief Planning Officer on the Administrative Environment for Planning

PETER J. HURST AND MARVIN W. PETERSON

*Institution-wide planning, to be effective, must
have the support of key administrators. Presidents, vice-presidents, deans, and directors
must feel that sufficient consensus can be
reached on explicit goals to make comprehensive
planning possible and worthwhile. While much
has been written about the importance of CEO
leadership in gaining broad support for planning, little has been said about the role of the
chief planning officer in this regard. This paper,
based on a national survey of administrators'
views of planning, studies the relationship between having a chief planning officer and administrators' perceptions of campus planning.
Its intended audience includes all those interested in institutional planning.*

The post-World War II growth, leveling-off,
and sporadic bursts of retrenchment in higher
education in the United States have been paral-
leled by a growth of interest in institutional
planning. This expanding interest is reflected
in the increasing memberships of the two associations related to institutional planning and
institutional research in higher education. The
Society of College and University Planners
(SCUP) has gone from a charter membership of
300 in 1966 to 2,820 members listed in the
1990–91 SCUP directory. The directory of the
Association for Institutional Research (AIR),
first published in 1966–67 with 392 names, lists
2,402 members in the 1990–91 AIR directory.
While the number of planning officers in
higher education institutions has continued to
increase, the number of studies of their role in
and impact on the planning process has not.
How does the central coordination of the insti-

tutional planning function affect the planning
process? Is the presence of a chief planning
officer (CPO) related to differences in administrator perceptions of and attitudes toward campus planning? This paper presents a data-
based exploration of the latter question.

Literature

Institutional planning has come to play a central role in the higher education management
literature. Descriptions and analyses of planning processes include those of Cope (1981,
1985); Hollowood (1981); Keller (1983); Kotler
and Murphy (1981); Parekh (1977); Peterson
(1980); Scott (1986); Shirley (1988); and Steeples
(1988). There is also a growing number of case
studies of planning available including Chaffee
(1983, 1984); Clugston (1986); Cope (1987);
Farmer (1987); Hyatt (1984); Lelong and Hinman (1982); Poulton (1980); Schmidtlein and
Milton (1990); Steeples (1988); Tack, Rentz, and
Russell (1984); and Zemsky, Porter, and Oedel
(1978). Although many authors have discussed
the importance of executive leadership and the
role of faculty participation, there is almost no
mention or evaluation of the presence of an increasingly prevalent and central participant in
the planning process—the chief planning officer. In addition, the literature that examines the
role and function of university institutional re-
search/planning offices and their leadership
(e.g., Brown and Yeager, 1977; Miselis, 1988; Peterson and Corcoran, 1985; Storrar, 1981; Saupe,
1990) includes no studies of the utility of the
CPO in the overall planning process.

"The Impact of a Chief Planning Officer on the Administrative Environment for Planning," by Peter J. Hurst and Marvin W.
Peterson, reprinted from *Research in Higher Education*, Vol. 33, No. 1, 1992. Human Sciences Press, Inc.

Conceptual Framework

Two important obstacles confront the study of CPOs. The first obstacle is the lack of homogeneity in title or job description of this position. The position may reside in any one of a number of functional areas of administration including: the president's office, finance or budget planning, academic affairs or academic planning, or institutional research. It may even be established as a separate function. Therefore, it is not surprising that titles for this position vary by institution as do reporting relationships and responsibilities. A second obstacle lies in the difficulty of isolating the impact of a CPO from other factors that influence institutional planning. These obstacles were removed in a recent national survey of institutional planning done by the National Center for Postsecondary Governance and Finance (NCPGF) under the direction of Dr. Frank Schmidtlein. The conceptual framework and the data for this study are drawn from the NCPGF research project.[1]

The dependent variables in this study, depicted in the conceptual framework in Figure 1, are (1) administrator perceptions of what current planning processes and values *are* on their campuses and (2) administrator attitudes about what planning processes and values *should* be. The framework for administrators' perceptions and attitudes was constructed from Schmidtlein's (1973) planning process paradigms, the "Comprehensive-Prescriptive" and the "Incremental-Remedial." The two paradigms were defined by Larson (1987, pp. 11–12) as follows:

Comprehensive-Prescriptive Planning is characterized by attention given to technical and analytical systems rather than to political or market processes. It is an approach in which means and ends are explicitly defined, are logically consistent, and cover a broad range of alternatives. This approach to planning usually entails formal analysis of costs and benefits and prescribes detailed goals and objectives that are often forecast into a long-range future (Churchman, 1983; Schultze, 1968).

Incremental-Remedial Planning is characterized by attention given to processes rather than to systems. It is an approach that usually focuses attention on the margins of the status quo, restricts consideration of the variety of alternatives and outcomes to a few, makes successive limited comparisons of means to ends, continually amends choices as trials require remediation, and fragments or pluralizes the decision process (Lindbloom and Braybrooke, 1965).

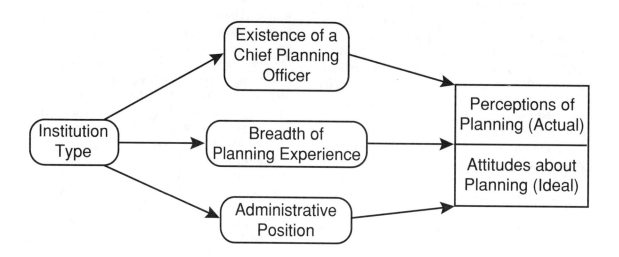

Figure 1. Conceptual framework of the relationship between existence of a CPO and administrator perceptions of and attitudes about planning.

While the central relationship being examined is of the presence of a CPO to administrator perceptions of and attitudes about institutional planning, other variables have been included in this study. Administrator attitudes toward planning may vary by administrative position (Takeuchi, 1984). Also, the breadth of administrator involvement with past and present planning activities may have an impact on current perceptions of and attitudes toward planning. Therefore, these three variables (presence of a CPO, administrative position, and breadth of planning experience of the respondent) are considered here for their direct and interactive relationships with administrator perceptions and attitudes. Finally, the effect of institutional type is examined in this study as a contextual variable. If CPOs are overrepresented in any of the institutional types, then a relationship between CPO and administrator perceptions and attitudes may be due at least in part to institutional type. The conceptual framework of the four independent and twelve dependent variables is presented in Figure 1.

Research Questions

The central research question of this study was, "Do administrators who indicate the existence of a CPO have different perceptions of actual campus planning and attitudes about ideal campus planning than do administrators who indicate that there is not a CPO on their campus?" The following subquestions were developed to guide the analysis:

1. Is there a relationship between institutional type and the other three independent variables (existence of a CPO, administrative position, breadth of planning experience)?

2. Is there a relationship between institutional type and the dependent variables (administrator perception of and attitudes about planning)?

3. Are there relationships between the three independent variables and the dependent variables?

4. What is the relative impact of the existence of a CPO, controlling for the other independent variables?

Data Sources and Methods

The NCPGF study involved a survey of 3,333 college administrators at 256 higher education institutions.[2] The institutions were randomly selected within two levels of stratification. The first level of stratification divided institutions by type—research university, state college, private liberal arts college, and community college. The second level subdivided each type by a set of major characteristics, for example, research universities into public and private, state colleges into unionized and not unionized, etc. Questionnaires were sent to administrators in 20 different positions at each institution and included trustees, CEOs, vice-presidents, deans, and directors. The overall response rate for the survey was 45.8 percent. The NCPGF study, while based on a stratified, random sample of institutions, was weighted toward larger institutions that tended to have more of the administrative positions that were being surveyed. For example, while research university and private college responses each represented 25 percent of the institutions surveyed, research universities alone accounted for 33.6 percent of the individual responses while liberal arts colleges accounted for only 18 percent. The authors of the study explained that the results were "not intended as definitive answers to planning questions but rather as stimulating suggestions for further qualitative study and evaluation" (Larson, 1987). Accordingly, the authors of this study wish to state the same caveat.

Data sources for the independent and dependent variables were:

1. *Existence of a CPO*—This variable is taken from a survey item worded as follows: "Does your institution have a senior administrative officer whose principal duty is to coordinate institution-wide planning?"

_____ Yes _____ No

Of the 1456 responses to this question, 841 answered "Yes" and 615 "No."

2. *Administrative Position*—A typology of administrative positions in the *Higher Education Directory* was used to identify the respondent's position. They were clustered into three position categories for this study:

(a) Executive Officers (CEO, chief academic officer, chief financial officer, chief student services officer, chief development officer, chief planning officer)

(b) Deans and Chairs

(c) Mid-level managers (registrar; head librarian; directors of admissions, counseling, financial aid, institutional research, computer center, and alumni relations)

3. *Breadth of Planning Experience*—One survey question asked, "Please check all of the planning activities listed below in which you have personally participated at any postsecondary education institution."

_____ College-wide planning committee member

_____ Evaluate and offer advice about a plan

_____ Provide statistical or other technical analysis of a planning issue

_____ Review and approve a plan

_____ Hold administrative responsibility for plan implementation

_____ Draft a plan proposal

_____ None of the above

The breadth of planning experience variable used in this study was a total of the number of activities participated in ranging from 0 to 6, broken into three categories as follows:

(1) 0–2 activities

(2) 3–4 activities

(3) 5–6 activities

4. *Institutional Type*—The four institutional categories represented in this study were:

(1) Research University

(2) Liberal Arts College

(3) State College

(4) Community College

5. *Administrator Perceptions of and Attitudes about Planning*—Administrators were asked to respond on a nine-point scale to six planning process and values topics. The response scale varied for each topic spanning statements drawn from Schmidtlein's planning paradigms. The

six topics and a shortened version of the statements are listed below:

1. *Response to change:*

(a) systematic and long-range vs. (b) incremental and short-range

2. *Reducing risks and uncertainty:*

(a) Quantitative analysis vs. (b) marginal adjustment

3. *Defining goals:*

(a) explicitly vs. (b) implicitly

4. *Reaching consensus on priorities:*

(a) by quantitative analysis of needs vs. (b) by bargaining and compromise

5. *The main objective of planning:*

(a) optimum choices vs. (b) satisfactory choices

6. *The better approach to planning:*

(a) comprehensive/prescriptive vs. (b) incremental/remedial

The nine-point scales connected the (a) and (b) positions so that, for example, a response of "I" on the scale for topic one indicated a systematic and long-range response to change (the C-P paradigm) while "9" indicated an incremental and short-range response to change (the I-R paradigm). For each of the six topics, respondents indicated what location on the nine-point interval scale best characterized their perception of actual institutional planning. On a second nine-point scale they indicated their attitude about how planning ideally should be done. The two scaled responses for each of the six items yielded twelve total responses: six planning perceptions and six planning attitudes. These comprised the dependent variables of the study.

At the core of the study is the strength of the relationship between having a CPO and administrator perceptions of and attitudes about planning. This relationship is studied relative to two other variables that may influence administrative perceptions of planning: administrative position and breadth of planning experience. These relationships are examined in the context of institutional type. If a relationship exists between institutional type and the other independent variables, institutional type must be controlled for in further analysis. If a relationship also exists between institutional type and the dependent variables, then the independent variables' relationships with the dependent variables must be considered in the context of institutional type. These considerations set the sequence of data analysis.

Analytic Results

1. *Existence of a CPO, Breadth of Planning Experience, and Administrative Position by Institutional Type*—Since three of the four variables are categorical, contingency table analysis was used. The data and the resulting chi-square analyses are presented in Table 1. There were significant differences in the distribution of all three of the independent variables by the contextual variable, institutional type. The ratio of respondents who indicated the presence of a CPO to those who indicated that there was not a CPO was much higher in community college respondents than respondents from the other institutional types. The breadth of planning experience was less in liberal arts colleges and state colleges than the other two types. Finally, administrative position categories were not evenly distributed across institutions. Liberal arts colleges and community colleges tend not to use dean titles to the extent that they are used by universities. The relationships between institutional type and the other independent variables dictate that institutional type must be controlled for when the relationships of these variables with the dependent variables are tested.

2. *Administrator Perceptions and Attitudes by Institutional Type*—A one-way analysis of variance was used to look for significant difference in administrator perception and attitude mean scores among the four institutional types. The results are presented in Table 2. Institutional type was related to only one of the six administrator perceptions of current institutional planning processes, how consensus is achieved (perception item #4). Research university administrator perceptions of how consensus is achieved were significantly closer to the bargaining and compromise end of the response scale than the perceptions of liberal arts college administrators. Administrator attitudes about how planning should ideally be done were related to institutional type for four of the six topics. The responses from liberal arts colleges and state colleges tended to be closer to the

Comprehensive/Prescriptive model. The relationship between institutional type and the dependent variables necessitated that it be considered in evaluating the relative strength of relationship of the three other independent variables with the dependent variables.

3a. *Effect of the Existence of a CPO on Administrator Perceptions and Attitudes by Institutional Type*—Having established the relationships between institutional type and both the other independent variables and the dependent variables, the analysis of the relationship between the existence of a CPO and administrator perceptions and attitudes, proceeded controlling for institutional type. Forty-eight T-tests were used to test the significance of differences between the group means of CPO-yes and CPO-no on the twelve perception and attitude variables for the four institutional types. The results are presented in Table 3. The relationship between the existence of a CPO and administrator perceptions of campus planning is striking. On all six of the perception variables, across all four institutional types, mean responses for CPO-yes were lower (closer to the Comprehensive/Prescriptive model) than were the mean responses for CPO-no. The differences were significant for 22 of the 24 tests (six perception variables by four institutional types).

A relationship also exists between the existence of a CPO and administrator attitudes about how planning should ideally be done. The CPO-yes group mean scores were lower than the CPO-no group mean scores for 22 of the 24 administrator attitude T-tests. Twelve of the 24 differences between means were significant. Community college administrator attitudes toward planning were not significantly related to the existence of a CPO.

3b. *Effect of Breadth of Planning Experience on Administrator Perceptions and Attitudes by Institutional Type*—The next step of the analysis was to test the relationship of the second independent variable, breadth of planning experience, with the dependent variables, perception of and attitude toward planning. A one-way analysis of variance of breadth of planning experience mean scores for the dependent variables was run for each institutional type. With the exception of some differences by experience for state college respondents, little relationship was found between breadth of plan-

**Table 1. Distribution of CPOs, Breadth of Planning Experience,
and Administrative Positions by Institutional Type**

| CPO | Chief Planning Officer | | | | |
	Research University	Liberal Arts College	State College	Community College	Totals
1. CPO-yes	278	133	221	209	841
	57%	51%	55%	69%	58%
2. CPO–no	212	129	178	96	614
	43%	49%	45%	32%	42%
Totals	490	262	399	305	1456
Chi Sq Sig = .000	34%	18%	27%	21%	100%

| Planning Activities | Breadth of Planning Experience | | | | |
	Research University	Liberal Arts College	State College	Community College	Totals
1. 0–2	87	70	89	54	300
	17%	26%	22%	18%	20%
2. 3–4	149	89	134	88	460
	30%	33%	33%	29%	31%
3. 5–6	267	114	183	166	730
	53%	42%	45%	54%	49%
Totals	503	273	406	308	1490
Chi Sq Sig = .007	34%	18%	27%	21%	100%

| Admin. Position | Administrative Position | | | | |
	Research University	Liberal Arts College	State College	Community College	Totals
1. Executive Officers	146	123	156	140	565
	30%	46%	38%	46%	38%
2. Deans	150	11	95	43	299
	34%	4%	24%	12%	20%
3. Directors	198	133	158	120	609
	40%	50%	39%	40%	41%
Totals	494	267	409	323	1473
Chi Sq Sig = .000	34%	18%	28%	22%	100%

ning experience and administrator perceptions of and attitudes toward institutional planning. The results are presented in Table 4.

3c. *Effect of Administrative Position on Administrator Perceptions and Attitudes by Institutional Type*—The final step in this stage of the analysis examined the relationship between administrative position and administrator perceptions and attitudes toward planning, controlling for institutional type. A one-way analysis of variance of the effect of administrative position on each of the dependent variables was run for each institutional type. Although some differences by administrative position were found for research universities, in general, little relationship existed between these

variables. The results are displayed in Table 5.

4. *Effect of the Existence of a CPO on Administrator Perceptions and Attitudes Controlling for All Other Variables*—The final analysis was a four-way ANOVA. The relationships of each of the three independent variables and of institutional type with the dependent variables were considered simultaneously. The resulting analysis is displayed as Table 6.

When all four variables were considered simultaneously (institutional type, administrative position, breadth of planning experience, and the existence of a CPO), the existence of a CPO made the most significant difference in administrator perceptions of how planning was actually being carried out. As was shown earlier (Table 3), the

Table 2. Administrator Perceptions and Attitudes About Institutional Planning by Institutional Type (One-way ANOVA and Comparisons of Means)

Perceptions and Attitudes	Significant. of F. (ANOVA)	Institutional Type (Mean Scores)				P. <.05 for Inst. Types
PERCEPTIONS:		Research University	Liberal Arts College	State College	Community College	
1. Response to Change 2. Reducing Risks and Uncertainty 3. Defining Goals 4. Reaching Consensus 5. Main Objective of Planning 6. Better Approach to Planning	.000	5.624	5.011	5.281	5.172	RU-LA
ATTITUDES:						
1. Response to Change 2. Reducing Risks and Uncertainty 3. Defining Goals 4. Reaching Consensus	.002	4.069	3.713	4.033	4.380	LA-CC
	.001	4.538	4.049	4.053	4.325	RU-LA RU-SU
5. Main Objective of Planning	.015	4.676	4.242	4.215	4.384	RU-SU
6. Better Approach to Planning	.000	3.966	3.532	3.669	4.208	RU-LA LA-CC SU-CC

difference favored the Comprehensive/Prescriptive paradigm. Breadth of planning experience was related to administrator perception of explicitness of goal definition (item #3) and institutional type was related to administrator perceptions of how consensus is achieved (item #4).

While the presence of a CPO also has a clear relationship with most of the administrator attitude variables, it does not stand out relative to the other independent variables to the same extent as it did for the perception variables. Table 6 suggests that both the existence of a CPO and institutional type have strong independent relationships with most of the administrator attitude variables. Various interaction terms also have significant independent relationships with some of the attitude variables.

Discussion and Conclusions

The results of this study that used a broad sample of administrators from diverse institutions surveyed in the NCPGF project suggest a relationship between the presence of a CPO and administrators' perceptions of and attitudes about institutional planning. In all four institutional types, the presence of a CPO was accompanied by an increase in the perception of more comprehensive and rational processes of campus planning. The presence of a CPO also seemed to increase the likelihood that administrators' attitudes about ideal planning would favor comprehensive processes to a greater extent than administrators who reported no CPO position on their campus. Most

Table 3. Differences in Administrator Perceptions and Attitudes by CPO-yes and CPO-no, Controlling for Institutional Type (T-Tests, Group Means, and Probabilities of T-Statistics)

Administrator Perceptions & Attitudes	Research University			Liberal Arts College			State College			Community College		
	CPO yes (means)	CPO no (means)	Sig. (P.)	CPO yes (means)	CPO no (means)	Sig. (P.)	CPO yes (means)	CPO no (means)	Sig. (P.)	CPO yes (means)	CPO no (means)	Sig. (P.)
PERCEPTIONS												
1. Response to Change	5.00	5.79	***	4.98	5.89	***	5.21	6.01	***	5.22	6.06	**
2. Reducing Risks and Uncertainty	5.09	5.35		4.99	5.70	**	4.98	5.57	**	5.04	5.65	**
3. Defining Goals	4.55	5.38	***	4.08	5.02	**	4.46	5.29	***	4.47	5.49	***
4. Reaching Consensus	5.35	5.97	***	4.61	5.44	***	5.00	5.57	**	5.02	5.47	
5. Main Objective of Planning	4.97	5.58	***	4.75	5.56	**	4.84	5.44	**	4.92	5.51	*
6. Better Approach to Planning	4.86	5.58	***	4.50	5.43	***	4.84	5.64	***	5.14	5.70	*
ATTITUDES												
1. Response to Change	3.88	4.30	*	3.48	3.89		3.96	4.05	4.32		4.48	
2. Reducing Risks and Uncertainty	4.51	4.66		4.21	4.89	**	4.13	4.56	*	4.66	4.84	*
3. Defining Goals	3.36	3.79	*	2.85	3.66	**	3.14	3.69	*	3.71	3.76	*
4. Reaching Consensus	4.42	4.68		3.87	4.25		3.81	4.27	*	4.35	4.25	*
5. Main Objective of Planning	4.44	4.98	**	3.91	4.59	*	3.94	4.51	*	4.24	4.68	*
6. Better Approach to Planning	3.78	4.23	**	3.38	3.74		3.36	3.94	**	4.26	4.06	**

* Probability of T statistic <.05
** Probability of T statistic <.01
*** Probability of T statistic <.001

importantly, the presence of a CPO had a greater effect on perceptions of how planning was handled on campus than did institutional type or administrative position or breadth of planning experience of the respondent.

The generalizability of these findings is limited by the fact that the unit of analysis was the individual administrator and not the individual campus. For example, in examining responses by institution, we were surprised to discover a lack of agreement among administrators about the presence of a CPO. We found that agreement about whether or not there was a senior administrative officer whose duty it is to coordinate institution-wide planning existed in only 57 percent of the institutions (82 of 143).[3] Even in surveyed institutions that had listed a chief planning officer in the *Higher Education Directory* ($n = 47$) and who had enough respondents to make the test of agreement meaningful ($n = 32$), only 63 percent ($n = 20$) agreed that there actually was such a person in the institution. The lack of agreement sug-

gested by these two attempts to verify the survey responses is striking and suggests the results need to be viewed tentatively.

However, the emphasis of these findings on the perceptions of the individual administrator is still important. Despite the limited agreement within an institution as to whether a CPO position exists, those administrators who think that there is a CPO are more likely to perceive the planning process as systematic, comprehensive, and rational than are their colleagues who say that there is no CPO. How might these findings be interpreted? The simplest, broadest interpretation is that CPOs actually do make institution-wide planning processes more comprehensive, systematic, explicit, etc. This interpretation is bolstered by the likelihood that administrators take the staffing of the CPO position as an institutional commitment to a comprehensive, analytical planning process. Thus, the CPO to some extent may symbolize the rationality of the process, thereby bringing it legitimacy and credibility.

Table 4. Administrator Perceptions and Attitudes by Breadth of Planning Experience, Controlling for Inst. Type (One-way ANOVA and Comparisons of Means)

Perceptions and Attitudes	Breadth of Planning Experience (1 = 0–2 activities, 2 = 3–4 activities, 3 = 5–6 activities)							
	Research Univ.		Liberal Arts Coll.		State College		Comm. College	
PERCEPTIONS:	Sig. of F	Group Means	Sig. of F	Group Means	Sig. of F	Group Means	Sig. of F	Group Means
1. Response to Change								
2. Reducing Risks and Uncertainty								
3. Defining Goals					.032	1 = 5.35 3 = 4.62		
4. Reaching Consensus								
5. Main Objective of Planning								
6. Better Approach to Planning								
ATTITUDES:								
1. Response to Change								
2. Reducing Risks and Uncertainty								
3. Defining Goals								
4. Reaching Consensus	.031				.043	1 = 4.47 3 = 3.80		
5. Main Objective of Planning								
6. Better Approach to Planning					.017	1 = 4.07 3 = 3.36		

Table 5. Administrator Perceptions and Attitudes by Administrative Position, Controlling for Institutional Type (One-way ANOVA and Comparisons of Means)

Perceptions and Attitudes	Administrative Position (1 = Executive Officers, 2 = Deans, 3 = Directors)							
	Research University		Liberal Arts College		State College		Community College	
PERCEPTIONS:	Sig. of F	Group Means	Sig. of F	Group Means	Sig. of F	Group Means	Sig. of F	Group Means
1. Response to Change								
2. Reducing Risks and Uncertainty								
3. Defining Goals	.029	1 = 4.60 3 = 5.24			.043			
4. Reaching Consensus								
5. Main Objective of Planning								
6. Better Approach to Planning								
ATTITUDES:								
1. Response to Change	.000	1 = 4.53, 2 = 4.18, 3 = 3.66						
2. Reducing Risks and Uncertainty	.006	1 = 4.91 3 = 4.26						
3. Defining Goals								
4. Reaching Consensus								
5. Main Objective of Planning								
6. Better Approach to Planning								

A more mundane explanation is also possible. The presence of a CPO may indicate that a particular campus is currently involved in a visible planning process. If that were the case, it would be likely that planning on that campus at that time would look more systematic and comprehensive than its status quo, the incremental alternative. Unfortunately, the NCPGF survey did not include a question asking if there was currently a formal, institution-wide planning process in place, so it is not possible to test this hypothesis.

Notes

1. Institutional Planning Project of the National Center for Postsecondary Governance and Finance, funded by a grant from the Office of Research. U.S. Department of Education.

The authors wish to express their gratitude to Frank Schmidtlein, Toby Milton, and Jon Larson for providing access to the data from their study.
2. The survey instrument, methodology, and results are presented in Larson (1987).
3. Institutions were included in this analysis if they were represented by three or more respondents from a group consisting of executive officers, deans, and directors of institutional research. Agreement was defined as at least 70 percent consensus among the respondents.

References

Brown, M. K., and Yeager, J. L. (1977). The impact of planning systems on managing and staffing an institutional research office. Paper presented at the Forum of the Association for Institutional Research, Montreal.

Table 6. Administrator Perceptions and Attitudes by CPO Institutional Type, Administrative Position, Breadth of Planning Experience, and Interactions

(ANOVA)

	Main Terms				Interaction Terms				
	CPO (A)	Inst. Type (B)	Admin Postn (C)	Plng. Exper. (D)	A B	B C	C D	A B C	A B D
PERCEPTIONS:									
1. Response to Change	***							*	
2. Reducing Risks and Uncertainty	***								
3. Defining Goals	***			**					
4. Reaching Consensus	***	**							
5 Main Objective of Planning	***								
6. Better Approach to Planning	***								
ATTITUDES:									
1. Response to Change		***						*	*
2. Reducing Risks and Uncertainty	**	*							
3. Defining Goals	**	*							*
4. Reaching Consensus	*	**							
5. Main Objective of Planning	***	*							
6. Better Approach to Planning	**	***							*

* Probability of F statistic < .05
** Probability of F statistic < .01
*** Probability of F statistic < .001

Chaffee, E. E. (1983). The role of rationality in university budgeting. *Research in Higher Education* 19(4): 387–406.

Chaffee, E. E. (1984). Successful strategic management in small private colleges. *Journal of Higher Education* 55(2): 212–241.

Churchman, C. W. (1968). *The Systems Approach.* New York: Dell.

Churchman, C. W. (1983). *The Systems Approach.* New York: Dell.

Clugston, R. M., Jr. (1986). Strategic planning in an organized anarchy: The emperor's new clothes? Paper presented at the Annual Meeting of the Association for the Study of Higher Education. San Antonio, TX: ED 268 902

Cope, R. G. (1981). *Strategic Planning, Management, and Decision Making.* AAHE-ERIC Higher Education Reports 9. Washington, DC: American Association for Higher Education.

Cope, R. G. (1985). A contextual model to encompass the strategic planning concept: Introducing a newer paradigm. *Planning for Higher Education* 13(3); 13–20.

Cope, R. G. (1987). *Opportunity from Strength: Strategic Planning Clarified with Case Examples.* ASHE-ERIC Higher Education Reports 8. Washington,

DC: Association for the Study of Higher Education.

Farmer, D. W. (1987). Taking charge of change through matrix management. *Planning for Higher Education* 15(2) 18–29.

Hollowood, J. R. (1981). College and university strategic planning: A methodological approach. *Planning for Higher Education* 9(4): 8–18.

Hyatt, J. (1984). *Reallocation: Strategies for Effective Resource Management.* National Association of College and University Business Officers.

Keller, G. (1983). *Academic Strategy.* Baltimore: Johns Hopkins University Press.

Kotler, P. R., and Murphy, Patrick (1981). Strategic planning for higher education. *Journal of Higher Education* 52(5): 470–489.

Larson, J. (1987). Senior administrator attitudes about planning. Paper presented at the annual meeting of the Association for the Study of Higher Education. Baltimore: ED 292390.

Lelong, D. C., and Hinman, Martha M. (1982). *Implementation of Formal Planning* (Publications in Higher Education 15). Ann Arbor: Center for the Study of Higher Education, University of Michigan.

Lindbloom, C. E., and Braybrooke, D. (1963). *The Intelligence of Democracy: Decision Making Through Mutual Adjustment*. New York: The Free Press.

Miselis, K. L. (1988). The organizational relationship between planning/institutional research and administrative information systems in higher education. Paper presented at the Forum of the Association for Institutional Research. Phoenix: ED 298 849.

Parekh, S. (1977). *Long Range Planning*. New York: Change Magazine Press.

Peterson, M. W. (1980). Analyzing alternative approaches to planning. In Paul Jedamus and Marvin Peterson (eds.), *Improving Academic Management* (pp. 113–163). San Francisco: Jossey-Bass.

Peterson, M. W., and Corcoran, M. (eds.) (1983). *Institutional Research in Transition*. New Directions in Institutional Research 46. San Francisco: Jossey-Bass.

Poulton, N. L. (1980). Impacts of planning activities in research universities: A comparative analysis of five institutional experiences. Unpublished doctoral dissertation, University of Michigan, Ann Arbor.

Saupe, J. L. (1990). *The Functions of Institutional Research*, 2nd edition. Tallahassee: The Association for Institutional Research.

Schmidtlein, F. A. (1973). The selection of decision process paradigms in higher education: Can we make the right decisions or must we make the decision right? *Ford Foundation Program for Research in University Administration* (P-42). Berkeley: University of California.

Schmidtlein, F. A., and Milton, T. H. (eds.) (1990). *Adapting Strategic Planning to Campus Realities*. New Directions for Institutional Research 67. San Francisco: Jossey-Bass.

Schultze, C. E. (1968). *The Politics and Economics of Public Spending*. Washington, DC: The Brookings Institution.

Scott, C. L. (1986). Launching successful planning efforts. *Planning for Higher Education* 14(2): 26–29.

Shirley, R. C. (1988). Strategic planning: An overview. In D. W. Steeples (ed.), *Successful Strategic Planning: Case Studies*. New Directions for Institutional Research 64. San Francisco: Jossey-Bass.

Steeples. D. W. (1988). Concluding observations. In D. W. Steeples (ed.), *Successful Strategic Planning: Case Studies*. New Directions for Higher Education 64. San Francisco: Jossey-Bass.

Storrar, S. J. (1981). Perceptions of organizational and political environments: Results of a national survey of institutional research/planning officers at large public universities. Paper presented at the Forum of the Association for Institutional Research. Minneapolis/St. Paul.

Tack, M. W., Rentz, A. M., and Russell, Ronald L. (1984). Strategic planning for academic programs: A strategy for institutional survival. *Planning for Higher Education* 12(4): 8–14.

Takeuchi, S. M. (1984). Planning support for the top: An application of "Miles' Law" (Where you stand depends on where you sit). *Planning for Higher Education* 12(2): 1–5.

Zemsky, R. W., Porter, R., and Oedel, L. P. (1978). Decentralized planning: To share responsibility. *Educational Record* 59(3): 229–253.

Peter J. Hurst, Office of Academic Planning and Analysis, University of Michigan, 520 E. Liberty St., Ann Arbor, MI 48109-2210. Marvin W. Peterson, Center for the Study of Higher and Postsecondary Education, University of Michigan.

Presented at the Thirty-first Annual Forum of the Association for Institutional Research, San Francisco, May 26–29, 1991.

The 21st Century University:
A Tale of Two Futures

JAMES J. DUDERSTADT

*It was the best of times, it was the worst of
    times,*
*It was the age of wisdom, it was the age of
    foolishness,*
*It was the epoch of belief, it was the epoch of
    incredulity,*
*It was the season of Light, it was the season of
    Darkness,*
*It was the spring of hope, it was the winter of
    despair,*

Charles Dickens
A Tale of Two Cities

To paraphrase Charles Dickens, these do indeed seem like both the best of times and the worst of times for higher education in America. On the one hand, in an age of knowledge in which educated people and their ideas have become the wealth of nations, the university has never been more important, and the value of a college education never higher. The educational opportunities offered by the university, the knowledge it creates, and the services it provides are key to almost every priority of contemporary society, from economic competitiveness to national security to protecting the environment to enriching our culture. There is a growing recognition that few public investments have higher economic payoff than those made in higher education. In 1997 the federal government made the largest commitment to higher education since the GI Bill through $40 billion of tax incentives to college students and their parents as part of the budget-balancing agreement. In 1998 thanks to our unusually prosperous economy, Washington took further action by proposing the largest increase in the funding of academic research in decades. Both the administration and Congress promise balanced budgets and generous support for years to come.

Yet, despite this vote of confidence, there is great unease on our campuses. The media continues to view the academy with a frustrating mix of skepticism, ignorance, and occasional hostility that erodes public trust and confidence. The danger of external intervention in academic affairs in the name of accountability remains high. Throughout society we see a backlash against earlier social commitments such as affirmative action, long a key mechanism for diversifying our campuses and providing educational opportunity to those suffering discrimination in broader society. The faculty feels the stresses from all quarters. There is fear that research funding will decline again when the economy cools and entitlement programs grow. They are apprehensive about the future of long-standing academic practices such as tenure. They express a sense of loss of scholarly community with increasing specialization, together with a conflict between the demands of grantsmanship, a reward structure emphasizing research, and a love and sense of responsibility for teaching.

To continue paraphrasing Dickens, while we may be entering an age of wisdom—or at least knowledge—it is also an age of foolishness. Last year, the noted futurist Peter Drucker

"The 21st Century University: A Tale of Two Futures," by James J. Duderstadt. Paper presented at the North American and Western European Colloquium on the Challenges Facing Higher Education, Glion, Switzerland. Copyright © by James E. Duderstadt, Prof. Emeritus, University of Michigan.

shook up the academy when, during an interview in *Forbes*, he speculated: "Thirty years from now the big university campuses will be relics. Universities won't survive. It's as large a change as when we first got the printed book" (Drucker, 1997). One can imagine the reactions still ricocheting across university campuses following Drucker's conjecture. It was fascinating to track the conversations among the University of Michigan deans on electronic mail. Some responded by blasting Drucker, always a dangerous thing to do. Others believed it to be moot. A few surmised that perhaps a former president of the University of Michigan might agree with Drucker. (He doesn't, incidentally.)

So what kind of future do our universities face? A season of light or a season of darkness? A spring of hope or a winter of despair? More to the point, and again in a Dickensian spirit, is higher education facing yet another period of evolution? Or will the dramatic nature and compressed time scales characterizing the changes of our time trigger a process more akin to revolution?

To be sure, most colleges and universities are responding to the challenges and opportunities presented by a changing world. They are evolving to serve a new age. But most are evolving within the traditional paradigm, according to the time-honored processes of considered reflection and consensus that have long characterized the academy. Is such glacial change responsive enough to allow the university to control its own destiny? Or will a tidal wave of societal forces sweep over the academy, transforming the university in unforeseen and unacceptable ways while creating new institutional forms to challenge both our experience and our concept of the university? Returning again to Dickens, this could be a time when revolution is in the air!

In this chapter, we will discuss two sharply contrasting futures for higher education in America. The first is a rather dark, market-driven future in which strong market forces trigger a major restructuring of the higher education enterprise. Although traditional colleges and universities play a role in this future, they are both threatened and reshaped by aggressive for-profit entities and commercial forces that drive the system toward the mediocrity that has characterized other mass-media markets such as television and journalism.

A contrasting and far brighter future is provided by a vision for higher education as a pervasive culture of learning in which universal or ubiquitous educational opportunities are provided to meet the broad and growing learning needs of our society. Using a mix of old and new forms, learners are offered a rich array of high-quality, affordable learning opportunities throughout their lives. Our traditional institutional forms, including both the liberal arts college and the research university, continue to play key roles, albeit with some necessary evolution and adaptation.

Although market forces are far more powerful than my faculty colleagues are willing to accept, we remain convinced that it is possible to determine which of these or other paths will be taken by higher education in America. Key in this effort is our ability as a society to view higher education as a public good that merits support through public tax dollars. In this way, we may be able to protect the public purpose of the higher education enterprise and sustain its quality, important traditions, and essential values.

If we are to do this, we must also recognize the profound nature of the rapidly changing world faced by higher education. The status quo is no longer an option. We must accept that change is inevitable and use it as a strategic opportunity to control our destiny, retaining the most important of our values and our traditions.

The Forces Driving Change

There are powerful forces driving an increasing societal demand for higher education products and services. In today's world, knowledge has become the coin of the realm, determining the wealth of nations. One's education, knowledge, and skills have become primary determinants of one's personal standard of living, the quality of one's life. We are at the dawn of an Age of Knowledge, in which intellectual capital—brainpower—is replacing financial and physical capital as the key to our strength, prosperity, and well being.

As knowledge and educated people become key strategic priorities, our societies have become more dependent upon those social institutions that create these critical resources, our colleges and universities. Yet there is growing concern about the capacity of our existing institutions to serve these changing and growing social needs—indeed, even about their ability to survive in the face of the extraordinary changes occurring in our world.

The forces of change of most direct concern to higher education can be grouped into three areas: i) financial imperatives, ii) changing social needs, and iii) technology drivers.

Financial Imperatives

Since the late 1970s, higher education in America has been caught in a financial vise (Dionne & Kean, 1997). On the one hand, the magnitude of the services demanded of our colleges and universities has greatly increased. Enrollments have grown steadily, while the growing educational needs of adult learners are compensating for the temporary dip in the number of high school graduates associated with the post-war baby boom/bust cycle. University research, graduate education, and professional service have all grown in response to societal demand. Yet the costs of providing education, research, and service have grown even faster, since these university activities depend upon a highly skilled, professional workforce (faculty and staff), require expensive new facilities and equipment, and are driven by an ever-expanding knowledge base.

While the demand for educational services has grown and the operating costs to provide these services have risen, public support for higher education has flattened and then declined over the past two decades (Breneman *et al.*, 1997). The growth in state support of public higher education peaked in the 1980s and now has fallen in many states in the face of limited tax resources and the competition of other priorities such as entitlement programs and prisons. While the federal government has sustained its support of research, growth has been modest in recent years, and it is likely to decline as discretionary domestic spending comes under increasing pressure from the impact of unconstrained entitlement programs on federal budget-balancing efforts. Federal financial-aid programs have shifted increasingly from grants to loans as the predominant form of aid, reflecting a fundamental philosophical shift to the view that education is a private benefit rather than a larger public interest. While the 1997 federal budget agreement provides over $40 billion in tax incentives to college students and their parents over the next several years, much of this federal support is likely to go into new consumption rather than to enhance access to or support of higher education.

Increasing costs and declining public support have forced most institutions to increase tuition and fees. This has provided short-term relief. It has also triggered a strong public concern about the costs and availability of a college education, and it has accelerated forces to constrain tuition levels at both public and private universities (Gumport & Pusser, 1997). Colleges and universities are looking for ways to control costs and increase productivity, but most are finding that their current organization and governance make this very difficult.

The higher education enterprise in America must change dramatically if it is to restore a balance between the costs and availability of educational services needed by our society and the resources available to support these services. The current paradigms for conducting, distributing, and financing higher education may be inadequate to adapt to the demands and realities of our times.

Societal Needs

The needs of our society for the services provided by our colleges and universities will continue to grow. Significant expansion is needed for the 30 percent growth in the number of traditional college-age students over the next decade. In addition, there will be an increasing number of adult learners in the workplace seeking the college-level education and skills necessary for their careers.

We are beginning to see a shift in demand from the current style of "just-in-case" education in which we expect students to complete degree programs at the undergraduate or professional level long before they actually need the knowledge, to "just-in-time" education through non-degree programs when a person needs it, to "just-for-you" education in which educational programs are carefully tailored to meet the specific lifelong learning requirements of particular students. The university will face the challenge of responding to other transitions: from passive students to active learners, from faculty-centered to learner-centered institutions, from teaching to the design and management of learning experiences, and from students to lifelong members of a learning community.

The situation is even more challenging at the global level, with over half of the world's population under the age of twenty. In most of the world, higher education is mired in a crisis of access, cost, and flexibility. Sir John Daniels, Chancellor of the Open University of the United Kingdom, observes that although the United States has the world's strongest university system, the American paradigm seems ill-suited to meeting global education needs (Daniel, 1996). Our colleges and universities continue to be focused on high-cost, residential education and to the outmoded idea that quality in education is linked to exclusivity of access and extravagance of resources.

Technology Drivers

As knowledge-driven organizations, it is not surprising that colleges and universities should be greatly affected by the rapid advances in information technology—computers, telecommunications, networks. In the past several decades, computers have evolved into powerful information systems with high-speed connectivity to other systems throughout the world. Public and private networks permit voice, image, and data to be made instantaneously available around the world to wide audiences at low costs. The creation of virtual environments where human senses are exposed to artificially created sights, sounds, and feelings liberate us from restrictions set by the physical forces of the world in which we live. Close, empathic, multi-party relationships mediated by visual and aural digital communications systems encourage the formation of closely bonded, widely dispersed communities of people interested in sharing new experiences and intellectual pursuits. Rapidly evolving technologies are dramatically changing the way we collect, manipulate, transmit, and use information.

This technology has already had dramatic impact on our colleges and universities. Our administrative processes are heavily dependent upon information technology—as the current concern with the approaching date reset of

Year 2000 has made all too apparent. Research and scholarship rely heavily upon information technology, e.g., the use of computers to simulate physical phenomena, networks to link investigators in virtual laboratories or "collaboratories," and digital libraries to provide scholars with access to knowledge resources. Yet, there is an increasing sense that new technology will have its most profound impact on the educational activities of the university and how we deliver our services.

We generally think of the educational role of our institutions in terms of a classroom paradigm, that is, of a professor teaching a class of students, who in turn respond by reading assigned texts, writing papers, solving problems or performing experiments, and taking examinations. Yet, the classroom itself may soon be replaced by learning experiences enabled by emerging information technology. Indeed, such a paradigm shift may be forced upon the faculty by the students themselves.

Today's students are members of the "digital generation." They have spent their early lives surrounded by robust, visual, electronic media—*Sesame Street*, MTV, home computers, video games, cyberspace networks, MUDs, MOOs, and virtual reality. Unlike those of us who were raised in an era of passive, broadcast media such as radio and television, they expect, indeed demand, interaction. They approach learning as a "plug-and-play" experience, unaccustomed and unwilling to learn sequentially—to read the manual—and inclined to plunge in and learn through participation and experimentation. While this type of learning is far different from the sequential, pyramid approach of the traditional university curriculum, it may be far more effective for this generation, particularly when provided through a media-rich environment.

Faculty of the 21st Century may be asked to adopt a new role as designers of learning experiences, processes, and environments. Today's students learn primarily on their own through solitary reading, writing, and problem solving. Tomorrow's faculty may need to develop collective learning experiences in which students work together and learn together, with the faculty member acting as a consultant or a coach. Faculty members will be less concerned with identifying and then transmitting intellectual content and more focused on inspiring, motivating, and managing an active learning environment for students. This will require a major change in graduate education, since few of today's faculty members have learned these skills.

One can easily identify similarly profound changes occurring in the other roles of the university. The process of creating new knowledge—research and scholarship—is evolving rapidly away from the solitary scholar to teams of scholars, spanning disciplines, institutions, and even national boundaries. There is increasing pressure to draw research topics directly from worldly experience rather than predominantly from the curiosity of scholars. Even the nature of knowledge creation is shifting somewhat away from the *analysis of what has been* to the *creation of what has never been*—stressing the experience of the artist rather than the analytical skills of the scientist.

Emerging information technology has removed the constraints of space and time. We can now use powerful computers and networks to deliver educational services to anyone, anyplace, anytime, no longer confined to the campus or the academic schedule. Technology is creating an open learning environment in which the student has evolved into an active learner and consumer of educational services, stimulating the growth of powerful market forces that could dramatically reshape the higher education enterprise.

Scenario #1: A Massive Restructuring of the Higher Education Industry

Universities have long enjoyed a monopoly over advanced education because of geographical constraints and their control of certification through the awarding of degrees. In the current paradigm, our colleges and universities are faculty-centered. The faculty is accustomed to dictating what it wishes to teach, how it will teach, and where and when the learning will occur. This faculty-centered paradigm is sustained by accrediting associations, professional societies, and state and federal governments.

This carefully regulated and controlled enterprise could be eroded by several factors. First, the growing demand for advanced education and training simply cannot be met by such a carefully rationed and controlled paradigm. Second, current cost structures for higher education are simply incapable of responding to the needs for high quality yet affordable education. Third, information technology is releasing higher education from the constraints of space and time (and possibly also reality). And fourth, all of these forces are driving us toward an open learning environment, in which the student will evolve into an active learner and empowered consumer, unleashing strong market forces.

Tomorrow's student will have access to a vast array of learning opportunities, far beyond the faculty-centered institutions characterizing higher education today. Some will provide formal credentials, others simply will provide knowledge, still others will be available whenever the student—more precisely, the learner—needs the knowledge. The evolution toward such a learner-centered educational environment is both evident and irresistible.

As a result, higher education is likely to evolve from a loosely federated system of colleges and universities serving traditional students from local communities into, in effect, a global knowledge and learning industry. With the emergence of new competitive forces and the weakening influence of traditional constraints, higher education is evolving like other "deregulated" industries, e.g., health care or communications or energy. These other industries have been restructured as government regulation has weakened. In contrast, the global knowledge-learning industry will be unleashed by emerging information technology that frees education from the constraints of space, time, and its credentialling monopoly.

Many in the academy would undoubtedly view with derision or alarm the depiction of the higher education enterprise as an "industry" or "business" operating in a highly competitive, increasingly deregulated, global marketplace. This is nevertheless a significant perspective that will require a new paradigm for how we think about postsecondary education. As our society becomes ever more dependent upon new knowledge and educated people, this global knowledge business must be viewed as one of the most active growth industries of our times. It is clear that no one, no government, no corporation, will be in control of the higher-education industry. It will respond to forces of the marketplace.

Will this restructuring of the higher education enterprise really happen? If you doubt it, just consider the health care industry. While Washington debated federal programs to control health care costs and procrastinated taking action, the marketplace took over with new paradigms such as managed care and for-profit health centers. In less than a decade the health care industry was totally changed. Higher education is a $180 billion a year enterprise. It will almost certainly be "corporatized" as was health care. By whom? By state or federal government? Not likely. By traditional institutions such as colleges and universities working through statewide systems or national alliances? Also unlikely. Or by the marketplace itself, as it did in health care, spawning new players such as virtual universities and for-profit educational organizations? Perhaps.

Several months ago, a leading information services company visited with my institution to share with us their perspective on the emerging higher education marketplace. They believe the size of the higher education enterprise in the United States during the next decade could be as large as $300 billion per year with 30 million students, roughly half comprised of today's traditional students and half of adult learners in the workplace. (Incidentally, they also put the size of the world market at $3 trillion.) Their operational model of the brave, new world of market-driven higher education suggests that this emerging domestic market for educational services could be served by a radically restructured enterprise consisting of 50,000 faculty "content providers," 200,000 faculty learning "facilitators," and 1,000 faculty "celebrities" who would be the stars in commodity learning-ware products. The learner would be linked to these faculty resources by an array of for-profit service companies, handling the production and packaging of learning-ware, the distribution and delivery of these services to learners, and the assessment and certification of learning outcomes. Quite a contrast with the current enterprise!

Unbundling

The modern university has evolved into a monolithic institution controlling all aspects of learning. Universities provide courses at the undergraduate, graduate, and professional level; they support residential colleges, professional schools, lifelong learning, athletics, libraries, museums, and entertainment. They have assumed responsibility for all manner of activities beyond education—housing and feeding students, providing police and other security protection, counseling and financial services . . . even maintaining power plants on many of our campuses!

Today comprehensive universities—at least as full-service organizations—are at considerable risk. One significant impact of a restructured higher education "industry" may be to break apart this monolith, much as other industries have been broken apart through deregulation. As universities are forced to evolve from faculty-centered to learner-centered, they may well find it necessary to unbundle their many functions, ranging from admissions and counseling to instruction and certification. We are already beginning to see the growth of differentiated competitors for many of these activities. Universities are under increasing pressure to spin off or sell off or close down parts of their traditional operations in the face of this new competition. Many of our other activities, e.g., financial management and facilities management, are activities that might be outsourced to specialists. Universities, like other institutions in our society, will have to come to terms with what their true strengths are and how those strengths support their strategies—and then be willing to outsource needed capabilities in areas where they do not have a unique competitive advantage.

The Emergence of a Commodity Market

Throughout most of its history, higher education has been a cottage industry. Individual courses are a handicraft, made-to-order product. Faculty members design from scratch the courses they teach, whether they be for a dozen or several hundred students. They may use standard textbooks from time to time—although most do not—but their organization, their lectures, their assignments, and their exams are developed for the particular course at the particular time it is taught. Our ability to introduce new, more effective avenues for learning—not merely new media in which to convey information—will change all that.

The individual handicraft model for course development may give way to a much more complex method of creating instructional materials. Even the standard packaging of an undergraduate education into "courses," required in the past by the need to have all the students in the same place at the same time, may no longer be necessary with new forms of asynchronous learning. Of course, it will be a challenge to break the handicraft model while still protecting the traditional independence of the faculty to determine curricular content. In this long-standing culture the faculty believes they own the intellectual content of their courses and are free to market these to others for personal gain, e.g., through textbooks or off-campus consulting services. Universities may have to restructure these paradigms and renegotiate ownership of the intellectual products represented by classroom courses if they are to constrain costs and respond to the needs of society.

As distributed virtual environments become more common, the classroom experience itself may become a true commodity product, provided to anyone, anywhere, at any time—for a price. If students could actually obtain the classroom experience provided by some of the most renowned teachers in the world, why would they want to take classes from the local professor—or the local teaching assistant? In such a commodity market, the role of the faculty member would change substantially. Rather than developing content and transmitting it in a classroom environment, a faculty member might instead manage a learning process in which students use an educational commodity, e.g., the Microsoft Virtual "Life on Earth" course starring Stephen I. Gould. This would require a shift from the skills of intellectual analysis and classroom presentation to those of motivation, consultation, and inspiration. Welcome back, Mr. Chips!

Mergers, Acquisitions, and Hostile Takeovers

Looking at the future of higher education as a deregulated industry has several other implications. There are over 3,600 four-year colleges and universities in the United States, characterized by a tremendous diversity in size, mission, constituencies, and funding sources. Not only are we likely to see the appearance of new educational entities in the years ahead as in other deregulated industries, but some colleges and universities will disappear. Others could merge. Some might actually acquire other institutions. One might even imagine a Darwinian process emerging with some institutions devouring their competitors in "hostile takeovers." All such events have occurred in deregulated industries in the past, and all are possible in the future we envision for higher education.

The market forces unleashed by technology and driven by increasing demand for higher education are very powerful. If they are allowed to dominate and reshape the higher education enterprise, we could well find ourselves losing some of our most important values and traditions of the university. While the commercial, convenience-store model of the University of Phoenix may be an effective way to meet the workplace skill needs of some adults, it certainly is not a model that would be suitable for many of the higher purposes of the university. As we assess these emerging market-driven learning structures, we must bear in mind the importance of preserving the ability of the university to serve broader public purposes.

The waves of market pressures on our colleges and universities are building, driven by the realities of our times: the growing correlation between education and quality of life, the strategic role of knowledge in determining the prosperity and security of nations, the inability of traditional higher education institutions to monopolize an open-learning marketplace characterized by active student-learner-consumers and rapidly evolving technology. Driven by an entrepreneurial culture, both within our institutions and across American society, the early phases of the restructuring of the higher education enterprise are beginning to occur.

We need a broader recognition of the growing learning needs of our society, an exploration of more radical learning paradigms, and an overarching national strategy that acknowledges the public purpose of higher education and the important values of the academy. Without these, higher education may be driven down roads that would indeed lead to a winter of despair. Many of the pressures on our public universities are similar to those which have contributed so heavily to the current plight of

K-12 education in America. Furthermore, our experience with market-driven, media-based enterprises has not been reassuring. The broadcasting and publicating industries suggest that commercial concerns can lead to mediocrity, an intellectual wasteland in which the least common denominator of quality dominates.

Scenario #2: A Culture of Learning

But there is also a spring of hope in our future. It is based on our inevitable and accelerating dependence upon knowledge and learning. We are beginning to realize that, just as our society historically accepted the responsibility for providing needed services such as military security, health care, and transportation infrastructure in the past, today education has become a driving social need and societal responsibility. It has become the responsibility of democratic societies to provide their citizens with the education and training they need throughout their lives, whenever, wherever, and however they desire it, at high quality and at an affordable cost.

Of course, in one sense this is just a continuation of one of the great themes of higher education in America. Each evolutionary step of higher education has aimed at educating a broader segment of society, at creating new educational forms to do that—private colleges, the public universities, the land-grant universities, the normal and technical colleges, the community colleges. But today, we must do even more.

The dominant form of higher education in America today, the research university, was shaped by a social contract during the last fifty years in which national security was regarded as America's most compelling priority, as reflected in massive investments in campus-based research and technology. Today, in the wake of the Cold War and at the dawn of the age of knowledge, one could well make the argument that education itself will replace national defense as the priority for the 21st Century. This could be the new social contract that will determine the character of our educational institutions, just as the government-university research partnership did in the latter half of the 20th Century. A social contract based on devel-

oping and maintaining the abilities and talents of our people to their fullest extent could well transform our schools, colleges, and universities into new forms which would rival the research university in importance.

So what might we expect over the longer term for the future of the university? It would be impractical and foolhardy to suggest one particular model for the university of the 21st Century. The great and ever-increasing diversity characterizing higher education in America makes it clear that there will be many forms, many types of institutions serving our society. But there are a number of themes which will almost certainly factor into at least some part of the higher education enterprise.

- *Learner-centered:* Just as other social institutions, our universities must become more focused on those we serve. We must transform ourselves from faculty-centered to learner-centered institutions.

- *Affordable:* Society will demand that we become far more affordable, providing educational opportunities within the reach of all citizens. Whether this occurs through greater public subsidy or dramatic restructuring of our institutions, it seems increasingly clear that our society—not to mention the world—will no longer tolerate the high-cost, low productivity model that characterizes much of higher education in America today.

- *Lifelong Learning:* In an age of knowledge, the need for advanced education and skills will require both a willingness to continue to learn throughout life and a commitment on the part of our institutions to provide opportunities for lifelong learning. The concept of student and alumnus will merge. Our highly partitioned system of education will blend increasingly into a seamless web, in which primary and secondary education; undergraduate, graduate, and professional education; apprentice and internships; on-the-job training and continuing education; and lifelong enrichment become a continuum.

- *Interactive and Collaborative:* We already see new forms of pedagogy: asynchronous (anytime, anyplace) learning utilizing information technology to break the constraints of time and space to make learning opportunities more compatible with lifestyles and career needs; and interactive and collaborative learning appropriate for the digital age and the plug-and-play generation.

- *Diverse:* Finally, the great diversity characterizing higher education in America will continue, as it must to serve an increasingly diverse population with diverse needs and goals.

We will need a new paradigm for delivering education to even broader segments of our society, perhaps beyond our society and to learners around the planet, in convenient, high quality forms, at a cost all can afford. It has become clear that most people, in most areas, can learn and learn well using asynchronous learning—"anytime, anyplace, anyone" education. Lifetime education is rapidly becoming a reality, making learning available for anyone who wants to learn, at the time and place of their choice. With advances in modern information technology, the barriers in the educational system are no longer cost or technological capacity but rather perception and habit.

But this may not be aiming enough. Perhaps we should instead consider a future of "ubiquitous learning"—learning for everyone, every place, all the time. Indeed, in a world driven by an ever-expanding knowledge base, continuous learning, like continuous improvement, has become a necessity of life.

Rather than "an age of knowledge," we could instead aspire to a "culture of learning," in which people are continually surrounded by, immersed in, and absorbed in learning experiences. Information technology has now provided us with a means to create learning environments throughout life. These environments not only transcend the constraints of space and time, but they, like us, are capable of learning and evolving to serve our changing educational needs. Higher education must define its relationship with these emerging possibilities in order to create a compelling vision for its future as it enters the next millennium.

Evolution or Revolution?

Despite all evidence to the contrary, many within the academy still believe that change will occur only at the margins of higher education. They see the waves of change lapping on the beach as just the tide coming in, as it has so often before. They stress the role of the university in stabilizing society during periods of change rather than leading those changes. This too shall pass, they suggest, if we demand that the university hold fast to its traditional roles and character. And they will do everything within their power to prevent change from occurring.

Yet, history suggests that the university must change and adapt in part to preserve these traditional roles. Many others, both within and outside the academy, believe that significant change will occur throughout the higher education enterprise, in each and every one of our institutions. Yet even these people see change as an evolutionary, incremental, long-term process, compatible with the values, cultures, and structure of the contemporary university.

There are a few voices, however, primarily outside the academy, who believe that both the dramatic nature and compressed time scale characterizing the changes of our times will drive not evolution but revolution. They have serious doubts about whether the challenges of our times will allow such gradual change and adaptation. They point out that there are really no precedents to follow. Some suggest that long before reform of the educational system comes to any conclusion, the system itself will collapse (Perelman, 1996).

As one of my colleagues put it, while there is certainly a good deal of exaggeration and hype about the changes in higher education for the short term—meaning five years or less—it is difficult to stress too strongly the profound nature of the changes likely to occur in most of our institutions and in our enterprise over the longer term—a decade and beyond. The forces driving change are simply too powerful.

Some colleges and universities may be able to maintain their current form and market niche. Others will change beyond recognition. Still others will disappear entirely. New types of institutions—perhaps even entirely new social learning structures—will evolve to meet educational needs. In contrast to the last several decades, when colleges and universities have endeavored to become more similar, the years ahead will demand greater differentiation. There will be many different paths to the future.

For the past decade we have led an effort at the University of Michigan to transform ourselves, to re-invent the institution so that it better serves a rapidly changing world. We created a campus culture in which both excellence and innovation were our highest priorities. We restructured our finances so that we became, in effect, a privately supported public university. We dramatically increased the diversity of our campus community. We launched major efforts to build a modern environment for teaching and research using the powerful tools of information technology. Yet with each transformation step we took, with every project we launched, we became increasingly uneasy.

We realized that the forces driving change in our society were stronger, more profound, that we had first thought. Change was occurring far more rapidly that we had anticipated. The future was becoming less certain as the range of possibilities expanded to include more radical options.

We concluded that in a world of such dynamic change, as we faced a future of such uncertainty, the most realistic near-term approach was to explore possible futures of the university through experimentation and discovery. Rather than continue to contemplate possibilities for the future through abstract study and debate, it seemed a more productive course to build several prototypes of future learning institutions as working experiments. In this way we could actively explore possible paths to the future.

Through a major strategic effort known as the Michigan Mandate, we significantly enhanced the racial diversity of our students and faculty, providing a laboratory for exploring the themes of the "diverse university." We established campuses in Europe, Asia, and Latin America, linking them with robust information technology, to understand better the implications of becoming a "world university." We launched major initiatives such as the Media Union (a sophisticated multimedia environment), a virtual university (the Michigan Virtual University), and we played a key role in the management of the Internet to explore the

"cyberspace university" theme. We launched new cross-disciplinary programs and built new community spaces that would draw students and faculty together as a model of the "divisionless university." We placed a high priority on the visual and performing arts, integrating them with disciplines such as engineering and architecture, to better understand the challenges of the "creative university." And we launched an array of other initiatives, programs, and ventures, all designed to explore the future.

All of these efforts were driven by the grass-roots interests, abilities, and enthusiasm of faculty and students. Our approach as leaders of the institution was to encourage a "let every flower bloom" philosophy, to respond to faculty and student proposals with "Wow! That sounds great! Let's see if we can work together to make it happen! And don't worry about the risk. If you don't fail from time to time, it is because you aren't aiming high enough!!!"

To be sure, some of these experiments were costly. Some were poorly understood and harshly criticized by those defending the status quo. All ran a very high risk of failure, and some crashed in flames—albeit spectacularly. While such an exploratory approach was disconcerting to some and frustrating to others, there were many on our campus and beyond who viewed this phase as an exciting adventure. And all of these initiatives were important in understanding better the possible futures facing our university. All have had influence on the evolution of our university.

The Questions Before Us

Many questions remain unanswered. Who will be the learners served by these institutions? Who will teach them? Who will administer and govern these institutions? Who will pay for them? What will be the character of our universities? How will they function? When will they appear?

Perhaps the most profound question of all concerns the survival of the university in the face of the changes brought on by the emergence of new competitors. That is the question raised by Drucker and other futurists. Could an institution such as the university, which has existed for a millennium, disappear in the face of such changes?

Most of us, of course, believe quite strongly that the university as a social institution is simply too valuable to disappear. On the other hand, there may well be forms of the university that we would have great difficulty in recognizing from our present perspective.

Let me suggest a somewhat different set of questions in an effort to frame the key policy issues facing higher education:

1. How do we respond to the diverse educational needs of a knowledge-driven society? While the educational needs of the young will continue to be a priority, we also will be challenged to address the sophisticated learning needs of adults in the workplace while providing broader lifetime learning opportunities for all of our society.

2. Is higher education a public or a private good? The benefits of the university clearly flow to society as a whole. But it is also the case that two generations of public policy in America have stressed instead the benefits of education to the individual student as a consumer.

3. How do we balance the roles of market forces and public purpose in determining the future of higher education? Can we control market forces through public policy and public investment so that the most valuable traditions and values of the university are preserved? Or will the competitive and commercial pressures of the marketplace sweep over our institutions, leaving behind a higher education enterprise characterized by mediocrity?

4. What role should the research university play within the broader context of the changes likely to occur in the higher education enterprise? Should it be a leader in change? Or should it simply strive to protect the important traditions and values of the academy during this time of change?

An Action Agenda

So where to next? How do we grapple with the many issues and concerns swirling about higher education? Let me suggest the following agenda for consideration and debate:

1. *Determine those key roles and values* that must be protected and preserved during this period of transformation, e.g.,

   Roles: education of the young, the transmission of culture, basic research and scholarship, critic of society, etc.

   Values: academic freedom, a rational spirit of inquiry, a community of scholars, a commitment to excellence, shared governance (?), tenure (?), etc.

2. *Listen carefully to society* to learn and understand its changing needs, expectations, and perceptions of higher education, along with the forces driving change.

3. *Prepare the academy for change and competition* by removing unnecessary constraints, linking accountability with privilege, reestablishing tenure as the protection of academic freedom rather than lifetime employment security, etc. Begin the task of transforming the academy by radically restructuring graduate education as the source of the next generation of the faculty.

4. *Restructure university governance*—particularly governing boards and shared governance models—so that it responds to the changing needs of society rather than defending and perpetuating an obsolete past. Develop a tolerance for strong leadership. Shift from lay boards to corporate board models where members are selected based on their expertise and commitment and held accountable for their performance and the welfare of their institutions.

5. *Develop a new paradigm for financing higher education* by first determining the appropriate mix of public support (higher education as a public good) and private support (higher education as a personal benefit). Consider key policy issues such as:

   • The appropriate burdens borne by each generation in the support of higher education as determined, for example, by the mix of grants versus loans in federal financial aid programs.

- The degree to which public investment should be used to help shape powerful emerging market forces to protect the public purpose of higher education.
- New methods for internal resource allocation and management that enhance productivity.

6. *Encourage experimentation* with new models of learning, research, and service by harvesting the best ideas from within the academy (or elsewhere), implementing them on a sufficient scale to assess their impact, and disseminating their results. Reward success while tolerating failure.

7. *Place a far greater emphasis on building alliances* among institutions that will allow individual institutions to focus on core competencies while relying on alliances to address the broader and diverse needs of society. Alliances should be encouraged not only among institutions of higher education (partnering research universities with liberal arts colleges and community colleges) but also between higher education and the private sector. Differentiation among institutions should be encouraged, while relying upon market forces rather than regulations to discourage duplication.

Concluding Remarks

We have entered a period of significant change in higher education as our universities attempt to respond to the challenges, opportunities, and responsibilities before them. This time of great change, of shifting paradigms, provides the context in which we must consider the changing nature of the university.

Much of this change will be driven by market forces—by a limited resource base, changing societal needs, new technologies, and new competitors. But we also must remember that higher education has a public purpose and a public obligation (Roundtable, 1996). Those of us in higher education must always keep before us two questions: "Who do we serve?" and

"How can we serve better?" And society must work to shape and form the markets that will in turn reshape our institutions with appropriate civic purpose.

From this perspective, it is important to understand that the most critical challenge facing most institutions will be to develop the capacity for change. We must remove the constraints that prevent us from responding to the needs of rapidly changing societies, clear away unnecessary processes and administrative structures, and question existing premises and arrangements. Universities should strive to challenge, excite, and embolden all members of their academic communities to embark on what should be a great adventure for higher education.

While many academics are reluctant to accept the necessity or the validity of formal planning activities, woe be it to the institutions that turn aside from strategic efforts to determine their futures. The successful adaptation of universities to the revolutionary challenges they face will depend a great deal on an institution's collective ability to learn and to continuously improve its core activities. It is critical that higher education give thoughtful attention to the design of institutional processes for planning, management, and governance. Only a concerted effort to understand the important traditions of the past, the challenges of the present, and the possibilities for the future can enable institutions to thrive during a time of such change.

Those institutions that can step up to this process of change will thrive. Those that bury their heads in the sand, that rigidly defend the status quo or, even worse, some idyllic vision of a past which never existed, are at very great risk. Those institutions that are micromanaged, either from within by faculty politics or governing boards or from without by government or public opinion, stand little chance of flourishing during a time of great change.

Certainly the need for higher education will be of increasing importance in our knowledge-driven future. Certainly, too, it has become increasingly clear that our current paradigms for the university, its teaching and research, its service to society, its financing, all must change rapidly and perhaps radically. Hence the real question is not whether higher education will be transformed, but rather *how . . .* and by *whom.* If the university is capable of transforming itself to respond to the needs of a culture of learning, then what is currently perceived as the challenge of change may, in fact, become the opportunity for a renaissance in higher education in the years ahead.

Book Publications:

Breneman, D. W., Finney, J. E., & Roherty, B. M. 1997 *Shaping the Future: Higher Education Finance in the 1990s.* California Higher Education Policy Center, San Jose, California.

Daniel, J. S. 1996 *Mega-Universities and Knowledge Media.* Kogan Page, London.

Dionne, J. L. & Kean, T. 1997 Report of the Commission on National Investment in Higher Education: *The Fiscal Crisis in Higher Education.* Council for Aid to Education, New York, New York.

Gumport, P. J. & Pusser, B. 1997 Academic Restructuring: Contemporary Adaptation in Higher Education. In: Peterson M., Dill D., & Mets, L. (eds.) *1997 Planning and Management for a Changing Environment: A Handbook on Redesigning Postsecondary Institutions,* Jossey-Bass, San Francisco, California, pp. 453–478.

Journal Articles:

Drucker, Peter F. 1997 Interview: Seeing things as they really are. *Forbes Magazine* 159 122–8.

Perelman, L. 1997 Interview: Barnstorming with Lewis Perelman. *Educom Review.* 32(2): 18–26.

Pew Higher Education Roundtable & California Higher Education Policy Center Roundtable on the Public and Private Finance of Higher Education 1996 Shaping the future. *Crosstalk* 4(3): pp. 1–8.

Understanding the Competitive Environment of the Postsecondary Knowledge Industry

MARVIN W. PETERSON AND DAVID D. DILL

"Drift." "Reluctant accommodation." And "belated recognition that while no one was looking, change had in fact taken place." Using these words, Frederick Rudolph concluded his scholarly, insightful, and entertaining history of American higher education prior to 1950 (Rudolph, 1962). But the history of change in higher or postsecondary education in the past four decades has been decidedly more guided. Federal, state, and institutional initiatives have all directed attempts to expand, guide, and even control our systems and our institutions. Planning at the state and institutional levels has received particular attention as attempts to devise plans and develop planning structures, processes, and approaches have become commonplace.

While our definitions of, perspectives on, and approaches to planning have been varied, the primary focus of planning has been to examine environmental change and to develop institutional strategies for *responding* or *adapting*. Our traditional approaches to long-range and strategic planning assume that we compete in a system or industry consisting of other higher and postsecondary institutions. From this perspective, institutional planning involves understanding these broader environmental changes and how to compete more effectively with other post-secondary institutions.

As we approach the twenty-first century, this chapter argues that the nature of our postsecondary system itself is changing, that major forces in the larger societal environment are reshaping the nature of postsecondary educa-

tion, changing it to a "postsecondary knowledge system" or industry that cuts across many of our traditional notions of system boundaries. These forces portend the growth of a postsecondary knowledge industry that delivers knowledge, information, and the capacity to teach and learn in a vast and flexible knowledge network. It also involves the active participation of many different types of institutions in the development and even educational use of this network. Postsecondary institutions are challenged not only to understand the nature of this new industry but to reconsider their institutional role and mission, their academic and administrative structure, and their academic processes.

This shift from a system of postsecondary institutions to one of a postsecondary knowledge system or industry suggests the need for a new paradigm in our thinking about the external and internal context of our institutions. Externally, it suggests competing and/or collaborating with non-postsecondary institutions and firms. Internally, it suggests potentially radical changes in the academic structure, the educational process, the conduct of research, and even the meaning of academic work in our institutions—the core of our institutional culture. A new approach to planning, *contextual planning*, is suggested (and elaborated in Chapter Seven). Chapter One provides a perspective on our changing postsecondary system. We examine the challenges reshaping postsecondary education, the nature of the emerging postsecondary knowledge network or industry, its internal and external insti-

"Understanding the Competitive Environment of the Postsecondary Knowledge Industry," by Marvin W. Peterson and David D. Dill, reprinted from *Planning and Management for a Changing Environment*, edited by M. W. Peterson, D. D. Dill and L. A. Mets, 1997. Jossey-Bass Publishers, Inc.

tutional implications for planning, and a new set of planning questions that suggest the need for a new approach to planning: contextual planning.

An Expanded Planning Perspective: Society, Industry, and Institution

The literature on higher and postsecondary governance, management, and planning has long recognized our institutions as complex organizations functioning as open systems and subjected to many external societal forces and conditions. Planning is often seen as the attempt to deal with issues of the fit between institution and environment. Similarly, as a country we have prided ourself on our diverse and decentralized higher and postsecondary system; we have often viewed it as a comprehensive, loosely defined national system made up of subsets or segments of differing institutional types with somewhat more formally organized state-level governance or coordinating systems. However, we seldom focus on the nature of our higher or postsecondary education system as an industry—and the implications for institutional planning. Yet industry—as a concept that clusters similar organizations in society and differentiates them from those in other industries, is an appropriate focus—especially when the structure of the industry within

which one exists is changing rapidly. Such is the case, this chapter argues, in postsecondary education today. The concept of an *industry* provides a useful tool for examining the changing, nature of competition among colleges, universities, and other organizations.

The industry concept is implicitly understood and seldom discussed, yet of critical importance to postsecondary education. An industry is often defined as a set of competing organizations that utilize similar resources or attract similar clients, and that produce similar products and services. There are two critical features to the notion of an industry. First, it helps us define our competitive market or segment of it. Second, it is often the focus of attempts at governmental control or regulation. Clearly, we can recognize our higher or postsecondary education system as a major industry in our society.

Changing Perspectives

In understanding our current and future contexts, it is important to note that our system or industry has not been stable. This is suggested in Figure 1.

Traditional Higher Education. Prior to 1950, the higher education system or in the public and private degree-granting, four-year, comprehensive, and university institutions in the country. Two-year institutions were still few in

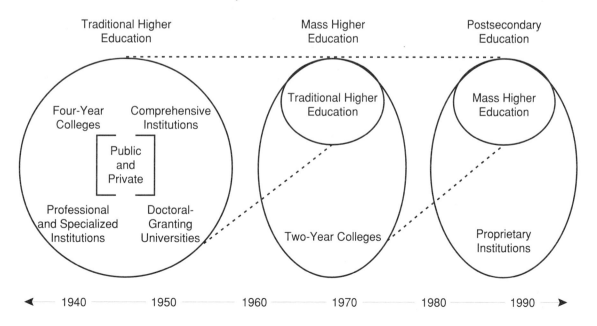

Figure 1. Redefining Our Industry.

number and not considered core competitors. Planning was not a major institutional function or activity.

Mass Higher Education. The release of the Truman Commission Report in 1948, which recommended higher education for everyone who graduated from high school (a population whose numbers were increasing rapidly), spawned the rapid expansion of community colleges from the 1950s through the mid-1970s, as well as increasing enrollments in most other types of institutions. The industry was expanded by including a broader array of students (clients) who were absorbed in the growth of existing institutions, in the rapid expansion of two-year institutions, and in the addition of many new public four-year and university institutions. Institutional planning became a focal concern as plans were developed for new institutions, and forecasting growth and resource needs gave rise to long-range planning efforts.

Postsecondary Education. The higher education amendments of 1972 redefined the system or industry in two important ways. First, they transferred federal student aid from institutions to students who could demonstrate financial need. Second, they broadened the definition of which institutions were eligible to receive students with federal aid by including nondegree-granting postsecondary institutions and proprietary institutions. The shift in government student aid policy from institutions to students and the expanded definition of which institutions could compete for students or clients who received federal funds redefined the competitive relationship and nature of the industry. The increasingly competitive market-oriented environment of the 1970s and the constrained resources of the 1980s reinforced institutional interest in planning and led to the expanded interest in strategic planning that continues into the 1990s.

These changes in the nature of our system and the structure of our industry, from traditional to mass higher education and then to postsecondary education, suggest the role of governmental action in redefining the "related organizations" in the industry and in increasing the array of "similar clients." The transitions to mass and then to postsecondary education both had the effect of expanding the industry. But it was still an industry of institutions delivering education beyond high school.

A Model of the Forces Reshaping Institutional Planning

In order to better comprehend the factors in our changing environment that will influence institutional and state-level planning in higher and postsecondary education, it is important to understand the shift from an industry composed of post-secondary educational institutions to a postsecondary knowledge system or industry. To do so it is helpful to examine both the forces that reshape an industry and the changing societal conditions that affect the industry itself (See Figure 2.) For example, the nature of competition in the postsecondary education industry will be affected by new customer or client needs for new educational services, by possible new entrants to the industry such as telecommunications companies seeking to offer degrees over the World Wide Web, and even by improvements within the industry itself. But the structure of the industry is being reshaped by larger forces: government regulation or deregulation, and the trend toward globalization of services and products.

While the planning challenges to individual institutions are clear, it is also important to examine their impact on the industry and less-direct implications for institution planning. To clarify the nature of these impacts, it is useful to examine the specific forces that govern competition in an industry. Porter (1980) has outlined a useful model for analyzing the structure of an industry (Figure 3). This schema, slightly revised to reflect education as a service industry, helps to reveal the forces that redefine the composition of an industry and reshape the competition within it. Those basic forces are (1) the threat of entry into the industry by new organizations, (2) the bargaining power of suppliers (for example, student clientele), (3) the bargaining power of customers (for example, employers, funding sources), and (4) the threat of substitute services. We have added a fifth force to Porter's model to reflect the potentially rapid changes occurring in how teaching, research, and service are being transformed by technology: (5) technical innovation in the core processes of the industry. Each of these forces in turn affects (6) the overall degree of rivalry or competition among institutions in the industry, which changes the external environment in which institutions must plan.

The model of institutional planning that emerges thus needs to reflect how changing societal conditions impact our industry as well as our postsecondary institutions directly. The institutional impacts of the societal changes affect both the internal nature of our institutions and the character of their external relationships. Thus, the planning perspectives institutions must have as we approach the twenty-first century are shaped both by the changing industry as well as the changing societal conditions.

This model guides the remaining discussion in this chapter. The next section examines changing societal conditions or challenges that are reshaping our industry and impacting our institutions. Then the nature of an emerging postsecondary knowledge industry and its institutional implications are discussed. The chapter concludes with a new set of institutional planning questions and suggests the need for a broader contextual approach to planning.

Societal Conditions and Challenges

It is beyond the scope of this chapter to deal with the infinite array of trends, issues, and possibilities that forecasters, scanners, and futurists have identified that can affect postsecondary institutions. However, many of them coalesce around a series of discrete challenges to postsecondary educational institutions. We present here six challenges that have emerged in the 1990s and that promise to continue into the new century. They are quite different in nature from the demands and challenges that reshaped our industry in its transition from traditional to higher education and then to postsecondary education. These challenges require us to revise our thinking extensively about postsecondary education, the basic nature or structure of our institutions, and the nature and meaning of academic work.

More importantly, these challenges impact postsecondary education at a time when our institutions face a common, critical condition that amounts to a seventh, overarching challenge: *constrained resources*. For example, the costs of higher education are exceeding the willingness of taxpayers, governments, parents, employers, or students to pay; there are

other societal priorities for funds; and many campuses are already financially strained. Resource-constraint issues are already so well documented that they are not discussed separately as a challenge in this chapter but rather are assumed. The following is a brief description of the six other challenges, their influence on the forces reshaping our industry, and their internal and external impacts on and implications for our institutions.

Changing Patterns of Diversity

The challenge of dealing with cultural diversity and its concomitant educational and economic deprivation is widely recognized as a social reality, a public policy issue, and an institutional reality. We have had some success in the past three decades in improving access to postsecondary education for various disadvantaged groups, but our record of successful retention and graduation is still inadequate in many fields and at the graduate level (Carter and Wilson, 1993; Mintz, 1993; Musil, 1995).

There are several lessons from our experience to date. First, the operant definition of cultural diversity is constantly changing. The initial concern for African American minorities in the 1960s has expanded to include numerous other racially underrepresented groups, and even to various subdivisions within them. Issues of gender, sexual preference, and economic or educational disadvantage have further expanded and/or fragmented the definition and focus of diversity as an issue. Second, our public policy and institutional responses have shifted: from separate-but-equal to nondiscrimination, to affirmative action, to preferences, and now to attempts to dismantle affirmative action. Third, members of most minority groups have become well organized and are gaining effective political voice both on campuses and in government.

While these lessons seem clear, so are the trends. The numbers of almost all of minority groups are increasing and will continue for the foreseeable future. Their differential rate of educational attainment or improvement is leading to conflict among disadvantaged groups. The debates about affirmative action are likely to be heated and continual. But the impacts both on our industry and in our institutions are revealing.

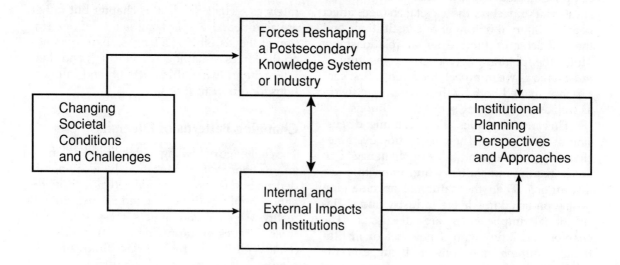

Figure 2. Influences on Institutional Planning

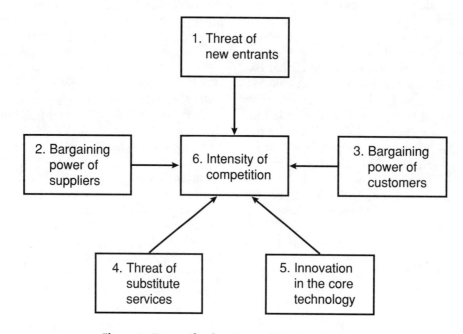

Figure 3. Forces Shaping Competition in an Industry

Source: Adapted from Porter, 1980.

At the *industry level* (Table 1), potential customers for postsecondary learning opportunities—both the number of individuals and the categories defined as educationally disadvantaged—continue to grow. As a client group influencing public policy, the increasing presence of minority political caucus groups at the institutional, state, and national levels makes them a more powerful force. Although there have been few new institutions of postsecondary education founded as minority institutions in recent decades (except those for American Indians), the number of institutions becoming de facto minority institutions is increasing rapidly: approximately one in five postsecondary institutions has an enrollment in which ethnic minority students exceed 50 percent. Several new minority-oriented professional associations have been founded to serve these institutions and groups and to represent their interests. Within postsecondary institutions, the increase of minority-oriented academic and support programs has often been seen as adding substitute services. Although not directly affecting the core technology of postsecondary education, the advent of minority programs, new faculty staffing patterns, new student interaction patterns, and new academic perspectives and research agendas have influenced the processes of teaching and research in significant ways. Clearly, pressure to enhance diversity has created intensive competition for scarce resources, among students seeking limited financial support and admission slots, and among institutions to attract increased numbers of more diverse students, faculty, and staff.

The *impacts on institutions* largely reflect the changes impacting the industry (Table 2). Externally, governmental and political issues reflect the growing number and influence of minority political groups that demand attention. Competition both from minority and nonminority institutions for minority students, faculty, and funds is now a reality. The lessons within our institutions are even more telling. Dealing with issues of racism, discrimination, and pluralism requires addressing not only student conduct and classroom behavior but also issues of course, program, and discipline content, of research agendas, and of faculty behavior and staffing.

Regardless of its definition, diversity is clearly a condition and challenge that will not abate soon. Indeed, the new debates about affirmative action force us to take a hard look at dealing with and responding to issues of educational disadvantage versus social, cultural, or economic disadvantage, and whether it is to be addressed as a group problem, an individual issue, or both. Diversity is an issue that is reshaping our industry and affecting its institutions. In addressing it, we need to be aware of how it is changing the nature of this postsecondary industry, the external political realities of our institutions, and the internal influences on curriculum, teaching, research, and tension over our "political ambivalence"' (Smelser, 1993) about the concept itself

The Telematics Revolution: Reinventing or Supplementing the Core Technology

Probably the most pervasive challenge to our industry and institutions is the rapid expansion and influx of interactive telecommunications networks, which link students and faculty to extensive data resources via workstations and computers capable of integrating information, sound, and video images. Whether it will lead to a sweeping reinvention of how students and faculty teach, learn, and conduct scholarship or whether it is merely a technical substitute is the source of heated debate on most campuses. There are several unique features about the current revolution: (1) its rapid development and rate of change, (2) the extent to which applications are being adopted in all areas of modern life beyond the campus, (3) its spread to national—even global—availability in a short time span, (4) its potential for use with few constraints of time and location, and (5) the increased affordability of ever more powerful technology. These features make it imperative that institutions adopt it as a tool of postsecondary education. But the capacity for use of telematics as a technology for learning (not just a teaching or communication technology) is perhaps the most critical challenge facing postsecondary institutions. The irony and difficulty is that this technology, which was spawned in universities, has taken on a life of its own. With so many societal as well as educational applications and implications, it has created its own in-

Table 1. Challenges and Forces Reshaping the Postsecondary Industry

Changing Societal Conditions or Challenges	Forces Reshaping an Industry					
	Bargaining Power of Customers	Bargaining Power of Suppliers	Threat of New Organization Entrants	Threat of Substitute Services	Innovation in Core Technology	Intensity of Competition
Patterns of Diversity	More defined groups; increasing numbers	Stronger and more numerous political groups	Minority institutions and associations	New programs and services	New academic and research perspectives	Among students and among institutions
Telematics Revolution	More access and numbers; individualized needs	Telematics firms control key educational resources	Telecommunications computing, and information firms	Training firms and merger of entertainment and telecommunications	New interactive, individualized T/L/R potential	New cross-industry competition
Quality Reform	Increased focus on learner needs	Increased attention to client demands	—	Minor new training options	New mode of management; limited use by academics	Improvements in efficiency and effectiveness
Economic Productivity	Increased career oriented pressure	Government and industry needs	New role or inter-organizational patterns	Many new groups and government agencies	May redirect teaching and research	New regional, state, or national
Postsecondary Relearning	New groups of post-secondary learners	Employer-based funding sources	Many new forms emerging	Corporate and governmental education programs	Emphasis on personalized content and delivery	Ill-defined market; potential of many sources
Globalization of Scholarship	Not clearly defined; highly specialized	Potentially, nations and institutions	Currently informal or limited arrangements	Emergent use of technology	Traditional or new technology	Yet to be determined

Table 2. External and Internal Institutional Impact of Changing Conditions

Changing Conditions and Challenges	Institutional Impacts	
	Internal	External
Changing Patterns of Diversity	Pluralism, curricular content, research perspectives, faculty role	Rise of minority political power groups, institutions, and associations
Telematics Revolution: Telecommunications, Computing, and Information Resource Firms	Teaching/research, delivery modes, new faculty and student roles	Cross-industry links: educational information, telecommunications and entertainment firms
Academic and Institutional Quality	Academic outcomes, value added and assessment; culture of academic quality improvements	Business-government collaboration; tide of TQM/CQI
Improving Societal Economic Productivity	Resource partner, or leadership role; new managerial and academic priorities	Business government, and higher education collaboration
Postsecondary Relearning markets	Client-driven modular content, external delivery, faculty role	Growing adult and professional postsecondary market; academic collaboration and new competitors
Globalization of Scholarship and Education	Interdisciplinary and transnational colleagues, problems, and research paradigms	Multidisciplinary cross-industry and transnational research groups; Multinational institutions

dustry as new computer hardware and software, telecommunications, and information-handling products and techniques are developed. The impacts on our postsecondary industry and our institutions will be extensive, and perhaps central, in the next decade (Green and Gilbert, 1995; Twigg, 1994; see also Chapter Twenty-Two, which provides a focused treatment of this challenge).

At the *industry level* (Table 1), this revolution has a vast potential for increasing the options for accessing electronic learning opportunities, for reaching a significant array of new customers (students or scholars), and for extending an institution's teaching potential. On the other hand, it has in many instances reversed the client relationship of postsecondary institutions with the telematics, firms. Rather than those firms being the client seeking an institution's research results or trained students, they have become both the creator and

supplier of information-handling tools, which makes the postsecondary institution the client—effectively reversing roles and making postsecondary institutions increasingly dependent on their former clients. An even bigger threat is the potential for new non-postsecondary institutions to enter the postsecondary educational arena. A small number of institutions offering postsecondary education via interactive telecommunications have emerged, and others are beginning to experiment with this mode. Large companies are adopting these technologies for their own internal postsecondary training programs. Of greater possible significance is the merger of entertainment and telecommunication firms, further enhancing the potential of the packaging and delivery of postsecondary knowledge. (Will they make education entertaining, or entertainment more educational?)

Clearly, what makes this change so revolutionary is that it constitutes an alteration of the core technology of teaching, learning, and research. Colleges and universities cannot afford *not* to utilize it. But the critical issue for faculty is whether that will be as a substitute service for some portions of their teaching and scholarly activities, or an adoption of it as a more central mode.

One of the things that make this technological revolution so critical is the extent to which it interacts with all the other societal challenges. It enhances the capacity to reach both new and current student-customers differently. It also influences the way academics work and students learn. This technology is just beginning to reshape the way postsecondary institutions compete with each other for students and compete or cooperate with firms in other industries (telematics, entertainment, training) to deliver their educational products. New patterns of competition and cooperation in delivering educational services with firms that were not part of our postsecondary industry are emerging as they and we become part of a postsecondary knowledge industry.

At the *institutional level* (Table 2), the implications are also extensive. Externally, universities will either find themselves collaborating with public and private educational corporations, telecommunications companies, and information-based firms and even entertainment enterprises in designing educational and knowledge-delivery systems, or competing with them. Already, researchers have the capacity to collaborate with scholars around the globe; they will increasingly do so.

Within the institution, students have access to extensive content material, educational resources, and other students and faculty without constraints of time or location. Such an educational network suggests a very different teaching-learning process. In addition to their traditional role, faculty may serve as learning facilitators, network guides, or learning-resource designers. The nature of the faculty role, the student-faculty relationship, and the course or classroom may change as the campus becomes part of a teaching-learning network.

While the investment in hardware and software for wide-scale use will strain the budgets of all institutions, its influence on faculty and the processes of teaching and research constitutes a major internal challenge to redefine the nature of academic work within the academy. The major external challenge is to develop new interinstitutional ties with various telematics firms.

Academic and Institutional Quality: A Focus on Learning and Improvement

Thus far in the 1990s, the demand for educational quality has already become pervasive (Ewell, 1991). The meaning of academic quality, however, has changed in recent decades. In the 1960s and 1970s, academic quality was associated with the level and nature of institutional resources. In the 1980s, a new meaning evolved: assessment, with a focus on assessing results (outcomes, goal achievement, value-added). In the mid-1990s, academic quality has become associated with public accountability and a focus on student learning, faculty productivity and performance, program effectiveness, and even institutional evaluation. The debate about the definition of, criteria for, and means of improving educational quality shows no signs of diminishing and will be a continuing challenge both in government policy circles and in academic and institutional discussions (Dill, 1995a).

A more recent focus on quality is the concern for Total Quality Management (TQM or Continuous Quality Improvement (CQI) (Dill, 1992). While those ideas emerged in the private sector and have had the support of political leaders, the primary emphasis and application in postsecondary education to date has been in administrative activities and functions. Unlike the more educationally focused notions of quality, this approach suggests a comprehensive emphasis on developing an institutional culture that stresses policies and practices promoting (1) an environment of continuous improvement, (2) customer- or client-centeredness, (3) a rational approach to decision making using intensive measurement and benchmarking, (4) a focus on process design, (5) collaboration and teamwork, and (6) individual empowerment. Such a comprehensive approach promises to clash with strong traditions of academic individualism when applied to academic areas. But if this perspective can be successfully adapted to academic settings, it may also lead to rethinking our teaching learning, and research processes and how we utilize the new technology for educational purposes. The fact that the Baldrige Award was recently extended in 1995 to postsecondary education suggests that TQM/CQI will have a continued emphasis in academic as well as administrative areas. (Chapter Twenty-Five addresses the concerns of planning for quality in greater detail.)

To date, the quality challenge has not had an extensive impact on our *postsecondary industry*, but it may increase as competition within the industry increases (Table 1). The quality challenge does force an institution to refocus on defining and differentiating its stakeholders (customers with needs and clients making demands) and designing its services (academic or administrative) with them in mind rather than with disciplinary, professional, or faculty concerns being primary. This particular challenge has not yet prompted new organizations to enter postsecondary education except in the narrow area of TQM/CQI training programs. Quality or continuous-improvement approaches initially seemed to represent a new mode of management rather than a revision of core academic technology or provision of a substitute service. However, as competition requires postsecondary institutions to attend more to cost and productivity, quality approaches may become associated with reengineering (a focus on process), downsizing, and/or prioritizing of services. As such, they are more a response to resource constraint designed to enhance institutional competitiveness than a force changing the competitiveness in the industry.

At the *institutional level* (Table 2), the major external dynamics suggest that as the public image of postsecondary education continues to decline, the emphasis both on educational quality and TQM/CQI will likely increase. Internally, the varying approaches to assessment, reinforced by accreditation and political pressures, are increasingly used for collegial accountability, redesign, or improvement (Romer, 1995). The advent of the Baldrige Award for education will no doubt also reinforce the use of TQM and CQI in administrative arenas. Whether concerns for educational quality and assessment can effectively merge with total-quality and continuous-improvement approaches will be a major management and planning challenge for the future.

Improving Economic Productivity: New Emphasis or New Function?

The contribution of postsecondary education to economic development has been the primary drive for the rapid and continuous expansion of postsecondary education (Leslie and Brinkman, 1988). Colleges and universities produced well-trained students, provided appropriate professional programs, and conducted pure and applied research that contributed to society's well-being and improvements in the standard of living. But the decline of US. economic fortunes, and particularly the loss of dominance in key manufacturing industries in the global marketplace, has led to a new emphasis on enhancing economic productivity both at the national and state levels.

In the development of federal government priorities and state-level plans for economic development, it has been implicitly assumed that higher education, government, and the private business community are all key players. Postsecondary institutions have historically played, and been satisfied with playing, a "knowledge development" function, serving as primary providers of academic and professional training and of pure and applied research. In recent decades, serving as consultants and as sites for campus research parks, they have participated more directly in the "technology transfer" function. A more recent and aggressive form of this function is reflected in the growth of campus-affiliated incubator parks for new-product and new-company development. Most recently, postsecondary institutions have participated in developing "state or regional economic development strategies" (Dill, 1995b). In all of these roles, their participation can vary from resource institution to partner, or to manager of the function (Peterson, 1995). Increasingly, institutions are pressured to take on all three roles and to become a leader of the effort. The difficulty is that becoming a manager of technology transfer or economic development may involve an institution in an activity for which it is not well suited and one in which it may not be able to succeed (Feller, 1990). Yet political and economic pressures to show greater institutional accountability for and contribution to this area is likely to increase as long as our economy falters or fails to meet political expectations or promises. (See Chapter Twenty-Two for an extended examination of this challenge.)

At the *industry level* (see Table 1), this challenge has little direct effect on our primary customers (students), but it is probably reflected in their career-oriented priorities and concerns about useful programs. However, it does subject the industry to increasing demands from its primary clients (government and industry), especially in the public sector. The expansion of concern for economic productivity also introduces new entrants into postsecondary education—public and private technology development organizations—that may be better positioned than postsecondary institutions themselves are to compete for public applied research and development funds, and better staffed to carry out such activities. It may also require institutions to subsidize risky economic development activities with other funds traditionally used for academic functions (Feller, 1990). In effect, a new mode of organization is created (the economic development agency or the technology transfer partnership) to provide a new service. In order to compete in this emerging service activity, institutions may be pressed to redirect effort away from some of the traditional postsecondary emphasis on teaching and research to supply the knowledge and trained students for economic development to active organizers of economic development activity. In most instances, this pressure for economic development involves postsecondary education directly in a new realm of competition: interregional, interstate, or even international, an arena in which it was previously only indirectly engaged.

At the *institutional level* (see Table 2), the press for economic development involves the institution in potentially different types of partnerships that cut across industry boundaries in order to engage in complex public-private corporate arrangements and to develop a new or previously peripheral function. These may be collaborative arrangements, or they may subject the institutions to new governmental controls and regulations. Internally, extensive involvement in economic development activity may require new managerial roles and approaches to engage in more entrepreneurial (for example, technology transfer) or political development activity. It may also realign faculty effort or require hiring of faculty more skilled in these less scholarly or academic realms (Fairweather, 1996).

Postsecondary Relearning: New Markets, Modes, and Models of Continuing Education

In recent decades, expanded educational services have been directed toward increasing traditional student enrollments and increasing service to underrepresented groups: minorities, women, older students. Modifications in schedules (evenings, weekends) or locale (off campus) were used to deliver traditional courses or programs to the part-time, nontraditional student. Continuing education was often an ancillary function, or primarily related to professional and occupational programs. Yet in today's increasingly competitive and technologically turbulent world, products, companies, and careers can change rapidly. The need for technological retooling and postsecondary reeducation is increasing in a wide variety of professions (Reich, 1991).

The demand for postsecondary relearning by older individuals is an exploding market. It comprises three identifiable groups. One is the post-high school but pre-baccalaureate group who need further education to reenter the job market or remain viably employed. One study (Grubb, forthcoming) suggests there are 20–30 million individuals between twenty-five and fifty years of age in this category. A second is the postbaccalaureate group who have college degrees but may need further education (but less than a full graduate degree) to remain viably employed or to change fields. While not as large as the previous group, it is rapidly growing as the proportion of degree holders continues to grow. Finally, there are the graduate and professional degree holders who need more than traditional continuing education to advance or change fields. In addition to their size and growth, these three market segments have much in common. Their educational interests and/or those of their employers often focus on professional competencies, individual educational needs, learning modules, off-campus delivery, and willingness to use distance-education modes of transmission (including technology) rather than on traditional courses, degrees, or programs.

At the *industry level* (see Table 1), these numbers suggest three substantial groups of potential customers for postsecondary reeducation. While some may pay for their own education, there is a sizable set of employer organizations that may be potential clients for such educational services for their employers. This market is currently served by internal corporate educational units, specialized training and development firms, and numerous postsecondary institutions, although often in traditional courses, programs, and delivery modes. (Eurich, 1985). It is a market with significant potential for new industry entrants and in which postsecondary institutions are expanding. But this market is still somewhat amorphous, with patterns of competition that are not well defined, especially by traditional postsecondary institutions.

At the *institutional level* (see Table 2), this is a substantial market. If traditional postsecondary institutions fail to respond, they risk losing a growing, sophisticated market for postsecondary, professional, and even postgraduate reeducation (beyond traditional continuing education in this field). But responding to this market requires working closely, even collaboratively, with the client and customer (or their employees). Within the institution, organizing, delivering, and financing customer-based education is often a complex new endeavor. It requires a responsive mode of curriculum design, new or individualized content modules, willingness to provide nontraditional delivery modes, and a substantial change of faculty roles.

Globalization: Breaking Bonds and Boundaries

The challenge of international and global perspectives as we approach the twenty-first century needs little exposition; nor is it a new phenomenon. Models of international student and faculty exchange programs, attempts to emphasize and improve foreign language instruction, and introducing global perspectives into our curriculum are widespread if not completely effective. But two emergent phenomena suggest that the need for greater global emphasis could take on new boundary-spanning forms in the near future.

While knowledge and scholars have already resisted regional and national boundaries, a new form of international network may be emerging. One author (Cohen, 1994) has coined the term "international civil societies" to describe a form of network consisting of university scholars, governmental policy researchers, and private-sector experts organized around major significant social problems or issues (for example, global warming, AIDS, human rights, etc.). These civil societies are interdisciplinary, cross-national, and cross-industry groups. Their work may combine research, learning, action or policy, and formulation. They often rely on technology and have access to a wide array of information and expertise, but they often have little managerial structure. In effect, they reflect how the knowledge and technology explosion can rewrite scholarly boundaries without institutional structure.

Another form of globalization that may emerge is more similar to the multinational corporation. While loosely structured, institutional exchange programs and research alliances crossing national boundaries are common, the prospects for a multinational university are worth contemplating. Some universities now have their own campuses in other countries. Many institutions have partnerships with multinational technology firms. Some countries such as those of the European Union have supported cross-national postsecondary alliances. A move to more formalized international consortia, degree-granting federations among institutions in different countries, and even the possibility of a multinational university, while a daunting challenge, are likely in the decade ahead. (See Chapter Twenty-Seven, which provides further insights on planning for this challenge.)

At the *industry level* (see Table 1), new forms of global organization would markedly intensify competition in postsecondary education (Dill and Sporn, 1995). Clearly, scholars, researchers, and many students who now participate in the less formal arrangements are a specialized customer group who could be attracted. Some countries as clients might support limited forms of cross-national organizations, and institutions with an extensive international mission or presence could emerge. A truly multinational focus would be an intriguing new entrant to our postsecondary industry, providing an alternate form of global and international opportunity for study and scholarship, and an interesting addition to the competitive mix.

At the *institutional level* (see Table 2), the prospect of organizing a multinational institution or participating in a multinational partnership requires development of new mechanisms for collaboration with or competition in different cultures and in dealing with multiple government bureaucracies. The problems of internal management require guiding a more entrepreneurial, multicultural network form of organization—a skill to be advanced by those who develop such enterprises.

The Emerging Postsecondary Knowledge Industry: A New Perspective

As we face the twenty-first century, the changing societal conditions discussed earlier are all likely to continue. Each promises to have a major impact on both our postsecondary institutions and our industry (Tables 1 and 2).

In the previous transitions from higher education to mass education to a postsecondary industry, only one or two societal conditions created the need for transition, and the necessary industry change was usually expansion of clientele (students) or institutions. However, the six societal conditions discussed above affect all of the forces that reshape an industry. The resulting alteration in our notion of a postsecondary industry promises to be extensive and to call for a new paradigm: the postsecondary knowledge industry. While the exact nature of this new industry is only nascent, a review of how the forces reshaping an industry are affected by societal conditions provides some glimpses into our industry's possible evolution (Table 3).

Core Technology

Perhaps the most influential force is the potential for innovation in our core technology: the development, transmission, and dissemination of knowledge in society and in turn in our postsecondary industry. Postsecondary institutions have long believed they were the preeminent knowledge industry for postsecondary teaching, learning, and research. However, the telematics revolution has introduced a powerful new interactive information-handling technology that offers potentially revolutionary changes in moving from traditional modes of teaching, learning, and research to varied, responsive, flexible, interactive, and individualized modes. More critically, the telematics revolution makes it easier to respond to most of the other societal conditions affecting the industry (diversity, quality, economic productivity, postsecondary relearning, and globalization); and the revolution enhances all the other forces acting upon the industry (new organizational entrants, the power of customers and suppliers, the threat of substitute services, and the intensity of competition).

New Organizational Entrants

While the extent of use and effectiveness of information technology is key to our core processes of postsecondary education, the threat of new organizational entrants is perhaps the most tangible way of visualizing the reconfigured industry. Figure 1 reflects the institutional changes as our industry moved from traditional to mass education and then to postsecondary concepts. However, all of these transitions have primarily added students (customers) and new types of postsecondary educational institutions. Postsecondary now includes a broad array of public, private, and proprietary educational organizations providing varied educational offerings. But all are primarily educational organizations. Focusing on the organizations that are critical to a postsecondary knowledge industry perspective suggests the addition of many types of organizations previously thought to be part of other industries: telecommunications companies; computer software and hardware firms; information resource organizations; corporate and governmental organizations engaged in education, training, and professional development; and, perhaps, even "entertainment" firms. Figure 4 portrays this new extended industry that includes all the organizations in the postsecondary knowledge network. As our previous discussion has suggested, these new organizations are often no longer either just suppliers to, or customers of, postsecondary institutions. They are now effectively part of our postsecondary knowledge development, dissemination, and education system and need to be viewed as potential collaborators or competitors.

The Power of Customers

The analysis of societal conditions also suggests a change in perspective on our potential customers for postsecondary education (students). The shift is from a focus on traditional and nontraditional students seeking regular courses and degree offerings via traditional delivery modes to a broader view of the entire market for postsecondary education, which includes those potential student customers who are interested in non-degree-oriented learning and often in nontraditional modes of delivery. The key shift in the postsecondary knowledge industry perspective is to focus on students as learners with individualized educational needs rather than as potential students for courses and programs designed and delivered by postsecondary institutions.

The Power of Suppliers and the Threat of Substitute Services

The inclusion of potential new organizational entrants in the new postsecondary knowledge industry both enlarges and suggests their in-creased power as suppliers. They are no longer just the customers who are employers of graduates and purchasers of our knowledge products and services or sources of funding. They are often key suppliers, providers of valuable information resources, new educational technology and advances, and access to critical communication networks. Another major shift is to recognize that in the new postsecondary knowledge environment suppliers may be not merely resource providers for and purchasers of services from postsecondary institutions but also sources of substitute (educational) services. Further, they are now potential pressure groups, educational partners, or competitors—not merely suppliers. It is clear that in a postsecondary knowledge environment other knowledge-based firms do have greater power, both as suppliers of resources or as sources of substitute services, because of the ease of access to knowledge and its utilization.

Competition

Finally, it is also apparent that in the postsecondary knowledge industry competition is

Table 3. A New Paradigm for the Postsecondary Knowledge Industry

Industry Forces	Postsecondary Industry	Postsecondary Knowledge Network
Innovation in core technology	Traditional teaching, learning, research modes	Interactive information technology network for T, L, & R
Threat of new organizational entrants	Traditional colleges, universities, and proprietary institutions	Telecommunications, computing hardware and software, information resource, corporate and government education and training, and entertainment firms
Bargaining power of customers (students)	Traditional and nontraditional degree students	Growing minority and postsecondary relearning markets for individual learning needs
Bargaining power of suppliers (clients)	Primarily as employers, funding sources, and purchasers of services	Providers of information resources, educational technology, and communications networks; as pressure groups, partners, or competitors
Threat of Substitute services	Limited	More extensive
Intensity of competition	Among existing postsecondary institutions or segments	Cross-industry more competitive

likely to intensify. Clearly, competition among existing postsecondary institutions is intensified by the challenges to increase diversity, to improve quality, to constrain costs, and to enter the expanding postsecondary relearning markets. What is likely to be qualitatively different is competition in the knowledge industry that cuts across old industry boundaries. For instance, competing in the knowledge industry with organizations from the telecommunications, computing, or the corporate education and training world is far more entrepreneurial and fast-paced than in the traditional postsecondary world. Also, competition to engage in economic development or new global arrangements may entail both creative risks and new governmental controls or regulatory environments.

Thus, it is apparent that a postsecondary knowledge industry is substantially different from one composed only of postsecondary educational institutions. Participating in this new environment or industry requires a continued attempt to understand its evolving character and the role that traditional postsecondary institutions will play in it.

Institutional Challenges: A Contextual Planning Perspective

Discussion of changing societal conditions has implicitly identified many of the internal and external impacts on postsecondary institutions and the forces that are shaping the emerging postsecondary knowledge industry (Tables 1 and 2).

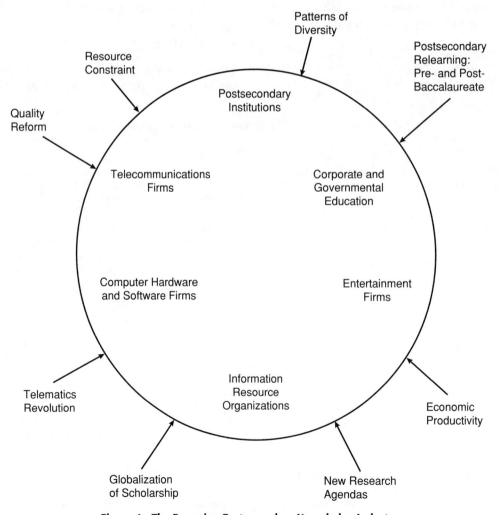

Figure 4. The Emerging Postsecondary Knowledge Industry.

A brief review highlights the challenges for institutional leaders and planners as they provide new perspectives to their institutions in the decade ahead. First, there is the need to plan for a period of substantial external change and uncertainty in which the nature not only of our postsecondary system but of our postsecondary knowledge industry is changing. The foremost challenge is to understand the critical societal conditions and forces that are reshaping our postsecondary knowledge industry. Second, one needs to understand how interactive, technology-based information and knowledge systems will reshape our industry and our institutions. Third, there is an even more diverse array of potential educational customers needing postsecondary educational services: the growing minority and educationally disadvantaged populations, new cadres of postsecondary learners, etc. Fourth, there is an increasingly diverse and powerful set of constituent groups and organizations demanding various educational services: a more proactive business community, more varied and changing governmental interest, and a complex labyrinth of telematics and information-resource firms. Fifth, many of these external business and governmental organizations are now also potential competitors for or collaborators with existing postsecondary institutions for both the new postsecondary markets and as an alternative or substitute for our more traditional undergraduate, graduate, and professional education and research functions. Sixth, the growing diversity of customers or student clientele includes postsecondary learners interested in or willing to use interactive technology as modes of educational transmission delivered to noncampus settings and packaged in nontraditional content or competency modules rather than traditional programs or degrees. Seventh, on the educational side, there is a shift in emphasis from teaching—from faculty and instructional development—to learning, learners, learning needs, and learning development. Eighth, the nature and bounds of research are likely to be more transdisciplinary and collaborative but less limited to geographic, institutional, or even national spheres. Finally, most of these challenges call for rethinking the basic educational delivery and research processes and functions. They focus more on change in the teaching-learning process, the research pro-

cess, and faculty-to-student and faculty-to-faculty relationships. They suggest extensive changes in faculty roles and behaviors—in essence, changing the academic culture of the workplace.

This set of planning challenges suggests extensive change in how we view our institutions both externally and internally. Externally it requires a planning perspective focused on the broader notion of a postsecondary knowledge industry or network rather than an industry or system of higher or postsecondary institutions. This suggests an external environment of increasing diversity and complexity, recognizing that many other types of organizations are engaged in the development, dissemination, and utilization of knowledge that is postsecondary in character. Internally, the planning perspective must recognize the potential need for extensive change in the academic structure and function and even in the nature of academic work. In essence the societal challenges to postsecondary institutions and this new paradigm of a postsecondary knowledge industry may require extensive institutional change. This suggests a need for planning which will address the following questions:

> *Redefinition*: What is the nature of a postsecondary knowledge industry, and what is our institution's role in it?
> *Redirection*: How should our institution's mission change to reflect these new realities, and what new external relationships should we develop?
> *Reorganization*: How should we redesign our academic processes and structures and reorganize our management functions?
> *Renewal*: How do we renew or re-create our academic workplace and institutional culture? Our preparation of future faculty?

In an environment of extensive and often unpredictable change that mandates rethinking the nature of our system or industry and considering the need for major institutional adaptation, current approaches to planning may be inadequate. Long-range and strategic planning typically begins with the assumption that one functions within an existing system of institutions or an industry, and that evolutionary change will allow an institution to adapt to environmental constraints and opportunities. However, in a situation in which the industry context is being reshaped and the institution may need to change drastically, a more proactive mode of planning that seeks to participate in shaping the industry and offers the possibility of more radical redesign of the institution may be called for. Contextual planning, discussed in Chapter Seven, offers an approach to addressing these broader questions of redefinition, redirection, reorganization, and renewal.

Further Reading

Those interested in exploring the changing nature of society and its implications for postsecondary education in the information age will find Peter Drucker's "The Age of Social Transformation" (1994) and *Managing for the Future* (1992) provocative and insightful. For a perspective on the changing nature of institutions as organizations, *Organizing for the Future*, by Jay Galbraith and others (1993), is an interesting generic treatment for those interested in planning postsecondary institutions. Two thought-provoking books that provide new ways of thinking about organizations in a postindustrial information age are Sally Hegelson's *The Web of Inclusion* (1995) and Margaret Wheatley's *Leadership and the New Science* (1992). Two edited volumes that focus more explicitly on our current and changing world of postsecondary education are David Dill and Barbara Sporn's *Emerging Patterns of Social Demand and University Reform: Through a Glass Darkly* (1995) and *Higher Education in American Society* (1994, third edition, but a fourth is planned), edited by Philip Altbach, Robert Berdahl, and Patricia Gumport. These volumes feature well-prepared chapter contributions that focus on the external conditions influencing postsecondary institutions (Dill and Sporn, 1995) and on a comprehensive examination of our current postsecondary system or industry and how it is changing (Altbach, Berdahl, and Gumport, 1994). Readers are also encouraged to identify a broadly focused publication or other information source that scans and examines external forces or internal changes in postsecondary education. *On the Horizon*, edited by James Morrison and published by Jossey-Bass, is such a useful resource focusing on education. Readers with more focused interests in the challenges to postsecondary education discussed in this chapter will want to identify a resource related to their particular interest.

References

Altbach, P. G., Berdahl, R. O., and Gumport, P. J. *Higher Education in American Society.* (3rd ed.) Amherst, N.Y: Prometheus, 1994.

Carter, D. J., and Wilson, R. *Minorities in Higher Education: American Council on Education Eleventh Annual Status Report.* Washington, D.C.: American Council on Education, 1993.

Cohen, D. W. "The Constitution of International Expertise." *Journal of the International Institute.* Ann Arbor, Mich.: University of Michigan International Institute, 1994.

Dill, D. D. "Quality by Design: Towards a Framework for Academic Quality Management." In J. Smart (ed.), *Higher Education: Handbook of Theory and Research,* Vol. VIII. New York: Agathon Press, 1992.

Dill, D. D. "Through Deming's Eyes: A Cross-National Analysis of Quality Assurance Policies in Higher Education." *Quality in Higher Education,* 1995a, *1*(2), 95–110.

Dill, D. D. "University-Industry Entrepreneurship: The Organization and Management of American University Technology Transfer Units." *Higher Education,* 1995b, *29*(4), 369–384.

Dill, D. D., and Sporn, B. "The Implications of a Postindustrial Environment for the University: An Introduction." In D. D. Dill and B. Sporn (eds.), *Emerging Patterns of Social Demand and University Reform: Through a Glass Darkly.* New York: Pergamon Press, 1995.

Drucker, P. *Managing for the Future: The 1990s and Beyond.* New York: Dutton, 1992.

Drucker, P. "The Age of Social Transformation." *Atlantic Monthly,* November 1994, pp. 53–80.

Eurich, N. P. *Corporate Classrooms, the Learning Business.* Princeton: Princeton University Press, 1985.

Ewell, P. T. "Assessment and Public Accountability: Back to the Future." *Change,* 1991, *23*(6), 12–17.

Fairweather, J. *Faculty Work and Public Trust. Restoring the Value of Teaching and Public Service in Academic Life.* Needham Heights, Mass.: Allyn & Bacon, 1996.

Feller, I. "Universities as Engines of R&D-Based Economic Growth: They Think They Can." *Research Policy,* 1990, *19*(4), 335–348.

Galbraith, J. R., Lawler, E. E., III, and Associates. *Organizing for the Future.* San Francisco: Jossey-Bass, 1993.

Green, K. C., and Gilbert, S. W. "Great Expectations: Content, Communications, Productivity, and the Role of Information Technology in Higher Education." *Change,* 1995, *27*(2), 8–18.

Grubb, W. N. *Working in the Middle: Strengthening the Sub-Baccalaureate Labor Force.* San Francisco: Jossey-Bass, forthcoming.

Hegelson, S. *The Web of Inclusion: A New Architecture for Building Great Organizations.* New York: Doubleday, 1995.

Leslie, L., and Brinkman, P. T. *The Economic Value of Higher Education*. New York: American Council on Education and Macmillan, 1988.

Mintz, S. D. (ed.). *Sources: Diversity Initiative in Higher Education*. Washington, D.C.: American Council on Education, 1993.

Morrison, J. L. (ed.). *On the Horizon: The Environmental Scanning Publication for Leaders in Education*. San Francisco: Jossey-Bass, 1996.

Musil, C. M. *Diversity in Higher Education: A Work in Progress*. Washington, D.C.: Association of American Colleges and Universities, 1995.

Peterson, M. W. "Images of University Structure, Governance, and Leadership: Adaptive Strategies for the New Environment." In D. Dill and B. Sporn (eds.), *Emerging Pattern of Social Demand and University Reform: Through a Glass Darkly.* New York. Pergamon Press, 1995.

Porter, M. E. *Competitive Strategy*. New York: Free Press, 1980.

Reich, R. *The Work of Nations: Preparing Ourselves for 21st Century Capitalism*. New York: Knopf, 1991.

Romer, R. *Making Quality Count in Undergraduate Education*. Denver: Education Commission of the States, 1995.

Rudolph, F. *The American College and University: A History*. New York: Random House, 1962.

Smelser, N. "The Politics of Ambivalence." *Daedalus*, 1993, *122*(4), 37–54.

Twigg, C. A. "The Need for a National Learning Infrastructure." *EDUCOM Review*, 1994, *29*(5),16–20.

Wheatley, M. J. *Leadership and the New Science: Learning About Organization from an Orderly Universe*. San Francisco: Berrett-Koehler, 1992.

Institutional Adaptation: Demands for Management Reform and University Administration

PATRICIA J. GUMPORT AND BARBARA SPORN

The writing of this chapter was, in part, supported under the Educational Research and Development Center program, agreement number R309A60001, CFDA 84.309A, as administered by the Office of Educational Research and Improvement (OERI), U.S. Department of Education. The findings and opinions expressed herein do not necessarily reflect the positions or policies of OERI or the U.S. Department of Education. The preparation of this chapter benefited considerably from research assistance by Marc Chun, John Jennings, Imanol Ordorika, Brian Pusser, Angela Schmiede and comments by David Dill.

Introduction

Higher education organizations around the world have always faced environmental changes. However, in the past decade altered societal expectations, new public policies, and technological innovations have created an unprecedented set of challenges for universities. Although the borders of universities have opened in new ways for their services and products, universities have been the subject of increased public scrutiny from diverse constituencies. While under such scrutiny, higher education institutions have been simultaneously identified for their potential as a key catalyst in the development of new knowledge organizations and the "digital" economy, especially in the Western world. Tending to these domains, their management has become increasingly significant at the turn of the century;

as Peter Drucker admonished in a recent analysis: "The most important area for developing new concepts, methods, and practices will be in the management of society's knowledge resources—specifically, education and health care, both of which are today overadministered and undermanaged." (Drucker, 1997)

These pressures on universities along with attendant opportunities are prominent features of the contemporary wave of accountability. Higher education organizations are being asked to solve problems of costs, quality, effectiveness, and access (Barrow, 1993; Cameron and Tschirhart, 1992; Kerr, 1994). The accumulation of pressures and opportunities prompts a reconsideration of the relationship between society at large and academic institutions, specifically determining the appropriate balance between independence and control, incentives and constraints, as well as costs and benefits (Berdahl and McConnell, 1994).

In this chapter, we characterize the cumulative challenge for universities as one of institutional adaptation to changing environments, a multifaceted phenomenon that is worthy of conceptual and empirical attention (Cameron and Tschirhart, 1992; Gumport and Pusser, 1997). We examine the prescriptions in this contemporary wave of accountability, specifically the demands on universities for management reform. Demands for management reform, including mandates to apply business-like strategies, are evident in higher education across a wide range of national systems and institutions

"Institutional Adaptation: Demands for Management Reform and University Administration," by Patricia J. Gumport and Barbara Sporn, reprinted from *Higher Education: Handbook of Theory and Research*, Vol. 14, edited by J. C. Smart, 1999. Agathon Press.

throughout Europe and the United States (Dill and Sporn, 1995a; Gumport and Pusser, 1997).

Within the higher education literature, researchers have examined several dimensions of institutional adaptation, including retrenchment (Cameron and Tschirhart, 1992; Hearn, 1996; Zusman, 1994), restructuring (Gumport, 1993; Rhoades, 1995; Slaughter, 1995), improved performance, redefined missions, reorganization (Cameron, 1984; Dill and Sporn, 1995a; Gumport and Pusser, 1997; Peterson, 1995), mandated change, governmental reforms, institutional autonomy and accountability (Berdahl and Millett; Van Vught, 1989), diversification of funds, strengthened administrative core, entrepreneurial periphery (Clark, 1996a; Clark, 1996c; Clark, forthcoming; Slaughter and Leslie, 1997), transformational leadership, and quality management (Cameron and Tschirhart, 1992; Dill, 1993b; Van Vught, 1995).

A close look at this literature reveals an implicit premise throughout: that university administrators are increasingly called upon to orchestrate that adaptation. We highlight this premise because we believe that it entails a potential shift of prevailing authority structures and decision-making procedures within universities (Barrow, 1993; Lazerson, 1997; Kogan, forthcoming). Although the literature attests to the changing nature of the academic environments, we find that prescriptions for the role of administration in university adaptation have been under-studied.

The literature on organizational adaptation is based on an open system perspective (Scott, 1992b) and focuses on an analysis of the environment and management challenges. The resulting approaches differ in their emphasis on internal as opposed to external forces shaping adaptation. Accordingly, we review a range of approaches (Cameron, 1984; Hrebiniak and Joyce, 1985) of externally controlled adaptation (Hannan and Freeman, 1977), of a combination of environmental and management imperatives for adaptation (Lawrence and Lorsch, 1986; Pfeffer and Salancik, 1978; DiMaggio and Powell, 1983), and of internal forces initiating adaptation (Child, 1972). As our review indicates, each of these approaches can be applied to adaptation by universities.

We think it is essential to examine the implicit role of administration in these literatures for several reasons. First, over the past several decades, administrative positions and expenditures have become prominent features of higher education organizations (Leslie, 1995; Leslie and Rhoades, 1995; Tolbert, 1985; Gumport and Pusser, 1995). Second, within management reform prescriptions, administrators are increasingly the key actors who mediate and even manage the relationships between the organization and its environments (Neave, 1997; Clark, 1996b; Peterson, 1997). Research on higher education organizations has neglected this topic, in spite of the widespread use of open systems perspectives in organizational theory over the past two decades. We believe that, as adaptation has become a major concern for higher education, it is increasingly essential to ask who is positioned to do it and with what consequences for the organization.

Based on this background of acknowledging changing environments and the role of administration in calls for management reform, this chapter is organized as follows. In part one, we describe the dynamics of the changing environment for higher education in the 1990s, concentrating on trends in Europe and the United States. Given the comprehensive nature of these environmental changes, some trends might be applicable to other national settings as well. Our review addresses features of the broader society (i.e., technology, politics, economy) and specific demands on institutions (i.e., cost, quality, effectiveness, access). In the second part, we review several approaches to adaptation within the relevant literatures on organizations and specifically on universities. We focus on open system perspectives that conceptualize environments and organizations as inextricably linked, in order to make analytical distinctions between the environment, the organization, and the role of administration in managing that relationship. In the third part, we draw together three theoretical perspectives to account for the increased centrality of administration in responding to environmental demands, and we examine implications for the changing organization of academic work. The last section of the chapter offers suggestions for further research.

The Environmental Changes for Universities

Observers from different vantage points concur on a profound shift: environmental forces have become so dynamic as to lead to a basic shift in the structure of higher education as an industry (Cameron and Tschirhart, 1992); the present era may be characterized as a point of revolutionary, rather than evolutionary, change (Kerr, 1987); and the demands of global capitalism hinder the university's ability to fulfill its cultural mission (Readings, 1996). The cumulative pressure amounts to a new environment for universities. Europe and the United States show several converging patterns (Dill and Sporn, 1995a):

- Financial crisis caused by decreased government support for students
- Devolution or decentralization of responsibility to the institutional level
- International competition for funds, faculty, and students
- Governmental regulations to improve quality in teaching and learning
- Changing student demographics
- New technologies

This new environment calls for increased accountability of universities. Pushed by economic, political, and technological forces of the wider societal environment, higher education institutions are increasingly held accountable for the resources they use and the outcomes they produce. Environmental pressures are translated into demands to solve problems of cost, quality, effectiveness, and access. The emerging discussion of possible solutions encompasses institutional management, restructuring, resource development and reallocation, quality assurance, and strategic planning. All of these prescriptions either implicitly or explicitly call for an expanded role for university administration. In this scenario, we argue, the domain of faculty authority is narrowed, as administrators are provided the resources to orchestrate various management reforms. Figure 1 depicts our approach visually.

The Societal Environment

Across national systems, the principal features of the societal environments impacting higher education are the economy, politics, and technology (Cameron and Tschirhart, 1992; Dill and Sporn, 1995a; Gumport and Pusser, 1995; Gumport and Pusser, 1997; Massy, 1996; Peterson and Dill, 1997). Economic issues include shortfalls in projected state appropriations alongside increased expectations for productivity and global competitiveness. Political parties and public decision making bodies determine higher education policies including the role of the state or the diversity of faculty and students. New technologies such as the Internet and telecommunications profoundly change the delivery of services by universities. Each set of forces warrants separate consideration.

Economy

Research universities in the United States have been challenged by changing economic conditions which shaped four major stages of development—from their origins in the late 1880s, to a period of slow growth until 1940, to dramatic expansion between 1940 and 1990 based on federal funding, and most recently to a period of constrained resources. Revenue from state appropriations have been an uncertain funding source during the 1990s (Williams, 1995; Leslie, 1995). The likelihood for stability in funding from government sources is not assured in the United States, even for flagship public universities, prompting them to diversify their revenue sources (Kerr, 1994; Gumport and Pusser, 1997).

In Europe state budgets for higher education are also under scrutiny. Regulations for introducing the common currency "Euro" by the European Union have contributed to a stagnating economy in many European countries. Pressure lies on state budgets, and cuts in the share for higher education are the consequence. In countries like France, Germany, Great Britain, and Austria, public expenditure per student has declined over the last decade (Dill and Sporn, 1995a). At the same time, the share of higher education funds from nonpublic sources is growing; as evidenced by an increased percentage of revenue from private sources for example in

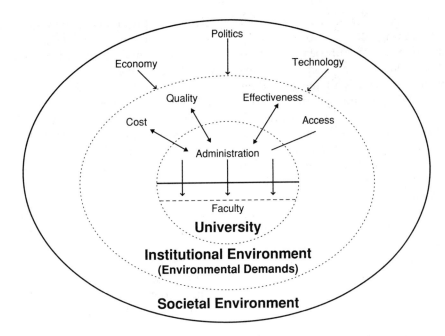

Figure 1. The role of university administration in adaptation

France, Germany, the Netherlands, and the UK (Williams, 1995). Generally, the pressure to diversify the funding base has led to the introduction of competitive markets within the higher education systems of many European countries (Clark, 1996b; Clark, 1996c; Dill and Sporn, 1995a; Gellert, 1993b; Teichler, 1993; Wasser, 1990). Reform processes aim at making institutions more independent from the state in order for them to raise additional funds through student fees and the private sector. At the same time, the need for efficient management structures and skills for fundraising and development become critical.

As observers have studied this financial vulnerability particularly for public universities around the world, they expect to see several trends for the future of higher education institutions: privatization, decentralization of authority, alternative financial resources, greater attention to effective use of resources, leadership on all levels, continued discussion of planning and restructuring alternatives. (Dill and Sporn, 1995a; Gumport and Pusser, 1997; Kerr, 1994; Nowotny, 1995; Peterson, 1995). Whether explicitly or implicitly, within such predictions, administration is called upon to implement these changes as well as to buffer their higher education institutions from selected environmental demands.

Another dimension of economic pressure is the expectation for higher education to contribute to a country's national productivity. Through academic research, universities are expected to innovate new products and services, as well as to collaborate in product development with industry. New trends show an increased need for technology transfer, for a combination of basic and applied research, and for professors contributing to spin-off or start-up companies (Goldstein and Luger, 1997). This environment can create a major revenue stream for universities as it simultaneously stimulates the economy (Goldstein, Maier, and Luger, 1995).

Higher education also contributes to national productivity through the production of a well-educated workforce (Peterson and Dill, 1997). With the emergence of the information age and a knowledge-based economy, qualified professionals increase the country's productivity and economic well-being. Aside from producing knowledge workers, colleges and universities also provide programs and training services to meet societal needs in other sectors.

Closely related to these expectations is the contribution of higher education to re-education (retraining) and continuing education (Peterson and Dill, 1997). New types of universities as well as new institutional forms (e.g. Fachhochschule in Germany specialized in vocational training) of advanced learning have been set up in several European countries (Gellert, 1993a). On the one hand, students need "hands-on" programs to increase their chances of finding a job, and companies need to update their knowledge through hiring university graduates on a regular basis. On the other hand, universities use re-education programs to raise additional revenue. Especially in the United States, the growing market for re-training has led to a shift in emphasis from undergraduate to professional education, and from liberal arts to vocational training in the community colleges. Even in Europe the trend is toward "professionalization" of general education (Teichler, 1993; Gellert, 1993a).

Politics

Budgetary pressures and conservative political trends in many countries have led to a movement of different political parties towards "middle of the road" policies. As a consequence, well-established concepts like "free" and "open" higher education are being questioned by politicians. In Austria, for example, the 20-year tradition of open access and no-tuition is increasingly discussed by ministers and policy makers. Generally in Europe, the role of the state has been changing from a control to a supervising model (Van Vught, 1994). The implications are more decentralization of responsibilities to the institutional level, stricter reporting systems and quality measures, as well as a need for better management and leadership skills at the institutional level.

An additional political factor of the higher education environment is the changing demographics of student populations towards greater diversity of society. New populations from different age groups and ethnic backgrounds are entering universities as students, faculty, or administrators (Hurtado and Dey, 1997). The challenge is to accommodate these different cultures. For example, California has been planning under the heading of "tidal wave II" to address the needs of a dramatic increase in the Hispanic student population. In Europe, countries are facing rising migration from Africa and Eastern Europe. From an institutional perspective, new programs for access and retention, new research agendas, and new

hiring and promotion systems have to be created (Peterson and Dill, 1997). As these minorities become majorities, institutional challenges will be pervasive.

Globalization trends are influencing the political environment as well. As one example, networks of scholars, policy makers, and private sector experts have formed around major social and political problems, such as human rights and AIDS. Such groups often have an interdisciplinary, cross national, and cross industry character. Another example are multinational universities with campuses in different countries and in some cases alliances with international firms and several academic institutions.[1] Such new ventures call for new management policies and practices, including expanded negotiation skills by those in the university (Peterson and Dill, 1997).

Technology

The technological revolution underway in all countries potentially entails significant changes for several institutions in modern society, particularly for higher education. The expansion of interactive telecommunications and the availability of relatively inexpensive computers and software have led to the widespread use of technology (Peterson and Dill, 1997; Sporn, 1996). The potential impact for how students learn, how professors teach and conduct research, and how administrators manage the institution is complex and not easily forecast (Gumport and Chun, forthcoming). New programs such as the virtual university, research collaboration between international scholars transcending the obstacles of time and location, and design of new administrative information systems are only a few examples.

Teaching improvements may be achieved through modern technologies. New forms of communication and collaboration between teachers and students become possible through on-line services like electronic mail. The creation of distance education programs or virtual universities[2] expands access to students in geographically remote regions. Academic programs can be customized to individual learning needs. Research activities can also be influenced by new technologies. A new form of international collaboration links industry, universities, and government agencies around the world to solve modern problems such as coping with global warming or enhancing social mobility (Gibbons, 1995; Nowotny, 1995; Peterson and Dill, 1997). Additionally, access to information is improved through CD-ROM and library servers with benefits to literature searches and analyses. The emergence of electronic publishing provokes controversy as an innovation in the distribution of research, with implications for the changing roles of university libraries and university publishers.

From an institutional perspective, technological changes have the potential to raise the organizational intelligence of universities (Senge, 1990). Sophisticated information systems enable academic organizations to learn about internal processes, markets, or customers and present a more comprehensive picture to the outside world. The feedback can be used for program development, marketing and decision making. A new form of "management by information" may make structures and processes more transparent[3] with possible increases in efficiency and effectiveness for the university (Green and Gilbert, 1995).

The Institutional Environment

Societal changes in technology, politics, and economy get translated into environmental demands for universities and, taken together, form an immediate institutional environment (see again Figure 1). Expectations on higher education abound, due not only to the significant contributions of higher education to society but also to the ambiguities of academic organizations (i.e., unclear mission and technology, gap between administrative and academic values) (Baldridge, 1983; Birnbaum, 1989; Clark, 1983; Weick, 1976). Increasingly higher education institutions are asked "to justify activities by demonstrating their contribution to objectives, and defend the cost of the enterprise" (Berdahl and McConnell, 1994, p. 70). In an effort to meet these demands for accountability, universities have developed strategies to achieve cost containment in addition to improvements in quality, effectiveness, and access.

Cost

The explosion of institutional costs and the dramatic increase in overall expenditures in

higher education have been widely discussed during the last decade (Leslie and Rhoades, 1995; Zemsky and Massy, 1990). It is not clear, though, if the cost escalation is due to the administrative or the academic domain (Gumport and Pusser, 1995; Leslie and Rhoades, 1995). In any case, accountability expectations have triggered numerous attempts to achieve cost containment through restructuring (Zemsky and Massy, 1990).

Generally, we can see a decline in government support for higher education in all OECD countries; advocates for a "market model" offer the American system as exemplary (Leslie, 1995; Williams, 1995): "The decline means that institutions are expected to raise more and more of their own revenues through such means as new or higher charges to students, research grants and contracts with business and industry, and special training programs for discrete groups" (Leslie, 1995, p. 6). Such trends can be observed in many European countries with the introduction of student fees, expensive postgraduate programs, and applied research projects with industry. In the United States, the recent trend points to tuition increases, corporate partnerships, and expanded continuing education programs.

These efforts to generate revenue have been accompanied by changes in operating functions and management structures, principally an increasing scale of administration (Bergmann, 1991; Gumport and Pusser, 1995; Guskin, 1994a; Leslie, 1995). Administrators have tended to respond to fiscal constraints in higher education differently in the 1990s, moving away from short-term crisis management to strategic planning for prolonged challenges (Barrow, 1993). And administration itself has been asked to change—to become leaner and more professional, through more vigilant leadership and more efficient uses of technologies (Guskin, 1994a).

Research shows that, with the necessity to cultivate funds from new sources, new organizational structures (including administrative ones) are created (Tolbert, 1985). Internal resource allocation is based on the centrality to mission and closeness to the market of the respective academic or administrative units (Hackman, 1985). Budgeting at the state or government level shifts from line-based budgets to block grants and will increasingly include target–based budgets for universities (Williams, 1995). Additionally, the quality and effectiveness goal favors cost containment through process analyses and a redefinition of core competencies (Prahalad and Hamel, 1990). It could follow that the turbulence in higher education finance explains the disproportionate increase in administrative expenditure over recent years and the decline in expenditure shares devoted to instruction (Gumport and Pusser, 1995; Leslie and Rhoades, 1995). This type of restructuring causes difficulties for academic areas with less market potential and for faculty within those fields or within the institution who resist such resource shifts.

Quality

The 1990s can be characterized as a quest for quality in higher education (Ewell, 1991). The notion of quality applied to higher education has over the years become more inclusive to encompass caring for clients, coherence in teaching and learning processes, and responsiveness to changing client needs. In universities, quality expectations focus on public accountability, student learning, faculty productivity and performance, program effectiveness, and institutional evaluation (Peterson and Dill, 1997). The demand for quality of academic products and services is seen to change the educational value of universities (Lozier and Teeter, 1993; Van Vught, 1995): "Management for quality in higher education institutions should consist of a deep caring for the fundamental values of the search for truth and the pursuit of knowledge, and of a sincere attempt to respond to the needs of present-day-societies" (Van Vught, 1995, p. 209).

The development of the quality movement led to the introduction of comprehensive concepts and tools of TQM (Total Quality Management) and CQI (Continuous Quality Improvement) on campus. As opposed to the educational quality movement, TQM or CQI concentrate on administrative structures and processes but might eventually reach the academic side of the institution as well. The main principles emphasize a culture of continuous improvement, a customer and client focus, a rational approach to decision making through performance indicators and benchmarking, more process design, teamwork, and individual empowerment (Cameron and Whetten,

1996; Lozier and Teeter, 1993; Peterson and Dill, 1997; Seymour, 1992).

Given the deteriorating public image of universities in many countries, TQM and CQI strategies may be seen as mechanisms to both increase accountability and provoke structural improvements and redesign (Ewell, 1997). Some examples are evidence of this trend. With the restructuring of the higher education market in the UK, a new unit "Quality Support Centre"[4] was founded, mainly concentrating its work on developing and disseminating concepts and tools for quality in higher education. In Austria and Germany[5], the ministries of science and research have created evaluation standards that have to be met by all public universities in order to secure quality of outputs. In the United States, the Baldridge Award[6] designed for excellent corporations was extended to institutions of higher education, signaling the increased call to use TQM and CQI in university administration (Peterson and Dill, 1997).

Effectiveness

Concerns over effectiveness have become prominent in discussions of higher education institutions and systems. While efficiency is an internal measure of goal achievement and resource usage that concentrates on "doing things right," effectiveness is an external measure focusing on "doing the right things" through establishing appropriate goals based on environmental needs and demands (Cameron and Whetten, 1996; Pfeffer and Salancik, 1978). The increased demand for accountability on universities expanded the focus from efficiency to effectiveness (Gumport and Pusser, 1997). The shift to effectiveness has some components of quality concerns, including emphasis on a client or customer perspective, prescriptions for management strategies to bring about organizational change, and reconsideration of adaptive structures, processes, and outcomes (Cameron and Whetten, 1996).

In some cases, the shift to questions of effectiveness has led to reorganization or restructuring of the institution. One typology of such initiatives has characterized them as of three types—reengineering, privatization, or reconfiguring (Gumport and Pusser, 1997). Generally, the goals are far reaching—to cut costs through reduced bureaucracy, to improve quality and enhance effectiveness, and in some cases to increase access. As new processes and services are created to serve ever more extensive outside needs, administration plays a critical role as mediator and change agent. Ironically, the increased centrality of administration to restructuring has occurred alongside demands to reduce administrative costs.

One study specifically analyzed the relationship between postindustrial environments and organizational effectiveness of United States universities (Cameron and Tschirhart, 1992). The results showed that certain environmental attributes (i.e., scarcity, competition, turbulence) have negative effects on organizational effectiveness. However, the study also showed that administration can mitigate these negative effects through participative bureaucratic systems of decision making, i.e., integration of all groups within the university in the decision process and communication of results through transparent channels. In general, the results of the study show that information sharing and the establishment of a learning culture are successful strategies to deal with the pressures of a postindustrial environment (Whetten and Cameron, 1985).

Access

In the United States, the expectation for universal access to higher education was initiated after World War II with the GI Bill. Universal access meant moving from mostly middle-income students to students of all income levels as well as expanding access to students in all geographic locations and later through affirmative action to previously underrepresented ethnic groups (Kerr, 1994). More recently, through the emphasis on lifelong learning, the expansion of access can be further achieved as increased numbers of adult learners expect access to higher education programs through technology-based services that can overcome the obstacles of location and time (Gumport and Chun, forthcoming; Mingle and Epper, 1997).

The financial pressures on higher education also have consequences for student access. In the United States, the shift from grants to loans for students in the contemporary period undermines the aim to expand access to more diverse populations of lower income students. "Given the reluctance of some ethnic groups to borrow large sums of money, a movement away from grants will reduce access to college for the groups that need it the most" (Hartle and Galloway, 1997, p. 35).

Access is only a first step, for once students arrive on campus they need to find a campus climate that will facilitate their retention and degree completion. The challenge for campuses to deal with multiculturalism and diversity will continue to increase (especially in Europe) and needs to be accommodated by universities (Hurtado and Dey, 1997). Public policies and governmental regulations may help retain a diverse student body (Peterson and Dill, 1997). Well–balanced systems of merit or need-based student support are commonly found mechanisms to achieve these goals. Unfortunately, recent votes against affirmative action policies in California and Texas signal increased difficulty in removing ethnic and class barriers to higher education.

Geographic barriers are easier for universities to overcome because of the new developments of technology. Strategies are designed to enhance the delivery of educational programs to students in remote locations. Referred to as distance education, distance learning programs or "virtual university" initiatives in the United States, the discussion in Europe focuses on international joint academic programs and voucher systems that enable students to change universities and move between countries easily and freely. The aim is to make geographic as well as cultural boundaries obsolete, so that students can choose programs and universities that are best suited to their needs.

Environmental Changes, University Responses, and Managerial Imperatives

In the previous paragraphs we showed how environmental demands for cost containment, quality, effectiveness, and access constitute the contemporary pressures for institutional accountability. As universities seek to respond to these pressures, we see attempts not only for organizational survival but also for organizational legitimacy. Their adaptation processes encompass strategies such as reorganization and restructuring, diversification of revenue sources, revised mission statements, a redefined role of the state between supervision and control, redesign of programs, evaluation and assessment of faculty, or total quality management. With the environment gaining more influence on the functioning of universities (Cameron, 1984: Dill and Sporn, 1995a; Gumport and Pusser, 1997; Kerr, 1987; Peterson, 1995) and the widespread directives for management reform, a major consequence is that more authority is given to administration to decide upon changes, distribute resources and implement decisions (Kogan, forthcoming; Trow, 1994). A comparative study of European countries confirms that while academic expertise remains dominant on the primary processes of teaching and research, "the role of the central institutional administration is an important component in higher education governance and management, especially for the nonprimary processes issues such as financial management" (De Boer and Goedegebuure, 1995, p. 4).

Thus, we think it essential to examine how, within institutional adaptation prescriptions, there is an implicit mandate for administration to play a central role as mediator and change agent. We believe this mandate entails concomitant shifts in the authority structure within universities that narrows the domain of professional expertise of faculty.

Following this argument, the first response to the new environment then is to strengthen hierarchical administrative structures (Kogan, forthcoming). We would suggest though that eventually the whole institution (and not one part being either administration or faculty) needs to be included in an analysis of observable weaknesses in existing collegial, professional, and administrative structures. Consequently, this would facilitate successful institutional adaptation.

We want to briefly describe how, from a historical and a comparative perspective, the division of labor between faculty and administration has looked quite different across time periods and national systems.

The University and the Role of Administration

In the context of this chapter, we focus on institutional adaptation to changing environments and the implications for the role of administration. Accordingly, we broadly define administration as the structure and processes within universities for implementing and executing decisions made by academic governance (Peterson and Mets, 1987). Additionally, we include functions and positions within a university which deal with mediating environmental demands. In our view, administration is inclusive of upper as well as middle management: i.e., we incorporate leadership in our definition of administration. This would include faculty who have become deans, provosts and presidents. We believe that this comprehensive definition—through the inclusion of all administrative tiers—permits a more comprehensive perspective on the role of administration.

According to Peterson, ten years ago, "the management of many institutions today involves modifying existing structures and processes or developing new ones to deal with problems of institutional change and innovation, quality and effectiveness, and decline and equity" (Peterson and Mets, 1987). We believe that this responsibility for adaptation has become even more prominent in management reform prescriptions for higher education throughout the late 1980s and into the 1990s, with the consequence of expanding the authority of administration. In order to examine this shift, we first provide a brief sketch of the historical development of university organization and administration (Burns, 1962; Duryea, 1962; Tyack, 1990).

Classic studies of university organization occurring in the 1970s provided the basics of organizational analysis in higher education (Baldridge, Curtis, Ecker, and Riley, 1977; Birnbaum, 1989; Blau, 1994; Cohen and March, 1974; Weick, 1976). Changes from elite to mass higher education produced two waves of changes in university organization and administration based on integration and differentiation (Clark, 1995; Dill, 1992b; Lawrence and Lorsch, 1986). Differentiation refers to the process of forming highly specialized units (i.e., basic academic units, departments) to address uncertain and dynamic environmental demands. Integration of differentiated units aims at coherence and effectiveness by investing time and resources in horizontal mechanisms of coordination (Lawrence and Lorsch, 1986). Integrating mechanisms emphasize lateral and reciprocal forms of communication such as face to face meetings, liaison roles, task forces, teams, and even integrating managers and departments (Dill, 1995b; Galbraith, 1977).

With the expansion of higher education in the 1960s, authority increased for professors on the continent (i.e., establishment of chair system) and nonfaculty in the United States (i.e., influence in decision making of nonacademic staff and students). "Ironically, this has also been accompanied by an increase in the number of academic administrators required to manage institutions of increased size and complexity. The transition from mainly oligarchic to mainly democratic structures created a need for administrators who can attend to conflicting interests" (Dill, 1992a, pp. 15/16).

The second wave of changes starting in the 1980s has influenced the organization of universities and their administrative structures through institutional competition, differentiation, and social responsiveness (Dill, 1992a). Adaptations include hierarchical integrating mechanisms of lateral groups consisting of administrators and faculty sharing information. Examples are task forces or strategy development teams. To be effective in a competitive environment, these mechanisms must be combined with market and collegial mechanisms. This means that environmental scanning and governance based on democratic representation are critical. Conflicting pressures of diminishing resources and expanding knowledge call for the articulation of collective professional values and priorities as a basis for decisions. "As specialization and differentiation are the universal characteristics of academic organization, so integration is the universal challenge of academic administration" (Dill, 1992a, p. 16).

Since most management reform processes aim at securing financial support, legitimacy, and thus organizational survival, the "external push" for adaptation draws our attention to the organization/environment interface. Internally, actions concentrate on institutional finance, mis-sion statements, and improved decision making processes. The responsibility mainly falls in the realm of administration and, we argue, entails a shifting authority structure within universities. In the next section we review theories of adaptation that depict alternative approaches to understanding the organization/environment relationship and their inherent prescriptions for administration's role.

Review of Relevant Theory of Adaptation

The study of adaptation has a long tradition in organizational analysis. Under the headings of organizational change (Goodman and Kurke, 1982; Huber and Glick, 1993), organizational development (Cameron and Quinn, 1983), organizational design (Galbraith, 1977), or organizational learning (Argyris and Schön, 1974; Argyris, 1982; Levitt and March, 1988) lies the concept that organizations need to adapt to their environment in order to succeed (Burns and Stalker, 1961; Hannan and Freeman, 1977; Lawrence and Lorsch, 1986; Pfeffer and Salancik, 1978). In general, most conceptual and empirical contributions to the theory of adaptation derive from research published in the business, economics, and sociology literature (Aldrich, 1979; Argyris, 1982; Child, 1972; Hannan and Freeman, 1977; Hrebiniak and Joyce, 1985; Lawler and Mohrman, 1996; Lawrence and Lorsch, 1986; March, 1991; March, 1994; March, 1996; Meyer and Rowan, 1992a; Meyer and Scott, 1992; Miles and Snow, 1978; Miller and Friesen, 1980; Perkins, 1973; Pfeffer and Salancik, 1978; Powell, 1990; Powell and Friedkin, 1987; Scott, 1992a; Thompson, 1967).

Adaptation research has been focused on an analysis of environments and their resulting management challenges. Approaches range from an emphasis on total external to total internal control of adaptations and they concentrate on either environmental (i.e., population ecology), organizational (i.e., resource dependence, contingency theory, institutional isomorphism), or internal forces (i.e., strategic choice) (Cameron, 1984; Hrebiniak and Joyce, 1985). These approaches share a commonality: they are based on an open system perspective (Scott, 1992b).

The concept of adaptation has been applied to higher education occasionally and not systematically. We identified authors in the field of higher education who have been interested in higher education adaptation as well as topics closely related to it like strategic planning, restructuring, resource allocation, innovation, or entrepreneurial universities (Balderston, 1995; Baldridge and Deal, 1983; Becher and Kogan, 1992; Blau, 1994; Cameron, 1984; Clark, 1983; Clark, forthcoming: Conrad, 1978; Dill and Friedman, 1979: Dill and Sporn, 1995b: Gumport and Pusser, 1995; Gumport and Pusser, 1997; Hardy, 1990; Hearn, 1988; Keller, 1983; Leslie, 1995; Levine, 1980; Massy, 1996; Peterson, 1995; Rhoades, 1995; Rubin, 1979; Salancik and Pfeffer, 1974; Slaughter, 1995; Slaughter and Leslie, 1997; Sporn, 1995a; Tolbert, 1985; Trow, 1983). Our chapter is mostly based on their work.

When studying adaptation to changing environments and the role of university administration, we need to analyze the societal and institutional environments, the relevant theories of adaptation, and the consequences for the organization. For this purpose, we use the following definition of adaptation:

> Organizational adaptation refers to modifications and alterations in the organization or its components in order to adjust to changes in the external environment. Its purpose is to restore equilibrium to an unbalanced condition. Adaptation generally refers to a process, not an event, whereby changes are instituted in organizations. Adaptation does not necessarily imply reactivity on the part of an organization because proactive or anticipatory adaptation is possible as well. But the emphasis is definitely on responding to some discontinuity or lack of fit that arises between the organization and its environment (Cameron, 1984, p. 123).

Accordingly, our emphasis lies on a process view of adaptation that aims at establishing a balance between environmental demands and internal structures. Organizational alterations may include strategies or positions to manage the relationship between the organization and the environment. Administration may function as a bridge as well as a buffer.

In the first part of this chapter we described how environmental changes have become more complex, turbulent, uncertain, and interconnected for higher education institutions (Cameron and Tschirhart, 1992). As a result, environmental demands for accountability cause major management challenges for universities (i.e., lower costs, higher quality, more effectiveness, open access). These demands get mitigated by administration in order to secure survival and legitimacy. Hence, the administration voices the reaction of the organization to the environment, guides the courses of adaptation, and thereby expands its scope of authority within the institution. Conflicts with faculty who see themselves as the professionals in charge of the institution are a consequence. One indicator of the potential for increased conflict is the rise in the number of administrators compared to faculty. In Europe, the ratio is starting to favor administration based on major "management reforms" and in the United States administration has a long history of being twice as large as faculty (Chronicle, 1997; Sporn, 1995b).

After a review of the major models of adaptation and their application to higher education, we provide an analysis of the changing role of professionals (faculty and administrators) based on the theory of the sociology of professions. For this purpose, we adopt a synergy of perspectives, i.e., an eclectic mix of approaches to account for the expansion of administration as an inherent part of university adaptation. Given the goal of this chapter, we selected approaches concentrating on the management of the organization/environment relationship and the role of administration. Generally all these approaches assume organizations as open systems that confront and respond to various challenges, demands, and opportunities in their environment. Hence, we first give an overview of open systems theory and then describe specific approaches relevant to higher education as shown in Figure 2 (i.e., contingency theory, population ecology, institutional isomorphism, strategic choice, resource dependence, network organization).

Open Systems Theory

Generally, systems are characterized by an assemblage or combination of interdependent parts. "That a system is open means, not simply that it engages in interchanges with the environment, but that this interchange is an es-

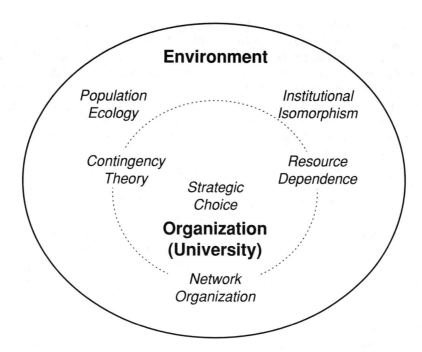

Figure 2. Major approaches to organizational adaptation based on open systems theory

sential factor underlying the system's viability." (Scott, 1992b, p. 83.) In open social systems like organizations the connections among the interacting parts become relatively loose. This means that less constraint is placed on the behavior of one element by the condition of the others. Through the importance of the environment and the relative freedom of elements, these systems are predicted to be more adaptive (Scott, 1992b). Loosely coupled systems persist due to environmental scanning and local adaptation of individual units. Actors are self-determined in their activities and coordination is kept to a minimum (Weick, 1976). Internally, organizations consist of participants not organized as a unitary hierarchy or as an organic entity, but as a loosely linked coalition of shifting interest groups (Cyert and March, 1992; Pfeffer and Salancik, 1978; Weick, 1976). Applied to higher education, universities have often been defined as loosely coupled systems (Weick, 1976) or organized anarchies (Cohen and March, 1974).

The environment is characterized by diversity and variety that causes uncertainty for organizations. Adaptation is defined as the process by which systems seek a dynamic equilibrium or "fit" with their relevant environment (Cameron, 1984; Lawrence and Lorsch, 1986; Weick, 1979). Systems are seen as self-maintaining; i.e., in order to strive they will find strategies of survival in accordance with their environment (Pfeffer and Salancik, 1979; Tolbert, 1985). In summary, loosely coupled systems (like universities) are likely to persist through external sensing mechanisms, fast localized adaptation, and the possibility to retain innovation on a subunit level. They have the advantage of isolating problematic areas and of minimal costs of coordination. But with increasing need for integration the independence of actors and only local innovations can impede an overall change process.

After more than ten years, Orton and Weick (1990) reconceptualized the theory of loosely coupled systems and argue for a dialectical application of the concept. Loose coupling theory should be used from two different and opposing perspectives. On the one hand, loose coupling helps the organization to create a potential for survival through innovations of independent and highly skilled units. On the other hand, the dysfunctions of loose coupling, such as lack of integration and identity, can be compensated for by activities in the "management arena" like enhanced leadership, focused attention, or shared values (Weick, 1976).

Orton and Weick (1990) found three types

of adaptability in their study of the literature on loose coupling: experimentation, collective judgment, and dissent. Experimentation refers to problem solving by curiosity, learning, and exploration (Orton and Weick, 1990). Collective judgment is translated into a structure of self-governing voluntary groups (or collegium) which promote "wise choices" (Rubin, 1979; Thompson, 1967). The preservation of dissent focuses on the concept of "unified diversity" as a powerful source of adaptation (Weick, 1976).

We adopt this open and loosely coupled system perspective and focus our attention on the role of administration. As we argue, universities as open systems adapt to their environment in order to reduce uncertainty and increase legitimacy. Given the nature of the environment, one form of this adaptation is the expansion of administration and the shift of authority structure within the institution. In order to provide a more detailed analysis of this proposition we need to review the relevant theories of adaptation. As some authors before (Cameron, 1984; Goodman and Kurke, 1982; Hrebiniak and Joyce, 1985; Scott, 1992b), we selected the following approaches because of their emphasis on the role of the environment and management.

Contingency Theory

Contingency theory claims that effective organizational structure and management are dependent upon the core technology and nature of the competition in the relevant industry (Lawrence and Lorsch, 1986). This implies that there is no one best way to organize (Scott, 1992b; Van de Ven and Drazin, 1985). In stable and certain environments, organizations develop "mechanistic" structures with centralized hierarchies and fixed procedures. Rapidly changing environments and uncertain technologies require "organic" structures characterized by horizontal and vertical communication, autonomous actors, and higher flexibility and adaptability (Burns and Stalker, 1961; Lawrence and Lorsch, 1986).

Actually, contingency theory is a branch of system design (Galbraith, 1977) emphasizing the contingent nature of organizations depending on environmental conditions. In their work, Lawrence and Lorsch (1986) concentrate on integration and differentiation as adaptation

mechanisms. They argue that adaptation takes place on two levels: the structure of the subunit to fit its environment and the organizational mode of integration and differentiation to meet the broader demands of the environment (Lawrence and Lorsch, 1986).

In a university setting differentiation and integration can help to understand university behavior (Clark, 1995; Dill, 1997a). With increased complexity of tasks like interdisciplinary teaching and research or diverse student bodies, institutions of higher education diversify their services (Dill, 1997b). As the production of new knowledge has become difficult, academic departments need to specialize even further (Clark, 1995; Clark, 1996c). The importance of integration through collaboration and cooperation among units and members intensifies as a competitive environment forces universities to increase quality, improve effectiveness, lower costs. and provide access to a diverse student body.

Contingency theory is useful if we want to explain the increased need of integration at universities caused by complex and rapidly changing environments (Clark, 1993; Clark, 1995; Dill and Sporn, 1995b). Administration has to play two roles. On the one hand, administrators and units serve as a buffer between the environment and the core activities of the institution. On the other hand, administration tries to integrate the differentiated units through mechanisms of communication like personal meetings, liaison offices. task forces, teams and committees (Dill, 1997b; Dill and Sporn, 1995b; Galbraith, 1977). For example, we found line administrators (i.e. vice president for planning) and offices of "professional liaison" to serve as a connection between central administration, schools and colleges, and trustees (Sporn, 1995b).

Population Ecology

Organizational adaptation according to the population ecology tradition (Aldrich, 1979; Hannan and Freeman, 1977; Hannan and Freeman, 1989) happens through natural selection by environmental demands. The population ecology approach only considers populations of organizations as the unit of analysis and views changes of individual organizations as rather arbitrary and irrelevant. The environment is viewed as a powerful force selecting those forms that have a chance of survival and other organizational forms vanish. Generally, Hannan and Freeman (1997, p. 946) suggest that "we ought to find specialized organizations in stable and certain environments and generalist organizations in unstable and uncertain environments."

This natural selection process derives from biology where the fittest survive because of their matching characteristics with the environment (Aldrich, 1979). "Most organizations adapt, therefore, not because of intelligent or creative managerial action but by the random or evolutionary development of characteristics that are compatible with the environment. Managerial discretion and influence is neither present nor relevant." (Cameron, 1984, p. 126.) Hence, "the ability to perpetuate one's form is the hallmark of successful adaptation" (Scott, 1992b, p. 22).

In summary, population ecology approaches aggregate organizations into populations, downplay the importance of managerial choice, and view the source of adaptation as an inconsequential artifact of evolution. It is meant to explain why certain types of organizations survive, e.g., the decline in teacher's colleges and the growth in the number of community colleges in the United States (Scott, 1992b).

In this chapter, population ecology has less importance since we concentrate on the role of administration (i.e., management). But it could be used to provide a critical discussion of the role of management vis-à-vis a dynamic environment focusing on the tendency of managers to overestimate their influence (Birnbaum, 1992; Cohen and March, 1974). Another application would be to analyze how much of the environmental demands are manageable or inescapable.

Institutional Isomorphism

Institutional theory, like population ecology, focuses on whole sets of organizations acting in relevant organizational fields (Meyer and Rowan, 1977; Meyer and Scott, 1992; Powell and DiMaggio, 1991). Adaptation is defined as isomorphism or the homogenization of organizational form in the same field of organizations. (DiMaggio and Powell, 1983). In general,

institutional isomorphism states that adaptation stems either from concerns about political power and legitimacy (i.e. coercive isomorphism), from imitating other organizations (i.e. mimetic isomorphism), or from the homogenization of management (i.e. normative isomorphism) (DiMaggio and Powell, 1983). Hence, this approach explains adaptation mainly in terms of values and politics.

The model of institutional isomorphism looks at organizations as a dynamic mix of participants, interests, and resources. Accordingly, organizations are dominated by coalitions of shifting interest groups which must adapt to their environment. The model focuses on an ecological level of analysis, i.e., relating organizational functioning to the larger society. Consequently, social and cultural values and policies are relevant factors for internal decision making (DiMaggio and Powell, 1983; Meyer and Rowan, 1992a; Meyer and Rowan, 1992b). In other words. "organizations experience pressure to adapt their structure and behavior to be consistent with the institutional environment in order to ensure their legitimacy and. hence, their chances of survival" (DiMaggio and Powell, 1983, p. 150).

As a result, organizations are increasingly homogeneous within given domains and increasingly organized around rituals of conformity to wider institutions. Accordingly the environment is interpreted as organizational fields and consists of technical and social/cultural elements. Technical environments include resources, information and know-how, and markets. Social and cultural environments encompass values, norms and politics of the larger society (Scott, 1992a).

We are especially interested in the role of professionals according to the institutional isomorphism model. Professionalization is interpreted as "the collective struggle of members of an occupation to define their working conditions and to establish a cognitive base and legitimization for their occupational autonomy" (DiMaggio and Powell, 1983, P. 152). Isomorphic processes are enhanced through two aspects: the cognitive base produced by university specialists and the growth and elaboration of professional networks (DiMaggio and Powell, 1983). Both aspects have relevance for universities (Cameron, 1984; Dooris, 1989; Hrebiniak and Joyce, 1985; Rhoades, 1995; Simsek and Louis, 1994; Tolbert, 1985).

If we focus again on the role of administration in adaptation, we can see that administrators are key players in mimetic as well as normative isomorphic processes. Given the complex and competitive environment for universities, business like strategies for managing universities become more common. Administrators are responsible for developing and implementing these strategies. Through their professional networks and associations the principles of "successful" universities are exchanged and strategies of imitation follow. This shows that through mimetic and normative isomorphism in today's higher education, the importance of administration perpetuates.

Strategic Choice

Strategic choice models of adaptation recognize the importance of environmental demands and the need to find a balance or fit between the environment and the organizational structure and processes (as in contingency theory). Here the major focus lies on the selection of strategies for managers that can modify the environment and determine the success or failure of adaptation.

One of the first proponents of this approach, John Child (1972). based his work on the definition of organizations as a dominant coalition of interest groups (Cyert and March, 1992; Thompson, 1967) and on the important role of management. He argues that strategic choice made by decision makers in the dominant coalition is essential for understanding how organizations adapt to their environments. The dominant coalition can adapt proactively rather than merely to accommodate to uncontrollable changes. For example, organizations can choose which environment or market to operate in, manipulate and control their environment, choose technologies that grant them subsequent control, employ control systems to deal with large size, and perceive and reevaluate their environments in ways that enable them to adapt creatively to contingencies (Child, 1972).

According to strategic choice approaches, adaptation is an active management responsibility. This has led to extensive applications in higher education starting in the 1970s (Hearn,

1988; Peterson, 1991: Schmidtlein, 1990). Hence, adaptation is defined as strategic planning (Chaffee, 1985) whereby organizational structure follows a strategy (Hardy et al., 1983) and the environment has a technical/task character (Kotler and Murphy, 1981). The role of administration lies in managing and implementing strategies and plans (Cameron, 1983; Chaffee, 1983; Sporn, 1996).

Universities have been subject to strategy formation and planning for more than two decades. A major goal has been to apply business approaches to higher education and advertise the development of skills of strategic management that help universities to become more effective and efficient. The book by George Keller, *Academic Strategy*, is an excellent example of this approach (Keller, 1983). Later authors started to work on organizational characteristics of universities and how these influence strategic planning (Chaffee, 1985; Chaffee, 1989; Dill, 1993a; Dill, 1994; Hearn, Clugston, and Heydinger, 1993; Keller, 1995; Peterson, 1997).

Another example of strategic choice approaches applied to higher education is Cameron's study of different forms of strategies of adaptation (i.e., domain defense, domain offense, domain creation) under conditions of decline (Cameron, 1983). Given the dynamic environment of higher education. the results may still be valid. "Although administrators may be required to be conservative and efficiency oriented, alternative strategies emphasizing effectiveness and innovation must also be considered" (Cameron, 1983, p. 377).

Recent developments in the 1990s concentrate on comprehensive "contextual" planning models which link policy and institutional environments with planning and process elements inside the institution to result in institutional transformation (Dill, 1997b; Keller, 1997; Peterson, 1997; Van Vught, 1997). During this process the industry, the institutional role, and its mission, as well as external relationships, are redefined. Academic and administrative structure and processes, and institutional culture are part of the assessment (Peterson, 1997). We can see that with these challenges mainly administration will be in the position to create adaptive institutions.

Resource Dependence

As in strategic choice approaches, resource dependence theory assumes an active role of individual organizations in their struggle for survival. Again this perspective is characterized by an open system framework, i.e., we cannot understand organizational structure or behavior without understanding the context within which it operates (Aldrich, 1979; Pfeffer and Salancik, 1978; Scott, 1992b). For their survival, organizations must engage in an exchange with the environment. The need to acquire resources creates dependencies between organizations and external units and the scarcity of resources determines the degree of dependency. These economic dependencies can lead to political problems followed by political solutions (Scott, 1992b).

Resource dependence defines adaptation as strategies to reach compliance with external constraints. Successful organizations are called effective (Pfeffer and Salancik, 1978). Pfeffer and Salancik suggest two adaptive responses to compensate for dependence. On the one hand, organizations can adapt and change to fit environmental requirements. On the other hand, organizations can attempt to alter the environment so that it fits the organization's capabilities. The main contribution of resource dependence theory is the detailed analysis of adaptation strategies. These include merging with other organizations, diversifying, coopting important others through interlocking directorates, or engaging in political activities to influence matters such as regulations (Pfeffer and Salancik, 1978).

Accordingly, organizations are viewed as active. Organizational participants—especially managers—scan the relevant environment, searching for threats and opportunities with the goal to find the most favorable and profitable solution. The selection of customers and the terms of exchange are partly determined by the organization. Effective managers acquire sufficient resources without creating too much dependence (Scott, 1992b). Pfeffer and Salancik promote a form of management that includes symbolic, responsive, and discretionary features (Aldrich, 1979; Pfeffer and Salancik, 1978). In general, resource dependency theory interprets organizations as "capable of changing, as well as responding to, the environment" (Pfeffer and Salancik, 1978, p. 83).

The environment plays a major role in resource dependence because of its affect on the organization. As with institutional isomorphism, it is defined as the major reason for dependence and includes a technical or task environment (e.g. resources, markets) and an environment of interest groups and political actors (e.g., policies, values).

External funds are becoming the most critical resource for universities. An important indicator is that most adaptation is based on a shift in the financial structure of universities. Based on resource dependence theory, authors have shown (Gumport and Pusser, 1995; Hackman, 1985; Leslie, 1995; Pfeffer and Salancik, 1978; Rhoades, 1995; Slaughter, 1995; Tolbert, 1985) that "structure follows resources" at universities; i.e., new sources of income make new structures to manage these dependencies necessary. As we are proposing, the current environment for higher education and the restructuring initiatives based on budget cuts in many Western countries have led to a shift in authority structure at the institutional level. Administrators become more important because they are mainly responsible for the development and implementation of strategies that help to reduce dependency relationships with the environment.

Network Organization

One of the more recent theories applied to organizations is the network approach (Gerstein, 1992: Nadler, Gerstein, and Shaw, 1992; Nohria, 1992; Nohria and Eccles, 1992; Powell, 1990; Scott, 1992a). This approach helps to understand power and influence in organizations, new organizing efforts, strategic alliances, and new competitive forces (Nohria, 1992). It mainly focuses on internal and external boundary spanning relationships that characterize organizational functioning. Organizations are defined as social networks and their environment consists of other organizations and relevant groupings. Actions, attitudes, and behaviors have to be analyzed as contingent upon the position in the network of relationships (Nohria, 1992).

Adaptation is influenced and shaped by linkages established inside and among institutions. Network organizations are committed to their network partners through trust and information sharing. Management is constrained to adapt quickly to purely economical pressures. But with increasing environmental complexity networks can be advantageous for adaptation (Dill, 1997a). The role of management is shaped by the position in the network and includes the establishment and maintenance of linkages or the production and distribution of information. We can differentiate between networks among and networks within organizations.

Networks among organizations provide a structure of lateral exchange with reciprocal lines of communication. Organizations conduct resource allocation through networks of individuals engaged in mutually supportive actions. Because one organization is dependent on the resource of another, advantages can be gained by pooling resources. These relationships need time to be established and sustained. Networks are good for circumstances where there is a need for efficient reliable information and they permit the exchange of "thick" descriptions (Powell, 1990). In conditions of uncertainty, network structures that encourage reciprocity, trust, and long-term commitments offer the best potential for adaptability and innovation.

Internally, network organizations differ in architecture from hierarchically designed structures (Gerstein, 1992; Nohria and Ghoshal, 1994). Resources are not concentrated in the center nor disbursed to basic units. Assets, knowledge, and competence are distributed throughout the institution, residing in multiple locations. Not all operating units interact with a comparable environment nor possess the same relative resources: they may play different roles within the organization. In developing new services or strategies, some units lead while others play a supportive role. Integration is facilitated through shared values, common standards, extensive horizontal communication and socialization. Some structures, such as project groups and teams are only temporary. Network organizations depend on strong but flexible planning and budgeting systems, and common incentives (Dill and Sporn, 1995b).

Academic institutions can experiment with network organizational structures to solve the problem of dynamically changing environments (Dill, 1997a; Dill and Sporn, 1995b). Tra-

ditionally, the university's capacity to innovate and adapt was built upon the formal network structure of the disciplines and professions, as well as the informal networks of academic work. Complex environmental demands upon the university at the end of the century require structural innovation at the overall university level. Here the traditional forms of academic networks need to be integrated and used as a comparative advantage for adaptation. To achieve this goal administration has to coordinate highly differentiated academic institutions, information technology, organizational structure, and management through, e.g., mission statements.

Based on this line of reasoning, we would expect network forms of academic institutions to proliferate. As cases have shown, the major motivation can be seen in the increased need of know-how, and the demand for speed and trust. Powell (1990) found the following comparative advantages of networks in his case studies:

- Cooperation can be sustained over the long run as an effective arrangement.

- Networks create incentives for teaming and the dissemination of information, thus allowing ideas to be translated into action quickly.

- The open-ended quality of networks is useful when resources are variable and the environment uncertain.

- Networks offer a highly feasible means of utilizing and enhancing tacit knowledge and technological innovation.

We can use the network approach to analyze how universities can make more use of their qualities as professional or collegial networks. Additionally, the approach explains how management plays a critical role in mediating lateral and horizontal communication patterns. Since overall university integration and management instruments are becoming more important, administrators rise to the new key players in the network. Through their internal and external linkages with essential constituencies, the power of their position increases.

The Expanding Role of Administration

Based on this review of relevant theoretical models of adaptation, we turn now to the discussion of the expanded role of administration. At the close of this century, there is an increased awareness and urgency about managing the environmental demands for higher education. At the same time, a prominent part of this discourse is a demand for the management of higher education to become leaner, more efficient, and more accountable. This creates an apparent paradox: essentially a demand to do more with less. Our interpretation is that this paradox is reconciled by changing the role of administration, by expanding the domain of administrative authority.

As prescriptions for management reform abound, both implicitly and explicitly in the relevant organizational approaches reviewed above, we think the expanded role for administration may be understood as a consequence of three distinct yet interdependent dynamics. They are as follows: (1) resource dependence that is primarily motivated by organizational survival, (2) institutional isomorphism that is motivated by legitimacy concerns, and (3) professional authority that is motivated by a struggle for control of the institutional enterprise. These three dynamics form imperatives to manage resources, sustain legitimacy, and ensure their own professional authority.

We identify these three converging dynamics as a conceptual scaffolding that generates propositions which may be examined in future research. It is interesting to note that data on change and expansion of higher education administration are scarce, even for something as basic as documenting the growth of administration in size and role across national settings. It is our hope that this thesis will break new ground for prompting empirical studies of how contemporary demands for management reform may have far reaching consequences for the changing organization of academic work.

Managing Resource Relationships

Building on our review of resource dependence theory in higher education, the administration may be seen as an active agent positioning the university in a struggle for survival. Focusing on an uncertain and turbulent environmental context, on which the organization is necessarily dependent for resources, the administration could spend all of its resources in the service of scanning, forecasting and repositioning itself within a changing environment. The primary motivation is for the organization to survive.

From this perspective, three challenges are most prominent: staying attuned to changes in resource dependencies; meeting expectations for compliance with environmental demands; and cultivating alternative resources to reduce existing dependencies. The imperative to manage these challenges provides a compelling rationale for expanded administrative roles. For survival, organizations and the agents who act on their behalf must attend to all three dimensions.

First, administrators in universities are prepared to elaborate their structures to stay attuned to changes in their resources. As primary examples of this focus of attention, public university officials give ongoing attention to forecasting enrollment changes, shifts in state appropriations, and how such changes are handled by their peer institutions that are competitors. It is essential to note that administrators must stay attuned to multiple environments, with primary attention paid to those resources on which the organization has had the greatest dependence.

Second, a key ongoing function of the administration is to ensure compliance with demands. There are various mechanisms in place for ensuring and then demonstrating that an academic organization is in compliance, some of which are expensive for the organization. Health and safety regulations abound, for example, as both public and private universities often attest. As new layers of expectations for reporting are relevant for universities, satisfactory compliance with these requirements is often tied to state and national funding (e.g., national funds for student financial aid, state general fund appropriations for institutions, etc.). And increasingly, additional layers of expectations have been identified for public higher education and tied to funding that is essential to organizational survival. These initiatives range from demonstrating faculty workload to assessment of student learning outcomes.

Third, and extremely visible in the contemporary era, is the cultivation of new resources to reduce existing dependencies. For public colleges and universities this takes the primary form of devising strategies that will generate revenue for the organization—whether it be seeking out new student markets, new sources for research funding, or cultivating new sources of private gifts. (The latter used to be called "development" activities, and is now commonly known as "institutional advancement.") The cultivation of a plurality of resources to reduce existing dependencies has long been seen a prudent cost for organizations, but has gained greater currency for public higher education in the contemporary era where primary dependence on funding from the state seems imprudent given fluctuations.

Across these dimensions, the common thread is that administrators and their staff of subordinates are responsible for maintaining the organization's exchange relationships and the ongoing transactions with its environments. Whether the administration functions as a bridge or a buffer, the main role is to manage these dependencies for the organization's very survival. From this perspective, in the best of all possible worlds, this role for administration would be welcomed by faculty, who would see their own functions primarily at the core of the organization—to teach and do research. In this way, the administration buffers the faculty by themselves performing key adaptive responses to threats and opportunities.

However, the management of resource dependencies in practice is more complex, as resource strategies ripple through the organization rather than being contained at one level or in one part of the organization. For example, the cultivation of revenue-generating strategies may involve programmatic changes that faculty may not support due to commitments that lie in educational criteria or values that run contrary to cost-effectiveness principles. Potential strain may also emerge within the organization, if faculty suggest the administration has cast environmental factors in an overly deterministic and disproportionately influential role. In the United States in the contemporary era, we see examples of this in Virginia where a legislative restructuring mandate tied to state funding was initially met with faculty resistance; it is important to note that adequate campus responses to the mandated change ultimately did occur in the requisite time frame

(Gumport and Pusser, 1999, this volume). These examples point to a key premise in the resource dependence perspective—that administrators can speak for and act for the organization as a whole in repositioning it within resource dependencies. If administrators have the responsibility to manage according to this premise, the path to organizational survival becomes more assured if administrators have ongoing access to information about the changing resources and have the ability to alter the strategies of the organization to respond to those changes.

Sustaining Institutional Legitimacy

Adaptation to environmental demands becomes even more complex when we focus on the organization's principle nonfinancial resource—its legitimacy. The key concern raised from the above section on resource dependence is twofold: Can the organization respond to whatever is demanded in order to survive? And how to reconcile conflicting demands. Implicit in this approach is a significant question: not only whether or not the organization can respond, but also whether it even *should* respond to demands.

Drawing on institutional isomorphism theory, we see university administrators as key players in mimetic as well as normative isomorphic processes. In the current climate, university administrators develop and implement business-like strategies in order to show that they are responsive to demands for management reform. Even a symbolic act can be sufficient to signal the organization's responsiveness and thus to accrue legitimacy. From this perspective, the primary motivation is to act for the organization to ensure that it will be seen as legitimate. Failure to do so may leave the organization vulnerable to judgments that it is not legitimate thus threatening its niche and its very survival.

At the core of this dynamic is a concern with organizational purpose. For universities this translates into mission, a broad notion of organizational goals that has proven to be exceedingly malleable over time. As Gumport and Pusser (1995) have suggested, in times of expansion, administrators have used mission as a stand-in for policy; while in times of contraction mission is less effective for helping administrators determine among the array of possible priorities (Dill, 1997b).

In the current climate, it is critical to ask not only whether the organization *can* adapt to whatever is demanded, but whether it *should* respond to what is demanded—for it is not clear if an entirely different kind of organization may result.

For example, consider a situation in which both a local community college and a liberal arts college are facing demands to offer more vocationally oriented programs, including electronic access through expanded distance learning programs. It is prudent for the community college to do so, given that those community colleges nationwide which are perceived to be cutting edge are doing precisely that and advertising through relevant media that can enthusiastically accommodate these demands. For the selective liberal arts college, however, the path is not clear. While some liberal arts colleges may come to add some vocationally oriented programs, the bulk of the academic program cannot shift too far afield from its liberal education mission. In fact, the institutional unwillingness to offer such programs may earn it greater legitimacy within a smaller elite niche for holding steadfast to its commitment to distinctive values in its mission. In this situation, it would be prudent to see what its peer institutions are doing, and even better if it can determine what the most successful liberal arts colleges are doing to respond to such demands[7].

Giving the primary attention to gaining and sustaining organizational legitimacy, this perspective sheds light on the possibility that changing environments may be constituted of conflicting demands. It is not that demands are inherently in conflict, but that the pursuit of them at the same time would call for strategies that are contradictory, or at cross-purposes. A classic illustration of contradictory demands is the demand on public universities to simultaneously reduce or contain costs, improve teaching and learning, become technologically current, and expand access. The demand to reduce or cut costs can be achieved in several ways, for example streamlining, budget discipline, elimination of programs that are not cost-effective, not investing in risky or expensive ventures, and trying to achieve economies of scale. Improvement of teaching and learning may be achieved by reducing the class size or providing more faculty attention to individual students, obtaining better state of the art equipment, and enhancing the learning environments to overcome various barriers. Similarly, upgrading technology may entail major overhauls of the institutional infrastructure and access to information systems in addition to providing students and faculty with state of the art equipment and training to use it. Finally, expanding access may involve admitting students who are under-prepared academically and thus would require expansion of extensive remedial programs across subject matters. Accomplishing any one of these four would be an outstanding feat, and any two in a resource-constrained environment unlikely. The planning dilemma for the organization is to determine which demands are the highest priority.

A compelling rationale for the management of these challenges positions the administrators in the central mediating role of determining the potential costs and benefits of any course of action (or nonaction) for the organization's legitimacy. In the absence of faculty involvement, administrators who occupy the most visible leadership roles in the university function as interpreters for the rest of the organization. In this capacity, they address such key concerns as: Who are the constituencies from whom the organization is seeking legitimacy? What are successful peer institutions doing to manage contradictory demands? Can some demands be responded to symbolically and superficially or minimally, as in a "satisficing" mode? What are the consequences for how the organization will be viewed vis-à-vis mission? Attending to these concerns, administrators can both symbolically manage the image of the organization to those in the environment and internally to organizational members as well as to the governing board. While it is unlikely that administrators can create a dissonance-free organization, their efforts on these dimensions can have powerful results for securing a sense of organizational identity as the organization navigates through times of environmental uncertainty and turbulence.

Expanding Professional Authority

While the management of resource relationships and sustaining legitimacy illuminates some of the dynamics underlying the major role of administration in the organization's response to changing environments, the two perspectives have a key premise that warrants careful scrutiny—that administrators are appropriately and effectively positioned to act for the organization. This premise is of course questionable: whether administrators should not only be acting as spokespersons for the institution, but whether they should and—even can—reposition the organization amidst changing environments. While the management of resource dependence and legitimacy provides a compelling post-hoc rationale for expanded administrative activities, an additional governance[8] dynamic is undergoing transformation within the organization. Administrators position themselves in an expanded role as managers having authority over a broader domain of organizational decision-making as well as in representing the organization's purposes and priorities to the environment. Drawing on literature from the sociology of professions and selected higher education scholars, we interpret this dynamic as a shift in the authority structure within academic organizations, that entails a narrowing of the domain of faculty's professional authority. Even though prescriptions for management reform entail such an expanded authority of the administrative domain, we suggest that this transformation is problematic in terms of appropriateness and effectiveness.

Within academic organizations, the basic structure of authority has been characterized as a combination of administrative and professional authority (Etzioni, 1964). Administrative authority is based in the responsibilities of the position that resides in a bureaucratic hierarchy, while professional authority is based in expert knowledge of individuals with accountability assured through self–regulation (Larson, 1977; Freidson, 1970, 1986, 1994). According to Etzioni (1964), in academic organizations, administrators are to offer advice about economic and organizational implications of various activities undertaken by professionals, but the professionals themselves and their decision-making bodies have the responsibility for the academic domain, on matters related to the core activities of teaching and research. Stated somewhat more as an admonishment to administrators' awareness of limits on their authority, Duryea (1962, p. 43) explained the ideal as follows: "In exercising authority, the administrator should stress collaborative effort, especially in his relations with professional personnel. He serves as a leader among scholars rather than an executive over employees." Thus, the ensuing locus of authority in academic organizations has been characterized as diffuse, with decisions made at several levels with little central steering, oversight and sanctions (Hearn, 1988). A domain of shared authority has long been acknowledged, stressing the mutual interdependence of faculty and administration and the ideal of working on a joint endeavor in matters that entail an intermingling of academic and fiscal concerns (Mortimer and McConnell, 1978). However, as Abbott (1988) notes, disputes over claims of jurisdiction are significant aspects of the social relations of professionals, both for the dynamics internal to the organization and for relations with external audiences.

Work on governance and strategy formation in higher education institutions (Cameron, 1984; Chaffee, 1985; Chaffee, 1989; Hardy et al, 1983; Peterson, 1981) shows how decisions at colleges and universities can be distinguished between administrative fiat, professional judgment, and collective choice (Hardy et al, 1983). While administrators and professionals only dominate certain areas (e.g. teaching and research; support services) of decision making, decisions based on collective choice often pertain to issues of the overall institution. These situations of collective choice are characterized by interactive processes which have the potential of creating consistencies through formal procedure and implicit habit, leading to (more or less) planned strategies based on consensus (Hardy et al, 1983). Ideally. decision making through collective choice would even compensate for shifting authority structures within academic institutions.

Over time, as academic organizations have become larger, with more complex and elaborated structures, there has been a growth of administrative expenditures and positions (Blau, 1994; Clark, 1993; Gumport and Pusser, 1995). With the increased visibility of administrators on campuses, they have developed their own specialized knowledge for running the organization. At the same time, administrators at several levels of the organization have also established professional identities through formal associations (e.g., AAU, SCUP, AIR, NASPA, NACAC—some of which have their own statements of "professional standards" for planners, institutional researchers, student personnel administrators, and college admissions counselors) and informal groups (e.g. ad hoc meetings of provosts from peer institutions). Observers of contemporary higher education have also acknowledged that there are different authority patterns by institutional type, with elite institutions retaining a larger domain of faculty authority than community colleges (Clark, 1983; Ruscio, 1997; Dill and Helm, 1988).

Based on Freidson (1986), the emergence of the administrative class could be seen as a new professional category. From this perspective, administrators and faculty compete for control over the enterprise and for resources within it. Evidence that substantiates the plausibility of this hypothesis can be found in Rhoades (1998), which identifies a new class of managerial professionals, middle management administrators who have expanded control over faculty.

In practice, the combination of shared authority principles has not been without strain, especially given the politics of scarce resources (Hearn, 1989; Gumport, 1993). Even since the 1960s where division of academic labor in universities gave faculty increased jurisdiction over academic matters and administrators the responsibility to coordinate the means of the major activities carried out by the professionals, over the past several decades there has been a move away from democratic faculty participation to strategic policymaking (Keller, 1983; Dill and Helm, 1988). Managerial prescriptions have positioned administrators as experts wielding tools of forecasting, cost-benefit analyses, and modeling techniques facilitated by access to technology that enables careful scrutiny of centralized data. The expansion of administrative authority has been facilitated by declaration of a crisis, in which longer range academic governance procedures could be bypassed in favor of swift centralized decision-making (Hearn, 1988; Gumport, 1993).

Observers of academic organizations have also noted the emergence of a new type of decision-making body constituted by ad hoc committees (Keller, 1983; Schuster et al, 1994). Harkening back to the ideal of joint endeavor, such a big decision committee can engage in deliberations about long range planning. Constituted by representatives from administration, faculty and students, this type of committee has been proposed as a structural and process solution that is capable of reconciling inherent tensions within planning and governance (Schuster et al, 1994).

However, in spite of the emergence of such ad hoc committees, there is also an emerging concern about an underlying shift in the organization of academic work. This critical concern falls under the general category of "the politics of professional work" (Rhoades, 1998). It is compatible with related critical analyses of "managerialism" (Enteman, 1993) and "the emergence of technocracy," a term that is intended to replace the simple bureaucracy-professionalism dualism that has been used to characterize academic organizations (Heydebrand, 1990). Building on the historical argument that universities have become more entrepreneurial through increased academic capitalism, scholars have proposed that so too universities have become more managerial in their governance and the division of labor (Rhoades and Slaughter, 1997). In particular, Rhoades (1998) has proposed that faculty have become "managed professionals," while middle-level administrators have become "managerial professionals."

A key rationale for this shift in authority has been the need for managerial flexibility and a concomitant need for discretion to make centralized resource allocation decisions. The consequences for the organization are all-important, as such decisions determine where and how the organization will invest its resources. The reach of such expanded administrative authority ranges from selecting among organizational priorities to determining the academic workforce and its characteristics (i.e., full-time vs. part-time, course load, etc.). Central to this argument is the proposition that such authority shifts and ensuing structural consequences should not necessarily be predetermined by environmental conditions. As Rhoades and Slaughter (1997, P. 33) argue: "The structural patterns we describe are not just inexorable external developments to which colleges and universities are subject and doomed. . . . The academy itself daily enacts and expresses social relations of capitalism and heightened managerial control grounded in a neo-conservative discourse."

Implicit in these accounts is a contest over control over the enterprise and calling into question the presumption that managerialism is a natural academic adaptation. The main issues with regard to administrators acting for the organization are appropriateness and effectiveness. Who should appropriately determine organizational priorities and purposes? Administrators, faculty, or governing boards chartered with the overall responsibility for the institution? Should participative forms of decision-making be preserved in spite of their inefficiency? Moreover, in an era where there is already an increased proportion of part-time faculty (Rhoades, 1996 and forthcoming), there is critical concern that traditional forms of faculty governance are de facto rendered ineffective. Are administrators effective at making decisions as to which academic programs and positions should be privileged in the name of selective excellence? As far as management of academic work, there are similar questions as to whether administrators should and can effectively manage faculty. While there has been considerable discussion of the potential for administrative incentives and sanctions to increase faculty productivity (Massy, 1996; Massy and Zemsky, 1994), there has been little discussion of whether such incentives and sanctions are appropriate. Recently, there has been emerging concern over the effect on faculty morale of performance-based initiatives (Gumport, 1997) as well as no-tenure contracts (Bess, 1998), that such institutional initiatives may be detrimental to the academic workplace.

Nonetheless, the climate of accountability is an ongoing pressure wherein administrators are asked to speak for their institutions and to respond to their governing boards and external constituencies. In this context, we find it revealing that the accountability discourse at the state level scapegoats faculty and asks for scrutiny of faculty workload and productivity more often than it does for administrators themselves. However, before concluding that administrators have become well-established as their own self-regulating professional interest group, it is essential to note a critical undercurrent that ranges from allegations of excessive expenditures to administrative incompetence (Gilley, 1997). Perhaps the lesson to be taken from the current climate is that no professional group—whether aspiring or long-established—is immune to criticism.

When examining the domain of professional authority, these concepts warrant further attention as well as empirical study. There are few empirical studies that have begun to document how contemporary demands for management reform may have far reaching consequences for the organization of academic work (the primary exception being Rhoades, 1998). Work that examines shifts in the structure of authority for academic organizations will be important for all stakeholders in the enterprise. For in all likelihood, the social division of labor in academic organizations will continue to be differentiated, elaborated, and contested. A number of unexplored themes need attention, including examining changes in the labor process (skilling and deskilling of academic workers), the ownership of academic work (the products of teaching as well as research), the role of gender, race and class, as well as concomitant changes in the distribution of power and autonomy.

Obviously, the contemporary academic organization is more complex than the characterization of a blend of professional and bureaucratic authority. It is essential to note that there is a long history of exhortations of the evils of bureaucracy in academic organizations and the potential for administrative mentalities to be detrimental to scholarship (Blau, 1994). In the context of the research for this chapter, we think it essential to note that administrators play a vital role in mediating a wide range of changing environmental demands. These are difficult positions that many academics would find unattractive, even distasteful. At the same time, however, we think the de facto expansion of the jurisdiction of administrative authority may have devastating educational consequences. While we are not arguing for decentralization of all decisions related to academic affairs, we are advocates of the valuable substantive role faculty must play in determining how to re-position the present and future course of academic organizations. Our sense is that the competing interests in these decisions need to be made more explicit, so that they can be carefully weighed, negotiated, and then implemented by the organization. As it stands, without acknowledging that there are competing interests alongside a struggle for control of the enterprise, attempts at wholesale management reform may further polarize the members of the organization and result in professional discord that is detrimental to the university's viability in the next century.

Conclusion

In this chapter, we have suggested that prescriptions for institutional adaptation to changing environments, either implicitly or explicitly, call for an expanded role of administration. Whether administrators are viewed as managers of the organization's resource dependencies, interpreters and promoters of the organization's actions as legitimate, the domain for administrative authority has expanded. Of course, this is not a *fait accompli*. And prescriptions for expanded administrative authority are not to be equated with actual expansion of administrative control. Furthermore, expanded administrative control of the institutional enterprise does not necessarily entail appropriate or effective control of the academic enterprise. Thus, we advocate proceeding with caution and identifying the conceptual possibilities and propositions that may or may not be borne out in data.

Based on our analysis, we would argue that successful processes and structures for adaptation can only be implemented through joint activities of administration and faculty. As we see it now, danger emerges that the expansion of administration leads to counterproductive forces, i.e., splitting the academy and impeding adaptation. Through more involvement, decentralization and networks which give back power and respect to professionals, the desired outcomes of organizational effectiveness and efficiency of the university would follow. We suggest further research on these structures and processes, as no detailed data exist and the results would aid university practice. In our chapter we concentrated on the dynamics of administrative expansion as adaptation, but further conceptual and empirical work on this topic is needed.

Much empirical work is yet to be done. We would like to see studies that document the growth of administration and administrative expenditures across types of institutions and across national settings. We would also like to see research that examines the emergence and the changing role of administration, including differences in types of administrative positions vertically in the hierarchy (provost, finance offices, deans) and horizontally with respect to different functions (student affairs, faculty affairs, government affairs). It is our hope that this thesis will break new ground for prompt-

ing empirical studies of how contemporary demands for management reform have far reaching consequences for the organization of academic work and ultimately for the organization itself.

References

Abbott, A. (1988). *The System of Professions: an Essay on the Division of Expert Labor*. Chicago and London: University of Chicago Press.

Aldrich, H. (1979). *Organizations and Environments*. Englewood Cliffs, NJ: Prentice-Hall.

Argyris, C. (1982). How learning and reasoning processes affect organizational change. In P. S. Goodman (ed.), *Change in Organizations*. San Francisco: Jossey-Bass

Argyris, C. (1994). *On Organizational Learning*. Oxford: Blackwell.

Argyris, C., and Schön, D. (1974). *Organizational Learning*. Reading, Mass.: Addison-Wesley.

Balderston, F. E. (1995). *Managing Today's University: Strategies for Viability, Change, and Excellence*. Second Edition. San Francisco: Jossey-Bass.

Baldridge, J. V. (1983). Organizational characteristics of colleges and universities. In J. V. Baldridge and T. Deal (eds.), *The Dynamics of Organizational Change in Education*. Berkeley: McCutchan.

Baldridge, J. V., Curtis, D. V., Ecker, G. P., and Riley, G. L. (1977). Alternative models of governance in higher education. In G. L. Riley and J. V. Baldridge (eds.), *Governing Academic Organizations*. Berkeley, CA: McCutchan.

Baldridge, J. V., and Deal. T. E. (1983). The basics of change in educational organizations. In J. V. Baldridge, T. E. Deal, and C. Ingols (eds.), *The Dynamics of Organizational Change in Education*. Berkeley, CA: McCutchan.

Barrow, C. W. (1993). Will the fiscal crisis force higher ed to restructure? *Thought and Action*: 7–24.

Becher, T., and Kogan, M. (1992). *Process and Structure in Higher Education*. Second Edition. London: Routledge.

Berdahl, R., and McConnell, T. R. (1994). Autonomy and accountability: Some fundamental issues. In P. Altbach, R. Berdahl, and P. Gumport (eds.), *Higher Education in American Society*. Amherst, NY: Prometheus Books.

Berdahl, R. O., and Millett, J. D. (1991). Autonomy and accountability in United States higher education. In G. Neave and F. A. Van Vught (eds.), *Prometheus Bound: The Changing Relationship Between Government and Higher Education in Western Europe*. Oxford: Pergamon.

Bergmann, B. R. (1991). Bloated administration, blighted campuses. *Academe* November-December: 12–15.

Bess, J. (1998). Contract systems, bureaucracies, and faculty motivation: The probable effects of a no-tenure policy. *Journal of Higher Education*. 69 (1) January/February: 1–22.

Birnbaum, R. (1989). *How Colleges Work: The Cybernetics of Academic Organization and Leadership*. San Francisco: Jossey-Bass.

Birnbaum, R. (1992). *How Academic Leadership Works: Understanding Success and Failure in the College Presidency*. San Francisco: Jossey-Bass.

Blau, P. M. (1994). *The Organization of Academic Work*. Second edition. New Brunswick: Transaction Publishers.

Burns, G. P. (ed.). (1962). *Administrators in Higher Education: Their Functions and Coordination*. New York: Harper and Row.

Burns, T., and Stalker, G. M. (1961). *The Management of Innovation*. London: Tavistock.

Cameron, K. (1983). Strategic responses to conditions of decline: Higher education and the private sector. *Journal of Higher Education* 54(4): 359–380.

Cameron, K. (1984). Organizational adaptation and higher education. *Journal of Higher Education* 55(2), 122–144.

Cameron, K. and Tschirhart, M. (1992). Postindustrial environments and organizational effectiveness in colleges and universities. *Journal of Higher Education* 63(1): 87–108.

Cameron, K. and Whetten, D. (1996). Organizational effectiveness and quality: The second generation. In J. Smart (ed.), *Higher Education: Handbook of Theory and Research*. Volume XI. New York: Agathon.

Cameron, K. S., and Quinn, R. E. (1983). The field of organizational development. In R. E. Quinn and K. S. Cameron (eds.), Classics in Organization Development. Oak Park, Ill.: Moore Publishing.

Chaffee, E. E. (1983). Three models of strategy. *Academy of Management Review*, 10(1), 89–98.

Chaffee, E. E. (1985). The concept of strategy: From business to higher education. In J. Smart (ed.), *Higher Education: Handbook of Theory and Research*. Volume I. New York: Agathon.

Chaffee, E. E. (1989). Strategy and Effectiveness in systems of higher education. In J. Smart (ed.), *Higher Education: Handbook of Theory and Research*. Volume V. New York: Agathon.

Child, J. (1972). Organizational structure, environment and performance: The role of strategic choice. *Sociology* 6: 1–22.

Chronicle of Higher Education. (1997, August 29). Almanac, pp. 24, 26.

Clark, B. R. (1983). The Higher Education System: Academic Organization in Cross-national Perspective. Berkeley, CA: University of California Press.

Clark, B. R. (1993). The problem of complexity in modern higher education. In S. Rothblatt and B. Wittrock (eds.), *The European and American University Since 1800*. Cambridge: Cambridge University Press.

Clark, B. R. (1993). Complexity and differentiation: The deepening problem of integration. In D. D. Dill and B. Sporn (eds.), *Emerging Patterns of Social Demand and University Reform: Through a Glass Darkly*. Oxford: Pergamon.

Clark, B. R. (1996a). Case studies of innovative universities: A progress report. *Tertiary Education and Management* 2(1): 52–61.

Clark, B. R. (1996b). Leadership and innovation in universities: From theory to practice. *Tertiary Education and Management* 1(1): 7–11.

Clark, B. R. (1996c). Substantive growth and innovative organization: New categories for higher education research. *Higher Education* 32: 417–430.

Clark, B. R. (1998). *Creating Entrepreneurial Universities: Organizational Pathways of Transformation*. Oxford: Pergamon.

Cohen, M. D., and March, J. G. (1974). *Leadership and Ambiguity: The American College President*, second edition, Boston: Harvard Business School Press.

Conrad, C. F. (1978). A grounded theory of academic change. *Sociology of Education* 51: 101–112.

Cyert, R. M., and March, J. G. (1992). *A Behavioral Theory of the Firm*, second edition. Englewood Cliffs, NJ: Prentice-Hall.

De Boer, H., and Goedegebuure, L. (1995). Decision-making in higher education—a comparative perspective. *Australian Universities' Review* 1: 41–47.

Dill, D. D. (1992a). Academic administration. In B. R. Clark and G. R. Neave (eds.), *The Encyclopedia of Higher Education*. Volume 2. Oxford: Pergamon.

Dill, D. D. (1992b). Organization and administration of higher education. In M. C. Alkin, M. Linden. J. Noel, and K. Ray (eds.), *Encyclopedia of Educational Research*. Volume 3. New York: Macmillan.

Dill, D. D. (1993a). Implementing a planning process: A problem in organizational design. Paper presented at Society for College and University Planning, Minneapolis, Minnesota, July 1993.

Dill, D. D. (1993b). Quality by design: Toward a framework for quality management in higher education. In J. Smart (ed.). *Higher Education: Handbook of Theory and Research*. Volume VIII. New York: Agathon.

Dill, D. D. (1994). Rethinking the planning process. *Planning for Higher Education* 22(2): 8–13.

Dill, D. D. (1997a). Effects of competition on diverse institutional contexts. In M. W. Peterson, D. D. Dill, and L. A. Mets (eds.), *Planning and Management for a Changing Environment: A Handbook on Redesigning Postsecondary Institutions*. San Francisco: Jossey-Bass.

Dill, D. D. (1997b). Focusing institutional mission to provide coherence and integration. In M. W. Peterson, D. D. Dill, and L. A. Mets (eds.), *Planning and Management for a Changing Environment: A Handbook on Redesigning Postsecondary Institutions*. San Francisco: Jossey-Bass.

Dill, D. D., and Friedman, C. P., (1979). An analysis of frameworks for research on innovation and change in higher education. *Review of Education Research* 49(3): 411–435.

Dill, D. D., and Helm, K. P. (1988) Faculty participation in strategic policy making. In J. Smart (ed.), *Higher education: Handbook of theory and research.* Volume IV. New York: Agathon.

Dill, D. D., and Sporn, B. (1995a). The implications of a postindustrial environment for the university: An introduction. In D. D. Dill and B. Sporn (eds.), *Emerging Patterns of Social Demand and University Reform: Through a Glass Darkly.* Oxford: Pergamon.

Dill, D. D., and Sporn, B. (1995b). University 2001: What will the university of the twenty-first century look like? In D. D. Dill and B. Sporn (eds.), *Emerging Patterns of Social Demand and University Reform: Through a Glass Darkly.* Oxford: Pergamon.

DiMaggio, P. J. and Powell, W. W. (1983). The iron cage revisited: Institutional isomorphism and collective rationality in organizational fields. *American Sociological Review* 48: 147–160.

Dooris, M. J. (1989). Organizational adaptation and the commercialization of research universities. *Planning for Higher Education* 17(3): 21–31.

Drucker, P. F. (1997). The future that has already happened. *Harvard Business Review* September-October: 20–24.

Duryea, E. D. (1962). The theory and practice of administration. In G. P. Burns (ed.), *Administrators in Higher Education.* New York: Harper and Row.

Enteman, W. (1993). *Managerialism: The Emergence of a New Ideology.* Madison: University of Wisconsin Press.

Etzioni, A. (1904). Administrative and Professional Authority. In A. Etzioni. *Modern Organizations.* Englewood Cliffs, NJ: Prentice-Hall.

Ewell, P. T. (1991). Assessment and public accountability: Back to the future. *Change* 23(6): 12–17.

Ewell, P T. (1997). Strengthening assessment for academic quality improvement. In M. W. Peterson, D. D. Dill, and L. A. Mets (eds.), *Planning and Management for a Changing Environment: A Handbook on Redesigning Postsecondary Institutions.* San Francisco: Jossey-Bass.

Freidson, E. (1970). *Profession Of Medicine: A Study of the Sociology of Applied Knowledge.* New York, NY: Harper and Row.

Freidson, E. (1986). *Professional Powers: A Study of the Institutionalization of Formal Knowledge.* Chicago, IL: The University of Chicago Press.

Freidson, E. (1994). *Professionalism Reborn: Theory, Prophecy and Policy.* Chicago: The University of Chicago Press.

Galbraith, J. R. (1977). *Organization Design.* Reading, MA.: Addison-Wesley.

Gellert, C. (1993a). Introduction: Changing patterns in European higher education. In C. Gellert (ed.). *Higher Education in Europe.* London: Jessica Kingsley.

Gellert, C. (1993b). Structures and functional differentiation—Remarks on changing paradigms of tertiary education in Europe. In C. Gellert (ed.), *Higher Education in Europe.* London: Jessica Kingsley.

Gerstein, M. S. (1992). From machine bureaucracies to networked organizations: An architectural journey. In D. A. Nadler, M. S. Gerstein, and R. B. Shaw (eds.), *Organizational Architecture: Designs for Changing Organizations.* San Francisco: Jossey-Bass.

Gibbons, M. (1995). The university as an instrument for the development of science and basic research: The implications of mode 2 science. In D. D. Dill and B. Sporn (eds.), *Emerging Patterns of Social Demand and University Reform: Through a Glass Darkly.* Oxford: Pergamon.

Gilley, J. W. (1997). Governors versus college presidents: Who leads? In L. Goodchild, C. Lovell, E. Hines, and J. Gill. (eds.) *Public Policy and Higher Education.* ASHE Reader Series. Needham Heights, MA: Simon and Schuster Publishing.

Goldstein, H., Maier, G., and Luger, M. (1995). The university as an instrument for economic and business development: U.S. and European comparisons. In D. D. Dill and B. Sporn (eds.), *Emerging Patterns of Social Demand and University Reform: Through a Glass Darkly.* Oxford: Pergamon.

Goldstein, H. A., and Luger, M. I. (1997). Assisting economic and business development. In M. W. Peterson, D. D. Dill, and L. A. Mets (eds.), *Planning and Management for a Changing Environment: A Handbook on Redesigning Postsecondary Institutions.* San Francisco: Jossey-Bass.

Goodman, P. S., and Kurke, L. B. (1982). Studies of change in organizations: A status report. In P. S. Goodman (ed.), *Change in Organizations.* San Francisco: Jossey-Bass.

Green, K. C., and Gilbert, S. W. (1995). Great expectations: Content, communications, productivity, and the role of information technology in higher education. *Change* 27(2): 8–18.

Gumport, P., and Pusser, B. (1995), A case of bureaucratic accretion: Context and consequences. *Journal of Higher Education* 66(5): 493–520.

Gumport, P., and Pusser, B. (1997). Restructuring the academic environment. In M. W. Peterson, D. D. Dill, and L. A. Mets (eds.), *Planning and Management for a Changing Environment: A Handbook on Redesigning Postsecondary Institutions.* San Francisco: Jossey-Bass.

Gumport, P. and Pusser, B. (1999). University restructuring: The role of economic and political forces. In J. Smart (ed.) *Higher Education: Handbook of Theory and Research,* Vol. XIV. New York: Agathon.

Gumport, P. J. (1993). The contested terrain of academic program reduction. *Journal of Higher Education* 64(3): 283–311.

Gumport, P. J., and Chun, M. (forthcoming). Technology and higher education. In P. Altbach, R. Berdahl, and P J. Gumport (eds.), *American Higher Education in the 21st Century: Social, Political and Economic Challenges*. Baltimore: Johns Hopkins University Press.

Guskin, A. E. (1994a). Reducing student costs and enhancing student learning: The university challenge of the 1990s. Part I: Restructuring the administration. *Change* 26(4): 23–29.

Guskin, A. E. (1994b). Reducing student costs and enhancing student learning: The university challenge of the 1990s. Part II: Restructuring the role of faculty. *Change* 26(5): 16–25.

Hackman, J. (1985). Power and centrality in the allocation of resources in colleges and universities. *Administrative Science Quarterly* 30: 61–77.

Hannan, M. T., and Freeman, J. (1977). The population ecology of organization. *American Journal of Sociology* 82(5): 929–964.

Hannan, M. T., and Freeman, J. (1989). *Organizational Ecology*. Cambridge, MA: Harvard University Press.

Hardy, C. (1990). "Hard" decisions and "tough" choices: The business approach to university decline. *Higher Education* 20: 301–321.

Hardy, C., Langley, A., Mintzberg, H., and Rose, J. (1983). Strategy formation in the university setting. *Review of Higher Education* 6(4): 407–433.

Hurtle, T. W., and Galloway, F. J. (1997). Federal guidance for a changing national agenda. In M. W. Peterson, D. D. Dill, and L. A. Mets (eds.), *Planning and Management for a Changing Environment: A Handbook on Redesigning Postsecondary Institutions*. San Francisco: Jossey-Bass.

Hearn, J. C. (1988). Strategy and resources: Economic issues in strategic planning and management in higher education. In J. Smart (ed.), *Higher education: Handbook of Theory and Research*. Volume IV. New York: Agathon.

Hearn, J. C. (1996). Transforming U.S. higher education: An organizational perspective. *Innovative Higher Education* 21(2): 141–154.

Hearn, J. C., Clugston, R. M., and Heydinger, R. B. (1993). Five years of strategic environmental assessment efforts at a research university: A case study of an organizational innovation. *Innovative Higher Education* 18(l): 7–36.

Hedberg, B. L. T., Nystrom, P. C., and Starbuck, W. H. (1976). Camping on seesaws: Prescriptions for a self-designing organization. *Administrative Science Quarterly* 21: 41–65.

Heydebrand, W. (1990). The technocratic organization of academic work. In C. Calhoun, M. W. Meyer, and W. R. Scott (eds.) *Structures of Power and Constraint: Papers in Honor of Peter M. Blau*. Cambridge, MA: Cambridge University Press

Hrebiniak, L. G., and Joyce, W. F. (1985). Organizational adaptation: Strategic choice and environmental determinism. *Administrative Science Quarterly* 30: 336–349.

Huber, G. P, and Glick, W. H. (eds.). (1993). *Organizational Change and Redesign*. New York: Oxford University Press.

Hurtado, S., and Dey, E. L. (1997). Achieving the goals of multiculturalism and diversity. In M. W. Peterson, D. D. Dill, and L. A. Mets (eds.). *Planning and Management for a Changing Environment: A Handbook on Redesigning Postsecondary Institutions*. San Francisco: Jossey-Bass.

Keller, G. (1983). *Academic strategy: The management revolution in American higher education*. Baltimore: The Johns Hopkins University Press.

Keller, G. (1995). The changing milieu for educational planning. *Planning for higher education* 23(2): 23–26.

Keller, G. (1997). Examining what works in strategic planning. In M. W. Peterson, D. D. Dill, and L. A. Mets (eds.). *Planning and Management for a Changing Environment: A Handbook on Redesigning Postsecondary Institutions*. San Francisco: Jossey-Bass.

Kerr, C. (1987). A critical age in the university world: Accumulated heritage versus modern imperatives. *European Journal of Education* 22(2): 183–193.

Kerr, C. (1994). Expanding access and changing missions: The federal role in U.S. higher education. *Educational Record* (Fall): 27–31.

Kogan, M. (forthcoming). The academic-administrative interface. In M. Henkel and B. Little (eds.), *Changing Relationships between Higher Education and the State*. London: Jessica Kingsley.

Kotler, P., and Murphy, P. E. (1981). Strategic planning for higher education. *Journal of Higher Education* 52: 470–489.

Larson, M. S. (1977). *The Rise of Professionalism: A Sociological Analysis*. Berkeley, CA: University of California Press.

Lawler, E., and Mohrman, S. A. (1996). Organizing for effectiveness: Lessons from business. In W. F. Massy (ed.), *Resource Allocation in Higher Education*. Ann Arbor: The University of Michigan Press.

Lawrence, P R., and Lorsch, J. W. (1986). *Organization and Environment: Managing Differentiation and Integration*. Boston: Harvard Business School Press.

Lazerson, M. (1997). Who owns higher education? The changing face of governance. *Change* March/April: 10–15;

Leslie, L., and Rhoades, G. (1995). Rising administrative costs: On seeking explanations, *Journal of Higher Education* 66(2): 187–212.

Leslie, L. L. (1995). What drives higher education management?: The new era in financial support. *Journal for Higher Education Management* 10(2): 5–16.

Levine, A. (1980). *Why Innovation Fails*. Albany, NY., State University of New York Press.

Levitt, B., and March, J. G. (1988). Organizational learning. *Annual Review of Sociology* 14: 319–340.

Lozier, G., and Teeter, D. (1993). Six foundations of total quality management. In D. Teeter and G. Lozier (eds.), *Pursuit of Quality in Higher Education: Case Studies in Total Quality Management*. San Francisco: Jossey-Bass.

March, J. G. (1991). Exploration and exploitation in organizational learning. *Organizational Science* 2(1): 71–87.

March, J. G. (1994). *Three Lectures on Efficiency and Adaptiveness in Organizations*. Helsingfors: The Swedish School of Economics and Business Administration Research Reports.

March, J. G. (1996). Continuity and change in theories of organizational action. *Administrative Science Quarterly* (41): 278–287.

Massy, W. (1996). Productivity issues in higher education. In W. Massy (ed.), *Resource Allocation in Higher Education*. Ann Arbor: The University of Michigan Press.

Massy, W. F., and Zemsky, R. (1994). Faculty discretionary time: Departments and the "academic ratchet." *Journal of Higher Education* 65(1): 1–22.

Meyer, J. W., and Rowan, B. (1977). Institutionalized organizations: Formal structure as myth and ceremony. In J. W. Meyer and W. R. Scott (eds.). *Organizational Environments: Ritual and Rationality*. London: Sage.

Meyer, J. W., and Rowan, B, (1992b). The structure of educational organizations. In J. W. Meyer and W. R. Scott (eds.). *Organizational Environments: Ritual and Rationality*. London: Sage.

Meyer, J. W., and Scott. W. R. (1992). *Organizational Environments: Ritual and Rationality*. London: Sage.

Miles, R. E., and Snow, C. C. (1978). *Organizational Strategy, Structure, and Process*. New York: McGraw-Hill.

Miller, D., and Friesen, P. H. (1980). Momentum and revolution in organizational adaptation. *Academy of Management Journal* 23(4): 591–614.

Mingle, J. R., and Epper. R. M. (1997). State coordination and planning in an age of entrepreneurship. In M. W. Peterson, D. D. Dill. and L. A. Mets (eds.). *Planning and Management for a Changing Environment: A Handbook on Redesigning Postsecondary Institutions*. San Francisco: Jossey-Bass.

Mohrman, S. A., and Mohrman, A. M. (1993). Organizational change and learning. In J. R. Galbraith and E. E. Lawler (eds.), *Organizing for the Future: The New Logic for Managing Complex Organizations*. San Francisco: Jossey-Bass.

Mortimer, K. and T. R. McConnell (1978). *Sharing Authority Effectively*. San Francisco: Jossey-Bass.

Nadler, D. A., Gerstein, M. S., and Shaw, R. B. (1992). *Organizational Architecture: Designs for Changing Organizations*. San Francisco: Jossey-Bass.

Neave, G. (1997). Back to the Future: or, a view on likely brain teasers with which university management is likely to be faced in a fin de siècle world. *Tertiary Education and Management* 3(4): 275–283.

Nohria, N. (1992). Introduction: Is a network perspective a useful way of studying organizations? In N. Nohria and R. G. Eccles (eds.), *Networks and Organizations: Structure, Form, and Action*. Boston: Harvard Business School Press.

Nohria, N., and Eccles, R. G. (eds.). (1992). *Networks and Organizations: Structure, Form, and Action*. Boston: Harvard Business School Press.

Nohria, N., and Ghoshal, S. (1994). Differentiated fit and shared values: Alternatives for managing headquarters-subsidiary relations. *Strategic Management Journal* 15(6): 491–502.

Nowotny, H. (1995). Mass higher education and social mobility: A tenuous link. In D. D. Dill and B. Sporn (eds.), *Emerging Patterns of Social Demand and University Reform: Through a Glass Darkly*. Oxford: Pergamon.

Orton, J. D., and Weick, K. E. (1990). Loosely coupled systems: A reconceptualization. *Academy of Management Review* 15(2): 203–223.

Perkins, J. A. (1973). Missions and organizations: A redefinition. In J. A. Perkins (ed.), *The University as an Organization*. New York: McGraw-Hill.

Peterson, M. W. (1981). Analyzing alternative approaches to planning. In P. Jedamus and M. W. Peterson (eds.), *Improving Academic Management: A Handbook for Planning and Institutional Research*. San Francisco: Jossey-Bass.

Peterson, M. W. (1995). Images of university structure, governance, and leadership: Adaptive strategies for the new environment. In D. D. Dill and B. Sporn (eds.), *Emerging Patterns of Social Demand and University Reform: Through a Glass Darkly*. Oxford: Pergamon.

Peterson, M. W. (1997). Using contextual planning to transform institutions. In M. W. Peterson, D. D. Dill. and L. A. Mets (eds.). *Planning and Management for a Changing Environment: A Handbook on Redesigning Postsecondary Institutions*. San Francisco: Jossey-Bass.

Peterson, M. W., and Dill, D. D. (1997). Understanding the competitive environment of the postsecondary knowledge industry. In M. W. Peterson, D. D. Dill, and L. A. Mets (eds.). *Planning and Management for a Changing Environment: A Handbook on Redesigning Postsecondary Institutions*. San Francisco: Jossey-Bass.

Peterson, M. W., and Mets, L. A. (1987). An evolutionary perspective on academic governance, management, and leadership. In M. W. Peterson and L. A. Mets (eds.). *Key Resources on Higher Education Governance, Management, and Leadership*. San Francisco: Jossey-Bass.

Pfeffer, J., and Salancik, G. R. (1978). *The external control of Organizations: A Resource Dependence Perspective*. New York: Harper and Row.

Powell, W. W. (1990). Neither market nor hierarchy: Network forms of organization. *Research in Organizational Behavior* 12: 295–336.

Powell, W. W., and DiMaggio, P. J. (eds.). (1991). *The New Institutionalism in Organizational Analysis*. Chicago: The University of Chicago Press.

Powell, W. W., and Friedkin, R. (1987). Organizational change in nonprofit organizations. In W. W. Powell (ed.), *The Nonprofit Sector: A Research Handbook*. New Haven: Yale University Press.

Prahalad, C. K., and Hamel, G. (1990). The core competence of the corporation. *Harvard Business Review* May-June: 79–91.

Readings, B. (1996). *The University in Ruins*. Cambridge: Harvard University Press.

Rhoades, G. (1995). Rethinking restructuring universities. *Journal of Higher Education Management* 10(2): 17–30.

Rhoades, G. (1996). Reorganizing the faculty workers for flexibility. *Journal of Higher Education* 67(6): 626–659.

Rhoades, G. (1998). *Managed Professionals*. Albany, NY. SUNY Press.

Rhoades, G., and Slaughter, S. (1997). Academic capitalism, managed professionals, and supply-side higher education. *Social Text* 15(2): 11–38.

Rubin, I. S. (1979). Retrenchment, loose structure, and adaptability in the university. *Sociology of Education* 52(October): 211–222.

Ruscio, K. (1987). Many sectors, many professions. In B. Clark (ed.), *The Academic Profession*. Berkeley and Los Angeles: University of California Press.

Salancik, G. R., and Pfeffer, J. (1974). The bases and use of power in organizational decision making: The case of a university. *Administrative Science Quarterly* 19: 453–473.

Schmidtlein, F. (1990). Responding to diverse institutional issues: Adapting strategic planning concepts. In F. Schmidtlein and T. H. Milton (eds.), *Adapting Strategic Planning to Campus Realities*. San Francisco: Jossey-Bass.

Schuster, J., Smith, D., Corak, K., and Yamada, M. (1994) *Strategic Governance: How to Make Big Decisions Better*. Phoenix, AZ: Oryx Press/American Council on Education.

Scott, W. R. (1992a). The organization of environments: Network, cultural, and historical elements. In J. W. Meyer and W. R. Scott (eds.), *Organizational Environments: Ritual and Rationality*. London: Sage.

Scott, W. R. (1992b), *Organizations: Rational, Natural, and Open Systems*. Third Edition. Englewood Cliffs, NJ: Prentice Hall.

Senge, P M. (1990). *The Fifth Discipline: The Art and Practice of the Learning Organization*. New York: Doubleday.

Seymour, D. T (1992). *On Q: Causing Quality in Higher Education*. New York: Macmillan.

Simsek, H., and Louis, K. S. (1994). Organizational change as paradigm shift: Analysis of the change process in a large, public university. *Journal of Higher Education* 65(6): 670–695.

Slaughter, S. (1993). Retrenchment in the 1980s. *Journal of Higher Education* 64(?): 250–282.

Slaughter, S. (1995). Criteria for restructuring postsecondary education. Journal for Higher Education Management 10(2): 31–44;

Slaughter, S., and Leslie. L. L. (1997). *Academic Capitalism: Politics, Policies, and the Entrepreneurial University*. Baltimore: Johns Hopkins Press.

Sporn, B (1995a). Adaptation processes at universities: Organizational implications of a complex environment. *Tertiary Education and Management* 1(1): 72–76.

Sporn, B. (1995b). Adaptive university structures: An analysis and comparison of U.S. and European universities in adapting to the current socioeconomic environment. Paper presented at Association for the Study of Higher Education, Orlando, Florida, November, 1995.

Sporn, B. (1996). Managing university culture: an analysis of the relationship between institutional culture and management approaches. *Higher Education* 32: 41–61.

Sporn, B., and Miksch, G. (1996). Implementing an information strategy—The case of the Vienna University of Economics and Business Administration. In IMHE (ed.), *Managing Information Strategies in Higher Education*. Paris: OECD

Teeter, D., and Lozier, G. (eds.). (1993). *Pursuit of Quality in Higher Education: Case Studies in Total Quality Management*. San Francisco: Jossey-Bass.

Teichler, U. (1993). Structures of higher education systems in Europe. In C. Gellert (ed.), Higher Education in Europe. London: Jessica Kingsley.

Thompson, J. D. (1967). *Organizations in Action*. New York: McGraw-Hill.

Tolbert, P. S. (1985). Institutional environments and resource dependence: Sources of administrative structure in institutions of higher education. *Administrative Science Quarterly* 30: 1–13.

Trow, M. A. (1983). Reorganizing the biological sciences at Berkeley. *Change* 15(8): 44–53.

Trow, M. (1994). *Managerialism and the Academic Profession: Quality and Control*. Higher Education Report 2. London: Quality Support Centre.

Tyack, D. (1990). "Restructuring" in historical perspective: Tinkering toward utopia. *Teachers College Record* 92(2): 170–191.

Van de Ven, A. H., and Drazin, R. (1985). The concept of fit in contingency theory. In L. L. Cummings and B. M. Straw (eds.), *Research in Organizational Behavior: An Annual Series of Analytical Essays and Critical Reviews*. Greenwich: JAI Press.

Van Vught, F A. (ed.). (1989). *Governmental Strategies and Innovation in Higher Education*. London: Jessica Kingsley.

Van Vught, F, A. (1994). Policy models and policy instruments in higher education: The effects of governmental policy-making on the innovative behavior of higher education institutions. In J. Smart (ed.), *Higher education: Handbook of Theory and Research*. Volume X. New York: Agathon Press.

Van Vught, F. A. (1995). The new context for academic quality. In D. D. Dill and B. Sporn (eds.), *Emerging Patterns of Social Demand and University Reform: Through a Glass Darkly*. Oxford: Pergamon.

Van Vugt, F. A. (1997). Using policy analysis for strategic choices. In M. W. Peterson, D. D. Dill, and L. A. Mets (eds.). *Planning and Management for a Changing Environment: A Handbook on Redesigning Postsecondary Institutions*. San Francisco: Jossey-Bass.

Wasser, H. (1990). Changes in the European university: From traditional to entrepreneurial. *Higher Education Quarterly* 44(2): 111–122.

Weick, K. E. (1976). Educational organizations, as loosely coupled systems. *Administrative Science Quarterly* 21: 1–19.

Weick, K. E. (1979). *The Social Psychology of Organizing*. Second Edition. New York: McGraw-Hill.

Weick, K. E. (1993), Organizational redesign as improvisation. In G. P. Huber and W. H. Glick (eds.). *Organizational Change and Redesign*. New York: Oxford University Press.

Whetten, D. A., and Cameron, K. S. (1985). Administrative effectiveness in higher education. *Review of Higher Education* 9(1): 35–49.

Williams, G. L. (1995). The "marketization" of higher education: Reforms and potential reforms in higher education finance. In D. D. Dill and B. Sporn (eds.), *Emerging Patterns of Social Demand and University Reform: Through a Glass Darkly*. Oxford: Pergamon.

Zammuto, R. F. (1994). Are the liberal arts an endangered species? *Journal of Higher Education* 55(2): 184–211.

Zemsky, R., and Massy, W. F. (1990). Cost containment: Committing to a new economic reality. *Change* 22(6): 16–22.

Zusman, A. (1994). Current and emerging issues facing higher education in the United States. In P. Altbach, R. Berdahl, and P. Gumport (eds.), *Higher Education in American Society*. Amherst, NY: Prometheus Books.

Notes

1. Examples of corporate partnerships and strategic alliances on the Internet: Corporate relations at the The University of Michigan: http://www.corporaterelations.umich.edu/ Worldwide locations of Webster University: http://www.webster.edu/worldwide_locations.html International MBA at Vienna University of Economics and Business Administration: http://www.wu-wien.ac.at/inst/imba/ International Management Institute of Universita Bocconi, Italy, in St. Petersburg, Russia: http://www.sda.uni-bocconi.it /pi/imisp.html

2. Examples of distance education and virtual universities on the Internet: The Open University, UK: http://www.open.ac.uk/ The Virtual University, European Union: http://136.201.8.7/vuniv/ERAShome.htm The Western Governor's University: http://www.westgov.org/smart/vu/vu.html

3. Examples of an open information policy on the Internet: Reengineering at MIT: http://web.mit.edu/reeng/www/ Committee structure and decisions at Vienna University of Economics and Business Administration: http://www.wu-wien.ac.at/englhome.html

4. Quality Support Center at the Open University, UK: http: //www. open.ac.uk /OU/Admin.html

5. Ministry of Science and Research, Austria: http://www.bmwf.gv.at/3unisys/12evalu.htm Ministry of Science and Research, Germany: http://www.bmbf.de/inhalt.htm

6. The Baldrige Award: http://www.quality.nist.gov/docs/97_crit/award.htm

7. Research by Zammuto (1984) revealed that the proportion of professional/vocational majors graduating from nonselective liberal arts colleges had skyrocketed. As a result the Carnegie Classification has changed their category of "Liberal Arts Colleges" to "Baccalaureate Colleges." Also, Cameron's (1983) framework of alternative strategies of adaptation, i.e., domain defense, domain offense, domain creation, can help to explain different strategic choices.

8. As defined by Balderston (1995, p. 55), governance "refers to the distribution of authority and functions among the units within a larger entity, the modes of communication and control among them, and the conduct of relationships between the entity and the surrounding environment."

PART II

NATURE AND ROLE OF INSTITUTIONAL RESEARCH

CHAPTER II

Nature and Role of Institutional Research

Institutional research is widely understood as a process that serves as an analytic resource for governance and management of an institution and informs operational, managerial and planning decisions. As institutional research has evolved over the past 40 years, there has been a continuous reinterpretation and broadening of the nature of institutional research and the role or function it plays in the institution. The many roles of institutional research were identified previously (see p. xiv). Articles on each of those are too numerous to be included here. The articles in this section, however, do provide broad examinations of the nature of the field, its institutional role, its methods, and some research-based evidence on how institutional research is organized and carried out.

Two selections reflect the field of institutional research's concern about the role of the institutional research process or function in a postsecondary institution and its professional nature. Saupe's "The Functions of Institutional Research," published by the Association for Institutional Research, provides an official statement on the nature and purpose, responsibilities, and role in institutional research in planning, decision making and policy formulation. The official "AIR Code of Ethics," adapted after years of debate, reflects the field's concern about ethical responsibility in data analysis and interpretation and also a concern for the status of IR as a profession.

Three articles deal more directly with the changing role of institutional research. In "Proliferation or Professional Integration" Peterson and Corcoran summarize an edited volume which recognized the fragmentation and proliferation of institutional research and the importance of viewing it as a process with a critical mediating role amongst institutional forces. Saunders chapter on "Policy Analysis" captures the recent emergence of this analytic approach in the field of institutional research. And in a more future oriented, speculative view, Peterson's "The Role of Institutional Research: From Improvement to Redesign" suggests a potential new institutional role or function for institutional research: the postsecondary knowledge industry analyst.

The methodological nature of institutional research is captured by two selections. Fincher in the "Art and Science of Institutional Research" provides an excellent depiction and examination of the methodological developments in the field and then suggests the need to view it as art as well as science. Hathaway's article, "Assumptions Underlying Qualitative and Quantitative Research," places an important recent debate about the growing role and use of qualitative methods in a broader context.

Finally, two research-based articles provide a recent picture of the practice of institutional research. In "The Role of Institutional Research In Higher Education," Delaney examines types of research projects actually being undertaken by offices. Knight, Moore, and Coperthwaite, in "Institutional Research: Knowledge, Skills, and Perceptions of Effectiveness," actually test a conceptualization of this topic proposed by Terenzini in an earlier paper.

The Functions of Institutional Research

JOE L. SAUPE

The Nature and Purpose of Institutional Research

Institutional research is research conducted within an institution of higher education to provide information which supports institutional planning, policy formation and decision making. The institution may be a single campus, a multi-campus system, a state or provincial system or an even larger grouping of colleges and universities. Although the activity of institutional research is commonly associated with the individual campus, it also is carried out within higher education systems to serve the governance responsibilities which reside there.

Institutional research can be distinguished from research on postsecondary education which has as its purpose the advancement of knowledge about and practice in postsecondary education generally. The subject of institutional research is the individual college, university, or system. While institutional research can involve data and analyses which contribute to wider knowledge about how colleges and individuals function, this type of result generally is not sought for its own sake.

Activities of institutional research are frequently undertaken in association with specific planning, policy, or decision situations. Information to answer specific questions is desired. How many sections of a specific course should be offered? By what amount should tuition rates be increased to produce a target amount of tuition income? Is attrition a problem at our institution? Are our faculty salaries competitive with those paid by peer institutions? Are the outcomes of our degree programs what the stated purposes of the programs suggest they should be? Institutional research designed to answer such questions is a form of *applied* research.

The assembling of the quantitative and qualitative information for use in periodic or ad hoc reviews of programs or organizational units illustrates the form of institutional research having characteristics of *evaluation*. Information on cost and productivity underlies judgements about efficiency. Information on other characteristics of programs and units and on outcomes leads to judgements about effectiveness or quality. Information on program purposes, on programs offered by other institutions, on the labor market and on potential demand produce judgements about the need for academic programs. Judgements of these types lead to decisions about program initiation, continuation, and improvement.

Occasionally institutional research leads to general information about the college or university and its environment and provides a comprehensive view of the institution which may inform planning, policy formulation, and decision making of a variety of types. Information of this type may arise as a by-product of institutional research on some specific question. For example, a study of student flow undertaken to guide enrollment projections may reveal that large numbers of juniors and seniors entered the institution as transfer students. This incidental finding may have a variety of implications.

"The Functions of Institutional Research," by Joe L. Saupe, reprinted from *The Functions of Institutional Research*, Second Edition, 1990. Association for Institutional Research.

Similarly, institutional research may be undertaken on a general topic and not be guided by a specific problem or question. The expectation is that the findings will be generally informative. For example, surveys of alumni and of members of the community in which the institution is located may reveal attitudes and impressions about the institution. These forms of institutional research have characteristics of *basic* research.

Some activities of institutional research may, intentionally or incidentally, identify situations within the institution which are causes for concern. A by-product of the routine tabulation of enrollment data by program or a special analysis of enrollment data designed to isolate patterns of retention and attrition may reveal that attrition appears to be a special problem for selected programs. Some form of administrative or academic attention, perhaps accompanied by additional study, may be suggested by such results. Thus, *problem identification* may be a result of institutional research.

Some projects of institutional research may be called *action research*, because the researcher and client work closely throughout the problem definition, research design, data collection, analysis, interpretation and implementation phases of the activity. The institutional researcher who is asked to serve on or as a resource to a task force charged with studying some matter and with making recommendations thereon can work closely with the task force and may then be able to follow up after the task force has reported to insure the recommendations of the task force are correctly understood and acted upon. Such an arrangement provides an excellent opportunity for institutional research to have impact.

Policy analysis is another phrase which applies to some forms of institutional research. Deliberations on matters of policy are often, or often should be, accompanied by analysis and that analysis is institutional research. Deliberations on admissions policies may require analysis of the impacts of policy changes on different segments of the potential student population as well as on the size and composition of the student body.

Clearly, the term research, as used here, has a broad meaning. Information about the college or university results from analyses of quantitative data and qualitative assessments.

Tabular displays of counts of fall-term students and of annual expenditures illustrate the simplest form of analysis. Comparisons of current with prior-year totals of such data provide a similar, still simple, form of analysis which conveys information. Cost analyses, space utilization analyses and teaching-load analyses are conventional types of institutional research. Statistical techniques ranging from the calculations of averages and percentages to the applications of complex multivariate procedures are included. A variety of prior-year, current and projected institutional data, along with quantitative representations of policy variables and assumptions, may be used to simulate institutional functioning in future years using techniques of mathematical modeling. Simulation is a form of analysis by which implications of alternative courses of action are assessed. The measurement of student outcomes and the examination of the measures in the context of student and institutional goals and quantitative and qualitative characteristics of academic programs is another form of analysis. The performance of administrative and support programs may be similarly analyzed.

Institutional research, like other types of research, should be objective, systematic and thorough. The outcomes of the research should be as free as possible from the influence of personal philosophy, political considerations or desired results. The information provided by institutional research is combined with academic and professional judgement in planning and other decision-making processes. Almost never is the final decision based solely on the findings of the research, nor should it be. Considerations of institutional philosophy and tradition, of priorities and of the environment in which the institution exists may be as important as the findings of the research in determining the course of action to be followed. For example, a study may suggest a technique of recruiting students which has considerable potential for increasing enrollment. The factors of judgement may lead to a rejection of the proposal that the techniques be used or to a major modification in it. Nonetheless, the research has served its purpose by bringing information to the decision-making arena and stimulating reflection about recruitment and the various factors involved in this institutional activity. The research might not have served this purpose if it had been of questionable validity or had been guided by some preconceived notion of what result was desired or expected.

This is not to say that institutional research should be undertaken or carried out in ignorance of the nature of the institution and the forces which guide its operation. An investigation of forms of "hard-sell" recruiting, for example, would not be useful in colleges and universities where this type of activity would be inconsistent with strongly held institutional values. The design and the presentation and interpretation of the findings of institutional research can be guided by the nature of the institution and its environment and the usefulness of the results thereby enhanced.

Institutional research, then, is an essential ingredient of sound college or university governance. It should occur throughout the institution wherever any sort of planning occurs, any type of policy issue is considered and any decision about some aspect of the institution is proposed. Institutional research has been described as an attitude of commitment to the institution's purpose in society and to the value of critical appraisal and careful investigation. Institutional governance is informed and rational to the degree that such an attitude pervades the institution.

The Place of Institutional Research in the Organization

Institutional Research is carried out in the individual academic and administrative units of the college or university in support of the information needs, planning and decision-making responsibilities which reside at the unit level. At some colleges and universities, a conscious decision had been made that each unit in central administration will be responsible for institutional research relating to the activities of that unit. There may be no formally identified offices for institutional research in these institutions, but this does not mean that the activity is absent. Rather, it is dispersed and carried out by persons who may have principal responsibilities other than institutional research. Economy and in-depth knowledge of the matters studied may be points in favor of such arrangements. Problems of dispersed institutional research are duplication, a lack of research exper-

tise in some or many institutional domains, an inability to deal with issues which cross organizational boundaries, and an absence of an institution-wide view in the research activities.

At other colleges and universities, offices of institutional research have been established in recognition of the fact that the activity requires specialized expertise and full-time attention. In some cases, the title Office of Institutional Research is given to an organizational unit which supports functions such as planning and budgeting wherever these occur within the institution. Elsewhere, the connection of institutional research with the activities of planning or budgeting has resulted in organizational units titled Office of Institutional Research and Planning, Office of Institutional Research and Budgeting or Office of Institutional Research, Planning and Budgeting. Names such as Office of Institutional Analysis and Office of Institutional Studies also are used.

Various administrative units may be charged with some responsibility for institutional research. The placement of the unit within the administrative organization determines the nature of the unit's responsibilities or type of institutional research it undertakes. In some colleges and universities, institutional research reports to the chief executive officer. The specific charges to such offices vary widely, but this organizational arrangement recognizes the function as one of central importance and so broad that to be effective it must be placed near the top. Placement at the top may indicate that institutional research on academic, administrative, financial and auxiliary matters are all important and cannot effectively be carried out in isolation from one another. This arrangement also recognizes that institutional research supports planning and resource allocation which crosses organizational boundaries.

Another model is that of an office of institutional research and planning which is responsible to a vice president for planning. Such an organization recognizes that information developed from research underlies institutional planning. Although the name of the activity may not include the designation "institutional research" because the principal responsibility is planning, the information development phase of the activity is institutional research nonetheless.

The office of institutional research may be a responsibility of the institution's chief aca-

demic officer in which case research and information on academic purposes, programs, program outcomes, policy and personnel will support academic planning, budgeting for
academic units and other responsibilities of
that officer. Such a unit may be responsible for
the institution's program evaluation and assessment activities. In this regard it may conduct surveys of graduates and former students.
It may be responsible for needs assessment
studies designed to guide the development of
new programs. The unit also will respond to requests for assistance from deans, chairpersons,
and faculty committees.

In many colleges and universities a unit
charged with leading efforts to improve instruction and academic programs has been established. Institutional research supports the
activities of such a unit. Research on teaching
methods and instructional media may be carried out there. Programs of student ratings of
instruction are often housed in such units and
are based upon research. Questions about testing and grading lead to research on these topics. Courses and curricula, and the interaction
of students therewith, are analyzed and evaluated. Data underlying periodic reviews of programs and academic units are assembled. Evaluations of special services (for example,
learning centers created to serve marginal or
disadvantaged students) are carried out. Responsibilities for program assessment may be
assigned to such a unit by virtue of its experience and expertise with regard to instructional
programs and testing.

Interests in institutional and program assessment for purposes of accountability and
program involvement, often stimulated by authorities external to the institution, have in
some institutions led to the designation of a
person or office responsible for leadership and
staff support for assessment activities. Assessment of institutional and program effectiveness
is a form of institutional research.

An office of student research may exist
within the institution's student affairs organization and be responsible for research on campus climates and subcultures, on the characteristics of various services provided students, on
residence hall life, and on factors involved in
retention and attrition. The student affairs' research office may investigate the development
of student attitudes and values. Market re-

search, designed to enhance the congruence between the offerings of the college or university
and the needs and expectations of its clientele,
may be carried out by this office or by units for
institutional research located elsewhere.

An office of financial analysis, analytical
studies or administrative research may be located within the organization of the institution's chief officer for business and finance.
Studies of business operations and budget and
cost analysis are likely to be principal responsibilities of such a unit, and financial planning
may be based largely upon the analysis of this
institutional research activity.

It is important to recognize that data descriptive of the operation of the college or university are by-products of various institutional
operating processes. Data about students are
acquired as a result of admissions, registration
and associated processes. Budget building and
financial transactions result in budget and accounting data. Personnel transactions generate
data about employees. The translation of these
various items of data into information useful to
planners and decision makers requires analysis
and, indeed, is a major activity of many offices
of institutional research. The products of this
translation and analysis have been referred to
as management information.

In colleges and universities of all sizes,
computers are used to facilitate the several operating processes and to manage the data involved in these processes. What were at one
time called administrative data processing systems are now called management information
systems. The applicability of the current designation depends upon the degree to which the
computer system, in fact, not only processes
the data for operational purposes but also includes capabilities for translating the data into
information. These capabilities cannot exist
without careful planning and management of
the data. Data administration is the function
that attempts to insure that the data captured
from the operational data systems are meaningful. The knowledge and perspectives of persons responsible for institutional research can
make important contributions to the function
of data administration.

The relationship between administrative
data processing systems and management information and a recognition of the importance
of data administration has resulted at some col-

leges and universities in a close association between the administrative computing organization and the office of institutional research. In these organizational arrangements, the activity of institutional research includes participation in the preparation of specifications for information systems as well as analysis and dissemination of the information handled by the systems.

Finally, in considering the various ways in which the college organization may incorporate institutional research, the fact that the activity often occurs within the standard organizational units bears emphasis. Information about students may be prepared in the office of admissions where research on admissions criteria may also be conducted. The office of registration and records may prepare reports and analyses of enrollment statistics and trends and may be responsible for enrollment projections. The accounting office prepares the annual report of income and expenditures which is important information for planning and decision making and may undertake analyses of trends and projections of financial variables. The physical plant or the space assignment office may be responsible for maintaining information on buildings and rooms, for analyses of the utilization thereof, for data and studies on facilities maintenance, for research on building and room accessibility for handicapped persons, for studies related to energy conservation efforts and for other activities which support campus and facility planning. Personnel offices study employee classification systems, salary scales and compensation policies. Any component of the college or university may have a responsibility for institutional research.

The dispersal of institutional research activities which has been multiplied by the widespread use of personal computers and personal computer networks and access to central computer data bases has introduced problems of data comparability. The data analysis of the dean of arts and science may conflict with that of the vice president for academic affairs simply because of differences in definitions and sources of basic data. Some offices of institutional research work with data administrators to develop official definitions and sources of data in order that decision makers can focus attention on the issues and the relevant management information rather than upon conflicting data analyses.

A benefit of an office of institutional research, based upon its in-depth comprehension of institutional data systems, should be its capacity to combine, analyze and interpret data resulting from the several operational activities of the college or university. The office need not be responsible for all varieties of institutional research, but it can serve as a reliable source for comprehensive and authoritative information about the institution.

Associated Responsibilities of an Institutional Research Office

By virtue of its responsibilities for data and information about the college or university, an office of institutional research typically will be assigned responsibilities which need not be considered research on the institution. The following are illustrative.

The office of institutional research is likely to have some responsibility for the institution's responses to national statistical surveys such as the Integrated Postsecondary Education Data System (IPEDS) of the National Center for Education Statistics in the United States or the surveys for *Statistics Canada* publications in that country. Similarly, the data forms which must be completed for the state or provincial agency with responsibility for higher education may be assigned the institutional research office. The nature of such responsibilities varies. At one extreme, the office simply serves as the point of coordination, receiving the packets of forms, distributing them to other offices where they are completed, then collecting and returning them. At the other extreme, many or all of the data forms may be completed in the office of institutional research itself, drawing upon whatever data files are necessary. Even in the former case, staff in the office are likely to be—and because of their expertise, should be—called upon for assistance in interpreting the standard definitions and instructions of such surveys. They may also be asked to assist in determining how the data in the institution's files should be processed in order to produce the required figures, and in general to insure that the institutional data provided are consistent and accurate.

There are two points to be made about reporting data to state, provincial and federal agencies. First, while there are few immediate rewards for filling out forms, the responsibility should be taken seriously. The data are collected for what may be presumed to be good reasons and should be as sound as the data assembled to serve purposes internal to the institution. The completed forms are products of the institution and, as with any institutional product, should be of high quality. Further, the accuracy of the data may affect perceptions of the credibility of the institution and thereby influence policy decisions important to it.

Secondly, the data reported to the agencies are descriptive of the college or university and the potential value to the institution of the data should not be overlooked. A caution in this regard, however, is that the data are reported in standard categories which may detract from their utility to the institution. Counts of degrees granted for standard subject field categories are less informative to the institution than are counts arrayed by specific institutional academic units and programs. Current fund expenditure amounts displayed in standard expenditure categories are less meaningful internally than are data displayed by the cost centers of the institution. Thus, in capitalizing on the availability of data produced for the external forms, attention needs to be given to displaying the data in categories that are meaningful to the institution.

A related responsibility often assigned to the office of institutional research is that of responding to questionnaires and other non-routine requests for data or information. Almost daily, a college or university receives some request for information from an agency of government, from the publisher of a higher education directory, from a doctoral student or from some other source. Some selectivity with regard to which inquiries merit responses must be exercised and, if it is decided that a response will be given, the response should be prepared carefully for the reasons previously cited. By virtue of its general responsibility for and understanding of data or information on the institution and because of its commitment to consistent data of high quality, it is natural that many or all such inquiries or questionnaires be referred to the office of institutional research. It is at least embarrassing when reports of apparently conflicting information about the college or university, made by different representatives of the institution, are found.

The dispersal of activities of institutional research within the college or university has led to a need for sharing information about the activity. The office of institutional research, by virtue of its responsIbilities for and expertise on institutional data and research, may provide the leadership in orienting others to the nature and sources of institutional data and their use. One purpose of the orientation is to encourage consistent use of the official institutional data in order to avoid conflicting data analyses. The other purpose is simply to provide education on the techniques of institutional research and, as appropriate, on research methodology generally.

The data and information managed by the office of institutional research may be used elsewhere in the college or university for purposes other than planning, policy formulation and decision making. For example, the office of public information may seek data to include in press releases or publications about the institution. Similarly, general or specific data may be required to support proposals for external funding for research or other purposes, and the office of institutional research may be asked to serve as the principal source of such data and information.

The office of institutional research often provides the continuing point of contact for the state or provincial agency for higher education on matters relating to institutional data. Institutional research staff may be asked to serve on agency committees where a central concern is institutional data. Persons from institutions provide advice on the development and refinement of state- or provincial-level information systems, on funding formulas and the data requirements for them, on studies of special issues in higher education, as well as on the information required for state- or provincial-level strategic or long-range planning. It is appropriate that the expertise of the person assigned to institutional research be drawn upon in such endeavors.

Quite often, by virtue of background and interest, the institutional researcher will keep abreast of the journals and books on postsecondary education and, particularly, the literature on research on postsecondary education. If this person has an academic background or is so inclined for some other reason, he or she may, on occasion, contribute to this literature. While the purposes of institutional research and research on higher education differ, the two forms of research contribute one to the other. The problems, methodology, and results of the general research can be applied and particularized in institutional research, and the findings of institutional research may merit generalization through broader studies. The interest of the institutional researcher in the literature on higher education often leads to the development of a library of publications maintained by the office of institutional research but available to others, particularly administrators.

Finally, the person responsible for institutional research may be called upon to provide advice on planning, policy and other issues facing the college or university. In one sense, this function is a natural consequence of the institutional research activity. The products of research need to be interpreted and their implications explained. The consequences of alternative courses of action, based upon the research, need to be described and qualified. The person who has done the research should be well qualified to describe its results and implications and to answer questions about it. When the director of institutional research participates in planning, policy formulation and decision-making deliberations at the stage in which considerations other than those raised by the research are brought to bear, it is important to recognize that participation is based upon the director's status as an expert on the institution and higher education rather than upon the director's responsibility as a researcher. The distinction suggested here may be difficult to identify in specific situations. The point is that the values and perspectives of the researcher are not identical to those of the decision maker. There is considerable merit in distinguishing the two roles. Just as the results of the research will seldom be the sole determinant of the decision, so the desired decision cannot be allowed to bias the outcomes of the research.

Characteristics of Effective Institutional Research

It is not within the scope of this monograph to describe or review all the methods and tools of research which are employed in institutional research. Numerous books describe applicable topics, such as descriptive statistics, sampling and statistical inference, questionnaire construction and survey research, experimental and quasi-experimental design, principles of operations research, procedures for program evaluation and methods of qualitative research. Not only is it beyond the range of competencies of any single individual or, even, office of institutional research, to possess expertise in the full array of these methodologies, such expertise is often unnecessary since at many colleges and universities there are qualified researchers on the faculty who can be called upon to advise on or to carry out selected projects.

Some of the fundamental requirements of good research merit mention as they apply to institutional research. The first is that of *purpose*. Each activity or project of institutional research should be guided by a purpose or set of purposes stated as specifically as possible. Normally the resources available for institutional research are inadequate to justify undertaking projects because "it would be interesting to know . . ." or "it might be useful to know . . ." (To some degree, this is regrettable because what *might* be useful to know could turn out to be, in fact, *very* useful to know.) In view of the applied nature of most institutional research, the guidance given to the research effort by a purpose can be enhanced by including consideration of what actions or decisions might be made on the basis of the results of the research. For example, the initial purpose of a project might be to determine attrition rates for various types of students. This can be done, but when the question becomes "What actions might be taken as a result of knowing the rates?" the nature of the project may change. The fundamental question turns out to be "What are the characteristics of the college or university which lead to attrition and what might be done to change these characteristics?"

Similarly, if the question is "What is the faculty-salary cost per student credit hour for the undergraduate courses of each department?" an analysis may provide the answer. However, the data collected and their analysis will differ depending upon whether the resulting unit costs will be used to project faculty-salary costs on the basis of projected student-credit-hour data or will be drawn upon in making budget decisions. If it is the latter, a more complete analysis may be needed. The linkage between institutional research and planning, policy formulation or decision making is provided by the purposes given to the former by the requirements of the latter.

Assumptions are involved in institutional research. If, in the previous example, a unit cost is multiplied by a projected count of student credit hours to produce a future year cost estimate, an assumption is that the unit cost is not a function of department size (or of any other variable which may change between the current and projected year). There are assumptions about the meaning and accuracy—validity and reliability—of the basic data, and the researcher needs to recognize the assumptions and to point them out to the consumers of the research. It is often useful to review the assumptions with the consumer before the project is begun. The interpretation and implications of the results of a project are typically influenced by the assumptions involved. An understanding of, and selection from among, alternative assumptions before the project is begun can help insure that the eventual results are interpreted properly and that implications are derived appropriately.

Communication of the findings of institutional research takes a variety of forms. Oral reports, in person or on the phone, are made to answer generally straight-forward questions. A table or two or a display of data in a chart or graph may constitute a sufficient report. Letters or memoranda are used as brief reports which do not merit or require general distribution. Written reports, including tables and, perhaps, graphs and charts, are produced for many projects. The audiences for reports of institutional research are typically administrators who often are served best by a concise report—an executive summary—which emphasizes the results and, perhaps, implications of the project. However, because faculty members are often consumers of institutional research, and because administrators have faculty backgrounds and perspectives, it is well to have a complete report in the file for use in answering questions of detail which may be raised. The more complete report includes relationships to previous research and a description of the methodology in sufficient detail that the study could be replicated. The more complete technical report is written as though intended for publication to serve an audience of other researchers.

Personal computers, local area networks, electronic mail, desk-top publishing, and advanced graphics capabilities have added options for the communication of results of institutional research. For example, a table of data or, even, a complete "fact book" may be stored in a computer data base to be retrieved by anyone with need for the data. Complete reports may be treated similarly. Data and reports stored electronically or on microfiche can save much space in file cabinets and be readily available. Questions about results may be asked and answered, and dialogues on the topic of the research may be carried out, by electronic mail. The existence of sophisticated graphics capabilities has drawn attention to this form of communication.

A consideration of the content of an institutional research report may illuminate the nature of the activity and the manner in which it aids planning, policy formulation and decision making. As already noted, institutional research consists of analysis which results in information. Data analysis yields *results*, generally quantitative, which constitute what may be considered an initial level of information. Results are, of course, included in the report. A next level of information may be added by means of an analysis of the results in the context of the purpose of the research, the assumptions used, and other factors. This analysis constitutes the *interpretation* of the research, may produce *generalizations* and adds meaning to the results. The analysis of the interpretations in the context of the institutional environment may produce *implications*. A final stage of analysis may result in *recommendations*. The extent to which this sequence of analysis applies to individual projects, of course, varies. The point is that the sequence represents a movement from analyses which are clearly institutional research toward analyses which are characteristic of planning, policy formulation and decision making. At each step, additional considerations are brought to bear. As the new considerations begin to depart from those of fact and evidence, the analysis loses characteristics of research. Certainly the researcher should illuminate the subject of the research to whatever degree the evidence and the researcher's experience and expertise permit. At the same time, the distinction between the roles of the researcher and the decision maker needs to be maintained.

While written reports are important products of institutional research, it is often desirable to attempt to ensure that research undertaken is relevant and research completed is useful. Some institutional research offices draw upon advisory committees or upon networks of users of research to ensure that the projects undertaken are relevant to the issues faced by the college or university. After a report is written and distributed, the contribution it makes often can be increased by some follow-up techniques designed to ensure that the research results are understood correctly and interpreted appropriately.

Basic Tools of Institutional Research

There are several techniques or tools of institutional research which deserve special attention because, even though they are not unique to institutional research, they are used frequently.

First, the conversion of data in the institution's operational data processing systems into *management information* frequently is a responsibility of the office of institutional research. The activity undertaken to fulfill this responsibility is not guided by a specific research purpose in the sense of a plan to be prepared, a policy to be established or a decision to be made. Rather, the purpose is to develop a set of data which provides a meaningful picture of the institution and its operation and which is comprehensive and flexible enough to provide answers to unanticipated questions. One product may be a set of summary reports which is prepared regularly and consistently and which, consequently, reveals trends in key institutional characteristics. Another product is a data

base from which ad hoc analyses may be produced on demand with relative ease.

Computer technology has enabled the development of such management information systems. This technology allows not only the accumulation of consistent subtotals (by department) and totals (for the institution) of various types of data describing students, courses, employees, finances, and facilities, but by combining the various types of data, it also allows reports of, for example, student credit hours per full-time-equivalent faculty member, expenditures per student, and square feet of space per student contact hour. By taking advantage of the capability of the computer to store, retrieve, and manipulate data, a variety of types of information descriptive of the institution and its functioning can be produced. Offices of institutional research are involved, sometimes centrally, in the development and operation of computer information systems, because these offices are expected to possess expertise in all types of institutional data and in their uses for planning, policy formulation and decision making.

It might appear that the task of converting data from the institution's operating data systems into management information requires only computer programming. Usually this is not the case. Inconsistencies between data systems sometimes seem to be the rule and not the exception. It is difficult to prepare a meaningful report of student credit hours per full-time-equivalent faculty by department when the student information system and the personnel or budget systems make use of differing sets of departments. The function of data administration, mentioned previously, exists because of the recognition of such difficulties. This function requires in-depth knowledge not only of the several operating data systems, but also of the nature of the information needed for planning, policy formulation, and decision making.

The *decision support system* (DSS) constitutes another method of carrying out institutional research. Fundamentally, a DSS is a data base and computer software for using the data base which are made available to the decision maker as an aid in making decisions. The central feature of the DSS methodology is that it enables the decision maker to do the analysis, rather than making use of analyses carried out by someone else. The decision maker decides what analysis to carry out and understands the implications and limitations of the information produced by the analysis. A decision support system is developed by a technical person, often a member of the institutional research staff, working closely with the decision maker. The development of a decision support system typically is a continuous process; as the system is used, features of it are refined and new features are added. The relationship between the institutional researcher and the decision maker is a close and continuing one.

A relative of the decision support system is the *executive support system* (ESS), also referred to as the executive information system (EIS). (Some authorities distinguish between executive support and executive information systems.) An ESS can be defined as the use of computer technology to serve (a portion of) the information needs of an executive officer, whose responsibilities are more general than those of the decision maker served by a DSS. An ESS may include the capabilities of a DSS, but can be expected to have such additional features as electronic mail, electronic conferencing, and powerful graphics. The executive may use the system principally to acquire information about the college or university, rather than as an aid in making specific decisions. Advanced computer technology which makes the system very easy to use is often involved. The ESS is developed in much the same manner as the DSS; the technician with institutional research expertise or support works with the executive in a mode which accommodates the limited amount of time the executive has available for the activity.

Modeling is also employed in institutional analysis. It involves the specification of mathematical relationships among variables of institutional operation. Parameters of the mathematical relationships are derived from historical data and are used to project variables of the model for future years. By varying values of model parameters, which reflect assumptions about future relationships, answers to "what-if" questions may be derived. Enrollment projections are developed using enrollment and student-flow models. Faculty-flow models are used to project numbers of faculty in various categories, particularly numbers on tenure, and elaborate cost and budget projection models are used. It is not unusual to find that the most difficult step in applying the sim-

ulation-model techniques is the development of the required (consistently defined and developed) historical or base-line data. Models often are included in the software components of decision support systems and executive support systems.

Another technique of institutional research is *comparative analysis*. Quantitative descriptions are given meaning by comparison. Several bases of comparison may be used. One basis is the comparable prior year value or the trend for a series of prior years. For example, meaning is added to an average class size of 36 for the history department by comparing this average with the averages for past years. A second basis is comparison with similar units. For example, how does the average class size for the history department compare with the averages for the sociology and economics departments.

The basis of comparison may be some predetermined standard. Using such considerations as student demand for history courses, the educationally desirable size of classes for different courses, and teaching-load policy, it may have been established that the average class size of the introductory courses should be 50 and of advance courses 20, for an overall average size of 32. The actual size of 36, then, will exceed the standard.

Other institutions provide yet another basis of comparison. How does the figure 36 compare with the average class sizes (calculated the same way!) for the history departments of other (comparable) colleges or universities?

Data exchange is a practice of institutional research which provides the data required to make comparison with other colleges or universities. The normal procedure is for a group of peer institutions to agree upon sets of data to be exchanged and the schedule for the exchange activities. Several approaches are used. At one extreme, fully analyzed data (e.g., unit cost or student-credit-hour-per-faculty-appointment ratios) are exchanged. At the other extreme, more basic data are exchanged in formats which permit each participating institution to conduct analyses in a manner tailored to local conventions, analytical procedures, and needs. Data exchanges which lead to peer institutional comparisons are frequently undertaken by public colleges and universities in order to generate information for use in supporting requests for governmental appropriations. A second purpose is to provide information to enlighten institutional planning, policy formulation and decision making.

Colleges and universities exchange information on policies and procedures as well as data. Deliberations on a policy issue often lead to the question "What is the policy at our peer institutions?" The data exchange mechanism can be used to answer this question. Data exchanges often take place electronically. Data are exchanged on floppy disks or over telephone lines. Comparisons of policies and procedures are facilitated by electronic mail.

A concern with *data definition* underlies almost all varieties of institutional research because the information resulting from analyzed data of any type can be only as meaningful as the definitions underlying the original data and the degree to which the definitions are observed in assembling the data. The definitions must lead to data that are meaningful to those who use the data and that are relevant to planning, policy and other decision issues of the college or university. The involvement of persons responsible for institutional research in data administration occurs, at least in part, because of the importance of the definitions underlying the information. The importance of the involvement of the ultimate user, the decision maker, in determining the definitions is recognized by the processes used in developing a decision support system. Agreement on, and use of, data definitions is a central concern in data exchange efforts and in all other forms of comparative analysis. The term "comparison" implies careful attention to data compatibility and comparability which are assured only by sound and complete definitions.

Contributions of Institutional Research to Planning, Decision Making, and Policy Formulation

The range and variety of problems, questions and issues which arise in higher education and for which institutional research is relevant defy categorization or enumeration. Any administrator and any committee may seek institutional research to inform plans, decisions and actions. In many cases the researcher can aid in specifying the information to be brought to bear on a problem or issue and, for this reason,

should be included at an early stage. The breadth of the potential applicability of institutional research is indicated by the following illustrations.

Institutional research can aid in determining how the institution's several publics perceive its missions and goals and in specifying new or altered missions, goals and objectives. It can assist in relating performance to goals by assessing institutional outcomes and accomplishments, can point to areas in which performance does not appear to meet expectations and can suggest strategies for improvement. Institutional research can facilitate institutional self-study and accreditation processes and can contribute evidence that the college or university is accountable for its use of resources and performance.

Institutional research can contribute to program planning and development by means of market research and needs assessment. It can support intensive reviews of programs or departments by providing relevant factual evidence and by summarizing qualitative information. It can illuminate reviews and revisions of curricula by producing information on students' course-selection behavior. Institutional research can provide information relevant to questions about the grade-giving behavior of faculty and the grade-earning behavior of students; such questions may arise from concerns about standards or about equity with students.

Institutional research can study the culture of the college or university, investigating the extent to which various values and norms are present among the faculty, students and administrators and the extent to which the culture is shared or in conflict. Information from such investigations can inform the direction of planning or policy and can provide an understanding of potential obstacles to moving in new directions.

Institutional research underlies the improvement of instruction. Procedures and specific instruments used in the evaluation of instruction, such as student rating-of-instruction forms, are selected or developed by means of research. The evaluation of instructional methods and media is a process designed to lead to improvement and is guided by evidence from research.

Institutional research can assist in identifying inefficiencies in instructional activities and in the allocation of resources. Data on class sizes, teaching loads and student-credit-hour productivity and data on the incidence of small classes and on the frequency of offering of individual courses are made available to academic administrators.

The admissions program can benefit from institutional research. Criteria for admissions can derive from relationships between measures of student ability and success in programs. Data on sources of students and the "yields" of alternative strategies of admissions officers and others can assist in tailoring the admissions program to the mission and goals of the college or university and of specific programs.

Institutional research not only can provide enrollment projections but also can provide analyses of enrollment trends and relationships which guide enrollment policy and suggest assumptions and strategies for enrollment planning. Data describing the student body can be related to enrollment goals. Data on retention and attrition can reveal problems. Institutional research on causes of attrition and on strategies for increasing retention can contribute to maximizing society's investment in education.

Institutional research can support efforts to provide education to special types of students by assessing their preferences, predispositions and academic behavior. In what regards do part-time students, minority-group students, women students, highly talented students, handicapped students, older students and others differ from the traditional student in ways which have implications for the achievement of the educational goals of such students and of the college or university? Students' program, course and scheduling behavior can be summarized, and attempts to achieve student and institutional goals can be evaluated.

Institutional research can assist with initiatives intended to foster access to the educational opportunities offered by the college or university and can contribute to attempts to ensure that the applicant's choice of the institution is an informed one. Institutional research can assist in developing the consumer information which should be available to prospective students. The financial affairs of students can be determined and used as consumer information as well as referents for the determination of financial aid programs and policies. The effectiveness of the program of financial aid in achieving the goals set for this program can be evaluated and the evaluation may lead to im-

proved use of financial aid resources.

Equal opportunity and affirmative action goals are established with the aid of information, and data are used to assess progress toward the goals. The establishment of salary and compensation goals, policies and guidelines can be informed by institutional research. Investigations of equity in salaries for faculty, administrators and support staff draw upon a wide variety of variables. Institutional research offices may also become involved in litigation on issues of affirmative action and salary discrimination by serving as the source of "official" data and analysis.

Institutional research can be applied in the evaluation and improvement of such programs as academic advising, counseling, career planning, placement, intercollegiate athletics, health services and housing.

Questions about faculty workload and considerations of policy pertaining to it can be illuminated by institutional research. Current workload patterns can be measured. Faculty preferences regarding workload patterns can be determined.

Questions about the size, composition and quality of the faculty can be subjects for institutional research. Promotion and tenure practices and rates can be displayed and analyzed, and a faculty-flow model can be used to project the effects of alternate assumptions or policies on numbers and characteristics of the faculty at points in the future. Characteristics and preferences of faculty members, described by institutional research, can be useful in planning programs of faculty development. Issues involved in the appraisal of faculty performance—whether arising from goals of faculty development or from questions about promotion, tenure and salary policies and procedures—can be subjects for institutional research. Information which is the subject of collective bargaining, where it exists, is assembled by institutional research.

The processes involved in resource acquisition and allocation rely on institutional research. Budgets are analyzed in the contexts of goals, priorities, workload and performance. Income and expenditure projections are made to guide budget planning. Costs analyses are carried out in support of various responsibilities of governance.

Institutional research can contribute to the institution's development program. It can provide and assist in organizing information about the institution used in proposals for external funding of specific projects; it can assist in building case statements for fund-raising campaigns; and it can contribute to designing information-based strategies for seeking donations from foundations, corporations, and individuals.

Institutional research can aid in the formulation of policies, structures and rates for student tuition and fees. Enrollment projections can be translated into projections of tuition and fee income.

Facilities planning, allocation and management are guided by institutional research. The inventory of buildings and rooms is maintained. Utilization of classrooms and other types of space is measured and compared with standards to guide reallocation decisions. Assessments of the condition, suitability and utilization of existing facilities combine with the requirements of programs to produce plans for maintenance, rehabilitation, remodeling and new building. Energy use and conservation are areas of study which have obvious applicability to problems facing colleges and universities.

Institutional research alone cannot lead to sound plans, appropriate policies, or correct decisions for the college or university. The wisdom, integrity, and courage possessed by those who share the responsibilities of governance are the principal determinants of the soundness of plans, the appropriateness of policies, and the correctness of decisions. Institutional research *can*, however, provide data and information which contribute to and, in some instances, are essential for maintaining the quality of governance expected of an institution whose existence is based upon principles of rationality, wisdom and truth.

Additional Sources

For additional information on the functions and methods of institutional research, the reader is referred to publications of or sponsored by the Association for Institutional Research and to selected other sources which, despite their dates of publication, are comprehensive, remain timely and can be highly recommended.

Publications of or Sponsored by the Association for Institutional Research

(Some issues of several of these publications are now out of print.)

A Declaration on Institutional Research, S. Suslow. Esso Education Foundation and the Association for Institutional Research, 1972.

A Primer on Institutional Research, J. A. Muffo & G. W. McLaughlin eds. Association for Institutional Research, 1987.

Annual Forum Proceedings. Association for Institutional Research. Published annually, 1963–1984; titles vary.

Annual Proceedings, European AIR Forum, EAIR Secretariate, University of Twente, The Netherlands (contact AIR for specifics).

Bibliography of Reference Sources, W. P. Fenstemacher & D. R. Coleman, eds. Association for Institutional Research, 1984.

General Session Presentations. Association for Institutional Research. Published annually since 1985; titles vary.

Higher Education: Handbook of Theory and Research, J. C. Smart, ed. New York: Agathon Press Inc. Published annually since 1985.

New Directions for Institutional Research. San Francisco: Jossey-Bass Inc. Published quarterly since 1974; titles vary.

Research in Higher Education, New York: Human Sciences Press, Inc. Published since 1973 (by APS Publications from 1973 to 1979 and by Agathon Press from 1979 to 1988); four issues a year, 1973–75; eight issues a year, 1976–1988; six issues a year since 1989.

The AIR Professional File. Association for Institutional Research, Published since 1978; up to four issues a year.

The Design, Production and Use of Computer Graphics: A Tutorial and Resource Guide, R. S. Mims. The Association for Institutional Research, 1987.

Other Sources

Improving Academic Management: A Handbook of Planning and Institutional Research, P. Jedamus, M. W. Peterson & Associates. San Francisco: Jossey-Bass Inc., 1980.

Institutional Research in the University: A Handbook, P. L. Dressel & Associates. San Francisco: Jossey-Bass Inc., 1971.

State-Wide Planning in Higher Education, D. K. Halstead. Washington, D.C.: U.S. Government Printing Office, 1974.

The Association for Institutional Research
Code of Ethics

ADOPTED BY THE MEMBERSHIP 12/18/92

Section I: Competence.

I(a) Claims of Competence. The institutional researcher shall not, in job application, resume, or the ordinary conduct of affairs, claim a degree of competency he/she does not possess.

I(b) Acceptance of Assignments. The institutional researcher shall not accept assignments requiring competencies she/he does not have and for which she/he cannot effectively rely upon the assistance of colleagues, unless the supervisor has been adequately apprised.

I(c) Training of Subordinates. The institutional researcher shall provide subordinates with opportunities for professional growth and development.

I(d) Professional Continuing Education. The institutional researcher has the responsibility to develop her/his own professional skills, knowledge, and performance.

Section II: Execution.

II(a) Use of Accepted Technical Standards. The institutional researcher shall conduct all tasks in accordance with accepted technical standards.

II(b) Initial Discussions. Before an assignment is begun, the institutional researcher shall clarify with the sponsor and/or major users the purposes, expectations, strategies, and limitations of the research.

II(b)(i) Special care shall be taken to recommend research techniques and designs that are appropriate to the purposes of the project.

II(b)(ii) Special care shall be taken to advise the sponsor and/or major users, both at the design phase and, should the occasion arise, at any time during the execution of the project, if there is reason to believe that the strategy under consideration is likely to fail or to yield substantially unreliable results.

II(c) Identification of Responsibility. The institutional researcher shall accept responsibility for the competent execution of all assignments which he/she, or a subordinate, undertakes, and shall display individual and/or office authorship, as appropriate, on all such reports.

II(d) Quality of Secondary Data. The institutional researcher shall take reasonable steps to insure the accuracy of data gathered by other individuals, groups, offices, or agencies on which he/she relies, and shall document the sources and quality of such data.

II(e) Reports. The institutional researcher shall ensure that all reports of projects are complete; are clearly written in language understandable to decision-makers; fully distinguish among assumptions, speculations, findings, and judgments; employ appropriate statistics and graphics; adequately describe the limitations of the project, of the analytical method, and of the findings; and follow scholarly norms in the attribution of ideas, methods, and expression and in the sources of data.

II(f) Documentation. The institutional researcher shall document the sources of information and the process of analysis in each task in sufficient detail to enable a technically qualified colleague

"The Association for Institutional Research Code of Ethics," by Association for Institutional Research Directory of Members for 1998–99. Association for Institutional Research.

to understand what was done and to verify that the work meets all appropriate standards and expectations.

Section III: Confidentiality.

III(a) Atmosphere of Confidentiality. The institutional researcher shall establish a general atmosphere of awareness about confidentiality issues within the institutional research office.

III(b) Storage and Security. The institutional researcher shall organize, store, maintain, and analyze data under his/her control in such a manner as to reasonably prevent loss, unauthorized access, or divulgence of confidential information.

III(c) Release of Confidential Information. The institutional researcher shall permit no release of information about individual persons that has been guaranteed as confidential, to any person inside or outside the institution except in those circumstances in which not to do so would result in clear danger to the subject of the confidential material or to others; or unless directed by competent authority in conformity with a decree of a court of law.

III(d) Special Standards for Data Collection.

III(d)(i) Balancing Privacy Risks Against Benefits. The institutional researcher shall, at the design stage of any project, thoroughly explore the degree of invasion of privacy and the risks of breach of confidentiality that are involved in the project, weigh them against potential benefits, and make therefrom a recommendation as to whether the project should be executed, and under what conditions.

III(d)(ii) Developing Specific Guidelines. The institutional researcher shall prepare or approve a written description of any specific steps beyond the regular guidelines within the institutional research office that are necessary during the execution of said assignment to insure the protection of aspects of privacy and confidentiality that may be at specific risk.

III(d)(iii) Disclosure of Rights. The institutional researcher shall insure that all subjects are informed of their right of refusal and of the degree of confidentiality with which the material that they provide will be handled, including

where appropriate, the implications of any freedom of information statute.

III(d)(iv) Appraisal of Implications. The institutional researcher shall apprise institutional authorities of the implications and potentially binding obligations of any promise to respondents regarding confidentiality and shall obtain consent from such authorities where necessary.

Section IV: Relationships to the Community.

IV(a) Equal treatment. The institutional researcher shall promote equal access and opportunity regarding employment, services, and other activities of his/her office, without regard to race, creed, gender, national origin, disability or other accidental quality; and in analysis, demeanor, and expression shall be alert to the sensitivities of groups and individuals.

IV(b) Development of Local Codes of Ethics. The institutional researcher should develop and promulgate a code of ethics specific to the mission and tasks of the institutional research office; and should strive to cooperate with fellow practitioners in the institution in developing an institution-wide code of ethics governing activities in common.

IV(c) Custody and Archiving. The institutional researcher shall apply all reasonable means to prevent irrevocable loss of data and documentation during its immediately useful life; and, being aware of the role of data as institutional historic resource, shall act as advocate for its documentation and systematic permanent archiving.

IV(d) Assessment of Institutional Research. The institutional researcher shall develop and implement regular assessment tools for the evaluation of institutional research services.

IV(e) Institutional Confidentiality. The institutional researcher shall maintain in strict confidence and security all information in her/his possession about the institution or any of its constituent parts which by institutional policy is considered to be confidential, and shall pursue from Section III of this Code all processes for that purpose as are appropriate.

IV(f) Integrity of Reports. The institutional researcher shall make efforts to anticipate and prevent misunderstandings and misuse of reports within the institution by careful presentation and documentation in original reports, and by persistent follow-up contact with institutional users of those reports. If an institutional research report has been altered, intentionally or inadvertently, to the degree that its meaning has been substantially distorted, the institutional researcher shall make reasonable attempts to correct such distortions and/or to insist that institutional research authorship be removed from the product.

IV(g) External Reporting. The institutional researcher has an obligation to the broader community to submit and/or report accurate data and professionally responsible interpretive material when requested by legitimate authority, including federal, state, and other governmental agencies and accrediting bodies. With respect to private inquiries, such as those from guidebook editors, journalists, or private individuals, the institutional researcher, should he/she respond, is bound by the same standards of accuracy and professionally responsible interpretation.

Section V: Relationships to a Craft.

V(a) Research Responsibilities. The institutional researcher shall seek opportunities to contribute to and participate in research on issues directly related to the craft and in other professional activities, and shall encourage and support other colleagues in such endeavors.

V(b) False Accusations. Institutional researchers shall take care not to falsely demean the reputation or unjustly or unfairly criticize the work of other institutional researchers.

V(c) Unethical Conduct of Colleagues. The institutional researcher shall take appropriate measures to discourage, prevent, or correct unethical conduct of colleagues when they are unwittingly or deliberately in violation of this code or of good general practice in institutional research.

Proliferation or Professional Integration: Transition or Transformation

MARVIN W. PETERSON AND MARY CORCORAN

The current state of the field and the impact of new environmental forces have substantial implications for the practice and profession of institutional research. They suggest that attention needs be given to the development of the profession, not just to the professional development of its members, and that the AIR needs a proactive, transformational leadership strategy.

This chapter asks three basic questions: First, what is the current state of institutional research? Second, what are the implications for institutional research of the current environmental changes? Third, what needs to be done if institutional research is to continue to be a viable institutional function that improves the performance of institutions of higher education?

The State of the Field

The current state of institutional research is perhaps best summarized as Cameron Fincher does in Chapter Two: It is a practicing art with commendable promise as a professional and technical specialty. However, as Peterson suggests in Chapter One, the field is currently subject to increasing fragmentation and uncertainty about its future direction.

As a field of practice, institutional research, despite some minor dissent, has evolved into a primarily management-oriented, applied, data-handling, analysis, and research function. The increased complexity of our institutions and systems, the increased accessibility of data, and the increased availability of analytic capability in many administrative offices have led over the past five years to considerable dispersion and fragmentation of institutional research activity on many campuses. This development can be contrasted with the full decade of movement toward more coordinated or consolidated office structures that preceded it. Recent institutional pressures for reduction have increased the political pressure on institutional research and encouraged interest in a political, advocacy-oriented stance to research as units seek to defend their own resources, and the renewed institutional interest in planning has focused attention on policy research that is sometimes conducted elsewhere than in traditional institutional research offices. Finally, the growth of institutional research and the increasing diversity of its members have led to a proliferation and fragmentation of state and regional and special-interest groups within the AIR itself.

The wide array of activities and responsibilities that have been associated with institutional research (data collection, information system design, administrative computer specialists, external studies, resource and reduction analysis), the often extensive list of types of studies, the diverse methodologies used and data sources tapped, have all heightened the uncertainty about what constitutes institutional research.

It is not surprising, then, that a major concern for institutional researchers as the members of a profession is how to deal with the varied and often specialized interests of individuals who represent different academic backgrounds and work in an increasingly diverse

"Proliferation or Professional Integration: Transition or Transformation," by Marvin W. Peterson and Mary Corcoran, reprinted from *Institutional Research in Transition, New Directions for Institutional Research*, No. 46, June 1985. Jossey-Bass Publishers, Inc.

array of institutions, agencies, and administrative offices. Concern for professional development (to keep abreast of an expanding field) and for personal advancement (where does this lead?) are central for many in the field.

As Cameron Fincher concludes, this highly interdisciplinary professional area lacks an integrative nexus of ideas or theories. Institutional research is an applied research field with a considerable repertory of methods, but it has as yet paid little attention to how well its array of methods serves higher education. There is a massive amount of data and information about institutions and institutional research practice, but there has been little synthesis of what we know or think is essential and most useful. Despite its scientific shortcomings, Fincher notes that practitioners in the field appreciate theory and practice and that they are concerned about the relevance and usefulness of their work and about enhancing their analytic and interpretive skills. With standards and norms of the field still emerging, practitioners need guidance in preparing for and entering the field and leadership in planning their professional development.

The AIR has grown with the practice and the profession. It has succeeded by growing and becoming more inclusive so as to accommodate new practitioners. In doing so, it has expanded its programs, its publications, and its membership subgroups to respond to the increasingly diverse interests of its members. Over time, it has added activities that broaden its functions. It began as a way of helping members to meet peers and share ideas (the early forums). Its functions broadened to include publications that captured new developments in the field and provided an outlet for member's work and activities that assisted members in keeping abreast and that furthered their professional development. The association's current concern about mission and direction reflects a sensitivity to the uncertainty and fragmentation that we have just invoked.

Impacts of the New Environment

The analyses contained in Chapters Three, Four, and Five suggest very different and contrasting pictures of the future of postsecondary education. These pictures have significant implications for institutional research. Table 1 depicts these implications.

Educational Environment. In Chapter Three, Heydinger portrays an educational reality in which fundamental shifts in the external environment may be occurring in demographic patterns, the basic values of youth, attitudes toward postsecondary education, costs of postsecondary education, retraining needs, patterns of educational competition and collaboration, the role of government, and communication technology. These changes suggest potentially extensive changes in the nature of postsecondary education and underscore the importance of examining educational futures. The primary roles of institutional research in this environment are those of educational and organizational future strategist and planner. Institutional research can play a critical role in providing research and analysis that assists in the formulation of comprehensive institutional and educational strategy. Such activity may be either centralized or carefully coordinated by a planning officer or function. It requires practitioners with a broad perspective, and it involves studying external environments, forecasting, assessing values and preferences, identifying internal strengths, creating scenarios, and assessing alternatives.

This perspective suggests a professional focus on educational and societal environments and on organization environment theories. The methodologies are both qualitative and quantitative and involve highly interdisciplinary modes of futures and planning research and policy analysis. Such research also relies heavily on the use of data bases from sources outside the institution and outside higher education. The emphasis is on broad educational and societal understanding, on ideas and enlightenment about possibilities and strategies, not on day-to-day operations or managerial responsibilities.

Governance and Management. In his views of governance and management, Schmidtlein shares some of Heydinger's and Sheehan's concerns. He sees management as being reshaped by the effects of external trends (particularly those causing institutional retrenchment) and by the rapid spread of microcomputer technology. He also is concerned about some emerging changes in the way we view

Table 1. Implications of the New Environmental Reality

	Postsecondary Education	Governance	Telematics
The New Environmental Reality	Broad fundamental shifts External influences critical Needs and demands, delivery modes, institutional forms perhaps reshaped Importance of alternative futures	Limits of rationality Environmental evidence Complexity of resources Limits of the goal and problem concepts	Convergence of computing and communications Microcomputer development Information accessibility Decentralized analysis capacity
Implications for Practice 1. Functions	Comprehensive, future educational strategist, institutional planner	Organizational integration, policy analyst, management analyst	Information expertise, telematics technologist, decision support intermediary
2. Structure	Centralized or coordinated with planning	Coordinated or dispersed	Centralized or coordinated
3. Content	Studies of environment, development of scenarios, assessment of alternatives	Studies of policy and managerial efficiency and effectiveness	Expertise in information and administrative computing systems, applications, and utilization
Implications for the Profession 1. Science	Organization environment theory Quantitative and qualitative interdisciplinary methods Relevance of external data and sources	Organizational behavior, management science Quantitative and qualitative methods Information for decisions with rationale	Information, communication, and decision sciences Emphasis on quantitative methods Building of information networks
2. Art	Broad understanding of society and education Enlightenment, not operational	Comprehensive understanding of organization Systematic managerial perspective	Technological sophistication Information expertise

the nature of organizations. His analysis identifies many of the issues that are attracting the attention of decision makers. He notes the increased reliance on data and information about external events, the importance of contextual factors in decision making, the increasingly broad range of resources to be considered when examining decision issues, the limitations of goals and problems as the focus of decision analysis, and the critical importance of the location of institutional research on its ability to influence decisions in a changing governance and management arena.

These observations suggest that the practice of institutional research will still be management oriented but that it will need to address these changing characteristics if it is to influence decisions effectively. The primary role or emphasis will be that of the policy analyst who informs broad planning and policy issues or of the management analyst who examines issues of institutional performance and complex decision issues. A major concern in times of tight resources is the improvement of organizational integration; institutional research needs to make this concern a criterion both of its research and of the organization of its own activities. Because management studies will continue to focus on efficiency and effectiveness in all areas of higher education, Schmidtlein sees a continued dispersal of institutional research and perhaps an increased need for coordination.

Schmidtlein's perspective rests on a theoretical view of organizational and administrative behavior and management science. The methodologies of these fields are probably not significantly different from the methodologies that institutional researchers employ; the emphasis on quality and on costs and benefits in planning, resource allocation, and evaluation suggests that both qualitative and quantitative methods are relied on. Also, while empirical studies are useful as information for decisions, they are likely to require extensive rationale and contextual or comparative data if they are to inform the difficult choices that must be made when resources are constrained. The perspective of professionals, he suggests, will be the perspective of individuals who have a comprehensive understanding of organizational or system dynamics and resources but whose orientation is to the concerns of management.

Telematics. In Chapter Five, Sheehan examines the convergence of computing and communications that is rapidly reshaping the information-handling and analysis capacity both of our institutions and of the field. The advent of microcomputers and the ease with which information can be stored and retrieved have already had one notable impact: decentralization of the capacity to do institutional studies to any office that has a microcomputer and access to institutional or other relevant data sets or the capacity to create its own. In Chapter One, Peterson noted that decentralization can fragment or politicize a college's institutional research capacity and undermine carefully integrated information systems and centralized or highly coordinated institutional research functions. In contrast, Sheehan suggests that decentralization can create two new role emphases or possibilities for institutional research: the telematics technologist or information center expert (chief information officer) who becomes the institution's expert on information-handling technology, and the decision support intermediary who serves decision makers. The first role suggests a centralized service function, while the second may involve coordination between decision makers and telematics technologists. In either role, the activities suggested by Sheehan's model involve either coordinating the development of information technology or applying it to decision support activities.

The professional implications of Sheehan's perspective suggest a strong conceptual base in information, communications, and decision science fields. The major emphasis is still on quantitative data and quantitative methods of analysis, although the techniques used for handling qualitative measures are expanding. One significant potential of this development lies in its ability to build information networks among institutional researchers that can enhance the exchange and synthesis of empirical findings. This area also suggests the potential merger of the art and science of this aspect of the profession, since the methodological sophistication is embedded in technology, and the standards (if not norms) are often dictated by the expertise required.

Contrasts and Common Themes. The relative importance of the three environments, the validity of the descriptions, and the analysis of their implications can be debated. The issue of primary concern for the development of institutional research as a field is the commonalities and differences among the three.

Clearly, the three environments suggest very different primary functions for the practice of institutional research: future strategist and institutional planner contrast with policy analyst and management analyst and with telematics technologist and decision support intermediary. As already noted, some environments suggest more centralized and others more coordinated or more dispersed structures, and the content or topics of analysis are highly varied.

The three environments suggest somewhat contrasting views of the science of institutional research. The concepts derive from societal perspectives, organizational environment theory, organizational and administrative behavior, management sciences, and information and communication sciences. The methodologies vary from the methods of interdisciplinary futurists, planning and forecasting, policy analysis, efficiency and effectiveness evaluations, organizational analysis, simulation and modeling, and information systems design to our traditional descriptive studies and reports. The empirical emphasis changes in each environment, but to varying degrees each environment includes quantitative and qualitative measures and methods; relies on internal data, external data, or both; and emphasizes both the use of information and the building of information networks.

When institutional research is viewed as an art, the three environments differ also in their levels of focus or analysis—societal, organizational, and technological—and in their sources of standards or norms—enlightened societal interest (values), management (process), and technical expertise (technology). Clearly, these contrasts do nothing to diminish current concerns about fragmentation in the field and uncertainty about the direction that it will take.

However, three common themes also emerge across the three environmental perspectives: First, although each new environmental reality implies different practical functions for institutional research, each new reality also stresses the importance of good information, analysis, and research in the future for viable educational strategy in a changing envi-

ronment, for sound management in periods of constraint, and for effective use of the rapidly changing telematics technology. Second, despite their quite different theoretical or conceptual emphases, each perspective seems to recognize the importance of relating its theory, methods, and empirical approaches to the unique nature of postsecondary education. Third, all three perspectives suggest the need for some sophistication in relating theory and practice and for broad guides (if not standards) for good practice.

Proliferation or Professional Integration: Transition or Transformation?

The current tendency toward fragmentation in institutional research and uncertainty about future directions in practice, the profession, and the association was suggested by Peterson. The potential limitations of institutional research as a professional field were discussed by Fincher. The potential for further fragmentation posed by the three key environmental forces was analyzed by Heydinger, Schmidtlein, and Sheehan, and it has been summarized here. The AIR's history of responding to members' concerns and of supporting professional development of the field has been discussed. Yet, the overwhelming evidence suggests that, if institutional research continues to evolve in its present pattern, proliferation and fragmentation are likely to continue. A heightened sense of professional direction and integration seems especially important in the years ahead.

The AIR's strategy has largely been reactive. It responds rapidly to new developments in the field and to new needs among its members. To date, this transitional strategy—assisting members to make transitions or adjustments to new developments—has been successful. One approach would be to continue this evolutionary or responsive transitional strategy. The AIR can seek out and incorporate as members practitioners who play the roles suggested by the three discussions of the environment in this volume. It can modify and expand its programs and publications so as to incorporate these new topics and interests (it already has to some extent), and it can plan professional development activities for the association that anticipate the interests of others in topics related to these developments.

Dealing with the current issues of uncertainty and fragmentation posed by Peterson will be critical. Dealing with Fincher's concerns about the need for development of the art and science of the field may require the association to adopt a more active role, providing professional leadership in defining the integrative themes. However, the challenge does not end there. As Heydinger, Schmidtlein, and Sheehan suggest, other forces promise to reshape institutional research even more extensively. Can reactive or responsive transitional strategy accommodate that reshaping? Or, will it require a more proactive transformation strategy, one that provides leadership by defining the direction of the profession as well as by identifying integrative themes and that reshapes the way we view the field of institutional research?

Our analysis leads us to conclude that the current responsive transitional strategy may not be sufficient. Both the current and impending changes are moving so rapidly and in so many different directions that a more action-oriented agenda is appropriate. Such an agenda would call for seeking a new level of professional identification and integration.

An Agenda for Development of the Profession

The previous analysis argues that the AIR should pay as much attention to development of the profession of institutional research (its direction and substantive integration) in the years ahead as it has to the professional development of its members in the past and that it needs to achieve a balance between these two emphases. Achieving that balance will involve the agenda depicted in Table 2.

Recognizing a New Reality. Institutions of higher education—their clientele, their delivery modes, and their programs, not just the institutional research function, could be very different within five to ten years. Both the changes in the educational environment and the educational implications of the telematics revolution, which Sheehan does not discuss, suggest that this is possible. Institutional researchers need to consider this possibility to understand both the context in which they work and their role and work itself. Like other faculty and administrators, they need to become serious students of the changing nature of their institutions, not just of their own offices and related activities.

An Intermediary Role. Similarly, institutional researchers need to recognize the critical intermediary role that their function plays between the educational, governance or managerial, and information or telematics functions of their institution. The research and analysis function is constantly shaped by all three, and it must relate to all three even if it serves primarily only one of these functions.

Need for a Common View of Practice. For a profession to develop, its members need to have a common understanding of their field of practice, if not of their theoretical endeavors. After early debates about the nature and nomenclature of institutional research, the term institutional research sufficed during the 1970s as practice became consolidated and as it was identified on many campuses with an office of institutional research. Recently, an influx of members not affiliated with such offices and changes in the name or location of many such offices on college campuses have renewed the debates about the meaning of the term. For a profession—even an applied profession—a commonly accepted view of practice is required. Without proposing a new name, it does seem appropriate to conceive of the practice of institutional research as encompassing the following: an institutional process (not structure or office) that includes the collection or development of information, analysis of research, and utilization activities designed to improve some aspect of an institution of postsecondary education. Under this conception, institutional research includes varying types of research designed to serve planning, policy development, resource allocation, and management or evaluation decisions in all functional areas.

The intent of this definition is to include the different models or functions of institutional research, the varied organizational arrangements for institutional research functions, and the diverse methods that are employed. It places the focus on applied research that is concerned with improving the institution, not just with improving planning, resource management, resource allocation, or evaluation. We may have lost sight of the fact that improving

Table 2. An Agenda for Professional Development

Dimension	Agenda Item
The New Institutional Reality	New forms of higher education possible Concern with their changing nature Institutional research in critical intermediary role
Institutional Research in Practice	Need for common view: institutional improvement
Function	Information collection, analysis, research, and utilization Related to planning, management, resource allocation, and evaluation
Structure	A process, not an office per se
Influence	Comprehensive strategies and methods More substantive knowledge (not information access and control)
Content	Varied studies and methods
Institutional Research as Profession	
Common Theme	Improvement of higher education Relating theory to practice Applied professional field Responsiveness to new roles and methods
Conceptual Base	Integrated interdisciplinary framework
Methodological Focus	Assessment of useful methods and techniques
Empirical Findings	Development of a substantive and methodological knowledge base
Sophistication	Relating of theory and practice
Standards and Norms	Examination of current patterns and needs
Other Developments	Telematics: development of information sharing and communication links Expansion of relationships with other researchers and administrative change leaders

the institution and its educational, research, and service function (not just its management functions and processes) is or should be our primary focus. In particular, the emphasis of this definition is on the process of institutional research, not on the structure of institutional research offices. Institutional research can be conducted in offices with different names or by individuals with different titles.

Shifting Bases for Influence. An applied activity like institutional research is supported only to the extent that it deals with critical institutional issues, that it is designed to help the institution function more effectively, and that it is credible. The chapters of this volume have suggested some important arenas for institutional research activity. Another implication is that the basis for influencing decisions may also be changing. During the 1960s and 1970s, one major source of an institutional researcher's influence and power was his or her access to and knowledge or control of institutional data. The advent of well-designed information systems and the spread of microcomputers removes to some extent this basis for influence. Skill in research methods and techniques, especially those involving complex computer simulations and models, has also been dispersed as new easy-to-use microcomputer software has placed powerful analytic capability within the reach of administrators concerned about influencing decisions that affect their own unit. The advent of concern for futures-oriented strategic policy or planning studies that use external data sources often allows individuals with different analytic skills and knowledge of external data sources to gain influence. In essence, these insights suggest that influence for institutional researchers is no longer as tied to knowledge and control of internal data or to sophisticated computer modeling skills as it once was; external sources and comprehensive research strategies that combine varied research methods and that use quantitative and qualitative data from internal and external sources are becoming increasingly important.

On another dimension, institutional researchers have often relied on research methods and techniques as their primary source of expertise. However, the role of substantive knowledge about postsecondary education may become more critical than methodological knowledge about institutional research methods and techniques. For example, executive officers considering a proposal for a new or alternative educational delivery mode may be more interested in knowing how effective it has been in attracting new students or in how it has affected learning. Answers to such questions should build on knowledge of the relevant research literature; both synthesis of existing studies and ad hoc institutional studies should be considered. Thus, access to other research findings and knowledge about substantive issues may be as critical in the future as good research design and methodological skills have been in the past.

A Common Professional Theme. For a profession to develop, it must have a common concern. One common view of the practice of institutional research has already been suggested. However, three elements appear to constitute the common bond for individuals participating in these various institutional research activities: First, they are concerned about institutional improvement in some specific area of institutional functioning, not about some kind of general improvement in management. Second, they share a concern for relating theory to practice. Institutional research is an applied field, yet the analysis of the three environments in this volume suggests that it is important to relate broad theoretical concepts to practice, and Fincher suggests that institutional researchers are aware of this need. Third, they identify institutional research as an applied professional field.

Responsiveness to New Roles and Methods. The history of institutional research suggests that the important institutional problems are constantly changing. If that is so, institutional research must use its data collection, analysis, and utilization skills to attack new problems or serve new needs and to continue to play new roles and adopt new methods as appropriate. The three environments examined in this volume suggest the need for new roles and methods such as these. It is important for a

developing profession not to lose sight of this important characteristic of the field.

An Integrative Framework. The concern for understanding the new reality of changing educational conditions; the fragmenting pressures exerted by the diverse functions, theoretical underpinnings, and methods identified in both the description of the evolution of institutional research and in the analysis of the three environments; and Fincher's analysis of the awareness of the need for a nexus of ideas all underscore the timeliness and importance of developing an integrative framework from which we can view institutional research. Such a framework might have the following characteristics: It views colleges and universities as complex human organizations that include students, faculty, administrators, and staff. It views education from an open systems framework that recognizes environmental forces and influences. It pays attention to the distinctive characteristics of institutions of postsecondary education, their primary functions, and how they operate. It links resources with primary educational, scholarly, and service outputs. It focuses on understanding and informing the primary planning, management, resource allocation, and evaluation decisions. And, it includes appropriate internal and external data and information flows. Such a framework would of necessity be extensive and interdisciplinary, but it would reflect the arena of institutional research activity in postsecondary education.

Useful Methodologies. The preceding discussions all highlight the extensive array of inquiry methods used in institutional research and underscore the continual need to develop or borrow others. However, as Fincher notes, we often borrow and use methods and techniques that do not seem to be very useful. (PPBS always comes to mind.) To develop as a field, institutional research must continue to recognize the validity of diverse methods of inquiry (including both qualitative and quantitative methods), but we also need to begin to assess which methods and techniques are useful, which are not, and which might better serve higher education if they were modified. Currently, this process proceeds largely by trial and error, and there is no attempt to systematically review and assess new inquiry methods and techniques used in practice.

The Knowledge Base. As Fincher notes, institutional research has generated masses of data and studies, but we know little about the patterns of findings or about the appropriate substantive and methodological knowledge that it might be useful for an institutional researcher to possess. Before the field proliferates further, such syntheses would be useful, particularly if they were associated with an integrative framework and with the assessment of methodologies that proved useful in the past.

Sophistication, Standards, and Norms. While conceptual and methodological sophistication varies in an applied field of practice, institutional research should probably focus on increasing our sophistication in relating theory to practice. Only in that way is the level of discourse on development of the field likely to improve. Although discussion of standards and norms of good practice has some proponents, it seems likely to occur much later in the development of institutional research.

Information Sharing and Communication Links. The discussion of educational and governance environments highlighted the need for external and comparative data that reinforce earlier data exchange interests. Fincher notes that there are few syntheses of relevant findings and few assessments of which methods work and which do not. The advent of telematics makes interinstitutional data sharing and cross institutional identification of studies of similar issues much more feasible and with them the synthesis of findings and the assessment of different methodological techniques. Developments in this area could help individual practitioners in their work and the profession in its synthesis of findings and assessment of methods.

An Old Dialogue. The distinction between institutional research, which focuses on applied findings in a particular setting, and higher education research, which focuses on general patterns and theoretical interests, has been largely dormant since the early AIR forums. The proponents of each emphasis have largely gone their own way. Researchers in higher education now primarily attend Association for the Study of Higher Education or American Educational Research Association Division J meetings. However, this analysis suggests that the two may again have reasons to renew their dialogue. Clearly, the profes-

sional concerns for establishing an integrative framework and for conducting research on the effectiveness of various modes of inquiry (methods and techniques) are agenda items that might appeal to researchers in higher education. Similarly, institutional researchers who have interests in comparative research for planning and evaluation studies and who have an increasing need for substantive as well as methodological research findings may find that their interests are now more in line with those of their counterparts in higher education research. Further, the increasing sophistication of research methods, the interest in relating theory to practice, and the three critical environmental changes are all topics of interest to higher education researchers. Improved dialogue could prove a mutual advantage.

An Association Role: Reactive or Proactive, Transition or Transformation?

As noted earlier, the AIR can help both the field and the profession to evolve and develop by adopting a transitional role: by reacting supportively and responsively to the new functions, to potential members, and to the needs identified in the analysis of the three changing environments. These aims can be accomplished by incorporating these interests into existing meetings, publications, and professional development activities. However, such an approach may not succeed with the current proliferation of changes and forces.

An alternative agenda involves seeking a new level of development for the profession. This requires a proactive leadership role in which the association seeks to transform the way in which the profession views itself, its direction, and its role. Such a transforming role requires the association to address a more difficult agenda that addresses such questions as these: How do we develop knowledge about an entire field? How do we define its substance? How does an association lead rather than respond to its members? A modest action agenda based on the professional agenda sketched in Table 2 would include the following:

1. Give greater attention to the changing environment of postsecondary educa-

tion and to the institutional context for institutional research.

2. Focus attention on the need for a common view of the practice of institutional research as an inclusive process of information collection, analysis, research, and utilization related to planning, management, resource allocation, and evaluation decisions. (This issue is singled out for attention in AIR's 1984 revised mission statement.)

3. Promote a professional theme focused on the improvement of institutions of postsecondary education through institutional research that relates theory to practice and that responds to new rational methods.

4. Take steps to develop an integrative framework for the field. There is none now. One could be prepared for the AIR's twenty-fifth anniversary.

5. Promote research activities and syntheses aimed at assessing the usefulness of methods and techniques. Current activities primarily identify and describe them.

6. Develop a knowledge base appropriate for the institutional research practitioner. Such a base would include substantive knowledge about postsecondary education, knowledge of important research methods and techniques, and information about important data and information sources. Such information probably exists, but synthesis and judgment about its importance are required.

7. Continue to stress relating institutional studies to theory or broader patterns of findings.

8. Assess current norms and standards of good practice among members.

9. Focus some current publication activities on systematic synthesis of useful methods, development of the knowledge base, and discussion of standards and norms of practice.

10. Make professional development activities more proactive by identifying new cutting edge areas for exploration. Continue to revise the annual AIR forum program and regional programs to reflect emerging interests and needs.

11. Actively promote membership among groups doing institutional research who do not have such titles.

12. Seek a more active involvement of and dialogue with education researchers and with administrative leaders interested in changing and improving institutions of postsecondary education.

13. Develop telecommunications and computerized information-sharing networks to serve members' professional and institutional needs more effectively.

It can be hoped that this agenda for the future will help to balance concern for the development of the profession with concern for the professional development of AIR members. It will limit the tendency toward proliferation, and we can hope that it will also assure that institutional research continues to he a major factor in the improvement of postsecondary education over the next twenty-five years.

Marvin W. Peterson is director of the Center for the Study of Higher Education at the University of Michigan. He is now president of the Association for Institutional Research.

Mary Corcoran is professor of higher education and educational psychology at the University of Minnesota. She is a former editor of AIR publications and a Distinguished Member of the association.

Policy Analysis: Neither Institutional Research nor Planning

Laura Saunders

Policy analysis is applied research and analysis conducted for policymakers to assist in the policy decision process. While there is overlap between institutional research, planning, and policy analysis, they are different. This chapter discusses the differences and similarities. Several volumes in the Jossey-Bass series New Directions for Institutional Research (NDIR) are examined to illustrate the differences. NDIR provides good examples of policy analysis as well as solid methodological guidance and information about data sources for the policy analyst.

Institutional Research Versus Policy Analysis

Institutional research has had a variety of definitions over the years and slowly seems to be coming together as a profession. Joe Saupe (1981, p. 1) defined institutional research as "research conducted within an institution of higher education in order to provide information which supports institutional planning, policy formulation, and decision making." An elaboration of this definition is given in the introduction to the Association for Institutional Research (AIR) publication *A Primer on Institutional Research* (Muffo and McLaughlin, 1987, p. iv): "processes and functions which can be, and are, performed in and on most functional areas of the institutions." Thus, institutional researchers are characterized by where they function—institutions and systems of higher education—and what they do.

These definitions are misleading, however, since institutional research in recent years has spread beyond a focus on institutions of higher education. The content of the papers presented at the annual meeting of AIR suggests the eclectic nature of the profession, with presentation topics including alumni research, outcomes assessment, ranking polls, graduation rates of athletes, and appropriate computer techniques. While traditional colleges and universities and state higher education systems remain a major focus of institutional researchers, vocational and technical schools, proprietary institutions, and national education policy also receive attention.

Institutional research emphasizes data and information: collection, analysis, appropriate methodologies, sources, and uses. This emphasis is particularly important to the policy analyst who frequently calls upon institutional research skills when examining a policy analysis problem. The sourcebooks and meetings of institutional researchers provide a wealth of information on appropriate data sources, the wit and wisdom of making comparisons of various kinds, techniques to find information in masses of data, and even the right questions to ask. Because of their central position as data managers in institutions, systems offices, and agencies, institutional researchers can often identify sources of data or information and may know of previous work that has been done related to the issue under review. In early stages of policy analysis development, the institutional researcher's perspective may help to define the study's objectives and its boundaries. The

"Policy Analysis: Neither Institutional Research nor Planning," by Laura Saunders, reprinted from *Developing Effective Policy Analysis in Higher Education*, Winter 1992, No. 76. Jossey-Bass Publishers, Inc.

institutional researcher will always be a strong member of the field-testing group.

Another area where the institutional researcher can make a contribution is in providing a road map to external institutional information sources. Institutional researchers, through their participation in regional and national meetings, connections to electronic networks, and constant review of publications, may be able to identify external sources of data, policy work, or methodologies. Many institutional research offices have access to the burgeoning number of electronic newsletters and lists that are sources of up-to-date information, as well as access to other institutions and settings. Questions are asked and answered, papers sent, and people identified for detailed discussion. The question "Does anybody know anybody who has done anything recently on . . .?" is a frequent query on the electronic networks, and because of the speed and ease of communication, they are a first-rate resource that the institutional researcher can share with the policy analyst.

Methodologies and appropriate data-handling techniques are the special expertise of the institutional researcher. Policy analysis may require data or information to test alternatives, describe problems, or select recommendations. In particular, institutional researchers can test data for statistical reliability so that policy analysts do not draw invalid inferences from their data. The skillful caution of the institutional researcher is useful to the policy analyst, who often works in a pressured and rushed atmosphere. Jumping to unwarranted conclusions based on incorrect use of data can be very costly to the credibility of the policy analyst. The practice of having the resident institutional researcher review data for validity and reliability may cause a momentary delay, but it can save a policy analyst from mistakes with long-run implications.

There is a delicate balance in the relationship between the data handler (institutional researcher) and the policy analyst. Too much caution may mean that policy work is sometimes not timely, too little may mean that the work is not valid. Typically, however, policy analysts cannot afford to leave the data and research experts out of their consultations.

Besides advice and input on data and methodologies, the institutional researcher is often useful in the initial formulation stages of a project, when the policy analyst is attempting to understand the dimensions of the problem. Because institutional researchers are often involved in a variety of campus projects, they may have unique insights into the institutional climate and environment. In addition, institutional researchers frequently function as local historians and have insights on what has and has not worked, which powerful or influential groups play an active role in the development and dissemination of policy, and which pitfalls exist for the unwary policymaker.

The distinctions, therefore, between institutional research and policy analysis are several: Institutional research focuses on data and information in institutions and systems, whereas policy analysis extends beyond data collection and analysis and makes use of many qualitative research methodologies as well as generous helpings of intuition. Institutional research usually does not point to recommendations or changes, while policy analysis almost always does. The reasons for doing policy analysis reflect real-world issues and the analysis has definite time constraints. Policy analysis takes place in an atmosphere where judgments and biases have already constrained the analysis. Institutional research may require the maintenance of long-term data bases and the production of periodic reports using agreed-on formats. Policy analysis has widely diverse outputs, may draw on a variety of sources of information, including institutional research data bases, and extends beyond the use of quantitative data. Policy analysis frequently includes recommendations for action or reinforcement of existing policies and strategies for implementation; these elements are usually not part of the institutional research agenda. Policy analysts may field-test and revise their recommendations a number of times, while the products of institutional researchers are reports written as of particular points in time. The policy analyst's work is messy, inexact, and grounded in the real world of trying to get things done. Political factors enter into the shaping of the policy analysis and the associated recommendations, while the institutional researcher's work is conducted more independently of political factors. The institutional researcher may often perform policy analysis, and the policy analyst may draw on the work of the institutional researcher, but these actions do not entail the same function.

How does the work of the policy analyst influence that of the institutional researcher? The policy analyst is usually involved in issues of concern to campus or systemwide management. The results of the policy analysis are needed immediately and may result in changes in the environment. The need of campus managers for policy analysis comes from both inside and outside the institution, from individual complaints, from government action, from demographic and social changes. The agenda of the decision maker is the source of the assignments for the policy analyst. Eventually, the policy analyst's need for data and information will influence the institutional researcher, initially in the development of short-term studies and investigations, and in the longer run in the refinement and evolution of institutional data systems that provide information suited to the analysis. The growth of interest in attrition rates is a good example. In studying program completion rates, policymakers have gone from occasionally requesting data to requiring continuous longitudinal studies.

Higher Education Planning Versus Policy Analysis

What is higher education planning? Is it a type of policy analysis or research? What is its relationship to institutional research? Donald Norris's (1991) excellent introduction to the field, *A Guide for New Planners*, describes the characteristics of various kinds of planning: strategic, long range, tactical, and operational. In a more extended discussion, Marvin Peterson (1980) defines planning as a key organizational process that may or may not be developed as part of the larger institutional management function. Peterson's definition assumes (1) that the institution and its members are concerned about the future as well as the current states of the institution and the means for achieving them, (2) that they choose to develop a planning process rather than rely on the whims of key individuals or sporadic responses to unpredictable external events, and (3) that an attempt to assess institutional strengths and weaknesses and to examine the environment for constraints and opportunities leads to changes that are beneficial to the institution's vitality.

Peterson emphasizes that planning is a process rather than a static view. Planners try to anticipate and shape the future through actions that take place in the present. They are watchful

of activity in the institution's environment that may impact on the college or university, influencing its future direction. Knowledge obtained from strategic planning activities can be very beneficial to the policy analyst's need for information on environmental issues.

Planners also stimulate policy analysis. As they develop institutional goals and strategic directions, planners may discover areas of unclear or missing policy or even unearth conflicts between existing policies. In looking to the future and planning for change, planners raise issues central to the college or university—anticipated demographic changes in enrollment may require new admissions policies, for example.

Policy analysis is used in the formulation of plans, and planning suggests questions or areas in which policy analysis is needed. Planning typically leads to plans, and plans often Suggest or lead to actions. Policy analysis may or may not lead to any changes, depending on the issue and the results of the analysis. Planning usually involves fairly large-scale, total system treatments; policy analysis is more focused on specific issues or questions. Planning produces plans that are finished as of particular points in time; policy analysis is repetitive and iterative as the issues and the environment change. Institutional research provides data for both planning and policy analysis, long-range forecasts, trends, and descriptions of the environment for planners, and topic- or issue-based data for policy analysts.

How does the policy analyst contribute to the work of the planner? In many cases, the policy analyst identifies issues that shape institutional goals and objectives. Because policy analysts work closely with and for decision makers, their work influences the framework that the decision maker uses to shape the planning process. Issues researched, analyzed, and studied by the policy analyst are the background of institutional planning. For example, policy analysts may identify changes in student demand as critical to the future of the institution, and the planners then incorporate into their plan a strategic emphasis on attracting a new and different market. The work of the policy analyst and the planner is interactive and interwoven, although their products may be quite distinct.

Overall, the above-named distinctions among the work of the policy analyst, the institutional researcher, and the planner may appear clear, but in day-to-day operations the distinctions blur. Many institutional researchers do all three functions, as confusing as that can sometimes be. The mindsets and assumptions required by each kind of work are different and the products differ accordingly. The harried staff member has to remember which cap is being worn and what the output should contain in order to meet the demands of the job; the ability of staff to rapidly shift administrative paradigms ensures some level of success.

Policy Analysis and the New Directions for Institutional Research Series

At present, there is no single journal for higher education policy analysis. The NDIR series is an informative source for policy analysts even though it focuses primarily on the field of institutional research. NDIR provides valuable references for data sources, techniques and tools, and descriptions of the higher education environment, including institutions and their participants. Occasionally, NDIR includes data analysis as well. We review three areas where NDIR volumes are a rich source of data, literature, and guidance to illustrate how an institutional researcher can use the series for policy analysis.

Data, Techniques, and Tools. The major strength that the institutional researcher brings to the policy analysis task is detailed student educational data: sources, methods for handling, and qualifications concerning its use. NDIR offers a number of volumes that focus on student data. For example, *Using National Data Bases* (Lenth, 1991) guides the policy analyst to major national resources. An excellent short guide to over fifty national data bases is provided in the last chapter. These national data bases are used in the first chapter to examine the policy issue of minority student participation. NDIR has not yet offered a similar volume on state-level data bases, but some of the resources cited in Lenth (1991) can be disaggregated to state-level summaries.

Besides the data sources, NDIR volumes frequently cover methodological topics, particularly new and emerging methodologies. The

use of statistical and other quantitative techniques is not always simple and straightforward. The volume *Applying Statistics in Institutional Research* (Yancey, 1988) is a balanced description of the problems and opportunities inherent to the use of statistical methods. Literature for more detailed study of the methodologies is also cited, and several relatively recently applied methodologies are described. Other data-oriented volumes include *Enhancing Information Use in Decision Making* (Ewell, 1989), which alerts the policy analyst to the problem of making data meaningful to decision makers in an institution, a problem of particular concern to the policy analyst. *Alumni Research: Methods and Applications* (Melchiori, 1988) deals with a specialized subject population but provides useful information for analysts concerned with follow-up studies or more general questionnaire issues. And *Conducting Interinstitutional Comparisons* (Brinkman, 1987) provides useful cautions to the policy analyst who has data from different institutions and wishes to compare them.

Educational Context. *The Chronicle of Higher Education* is the analyst's most useful source of data on current policy problems, issues, struggles, and resolutions in higher education. Policy issues and assignments to policy analysts arise from the current events of the day. The *Chronicle* reports on those issues in a faithful and timely manner. The *Chronicle* also records the history of higher education in its making, and the longer, thoughtful analyses of current issues are the first places to look for information on educational context.

The NDIR volumes also contain descriptive information on the educational setting, particularly in relation to the central topic of each volume. Slightly dated perhaps, but still relevant for any policy analyst dealing with funding issues, is the volume *Responding to New Realities in Funding* (Leslie, 1984). Specific funding strategies and related external conditions have changed only slightly, and the organizational scheme for studying them remains relevant and current. Other, even older volumes deal with more specific events in budgeting for declining resources.

Another volume that contributes to our understanding of educational setting and context is *Assessing Academic Climates and Cultures* (Tierney, 1990). This volume contains a number of chapters that describe how to analyze an academic culture: George Kuh's chapter on student culture is particularly useful, as is Ann Austin's chapter on faculty cultures and values. Any policy analyst proposing a change in faculty governance, hiring, or compensation policy needs to have a sophisticated understanding of faculty cultures and of how to go about understanding the culture at the particular institution under study. Faculty culture at research universities is quite different from faculty culture at community colleges, but they can be analyzed and understood with some of the same tools. Estela Maria Bensimon's chapter offers the perspective of an outsider coming to a campus as the new president and illustrates a good starting point for any policy analysis.

The use of these volumes requires caution since conditions change. But the quarterly appearance of volumes in the series ensures a measure of timeliness in the topics addressed.

Other excellent discussions of academic context include those found in the Jossey-Bass series New Directions for Higher Education as well as *Academe* and more specialized journals.

Policy Analysis. NDIR volumes also include actual policy analyses. *Issues in Pricing Undergraduate Education* (Litten, 1984) studies a topic that is still of vital concern to the policy analyst. The question of how institutions should determine their undergraduate tuition levels remains a central concern of every independent institution and, increasingly, of every public institution. This volume summarizes several conceptual approaches to pricing issues, including the point of view of an economist who sees prices (tuition) reflecting enrollment or market demand. Pricing is also examined as a political decision—who pays and who should pay? Another volume, *The Effect of Assessment on Minority Student Participation* (Nettles, 1990), examines the twin issues of assessment and minority student participation and illustrates the interrelationships among policy issues and the impact of one policy area on another.

References

Brinkman, P. T. (ed.). *Conducting Interinstitutional Comparisons.* New Directions for Institutional Research, no. 53. San Francisco: Jossey-Bass, 1987.

Ewell, P. T. (ed.). *Enhancing Information Use in Decision Making.* New Directions for Institutional Research, no. 64. San Francisco: Jossey-Bass, 1989.

Lenth, C. S. (ed.). *Using National Data Bases.* New Directions for Institutional Research, no. 69. San Francisco: Jossey-Bass, 1991.

Leslie, L. L. (ed.). *Responding to New Realities in Funding.* New Directions for Institutional Research, no. 43. San Francisco: Jossey-Bass, 1984.

Litten, L. H. (ed.). *Issues in Pricing Undergraduate Education.* New Directions for Institutional Research, no. 42. San Francisco: Jossey-Bass, 1984.

Melchiori, G. S. (ed.). *Alumni Research: Methods and Applications.* New Directions for Institutional Research, no. 60. San Francisco: Jossey-Bass, 1988.

Muffo, J., and McLaughlin, G. *A Primer on Institutional Research.* Tallahassee, Fla.: Association for Institutional Research, 1987.

Nettles, M. T., (ed.). *The Effect of Assessment on Minority Student Participation.* New Directions for Institutional Research, no. 65. San Francisco: Jossey-Bass, 1990.

Norris, D. *A Guide for New Planners.* Ann Arbor, Mich.: Society for College and University Planners, 1991.

Peterson, M. W. "Analyzing Alternative Approaches to Planning." In P. Jedamus, M. Peterson, and Associates, *Improving Academic Management: A Handbook of Planning and Institutional Research.* San Francisco: Jossey-Bass, 1980.

Saupe, J. L. *The Functions of Institutional Research.* Tallahassee, Fla.: Association for Institutional Research, 1981.

Tierney, W. G. (ed.). *Assessing Academic Climates and Cultures.* New Directions for Institutional Research, no. 68. San Francisco: Jossey-Bass, 1990.

Yancey, B. D. (ed.). *Applying Statistics in Institutional Research.* New Directions for Institutional Research, no. 58. San Francisco: Jossey-Bass, 1988.

Laura Saunders is dean of administration at Highline Community College, Des Moines, Washington.

The Role of Institutional Research: From Improvement to Redesign

Marvin W. Peterson

The nature and role of institutional research has expanded and progressed by helping institutions adapt to new challenges and conditions. As a postsecondary knowledge industry emerges and institutions consider redesigning themselves, institutional researchers need to become knowledge industry analysts.

Any discussion of the evolution of institutional research and its future direction will inevitably reflect the perspective the author brings to the task. The previous authors have each provided theirs. In this chapter, I incorporate four perspectives: professional self reflection, institutional adaptation, contingency, and industry as we look both to the past and future.

First, *professional self reflection,* examining the role and function of institutional research, has historically been a major preoccupation of this field ever since the first national forum in 1961. What is I.R.? What is its institutional role? How is it defined? What are its primary functions and activities? How is it organized? What skills and expertise does it require? Is it a profession? These have all been the focus of continuous debate in our forums, our workshops, and our publications. Our literature reflects the endless debate over the nature and role of institutional research. The role has been variously described as a management service function (Brumbaugh, 1960), an autonomous institutional critic (Dressel, 1971), an organizational intelligence officer (Tetlow in Cope, 1979), a change agent and action researcher (Lindquist, 1980), an institutional advocate or political partisan (Firnberg-Lasher, 1983), a telematics technologist (Sheehan in Peterson & Corcoran, 1985), a mediator of institutional environments (Peterson & Corcoran, 1985). a management and decision support function, (Saupe, 1990). a policy analyst (Gill & Saunders, 1992; Terenzini, 1995). and many other variations. The evolving nature of institutional research as a profession (Peterson & Corcoran, 1985), whether it is "act or science" (Fincher in Peterson & Corcoran, 1985), how professional development for the field occurs (Cope, 1979) and what its ethics and standards are or should be (Schiltz, M. E., 1992) have been examined and discussed. This practice of professional self reflection has served us well both as a professional field, as an association, and as individual professionals. Hopefully this volume and this chapter will aid our understanding of our past and future.

Second, while I concur with AIR's official definition of institutional research as: "research leading to improved understanding, planning and operating of institutions of postsecondary education" and "to its utilization in planning, management and resource allocation to improve postsecondary education." In my view, institutional research has been more than a servant of institutional improvement and management. From my perspective, institutional research has flourished as an institutional function and a profession because it has contributed to an institution's *adaptive function* and played a major role in fostering and assisting institutional change. As I look back briefly on the development and contribution of the field, institutional research may best be understood by examining how we tackled the major issues facing our institutions and helped them accommodate to them. As I look ahead, I will suggest the major challenge facing institutional research may be more daunting—to assist our institutions in addressing changing conditions that require not just institutional improvement but the need to redesign and transform themselves.

Third, to understand both the evolution of institutional research and its future challenge, a *contingency* perspective is useful. This suggests we can best understand the changing role and contribution of institutional research by examining the interface between an institution and its environment and how institutions adapt to challenges at that interface.

And finally in looking ahead, this chapter takes an *industry* perspective. While this term maybe as threatening to some college administrators today as management was an anathema to them twenty five years ago, it is a useful analytic perspective which helps in gaining insight into today's institutional challenges. Adopting these perspectives, this chapter will review briefly the evolving role and contribution of institutional research to institutional adaptation, how societal conditions are reshaping our postsecondary industry, and suggest some implications for institutional research as institutions respond to emerging new postsecondary knowledge industry.

A Brief History of the Evolution of Institutional Research

While there were institutional research studies prior to World War II, the development of institutional research as an administrative process or function is primarily a post 1950's development, so our analytic interpretation begins here. The contingency argument is quite simple. As external conditions affecting higher or postsecondary education have changed in the past forty years, the primary press on institutional management, how institutions were viewed as organizations, and the primary focus of institutional performance has shifted. Institutional research developed concurrently, helped our institutions adapt to meet these

challenges and has been shaped by the same forces. (See Table 1).

1950s and 60s Growth and Expansion: Following World War II and continuing through the 1960s, U.S higher education experienced an unprecedented period of growth and expansion which reflected strong public support, expanding enrollment demands, and increasing government financial support. During this period, the pressure on institutional management was to provide a sense of direction for their growing institution and to account for the extensive human, financial, and physical resources they were absorbing to justify that support.

Two internally oriented models of organization emerged at this time to help us understand and manage our growing institutions. First was the notion of a formal rational or bureaucratic organization (Stroup, 1966) which focuses on building rational structures to administer and mechanisms to account for growing resource flows and needs. The second was the collegial model which viewed them as communities of learners (Goodman, 1964), professionals (Clark, 1962) or constituents with a common community of interests (Millett, 1962). Both reflected our notions of colleges and universities as self contained educational organizations.

Institutional performance during this era focused primarily on accounting for resources. With encouragement from ACE, WICHE, NEBHE, and SREB workshops on institutional research were held and spawned the formal development of our emerging field (Doi in Cope, 1979). The focus was on developing means of accounting for resources and on conducting studies of student characteristics; faculty work and activities; admissions, enrollment and placement; space utilization; and income and expense analysis. These studies were basic descriptive data crunching by current standards. During the 1960s, issues of institutional size, complexity and concerns about standards also gave rise to more complex institutional self studies and increasingly data driven accreditation reviews.

The first AIR forum in 1961, which was convened by invitation, was opened to broader participation the following year in response to institutional interests. The rapidly growing interest and expansion led to the founding of AIR in 1964 (Doi in Cope, 1979). Most of the early institutional research directors reported to the President. Clearly institutional research was contributing to managing growth and expansion. Rourke and Brooks' book, *The Managerial Revolution* (1966), summarized this expanding era and the development of institutional research as a critical management function.

Disruption and Demands. In the late 1960s and early 1970s, higher education's bubble burst. Disruptions emanated both from inside and outside the university. Students were dissatisfied with the increasingly large, impersonal and formally structured institutions and with increasingly professionalized faculty with scholarly rather than teaching interests. Societal issues such as the U.S. role in the Vietnam War, the civil rights movement and the free speech movement found fertile ground among liberal and disaffected faculty and students who wanted a forum to express their views. The pressure on institutional management was to keep order or control on campus and to assure greater access for minority and less traditional students.

Our models of colleges and universities as organizations, reflecting the general organizational literature (Katz and Kahn, 1978), began to recognize them as open system. More importantly, they were viewed as political organizations (Baldridge, 1971) made up of competing constituencies. This era also coincided with the growth of state systems which brought public institutions increasingly under political scrutiny (Berdahl, 1971) and added a new layer of complexity to institutional governance and external reporting.

Interestingly, while the emergent internal political governance model attempted to incorporate and mollify the conflicting constituents, the external emphasis on performance shifted to enhancing the external reputation of higher education. Indeed, the first reputational studies of higher education were sponsored by the American Council on Education (Cartter 1966; Roose and Anderson, 1970) and focused primarily on graduate research universities. This emphasis on reputational quality determined by peer judgment later expanded to include most institutional types and many professional or disciplinary segments. Of course, today we have reputational ratings done by magazines and non-educational organizations based on

the judgment of our business and consumer customers At the state level interest in financial cost issues, program review, and institutional duplication intensified. An institution's political reputation demanded more detailed accounting and reporting for all resources.

While institutional researchers did not start reputational studies nor create the state pressures, they responded. They became more analytic and comparative in their approach rather than relying on descriptive reports. They were eager to examine the correlates of quality programming, deepened their interest in studies of student behavior, strengthened their resource reporting capacity, and become aware of the potential uses, value and abuses of such studies.

Recession and Constraint. From the mid 1970s to the early 1980s, an economic recession and the realization that the end of the post war baby boom would dampen enrollment growth forced a new reality on many campuses. State, federal, and other external agencies were also responding to their own resource constraints. They demanded greater institutional accountability for resources and were becoming more sophisticated in collecting and analyzing data and asking tough management questions. At the same time the 1972 Higher Education Amendments shifted federal student aid distribution from institutions directly to the student and began using the term postsecondary education. This vastly increased the number of institutions and students eligible for student aid. These changes pressed institutional management to focus on improving internal efficiency and to seek new markets for students.

New organizational models now began to emphasize colleges and universities either as managerial models built on more comprehensive information systems which used resource simulation models to inform decisions (Lawrence & Service, 1977) or as market oriented models (Kotler, 1975) designed to identify and attract new students.

This new reality led to a new emphasis on performance based on results—not just on inputs or resources used. Initially this focused primarily on quantitative measures of productivity (output measures of numbers of graduates, degrees granted, etc.) or efficiency (indices of cost per degree or course, faculty workload, space utilization etc.). Cameron

Fincher (1985) has chronicled the increased use of evaluative research approaches, as institutional researchers developed and implemented MIS systems, and added MBO studies, demographic forecasting, PPB and Zero based budgeting, cost studies, resource utilization studies and even economic benefit analysis to their repertoire during this period.

Enrollment and Financial Constraints. By the mid 1980's, it became apparent that improved management, marketing, and efficiency would not be sufficient. Economic constraints continued and new demands for public funds grew. Demographic characteristics suggested real declines in traditional aged students and likely changes in their economic, ethnic, and educational background. Competition increased as proprietary institutions and other organizations competed with more traditional higher education institutions for students and funds. The management press was to reduce, reallocate and retrench (Mortimer and Tierney, 1979); to carefully examine programs and to focus on more limited or purposes; and to become more effective not just efficient.

Colleges and universities were now being viewed not just as more open institutions that responded to their environment. They were now strategic organizations (Keller, 1988; Peterson, 1981) which could revise purposes and priorities, change clientele and program mixes, and seek a strategic market niche within the higher education industry. Other new organizational models viewed them as flexible, decentralized conglomerates, as matrix organizations (Alpert, 1986), as organized anarchies (Cohen and March, 1974) and as unique cultural entities (Tierney, 1990).

The latter part of the 1980s and early 199's has brought a curious twist to this era of constraints. Criticism of U.S. education, first at the K-12 level (National Commission on Excellence in Education, 1983) and then at the higher education level (Study Group on Conditions of Excellence in American Higher Education, 1984), led some academic leaders and many public policy officials to challenge colleges and universities to measure performance results in terms of educational and instructional quality and of student learning outcomes and to encourage the use of student and academic assessment in a variety of modes and purposes. The Quality Improvement movement, popular in U.S. business and industry as a way to recapture economic supremacy, also added another dimension to performance assessment focusing on total institutional functioning.

Once again institutional researchers were in the foray. Strategic planning studies and mission reviews; marketing, recruitment and need and demand studies; student, faculty and program evaluation and assessment; studies of utilization and condition or capital facilities; design of decision support systems; administrative staff studies; and policy analysis were all added to the I.R. arsenal (Fincher, 1985). Most recently, the elusive performance indicators have been a focus of attention. In expanding these efforts, institutional researchers have also come to rely more on qualitative approaches.

Implications. This history has several useful themes as we approach the 21st Century. First, the major challenges that have shaped our institutional management press, organizational models, and performance criteria were primarily external. Second, those challenges reflect an environment that has become more complex, less munificent and more critical or threatening. Third, the challenges have been dealt with primarily by managerial responses in institutional governance, management, and performance patterns. While program offerings have been modified and student clientele changed, the basic teaching and learning processes and academic functions have been affected very little. Fourth, institutional research has played a critical role in helping institutions respond, and in the process, has expanded its role and array of activities (although often through a more dispersed set of institutional offices and activities—not necessarily from a central institutional research office). And finally, the new models or patterns, including our institutional research activities, do not supersede the earlier ones. Rather understanding institutional research can be seen as part of a more complex picture of how we understand the organizational, management and performance patterns in our institutions. These contextual insights are helpful as we look to the future.

Challenges of the 21st Century

The decade ahead will pose serious challenges both for our institutions and for institutional researchers that are quite different from our past four decades. In facing these challenges, I side neither with Peter Drucker (1995) who speculates universities, as we know them will seek to exist in 20 years or with our traditional view that colleges and universities—only slightly modified—will always exist. The argument is that a more fundamental change is occurring than we have not faced in the past—a *redefinition* of our industry that could lead to institutional *redesign*.

An Industry perspective. Industry reflects a "set of related organizations which utilize similar resources, attract similar clients, and produce similar services." Clearly higher or postsecondary education is a definable segment of the education industry. Porter (1981) in his study of forces reshaping competition in an industry posits four key forces. 1) the bargaining power of customers (students); 2) the bargaining power of suppliers; 3) the threat of new organizational entrants; and 4) the threat of substitute services. A fifth force, innovation in the core processes of the industry, is also suggested as critical.

Viewed as an industry, over the past 50 years we have undergone two transitions: from an industry of traditional higher education to mass higher education and from mass to postsecondary education. These transitions occurred primarily as a result of only two of the five forces: 1) the addition of new organizations to the competitive mix (the expansion of public colleges and universities and growth of the community college sector in the transition from traditional to mass higher education and the addition of the proprietary sector as a result of government policy change as we moved from mass to postsecondary) and 2) the bargaining power of consumers of postsecondary education as their numbers increased and the control of financial aid shifted to them. But after both transitions, we are still competing with other institutions whose primary business is education and we have only minimally modified the process of delivering education.

As we approach the 21st century, much at-

tention is directed at the rapid technological changes affecting education, but my argument is that at least six societal conditions are affecting all five forces reshaping an industry. A seventh, resource constraint, is a condition which both affects how we respond and enhances competition. Since it is one we all clearly understand, it is not discussed. While we understand the impact of these conditions on our institutions individually, it is the collective impact on our industry that is addressed here. Therefore, the nature of each condition and how it affects the forces on our postsecondary industry will be discussed briefly.

Changing Patterns of Diversity. The challenge of dealing with cultural diversity and its concomitant educational and economic deprivation is widely recognized as a social reality, a public policy issue and an institutional reality. We have had some success in improving access to postsecondary education for various disadvantaged groups but our record of successful retention and graduation is still inadequate in many fields and at the graduate level. (Carter and Wilson, 1993; Mintz, 1993; Musil, 1995).

There are several lessons from our experience and trends. First, the operant definition of cultural diversity is constantly changing. The initial concern for African-American minorities in the 1960s has expanded to include numerous other racially under represented groups. Issues of gender, sexual preference and economic or educational disadvantage have further expanded and/or fragmented the focus of diversity as an issue. Second, the numbers of almost all of our minority groups are increasing and will continue for the foreseeable future. Third, members of most minority groups have become well organized and are becoming more effective political voices both on campuses and in the public policy arena. Fourth, our public policy and institutional response strategy has shifted—from separate but equal, to nondiscrimination, to preferences, to affirmative action, to multicultural emphasis. The current debates about and attempts to dismantle affirmative action are likely to be heated and to continue. But the impacts on the forces reshaping our industry and are more revealing.

Industry. (See Table 2). Both the number of individuals and categories defined as educationally disadvantaged continues to grow. As potential learning customers influencing public policy, the increasing presence of minority political caucus groups at the institutional, state and national level makes them a more powerful force influencing our resource suppliers. Although there have been few minority postsecondary institutions founded as new organizational entrants in recent decades, the number of existing institutions becoming de-facto minority institutions is increasing rapidly (approximately one in five postsecondary institutions now have an enrollment in which ethnic minority students exceed 50% of the student body). Several new minority-oriented professional associations have been founded to serve these institutions and to represent their constituent interests. The increase of minority-oriented academic and support programs have often been seen as adding substitute services. Although not directly affecting the core technology of postsecondary education, the advent of minority programs, new faculty staffing patterns, student and faculty interaction patterns and new academic perspectives and research agendas have influenced the processes of teaching and research in significant ways. Clearly pressure to enhance diversity affects all five forces and has created intense competition among institutions attempting to attract increased numbers of more diverse students, faculty and staff.

The Telematics Revolution. Probably the most pervasive challenge to our industry and institutions is the rapid expansion of interactive telecommunications networks linking student and faculty to extensive data resources via workstations capable of integrating information, sound and video images. It is expanding rapidly in areas such as distance and continuing education to serve older students but also is serving more traditional students. The extent to which traditional institutions will enter this market and whether it will lead to a sweeping reinvention of how students and faculty teach, learn, and conduct scholarship or whether it merely is a technological resource is the source of heated debate on most campuses. There are several unique features about the current revolution: 1) its rapid development and rate of change, 2) the extent to which applications are being adopted in all areas of our modern life beyond the campus; 3) its widespread availability nationally—even globally—in a short time span; 4) its potential for use with few con-

straints of time and location; and 5) the increased affordability of more powerful technology. These features make it imperative that institutions adopt it as a tool, but their capacity to use technology for educational purposes is perhaps the most critical challenge which postsecondary institutions must face. The irony is that this technology, which was spawned in universities, has taken on a life of its own. With so many societal as well as educational applications and implications, it has created its own industry as new computer hardware and software, telecommunications, and information-handling products and firms are developed. The impacts on our postsecondary industry and our institutions will be extensive, and perhaps central, in the next decade (Green and Gilbert, 1995; Twigg, 1994).

Industry. (See Table 2). This revolution has a vast potential for increasing the array of options for accessing electronic learning opportunities, for reaching a significant array of new customers (students or scholars), and for extending an institution's potential to serve. On the other hand, it has in many instances reversed the client relationship of postsecondary institutions with the telematics firms. Instead of being the customer seeking an institution's research results or trained students, they have become both the creator and supplier of information handling tools making the postsecondary institutions increasingly dependent on their former clients. An even bigger threat is the array of postsecondary and non-postsecondary organizations as both new entrants and substitute suppliers in our current postsecondary educational industry. A rapidly growing number of institutions and organizations offering postsecondary education via interactive telecommunications have emerged and others are beginning to experiment with this mode (Marchese, 1998). Large companies are adopting these technologies for their own internal postsecondary training programs. Of greater significance is the possible merger of entertainment and telecommunication firms which further enhance the potential of delivering postsecondary knowledge (Will they make education entertaining or entertainment more educational?). For current postsecondary institutions this revolution has the potential to alter significantly the core technology of teaching, learning and research. The availability and control of information, the role of faculty, the role of the learner, the process of learning, and even the process of research can all be changed radically.

Clearly, what makes this change so revolutionary is that it also interacts with all the other societal challenges. Despite often high initial investment costs, colleges and universities cannot afford *not* to utilize it. It enhances the capacity to reach both new and current customers/students differently. It also influences the way academics work and students learn. This technology is just beginning to reshape the way postsecondary institutions compete with each other for students and compete or cooperate with firms in other industries (telematics, entertainment, training) to deliver their educational products. New patterns of competition and cooperation in delivering educational services with firms that were not part of our postsecondary industry are emerging as they and we become part of a postsecondary knowledge industry. The major challenge is to develop new interinstitutional ties with telematics firms in appropriate educational ventures.

Academic and Institutional Quality. The challenge to academic and institutional quality are somewhat separate conditions. In the 1990s, the demand for educational quality has become pervasive (Ewell, 1997) but has been changing over the recent decades. In the 1960s and 70s, it was associated with the level and nature of institutional resources. In the 1980s, the focus shifted to assessing results (outcomes, goal achievement, value-added). In the mid 1990s, academic quality has become associated with public accountability and with a focus on student learning, faculty productivity and performance, program effectiveness, and even institutional performance indicators. The debate about the definition of, criteria for, and means of improving educational quality shows no signs of diminishing and will be a continuing challenge both in government policy circles and in institutional discussions. (Dill, 1995a).

A more recent focus on institutional quality is the concern for Total Quality Management (TQM) or Continuous Quality Improvement (CQI) (Dill, 1992) which emerged in the private sector. Unlike the more educationally focused notions of quality, this approach suggests a more comprehensive emphasis on developing an institutional culture that stresses policies and practices promoting: 1) an environment of continuous improvement; 2) customer or client centeredness; 3) a rational approach to decision making using intensive measurement and benchmarking; 4) a focus on process design; 5) collaboration and teamwork; and 6) individual empowerment. Such a comprehensive approach clashes with our strong traditions of academic individualism but may also lead to rethinking our teaching, learning and research processes and how we utilize the new technology for educational purposes. The fact that the Baldridge Award was extended in 1995 to include postsecondary education suggests that it may have a continued emphasis in academic as well as administrative areas.

Industry (See Table 2). To date, the two quality challenges have had only limited but differing impacts on our postsecondary industry. However, that may increase as competition within the industry, public scrutiny, and cost pressures increase. Both force institutions to refocus on defining and differentiating its stakeholders (customers needs and demands) and designing its services (academic or administrative) with them in mind rather. While neither have yet prompted the entry of new organizations to enter postsecondary education, numerous assessment and evaluation groups all providing services for our institutions. More importantly many of the new forms of technology–based institutions emphasize both assessment and quality principles. This challenge may shape public support and the competition for students.

Improving Economic Productivity: New Emphasis or New Function. Economic development has always been a factor in the rapid and continuous expansion of postsecondary education (Leslie & Brinkman, 1988). Colleges and universities produced well trained students, provided appropriate professional programs, and conducted pure and applied research which contributed to society's well being which, we argued, led to improvement in our standard of living. But the decline of U.S. economic fortunes in the past two decades and the loss of dominance in key manufacturing industries in the global marketplace has led to a new emphasis on enhancing economic productivity at the national, state, and regional level.

In the development of federal priorities and state level plans for economic development higher education institutions, government agencies and the private business organizations are all viewed as key players. Postsecondary institutions have historically played and been satisfied with playing a "knowledge development" function as primary providers of academic and professional training and of pure and applied research. In recent decades, as consultants and as sites for campus research parks, they have participated more directly in "technology transfer." A more recent and aggressive form of this activity is reflected in the growth of campus affiliated incubator parks for new product and new company development. Most recently, postsecondary institutions have participated in developing "state or regional economic development strategies". In all of these roles, their participation can vary from resource institution, to partner, to manager of the function. (Peterson, 1995). Increasingly, institutions are pressured to take on all three roles and even to become a leader of the effort. The difficulty is that becoming a manager of technology transfer or economic development may involve an institution in an activity for which it is not well suited and one in which it may not be able to succeed (Feller, 1990). Yet political and economic pressures to show greater institutional accountability for and contribution in this area is likely to increase if our economy falters or fails to meet political expectations or promises.

Industry (See Table 2). This challenge has little direct affect on students as our primary customers, but some argue is reflected in their career-oriented priorities and concerns about useful programs. However, it does subject the industry to increasing demands from its primary government and industry suppliers, especially in the public sector. The growing concern for economic productivity, also attracts public and private technology development organizations, both as new entrants and as substitute sources of this activity, that may be better positioned than postsecondary institutions to compete for applied research and development funds and better staffed to carry out such activities. Existing postsecondary institutions who decide to participate may need to subsidize risky economic development activities, create an economic development alliance, a technology transfer partnership, or a joint venture to provide this new service. In doing so,

they may be pressed to redirect funds and effort away from some of the traditional postsecondary emphasis on teaching and research to supply the needs of economic development activity. In most instances, this pressure for economic development involves postsecondary education directly in a new realm of competition: interregional, interstate, or even international—an arena in which it was previously only indirectly engaged.

Postsecondary Relearning: New Markets, Modes, and Models. In recent decades, expanded educational services have been directed towards increasing traditional student enrollments and increasing service to under represented groups such as minorities, women, and older students. Modifications in schedules (evening, weekends) or locale (off campus) were used to deliver traditional courses or programs to the part time, non-traditional student. Continuing education was often an ancillary function or primarily related to professional and occupational programs. Yet in today's increasingly competitive and technologically turbulent world, products, companies, and careers can change rapidly. The need for technological retooling and postsecondary re-education is increasing in a wide variety of professions. (Reich, 1991).

The demand for postsecondary relearning by older individuals is an exploding market consisting of three identifiable groups. One is the post high school but pre-baccalaureate group who need further education to reenter the job market or remain viably employed. One study (Grubb, Forthcoming) suggests there are 20–30 million individuals between 25 and 50 years in age in this category. A second is the post-baccalaureate group who have college degrees but may need further education but not necessarily degree education to remain viably employed or to change fields. While not as large as the previous group, it is rapidly growing as the proportion of degree holders continues to grow. Finally, there are the graduate and professional degree holders who need more than the traditional continuing education in their professional field to advance or change fields. In addition to the size and growth of these three market segments, they share much in common. Their educational interests and/or those of their employer often focus on professional competencies, individual educational needs, learning modules, off campus delivery and willingness to use distance education modes of transmission (including technology) rather than on traditional courses, degrees or programs.

Industry (See Table 2). These numbers suggest three substantial groups of potential customers for postsecondary re-education. While some may pay for their own education, many employer organizations are clients for such educational services for their employees. Indeed some large companies or industries are either supporting or developing their own providers. It is a market which many in the proprietary sector see as economic opportunity as well as a large underserved educational market. It has begun to attract many competing organizations either as new entrants or as substitute sources. Some are existing postsecondary institutions; some are new postsecondary institutions, education and training firms; entertainment and telecommunication firms are involved; and there are various alliances. In some instances, political entities such as the Western Governors or individual states are promoting these developments. Virtual institutions of varied types are also emerging. (Carchidi & Peterson, 1998; Marchese, 1998). Almost all emphasize new modes of packaging and delivery and emphasize learner centered education. But this market is still somewhat amorphous. Patterns of market demand, financing and competition are not well defined, especially the role to be played by traditional postsecondary institutions.

Globalization: Breaking Bonds and Boundaries. As we approach the 21st century, the challenges of international and global perspectives need little exposition. International student and faculty exchange programs, emphasis on foreign language instruction, and introducing global perspectives into our curriculum are widespread if not completely effective. But two emergent phenomenon suggest the globalization in postsecondary education could take on new institutional boundary spanning forms in the near future.

While knowledge and scholars have always resisted regional and national boundaries, a new form of international network or "international civil societies" (Cohen, 1997) are emerging. These are networks of university scholars, governmental policy researchers, and private sector experts organized around major

significant social problems or issues (e.g. global warming, AIDS, human rights, etc.). These civil societies are interdisciplinary, cross-national, and cross-industry groups. Their work may combine research, learning, policy making and action. They often rely on technology and can have access to a wide array of information and expertise, but with little managerial structure. In effect, they reflect how the knowledge and technology explosion can rewrite scholarly boundaries without depending on institutional structure.

Another form of globalization that may emerge is more similar to the multi-national corporation. While loosely structured institutional exchange programs and research alliances which cross national boundaries are common, the prospects for a multinational university are worth contemplating. Some universities now have their own campuses in other countries. Many institutions have partnerships with multi-national technology firms. Some countries such as the European Union have supported cross-national postsecondary alliances. A move to more formalized international consortia, degree granting federations among institutions in different countries, and even the possibility of a multi-national university, while a daunting challenge, are possible in the decade ahead.

Industry (See Table 2). Clearly, scholars, researchers and many students who participate in the less formal arrangements are a specialized customer group who could be attracted. Some countries as clients might support limited forms of cross-national alliances and embrace institutions with an extensive cross-national mission or presence. Currently some postsecondary institutions do function on a multi-national basis to a limited degree and some of the emerging institutions which focus on distance education via technology have identified this as their niche. But truly multinational, postsecondary educational organizations would be an intriguing new entrant to our postsecondary industry and provide an alternate form of global and international opportunity for study and scholarship. As some authors note, these new forms of global organization may markedly intensify competition in postsecondary education (Dill and Sporn, 1995).

The Emerging Postsecondary Knowledge Industry

As we face the 21st century, the changing societal conditions are all likely to continue. Each promises to have a major impact on the forces reshaping our postsecondary industry into a postsecondary knowledge industry. A brief summary highlights the paradigm of the new industry from the previous discussion (see Table 3).

Core Technology. Perhaps the most influential force is the potential for innovation in our core technology—the development, transmission and dissemination of knowledge in society and in turn in our postsecondary industry. Postsecondary institutions have long believed they were the preeminent knowledge industry for postsecondary teaching, learning, and research. However, the telematics revolution has introduced a powerful new interactive information-handling technology that offers potentially revolutionary changes in moving from more traditional modes of teaching, learning and research to varied, responsive, flexible, interactive and individualized modes. The technology revolution has allowed institutions from outside traditional postsecondary education to become leaders in reshaping both our basic technology and our industry. More critically the telematics revolution makes it easier to respond to all of the other societal conditions affecting the industry (university, quality, economic productivity, postsecondary relearning, and globalization) and the revolution enhances all of the other five forces acting upon the industry (new organizational entrants, the power of customers and suppliers, the threat of substitute services and the intensity of competition).

New Organizational Entrant. The threat of new organizational entrants is suggested by five of the six societal conditions (telematics, diversity, economic productivity, relearning and globalization). Perhaps the most tangible way of visualizing the reconfigure industry is by focusing on the organizations that are becoming part of a postsecondary knowledge industry. Postsecondary now includes a broad array of public, private and proprietary educational organizations from associate degree granting to doctoral level. A postsecondary knowledge industry suggests the addition of many organizations previously thought to be part of other industries—telecommunication companies; computer software and hardware firms; information resource organizations; corporate and governmental organizations engaged in education, training, and professional development; and, perhaps, even "entertainment" firms. As our previous discussion has suggested, these new organizations are often no longer either just suppliers to, or customers of, postsecondary institutions. They are now effectively part of our postsecondary knowledge development, dissemination and education system and may be viewed as potential collaborators or competitors.

The Power of Customers. The analysis of all six societal conditions also suggests implications for our potential student markets for postsecondary education. In addition to traditional and non-traditional students seeking regular course credits and degree offerings via traditional delivery modes to a more broadly defined market for postsecondary education, there are potential new student customers who are interested in non-degree oriented learning and, often, in non-traditional modes of delivery. The key shift in the postsecondary knowledge industry perspective is to focus on students as learners with individualized educational needs rather than as students for courses and programs designed and delivered by postsecondary faculty or institutions. This shift is captured in moving from "just-in-case," to "just-in-time" to "just-for-you" education (Duderstadt, 1998).

Power of Suppliers and Threat of Substitute Services. The inclusion of potential new non-educational organizational entrants to the emerging postsecondary knowledge industry is implied by each of the societal conditions. It not only enhances their role as customers but also changes their role as suppliers. As customers for particular types of postsecondary education for their employees, they are now more active and aggressive in defining and demanding their educational needs and learning experiences. But they are no longer just customers who employ graduates, purchase our knowledge products and services or provide sources of funding. They are often key suppliers who are also providers of valuable information resources, new educational technology and advances, and access to critical communication networks. Another major shift is to recognize that in the new postsecondary knowledge environment these non-educational participants may be sources of substitute (educational) services. Further, they are not potential pressure groups, educational partners or competitors—not merely customers or suppliers. It is clear that in a postsecondary knowledge environment other knowledge based firms do have greater power as suppliers of educational resources and as customers for or sources of substitute services because of their control of educational information technology and access to customers for learning.

Competition. Finally, it is apparent that the level of competition in the postsecondary knowledge industry competition is likely to increase. clearly, competition among existing postsecondary institutions is intensified by the challenges to increase diversity, to use technology, to improve quality, to contribute to economic productivity, to become more global, and to enter the expanding postsecondary relearning markets while constraining costs. However, what is likely to be qualitatively different is competition in the knowledge industry that cuts across old industry boundaries. For instance competing with organizations whose primary function is not education from the telecommunications, computing, information resource, corporate education and training or entertainment industry world is far more entrepreneurial and fast paced than in the traditional postsecondary world. Also competition to engage in economic development or new global arrangements may entail both creative risks and new governmental controls or regulatory environments.

Clearly, no one knows the exact direction, comprehensiveness, or rate at which the postsecondary knowledge industry will emerge and the full extent of its impact on our current postsecondary institutions. Neither do we know whether those changes will be evolutionary and manageable or revolutionary and chaotic. It will, no doubt, affect different types of institutions differently and some will see it as opportunity and others as threat.

Implications: The New Management, Organization and Performance Focus. While the likelihood and implications of this emerging industry maybe unclear, it is different in magnitude from our previous industry transactions and too critical for institutional leaders and researchers not to address. The challenges of this emerging industry will require institutions to consider whether to take a proactive, adaptive, or responsive strategy toward the emerging industry and their institution's role in it. They will need to consider the managerial challenge to *redesign* their institution. New *organizational models* reflecting institutional responses to this new industry are already emerging. Those include entrepreneurial, network and virtual organizations and new forms of strategic alliances and joint ventures with non-educational partners in the design, dissemination, and discovery of knowledge. In addressing redesign the long term performance criteria for our institutions will also change. These may be assessed by how well we address and answer those four R's of the next decade. How well have we:

> *Redefined* the nature of a postsecondary knowledge industry and our institution's role in it?
> *Redirected* our institution's mission and developed new external relationships to reflect these new realities.
> *Reorganized* or restructured our academic processes and delivery systems?
> *Reformed* our academic workplace and institutional culture?

Institutional Research for Institutional Redesign

The implications for an institutional research office whose institutional leadership focuses on this emerging new industry and examines the need for institutional redesign suggests a new role or function and several related activities.

Knowledge Industry Analyst. In an emergent industry with rapidly changing participant and dynamics, institutional leadership will need to understand this new environment and its institutional implications. Becoming a postsecondary knowledge analyst will involve becoming the institution's expert on the various segments of the postsecondary relearning markets for both degree and non-degree nontraditional and older student consumers; on what postsecondary institutions and non-postsecondary organizations are offering postsecondary learning experiences for those markets;

on the varied strategies and methods for delivering postsecondary learning on and off campuses; on the new forms of technology based delivery including the virtual learning systems; and on the forms of strategic alliances, joint ventures or other forms of interinstitutional linkages developed to deliver postsecondary education, promote knowledge dissemination and support research. While this role may be analogous to an institutional researcher's role in environmental analysis for planning, it is focused more specifically on the emerging industry. The intent is not merely to inform institutional leaders but to assist them in developing new roles and strategies for the institution in this new industry—to become the institution's source of expertise on this new industry paradigm, its dynamics and its implications for the institution. Implicit in this new function or role are several more specific activities.

Monitoring Societal and Industry Conditions. This chapter has suggested several changing societal conditions that influence the emerging postsecondary knowledge industry that might be monitored. Other areas that impact the emerging industry also come to mind: the role states and accrediting agencies adopt in regulating the industry; changes in patterns of financial support for older students and for those pursuing non-degree as well as degree oriented education (financial aid, tax credits or vouchers, company employment benefits, etc.); the cost structure of access to the internet; the financial structure of new technology-based providers (technology investment, course development costs, student fees and charges), and others. While this may be similar to environmental scanning, the key is to focus on conditions that have implications for the entire industry as well as for your institution. A major contribution will be to develop indicators for these conditions and for the emerging industry. A major complicating factor is knowing how to define the scope of such indicators when markets, participating organizations and delivery systems are becoming less geographically bounded with the advent of technology based delivery systems.

Reviewing strategic options. As institutions redefine the role they intend to play in this emerging industry, reshape their external

relationships and reorganize their delivery systems, proposed new joint ventures, strategic alliances, and other interinstitutional arrangements with non-postsecondary partners will emerge. These will need to be compared with existing or more institutionally controlled approaches. These new approaches may involve major new investments—not simple modifications or small pilot efforts. Reviews of such strategic options might include careful examination of market potential for the proposed venture (in markets that are being created or are ill defined); examining the organizational, legal and fiscal requirements of joint efforts and the managerial capacity to run them; conducting institutional impact studies of new ventures on the current institution; and doing a careful resource investment and risk analysis. These are no longer simple program reviews of new academic programs with marginal resource reallocations.

Monitoring the Periphery. Robert Zemsky (1997) has pointed out that in many postsecondary institutions the changes that respond to the new postsecondary knowledge industry demands are on the periphery of the institution. Most institutions continue to manage their traditional core degree programs and research activities and give little attention to the new ventures until they become dominant or the source of mismanagement or embarrassment. Monitoring an institution's "peripheral" activities as a good management servant would include keeping track of things such as: 1) the extended delivery academic programs and joint ventures or alliances in research education and service; 2) the growing enrollment and employment patterns of these activities; and 3) their revenue and expense patterns. Some have also suggested the need for a fiscal vulnerability audit related to these activities. More basically there is a need to understand the balance of an institution's core and periphery efforts and its shifting priorities in relation to its mission, role and managerial capacity.

Assessment and Program Reviews. Many of the new educational, research, and service ventures which respond to this new industry will require new performance criteria, new management approaches, and new external partners. Programs delivered by technology or based on a specialized or individualized design are especially problematic. Extending assessment and program review to such new ventures and perhaps conducting them with new external and non-educational partners is critical to the assuring quality of the efforts, will be challenging to undertake and will require new approaches to assessment and program review.

Institutional Change Assessment. An institution undergoing extensive change or transformation, particularly if it is an intentional redesign, needs to mount efforts to assess the academic and administrative capacity to undertake the planned changes, to understand the tensions between traditional or core programs and new more peripheral ones, and to understand the changing external image resulting from intentional institutional mission and role changes. Assessing both the readiness and capacity for institutional change will become central to successful redesign.

Proactive Management Guide. In sum, this new role of postsecondary industry knowledge analyst and the suggested agenda provides institutional researchers with a substantial new role and set of activities. Clearly, the extent of this role will vary by institutional type, size and current mission; by the way in which planning and institutional research are organized; and by the interest in and willingness of key institutional leaders to address the challenge of an emergent postsecondary knowledge industry and the possibility of institutional redesign. Whether the actual shift will be evolutionary or revolutionary is unclear. But institutional research once again has the opportunity of assisting in and shaping the institutional response to a major challenge and of going beyond its traditional management service and institutional improvement function. By becoming a proactive management guide to this new industry and environment, institutional research will once again have played its adaptive function—benefiting both the institution and the profession.

References

Alpert, D. "Performance and Paralysis: The Organizational Context of the American Research University." *Journal of Education,* 1986, 56(3).

Baldridge, J. V. *Power and Conflict in the University.* New York: Wiley, 1971.

Berdahl, R. O. *Statewide Coordination of Higher Education.* American Council on Education. Washington, D.C., 1971.

Bowen, H. R. *Evaluating Institutions for Accountability.* New Directions for Institutional Research. Jossey-Bass Vol. 1, 1974.

Brumbaugh, A. J. *Research Designed to Improve Institutions of Higher Learning.* Washington, D.C. American Council on Education, 1960.

Carchidi, D. M. and Peterson, M. W. "The Emerging Organizational Landscape of Postsecondary Education." Center for the Study of Higher and Postsecondary Education, University of Michigan, 1998.

Cartter, A. An *Assessment of Quality in Graduate Education.* Washington, D.C.: American Council on Education, 1966.

Cohen, M. D., and March, J. B. *Leadership and Ambiguity: The American College President.* York: McGraw-Hill, 1974.

Cope, R. G. *Professional Development for Institutional Research.* New Directions for Institutional Research. Jossey-Bass. Vol. 23. 1979.

Dill, D. D., and Sporn, B. "University 2001: What Will the University of the Twenty-First Century Look Like?"' In D. D. Dill and B. Sporn (Eds.), *Emerging Patterns of Social Demand and University Reform: Through a Glass Darkly."* New York: Pergamon Press, 1995.

Dressel, P. L. and Associates. *Institutional Research in the University.* Jossey-Bass, 1971.

Drucker, P. "Interview," *Forbes Magazine, 1997.*

Duderstadt, J. J. "The 21st Century University: A Tale of Two Futures." Paper presented at the North American and Western European Colloquium on the Challenges Facing Higher Education, Glion, Switzerland, May 13–17, 1998.

Fetterman, D. M. *Using Qualitative Approaches in Institutional Research.* New Directions for Institutional Research. Jossey-Bass. Vol 72, 1991.

Firnberg, J. W. and Lasher, W. F. *The Politics and Pragmatics of Institutional Research.* New Directions for Institutional Research. Jossey-Bass. Vol. 38, 1983.

Gill, J. I. & Saunders, L. *Developing Effective Policy Analysis.* New Directions in Institutional Research. Jossey-Bass, 1992.

Goodman, P. *Community of Scholars.* New York: Random House, 1964.

Katz, D., and Kahn, R. *The Social Psychology of Organizations.* (2nd ed.) New York: Wiley, 1978.

Keller, G. *Academic Strategy: The Management Revolution in American Higher Education.* Baltimore, MD.: Johns Hopkins University Press, 1983.

Kotler, P. *Marketing for Non-profit Organizations.* Englewood Cliffs, NJ. Prentice-Hall, 1975.

Lawrence, G. B., and Service, A. L. (Eds.) *Quantitative Approaches to Higher Education Management: Potential, Limits, and Challenge.* AAHE-ERIC Research Report, no. 4. Washington, D.C.: American Association of Higher Education, 1977.

Marchese, T. "Not-So-Distant Competitors". *AAHE Bulletin*. Vol. 50. No., 9, 1998.

Millett, J. D. *The Academic Community*. New York: McGraw-Hill, 1962.

Mortimer, K. P., and Tierney, M. L. *The Three Rs of the Eighties: Reduction, Reallocation, and Retrenchment*. ASHE-ERIC Research Report, No. 4. Washington, DC: American Association for Higher Education, 1979.

National Commission on Excellence in Education. *A Nation at Risk*. Washington, D.C.: U.S. Department of Education, 1983.

Norris, D. M. and Morrison, J. L. *Mobilizing for Transformation*. New Directions for Institutional Research. Jossey-Bass Publishers. Vol 94, 1997.

Peterson, M. W. "Analyzing Alternative Approaches to Planning." In P. Jedamus, M. W. Peterson, and Associates (eds.), *Improving Academic Management: Handbook of Planning and Institutional Research*. San Francisco: Jossey Bass, 1980.

Peterson, M. W. and Corcoran, M. *Institutional Research in Transition*. New Directions for Institutional Research. Jossey-Bass. Vol. 46, 1985.

Peterson, M. W.; Dill, D. D. and Mets, L. A. *Planning and Management for a Changing Environment*. Jossey-Bass. 1997.

Porter, M. *Competitive Strategy*. Free Press, 1980.

Reich, R. *The Work of Nations: Preparing Ourselves for 21st Century Capitalism*. New York: Knopf, 1991.

Roose, K. D., and Anderson, C. J. *A Rating of Graduate Programs*. Washington, D.C.: American Council on Education, 1970.

Rourke, F. E. and Brooks, G. E. Johns Hopkins Press. *The Managerial Revolution in Higher Education*. Baltimore, Md. 1966.

Saupe, J. L. *The Functions of Institutional Research*. Tallahassee, Florida: AIR, 1990.

Schiltz, M. E. *Ethics and Standards in Institutional Research*. New Directions for Institutional Research. Jossey-Bass. Vol. 73, 1992.

Sheehan, B. S. *Information Technology*. New Directions for Institutional Research. Jossey-Bass. Vol. 35, 1982.

Stroup, H. *Bureaucracy in Higher Education*. New York: Free Press, 1966.

Study Group on the Condition of Excellence in American Higher Education. *Involvement in Learning*. Washington, D.C.: National Institute of Education, 1984.

Terenzini, P. "AIR Presidential Address." AIR Annual Forum. Boston, Mass, 1995.

Tetlow, W. L. *Using Microcomputers for Planning and Management Support*. New Directions for Institutional Research. Jossey-Bass. Vol. 44, 1984.

Tierney, W. G. *Assessing Academic Climates and Cultures*. New Directions for Institutional Research. Jossey-Bass. Vol. 68, 1990.

Zemsky, R. "AIR Forum Address". AIR Annual Forum. Albuquerque, New Mexico, 1996.

Marvin W. Peterson is professor of higher education at the Center for the Study of Higher and Postsecondary Education at the University of Michigan and research program director for the National Center for Postsecondary Improvement.

TABLE 1: EVOLUTION OF I.R.: ADAPTING TO INSTITUTIONAL CHALLENGES

	EXTERNAL CONDITIONS →	MANAGEMENT PRESS →	ORGANIZATION & GOVERNANCE →	PERFORMANCE FOCUS →	PRIMARY ROLE OF I.R. →
1950	Growth & Expansion	Direction & Accountability	Formal & Collegial	Resources:	Descriptive, Developmental
1960	Disruption & Demands	Order, Control & Access	Political & Open Systems	Reputation:	Analytic, Comparative
1970	Economic Recession	Efficiency & Market Orientation	Managerial & Market	Results: Productivity & Efficiency	Evalative - Quantitative
1980	Constraint & Quality	Reduction, Reallocation & Retrenchment; Effectiveness & Quality	Organized Anarchy, Cultural & Conglomerate	Results: Goal Achievement; Student Performance Re-engineer & Structure	Evaluative- Qualitative, Planning and Policy Analysis
1990					
2000	Educational Challenges and New Constituents	Redesigning Institutions	Entrepreneurial, Networks, Alliances & Jt. Ventures, Virtual Organ.	Redefine Industry & University Role Redirect Mission & Relationships Reorganize Processes & Structures Reform Workplace Culture	Knowledge Industry Analyst Anticipatory- Proactive

TABLE 2. CHALLENGES AND FORCES RESHAPING THE POSTSECONDARY INDUSTRY

SOCIETAL CONDITIONS OR CONDITION CHALLENGES	FORCES RESHAPING AN INDUSTRY					
	BARGAINING POWER OF CUSTOMERS	BARGAINING POWER OF SUPPLIERS	THREAT OF NEW ORGANIZATION ENTRANTS	THREAT OF SUBSTITUTE SERVICES	INNOVATIONS IN CORE TECHNOLOGY	INTENSITY OF COMPETITION
DIVERSITY	More defined groups. Increasing numbers.	Stronger and more numerous political groups.	Minority Institutions and Associations.	New programs and services.	New academic and research perspectives.	Among students and among institutions.
TELEMATICS REVOLUTION	More access and numbers. Individualized needs.	Telematics firms control key educational resources.	Telecomunications, computing and information firms	Training firms and merger of entertainment & telecomm.	New interactive, individualized T/L/R potential.	New cross industry competition.
QUALITY REFORM	Increased focus on learner needs.	Increased attention to client demands.		Minor new training options.	New mode of management. Limited use by academics.	Improvements in efficiency and effectiveness.
ECONOMIC PRODUCTIVITY	Increased career-oriented pressure.	Government and industry needs.	New role or inter-organization patterns.	Many new groups and government agencies.	May redirect teaching and research.	New regional, state or national agencies.
POSTSECONDARY RELEARNING	New groups of postsecondary learners.	Employer based funding sources.	Many new forms emerging.	Corporate and governmental education programs.	Emphasis on personalized content and delivery.	Ill defined market. Potential of many sources.
GLOBALIZATION	Not clearly defined. Highly specialized.	Nations & institutions potentially.	Currently informal or limited arrangements.	Emergent use of technology.	Traditional or new technology.	Yet to be determined.

TABLE 3. PARADIGM OF AN EMERGING POSTSECONDARY KNOWLEDGE INDUSTRY

INDUSTRY FORCES	POSTSECONDARY INDUSTRY	POSTSECONDARY KNOWLEDGE NETWORK
Innovation in Core Technology	Traditional Teaching, Learning, Research Modes	Interactive Information Technology Network for T, L, & R.
Threat of New Entrants	Traditional Colleges, Universities and Proprietary Institutions	Telecommunications, Computing Hardware and Software, Information Resource, Corporate & Government Education & Training, and Entertainment Firms
Power of Customers (Students)	Traditional and Non-Traditional Degree Students	Growing Minority and Postsecondary Relearning Markets for Individual Learning Needs
Power of Suppliers (Clients)	Primarily As Employers, Funding Sources and Purchasers of Services	Providers of Information Resources, Educational Technology and Communications Networks; As Pressure Groups, Partners or Competitors
Threat of Substitute Services	Limited	More Extensive
Intensity of Competition	Among Existing Postsecondary Institutions or Segments	Cross Industry More Competitive & Entrepreneurial

The Art and Science
of Institutional Research

CAMERON FINCHER

There are two undeniable facts about higher education: Colleges and universities must keep numerous records, and they must report voluminous data to governing, funding, accrediting, and regulating authorities. The analysis and interpretation of institutional records and data, plus the occasional or periodic studies that are necessary to supplement routine record keeping and reporting, would thus seem to be what institutional research is all about.

The origins of institutional research are embedded, therefore, in institutional functions and activities. The organization and governance of English colleges were no doubt an object of study by the colonial colleges established in America, but there was no concept of systematic research to give guidance to such efforts. Tom Dyer (1978) calls historians the first institutional researchers, because they were the first to study charters, presidential correspondence, recorded minutes, and other institutional records for the purpose of depicting the historical development of institutions.

Institutional research as a specialized administrative function begins with the efforts of institutions to use tools and techniques developed in other fields of specialization to study their internal activities and processes. The University of Minnesota, the prime example, established in 1924 a committee on educational research to study the problems of curriculum, student attrition, counseling, and test performance (Gray, 1951). In the following decade, a bureau of institutional research was established for the explicit purpose of conducting studies to facilitate administrative and instructional effectiveness.

Of all the documents pertaining to institutional research, Brumbaugh's (1960) monograph for the American Council on Education (ACE) is the one undeniable classic. A statement issued by the ACE's Office of Statistical Information and Research, headed at that time by Elmer D. West, it specifies the purposes and intents of institutional research. Brumbaugh was appreciative of the forthcoming increase in enrollments that colleges and universities had to prepare for, the rising costs of higher education, the increased complexity of administration, the expansion of institutional programs and services, and the need to convince state legislators that increases in appropriations would be needed.

Administrative effectiveness in dealing with the changing conditions of higher education was, according to Brumbaugh, a matter of asking the right questions and of finding the right answers. Whether the right answers were specific or comprehensive, they depended on the kind of data that only institutional research could provide. Thus, institutional research should play an important role in institutional policy making, planning, management, and evaluation. Institutional research was needed in these areas: goals and objectives, student characteristics and achievement, faculty characteristics and conditions of service, curricular change and effectiveness, institutional administration and organization, funding and financing, and public relations.

"The Art and Science of Institutional Research," by Cameron Fincher, reprinted from *Institutional Research in Transition*, edited by M. W. Peterson and M. Corcoran, 1985. Jossey-Bass Publishers, Inc.

A Science of Institutions?

Six years after Brumbaugh's espousal of institutional research, Henry Dyer (1966) asked whether institutional research could ever lead to a science of institutions. Dyer noted the published research dealing with institutional concerns and issues and mentioned the newly formed Association for Institutional Research (AIR) as a professional society. Dyer thought there was cause for optimism if institutional research could reconcile the conflicting points of view represented by Nevitt Sanford (1962) and John Dale Russell. Sanford (1962) was cited as the foremost exponent of long-term, theoretically oriented research into institutional processes and outcomes, while Russell's many writings were typical of studies concerned with practical and purely operational problems. It was Dyer's judgment that institutional research had nowhere to go if it remained purely operational. At the same time, institutional research would be of little help to policy makers and decision makers if it served only to spin theories.

In many respects, the distinction that Dyer was making was a distinction between discipline-oriented and mission-oriented research. However, a bridge could be built between the two by recognizing the centrality of measurement and by developing suitable instruments for the assessment of institutional goals and the degree to which they were being met. Dyer wrote at a time when the Educational Testing Service had launched an ambitious program involving measures of campus climate, faculty and student perceptions of instructional effectiveness, and factors facilitating or impeding institutional progress toward the fulfillment of its goals. His concluding point was that institutional research could lead to a science of institutions if it could deal with "the real problems of particular institutions" and if it endeavored "to fit these problems into some sort of evolving generalizations" (Dyer, 1966, p. 466).

Unfortunately, Dyer did not inquire into the nature of institutions, and he was not explicit about science as either a body of organized facts or an organized search for explanatory concepts and principles. He doubted that institutional research could use experimental methods to good advantage, and he suggested that institutional researchers could serve well by reminding college administrators and faculty of the many blind assumptions on which their work was based. Dyer's contribution is best regarded, therefore, as the challenge he issued and as the support that he gave to the development of assessment instruments and methods.

Changing Problems and Issues. The challenge that Dyer issued was not heard by institutional researchers for many reasons. Neither the 1960s nor the 1970s proved to be years in which a science of educational institutions could be developed. By 1968, other concerns and issues were dominant, and as the 1970s opened, the political, legal, and financial problems of higher education dominated institutional research, just as they dominated other educational functions and activities. Virtually all institutions sought economic, judicial, and technological solutions to their problems, not the self-understanding or self-enlightenment that a science of institutions would presumably bring. The purely operational problems of institutional accountability, management, financing, and evaluation pushed studies of student and faculty characteristics, institutional missions and goals, instructional improvement, and curricular change to the side. Theoretically oriented research became a luxury that few institutions could afford, and administrative officials cited economists, lawyers, and engineers more often than they did the social and behavioral scientists who had contributed to Sanford's (1962) ambitious volume.

Although the federal government continued to support the development of offices of institutional research in smaller institutions, it shifted its funding policies and priorities to planning, management, and evaluation. Many institutional researchers settled into supportive or technical assistance roles that were necessary for crisis management, the demands of annual budgeting cycles, and the incessant requests for information from governing boards and regulatory agencies. Some directors of institutional research were promoted to vice-presidencies in charge of institutional research and planning, but a large number of institutional researchers became troubleshooters, brushfire fighters, or faceless technocrats. If a few recovered from their newfound obscurity in time to become members of the anonymous leadership described by Lyman Glenny (1972), too many institutional researchers remained the captives of national and statewide demands for data that were uniformly reported for purposes of aggregation. Analytic and interpretative skills did not become tools of the trade for many institutional researchers, and the massive data reported to external authorities did not become a body of knowledge common to all members of a research specialty or profession.

Changing Methods of Inquiry. The early emphasis on student behavior and performance was one of the first casualties for the first generation of institutional researchers. The evaluation of student performance by teaching faculty gave way to the evaluation of teaching effectiveness by student ratings. The personal, social, and academic characteristics of students became objects of large-scale research efforts by national agencies and associations, and predictive studies of academic performance became a service rendered routinely by national testing agencies. If their institutions participated, institutional researchers could obtain far more data on students from the American Council on Education's Cooperative Institutional Research Program than they could by their own methods. And, as more institutions adopted open-door or nonselective admissions policies, the determinants of academic performance became less an object of research at the institutional level.

Faculty work load studies continued to show occasional interest in instructional methods and outcomes but more or less stabilized as analyses of faculty activities. Assigned time for instruction, research, and public service became a standardized form of reporting to centralized governing or coordinating bodies, and faculty contact hours, student credit hours, or both became the sole measure of faculty productivity at too many institutions. Analyses of financial budgetary data, space utilization, and enrollment projections became the dominant if not exclusive concern of many offices of institutional research. And, a generation of institutional researchers became quite productive in the 1970s without ever having read or even heard of Sanford's (1962) psychological and social interpretation of higher learning in America.

Seen in this light, the development of institutional research in the years following its early, enthusiastic beginnings was greatly influenced by events and forces outside offices of institutional research. The centralization of administrative and governing authority within the separate states, the presence of the federal government as a funding and regulatory agency, and the extensive analysis of higher education by national commissions were potent forces influencing the data-collecting and reporting activities of institutional researchers. Also relevant to objective and systematic research at the institutional level was the changing climate in which institutional studies had to be conducted. Student protests and faculty dissent placed many barriers between researchers and those who were no longer willing to be objects of research. Court rulings and fears of litigation declared many interesting research questions out of bounds.

Models of Varying Influence

The advocacy of other models and paradigms was particularly strong in the late 1960s and early 1970s. Unifying or organizing themes for institutional research as a developing professional specialty were not highly visible, and institutional research was regarded by some observers as floundering in its efforts to become a specialized function in academic administration and governance. Institutional researchers were greatly diversified in background and experience, and the success with which they applied various tools of their trade to institutional problems varied even more. Depending on their professional education and training, institutional researchers were inclined to define institutional problems in familiar terms and thereby to advocate the application of methods and techniques that made personal sense. The proceedings of the AIR annual forums thus reflect a variety of insights and viewpoints concerning the future development of institutional research. Insofar as the professional development of institutional research can be traced, institutional researchers seem to have been reluctant to chart courses that would carry them too far from their original moorings.

Educational Research. The oldest role model for institutional researchers was the traditional model of educational research. Despite many efforts to introduce concepts and principles of experimental inquiry into institutional studies, institutional researchers did not identify strongly with educational researchers, and many of them gave up their membership in the American Educational Research Association as they became increasingly active in the Association for Institutional Research. Educational researchers continued to be enamored of basic or fundamental processes in education that were best investigated with experimental or quasi-experimental methods of inquiry and analysis. In contrast, institutional researchers have seen their responsibilities as related to practical, applied, mission-oriented forms of research, and they have been particularly aware of profound differences between the problems of elementary education, where the interests of educational researchers are concentrated, and the problems of higher education. To no small extent, educational research has remained a captive of the natural sciences, although it has yet to produce a science of education. Efforts during the 1960s to redirect educational research to applied, mission-oriented, policy-related forms of research were not successful, despite lavish financial support for regional laboratories, research and development centers, and other extradepartmental research agencies.

From later perspectives, it would appear that institutional researchers were wise not to tie their destiny to that of educational researchers. Neither regional laboratories nor research and development centers could free educational research from orthodoxy, and educational research lost much of its credibility as a means of influencing educational policy. Further retrospection suggests that different funding policies and priorities for educational and institutional research on the part of the federal government virtually assured that the two would not develop along parallel paths (Cronbach and Suppes, 1969; Fincher, 1974; Gideonse, 1968).

Measurement and Assessment. As Dyer (1966) suggested, measurement did not prove to be central for institutional research. Although commendable progress has been made in the development of instruments for the assessment of institutional characteristics, the usefulness of those instruments in the improvement of institutions still remains to be proved. Each college and university has a personality and character of its own, but the extent to which personality and character are accurately depicted in mea-

sures of campus climates or environments is unknown. Many crucial features of colleges and universities remain obscure or otherwise concealed from the perceptions of trustees, administrators, faculty, and students as they respond to such instruments as the College and University Environment Scales (CUES), the Institutional Goals Inventory (IGI), and the Institutional Functioning Inventory (IFI). The uses of such instruments depend on the differential weighting that is necessary when the averages of different groups are computed and studied. The significance or importance to be attached to the various dimensions of institutional life raises further questions. And, there are numerous reservations concerning the relevance of national or regional norms for the institution being studied.

Nonetheless, the premises on which the CUES, IGI, and IFI measures were based are sound. Such inventories reflect perceptions, judgments, opinions, or beliefs that are more systematic and objective than the journalistic or impressionistic reports so often publicized in the news media. There are also reasons to believe that, if valid, reliable measures of institutional characteristics can be developed, the possibility of matching institutions and individuals for their mutual benefit improves. If such measures are used wisely in advising and counseling students, they should facilitate the educational accomplishment of those students. Unfortunately, the institutional characteristics tapped by such instruments may be more subtle and thereby less accessible to systematic inquiry than the developers expected.

Systems Analysis. The influence of systems analysis on the development of institutional research is appreciable, but a high level of sophistication in systems thinking is not obvious in many institutional researchers. Systems concepts and principles were evident in the centralization of administration and governance during the 1960s and in the need for geographical distribution of educational resources and opportunities. Systems analysis also laid the groundwork for the computer and communications revolution that swept college campuses at the same time. Cutbacks in the nation's space program presumably brought more systems analysts to college campuses and thereby fostered further adaptation of systems thinking for institutions of higher education (Hoos, 1972).

For institutions of higher education, the introduction of systems theory and concepts may be the best example of efforts to transfer technology from one organizational setting to another. In whatever way systems design and engineering may have been serviceable for corporate industry and for the nation's space program, much of their effectiveness was lost on institutions that had other kinds of traditions and commitments. Sufficient attention was not always paid to the differences between corporate industry or business and educational institutions, and efforts to transfer specific concepts and techniques without modification or adaptation resulted in noticeable contradictions. For example, traditions of autonomy and independence prevented units of statewide systems of higher education from functioning as systems theory suggested. Many institutions were members of a statewide or multicampus system for reasons of funding and public support, not because each was an interrelated part of a closed system. Systems thinking may have been more beneficial in defining and discussing the common problems of colleges than in finding solutions to those problems.

Operations Research. Closely related to systems analysis—and rejected for many of the same reasons—are the specialties of operations research and management science. Institutional management and governance have been the subject of occasional research by operations researchers and management scientists, but there is little evidence of an enduring impact on institutional operations and practices. Institutional researchers may remain impervious to influence because they seldom read the professional literature of operations research and management science, and they rarely belong to professional associations representing such research interests. Another reason may be that both operations research and management science are too specialized to serve the practical needs of institutional researchers. Particular tools and techniques may be borrowed when appropriate, and a few concepts would seem to be common to the three fields, but for the most part institutional researchers have not identified their own interests with those of operational researchers or management scientists. Neither the research skills nor the research interests of institutional researchers would appear to be as tightly knit as those of operational

researchers and management scientists. However, operations research and management science do involve resources, methods, and facilities that institutional researchers believe to be missing from their own field (Schroeder and Adams, 1976).

Evaluation Research. The influence of evaluation research as a role model is difficult to assess. The evaluation of educational programs and services is not incompatible with institutional research, but evaluation research on college and university campuses has not originated in offices of institutional research. The concern for evaluation research dates from the specific requirements for program evaluation contained in federal legislation of the 1960s. Many aspects of evaluation have always been indigenous to education and a visible component of educational research, with the result that institutional research has sometimes been perceived by faculty as evaluation in another guise. Nonetheless, the relevance of evaluation research for institutional researchers may be found in its differences from traditional modes of educational research and in its immediate applications to many problems and issues in institutional research. By 1980, there was no doubt that evaluation research had emerged as a research specialty in its own right, while institutional research was still uncertain about many of its merits. The need for program and project evaluation in higher education was quite evident when higher education was in its period of rapid growth, but that need was not recognized fully until institutions were confronting uncertain enrollments and possibilities of retrenchment. A continuing demand for evaluation thus may mean that institutional researchers will become increasingly involved in program evaluation and assessment regardless of how much they prefer other duties and responsibilities (Fincher, 1981).

Computer Modeling. Although computer modeling is closely related to operations research and management science, it has had a different kind of relationship with institutional research. During the late 1960s, the promise for computer-based models of colleges and universities was quite high, and as early as 1965, CAMPUS (Comprehensive Analytical Methods for Planning in University/College Systems) was discussed in institutional research circles. By the early 1970s, HELP/PLANTRAN (Higher

Education Long-Range Planning/Planning Translator), SEARCH (System for Evaluating Alternative Resource Commitments in Higher Education), and RRPM (Resource Requirements Prediction Model) were on the scene. Computer models had three advantages: They made it possible to forecast or project future conditions in institutional development, they allowed researchers to ask questions about contingent events or situations, and they promoted the understanding of the many complex variables that were involved in institutional management. By simulating institutional activities and functions, computer models foreshadowed a science of institutional management that would enable institutional leaders to study the cause-and-effect relations of their administrative decisions and policies. With the development of realistic simulation models, administrators could anticipate changes in financing, student enrollments, faculty supply and demand, curricular needs, and public expectations. A means of monitoring and managing complex and interrelated institutional functions was almost at hand (Mason, 1976).

Computer modeling failed to live up to its promise for many reasons (Greenberger and others, 1976). The difficulties of updating models and keeping them current were sufficient to explain most failures, but even more obvious explanations are found in the changing environment of higher education and in the lack of receptivity shown by institutional leaders. The financial crisis of the early 1970s called attention to the high cost of simulation and modeling, and the downturn in student enrollments was a disrupting variable that enrollment-driven models could not easily accommodate. The data banks of such models reflected institutional growth and expansion, not conditions of decline or steady state. Many academic administrators remained optimistic about the uses of computer models but did not report extensive use of computer-based information in the administrative decisions of their own institutions (Plourde, 1976). However, the advent of microcomputers in recent years has revitalized computer applications on college campuses, and the promise for decision support systems reached an all-time high in the 1980s.

Planning Models. Although institutional researchers have never identified themselves explicitly as planners, they have been influenced by planning principles and practices. As campus planning agencies fulfilled their mission in the 1970s, mergers with offices of institutional research were not unknown. Despite their many affinities, the AIR and the Society for College and University Planning (SCUP) did not seriously consider merger, but the continued separateness was a function of leadership, not of incompatible purposes and programs. Both the AIR and the SCUP owe much to the statewide master planning that was prominent in the 1960s, and they both reflect a renewed interest in program planning and development as conditions in higher education signal a return to systemwide and even statewide needs and considerations.

Program Budgeting. Also evident in the early 1980s was a continuing need for financial and budgetary analyses that supported institutional and program planning. For many years, institutional research documented the declining support for higher education from the federal government, the low probability that institutions of higher education would obtain an increased proportion of state and local resources, and the widespread need for colleges and universities to seek other sources of funding for continued institutional development. The formula budgeting that had prevailed in the 1960s was no longer the fortunate means of financing public higher education, and different funding methods were needed to cope with the conditions that adversely affected institutions in financial or budgetary difficulty. The analysis of institutional income and expenditures, one of the first responsibilities of offices of institutional research, again became a challenge. Uncertain student enrollments, the rising cost of education, government regulations, competition among institutions and agencies, and threats of a taxpayer revolt were the obvious features of that challenge (Gross, 1983; Mingle and others, 1981).

Measured Outcomes. As institutional researchers became increasingly involved in financial and budgetary analysis, they became increasingly concerned about measured outcomes that could be related to educational costs. The public demand for good measures of educational outcomes can be dated from the Equal Educational Opportunity Study (Coleman and others, 1966) and the various reanalyses of the data collected in that study (Jencks and others, 1972; Mayeske and others, 1972). The financial crisis of the early 1970s added impetus to the accountability movement and placed institutional researchers under considerable pressure to adopt the tools and techniques of econometrics. There was a strenuous challenge to measure in economic terms the outcomes of higher education and to demonstrate their cost-effectiveness in ways that would satisfy national leaders and critics. Among the techniques recommended for this responsibility were input-output analysis, linear programming, game theory, and econometric modeling.

Efforts to study the productivity of colleges and universities with economic methods were less than satisfactory for both institutional researchers and institutional leaders. The cost-effectiveness of a college education was not easy to compute, because neither costs nor indicators of effectiveness could be systematically and consistently derived. Institutions of higher education were not industrial plants, and the productive function studied by economists in other organizational settings did not make sense for colleges and universities. Bowen (1977) effectively answered econometric critics by demonstrating the importance of nonmonetary outcomes in the form of numerous benefits and advantages to both society and individual college graduates. However, the analysis of educational outcomes in terms of input and process variables remained a challenge that institutional researchers should learn to understand. Cost-benefit analysis is still a worthy application of the institutional researcher's time, and the demonstration of educational benefits and advantages is still the most effective argument that can be made to the critics of education.

Policy Research and Analysis. Throughout the 1970s, there was growing awareness that the functions and activities of institutional research were determined for the most part by public policy at national, regional, and state levels. Federal policies and funding changed drastically as national administrations changed and as national priorities shifted to economic, energy, and environmental issues. State policies and priorities underwent similar changes as state governments and coordinating boards assumed additional financial burdens for education, coped with stagflation, and addressed their own energy and environmental issues. Institutional policies changed as national and state policies required attention to diminishing public resources and to reallocation of resources among competing sectors of the economy and competing institutions of higher education.

Unfortunately, institutional researchers were seen in too many institutions as data collectors who could contribute neither substance nor style to institutional policy making. They were, in Wilensky's (1969) terminology, facts-and-figures people, not internal communications specialists or contact people. By this time, many directors of institutional research were removed from the top level of administration and reported to vice-presidents who were not always involved in the formation of crucial institutional policy. Whenever institutional researchers were participants in institutional policy making or influential with administrators who were, their participation and influence could often be attributed to personal working relations that had been established in the past.

Nonetheless, policy research and analysis gave institutional research a focus that Brumbaugh (1960) and others had specified. Policy-related research in particular offered a context in which institutional researchers could assert their professional status and in which their specialized skills and competencies could come into play. There were excellent reasons to believe that the meaning and significance of institutional research could be found in the systematic, empirical technical assistance that institutional researchers could provide in the formation of viable institutional policy. It was again possible to think of institutional researchers as problem solvers who, by virtue of the data and information at their disposal, could contribute to policy and decision making as deliberative processes. As Table 1 shows, the methodological influences on institutional research have varied appreciably with time and circumstances.

Institutional Research as Science

If institutional research is correctly identified as a specialized administrative function that dates from 1960, give or take three or four years, what can be said about its specialized, advanced, or professional status a quarter of a century later? Institutional researchers would be reluctant to claim prominent status among traditional fields of disciplined inquiry, but they could point to an appreciable array of methods, skills, and competencies that are applied in pursuit of interesting knowledge. They could contend seriously that institutional research has not aspired to be a science as physics, chemistry, and biology are. On the contrary, institutional research has not been influenced by the natural sciences as much as it has applied the concepts and methods of other sciences to various institutional problems. Thus, few institutional researchers would claim that Henry Dyer's (1966) goal of a science of institutions has been achieved, and most would be skeptical that such as aspiration is a worthy one.

There are reasons, nonetheless, to examine the scientific underpinnings of institutional research. Other fields of specialization are judged by the sophistication of their theoretical bases, methods of investigation, and the empirical findings that systematic inquiry has netted; institutional research need not be an exception. There was a need for theoretically based studies in 1983, as there was in 1963. There is also a need for sophisticated methods of inquiry and analysis that can derive right answers for the right questions, as Brumbaugh (1960) indicated

twenty-five years ago. And, there are many reasons for assessing the current state of knowledge in institutional research as the outcome of twenty-five years of investigation into the internal operations and processes of higher education.

Theoretical Bases. The conceptual, ideational bases of institutional research would be judged by most knowledgeable critics as lacking strength and internal consistency. The efforts of institutional research to solve institutional problems and to study internal processes are not guided by a conspicuous network of hypotheses and conjectures that could be called theory. Colleges and universities are remarkably diverse institutions, and despite many similarities in structure and functions, there are few useful generalizations that would apply to all. Although occasional attempts are made at theory building in higher education, most institutions have a justifiable claim to the uniqueness that they profess in the presence of evaluation committees, prospective students, and newspaper reporters. Given the premise that institutional research should be the systematic, objective study of internal operations and processes, it follows that neither institutional research nor its object of study is best described by its nomothetic or lawlike characteristics. The idiosyncratic features of institutional

Table 1. Methodological Influences in Institutional Research

The Early Years: 1958–1967	The Crisis Years: 1968–1973	The Later Years: 1974–1985
Long-range planning	Planning, programming, budgeting systems	Strategic planning
Student characteristics	Evaluation research	Student program needs
Faculty activities	Faculty evaluation	Mission review, marketing, recruitment
Enrollment studies	Demographic forecasting	Measured outcomes
Admission and placement studies	Economic benefits	Utilization of capital facilities
Space utilization studies	Cost studies	Needs assessment
Institutional studies	Management information systems	Effective information systems
Self-studies for accreditation	Management by objectives	Program assessment
Income/expenditures analysis	Zero-based budgeting	Reduction-in-force
	Resource allocation and utilization	Policy analysis
		Budgeting strategies and priorities
		Decision support systems
		Administrative staff needs

research dominate, and institutional researchers are better prepared to analyze and interpret specific events and processes within their institutions than they are to explain complex institutional behavior in theoretical terms.

Methods of Inquiry. The strength of institutional research must be found in the methods that institutional researchers have adopted or devised for the analysis and interpretation of institutional data. As institutional records have become increasingly computerized, institutional researchers have gained commendable proficiency as information specialists. Various methods have been developed for the routine reporting functions of colleges and universities, and the aggregation of institutional data for uniform reporting to external authorities is now taken for granted. Methods of statistical, demographic, financial, and budgetary analysis have been applied to the numerous problems of institutional life with valuable results for institutional planning, management, and evaluation. Many institutional researchers are able to deal with the diversities of administrative, business and financial, faculty, and student records, and some have a remarkable expertise in relating computer applications to the problems and issues of higher education.

The extent to which institutional researchers have developed their own methods and techniques is an open question. Other fields have developed the statistical and quasi-experimental methods that institutional researchers use. Their methods of financial and budgetary analysis were developed elsewhere, and their measures of student characteristics, performance, and academic progress have been developed mostly by national testing or research agencies. However, the products of the National Center for Higher Education Management Systems (NCHEMS) have been influenced by institutional researchers (Lawrence and Service, 1977), and some institutional researchers have been particularly resourceful in the analysis of faculty work loads and productivity, in studies of student development, and in the development of planning methods and models. Given the reactive stance that colleges and universities assumed during the years in which institutional research developed, it is easy to infer that institutional researchers have not been encouraged to design and improve their own methods of inquiry and analysis into institutional problems.

Empirical Findings. Institutional research has produced volumes of institutional studies, research reports, journal articles, conference proceedings, workshop manuals, hardback books, and handbooks, but only reservations can be expressed concerning the establishment of an organized body of knowledge common to all practitioners in the field. Several sources of knowledge based on institutional research are national in scope and provide both cross sectional and longitudinal data for institutional analysis. The Cooperative Institutional Research Program (CIRP) launched by the American Council of Education in 1964, the Higher Education General Information Survey (HEGIS) conducted by the federal government, and other national surveys, such as the digests and projections of educational statistics produced by the National Center for Education Statistics, provide valuable backgrounds against which institutional trends and developments can be viewed. The AIR forum proceedings, its *Professional File* series, the journal *Research in Higher Education*, and the Jossey-Bass *New Directions in Institutional Research* sourcebooks give institutional researchers an opportunity to publish research results and findings of common interest. An annual forum for European AIR members provides further opportunities for the discussion of common interests and reflects the diversity of research findings.

However, despite the mass of data and information now available, institutional research is still not characterized by empirical findings that resemble the uniformities and regularities found in other areas of specialization. Institutional researchers share many common research skills and interests, but there is no core of hard-and-fast, systemic truths that each must master in becoming an institutional researcher. Newcomers to the field are still drawn from various academic and professional backgrounds, and, despite appreciable efforts by the AIR to provide training and developmental opportunities through workshops and forums, institutional researchers remain a highly diverse collegial group (Schietinger, 1968; Dressel and Associates, 1971; Dressel and Pratt, 1971; Jedamus and others, 1980).

Institutional Research as Art

If institutional research has been slow to develop as a specialty with scientific underpinnings, what can be said about its growth as a professional or technical specialty that might qualify as a performing art? Since *art* means "a specific skill or its application" and "any craft, trade, or profession" as well as the "making or doing of things that display form, beauty, and unusual perception" (*Webster's New World Dictionary*, 1980), the question is not out of order.

As an art, craft, or profession, there is much about institutional research that is not in doubt. Most institutional research studies are applied, mission-oriented investigations of practical institutional problems. As a rule, they address specific concerns or issues within the institution, and they are said to be conducted on an ad hoc basis. Thus, the results or outcomes of institutional research are usually specific to the institution, and they may not be generalizable to other institutions of similar size or structure. As institutional researchers quickly learn, the findings and conclusions of institutional studies at one institution may not be transferable to other institutions even within the same statewide system.

The professional and technical status of institutional research as an art can be examined in several ways. The methodological sophistication of institutional researchers can be examined in this light, and other characteristics of professional status, such as standards, norms, and institutional impact, should throw additional light on the subject. The conclusions and implications reached in addressing such questions are more or less a definition of the role and functions of institutional research in the 1980s.

Methodological Sophistication. As one form of policy-related research, institutional research in the 1980s is greatly different from the institutional studies conducted in the 1960s. An impressive array of tools and techniques is now available to institutional researchers, and greatly enhanced capabilities in computation and communications permit studies of a scope and depth that were not possible two decades ago. Conceptual distinctions between theory and policy give a better grasp of the methodological differences between theory-based and policy-related research. Theory is now accurately per-

ceived as a conceptual framework of hypotheses and empirical findings that can help to explain observed events and processes. Physical, biological, behavioral, and social sciences traditionally seek to explain significant events or outcomes in terms of their antecedents, and the construction or development of theory is often identified as an attempt to answer the question, How? The preferred outcome of theory is usually a conclusion that extends or elaborates what is known about the objects, conditions, and results being investigated.

In contrast, policy is best perceived as a logical, coherent rationale providing guidance for administrative decisions and actions. The outcome of policy-related research is likely to be an interpretation of observed events, followed by recommendations for improvements, redirection, or other modifications. Frequently, alternatives for action are delineated or fashioned, and the suitability of those alternatives is then judged in terms of their consequences. In this way, there is an active concern for decisions or choices, and policy-related research often seeks an answer to the question, Which? Plans, programs, and deliberate action are typical outcomes of policy-related research in higher education.

Multiple regression techniques give institutional researchers a powerful tool for the analysis of policy variables when policy-related research is clearly their intent. Computer capabilities in most offices of institutional research permit analysis-of-effects designs that relate dependent research variables to the multiple independent variables that are often operative in institutional problems. Whenever the researcher's intent is theory-based research, multiple regression techniques provide partitioning-of-variance designs that are equally helpful in specifying the variance in research outcomes that can be attributed to the researcher's independent or experimental variables. The choice of research models is crucial, therefore, and institutional researchers must take as much care in the definition and measurement of their policy variables as they take in the analysis of their data.

The possibilities for policy-related research are particularly promising to institutional researchers because institutions of higher education are so complex. However, *policy-related research*, not *policy research* or *analysis*, is the correct term, because of the manner in which policy is formulated in educational institutions. Policy is seldom determined by research findings alone, and it is not merely a matter of politics, despite appearances. Whatever the policy-making process is in higher education, it is a deliberative process that pays considerable attention to factual, empirical information. In the absence of such information, most policy makers will fall back on preferences and suppositions. No small challenge to institutional researchers, therefore, is policy-related research that will keep policy makers honest.

In addition to policy-related research, institutional researchers are showing increasing sophistication about funding, financing, and budgeting. The competition of institutions for outside funding adds impetus to the organizational intelligence role of some offices of institutional research. Institutional image is not unrelated to success in fund raising, and institutional research is not irrelevant to the image building of colleges and universities. More important, however, is the sophistication that comes from historical, developmental, and comparative perspectives in higher education. There is appreciable awareness that institutions of higher education must be understood and interpreted in terms of their historical development as well as of their structural and functional features. Institutional reputations are seldom changed dramatically by reorganization, new presidents, curricular revisions, or faculty and student recruitment. On the contrary, reputations can lag behind institutional performance or live on long after performance has declined. Institutional reputations are the results of historical developments, just as institutional research and other institutional functions are.

Standards and Norms. The standards and norms that would accurately reflect the status of institutional research as a profession are still in the process of becoming. The Association for Institutional Research serves many purposes of a professional society, but it has not established standards of training and preparation that can be enforced. Entry into the field of institutional research is still a matter of appointment by presidents or vice-presidents who designate newcomers institutional researchers. Membership in the AIR is still a matter of professional or personal preference, not of professional per-

formance. Although the AIR has made commendable efforts to introduce new members to institutional research concepts and methods, no performance standards have been set for the application and use of those concepts and methods.

Professional norms in institutional research are almost as difficult to establish as professional standards. Several surveys have dealt with the demographics of institutional researchers, and one or two have tapped the functions or activities that constitute their duties and responsibilities. However, the norms of institutional research are difficult to delineate, because they are still in their formative stages. The ambiguity of professional norms strikes many institutional researchers as both typical and healthy.

Institutional Impact. The influence that institutional research has had on the nation's institutions of higher education is, of course, a matter of judgment. Institutional researchers have seen their professional and personal influence ebb and flow with changes in the president's or chancellor's office. Some have witnessed immediate and direct consequences of their influence, while others have served long and diligently without seeing noticeable results of any kind. Yet, it is altogether possible that the most significant and enduring impact of institutional research on institutional operations and practices has been in areas little affected by changes in presidents. This is to say that the impact of institutional research may be more noticeable in institutional operations than in institutional policy.

There are numerous early changes in institutional operations that can be attributed to institutional research and to the presence on campuses of individuals directly concerned with the institution's internal processes. At least one generation of institutional researchers had appreciable influence through their enrollment projections. Others can claim improved efficiency in course sectioning and scheduling, reduction of overlap in course content and requirements, and elimination of small, costly courses. Some can point to improved admission standards and procedures, changes in retention policies and practices, and improvements in use of part-time faculty. Without doubt, institutional research has influenced faculty assignments, the uses of instructional space and facilities, and the specification of faculty and staff workloads.

Later changes that can be attributed to institutional research pertain to institutional planning, management, and evaluation. In planning, institutional research had a noticeable impact on the kinds of data or information gathered for planning purposes and on the manner in which the data were collected. Many of these changes were subtle, and some may have been unavoidable, but systematic planning efforts have always involved the gathering of data, and those who gather data are participants in the planning process. Influence has also been seen in the uses made of data by planning committees or commissions. The interpretation of data often suggests the uses to which they will be put, and planning committees are notoriously weak in analytic and interpretative skills.

There are many ways in which institutional research may have influenced administrative or managerial decisions during the 1960s and 1970s. Much of this influence may have more to do with style than with substance, but the influence has nonetheless been effective. Administrators who were infatuated with management information systems needed help in deciding the kinds of data that should be stored for later retrieval and use. And, as in the case of planning committees, administrators often needed assistance in the interpretation of management information stored and retrieved at their own request. However, the most substantive impact of institutional research is likely to have been on the ways in which administrative decisions were ostensibly made. Some institutional research confirmed more administrative decisions than it informed, but increasingly few administrative decisions were made without some semblance of fact finding.

The influence of institutional research on evaluation is more difficult to trace, but it can be seen in its effect on program review or assessment procedures. The review, assessment, and evaluation of academic programs and funded projects inevitably require some kind of descriptive data that are historical in nature. Institutional researchers often provide this kind of information when registrars, directors of admissions, deans, and department heads cannot. The storage and retrieval of historical data that

can serve descriptive, comparative purposes exert a subtle but nonetheless relevant influence on program review or assessment.

Potential if not actual impact is very much the case in the provision of student and academic services, such as academic advisement, student counseling, and career placement. As student demands for these services increase at many colleges, the need for systematic, ongoing review will be intensified. Universities in particular may be under pressure to evaluate student services as the cost and the demand for them increase. Academic support services, as components of faculty development programs and as new commitments at many institutions, will also be reviewed or monitored as their costs become visible in institutional budgets and financial reports.

In brief, the institutional impact of institutional research over a twenty-five-year period is pervasive if not prominent. The influence of institutional research is more visible in operational or procedural matters than in administrative decision making and institutional policy, but influence in the last two areas, is nonetheless present. Institutional research is undoubtedly one of several forces that have encouraged and facilitated participatory decision making in administrative councils and open policy deliberations in academic governance.

The Potential for Continued Development

A careful review of the development on institutional research since 1960 undoubtedly discloses its hesitant but commendable progress as a specialized administrative function. Table 2 summarizes the features that suggest the emerging status of institutional research as a practicing profession, and the continuing challenges to the institutions of higher education imply that it may indeed be an indispensable support service for administrative decision making and institutional policy formation. In the 1980s, institutional research is best described as a professional, technical specialty with strong resources and capabilities for policy-related research in institutions of higher education. There is no less need for policy-related research in the 1980s than there was in the 1960s. On the contrary, the need for such research has increased, and institutional researchers should never hesitate to quote or cite Brumbaugh's (1960, p. 34) admonishment: "To make wise decisions, data that only institutional research can provide are indispensable."

However, if institutional research is to realize its potential for continuing professional development, there are numerous challenges that must be met. Institutional research perspectives must be broadened, and they must include more in-depth analyses of colleges and universities as educational institutions and national resources. The historical, developmental, and comparative dimensions of higher education must be better appreciated, and there must be less infatuation with business corporations, government agencies, and other organizations that cannot provide a viable model for colleges to emulate. Henry Dyer's (1966) challenge should again be considered, and the contributions of institutional research to the systematic, coherent study of collegiate institutions should be greatly strengthened.

Institutional research could make an essential contribution by helping to create a climate wherein the study of colleges and universities as societal and cultural institutions would be worthy of its own theoretical bases, methods of inquiry, and empirical findings. Such a contribution should not be made at the expense of the policy-related research that institutional researchers must provide, but a more positive attitude toward theory-related research would accomplish much in the continued development of institutional research.

In conclusion, the merits of institutional research depend not on its scientific underpinnings but on its relevance and influence in decision and policymaking. In its young adult years, institutional research makes a substantive contribution to institutional planning management, and there are many conspicuous indications that it is capable of contributing even more.

Table 2. The Developmental Status of Institutional Research

As a Science	
Theoretical Bases	Increasing awareness that institutional research needs a unifying or integrative nexus of ideas that would provide a good theoretical foundation; an absence of well-formulated hypotheses or theorems to be tested experimentally or quasi-experimentally
Methods of Inquiry	Many applications and uses of statistical methods and quasi-experimental design for institutional and program analysis, but an increasing need for methods of inquiry, analysis, and verification that serve institutions of higher education well
Empirical Findings	Massive data and detailed information about institutional activities and functions, but no body of knowledge commonly accepted by institutional researchers as essential to mastery of the field, and limited knowledge of institutional outcomes, productivity, and effectiveness
As an Art	
Methodological Sophistication	Increasing appreciation of both theory and policy, their distinctions, and their relevance for institutional research; methods and techniques that can greatly enhance institutional researchers' analytic and interpretative capabilities
Standards and Norms	Still in the process of becoming, but nonetheless important; a continuing need for AIR leadership in setting standards of preparation, training, and entry to the professional field and in providing newcomers with in service developmental opportunities
Institutional Impact	Appreciable influence on institutional record keeping and data reporting, with significant impact on style of administrative decision making in large institutions and in centralized boards of governance or coordination; slight influence on faculty governance and participation in institutional management; increasing influence on program planning, review, and evaluation

References

Bowen, H. R. *Investment in Learning: The Individual and Social Value of American Higher Education*, San Francisco: Jossey-Bass, 1977.

Brumbaugh, A. J. *Research Designed to Improve Institutions of Higher Learning.* Washington, D.C.: American Council on Education, 1960.

Coleman, J. S., and others. *Equality of Educational Opportunity.* Washington, D.C.: U.S. Government Printing Office, 1966.

Cronbach, L. J., and Suppes, P. (Eds.). *Research for Tomorrow's Schools: Disciplined Inquiry for Education.* New York: Macmillan, 1969.

Dressel, P. L. "The Shaping of Institutional Research and Planning." *Research in Higher Education*, 1981, 14, 229–258.

Dressel, P. L., and Associates. *Institutional Research in the University: A Handbook.* San Francisco: Jossey-Bass, 1971.

Dyer, H. S. "Can Institutional Research Lead to a Science of Institutions?" *Educational Record*, 1966, 47, 452–466.

Dyer, T. G. "Institutional Research and Institutional History." *Research in Higher Education*, 1978, 8, 283–286.

Fincher, C. "COBRE and the Dilemma of Basic Research in Education." *Educational Researcher*, 1974, 3 (2), 11–13.

Fincher, C. "The Literature of Evaluation Research." *Research in Higher Education*, 1981, 14, 277–280.

Fincher, C. "The Return of Grand Strategy." *Research in Higher Education*, 1983, 19, 125–126.

Gideonse, H. D. "Research, Development, and the Improvement of Education." *Science*, 1968, 162, 541–545.

Glenny, L. A. "The Anonymous Leaders of Higher Education." *Journal of Higher Education*, 1972, 43, 9–22.

Gray, J. *The University of Minnesota: 1851–1951.* Minneapolis: University of Minnesota Press, 1951.

Greenberger, M., Crenson, M. A., and Crissey, B. L. *Models in the Policy Process: Public Decision Making in the Computer Era.* New York: Russell Sage Foundation, 1976.

Gross, F. M. "Formula Budgeting and the Financing of Public Higher Education: Panacea or Nemesis for the 1980s?" In *Institutional Research Issues and Applications 1978–1983.* AIR Professional File 1–16. Tallahassee, Fla.: Association for Institutional Research, 1983.

Hoos, I. R. *Systems Analysis in Public Policy: A Critique.* Berkeley: University of California Press, 1972.

Jedamus, P., Peterson, M. W., and Associates. *Improving Academic Management: A Handbook of Planning and Institutional Research.* San Francisco: Jossey-Bass, 1980.

Jencks, C., and others. *Inequality: A Reassessment of the Effect of Family in America.* New York: Basic Books, 1972.

Lawrence, G. B., and Service, A. L. (Eds.). *Quantitative Approaches to Higher Education Management.* ERIC/Higher Education Research Report No. 4. Washington, D.C.: American Association for Higher Education, 1977.

Mason, T. R. (Ed.). *Assessing Computer-Based System Models.* New Directions for Institutional Research, no. 9. San Francisco: Jossey-Bass, 1976.

Mayeske, G. A., and others. *A Study of Our Nation's Schools*, Washington, D.C.: U.S. Government Printing Office, 1972.

Mingle, J. R., and Associates. *Challenges of Retrenchment: Strategies for Consolidating Programs, Cutting Costs, and Reallocating Resources.* San Francisco: Jossey-Bass, 1981.

Plourde, P. J. "Institutional Use of Models: Hope or Continued Frustration?" In T. R. Mason (Ed.), *Assessing Computer-Based System Models.* New Directions for Institutional Research, no. 9. San Francisco: Jossey-Bass, 1976.

Sanford, N. (Ed.). *The American College: A Psychological and Social Interpretation of the Higher Learning.* New York: Wiley, 1962.

Schietinger, E. F. (Ed.). *Introductory Papers on Institutional Research.* Atlanta: Southern Regional Education Board, 1968.

Schroeder, T. G., and Adams, C. R. "The Effective Use of Management Science in University Administration." *Review of Educational Research*, 1976, 46, 117–131.

Webster's New World Dictionary of the American Language: Second College Edition. New York: Simon & Schuster, 1980.

Wilensky, H. L. *Organizational Intelligence: Knowledge and Policy in Government and Industry.* New York: Basic Books, 1969.

Cameron Fincher is regents professor and director of the Institute of Higher Education at the University of Georgia. He is associate editor for the AIR of Research in Higher Education and a Distinguished Member of the Association for Institutional Research.

Assumptions Underlying Quantitative and Qualitative Research: Implications for Institutional Research

RUSSEL S. HATHAWAY

For institutional researchers, the choice to use a quantitative or qualitative approach to research is dictated by time, money, resources, and staff. Frequently, the choice to use one or the other approach is made at the method level. Choices made at this level generally have rigor, but ignore the underlying philosophical assumptions structuring beliefs about methodology, knowledge, and reality. When choosing a method, institutional researchers also choose what they believe to be knowledge, reality, and the correct method to measure both. The purpose of this paper is to clarify and explore the assumptions underlying quantitative and qualitative research. The reason for highlighting the assumptions is to increase the general level of understanding and appreciation of epistemological issues in institutional research. Articulation of these assumptions should foster greater awareness of the appropriateness of different kinds of knowledge for different purposes.

There are few subjects that generate as much passion among scientists as arguments over method. (Shulman, 1981, p. 5).

Institutional researchers are continually involved with implementing research agendas for various campus constituencies. Institutional research offices provide important technical and informational support for central decision makers in higher education by engaging in research-oriented activities such as tracking enrollment patterns, surveying incoming students, documenting faculty workloads, and assessing staff job satisfaction. Research methods that institutional researchers employ range from basic quantitative statistical analyses to interviews and case studies (Bohannon, 1988;

Bunda, 1991; Fetterman, 1991; Hinkle, McLaughlin, and Austin, 1988; Jennings and Young, 1988; Sherman and Webb, 1988; Tierney, 1991). Some institutional researchers advocate integrating quantitative and qualitative approaches to institutional research (Marshall, Lincoln, and Austin, 1991; Peterson, 1985a). Often, the driving forces behind the choice of methods are time, money, resources, staff, and those requesting the study. The choice to use a quantitative approach (e.g., survey and statistical analysis of responses) versus a qualitative approach (e.g., transcription analysis of interviews) is generally decided at the level of methods. Although the choice of methods is often a difficult one, institutional researchers generally make the decision with relative ease, choosing the method that will garner the information they seek. However, they often make their decisions without giving much thought to the assumptions underlying research methods.

Over the past decade, educational researchers have been engaged in an ongoing polemic concerning quantitative and qualitative research. They have been arguing over philosophical commensurability,[1] the concern that qualitative research has been seen as a methodological variation of quantitative research, and whether researchers should combine quantitative and qualitative research methods when pursuing research interests (Donmoyer, 1985; Eisner, 1981, 1983; Firestone, 1987; Howe, 1985, 1988; Shulman, 1981).

Although the intricate details of this debate are not of paramount concern for institutional researchers, the general discourse over the fun-

"Assumptions Underlying Quantitative and Qualitative Research: Implications for Institutional Research," by Russel S. Hathaway, reprinted from *Research in Higher Education*, Vol. 36, No. 5, 1995. Human Sciences Press, Inc.

damental philosophical grounds guiding research methods is relevant. Some of those involved in the debate argue that the choice to use a quantitative or qualitative research approach should not be made at the method level (Guba and Lincoln, 1981).[2] This concern has direct relevance for those making methodological choices in an applied field such as institutional research. The decision to use quantitative or qualitative methods is replete with assumptions concerning the nature of knowledge and reality, how one understands knowledge and reality, and the process of acquiring knowledge and knowledge about reality. When one chooses a particular research approach, one makes certain assumptions concerning knowledge, reality, and the researcher's role. These assumptions shape the research endeavor, from the methodology employed to the type of questions asked.

When institutional researchers make the choice between quantitative or qualitative research methods, they tacitly assume a structure of knowledge, an understanding and perception of reality, and a researcher's role. The purpose of this paper is to clarify and explore the underlying assumptions contained within quantitative and qualitative research. It is important for institutional researchers to understand the philosophical grounding of the two approaches so that they may reflect on those assumptions while engaging in institutional research. In addition, understanding the philosophical grounding also highlights the strengths and weaknesses of both approaches. The reason for contrasting the two paradigms is to increase the general level of understanding and appreciation of epistemological issues in the institutional research profession. Articulation of the epistemological differences should foster greater awareness of the appropriateness of different kinds of knowledge for different purposes; it may thereby help legitimate the adoption of alternative and more appropriate knowledge-yielding paradigms in institutional research. It should also help reduce conflicts within the field by justifying and providing a basis for tolerance of diversity and multiplicity in research design.

Greater epistemological appreciation seems to be an essential prerequisite to developing an appropriate inquiry approach whereby researchers would explicitly select a mode of inquiry to fit the nature of the problematic situation under study, the state of knowledge, and their own skills, style, and purpose (Donmoyer, 1985; Smith, 1983a). In addition, appreciation of epistemological issues has implications for the evaluation of institutional research products. It leads to a belief that the quality of a piece of research is more critically indicated by the appropriateness of the paradigm selected than by the mere technical correctness of the methods used (Donmoyer, 1985; Eisner, 1981; Herriott and Firestone, 1983; Smith 1983a).

The debate that has been going on among educational researchers will be highlighted in brief, emphasizing the major points that have been raised by proponents of quantitative and qualitative research, as well as the arguments for those who advocate the combination of the two approaches. This debate will be used as a stepping stone into a discussion of the underlying philosophies of quantitative and qualitative research. An example program review will be used to describe how the two approaches might structure the program investigation and evaluation. This example is not meant to represent an ideal, or even typical, method of conducting a review, but rather to provide a vivid sense of the distinctions between the two approaches. Finally, differences between the paradigms will be identified and discussed followed by a conclusion highlighting implications for conducting inquiry in institutional research.

Debates Over Disciplined Inquiry

Early Debate

The educational research community is engaged in a heated debate over quantitative and qualitative approaches to disciplined inquiry. The crux of the debate centers on the incommensurability of the underlying assumptions structuring the approaches (Donmoyer, 1985; Eisner, 1981; Firestone, 1987; Howe, 1985).[3] This debate in educational research, however, followed a crisis in the social sciences concerning identical philosophical issues (Bernstein, 1976, 1983; Rabinow and Sullivan, 1987). Bernstein (1976) has provided one of the most comprehensive summaries of the history of the social science debates, as well as a rich description of the various research paradigms that were, and still are, being discussed.

The debate over quantitative and qualitative research arose out of the social and political unrest of the 1960s during which the foundations of the social disciplines came under radical criticism (Bernstein, 1976; Rabinow and Sullivan, 1987). Bernstein argues that these critiques came at a time when the social disciplines had arrived at a tentative agreement on an empirical foundation where they could begin a stable expansion of the scientific knowledge of society. Critics argued, and continue to argue, that the foundations of the social sciences were replete with weakness; that what was believed to be objective scientific knowledge was a veiled form of ideology that supported the status quo (Bernstein, 1976; Gordon, Miller, and Rollock, 1990; Stanfield, 1985). Others argued that the social sciences did not provide the critical perspectives on what was happening in society, nor did they provide solutions to the problems they set out to solve (Bernstein, 1976). The belief that a rational, systematic study of societal problems would result in policies and programs that would address them was doubted (Bernstein, 1976).

As the social sciences began to experience profound criticism and self-doubt, newly discussed approaches arose to rescue social science research from the depths of angst. Bernstein (1976) argues that linguistic philosophical inquiries were used to challenge the epistemological foundations of the social sciences. Phenomenology and hermeneutics also became more welcome in social scientific circles. These disciplines, often characterized as soft and subjective by empirical researchers, were perceived as panaceas for the ills facing social research (Bernstein, 1976). Advocates of phenomenology and hermeneutics believed that these approaches could provide elucidative insight into social processes that was not being acquired with empirical inquiry methods (Bernstein, 1976).

The literature produced in this period concerning the nature of research can best be described as muddled. Bernstein (1976) reports that there was no agreement during the 1960s and 1970s about what were provable results, what were the proper research methods, what were important problems to address, or what were "the most promising theoretical approaches" in the study of social science. It was during this confusing period that the educational community began questioning its approaches to disciplined inquiry.[4]

Educational Debate

Closely following what could be called the "angst" period in social science research, the educational research community began to experience a similar debate, beginning in the late 1970s and continuing today (Donmoyer, 1985; Eisner, 1981, 1983; Firestone, 1987; Garrison, 1986; Giarelli and Chambliss, 1988; Howe, 1985, 1988; Hutchinson, 1988; Lincoln and Guba, 1985; Marshall, Lincoln, and Austin, 1991; Sherman and Webb, 1988). Throughout this period, educational researchers have engaged in a heated debate over the degree to which quantitative and qualitative methods can be combined. This discourse revolved around defining different facets of qualitative and quantitative research along with the debate focusing on the pros and cons of combining the two approaches. In general, researchers fall into three perspectives in this discussion: the purists, the situationalists, and the pragmatists (Rossman and Wilson, 1985). The purists would not entertain the notion of discussing combining the two approaches. Educational researchers within this perspective focus on the incommensurability between the two approaches and argue that the philosophies grounding the two approaches are so divergent in terms of assumptions about the world, truth, and reality that one should not even consider combining quantitative and qualitative research (Guba, 1987; Smith, 1983a, 1983b; Smith and Heshusius, 1986). The concern is that by combining approaches, researchers neglect to acknowledge that the different approaches make vastly different assumptions concerning knowledge and reality. Others have discussed the problems involved in ignoring the issue of underlying assumptions and focusing only on the benefits of combining both approaches (Donmoyer, 1985).

In contrast, those falling within the situationalist perspective focus on the level of method and argue "that certain methods are most appropriate for specific situations" (Rossman and Wilson, 1985, p. 630). The choice of method for the situationalist is partially determined by the questions to be answered. Furthermore, situationalist researchers also alternate between qualitative and quantitative methods as they engage the research process (Rossman and Wilson, 1985). In other words, researchers adhering to this perspective may use a survey to generate information that could assist in the development of an interview protocol.

For the pragmatist, quantitative and qualitative methods are viewed as capable of informing one another throughout the research process. In contrast to the situationalist, who alters between the two approaches, the pragmatist views the two approaches capable of simultaneously bringing to bear both of their strengths to answer a research question. Using interviews, surveys, questionnaires, and observation techniques within one study is as an example of a pragmatic approach to integrating or combining research methods.

Institutional Research Debate

Throughout the past decade of discussion, the educational research debate has highlighted many of the strengths and weaknesses of quantitative and qualitative research, and it has brought to light the philosophies underlying the two approaches. For institutional researchers, the debate follows closely on the heels of the evolution of the profession, a profession that has slowly moved from engaging primarily in descriptive quantitative studies in the 1970s and 1980s (Peterson, 1985a, 1985b) to more multimethod studies in the 1990s (Peterson and Spencer, 1993). Institutional researchers have engaged in debates similar to those of educational researchers, but not to the same extent. Institutional researchers have primarily discussed quantitative and qualitative differences at the method level (Bohannon, 1988; Fetterman, 1991; Fincher, 1985; Hinkle, McLaughlin, and Austin, 1988; Jennings and Young, 1988; Marshall, Lincoln, and Austin, 1991; Tierney, 1991) and how different methodologies yield different information (Peterson and Spencer, 1993). At this level, institutional researchers have been attending, correctly so, to assumptions supporting specific statistical procedures (Bohannon, 1988; Yancey, 1988a, 1988b), such as having random selection when performing multiple regression, having a sample size larger than five in each cell of an ANOVA, or assuming a normal distribution. By attending to the assumptions at this level, insti-

tutional researchers have produced studies that have rigorous application of methods.

Institutional researchers advocating qualitative approaches have also appropriately focused attention on the assumptions guiding good qualitative research. Qualitative institutional researchers have tended to address data collection procedures, such as having an interview protocol composed of nonleading questions and accurate transcripts of observation or taped accounts (e.g., Miles and Huberman, 1984), but they fail to discuss or acknowledge the scientific philosophies (i.e., phenomenology, hermeneutics, positivism) in which they are grounded. Those using quantitative approaches also neglect to mention the philosophical grounds on which their approaches are based. It is important for institutional researchers to be cognizant of the philosophical assumptions guiding both quantitative and qualitative approaches. It is important not only because it is good practice, but because institutional research is an applied field in which much of what is done is used for policy decisions. These policy decisions, once implemented, make assumptions concerning the reality of campus life. These realities are defined, in part, by the underlying philosophies structuring the approach used by the institutional researcher. For example, a statistical analysis performed on survey results may describe certain aspects of the campus, but these aspects have been shaped by the people who developed the survey and may not reflect the reality as understood and experienced by those who answered the survey.

Paradigms Underlying Quantitative and Qualitative Research

Defining Paradigm

A framework is needed to discuss the differences between philosophies underlying the quantitative and qualitative research approaches. The distinction between the philosophies can be made by using the concept of paradigm. The work of a number of philosophers (Bernstein, 1976; Firestone, 1987; Gubrium, 1988; Kuhn, 1962, 1970, 1974) is quite useful in defining the idea of a paradigm. Kuhn defines scientific paradigm as a theoretical framework, or a way of perceiving and understanding the world, that a group of scientists has adopted as their worldview. For Bernstein, the underlying paradigm dictates a level of generally unexamined common assumptions, attitudes, and expectations, and a framework within which inquiry operates. This paradigm guides a shared sense of what scientific inquiry is and could be the kind of reality being investigated, the proper form of inquiry, and a general orientation for perceiving and interpreting the world (Bernstein, 1976). The paradigm from which one operates has consequences for views of the nature of empirical knowledge, the relations of theory and practice, the relations of fact and perception, and the education and role of the theorist (Bernstein, 1976). When a scientist observes a phenomenon and interprets what this observation means, that scientist is using a particular paradigm to give that observation meaning. Gubrium (1988) defines paradigm as a way of structuring everyday experience, a way of framing events, a sense of what is real and how to prove it, and an implicit stance on ontology and epistemology (i.e., being and knowing). This paradigm also influences the methods chosen (Firestone, 1987) and implies policy and action (Banks, 1988).

In essence, scientific paradigms act as lenses through which scientists or researchers are able to perceive and understand the problems in their field and the scientific answers to those problems. Paradigms dictate what researchers consider data, what their role in the investigation will be, what they consider knowledge, how they view reality, and how they can access that reality. A scientific paradigm provides a group of scientists or researchers with a way of collectively making sense of their scientific world. It is this framework of everyday assumptions about knowledge, reality, and the proper methodology that will be summarized in the remainder of this paper.

Distinguishing the Paradigms

Quantitative and qualitative approaches can both serve research purposes, but in different ways and with different effects. The ways in which they are used and the insights provided are a function of the underlying assumptions of the paradigms grounding the approaches. The attempt here is to systematically articulate the paradigms underlying both these approaches by direct description and by contrast with a recognizable alternative. The two paradigms will be contrasted on a number of dimensions (summarized in Table 1).

Before discussing the differences between the two paradigms of inquiry, it may be useful to comment on the paradigms underlying the distinction between quantitative and qualitative research approaches. A review of the literature yields a wide array of distinctions between the philosophies undergirding the two approaches.[5]

Included among these are Geertz's (1973) distinction between thin and thick description; Hall's (1976) low context and high context; Pike's (1967) etic and emic; Kaplan's (1964) logic-in-use and reconstructed logic; Smith's (1983a) realist and idealist continuum; Smith and Heshusius's (1986) rationalist and naturalist distinction; Habermas's (1988) and Bernstein's (1976) empirical-analytic and interpretive distinction; and the distinctions between acquaintance with and knowledge about as variously construed by James (1918), Dewey (1933), Schutz (1967), and Merton (1972). For the purposes of this paper, the term *empirical-analytic* will be used to describe the paradigm structuring quantitative research, and the term *interpretive* will be used to describe the paradigm underlying qualitative research.

Most commonly, the empirical-analytic paradigm has been associated with positivism. There are many varieties of positivism (Phillips, 1983). Comptean positivism holds that the scientific method can be applied to human experiences (Phillips, 1983). Thus, researchers within the Comptean tradition focus upon observable, objectively determinable phenomena. In contrast, logical positivism is marked by an intense dislike of metaphysics and aims to remove the idea from both the natural and the human sciences (Phillips, 1983). Logical positivists also believe in the verifiability principle of meaning, which states that something is meaningful if and only if it is verifiable empirically—directly by observation through the senses. From the verifiability concept arose the idea of operational definitions (Phillips, 1983). Other terms used to describe this paradigm include hypothetico-deductive and objectivist (Moss, 1990).

Table 1. The Paradigm Framework Underlying the Two Approaches

	Empirical-Analytic (quantitative)	Interpretive (qualitative)
Methodology	Begin with hypothesis of a relationship between cause & effect (program & outcome). Test hypothesis. Develop instruments. Identify sample (random). Measure/code phenomenon. Aggregate data. Generalize: theory that has withstood this test. Researcher should have objective stance.	Formulate a question. Identify sample (purposive). "Fix" phenomenon (interview, observe, tape record). Narrative articulation and interpretation of themes. Compare data types; integrate material (as parts of a whole). Hypothesis generating. Write case descriptions. Generalize? Researcher should have participatory stance.
Ontology (Reality)	Public events (e.g., discussion, utterances, etc.) reflect a reality. Private perceptions (e.g., beliefs, perceptions, etc.). Subjects and objects exist separate from the perception of them. Objective events, subjective states. Governed by laws.	Public events. People have different aims, attitudes. People interact within, and can change, a local setting. Subjects and objects located in intersubjective communities. People construct and act within a context which structures and constrains that activity.
Epistemology (Knowledge)	Knowledge = objective reports of measured dimensions of the phenomenon. Compared against (tacit) norms ("skills"). Compared over time. Differences/no differences attributed to hypothesized causal relationship, to lack of validity of instruments, or to alternative causes. General statements of regularities among objective properties that are internally consistent and that correspond to the way things really are.	Knowedge = understanding of participants' aims, perspectives, assumptions: the terms in which their everyday life is grasped. Plus articulation of the local social context of interaction. Description of specific cases (persons & communities): people employ interpretive schemes that must be understood before action can be described. Character of the local context must be articulated.

The description of the interpretive inquiry paradigm has a wider range of descriptors. Interpretive inquiry can be described as phenomenological, hermeneutical, experiential, and dialectic. Naturalistic, inductive, and relativist are some of the other terms used to describe the interpretive paradigm (Moss, 1990). Each of these terms is difficult to describe in brief or with precision. It needs to be made clear that although many of these terms can be identified as interpretive research, caution is required from equating it with any one of them. This is due to the slight variation in assumptions concerning different interpretive approaches.[6] As will be seen later, all the interpretive research traditions, however, generally share common assumptions about methodology, ontology, and epistemology.[7]

Methodological and Ontological Differences

The description of the paradigms begins by comparing the researcher's role and relationship to the setting under the two paradigms, and by identifying the epistemological and validity assumptions underlying the choice of role and relationship.[8] Knowledge and understanding of a college or university situation can be acquired in two ways: (1) by studying, "objectively," data generated by the situation, and (2) by becoming part of the situation by understanding participant views of it. We can come to "know" the chemistry and psychology departments by examining faculty research productivity, enrollment statistics, questionnaire results, or GRE subject tests; or, alternatively, by functioning within these departments for a period of time talking with faculty, students, and staff.

Empirical-analytic inquiry is characterized by the researcher's detachment from the organizational setting under study (Eisner, 1981; Phillips, 1983; Smith, 1983a, 1983b). The detachment derives, in part, from the assumption that the object under study is separate from, unrelated to, independent of, and unaffected by the researcher (Eisner, 1981; Smith, 1983a, 1983b). The mind is separate from reality (Smith, 1983a, 1983b) and truth is defined as a correspondence between our words and that independently existing reality (Smith and Heshusius, 1986). In other words, "there are social facts with an objective reality apart from the beliefs of individuals" (Firestone, 1987, p. 16). Physics provides an ideal example. The objects of interest are measured with instruments, the data are analyzed to determine if logical patterns seem to exist, and rational theories are constructed to integrate, explain, and perhaps predict a multitude of facts. Underlying the detachment of the researcher inquiring from an empirical-analytic perspective are critical ontological assumptions: the researcher is guided by belief in an external reality constituted of facts that are structured in a law-like manner (Firestone, 1987). In essence, researchers conducting inquiries within this paradigm are hoping to document laws that structure reality.

In contrast, inquiry for the interpretive paradigm carries with it the assumptions that the researcher can best come to know the reality of a situation by being there: by becoming immersed in the stream of events and activities, by becoming part of the phenomenon of study, and by documenting the understanding of the situation by those engaged in it (Firestone, 1987; Herriot and Firestone, 1983; Howe, 1985; Jacob, 1988; Smith, 1984). Jacob (1988) states, "Qualitative research has been charac-

terized as emphasizing the importance of conducting research in a natural setting, as assuming the importance of understanding participants' perspectives, and as assuming that it is important for researchers subjectively and empathetically to know the perspectives of the participants" (p. 16). Knowledge is validated experientially (Firestone, 1987; Herriot and Firestone, 1983; Howe, 1985; Jacob, 1988; Smith, 1984). Underlying the interpretive paradigm is a very different set of epistemological assumptions from those of the empirical-analytic paradigm. Fundamental to the interpretive paradigm is the belief that knowledge comes from human experience, which is inherently continuous and nonlogical, and which may be symbolically representable (Firestone, 1987; Herriot and Firestone, 1983; Howe, 1985; Jacob, 1988; Smith, 1984). Reality is constructed by those participating in it, and understanding the reality experienced by the participants guides the interpretive researcher. Truth is "a matter of socially and historically conditioned agreement" (Smith and Heshusius, 1986, p. 6). An interpretive researcher would not look for the laws governing reality because, ultimately, reality is constructed and understood differently for each individual (Taylor, 1987). For example, an interpretive researcher could not describe the "objective" culture of an academic department, but could describe the culture as seen by those participating in it. Some would argue that one can never understand the reality of others, but only be able to articulate one interpretation of it (Cziko, 1989; Dilthey, 1990; Kent, 1991).

The researcher's role in empirical-analytic inquiry can be best described as that of onlooker. Since researchers operating from an empirical-analytic paradigm adhere to the concept of a mind-reality duality, researchers simply need to look around in the environment to document objective reality. Quantitative researchers are detached to avoid personal bias infringing on the description of reality (Firestone, 1987). Empirical-analytic research presupposes an independent reality and then investigates how we are a part of that reality and how we can know that reality (Firestone, 1987; Smith 1983a, 1983b; Smith and Heshusius, 1986). Subsequently, the researcher is a detached observer, looking at reality and attempting to understand its complexities and relationship to those doing the observation. The researcher may use a telescope, microscope, survey, or assessment instrument when viewing a selected piece of the world; such use allows the researcher to remain detached, an essential feature of empirical-analytic inquiry. What the researcher sees (i.e., data, coded interviews) are taken *prima facie* as indicators of "reality."

For interpretive inquiry, the researcher becomes an actor in real situations.[9] The researcher must attend to the total situation and integrate information from all directions simultaneously—interviews, observations, and collected cultural artifacts (Denzin, 1971; Herriot and Firestone, 1983; Howe, 1988; Smith, 1984; Taylor, 1987). The relevant world is the field surrounding the individual actor/researcher (Denzin, 1971; Herriot and Firestone, 1983; Howe, 1988; Smith, 1984). Researchers engage what is being researched to understand what is taking place. They identify what they know about what they are studying to elucidate the understanding they are bringing to the situation (see e.g., McCracken, 1988; Rabinow and Sullivan, 1987). "It is by drawing on their understanding of how they themselves see and experience the world that they can supplement and interpret the data they generate" (McCracken, 1988, p. 12). The researcher's knowledge can be used as a guide, directing the researcher to possibilities and insights into that which is being researched (McCracken, 1988). For this reason, universal law and generalizability is limited because reality is a constructed concept and a researcher's interpretation is also a constructed part of the reality observed. Reality for those being studied is different for everyone in the researcher's field of vision.

Another difference between the two paradigms is the source of the analytical categories around which data are organized. In a typical piece of empirical-analytic research, the investigator uses a theoretical framework from which to preselect a set of categories that will guide the inquiry (Firestone, 1987; Howe, 1985; Smith, 1983a, 1983b; Smith and Heshusius, 1986). The goal is to isolate and define categories precisely before the study is undertaken, and then to determine the relationships between them (Firestone, 1987; Howe, 1985; McCracken, 1988; Smith, 1983a, 1983b; Smith and Heshusius, 1986). Hypotheses are phrased in terms of these categories, and only those data

pertaining to them are collected (Howe, 1985; McCracken, 1988). The life of a college or university microenvironment (i.e., academic department, student affairs office) is viewed through the lens of a limited number of categories. For example, when investigating the supervisory style of student affairs middle managers, an institutional researcher could apply categories of human development to see if these managers engage in situational supervision. At the extreme, some might argue that the reality being viewed is being actively structured by the categories employed by the researchers to investigate the phenomenon of interest.

Empirical-analytic researchers may derive their a priori categories from personal beliefs or experience, from theoretical formulation, or from their own or others' interpretive research (Heyl, 1975; McCracken, 1988). In the case of interpretive inquiry, there are, generally, no intentionally prescribed categories to constrain the researcher (Denzin, 1971; Eisner, 1981; Howe, 1988; Shulman, 1981; Smith, 1983a, 1983b). Instead, the interpretive researcher attempts to identify emergent themes within an understanding of the respondent's viewpoint of the context (Denzin, 1971; Eisner, 1981; Shulman, 1981; Smith, 1983). Features are noticed and identified through an interpretive, iterative process whereby data and categories emerge simultaneously with successive experience (McCracken, 1988). The process represents an experiential exploration and is particularly suited to early inquiry into new research territory (Denzin, 1971; Firestone, 1987; Smith and Heshusius, 1986). Interpretive inquiry is useful for generating tentative categories grounded in the concrete circumstance of a particular situation. Such emergent categories may subsequently be used as the a priori categories guiding the more deductive, hypothesis-testing empirical-analytic approach.

A caveat must be noted to the process just described. Some may argue that the idea of viewing a situation or phenomenon for "emergent" themes is unattainable. Phenomenologists and hermeneuticists might disagree with the description just provided. For them, a situation or occurrence cannot be comprehended without one's own knowledge about the situation. Everyone has some idea of the phenomenon at which they are looking and these ideas shape what is being seen. In other words, the "emergent" themes that are being observed may be seen because of the particular knowledge or ideas possessed by the researcher before the start of the research. Phenomenologists believe that the researcher's preknowledge can be identified and bracketed out when viewing a phenomenon (McCracken, 1988). In contrast, a hermeneuticist would disagree and argue that one can never remove one's own preknowledge from the investigation (Kvale, 1983; Packer and Addison, 1989). One cannot understand the situation without preknowledge, because preknowledge assists in understanding what is being seen.

A further difference is the aim of inquiry. The aim of inquiry for the empirical-analytic paradigm is to generalize from the particular to construct a set of theoretical statements that are universally applicable (Donmoyer, 1985; Firestone, 1987; Garrison, 1986; Howe, 1988; McCracken, 1988; Smith, 1983a, 1983b; Smith and Heshusius, 1986). The institutional research done in the empirical-analytic paradigm aims to develop understanding of classes of higher education phenomena, rather than to focus on particular instances in particular settings. Interpretive inquiry, however, is directed toward the unique situation or what Lewin (1951) calls a focus on the whole and the individual's present situation. The aim of interpretive inquiry is to describe in detail a specific situation or phenomenon under study. The situationally relevant products of qualitative inquiry serve both practical and theoretical purposes (Jacob, 1988; McCracken, 1988). They can provide guides for action in the immediate situation and ideas for developing hypotheses to guide quantitative inquiry (Miles and Huberman, 1984).[10]

Epistemological Differences

The different paradigms are also associated with different types of knowledge. The aim of situation relevancy pursued in interpretive research is served by knowledge of the particular phenomenon (i.e., college or university, academic department, etc.) under study (McCracken, 1988; Mishler, 1986). The aim of generalizability sought by empirical-analytic research is served by the development of universal knowledge. Interpretive inquiry focuses on the particular: the knowledge that is infused

with human organization and human interest, as represented by the situation under study (Bernstein, 1976, 1983; McCracken, 1988; Mishler, 1986). For the interpretive paradigm, knowledge is knowledge only as understood within the social context in which it takes place (Guba, 1987; Guba and Lincoln, 1981; McCracken, 1988; Mishler, 1986; Smith, 1983a, 1983b; Smith and Heshusius, 1986). The meaning of a particular utterance or interaction can be understood and has meaning only within the specific context in which it occurred (McCracken, 1988; Mishler, 1986). In the extreme, generalizability within the empirical-analytic inquiry implies a dissociation of universal knowledge from human interest (Habermas, 1971). And, at the other extreme, qualitative inquiry implies a preoccupation with the idiosyncratic.[11]

Knowledge for both paradigms is further differentiated by what researchers consider to be data and the level at which they consider issues of meaning. In interpretive inquiry, the aim of understanding a particular situation requires that researchers make direct experiential contact with the phenomena under study (e.g., classroom, academic department, etc.). Understanding the events, activities, and utterances in a specific situation requires a complex appreciation of the overall context in which the phenomenon occurs (McCracken, 1988; Mishler, 1986). Context refers to the complete fabric of local culture, people, resources, purposes, earlier events, and future expectations that constitute time-and-space background of the immediate and particular situation (Denzin, 1971; Guba, 1987; Guba and Lincoln, 1981; McCracken, 1988; Mishler, 1986; Smith, 1984). Facts have no meaning in isolation from the setting (Herriott and Firestone, 1983; McCracken, 1988; Mishler, 1986). Meaning is developed from the point of view of the participant (Firestone, 1987; McCracken, 1988; Mishler, 1986; Smith, 1983a, 1983b). Interpretive research yields knowledge that is connected to the participant's definition or perspective of the situation, what Rogers (1951) has termed the "phenomenal field" of the person. Researchers involve themselves directly in the setting under study in order to appreciate organizational phenomena in light of the context in which they occur and from the participants' point of view.

In empirical-analytic inquiry, the aim of developing universal principles of institutional life necessitates stripping away the idiosyncrasies of the particular phenomenon studied to reveal what is generally applicable to all similar situations (Firestone, 1987; Garrison, 1986; Howe, 1985; Smith, 1983a, 1983b; Smith and Heshusius, 1986; Soltis, 1984). The separation of the universal from the particular is accomplished through several processes. With the aid of sampling, aggregation, and other analytic techniques, the uniqueness of individual academic departments or classrooms is randomized, controlled for, and otherwise "averaged," revealing the core of presumed common truths. The validity of such efforts relies on the comparability of measurements across observations, settings, and times, as well as the completeness with which the observational procedures and situations are documented. Hence, the concern with instrumentation, specification, precision, and adherence to methodological assumptions (i.e., sampling is random, variables are normally distributed).

Empirical-analytic research is designed to be detached from, and independent of, a specific situation under study in a particular organization, academic department, or classroom. The researcher determines the frequencies of, and associations among, events with respect to a set of hypothesized categories and relationships (Firestone, 1987; Garrison, 1986; Howe, 1985; Smith, 1982a, 1983b; Smith and Heshusius, 1986; Soltis, 1984). Meaning is assigned to events on the basis of a priori analytic categories and explicit researcher-free procedures. The spectrum of a phenomenon is filtered through the researcher's preset categories; elements related to the categories are selected, coded as data, and simultaneously given meaning by the categories (Firestone, 1987; Garrison, 1986; Howe, 1985; Smith, 1983a, 1983b; Smith and Heshusius, 1986; Soltis, 1984). As a result, data are considered factual when they have the same meaning across situations and settings. That is, they are context-free.

An Academic Program Review Example

To illustrate how the underlying philosophical grounds of the two paradigms shape an ap-

proach to an institutional research question, a hypothetical example of an academic program review is presented. The example developed focuses on an English department's interest in whether it has successfully implemented its new focus on critical thinking skills and what impact the focus has on various outcomes of interest, including faculty workload. The assumption behind the design is the belief that interactive and collaborative class discussion will facilitate critical thinking skills more so than the normal faculty lecture format. By engaging with their classmates over course-assigned texts, the department hopes that the students will reflect on their own perspectives and interpretations, but also be challenged to better articulate what they believe the texts to be saying. In addition, the department hopes that the increase in skills of articulation will translate into better writing and better academic performance in other writing-based classes as well as better job placement upon graduation.

Table 2 highlights some of the major differences between an empirical-analytic and an interpretive approach to this study. Comparing the aims of the study, one notices that empirical-analytic institutional researchers would look to document the implementation of classroom discussions. They would hypothesize prior to the study what they think would occur, for example, what "types" of interactions they would see. In this case, they would hypothesize that discussions would facilitate the writing skills of those students participating in the study and compare them to a group of students in a control group who were exposed to the traditional lecture format. They would want to describe changes that occur, whether they be the presence or absence of what they expected to occur. In contrast, interpretive researchers' intention would be to explain the content and the processes of the discussions occurring in the classroom with the discussion intervention. They want to document the understanding of the intervention from the participants' viewpoints and explicate any unpredicted and emergent themes.

The aims of the study are structured by the underlying assumptions guiding the paradigms. On the interpretive side, the assumption that reality is constructed directs the researchers to attempt to document how the participants understand and experience the critical thinking focus of the department and how faculty view the impact on their workload. In contrast, the empirical-analytic researchers' assumption that there is a "true" reality Would direct them to determine patterns of relationships among numerous variables (race, gender, previous English classes, as well as course grades, postgraduation job placement and performance) and critical thinking and generate laws explaining how the critical thinking is having an impact (e.g., documenting any increase or decrease in faculty workload hours). The interpretive researchers would resist generating explanations about how students are experiencing the component, arguing that each student and faculty member constructs a different understanding and, therefore, generalized explanations are not possible.

The two paradigms also have different design details. The goal of interpretive research is to get as close to describing the participants' understanding as possible. Observing three classes and interviewing a select few students, faculty, and graduates provides researchers with an opportunity to analyze transcripts in detail. Subsequently, they can compare transcript analysis (1) to see if the intervention was implemented the same way by faculty, (2) to document how the students and faculty understood the intervention, and (3) to document participant understanding of the impact of the critical thinking focus. In contrast, empirical-analytic researchers may observe five classes and code observation by a priori "indicators" of interactive/collaborative learning (i.e., coding certain types of interactions and comparing between classes). By approaching classroom observations in such a manner (i.e., a priori indicators), these qualitative methods (interviews) are being done from within empirical-analytic framework. This highlights the point that just doing an interview does not necessarily indicate one is engaged in qualitative (interpretive paradigm) research. It is the assumptions being made about methodology, ontology, and epistemology that determine whether the interview is truly qualitative. Faculty interviews would be coded the same way as well.

One of the major differences between the two approaches is the implementation of an assessment instrument. Within the empirical-

analytic paradigm, the assessment instrument items would be constructed beforehand from the researchers' ideas of what is critical thinking and what they think should be important outcomes, of the new component. For this example, the assessment would be a pretest and posttest comparing critical thinking skills between the critical thinking group and control group. Following the administration of the tests, the researchers could compare scores between the control and experimental groups. They then would compare the "critical thinking" group with a control group to document any statistically significant differences between the two groups on critical thinking.

As one can see from Table 2, the type of material obtained also differs. As mentioned previously, the interpretive approach would yield transcripts of class discussions and faculty interviews. For the empirical-analytic approach, we would get observation notes coded for indicators of interactive/collaborative leaning in addition to the survey and assessment instrument information.

The form of analysis is one main area of difference between the two approaches. Empirical-analytic researchers would perform statistical analyses comparing the assessment and survey scores of the control group with that of the critical thinking group. The faculty interviews would be taken at face value as a statement of the faculty members' beliefs, attitudes, and perceptions. In addition, a mean for specific codes could be calculated and correlations among other variables of interest could be attained, therefore indicating that the researchers were operating within the empirical-analytic paradigm. In contrast, interpretive researchers would analyze the classroom discussion tapes and attempt to articulate the goals, aims, and feelings of the participants. Interpretive researchers would look to identify preexisting assumptions on the part of the participants and document where they see adherence to the critical thinking component guidelines and where they see instances of interactive/collaborative discussion. An interpretive analysis would attempt to identify how the students and faculty understood the class discussion and the critical thinking emphasis.

For this hypothetical program review, let us say that there were no differences between the classes who engaged in the discussion

Table 2. Hypothetical Academic Program Review

	Empirical-Analytic *(quantitative)*	*Interpretive* *(qualitative)*
Stated aims of the study	To document implementation of critical thinking component. To chronicle (presence or absence of predicted) changes. Summative evaluation (decision making and accountability).	Explanation of participant and processes of discussion. Document understanding of goals from participant perspectives. To articulate unpredicted, emergent themes. Formative evaluation (program improvement).
Design details	Observation of classes for 3 months. Interviews with 6 faculty. Surveys of faculty, students, and graduates. 3 focus group discussions.	Observation, interviews, field notes in 3 classes—selected to contrast for 12 months. Interviews with 6 faculty, 6 students, 6 graduates. 3 focus group discussions.
Material obtained	Observation notes of conversation "gist." Coded for "indicators" of goal attainment (a priori categories). Multiple-choice survey questions (a priori categories). Course grades.	Transcripts of focus group discussions and interviews.
Form of the analysis	Statistical assessment of change over time in coded observations, collapsed over interview and group discussions. Statistical comparison of survey responses. Interviews taken at face value as statement of beliefs, attitudes, perceptions. Documentation of faculty workload hours.	*Articulation of* goals, aims, feelings. Unconscious, preexisting assumptions. Rule enforcement—encouragement, modeling of goal-directed behavior. *Creation of* social contexts that encourage goal-directed behavior, safe atmosphere, sense of purpose. Discussion of how participants "understand" the goals.
Findings	No observed differences among faculty, staff, and students. No significant difference in course grades between critical thinking and control groups. Increase in faculty workload hours.	Goal-directed behavior is enacted differently by different faculty, staff, and students, due to preexisting assumptions about department, and different focus of attention. Change in type of preparation and feedback given to students, thereby altering faculty perceptions of workload.
Norms	"Indicators" of successful goal-directed behavior are treated as factual. Normative findings: decrease in faculty utterances in class discussions, increase in participant-interactions, number of participants speaking, increase in categories such as "substantive," "probing-monitoring," "management," etc. Increase in faculty/student interactions outside of class.	Empirical evidence sought of goal-directed behavior. Normative findings: interpretive authority based on persuasive justification (use of evidence and explanation; questioning), and a sense that text is open to different readings, vs. faculty as authority and guide, with the sense that there is a single text meaning.

experience and those who did not. In the empirical-analytic paradigm, this result would be indicated by no significant difference between the two groups on the assessment instrument. In addition, student grades in other writing-based courses were not significantly different between the two groups and graduates. The interpretive researcher would note that the intervention was implemented differently by different faculty due to preexisting assumptions about the text and the intervention, and the focus within the intervention of each faculty member. The empirical-analytic researcher would conclude that the critical thinking focus was not significantly improving upon what was already being done in the department whereas the qualitative researcher would conclude the focus was not implemented the way it was intended or that it was implemented differently depending on the faculty member involved and student perception of the department.

Finally, the norms adhered to are different between the two paradigms. For empirical-analytic researchers, the indicators for successful impact of the critical thinking focus are treated as factual. The evidence sought are indicators whereas interpretive researchers would look for empirical evidence (observations) of critical reflection and how critical reflection is "understood" by departmental participants. For this example, let us say that there were changes in the discussion dynamics over the course of the observation period. Empirical-analytic researchers would see a decrease in faculty comments over the three months of observations with a concomitant increase in student-student interactions. There is also a corresponding increase in different coding categories. On the other hand, interpretive researchers would notice that those assuming the authority during the discussion are the ones able to build more persuasive argument for their text interpretations. Interpretive researchers would note that the intervention was implemented in slightly different ways with one group assuming responsibility and believing the texts to be open to multiple interpretations. Other groups would believe the text has one meaning and would then rely on the faculty to guide them to that meaning.

Overall, therefore, empirical-analytic researchers may conclude that the critical thinking focus was not successful as indicated by the nonsignificant findings. In addition, they would see the increase in faculty workload and might conclude that the time invested in faculty is not translated into the hoped-for positive outcomes. In contrast, interpretive researchers would indicate that they found that different faculty articulated different understandings of the critical thinking focus, and therefore, implemented it differently. In addition, interpretive researchers would articulate faculty perceptions of how their workload hours changed in terms of quality, that they were not just spending more time, but that time entailed more intense preparation for class to ensure critical engagement during discussion, as well as more attention to the type of feedback given to students to facilitate their critical thinking skills.

Implications for Institutional Research

As in everyday life, institutional researchers need both modes of inquiry, both ways of knowing, and both kinds of knowledge to advance understanding of our specific college or university. Most social scientists and educational researchers have typically advocated the use of one or the other mode of inquiry. In contrast, institutional researchers tend to rely on empirical-analytic research more regularly (Peterson, 1985a, 1985b). The reasons for the preference for empirical-analytic research are elusive. Perhaps it stems from an artifact left over from the social sciences or that the interpretive paradigm has not yet been seen as a viable and useful tool for understanding colleges and universities. This artifact entails the drive for institutional researchers to have their work viewed as based on "true science." Despite the success and usefulness of empirical-analytic research in institutional research, its limitations for the social sciences—and institutional research— have become increasingly apparent and of concern recently (Donmoyer, 1985; Eisner, 1981, 1983; Firestone, 1987; Garrison, 1986; Giarelli and Chambliss, 1988; Howe, 1985, 1988; Hutchinson, 1988; Lincoln and Guba; 1985; Marshall, Lincoln, and Austin, 1991; Peterson and Spencer, 1993; Sherman and Webb, 1988).

Empirical-analytic research systematically overlooks critical features that often render the results epistemologically limited (Guba, 1987; Guba and Lincoln, 1981). Such features include the definition of human action in specific settings, the actor's particular definition of his/her situation, the human interest of the actor, and the historical context of the situation. These issues are exemplified by the program review example described previously, particularly in reference to how the faculty and students understood the critical thinking focus. Each faculty member had different perceptions of the component, perceptions possibly influenced by institutional culture and climate. The empirical-analytic approach neglects this information. These shortcomings can be overcome by qualitative research techniques.

Interpretive research, however, may appear replete with subjectivism and be viewed by university administrators as having questionable precision, rigor, or credibility. It may be easier for an administrator to make a decision based on findings from a large sample rather than trust a description of five case studies or five in-depth interviews. University administrators need to make decisions on what they think is a "typical" or "average" case that holds true across various university environments or in particular departments. One cannot fault an administrator for being uncomfortable basing a policy decision on five or six well-described cases when an empirical-analytic approach (with accompanying large database) might provide a better opportunity to generalize. However, these shortcomings can be overcome by empirical-analytic research.

Institutional research is currently characterized by two broad approaches. One is based on the assumptions that there exists a true reality, whereas the other is based on the assumption that there is no true reality but a reality that is constructed by shared understandings of participants. Both are methodologically precise. One utilizes techniques that produce results generalizable across contexts, but neglects the reality of institutions; and the other provides the researcher with in-depth knowledge that often is not generalizable. Although educational researchers and social scientists have debated the merits of combining the approaches, for institutional researchers, using both approaches can only strengthen the rigor

from which they approach their assigned tasks. However, as we have seen, the choice embodies not a simple decision between methodologies, but an understanding of the philosophical assumptions concerning reality, the role of the researcher, what is knowledge, and what are data. By using both approaches, institutional researchers can strengthen the results of their endeavors. Institutional researchers need to identify and refer to exemplars of good research—research that is both methodologically precise and grounded in understanding of the philosophical assumptions undergirding both approaches.

Empirical-Analytic and Interpretive Research Used Together

Institutional research studies require that both approaches be simultaneously pursued, either by different researchers or by a single researcher. Of course, it must be acknowledged that some questions are more amenable to being investigated by one approach, but using both enhances institutional researchers' ability to understand "what is going on." Each mode offers distinctive advantages, suggesting circumstances (type of problem, state of knowledge, unit of analysis, researchers' role and purpose) in which one may be more appropriate. Qualitative research is more useful for exploring institutional phenomena, articulating participants' understandings and perceptions, and generating tentative concepts and theories that directly pertain to particular environments (e.g., academic departments, specific residence halls). By yielding in-depth knowledge of particular situations, it also more directly serves practitioners' and administrators' needs. The policies and/or decisions based on this type of interpretive information may be more directly suited to the specifics of the milieu from which it was derived. Quantitative research is suited to theory testing and developing universal statements. It also provides a "general" picture of an institutional situation or academic department climate.

The choice of approach will depend on a number of factors. First, the choice will depend on the institutional researcher's personal training, cognitive style, and preference. Second, the choice will no doubt depend on those being researched. For example, some individuals may be particularly uncomfortable with the idea of being interviewed and others may not like being filmed so that their interactions with students can be analyzed. Third, the choice could also depend on the intended audience for the research. Some audiences may want a concise summary of findings more easily produced by empirical-analytic inquiry than in-depth articulations of subjects' realities. Fourth, the choice may depend on time and money—issues often on the minds of institutional researchers. Often, people assume that qualitative research involves a larger investment of time. In reality, the time needs for both quantitative and qualitative research may be close to equal, just distributed differently. For quantitative research, much of the time is spent developing surveys, distributing them, compiling the data, analyzing the data, and presenting the results. Interpretation of the results is a relatively small portion of the overall time spent on a quantitative study. On the other hand, the majority of time in qualitative research is spent on interpretation, analyzing pages of transcripts, viewing videotapes over and over, while the time spent on the collection of data is a relatively small portion of the overall time commitment. Finally, one cannot ignore the history of the institutional research office, what is the preferred research approach, and what those using the office prefer in terms of research. One cannot suddenly switch from quantitative to qualitative methods without checking the political ramifications of doing so.

In contrasting the two research approaches, the attempt has been to discuss the limitations associated with different ways of knowing. In light of these limitations, to continue the exclusive use of one approach that has characterized institutional research will produce limited results—that is, results that are methodologically rigorous but at times inappropriate. Institutional researchers' abilities to grasp the breadth, depth, and richness of college and university life are hampered by allegiance to a single mode of inquiry. Institutional researcher efforts to develop comprehensive pictures of college and university phenomena are handicapped when only one (either quantitative or qualitative) approach is advocated and practiced. We can survey regarding the benefits of a new departmental focus and find that the new approach is not increasing student

performance on particular skills. We could find out that there is no improvement, but we will not know exactly why there is no improvement. A survey could point an institutional researcher to the problem, and in-depth interviews with some students could provide the information necessary to begin to explain the "no improvement" finding.

Institutional researchers can alternate between the two approaches. Peterson (1985a) advocates alternating between quantitative and qualitative research, using findings generated from one approach to generate research questions for the other. In the previous example, there was no significant improvement in skills following a new departmental focus. Using this information, an institutional researcher could interview students to see how they experienced the new focus. Through these interviews a researcher could identify common themes (e.g., students feel positive about the focus; however, it is not being implemented consistently) that could be used to generate questionnaire items for additional surveys. By alternating between the two modes, an institutional researcher could get a more accurate picture of the new departmental focus that may not have been possible using only one approach.

Conclusion

A major reason why research methodology in institutional research is such an exciting area is that institutional research is not itself a discipline. Indeed, it is hard to describe institutional research. However, it is a field containing phenomena, events, institutions, problems, persons, and processes, which themselves constitute the raw material for inquiries of many kinds. Many of these inquiries provide the foundation from which to develop policies and institutional interventions.

Due to the complexity of institutional research, the choice of research approach to a question should not be taken lightly. Each approach to an institutional research problem or question brings its own unique perspective. Each sheds its own distinctive light on the situations and problems institutional researchers seek to understand (Peterson and Spencer, 1993). The issue is not choosing a qualitative or nonqualitative approach, but it is deciding how an institutional researcher approaches the world. Choosing an approach is not a decision between methods; each choice is replete with underlying assumptions about reality. Research methods are not merely different ways of achieving the same end. They carry with them different ways of asking questions and often different commitments to educational and social ideologies. The attempt here has been to clarify the distinction between the two approaches so that the two approaches are viewed as more than simply alternative methods.

As institutional researchers employ their crafts, they make a multitude of decisions concerning research methods. These decisions have a direct impact on how they make meaning and how reality is structured and understood by institutional researchers and their constituencies. In some ways, the choice of quantitative and qualitative approaches creates the reality we are attempting to discover. By making a choice between quantitative or qualitative inquiry, "to a significant extent, we choose our world view" (Allender, 1986, p. 188). For institutional researchers, it is not just a choice between "doing interviews" or "conducting a survey"; it is a choice between assumptions about the world.

Notes

1. Definitions of some terms are in order here. *Commensurability* refers to the ability to compare philosophical underpinnings without a neutral frame of reference. *Epistemology* is the investigation or study of the origin, structure, methods, and validity of knowledge (Runes, 1983). *Ontology* is a theory as to what exists (Urmson and Ree, 1989) or the assumptions about existence underlying any conceptual scheme, theory, or system of ideas (Flew, 1984). *Phenomenology* is the study of how the world is experienced from the actor's/subject's own frame of reference (Patton, 1980). *Hermeneutics* is the art and science of interpreting the meaning of texts which stresses how prior understandings and prejudices shape the interpretive process (Runes, 1983). *Dialectic* refers to a process through which what is known emerges within an interaction between the knower and what is to be known.
2. Please see Guba and Lincoln (1988) for an in depth treatment of the distinction between method and methodology.
3. Moss (1990) provides a brief and useful discussion about the distinction among the terms *incompatible, incommensurable,* and *incompara-*

ble. The reader is directed to Moss's comments as well as to Bernstein's (1983) in-depth discussion concerning the definitions of these terms.
4. With the advent and development of critical theory and postmodernism, some (Lather, 1991a, 1991b) would argue that we are currently immersed in a crisis over what it means to do research. The reader is directed to Darder (1991), Giroux (1988), and Gore (1993) for descriptions of critical theory, and Bauman (1992), Giroux (1991), and Rosenau (1992) for descriptions of postmodernism.
5. For this paper, the distinction between the quantitative and qualitative paradigms is being used as a heuristic device. One must note, however, that this distinction may oversimplify the various philosophical differences even within the two paradigms.
6. To distinguish the different interpretive approaches is beyond the purview of this paper. The reader is directed to Denzin and Lincoln's (1994) *Handbook of Qualitative Research* and Lancy (1993) for in-depth explorations of the distinctions.
7. Firestone (1987) argues that the two paradigms can also be distinguished by differing rhetoric. In essence quantitative and qualitative methods "lend themselves to different kinds of rhetoric" (p. 16). Subsequently, each method type uses different presentation techniques and means of persuasion to express assumptions about methodology, ontology, and epistemology and to convince readers about conclusions.
8. For the sake of this paper, methodology, ontology, and epistemology have been separated for convenience and clarity. Generally, however, these concepts are so intertwined that discussing one almost necessitates discussing one or both of the other. For example, discussing what each paradigm believes to be "reality" (ontology) almost dictates what can be known (epistemology) about that reality and how that reality can be measured (methodology).
9. The degree of engagement varies depending on the qualitative approach being used. For example, nonparticipant observers are not actively involved in the situation whereas participant observers attempt to assume a role to understand the reality as constructed and comprehended by those in the situation.
10. Smith and Heshusius (1986) raise a common concern among many educational researchers that qualitative research should not be thought of as just a procedural variation of quantitative research. The reader should note this caveat when entertaining the notion of using qualitative data collection and analysis as an avenue from which to generate categories for quantitative research.

11. It would be misleading to imply that qualitative research is not concerned with generalizability. Firestone (1993) highlights the various arguments for, and the types of generalizability within, qualitative research, and Kirk and Miller (1986) discuss reliability and validity in qualitative research.

References

Allender, J. S. (1986). Educational research: A personal and social process. *Review of Educational Research* 56(2): 173–193.

Banks, J. A. (1988). *Multiethnic Education*, 2nd ed. Boston: Allyn & Bacon.

Bauman, Z. (1992). *Intimations of Postmodernity.* New York: Routledge.

Bernstein, R. J. (1976). *The Restructuring of Social and Political Theory.* Philadelphia: The University of Pennsylvania Press.

Bernstein, R. J. (1983). *Beyond Objectivism and Relativism. Science, Hermeneutics, and Praxis.* Philadelphia: The University of Pennsylvania Press.

Bohannon, T. R. (1988). Applying regression analysis to problems in institutional research. In B. D. Yancey (ed.), *Applying Statistics in Institutional Research*, 43–60. San Francisco: Jossey-Bass, Publishers.

Bunda, M. A. (1991). Capturing the richness of student outcomes with qualitative techniques. In D. M. Fetterman (ed.), *Using Qualitative Methods in Institutional Research*, pp. 35–47. San Francisco: Jossey-Bass, Publishers.

Cziko, G. A. (1989). Unpredictability and indeterminism in human behavior: Arguments and implications for educational research. *Educational Researcher* 18(3): 17–25.

Darder, A. (1991). *Culture and Power in the Classroom. A Critical Foundation for Bicultural Education.* New York: Bergin & Garvey.

Denzin, N. K. (1971). The logic of naturalistic inquiry. *Social Forces* 50: 166–182.

Denzin, N. K., and Y. S. Lincoln (1994) (eds.). *Handbook of Qualitative Research.* Thousand Oaks, CA: Sage Publications, Inc.

Dewey, J. (1933). *How We Think.* Massachusetts: D. C. Heath.

Dilthey, W. (1990). The rise of hermeneutics. In G. L. Ormiston and A. D. Schrift (eds.), *The Hermeneutic Tradition. From Ast to Ricoeur* (pp. 101–114). Albany: State University of New York Press.

Donmoyer, R. (1985). The rescue from relativism: Two failed attempts and an alternative strategy. *Educational Researcher* 14(10): 13–20.

Eisner, E. W. (1981). On the differences between scientific and artistic approaches to qualitative research. *Educational Researcher* 10(4): 5–9.

Eisner, E. W. (1983). Anastasia might still be alive, but the monarchy is dead. *Educational Researcher* 12(5): 13–14, 23–24.

Fetterman, D. M. (1991). Qualitative resource landmarks. In D. M. Fetterman (ed.), *Using Qualitative Methods in Institutional Research*, pp. 81–84. San Francisco: Jossey-Bass, Publishers.

Fincher, C. (1985). The art and science of institutional research. In M. W. Peterson and M. Corcoran (eds.), *Institutional Research in Transition*, pp. 17–37. New Directions for Institutional Research. San Francisco: Jossey-Bass Inc., Publishers.

Firestone, W. A. (1987). Meaning in method: The rhetoric of quantitative and qualitative research. *Educational Researcher* 16(7): 16–21.

Firestone, W. A. (1993). Alternative arguments for generalizing from data as applied to qualitative research. *Educational Researcher* 22(4): 16–23.

Flew, A. (1984). *A Dictionary of Philosophy.* London: The Macmillan Press Ltd.

Garrison, J. W. (1986). Some principles of postpositivistic philosophy of science. *Educational Researcher* 15(9): 12–18.

Geertz, C. (1973). *The interpretation of Cultures.* New York: Basic Books.

Giarelli, J. M., and Chambliss, J. J. (1988). Philosophy of education as qualitative inquiry. In R. R. Sherman and R. B. Webb (eds.), *Qualitative Research in Education: Focus and Methods*, pp. 30–43. New York: The Falmer Press.

Giroux, H. A. (1988). *Schooling and the Struggle for Public Life. Critical Pedagogy in the Modern Age.* Minneapolis, MN: University of Minnesota Press.

Giroux, H. A. (1991) (ed.). *Postmodernism, Feminism, and Cultural Politics.* Albany, NY: State University of New York Press.

Gordon, E. W., F. Miller, and D. Rollock (1990). Coping with communicentric bias in knowledge production in the social sciences. *Educational Researcher* 19(3): 14–19.

Gore, J. M. (1993). *The Struggle for Pedagogies. Critical and Feminist Discourses as Regimes of Truth.* New York: Routledge.

Guba, E. (1987). What have we learned about naturalistic evaluation? *Evaluation Practice* 8(1): 23–43.

Guba, E., and Y. Lincoln (1981). *Effective Evaluation.* San Francisco: Jossey-Bass.

Guba, E. G., and Y. S. Lincoln (1988). Do inquiry paradigms imply inquiry methodologies? In D. M. Fetterman (ed.), *Qualitative Approaches to Evaluation in Education: The Silent Scientific Revolution*, pp. 89–115. New York: Praeger Publishers.

Gubrium, J. (1988). *Analyzing Field Reality.* Newbury Park, CA: Sage.

Habermas, J. (1971). *Knowledge and Human Interest.* Boston, MA: Beacon.

Habermas, J. (1988). *On the Logic of the Social Sciences* (S. W. Nicholsen and J. A. Stark, trans.). Cambridge, MA: The MIT Press.

Hall, E. T. (1976). *Beyond Culture.* New York: Double-day.

Herriott, R. E., and W. A. Firestone (1983). Multisite qualitative policy research: Optimizing description and generalizability. *Educational Researcher* 12(2): 14–19.

Heyl, J. D. (1975). Paradigms in social science. *Society* 12(5): 61–67.

Hinkle, D. E., G. W. McLaughlin, and J. T. Austin (1988). Using log-linear models in higher education research. In B. D. Yancey (ed.), *Applying statistics in Institutional Research,* pp. 23–42. San Francisco: Jossey-Bass, Publishers.

Howe, K. R. (1985). Two dogmas of educational research. *Educational Researcher* 14(8): 10–18.

Howe, K. R. (1988). Against the quantitative-qualitative incompatibility thesis or dogmas die hard. *Educational Researcher* 17(8): 10–16.

Hutchinson, S. A. (1988). Educational and grounded theory. In R. R. Sherman and R. B. Webb (eds.), *Qualitative Research in Education: Focus and Methods,* pp. 123–140. New York: The Falmer Press.

Jacob, E. (1988). Clarifying qualitative research: A focus on traditions. *Educational Researcher* (17(1): 16–24.

James, W. (1918). *The Principles of Psychology.* New York: Dover.

Jennings, L. W., and D. M. Young (1988). Forecasting methods for institutional research. In B. D. Yancey (ed.), *Applying Statistics in Institutional Research,* pp. 77–96. San Francisco: Jossey-Bass, Publishers.

Kaplan, A. (1964). *The Conduct of Inquiry.* San Francisco: Chandler.

Kent, T. (1991). On the very idea of a discourse community. *College Composition and Communication* 42(4): 425–445.

Kirk, J., and M. L. Miller (1986). *Reliability and Validity in Qualitative Research.* Beverly Hills, CA: Sage Publications, Inc.

Kuhn, T. S. (1962). *The structure of Scientific Revolutions.* Philadelphia: The University of Pennsylvania Press.

Kuhn, T. S. (1970). *The Structure of Scientific Revolutions,* 2nd ed. Chicago: University of Chicago Press.

Kuhn, T. S. (1974). Second thoughts on paradigms. Reprinted in *The Essential Tension: Selected Studies in Scientific Tradition and Change.* Chicago: University of Chicago Press.

Kvale, S. (1983). The qualitative research interview: A phenomenological and a hermeneutical mode of understanding. *Journal of Phenomenological Psychology* 14(2): 171–196.

Lancy, D. (1993). *Qualitative Research in Education.* New York: Longman.

Lather, P. (1991a). *Getting Smart: Feminist Research and Pedagogy Within the Postmodern.* New York: Routledge.

Lather, P. (1991b). Deconstructing/deconstructive inquiry: The politics of knowing and being known. *Educational Theory* 41(2): 153–173.

Lewin, K. (1951). *Field Theory in Social Science.* New York: Harper.

Lincoln, Y. S., and E. G. Guba (1985). *Naturalistic Inquiry.* Beverly Hills: Sage Publications.

Marshall, C., Y. S. Lincoln, and A. E. Austin (1991). Integrating a qualitative and quantitative assessment of the quality of academic life: Political and logistical issues. In D. M. Fetterman (ed.), *Using Qualitative Methods in Institutional Research,* pp. 65–80. San Francisco: Jossey-Bass, Publishers.

McCracken, G. (1988). *The Long Interview.* Newbury Park, CA: Sage Publications, Inc.

Merton, R. (1972). Insiders and outsiders: A chapter in the sociology of knowledge. In *Varieties of Political Expression in Sociology.* Chicago: The University of Chicago Press.

Miles, M. B., and A. M. Huberman (1984). Drawing valid meaning from qualitative data: Toward a shared craft. *Educational Researcher* 13(5): 20–30.

Mishler, E. G. (1986). *Research Interviewing. Context and Narrative.* Cambridge, MA: Harvard University. Press.

Moss, P. A. (1990, April). *Multiple Triangulation in Impact Assessment: Setting the Context.* Remarks prepared for oral presentation in P. LeMahieu (Chair), Multiple triangulation in impact assessment: The Pittsburgh discussion project experience. Symposium conducted at the annual meeting of the American Research Association, Boston, Massachusetts.

Packer, M. J., and R. B. Addison (1989). Introduction. In M. J. Packer and R. B. Addison (eds.), *Entering the Circle: Hermeneutic Investigation in Psychology,* pp. 13–36. Albany: State University of New York Press.

Patton, M. Q. (1980). *Qualitative Evaluation Methods.* Beverly Hills, CA: Sage Publications, Inc.

Peterson, M. W. (1985a). Emerging developments in postsecondary organization theory and research: Fragmentation or integration. *Educational Researcher* 14(3): 5–12.

Peterson, M. W. (1985b). Institutional research: An evolutionary perspective. In M. W. Peterson and M. Corcoran (eds.), *Institutional Research in Transition,* pp. 5–15. *New Directions for Institutional Research,* no. 46. San Francisco: Jossey-Bass Inc., Publishers.

Peterson, M. W., and M. G. Spencer (1993). Qualitative and quantitative approaches to academic culture: Do they tell us the same thing? *Higher Education: Handbook of Theory and Research,* Vol. IX, pp. 344, 388. New York: Agathon Press.

Phillips, D. C. (1983). After the wake: Postpositivistic educational thought. *Educational Researcher* 12(5); 4–12.

Pike, K. L. (1967). *Language in Relation to a Unified Theory of the Structure of Human Behavior.* The Hague: Mouton.

Rabinow, P., and W. M. Sullivan (1987). The interpretive turn: A second look. In P. Rabinow and W. M. Sullivan (eds.), *Interpretive Social Science. A Second Look,* pp. 1–30. Berkeley, CA: University of California Press.

Rogers, C. R. (1951). *Client-Centered Therapy.* Boston: Houghton.

Rosenau, P. M. (1992). *Post-Modernism and the Social Sciences: Insights, Inroads, and Intrusions.* Princeton, NJ: Princeton University Press.

Rossman, G. B., and B. L. Wilson (1985). Numbers and words. Combining quantitative and qualitative methods in a single large-scale evaluation study. *Evaluation Review* 9(5): 627–643.

Runes, D. D. (1983). *Dictionary of Philosophy.* New York: Philosophical Library, Inc.

Schultz, A. (1967). *The Phenomenology of the Social World.* Evanston, IL: Northwestern University Press.

Sherman, R. R., and R. B. Webb (1989). Qualitative research in education: A focus. In R. R. Sherman and R. B. Webb (eds.), *Qualitative Research in Education: Focus and Methods,* pp. 2–21. New York: The Falmer Press.

Shulman, L. S. (1981). Disciplines of inquiry in education: An overview. *Educational Researcher* 10(6): 5–12, 23.

Smith, J. K. (1983a). Quantitative versus qualitative research: An attempt to clarify the issue. *Educational Researcher* 12(3): 6–13.

Smith, J. K. (1983b). Quantitative versus interpretive: The problem of conducting social inquiry. In E. House (ed.), *Philosophy of Evaluation,* pp. 27–52. San Francisco: Jossey-Bass Publishers.

Smith, J. K. (1984). The problem of criteria for judging interpretive inquiry. *Educational Evaluation and Policy Analysis* 6(4): 379–391.

Smith, J. K., and L. Heshusius (1986). Closing down the conversation: The end of the quantitative-qualitative debate among educational inquirers. *Educational Researcher* 15(1): 4–12.

Soltis, J. F. (1984). On the nature of educational research. *Educational Researcher* 13(10): 5–10.

Stanfield, J. H. (1985). The ethnocentric basis of social science knowledge production. In E. W. Gorden (ed.), *Review of Research in Education,* vol. 12, pp. 387–415. Washington, DC: American Educational Research Association.

Taylor, C. (1987). Interpretation and the science of man. In P. Rabinow and W. M. Sullivan (eds.), *Interpretive Social Science. A Second Look,* pp. 33–81. Berkeley, CA: University of California Press.

Tierney, W. G. (1991). Utilizing ethnographic interviews to enhance academic decision making. In D. M. Fetterman (ed.), *Using Qualitative Methods in Institutional Research,* pp. 7–22. San Francisco: Jossey-Bass, Publishers.

Urmson, J. O., and J. Ree (1989) (eds.). *The Concise Encyclopedia of Western Philosophy and Philosophies.* Boston: Unwin Hyman.

Yancey, B. D. (1988a). Exploratory data analysis methods for institutional researchers. In B. D. Yancey (ed.), *Applying Statistics in Institutional Research,* pp. 97–110. San Francisco: Jossey-Bass, Publishers.

Yancey, B. D. (1988b). Institutional research and the classical experimental paradigm. In B. D. Yancey (ed.), *Applying Statistics in Institutional Research,* pp. 5–10. San Francisco: Jossey-Bass, Publishers.

The Role of Institutional Research in Higher Education: Enabling Researchers to Meet New Challenges

Anne Marie Delaney

Based on a survey of 243 New England colleges and universities, this article is designed to contribute to an understanding of the current and projected roles of institutional research and to discuss the implications of these roles for the education and training of future institutional researchers. Results from this study reveal the strongest relationships between the institution's size and the scope of the institutional research function, the reporting relationship, and the size and the qualifications of the institutional research staff. Multivariate analysis identifies the size of the institutional staff and the qualifications of the institutional director as significant predictors of involvement in planning and policy studies. These data indicate the need to enhance the presence, qualifications, and level of activity of institutional researchers in order to enhance the contribution to institutional decision making particularly among small institutions. Recommendations are offered to achieve these goals and prepare the institutional research profession for the challenges confronting higher education now and in the 21st century.

This article is intended to contribute to an understanding of the current roles of institutional research across diverse institutions. In addition, the article discusses the implications of these roles for the education and training of institutional researchers and proposes how the institutional research profession might prepare to meet the challenges confronting higher education now and in the 21st century.

Higher education theorists and practitioners claim that institutional research is essential to effective decision making in colleges and universities. Further, recent developments—including growing competition, rising costs, the need for cost containment, public demand for accountability, federal reporting requirements, and declining enrollment and graduation rates among certain student segments—have expanded the need both for institutional research and for effective collaboration between researchers and administrators. In colleges and universities throughout the country, institutional research is being called upon increasingly to serve critical roles informing decision making, planning, and policy formulation. Although many leaders and decision makers in the higher education community recognize the need for institutional research to guide their planning, some have not yet developed the capacity within their institutions.

The potential contribution and evolving nature of institutional research to college and university planning and policy development have been well documented in the literature. Saupe (1990) identified institutional research as an essential component of sound college and university governance that should occur whenever any planning initiatives, policy issues, or institutional decisions are proposed. In 1985, Peterson observed that institutional research continues to evolve as a consequence of state and federal policy decisions, the changing student clientele, advances in computing and telecommunications, the shifting budgetary climate and the growing internationalization of higher education, the increasing complexity and sophistication of decision making, and the growing number and volume of calls for in-

"The Role of Institutional Research in Higher Education: Enabling Researchers to Meet New Challenges," by Anne Marie Delaney, reprinted from *Research in Higher Education*, Vol. 38, No. 1, 1997. Human Sciences Press, Inc.

creased institutional effectiveness. More recently, Matier, Sidle, and Hurst (1994) advocate expanding the scope of institutional research to encompass the roles of information architect, change agent, and consultant of choice within higher education institutions.

Preparation for these new roles and the continued growth of institutional research as a profession require information about the functioning of institutional research at different colleges and universities, the identification of existing needs for professional training and development, and the creation of structures and plans to meet the emerging needs and fulfill these new roles. Clyburn (1991) reports that the current models of institutional research and the emerging roles and activities of the director of institutional research have received limited investigation; the need is particularly acute with respect to small, private colleges. Volkwein (1990) provides a rationale for documenting the diversity of institutional research across institutions. "The effectiveness and efficiency of the institutional research profession can only be improved by recognizing the wide diversity of structures and tasks that characterize campus practice and by designing the kind of collaborative support that is consistent with this diversity" (p. 26).

Data Source

This article is based on a survey of 243 New England colleges and universities including 80 two-year institutions and 163 four-year colleges and universities. Responses were obtained from 127 of the 243 institutions, yielding an overall response rate of 52%–41% for the two-year institutions and 58% for the four-year colleges and universities.

The sample is comprised of diverse institutions including community colleges, liberal arts colleges, and universities. The majority of responding institutions, 64%, are private and the vast majority, 74%, are four-year colleges and universities. Most of the responding institutions are relatively small colleges and universities. Approximately 60% have enrollments of less than 2,000.

The survey was designed to assess the current level of institutional research at New England colleges and universities; to elicit ideas regarding how the role of institutional research might be expanded to increase the influence on institutional decision making and policy development; and to identify the resources and training required to achieve the maximum potential from institutional research in various higher education institutions.

Results

Configuration of the Institutional Research Function at Responding Institutions

The scope and characteristics of the institutional research function vary substantially at these institutions. Of the 127 responding institutions, 40% report they have an institutional research office; another 45% have a person or other office engaged in institutional research activities, but no office; and the remaining 15% have neither an institutional research office nor an institutional research function. Among the 80 institutions who identified the reporting relationship, the largest number, 27, indicated that the institutional research office or function reports to the president and 16 and 14, respectively, report to the provost/vice chancellor and vice president.

There is also considerable diversity in terms of the levels of positions held by those doing institutional research, their level of experience, and academic background. The title of individuals doing institutional research ranges from vice president to research assistant. Some 53 institutions reported they have an institutional research director and 25 institutions have an associate or analyst doing institutional research. It is interesting to note that in nine institutions, individuals conducting institutional research hold the title of vice president or assistant vice president and another 14 hold the title of dean or assistant dean.

The level of experience for those doing institutional research reflects a substantial range from two or fewer years to 11 or more years of experience. With respect to the academic background of those doing institutional research, most hold a master's degree in the social sciences or in education.

Role of Institutional Research

Typical Institutional Research Projects

In an effort to identify the role of institutional research at various institutions, respondents were asked to describe the typical research projects they conducted. The descriptions of the research projects were then classified into the following eight categories:

Reports: institutional statistics, internal and external administrative reports;

Research, Planning & Policy Analysis: planning and policy analysis studies, forecasting/statistical projections, longitudinal research, and market and survey research;

Financial Studies: cost analysis, budget planning, and financial projections;

Enrollment Management Studies: admission, financial aid, and retention studies;

Student Surveys: student and alumni/ae surveys;

Faculty Studies: faculty evaluations, faculty workload studies, and salary analyses;

Academic Studies: academic program review, academic program evaluation, assessment of placement tests and outcomes assessment; and

Other Projects: space utilization studies, transfer studies, and other miscellaneous projects.

Table 1 displays the frequency and percent of responding institutions engaged in these various activities. Clearly, enrollment management studies are the most frequently reported activity. Approximately two-thirds of the institutions reported they were doing one or more

studies in this area including admission, financial aid, enrollment, and retention studies. Close to 50% report they typically are responsible for institutional reports that involve generating statistics for internal audiences and providing data to external audiences. Slightly more than 25% report involvement in research, planning and policy studies.

As illustrated in Table 1, relatively few institutions ($N = 11$) report they typically conduct financial studies such as cost analysis, budget planning, financial projections, or resource allocations studies. Similarly, only a small number of institutions ($N = 10$) report they typically conduct faculty studies such as faculty evaluations, faculty workload studies, and faculty salary analyses.

Typical Audiences for Institutional Research Projects

Survey responses indicate that institutional researchers conduct studies for diverse audiences both within and outside the institution. Over 50% typically report the results of their studies to various administrative offices within the institution. Some 14% report that the president, vice president, and trustees comprise a typical audience for their studies and another 14% identify deans, chairpersons, and faculty as typical audiences for their reports.

Future Directions for Institutional Research

To provide a perspective on the future of institutional research at New England's colleges

Table 1. Typical Institutional Research Projects

Type of Institutional Research Projects	Number	Percent[a]
Enrollment management	85	66.9%
Institutional reports	62	48.8
Research, planning & policy analysis	35	27.6
Academic studies	23	18.1
Student surveys	20	15.7
Financial studies	11	8.7
Faculty studies	10	7.9
Other	59	46.5
		($N = 127$)

[a]The cumulative percentage exceeds 100 since some institutions conduct more than one type of institutional research project.

and universities, survey respondents were asked to identify the kinds of institutional research studies their institution would like to do that they currently are *not* doing and to specify the staff, financial, and computer resources that would be needed in order to do these studies. In addition, respondents were asked to indicate the types of technical training and professional development experiences that would be most helpful in achieving the maximum potential from institutional research at their institution.

Using the previously defined categories, Table 2 displays the types of institutional research studies institutions would like to do. Similar to the report on typical projects currently being done, the largest number of institutions would like to do more enrollment management studies. However, in contrast to the distribution of current projects, a higher proportion of institutions, 38.6%, express interest in doing more academic studies including academic program reviews, academic program evaluations, and outcomes assessment studies. Close to 20% also reported interest in conducting more student surveys.

Seventy-eight respondents reported they would need additional staff to complete the desired institutional research studies. Four respondents projected that an institutional research office would be needed while most respondents recommended increasing the professional research staff to conduct the desired studies. In addition to projecting additional staff, some 30 respondents also indicated that more computer resources would be needed. Their recommendations ranged from upgrading current systems to establishing new computer networks.

Results from Bivariate Analyses: the Relationship of Institutional Characteristics to Institutional Research

Institutional Size and the Institutional Research Function

Bivariate analyses of the relationship between institutional characteristics and the institutional research function revealed the strongest relationship with the institution's size. As shown in Table 3, the scope of the institutional research function, the reporting relationship, the size and the qualifications of the institutional research staff vary significantly in relation to the institution's size. All of the institutions with enrollment of 5,000 or more, compared with only one-fifth of the institutions with enrollments of less than 1,000, had an institutional research office. Reporting relationships also vary in relation to size; over 90% of the larger institutions report at the vice presidential, provost, or presidential level whereas the smaller institutions report at many different levels. As expected, larger institutions had larger institutional research staff and were much more likely to have an institutional research director with a doctorate; 54.5% of the largest institutions, compared with only 7.5% of the smallest institutions, had a research director with a doctorate.

Table 2. Desired Institutional Research Studies

Type of Institutional Research Projects	Number	Percent[a]
Enrollment management	67	52.8%
Academic studies	49	38.6
Student surveys	24	18.9
Planning & policy analysis	19	15.0
Financial studies	11	8.7
Institutional reports	7	5.5
Faculty studies	5	3.9
Other	46	36.2
		(N = 127)

[a]The cumulative percentage exceeds 100 since some institutions desire to conduct more than one type of institutional research study.

Institutional Characteristics and the Role of Institutional Research

Results from bivariate analyses reveal several meaningful relationships between the role of institutional research and selected characteristics of the institution. Larger, four-year and private institutions were more likely to engage in projects involving social science research methodology, such as planning, forecasting, and research on faculty and academic issues. Also, compared with public institutions, private institutions were more likely to engage in advanced research projects and in studies focused on academic issues.

Several statistically significant relationships were also found. The presence of an institutional research director with a doctorate was found to be significantly related to involvement in planning studies ($\chi^2 = 14.83$, $p \leq .001$)

and enrollment management studies ($\chi^2 = 4.61$, $p \leq .05$). Institutions with larger research staff were also more likely to engage in planning, policy analysis, and forecasting ($\chi^2 = 8.41$, $p \leq .05$). As shown in Table 4, chi-square analysis revealed a statistically significant relationship between institutional size and involvement in research, planning, and policy studies ($\chi^2 = 8.12$, $p \leq .05$).

Compared with two-year institutions, four-year institutions also conducted more research, planning, and policy studies ($\chi^2 = 4.35$, $p \leq .05$).

Institutional Characteristics and Perspective on Institutional Research Topics

Respondents were asked to estimate the importance of various institutional research topics in

Table 3. Variations in the Institutional Research Offices by Institutional Size

A. Institutional Research Presence

Institution Size	Institutional Research Office	Institutional Research Function	No Office or Function	Total
5,000 or More	100.0%	—	—	100% (N = 11)
2,000–4,999	53.3	43.4	3.3	100% (N = 30)
1,000–1,999	41.7	41.7	16.6	100% (N = 24)
Less than 1,000	20.8	56.6	22.6	100% (N = 53)
$\chi^2 = 29.22, p \leq .001$				Total N = 118

B. Reporting Relationship

Institution Size	Provost/Vice President	Vice Chancellor	President	Dean	Other Offices	Total
5,000 or More	9.1%	72.7%	9.1%	9.1%	—	100% (N = 11)
2,000–4,999	28.0	24.0	8.0	16.0	24.0	100% (N = 25)
1,000–1,999	25.0	16.7	33.3	8.3	16.7	100% (N = 12)
Less than 1,000	48.1	—	22.3	11.1	18.5	100% (N = 27)
$\chi^2 = 30.87, p \leq .01$						Total N = 75

C. Size of Full-Time Institutional Research Staff

Institution Size	Two or more	One	None	Total
5,000 or More	81.8%	18.2%	—	100% (N = 11)
2,000–4,999	13.0	78.3	8.7	100% (N = 23)
1,000–1,999	22.2	77.8	—	100% (N = 9)
Less than 1,000	—	54.5	45.5	100% (N = 11)
$\chi^2 = 34.41, p \leq .001$				Total N = 54

D. Presence of Institutional Research Director with a Doctorate

Institution Size	A Director with Doctorate	No Director with Doctorate	Total
5,000 or More	54.5%	45.5%	100% (N = 11)
2,000–4,999	23.3	76.7	100% (N = 30)
1,000–1,999	16.7	83.3	100% (N = 24)
Less than 1,000	7.5	92.5	100% (N = 53)
$\chi^2 = 14.61, p \leq .01$			Total N = 118

Table 4. Variation in the Role of Institutional Research by Institutional Characteristics

Institution Size	A. *Variation by Institutional Size*		
	Research & Planning	Nonresearch & Planning	Total
5,000 or More	54.5%	45.5%	100% (*N* = 11)
2,000–4,999	26.7	73.3	100% (*N* = 30)
1,000–1,999	25.0	75.0	100% (*N* = 24)
Less than 1,000	15.1	84.9	100% (*N* = 53)
$\chi^2 = 8.12, p \leq .05$			Total N = 118

Institution Type	B. *Variation by Institutional Type*		
	Research & Planning	Nonresearch & Planning	Total
4 Year	26.6%	73.4%	100% (*N* = 94)
2 Year	9.1	90.9	100% (*N* = 33)
$\chi^2 = 4.35, p \leq .05$			Total N = 127

relation to the needs of their institution. The list of topics included the Role of Institutional Research in Higher Education, Organizing an Institutional Research Office, Building Institutional Research Databases, Admission Research Issues, Financial Aid Research Issues, Retention Studies, Using Institutional Research to Enhance Academic Life, Using Institutional Research to Improve Student Life, Outcomes Assessment, Use of Quantitative Methods in Institutional Research, Use of Qualitative Methods in Institutional Research, and the Use of Survey Research in Institutional Research.

Chi-square analyses revealed statistically significant relationships between selected institutional characteristics and the perceived importance of these various institutional research topics. Respondents at four-year institutions attributed more importance to conducting financial aid studies ($\chi^2 = 4.53$, $p \leq .05$); approximately 70% of those at four-year colleges and universities, compared with only 48% at two-year colleges, perceived financial aid to be an important or very important topic. Conversely, those at two-year institutions ascribed more importance to survey research ($\chi^2 = 4.52$, $p \leq .05$); approximately three-quarters of the respondents at two-year colleges, compared with about one-half of those at four-year colleges, perceived survey research to be an important or very important topic. Variations were also found between public and private institutions put more emphasis on financial aid studies ($\chi^2 = 5.34$, $p \leq .05$) while public and private institutions placed more importance on outcomes assessment ($\chi^2 = 4.81$, $p \leq .05$).

Results from Multivariate Analysis: Predicting Institutional Research Involvement in Planning and Policy Development

Discriminant analysis results, presented in Table 5, identified both research staff and institutional characteristics as predictors of the types of institutional research conducted in different colleges and universities. For example, four variables were found to predict successfully whether or not institutional research staff engaged in research, planning, and policy analysis studies. The structure coefficients were .75 for institutional research staff size; .61 for institutional research office or function; .49 for institutional research staff qualifications; and .18 for the type of institution—public or private. The canonical correlation of .52 indicates that the function explains 27% of the variance in the nature of institutional research projects.

Discussion

Findings from this research provide a perspective on the role of institutional research at various colleges and universities. The information may be most revealing for smaller institutions since 60% of the responding institutions have enrollments of less than 2,000. The data identify various aspects of the institutional research function including the scope of the institutional research presence in the institution; the qualifications of those doing institutional research;

Table 5. Predicting Institutional Research Involvement in Planning and Policy Development

Predictors	Structure Coefficients	Percent Correctly Classified
Institutional Research Staff Size	.75	71.7%
Institutional Research Office or Function	.61	
Institutional Research Staff Qualifications	.49	
Type of Institution (Private versus Public)	.18	
Canonical Correlation	.52	$\chi^2 = 15.62$, $df = 4$, $p \le .01$

the nature of their professional activity; and the audiences for whom institutional researchers conduct their studies.

Institutional Research Presence. Among all the responding institutions, only 40% have an institutional research office and only 45% report at the vice presidential or higher level of the organization. Similar to Volkwein's (1990) finding, the existence of an institutional research office varies substantially by the size of the institution; 100% of the larger institutions compared with only 21% of the smaller institutions have an institutional research office.

Qualifications. With regard to academic qualifications, the largest proportion of those doing institutional research have a master's degree. Only 23 of the 127 responding institutions have an institutional research director with a doctorate. The qualifications of those doing institutional research are critical if institutional research is going to have a significant impact on decision making. Results from this research reveal statistically significant relationships between the qualifications of institutional research staff and involvement in planning and policy studies; doctoral-level institutional research directors were significantly more likely to engage in planning and policy development studies. In reporting the results from a previous study of institutional research structures and functions, Volkwein (1990) also commented on the positive influence of academic qualifications on the nature of the work performed by institutional researchers.

Nature of Institutional Research Activity. Institutional researchers responding to this survey report that they are engaged extensively in doing institutional reports and conducting various enrollment management studies. However, only a minority report they are conducting planning and policy studies, academic studies, and financial studies. Identification of

the audiences indicates that these institutional research reports and studies are generally not conducted for the highest-level decision makers within the institutions. While a majority report they conduct studies for various administrative offices, only a small minority identify the president, vice president, or board of trustees as an audience for their research. Reflecting the limited involvement in academic studies, very few identify deans, chairpersons, and faculty as audiences for their research.

The nature of the work conducted by institutional researchers also determines the extent to which the research may impact decision making. Results from this study indicate that institutional researchers, particularly at small colleges, should strengthen their capacity and develop political support for conducting more research on academic policies and the financial implications of these policies. Decision making at colleges and universities frequently involves coping with tensions between academic issues and financial concerns. By addressing such tensions in the study design, institutional researchers may offer a unique and critical contribution to planning and policy development.

Enhancing the Role of Institutional Research. These data indicate the need to enhance the presence, qualifications, and level of activity of those doing institutional research, particularly at small colleges and universities. While support from administrators is essential, institutional researchers might also exercise initiative to enhance the institutional research presence in institutional decision-making contexts. Possible approaches include establishing formal and informal relationships with executive-level administrators; continually seeking out information regarding decision makers' information needs; taking the initiative in informing decision makers regarding the relevance of data and studies to inform their decisions; and developing political support for establishing executive-level audiences for institutional research studies.

Future Plans. Vision, competence, and commitment are required if institutional research is to evolve to a new role in the 21st century. Institutional researchers may first need to become more aware of the importance of their contribution to the university decision-making process in critical policy areas. When respondents in this study were asked to identify the kinds of institutional research studies their institutions would like to do that they are currently not doing, a minority expressed an interest in doing more policy and planning studies, more financial studies, and more academic studies.

Professional Development Needs. Respondents may have expressed limited interest in conducting such studies due to a perceived lack of relevant expertise and required resources. Relevant knowledge and skills are essential prerequisites for effective institutional research. Terenzini (1993) conceptualizes the types of knowledge and skills required for competency in institutional research in terms of three tiers of organizational intelligence: technical/analytical, issues, and contextual intelligence.

Respondents in this study express strong interest in further training primarily in technical/analytical areas, with a majority seeking further training in statistical analysis, research design, data management, and personal computer applications. The perceived need is even stronger among institutional researchers who work at institutions where there is no doctoral-level institutional research director.

Perspective on Training. Policy issues confronting colleges and universities are increasingly complex; studies designed to address these issues require extensive and sophisticated methodological expertise and substantive knowledge. Those doing institutional research should continually expand their technological and statistical skills to handle institutional data effectively, and when necessary they should employ relevant technical consultants to ensure that the studies are methodologically sound to produce valid and reliable information.

Insights gained from analyses of these study findings are reflected in the following recommendations. These recommendations are intended to generate reflective discussion regarding how the role of institutional research might be configured and how institutional researchers might be prepared to meet the challenges of the 21st century.

Recommendations

Enhance the Capacity for Conducting Complex Research Studies

Results from this research document limited resources and possibly limited methodological and technical expertise among many of the responding institutional research offices. These limitations potentially constrain the ability of institutional researchers to conduct effective research and policy studies. Given the complex factors involved in institutional decisions, institutional researchers need to possess sophisticated research skills including substantial knowledge of research design and advanced statistics; extensive skills in data analysis; and experience and expertise in translating the results of institutional research studies into planning and policy documents. To address complex policy questions, institutional researchers will need to possess or expand their methodological and technical competence.

Presley (1990) discussed the essential role of professional competencies and expertise in creating effective institutional research offices. She observes that effective institutional research offices possess researchers with strong quantitative skills, superb oral and written presentation skills, and excellent communication skills. In addition, effective institutional research offices often involve specialists in technology and other experts in areas such as measurement, testing, and survey research. In their projection of how institutional research ought to be in the 21st century, Matier, Sidle, and Hurst (1994) observe that the environment in which all of higher education functions is becoming more and more complex. To perform effectively in such an environment, institutional researchers will need to become the information architects, change agents, and consultants of choice in their institution. Such a mandate requires advanced knowledge and expertise.

Develop Creative Ways to Shift the Focus from Mere Reporting to Research

Findings from this study reveal that institutional researchers, particularly at small colleges, are much more involved in routine reporting than they are in research and planning studies designed to inform policy decisions. If institutional researchers are to have an impact on decision making, they need to reallocate time and resources to focus on areas of critical importance to higher education. Given limited resources, the shift may need to be gradual, but it might be achieved by enhancing the capacity for conducting research through collaboration with institutional researchers at other institutions; participation in research-related professional development programs; and selective use of methodological and technical consultants. In addition, institutional researchers might exercise more discretion in responding to requests for information and seek external funding to expand the resources for institutional research.

In her discussion on creating effective institutional research offices, Presley (1990, p. 106) addresses the issue of reporting versus research. "When institutional research is perceived simply as a number-crunching activity, not only does the profession lose, but so does each and every institution where this attitude prevails. Even if limited staffing prevents an office from undertaking major second-order activities, it is possible to turn first-order reporting into an interesting and important activity." This could be accomplished in part by not simply providing an answer in response to a question, but by seeking to understand the question and provide a context for the answer. Institutional researchers in small offices might also expand their involvement in research and policy analysis by creating teams of helpers throughout the institution from the registrar to computing support personnel to the faculty themselves.

In their presentation of a model approach to studying student retention, Kinnick and Ricks (1993) also identify skills and requirements necessary to achieve the transformation from mere "number crunching" to policy-related research. The proposed skills include strong technical skills, mastery of both quantitative and qualitative research methodologies, knowledge of the organization, and the ability

to function in the political arena. In order to advance to a higher order of functioning, institutional researchers need to increase their understanding and awareness of the political functioning of the organization; use multiple approaches and sources for gathering information; utilize training opportunities available through professional organizations to acquire necessary methodological knowledge and technical skills; increase the client-centered focus of institutional research and communicate the student voice to policymakers; and, finally, use case analysis to reflect on practice within their own institution. Kinnick and Ricks propose that such case analyses may serve to examine the usefulness of current theory in light of practice and thus help to develop better theory to guide the practice of institutional research.

Strengthen the Capacity for Conducting Institutional Research, Particularly at Small Colleges

Resources and expertise for conducting institutional research appear quite limited particularly at the small colleges and universities participating in this study. Only a minority of institutions have an institutional research office and very few have a doctoral-level institutional research director. In a previous study, Clyburn (1991) also found that most small, private colleges lacked an effective institutional research operation; institutional research received inadequate institutional commitment and support; and institutional research activities were primarily dispersed, disjointed, and characterized by report generation for external organizations.

Clyburn (1991) proposes a model that would expand the scope and function of institutional research at small colleges. He recommends that the institutional research director exert ongoing leadership for systematic institutional evaluation and create a service philosophy encouraging individuals and departments to utilize the office of institutional research.

The author suggests that the potential for conducting quality institutional research studies at small institutions might also be improved by implementing professional development training opportunities for institutional researchers at small colleges; by establishing networks of consultants who might assist these institutional researchers; and by creating consortia so that smaller institutions might share knowledge, resources, and the cost of consultants and training.

Create and Support High-Level Audiences for Institutional Research Studies

A primary criterion of success for institutional research is the extent to which it promotes action and influences decision making. To achieve this goal, institutional researchers must create and maintain a vital connection with the decision makers at the institution. Through these relationships, they can work to integrate the work of the institutional office into the fabric of the institution. "Integrating institutional research is vital to the success of the institution. First, successful integration maximizes the use of information. . . . Second, introducing information into the layers of the organization focuses decision making on actual knowledge rather than on conventional wisdom" (Billups and DeLucia, 1990, p. 95).

The location of the institutional research office is also critical to establishing and maintaining strong relationships with key decision makers. The institutional research office needs to be placed high enough in the organizational structure for the staff to be cognizant of the major issues and decisions facing senior management. Such proximity to key decision makers enables institutional researchers to anticipate and respond to management needs for information in a timely and effective manner (Presley, 1990).

Increase Involvement in Academic Studies

While institutional research traditionally has made substantial contributions to various administrative areas, involvement has been somewhat less extensive in academic areas. This may be due in part to the organizational location of the institutional research office and to the faculty culture which places a high priority on academic freedom.

In the future, institutional research can make significant contributions to the academic life of the university by conducting research to inform academic policies and by providing research support to various constituents. Relevant constituencies include accrediting boards, university academic councils, educational policy committees, academic deans, chairpersons, and individual faculty members. The intellectual climate of a university, the quality of academic programs, academic standards in courses and programs, and the academic performance of students are topics that might be addressed by institutional research.

Expand the Focus of Institutional Research Studies to Include Relevant Factors and Trends in the External Environment

In discussing the changing role of institutional research, Chan (1993) proposed that institutional research must shift the focus from the internal context only to include the external context in order to provide effective support for strategic management. More recently, in his keynote address to the 1995 AIR Forum, Terenzini also commented on the significance of developments in the external environment to the evolution of institutional research. He noted that while an understanding of the internal culture and politics is essential, the significance of the external context and climate for higher education and institutional research have increased due to the state's and the federal government's views of education as a strategic public investment. Consequently, institutional researchers need to identify the demographic, financial, political, and technological developments in the external environment that will impact the college's future. Fulfilling this recommendation requires that institutional researchers expand the vision of their role, the scope of their studies, and the level of their methodological and technical competence to accommodate a complex array of external as well as internal factors that will impact the growth and development of colleges and universities in the 21st century.

Acknowledgment. The author gratefully acknowledges Ce Shen for the technical assistance he provided for this study.

References

Billups, F. D., and DeLucia, L. A. (1990). integrating institutional research into the organization. In

P. T. Terenzini and E. E. Chaffee (series eds.) and J. B. Presley (vol. ed.), *New Directions for Institutional Research: No. 66. Organizing Effective Institutional Research Offices* (pp. 93–102). San Francisco: Jossey-Bass.

Chan, S. S. (1993). Changing roles of institutional research in strategic management. *Research in Higher Education* 34(5): 533–549.

Clyburn, M. (1991, May). *An Investigation of Institutional Research in Small, Private Colleges in the Southeastern United States.* Paper presented at the annual forum of the Association for Institutional Research, San Francisco, CA (ERIC Document Reproduction Service No. ED 336 030).

Kinnick, M. K., and Ricks, M. F. (1993). Student retention: Moving from numbers to action. *Research in Higher Education* 34(1): 55–69.

Matier, M. W., Sidle, C. C., and Hurst, P. J. (1994, May). *How It Ought to Be: Institutional Researchers' Roles as We Approach the 21st Century.* Paper presented at the annual forum of the Association for Institutional Research, New Orleans, Louisiana.

Peterson, M. W. (1985). Institutional research: An evolutionary perspective. In P. T. Terenzini and M. W. Peterson (series eds.) and M. W. Peterson and M. Corcoran (vol. eds.), *New Directions for Institutional Research: No. 46. Institutional Research in Transition* (pp. 5–15). San Francisco: Jossey-Bass.

Presley, J. B. (1990). Putting the building blocks into place for effective institutional research. In P. T. Terenzini and E. E. Chaffee (series eds.) and J. B. Presley (vol. ed.), *New Directions for Institutional Research: No. 66. Organizing Effective Institutional Research Offices* (pp. 103–106). San Francisco: Jossey-Bass.

Saupe, J. L. (1990). *The Functions of Institutional Research* (2nd ed.). Tallahassee, Florida: Association for Institutional Research (ERIC Document Reproduction Service No. ED 319 327).

Terenzini, P. T. (1993). On the nature of institutional research and the knowledge and skills it requires. *Research in Higher Education* 34(1): 1–10.

Terenzini, P. T. (1995, Fall/Winter). Evolution and revolution in institutional research. *Air Currents* 33: 7.

Volkwein, J. F. (1990). The diversity of institutional research structures and tasks. In P. T. Terenzini and E. E. Chaffee (series eds.) and J. B. Presley (vol. ed.), *New Directions for Institutional Research: No. 66. Organizing Effective Institutional Research Offices* (pp. 7–26). San Francisco: Jossey-Bass.

Institutional Research:
Knowledge, Skills, and Perceptions of Effectiveness

WILLIAM E. KNIGHT, MICHAEL E. MOORE,
AND CORBY A. COPERTHWAITE

Terenzini (1993) approached the issue of institutional research effectiveness by articulating three tiers of organizational intelligence necessary for effective institutional researchers. Responses (n = 601) from a nationwide survey of AIR members provided for an empirical investigation based on this concept. The study examined the existence and acquisition of examples of institutional research knowledge and skills and how they relate to perceptions of effectiveness. Participants indicated that they were effective in their functions and reported that they possessed examples of the technical, issues, and (to a lesser extent) contextual knowledge and skills articulated by Terenzini. Multiple regression revealed the relationships between background characteristics, knowledge and skills in institutional research, and perceptions of effectiveness to be minimal, however. The authors conclude that an institutional researcher's effectiveness can perhaps only be adequately evaluated relative to institutional culture and expectations and leaders' personalities and orientation toward decision making.

Gaither, Nedwek, and Neal (1994) note that growing costs, reduced public confidence, and eroding state support for higher education are among the reasons for increased concern over accountability, quality, and productivity within academe. Internal and external pressures calling for the assessment of college student learning and development have been joined by concerns over the effectiveness of administrative offices and functions. Recent higher education conferences and publications abound with discussions of performance indicators, such as the National Association of College and University Business Officers' National Benchmarking Project, the National Study of Instructional Costs and Productivity, and the Peterson's Guides/Association of Governing Boards' Strategic Indicators Project.

The institutional research function has not evaded these concerns. Most of the regional accrediting associations now have strong provisions for institutional effectiveness regarding administrative functions such as institutional research. For example, the Commission on Colleges of the Southern Association of Colleges and Schools (1995) prescribes within its criteria on institutional effectiveness that "an institution must regularly evaluate the effectiveness of its institutional research process" (p. 20). While institutional research has not yet been the subject of externally imposed empirical performance indicators, its effectiveness has been a subject of ongoing interest among its community of practitioners (Billups and DeLucia, 1990; Dressel, 1981; Fincher, 1978, 1985; Harrington, 1995, Hearn and Corcoran, 1988; Presley, 1990; Sheehan, 1980, Volkwein, 1990).

Given this context, it is surprising that few studies exist that explore the effectiveness of institutional research and the means by which it can be improved. Opportunities such as the Association for Institutional Research (AIR) Forum, the *AIR Professional File*, and, most recently, the AIR Institutes, are available for institutional research professionals to explore and

"Institutional Research: Knowledge, Skills, and Perceptions of Effectiveness," by William E. Knight, Michael E. Moore and Corby A. Coperthwaite, reprinted from *Research in Higher Education*, Vol. 38, No. 4, 1997. Human Sciences Press, Inc.

develop technical and analytical skills and to promote understanding of issues relevant to the function. Also, occasional efforts, such as Coburn, Field, Hunter, Lindquist, Meredith, and Olomon's 1990 AIR panel session, have explored some common institutional research problems and their solutions. Unfortunately, however, these ideas about improving effectiveness tend to be based on the experiences of one or more individuals; they do not result from a systematic study of practitioners in the field.

One exception to this paucity of empirical research was a study by Huntington and Clagett (1991) that explored institutional researchers' concerns about effectiveness and productivity by means of a national survey. The core of the survey was comprised of open-ended questions about office effectiveness, productivity, and innovations. The question about office effectiveness asked respondents to list the biggest obstacle to increasing the effectiveness of their offices. In addition to inadequate staff size and expertise (the greatest obstacle noted by 15% of the 123 directors of institutional research responding to the survey), other obstacles included lack of appreciation for data and research by campus leaders, inadequate technical resources, lack of access to decision makers by institutional researchers, external reporting demands and (relatedly) lack of time, institutional research not being seen as part of the institution's leadership team, lack of identification of the institution's most important issues by executives and discussion of these issues with institutional researchers, campus politics, and insufficient lead time. While many of the ideas proposed by respondents for increasing institutional research office productivity were related to resources (e.g., "add more staff"), the survey results frequently cited skill training for institutional research staff, "early identification of key issues by management," and "regular communication with top management" as possible means for institutional researchers to overcome obstacles to their effectiveness. Clagett and Huntington (1993) built upon these results to offer a follow-up monograph on knowledge and skills that institutional researchers can develop to increase their professional effectiveness.

Terenzini (1993) approached the issue of institutional research effectiveness in terms of the requisite professional characteristics of effective institutional researchers. He drew upon numerous sources to articulate three tiers of "organizational intelligence." Technical and analytical intelligence (e.g., familiarity with institutional data files, statistical analysis skills) concerns the basic analytic processes of institutional research. Issues intelligence involves understanding of substantive institutional management issues such as faculty workload analysis or assessment. Contextual intelligence requires familiarity with the history, culture, and unique aspects of the institution at which institutional research professionals are employed (e.g., political structures, decision-making processes). Terenzini further discussed the ways in which each domain of institutional research knowledge and skills may best be acquired (i.e., through graduate course work, through on-the-job training, and through interaction with institutional decision makers and those "in the know" about the history and culture of the institution).

Terenzini's (1993) ideas about the knowledge and skills necessary for institutional research professionals to be fully effective in their jobs seem eminently logical and are in accordance with established principles of management and human resource development. However, they have not been empirically validated, either in terms of the existence or interrelationships of these types of knowledge and skills among practitioners, or in terms of the relationship between them and indicators of effectiveness. An analysis of Terenzini's article and other literature suggests that an empirical study of the relationship between institutional researchers' knowledge and skills, their experiences and activities by which they might gain such knowledge and skills, and their effectiveness in their function could benefit the professional development of institutional research practitioners. This is the purpose of the current study. The specific research questions are:

1. To what extent do institutional research professionals possess examples of the three types of knowledge and skills (technical/analytical, issues, and contextual) proposed by Terenzini?

2. To what extent do underlying subsets among institutional research knowledge and skills determined through factor analysis validate or conform to those proposed by Terenzini?

3. How do the experiences and activities of institutional research professionals predict or explain the degree to which they report having these types of knowledge and skills?

4. How do the knowledge and skills of institutional research professionals and their experiences and activities predict or explain their self-reported effectiveness?

Method

Participants

Mailing labels ($N = 2,429$) were obtained from the AIR Executive office for all registered members as of December 1994. Full-time faculty, students, retired members, campus executives, and individuals with titles such as Director of Computer Services or Director of Business Affairs, as they could be determined by title, were excluded. Surveys were mailed to the remaining 1,234 persons. Thirty-five persons stated that the

requested information was not applicable to them. Six hundred ninety-five of the remaining 1,199 surveys were returned, resulting in a response rate of 58%. The profile of the participants was quite similar to that resulting from a recent AIR membership survey (Lindquist, 1995); the percentages of participants by categories of experience in institutional research, institutional type, highest academic degree, and reporting relationship never varied between the two surveys by more than 5%.

Recognizing the fact that, regardless of title, some respondents perform multiple job functions, an initial survey question asked for the percentage of time individuals spent performing institutional research-related tasks as opposed to activities such as teaching, fund-raising, etc. Ninety-four respondents were excluded from subsequent analyses since they reported spending less than 50% of their time doing institutional research. No significant differences were found between these 94 persons and the remaining 601 participants with respect

Table 1. Characteristics of the Study Participants

Job Title	Time Spent Doing IR Tasks	Years in IR	Years at Institution
57% director	median 88%	median 7	median 8
22% research analyst	range 50–100%	range 1–35	range 1–41
10% asst./assoc. dir.			
11% other			
Institution Type	Reports to	FTE Professional Staff	FTE Clerical Staff
26% two-year	51% vice president	median 2	median 1
24% masters/comp.	23% president	range 0–15	range 0–20
18% research univ.	26% IR director		
14% bacc./liberal arts		Hours/Month Reading Institutional Publications	Hours/Month Reading Professional Publications
13% doctoral univ.			
5% system offices			
		median 5	median 5
		range 0–150	range 0–60
Highest Degree	Degree Field		
46% doctorate	34% social sciences		
41% masters	31% education	Hours/Month Attending General Meetings	Hours/Month Talking with Experienced Staff
10% bachelors	16% business		
3% other	13% math/science		
	6% other	median 4	median 5
		range 0–65	range 0–125

Most Important Source of IR Knowledge/Skills

88% on-the-job experience
9% course work
8% professional development opportunities

Table 2. Factor Analysis Results of Institutional Research Knowledge and Skill Items

Items			Factors			
	1	2	3	4	5	h²
Written communication skills (79%)	.85	.10	.09	.21	-.05	.78
Knowledge and skills in data presentation and reporting (81%)	.85	.06	.05	.18	.13	.78
Knowledge of how to work successfully with other people (79%)	.82	.17	.07	.20	-.02	.74
Familiarity with standard variable categories and definitions (81 %)	.82	.07	.21	-.06	.25	.79
Knowledge of basic counting rules and formulae (78%)	.79	.08	.24	-.08	.29	.77
Oral communication skills (70%)	.78	.12	.08	.26	-.07	.69
Knowledge of organizational and governance structures in general (72%)	.75	.22	.25	.08	.00	.68
Familiarity with the structures, definitions, etc., of institutional data files (70%)	.69	.05	.19	-.08	.33	.63
Knowledge and skills with respect to computer application software (66%)	.68	-.07	.01	-.03	.24	.53
Knowledge of the need for prior consultation with important opinion makers (70%)	.67	.27	.30	.22	-.09	.66
Library research skills (57 %)	.63	.08	.01	.36	.00	.54
Knowledge of the local community political environment and how it impacts the institution (41%)	.13	.85	.06	.08	.00	.75
Knowledge of the state political environment and how it impacts the institution (42%)	.15	.83	.12	.01	.10	.74
Knowledge of the perspectives, values, and attitudes of important legislators (28%)	2.13	.78	.13	.10	.19	.68
Knowledge of the national political environment and how it impacts the institution (35%)	.14	.72	.13	.12	.11	.58
Knowledge of the importance of and rationale for faculty workload analysis (49%)	.19	.17	.82	.04	.29	.82
Knowledge of the importance of and rationale for salary equity studies (46%)	.15	.16	.80	.08	.20	.73
Technical knowledge and skills in instructional evaluation (31%)	-.12	.08	.22	.78	.15	.70
Technical knowledge and skills in assessment and program evaluation techniques (50%)	.33	.11	.12	.72	.15	.67
Technical knowledge and skills in enrollment forecasting (41%)	.16	.15	.25	.14	.77	.72
Technical knowledge and skills in student flow modeling (38%)	.00	.10	.31	.18	.72	.65
Knowledge and skills in quantitative research methodologies (61%)	.62	-.02	.04	.41	.43	.74
Knowledge and skills in qualitative research methodologies (40%)	.25	.18	-.13	.55	.40	.57
Technical knowledge and skills in faculty workload analysis (42%)	.07	.11	.65	.04	.51	.70
Knowledge of the importance of and rationale for enrollment goal setting (56%)	.40	.23	.50	.17	.30	.57
Knowledge of the importance of and rationale for student assessment (65%)	.52	.14	.40	.50	.00	.70
Knowledge of the importance of and rationale for institutional self-study (70%)	.59	.18	.43	.39	-.05	.72
Knowledge of the importance of and rationale for faculty evaluation (56%)	.30	.13	.62	.45	-.10	.70

	1	2	3	4	5	
Knowledge of the decision process in academe (53%)	.47	.33	.42	.30	-.02	.60
Knowledge of the perspectives, values, and attitudes of the executives of the institution (66%)	.66	.43	.19	.25	-.04	.72
Knowledge of the perspectives, values, and attitudes of students at the institution (53%)	.44	.36	.02	.42	.08	.50
Knowledge of the perspectives, values, and attitudes of faculty at the institution (51%)	39	.45	.23	.44	.00	.61
Knowledge of the history and unique characteristics of the institution (65%)	. 62	.45	.15	.09	2.06	.62
Knowledge of political environment of the institution (60%)	.51	.63	.17	.15	-.05	.71
Percent of Variance	41%	10%	7%	5%	4%	

Factor 1 = General Institutional Research Knowledge and Skills; Factor 2 = Knowledge of the External Political Environment; Factor 3 = Faculty-Related Institutional Research Knowledge; Factor 4 = Technical Knowledge and Skills in Assessment and Instructional Evaluation; Factor 5 = Technical Knowledge and Skills in Enrollment Management Research. Percentages in parentheses indicate participants who agreed or strongly agreed that they possess each type of knowledge and/or skill.

to a variety of background characteristics. Additionally, no significant differences were found in preliminary analyses between respondents and nonrespondents with respect to type and location of institution and highest degree held.

Procedure

Data were collected by means of a survey developed specifically for this study. The first portion of the survey asked participants about some of their experiences and activities, which were suggested by Terenzini (1993) as being related to the acquisition of institutional research knowledge and skills. Data concerning participants' years employed in institutional research, years employed at their current institution, type and field of their highest academic degree and time since it was earned, their job title and supervisor's title, type of institution where they are employed, and the number of full-time-equivalent professional and clerical staff in their offices were elicited. Also, the number of hours per week participants spend in activities such as reading internal and professional publications, attending general institutional meetings and talking informally with people with a long employment history at the institution, and the importance of on-the-job experience, course work, and professional development opportunities as sources of IR knowledge and skills were collected. These items are listed in Table 1. Finally, participants indicated the number of courses they have completed in 14 areas related to higher education administration, research, and statistics.

The second part of the survey included items related to institutional research knowledge and skills. These were developed from the full set of examples of the three tiers of organizational intelligence articulated by Terenzini (1993). The items are listed Table 2, although not according to Terenzini's *a priori* specification. Respondents were asked to indicate the degree to which they believed they possessed each knowledge or skill utilizing a five-point scale (from "I do not possess this knowledge or skill at all" to "I am an expert with respect to this knowledge or skill").

The last item of the survey requested that participants rate their overall effectiveness as an institutional research professional using a five-point scale (from "very effective" to "very ineffective"). As no specific, broadly recognized measure of institutional researcher effectiveness appears in the literature, this single-item measure was the only means readily available to serve as a dependent variable in the analyses.

A pilot study of the survey was carried out by a group of institutional researchers in Georgia. In order to ensure the quality and to establish and enhance the validity of the survey, the revised instrument was then critiqued by a group of experts who have extensive experience as both theorists and practitioners of institutional research. The final edition of the survey was mailed to the participants in January 1995 along with a cover letter and postage-paid return envelope. Follow-up letters were sent to nonrespondents two weeks later.

Results

Characteristics of the Participants

Responses to questions about participants' experiences and activities are shown in Table 1. As stated earlier, these are quite similar to the results of a recent AIR membership survey (Lindquist, 1995). In addition to the questions addressed in the table, participants were asked to indicate how many of the 11 courses in higher education administration and research listed in the survey they had completed. They most often completed none of those courses at all. This is not surprising given that only 31% of the participants held degrees in education, only 13% stated they held degrees specifically in higher education, and not all graduate programs in higher education offer all of the courses listed. About one-half of the participants took three or more courses each in quantitative research methods and statistics; 71% took no courses or one course only in qualitative research methods. It is understandable that larger percentages of institutional researchers took courses in research and statistics since such courses are available through a variety of graduate programs, such as business and the social sciences, as well as education.

Institutional Research Knowledge and Skills

In response to the first research question, participants indicated that they possessed to a large extent examples of technical/analytical and issues knowledge and skills posed by Terenzini (1993). To a lesser extent they reported having the contextual knowledge described. The percentage of participants who agreed or strongly agreed that they possessed each of these types of knowledge and skills listed in the survey is given in parentheses after each item in Table 2.

The majority of institutional researchers agreed or strongly agreed that they had a strong grasp of 10 of the 16 indicators of technical/analytical knowledge and skills articulated by Terenzini (1993). Participants were most likely to agree that they were knowledgeable about standard variable categories and definitions, and reporting, and basic counting rules and formulae, and that they possessed strong written communication skills. They were least likely to agree that they possessed technical knowledge and skills in instructional evaluation and student flow modeling.

Similarly, the majority of the participants felt they strongly possessed seven of the nine examples of issues knowledge suggested by Terenzini (1993). They reported being most knowledgeable about how to work successfully with other people, the need for prior consultation with important opinion makers, and the importance of and rationale for institutional self-study. They were least knowledgeable about the importance of and rationale for salary equity studies and faculty workload analysis.

Finally, the majority of institutional research practitioners responding to the survey purported to strongly possess about one-half of the survey items that reflected contextual knowledge. They were most familiar with the perspectives, values, and attitudes of campus executives and the history and unique characteristics of their institutions. They were least familiar with the perspectives, values, and attitudes of legislators who are important to their institutions and the national political environment and how it affects their college or university.

The second research question (i.e., to what degree were Terenzini's [1993] proposed three tiers of organizational intelligence actually reflected in the empirical data) was addressed by performing a factor analysis on the 34 institu-

tional research knowledge and skill items listed in the survey. Principal components extraction was used with varimax rotation. Factor loadings, communalities (h^2), and percents of variance for the principal factors are shown in Table 2. Items are ordered and grouped by size of loadings to facilitate interpretation. Boxes in the table indicate the items associated with each factor. The 13 items that loaded at .40 or above on more than one factor are listed at the bottom of the table; they are included only in order to display the full factor analysis results.

Five factors were extracted that explained 67% of the total variance. Factor 1, which explained 41% of the total variance, is interpreted and titled as General Institutional Research Knowledge and Skills. Eleven items—nine of the examples of technical/analytical knowledge and skills suggested by Terenzini (1993) and two examples of issues knowledge and skills—showed high loadings on this factor. Factor 2, which explained 10% of the total variance, is interpreted as Knowledge of the External Political Environment, since it comprises four items dealing with the local community, state, and national political environment, and the perspectives of legislators important to the institution. This factor corresponds to a portion of Terenzini's examples of contextual knowledge and skills; interestingly, only the external, not the internal, context is represented. Factor 3 (accounting for 7% of the total variance) is termed Faculty-Related Institutional Research Knowledge, since it deals with knowledge of the importance of and rationale for faculty workload analysis and salary equity studies. Both of the items for this factor fall within Terenzini's examples of issues knowledge and skills. Factor 4, which explained 5% of the total variance, seems to represent Technical Knowledge and Skills in Assessment and Instructional Evaluation. These items are included in the examples of technical/analytical knowledge and skills. Factor 5 (accounting for 4% of the total variance) is interpreted as Technical Knowledge and Skills in Enrollment Management Research. Again, these items are included in the examples of technical/analytical knowledge and skills.

Relationships Between Participants' Experiences and Activities and Their Institutional Research Knowledge and Skills

Stepwise multiple regression was carried out in order to determine how participants' experiences and activities related to their self-reported institutional research knowledge and skills in response to the third research question. Based on the previous results, only one factor (General Institutional Research Knowledge and Skills) was found to represent a substantial number of knowledge and skill items (11) possessed by a large number of participants, and only this factor explained a substantial amount of the total variance (41%). Therefore, a summed scale score (coefficient alpha = .94) of the items encompassing this factor was used as the one and only dependent variable. All of the participant experiences and activities served as independent variables; job title, supervisor's job title, type and field of highest degree, and type of institution where participants were employed were dummy coded. Table 3 provides the multiple regression results. Only the number of years participants were employed in institutional research and the number of courses they completed in planning were significantly related to the dependent variable; they accounted for only 3% of its variance. None of the other background characteristics (e.g., educational background, hours per week engaged in various activities, job title, type of institution where employed) served as significant predictors of General Institutional Research Knowledge and Skills.

The inability of educational background to predict the extent to which participants possessed technical skills is perhaps explained by the fact that on-the-job training was viewed as a greater contributor to the acquisition of those skills than was course work. The significance of the number of courses taken in planning may

be attributed to the fact that such courses are available in a wide variety of graduate programs (e.g., business and the social sciences); they are not available solely to individuals with a higher education administration background.

Perceptions of Effectiveness

In response to the fourth research question, stepwise multiple regression analysis was performed in order to determine the relationship between the self-reported effectiveness of institutional researchers, their professional knowledge and skills, and their experiences and activities. The results are shown in Table 4. The five-point self-rating of effectiveness served as the dependent variable. All items concerning the experiences and activities of the participants and the General Institutional Research Knowledge and Skills scale score served as independent variables. As with the previous multiple regression analysis, only the single knowledge and skill factor served as an independent variable because only this one factor of the five identified was found to represent a substantial number of knowledge and skill items possessed by a large number of participants, and only this factor explained a substantial amount of the total variance in the overall factor solution.

Participants who have been employed in the field for a greater number of years, those holding the doctorate, those who are associate directors of institutional research, and those who report directly to their institution's president were more likely to consider themselves to be effective. Those who held a bachelor's as their highest degree, whose highest degree was in the field of education, and who had a greater level of general institutional research knowledge and skills were less likely to consider themselves to be effective. These seven variables accounted for 17% of the variance in self-reported effectiveness.

Table 3. Summary of Stepwise Regression Analysis for General Institutional Research Knowledge and Skills

Independent Variable	B	SE B	ß
Years Employed in Institutional Research	.16	0.06	.12**
Number of Graduate Courses: Planning	1.09	0.43	.11*

R^2 = .03. The dependent variable is the General Institutional Research Knowledge and Skills factor.
*$p < .05$
**$p < .01$

Table 4. Summary of Stepwise Regression Analysis for Institutional Research Effectiveness

Variable	B	SE B	ß
Years Employed in Institutional Research	.02	0.01	.19**
Highest Degree: Doctorate	.25	0.06	.11**
Title: Associate Director	.32	0.13	.10*
Reports to President	.15	0.07	.09*
Highest Degree: Bachelor's	−.28	0.11	−.12**
Highest Degree Field: Education	−.21	0.08	−.11*
General IR Knowledge and Skills	−.01	0.00	−.11*

$R^2 = .17$
*$p < .05$
**$p < .001$

Limitations

While the survey items were tied very closely to Terenzini's (1993) examples of knowledge and skills necessary for effective institutional researchers, and the instrument was pilot tested and reviewed by a panel of experts, it nevertheless remains exploratory in nature. Terenzini's examples of knowledge and skills were intended only to clarify the nature of his three tiers of organizational intelligence; they do not comprise a comprehensive taxonomy and there are probably other specific institutional research knowledge and skills that were not identified or examined. For example, knowledge and skills in using the World Wide Web for institutional research and knowledge of data warehousing and geodemography are recently developed examples of types of organizational intelligence not accounted for by Terenzini. The results of self-reported knowledge and skills may differ from results gained from an external, objective measure. There may be severe constraints on the reliability and validity of the complex construct of institutional research effectiveness as measured by a single item. This may well be the most serious limitation of the current study; as noted earlier, however, no comprehensive, broadly recognized measure appears to be available at this time. Finally, the study participants may not be fully representative of the entire AIR membership or of all persons engaged in institutional research.

There may be a difference between individual institutional researchers and an entire institutional research office staff with regard to knowledge, skills, and effectiveness. It seems likely that a collective office staff will display a broader array of knowledge and skills as well

as greater effectiveness than will individual researchers. The nature of the current study, however, was such that the individual researcher constituted the unit of analysis; further studies focusing on entire office staffs remain an area of future inquiry.

The authors also considered the idea that separate analyses involving only directors of institutional research might lend greater support for Terenzini's (1993) construction. Subsequent factor analysis restricted to directors only, however, revealed a less "clean" six-factor solution that was even less similar to the tiers of organizational intelligence proposed by Terenzini. Such an analysis was also less appropriate to the current study, the goal of which was to collect and analyze data representing institutional research professionals with a broad range of experience.

Discussion

Within these constraints the current study provides some interesting conclusions for those interested in the professional development of institutional researchers. Most of the study participants believed that they possessed the examples of technical/analytical and issues intelligence articulated by Terenzini (1993). They believed they possessed to a lesser extent the examples of contextual intelligence. Many of Terenzini's examples of technical/analytical intelligence were found to be interrelated in terms of a General Institutional Research Knowledge and Skills factor, but additional examples of organizational intelligence were found associated with other distinct factors. Only two variables (years employed in institutional research and number of courses completed in planning) were found to be significantly related to General Institutional Research Knowledge and Skills. Finally, only longevity, type and field of participant's highest degree, General Institutional Research Knowledge and Skills, being an associate director, and reporting directly to the president significantly predicted self-reported effectiveness.

The existence of institutional research knowledge and skills factors distinct from the general factor suggests that there are separate areas of institutional research abilities (e.g., knowledge and skills in assessment, faculty and enrollment management-related research) that are not exhibited by (or perhaps needed by) all institutional researchers. The relationship of knowledge and skills with almost nothing but longevity suggests that no specific educational or experiential background is requisite for these general abilities. The finding that 88% of the participants reported that on-the-job experience was their most important source of professional knowledge and skills suggests that experience may be a necessary, but not sufficient, source of General Institutional Research Knowledge and Skills.

The paucity of variables related to institutional research effectiveness again suggests few specific experiences seem requisite for self-rated effectiveness. The relationship between effectiveness and being an associate director of institutional research (especially since none of the other education and experience variables were substantially correlated with being an associate director) remains unexplained. The negative relationship between effectiveness and the general knowledge and skills factor suggests that general knowledge and skills may be a necessary but not sufficient condition for effectiveness. In order to be truly effective, in the broad sense, institutional researchers need contextual as well as the more basic types of knowledge and skills.

These conclusions suggest that a quantitative study focusing on the relationships between global effectiveness and preselected examples of knowledge, skills, and experiences simply may not be adequate for the goal of providing meaningful suggestions for improving institutional research. The authors' own experiences, Fincher's (1978) and Hearn and Corcoran's (1988) discussions about successful institutional research, and a logical extension of

Terenzini's (1993) thesis of contextual intelligence to the idea of "contextual effectiveness" all lead to one conclusion. The effectiveness of institutional research can perhaps be evaluated only relative to the capabilities, experiences, and orientation of the institutional researcher and the expectations, experiences, orientation toward information and rational decision making, and personalities of the institutional leadership. The institutional researcher whose tasks are limited to responding to external surveys and carrying out the annual student satisfaction survey or faculty salary study might (quite correctly) feel that he or she is very effective and possesses the requisite knowledge and skills for these tasks. This sense of effectiveness is confirmed in a context where these activities comprise all that is expected or even wanted from institutional research. At the same time the institutional researcher who is heavily engaged in campus planning, who maintains an extensive executive information system, who is greatly involved in a comprehensive assessment program, etc., might also consider himself or herself to be effective and to possess the necessary knowledge and skills for the tasks at hand. Again, this sense of effectiveness would be confirmed if institutional leaders rely heavily on institutional research as a tool for decision support and have very high expectations for the function. The sense that institutional research is not up to the task and that institutional researchers do not possess the necessary competencies, or the sense that the function is not being used to its fullest extent, might occur when there is a mismatch between leaders and institutional researchers about the role of and expectations for the function.

If this scenario is representative of the ways in which institutional research may or may not be viewed as effective, and the ways in which the knowledge and skills of its practitioners may or may not be perceived is adequate, then it seems that further inquiry into this topic cannot be accomplished through use of a descriptive survey of a large number of practitioners. The next step in the investigation may involve multiple detailed case studies designed to promote better understanding of the congruence between institutional decision support processes and the perceived role and effectiveness of institutional research.

References

Billups, Felice D., and DeLucia, Lenore A. (1990). Integrating institutional research into the organization. In Jennifer B. Presley (ed.), *Organizing Effective Institutional Research Offices*, pp. 93–102. New Directions for Institutional Research No. 66. San Francisco: Jossey-Bass.

Clagett, Craig A., and Huntington, Robin B. (1993). *Making a Significant Difference with Institutional Research*. Largo, MD: The Maryland Association for Institutional Research/Prince George's Community College.

Coburn, Kari, Field, Tom, Hunter, Larry, Lindquist, Sarah, Meredith, Mark, and Olomon, Jim (1990). *Common Institutional Research Problems and Their Solutions—or "Institutional Research Can Be Trying."* Panel presentation at the Association for Institutional Research Forum, Louisville, KY.

Commission on Colleges of the Southern Association of Colleges and Schools (1995). *Criteria for Accreditation* (9th ed.). Decatur, GA: Author.

Dressel, Paul L. (1981). The shaping of institutional research and planning. *Research in Higher Education* 14(3): 229–258.

Fincher, Cameron (1978). Institutional research as organizational intelligence. *Research in Higher Education* 8(2): 189–192.

Fincher, Cameron (1985). The art and science of institutional research. In Marvin W. Peterson and Mary Corcoran (eds.), *Institutional Research in Transition*, pp. 17–38. New Directions for Institutional Research, No. 46. San Francisco: Jossey-Bass.

Gaither, Gerald, Nedwek, Brian P., and Neal, John E. (1994). *Measuring Up: The Promise and Pitfalls of Performance Indicators in Higher Education*. ASHE-ERIC Higher Education Report No. 5. Washington, DC: The George Washington University, Graduate School of Education and Human Development.

Harrington, Charles F. (1995). *Assessing Institutional Research: A Practical Guide to Assessment Strategy*. Paper presented at the Association for Institutional Research Forum, Boston, MA.

Hearn, James C., and Corcoran, Mary E. (1988). An exploration of factors behind the proliferation of the institutional research enterprise. *Journal of Higher Education* 59(6): 634–651.

Huntington, Robin B., and Clagett, Craig A. (1991). *Increasing Institutional Research Effectiveness and Productivity: Findings from a National Survey*. Paper presented at the meeting of the North East Association for Institutional Research, Boston, MA.

Lindquist, Sarah H. (1995, July 11). AIR membership profile from AIR membership survey: Fall 1994. *The Electronic AIR* [On-line serial]. Available: 15(9).

Presley, Jennifer B. (1990). Putting the building blocks into place for effective institutional research. In Jennifer B. Presley (ed.), *Organizing Effective Institutional Research Offices*, pp. 103–106. New Directions for Institutional Research No. 66. San Francisco: Jossey-Bass.

Sheehan, Bernard S. (1980). Developing effective information systems. In Paul Jedamus, Marvin W. Peterson, and Associates (eds.), *Improving Academic Management: A Handbook of Planning and Institutional Research*, pp. 510–538. San Francisco: Jossey-Bass.

Terenzini, Patrick T. (1993). On the nature of institutional research and the knowledge and skills it requires. *Research in Higher Education* 34(1): 1–10.

Volkwein, J. Fredricks (1990). The diversity of institutional research structures and tasks. In Jennifer B. Presley (ed.), *Organizing Effective Institutional Research Offices*, pp. 7–26. New Directions for Institutional Research No. 66. San Francisco: Jossey-Bass.

PART III

PLANNING DOMAINS, ELEMENTS, AND ISSUES

CHAPTER III

PLANNING DOMAINS, ELEMENTS, AND ISSUES

Planning in an institution is often discussed in terms of *domains* (segments of the institution for which planning is done), *elements* (activities usually associated with the planning process) and *issues* (problems or challenges of running the planning process itself). Planning is often organized by domains or segments of the institution, such as academic programs, curriculum or instruction; enrollment and student life; faculty and staff as human resources; finances including operating revenue and expenses and capital needs; campus and facilities; information technology infrastructure; research; and service. Planning domains may also be focused on organizational sub-units such as schools or colleges, departments or divisions, programs, and management functions or offices. It is neither feasible nor the intent of this Reader to provide readings relevant to each domain. The models of or approaches to planning, elements of the planning process, and issues faced in planning for each of these domains are similar. Individuals designing a course or seminar on planning who want to focus on planning in one or more of these domains may wish to consult chapters in the Recommended Texts (Part V-A1. of this *Reader*), one of the Related Reference Texts (Part V-A2.), or the *ASHE Reader on Curriculum* (C. F. Conrad and J. G. Grant, 1990) and on *Finance* (L. L. Leslie and R. E. Anderson, 1990) for useful references.

The elements or activities associated with a planning process often include environmental analysis; establishing vision, mission, goals and/or priorities; restructuring; program planning; resource allocation; and assessment or evaluation. The readings in this section relate primarily to the first three elements of the planning process. Those interested in academic program planning, resource allocation, or assessment and evaluation should also consult chapters in the Related Higher Education Reference Books (Section V-A) or appropriate sections of the *ASHE Reader on Curriculum* (Conrad and Grant, 1990), *Finance* (Leslie and Anderson, 1990), and *Assessment and Program Evaluation* (Stark and Thomas, 1994).

The role of external environments in the planning process is the focus of two readings. In "Managing Uncertainty: Environmental Analysis/Forecasting in Academic Planning," Morris and Mecca discuss the process of environmental analysis and relate it to academic planning. Whitely, Porter, Morrison, and Moore are more concerned with linking "Environmental Scanning and Strategic Planning" and the process of scenario development.

Establishing direction for an institution is discussed by three authors. Keller, in "The Vision Thing In Higher Education," addresses this most amorphous notion of direction and addresses how to make it useful in the planning process. Lang and Lopers' "The Role of Statements of Institutional Purpose" examines several institutional and system plans and discusses ways to use them in the mission setting process. On a more specific dimension, Massy addresses the use of goals in "Measuring Performance: How Colleges and Universities Can Set Meaningful Goals and Be Accountable."

Planning that leads to major change often involves restructuring or other modes of reorganization. Dill examines this phenomenon in "Academic Planning and Organizational Design: Lessons from Leading Research Universities" and suggests characteristics of such a process. Schmidtlein and Taylor's "Responses of American Research Universities to Issues Posed by the Changing Environment of Higher Education" provides new insights into how these institutions experience their environments and engage in issue-oriented planning. Massy shifts the focus from academics in "Improvement Strategies for Administration and Support Services" and suggests a process for improving and/or restructuring this important non-academic area of institutional functioning.

Three articles address perennial planning issues. Dill and Helm provide an examination of varying approaches to a critical process issue, "Faculty Participation In Strategic Policy Making." Jones addresses the link between planning and the need for useful information in "Expanding Information and Decision Support Systems." A major unresolved issue in planning is always that of productivity: what it is and how to achieve it. Massy and Wilger provide a comprehensive look at this critical planning issue in "Productivity In Postsecondary Education: A New Approach."

Managing Uncertainty: Environmental Analysis/Forecasting in Academic Planning

James L. Morrison and Thomas V. Mecca

The external environment of institutions of higher education can be characterized by change and turbulence. Administrators of colleges and universities have witnessed major shifts in the demographics of their institutions' clientele. External agencies have tightened their control of policymaking and fiscal decisions made by the institutions' administrations. There has been a growing criticism of the value of the curriculum offered and the quality of instruction provided by many institutions of higher education, particularly in view of the importance of education in the increasingly competitive environment of the global economy. Less obvious, but no less significant, there has been a pervasive spread of electronic technologies through American society, challenging the dominant instructional and managerial paradigm found in the majority of American higher education institutions. In short, the accelerating rate, magnitude, and complexity of change occurring in all sectors of American society have created vulnerabilities and opportunities across the higher education "tableau" (Keller, 1983).

The rapidity and volume of changes have resulted in less lead time for administrators to analyze changes in their institutions' external environment and to formulate appropriate strategies. In addition, the risks and uncertainty involved in implementing a particular strategy or set of strategies have intensified. In summary, the turbulence in higher education's external environment challenges the capability of decision-makers to effectively anticipate changing conditions.

This phenomenon of rapid environmental shifts led to a recognition among administrators and organizational theorists of the need for a comprehensive approach to institutional planning that emphasizes sensitivity to the effects of environmental shifts on the strategic position of the institution (Ellison, 1977; Cope, 1988). An administrator's analysis of the organization's environment is critical in accurately assessing the opportunities and threats that the environment poses for the institution and in developing the strategic policies necessary to adapt to both internal and external environments.

All organizations, including colleges and universities, are perceived by contemporary organizational theorists as social systems existing in and interacting with their environment (Aldrich, 1979; Scott, 1981). An organization's environment is essentially all those external factors that affect it or are perceived to affect it. Hall (1977) divides an organization's environmental factors into two categories: the limited number of factors that directly affect it (the task environment) and the almost unlimited number of factors that influence all organizations in the society (the general societal environment). In essence, the task environment is composed of the set of factors that are unique to each organization, while the general societal environment includes environmental factors that are the same for all organizations.

Factors in the task environment are readily apparent to college and university administrators (e.g., clients/students, revenue sources, and government educational policies and regulations). However, the distinction between the

"Managing Uncertainty: Environmental Analysis/Forecasting in Academic Planning," by James L. Morrison and Thomas V. Mecca, reprinted from *Higher Education: Handbook of Theory and Research*, Vol. 5, edited by J. C. Smart, 1989. Agathon Press.

organization's task environment and the general societal environment is not always clear. Particularly under turbulent conditions, factors in the general societal environment "break through" into the organization's task environment (Kast and Rosenzweig, 1979). Consequently, changes in the general societal environment can, and often do, have significant effects on the organization, effects well documented in the literature of organizational analysis (Osborne and Hunt, 1974; Hall, 1977; Kast and Rosenzweig, 1979; Scott, 1981).

The uncertainty faced by a decision-maker in planning strategically is compounded by an increasingly dynamic and uncertain environment (Emery and Trist, 1965). Terreberry (1968) concluded that organizations must be prepared to adapt even more to the influence of external forces. Most environments are dynamic and, consequently, rich in possible opportunities as well as possible threats to the organization. Therefore, the strategic planner and policymaker cannot analyze the condition of the future environment by assuming that it will remain in a readily predictable state (i.e., in an orderly and incremental progression into the future).

Contingency approaches to organizational theory have focused upon the effect of environmental change in creating uncertainty for policymakers formulating organizational strategy (Anderson and Paine, 1975; Lindsay and Rue, 1980; Boulton et al., 1982; Miller and Friesen, 1980; Jauch and Kraft, 1986; Kast and Rosenzweig, 1984). Duncan (1972) describes three factors that contribute to this sense of uncertainty: (a) a lack of information about environmental factors that would influence a given decision-making situation; (b) a lack of knowledge about the effects of an incorrect decision; and (c) the inability of the decision-maker to assess the probability that a given environmental factor will affect the success (or failure) of the organization or one of its subsystems in fulfilling its mission. In a later study, Leblebici and Salancik (1981) also found that the uncertainty experienced by a decision-maker arises from his or her inability to predict the outcomes of certain actions. This inability to predict decision outcomes is derived from two sources. The first is the nature of the world in which we live—multivariate, complex, and interrelated. The second is the probabilistic quality of our world—an event can occur tomorrow, next week, or next year that could affect the interrelationships of variables, trends, and issues. In essence, the more turbulent and complex the organization's environment appears, the less able an administrator is to anticipate the probability of success in implementing a particular strategy.

Traditional planning models are weak in identifying environmental changes and in assessing their organizational impact. In his analysis of the approaches to planning exhibited by American educational institutions, Ziegler (1972) identified two primary assumptions that characterize the weakness of these models: (a) the organization's environment will remain essentially static over time; and (b) the environment is composed of only a few variables that impact education. In essence, the underlying assumption of most current educational planning is that environmental change will be a continuation of the rate and direction of present (and past) trends. These trends are manifested in the "planning assumptions" typically placed in the first part of an institution's strategic or long-range plan. Therefore, many administrators implicitly expect a "surprise-free" future for their institutions. We know, however, that change, not continuation, will be the trend, and the further we go out into the future, the more true this will be. An approach is needed that enables administrators to detect signals of change in all sectors of the environment and to link environmental information to the organization's strategic management (Ansoff, 1975; Weber, 1984; Chaffee, 1985; Levy and Engledow, 1986; McConkey, 1987; Dutton and Duncan, 1987; Hearn, 1988).

The purpose of this chapter is to describe an approach to environmental analysis and forecasting that educational policymakers can employ in dealing with the level of uncertainty associated with strategic decision-making. Unlike traditional models of planning, such an approach does not lead decision-makers to conclude that the uncertainty they perceive in the external environment has been reduced. Rather, the focus of this approach is to enhance their capability to deal with a changing environment by making the perceived uncertainty in that environment explicit (Fahey, King, and Narayanan, 1981). This is accomplished through the analysis and evaluation of possible alternative future states of an organization's environment and the sources of change within it. In this chapter, we will explain one model of this approach and demonstrate its application in a case study. We conclude with an examination of the issues and questions posed by the application of this model to educational institutions, and we suggest directions for future research in this emerging methodological domain.

Environmental Analysis and Forecasting

Environmental analysis and forecasting are based upon a number of assumptions, among them the following (Boucher and Morrison, 1989):

- the future cannot be predicted, but it can be forecasted probabilistically, taking explicit account of uncertainty.

- Forecasts are virtually certain to be useless or misleading if they do not sweep widely across possible future developments in such areas as demography, values and lifestyles, technology, economics, law and regulation, and institutional change.

- Alternative futures including the "most likely" future are defined primarily by human judgment, creativity, and imagination.

- The aim of defining alternative futures is to try to determine how to create a better future than the one that would materialize if we merely kept doing essentially what is presently being done.

A model based upon assumptions like these is shown in Figure 1. Basically, the model states that from our experiences or through environmental scanning we identify *issues or concerns* that may require attention. These issues/concerns are then defined in terms of their component parts—*trends* and *events*. Univariate forecasts of trends and events are generated and subsequently interrelated through *cross-impact analysis*. The "most likely" future is written in a scenario format from the univariate trend and event forecasts; outlines of alternative scenarios to that future are generated by computer simulations from the cross-impact matrix. In turn, these *scenarios* stimulate the development of

policies appropriate for each scenario. These policies are *analyzed* for their robustness across scenarios. The purpose of the entire exercise is to derive a final list of *policies* that effectively address the issues and concerns identified in the initial stage of the process. These policies are then implemented in *action plans*.

Issue Identification

A wide range of literature provides insights into how issues are recognized by decision-makers. Included is literature related to problem sensing and formulation (Kiesler and Sproull, 1982; Lyles and Mitroff, 1980; Pounds, 1969), normative strategy development (Nutt; 1979), decision-making (Alexis and Wilson, 1967; Mintzberg, Raisinghani, and Theoret, 1976; Segev, 1976), and environmental scanning (Aguilar, 1967; Kefalas and Schoderbeck, 1973; King, 1982). Regardless of how issues are identified, there is agreement that inconsistencies perceived within the environment stimulate the decision-maker to further examine the issue (Dutton and Duncan, 1987).

The articulation of issues/concerns is particularly critical for effective strategic planning. A central tenet of strategic management pervading both the literature of organizational theory (Lawrence and Lorsch, 1967) and traditional business policy (Andrews, 1971) is that the proper match between an organization's external conditions and its internal capabilities is critical to its performance. Accordingly, the primary responsibility of the organizational strategist is to find and create an alignment between the threats and opportunities inherent in the environment and the strengths and weaknesses unique to the organization (Thompson, 1967).

A number of writers have recognized that the strategist's perceptions of the environment and the uncertainty it represents to the organization are key to the strategy-making process (Aguilar, 1967; Anderson and Paine, 1975; Bourgeois, 1980; Hambrick, 1982). Hatten and Schendel (1975) and Snow (1976) further suggest that the effectiveness of the strategy an organization pursues is dependent upon the strategist's ability to identify and evaluate major discontinuities in the environment. This ability is dependent upon the experience the strategist brings to this task as well as his or her ability to systematically scan the contemporary external environment.

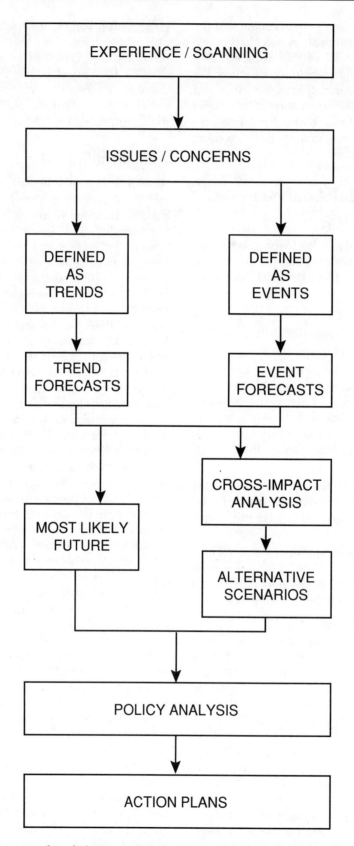

Figure 1 Environmental Analysis/Forecasting Model (modified from Boucher and Morrison, 1989)

Scanning

A major tool to identify discontinuities in the external environment is environmental scanning. Aguilar (1967) defined environmental scanning as the systematic collection of external information in order to lessen the randomness of information flowing into the organization. According to Jain (1984), most environmental scanning systems fall into one of four stages: primitive, *ad hoc*, reactive, and proactive. In the primitive stage, the environment is taken as unalterable. There is no attempt to distinguish between strategic and nonstrategic information; scanning is passive and informal. In the *ad hoc* stage, areas are identified for careful observation, and there are attempts to obtain information about these areas (e.g., through electronic data base searches), but no formal system to obtain this information is instituted. In the reactive stage, efforts are made to continuously monitor the environment for information about specific areas. Again, a formal scanning system is not utilized, but an attempt is made to store, analyze, and comprehend the material. In the proactive stage, a formal search replaces the informal searches characteristic of the earlier stages. Moreover, a significant effort is made to incorporate resulting information into the strategic planning process.

Aguilar suggests that environmental assessment is more effective where a formal search replaces the informal search of the environment. The formal search uses information sources covering all sectors of the external environment (social, technological, economic and political) from the task environment to the global environment. A comprehensive system includes specifying particular information resources (e.g., print, TV, radio, conferences) to be systematically reviewed for impending discontinuities. Examples of such systems are found mainly in the corporate world (e.g., United Airlines, General Motors); less comprehensive systems are now appearing in colleges and universities (Hearn and Heydinger, 1985; Morrison, 1987), although recent literature advocates establishing formal environmental scanning systems to alert administrators to emerging issues (Cope, 1988; Keller, 1983; Simpson, McGinty, and Morrison, 1987).

Structuring Issues

Issues may be *structured* by identifying their parts as trends or events. *Trends* are a series of social, technological, economic, or political characteristics that can be estimated and/or measured over time. They are statements of the general direction of change, usually gradual and long-term, and reflect the forces shaping the region, nation, or society in general. This information may be subjective or objective. For example, a subjective trend is the level of support for a public college by the voters in the state. An objective trend would be the amount of funding provided to all public institutions in the state. An *event* is a discrete, confirmable occurrence that makes the future different from the past. An example would be: "Congress mandates a period of national service for all 17–20-year-olds."

Structuring the issues involved in the planning problem includes developing a set of trends that measure change in individual categories, along with a set of possible future events that, if they were to occur, might have a significant effect on the trends, or on other events. The trend and event set is chosen to reflect the complexity and multidimensionality of the category. Ordinarily, this means that the trends and events will describe a wide variety of social, technological, economic, and political factors in the regional, national, and global environment.

Forecasting

Having defined the trend and event sets, the next step is to forecast subjectively the items in each of these sets over the period of strategic interest (e.g., the next 15 years). For trends, the likely level over this period is projected. This is an *exploratory forecast*. It defines our expectation, not our preference. (*Normative forecasts* define the future as we would like it to be with the focus on developing plans and policies to attain that future.) Similarly, the cumulative probability of each event over the period of interest is estimated, again on the same assumption.

It is important to distinguish between the terms *prediction* and *forecast*. Science depends upon theoretical explanation from which predictions can be made. With respect to the future, a prediction is an assertion about how some element of "the" future will, in fact, materialize. In contrast, a forecast is a probabilistic statement about some element of a possible future. The underlying form of a forecast statement is, "If A occurs, plus some allowance for unknown or unknowable factors, then maybe we can expect B or something very much like B to occur, or at least B will become more or less probable."

It is also important to distinguish the criteria for judging predictions and forecasts. Predictions are judged on the basis of their accuracy. Forecasts are judged, according to Boucher (1984, as reported in Boucher and Morrison, 1989), on the following criteria:

1. *Clarity.* Are the objects of the forecast and the forecast itself intelligible? Is it clear enough for practical purposes? Users may, for example, be incapable of rigorously defining "GNP" or "the strategic nuclear balance," but they may still have a very good ability to deal with forecasts of these subjects. On the other hand, they may not have the least familiarity with the difference between households and families, and thus be puzzled by forecasts in this area. Do users understand how to interpret the statistics used in forecasting (i.e., medians, interquartile ranges, etc.)?

2. *Intrinsic credibility.* To what extent do the results "make sense" to planners? Do the results have "face validity"?

3. *Plausibility.* To what extent are the results consistent with what the user knows about the world outside of the scenario and how this world *really* works or *may* work in the future?

4. *Policy relevance.* If the forecasts are believed to be plausible, to what extent will they affect the successful achievement of the user's mission or assignment?

5. *Urgency.* To what extent do the forecasts indicate that, if action is required, time must be spent fairly quickly to develop and implement the necessary changes?

6. *Comparative advantage.* To what extent do the results provide a better foundation now for investigating policy options than other sources available to the user *today*? To what extent do they provide a better foundation now for future efforts in forecasting and policy planning?

7. *Technical quality.* Was the process that produced the forecasts technically sound? To what extent are the basic forecasts mutually consistent?

These criteria should be viewed as filters. To reject a forecast requires making an argument that shows that the item(s) in question cannot pass through all or most of these filters. A "good" forecast is one that survives such an assault; a "bad" forecast is one that does not (Boucher and Neufeld, 1981).

Boucher and Neufeld stress that it is important to communicate to decision-makers that forecasts are transitory and need constant adjustment if they are to be helpful in guiding thought and action. It is not uncommon for forecasts to be criticized by decision-makers. Common criticisms are that the forecast is obvious; it states nothing new; it is too optimistic, pessimistic, or naive; it is not credible because obvious trends, events, causes, or consequences were overlooked. Such objections, far from undercutting the results, facilitate thinking strategically. The response to these objections is simple: If something important is missing, add it. If something unimportant is included, strike it. If something important is included but the forecast seems obvious, or the forecast seems highly counterintuitive, probe the underlying logic. If the results survive, use them. If not, reject or revise them (Boucher and Morrison, 1989).

A major objective of forecasting is to define *alternative* futures, not just the "most likely" future. The development of alternative futures is central to effective strategic decision-making (Coates, 1985). Since there is no single predictable future, organizational strategists need to formulate strategy within the context of alternative futures (Heydinger and Zenter, 1983; Linneman and Klein, 1979). To this end, it is necessary to develop a model that will make it possible to show systematically the interrelationships of the individually forecasted trends and events.

Cross-Impact Analysis

This model is a *cross-impact model*. The essential idea behind a cross-impact model is to define explicitly and completely the pairwise causal connections within a set of forecasted developments. In general, this process involves asking how the prior occurrence of a particular event might affect other events or trends in the set. When these relationships have been specified, it becomes possible to let events "happen"—either randomly, in accordance with their estimated probability, or in some prearranged way—and then trace out a new, distinct, plausible and internally consistent set of forecasts. This new set represents an alternative to the comparable forecasts in the "most likely" future (i.e., the "expected" future). Many such alternatives can be created. Indeed, if the model is computer-based, the number will be virtually unlimited, given even a small base of trends and events and a short time horizon (e.g., the next ten years).

The first published reference to cross-impact analysis occurred in the late 1960s (Gordon, 1968), but the original idea for the technique dates back to 1966, when the coinventors, T. J. Gordon and Olaf Helmer, were developing the game FUTURES for the Kaiser Aluminum Company. In the first serious exploration of this new analytic approach, the thought was to investigate systematically the "cross correlations" among possible future events (and only future events) to determine, among other things, if improved probability estimates of these events could be obtained by playing out the cross-impact relationships and, more important, if it was possible to model the event-to-event interactions in a way that was useful for purposes of policy analysis (Gordon and Haywood, 1968). The first of these objectives was soon shown to be illusory, but the second was not, and the development of improved approaches of event-to-event cross-impact analysis proceeded (Gordon, Rochberg, and Enzer, 1970), with most of the major technical problems being solved by the early 1970s (Enzer, Boucher, and Lazar, 1971).

The next major step in the evolution of cross-impact analysis was to model the interaction of future events and trends. This refinement, first proposed by T. J. Gordon, was implemented .in 1971–1972 by Gordon and colleagues at The Futures Group and was called *trend impact analysis,* or TIA (Gordon, 1977). Similar work was under way elsewhere (Helmer, 1972; Boucher, 1976), but TIA became well established, and it is still in use, despite certain obvious limitations, particularly its failure to include event-to-event interactions.

Two strands of further research then developed independently and more-or-less parallel with the later stages in the creation of TIA. Each was aimed primarily at enabling cross-impact analysis to handle both event-to-event and event-to-trend interactions and to link such a cross-impact modeling capability to more conventional system models, so that developments in the latter could be made responsive to various sequences and combinations of developments in the cross-impact model. One strand led to the joining of cross-impact analysis with a system dynamics model similar to the one pioneered by Jay Forrester and made famous in the first Club of Rome study (Meadows et al., 1972). This line of research—again directed by T. J. Gordon—produced a type of cross-impact model known as *probabilistic system dynamics,* or PSD.

The second strand led to a cross-impact model known as INTERAX (Enzer, 1979), in which the run of a particular path can be interrupted at fixed intervals to allow the user to examine the developments that have already occurred. The user can also examine the likely course of developments over the next interval and can intervene with particular policy actions before the run is resumed. Since the development of INTERAX, which requires the use of a mainframe computer, some work has been done to make cross-impact analysis available on a microcomputer. The Institute for Future Systems Research (Greenwood, SC) has developed a simple cross-impact model (Policy Analysis Simulation System—PASS) for the Apple II computer and an expanded version for the IBM AT. A comprehensive cross-impact model, *Bravo!,* will be released in mid-1989 by the Bravo! Corporation (West Hartford, CT) for an IBM AT (Morrison, 1988, July–August). These microcomputer based models greatly enhance the ability to conduct cross-impact analyses and, therefore, to write alternative scenarios much more systematically.

Alternative Scenarios

Scenarios are narrative descriptions of possible futures. A single scenario represents a history of the future. The "most likely" future, for example, contains all of the forecasts from the forecasting activity in a narrative weaving them together from some point in the future, describing the history of how they unfolded. Alternatives to this future are based upon the occurrence or nonoccurrence of particular events in the event set. Such alternatives define unique mixes of future environmental forces that may impact on a college or university. The range of uncertainty inherent in the different scenarios (which are, themselves, forecasts) changes the assumption that the future will be an extrapolation from the past (Zentner, 1975; Mandel, 1983). Within the context of an alternative future depicted by a scenario, the decision-maker can identify causal relationships between environmental forces, the probable impacts of these forces on the organization, the key decision points for possible intervention, and the foundations of appropriate strategies (Kahn and Wiener, 1967; Sage and Chobot, 1974; Martino, 1983; Wilson, 1978). By providing a realistic range of possibilities, the set of alternative scenarios facilitates the identification of common features likely to have an impact on the organization no matter which alternative occurs. It is conventional to create from three to five such histories to cover the range of uncertainty.

Numerous approaches can be taken in writing the scenarios, ranging from a single person writing a description of a future situation (Martino, 1983) to the use of an interactive computer model that uses cross-impact analysis to generate outlines of the alternatives (Enzer, 1980a,b; Mecca and Adams, 1985; Goldfarb and Huss, 1988). A broader range of scenario writing approaches is described by Mitchell, Tydeman, and Georgiades (1979), Becker (1983), and Boucher (1985).

Any of a number of scenario taxonomies, each with its own benefits and limitations, may be used to guide the development of a scenario logic (Bright, 1978; Ducot and Lubben, 1980; Hirschorn, 1980; Boucher, 1985). The most comprehensive of the taxonomies, however, is that of Boucher (1985) which has been updated in Boucher and Morrison (1989). In this taxonomy

there are four distinct types of scenarios: the demonstration scenario, the driving-force scenario, the system change scenario, and the slice-of-time scenario. The first three types are characteristic of "path-through-the time" narratives; the fourth is a "slice of time" narrative. The following descriptions are derived from Boucher (1985) as updated in Boucher and Morrison (1989).

The *demonstration scenario* was pioneered by Herman Kahn, Harvey De Weerd, and others at RAND in the early days of systems analysis. In this type of scenario, the writer first imagines a particular end-state in the future and then describes a distinct and plausible path of events that could lead to that end-state. In the *branch-point* version of this type of scenario, attention is called to decisive events along the path (i.e., events that represent points at which crucial choices were made—or not— thus determining the outcome). Thus the branch points, rather than the final outcome, become the object of policy attention. As Kahn and Wiener (1967) point out, they answer two kinds of questions: (a) How might some hypothetical situation come about, step by step? and (b) What alternatives exist at each step for preventing, diverting, or facilitating the process?

The major weakness of the demonstration scenario, as Boucher (1985) points out, is that it is based upon "genius" forecasting and is, therefore, dependent upon the idiosyncrasies and experiences of individuals. However, this type of scenario (like all methods and techniques in this field) is useful in both stimulating and disciplining the imagination.

The *driving-force scenario*, perhaps the most popular type of scenario in governmental and business planning (Goldfarb and Huss, 1988; Ashley and Hall, 1985; Mandel, 1983), is exemplified by Hawken, Ogilvy, and Schwartz's *Seven Tomorrows* (1982). Here the writer first devises a "scenario space" by identifying a set of key trends, specifying at least two distinctly different levels of each trend, and developing a matrix that interrelates each trend at each level with each other. For example, two driving forces are GNP growth and population growth. If each is set to "high," "medium," and "low," there are nine possible combinations, each of which defines the scenario space defining the context of a possible future. The writer's task is to describe each of these futures, assuming that the driving-force trends remain constant.

The purpose of the driving-force scenario is to clarify the nature of the future by contrasting alternative futures with others in the same scenario space. It may well be that certain policies would fare equally well in most of the futures, or that certain futures may pose problems for the institution. In the latter case, decision-makers will know where to direct their monitoring and scanning efforts.

The major weakness of the driving-force scenario is the assumption that the trend levels, once specified, are fixed—an assumption that suffers the same criticism directed to planning assumptions in traditional long-range planning activities (i.e., they ignore potential events that, if they occurred, would affect trend levels). The advantage of this type of scenario, however, is that, when well executed, the analysis of strategic choice is simplified—a function of considerable value at the beginning of an environmental or policy analysis when the search for key variables is most perplexing.

The *system-change scenario* is designed to explore systematically, comprehensively, and consistently the interrelationships and implications of a set of trend and event forecasts. This set, which may be developed through scanning, genius forecasting, or a Delphi, embraces the full range of concerns in the social, technological, economic and political environments. Thus, this scenario type varies both from the demonstration scenario (which leads to a single outcome and ignores most or all of the other developments contemporaneous with it) and from the driving-force scenario (which takes account of a full range of future developments but assumes that the driving trends are unchanging), in that there is no single event that caps the scenario, and there are no *a priori* driving forces.

The system-change scenario depends upon cross-impact analysis to develop the outline of alternative futures. The writer must still use a good deal of creativity to make each alternative intriguing by highlighting key branch points and elaborating on critical causal relationships. However, this scenario suffers from the same criticisms that may be leveled at driving-force and demonstration scenarios: although everything that matters is explicitly stated, all of the input data and relationships are judgmental. Moreover, the scenario space of each trend pro-

jection is defined by upper and lower envelopes as a consequence of the cross-impacts of events from the various scenarios that are run. Although it is valuable to know these envelopes, this information by itself provides no guidance in deciding which of the many alternative futures that can be generated should serve as the basis for writing scenarios. This choice must be made using such criteria as "interest," "plausibility," or "relevance."

The *slice-of-time scenario* jumps to a future period in which a set of conditions comes to fruition, and then describes how stakeholders think, feel, and behave in that environment (e.g., 1984, *Brave New World*). The objective is to summarize a perception about the future or to show that the future may be more (or less) desirable, fearful, or attainable than is now generally thought. If the time period within the "slice of time" is wide, say from today to the year 2000, it is possible to identify the macrotrends over this period (e.g., Naisbitt's *Megatrends*, 1982). In this sense, a slice-of-time scenario is the same as the "environmental assumptions" found in many college and university plans. The weakness of this approach is that there is no explanation as to the influences on the direction of these trends, no plausible description of how (and why) they change over time.

Variations in these types of scenarios occur according to the perspective brought to the task by scenario writers. Boucher (1985) points out that writers using the *exploratory* perspective adopt a neutral stance toward the future, appearing to be objective, scientific, impartial. The approach is to have the scenario begin in the present and unfold from there to the end of the period of interest. The reader "discovers" the future as it materializes. The most common version of this mode, "surprise-free," describes the effects of new events and policies, although only likely events and policies are used. A second version, the "play-out" version, assumes that only current forces and policy choices are allowed to be felt in the future (i.e., no technological discoveries or revolutions are permitted).

Writers using the *normative* perspective focus on the question, "What kind of future might we have?" They respond to this question from a value-laden perspective, describing a "favored and attainable" end-state (a financially stable college and the sequence of events that show how this could be achieved) or a "feared but possible" end-state (merger with another institution).

In the *hypothetical* or *what-if?* mode, writers experiment with the probabilities of event forecasts to "see what might happen." In this mode, the writer explores the sensitivity of earlier results to changes in particular assumptions. Many "worst case" and "best case" scenarios are of this sort.

Boucher (1985) maintains that all scenarios may be placed in a particular type/mode combination. The current business-planning environment, for example, with its emphases on multiple-scenario analysis (Heydinger and Zenter, 1983), places a "most likely" future (exploratory, driving-force) surrounded by a "worst case" (normative—feared but possible, driving-force) and a "best case" (normative—desired and attainable, driving-force) scenario. Unfortunately, such a strategy ignores potentially important alternative futures from such type/mode combinations as the exploratory system change or exploratory driving-force scenarios. The choice of which scenario to write must be made carefully.

Policy Analysis

Policy analysis is initiated when the scenarios are completed. Since a scenario represents a type of forecast, it is evaluated by the same criteria described earlier (i.e., clarity, intrinsic credibility, plausibility, policy relevance, urgency, comparative advantage, and technical quality). Once these criteria are satisfied, each scenario is reviewed for explicit or implied threats and opportunities, the objective being to derive policy options that might be taken to avoid the one and capture the other. It is here that the value of this approach may be judged, for the exercise should result in policies that could not have been developed without having gone through the process.

Action Plans

Action plans are directly derived from the policy options developed through reformulating each option as a specific institutional objective. Responsibilities for developing detailed action plans and recommendations for implementation may be assigned members of the planning team. Typically, these staff members have knowledge,

expertise, and functional responsibilities in the area related to and/or affected by the implementation of the strategic option. The resulting action plans are incorporated into the institution's annual operational plan as institutional objectives assigned to appropriate functional units with projected completion dates (Morrison and Mecca, 1988).

A Case Study

The brief case study that follows illustrates the application of this approach to the strategic planning process of a two-year college. The institution, a public technical college located in the southeastern United States, is charged with offering a comprehensive program of technical and continuing education in concert with the economic and industrial development needs of its seven county service area. Like most two-year colleges, the institution's mission, role and program scope are greatly determined by the totality of its external relationships (Gollattscheck, 1983).

Several years ago, recognizing the institution's sensitivity to external change, the administration adopted a strategic planning process, ED QUEST, which incorporates the external analysis and forecasting approach described in this chapter. The participants in the process were drawn from across the college's administrative and instructional staff. The 15 members of the institution's planning team represented many of the functional areas of the college (e.g., instruction, continuing education, finance, and student services). The president and the three vice-presidents of the college were also members of the planning team. In addition to the 15 members of the planning team, 16 other staff members were selected based upon their expertise in a particular curriculum content area (e.g., business, engineering technology, industrial crafts) or for the "boundary-spanning" nature of their institutional role (e.g., admissions, job placement, financial aid, management development programs). Together, these individuals participated in environmental scanning and constituted a Delphi panel tasked to forecast relevant trends and events. The membership of this panel represented as broad a range of functional areas and organizational specialities as feasible.

Scanning the External Environment

The information and forecasts about environmental trends, issues, and developments that might have impact on the college's future were drawn from a variety of sources. Materials were obtained not only from education sources (e.g., *Chronicle of Higher Education, Change, Community College Journal*), but also from

- General sources (e.g., *US News and World Report, Newsweek, New York Times, Atlanta Journal*);

- "Fringe" publications (e.g., *Mother Jones, New Ages*);

- Periodicals covering four major areas— social, technical, economic and political (e.g., *Working Woman, American Demographics, High Technology, Business Week, Computer World*);

- Future-focused journals/newsletters (e.g., *The Futurist, What's Next, and the Issue Management Newsletter*);

- Additional information obtained from the institutional research office, including data on variables descriptive of the college's task environment (e.g., college-going rates of high school graduates, state revenues, demographic profile of state and region).

The intent of this information was to stimulate readers to identify possible future changes in the environment (i.e., trends, events, or issues) that would affect the college's future. The material was selected to provide an "information gestalt," within which members of the Delphi panel could begin to see patterns of change in the external environment. Using this material and personal experience, the members of the Delphi panel completed an open-ended questionnaire. This represents Round One (R1) of the Delphi survey. The questionnaire asked each respondent to identify several trends that would have major consequences for the college during the period of the next 11 years and to identify several events believed to have both a high likelihood of occurring at some time during the same period and, if occurring, a significant impact on the institution.

Forecasting External Changes

The R1 responses were used to develop the second-round (called R2) questionnaire. Typically, R1 responses reflected a general concern, "The demographics of our student body are changing rapidly." This concern needed to be restated into measurable trend statements, such as "the percentage of black students," "the percentage of Asian students," and "the percentage of those students older than 25 years of age." A related potential event statement was "The percentage of minority first graders in our area is greater than 50%."

The R2 questionnaire provided the Delphi panel members with the opportunity to forecast the set of trends (N = 78) and events (N = 60) over the period of the next 11 years (e.g., 1987 to 1997.) Representative trends on this questionnaire were as follows:

- Annual number of manufacturing jobs moving to the developing countries (e.g., Mexico, Korea) from the U.S.;

- Number of new jobs annually created by industrial development and expansion in the state;

- Number of industries in the southern U.S. using robots;

- Number of four-year colleges in the U.S. offering technical programs at the baccalaureate level.

Representative events on this questionnaire were as follows:

- A national opinion poll reveals that over 40% of the public believe that a general/liberal arts education is the best preparation for entering the job market.

- The federal government requires an 800 SAT or comparable ACT score for persons to be eligible to receive federal student aid.

- The state legislature mandates articulation policies and procedures among two-year colleges and four-year colleges.

- A major depression occurs in the U.S. (unemployment exceeds 15% for two consecutive years).

Panel members forecasted the level of each trend at two points in the future, 1992 and

1997, and estimated the probability that each event would occur at some time between 1987 and 1997. In order to relieve their anxiety about forecasting, they were instructed to provide their "best guess," and to indicate their first impressions. The purpose of requesting their forecasts as opposed to relying solely on forecasts of experts was to obtain the thinking of the chief decision-makers of the college as to their version of the "most likely" future. It is entirely possible that when faced with making these forecasts they may turn to the information initially provided, or they may seek other information. The assumption is that by having the decision-makers participate in the analysis, they "own" the analysis and, therefore, will find it creditable for developing policy options on the basis of the analysis.

In addition, panel members assessed the positive and negative consequences of each trend and event. This latter information was used to reduce the size of the trend and event set by eliminating those variables with lesser impact upon the institution.

Refining the Forecast

The forecasts of trends represented the panel's view of the "most likely" future of the college. In order to develop alternative scenarios to this future, it was necessary to conduct a third round (R3) Delphi, which focused on refining the probability estimates from the previous round (R2). This refinement was conducted using small groups from the Delphi panel. Initially, it was planned to use the Delphi panel to make these estimates as well as those estimates required to develop the cross-impact model (see below). This required each member of the Delphi panel to potentially make an enormous number of estimates. Although having the entire membership of the Delphi panel make all the estimates would have resulted in a single vision of the future of the group, it was decided that this task would be overwhelming to the individuals on the panel and would lead to panel "dropouts," a recurring problem in a large Delphi.

Therefore, to refine the forecast of events, the panel was divided into smaller groups, each being assigned a set of events and required to complete several estimates for each event: the earliest year the event's probability would first exceed zero and the event's probability of occurring by 1990 and by 1994. The procedure was for team members to (a) review R2 estimates for the median and interquartile range; (b) make a decision if, on the bases of earlier discussion, these estimates needed revision; (c) discuss the rationale for reestimation with other members of the group; and (d) make individual reestimations.

Developing the Cross-Impact Model

These groups were used to develop a cross-impact model that defined the interrelationships of events-on-trends and events-on-events. The events-on-trends model required the group to determine the impact of an event on the level of each trend. This was accomplished by the group providing both estimates of the magnitude of the event's maximum and "steady-state" impact on the trend's forecasted level (i.e., how long the maximum impact would remain to affect the trend level). In addition, group members estimated the number of years it would take from the initial occurrence of the event until it affected the trend, how long it would take for the effect of the event to reach its maximum effect, how long the maximum effect would last, and how long it would take for the impact of the event to decline until the trend reached a "steady state." For example, one event in the set was "voice-activated microcomputers available in the U.S." The impact of this event on the level of automation in U.S. offices was as follows: It would be five years before voice-activated microcomputers would begin to influence the level of office automation, and another two years before the maximum impact of a 40% increase in office automation would be reached. It was estimated that the maximum impact would continue for four years after which the impact would decrease over a three-year period to 30% steady-state impact.

The process of making these estimates was initially slow. After panel members grasped the concept of cross-impact analysis, however, the process proceeded at a smooth pace. The estimates from all teams were then reviewed by selected panel members. This step was necessary to ensure that there was consistency in the vision of the future represented by the cross-impact model's estimates.

Development of Alternative Scenarios

Once the cross-impact model was complete, a series of scenarios showing possible alternative future environments of the college were developed. The first scenario developed represented the college's "most likely" future. It described the content of the "expected futures" as defined by those trends identified as critical to the college's future. The specific character of this future was represented by the forecasted level of the trend based upon the implicit assumptions of each member of the panel. In this sense, the "most likely" future was a compilation of the planning assumptions used in most planning models, written in the form of a scenario.

Three other scenarios were created showing the alternative futures that could occur, should specific events happen in the future. Each of these scenarios described the changes in the level of the trends resulting from the impacts of a particular sequence of events over the period of the future which defined the strategic planning horizon for the college (10 years). In essence the alternative futures depicted in these scenarios represented a variation of the external environment described in the "most likely" scenario. The alternative scenarios were generated using PASS, an event-to-event and event-to-trend cross-impact model implemented on a personal computer. Within PASS, the "hits" for the event-to-event and event-to-trend sections of the model were determined from the cross-impact estimates made by the analysis teams. These estimates represented how the probability of a particular event would change, given the prior occurrence of an impacting event and how the level of a trend would change given the impact of a particular sequence of events. The result outlined a single path of development over time. Such paths were instructive to the planning teams, not only because they integrated the input estimates of the cross-impact model, but also because they described the alternative paths of developments that were, in fact, possible and redefined the context of the "most likely" future as represented by the changes in the levels of the impacted trends.

Conducting the Policy Analysis

The analysis of the implications of the four scenarios represented the policy analysis phase of the process. The planning team first evaluated the scenarios using the criteria previously mentioned in this chapter for judging forecasts. These criteria allowed the team to maintain the perspective that no scenario was to be viewed as a prediction of a future state of affairs of the college. Instead, there were an infinite number of possible alternative futures, each varying because of interactions among human choice, institutional forces, natural processes, and unknowable chance events. Each scenario, therefore, represented a probabilistic statement about some element of a possible future (i.e., forecast).

After the group had rigorously examined the scenarios, they assessed how the institution would be affected if the particular future described by the scenario materialized. This step was a critical part of the team's strategic planning process, because forecasts are of little or no value unless decision-makers estimate the degree and nature of the impact of change on the organization (Halal, 1984). Team members assessed the consequences of the scenario for the current and future mission of the organization. Also explored was the impact of the scenario on the institution's key indicators—factors that were perceived to make the difference between institutional success or failure (Rockart, 1979).

Once all scenarios had been reviewed, a list of implications was developed. These implications, common to all scenarios, represented those of critical importance to the establishment of institutional strategy (e.g., the demand for the college to develop more and varied outreach services, to provide both technical education and technology transfer activities, to adapt a core approach to its engineering curriculum, to demonstrate quality and excellence, and to operate in a context of more centralized governance at the state level). Those implications unique to a particular scenario represented possible conditions for which contingency strategies might have to be developed should the future described in the particular scenario emerge.

From these implications the planning team developed a list of institutional strategies. To ensure that strategies were appropriately focused, team members were directed to think of strategy as defining the relationship of the college to its external environment and as providing guidance to the institution's staff in carrying out their administrative and operational activities in six key decision areas: (a) basic mission; (b) array of programs and services; (c) types of students served; (d) geographic area served; (e) educational goals and objectives; and (f) competitive advantage(s) over competitors (e.g., low tuition, location). A strategy that affected one or more of these decision areas or the relationship between the college and the environment was considered a good candidate for adoption by the planning team. The potential of each strategy was assessed as to the degree it enhanced or inhibited institutional strengths and weaknesses previously identified by the planning team.

Those strategies estimated to enhance strengths or reduce weaknesses were examined as to their effectiveness across scenarios and then categorized with respect to the external implications they address. For example, a number of strategies focussed on the issue of educational excellence. Members of the team believed this issue would continue to grow as a public concern based upon the analysis of several of the scenarios; consequently, it was deemed important to make the college's community and staff perceive "quality" and "excellence" as important institutional values. Specific strategies identified by the planning team to accomplish this included:

- Publicizing institutional and faculty awards, honors, and innovative projects;
- Publicizing student achievements;
- Establishing a task force on institutional excellence to examine and make appropriate recommendations for improving any aspect of those educational programs and operations deemed "less than excellent";
- Expanding the number of major national conferences and meetings annually hosted by the college;
- Encouraging greater faculty participation in regional and national professional associations;
- Improving the quality of the college's adjunct faculty through increased salaries

and involvement in the college's activities;

- Establishing an endowment fund to expand professional development opportunities available to the college's faculty and staff to ensure that all personnel remain current in their field of specialization;
- Establishing an instructional resource center in the college to provide support and training for all part-time and full-time faculty to maintain their instructional skills.

Another category of strategies was intended to reaffirm the institution's role as a catalyst for regional economic development. Strategies included:

- Expanding the capability of the college's continuing education program to provide start-up and ongoing job training and technical assistance for small business and service industries;
- Establishing a technology transfer consortium to assist businesses and industries in the region to improve their productivity through the application of new technologies for existing production processes;
- Establishing an ongoing program of conferences and workshops for local and community groups to foster regional economic and community activities;
- Establishing an advanced technology education center for the "factory of the future" to provide technical training and technology transfer services to industries in the region.

Incorporating the Strategies into the College's Ongoing Activities

The planning team was asked to discuss these strategies with members of their staffs. The vice president for planning circulated this list of strategies and their corresponding objectives to all members of the planning team. At a half-day meeting, the team reviewed suggested objectives for each strategy and selected those objectives they believed the college should emphasize in its annual operational plan, allocating appropriate resources. Periodically during the year the president and the vice presidents reviewed the progress made in accomplishing the objectives.

Benefits and Limitations

An evaluation of the process by the members of the planning team indicated that the planning process was successful in producing information describing changes in the external environment relevant to the future of the college and in stimulating strategies that would not have been developed without going through the process. More specifically, team members felt that the process provided a systematic approach to the identification and analysis of external information. This viewpoint was best summarized by several members of the team who said that the process caused the team "to look at the future in an organized manner," and it "gave order to all the data that are out there" by helping the college's planning team to "structure the data so they can be matched with what we are about [and] what we are trying to do."

Overall, the team members thought that this planning approach increased their awareness and ability to assess the implications of external changes for the institution's future. Several members of the team said that it, "forces members [i.e., the planning team] to look at issues which would be overlooked and . . . aids in broadening the participant's perspective." Members of the planning team also indicated that the alternative scenarios were useful in developing a number of strategies and that the process provided a systematic approach for identifying those strategies that were to be given priority for implementation.

The incorporation of the strategies selected for implementation into the college's ongoing management activities, however, did not go smoothly. This was not surprising in that Gray (1986) found that the difficulties encountered in the implementation of strategic plans were the source of the greatest discontent among corporate executives (p. 90). In this case, planning-team members felt that there was a gap between the college's strategic planning process and its operational planning. The perception of a number of members was that the results of the process were not used in their entirety. Members also noted that the strategies were added to previously determined priority assignments

of staff, thus increasing work loads and resulting in incompatible demands. In other words, the new strategies were implemented without work assignments being "uncoupled" from strategies previously developed by the administration (Hobbs and Heany, 1977).

The problem of implementation was also related to what team members viewed as another problem—the lack of wider participation in the process among other members of the faculty and staff. While team members believed that the process facilitated the development of a consensus regarding the strategic directions of the institution among members of the planning team, they generally did not perceive this consensus reaching other members of the faculty and staff. Consequently, the results of the strategic planning process were perceived to be mandated by some staff. The importance of this problem is supported by the conclusion that Cleland and King (1974) draw that an organization's success in strategic planning is more sensitive to the overall organizational culture within which the planning is accomplished than the planning techniques and processes used (p. 70).

Some planning-team members were critical about the techniques and procedures used during the process. Several individuals believed that the scope of the environmental scan was too narrow and concentrated too heavily on technological and economic changes in the environment. There was far from unanimity on this point. One team member's sole criticism of the process was that the information from the scan was of little value and should rather have concentrated on the economic and employment data reflective of the local economy of the college's service area. Most team members thought, however, that the environmental scan and the trend and event statements contained on the Delphi's R2 questionnaire reflected changes in all sectors of the environment affecting the college.

Lastly, team members thought the procedures followed for evaluating the robustness and probable effectiveness of the strategies needed to be strengthened. More specifically, it was pointed out that short of a subjective assessment of the impact on college expenditures, the complete financial implications of implementing a particular strategy would not be known until after it was selected. Also, several individuals believed that in addition to assessing the strategies' impact on the institution's strengths and weaknesses, it would have been useful if the strategies had also been assessed as to their impact on the college's key indicators. With the availability of the PASS model, such an assessment was technically feasible, as it allows the user to incorporate policies (i.e., strategies) and trend data for each indicator into the cross-impact model of the institution's future environment.

Problems, Issues, and Needed Research

This approach to planning and associated research methods and techniques is derived from the development of technological forecasting by military planners in the years that followed World War II in an attempt to avoid being unprepared for future wars. Technological forecasting differed from traditional planning methods in that findings were based upon judgments about the future and were used to develop complex scenarios (as opposed to identifying only the next generation of military-related breakthroughs). However, according to Enzer (1983), it was not until the mid-1960s that technological forecasting was placed into an analytical framework with such supporting methods as the Delphi, scenario writing, cross-impact analysis, and system dynamics, through the work of Gabor (1964), Jantsch (1967), Kahn and Wiener (1967), and de Jouvenel (1967).

As one might expect with such a newly developing field, there are a variety of problems and issues associated with external analysis and forecasting. Indeed, Boucher (1977) identified some 300 unique problems and issues in this emerging area in a survey of the literature and of leading researchers in the futures field; Coates (1985) identified almost as many in a survey of issues managers. Space permits only a limited description of the most pressing issues for further research in this area.

Methodological Issues

Forecasting the "most likely" and alternative futures using the approach described here is based on soft, judgmental data, data based upon intuitive, often theoretically unstructured insights into real-world phenomena. Indeed, one of the major problems in this area of inquiry is the inadequacy of current theories of social change. Boucher (1977) found that none of the competing theories existing then or now (personal communication, August 1988) had predictive value. If our understanding of social change were more highly developed, forecasting the future would be much less problematic.

Improving methods of forecasting involves the question of how the validity of results obtained by the construction of a simulation model about the future can be measured. Of course, the concept of validity is difficult to apply to the study of the future. For this reason, many forecasters emphasize that accuracy is not a criterion for evaluating forecasts, for it is impossible to identify and assess the impact of all future events. Therefore, the best criteria we can develop at present are that forecasts be credible, plausible, and internally consistent given the information we have as a result of our scan and given our state of knowledge vis-á-vis social change.

Reliability and validity are also problems in judgmental forecasting. There has been some research on the extent to the same methods produce the same results. Martino (1983) reviewed a number of studies that reported a similarity of results across different Delphi studies. However, Sackman (1974) found that the similarity of forecasted median dates for events from some of these Delphi studies were statistically low. The effect of expert and nonexpert panels on the potential validity of judgmental forecasting has also been difficult to assess. Proponents argue that there is evidence that the more expertise panel members have, the better the forecast. Sackman (1974) reviewed a variety of Delphi studies comparing forecasts of experts with those of nonexperts and found that there was no difference. Studies by Campbell (1966) and Salancik, Weger, and Helfer (1971) came to essentially the same conclusion. Unfortunately, there has been little recent research on reliability and validity in judgmental forecasting.

Moreover, there has been little research on the relative advantages of different methods of eliciting forecasts from a group (e.g., questionnaires, interviews, computer terminals, face-to-face discussion), and on the extent to which forecasts derived through the use of these different techniques differ (Boucher, personal communication, August 1988). Perhaps one reason for the lack of research on these questions is the paucity of university-based programs that incorporate a responsibility for developing the concepts and methodology of forecasting. Another reason may be due to the pragmatic use of this approach to planning. That is, a major function of this approach to planning is to involve decision-makers in thinking about the future in ways that they have not thought previously. Ideally, they should be involved in all forecasting activities so that they "own" the products of the analysis and, therefore, are comfortable in using this analysis to stimulate the development of policy options that can be implemented in action plans. They use forecasts by experts (as reported in the literature or through personal communications) to assist them in making their own forecasts. In so doing, they become "smart" about current and forecasted changes and use this increasing alertness to conduct their managerial and planning responsibilities. The process of scanning, forecasting, and planning, therefore, may be more important to the future of the organization than the product of any particular round of forecasting or planning. Consequently, the validity of the analysis is not as crucial as it would be in other research activity.[1]

There are a number of questions related to one of the major tools used by forecasters—the Delphi. Olaf Helmer (1983), one of the developers of the Delphi technique, has posed the following research questions (fp 118): What degree of anonymity is most helpful to the performance of a panel? How should the questioning process be structured? How can information from a variety of individuals from a variety of disciplines be best used? How stable is a panel's judgment over time? What is the optimal panel size? How can the performance of forecasters be calibrated? Be enhanced? What data, data-processing facilities simulations, communication devices or models would be most helpful to forecasters? How can control for the systematic bias of forecasters be obtained?

There are also a number of issues related to a tool essential to forecasting alternative scenarios—cross-impact analysis. For example, the cross-impact matrix is constructed in a bi- variate, first-order impact fashion (if Event A occurs, does it affect the probability of Event B occurring and, if so, to what extent?). It is too unwieldy and complex for this technique to handle the possibility of two or more events jointly affecting the probability of another event. Too, Helmer (1983) notes the problem of "double-accounting"; i.e., "if event A has a direct impact on event C but also has an indirect impact on it via another event, B, how can we make sure that this indirect impact is not also reflected in the direct impact of A on C and thus counted twice?" (p. 120).

Implementation Issues

Most educational leaders can readily identify pressing concerns and issues facing colleges and universities on the basis of their reading, experience in managing issues, and discussions with colleagues, both at home and around the world. Frequently, however, this identification is limited without the benefit of a comprehensive environmental scan of critical trends and potential events in the social, technological, economic, or political environments from the local to the global levels. Moreover, a systematic and continuous scanning process is crucial to the successful implementation of an external analysis/forecasting approach to planning in order to reevaluate the forecasts to determine if they need to be reestimated on the basis of new information generated in the scan.

Developing and institutionalizing a systematic, comprehensive environmental scanning function requires a commitment of time and resources that at present only major corporations (e.g., General Motors), trade associations (e.g., American Council of Life Insurance), think tanks (e.g., Standford Research Institute) and some philanthropic organizations (e.g., United Way of America) have been willing to do. A number of colleges (e.g., St. Catherine) and universities (e.g., Arizona State, Colorado, and Minnesota) have conducted periodic scans, but the only comprehensive, ongoing system reported in the literature is at the Georgia Center for Continuing Education (Simpson, McGinty, and Morrison, 1987). There may be several reasons for this state of affairs. One is the resource commitment required in (a) obtaining sufficient readers to regularly scan a variety of information sources, (b) maintaining the files manually and electronically, and (c) obtaining time of busy administrators and faculty members to review, discuss, and use the pertinent information developed in the process. Pflaum (1985) argues, for example, that many scanning processes do not survive because of the time and energy required to sustain them by volunteers. Ptaszynski, in applying the ED QUEST model in the School of Management at Wake Forest University, reported that their planning team thought that they were wasting valuable professional time scanning irrelevant material, time that detracted from the more important analysis phase (personal communication, May 28, 1988).

There are attempts under way to develop environmental scanning consortia. United Way of America, for example, encourages colleges and universities to participate in its electronic environmental scanning network, although it has not yet established a separate subnet for higher education (Morrison, 1987). Even with such assistance in maintaining a shared data base, however, the question of how to best use the scarce time available for the major decision-makers remains an issue.

Studies Needed

In addition to the research implications of the discussion above in the advancement of this important area of inquiry, there are a number of specific studies needed. For example, the general approach to external analysis and forecasting advanced here has been applied only in a small two-year technical college. How applicable is this model to other types of educational organizations and units (e.g., academic departments, four-year colleges, research universities, state systems of higher education)? A number of case studies are under way that apply this approach to a learning resources center in a dental school (Raney, personal communication, August 1988), to the admissions program of a school of management (Ptaszynski, 1988), to a department of training and development in a university hospital (Clay, personal communication, August 1988), to a consortium of church-related colleges (May 1987), and to a doctoral-degree-granting university (Porter, personal communication, May 1988). More are needed. Such studies could include a focus on actual decision-making behaviors of educational

leaders engaged in formal analysis, forecasting, and planning activities. Others could focus on comparisons of effectiveness (as measured by outcomes) of those institutions using this approach to those not using the approach, controlling on relevant third variables (e.g., selectivity, type of control, institutional size, financial support).

Winkler (1982) identified several promising research directions when considering modeling decision-making problems under uncertainty that are relevant to the approach described in this chapter. First, the link between the creative process and the model-formulation stage of decision-making under uncertainty has not been explored, although Mendell (1985a) has developed a set of rules for improving an individual's ability to create mental scenarios of the future and a framework of questions designed to stimulate consciousness of the future implications of current phenomena (1985b).

Winkler (1982) also suggested the development of decision-aids involving user-friendly computer software for modeling decision-making problems under uncertainty, preferably in an interactive mode. The cross-impact models noted in this chapter such as PASS and *Bravo!* are designed to enable users to generate outlines of scenarios of future environments and of organizational performance simultaneously. It is possible to examine each alternative scenario for developments that give the future its special character and, thereby, to identify those events that are particularly "bad" or "good." Policy options may then be designed to increase the probability of "good" events and decrease the probability of "bad" events. By including these policies in the cross-impact model, it is possible to treat them analytically in the same manner as events (i.e., estimate their effects on the events and trends in the model), and to rerun the computer simulation to create alternative scenarios that contain policies as well as events and trends. This is known as *policy-impact analysis* (Renfro, 1980). Although such decision-aids are available, there is no evidence in the literature that they are being used in external analysis and forecasting in colleges and universities. As Norris and Poulton (1987) note, there is a dire need for case studies to illuminate the applicability of this approach to educational planning.

The applicability of catastrophe theory to sociopolitical forecasting is another direction for possible research. Catastrophe theory defines sudden changes and discontinuities in the behavior of natural and social systems (Woodcock and Davis, 1978). Zeeman (cited in Smith, 1980) points out that catastrophe theory "can be applied with particular effectiveness in those situations where gradually changing forces or motivations lead to abrupt changes in behavior" (p. 26). Although a relatively young science, catastrophe theory is beginning to be applied in planning. For example, analysts at a major corporation adapted the approach for modeling alternative "catastrophes" of discontinuous and divergent change in the motivational forces of growth and profit that control business behavior (Smith, 1980). One can only speculate as to the value in the decision-making process of alternative scenarios generated by computerized cross-impact models incorporating the mathematical modeling approach of catastrophe theory.

There are dozens of other research possibilities to improve this approach to academic planning, of which only two additional ones will be mentioned here. First, there is a need for a current handbook on external analysis and forecasting that can guide college and university institutional researchers and planners in this promising methodology. The only published guides (Fowles, 1978; Henckley and Yates, 1974), although good, are dated. Second, there is a need for a national research effort on the future of higher education, with corresponding implications for academic planning in America's diversified system of colleges and universities. This effort should include an environmental scanning/forecasting data base, housed either with the U.S. Department of Education or at one of the major professional associations (American Association for Higher Education, American Council on Education, Association for Institutional Research, or the Society for College and University Planning). This data base should be electronically accessible to the higher education research and planning community. Moreover, portions of the annual meetings of professional associations could focus on the implications of this evolving data base for academic planning and provide professional development opportunities in current techniques of external analysis and forecasting.

Conclusions

The purpose of environmental analysis/forecasting in academic planning is to provide college and university administrators information that can facilitate better decision-making, particularly in making decisions affecting the long-range future of their institutions. Given that we live in an age of "future shock," when changes in the external environment occur with ever-increasing rapidity, educational leaders are faced with a future that most assuredly will be different from the present. This chapter has reviewed the salient literature describing a basic approach used to manage this uncertainty—identifying issues/concerns based upon experience and upon environmental scanning, structuring issues in the form of trends and events, forecasting the "most likely" future of these trends and events, assessing the interrelationships of these trends and events through cross-impact analysis, and producing alternative scenarios of plausible futures that stimulate the development of viable and robust strategic options that can be incorporated in specific institutional plans. This approach varies from a traditional long-range planning approach based upon a single set of environmental assumptions about the future in recognizing that, although the future is a continuation of existing trends, it is subject to modification by events that have some probability of occurrence. Indeed, environmental uncertainty is caused by potential events. We cannot predict the future, because uncertainty is a product of our incomplete understanding of trends, potential events and their interrelationships. However, by using the best available information we have, we can anticipate plausible alternative futures and, thereby, limit the number of unanticipated possibilities to the smallest possible set.

Acknowledgments. Many of the ideas expressed in this chapter were developed in earlier field work by the first author with Wayne I. Boucher, who continued to provide advice, and encouragement while this manuscript was being prepared. In particular, the sections on cross-impact analysis and scenarios draw heavily on his work as reported in Boucher and Morrison, 1989. In addition, the authors would like to express appreciation to Blanche Arons, Carol

Binzer, Maria Clay, Joseph Coates, Robert Cope, Gay Davis, David Dill, Christopher Dede, William Held, Lee May, Elizabeth Markham, Sherry Morrison, and James Ptaszynski for their helpful comments on earlier versions of the manuscript. Of course, the views expressed here, and any errors, are solely the responsibility of the authors.

Notes

1. This view is not shared by everyone, however. James Ptaszynski (personal communication, May 28, 1988) and David Snyder (personal communication, January 29, 1989) argue that college and university planning teams should not engage in forecasting, but rely solely on forecasts produced by experts.

References

Aguilar, F. J. (1967). *Scanning the Business Environment.* New York: Macmillan.

Aldrich, H. (1979). *Organizations and Environments.* Englewood Cliffs, NJ: Prentice-Hall.

Alexis, M., and Wilson, C. Z. (1967). *Organizational Decision Making.* Englewood Cliffs, NJ: Prentice-Hall.

Alter, S., Drobnick, R., and Enzer, S. (1978). A modeling structure for studying the future. (Report No. M-33). Los Angeles, CA: University of Southern California, Center for Futures Research.

Anderson, C. R., and Paine, F. T. (1975). Managerial perceptions and strategic behavior. *Academy of Management Journal* 18: 811–823.

Andrews, K. R. (1971). *The Concept of Corporate Strategy.* Howewood, IL: Dow Jones-Irwin.

Ansoff, H. I. (1975). Managing strategic surprises by response to weak signals. *California Management Review* 18(2): 21–33.

Armstrong, J. S. (1978). *Long-Range Forecasting.* New York: Wiley.

Asher, W. (1978). Forecasting: an appraisal for policy makers and planners. Baltimore, MD: Johns Hopkins University Press.

Ashley, W. C., and Hall, L. (1985). Nonextrapolative strategy. In J. S. Mendell (ed.), *Nonextrapolative Methods in Business Forecasting* (pp. 61–76). Westport, CT: Quorum Books.

Ayres, R. V. (1969). *Technological Forecasting and Long-Range Planning.* New York: McGraw-Hill.

Barton, R. F. (1966). Realight and business policy decisions. *Academy of Management* (June), pp. 117–122.

Becker, H. S. (1983). Scenarios: importance to policy analysts. *Technological Forecasting and Social Change* 18: 95–120.

Berquist, W. H., and Shumaker, W. A. (1976). Facilitating comprehensive institutional development. In W. H. Berquist and W. A. Shumaker (eds.), *A Comprehensive Approach to Instructional Development* (pp. 1–48). New Directions for Higher Education No. 15. San Francisco, CA: Jossey-Bass.

Blaylock, B. K., and Reese, L. T. (1984). Cognitive style and the usefulness of information. *Decision Science* 15: 74–91.

Boucher, W. I. (1976). *An Annotated Bibliography on Cross-Impact Analysis.* Glastonbury, CT: Futures Group.

Boucher, W. I., ed. (1977). *The Study of the Future: An Agenda for Research.* Washington, DC: U.S. Government Printing Office.

Boucher, W. I. (1982). Forecasting. In J. S. Nagelschmidt (ed.), *Public Affairs Handbook: Perspectives for the 80's* (pp. 65–74). New York: AMACOM.

Boucher, W. I. (1984). *PDOS Technical Advisors' Final Report: Chapters Prepared by Benton International, Inc.* Prepared for the Futures Team of the Professional Development of Officers Study (PDOS), Office of the U.S. Army Chief of Staff. Torrance, CA: Benton International.

Boucher, W. I. (1985). Scenario and scenario writing. In J. S. Mendell (ed.), *Nonextrapolative Methods in Business Forecasting* (pp. 47–60). Westport, CT: Quorum Books.

Boucher, W. I., and Morrison, J. L. (1989). *Alternative Recruiting Environments for the U.S. Army.* Alexandria, VA: Army Research Institute.

Boucher, W. I., and Neufeld, W. (1981). Projections for the U.S. consumer finance industry to the year 2000: Delphi forecasts and supporting data, Report R-7. Los Angeles: Center for Futures Research, University of Southern California.

Boucher, W. I., and Ralston, A. (1983). Futures for the U.S. property/casualty insurance industry: final report, Report R-11. Los Angeles: Center of Futures Research, University of Southern California.

Boulton, W. R., Lindsay, W. M., Franklin, S. G., and Rue, L. W. (1982). Strategic planning: determining the impact of environmental characteristics and uncertainty. *Academy of Management Journal* 25: 500–509.

Bourgeois, L. J. (1980). Strategy and environment: a conceptual integration. *Academy of Management Review* 5: 25–39.

Bright, J. R. (1978). *Practical Technology Forecasting Concepts and Exercise.* Austin, TX: Sweet Publishing Company.

Cameron, K. (1983). Strategic responses to conditions of decline. *Journal of Higher Education* 54: 359–380.

Campbell, G. S. (1971). Relevance of signal monitoring to Delphi/cross-impact studies. *Futures* 3: 401–404.

Campbell, R. M. (1966). A methodological study of the utilization of experts in business forecasting.

Unpublished doctoral dissertation, University of California at Los Angeles.

Chaffee, E. E. (1985). The concept of strategy: from business to higher education. In J. C. Smart (ed.), *Handbook of Theory and Research in Higher Education* (pp. 133–172). New York: Agathon Press.

Cleland, D. I., and King, W. R. (1974). Developing a planning culture for more effective strategic planning. *Long-Range Planning* 7(3): 70–74.

Coates, J. F. (1985). Scenarios part two: alternative futures. In J. S. Mendell (ed.), *Nonextrapolative Methods in Business Forecasting* (pp. 21–46). Westport, CT: Quorum Books.

Coates, J. F. (1986). *Issues Management: How You Plan, Organize, and Manage Issues for the Future*. Mt. Airy, MD: Lomand.

Cope, R. G. (1978). *Strategic Policy Planning: A Guide for College and University Administration*. Littleton, CO: Ireland Educational Corporation.

Cope, R. G. (1981). *Strategic Planning, Management, and Decision Making*. Washington, DC: American Association for Higher Education.

Cope, R. G. (1988). *Opportunity from Strength: Strategic Planning Clarified with Case Examples*. Washington, DC: Association for the Study of Higher Education.

Dalkey, N., and Helmer, O. (1963). An experimental application of the Delphi method to the use of experts. *Management Science* 9(3): 458–467.

Dede, C. (1989). Strategic planning and future studies in teacher education. In W. Robert Houston (ed.), *Handbook of Research on Teacher Education*. New York: Macmillan.

de Jouvenel, B. (1967). *The Art of Conjecture*. New York: Basic Books.

Dill, W. R. (1958). Environment as an influence on managerial autonomy. *Administrative Science Quarterly* 2: 409–443.

Dube, C. S., and Brown, A. W. (1983). Strategy assessment: a rational response to university cutbacks. *Long-Range Planning* 17: 527–533.

Ducot, C., and Lubben, G. J. (1980). A topology for scenarios. *Futures* 12(1): 51–59.

Duncan, O. D. (1973). Social forecasting: the state of the art. *The Public Interest* 17: 88–118.

Duncan, R. B. (1972). Characteristics of organizational environments and perceived environmental uncertainty. *Administrative Science Review* 17: 313–327.

Duperrin, J. C., and Godet, M. (1975). SMIC 74—A method for constructing and ranking scenarios. *Futures* 7: 302–341.

Durand, J. (1972). A new method for constructing scenarios. *Futures* 4: 323–330.

Dutton, J. E., and Duncan, R. B. (1987). The creation of momentum of change through the process of strategic issue diagnosis. *Strategic Management Journal* 8: 279–295.

Ellison, N. (1977). Strategic planning. *Community and Junior College Journal* 48(9): 32–35.

Emery, F. E., and Trist, E. L. (1965). The causal texture of organizational environments. *Human Relations* 18: 21–32.

Enzer, S. (1970). A case study using forecasting as a decision-making aid. *Futures* 2: 341–362.

Enzer, S. (1977). Beyond bounded solutions. *Educational Research Quarterly* 1(4): 21–33.

Enzer, S. (1979). *An Interactive Cross-Impact Scenario Generator for Long-Range Forecasting, Report R-1*. Los Angeles: Center for Futures Research, University of Southern California.

Enzer, S. (1980a). INTERAX—An interactive model for studying future business environments: Part I. *Technological Forecasting and Social Change* 17(2): 141–159.

Enzer, S. (1980b). INTERAX—An interactive model for studying future business environments: Part II. *Technological Forecasting and Social Change* 17(3): 211–242.

Enzer, S. (1983). New directions in futures methodology. In James L. Morrison and Wayne I. Boucher (eds.), *Applying Methods and Techniques of Futures Research* (pp. 69–83). San Francisco: Jossey-Bass.

Enzer, S., Boucher, W. I., and Lazar, F. D. (1971). *Futures Research as an Aid of Government Planning in Canada, Report R-22*. Menlo Park, CA: Institute for the Future, August.

Etzioni, A. (1968). *The Active Society: A Theory of Societal and Political Processes*. New York: Free Press.

Fahey, L., King, W. R., and Narayanan, V. K. (1981). Environmental scanning and forecasting in strategic planning: the state of the art. *Long-Range Planning* 14: 32–39.

Fisher, G. (1987). When oracles fail: A comparison of four procedures for aggregating probability forecasts. *Organizational Behavior and Human Performance* 28: 96–110.

Fowles, J., ed. (1978). *Handbook of Futures Research*. Westport, CT: Greenwood Press.

Gabor, D. (1964). *Inventing the Future*. New York: Knopf.

Gibson, R. (1968). A general systems approach to decision-making in schools. *The Journal of Educational Administration* 6: 13–32.

Goldfarb, D. L., and Huss, W. W. (1988). Building scenarios for an electric utility. *Long-Range Planning* 21: 79–85.

Gollattscheck, J. F. (1983). Strategic elements of external relationships. In G. A. Myran (ed.), *Strategic Management in the Community College* (pp. 21–36). New Directions for Community Colleges, No. 44. San Francisco: Jossey-Bass.

Gordon, T. J. (1968). New approaches to Delphi. In J. R. Wright (ed.), *Technological Forecasting for Industry and Government* (pp. 135–139). Englewood Cliffs, NJ: Prentice-Hall.

Gordon, T. J. (1977). The nature of unforeseen developments. In W. I. Boucher (ed.), *The Study of the Future* (pp. 42–43). Washington, DC: U.S. Government Printing Office.

Gordon, T. J., and Haywood, A. (1968). Initial experiments with the cross-impacts matrix method of forecasting. *Futures* 1(2, December): 100–116.

Gordon, T. J., Rochberg, R., and Enzer, S. (1970). *Research on Cross-Impact Techniques with Applications to Selected Problems in Economics, Political Science, and Technology Assessment, Report R-12*. Menlo Park, CA: Institute for the Future, August.

Gray, D. H. (1986). Uses and misuses of strategic planning. *Harvard Business Review* 64(1): 89–97.

Guerjoy, H. (1977). A new taxonomy of forecasting methodologies. In W. I. Boucher (ed.), *The Study of the Future: An Agenda for Research*. Washington, DC: U.S. Government Printing Office.

Guild, P. B. (1987). How leaders' minds work. In L. T. Sheive and M. B. Schoenheit (eds.), *Leadership: Examining the Elusive* (pp. 81–92). Washington, DC: 1987 Yearbook of the Association for Supervision and Curriculum Development.

Gustafson, D. H., Shulka, R. K., Delbecq, A. L., and Walster, G. W. (1973). A comparative study of difference in subjective likelihood estimates made by individuals, interactive groups, Delphi groups, and nominal groups. *Organizational Behavior and Human Performance* 9: 280–291.

Halal, W. E. (1984). Strategic management: the state-of-the-art and beyond. *Technological Forecasting and Social Change* 25: 239–261.

Hall, R. H. (1977). *Organizations: Structure and Process*. Englewood Cliffs, NJ: Prentice-Hall.

Hambrick, D. C. (1982). Environmental scanning and organizational strategy. *Strategic Management Journal* 2: 159–174.

Hatten, K. J., and Schendel, D. E. (1975). Strategy's role in policy research. *Journal of Economics and Business* 8: 195–202.

Hawken, P., Ogilvy, J., and Schwartz, P. (1982). *Seven Tomorrows*. New York: Bantam.

Hearn, J. C. (1988). Strategy and resources: Economic issue in strategic planning and management in higher education. In J. C. Smart (ed.), *Handbook of Theory and Research in Higher Education* (pp. 212–281). New York: Agathon Press.

Hearn, J. C., and Heydinger, R. B. (1985). Scanning the university's external environment. *Journal of Higher Education:* 56(4) 419–445.

Helmer, O. (1972). Cross impact gaming. *Futures* 4: 149–167.

Helmer, O. (1983). *Looking Forward: A Guide to Futures Research*. Beverly Hills, CA: Sage.

Helmer, O., and Rescher, N. (1959). On the epistemology of the inexact sciences. *Management Science* 1: 25–52.

Henckley, S. P., and Yates, J. R., eds. (1974). *Futurism in Education: Methodologies*. Berkeley, CA: McCutchan.

Heydinger, R. B., and Zenter, R. D. (1983). Multiple scenario analysis as a tool for introducing uncertainty into the planning process. In J. L. Morrison, W. L. Renfro, and W. I. Boucher (eds.), *Applying Methods and Techniques of Futures Research* (pp. 51–68). New Directions for Institutional Research No. 39. San Francisco: Jossey-Bass.

Hirschorn, L. (1980). Scenario writing: a developmental approach. *Journal of the American Institute of Planners* 46: 172–183.

Hobbs, J. M., and Heany, D. F. (1977). Coupling strategy to operating plans. *Harvard Business Review:* 55(3): 119–126.

Hogarth, R. M. (1978). A note on aggregating opinions. *Organizational Behavior and Human Performance* 21: 40–46.

Hogarth, R. M., and Makridakis, S. (1981). Forecasting and planning: an evaluation. *Management Science* 27(2): 115–138.

Ireland, R. D., Hitts, M. A., Bettsm, R. A., and DePorras, D. A. (1987). Strategy formulation processes: differences in perceptions of strengths and weaknesses indicates and environmental uncertainty by managerial level. *Strategic Management Journal* 8: 469–485.

Jain, S. C. (1984). Environmental scanning in U.S. corporations. *Long-Range Planning* 17:117–128.

Jantsch, E. (1967). *Technological Forecasting in Perspective*. Paris: Organization for Economic Cooperation and Development.

Jauch, L. R., and Kraft, K. L. (1986). Strategic management of uncertainty. *Academy of Management Review* 11 (4): 77–790.

Jones, J., and Twiss, B. (1978). *Forecasting Technology for Planning Decisions*. New York: Petrocelli.

Joseph, E. (1974). An introduction to studying the future. In S. P. Henchley and J. R. Yates (eds.), *Futurism in Education: Methodologies* (pp. 1–26). Berkeley, CA: McCutchen.

Kahn, H., and Wiener, A. (1967). *The Year 2000*. New York: Macmillan.

Kahneman, D., Slovic, P., and Tversky, A. (1982). *Judgment Under Uncertainty: Heuristics and Biases*. New York: Cambridge University Press.

Kane, J., and Vertinsky, I. B. (1975). The arithmetic and geometry of the future. *Technological Forecasting and Social Change* 8: 115–130.

Kast, F. L., and Rosenzweig, J. (1979). *Organization and Management: A Systems Approach*. New York: McGraw-Hill.

Kefalas, A., and Schoderbeck, P. P. (1973). Scanning the business environment: some empirical results. *Decision Science* 4: 63–74.

Keller, G. (1983). *Academic Strategy: The Management Revolution in American Higher Education*. Baltimore: Johns Hopkins University Press.

Kiesler, S., and Sproull, L. (1982). Managerial response to changing environments: perspectives on problem sensing from social cognition. *Administrative Science Quarterly* 27: 548–570.

King, W. (1982). Using strategic issue analysis in long-range planning. *Long-Range Planning* 15: 45–49.

Klein, H. E., and Newman, W. H. (1980). How to integrate new environmental forces into strategic planning. *Management Review* 19: 40–48.

Kotler, P., and Murphy, P. (1981). Strategic planning for higher education. *Journal of Higher Education* 52: 470–489.

Lawrence, P., and Lorsch, J. (1967). *Organization and Environment*. Boston: Harvard Business School.

Leblebici, H., and Salancik, G. R. (1981). Effects of environmental uncertainty on information and decision processes in banks. *Administration Science Quarterly* 26: 578–598.

Lee, S. M., and Van Horn, J. C. (1983). *Academic Administration: Planning, Budgeting and Decision Making with Multiple Objectives*. Lincoln: University of Nebraska Press.

Lenz, R. T. (1987). Managing the evolution of the strategic planning process. *Business Horizons* 30: 74–80.

Lenz, R. T., and Engledow, J. L. (1986). Environment analysis: the applicability of current theory. *Strategic Management Journal* 7: 329–346.

Lindsay, W. M., and Rue, L. W. (1980). Impact of the organization environment on the long-range planning process: a contingency view. *Academy of Management Journal* 23: 385–404.

Linneman, R. E., and Klein, H. E. (1979). The use of multiple scenarios by U.S. industrial companies. *Long-Range Planning* 12: 83–90.

Linstone, H. A., and Simmonds, W. H., eds. (1977). *Futures Research: New Directions*. Reading, MA: Addison-Wesley.

Linstone, H. A., and Turoff, M., eds. (1975). *The Delphi method: techniques and application*. Reading, MA: Addison-Wesley.

Lozier, G. G., and Chittipedi, K. (1986). Issues management in strategic planning. *Research in Higher Education* 24(1): 3–13.

Lyles, M., and Mitroff, I. (1980). Organizational problem formulation: an empirical study. *Administrative Science Quarterly* 25: 102–119.

Mandel, T. F. (1983). Futures scenarios and their use in corporate strategy. In K. J. Albert (ed.), *The Strategic Management Handbook* (pp. 10–21). New York: McGraw-Hill.

Martino, J. P. (1983). *Technological Forecasting for Decision-Making* (2nd ed.). New York: North-Holland.

May, L. Y. (1987). Planning for the future of United Methodist education. Draft Ph.D. dissertation proposal, School of Education, University of North Carolina at Chapel Hill.

McConkey, D. D. (1987). Planning for uncertainty. *Business Horizons* 00: 40–45.

McKenney, J. L. and Keen, P. (1974). How managers' minds work. *Harvard Business Review* 52: 79–90.

Meadows, D. H., Meadows, D. L., Randers, J., and Behrens, W. W., III (1972). *The Limits to Growth*. New York: Universe Books.

Mecca, T. V., and Adams, C. F. (1981). *The Educational Quest Guide: Incorporation of Environmental Scanning into Educational Planning*. Greenwood, SC: Institute for Future Systems Research.

Mecca, T. V., and Adams, C. F. (1982). ED QUEST: an environmental scanning process of educational agencies. *World Future Society Bulletin* 16: 7–12.

Mecca, T. V., and Adams, C. F. (April, 1985). Policy analysis and simulation system for educational institutions. Paper presented at the Annual Meeting of the American Educational Research Association, Chicago, April. (ERIC Document Report Reproduction Service No. ED 265–632)

Mendell, J. S. (1985a). Putting yourself in the scenarios: a calculus of mental manipulations. In Jay S. Mendell (ed.), *Nonextrapolative Methods in Business Forecasting* (pp. 77–80). Westport, CT: Quorum Books.

Mendell, J. S. (1985b). Improving your ability to think about the future: training your consciousness. In Jay S. Mendell (ed.), *Nonextrapolative Methods in Business Forecasting* (pp. 81–90). Westport, CT: Quorum Books.

Merriam, J. E., and Makover, J. (1988). *Trend Watching*. New York: AMACOM.

Michael, D. H. (1973). *On Planning to Learn and Learning to Plan*. San Francisco: Jossey-Bass.

Miller, D., and Friesen, P. H. (1980). Archetypes of organizational transitions. *Administrative Science Quarterly* 25: 268–299.

Miller, D., and Friesen, P. H. (1983). Strategy-making and environment: the third link. *Strategic Management Journal* 4: 221–235.

Milliken, F. J. (1987). Three types of perceived uncertainty about the environment: state, effect, and response uncertainty. *Academy of Management Review* 12(1): 133–143.

Miner, F. C. (1979). A comparative analysis of free diverse group decision-making approaches. *Academy of Management Journal* 22(1): 81–93.

Mintzberg, H. (1978). Patterns in strategy formation. *Management Science* 24(9): 934–948.

Mintzberg, H., Raisinghani, D., and Theoret, A. (1976). The structured of unstructured decision processes. *Academy of Management Review* 21: 246–275.

Mitchell, R. B., and Tydeman, J. (1978). Subjective conditional probability modeling. *Technological Forecasting and Social Change* 11: 133–152.

Mitchell, R. B., Tydeman, J., and Georgiades, J. (1979). Structuring the future application of a scenario generating procedure. *Technological Forecasting and Social Change* 14: 409–428.

Morrison, J. L. (1987). Establishing an environmental scanning/forecasting system to augment college and university planning. *Planning for Higher Education* 15(1): 7–22.

Morrison, J. L. (1988). Developing an environmental scanning/forecasting capability: implications from a seminar. Paper presented at the meeting of the Society for College and University Planning, Toronto, Canada, July–August.

Morrison, J. L., and Mecca, T. U. (1988). *ED QUEST—Linking Environmental Scanning for Strategic Management.* Chapel Hill, NC: Copytron.

Morrison, J. L., Renfro, W. L., and Boucher, W. I. (1983). *Applying Methods and Techniques of Futures Research.* New directions in institutional research, No. 39. San Francisco: Jossey-Bass.

Morrison, J. L., Renfro, W. L., and Boucher W.I. (1984). *Futures Research and the Strategic Planning Process: Implications for Higher Education.* ASHE-ERIC Higher Education Research Report No. 9, 1984. Washington, DC: Association for the Study of Higher Education.

Morrison, J. L., Simpson, E., and McGinty, D. (1986). Establishing an environmental scanning program at the Georgia center for continuing education. Paper presented at the 1986 annual meeting of the American Association for Higher Education, Washington, DC, March.

Nanus, B. (1979). *QUEST—Quick Environmental Scanning Technique* (Report No. M34). Los Angeles: University of Southern California, Center for Futures Research.

Naisbitt, John (1982). *Megatrends.* New York: Warner Books.

Nelms, K. R., and Porter, A. L. (1985). EFTE: An interactive delphi method. *Technological Forecasting and Social Change* 28: 43–61.

Norris, D. M., and Poulton, N. L. (1987). *A Guide for New Planners.* Ann Arbor, MI: The Society for College and University Planning.

Nutt, P. (1979). Calling out and calling off the dogs: managerial diagnosis in public service organizations. *Academy of Management Review* 4: 203–214.

Nutt, P. (1986a). Decision style and its impact on managers and management. *Technological Forecasting and Social Change* 29: 341–366.

Nutt, P. (1986b). Decision style and strategic decisions of top executives. *Technological Forecasting and Social Change* 30: 39–62.

Osborne, R. N., and Hunt, J. L. (1974). Environment and organization effectiveness. *Administrative Science Quarterly* 18: 231–246.

Pflaum, A. (1985). External scanning: an introduction and overview. Unpublished manuscript, University of Minnesota, March.

Porter, A. L. (1980). *A Guidebook for Technology Assessment and Impact Analysis.* New York: Elsevier Science.

Pounds, W. F. (1969). The process of problem finding. *Industrial Management Review* 2: 1–19.

Ptaszynski, J. G. (1988). ED QUEST as an organizational development activity. Ph.D. dissertation proposal, School of Education, University of North Carolina at Chapel Hill.

Pyke, D. L. (1970). A practical approach to delphi. *Futures* 2(2): 143–152.

Quade, E. S. (1975). *Analysis for Public Decisions.* New York: American Elsevier.

Renfro, W. L. (1980). Policy impact analysis: a step beyond forecasting. *World Future Society Bulletin* 14: 19–26.

Renfro, W. L. (1983). *The Legislative Role of Corporations.* New York: American Management Association.

Rockart, J. F. (1979). Chief executives define their own data needs. *Harvard Business Review* 57: 81–93.

Sackman, H. (1974). *Delphi Assessment: Expert Opinion, Forecasting, and Group Process. Report R-1283-PR.* Santa Monica, CA: Rand Corporation.

Sage, D. E., and Chobot, R. B. (1974). The scenario as an approach to studying the future. In S. P. Henckley and J. R. Yates (eds.), *Futurism in Education: Methodologies* (pp. 161–178). Berkeley, CA: McCutchen.

Salancik, J. R., Wenger, W., and Helfer, E. (1971). The construction of Delphi event statements. *Technological Forecasting and Social Change* 3: 65–73.

Scott, W. R. (1981). *Organizations: Rational, Natural and Open Systems.* Englewood Cliffs, NJ: Prentice-Hall.

Segev, E. (1976). Triggering the strategic decision-making process. *Management Decision* 14: 229–238.

Shane, H. G. (1971). Future-planning as a means of shaping educational change. In *The Curriculum: Retrospect and Prospect.* Chicago: National Society for the Study of Education.

Shirley, R. C. (1982). Limiting the scope of strategy: a decision based approach. *Academy of Management Review* 7: 262–268.

Simpson, E., McGinty, D., and Morrison, J. L. (1987). The University of Georgia continuing education environmental scanning project. *Continuing Higher Education Review* (Autumn), pp. 1–19.

Slocum, J. W., and Hellriegel, D. (1983). A look at how managers' minds work. *Business Horizons* 26: 56–68.

Smith, W. C. (1980). Catastrophe theory analysis of business activity. *Management Review* 6: 27–40.

Snow, C. C. (1976). The role of managerial perceptions in organizational adaption: an exploratory study. *Academy of Management Proceeding* 249–255.

Steiner, G. A. (1979). *Strategic Planning.* New York: Free Press.

Taggart, W., Robey, D., and Kroeck, K. G. (1985). Managerial decision styles and cerebral dominance: an empirical study. *Journal of Management Studies* 22: 175–192.

Tanner, G. K., and Williams, E. J. (1981). *Educational Planning and Decision-Making.* Lexington, MA: D. C. Heath and Co.

Terreberry, S. (1968). The evolution of organizational environments. *Administrative Science Quarterly* 12: 590–613.

Terry, P. T. (1977). Mechanisms for environmental scanning. *Long-Range Planning* 10: 2–9.

Thomas, P. S. (1980). Environmental scanning: the state of the art. *Long-Range Planning* 13: 20–25.

Thompson, J. D. (1967). *Organizations in Action.* New York: McGraw-Hill.

Uhl, N. P. (1983). Using the Delphi technique in institutional planning. In N. P. Uhl (ed.), *Using Research for Strategic Planning: New Directions for Institutional Research No. 37.* San Francisco: Jossey-Bass.

Utterbach, J. M. (1979). Environmental analysis and forecasting. In Dan E. Schendal and Charles W. Hoffer (eds.). *Strategic Management: A New View of Business Policy and Planning.* Boston: Little, Brown.

Van de Ver, A. H., and Delbecq, A. L. (1974). The effectiveness of nominal, Delphi and interacting group decision making processes. *Academy of Management Journal,* 17(4): 605–621.

Vanston, J. H., Frisbie, W. P., Lopreato, S. C., and Poston, D. L. (1977). Alternate scenario planning. *Technological Forecasting and Social Change* 10: 159–88.

Van Vught, F. A. (1987). Pitfalls of forecasting: Fundamental problems for the methodology of forecasting from the philosophy of science. *Futures* (April), pp. 184–196.

Wagschall, P. H. (1983). Judgmental forecasting techniques and institutional planning. In J. L. Morrison, W. L. Renfro, and W. I. Boucher (eds.), *Applying Methods and Techniques of Futures Research: New Directions for Institutional Research No. 39.* San Francisco: Jossey-Bass.

Weber, C. E. (1984). Strategic thinking—dealing with uncertainty. *Long-range Planning* 17: 61–70.

Wheelwright, S., and Makridakis, S. (1980). *Forecasting Methods for Management* (3rd ed.) New York: Wiley.

Wilson, I. A. (1978). Scenarios. In J. Fowles (ed.), *Handbook of Futures Research* (pp. 225–247). Westport, CT: Greenwood Press.

Winkler, R. L. (1982). State of the art: research directions in decision-making under uncertainty. *Decision Science* 13: 517–533.

Woodcock, A., and Davis, M. (1978). *Catastrophe Theory.* New York: Avon Books.

Woodman, R. W., and Muse, W. V. (1982). Organization development in the profit sector: lessons learned. In J. Hammons (ed.), *Organization Development: Change Strategies* (pp. 22–44). New Directions for Community Colleges No. 31. San Francisco: Jossey-Bass.

Zentner, R. D. (1975). Scenarios in forecasting. *Chemical and Engineering News* 53: 22–34.

Ziegler, W. L. (1972). *An Approach to the Futures-Perspectives.* Syracuse, NY: Syracuse University Research Corporation, Educational Policy Research Center.

Developing Scenarios: Linking Environmental Scanning and Strategic Planning

MEREDITH A. WHITELEY, JOHN D. PORTER, JAMES L. MORRISON AND NELLE MOORE

The 21st century has been the frequent setting for fantastic tales painted by science fiction writers, imaginative comic books, and the movies. By now, however, planners for the nation's businesses, government, colleges and universities need little reminder that the 21st century is within our strategic-planning horizons. The nineties are a critical transition decade, frequently characterized by an acceleration of technological, economic, and social change, increasing uncertainty, and growing international interdependency.

Planning in this age of change, transformation, and uncertainty takes on a number of new dimensions, calling for methods that are not mere extrapolations of past trends but that take into consideration how the future will be different, or "discontinuous," from the past. A central objective of this planning is to place the organization in a strategically flexible position in order to alter its strategies as the contextual conditions of the organization change (Becker and van Doorn, 1987; Godet, 1987).

For some time, planners in large businesses, marketing, and the defense and energy industries have recognized the need for nonextrapolative planning methods better suited for a time of rapid change and discontinuity. Many of the new methods they devised are based on group or expert judgment techniques and result in the development of alternative scenarios of the future. A recent "Manager's Guide to Forecasting" notes that, of the many nonextrapolative methods now in use, the scenario method is a popular and strong choice in developing strategies for the future. A 1983 sur-

vey of Fortune 1000 companies, for example, found that 35 percent of these large and mostly multinational firms use the Multiple Scenario Analysis technique. This figure more than doubled in the four years between 1977 and 1981 (Georgoff and Murdick, 1986; Godet, 1987; Linneman and Klein, 1983).

A critical goal of the scenario method is to guide managers and executives in the organization in their thinking about the future and the implications of the future for the organization. The impetus for much of the move away from planning based on extrapolative methods has been the errors of past extrapolative forecasting. A notable example was the failure of the energy industry to conceive of and plan for the energy crisis of the 1970s. The principal error of extrapolative planning of the type conducted in the energy industry was the assumption that the future will be a continuation of the past (Hankinson, 1986; Millett and Randles, 1986).

In this article, we discuss a method for developing and writing scenarios for a college or university. We begin by reviewing the general literature on scenarios; we then detail a scenario development project at Arizona State University. This project, conducted in 1988–89, was Arizona State University's first institution-wide, futures-based planning and scenario development effort. The focus of the project for Arizona State University was planning and programming for affirmative action. An outside consultant facilitated the group-process portion of the project and instructed university staff in scenario development. Staff in the uni-

"Developing Scenarios: Linking Environmental Scanning and Strategic Planning," by Meredith A. Whiteley, John D. Porter, James L. Morrison and Nelle Moore, reprinted from *Planning for Higher Education*, Vol. 18, No. 4, 1989–90. Society for College and University Planning.

versity's Office of Institutional Analysis then developed and wrote a set of three scenarios to guide the university's affirmative action programming and planning during the decade of the nineties.

What Are Scenarios?

Definitions of scenarios vary. The person most often attributed with the founding of the scenario method in the early 1950s, Herman Kahn, defined the scenario as "a hypothetical sequence of events constructed for the purpose of focusing attention on causal processes or decision points" (Kahn and Weiner, 1967, p. 6).

More recently, Georgoff and Murdick (1986), in their comparison of forecasting techniques, defined scenarios "as smoothly unfolding narratives that describe an assumed future expressed through a sequence of time frames or snapshots" (p.113).

Scenarios, generally written as a group, provide a range of possible futures. The optimum number of scenarios and whether the set should include a "most likely" (i.e., steady state) scenario are issues of debate. The focus of scenarios is on conditions and changes resulting in a future state, identifying threats and opportunities along the way. While scenarios may include elements of an organization's internal environment, most deal primarily with describing the external context within which the organization operates. The use of scenarios allows for the integration of both quantifiable economic and demographic data, along with a wider variety of information on technological environments, social attitudes, and political trends not usually incorporated in more traditional forecasting processes. A critical element of scenario development is specification and analysis of the interrelationships of factors often viewed as discrete entities in other planning methods (Godet, 1987; Hankinson, 1986; Linneman and Klein, 1983; Mendell, 1985; Schnaars, 1987).

Writing Scenarios

Numerous approaches can be taken in writing scenarios, ranging from a single person writing a description of a future situation to the use of an interactive computer model that uses cross-impact analysis to generate outlines of the al-

ternatives (e.g., Becker, 1983; Boucher, 1985; Enzer, 1980; Goldfarb and Huss, 1988; Martino, 1983; Mecca and Adams, 1985; Morrison and Mecca, 1989).

The process of constructing and writing scenarios is often described as something of an art form in which the "artist" (i.e., unsuspecting strategic planner) must weave a number of interrelated events and trends into a coherent picture of the future, complete with strategic options. However, over the past thirty years of scenario use, both constructing and writing scenarios have evolved into a fairly standardized process with several defined steps:

- identifying factors expected to affect the forecasting situation or issue
- postulating sets of plausible future values for these factors
- combining large numbers of values and interrelationships of these factors into a multiple set of scenarios or alternative futures (Linneman and Klein, 1983; Morrison, Renfro and Boucher, 1984; Schnaars, 1987).

Typically, the scenario development process involves a Delphi or mini-Delphi process to identify systematically the factors expected to affect the organizational planning issue and to establish future values for these factors (Godet, 1987; Morrison, Renfro and Boucher, 1984; Schnaars, 1987). As Morrison, Renfro, and Boucher note in their *Futures Research and the Strategic Planning Process: Implications for Higher Education* (1984), "Delphi was designed to obtain consensus forecasts from a group of 'experts' on the assumption that many heads are indeed often better than one, an assumption supported by the argument that a group estimate is at least as reliable as that of a randomly chosen expert" (p. 47).

However, as Michael Godet (1987) recently warned, the use of Delphi is limited by the fact that, "the history of forecasting errors shows rather, that we should distrust predominant ideas; the correct viewpoint is often to be found in the minority view" (p. 66).

The product of group identification and estimation of factors thought to affect the future context of an organization's planning is a large set of interrelated variables, each with a number of future data points. These variables usually include trends with a number of future values as well as events judged on the basis of their probabilities of occurring by a certain future date.

Cross-Impact Analysis

Cross-impact analysis was developed during the 1950s by Olaf Helmer of the Rand Corporation to aid in the organization and assessment of large sets of variables into scenarios. Cross-impact analysis builds on the convergence of opinions obtained through a Delphi process by considering interactions between trends and events. For example, consider how substantial curtailment of federally funded student financial aid might affect enrollments or minority student access at public colleges and universities across the country. Or, in the larger environment, consider how the defaulting of Mexico on loans made by American banks might affect key economic factors in the United States. Cross-impact analysis considers the interdependence of factors, netting an interpretation grid, or "matrix of discovery," from which alternative scenarios can be developed (Godet, 1987; Millett and Randles, 1986; Schnaars, 1987).

One difficulty in using cross-impact analysis is its complexity. Even a small group of ten trends and ten events has many potential cross impacts. Further, the specification of the cross impact can range from a consideration of the direction (+ or –) and degree of impact to include an estimation of the duration of impact or even estimations of the nature/intensity of impact in each year of the planning period. How much interaction occurs in cross-impact analysis depends on which trends and events are included and the assumptions made concerning the direction and order of the interactions. Quite simply, getting people in the organization to commit time and effort to specifying cross impacts is extremely difficult.

The advantage of including cross impacts in developing scenarios is that the process of specifying cross impacts illuminates relationships among factors that may not be considered otherwise. It also enables the planner to visualize a more complete future because reality is a complicated blending of trends and events.

Because of the complications inherent in cross-impact analysis, assumptions must be made to facilitate the process. Over the past twenty years, several computer algorithms have been developed to simulate cross impacts based on differing methodologies for determining whether or not an event occurs (e.g., Monte Carlo or closed-form cross-impact models). However, these models tend to be complex and subject to severe limitations because of computer-programming exigencies.

Attempting to perform cross-impact analysis also can be accomplished qualitatively by focusing on a reduced set of trends and events identified in the Delphi process as most critical to the organization's future. However, regardless of the complexity, the cross impacts of significant trends and events must be considered for the scenarios to become living tools for strategic-planning purposes. Only through interaction of trends and events does the richness of the scenario emerge.

Scenario Development at Arizona State University

In the spring of 1988, Arizona State University launched a futures-based planning project based on the Delphi judgments of approximately eighty faculty, administrators, and students. We then used cross-impact analysis to produce data from which we developed three alternative futures: the Stable Future, the Turbulent Future, and the Chaotic Future. This paper focuses on the development of these three scenarios, using the output generated by cross-impact analysis.

The Setting

Arizona State University is in a dynamic environment not unlike many other colleges and universities, particularly in the growing West. The next ten years are expected to be as increasingly dynamic. Coupled with this growth are significant transformations of the metro-Phoenix economy and lifestyle. Phoenix is, and will continue to be, influenced by changes affecting the United States and world society, including the following:

- accelerating rate of change
- increasing domination of technology in business and education

- shifting patterns in how and where people work
- increasing international interdependency
- changing demographics

The Project

The focus of the Arizona State University project was the university's affirmative action program and policies for students, faculty, and staff. We chose the scenario method to achieve several objectives:

- to identify trends and potential events in the external environment impacting ASU's affirmative action program
- to link these indicators to affirmative action policy evaluation and program planning
- to identify strategic decision points
- to provide a participative input mechanism.

In addition, we hoped to provide a vehicle to institutionalize, within the organizational culture of the university, futures-oriented planning.

The Delphi Process

We developed a questionnaire including fifty-four trends and forty-three events. This set included international trends and events such as the possibility that "a major regional conflict involving U.S. military troops erupts," local trends and events such as "the resale value of homes in the metro-Phoenix area," and internal university trends and events such as the "enrollment caps are implemented." We asked participants to do three things:

- estimate trend levels over the next ten years
- estimate the probability of an event occurring in the next ten years
- nominate additional trends and events they felt might affect the university's affirmative action planning.

Using a Delphi approach, we provided participants with group medians and interquartile ranges and asked individuals to re-vote. This process included a half-day workshop and another round of the Delphi questionnaire.

Estimating Cross Impacts

We estimated the cross impacts of events on events and events on trends. The objective of cross-impact analysis is to examine systematically the interrelationships in the trends and events set, a process that involves asking how the prior occurrence of a particular event might have an impact on other events or trends in the set. For example, for the trend "Enrollment at Arizona State University," suppose that the event "All non-military federal government student financial aid funds are cut by 50 percent" occurs. We then ask the question, How would the occurrence of this event affect this trend? Would the enrollments decrease by 10 percent? Or would enrollments remain unchanged?

With respect to the relationship of events to events, suppose the following event occurs: "A major regional conflict involving U.S. military troops erupts." We ask the question, How will the occurrence of this event affect another event, such as, "A major depression occurs." Would such a conflict decrease the probability of a depression? If so, by how much?

These cross-impact judgments were elaborated in terms of the direction (+ or −) of the impact in the trend value or event probability, the magnitude of the impact, and the duration of the impact. Figure 1 illustrates how the trend "level of federal student financial aid" is impacted by three events: major depression, balanced budget amendment, and regional conflict. For example, if a major depression occurs, the estimated impact on student financial aid would be a 5 percent decrease in the year following the year in which the depression occurs. By the beginning of the third year, the effect of a depression on the level of student financial aid, however, was estimated to be zero. On the other hand, a regional conflict was estimated to increase the level of student financial aid by 2 percent in the year after this event occurs, increasing the trend level by 10 percent five years after occurrence. By the seventh year, the influence of this event on the trend return was estimated to return to zero.

The values of the cross-impact judgments were then used to adjust the Delphi values for interacting events and interacting events and trends. Figure 2 illustrates the change in trend level showing the effects on level of student financial aid if the three events occur.

The Delphi values, with the cross-impact judgment alterations for impacted events and trends, then became the data used to generate our three scenarios.

Generating Scenarios

In our application of cross-impact analysis, we defined each of our three scenarios—Stable, Turbulent, and Chaotic—in terms of a trigger probability value. For example, we set the trigger value for the Stable Scenario at a probability level of .80. All events with a probability of .80 or greater were said to occur in the year their probabilities reached the .80 threshold. Each event's occurrence then set off a chain of alterations in the values of other impacted events and trends.

We manipulated trigger values to obtain rich data sets for each scenario. For the Turbulent Scenario, we set the trigger probability value at .60 and set the trigger value for the Chaotic Scenario at .35. The trigger values then produced scenarios defined by the events in the environment.

Writing ASU's Scenarios

We approached the task of writing scenarios from the vantage point of contemporary insti-

tutional historians in the year 2000 writing about the university's environment and internal developments during the 1990s. Our starting point for each scenario was the event history.

In developing scenarios, we established an organizational and conceptual pattern that we followed throughout the scenario writing. First, we separated our discussion of events and trends. Events were handled as the driving forces of the scenarios, with trends as the descriptors. We began our scenarios with a narrative overview, laying out the major events that occurred over the decade of the nineties. For example, in the Turbulent Scenario, we described the events occurring during the nineties in the following overview:

> This report surveys the history of developments affecting Arizona State University and its affirmative action efforts over the decade of the 1990s. The report chronicles the interplay of broad external forces, as well as the more specific socioeconomic and demographic factors shaping the environment for ASU's recruitment and retention of racial/ethnic minority and female students, faculty, and staff.
>
> Economic depression was the dominant theme of the decade. Starting in 1994, the depression had wide-ranging impact lasting throughout the rest of the decade.

IMPACTED TREND ____Level of federal student financial aid.____

Year since occurrence:	0	1	2	3	4	5	6	7	8	9	10
Impacting Events:											
MAJOR DEPRESSION		-5%		0%							
BALANCED BUDGET AMENDMENT		-5%	-10%	-15%						0%	
REGIONAL CONFLICT		+2%				+10%	0%				

Figure 1 Cross-impact estimations

PERCENT

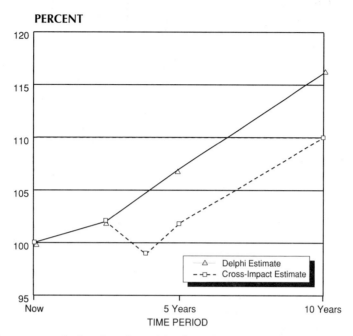

Figure 2 **Level of student financial aid—Delphi and cross-impact estimates**

One effect of the depression was the significant rise in demand for public-funded human services . . . and rising gang activity. . . .

The Arizona legislature responded to the problems of increased demand and lower revenues by focusing on accountability and increasingly intervening in the operations of state agencies . . .

Nationwide, demands for increased accountability, educational outcomes, and raised academic achievement standards were major educational policy issues throughout the decade. . . . As the decade closes, debate continues on the issues of the impact of financial aid cuts on minority student access and the racial bias of new eligibility requirements.

Against this backdrop, Arizona State continued its enrollment growth pattern.

The body of the scenario then dealt with trends, describing their levels and interrelationships over the decade in both narrative and graphics. To handle the large number of trends in our Delphi process, we organized our scenarios into five subsections: Economics, Demographics, Characteristics of the Workforce and Workplace, Education, and Focus on ASU. Here we discussed the implications for the organization of the contextual trends described in other

sections, setting the stage for strategic policy analysis and planning.

Dealing with Contradiction

Our task was to weave this large group of trends into a coherent image of the decade. In preparing our scenarios, however, we were struck immediately with a number of trends that appeared to be contradictory and even conflicting. For example, the trend levels for one scenario indicated a substantial increase in the number of women head-of-household families living below the poverty level—a not surprising, negative picture of women's economic status. At the same time, however, trend levels for the same scenario painted a more positive picture of substantially more women in graduate programs. Added to this were a number of other trends, some indicating a worsening in the economic and career status of women, others indicating improvement.

Our first reaction to contradictions of this kind was to check our data. Finding that our output correctly reflected the Delphi judgment values plus the cross-impact estimations, we then were left to puzzle over issues involved in the economic status of women. What we concluded was that trend projections in our output might well reflect a widening opportunity gap, separating the futures of those women with marketable skills and education from the futures of those with little skills or training.

Characteristics of the Three Scenarios

The Stable Scenario

The Stable Scenario generally portrayed a steady state future. Only six events occurred in this scenario, generating few cross-impact alterations of the Delphi estimations of trends. Three of these events related directly to higher education. In this scenario, the economy remained relatively stable, with only a slight downward trend in 1994–95. Demographic trends in the Stable Scenario included a rise in the numbers of the local population living below the poverty level and an increase in the proportion of women head-of-household families. These and other trends resulted in a dramatic rise in demand for social services. Characteristics of the Workforce and Workplace reflected the widening opportunity gap for both racial/ethnic minorities and women between those with marketable skills and education and those without. Throughout the decade, the latter group was portrayed as experiencing an increasing dislocation and economic instability.

Education in the Stable Scenario reflected rising college tuition costs and declining federal financial aid dollars. While Arizona's racial/ethnic minority student college enrollments rose substantially in this environment, most of this increase was in the state's community colleges. The state's universities garnered only a small 10 percent of this gain. In this environment, the Focus on ASU section described how Arizona State University faced the decision of whether to cap enrollment and the question of whether this decision would affect minority student access.

The Turbulent Scenario

The Turbulent Scenario portrayed a decade characterized by an economic recession/ depression and its related social problems. In this decade, fourteen events occurred, including a major depression in 1994, a fossil fuel crisis of

1973–74 proportions in 1999, and legislation passed by the Arizona legislature tying funding increases in education to educational outcomes in 1998. One result of the economic recession/depression was a dramatic increase in demand on publicly funded social services. The Arizona legislature responded to increased demand and lower revenues by focusing on accountability and by increasingly intervening in agency operations, including the state's universities.

Demographic trends reflected the economic downturn in a dramatic increase in homelessness and poverty. Characteristics of the Workforce and Workplace in the Turbulent Scenario reflected the economic depression with an increase in unemployment and a widening of the opportunity gap. The impact of the depression on the individual, however, was buffered partly by education, experience, and/or skills. The Focus on ASU section of the scenario included the following narrative:

> The effects of the depression on ASU were complex. While the decline in federal financial aid put the university out of reach for the severely economically disadvantaged, overall enrollment continued to climb during the first half of the decade. As enrollments climbed, debate centered around the decisions to cap main campus enrollments and establish a second branch campus in the East Valley . . .
>
> In this environment, ASU's affirmative action hiring tasks became more complex. On the one hand, the depression improved the size of the pools of racial/ethnic minority and women faculty and management personnel by as much as 33% during the period. Yet, on the other hand, salaries in the higher education sector became less competitive with the outside marketplace during the decade. While the effects of the depression on ASU were perhaps less severe than for many higher education institutions, the decline in appropriations and enrollment caps translated into only a few new positions and minimum hiring opportunities.

The Chaotic Scenario

In the Chaotic Scenario, we portrayed the decade of the nineties as a time of dislocation and disruption. Driving the Chaotic Scenario were nineteen events, including "a major depression occurs," "all non-military federal government student financial aid funds are cut by at least 50 percent," "a major regional conflict involving U.S. military troops erupts," and "the U.S. experiences a dramatic flood of refugees from Mexico, Central, and/or South America." The background section of the scenario described government's response:

> Confronted with problems of unprecedented magnitude, state and local governments responded with haphazard and often drastic policies and measures . . . in an environment of dwindling resources for higher education, demands for increased accountability, educational outcomes measures, and raised academic achievement standards were major educational policy responses.

The depression of the Chaotic Scenario was reflected in a number of trends described in the Economics section of the scenario. The rate of new job creation in Arizona, for example, fell by 20 percent over the decade. At the same time, business relocation to the Sunbelt fell by 26 percent, and the resale value of homes in metro-Phoenix declined by 27 percent. Not surprisingly, the social problems described in the Stable and Turbulent Scenarios deepened in the Chaotic nineties. In the Characteristics of the Workforce and Workplace section of the Chaotic Scenario, we detailed how the worldwide depression in an era of technological revolution brought changes to the workforce by raising the social security retirement age to 70 and changing the distribution of industry in the metro-Phoenix area. In addition, the depression of the Chaotic Scenario reflected a substantial change in the opportunity gap described in the Stable and Turbulent Scenarios. While opportunities remained steady throughout this decade for skilled and educated women, opportunities for skilled and educated minorities declined substantially.

The impact of the Chaotic Scenario conditions on education and Arizona State University was catastrophic. Tuition and funding cuts not only took their toll on the disadvantaged, but also devastated enrollments of whites and racial/ethnic minorities throughout the higher education system. For Arizona State University, the severe depression conditions of the Chaotic Scenario brought faculty and staff layoffs, a downscaling of programs, and an abandonment of earlier affirmative action goals and strategies.

Conclusion

The development and use of scenarios at Arizona State University was an experiment for us in terms of both (1) the dynamics of the process within our organization and (2) the methodology of writing scenarios. Our experience developing scenarios taught us a number of lessons that may be helpful to other institutions contemplating the development of scenarios for strategic planning.

Scenarios and the Organization

Significant changes within the university over the course of the project made it difficult for us to assess fully how the process works within the organization. Early in the project, the associate vice president for student affairs, a key supporter and organizer of the process, took a position as a vice president at another university. At about the same time, after eight years, the university president announced his retirement. However, despite the administrative disruption during the project, in the year since the project's completion, we see that several of our organizational objectives were met. The process of developing and using scenarios accomplished the following:

- focused and expanded our environmental-scanning efforts
- provided an input vehicle for a large number of people into the process of thinking about and planning for the future
- identified strategic decision points for the affirmative action program and highlighted many linkages between programs and the external environment

Writing Scenarios

There is no cookbook for writing scenarios. While we rather facetiously noted earlier that scenario writing is often referred to as an "art form," it is a highly creative process. Scenario writing requires a narrative writer unafraid of taking risks, making generalizations, and going out on a limb. While cross-impact analysis does provide an organized set of data for scenario writing, there is a creatively ambiguous gap still remaining between the data and the written story. From the vantage point of hindsight, we see that our scenario development and writing would have been aided if we had

- *specified critical factors more clearly.* Our Delphi questionnaire was far from perfect. In writing the scenarios from the results of this questionnaire, we frequently wished we had stated our factors more clearly. For example, our questionnaire included a trend we phrased as "percent of minority teens in Arizona entering the workforce rather than continuing their education." What we meant and should have said was "Arizona minority student high school dropout rate."

- *expanded the national, state, and local ranges of critical factors.* We frequently found the regional range of our factors too limiting, i.e., factors covered either too broad or too narrow an area. For example, our Delphi questionnaire included the trend "amount of Arizona student financial aid targeted specifically for minorities." We frequently wished in writing our scenarios that we also had this trend specified on a national level so that we could relate it to the trend in all federally funded financial aid.

- *controlled for the negative outlook.* Our scenarios portrayed ranges of "gloom and doom," primarily because of the closed-form, cross-impact methodology used in the project. This methodology, coupled with specifying a negative event (e.g., "a major economic depression occurs"), overshadowing all other events, produced these negative results.

Planning with Scenarios

In addition, we discovered that development and use of scenarios add a number of dimensions that are particularly important to planning in a time of rapid change:

- delineating the interrelationships between the organization's internal operations and the external context, thus placing a new emphasis on the organization's continuous environmental scanning.

- exposing the interrelationships between factors, often in ways not easily apparent, thus challenging the assumptions and

traditional thinking of planners and decision makers within the organization.

- simultaneously focusing and expanding the view of the organization's environmental-scanning effort. A number of factors previously thought to be important are shown to have less importance; at the same time, however, other factors are stressed, and new factors are shown to have high potential impact.

- defining critical strategic decision points, providing "lead time" and the opportunity for the organization to take a more proactive position in shaping its future.

- providing a mechanism for input. By utilizing group processes and feedback, scenario development facilitates communication both vertically and horizontally throughout the organization.

In sum, our experience at Arizona State University showed us that scenario development is a viable tool, particularly for expanding the thinking of planners and focusing the environmental-scanning effort. However, the institutionalization of scenario development and use across the organization is, for us, still a question. If the process can be streamlined and the benefits more directly related to specific decisions, we believe scenarios can make an important contribution in better preparing colleges and universities for a new era that promises to be dramatically different from the past.

Meredith A. Whiteley *is a senior researcher,* John D. Porter *is director, and* Nelle Moore *is research analyst, all in the Office of Institutional Analysis at Arizona State University.* James L. Morrison *is professor of education at the University of North Carolina, Chapel Hill.*

References

Becker, Henk A. and van Doorn, Joseph W. M. "Scenarios in an Organizational Perspective." *Futures, 19,* 1987, 669–677.

Becker, Howard S. "Scenarios: Importance to Policy Analysts." *Technological Forecasting and Social Change, 18,* 1983, 95–120.

Boucher, Wayne I. "Scenarios and Scenario Writing." *Nonextrapolative Methods in Business Forecasting: Scenarios, Vision, and Issues Management.* Edited by Jay S. Mendell. Westport, CT: Quorum Books, 1985.

The Council of State Governments. *The Dynamic West: A Region in Transition.* IL: Westrends, The Council of State Governments, 1989.

Enzer, Selyn. "INTERAX–An Interactive Model for Studying Future Business Environments: Part I." *Technological Forecasting and Social Change, 17,* 1980, 141–159.

Georgoff, David M. and Murdick, Robert G. "Manager's Guide to Forecasting." *Harvard Business Review, 64,* 1986, 110–120.

Godet, Michael. *Scenarios and Strategic Management.* Boston, MA: Butterworths, 1987.

Goldfarb, David L. and Huss, William R. "Building Scenarios for an Electric Utility." *Long Range Planning, 21,* 1988, 79–85.

Hankinson, G.A. "Energy Scenarios—The Sizewell Experience." *Long Range Planning, 19,* 1986, 94–101.

Kahn, Herman and Weiner, Anthony J. *The Year 2000.* London: Macmillan, 1967.

Linneman, Robert E. and Klein, Harold E. "The Use of Multiple Scenarios by U.S. Industrial Companies: A Comparison Study, 1977–1981." *Long Range Planning, 16,* 1983, 94–101.

Martino, Joseph P. *Technological Forecasting for Decision-Making,* 2d ed. New York, NY: North-Holland, 1983.

Mecca, Thomas V. and Adams, Charles F. "Policy Analysis and Simulation System for Educational Institutions." Paper presented at the annual meeting of the American Educational Research Association, Chicago, IL, 1985. (ERIC Document Reproduction Service No. ED 0265 632).

Mendell, Jay S. *Nonextrapolative Methods in Business Forecasting: Scenarios, Vision, and Issues Management.* Westport, CT: Quorum Books, 1985.

Millett, Steven M. and Randles, Fred. "Scenarios for Strategic Business Planning: A Case History for Aerospace and Defense Companies." *Interfaces, 16,* 1986, 64–72.

Morrison, James L. and Mecca, Thomas V. "Managing Uncertainty: Environmental Analysis/Forecasting in Academic Planning." *Higher Education: Handbook of Theory and Research,* Volume V. Edited by John C. Smart. New York, NY: Agathon Press, 1989, 354–390.

Morrison, James L., Renfro, William L., and Boucher, Wayne I. *Futures Research and the Strategic Planning Process: Implications for Higher Education. ASHE/ERIC Higher Education Research Reports,* Number 9, 1984.

Schnaars, Steven P. "How to Develop and Use Scenarios." *Long Range Planning, 20,* 1987, 105–114.

The Vision Thing in Higher Education

George Keller

Lately there has been expanding talk about how the planners and leaders in higher education need to "reinvent" America's colleges and universities for the changed conditions in the nation. If any educational group intends to reinvent its university or college it will need to have some idea of what the newly invented institution might look like. It is not sufficient to move away from existing problems, inefficiencies, and outmoded structures and programs. Toward what new directions should the group move? They will require a vision of what the renovated university or college could or should become.

The need for vision seems so obvious. Individually we have visions of becoming firemen, great violinists, major league pitchers, fashion models, famous authors, competent doctors or nurses, or owners of our own store or business. We labor to make ourselves more physically fit or financially shrewd. We struggle to have a happy family life or a merry circle of friends. Collectively we often work to make the town we live in one of the loveliest and best run, to have our college be the friendliest and best teaching institution in the region, or to see that the United States is a land of opportunity and freedom for all citizens, as Martin Luther King, Jr. did so magnificently. Nearly all humans carry a dream in their pockets, a vision of what could be one day in the future.

Somehow through evolution, mysteriously, human beings have been provided with two kinds of vision. One is the animal recognition of material objects and movements with our

eyes. The other is the ability to see with our minds, to imagine a new political condition, an ideal vegetable garden, a novel law school program. We can look back in time as we do with reflection, regret, or reevaluation; and we can look forward to conceive of a larger or smaller institution, a different organizational structure, a more strategic mode of operating in the decade ahead, or a new kind of international society linked by electronics and clever software. We are intelligent animals, intricately equipped for both sight and imagination. As one essayist recently wrote:

> Our bodies demonstrate, albeit silently, that we are more than just a complex version of our animal ancestors to which a little dab of rationality has been added; and conversely that we are also more than an enlarged brain, a consciousness somehow grafted onto or trapped within a blind mechanism that knows only survival. The human form as a whole impresses on us its inner powers of thought (or awareness and action). Mind and hand, gait and gaze, breath and tongue, foot and mouth—all are isomorphically part of a single package, suffused with the presence of intelligence.[1]

The history of U.S. higher education is replete with stories of persons who imagined, who saw ahead in their minds a new kind of college or university: Charles William Eliot and Nicholas Murray Butler who transformed urban colleges for gentlemen into great universities at Harvard and Columbia; Emma Hart Willard, who envisioned young women study-

"The Vision Thing in Higher Education," by George Keller, reprinted from *Reinventing the University*, 1995. John Wiley & Sons, Inc. Also published in *Planning for Higher Education*, Vol. 23, 1995.

ing as undergraduates as young men did; the Holy Cross fathers who imagined a Roman Catholic university in the wilds of northern Indiana at South Bend; president Wallace Sterling and provost Fred Terman who envisioned a postWorld War II, Harvard-like university at Stanford for people on the West Coast; U.S. Congressman Justin Morrill of Vermont who imagined and fought for a new kind of public college in every state "to promote the liberal and practical education of the industrial classes"—the land-grant college; and Frank Aydelotte who envisioned an Oxfordlike college in Swarthmore, Pennsylvania.

As I said, the need for vision seems obvious, and natural. Human beings are imaginative, envisioning creatures. Civilizations, and colleges and universities, are built and maintained and improved by people who possess a vision about a kind of life or institution different from the one that exists.

Phooey on Vision

Yet in the 1990s there is a growing cynicism about vision. When IBM's new chairman, Louis Gerstner, was questioned at a press conference about how he intended to halt the decline of the corporation, he responded:

> There have been a lot of questions as to whether I'm going to deliver a vision for IBM. I would like to say that the last thing IBM needs right now is a vision. What it needs is very tough-minded . . . strategies for each of its businesses.

And Robert Eaton, the new chairman of the Chrysler Corporation, told the *Wall Street Journal*, "Internally we don't use the word vision. I believe in quantifiable short-term results—things we can all relate to, as opposed to some esoteric thing no one can quantify." Billionaire William Gates, chairman of Microsoft Corporation, has sneered, "Being a visionary is trivial."

In higher education, a similar, growing disdain for vision can be heard. The new mood was perhaps best expressed in Richard Chait's opinion article in the September 22, 1993 *Chronicle of Higher Education*. In his view, "The 'vision thing' has been elevated nearly to the level of religion in higher education." But Chait contends, "The virtues of vision have been exaggerated. The concept should be enshrined in

the pantheon of panaceas that already includes management by objectives, zero-based budgeting, quality-control circles, and TQM." Chait believes "these are not the times for heady visions," and he argues for an Adam Smith-like *laissez-faire* approach by campus administrators:

> For all the emphasis placed upon vision, observers of higher education would be hard pressed to cite more than a dozen or two colleges . . . that have been successfully "reinvented . . ." More often institutional priorities and opportunities emerge from individual and departmental initiatives . . .
>
> Freed of the obligation to craft a compelling and comprehensive vision college presidents can concentrate on crucial, if mundane, tasks like controlling costs, increasing productivity, diversifying their work forces, assessing quality and streamlining operations . . .
>
> Few professors are disposed to be guided, let alone summoned, by the North Star of a presidential vision . . . Presidents may do better to nip at the heels of the laggards, to contain the strays to the extent possible, and wait importantly, to nudge the entire herd along.[2]

Richard Chait is a member of the higher education faculty at the University of Maryland's School of Education, along with scholars Robert Birnbaum and Frank Schmitlein. Chait and his colleagues at Maryland have been leaders in the higher education studies field in deriding attempts to improve leadership, strategic planning, quality of service enhancement, and vision in academe. Adhering to the incrementalism of political scientist Charles Lindblom, who wrote that, "Patching up an old system is the most rational way to change it, for the patch constitutes about as big a change as one can comprehend at a time,"[3] the Maryland school of skeptics believes in the beneficent "hidden hand" of multifold and scattered initiatives, chiefly by the faculty.

In this the Maryland scholars reflect the views of dozens of college and university presidents I have met who feel they are able to be little more than highly paid janitors and dignified spokespersons, and who are convinced that passive, unobtrusive administration of the semi-anarchic status quo is the only "realistic" course. They also concur with the view of

Clark Kerr and others who argue that the new power of federal grant agencies, state commissioners of higher education, ambitious scholar-entrepreneurs in their midst, the courts, special-interest racial, gender, and ethnic groups, and the accrediting bodies prevent academic executives from having a vision of their own for their institution. In the words of Clark Kerr during his 1963 Godkin lectures at Harvard:

> There is a "kind of lawlessness," in any large university . . . and the task is to keep this lawlessness within reasonable bounds . . . The president becomes the central mediator . . . among groups and institutions moving at different rates of speed and sometimes different directions . . . He has no new and bold "vision of the end." He is driven more by necessity than by voices in the air.[4]

This Ronald Reagan-like perspective on modern academic leadership is, I think a salutary caution, particularly against the sometimes hyperbolic claims for "reinventing" the university and those academic management texts which assume that campus deans and presidents have the charisma and power of England's Henry IV. To "reinvent" is to make over completely, or to reestablish in a very different form an already established institution. This is not very likely to happen. Universities are among the oldest, most conservative, and slowly adaptive organizations in Western civilization.[5]

The New Demands

But the caretaker view of college leadership—administration without vision, patching up and nipping at the heels of the professorial laggards—has become a perilous one to advocate at the end of the 20th century. It is also flawed in its analysis and suppositions.

For one thing not having a vision is a kind of vision. To imagine that a college will remain pretty much the same over the next 15–20 years in the face of radical changes in demography, technology, and finances is an apparition—and a decision about the future—as much as a vision to double in size or to become more multicultural.

For another thing, if an institution has no vision, other persons or outside agencies may

force a new mission, usually a more restricted or specialized one, on the institution. For a third item, a concentration on the basics—"good, solid blocking and tackling," as IBM's Louis Gerstner puts it—is quite appropriate for an organization that is badly run and in trouble because of ineptitude and neglect, and its lack of vision. The first priority for poorly run colleges, after all, is to get their house in order. TQM, well done, has been a considerable help to some colleges in this situation. But if a university is functioning fairly well, the priority becomes: what should it do in the future to maintain its position and excellence? Or to move to a slightly higher level of quality?

There are larger reasons for vision in higher education, however. It is not an historical accident that the calls for greater attention to the future began in the late 1960s and reached an almost nagging emphasis in the 1970s and 1980s. Herman Kahn and Daniel Bell (who invented the term "post-industrial society") in 1967, Michael Young in 1968, and Peter Drucker in 1969 were prominent among those who pointed out that North America and Western Europe were at the edge of major social, technological, demographic, and economic changes.[6]

After the 1965 amendments to the Immigration and Nationality Act, the United States began admitting more immigrants (including 150,000 to 300,000 illegal entries) each year than all the rest of the developed world combined, ushering in a new period of multiculturalism. The personal computer was introduced. The traditional two-parent family began disintegrating. Since the family has long been the co-educator of children, the change has meant new problems for the schools and cities. Out-of-wedlock births have increased rapidly to the point where 30 percent of all babies are now born in that way. Adult education has become a giant, growing addition to the customary youth education for many colleges and universities. And America faces new financial pressures from Japan and other countries abroad and from escalating expenses for crime prevention and prisons, pollution, pensions for the elderly, and health care from inside the nation. In short, the environment has become very turbulent, and educators are increasingly being asked to respond to the radical changes and "reinvent" their structures and services for the new environment.

A second source of pressure for greater vision is from those who think that the increasing decentralization and fragmentation of universities and many colleges demands something to hold the institution together—what two business professors have called "superordinate goals." These are "significant meanings or guiding concepts that an organization imbues in its members."[7] In effect, a vision of where the institution is going seems necessary to bind together the loose coupling of many campus parts.

As colleges grew larger, and as numerous universities (and some community colleges) expanded to 25,000 to 40,000 students in the 1970s, educational leaders pushed decisions out of the president's and academic vice president's office to the schools, departments, and divisions. This frequently resulted in quasi-independent medical, business, or law schools, or departments of physics or economics, or maintenance or student affairs divisions. The question thus becomes: How can a university decentralize and at the same time have a coordinated effort? As two scholars put it:

> How can people in the far reaches of these flatter organizations know where it is heading? The development of a shared organizational vision represents a response to this problem.[8]

There are other pressures to create a vision. Colleges and universities have long lead times. Change at most campuses is remarkably slow, with long debates over the processes, details, and educational policies. New facilities often have to be planned for five to eight years in advance. And students are preparing for work in society 10 to 20 years from the present. Therefore, a vision that imagines the institution 10 years hence is an enormous help. Also, arriving at a desirable vision for the institution's future circumvents some of the fierce discussion about the details of the present situation and immediate reallocations. A vision enables academics to think seriously about the purposes, priorities, and distinctiveness of their college or university without threats to current positions and arrangements.

Then too, Henry Mintzberg of Canada's McGill University has argued that strategic planning is largely instrumental. It provides reasonable priorities and detailed steps after the leaders have formulated a vision. For him, "Planning does not promote significant change in the organization so much as deal with it when it is introduced by other means." To him "A plan as vision—expressed in imagery, or metaphorically—may prove a greater incentive to action than a plan that is formally detailed, simply because it is more attractive and less constraining."[9] A vision with some emotional content is often more likely to spur action toward a rearranged college than a well-conceived strategy; and it gives faculty members a greater freedom to invent.

Vision's Key Ingredients

Vision is not the same as a mission statement, which is almost always a bland stew of platitudes, beliefs, and vague goals. Vision is a combination of gut values and a tangible goal.

The gut values need to be ones that are part of the college's tradition and that at least a large minority of people on campus already subscribe to. If the values articulated in a vision are too idealistic or vague, the vision will be treated cynically. The values must be genuine and specific. For example, a rigorous, historic liberal arts college might say, "Our college will continue to educate a small number of very able undergraduates for the highest positions in society through intense and scholarly study with exceptional scholar-teachers." Or, a major, large state university might advocate something like benefactor Ezra Cornell did when he established Cornell University: "I would found an institution where any person can find instruction in any study," thus giving equal value to poultry science, forestry, and labor relations and to history, literature, and science.

But if a college proclaims it will be a place giving primary importance to the cultivation of every individual's personal and intellectual growth—as half of America's colleges seem to do in their catalogs—when faculty union members, the director of athletics, or the dean of students actually have other priorities, the values will be only a fanciful bromide rather than an authentic expression of gut values. L. L. Bean, the Maine clothing and camping merchant, said in 1947: "Sell good merchandise at a reasonable price, and treat your customers as you would your friends, and the business will take care of itself." These were Bean's gut values.

But it is not enough to express one's deepest values in the vision statement. The vision must also have a tangible outcome. It should be an inspiring picture of a different future, something that seems slightly out of reach but achievable if enough people work on it, as when President John Kennedy proclaimed in 1961 as a vision, "before this decade is out, of landing a man on the moon and returning him safely to earth."

The tangible outcome is tricky. It should not be too definite and detailed, yet vivid enough to allow persons to imagine a new and better set of conditions and services and to strive toward their fulfillment. For instance, in 1909 Henry Ford said his vision was, "to democratize the automobile." The statement did not suggest the Model T but made it clear that the Ford Motor Company would concentrate on low-cost cars, not Cadillac-like vehicles. The vision implied a target audience and the kind of automobile with which the company would seek preeminence.

There are two kinds of tangible outcomes. One is that of setting a clear, unambiguous target. Here are some fictional examples of targeting:

"Within the next 20 years our university will become the near-equal of Harvard for Southern youths and adults."

"We will become widely known as the best managed and financially open private college in our region."

"The college will in the next 10 years be the finest teaching institution among state colleges in our state."

"Our state university will be smaller, more focused, and regarded as one of the top 10 or 12 public universities in the nation."

The other kind of tangible outcome is that of institutional transformation, of picturing a slightly "reinvented" institution to meet the emerging realities of the next decades. Again, some fictional examples:

"The university will have more Blacks, Latinos, and Asians among its students and faculty, and reorient its curriculum and scholarship to be more international and multicultural."

"Our university will employ the most advanced technology for teaching, financial planning and controls, and new linkages with other academic, cultural, and scientific entities."

"Recognizing the increase in state and community colleges, this historic state university will enlarge its graduate education, research, and leadership in professional education, admitting fewer undergraduates and chiefly those of demonstrated scholarly interests."

Misconceptions and Fallacies

One of the most common errors that critics of vision make is their assertion that vision requires a charismatic or exceptionally clairvoyant president. This is patently untrue. Some department chairpersons have created extraordinary collections of scholars in their department. I have often been told that a "visionary" financial officer has kept some institution's eyes on long-term financial strength rather than short-term expenditures. Three times in my travels I have encountered directors of buildings and grounds who take unusual pride in their work and staff and have a vision of what the campus grounds and horticulture will look like in the next decade.

Another error is that visionaries are dreamers, ambitious utopians who can't and won't pay attention to costs, details, and current problems. They lack realism, with realism usually defined as accommodation to the status quo and small, incremental changes at the edges. The fact is that good visions usually emerge from attention to the myriad workings of the institution, not a neglect of such attention. And even small changes can't be carried out effectively unless one has a vision of the direction toward which the small changes should be made.

Some of the most acerbic critics of "vision" have an implicit vision of their own about where the college or university should be going, although there is also a small but growing band of higher education scholars who seem resigned to drift, semianarchy, and lack of fiscal priorities or controls as the only satisfactory way of administering a varied, rambunctious, and quarrelsome collection of specialized scholars. To them, a vision seems confining rather than a bonding agent which provides purpose and distinctiveness to an institution competing with numerous others of the 3,500 colleges and universities in the United States.

However, there are several key ingredients that educators who would develop and promote a vision must possess. One is a sense of history, of what works and doesn't in social organizations, especially during times of change. Another is a willingness to understand the public's view as well as the parochial campus interests. Peter Drucker once expressed it this way:

> [The visionary leader] has to establish himself as a spokesman for the interest of society in producing, in performing, in achieving ... He has to become the proponent, the educator, the advocate. The manager, in other words, will have to learn to create the "issues."[10]

The vision of an education leader should connect the private interests of the professors and staff to the public urgencies of society in the years ahead.

Educators and planners also need to sharpen their imaginative thinking. Faculty members are passionately devoted to "critical thinking" but they say very little about *creative thinking*, which in our time has become essential. Our colleges and universities, as well as America's other institutions, lack sufficient powers of social invention. No one ever used creative thinking about social life better than Alexis de Tocqueville, when he observed Americans, identified the central features of young America, and constructed a pattern for future developments in this country.[11] In recent years more strategic planners and educators have become adept at analyzing the thrusts and novel features of society and have begun to help create visions and strategic plans to implement the visions.[12]

An Emotional Lever for Change

In a remarkable new book Antonio Damasio, one of the world's leading neuroscientists, has provided scientific evidence of "Descartes' error," the notion that there is an area of the brain that is capable of pure, objective thought.[13] Damasio and others have demonstrated in the past decade that every part of the brain is tied to emotion and to physical movements. People are creatures of their genetic material, their environmental conditioning, and their emotions.

Visions have emotional power. They help us organize our knowledge and supply hope, passion, and direction. They help give meaning to our lives. Visions speak to our entire selves rather than just to dry-as-felt goals or quantifiable objectives.

If colleges and universities are to reform their structures, finances, and services they will have to possess some vision of how they will do so, and why. The vision for any institution should combine its tradition, culture, and core values with the emerging conditions in society and with the public's expectations about higher education's role and behavior in the new environment.

The vision may take root in one of a university's colleges which is led by a farsighted dean. It can originate with department or division chairs, or with a courageous vice president. It can be forced by a strong, forward-looking Board of Trustees if the president and faculty drag their feet. Whatever its source, each college and university should design a vision for itself. David Riesman once wrote,

> There has always been room for innovation and fresh starts in American higher education, even if this freedom, which rested partly on expanding enrollments and funds, is more circumscribed now. What is really lacking is strong and visionary academic leadership.[14]

George Keller is editor of Planning for Higher Education. An award-winning author and editor, and recipient of SCUP's Casey Award for "distinguished achievements in the field of education planning," he is working on a book about designing colleges and universities for the 21st century. This article is reprinted with permission from the just published book, Reinventing the University, edited by Sean Rush and Sandra Johnson, and published by John Wiley & Sons.

Notes

1. Leon Kass, *The Hungry Soul: Eating and the Perfecting of Our Nature* (Free Press, 1994), 75–76. See also George Keller, "Neuroscience and the New Foundations of Transformational Planning." Paper presented at the 29th Annual Conference of the Society for College and University Planning, on July 26, 1994, in San Francisco.

2. Richard Chait, "Colleges Should Not Be Blinded by Vision," *Chronicle of Higher Education*, September 22, 1993, B1, B2.

3. Robert Dahl and Charles Lindblom, *Politics, Economics, and Welfare* (University of Chicago Press, 1976), 86.

4. Clark Kerr, *The Uses of the University* (Harvard University Press, 1963), 35, 37.

5. It is instructive to read medieval historian Charles Homer Haskins. *The Rise of Universities* (Cornell University Press, 1957).

6. Herman Kahn and Anthony Weiner, *The Year 2000: A Framework for Speculation* (Collier Macmillan, 1967); Daniel Bell, "Notes on the Post-Industrial Society," *Public Interest*, No. 6 (1967): 24–35, No. 7 (1967): 102–118; Michael Young (ed.). *Forecasting and the Social Sciences* (London: Heinemann, 1968); Peter Drucker, *The Age of Discontinuity* (Harper & Row, 1969).

7. Richard Tanner Pascale and Anthony Athos, *The Art of Japanese Management* (Warner Books, 1982), 125.

8. James Collins and Jerry Porras, "Organizational Vision and Visionary Organizations," *California Management Review* 34 (Fall 1991): 1.

9. Henry Mintzberg, *The Rise and Fall of Strategic Planning* (Free Press, 1994), 292–293.

10. Peter Drucker, *Managing in Turbulent Times* (Harper & Row, 1980), 218.

11. Alexis de Tocqueville, *Democracy in America* (Oxford University Press, 1947).

12. George Keller, *Academic Strategy* (Johns Hopkins University Press, 1983).

13. Antonio Damasio, *Descartes' Error: Emotion, Reason, and the Human Brain* (G. P. Putnam's Sons, 1994).

14. Quoted in Keller, 164.

The Role of Statements of Institutional Purpose

Daniel W. Lang and Rosanne Lopers-Sweetman

This paper assesses the utility and role of institutional purpose statements. If they are as effective as one is led to believe, what intrinsic facts or elements make them so? Is there value in having a purpose statement, or is the value attributed to the exercise of creating and discussing it? If there is such a value, what forms and circumstances create the value? What forms do mission statements usually take? Do different forms have different attributes? In addressing these questions, two methods are employed. One is conventional in that literature documenting the theory and research of others has been carefully reviewed, but from the particular perspectives of form and effectiveness. The other is to examine a series of actual statements of institutional purpose, with particular regard to form, content, and context of planning. To elucidate the context of planning, a series of master plans and mission statements for systems of higher education are also examined. In total, 32 institutional statements and 12 system plans or statements are examined. (The plans that are examined are listed in Appendixes A and B.) The paper observes that mission statements are effective in some situations, but not in all. In some situations they may be disadvantageous. Although planning theorists suggest that mission statements follow an approximately common form, the study of actual statements indicates several different types.

There are typically two views of the institutional mission, or purpose, statement. The first is a caricature:

[It] is the foundation on which the House of Intellect stands. And lofty are the utterances that express the importance of our mission. Indeed, they float like puffy clouds over our solidly positioned edifice. Broad is the applicability assigned these statements; so broad that they are thought to cover every contingency. Yet, narrow is the gate to understanding them, and few there be that find it.... [It is treated] like the House of Lords—all sound and fury, signifying nothing. (Martin, 1985, pp. 40–41)

The second view is a defense of such statements:

Why spend time on the statement of an idea, as in a mission statement, when we can predict that practice will fall short of it? Because actual practice, procedures, arrangements, settings, and appearances must always be measured against an ideal. A statement of institutional mission, at its best, formally represents assumptions and purposes that will guide the planning, as well as the activities, of a college or university. Despite its flights of rhetoric and sweeping generalizations, a good mission statement informs behavior and helps members of the community decide when to say no and when to say yes. It is a statement of intention that affects practice. It is informed by tradition and experience and yet transcends both. It relates to reality but is basically an ideal. And we need ideas and ideals even more than techniques and dollars. (Martin, 1985, pp. 60–61)

A growing number of colleges and universities, acting mainly in response to the first of the two views cited above, either have or have decided to have formal mission statements to

"The Role of Statements of Institutional Purpose," by Daniel W. Lang and Rosanne Lopers-Sweetman, reprinted from *Research in Higher Education*, Vol. 32, No. 6, 1991. Human Sciences Press, Inc.

gain clarity about their own purpose. The number of institutions with such statements in the United States seems to be on the order of 60 percent (Newsome and Hayes, 1991). There is an expectation that defining mission is critically important because it has the potential to affect virtually everything else. In some respects this is a re-realization. Statements of institutional mission were of considerable interest in the late 1960s and early 1970s, usually in public systems of postsecondary education in North America that were seeking greater differentiation between the various institutions they comprised. More recent interest in mission statements is part of a broader interest in strategic planning, mainly at the institutional (as opposed to system) level.

The statement of purpose or, more popularly, the mission statement of an institution of higher education encapsulates its peculiar raison d'être, what it seeks to accomplish in the larger environment. It may be a statement of direction, of priorities, of guidelines. It may be confined to a particular period or set of circumstances, or it may be for an indefinite period. Because all colleges and universities have a mission, whether or not it is articulated, certain elements are often the same for each postsecondary institution: the commitment to the teaching of basic skills, education in certain advanced skills, and the socialization of students (Martin, 1985, pp. 43–44). Thus, a statement of mission may indicate how institutions are alike as well as how they are different, with all of the ambivalence that such a dual role engenders. A purpose or mission statement, then, is simply a declaration—usually public—of how the university perceives its role, which is often closely tied with how others perceive its role. The question, "What is our mission?" must bring with it such questions as "Whom do we serve?" "What is our value to those we serve?" These questions sound simple, but are probably the most difficult any organization ever has to answer. They are also the most important for they inform all others. A question that follows, however, is whether or not institutional mission statements are effective means of answering these questions and informing institutional planning. There is some evidence that although mission statements are becoming ubiquitous they are not necessarily widely used in planning (Newsom and Hayes, 1991).

This study attempts to assess the actual utility and functional roles of institutional purpose statements as they relate to plans and planning. If they are as effective as one is led to believe, what intrinsic factors or elements make them so? Is there value in having a purpose statement, or is the value only in the exercise of creating and discussing it? And is the outcome worth the investment of substantial resources? What forms do mission statements typically take? Do different forms have different attributes and rely on different processes for development?

In addressing these questions, two methods are employed. One is conventional in that literature documenting the theory and research of others has been carefully reviewed, but from the particular perspectives of form and role. The other is to examine a series of actual statements of institutional purpose, with particular regard to form, content, and context of planning. To elucidate and broaden the context of planning within which institutional mission statements function, several master plans and mission statements for systems of higher education are also examined. In total, 32 institutional statements and 12 system plans or statements are examined. (The plans examined are listed in Appendixes A and B).

The Importance of Process in Developing Mission Statements

Many will point to the conclusion that the way in which a planning exercise is conducted is at least as important as why it is done, and perhaps more important than the actual product. Outcome depends on process. There are many sources that describe the value and importance of the process by which administrative activities such as the generation of an institutional purpose statement are carried out (Richman and Farmer, 1974; Jedamus and Peterson, 1980, Baldridge, 1980; Boxx and Johnson, 1980; Brown, 1980; Scott, 1986; Keller, 1983; Bean and Kuh, 1984; Alexander, 1986; Dressel, 1987).

A fundamental premise of some concepts of corporate planning is that the process of planning is probably more important than any document or plan produced (Bean and Kuh,

1984; Bryson, 1988). Planning refers not only to the end product but to the activities that enable members of the institution to create their own picture of the organization's place and future. The ideas generated in the planning process may be more directly linked to the future of the organization than changes in the structure or roles of the institution. Goal displacement may occur, however, if the means—the planning process—are substituted for the ends—a new institutional plan (Bean and Kuh, 1984, p. 42).

At this point it is important to observe that there are many different notions of what planning for higher education actually is. There are, perhaps, as many definitions as there are planners, or at least as many as the number of institutions with plans. Richardson and Gardner (1983), for example, describe a *planning continuum* with four different approaches to planning: adaptive, comprehensive, disjointed, and strategic. Within such a continuum one might then locate other forms of planning, such as master plans, complement plans, and program plans (Lang, 1988).

Mission statements more often than not are categorized as a form of strategic planning (Ackoff, 1970; Kotler and Murphy, 1981; Bryson, 1988; Hines, 1988; Schmidtlein, 1989). There is considerably less consensus about what strategic planning itself is in relation to colleges and universities and their missions. There are two quite opposing positions insofar as the role and utility of mission statements are concerned. Bryson expresses one of the positions particularly well: "Ultimately strategic planning is about purpose, meaning, values, and virtue, and nowhere is this more apparent than in the clarification of mission" (Bryson, 1988, p. 96). Consider, then, in juxtaposition this definition: "Strategic planning is defined as the process of developing and maintaining a strategic fit between the organization and its changing market opportunities" that is followed further by: "An effective mission statement should be market-oriented, feasible, motivating, and specific" (Kotler and Murphy, 1981, pp. 471, 479). The second definition is essentially an expression of the private corporate sector's view of strategic planning and mission.

There is no pressing theoretical reason to resolve the differences in viewpoint toward strategic planning and mission statements. There is, however, a practical reason to recog-

nize at least the differences. For example, process could transcend product in a mission statement that is developed from the point of view expressed by Bryson. The definition advanced by Kotler and Murphy, on the other hand, places much greater emphasis on product. Moreover, the concept of a *fit* with markets implies a transience and fluidity that is usually not associated with the relative permanence of roles, goals, and values typically associated with mission statements.

Thus, one of the most important aspects of planning as an expression of institutional mission is flexibility. Flexibility in turn requires plans that are developed more as guidelines than as blueprints (Kilmann, 1977). Flexibility can be ensured by allowing plans to be adapted incrementally at the department or program level to accommodate the demands and realities of limited resources (Van de Ven, 1980). In other words, plans as mission statements should be developed from the bottom up.

But to be taken seriously, plans must also have a high level of endorsement and acceptance by those persons and agencies that ratify and ultimately fund the roles, capacities, and activities defined by statements of mission. Although in terms of process some types of planning can be and remain bottom up, for mission statements top-down planning must at some point converge with bottom-up planning. The *top* in top-down planning, depending on one's view of strategic planning and the circumstances of a given institution, may either be an external agency, a governing board, a strong active president, the environment, or the market. It seems mistaken, therefore, to advocate and place a great deal of confidence in a process that assigns a predominant role to grass-root participants in the determination of mission statements that are genuine plans as opposed to "wish lists" regardless of the high degree of consensus that such lists engender.

It could perhaps go without saying that available resources are essential to the success of a stated plan. The planning process must be able to be supported and the implementation costs—both direct and indirect—of the proposed plan must be accurately assessed (Bean and Kuh, 1984, p. 50). But the expression of plans through a mission statement only infrequently does this. Of the mission statements we examined, only one (from the University of Hull) fully displayed resource requirements.

Resources can have a lot to do with consensus. An especially astute observation by Sibley is that while a sense of community is essential to the effectiveness of planning, a sense of community may permit no more than just a nominal consensus about shared values. "[I]nstead of being bound together by ideas, we are more and more bound only by interests, chiefly of an economic kind," which makes for fragile connections indeed (Sibley, 1986, p. 100).

If consensus depends on the resolution of competing economic interests, and if a key element in mission statements is a determination of what an institution will not do, the process of development of mission statements must somehow include information about the level and kind of resources that various alternative missions will require, yet in terms of either process or product the consideration of costs seems on the basis of the statements examined here to play at most a small role in the determination of mission for colleges and universities.

The absence from mission statements of factors that involve cost may be one result of a misfit between the ways colleges and universities are governed and the planning processes demanded by mission statements. Cohen and March (1974), in describing universities, coined the term *organized anarchies,* where management practices a "garbage-can model" of decision making. Keller (1983) calls for radical reform in university governance to a more active, change-oriented style. The "era of academic strategy has begun" (p. 26). The burden of this change will fall on the president of the university, who must "restore clear authority in some fresh form to American higher education" (p. 36). Many of the mission statements examined here begin with the recognition and acceptance of such a responsibility. But there is an inherent irony in linking the responsibility for mission statements with a senior administrator.

The relatively short terms of college and university presidents reduce the opportunity and the incentive to plan for the future. Instead they are consumed by more pressing current problems and more constraints in responding to them, which may moderate their ambitions for comprehensive strategic planning through mission statements (Sibley, 1986). We would observe on the basis of the plans that we exam-

ined that the processes for defining institutional mission are often highly personalized, relying heavily on the leadership of the president. This may explain why even well-devised mission statements sometimes are surprisingly ephemeral or are ignored in a waiting game between faculty and administrators.

Martin's advice in approaching institutional purpose statement development is that it must be a conscious and deliberate effort. "Otherwise it will be improvised or imposed," and if the institution is to be outstanding in periods of fiscal restraint, the "mission or culture must give that institution an added dimension, a certain distinctiveness and character" (1985, p. 59). The institutional culture is drawn from what has gone before, combined with what is, and pointed toward what might be appropriate for the next stage in the institution's life. From this institutional pattern, salutary distinctions can be considered. If no obvious distinctions present themselves, "weight institutional resources and canvass the aspirations of the people most committed" to the institution (p. 60). So, again, there is some reason to reconsider the degree to which resources should be taken into account in the processes by which mission statements are developed.

The Possible Roles of Institutional Mission Statements

The utility of statements of institutional purpose depend on separate planning mechanisms for adoption, adaptation, and refocusing, or in technical terms, other types of planning. The utility of a mission statement depends in the first instance on the constituency using it. Faculty, students, administrators, governors, legislators, and coordinating agencies may and often do view the same mission statement in widely varying ways.

Statements of institutional purpose are almost always highly official. They have to be. But because they are official, they are also, in either reality or perception, abstract. Most university faculty and students want to know how things work in practice. So do many of the institution's political and financial patrons. A statement of institutional purpose must be rational, even when it is employed to resolve severe crises. But universities are as susceptible to Murphy's Law as is any other organization. Thus, it would be unrealistic to expect a perfect symmetry between what should be and what is. Many of the decisive elements of institutional choice elude measurable assessment. A truly effective statement of institutional purpose may then be one that candidly acknowledges its limitations.

There are many different conditions that could give rise to the development of a statement of institutional purpose. There may be new and different internal or external expectations of the university's programs, services, and policies. The evolution of academic disciplines may call into question the organization of the curriculum. New research initiatives may create new opportunities and new requirements. Federation or affiliation, or other changes in the governance and administration of a university, may alter its profile and demand corresponding changes to its statement of purpose. Budget pressures, funding changes, enrollment growth, and change in the enrollment distribution might all be cause for an institution to examine or reexamine its primary roles and functions (Dressel, 1987, pp. 103–106).

Particularly within the current political and financial context for higher education, the identification of goals and institutional purpose appears to be at least desirable, if not necessary. For example, Fleming (1980) predicted that provincial governments in Canada would continue to curtail the growth rate of expenditures for higher education. In the decade that followed, virtually all of them did. Governments are ensuring universities' accountability for their expenditure of public funds (McKelvie, 1986, p. 162). Thus, there has been a series of external events that demand, either expressly or implicitly, that universities declare what roles they play and, over time, wish to play in terms of a larger sphere of public policy.

Mission Statements as Goal Clarification

Universities must therefore make their purpose known to the public if they hope to gain the support of the public in matters concerning them. "To survive the difficult years ahead the institutions of higher education must reassess the value of clarifying their own institution's goals. What better defense than to know where

you have been, where you are going, and precisely how you intend to get there" (McKelvie, 1986, p. 162). These, however, are rhetorical questions that presume a positive response. Perhaps universities should be less sanguine about the role and value of mission statements.

Among organizational theorists a common belief is that clearly defined missions are essential to the well-being of institutions (Davies, 1986, p. 90). Drucker (1973) declares that only a clear definition of the mission and purpose of the business makes possible clear and realistic business objectives. Without firm goals, organizations are subject to vagrant pressures from within and without, even as they may grow and prosper. Although the institution may have flexibility, there are few resources for unusual and concerted efforts (Perrow, 1970).

Within college and university administrations and among scholars of higher education, mission statements and the clarification of goals have been the focus of much attention. Richman and Farmer (1974, p. 335) claim that systematic consideration of the goals of an institution is the most important thing that an academic administrator should be doing. According to Konrad and McNeal (1984), defining the goals of an organization clarifies the very nature of its essence. Keller (1983) advises that a key to success in both internal and external campus relations is to possess a distinctive mission, to project a clear, forceful image. Cosand (1980) charges that educational institutions are grossly negligent if they do not have a clear understanding of the essential need for comprehensive "master planning"—which begins with mission definition—at the institutional and state levels. Another, corollary view (Parker, 1986) is more specific: that institutions with a high degree of internal commitment to an expressly stated mission can respond selectively to conditions of decline. Parker's study identifies certain circumstances that display a strong presence of a determined sense of institutional purpose among recovering and surviving institutions that was absent in institutions that had failed and closed.

All of these theories and others like them seem to operate on the assumption that once the goals are known and presumably made public, the efficiency and effectiveness of the organization will automatically follow. But will they? And more importantly, if they will, how?

Sizer (1982) observes that to assess its purpose or mission and proceed to formulate an effective mission statement, an institution must first engage in environmental scanning, a term strategic planners use to describe systematic examination of the future context in which the institution will be functioning. Threats and opportunities are identified. The institution must then understand and communicate the implications of this future environment to its constituencies. It must evaluate its current array of programs and critical resources. Through consensus-building techniques it must then develop statements of purpose for itself and its constituent parts, and the measures for monitoring progress toward the fulfillment of the mission, including long-term strategies and alternative plans. R. G. Cope, a frequent contributor to literature about strategic planning for higher education, declares that establishing "the mission and goals of the institution is the first step toward the effective use of resources" (1978, p. 71). In this context, a mission statement is, first, a plan, and second a plan oriented toward a match between resources and various external conditions. The plan is a plan for action.

Mission statements when viewed as statements of goal clarification are one obvious place to begin the process of self-assessment that public calls for accountability are forcing institutions of postsecondary education to undergo. Among self-assessment approaches, the Institutional Goals Inventory (IGI) of the Educational Testing Service is a popular instrument, so much so that separate materials have been prepared specifically for use by community colleges and small institutions (Fenske, 1980). The IGI approach to goal studies results in descriptive data that are used to interpret what certain institutional constituencies perceive the actual goals of the organization to be and what they think they should be. Twenty years ago attempts to measure institutional vitality—or functioning—resulted in the well-received Institutional Functioning Inventory instrument. Dimensions of institutional vitality were also regarded as legitimization dimensions, that is, dimensions by which an institution could justify its existence to various relevant assessors (Peterson and Loye, 1967, p. 5). As a means of clarifying goals and purposes, the mission statement is neither necessarily a plan nor a means of setting a plan. It can in

consequence constitute an agenda for planning by defining issues that require resolution and in turn indicating those planning processes that are most likely to resolve the issues thus identified. In this context, a mission statement is a plan for planning.

Mission Statements as Smoke Screens for Opportunism

There are a variety of ways in which a mission statement can be viewed or construed. It can be a snapshot depiction of the current state of the institution, a desired image of it, or a view combining past and present conditions with future intentions. Davies points out that there is a great deal of discrepancy between what scholarly literature says that mission definition and what is practiced on university campuses. The prevailing incentives are to avoid a too rigorous definition of mission; the tendency is to "remain flexible and alert to every opportunity" (Davies, 1986, p. 88). This posture is obviously pragmatic. It may be due to two quite separate sets of circumstance. One set is internal: The mission really did not resolve all of the issues before the institution. The statement thus is only a proximate solution. The second set is external: Government or its agencies have not made a firm commitment to mission statements or to the public policies that support them. The result is caution instead of confidence about the utility of mission statements.

Davies also describes a chameleonlike tendency that has come to characterize many academic institutions, particularly universities. That description, upon further consideration, suggests that universities may not stand as much for clarity of purpose as they do for deliberate opportunism in the form of vague, shifting statements of purpose. Under these circumstances, the institution recasts its identity to suit its environment or context. The result is an increasingly bland picture of colleges and universities as, by homogenization, they come to look more and more like one another. Left entirely to themselves in such circumstances, colleges and universities fall victim to the law of entropy (Davies, 1986, p. 91): They progressively define themselves in reference to a common model, which in turn causes them to claim missions that are not individually distinctive.

There are several explanations for this phenomenon. One has to do with the evolution of the academic profession. As the professoriate becomes more oriented to disciplines (Clark, 1987) it must necessarily become less oriented to institutions. To the extent that the faculty determines an institution's identity, it will look more like other institutions with similar faculties and arrays of disciplines. Research-intensive universities are most typical of the paradigm because they train the scholars who typically constitute the faculties of most colleges and universities, whether or not these institutions are or could reasonably aspire to be research universities.

Thus, a mission statement may often be more a statement of means than ends. If all or most institutions aspire to replicate an ideal form, their mission statements will have common goals, and will differ only in how those goals should be realized.

As resources become scarce, even the means may not be very different because of the growing tendency to compare institutions in terms of measurable costs and benefits, more usually costs. The demand for visible equity in funding is so great for public colleges and universities that few jurisdictions have funding formulas that differentiate at the institution level. Most, if they differentiate at all, do so at the program level. Thus, there is little financial incentive in producing highly differentiated statements of institutional mission. To the extent that costs define programs, program differentiation may not be notably differentiated either (CUDEC, 1985–86).

One might also observe that the motivation for planning at the system or state level is not always friendly toward colleges and universities. An interest at the system or state level in institutional statements of purpose can be and sometimes is motivated by a desire to force universities to declare themselves in ways that expose their plans to external examination and manipulation.

One should consider as well that good planning, particularly that which leads to an effective, realistic mission statement, has costs. It takes time and effort, usually at senior levels of leadership and management. If public jurisdictions require and value statements of institutional purpose mainly to demonstrate that their universities have plans, and therefore are

managed well and are doing what they are supposed to be doing, the benefits that might be set against those costs may not be sufficiently large. Sooner or later this realization discourages serious planning via institutional mission statements. Thus, there are systemic forces that, at least, do not encourage colleges and universities to express highly differentiated roles and that, at most, force institutions into a common academic mold, which in practice separate mission statements from plans and planning.

Mission Statements as Descriptions of Things as They Are

Yet another approach to mission statements is that above all an institution must describe itself "as is," and not try to mirror some distant, abstract model or ideal (Carruthers and Lott, 1981). Included in the mission definition must be descriptions of the past and of the future: It should report what the institution has been (its past), what it shall become (its destiny), and what it does not believe itself to be.

A mission statement that declares what the institution is not is recommended by others as well. Popular organizational theorists Thomas J. Peters and Robert H. Waterman (1982) identify as a quality in excellent companies the ability to know what they are not about, to "stick to the knitting." They mean that successful organizations—organizations that last—build on some central, declared skill or strength. They may branch out somewhat, but they maintain a basic stability because they stick very close to their central purpose. Diversification for its own sake, in areas where the organization may not have strengths, is folly. Adaptation must occur around the core. Again, an approach that declares what the institution is not inhibits opportunism.

Mission statements frequently start from some formulation of the institution's set of general goals and endeavor to move from such principles to the articulation of specific courses of future action. Sibley (1986) warns against falling into the belief that once objectives have been clarified and determined, the institution will be able to discern immediately what specific choices have to be made. One cannot, in Sibley's view, work with principles and objectives in isolation from the operational realities of the enterprise. As Burton Clark put it, broad statements are "inappropriate when used as guides to action" (1983, p. 22). If these views are correct, mission statements preclude some forms of planning and reinforce others. They may explain why, of the mission statements examined in this study, only a few could be characterized as plans for action.

Mission statements as plans should be more than formal expressions of official policy in regard to, for example, accessibility and quality—topics addressed by virtually every mission statement studied here. They must comprehend how broad, general policy objectives are finding actual expression in the classroom and laboratory, how the enterprise is actually functioning, and what the institution is really choosing to do. By "marrying" the overarching principles of the institution with the specific actualities, a pattern will emerge to which we can adhere in our decision making (Sibley, 1986, pp. 96–97).

But there can be forces that act against the emergence of such patterns. If the purpose of a mission statement is essentially promotional and oriented to an external audience, particularly an audience that in some way determines funding, assessments of actual performance could undermine the purpose of the statement by indicating that the institution is not entirely what it purports to be. Conversely, a mission statement that is mainly internally oriented will itself demand assessment of performance.

Sibley talks about the "dialectic" in academic planning and management that must be sustained in the process of articulating a sense of identity. Our identity lies in realizing what distinctive set of values we are called upon, in our historical situation, in our own context, to choose and act upon (p. 100). This dialectic also needs to be sustained as change forces us to redefine our pattern. As circumstances change, our guiding pattern may have to be altered. Just as a good constitution provides means for its own amendment, the operation of an institutional purpose statement allows for its own alteration. Such a view brings the concept of a mission closer to a strategic plan and further from a master plan.

We would observe that the real question should not be about the symmetry between mission statements and actual patterns of institu-

tional behavior but about which should take precedence. It is not impossible or even unlikely that institutional research and assessment might not in some instances reveal patterns. Even when they do, the patterns may be undesirable. In that case, Clark's observation about the inappropriateness of mission statements as guides to action might apply accurately to present realities but not to future realities. If the future is not to be a replication of the past, a mission statement may become a necessity.

Richardson and Doucette (1984) also assert that the abstractions that typify mission statements cannot readily be translated into concrete terms, that is, highly specific objectives. They see missions as "the expectations that external constituencies have for colleges and universities . . . thus missions exist at the interface between an institution and its environment." Goals, which are the next step in the standard hierarchy, "are the aspirations that a college or university has for itself." They propose that mission definition begin with an analysis of institutional activities and clientele, and suggest the use of surveys to set operational priorities and funding levels. The drawback to this approach is that the governing body might set a mission based solely on what the surveyed populations would support—assuming, of course, that some consensus emerged from the survey (in Davies, 1986, pp. 90–91).

Mission Statements as Aspirations

Another common feature of mission statements is that they tend to focus on what the institution aspires to become. The generalization is probably less true of flagship universities than of other institutions (Davies, 1986, p. 95), although when every other institution justifies its funding by what it intends to be, the flagships are forced to do likewise. Aspirations generally are not useful in resource allocation except that they are often seen, particularly by faculty, as powerful tools in making cases for more government funding. There is, however, an irony in such a view. A study underway under the aegis of the National Center for Postsecondary Governance and Finance in the United States has observed that because in most public jurisdictions funding for colleges and universities increases incrementally, with only infrequent changes in base funding for new programs or major expansion, planning is often viewed as ineffective, particularly when based on "wish lists" (Schmidtlein, 1989).

Institutional "wish lists" present another problem in that they are difficult to justify. Aspirations can be judged realistic or unrealistic, but clarification of values becomes an extremely delicate procedure. For example, the desire to "have the best research facilities available" can be verified in multiple ways, depending on who does the evaluation, when, and with what means. Arguments about statements of aspiration can become highly charged, politically and personally. "Disputes over aspirations are inevitable, and they are not particularly rational because they rarely connect with reality [and are] often decided by political strength" (Davies, 1986, p. 96). Whether or not "wish lists" engender dispute and disagreement, they seem rarely to function as effective plans and mission statements within institutions. Most faculty and even planners themselves (Schmidtlein, 1989) take such plans for what they are—promotional devices aimed at external agencies—and largely ignore them for the purposes of making decisions internally.

Etzioni (1964), one of the forerunners of modern management practices, cautioned that the desire to establish specifically how we are doing, and to find ways of improving ourselves through goal setting, has the undesired effect of distorting the organization, since some aspects or outcomes are simply more measurable than others. One thus tends to do that which is the highly measurable and neglects the less quantifiable. Clearly, anything that is not quantifiable—teaching and learning are notable examples—is difficult to hold up to this model.

The problems of quantitative measurement, and the failure to solve them, are of obvious significance. But they may be less significant than another, almost invisible problem. The word *program* is used ubiquitously with casual acceptance in discussions of goals, plans, and objectives for higher education. Mission statements usually employ the word *program* in two not entirely consistent ways.

One is borrowed from the PPBS concept—planning-programming-budgeting-systems (Balderston and Weatherly, 1972). Thus, in declaring institutional purposes, mission statements often use the idiom of broad programs, for example, *graduate education in technology*, to

describe sectors of activity in which the institution proposes to play a role. That concept of program, however, has little or no organizational meaning within colleges and universities. Organizationally, programs identify degrees, series of courses, or areas of research concentration. Neither of these concepts of program is invalid, but they are so substantially different from each other that one should not expect them to establish an operational link between mission statements and day-to-day institutional performance.

Mission Statements as Marketing Tools

Statements of institutional purpose can also be construed as marketing tools. Kotler and Murphy (1981) maintain that, to be effective, a mission statement should be market-oriented, feasible, motivating, and specific. The very number and variety of postsecondary options available to the decreasing pools of prospective North American students has forced institutions in many areas, particularly private schools, to carve out for themselves a distinct corner of the market, to position themselves (Willmer, 1981). Mission statements are therefore developed to distinguish one institution from other similar ones. Davies (1986, p. 90) warns, however, that "such explicit statements as may be contained in recruiting, fund-raising or other promotional materials may bear little resemblance to what an institution actually does, and therefore is." They may overreach an institution's capability in terms either of resources or of demographic possibility.

Closely related to the marketing approach is the tendency for institutions to emphasize the economic rationality of their missions, and thereby justify the continued existence and support of their institution. "Schools become important only to the degree that they can provide the forms of knowledge, skills, and social practices necessary to produce the labor force for an increasingly complex, technological economy" (Giroux, 1984, p. 188). Here an imitation of corporations on the level of management systems and marketing strategies has taken place. It is almost as if academic administrators have been willing to strike a deal with corporate leaders: If the corporations would show the university how to survive by overcoming management deficiencies, the programs of study would especially emphasize how students are being prepared for business and industry and how faculty cooperate with corporations in contract research (Martin, 1985, pp. 52–53). Such economic reality, however, is extremely difficult to demonstrate. Few mission statements actually do.

Mission statements are sometimes developed to herald a change in administrative leadership or approach. Thus, it is sometimes the mission statement itself that is being marketed. It may be perceived merely as a symbol to appease an external group or a constituency. On the other hand, the statement may be taken literally, internally and externally. The value of plans as advertisements of a change in direction to mollify external audiences must be weighted carefully against the value of plans used to guide internal constituencies into the future (Bean and Kuh, 1984, p. 49; Clark et al., 1980).

The Content of Mission Statements: Toward a Taxonomy

Most planners in higher education recognize that the taxonomy of planning is large. At virtually any established college or university one can find in various planning documents since the mid-1950s references to academic planning, divisional planning, strategic planning, institutional planning, master planning, long-range planning, sectoral planning, facet planning, program planning . . . the list goes on. And for each type of planning there is its own body of theory and applied methodology (Lang, 1988). Where do mission statements fit in the lexicon of planning? On the basis of this study it is evident that in terms of content and form, mission statements can and do vary widely. Moreover, no mission statement examined in this study expressly declared its theoretical or methodological premise. In other words, mission statements do not classify themselves. On the basis of this study, the content and form of mission statements can, with comparatively few exceptions, be empirically organized into a few generic classifications. Some have links to formerly recognized planning methodologies, but most do not. The generic classification therefore had in the end to be sui generis.

An especially common model might be called the *historical-philosophical* statement. This type of mission statement concentrates heavily on what the institution is, and how it came to be that way. Such a mission statement has a strong tone of self-justification and implied superiority. Although such mission statements seem intended to lead to a conclusion that the university in question is better than and different from other universities, they usually do not draw direct comparisons with other institutions. The emphasis is on roles and responsibilities. That emphasis is a strength internally since it can be a focus for consensus. Externally it permits only a general level of accountability and differentiation. On the one hand, that protects institutional autonomy. On the other hand, it does not guide governments or other public agencies toward specifications in support of the institution. Yet, ironically, this type of mission statement usually calls more for external change—for example, a different treatment by government—than for internal change.

Other mission statements can be categorized as *action plans*. Mission statements of this sort usually are provoked by rather definite, intimidating external circumstances. They begin with careful, quite definite assessments of internal and external environments. The assessments usually are not self-critical, but they ultimately do result in an expression of facts that the institutions must take as given for the purposes of planning. The mission statement then describes the ways and means of coming to terms with those facts. Mission statements thus developed address both goals (or ends) and objectives (or means). In some mission statements of this type, the facts of the institution's environment are so compelling and so unavoidable that the institution must change its goals. Where goals remain largely unchanged, the mission statement concentrates on new means of achieving the goals. This type of mission statement ultimately accepts a need for change and sets a course for making change.

It may be surprising that a considerable number of mission statements can be categorized as *interrogative* or *optional*. These mission statements are heavily oriented toward process, which in turn places great emphasis on consultation. Such plans carefully frame questions of policy and philosophy. They often state, for example, that the institution will be committed to excellence, and then ask how excellence should be measured. What then follows are various optional responses to the question. The options are developed with considerable elaboration and detail. But these mission statements stop with the question or the option; they do not select the preferred answer or option. Where the future is unusually uncertain, this type of mission statement may be prudent and effective. It is not, however, a type of mission statement that leads to decisions about change, either on the part of the institution or on its public patrons. This type of mission statement seems particularly attractive to Canadian universities. The mission statements examined in this study from several major Canadian institutions—Toronto, Queen's, Saskatchewan, and Alberta—are best categorized as being interrogative and optional.

In highly organized and centralized systems of postsecondary education, mission statements are often mainly expressions of *scale* and *capacity.* Mission statements of this type focus on enrollment and physical requirements. They differentiate among institutions to the extent that they demonstrate a demand or need for certain levels of enrollment in certain programs. These mission statements sometimes address institutional role, but when they do, they focus on demonstrations of a demand or need for particular programs in particular geographic areas. When governments or governmental agencies request mission statements—as, for example, has been done in the Maritime Provinces and Ontario in Canada and throughout Australia in the last decade—they tend toward scale and capacity.

There are as well statements of mission that can be best described as *messianic tablets.* These statements are usually closely identified with the president of the institution, and are expressed in personal terms. They have a philosophical bent and typically describe a plan for institutional reformation or reorganization. The practical intention of these statements appears to operate on an assumption that once problems are identified and analyzed, they will be acted on and solved. The result is a statement of mission that can encourage self-reflection and perhaps a confessional catharsis, and can in turn orient the institution toward constructive change. But a corollary result is often a statement that is very difficult to

translate into action and one that is so closely associated with a particular individual that it is inherently ephemeral.

The messianic tablet form of mission statement implies a peculiar twist for the top-down, bottom-up approach to planning. It in practical terms assumes that the top-down element in the development of a mission statement will precede the bottom-up element in timing. The mission statement thus produced is not so much a plan or mission statement itself but instead is a sort of herald and agenda for planning that will be done in consequence of the statement.

Because the messianic mission statement is usually highly personalized, it depends on the persuasive and political strength of the president. It rarely can stand as a statement of institutional purpose on its own. This type of statement depends a lot on timing. It must appear early enough in a president's term to allow him or her to carry through the implementation of the statement. It is not a type of statement that can be easily carried forward to a new administration, nor is it a type of statement that is likely to bring focus and consensus to a fractious situation.

Finally, there are mission statements that can be described best as *anthologies of missions.* They are, in effect, compilations of plans of various units within a university. They are, thus, characteristic of large, heterogeneous institutions in which the formation of consensus is particularly difficult and contentious. While mission statements of this ilk display a large measure of realism about what is possible in university management and leadership, they are highly susceptible to intrusion by external agencies that, in effect, say, "If the university cannot sort out its mission, we will choose the mission we prefer."

The Utility of Mission Statements in Planning

The nagging question in any discussion about institutional mission statements concerns their ultimate good. As previously shown, organizational theorists believe that a clear definition of the purpose of an organization makes possible clear and realistic objectives. But, as this examination of actual mission statements indicates, not all statements are clear (some are deliberately vague and flexible) and some do not answer questions that they raise about objectives.

The mission statement itself can be used in a variety of ways. A university president may use a mission statement to inspire and motivate the constituencies that are vital to the institution, to direct effort toward whatever objectives can be reached at the moment, and to engender feelings of potential within the academic community and beyond it (Davies, 1986, p. 91). It can be a "sales and public relations tool" both internally and externally.

It can be a bludgeon used within the institution, by it, or on it. The governing board and administration can justify a favorable allocation with it, or they can pummel funding bodies on the basis of their declared mission. On the other hand, funding bodies can withhold approval of a certain development if it does not appear to fall under the institutional mission. They can also measure enrollment, degrees conferred, research volume, and space use to ensure that the university is doing what it claims to be doing.

Sources are not plentiful that indicate a formal or even informal recognition and use of a purpose statement in decision making, particularly by a governing or coordinating agency (Micek and Arney, 1973; Fincher, 1978; Romney, 1978; Davies, 1986). In Canada, for example, the Maritime Provinces Higher Education Commission in 1980–81, the Bovey Commission (Ontario) in 1984–85, and the Ontario Council on University Affairs in 1987–88 asked universities in various ways to make statements of institutional purpose. Virtually all did, but none appears to have been used to make critical decisions about, for example, base operating funding at the institutional level. This omission, although factually simple, is extraordinarily important. It suggests a severe limitation on the utility of mission statements that are aimed primarily at external audiences.

This limitation becomes even more severe when one considers that most mission statements are aimed at external audiences. A logical sine qua non in an assessment of the mission statement as a means of strategic planning should be its fit with the public decision-making processes that affect the college or university. Where those processes are uncertain, or where they make no formal provision for recognizing institutional mission statements, it is question-able that any form of mission statement would be a good choice for strategic planning.

In *Strategic Planning, Management and Decision Making* Robert Cope (1981) talks about "conventional long-range planning" in contrast to strategic planning. The former, in his view, looks inward and tends to be scientific, whereas the latter looks outward and is more an art than a science. Strategic planning is a process that involves the skills of environmental scanning, construction of probability diffusion matrices, and diagnosis of value-system changes. It typically brings with it a proactive relationship to the environmental context of the institution, and emphasis on master planning.

Marvin Peterson also promotes strategic planning (1980) for academic management. He includes under this rubric environment (context) assessment or scanning, institutional (self-) assessment, values assessment, and master plan creation. The *Report of the Steering Committee for Efficiency Studies in Universities* (1985) in the United Kingdom referred to strategic planning as the setting of objectives for the university as a whole and its constituent parts, which take account of relevant long-term trends; and the preparation of plans, with stated priorities and options for achieving the objectives (p. 17). This is a process necessitated by conditions of uncertainty, a process other organizations have adopted in order to survive.

George Keller's *Academic Strategy* (1983) is one of the best-known works on strategic planning for postsecondary education. He describes academic strategies as a means of moving beyond the limitations of normative, rigid planning on the one hand, and traditional incrementalism on the other. He provides excellent discussions of the contextual and historical development of planning in higher education, the strengths and limitations of incrementalism and prescriptive planning, and the importance of leadership. He offers an account of strategic planning that is highly entrepreneurial and dynamic in character, and that emphasizes competition, differentiation, adaptability, and the drive for quality as its distinguishing features.

Keller's first theme is that universities are now faced more than ever before with the need to compete because higher education is faced with scarcity. The "specter of decline and bankruptcy" is haunting higher education (p. 3). Strategic planning, therefore, must concentrate on a Darwinian struggle for survival within the historical forces of the environment.

Like other strategic planning advocates, Keller advises universities to "scan the environment." While admitting to the limitations of this type of assessment, planners must engage in forcasting—of technological change and its impact, of the economy, of demographics, of political and legal developments, and of sociocultural changes. He cites Richard Cyert, who said strategic planning is an attempt to give organizations "antennae" to sense the changing environment. Sibley (1986) doubts the utility of environmental scanning since no technique is capable of predicting with any degree of certainty such critical things as the price of money, or the size of the enrollment or the composition of the student body in five years.

This advice poses two technical problems for the utility of mission statements. One is that although various planning techniques are available for scanning an institution's environment effectively, the environments themselves may be chaotic and uncertain. Thus, to presume that good environmental scanning will bring clarity to a statement of mission or other strategic plan is not necessarily correct. The external environment may be no more orderly and rational than the institution's own internal environment. No Canadian province or American state, for example, announces base funding levels for more than two years at a time. The longest advance funding commitment appears to be in Australia, where the commonwealth government assures institutional "educational profiles" for three years.

The second technical problem is that while the mission statement is in essence a form of strategic planning, its efficacy often depends on an institution's capability to make sound operational or logistical plans, such as projections of enrollment, and in terms of a constant fit with the environment or market it presumes a degree of flexibility and quick central decision making that few colleges and universities possess.

State and Provincial Systems and Purpose Statements

Many American states and some Canadian provinces have attempted to control duplica-

tion of programs and services within their systems of publicly supported institutions. They have classified their institutions, for example, as a major research university, regional university, undergraduate college, and so on, while affirming that these differing roles do not imply more or less important roles. Where this approach fails, however, is in the differential funding that is awarded to the different types of institutions. Davies calls this an *oblique* planning technique (Davies, 1986, p. 88). This approach is less common but not absent in Canada. It was proposed in Ontario by the Fisher Committee and the Bovey Commission. And it is currently the topic of a committee of the Royal Society of Canada.

Despite an almost automatic acceptance of the value of mission statements, there are some good reasons not to define institutional missions, especially within public systems of higher education. The planning that goes on in universities is often neither acknowledged nor endorsed by state or provincial authorities. Governments frequently provide money for missions that they want, and disregard institutional plans and priorities as self-promotional rhetoric not to be taken seriously. Moreover, whether honored in word or deed, the price of precision about mission can be very high for an institution and its leaders: Institutional constituencies may feel betrayed and the legislators that determine funding levels may steer the institution by referring to the language of the mission statement.

Legislative bodies can try to force differentiation through control of the funds to which each institution has access, thereby controlling institutional mission. The use of *earmarked* or *designated* funds is becoming prevalent in Canada in Ontario, British Columbia, and Alberta. Profiling the curricular mix of an institution, approving degree programs, setting enrollment caps, or stalling on decisions are other, indirect means. In Australia, education profiles are negotiated annually directly between each university and the minister for employment, education, and training. The profiles negotiated thus become statements of institutional purpose, albeit for a comparatively short (three-year) term.

Funding mechanisms are often regarded as being neutral insofar as planning and policy are concerned, but in practical effect they rarely are. Funding formulas can encourage like behavior among institutions or promote differentiation. They can either encourage or discourage risk and innovation (Darling, Lang, England, and Lopers-Sweetman, 1989).

The National Governors' Association (August 1986) report *Time for Results: The Governors' 1991 Report on Education* recommends, among other things, that "governors, state legislatures, state coordinating boards, and institutional governing boards should clearly define the role and mission of each public higher education institution in their state. Governors also should encourage the governing boards of each independent college to define clearly their missions" (p. 160). This recommendation results from their conviction that institutions of higher education must be accountable for the substantial public and private funds they receive. They go on to recommend that state and institutional governing bodies assess institutional accomplishment of mission, going so far as to suggest that institutions be rewarded fiscally as they take the time to evaluate their progress toward the goals of their mission statements. Setting aside the political advisability of such a scheme, it presumes a quite particular form of mission statement. The mission statement must be cast in terms that are specific and measurable.

It is, of course, also a contradictory recommendation for it directs both the public agencies and the institutions to define and evaluate institutional roles and missions. The contradiction, in addition to creating confusion, also begs an important question about the planning and coordination of public systems of higher education. Do they plan or do they coordinate?

Coordinating boards sometimes publish institutional mission statements without endorsement. The preface to Alabama's system document in 1985 stated that the sections on mission were written by the institutions themselves and left largely as submitted. Virginia's state plan for higher education, revised every two years, includes statements of institutional aspiration, clearly differentiating them from mission. "The state-supported mission description (of each institution) is followed by a statement of institutional aspiration. The Council does not necessarily endorse the aspirations described, but includes them ... to indicate how an institution hopes to develop" (quoted in Davies, 1986, p. 91).

If as it seems, coordinating boards and agencies are ambivalent about the status of statements of institutional purpose—either because they fail to endorse them formally or because they override them with their own plans for the institutions within their purview—it should not be surprising that many mission statements are in fact more statements of aspiration than of purpose. Nor should it be surprising that, as Davies (1986, pp. 92–93), Birnbaum (1983, p. 77), and the Carnegie Council (1980, p. 22) have pointed out, diversity and differentiation in higher education are on the decline as each institution seeks to become more and more like its competitors. To the extent that coordinating boards, grants councils, and other such "buffer bodies" rely on a single institutional paradigm and hierarchical pyramid in envisioning systems of higher education, and in directing and evaluating institutional statements of purpose, all institutions in a system will continue to gravitate toward homogeneity. The trend, if one considers its long-term implications, moves away from differentiation and, in turn, away from individual statements of mission and purpose. Of the several categories of mission statement identified in this study, only the scale and capacity type will remain useful and germane.

Concluding Observations

To the planning gourmet, the literature and experience about statements of institutional purpose are a smorgasbord. There are some delicacies of which any institution seriously interested in planning would be well advised to partake. There are some recipes and ingredients that are nutritional and good for institutional health, but unappetizing and difficult to digest. And then there are some that are indigestible and empty of nutritional value. It would be easy to conclude, *chacun à son gout*, but it is not that simple.

The utility and form of the institutional mission statement depends on the circumstances that prompt it and on the audiences that will receive it. In the first instance, mission statements are expressions about the future. But the future may be one that is imposed, in terms either of time or agenda. A mission statement may therefore address several kinds of future: the future that the institution prefers, the future that the institution wishes to create, the future that the institution wishes to avoid. For each future, the form of the mission statement may be different, as may be the planning processes and techniques by which the statement is developed.

The capability of mission statements to cope with these different futures also varies. They work well for some, but not for others. The same may be said about systems of higher education, some of which strongly promote and reinforce the institutional mission statement whereas others ignore or subvert it.

The institutional planner, before dining at the mission statement smorgasbord, should read the menu carefully, decide what type of future the institution should or must address, and determine how or whether the system of higher education in which the institution is located will receive the mission statement. As well the planner should recognize that the term *mission statement* is at best broadly generic. There are at least six quite different types of mission statement. Each type takes a different form and serves a different purpose. Some types may complement institutional planning processes. Some may operate outside those processes. And some may never function as plans at all.

References

Balderston, F. E. and Weatherly, G. B. (1972). PPBS in higher education planning and management: From *PPBS* to policy analysis. Office of the Vice-President—Planning, University of California.

Bean, John P., and Kuh, George D. (1984). Typology of planning problems. *Journal of Higher Education* 55(1): 35–55

Bovey, Edmund C., Chairman (December 1984). *Ontario Universities: Options and Futures. Report of the Commission on the Future Development of the Universities of Ontario.* Toronto, Ontario: Ministry of Colleges and Universities.

Bryson, John M. (1988). *Strategic Planning for Public and Nonprofit Organizations.* San Francisco: Jossey-Bass.

Cadwallader, Mervyn L. (1983). Open planning: A case study in educational change. *Planning for Higher Education* 11(2): 21–26.

Carnegie Council on Policy Studies in Higher Education (1980). *Three Thousand Futures: The Next Twenty Years for Higher Education.* San Francisco: Jossey-Bass.

Carruthers, J. Kent, and Lott, Gary B. (1981). *Mission Review: Foundation for Strategic Planning.* Boulder, CO: National Center for Higher Education Management Systems.

Clark, B. R. (1983). *The Higher Education System.* Berkeley, CA: University of California Press.

Clark, B. R. (1987). Planning for excellence: The condition of the professoriate. *Planning for Higher Education* 16(1): 1–8.

Clark, D. L., et al., eds. (1980). *New Perspectives on Planning in Educational Organizations.* San Francisco: Far West Laboratory.

Committee of Vice-Chancellors and Principals (March 1985). *Report of the Steering Committee for Efficiency Studies in Universities.* United Kingdom.

Cope, Robert G. (1978). *Strategic Policy Planning: A Guide for College and University Administrators.* Littleton, CO: The Ireland Educational Corporation.

Cope, Robert G. (1981). *Strategic Planning, Management and Decision Making.* Washington, DC: American Association for Higher Education.

Cosand, Joseph P. (1980). Developing an institutional master plan. *Improving Academic Management,* P. Jedamus and M. Peterson and Associates (eds.). San Francisco: Jossey-Bass, pp. 164–176.

CUDEC (Canadian Universities Data Exchange Consortium), 1985–86.

Darling, A. L., Lang, D. W., England, M. D. and Lopers-Sweetman, R. (1989). Autonomy and control: A university funding formula as an instrument of public policy. *Higher Education* 18(5).

Davies, Gordon K. (1986). The importance of being general: Philosophy, politics, and institutional mission statements. *Higher Education: Handbook of Theory and Research,* vol. 2. John C. Smart (ed.). New York: Agathon Press, pp. 85–108.

Dressel, Paul M. (1987). Mission, organization, and leadership. *Journal of Higher Education* 58(1): 101–109.

Drucker, Peter (1973). *Management: Tasks, Responsibilities, Practices.* New York: Harper & Row.

Etzioni, A. (1964). *Modern Organizations.* Englewood Cliffs, NJ: Prentice-Hall.

Fenske, Robert H. (1980). Setting institutional goals and objectives. *Improving Academic Management,* P. Jedamus and M. Peterson and Associates (eds.). San Francisco: Jossey-Bass, pp. 177–199.

Fleming, T. (1980). Beyond survival: Policies for academic revitalization in an uncertain environment. *Canadian Journal of Higher Education* 10(2): 103–115.

Giroux, H. (1984). Public philosophy and the crisis in education. *Harvard Educational Review* 54: 188.

Hines, Edward R. (1988). *Higher Education and State Governments.* Washington, DC: Association for the Study of Higher Education.

Jedamus, Paul, and Peterson, M. W. eds. (1980). *Improving Academic Management. A Handbook of Planning and Institutional Research.* San Francisco: Jossey-Bass.

Keller, George (1983). *Academic Strategy. The Management Revolution in American Higher Education.* Baltimore, MD: Johns Hopkins University Press.

Kerr, Clark, director. Commission on Strengthening Presidential Leadership (October 1984). *Presidents Make a Difference: Strengthening Leadership in Colleges and Universities.* Sponsored by the Association of Governing Boards of Universities and Colleges.

Konrad, A. G., and McNeal, Joanne (1984). Goals in Canadian universities. *Canadian Journal of Higher Education* 14: 31–40.

Kotler, Philip, and Murphy, Patrick E. (1981). Strategic planning for higher education. *Journal of Higher Education* 52(5): 470–489.

Lang, Daniel (Fall 1988). Planning and decision-making in universities. Canadian Society for the Study of Higher Education. *Professional File*, no. 4.

Martin, Warren Bryan (1985). Mission: A statement of identity and direction. In *Opportunity in Adversity*, J. S. Green and A. Levine (eds.). San Francisco: Jossey-Bass.

McKelvie, Brenda D. (1986). The university's statement of goals. An idea whose time has come. *Higher Education* 15: 151–163.

National Governors' Association (August 1986). *Time for Results: The Governors' 1991 Report on Education.* Washington, D.C.

Newsom, Walter, and Hayes, C. Ray (1991). Are mission statements worthwhile? *Planning for Higher Education* 19(2): 28–31.

Parker, Barbara (1986). Agreement of mission and institutional responses to decline. *Research in Higher Education* 25(2): 164–181.

Peters, T. J., and Waterman, R. H., Jr. (1982). *In Search of Excellence.* New York: Harper & Row.

Peterson, R. E., and Loye, D. E. (1967). *Conversations Toward a Definition of Institutional Vitality.* Princeton, NJ: Educational Testing Service.

Regents of the University of the State of New York (1979). *The Bulletin of the Regents 1980 Statewide Plan for the Development of Postsecondary Education.* Albany, N Y: The State Education Department.

Richardson, Richard C., and Doucette, Donald S. (1984). An empirical model for formulating operational missions of community colleges. Unpublished paper.

Richardson, Richard C., and Gardner, Don E. (1983). Avoiding extremes in the planning continuum. *Journal of Higher Education* 54(2): 180–192.

Richman, B. M., and Farmer, R. N. (1974). *Leadership, Goals, and Power in Higher Education: A Contingency and Open Systems Approach to Effective Management.* San Francisco: Jossey-Bass.

Schmidtlein, F. A. (1989). Center findings reveal planning problems. *News from SCUP* 19(4).

Schmidtlein, F. A., and Milton, T. H. (1988). Campus planning in the United States: Perspectives from a nationwide study. Unpublished paper.

Sibley, William M. (1986). Strategic planning and management for change. *Canadian Journal of Higher Education* 16(2): 81–101.

Sizer, J. (1982). Assessing institutional performance and progress. *Agenda for Institutional Change in Higher Education*, L. Wagner, (ed.). Surrey, England: Society for Research into Higher Education.

Willmer, Wesley Kenneth, ed. (September 1981). *Advancing the Small College.* New Directions for Institutional Advancement 13. San Francisco: Jossey-Bass.

Appendix A: Institutional Statements of Mission

"Statement of Roles and Goals [of Acadia University]" (1980)

"The Next Decade and Beyond: A Plan for the Future [of the University of Alberta]" (1986)

"The Mission of the University of British Columbia" (1979)

"The Role and Goals of Dalhousie University in the 1980s" (1981)

"Aims of the University of Guelph" (1985)

"350th Speech [Harvard University]" (1986)

"Academic Plan [of the University of Hull]" (1987)

"Our [Indiana] University in the State" (1987)

"The University [of Lethbridge] to the Century's End" (1985)

"McGill's Priorities" (1979)

"A Plan for McMaster University" (1977)

"Strategy for the Future [of Monash University]" (1988)

"Statement of Roles and Goals [of the University of New Brunswick]" (1980)

"Mission, Programs, and Priorities for Action [at SUNY–Albany]" (1977)

"Missions Statement [of the University of Ottawa]" (1987)

"Penn State" (1986)

"The University [of Pittsburgh] Plan" (1985)

"Towards a University [of Prince Edward Island] Community—Goals in Perspective" (1975)

"The Mission of the University [Queen's University]" (1984)

"A Statement of the Roles and Goals of St. Francis Xavier University" (1981)

"Directions for St. Lawrence University" (1984)

"The Aims of the University of Saskatchewan" (1975)

"Issues and Options [for the University of Saskatchewan]" (1986)

"A Statement of Mission for Simon Fraser University" (1979)

"General Objectives of the University [of Toronto]" (1973)

"Statement of Institutional Purpose [for the University of Toronto]" (1988)

"Planning for the Third Decade [of the University of Waterloo]" (1979)

"Planning for the Fourth Decade [of the University of Waterloo]" (1985)

"The University of Western Ontario: The Current Situation and a Strategy for the Future" (1983)

"Statement of Mission [for the University of Western Ontario]" (1984)

"A Report from the Campus [Wesleyan University]" (1986)

"A Proud Tradition Continues [the University of Winnipeg]" (1987)

Appendix B: System Master Plans and Statements of Mission

"A Master Plan for Higher Education in California, 1960–1975" (1960)

"The Challenges Ahead: A Planning Agenda for California Postsecondary Education, 1982–1987" (1982)

"The Regents [of New York] Statewide Plan for the Development of Postsecondary Education" (1976, 1980)

"The Challenge and the Choice [for the State University of New York]" (1985)

"Higher Education in Ohio: Master Plan" (1976)

"Master Plan for Higher Education [in Ohio]: Opportunity in a Time of Change" (1982)

"The Ontario University System: A Statement of Issues" (1978)

"[Ontario] System Rationalization: A Responsibility and an Opportunity" (1980)

"Report of the Commission on the Future Development of the Universities of Ontario" (1985)

"A Master Plan for Higher Education in Pennsylvania" (1967, 1971, 1978)

"Master Plan for Pennsylvania Higher Education" (1986)

"The Virginia Plan for Higher Education" (1967, 1974, 1981, 1985)

Measuring Performance: How Colleges and Universities Can Set Meaningful Goals and Be Accountable

WILLIAM F. MASSY

The headline for a recent article in *The Economist* opened with this encouraging thought: "Academia is the one bit of education in which America still leads the world." Then it dropped the other shoe: "But for how much longer?"[1]

According to *The Economist*, and a great many contemporary critics of U.S. higher education, colleges' and universities' costs are too high, and their ability to deliver value for money is problematic. In addition to the well-known problem of labor intensity, the high costs are due to a faculty labor market that is out of control, soaring research expense, and the fact that internal and external constituencies expect—and demand—that their institutions be all things to all people. The result is dwindling affordability, erosion of faculty accountability, and proliferation of programs and ideologies to the point where the general public has begun to question the whole enterprise. No wonder a populist backlash threatens deeply held academic values and leaves many academics with feelings of bewilderment and anger.

These problems will not go away. The affordability crunch is rooted in long-term pressures on the standard of living for the middle class: because of the diffusion of productive capacity around the world, and the resulting increase of international competition, today's young people can no longer look forward to automatic real income enhancements. A global tide of "deprotectionism," withdrawal of special privilege in both the social and economic spheres, fuels resentment over perceived faculty life-styles, perquisites, and freedom from accountability. Fragmentation of values in the larger society and the rise of in-your-face activism reinforce program proliferation on the one hand and popular resentment about particular programs and ideologies on the other. These forces are too strong—and too rooted in real ills—for the problem to be simply ridden out or assuaged by rhetorical and political defenses.

Colleges and universities must change their behavior. They must become more productive. They must learn to set meaningful goals and be accountable for achieving them.

A Program for Accountability

There is nothing particularly mysterious about accountability, even in higher education. The Presidential Commission on the Responsibility for Financing Higher Education put forward this four-point program:

1. Decide on the tasks that need to be accomplished, i.e., the goals of the enterprise.

2. Ensure that the available resources are sufficient to complete the tasks successfully.

3. Provide the enterprise with the authority it needs to be effective, and then let it do the job without interference.

"Measuring Performance: How Colleges and Universities Can Set Meaningful Goals and Be Accountable," by William F. Massy, reprinted from *Measuring Institutional Performance in Higher Education*, edited by W. F. Massy and J. W. Meyerson, 1994. Peterson's Guides, Princeton, NJ.

4. Define a set of measurements to indicate how well the enterprise is doing relative to its goals, and follow up by tracking these measurements.[2]

These principles apply at every level of the accountability stream: in higher education, the stream runs from state governments (for public institutions) to governing boards, to system and campus administrations, to academic units like schools and departments, and finally to individual faculty. No level should be exempt, but no level should feel disempowered either. Decisions about goals should be participatory, for example, although the authority for goal-setting must ultimately reside with those who provide funds and are held accountable by others for their use. (This authority locus is mandated by the third principle, applied one level up the chain.) Assessment of resource sufficiency and the design of measurements also should be participative, since the downstream units know more about productivity methods and measures than the upstream ones. Once again, however, the upstream unit needs to stay close enough to the action to be sure that the assessments and measures are reasonable. Finally, the local unit's authority to act autonomously to achieve the agreed goals provides the ultimate empowerment needed to motivate and enable the needed productive capacity.

Apologists for higher education will argue that accountability is inappropriate because only academicians know what is good in education and research, and because it is impossible to measure success in achieving the "good." We must reject that way of thinking. The first proposition is false on its face, since funds are spent on education and research in order to achieve certain educational and social objectives—which in turn must be traded off against other goods. Like medicine, higher education has become too large and costly to warrant delegation of goals and resource needs to the self-interested professionals within the enterprise. (This is one of the tenets of deprotectionism.) The second proposition is false as well, as I shall demonstrate in the remainder of this paper.

Prestige as Goal and Problem

The criticism of colleges and universities does not arise from an inability to define goals and measure performance, but rather because too many institutions have defined the wrong goal and have been all too effective in measuring progress toward achieving it. According to Harvard emeritus president Derek Bok:

> As we all know, the prizes, the media recognition, the extra income do not come from working with students or engaging in exemplary teaching. And it is not just the professors' incentives that are out of whack, but also those of administrators. What presidents and deans are held accountable for is improving the prestige of their institutions, and the *prestige* of their institutions comes from the research reputation of their faculties.[3]

Put in the best light, prestige has come to be viewed as a surrogate for higher education's contribution to society. Research is a "good" because it opens the way for new solutions and opportunities, and the prizes, media recognition, and extra income simply reflect its value. Prestige brings the institution comparative advantage in the competitive market for faculty as well as intrinsic pride in accomplishment and recognition. Successful prestige-building reinforces the importance of research (and its close cousin, graduate education), and failure brings both tangible and intangible penalties. Institutions compete for prestige, and over time the quest becomes self-fulfilling and regenerating.

While there is nothing wrong with prestige-building per se, an expanding body of opinion holds that the process has gone too far and that many of higher education's ills can be attributed to this fact. Unbridled competition for prestige—at least as traditionally defined in terms of research—leads to "mission creep," as evidenced by the drive of many institutions to become "universities." It increases cost per student as the "academic ratchet" adds to institutionally funded faculty discretionary time, which in turn is deployed to produce yet more research and scholarship.[4] It overwhelms researchers and libraries with exponentially growing volumes of research output—much of dubious quality—often promulgated in journals created more to meet faculty needs for publication than to disseminate information demanded by readers. It puts a "whatever-it-takes" premium on the recruitment and retention of faculty research stars and places promising young educators who do not excel

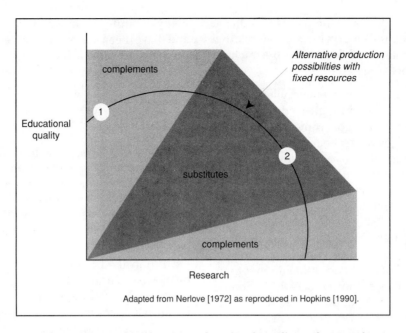

Figure 1 The Tradeoff between Educational Quality and Research

at research in counterproductive "publish or perish" situations. It adds to the proliferation of support services as more tasks are offloaded from faculty. Finally, it deprives undergraduate and professional students of faculty "quality time" that otherwise could be used for the modernization of educational goals, the design of new curricula and teaching methods, and teaching itself.

These problems are not unique to research universities. To quote Carnegie Foundation for the Advancement of Teaching President Ernie Boyer:

> The pressure to publish, while found to one degree or another in all types of institutions in our study, was especially apparent at those universities or doctorate-granting institutions that see themselves as "being in transition." The goal, as an administrator at one such institution put it, is "to be in the top twenty, or certainly in the top fifty." Meanwhile, the same institutions enroll large numbers of undergraduates, and members of the faculty—especially young faculty members—often feel caught in the middle.[5]

Small liberal arts colleges may have a culture of their own. Faculty may teach more and spend more time with their students. But even these institutions live in the shadow of the research university. They value good teaching but are likely to re-

ward most handsomely those members of the faculty who have scholarly reputations. A paper read at a national convention nets more praise than a splendid lecture to undergraduates. A published article in a prestigious journal or a major book is valued most of all.[6]

Defenders of research's primacy among institutional goals argue that research excellence is a necessary condition for excellence in teaching, and that by maximizing research (and its surrogate, prestige) the benefits conferred on undergraduates also will be maximized. For many institutions this was the original justification for upgrading research. The assertion is correct up to a certain point, especially if the definition of research is broadened to include general scholarship and keeping up with one's field. However, the process has gone too far in a growing number of institutions, to the point where research substitutes for education to an alarming degree. Worse yet, too many institutions strive to emulate this overcommitment to research.

Figure 1 depicts the various combinations of educational quality and research that could be produced by a hypothetical academic unit, given that faculty and other resource levels are fixed.[7] (I consider the quantity of education as fixed for purposes of the illustration but make no distinction between the quantity and quality of research.) Research and education are *complements in production* up to a certain point, as depicted in the figure's first gray triangle. At the low research levels depicted by point 1, increments to research improve educational quality for the traditional reasons of intellectual currency and excitement. However, successive increments to research bring diminishing returns. The conventional wisdom holds that the emphasis on research is about right or perhaps even too low. However, as research is pushed further the time demands on faculty and support staff take their toll. Educational quality and research become *substitutes* as one passes into the figure's second gray triangle. The research environment is competitive and open-ended, so the pressure on research time never lets up. Hence the amount of effort devoted to teaching must increase disproportionately as one moves downward toward point 2. While not relevant to the present discussion, it is worth noting that research and education become complements again at low levels of educational output, for example, in pure research institutes that do not benefit from the students' paradigm-breaking questions and inexpensive research labor.

Outside funding may reduce teaching loads and allow extra faculty to be hired, but it also brings new tasks such as proposal-writing and meeting sponsor-imposed deadlines. Faculty with significant research programs shift their allegiance from the institution outward toward their discipline and sponsors, breaking down the academic work-unit's sense of community. I am convinced that on balance, the cross-pressures generated by sponsored research programs put more pressure on undergraduate teaching performance than the extra funding alleviates through contributions to the institution's fixed cost. Higher education's critics believe with some justification that too many institutions have moved well into the substitutability region—where increments to research crowd out quality teaching time.

But maximizing prestige can lead to even more pernicious consequences than missing the optimal point in the difficult tradeoff between research and educational quality. It can undermine financial discipline and end up exploiting the institution's future stakeholders, as well as current undergraduates, to benefit today's faculty and administrators. Calls for

deficit spending in hard economic times to avoid degrading faculty morale are all too familiar. Losing prestigious faculty members erodes prestige to an extent disproportionate to the effect on educational quality. No institutional leader wants the responsibility (or the accountability) for such losses; many will go to extraordinary lengths to avoid them, regardless of the long-term consequences. These pressures also distort facilities maintenance decisions, transfers to capital budgets, and endowment payout rates.

Performance-measure asymmetry biases decisions away from educational quality and increases cost. Research accomplishment tends to be easier to measure than educational accomplishment—the work product is tangible and can be subjected to peer review, and it does not depend so much on the quality and motivation of the "raw material." Furthermore, faculty research productivity can be transferred more easily from institution to institution than can educational productivity. (The latter depends more on school-specific characteristics like curriculum, student attributes, and culture.) Hence the research marketplace has become very competitive, whereas the educational marketplace remains quite imperfect. Competition bids up the price of the research stars, as manifested in compensation, reduced teaching loads, and better support services and facilities. Institutions must appropriate an ever-larger fraction of their resources—including those intended for undergraduate and professional education—to sustain or improve their standing in the faculty marketplace.

Higher education's leaders and faculty did not set out to charge more for undergraduate education while providing less. Originally, the goal was to increase instructional quality by moving up the ascending portion of the curve in Figure 1. But, lacking explicit goal definitions, performance measures, and accountability for undergraduate educational quality and cost-effectiveness, the "researchification" process has encountered no natural stopping point. It has proceeded to ratchet along under its own power, producing these consequences:

- less time devoted to undergraduate and professional education
- less concern about the structure and coherence of the curriculum

- larger budgets and higher tuition
- greater pressure to transfer resources from future to present stakeholders

The juxtaposition of these consequences worries students, parents, donors, state and federal officials, and others who fund undergraduate and professional education.

The conclusion is simple and inescapable. To regain the public trust, colleges and universities must redefine their goals to emphasize more than prestige and its main driver, faculty research. The new goals must focus on the needs of the undergraduate and professional clients whose education represents the primary mission for most institutions and the objectives of those who provide the funding for them. While research should continue to be important, accountability requires that institutions demonstrate a reasonable balance between the resources dedicated to research and those used for education. This, in turn, requires that colleges and universities develop new success measures, that the media and other opinion leaders start publicizing and using them, and that institutional stakeholders accept the broader measures—and the goals from which they are derived—as a valid basis for accountability. Higher education should heed *The Economist*'s final dictum: "For once, a little more introspection on the part of the academic community seems to be in order."[8]

Improving Institutional Performance

To restore the public trust, academia's new introspection will have to improve the quality and cost-effectiveness of undergraduate education and demonstrate value for money. Table 1 outlines the dimensions of the task. The horizontal dimension divides the institution along academic and nonacademic lines, the vertical dimension articulates two classic quality-efficiency questions[9] plus the need to maintain financial discipline, and the cells contain examples of the kinds of tasks that need to be accomplished.[10] I shall focus here on cells I and III, plus the cost-control element of cell IV. I also have been working on issues pertaining to cell V.[11] Cells II and IV have been addressed elsewhere.[12]

Restoring the balance between teaching and research does not mean turning back the clock to the preresearch era, nor does it mean turning faculty into high-volume teaching machines. To attempt either would be to throw away an important element of college and university competence; indeed, it would negate the comparative advantage of the tertiary education sector. We need better balance, not a new overreaction that takes us back to the northwest corner of Figure 1.

Controlling costs and maintaining financial discipline need not diminish quality. Cost control means doing things efficiently, and more effective resource allocation can concentrate

---

Table 1 Approaches to Institutional Performance Improvement

	Educational tasks	Administrative and support tasks
	I	II
Do the right things	Develop new faculty incentives	Design appropriate services, incentives, and management systems
	Restore the balance between teaching and research, and design a more effective curriculum	
Do things right	III	IV
	Deliver effective teaching and advising	Insure effective program implementation
	Control costs	Control costs
	V	
Maintain financial discipline	Allocate resources effectively Maintain financial equilibrium	

money where it can make the biggest difference. By maintaining financial equilibrium, institutional leaders can avoid overspending endowment and reserve funds and building liabilities for their successors—the two classic methods for exploiting future stakeholders. Successful businesses have learned that a good restructuring program can improve quality *and* reduce cost, and we should aspire to do no less in higher education.

Educational quality is like industrial quality in another very important respect: it must be built in from the beginning, it cannot be "inspected in" afterwards. Effective service providers put the client first during the design phase, insist on total dedication to client needs during the service encounter, and then obtain and carefully analyze feedback from clients to maintain a process of continuous improvement. In higher education this means designing a meaningful curriculum, delivering effective teaching, carefully monitoring results, and making continuous adjustments to curriculum and teaching methods in response to client feedback and new technological opportunities. Such a program is not incompatible with striving for excellence in research and scholarship, but it will require a change in culture at many institutions.

Businesses have learned that the best way to achieve quality is to provide clear goals and appropriate resources, decentralize to self-directed work teams, and insist on effective performance feedback. (It is no accident that these stand in one-to-one correspondence with the four necessary conditions for accountability.) Higher education has gotten the formula partly right: over the last forty years we have marshaled the resources needed to do an effective job of education, and we have given institutions and their faculty the independence needed to do the job. We even began with a clear vision: that by upgrading research we would, ipso facto, improve educational quality. Unfortunately, however, our vision was not clear enough to foresee the consequences of carrying research to an extreme or to predict that combining ample resources and heavy decentralization with fuzzy educational goals and one-sided performance measures would unleash the prestige-maximization monster.

Colleges and universities should reflect on their mission and its implications for the edu-cation-research balance, redefine undergraduate education in terms of client need and value for money, redouble their efforts to maintain financial discipline, and develop appropriate performance measures. The objective should be significant quality improvements and cost reductions in areas not essential to the central academic mission—in other words, institutional restructuring.

Restructuring Tasks and Performance Measures

Restructuring requires the design and implementation of specific programs—high-sounding generalities won't do. The requirements follow the four-point program for accountability described earlier; however, restructuring necessitates a richer mixture of leadership, incentives, motivation, and assistance than does simple accountability. The following recommendations apply to both the academic and nonacademic sectors in all kinds of colleges and universities.

1. *Vision:* develop a clear vision for the changes that need to be accomplished and why they are important. Success becomes more likely when people understand clearly what is desired and why they should change their habitual ways of thinking and behaving. It should go without saying that institutional leaders must be strongly and visibly committed to the vision and demonstrate that commitment by actions as well as words.

2. *Resources:* ensure that needed resources are available in a timely and nonbureaucratic way. Investments in new equipment and technical assistance can be important for their own sake and also because they demonstrate commitment to the restructuring program and trust in the teams that drive it. Nothing will kill restructuring faster than achieving buy-in on the vision and then stifling initiatives with bureaucratic approval processes and "can't-do" managerial attitudes.

3. *Autonomy:* provide employee groups with (a) the autonomy they need to identify and implement the specific

changes needed for restructuring, and (b) clear statements about goals and limits, plus meaningful incentives based on the goals. In academic units the faculty already are largely self-directed, but too many fail to focus sufficiently on education, and there is too much fragmentation for effective teamwork.[13] The emphasis in academic work units should be on goals, limits, and incentives rather than autonomy per se; however, one should not try to micromanage faculty time.

4. *Performance measures:* agree on performance measures for each restructuring task, and then follow up to ensure that work groups are paying attention to the measures. Performance measures should represent aids to self-directed work improvement, not something unilaterally imposed and monitored by "the boss." While those with upstream accountability must track downstream performance and frequently discuss it with the responsible work teams, the relationship should be "win-win" rather than "gotcha."

Performance measures should focus on process and inputs as well as output assessment. For example, the way a work group approaches its task sometimes can be a good predictor of effectiveness: certain kinds of processes increase the probability of success, while others may virtually preclude it. Observing the input to a process will be important when time-on-task is problematic—as it is in the case for teaching-related activities, for example. This does not mean installing time clocks; it does mean learning to ask probing questions about priorities and time allocations.

The tendency for institutions and the press to use expense per student as a quality surrogate has produced some well-justified criticism about input and process measures as predictors of quality. I do not wish to argue against measuring output quality and cost-effectiveness whenever and wherever one can. On the other hand, the difficulty of measuring higher-education output quality means we will have to rely heavily on input and process measures for the foreseeable future. Furthermore, a closer look at the facts behind the criticisms reveals that much of the so-called "expense per

student" does not get applied to education at all but rather to faculty research and unneeded administrative and support services. A true accounting probably would indicate a better correlation between education input levels and output quality.

The mutually reinforcing character of output, process, and input measures becomes more apparent when we look at the cascading relationship among workplace processes. The outputs of certain processes become inputs to others, forming a complex network of dependence relationships. (This is one reason why flow-charting is included in so many industrial work-team training programs.) Examining the quantity and quality of inputs needed for one process informs output-specification writing for other processes. My experience indicates that it doesn't make much difference whether one starts by looking at inputs, processes, or outputs—all will have to be confronted sooner or later. Indeed, the categories tend to run together in academic work units, as we will see in the examples presented later.

Performance-measure design should be addressed in a practical, not a strictly "scientific" way. Social scientists tend to approach higher-education outcomes assessment too rigorously, for example, by trying to solve a narrow slice of the problem according to the standards of scientific proof or else throwing up their hands because the whole problem refuses to yield to such standards. Managers in business and government organizations know that one has to take a "what seems right, what seems to work" point of view. This does not mean that scientific method and insight should be cast aside—there is, after all, nothing so practical as a good theory. One should carry rigorous research as far as possible, but be prepared to make leaps of commitment to imperfect but implementable measures that offer a reasonable promise of improving the status quo.

The performance-measure design problem can be addressed by asking two different kinds of questions.

1. "If I were a hands-on work-team member, what would I need in order to track and improve my performance?" For example, how might professors gain better insight into how well their teaching is "going over" and how well the curricu-

lum meets the needs of nontraditional students? How might support service customers gauge the quality of the outputs they receive and provide feedback to the suppliers so that their own performance can be improved?

2. "How do the cost and quality of particular final and intermediate outputs compare with roughly similar outputs provided by other institutions?" What kinds of unit-cost comparisons would be most useful? How could reasonably common definitions be assured, and how should the set of "roughly similar" institutions be defined? Should one base the comparisons on "best practice" in a given institutional segment—on the grounds that one should aspire to be the best—or on a measure of central tendency?

The first type of question digs deeply into one's own organization. The second seeks more aggregate comparisons among a group of peer institutions. In-house information may be obtained by consultants, but the most effective source is the membership of the work units themselves. Comparability data, usually called "benchmark data," often are developed by consortia of institutions or by commercial suppliers. A hybrid, known as "best-practice benchmarking," has been popularized in connection with the Malcomb Baldridge business quality awards: the "best" firm at performing a given function is identified and its methods used as a model for others.

Performance Measures for Teaching Quality

The preceding discussion was necessarily rather abstract, so I will illustrate what I have in mind by means of examples, beginning with the issue of educational quality as it applies to question 1. The broad subject of outcomes assessment is beyond the scope of this paper. However, I hope to show that defining and measuring performance is not as difficult as the conventional wisdom suggests, and that meaningful progress is possible.

It is difficult to achieve consensus on a comprehensive definition of teaching, yet most people believe they "know it when they see it."

The following statement by the Committee on Inquiry of England's Polytechnics & Colleges Funding Council (now merged into the Higher Education Funding Council) captures the essence of good teaching:

> The Committee agreed that teaching must be interpreted broadly, as the initiation and management of student learning by a teacher; we also agreed that it must be responsive to student needs; and the conditions necessary for good teaching must be a priority at every level of the institution. We did not identify one definition of "good" teaching, but rather agreed that teaching must be judged good by whether it contributes to the purposes of higher education—the life-chances of the student. However, we also agreed that for excellence in teaching, it was vital to look to the ethos of the institution as a whole, to the sense of excitement amongst students, teachers, and visitors.[14]

The definition delineates the behavior we wish to encourage in order to improve teaching: in this case whether the teacher manages the learning process (as opposed to being passive or reactive), and whether responsiveness to student needs is a priority at every institutional level. The need to determine whether these behavior patterns are being achieved provides the basis for a first round of performance-measure design.

Analyzing the desired behavior in detail provides material for designing a richer set of measures. Teaching is, in effect, the delivery of a service, and the behaviors needed for effective service delivery also are necessary for effective teaching. Research on service delivery shows that two conditions are required to achieve excellence:

1. The provider must care about the client, engaging fully in the task and doing his or her best to understand and adapt to the client's needs.

2. The provider must arrange for feedback about the service encounter—from the client, from knowledgeable observers, or both—and then use the feedback to improve performance.

Effective service delivery requires a high degree of attention and caring, and the difficulty of putting oneself in the client's shoes requires systematic feedback and conscious adaptation. The need for feedback does not imply that a professional service provider must abdicate to the client's whims; it is up to the professional to apply his or her expertise in the client's service. The client also has a duty: students, for example, should strive to learn. However, the teachers' greater expertise makes them the "team captains" of the learning process. Input-type performance measures can assess the captains' commitment and attention, and process-type measures can assess the feedback arrangements.

The need for redefining the faculty "equity ethic" to encompass the principle of comparative advantage offers additional possibilities for performance-measure design. Though almost anyone can improve his or her performance through sustained effort, all professors do not have the same innate talents. Every institution's faculty can be arrayed according to relative ability in teaching and research. Some professors are outstanding in both—the "stars" that every school seeks to recruit and retain. Some turn out to have more research talent than teaching talent, and for some the balance will be reversed. Ideally only a few—mistakes in selection and promotion—turn out to lack sustainable ability in either research or teaching. An effective program for improving teaching quality would encourage professors who turn out better at teaching than research to focus their attention on teaching and be rewarded for so doing. This application of the comparative advantage principle is frustrated by the low status of teaching in many institutions. Improving the status of teaching would improve quality and, at the same time, relieve a source of tension for many faculty members. Teaching status is a measurable quantity and an important performance variable.

Good teaching encompasses exemplary classroom performance, but that is not all. The "initiation and management of student learning" begins with the development of a coherent curriculum. It continues with advising students about which curricular options can best meet their individual needs and mentoring them in ways that facilitate learning. Classroom performance also includes packaging and presenting materials in ways that make sense to the kinds of students being taught. For example, nontraditional students and disad-

vantaged minority students require different approaches than well-prepared traditional students. Finally, learning facilitation must include feedback to students about their performance. The findings from Berkeley professor Patricia Cross's classroom research project support the importance of feedback for students as well as faculty.[15] Once again, characterization of the desired behavior illuminates new possibilities for performance-measure design.

Table 2 lists some of the actions that faculty work-groups and institutions might take to promote good undergraduate teaching. The list is not exhaustive, nor do I suggest that all the actions should be required—mere bureaucratic compliance would not be useful, for instance. Nevertheless, good-faith efforts to improve performance, pursued consistently for a period of years, do seem likely to improve educational quality. The actions are within reach of most faculties and institutions, and thoughtful observers can determine how things are going without using special tests or techniques. Each item in the list begins with an action verb, which carries the basis for eventual performance evaluation. The list demonstrates that colleges and universities do not lack ways to assess progress toward educational quality—in fact, there may be an embarrassment of riches.

Benchmarks

The myth of incomparability has bedeviled higher education for a long time. Many college and university leaders believe that their institutions possess such unique characteristics that efforts to compare one with another will be self-defeating if not damaging. This can represent a self-fulfilling prophecy: for example, there is little standardization among management information system designs or data element definitions. Despite the guidelines promulgated by NACUBO, the Financial Accounting Standards Board (for private institutions), and the Government Accounting Standards Board (for public institutions), accounting methods remain differentiated to the point where meaningful comparisons are difficult or impossible. Institutional representatives fight standardization efforts tooth and nail, partly because of the expense and disruption associated with change and partly, one sus-

Table 2 Actions That Might Be Taken by Faculty Work-Groups and Institutions to Promote Good Teaching

Faculty work-groups

Develop clear goals and objectives related specifically to teaching and to the needs of the different kinds of students.

Develop strategies to make teaching a subject of vibrant discussion in faculty meetings and informal conversations, and to make good teaching a source of individual and collective satisfaction.

Encourage senior faculty to play exemplary teaching roles; shun systematic relief from teaching for senior faculty based on seniority.

Develop and maintain effective programs for (a) instructing doctoral students on effective teaching, (b) inculcating attitudes conducive to good teaching, and (c) providing knowledge about how faculty leaders can stimulate good teaching in their work groups.

Establish and enforce criteria for ensuring that junior faculty demonstrate good teaching as well as good research in order to be eligible for promotion.

Arrange for systematic feedback from students, and evaluation of faculty teaching by peers, in relation to goals.

Relate faculty salary increases to good teaching as well as to research; make sure the unit's best teachers' salaries keep pace with those of the best researchers, despite the latter's greater external visibility.

Work through retreats, resource people, and persuasive communication by senior faculty to develop group norms for continuing professional development of teaching skills by all faculty. Develop incentives for individual faculty to meet or exceed the group norms.

Regularly assess all aspects of the teaching program in a systematic way (e.g., using ideas presented earlier in this chapter), by self-study and use of external resources.

Institutions

Engage work groups in serious dialogue about their teaching goals and performance; require serious planning for better teaching.

Make sure that work groups develop effective mechanisms for assessing teaching quality on an ongoing basis.

Require periodic departmental self-studies of teaching and arrange for external reviews of departmental performance, including teaching.

Provide resources for professional development of teaching skills, such as teaching and learning centers. Make sure work groups develop appropriate norms and incentives for using these resources.

Reward exemplary teachers with institutional prizes or other forms of recognition.

Adjust the criteria for promotion and tenure review (a) to require demonstration of good teaching and (b) to limit the quantity (but not the quality) of research output considered, to make it possible for junior faculty to invest time in teaching.

Monitor effective teaching loads carefully; prevent unintended upward creep of departmental research.

Relate discretionary budget allocations to work-group performance on all of the above.

---

pects, because these efforts challenge the incomparability myth.

Even the well-known OMB circular A-21, on which research overhead recovery has been based for many years, is loaded with escape clauses. The resulting "flexibility" permits institutions to define data their own way—and thus escape comparability even on so basic a quantity as an overhead rate. Some modest recommendations on ways to improve the situation, put forth by the AAU Committee on Indirect Cost Recovery a few years ago,[16] were greeted with strong opposition from institutional accounting and financial officers. I outlined the dangers of incomparability in a 1990 presentation.[17] Ironically, government agencies and the press proceeded to make comparisons anyway—on the basis of fragmentary information and anecdotal evidence—and drew flawed

and damaging conclusions.

However understandable its genesis, the incomparability myth has taken on the same coloration as the prestige-maximization monster. That is, higher education's critics are coming to view it as an oversimplification or even as a device to enhance market power. Believers in the oversimplification argument hold that comparability can be improved if one is willing to analyze the situation deeply enough, and that there is no excuse for failing to do so. Careful attention to definition, and systematic data analysis and modeling where applicable, can produce valid comparisons in the financial arena—as Gordon Winston points out, for instance.[18] The same is true even in the difficult area of faculty teaching loads and discretionary time.[19]

The idea that incomparability enhances market power derives from the economic principle that pure competition (the antithesis of incomparability) precludes economic exploitation, whereas incomparability makes every entity a monopolist to some degree. Holding an enterprise accountable for efficiency and quality is difficult without good benchmarks. The market provides the needed benchmark in the competitive situation, but when markets are imperfect (as in the case of educational outputs) or nonexistent (as for many administrative and support services), derived benchmarks must be constructed to achieve comparability.

Benchmark information for colleges and universities can be obtained from a number of sources. The federal government collects aggregate information on a number of variables and distributes them at modest cost via the HEGIS/IPEDS and CASPAR databases. The Higher Education Data Sharing (HEDS) organization collects and disseminates more detailed information for member institutions on a cooperative basis. The Association of Governing Boards of Universities and Colleges (AGB) published a book of strategic indicators last year[20] and has updated and significantly enhanced the collection in a publication produced in collaboration with Peterson's Guides. I will conclude this paper by describing the latter effort, with which Joel Meyerson and I have been closely associated.

To be effective, benchmark data must deal with managerially meaningful variables. Hence the design of benchmark surveys must be guided by an implicit or explicit model delineating the important inputs, processes, and outputs for the type of enterprise in question. It will come as no surprise that my preference is for explicit models, ones that can at least potentially be defined in quantitative terms. Explicit models offer the dual advantages of being (a) relatively unambiguous and (b) capable of assessment in terms of internal consistency and completeness on important issues.[21]

Table 3 presents the categories and selected first-level subcategories used in the Peterson's-AGB survey. The first category, "financial profiles," generally follows the IPEDS format, but we added detail in many categories. For example, the figures for "expenditures by function" include the following breakouts (in addition to an "other" category), which we based on budgeting experience, indirect cost analysis, and production function modeling:

Academic support

- libraries
- academic computing

Institutional support

- government, public, and alumni relations; development
- telecommunications and administrative computing

Student services

- admissions and financial aid administration
- student health

Plant operation and maintenance

- plant and grounds maintenance
- utilities

Additional models informed our specification-writing for the other variables: e.g., models for (a) the interinstitutional comparison of indirect costs,[22] (b) the relation of endowment, plant, and maintenance expenditures to long-run financial equilibrium,[23] and (c) faculty age and tenure distributions.[24] More than seven hundred institutions responded to the survey.

The Peterson's-AGB strategic-indicators survey serves the dual objective of focusing attention on important strategic quantities and providing benchmarks for performance assessment. To our knowledge, this is the most comprehensive effort of its kind ever undertaken in higher education. Current plans are to replicate the survey approximately every two years, so that data series can be accumulated and trends evaluated. (The variable set will be refined as we gain experience with modeling and data usage.) We seek increased participation in the survey—especially from the research universities, which are underrepresented in the current dataset.

The survey provides sufficient detail and a large enough sample size to permit a richer set of comparisons than can be covered in any publication. One could design a microcomputer database to aid survey respondents in making the best use of the data. Provided annually on a subscription basis, the database would allow institutional researchers to compare their own data for any survey variable against a profile for either predefined or custom-tailored institutional segments. A more advanced decision-support system would incorporate models to combine, transform, and

**Table 3 Peterson's-AGB Strategic Indicators Survey Questionnaire
Major Headings and Selected Subheadings**

Financial Profile
Revenue
Tuition and fee income
Government appropriations
Government grants and contracts
Private gifts, grants, and contracts
Endowment support for operations (payout or yield)
Sales and services of educational activities
Sales and services of auxiliary enterprises
Sales and services of hospitals
Other sources
Independent operations
Total revenue
Current expenditures by Function
Instruction (including departmental research)
Organized research
Public service
Academic support
Student services (excluding student aid awards)
Institutional support
Plant operation and maintenance
Expenditures on auxiliaries
Expenditures on hospitals
Expenditures on independent operations
Student financial aid
Total expenditures
Current expenditures by object
Wages and salaries [by type of employee]
Fringe benefits
Interest payments to outside entities
Balance Sheet
Assets
Current funds
Endowment book value
Plant and equipment
Other assets
Total assets
Liabilities and funds balances
Current liabilities
Short-term debt to outside entities
Long-term debt to outside entities
Funds balances
Total liabilities and funds balances

Physical Plant Detail
Financial
Beginning-of-year value
Depreciation for the year
Retirement of plant
Additions to plant (new construction)
End-of-year value
Plant Inventory and Condition
Gross square feet [by type of facility]
Estimated deferred maintenance backlog ($)

Libraries and Information Resources Detail
Library holdings
Book and monograph volumes
Journal subscriptions
Information resources
Microcomputers supplied for student use

Endowment Detail
Beginning-of-year market value [by fund type]
Return on investment [by type of return]
Other additions to endowment [by type]

Subtractions from endowment
Normal support for operations (from line 1.A.4)
Special uses (e.g., to cover deficits)
Total
End-of-year market value [by fund type]

Students
Fall enrollment [headcount & FTE, by level]
Fall FTE enrollment by EEOC category and level
Fall FTE enrollment by gender and level
Fall FTE enrollment by field of study and level
Degrees awarded by level
Admissions data for the full year
Number of applications
Number of offers of admission
Number of matriculants
Geographic dispersion of entering students by level
Number of states represented
Student headcount from home state
Students from outside the U.S. and Canada
Tuition and financial aid
Published charges
Financial aid headcounts by type of aid
Financial aid dollars by type of aid

Faculty and Staff
Faculty numbers [full and part time, by rank]
Regular faculty FTE
By field and rank
By EEOC category and rank
By gender and rank
Percent faculty over 60 years old
Faculty gains and losses for the year by rank
Headcount at the beginning of the year
In-hire
Voluntary termination
Termination by death or disability
Termination by the institution
Change category (e.g., non-tenured to tenured)
Headcount at the end of the year

Sponsored Research
Expenditures for organized research
U.S. Government [direct and indirect, by major
agency]
State and local government agencies
Domestic corporations & corporate foundations
Other domestic private foundations
Foreign governments, corporations, foundations
Bequests and gifts from living individuals
Other outside sponsors
Institutional funds
Academic-year faculty salary offsets
Percent of regular faculty members who are principal
investigators on sponsored projects
Research proposal and award statistics
Proposals sent to potential outside sponsors
Awards received from outside sponsors

Fund Raising [Other Than for Sponsored Projects]
Dollars raised during the year by source
Dollars raised during the year by use
Designated or restricted for current operations
Designated or restricted for student financial aid
Designated or restricted for endowment
Designated or restricted for plant
Percent of living alumni who are active donors (e.g.,
have given during the last five years)

project the data elements for single schools or institutional segments. For example, a dynamic faculty cohort model could combine and transform data on hiring, tenure-granting, and retirement rates to project future tenure ratios, faculty age distributions, and longevity-based salary growth. Such models are well within the current state of the art.

Concluding Comments

This book's purpose is to raise issues of importance to higher education and to suggest ways for dealing with them. We are particularly interested in strategic issues that involve or should involve institutional leaders, and we will pursue these issues even when they challenge the conventional wisdom or threaten the industry status quo. Performance measurement and accountability represent quintessential examples of such issues.

I have argued that accountability is possible in higher education, that it is being mandated by our clients and sponsors, and that it is not incompatible with institutional, departmental, and faculty autonomy. I have raised questions about prestige maximization and the primacy of faculty research, and I hope that I have provided some useful ideas about how to evaluate quality and some insights about quantitative benchmark data. Although the ideas presented here represent only a beginning, I believe that the performance measures needed to track improvements in educational quality and institutional cost-effectiveness are well within our reach. Sustained creative effort and hard work by institutional leaders and their staffs will be required before colleges and universities can regain the public trust.

Notes

1. *The Economist,* 1992, p. 18.
2. National Commission on Responsibilities for Financing Postsecondary Education, 1993, p. 56.
3. Bok, 1992, p. 16, emphasis added.
4. Massy and Zemsky, 1992; Policy Perspectives 1990; Zemsky and Massy 1990.
5. Boyer, 1987, p. 122.
6. Ibid., p. 121.
7. For further discussion, see Hopkins, 1990; Nerlove, 1972.
8. *The Economist,* 1992, p. 20.
9. Cf. Hammer, 1990.
10. Cell I: Boyer, 1991; Hoenack, 1974; Hoenack and Berg, 1980; Massy, 1989b; Policy Perspectives, 1989; Policy Perspectives, 1992.
    Cell II: Massy, 1989a; Massy and Warner, 1991.
    Cell III: Brown, 1988; Eble, 1972; Levin, 1989; Sherman, 1987; Stevens, 1988.
    Cell IV: Baldridge, 1980; Griffin and Burks, 1976.
    Cell V: Hyatt et al., 1984; Jedamus and Peterson, 1980; Massy, 1990a; Massy, 1990b; McGovern, 1988.
11. Massy, 1992.
12. Massy, 1989a.
13. Policy Perspectives, 1992.
14. "Teaching Quality," 1990, p. 5. The current controversy over educational quality measures in Britain postdates this inquiry.
15. Cross and Angelo, 1988.
16. AAU, 1988.
17. Massy, 1990c.
18. For an example in the overhead-rate domain, see Massy and Olson, 1991.
19. Massy and Zemsky, 1992.
20. Taylor et al., 1991.
21. See Little, 1970 for a classic discussion of the case for using explicit models even in qualitative situations.
22. Massy and Olson, 1991.
23. Hopkins and Massy, 1981, ch. 6, and Massy, 1990b.
24. Hopkins and Massy, 1981, ch. 8.

Bibliography

"Teaching Quality: Report of the Committee of Enquiry Appointed by the Council." (1990). Polytechnics and Colleges Funding Council, Great Britain.

"Poisoned Ivy." (1992) *The Economist*, August 15, 18–20.

AAU (1988). "Indirect Costs Associated With Federal Support of Research on University Campuses: Some Suggestions for Change." AAU.

Baldridge, J. Victor (1980). "Managerial Innovation. Rules for Successful Implementation." *Journal of Higher Education* 15:117–134.

Bok, Derek (1992). "Reclaiming the Public Trust." *Change* (July–August): 13–19.

Boyer, Ernest L. (1987). *The Undergraduate Experience in America.* New York: Harper & Row.

Boyer, E. L. (1991). *Scholarship Reconsidered: Priorities of the Professoriate.* Princeton, NJ: Carnegie Foundation for the Advancement of Teaching.

Brown, George (1988). *Effective Teaching in Higher Education.* London: Methuen.

Cross, K. Patricia and Thomas A. Angelo (1988). "The Classroom Research Project: Results of the First Ten Months. Progress report prepared for The Classroom Research Project." University of California, Berkeley.

Eble, Kenneth E. (1972). *Professors as Teachers.* San Francisco: Jossey-Bass.

Griffin, Gerald and David R. Burks (1976). *Appraising Administrative Operations: A Guide for Universities and Colleges.* Berkeley, CA: University of California.

Hammer, Michael (1990). "Reengineering Work: Don't Automate, Obliterate." *Harvard Business Review* (July–August): 104–112.

Hoenack, S. A. (1974). "Incentives and Resources Allocation in Universities." *Journal of Higher Education* 45:21–37.

Hoenack, Stephen A. and David J. Berg (1980). "The Roles of Incentives in Academic Planning." *New Directions for Institutional Research* 28:73–95.

Hopkins, David S. P. (1990). "The Higher Education Production Function: Theoretical Foundations and Empirical Findings." In Stephen A. Hoenack and Eileen L. Collins (Eds.), *The Economics of American Universities,* pp. 11–32. Albany, NY. SUNY Press.

Hopkins, David S. P. and William F. Massy (1981). *Planning Models for Colleges and Universities.* Stanford, CA: Stanford University Press.

Hyatt, James A., Carol H. Shulman, and Aurora A. Santiago (1984). "Reallocation: Strategies for Effective Resource Management." National Association of Colleges and Business Officers.

Jedamus, Paul and Marvin W. Peterson (1980). *Improving Academic Management. A Handbook of Planning and Institutional Research.* San Francisco: Jossey-Bass.

Levin, Henry (1989). "Raising Productivity in Higher Education." Higher Education Research Program of the University of Pennsylvania and the Pew Memorial Trusts.

Little, John D. C. (1970). "Models and Managers: The Concept of a Decision Calculus." *Management Science* 16:466–85.

Massy, William F. (1989a). "Productivity Improvement Strategies for College and University Administrative and Support Services." Presented at the Forum for College Financing, held in Annapolis, MD (November).

Massy, William F. (1989b). "A Strategy for Productivity Improvement in College and University Academic Departments." Presented at the Forum for Postsecondary Governance, held in Santa Fe, NM (November).

Massy, William F. (1990a). "Budget Decentralization at Stanford University." *Planning For Higher Education* 18(2):39–55.

Massy, William F. (1990b). *Endowment: Perspectives, Policies, and Management.* Washington, DC: Association of Governing Boards of Universities and Colleges.

Massy, William F. (1990c). "Financing Research." In Richard E. Anderson and Joel W. Meyerson (Eds.), *Financing Higher Education in a Global Economy.* New York: ACE/Macmillan, pp. 41–56.

Massy, William F. (1992). "Beyond Responsibility Center Budgeting (working title)." Presented at the Conference on Resource Allocation and University Management in University of Southern California, Finance Center of the Consortium for Policy Research in Education, November 19–20.

Massy, William F. and Jeffery E. Olson (1991). "Overhead Diversity: How Accounting Treatments, Facilities Economics, and Faculty Salary Offsets Affect University Indirect Cost Rates." Stanford Institute for Higher Education Research, Stanford University, Discussion Paper.

Massy, William F. and Timothy R. Warner (1991). "Causes and Cures of Cost Escalation in College and University Administrative and Support Services." Presented at the National Symposium on Strategic Higher Education Finance and Management Issues in the 1990s in Washington DC, OERI and NACUBO, January 25,1991.

Massy, William F. and Robert Zemsky (1992). "Faculty Discretionary Time: Departments and the Academic Ratchet." Stanford University, Stanford Institute for Higher Education Research, Academic Modeling Project Discussion Paper 4.

McGovern, James J. (1988). "Perspectives for Management Control and Program Budgeting." Medical College of Virginia, Virginia Commonwealth University, Report to the Deans.

National Commission on Responsibilities for Financing Postsecondary Education (1993), "Making College Affordable Again." Washington, DC: Final Report of the Commission (February).

Nerlove, Marc (1972). "On Tuition and the Costs of Higher Education: Prolegomena to a Conceptual Framework." *Journal of Political Economy,* Part II 3:S178–S218.

Policy Perspectives (1989). "The Business of the Business." 2(1). Philadelphia, PA: University of Pennsylvania, Pew Higher Education Research Program (May).

Policy Perspectives (1990). "The Lattice and the Ratchet." 2(4). Philadelphia, PA: University of Pennsylvania, Pew Higher Education Research Program (June).

Policy Perspectives (1992). "Testimony from the Belly of the Whale." 4(3). Philadelphia, PA: University of Pennsylvania, Pew Higher Education Research Program (September).

Sherman, Thomas, et al. (1987). "The Quest for Excellence in University Teaching." *Journal of Higher Education* 58:66–84.

Stevens, Ellen (1988). "Tinkering with Teaching." *Review of Higher Education* 12:63–78.

Taylor, Barbara E., Joel W. Meyerson, Louis R. Morrell, and Dabney G. Park (1991). *Strategic Analysis.* Washington, DC: Association of Governing Boards of Universities and Colleges.

Zemsky, Robert and William F. Massy (1990). "Cost Containment." *Change* 22(6):16–22 (November–December).

Academic Planning and Organizational Design: Lessons From Leading American Universities

DAVID D. DILL

Abstract

The emerging competitive environment of higher education, both within and between countries, is requiring universities in Europe and other parts of the world to emulate American institutions by becoming corporate entities with an independent capacity to make strategic choices among academic programmes and activities. A number of the leading American universities have developed comprehensive planning processes that offer suggestive guidance for managing in this new environment. These processes have emphasized: clarifying and articulating norms essential to the legitimacy of planning; grouping and consolidating functions; promoting reciprocal communication; encouraging the development of a planning capacity within each strategic unit; and increasing direct communication and the sharing of information among members of the academic community. Essentially these universities have conceived of comprehensive planning as a problem of organizational design, systematically seeking means of promoting integration in a highly differentiated organization. The specific mechanisms by which this integration has been accomplished are reviewed.

Introduction

Observers of higher education on both sides of the Atlantic are in agreement that the rapidly changing environment for universities requires more effective means of strategic choice making in institutions of higher education (Benjamin, *et al.*, 1993; Cameron and Tschirhart,

1992; Neave, 1995). Changing demands from government for research and service, the introduction of competitive market conditions to state systems which have traditionally operated as public monopolies, declining public revenues per student in the majority of developed countries, and the increasingly vocational and professional ambitions of students now pursuing higher education will oblige institutions of higher education to focus their missions by clarifying their priorities and implementing difficult choices. Strategic analysis will be necessary, and will need to be taken more rapidly, to identify those programmes which are critical to the comparative advantage of an institution and need to be maintained or strengthened, those that are less critical and can be reduced or eliminated, and those new programmes in which investments must be made. Correspondingly, the new fiscal realities mean that resources for quality improvement and innovation must be derived increasingly from internal resource reallocation.

The actual experience of universities on both sides of the Atlantic in developing and effectively implementing such strategic choice processes, despite much discussion in the literature, is quite limited. European universities have historically lacked institutional-level capacity for strategic choice making because of the decisive role of state ministries of education in programme approval and resource allocation. British universities, which unlike their continental peers possessed greater autonomy and a tradition of institutional-level governance, have,

"Academic Planning and Organizational Design: Lessons From Leading American Universities," by David D. Dill, reprinted from *Higher Education Quarterly*, Vol. 50, No. 1, January 1996. Copyright © Basil Blackwell (US).

since the end of the Second World War—like most universities in the developed countries—experienced increasing levels of financial resources. Therefore, incremental rather than strategic choice making was the historic norm in the British university system. While the radical changes in government and direction since the early 1980s have encouraged British universities to implement executive styles of management and new internal mechanisms for planning and resource allocation, the government's emphasis on performance indicators for purposes of accountability has arguably retarded the successful implementation of institutional mechanisms for strategic choice making (Sizer, 1990). In the U.S., whose universities have always been theoretically subject to market forces, institutional strategic choice-making processes have been much discussed, but in many cases have been more symbolic than real. In a recent national survey of planning at American colleges and universities, Schmidtlein and Milton (1989) could find little evidence of processes that led to strategic choices. Planning processes were often superficial exercises which attempted to avoid difficult decisions; serious attempts at strategic choice making often foundered over conflicts between core constituencies.

Less noted, however, has been the success of several leading American research universities in implementing and sustaining over time collegially derived processes for the identification of priorities and regular reallocation of financial resources. As Trow (1983) has pointed out, these successful examples have been obscured by a tendency in American research on planning and resource allocation in higher education to ignore critical variables of culture and context:

> . . . in the United States students of leadership have looked . . . across a wide range of institutions, and have been more impressed with the constraints on them than with their resources for accomplishment. On the whole, such analysis may be right: in most American colleges and universities there is not a consensus on the values of competitive excellence nor the discretionary resources to develop programmes in the service of those values. Instead, many interests . . . push and pull the college presidents in ways that make difficult the initiation of sustained purposeful programmes

of any kind. The leading research universities, both public and private, remain an exception to this generalization (p. 51).

Leading public and private research universities such as Michigan, Minnesota, Princeton, and Stanford—institutions which are both clearly committed to competitive excellence in research and scholarship, and possess the autonomy to raise and to reallocate revenues—have implemented strategic choice making processes which promoted internal change and have lasted over time. These institutional examples are not without problems, conflicts, and inconsistencies, but their relative success, and the process by which they were achieved, provide potential benchmarks for other universities that wish to successfully implement effective strategic choice making.

An underlying reason for the relative success of the planning processes of these universities is their implicit attention to critical variables of organizational design (Nadler and Tushman, 1988). When college and university planning processes are well designed, they harmonize with and support the academic organizations in which they are embedded. When poorly designed, they undermine the decision processes necessary for institutional adaptation, creating administrative overhead, wasteful paperwork, and distrust.

There appear to be three primary reasons for the ineffective design of university planning processes. First, when resources were plentiful, universities did not need to master the discipline of good design. Higher education institutions grew incrementally, often in a redundant fashion. The planning processes by which this growth was managed were often informal. Second, design fails when narrow self-interest and individualism overcome the community interest. Universities are among the most segmented organizations in contemporary society. Academic organizations are fragmented into departments, disciplines, programmes, and research centres which pursue their own goals frequently at the expense of the larger organization. A well designed, comprehensive planning process must encourage individuals and units to value the normative bonds that bring them together and hold them together. Third, a good planning design must be sensitive to the governance tradition of each institution, respecting the processes of decision making which have evolved over many years. Attempts to insert the planning process of another institution into a particular culture and place encourages distrust and sows confusion.

In the sections that follow a framework for improving the design of comprehensive planning processes in universities will be outlined. This framework is drawn from the planning experiences of leading American universities as recorded in their planning documents, in published research on these processes, and as reported in interviews with administrators responsible for planning. In the first section the essential concepts of organizational design will be introduced. In the second section general principles for promoting good design in academic planning processes will be reviewed. A major goal of the paper is to contribute to the development of a body of practice knowledge regarding the design and implementation of academic planning processes. Such knowledge in use can help others in turn continually improve their strategic choice processes over time.

Organizational Design

In the simplest terms, there are three essential concepts of organizational design: *differentiation, integration,* and *contingency* (Lawrence and Lorsch, 1986). *Differentiation* represents the separating and grouping of individuals into units to carry out the organization's tasks. *Integration* represents the degree of collaboration among existing units.

All organizations are characterized by both differentiation and integration, but the balance between the two is *contingent* upon the type of task being performed and the nature of the environment. For example, a group psychiatric practice is highly differentiated into separately practising professionals. The psychiatrists have a low degree of integration, limited to collaboration on the management of a common facility and common services such as billing. In contrast, a rugby team has low differentiation into specialties—unlike American football, all rugby players must be able to run, kick, and handle the ball—and high integration in the form of practised teamwork. The image of a rugby team weaving its way down field is a perfect example of collaboration. Thus the tasks performed by each respective group affect the design of the organization. But the design is also influenced by the nature of the environment. Increasing competition in the psychiatric profession has made solo practice less efficient and created a need for group practices. Applying these three concepts to traditional practices of university planning processes reveals several key points (Figure 1).

First, the environment of universities in the early 1960s was the greatest growth market in the history of American higher education, characterized by plentiful resources and rapidly increasing student enrollments (Ben-David, 1972). While competition among academic institutions existed it was made largely invisible by the unusual opportunities for programme expansion. In this *growth* environment academic structure was characterized by high differentiation and low integration. The operative word for academic organization was *loosely-coupled* (Weick, 1976). The problem of conflict between units, and the need for collaboration,

Organization Design		
	1970s	**1990s**
Environment	Growth	Post-Industrial
Structure	High Differentiation	High Differentiation
	Low Integration	High Integration
	(Loosely-Coupled)	
Resources	Slack	Scarce
Decision Making	Garbage Can	Strategic Choice
	(Strategic Certainty)	(Strategic Uncertainty)

Figure 1 Organizational design changes from the 1970s to the 1990s

could be ignored because differentiation appeared to solve most problems of organization design. If faculty members in applied and pure mathematics did not get along, create a separate department of operations research; if the economics department will not collaborate with the business school, let the business school appoint its own economists. Given this munificent environment programme development was predictable—*strategically certain.* Consequently academic decision making at many campuses degenerated to a form of theatre. Cohen and March (1986) characterized this academic choice making as a *garbage can* process in which problems, solutions, participants, and choices flowed together randomly. In this process few problems were solved and few choices made.

Critical to Cohen and March's decision making model, however, and little emphasized in subsequent research, was the necessary condition of *organizational slack* or slack resources. In short, the choice making process of the American college and universities of the 1970s was *contingent* upon a predictable, growth-oriented, relatively non-competitive environment.

In the 1990s, as Cameron and Tschirhart (1992) suggest, colleges and universities face a *post-industrial environment* characterized by high competition among institutions, scarcity of resources, and unpredictable fluctuations in enrolments and revenues. By definition, programme development in a post-industrial environment is *strategically uncertain.* Strategic choices must be made among programmes and activities. In this environment greater attention will therefore need to be given to decreasing costs, increasing the efficiency of decision making, and improving programme quality—or, as Massy and Wilger (1992) emphasize, increasing productivity. If the design of academic decision making processes in the 1970s was contingent upon its munificent environment, then the design of academic decision making in the 1990s will be similarly contingent upon our new competitive environment. Cameron and Tschirhart assert that in this new context decision making will need to be more participative, more integrated on both the vertical and horizontal dimension, with greater delegation of authority and responsibility to the strategically appropriate level. In

short, there will need to be much greater *integration* and collaboration among differentiated units. While the segmentation of academic work cannot be eliminated—research and discovery require academic specialization—differentiation will have to be matched by mechanisms promoting integration.

To summarize, in order for an academic institution's planning process to become a strategic choice process, it must be designed as a primary means of organizational *integration.* If the process is not designed to promote collaboration, it cannot hope to effectively promote strategic choice. The means for achieving integration in an organization are often related to an organization's culture (Dill, 1982). Organizational culture can best be understood as a normative system, which is communicated through communication processes that follow both the informal and formal structure of an organization. Thus the design of a planning process must first address the means for articulating and communicating norms which will guide the specific interests of individuals and groups toward the common interest. Second, the design must consider those structural arrangements that support these norms by encouraging communication and contact among organizational members. Third, the design must encourage individual units themselves to develop the collective capacity to adapt to changes in the environment brought about by increasing competition. In the context or academic planning processes these design elements can be organized into five general categories (Dill, 1994):

- clarifying and articulating norms essential to the legitimacy of the planning process;
- grouping and consolidating functions where necessary;
- promoting reciprocal (down-up) communication;
- encouraging the development of a planning and choice making process within each strategic unit; and
- increasing direct communication and the sharing of information among members of the overall academic community.

Design Elements Promoting Norms Essential to Planning

Numerous studies on academic decision processes have argued that their effectiveness depends upon community perceptions of trust, fairness, and openness (Chaffee, 1983; Schmidtlein and Milton, 1989). What is less frequently stated is that essential norms must both be articulated verbally *and* manifested visibly in the design of a planning process. It is cruel, but true, that trust, fairness, and openness are not naturally occurring phenomena in the world. They must be developed and nurtured through the public actions of academic leaders and the design of organizational processes.

For example, Chaffee (1983) discovered that the perceived legitimacy of Stanford's planning and budgeting process derived in part from the public statements of the university's Provost as well as from the subsequent products of the planning process. The Provost first articulated to the community a set of academic criteria to be used as a basis for planning choices. These criteria were then applied in a publicly demonstrable manner in the process of establishing planning priorities. Finally, these same criteria were clearly connected to the publicly announced budgetary allocations which were an outcome of the planning process. In addition to Stanford similar criteria have been utilized in the planning processes of universities such as Michigan, Minnesota, and Princeton (Herring, *et al.*, 1979; Heydinger, 1982; University of Michigan, 1979).[1]

Figure 2 summarizes the criteria identified for strategic choice making respectively at Michigan, Minnesota, Princeton and Stanford. These generic criteria represent universal values underlying the stated institutional criteria: 1) the *quality* of the programme or activity; 2) the *centrality* of the programme or activity, that is, whether it is an essential condition of the enterprise; 3) the *demand* for the programme or activity on the part of students, other programmes, and the larger society; 4) the *cost-effectiveness*, or relative efficiency, of the programme or activity; and 5) the *comparative advantage* of the programme or activity, that is the extent to which it is a unique offering.

These universal expressions of institutional values attempt to communicate a collective basis for choice grounded in the ethos of each institution. One of the more corrosive effects of differentiation on a university community is the segmentation, not only of structure, but of faculty value orientations (Becher, 1989). Thus, attempts by administrators to appeal to the common good when making strategic choices may fall victim to conflicting disciplinary interests. In a number of the universities, such as Michigan, and Minnesota, where strategic choices were successfully implemented, essential academic criteria were developed by, or in close consultation with, broad-based faculty groups, prior to the initiation of a planning process (Dill and Helm, 1988). These academic communities thereby reestablished normative bonds which they could call upon in subsequent difficult choices.

These institutional examples also suggest how the norms of trust and fairness are manifested in a planning process. If planning processes are designed at the outset to ensure favorable access and influence to the existing feudal baronies, kingdoms, and fiefdoms that compose any college or university, then community concern over fairness and openness is

Criterion	Michigan	Minnesota	Princeton	Stanford
Quality	♦	♦	♦	
Centrality	♦	—	♦	♦
Demand	♦	♦	♦	♦
Cost-Effectiveness	♦	♦	♦	
Comparative Advantage	♦	♦	♦	—

Figure 2 Strategic Choice Making Criteria at Selected Universities

predictable. For example, research on university decision making processes in the growth period of the 1970s emphasized the influence of unit power in resource allocations (Hackman, 1985). Wealthy and established departments were consistently over-represented on key resource allocation committees, and received disproportionate shares of available revenues. If, instead, the composition of decision-making groups central to the planning process is designed to represent the interests of the larger community rather than the interests of particular factions—for example, through the appointment of representatives of the faculty and staff at large, and/or through the appointment of representative deans on a rotating basis—then the norms of openness and fairness essential to effective strategic choice making, can be better achieved.

As the Stanford example also makes clear, the constant concern in colleges and universities over the relationship between planning and budgeting is not simply an operating issues, but also a normative one—can the consistency of the planning process be trusted, or will budgetary allocations reflect hidden agendas or special influence? Trust in the planning process can be fostered by design elements that address the relationship between planning and budgeting. For example, the integration of planning and budgeting will depend to some extent on whether the planning calendar is appropriately sequenced in time with the operating and/or capital budget calendars, thereby providing sufficient opportunity for planning priorities to inform operational decisions. If these respective processes are not properly related, planning and budgeting may at best conflict, at worst become irrelevant to each other. Similarly, if the line administrators central to a planning process are the same as those responsible for budgeting and resource allocation, then some relationship between the two processes reasonably can be expected. If the two processes involve different administrators, then trust in the processes clearly diminishes.

Whether *both* planning and resource allocation information are made broadly available to the academic community also will effect the integration of planning and budgeting. As will be discussed below, the provision of both types of information to *all* members of the academic community on a regular basis permits the community members to judge the integrity of the process. The withholding of planning and/or budgeting information often has been justified on the grounds of retaining administrative flexibility or avoiding political ramifications, particularly in public institutions (Schmidtlein and Milton, 1989). However, the lack of consistent information on planning priorities and resource allocations also promotes suspicion regarding the legitimacy of the planning process, and thereby undercuts efforts to implement strategic choices.

Finally, the norm of fairness can be promoted by the extent to which a planning process, at least in its initial phase, is designed to be comprehensive rather than selective in its approach. Although a comprehensive planning process involving all academic and support units is costly in time and energy, it promotes a sense of openness, and equity among an institution's many internal stakeholders—*all* are included. In contrast, planning processes which focus sequentially on different units in different years, or encourage the development of plans for academic units prior to support units—rational as this ordering may be from a planning perspective—connote to the community a favoritism or selective concern that can be divisive.

Design Elements for Designating and Grouping Units

In complex universities with many different academic programmes, the design of a planning process can either lessen or increase differentiation, conflict, and organizational inefficiency. That is, any planning process must designate who, or which units will develop plans subject to review at higher levels. This is not a superficial design choice. If the unit designation is placed too low in the organization, for example at the department level, the planning process may compromise the authority of deans, increase pressures for differentiation, as well as overwhelm with information those ultimately responsible for the review and evaluation of unit plans.

At one highly differentiated professional school the planning process designated each programme as a planning unit, even though many programmes were composed of two or three faculty members. As a result of this design all of the faculty in the school were intensively involved in developing unit plans, the unit plans produced rarely considered coordination with other units as a means of enhancing strength, the process of reviewing the numerous plans was extremely time consuming, and the overall experience increased differentiation and conflict between units. In contrast, a design which selects planning units with too broad a span of control may lead to the preparation of meaningless reports which fail to stimulate strategic thinking and collective choice within core units. Unless careful thought is given in the planning design to identifying those programmes of an institution which need to develop their own strategic choice making process, the potential of a planning process to encourage organizational adaptation will be lost. As Cameron and Tschirhart (1992) argue, an environment of strategic uncertainty and resource scarcity requires that responsibility and accountability for strategic choices be delegated to the level where programmes, technologies, and customers interact and where assessments of quality and cost can be effectively made.

A related design element is the issue of grouping selected units in the planning process in order to promote consolidation and an integrative strategic focus. Units which share a similar technology (e.g. administrative and academic computing), or share similar customers (e.g., admissions, financial aid, and registrar) might be urged to develop plans in concert with each other as a means of encouraging communication, collaboration, and efficiency. Two examples of this design consideration are evident in the planning processes at Northwestern University and the University of North Carolina at Chapel Hill (UNC-CH). The second cycle of a comprehensive programme planning process at Northwestern University has been revised to schedule reviews by clusters of related academic fields such as the basic life sciences and modern language and literature programmes. Chapel Hill traditionally operated with three separate libraries: academic affairs, health affairs, and the law library. The decision to group all three libraries as a planning unit in a recently completed comprehen-

sive planning process led to a pan-university strategic library plan, and fostered increased communication and collaboration between the libraries which continues today.

Design Elements Promoting Reciprocal (Down-Up) Communication

One predictable reaction to scarce resources and strategic uncertainty is the centralization of authority and the one-way (i.e., top-down) flow of information. Research on college and university decision-making suggests that many colleges and universities have reacted to the post-industrial environment in this fashion, thus decreasing both their flexibility, as well as their ability to innovate and compete (Dill and Helm, 1988; Schmidtlein and Milton, 1989; Cameron and Tschirhart, 1992). In contrast, most organizational analysts argue that increased competition and uncertainty will require greater horizontal and vertical participation in decision-making, and more reciprocal, down-up, forms of communication and information sharing (Lawrence and Lorsch, 1986). The amount of reciprocal communication in the planning process is a function of the planning design. For example, did the proposed planning process leap, like Athena, fully armoured from the head of Zeus (i.e., the President), or was the planning design itself the product of a consultative process in which those who will be asked to produce plans participate in the design development?

As will be discussed in more detail below, the call-to-plan document, which initiates a comprehensive planning process and is usually issued by the president or chancellor of an American university, is another critical instrument for stimulating down-up forms of discussion and debate. The planning protocols developed at Stanford, Minnesota, UNC-CH, and Virginia suggest that departments and schools develop their strategies within directions set by university leaders. Consistent with research on planning processes (Dill and Helm, 1988), these examples illustrate that priorities do not emerge from meetings and discussions, they are first asserted by individuals, then are criticized, modified, and reshaped through the reciprocal processes of communication and negotiation over unit strategic plans.

A third means of incorporating reciprocal communication into the planning process is the procedure used for reviewing unit plans and providing feedback. Plans may be reviewed incrementally—first the review of mission statements, then the review of an initial draft plan, then the review of the final planning document—a process which encourages socialization and learning. Plans can be reviewed hierarchically, principally by line administrators, or by a process that emphasizes collegial structures, thereby promoting horizontal communication. The failure to think carefully about this aspect of the design often limits the degree to which a planning process can be used to increase integration in academic organizations. Although expensive in terms of administrative time, institutions such as Virginia and UNC-CH have required, in addition to formal planning documents, scheduled presentations or hearings as part of their planning or budgeting process. This design element promotes direct, two-way communication between central administrators and unit heads. Depending upon the composition of reviewing bodies, these presentations can also provide the opportunity to solicit the views of other constituencies as well.

Finally, most planning processes stipulate that units must submit written plans to a particular office, by a particular date. However, obvious as it may appear, not all planning calendars also stipulate that each unit that develops a plan will in turn receive a written response to their plan, from a particular person, by a particular time (Schmidtlein and Milton, 1989). Through these and other specific assignments of responsibility a planning process can be designed to increase reciprocal, vertical communication.

Design Elements Promoting Planning in Strategic Units

The organization of most American universities is analogous to a multidivisional firm that operates many differentiated programmes. Each of these programmes—for example arts and sciences, engineering, law—involves different markets, academic technologies, and programme components. The academic strate

gies for these diverse programmes cannot be established centrally. Instead, each programme must develop its own strategic choice making process. Encouraging the development of this capacity for planning should be a major objective of a well designed, comprehensive planning process.

Each unit may be encouraged to develop, as at Northwestern University, a proposed plan which represents the *collective* choice of the members of the unit. To reinforce this emphasis, units may be asked to provide both their proposed plans, and a brief description of the process by which plans were developed. If appropriate, large units might be offered recommendations on external planning consultants who could assist them in implementing an ongoing planning process. Alternatively, individuals within units that have already implemented successful planning processes might be encouraged to work with units new to the activity, or an experienced faculty or staff member might be designated as an internal consultant to facilitate planning discussions at the unit level.

A second means of encouraging planning within strategic units is through the distribution of data oriented toward planning and management at the unit level. One concrete axiom of organizational design is that a felt need for change is a necessary condition for organizational adaptation (Dill and Friedman, 1979). The implementation of a comprehensive planning process, in which selected organizational units must develop plans, provides a momentary need for planning data within schools and key support units. Many universities such as Penn State and UNC-CH as part of a comprehensive planning process have developed standard unit data profiles or formats for each of their planning units. These centrally produced profiles provide trend information on academic and service unit budgets, personnel resources, and relevant activity indicators, and critical ratios, as well as intrinsic criteria, which contribute to the integration of the institution. Chapel Hill, for example, developed planning data sheets that summarize in four pages for each academic and support unit critical planning information on students, academic performance (i.e., student credit hours), space utilization, contract and grant activity, and expenditures by fund source and purpose.

Data was provided with three-year trends, where possible. The sheets were designed in a *roll-up* format; similar sheets could be produced at every level of the University: all university, division, school, and department. Institutions designing a comprehensive planning process can also *benchmark* a number of peer institutions and identify the types of planning data that have already proven useful to these organizations at the institution-wide as well as unit level. By developing, disseminating, and refining these planning data in coordination with a comprehensive planning process, a more reflective, data-based process of choice making can be encouraged throughout a college or university.

Finally, the implementation of planning at the strategic unit level will also be influenced by the components of the unit planning report itself. Many institutions design comprehensive planning processes to produce information that will assist central decision makers in allocating scarce resources. Thus, the rationale for the classic planning report outline of mission and goals over some period of time. If, however, an important purpose of a comprehensive planning process is to encourage responsibility and accountability for strategic choice making at appropriate levels of an organization, rather than simply producing a *shelf document*, then this should be reflected in the requested outline for unit planning reports. Stanford University, for example, has gradually revised a planning process oriented toward operational budget planning toward one that also now encourages strategic thinking at the unit level. Planning reports are required to include formal assessments of the state of each school or administrative area with emphasis on programme, financial, and managerial strengths and weaknesses. Statements of programmematic plans are expected to identify anticipated linkages with other units, human resource implications, measures that can be used to assess progress toward stated goals, and the expected sources of funds to be used in carrying out the plan.

Similarly, Northwestern's programme review process is explicitly intended to develop the capacity of each unit to chart and manage a strategic course. Thus the planning outline for both academic and administrative areas requires the unit to select the five top competitive units in its field, identify the reason for their

preeminence, rank the focus unit in relationship to these competitors, and articulate the unit's distinctive strengths. Similar to Stanford, units are asked to report on the quality of their programmes and components. Plans for implementation include efforts to relate to, or cooperate with, other units at the university. Finally, reports must identify means of *re-marshaling* existing resources to achieve the changes advocated.

At Chapel Hill, the complexity of the University and the concern with developing a strategic choice capacity at every level of the institution led to the following framework:

Unit Assessment

- strengths/weaknesses of the unit
- status of unit's human, financial and physical resources
- significant new developments in the area or field
- opportunities that exist for the development of new or enhanced programmes, services, and activities with other units in the University.

Specific Goals for a Five-year Period

Programme Strategies

- actions to be taken in the next biennium to achieve stated goals
- listed in priority order
- indicating source of funding and other units affected.

The emphasis in the requested planning documents was to be on collective judgments at the unit level, 'on decisions, actions, and constructive communication, both vertical and horizontal.' Therefore plans were meant to be *brief* documents, between five and ten pages. Further, the focus was to be on a *five-year* planning horizon, to encourage collective, creative thought.

These examples, drawn primarily from private institutions that have attempted to cope with the effects of the post-industrial environment, suggest the importance of designing planning processes that foster choice making at different levels of academic organization. Differentiation has led to an organizational complexity which cannot be eliminated. Planning in these settings entails broad institutional direction, managing essential support services, and encouraging strategic choice at the appropriate unit level.

Design Elements Promoting Direct Communication and the Sharing of Information

Given the fluid nature of participation in the academic community, and the high degree of differentiation that is essential to academic organization, forms of socialization and communication that rely primarily on the organizational hierarchy are ineffective in promoting commitment and continuity. Greater reliance must be placed upon direct communication, including open meetings, reports through campus newspapers, direct mailings, and special reports disseminated to individual members of the academic community.

A critical design element in promoting the sharing of information is the content of the call to plan. At most American universities the planning process is initiated by a planning protocol from the president or chief academic officer. This document provides a decisive opportunity to build and sustain a common culture of information, ideas, language, and norms necessary for planning. The protocol typically includes:

- perceptions of the institution's environment;
- planning assumptions on enrolment, budget, or space;
- suggested critical institution-wide priorities; and
- criteria that will be employed throughout the planning process.

As at Minnesota, Michigan, and Stanford, the document can articulate institutional criteria which can become the normative basis, at every level, for choices regarding priorities and budgetary allocations. The planning document can also provide perceptions of the environment shared by all planning units as well as outline institutional priorities, needs, and plan-

ning assumptions to guide the development of unit plans. In its language, and in its conception of planning, the initial planning document can establish the extent to which trust, fairness, and openness will prevail.

A second means of promoting direct communication is by the inclusion of faculty members, students, and staff along with central administrators, in the process of examining and reviewing unit plans. This may be accomplished, as at the University of Minnesota and Northwestern, by submitting unit plans to a faculty committee for analysis and comment, by utilizing a planning committee composed of administrators, faculty, staff, and students as at Stanford, or by some combination of these devices (Dill and Helm, 1988).

Finally, as discussed earlier, the means of communicating planning outcomes to the broader academic community is a critical feature of planning design. Stanford University has annually distributed to all members of the institution a document titled, *Operating Budget Guidelines*, which presents the issues and planning priorities intrinsic to the budget, and provides extensive discussion and analysis of all operating revenues and expenditures for the university. As stated, the 'distribution of this document is made in the interest of greater understanding of the University's Operating Budget and the annual process through which it is developed' (Stanford University, 1988). During its planning and resource reallocation efforts in the 1980s, the University of Minnesota regularly disseminated a planning priorities document to all members of the academic community, that not only articulated university-wide priorities in planning, but also presented the proposed plans of academic units, *and* the administration's explicit response to each proposed plan.

Direct contact is needed to communicate institutional norms for planning, the data upon which decisions are made, and the strategic choices to be implemented. Fostering a common culture by communicating with the individual members of the academic community about planning and budgeting is a critical means of integrating highly differentiated academic communities.

Conclusion

Institutions of higher education are among the most differentiated organizations in contemporary society. Academic organizations are fragmented into departments, and units that are frequently in conflict over goals and resources. But the post-industrial environment characterized by increasing competition and decreasing resources requires that academic institutions both encourage the planning capacity of subunits as well as better integrate these differentiated segments to achieve unity of effort, efficiency, and quality. As Burton Clark (1995) has recently observed:

> Effective institutional leadership then means the recognition of the primacy of the professional clusters—the historians in their subdomain, the physicists and economists in theirs—and the construction of new tools for making those clusters more effective in research and teaching. Compared to the old style state-led segmental budgeting, this may necessitate a radical combination of lump-sum financing for the decentralization from university administration to basic units, with integration of the whole fashioned by new forms of dialogue, information tracking, and periodic full-scale review.

The process of planning, properly understood, can be a powerful instrument for achieving integration in highly differentiated academic organizations. By articulating the criteria by which collective decisions will be made, promoting consolidation among units where necessary, encouraging reciprocal communication and debate, facilitating strategic planning within academic and service units, and increasing direct communication on these matters to all members of the academic community, a comprehensive planning process can make a tangible contribution to the capacity of a university to make strategic choices. If a planning process also attends to the better instincts of an academic community by reflecting in its design the norms of openness and fairness, it may additionally inspire over time trust in its outcomes. As with the design of a building, however, the design of a planning process is an art. How one develops and implements an integrated planning process in a highly fragmented organization is a classic, and challenging, problem of organizational design.

Note

1 During this same period a number of public and private American universities developed such criteria. See, for example, Shirley and Volkwein, 1978, and Mingle and Norris, 1981. Sizer (1982) has discussed the applications of similar models in the U.K. context. For an argument comparable to what follows regarding the universal nature of these criteria for university planning, see Benjamin et al., 1993.

References

Becher, T. (1989), *Academic Tribes and Territories: Intellectual Enquiry and the Cultures of Discipline* (Milton Keynes: SRHE and Open University Press).

Ben-David, J. (1972), *American Higher Education* (New York: McGraw-Hill).

Benjamin, R., Caroll, S., Jacobi, M., Krop, C. and Shires, M. (1993), *The Redesign of Governance in Higher Education* (Santa Monica: Rand).

Cameron, K. and Tschirhart, M. (1992), 'Postindustrial Environments and Organizational Effectiveness in Colleges and Universities,' *Journal of Higher Education*, pp. 87–108.

Chaffee, E. E. (1983), 'The Role of Rationality in University Budgeting,' *Research in Higher Education*, pp. 387–406.

Clark, B. R. (1995), 'Complexity and Differentiation: The Deepening Problem of University Integration,' In D. D. Dill and B. Sporn (eds.), *Emerging Patterns of Social Demand and University Reform: Through a Glass Darkly* (Oxford: Pergamon Press).

Cohen, M., and March, J. (1986), *Leadership and Ambiguity: The American College President* (2nd ed.) (Boston: Harvard Business School Press).

Dill, D. D. (1982), 'The Management of Academic Culture: Notes on the Management of Meaning and Social Integration,' *Higher Education*, pp. 303–320.

Dill, D. D., and Friedman, C. (1979), 'An Analysis of Frameworks for Research on Innovation and Change in Higher Education,' *Review of Educational Research*, pp. 411–435.

Dill, D. D. and Helm, K. P. (1988), 'Faculty Participation in Strategic Policy Making.' In J. Smart (ed.), *Higher Education: Handbook of Theory and Research*, Vol. 4 (New York: Agathon Press).

Dill, D. D. (1994), 'Rethinking the Planning Process,' *Planning for Higher Education*, pp. 8–13.

Hackman, J. (1985), 'Power and Centrality in the Allocation of Resources in Colleges and Universities,' *Administrative Science Quarterly*, pp. 61–77.

Herring, C. P., Lemonick, A., McCrudden, C., Schafer, C. and Spies, R. R. (1979), *Budgeting and Resource Allocation at Princeton University: Report of a Demonstration Project Supported by the Ford Foundation*, 2 (N.J.: Princeton University Press).

Heydinger R. B. (1982). *Using Program Priorities to Make Retrenchment Decisions: The Case of the University of Minnesota* (Atlanta: Southern Regional Education Board).

Lawrence, P. and Lorsch, J. (1986), *Organization and Environment* (Rev. ed.) (Boston: Harvard Business School Press).

Massy, W. F. and Wilger, A. K. (1992), 'Productivity in Postsecondary Education: A New Approach,' *Educational Evaluation and Policy Analysis*, pp. 361–376.

Mingle, J. R. and Norris, D. M. (1981), 'Institutional Strategies for Responding to Decline'. In J. R. Mingle (ed.), *Challenges of Retrenchment* (San Francisco: Jossey-Bass).

Nadler, D. and Tushman, M. (1988), *Strategic Organization Design* (Glenview, Ill.: Scott, Foresman and Company).

Neave, G. (1995), 'The Stirring of the Prince and the Silence of the Lambs: The Changing Assumptions Beneath Higher Education Policy, Reform, and Society'. In D. D. Dill and B. Sporn (eds.), *Emerging Patterns of Social Demand and University Reform: Through a Glass Darkly* (Oxford: Pergamon Press).

Shirley, R. and Volkwein, J. (1978), 'Establishing Academic Program Priorities,' *Journal of Higher Education*, pp. 472–489.

Sizer, J. (1982), 'Institutional Performance Assessments Under Conditions of Changing Needs,' *International Journal of Institutional Management in Higher Education*, pp, 17–28.

Sizer, J. (1990), 'Funding Councils and Performance Indicators in Quality Assessment in the United Kingdom'. In L. C. J. Goedegebuure, P. A. M. Maassen, and D. F. Westerheijden (eds.), *Peer Review and Performance Indicators* (Utrecht: Lemma).

Schmidtlein, F. and Milton, T. (1989), 'College and University Planning: Perspectives from a Nation-Wide Study,' *Planning for Higher Education*, pp. 1–20.

Stanford University (1988) *1988–89 Operating Budget Guidelines* (Stanford, CA: Stanford University).

Trow, M. A. (1983), 'Organizing the Biological Sciences at Berkeley,' *Change*, pp. 28–53.

University of Michigan. (1979), *Regents Meeting of October*. Ann Arbor: University of Michigan.

Weick, K. (1976). 'Educational Organizations as Loosely-Coupled Systems,' *Administrative Science Quarterly*, pp. 1–19.

Responses of American Research Universities to Issues Posed by the Changing Environment of Higher Education

FRANK A. SCHMIDTLEIN AND ALTON L. TAYLOR

There are 31 public and 28 private universities who are members of the Association of American Universities (AAU) in the United States. They are the most prestigious of the country's 156 graduate/research universities. These 156 universities comprise only 4.2 per cent of the existing 3,688 colleges and universities but enroll approximately 21 per cent of the students.[1] In 1994–96 the National Science Foundation supported a study of issues confronting members of the AAU and the processes they were employing to respond to them.[2] Information was gathered through a survey of administrators at 35 member institutions and site visits to nine of these universities, five public and four private. Two of the nine universities visited were among the top 15 in terms of the amount of federal research support they obtained, four others were in the top 50, and three more were in the top 60.[3]

Much has been written about issues confronting graduate/research universities, most of it is based on the experiences of senior university administrators. A small number of articles are by scholars examining the changing environment of higher education or describing institutional responses to current challenges. However, there have been very few systematic examinations of the issues. We sought to address this gap by interviewing institutional staff to gain their perspectives on the issues confronting their own universities and descriptions of the means employed to resolve them. The issues identified by the interviewees were categorized into two groups: those related to the changing external environment and those related to changing internal cultures, structures and processes. Comments were often prefaced with general observations about the difficulties of singling out the specific issues confronting universities; these issues were described as intertwined and interrelated. Several noted that the list is almost limitless; one commented that the issues are clear but the solutions remain puzzling. Frequently, the issues described by interviewees appeared to be related to their university responsibilities. There were small differences in emphasis by staff at the private and the public universities, but generally the degree of consensus was remarkable.

The issues mentioned most often related to significant environmental changes now taking place, particularly the prospect of shrinking resources. However, interviewees were also concerned about the demise of a well-articulated federal science policy, burdensome federal grant management practices, state procedural impediments to administrative efficiency, changing demographics and equity matters, increasing institutional and international academic competition, declining public goodwill with consequent calls for accountability, and shifting university missions. The changing environment and changing expectations were seen as the biggest challenges now confronting universities. Most agreed with one official's comment that "The halcyon days of higher education are at an end."

"Responses of American Research Universities to Issues Posed by the Changing Environment of Higher Education," by Frank A. Schmidtlein and Alton L. Taylor, reprinted from *Minerva*, Vol. 34, 1996. Kluwer Academic Publishers (NL).

Shrinking Resources

Data on the resources devoted to higher education indicate that overall funding has increased each year, even when inflation is taken into consideration.[4] These increases have lessened in recent years and current small increases do not reveal the substitutions taking place among sources of funds, nor trends such as the growing use of revenues from tuition fees to fund student grants. Individual institutions have had decreases in their total funding—for example, state appropriations at the University of Maryland at College Park declined by $24 million in fiscal years 1990 to 1994; this decrease of 10.7 per cent was partially offset by substantial increases in tuition fee levels. Total revenues for all public colleges and universities totalled $69.6 billion, and for private institutions, $39.2 billion in 1992–93. The table illustrates the principal sources of revenues for colleges and universities and changes in the percentage distribution of these resources between 1986–87 and 1992–93.

Particularly striking is the decrease of 6.9 per cent in the states' share of support for public higher education, with a 3.3 per cent increase in the share covered by income from tuition fees. The most significant shifts for private institutions were a 2.1 per cent decline in the share of revenues from federal sources—principally research grants and contracts—and a 1.6 per cent increase in the share covered by tuition fees. Published reports do not provide data on the comparable trends among the AAU members. Public AAU institutions are likely to have experienced the same shifts, and, since the private members rely particularly heavily on federal research support, they have probably experienced greater than average shifts. Thus AAU universities were adjusting to changes in their traditional combination of revenue sources, while also confronting further long-term reductions in federal and state revenues as a result of national economic circumstances.

Staff at all the universities thought the constraints imposed by shrinking resources would be the dominant factor affecting them over the next decade or more. In an earlier study of strategic planning,[5] several respondents reported that many faculty at their institutions doubted that financial difficulties were imminent. However, respondents in the present study reported broad recognition by academic staff, as well as by administrators, that an impending long-term financial crisis faced the universities and would cause painful financial contractions. As one administrator said, "We are now out of the denial stage."

Efforts to contain the growing federal deficit, and changes resulting from the end of the Cold War, growing international competition, and sluggish national and state economies, were seen as major reasons for continued reductions in federal and state funding. Recent developments in health care, and their implications for university hospitals and medical programmes, were also of great concern. Nearly everyone believed these circumstances herald long-term economic adjustments that will force American universities to make major changes.

Federal revenues: Respondents in all the universities foresaw major reductions in the revenues available from federal sources. More

Table 1 Changes in Sources of Current-Fund Revenue for Public and Private Institutions of Higher Education: 1986–1987 to 1992–1993

	Public			Private	
Sources of revenue	86–87	92–93		86–87	92–93
		(Percentages)			
State governments	43.7	36.8		2.2	2.3
Federal government	10.4	10.8		17.0	14.9
Local government	3.6	3.7		0.7	0.6
Tuition	14.7	18.0		39.6	41.2
Sales and services	21.2	23.4		21.7	23.2
Endowment income	0.5	0.6		5.2	4.7
Private sources	3.3	4.0		9.3	8.5
Other	2.6	2.7		4.3	4.4

Sources: US Department of Education, National Center for Education Statistics, Integrated Postsecondary Education Data System: "IPEDS," "Finance, FY 1987" and "Finance, FY93" surveys.

specifically they were concerned that: federal student aid will fall or at best increase more slowly than student numbers; support for research will decline, particularly research supported by the Department of Defense; falling indirect cost recovery rates—the basis for reimbursements to universities for the overhead costs of research—will particularly damage private universities' ability to do research since they usually lack other sources of support for the indirect costs of research; support for graduate students and young scientists is declining, affecting the country's capacity to remain at the forefront of science; support for health care is declining while costs increase and efforts to contain them threaten university provision of high-quality medical education; and federal laws and regulations are creating "unfunded mandates" which require universities to expend funds for social purposes, such as safety and environmental protection, for which they are not reimbursed.

Concern was expressed that these anticipated reductions in federal support would reduce access to higher education and restrict the range and quality of research. Federal support of research is already declining in a number of areas. One university noted that, having dealt with an $83 million budgetary shortfall three years ago, it now confronts revenue cuts resulting from efforts to balance the federal budget. There was particular concern about the federal government's tendency to support applied, short-term research at the expense of the basic research which provides the foundation for continued scientific progress.

Another cause for concern was the fact that federal research support seemed increasingly to go to large centres, without peer review of their individual projects, rather than being awarded competitively to individuals or to projects of small research teams. This was thought to result in less peer review of projects and, potentially, lower quality research. Evidence was cited that younger researchers were finding it more difficult to get grants and contracts. Consequently, development of the United States' base of scientific talent might not keep pace with emerging opportunities or provide sufficient support to unconventional areas of research. Indirect cost recovery rates were reported to be less than actual costs and officials believed further reductions would harm their research infrastructures.

It was predicted that declining federal support for research would mean several private universities having to reduce their research drastically. One person suggested that only 50 graduate/research universities might survive at prospective funding levels.

State revenues: In most states, the percentage of public universities' budgets supported by state appropriations has declined over the past five years. One institution reported receiving only 20 per cent of its funds from its state; another reported a figure of 30 per cent. These declines were seen as likely to continue, particularly since the federal government will probably pass on more of its programme costs to the states. One official described how, as the percentage of state funding fell, his state continued to require procedures that impeded the university's use of technology to increase administrative efficiency. A number of state procedures were seen as time-consuming and costly and without commensurate public benefits. A private university also anticipated reductions in funds received from its state.

Institutionally generated revenues: It has been suggested that declining governmental appropriations might be considerably offset if universities increased other sources of revenues and became more efficient. However, increases in tuition fees were no longer seen as a practical option because students and their families are less able to pay and because of public resistance to high tuition fees. The universities all provided substantial aid to students from their own resources in order to enroll qualified students irrespective of ability to pay. However, they were reaching the limits of such aid and some suggested they might have to enroll a higher percentage of students who could pay their own way. None believed that sufficient economies could be found to offset a significant portion of the prospective reductions in funding.

Business and industry were seen to be cutting back sharply on in-house research. "Downsizing," and other efforts to contain costs, were thought to be reducing support for joint research ventures. Some expressed concern about fund-raising prospects in the current economic climate and expected declining returns from their endowments. However, officials at the public institutions said they were placing considerably more emphasis on private fund raising. All were moving rapidly to realize more income from "intellectual property" and technology transfer.

Universities, and their faculty, are often criticized for resisting change and being slow to adopt new technology which could improve teaching and reduce administrative and teaching costs—despite the fact that most of this technology owes its existence to university research! New communications technology was seen as a way to overcome constraints of time and place, and thereby significantly improve productivity and quality. In a frequently cited example, the use of interactive video could allow students throughout the United States to be taught by an outstanding Harvard professor rather than by many different professors, some of them probably less experienced and less competent.

There was concern that unless universities exploited the potential of communications technology other organizations would fill this void. The benefits of technology were recognized, but there was great uncertainty about the directions new technologies will take. Interviewees commented on the large investments in infrastructure, the rapid obsolescence of equipment and software, and the need for more standardization. As well as regularly having to upgrade equipment, there were the high costs of maintenance, providing technical support staff, purchasing software, developing educational software applications, adapting courses to utilize the technology and—perhaps most expensive—training staff to use it. Consequently, none believed that the rapid adoption of technology would save much money, at least in the foreseeable future. They saw the potential of communications technology for improving the quality of education, but were skeptical that it would reduce costs.

Fragmenting Federal Science Policy

After the Second World War, the federal government, led by Vannevar Bush and others, developed a general policy framework for the federal support of university science. Those involved in university research observed that this science policy disintegrated with the end of the Cold War and with more serious efforts to contain the federal budget deficit. A new

policy has yet to emerge. As a consequence, decisions were seen as being made on a fragmented and *ad hoc* basis, usually in the context of budgetary decisions: only the rare congressional staff member was thought to understand the implications for science policy. The federal government's dealings with universities were regarded as unsystematic; it was suggested that government should recognize that universities needed to be funded in ways consistent with their institutional interests.

The federal government was viewed as "schizophrenic" with respect to the balance between teaching and research, with policies pursuing conflicting objectives. Examples cited declining support of graduate students, increasing support of large research centres rather than individuals, over-reliance on documenting expected research results instead of relying more on investigators' "track records," categorizing basic and applied research separately when scientists do not see this distinction, and slowness to support important new initiatives in the laboratory sciences. Underqualified federal staff in some agencies were thought to be contributing to these problems.

Changing Demographics and Achieving Greater Equity

Considerable concern was shown on how universities could meet the needs posed by demographic changes. The pool of potential students will increase over the next ten years, although a larger proportion will be from racial minorities with lower than average participation in higher education. Numbers of eligible students will increase as proportionately less funds are available, creating tensions between the goals of quality and access. A university president suggested that heavy emphasis on access, equity and multiculturalism was reducing the attention given to maintaining and enhancing quality. He believed more attention will be given to academic quality in future.

Officials at two private universities considered increasing the number of undergraduates, especially since they needed more income from tuition fees. However, most institutions did not plan to increase undergraduate numbers, and a public university had substantially reduced its enrolment.

Problems were anticipated in achieving a diverse student body and faculty that mirrored the increasing diversity in American society, while avoiding "Balkanizing" institutions. Private universities, particularly, feared they might not be able to attract middle-class students because of the heavy financial burden imposed by their tuition fees.

Increasing Competition

Higher education was thought to face a far more competitive environment than in the past. Not only was competition among institutions growing but they were seen as facing more competition from other nonprofit organizations and from business. Competition seemed likely to increase with the expanding use of communications technology. Furthermore, many believed that the pre-eminence of American universities—particularly in the physical sciences—will be challenged by institutions in other countries.

Increasing institutional competitiveness was noted. Competition for students, faculty and funds was seen as becoming more intense between universities. One official even expressed concern about sharing the university's strategic plan with competitors, a precaution traditionally more typical of business. Competition to employ leading academics, and thus to raise faculty salary levels, was much discussed, together with the resulting disparate salary levels within universities. Several institutions wanted to expand continuing education and distance learning, both to generate revenue and to pre-empt competition from other institutions and businesses.

International competition and the globalization of education was discussed, as well as that of business, and there was concern that economic problems confronting graduate/ research universities could, in time, cause the United States to relinquish its leading position in science. They noted the "information revolution," with knowledge being disseminated quickly all over the world. The United States does not have a monopoly on talent, and investment in science is high in many Far East countries, with salaries also competitive. Some noted that universities now serve the world, not just their own country. Students will in-creasingly seek employment abroad, but without sufficient instruction in foreign languages. The benefits gained from educating foreign leaders were noted, but there was concern about over-reliance on foreign graduate students, particularly in the sciences.

Declining Public Esteem and Clarifying University Missions

The interviewees observed that higher education in the United States has received increasing public criticism in recent years. One suggested that this trend, in part, results from the emergence of mass higher education. A bachelor's degree has become common and a master's degree is the entry requirement for professional fields. Higher education was described as vulnerable to the kinds of criticisms levelled at elementary and secondary education.

University officials described public concern over the balance between research and teaching and the lack of emphasis on undergraduate education. The graduate/research universities have a primary responsibility for research. Consequently, their research is expected to contribute to national objectives, ranging from health and defence to economic development. At the same time they are among the most visible institutions and are expected to provide the highest quality undergraduate education. Many observed the public failure to connect support for basic science with the advances in, for example, medicine and communications technology that have transformed the American economy.

The public's concern about the productivity of universities, particularly public universities, was much discussed; one person noted that it was not about the amount of work but rather about what academics were working on. A university president said higher education would have to confront the "productivity" issue just as industry has done. Another president suggested that universities have been negligent in dealing with faculty teaching loads, which tend to be assigned without sufficient regard to the extent of individual research commitments: the degree of engagement in research was distinguished largely by varying salary levels, not by varying teaching loads.

As a result of these public concerns, faculty were seen as under growing pressure to maintain current levels of research while also being urged to increase time devoted to teaching undergraduates and to public service. These pressures were adding to faculty frustration and stress. Young assistant professors, trying to establish their research, were particularly affected.

There were several concerns about maintaining and clarifying university missions. One public university president commented on the difficulties states encounter in maintaining differences between their public institutions. The drive by primarily teaching institutions to emulate the salaries, teaching loads and research at graduate/research universities was seen as potentially having a "levelling down" effect on the quality of research universities.

Universities, historically, have valued their comprehensive array of programmes. However, the interviewees observed that no universities can offer a full range of academic topics or engage in every field of research; priorities must be set, particularly in view of restricted resources and growing disciplinary specialties. Several noted difficulties: priorities can be set for maintaining and expanding academic programmes and disciplinary specialties but, in recruiting faculty, generally the best available candidate should be appointed since several fields may be compatible with and important for achieving a university's aims.

Issues Related to Internal Cultures, Structures and Processes

The second set of issues were related to conditions within the universities that hindered their responses to environmental changes. These concerned universities' cultures and attitudes, allocation of resources, condition of infrastructure, appropriateness of curriculum and quality of instruction, utilisation of faculty, governance and leadership, and the effectiveness of internal processes.

Institutional cultures and norms which developed after the Second World War—in a period of relative affluence—were believed by some to be inconsistent with present realities.

They suggested that faculty and staff should recognise the changing character of the environment, and its implications for higher education, and accept new approaches. Some mentioned the need to create a "culture of change." Changing cultural values and shrinking resources were seen as having negative effects on the quality of universities. It was necessary to reassert higher standards and guard against compromising quality when faced with reduced budgets.

With regard to reallocating resources, it was recognised that priorities must be set and difficult decisions made, in order to phase out activities and programmes of low priority or quality and transfer resources so as to improve other programmes and to finance new initiatives. Nearly all the universities had recently reviewed and eliminated some programmes and activities.

Deteriorating infrastructures were an area in which staff frequently described the need for extensive investment. A public university president observed that most of their buildings had been constructed 30 to 40 years previously during the period of rapid growth in student numbers. The buildings needed renovation and the installation of modern communications technology and utility systems. Laboratories required refitting to incorporate new advances in scientific equipment, and costs of operating and maintaining buildings and land were growing. A shift in emphasis in capital budgets towards renovating buildings, rather than constructing new ones, was seen as a means of avoiding increased costs.

Improving the Quality of the Curriculum and Instruction

The increasing proliferation and specialisation of knowledge, and difficulties in pursuing cross-disciplinary studies, were noted. Several commented on tensions between "problem focused" centres and "discipline focused" departments. They noticed a trend towards cross-disciplinary scholarship and increased postdoctoral training to enable new doctorates to compete more effectively for limited vacancies.

All the universities were concerned about improving the quality of their undergraduate curriculum and becoming more "student centred." Many had completed, and/or were undertaking studies in this area. However, they wanted to improve their undergraduate programmes without reducing emphasis on research and scholarship, and they were struggling with the considerable costs of making substantial improvements.

Most institutions were seeking to limit the scope of their graduate programmes so as to maintain quality and keep attuned to markets for their graduates. The graduate programme at one university was said to have slipped in quality over the past 25 years and efforts were under way to arrest the process. Several persons described the implications of having to prepare students for careers not previously considered by graduates in their disciplines or professions. One dean pointed out that fewer doctoral graduates will be "bench scientists" in the future. Most will work in industry. Consequently, doctoral programmes will have to be modified. A physicist observed that many recent recipients of doctoral degrees in physics were now employed in the securities industry where their outstanding analytic skills were in demand. Sensitivity to national concern about the quality of university teaching was highly evident. One provost listed the improvement of instruction as a major concern of his public university. He believed universities had been slow to address concerns about teaching, though some had moved boldly. He knowledgeably discussed collaborative and active learning strategies and what had been learned from the assessment literature.

More effective use of faculty was thought necessary. Several interviewees described problems associated with using non-tenured faculty. They believed institutions needed to take a thorough look at the status of these faculty to ensure they are employed effectively and treated appropriately. Some were concerned by the implications of the growing use of postdoctoral fellows, and that the law eliminating mandatory retirement at the traditional age might restrict their flexibility to realign programmes, to release unproductive faculty members, and to employ younger staff.

Governing and Providing Leadership

Problems related to governing their universities and the role of faculty in governance were frequently described. It was believed these processes were not understood, nor their importance sufficiently appreciated, by those outside the universities. All affirmed the important role faculty play in governance but, at the same time, noted the constraints this places on rapid and decisive decision-making. They commented on the relatively high degree of faculty independence, the lack of clarity about who could make and who could veto decisions, and the "loose coupling" among units. Some mentioned that, in the collegial environment, those who make controversial decisions without first gaining faculty support often lasted only a short time in office.

There was concern about complex and inefficient internal administrative processes, including budgeting, procurement, personnel management, and relations with students on such matters as financial aid and registration. The inefficiencies, in some cases, were attributed to slowness in adopting new technologies.

Responding to the Issues: Strategic Planning

These universities were acting both to address several issues simultaneously and also to target specific issues. Their approaches fell into several categories: various types of planning, reviewing and assessment of programmes, seeking to contain costs and increase revenues, restructuring and rationalizing processes, and improving communications with a variety of audiences.

Comprehensive strategic planning: A considerable body of literature promotes strategic planning as an effective means of addressing the broad range of issues confronting universities. Most of the universities visited had carried out such processes, although in two cases these were suspended in order to concentrate on more immediate concerns. The interviewees discussed both the benefits sought from strategic planning and the factors limiting their success, including problems encountered when implementing plans.

Assessing benefits: Interviewees generally viewed strategic planning more positively than had those interviewed seven years earlier.[6] Current university planning processes seem to have benefited from earlier mistakes, and are carried out in a very different environment of financial retrenchment. During the earlier study, units often saw planning as a means to increase their resources, so plans might include many proposals whose costs exceeded available resources. In this study, however, planning generally appeared to recognise financial constraints and the fact that additional funds would probably have to come from reallocation. Plans seemed to have become more realistic. For example, one public university had established a strategic planning process many years before that was the first we had come across to have survived, in recognised form, changes in an institution's presidency through constant modification of approaches and procedures.

Some of the benefits perceived to be accruing from strategic planning included: creating a clearer, more comprehensive vision of the university's aims, opportunities and strengths; identifying its comparative advantages; providing guidance for budget reductions; clarifying the context of decision-making; fostering awareness of issues; setting broad priorities for resource allocation; and improving communications with and among units.

Strategic planning processes typically appeared to help define the broad context within which decisions were made. However, most operational decisions apparently came from various committees and task forces appointed to address a specific issue in depth. Major decisions on eliminating programmes or units were always determined by committees and processes specifically designed for that purpose. At one public university the planning process seems to have made units exceptionally aware of each other's plans and priorities. Such broadly shared knowledge probably contributed to greater understanding of the wider university context and informed them about potential areas of collaboration.

Assessing costs and limitations: Many factors were described as limiting the effectiveness of strategic planning. Frequently, interviewees' enthusiasm for planning was qualified. Most descriptions of impediments to planning reiterated earlier descriptions.[7] Difficulties included

distinguishing among worthwhile aims—decisions might be postponed in the hope that new information or circumstances would make choices easier; countering faculty demands for an "inclusive" plan covering all their activities; avoiding over-detailed plans which lacked guidance on strategic choices; avoiding overemphasis on income generation strategies; and creating overlapping committees. They stressed the need to recognise that most improvements result from seized opportunities, that monetary considerations and external constraints "run things," that the "form" of a process is far less important than the quality of managers, and that a "reward structure" is necessary. Recognising the constraints imposed by changes in federal policy and funding, and avoiding overcomplicated and time-consuming processes, were also mentioned.

Problems in implementing plans were frequently described. The reasons for difficulties included failure to link planning to budgetary and fund-raising decisions or to recognise the importance of budgetary constraints when decision-making; and failure to implement plans incrementally, or recognise that events quickly overtake plans which may need revision. Other difficulties were failure to involve key persons, or to realise that implementation depends on the individuals available—committees do not implement plans so the gap between those who make and those who carry out plans must be bridged. In addition, the loosely-coupled, complex nature of university structures has to be taken into account.

Responding to the Issues: Issue-oriented Planning

Most of the important decisions being made by the universities appeared to result from processes addressing specific issues. All had numerous task forces and committees at work on a variety of topics. Processes and participation were tailored to meet the characteristics of each issue. The narrow focus permitted deeper analysis and consideration of alternatives than was feasible for more comprehensive planning. Strategic plans were viewed as providing a general context for issue-oriented processes.

None of the universities used their strategic planning processes as the immediate vehicle for identifying programmes or departments for major cuts or closure. In all cases such decisions were made by committees or task forces appointed specifically for that purpose. For example, a new provost at one institution had suspended its comprehensive strategic planning process and now had a group examining narrower questions about the future character and operation of the university. The topics addressed included clarifying the university's mission, redefining missions more precisely and/or more narrowly, and reviewing specific programmes for development or for reduction.

All the universities visited were engaged in activities designed to improve their teaching. It was widely believed that they had not placed sufficient emphasis on undergraduates and they were now seeking, as one person put it, to become much more student centred. Two institutions were considering reducing the scope of their graduate programmes and, while all emphasised the importance of research and its centrality to their role, many also indicated that their universities were paying increased attention to teaching. A few persons suggested that, given the anticipated decline in resources for university research, several private universities would undoubtedly have to curtail their research substantially. Many noted the teaching possibilities presented by communications technology and its potential for eliminating barriers of time and space and giving "place bound" students greater educational opportunities.

Reviewing and assessing programmes: All the universities had a variety of institution-wide methods of evaluating students and faculty, and their academic programmes. In addition, two had formal processes for evaluating administrative offices. One private university had no strategic planning process; instead, an extensive evaluation of academic and administrative programmes formed the basis for both strategic and tactical decisions. Some universities had appointed external advisory committees, particularly for their professional schools.

Containing costs and seeking new revenues: All the universities had tried to reduce costs and find new sources of revenue. The areas addressed included reducing administrative costs, containing "fringe benefits," "privatising" activities and contracting out for services; studying faculty workloads and tightening up policies on assignments; instituting tougher budgetary controls and restricting growth even during relatively "good" times; restricting the number of committees, eliminating unnecessary meetings, and using communications technology to create a "paperless" environment and reduce secretarial staffing.

Efforts to obtain additional resources included increasing undergraduate numbers to obtain greater tuition fee income and seeking more "self-supporting" students; increasing fund-raising from private sources, including the addition of foreigners to governing and advisory boards and developing links with foreign alumni; increasing income from technology transfer and intellectual property; extending capital campaigns beyond original completion date; emphasising candidates' potential for obtaining grants when making appointments, and generally fostering faculty entrepreneurship.

Responding to the Issues: Restructuring and Rationalising

A number of writers have suggested that, to succeed in a changing environment, American universities will have to adapt in major ways comparable to the changes when land-grant institutions and graduate/ research universities were created. Although none of the universities visited were inventing a radically new type of institution, they were examining their missions and had started to restructure various operations and to rationalise their processes. Several were employing "total quality management" techniques—but terming them "continuous quality improvement"—to streamline operations and to become more "customer friendly," particularly in serving students. Some were employing "re-engineering" teams. One university used a *pro bono* industry consultant to examine its purchasing operations.

Many of these universities were eliminating or reducing the size of academic departments, decentralising administrative processes, reducing excessive bureaucracy through greater use of technology, and restructuring business methods. Several were also attempting to streamline through, for example, creating a more effective role for faculty in governance and reducing the time faculty spent on unproductive committees.

Nearly all the universities were re-examining and redesigning their budgetary processes and, in some cases, linking decisions more closely to planning. They wanted them to help set and implement priorities, promote interdepartmental co-operation, create a sense of financial realism at unit level by confronting units with "fiscal trade-offs," and provide units with the flexibility needed to manage their resources well. They sought ways to involve faculty more effectively in setting budgetary priorities and were trying to increase their awareness of financial constraints and opportunities. They were reducing the complexity of processes and revising policies and procedures for distributing funds to units. Techniques were employed to increase flexibility in reallocating funds, including withholding percentages of unit budgets for reallocation and having vacant faculty positions revert to deans or provosts for determination of priorities and possible reallocation. Some sought to increase the analytic capacity of their budget staffs. One university was "banking" unanticipated unit revenues to meet contingencies and for potential reallocation.

Two universities used systems that assigned revenues to the units generating them and gave these units considerable latitude in spending— "resource centre budgeting." Some thought such systems inhibited cooperative ventures between units. These decentralised systems were said to make reallocations more difficult and time-consuming, and to cause conflicts over the "tax" formulas for funding common services and vital activities which were unable to generate sufficient resources for their own support. Several persons noted that some "fee for service" arrangements had unsatisfactory results. One claimed resource centre budgeting harmed units that could not generate sufficient income to cover expenses, and transferred the focus from university goals on to formulas for distributing resources. On the other hand, many noted that it increased units' sense of fiscal responsibility, gave them greater flexibility to respond to new opportunities, and promoted efficiency.

Strengthening leadership: A number of persons discussed the role of leadership and the efforts their institutions were making to improve it. They emphasised the importance of a competent and tough president and the need to make strategic decisions and then delegate. However, they also described the need to obtain faculty support for initiatives and to avoid the "top-down" bureaucratic model. They described efforts to replace ineffective deans and chairmen and women and the importance of appointing and developing leaders at lower levels; for example, most had programmes for developing the competence of department heads. In one case, a university had placed an ill-led department in "receivership."

Improving dissemination of information: A major concern of nearly everyone interviewed was what they viewed as major misperceptions of universities by the public, press and government officials. Many also thought their universities needed to do a better job of informing their faculty, students and parents about the difficulties confronted. The activities under way to "educate" external audiences included increasing efforts to inform federal and state officials about the effects of governmental policies and decisions, and acting more aggressively to correct misrepresentations in the press.

Efforts to improve understanding within the university included increasing communications with faculty and students. One president was bringing in speakers to help acquaint faculty with the "new realities." A provost brought in a variety of outsiders to speak on issues related to the university's strategic planning process. Annual reports were used to describe achievements and needs.

University councils: All the universities had bodies such as president's cabinets, dean's councils and budget priority committees that met regularly to review progress, exchange information and advice, and make policy and planning decisions. These bodies appeared to have a substantial role in planning, both apart from and related to other formal planning processes.

Sources of the Issues

The major issues confronting graduate/ research universities appear to have resulted from the profound economic and social changes taking place in American society—first and foremost, from the efforts of the federal and state governments to deal with the consequences of the large federal deficit by restricting budget growth. This task will be complicated by strong public resistance to raising taxes. At the same time the United States is adjusting to a global economic market, with companies shifting manufacturing overseas, meeting increased competition by "downsizing" and restructuring, and with large numbers of employees becoming redundant. Those interviewed believed there would be fewer resources for universities, but many also thought it essential to maintain or increase investment in higher education in light of other contemporary trends. Society is becoming increasingly "knowledge based" and requires a highly educated work force. Research is becoming more important in maintaining national economic status in an increasingly competitive international economy, and investments in technology seem likely to make possible significant improvements in educational and administrative processes.

Second, at the same time as the average age of Americans increases and older people incur higher health and retirement costs, numbers of prospective students will increase—although many will come from minority groups whose participation in higher education has been lower than average. Because of contemporary societal changes, there are calls for major changes in universities in both the academic and popular presses. However, these rarely suggest the substantive nature of such changes, or acknowledge the substantial costs involved. In addition, the consequences of these trends may differ according to universities' varying circumstances and the quality of their leadership.

Consequences of the Issues

The conflict between declining resources and growing needs are likely to force painful choices between the important social goals of student access and educational quality. Most of the universities visited appeared to be choosing to maintain and increase quality by restricting growth—although two private institutions were considering increased undergraduate enrollment. If universities maintain quality by restricting access, then pressures may mount on teaching institutions to increase student numbers without a commensurate increase in re-

sources. This could create a bimodal higher education system with graduate/research universities limiting enrolments to maintain quality, and primarily teaching institutions increasing enrolment while their quality erodes. Voices questioning the current commitment to broad access are likely to grow louder.

Many critics believe these problems can be avoided if institutions refocus their aims and become more efficient. States are using assessment and accountability reporting, promoting strategic planning and techniques such as "continuous quality improvement," and encouraging communications technology. But important as greater efficiency is, there is little evidence that the savings gained will offset the predicted decline in resources.

Unless, for unanticipated reasons, the performance of its economy significantly improves, the United States will have to strengthen its efforts to live within its means. Politically difficult decisions on priorities will have to be made. Universities, unless they convince the public that they deserve a higher place in the competition for resources, will confront growing financial constraints. They will be competing with areas such as health care, retirement security, public safety and the environment. They have a very difficult case to make, although they may legitimately proclaim the importance of their role in addressing these issues.

Nature of the Universities' Responses to the Issues

The universities visited all sought to understand the implications of the circumstances they confronted and to clarify their options for dealing with them. They were pursuing many typical components of strategic planning though not primarily through formal, comprehensive planning processes. They had all obtained information on external and internal conditions and trends and interpreted this information to assess its significance. Using these insights, they were—explicitly or implicitly—developing "visions" about the directions in which to evolve. To a greater or lesser extent, they were creating strategies for achieving their aims. Policies and plans were being developed and resources sought to carry them out.

However, these efforts were pursued through a variety of means that usually had no formal links. The universities were undertaking incremental, "emergent" strategies,[8] rather than relying primarily on highly articulated, comprehensive, formal approaches. There were several reasons for their modes of response to their existing and anticipated situations.

Broad "strategic visions," while important for creating common understanding and clarifying the context of decision-making, apparently provided only modest guidance for resolving specific issues. Strategies often seemed to emerge during the process of resolving specific issues, rather than from deliberate attempts to devise a framework for decisions.

This difficulty in linking strategies and plans directly to action was evident in the numerous comments emphasising that the important factor was "strategic thinking," not a particular plan or planning process. Many shared the view of planning as learning,[9] rather than as a specific process, and were primarily concerned that participants shared a common understanding of university circumstances and priorities and based their decisions on a consistent set of premises and accurate information. This approach was seen as more consistent with the decentralised, loosely-coupled nature of university decision-making. Most of the complexities and constraints affecting operational decisions appeared to defy advance identification and resolution through a single university-wide planning process.

The variety of processes and techniques employed to address issues was revealing. The literature on planning seems to undervalue the issue-oriented planning that was most commonly used to deal with specific concerns. This type of planning focuses on an issue, recognises various priorities among issues, and deals with the most salient, permitting in-depth analyses and detailed consideration of solutions. However, unless guided by strategic perspectives, this approach risks creating solutions for the wrong problems.

Conclusions

This study clearly reveals that the benefits ascribed to strategic planning typically are achieved through a variety of means. A formal process that seeks to plan in a comprehensive, linear fashion is likely to be too complicated, politically divisive, expensive and inflexible, and to ignore how decisions are made in a complex, highly decentralised university. While many approaches to planning are used, universities must ensure they provide periodically opportunities for university staff—freed from daily responsibilities—to consider strategic concerns. Accurate and relevant information must be available to all who make and carry out decisions. Planning should be viewed as a learning process rather than a document producing exercise. Extensive communication among university staff and faculty is needed to ensure informed debate and substantial acceptance of decisions—otherwise they are unlikely to be implemented. Perhaps most important is not the process employed but the decision-maker's breadth of perspective and sophistication. No process will overcome lack of competent leadership. The importance of daily decision-making in various councils and committees on issues such as cost containment and budgetary priorities is underestimated in the literature on planning.

Critics have doubted whether universities' structures and processes permit them, or their leaders have the resolve, to confront the emerging issues. However, in many respects, the universities' decentralised, multiple decision-making practices may suit them well. They face the same challenging societal changes as other sectors of society. Their staff include some of the most capable individuals in the United States, and in the past they have been highly adaptable during periods of profound social change.

Universities do not appear to be less aware of the need to adapt, nor more constrained in adapting to new conditions, than other sectors of society. In fact, university research and scholarship will be highly important in pointing the way for the whole of society to meet this era's challenges. If pessimistic predictions about current trends turn out to be accurate, universities no doubt will adapt at least as well as other kinds of institutions. The travails of business in this environment are daily news! There will be occasional casualties among the universities, as frequently occurs during major social transitions, but institutions that have grown in importance for over 1,000 years, will doubtless emerge from this period perhaps somewhat changed but still performing their historic social functions.

Notes

1. National Center for Educational Statistics, *Digest of Education Statistics 1995* (Washington, DC: Office of Educational Research and Improvement, US Department of Education, 1995).
2. Taylor, A. L., Schmidtlein, F. A., Viswadoss, A. and Karr, S., "Issues Posed by the Changing Higher Education Environment and Responses of Graduate/Research Universities." Paper presented at the 17th Annual Forum, European Association for Institutional Research, Zurich, Switzerland, 1995.
3. National Center for Educational Statistics, *Digest of Education Statistics 1995*, op. cit.
4. *Ibid.*
5. Schmidtlein, F. A. and Milton, T. H., "Campus Planning in the United States: Perspectives from a Nation-Wide Study," *Planning for Higher Education*, XVII, 3 (1989), pp. 1–19.
6. *Ibid.*
7. Wildavsky, A., "If Planning is Everything, Maybe it's Nothing," *Policy Sciences*, IV, 2 (1973), pp. 127–153; Schmidtlein, F. A. and Milton, T. H., "Campus Planning in the United States," *op. cit.*; Mintzberg, H., *The Rise and Fall of Strategic Planning* (New York: Free Press, 1994).
8. Mintzberg, H., *The Rise and Fall of Strategic Planning, op. cit.*
9. De Geus, A. P., "Planning as Learning," *Harvard Business Review* (March-April 1988), pp. 70–74.

Improvement Strategies for Administration and Support Services

WILLIAM F. MASSY

In a report on the problem of increased research overhead published in the late 1980s, the Association of American Universities brought attention to the need to hold the line on administrative and support costs. Picking up where the AAU left off, William Massy acknowledges the necessity for administrators to improve their own area before they can address the question of productivity in academic departments. In this chapter, Dr. Massy responds to the problem by discussing factors that reduce productivity in administrative and support areas, presenting a step-by-step process for diagnosing such problems and laying out the elements of an effective productivity improvement strategy.

We are all familiar with the history of cost escalation in colleges and universities and the negative impression this has made on the general public. For example, an article entitled "The Untouchables" in the November 30, 1987, issue of *Forbes* asked the question: "Are colleges picking our pockets?" According to this piece, "Efficiency and cost cutting are demanded of unions and industry. Even government is under pressure to deliver value for the dollar. Why then does higher education get away with delivering a deteriorating product at ever increasing prices?" As Chester E. Finn Jr. has stated in "Judgment Time for Higher Education: In the Court of Public Opinion," the court of public opinion is concluding that institutions of higher education are not as efficient or productive as they should be.

Parents are becoming more and more concerned about whether they will be able to af-

ford college, and, indeed, many are asking themselves whether the financial sacrifice associated with sending a child to a high-priced private college is warranted. Cost increases at public institutions often trigger sharp political debates, and students everywhere demonstrate against tuition hikes at their schools. Higher education officials argue that the money is needed to maintain or increase quality, but they are challenged by those who demand to know if the quality gained is worth the price.

There are two general explanations of why education costs keep rising. They are higher education's "cost disease" and its "growth force."

Cost disease accounts for expenses escalating faster than the rate of inflation. Most operating costs in education are wage driven, and competition in the labor market links a school's salary increases to the rate of productivity improvement in the national economy. The theory is borne out by the behavior of the higher education price index (HEPI) in relation to the consumer price index (CPI). The former rose at an annual rate of 6.4 percent for the period 1961–86, while in the same period the latter rose by 5.3 percent—a difference of 1.1 percent. (The differential was 1.0 percent for the decade of the 1960s; 1.0 percent for the 1970s when, in an effort to cope with the oil crisis, higher education allowed salaries to lag; and 2.3 percent for the 1980s, when salaries caught up.) The cost-disease explanation points out that as long as a school's student-faculty ratio remains constant, its unit costs will tend to grow in real

"Improvement Strategies for Administration and Support Services," by William F. Massy, reprinted from *Productivity and Higher Education*, edited by R. E. Anderson and J. W. Meyerson, 1992. Peterson's Guides, Princeton, NJ.

terms. Steady erosion of student-faculty ratios will have adverse effects on quality.

Growth force applies to the phenomenon of budgets growing faster than can be accounted for by mere cost increases. It is usually due to the addition of new academic programs and the reluctance of administrators to dismantle old programs and reallocate funds to the new ones. The need for new academic programs springs from the dynamism of knowledge development and the creativity of college and university faculty and students. An institution that fails to innovate will soon fall behind—an outcome that university officers rightly seek to avoid. Add-ons are also the rule in administration and support services. The cost of meeting a new government regulation, for instance, or supplying a newly demanded service is usually layered on top of existing costs.

More specific reasons why college and university costs are continually increasing include the constant need for new technology, rising utility costs, and, of course, the accretion of organizational slack. Whatever the causes, current fund expenditures per full-time equivalent (FTE) student in all higher education institutions grew at an annual rate of 1.4 percent over the HEPI between 1975–76 and 1985–86. (The figures for public and private institution were 1.2 percent and 1.6 percent, respectively.) Much ingenuity, energy, management skill, and motivation are needed to innovate and meet new requirements with constant or declining resources, and it appears to critics of higher education that these have not been forthcoming.

Why, they ask, are new programs, functions, and services usually add-ons to budgets instead of replacements for existing activities?

Why don't investments in new facilities and equipment reduce costs rather than add to them? Why don't institutional leaders put more emphasis on productivity? Why is there so much pressure to increase quality and so little to improve cost effectiveness? Why do support-service departments seem to suffer the same productivity malaise as the academic departments with seemingly less justification?

I have chosen to focus on this last question and offer some suggestions for improving administrative and support service productivity.

Growth of Administration and Support Costs

Administration and support costs amount to some 30 percent of education and general (E&G) expenditures at public institutions and over 40 percent at private institutions, according to Arthur M. Hauptman's report, "Why Are College Charges Increasing? Looking into the Various Explanations." As shown in Table 1, most indirect costs (other than for libraries) are growing faster than direct costs. Administration and student services are the growth-rate leaders in both public and private institutions, and their effect on budgets is compounded by the fact that between them they account for 25 percent of E&G expenses. Most institutions would do well to focus on these service areas when looking at costs. Although all the categories in the table are important to consider, demonstrable progress in containing administration and support costs is a necessary precursor to addressing the question of productivity in academic departments.

Table 1 Growth Rates of Key Expense Categories for Public and Private Higher Education 1975/1976 to 1985/1986.

	Public	Private
Indirect		
Administration	5.0%	7.6%
Student Services	4.9%	8.3%
Libraries	0.4%	1.6%
Operations and maintenance	3.4%	5.0%
Direct		
Instruction	2.7%	4.5%
Research	5.1%	3.5%
Public service	3.6%	7.0%

Computed from "Why Are College Charges Increasing? Looking into the Various Explanations," Table 4, by Arthur M. Hauptman.

Growth-Rate Analysis

The first step in getting a grip on administrative and support costs is to systematically observe the pattern of cost increases during the preceding three to five years. (A variation on this procedure is to calculate increases in FTE employees by organizational unit, based on payroll records for a fixed date in each benchmark year.) The analysis can proceed as follows: (1) from the pattern of cost increases, develop a chart outlining the administration and support services organization; (2) extract data for two or more benchmark years according to this chart; (3) calculate the annualized growth for each organizational unit in the tree; and (4) focus attention on the high-growth units. If no assignable cause for high growth can be found, the unit is a prime candidate for cost reduction. It is hard to determine in advance what organizational level to look at, so it is best to start at a fairly minor level in the organization and then look at more levels until you can reach conclusions about what is meaningful growth.

The Cambridge, Massachusetts-based MAC Group of management consultants performed such an analysis for a midwestern research university a few years ago. The operating units were ranked according to growth rate in expenditures, and attention was focused on those that fell outside the norm for the organization—the outliers. Special study was made of the outliers that showed higher-than-average expenses. On closer investigation, it turned out that some of the extremes were due to readily assignable causes such as reorganization or a high-level management decision to add to service levels. In other cases, the growth seemed to be due to steady accretion.

Marginal Cost

Sometimes indirect costs are driven by changes in the scale of direct activities like instruction and research. The slope of this relation is, of course, the marginal or incremental cost of the indirect activity with respect to the direct one. Everyone who has taken an economics course knows about marginal costs, but there seem to be few applications for the concept in colleges and universities. There are, however, three ways in which one can examine higher education's marginal costs: the regression method,

the fixed- and variable-cost method, and the incremental-cost method. Briefly, the first is a statistical procedure usually based on time-series data. The second assigns each element of expense into a fixed or variable (i.e., marginal) component based on a detailed understanding of the process involved. The third attempts to identify and quantify the components of cost that vary with a given external variable.

Information about marginal costs helps interpret the growth-rate analysis results described earlier. It may be possible, for instance, to normalize some of the growth rates for changes in the cost-driving activities. As an example, when looking at growth rates in an accounting office, one might observe that transactions (T) are growing at x percent per year, that costs (C) are growing at y percent over the university's index of cost rise for continuing activities, and that marginal costs (MC) are about z percent of total cost. The following formula can be used to calculate the change in cost expected in that accounting office on the basis of the changed transaction volume.

$$\Delta T = xT$$
$$\Delta C = yC$$
$$MC = z\, C/T$$
$$\Rightarrow \text{normalized } y = (1+y)/(1+xz)$$

Suppose x = 3 percent, y = 1.5 percent, and z =30 percent. Substituting these numbers in the above formula yields normalized y = 1.0151/(1 + 0.03 × 0.30) = 1.006, a growth rate of only 0.6 percent. The difference between 1.5 percent net expansion and 0.6 percent net expansion adjusted for volume growth would make a big difference in one's thinking about what has been happening in that office.

This example assumes that there is only one cost-driving variable. Of course there may be multiple variables, in which case, to separate their individual effects the regression method may be required. It is best, however, to begin with a single cost-driver variable for each organizational unit. (It may be necessary to disaggregate another level or two to find a unit with one main driver.) There is, of course, no harm in having different cost drivers for different organizational units—it is required if the analysis is to be comprehensive. The preliminary specifications for an institution-wide cost study at Stanford, for instance, include the following cost drivers.

- Employee head count—used in the controller's office for payroll and in personnel services.
- Accounting transactions—used in the controller's office for general accounting.
- Number of separate funds—used for fund accounting and in the treasurer's office.
- Building square footage—used in operations and maintenance, security, and health and safety.

Remember, these are not the only cost drivers. The important thing is to start somewhere and build an internally consistent set of measures that can normalize observed and requested expense growth rates. The model can be refined according to individual needs, but even rough marginal cost measures are useful.

How can conclusions be reached about growth-rate outliers that cannot be explained by cost drivers? First, identify some other assignable cause that is acceptable from the standpoint of productivity—for example, new regulations. It is important not to accept rationalizations. Much of what is explained away as increased complexity turns out to be bureaucratic accretion, the nemesis of productivity. The rule should be to take a hard look at all the outliers and some units that are not outliers but, because of known external forces that might have been expected to reduce their work load, should have been. The second step is to examine the units for productivity-degrading factors.

Factors That Degrade Productivity

Left to themselves, most organizations are not only sluggish in adopting productivity-enhancing innovations but actually tend to self-destruct in regard to productivity. This self-destruction can be compared to the thermodynamic concept of entropy. In the state of lowest potential, any closed system will "run down" in the sense that its energy will eventually distribute itself evenly. The only way to counter this tendency is to introduce new energy from the outside to keep the system efficient. Before discussing ways that leaders in higher education can introduce energy and information to

their organizations and avoid running down productivity, however, I'd like to first examine the three main destructive forces.

Organizational Slack

Organizational slack can stem from simple inattention to efficiency—in which case "fat" is an apt descriptor. Slack can also arise when employees are prevented from performing effectively or when their personal goals are inappropriately substituted for those of the organization. The latter situation, known as resource diversion, gives rise to the view that people will pursue their own interests at the expense of the organization's at every opportunity. Substitution of personal for organizational goals can take the form of loafing, appropriating the organization's resources for personal use, or, perhaps, becoming obsessed with one's own rights and privileges.

Slack is not always bad. Too strong an emphasis on efficiency can demotivate employees and possibly stunt innovation. The beneficial aspects of slack are even more important in higher education than in industry, and they are most important in research universities where innovation must be a way of life. This is why faculty sometimes question the overzealous pursuit of efficiency in academic departments. (Their concerns are reinforced by the fact that what may seem like slack to an outsider is actually the contemplation necessary to produce new discoveries.)

On the administrative and support side of colleges and universities though, the value of slack is about the same as it is for business and government—some slack is a good investment for the future but too much is an unacceptable drag on current operations. James March, in his article "Emerging Developments in the Study of Organizations," put it well when he wrote:

> Under good conditions, slack search generates ideas, many of them too risky for immediate adoption. When conditions change, such ideas are available as potential solutions to new problems. An organization is able to meet brief periods of decline by drawing on discoveries generated, but overlooked, during better times. A prolonged period of adversity or of exceptional efficiency in avoiding slack depletes

the reservoir and leaves the organization vulnerable.

Slack tends to build up in good times and be squeezed out when times turn bad. J. Paul Austin, chairman of the United States Steel Corporation during the 1950s, once told me that U.S. Steel was "like a big bear—building up fat during economic booms and then hibernating, maintaining itself by shedding fat, during recessions." The cyclical process seems inevitable, but if it is not controlled, the slack may build to dysfunctional levels during good times and the eventual squeezing out may be incomplete. An organization should restructure itself to improve during the course of each cycle rather than simply allow history to repeat itself over and over again.

Accretion of Unnecessary Tasks

Everyone can be busy performing his or her assigned duties with energy and intelligence, and yet the organization as a whole may lack productivity. The key is in deciding what tasks are to be performed or, more precisely, in determining whether the tasks, taken separately and as an ensemble, contribute optimally to the long-range purpose of the whole organization.

Productivity is a measure of effectiveness. It reflects an assessment of the usefulness of what is being done, as well as the ratio of outputs to inputs, per se. Effectiveness, however, is not the same as efficiency, which is based on the narrower measure of the resources required to accomplish a particular task without regard to the task's ultimate value.

There are many reasons for the accretion of tasks. Workers or managers may lack competence and thus create unnecessary work for others—when a personnel department must clean up an employee relations mess left by an overbearing supervisor, for instance. A work unit might create unnecessary tasks by suboptimizing their resources, which can result in a redundancy of effort—as when two departments teach the same subject, each to half the optimal number of students. If not corrected decisively, certain types of incompetence and suboptimization can become the organizational norm.

Escalating spirals of administrative interactions are another prime cause of task accretion. A good person is hired to perform a certain task.

That task results in the discovery of new problems, creating the need to perform additional tasks. Others in the organization are drawn in since they must respond to the new initiatives. Coordinating everyone's efforts means that time is being spent in meetings. Soon, additional people must be hired to keep up with the increased work load. They, in turn, find new problems and create work for others—thus perpetuating the spiral. As Jane Hannaway phrased it in her study *Supply Creates Demands: An Organizational Process View of Administrative Expansion,* "The supply of administrators creates its own demand." This problem can be seen not only in education but in all sectors of business and government, For example, government bureaucracies grow inevitably and inexorably as they respond to new sets of problems. These problems beget new organizations or increase the number of layers in existing organizations. This is one reason why heavily regulated industries have many layers of management.

Instituting procedures to correct problems without periodically examining how the procedures can be refined is a common cause of task accretion. Another cause can be two procedures developed for different purposes that cover much of the same ground. Whatever the situation, it is certain that continual layering of new procedures to address new problems will in time degrade productivity. Conscious decisions and much energy are required to reverse the trend and strip away the layers or their cumulative effect will stifle organizational effectiveness at an ever-increasing rate.

Function Lust

Controllers think that their job is important and tend to want to do more of it. The same is true for auditors, planners, builders, landscape architects, lawyers, and even minute-takers in the myriad meetings that characterize colleges and universities. Student-service professionals, librarians, and computer experts are not exempt either. All can make a perfectly plausible case for how the institution could benefit by more being produced from their specialty. While the phrase "function lust" is perjorative, the motives of those who perpetuate the notion are, at least in their own eyes, pure. All these functions are important; otherwise the institution would not have created job openings for them in the first place. The problem is that specialists are not necessarily in the best position to gauge their own importance in relation to other institutional needs. They can do a good job of assessing absolute importance but are less successful in determining relative priorities and in negotiating trade-offs with other functions.

An outgrowth of function lust is the incentive to increase one's job responsibilities and get promoted, which also contributes to administrative task accretion. Job classification systems that offer advancement on the basis of budget size or the number of people supervised are particularly prone to this malady. Organizations whose managers permit "turf wars" invite accretion because the incentives are to staff up in order to beat competing departments instead of trying to cooperate with them. A certain amount of competition can be healthy, but too much is wasteful.

Diagnosing Problems

While information about expenditure or staff growth rates for organizational units can point toward areas where productivity is suspect, these quantitative measures cannot provide information on *why*. Informal managerial evaluation is the method of choice for diagnosing problems. There is no substitute for "management by walking around," especially in areas where there is reason to suspect subtly hidden difficulties. Unfortunately, though, even the most perceptive managers may well miss systemic issues—i.e., those that involve more than one function or unit—if they rely solely on intuitive processes. More formal approaches can be of greater effectiveness, especially if the organization is embarking on a major productivity enhancement effort.

The Process-by-Function Matrix

Certain key administration and support operations are common to all colleges or universities of a given size and type, regardless of how they are organized. These operations can be displayed in a process-by-function matrix where function refers to activities generally associated with an organizational unit. A hypothetical example of such a matrix is presented in Table 2.

The important processes of hiring and paying people are depicted in the first two columns of the matrix. Each process is initiated by an operating department. (The initiating department may be either academic or non-academic.) The action must then be approved by the appropriate dean or, in the case of nonacademic units, the vice president or his or her delegate. Actions on high-level positions must be approved by the president or by the provost's office. In many cases, the Affirmative Action officer must approve the new hire as well. The personnel department will review and render an opinion sometime during the process. Though personnel may not have the last word, its view is taken into account by the aforementioned decision makers. The payment screening section of the controller's office may be asked to verify that funds are available and that the hiring or salary is consistent with the project budget and with other contractual requirements if this is a sponsored agreement. Of course, the payroll department and the general accounting department get involved in processing the transaction when it finally comes to pass.

Often the process will loop back to involve a given function more than once. Consider the process of purchasing, for example. This is done many thousands of times annually and, while it would seem to be a simple task, it actually is very complicated. The transaction usually originates in an academic or operating department. The typical pattern is for a purchase order to be checked for fund availability by the payment screening group and then be sent to procurement for vendor selection and, if applicable, negotiation of price and terms. Procurement writes a purchase order and notifies the vendor, the originating department, and accounts payable. The order is shipped directly to the originating department which is responsible for matching the purchase order to the packing slip and notifying procurement and accounts payable that the desired goods have been received and are satisfactory. In the meantime, the vendor sends a bill to accounts payable, which matches it to the appropriate receiving notice. The bill is paid (perhaps after a lag to optimize the financial float) and the transaction is entered into the general ledger. It then appears on the originating department's budget and expenditure statement. Is it any wonder that faculty complain about slow turnaround and departmental administrators are driven to their

Table 2 A Hypothetical Process-by-Function Matrix.

Function	Human Resources		Purchasing (general)	Purchasing (equipment)		Submitting Research Proposals	Procurement Contracts	
	Hiring People	Paying People		Gov't. Projects	Univ. Funds		Govt. Projects	Univ. Funds
Academic or operating department	✓	✓	✓	✓	✓	✓	✓	✓
School dean or vice president	✓	✓	✓	✓	✓	✓	✓	✓
President or provost	✓	✓			✓			✓
Dean of research				✓		✓	✓	
Affirmative Action office	✓	✓						
Personnel office Employment	✓							
Compensation		✓						
Employee relations		✓						
Controller's office Payment screening	✓		✓	✓	✓		✓	✓
Accounts payable			✓	✓	✓		✓	✓
Payroll	✓	✓						
General accounting	✓	✓	✓	✓	✓		✓	✓
Sponsored projects office						✓		
Legal office							✓	✓
Facilities office							✓	✓
Procurement department			✓	✓	✓			

Computed from "Why Are College Charges Increasing? Looking into the Various Explanations," by Arthur M. Hauptman.

wits' end trying to keep track of outstanding expenditure commitments?

Similar descriptions could be given for the other processes in the matrix. Though this is only a hypothetical example, most people who know colleges and universities will recognize it as a familiar pattern.

Process Flowcharts

The next step is to develop flowcharts for the processes shown in the matrix. Flowcharts help to organize information about the order in which activities are typically or necessarily performed. Useful insights can be added by showing the range of delay times and perhaps the number of man-hours required to transact each step. The approach should be pragmatic; use a level of detail that illuminates the process, not one that obfuscates it into a maze of unimportant detail. Remember, these are *management displays,* not engineering or computer program specifications. Their purpose is strategic. They are not meant to provide detailed instructions for workers or first-line supervisors. In short, the process flowchart provides essential information about the order in which the gross tasks that make up a process are (or should be) performed, not about how each task should be performed. Each flowchart should take up no more than a single letter-sized page, so that it will fit into a ring binder.

Importance, Reliability, and Redundancy

With the flowchart created, I am ready to turn to diagnosis, which begins with the analysis of importance, reliability, and redundancy. (I have decided to call this IRR, partly because it does provide an "internal rate of return.") The IRR tests are applied to each element of the flowchart.

Because it was included in the process-by-function matrix, the process as a whole has already passed a general test determining its importance. But this is not necessarily the case for its individual elements. The first stage is to scrutinize each step of the process. Tasks that have accreted into the system will not automatically pass if the test is performed rigorously.

One of the main impediments to purging tasks is the argument that deleting a step will degrade the quality of the process. Quality is a loaded word at colleges and universities, and one should not allow that assertion to trump the question of importance—even if the assertion is demonstrably true. The answer lies in recognizing that there are two kinds of quality.

- *Design quality* is the quality designed into the product or service. A BMW has greater design quality than, say, a Ford, and it is more expensive. For some purposes and purses, the BMW represents the best price-quality trade-off; for others, the Ford wins out. It is possible even to construct examples where the Ford is better in absolute terms—regardless of price. Driving in high crime areas or where parts and specially trained mechanics are hard to find are two cases in point. The key idea is that more design quality is *not* always better; it needs to be calibrated to the task or situation at hand.

- *Implementation quality* deals with how well the product or service meets its specifications. If the product is to be a Ford, let it be a well-built Ford. It should be the same whether assembled Monday morning or Wednesday afternoon—no lemons allowed. American industry has learned the hard way that implementation quality should always be maximized. "Do it right the first time" is

an important principle both for customer satisfaction and for productivity. Everyone can take pride in producing the best possible implementation quality, but not everyone need aspire to build BMWs.

Taking advantage of higher education's reverence for quality in order to enhance implementation quality is a good thing. Allowing this reverence to mandate unneeded levels of design quality in administration and support services is not. Therefore, one should go through each process flowchart and ask whether the tasks are specified at the minimum acceptable level of design quality. High implementation quality should be insisted on, but academic program needs should rule out unnecessarily expensive work specifications in the administrative and support areas. Implementation quality rarely increases costs significantly. Indeed, an institution probably is paying for this kind of quality anyway, and the only question is whether it is getting its money's worth. Implementation quality is obtained by hiring good people, training them well, and providing good leadership and supervision.

Although reliability is related to design quality and implementation quality, it is worthy of separate consideration for two reasons. First, certain designs will be unreliable even with perfect implementation—these should be avoided if the penalty for failure is even remotely high. Second, issues of reliability tend to be systemic rather than oriented toward the individual process elements.

The assessment of total quality cost (TQC) is being used by many companies as a way to consider the reliability question. The objective is to understand what is being spent on maintaining reliability (that is, preventing failures) and correcting failures. Only by looking carefully at both sides of the equation can a reasonable judgment be made about the optimal reliability. In one case, some 80 percent of cost was due to failure, suggesting that the best trade-off might be to spend more on prevention. The trade-off can go the other way, too. An occasional accounting error that can be corrected later is not as consequential as having a part not work as designed or, worse yet, fail in use. Health and safety, systemic financial control weaknesses, and personnel-policy problems are probably the most worrisome risks— the first for obvious reasons, the second because disallowances and defalcations can be very costly, and the last because of the possibility of class-action lawsuits. The total cost of quality should be assessed for each of the processes included in the matrix.

Redundancy is a clear waste of resources unless it is needed for reliability. Redundancy tends to build up as a by-product of administrative task accretion, and it takes conscious effort and energy to identify and eliminate it. This is basically a common-sense matter: go through the process flowchart and simply ask whether each task is also done somewhere else. If the answer is yes, then question whether the redundancy is needed to contain risk (i.e., for reliability) and how much the risk would be increased if it were eliminated. Often the same risks are mitigated several times in complex systems. One can be more vigorous in rooting out redundancies in processes where the risks of failure are in terms of individual transactions rather than systemic operations.

It is also important to determine whether each process should be centralized or decentralized. Some processes are so critical in terms of the need for precise procedures and quality control that they must be centralized in order to achieve the best performance or to contain risks. Others are better left to the creativity and initiative of those closest to them. More situations probably fall into the latter category than one might think, but each instance requires careful analysis. Generally, one dictum is applicable: decide whether a process must be centralized or whether it can be decentralized and then insist that things be done that way. Do not allow a decentralized process to drift toward centralization because of task accretion by staff groups or second-guessing by upper-level line managers. Such behavior can produce a heavy drag on productivity.

Technology

Once it is clear that only essential tasks are being performed, the next question is whether they can be performed more efficiently. Given a fixed set of tasks, substituting capital for labor is the classic approach for improving productivity, and the second industrial revolution (a phrase coined by Herbert A. Simon in the article "The Steam Engine and the Computer: What Makes Technology Revolutionary") represented by information technology provides unusual opportunities. Volumes have been written about the advantages and pitfalls of office automation, so I will limit myself to only a few points.

- Don't try to automate work processes exactly as they are being done by conventional means. The result will nearly always be a more expensive and less satisfactory product than can be obtained by changing work flows to fit the new opportunities. (This is true especially if packaged software is available to do some or all of the job.)

- Strive to input data once only, as close to their original source as possible. Also, minimize paper flow and the need for multiple files. This not only increases the original cost of the job, but adds additional costs if conflicting information requires reconciliation.

- Don't try to get the process exactly right the first time. Modern software development tools permit systems to evolve as people gain experience with them. Often it is best to build a working prototype that will evolve during the project. This avoids endless arguments about once-and-for-all decisions that are so familiar in traditional development environments.

In the long run, automation can cure the cost disease by substituting a resource whose unit cost is declining in real terms for one whose unit cost is constantly increasing. Sometimes the up-front investment is hard to justify, and it certainly is necessary to be discriminating in terms of proposals. Still, the college or university that is not investing in information technology is likely to be left behind in terms of productivity.

Optimizing Staff Allocations

As with law, accounting, and consulting firms, colleges and universities rely on the services of highly trained professionals—in their support staff as well as their faculty. Productivity improvement in professional-service firms is obtained mainly by substituting less expert and hence less costly people for those with higher levels of expertise. Senior partners leverage their time with that of partners, associates, and research assistants. The cardinal rule is "Always use the least-expert resource that can do the job." Many colleges and universities spend substantial sums on support staff who directly leverage faculty time. Additional sums are spent for lower-level staff who support higher-level people all through administrative and support areas.

Time leveraging in colleges and universities is a double-edged sword. The advantages are the same as in the case of professional firms. However, more leverage is not desirable unless it leads to savings elsewhere. Under what circumstances do such substitutions increase productivity? The answer is easy when talking about for-profit enterprises such as law or consulting firms; the substitution is productive if and only if it increases the partners' income. For colleges and universities the problem is much more difficult because there is no profit measure and, of course, most administrative and support-service outputs are intangible. Individuals often want additional support in order to ease their burdens or to enrich their jobs by unloading repetitive tasks they feel they have fully mastered. The potential for task accretion furthers this phenomenon by offering a ready menu of interesting additional things to do.

The Need for Management Intervention

Insights into how to diagnose the factors that inhibit productivity in administrative and support services lead to the question "What can be done about them?" What are needed are managerial interventions that afford the possibility of mitigating or reversing the inhibiting factors and that unleash the forces that will enhance productivity and allow more resources to flow to academic operations.

Many of the diagnostic steps discussed in the previous section contain, within themselves, a blueprint for management intervention. The solutions for certain problems are obvious once their existence is understood.

Unfortunately, however, a straightforward problem-by-problem attack on productivity often fails to achieve the expected result. The complex interactions among the productivity-inhibiting factors and the people problems associated with change require a carefully thought-out and integrated management intervention strategy.

The growth of medical costs could not be contained until the cost-plus rules of Medicare and Medicaid were amended to establish limits on how much the government would pay for a given procedure or hospital stay. Airline, railroad, and phone companies could not strip away unneeded layers of management and other impediments to productivity until deregulation converted cost-plus into competitive pricing. U.S. industry as a whole could not streamline itself until foreign competition made it a virtual necessity. Similarly, the add-on spiral in higher education must be broken if costs are to be contained. The continued layering of program on program, cost on cost, will sooner or later cause critics of higher education to shift from rhetoric to action. It is better for correction to be accomplished within the academy than imposed from outside. The experience of the medical profession, which a decade ago was seen as singularly unresponsive to the issue of cost containment, supports this thesis.

To arrest the cost-plus spiral higher education must:

- end cost-plus pricing and place strict limits on spending growth, which, in effect, will simulate the discipline of the marketplace; and
- establish planning and resource-allocation processes and incentives to enhance innovation and stimulate resource reallocation from areas with low productivity to those with greater potential.

In other words, the message is "say no, but don't *just* say no." Higher education must simultaneously enforce spending constraints and make sure that its governance and management processes can generate productivity improvement to fund needed innovation.

College and university managers must provide the transitional leadership needed to give productivity high priority—high enough to offset inevitable bureaucratic forces. This requires vision and team building as well as the more traditional applications of legitimate power, tangible incentives, and analytical problem solving. It amounts to answering the question "What must be done in addition to saying no for the institution to change positively?"

The lesson from industry is that while resource constraints are a necessary condition for unleashing productivity improvement and innovation, they are not sufficient. Financial pressure by itself can crush initiative or create conflict over shares of a fixed or shrinking pie. The challenge is to mitigate these effects and turn the financial pressure into a driving force instead of a crushing burden.

Presentation of a coherent and integrated management intervention strategy is beyond the scope of this chapter, but I will describe some of the elements that have to be included in such a strategy. I hope that this will provide practical advice to higher education executives who are charged with productivity enhancement in the administrative and support service areas.

Elements of a Productivity-Enhancing Strategy

Table 3 provides a paradigm for gaining productivity improvement. It sets forth the interactions among four elements: resource constraints; strategic thinking (visions, plans, measures); incentives, recognition, and rewards; and individual and group empowerment.

Resource Constraints

Approaching the illustration in Table 3 from the nine-o'clock position immediately reveals the problem—in this context, it might better be described as the "opportunity" of resource constraints. Meeting these constraints must become a major organizational objective, in effect the enactment of environmental limits by the organization.

Strategic Vision

Organizations, especially complex ones, need a common sense of direction, a way for the organization to manage what Stanley M. Davis in

Future Perfect has called its "beforemath." A good strategic vision can provide this, exerting a pull to the future that permits people to move with sufficient common purpose to accomplish complex goals over a long period of time. Likewise, a shared paradigm about the organization's technological, market, and financial settings and its internal dynamics and management processes allows individuals to work toward a common goal with more independence than would be possible if they operated on different theories.

One of the most important advantages of a shared strategic vision is that it makes large-scale organizational change possible over a much longer period of time than would otherwise be possible. Such changes are more likely to require cultural adaptation than simpler changes that deal with individual operations or specific skills and routines. Cultural adaptation requires more time to accomplish. Sometimes the time scale is measured in years, during which memories fade and management turns over. A good strategic vision, well articulated and fully internalized as part of the organization's sense of subjective reality, provides the compass to keep the change process on course.

Strategic vision can be externally oriented or internally oriented, and, according to James L. Heskett's "Lessons from the Private Sector," most organizations need both. The former is usually concerned with what is to be accomplished vis-a-vis the outside environment—i.e., clients, competitors, or suppliers of capital. The latter concerns itself more with how the work will be accomplished and the organization's planning and management processes. Some examples of external and internal vision elements based on the service industry are presented in Table 4. Service-industry experience has much relevance for college and university administration and support services, which are dedicated to serving clients both inside and outside the academy.

Vision is created and promulgated through analysis and communication and by acting out the vision. For mid-level managers and rank-and-file employees, the latter can be furthered through carefully designed training sessions. On the next page, Table 5 presents the results of service training in the Stanford finance division as reported to me by my staff. The benefits of

Table 3 Gaining Productivity.

It is not easy for colleges and universities to increase productivity. The incentives in an academic culture point toward improving quality; there are few obvious incentives for focusing on efficiency and cost effectiveness. It is possible, however, for institutions to contain costs. Under the right conditions, cost containment can trigger increased productivity, thereby helping to achieve improvement in quality.

I believe that there are four conditions necessary for improving productivity.

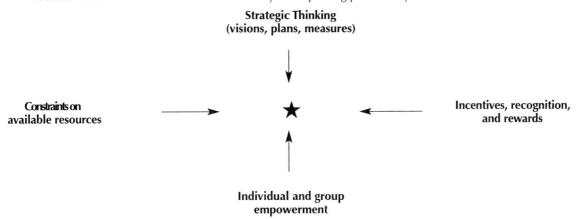

Resource Constraints

Resource constraints can be the driving force behind an institution's decision to increase efficiency and productivity. Most educational leaders press hard to enhance quality, but without the effect of resource constraints there is no incentive to consider cost effectiveness in relation to quality. It is no accident that institutions that regard themselves as relatively well-off financially find it hard to increase productivity, even though they have some of the best human and technological resources for tackling the problem.

Individual and Group Empowerment

Productivity improvement depends on the initiatives and skills of faculty and staff on both the individual and the group levels. They are the ones who are most familiar with the work process and who will implement any day-to-day changes. Faculty and staff must be empowered to lead the institution through its difficult choices. Empowerment means believing that one *can* and *should* make a difference and possessing or having access to the skills and resources needed to do the job.

Incentives, Recognition, and Rewards

Incentives and rewards can be offered in the context of tight resource constraints. In fact, they do not need to be monetary or even tangible. They should, however, be devised to encourage workers to think positively about productivity. It is very important to avoid inadvertently creating incentives that undermine productivity. Personnel reductions that are directly attributable to productivity improvement often decrease the potential for additional gains. Recognizing and celebrating a good result or a good effort is also essential. For example, school administrations should recognize faculty efforts to develop new and more productive teaching methods when setting salaries and making promotion and tenure decisions.

Strategic Thinking

The institution's leaders must engage in strategic thinking about productivity improvement. They must define what they mean by gaining productivity and make clear that it is an important part of their vision for the institution. They must develop plans and programs for embedding the vision in the organizational culture at the working level. They must also provide the concepts and support necessary for empowering people to develop and implement productivity-enhancing initiatives. They must arrange for the right incentives, recognition, and rewards and make sure there is follow-through across the organization.

All four conditions are necessary. Without incentives there will be few faculty and staff initiatives. Without strong conceptual leadership, those initiatives will lack focus, coherence, and staying power. Without faculty and staff initiatives, central visions and plans will stagnate because they lack connection to the actual work process and saliency for the people who would have to implement change. Finally, without a clear and binding resource constraint, the drive for quality and the incentives, recognitions, and rewards associated with quality dominate the objective of gaining productivity.

Adapted from the author's contribution to the article "Double Trouble," which was published in the September 1989 issue of *Policy Perspectives*.

Table 4 Sample Vision Elements from the Service Industry.

Externally-oriented Elements	Internally-oriented Elements
• How does the service concept propose to meet customer needs?	• What are common characteristics of employee groups?
• What is good service? Does the proposed concept provide it?	• How important are each of these groups to the delivery of service?
• What efforts are required to bring client service expectations and capabilities into alignment?	• What needs does each group have?
• What are the important features of the delivery system?	• How does the service concept propose to meet employee needs?
• How can the actual and perceived differences between the value and cost of services be maximized?	• To what extent are the concept and the delivery system for serving important employee groups internally consistent?
• Where will investments be made and efforts concentrated?	• To what extent have employees been involved in the design of the concept and the delivery system?

Adapted from Exhibits I and II in James L. Heskett's "Lessons from the Private Sector."

the session included empowerment through confidence building and skill development as well as the creation of a more powerful shared vision of the what, why, and how of providing good service. Extensive feedback from the participants and from their clients confirmed management's assessment that the program was highly successful.

Empowerment

While strategic vision provides a shared sense of what should be done, empowerment provides a powerful force for making things happen—thus providing a new way to think about productivity and change. A recent retreat for my senior finance staff began with a discussion entitled "Empowering Ourselves: What Can I Do to Create a Stanford of the Future to Which I Am Committed?" The investigation began with the meaning of work. Participants learned that most people work in order to meet some combination of the following objectives:

- To make a living
- To express deepest values
- To create an organization of one's own choosing
- To fulfill potential
- To discover identity

Only the first entry on the list regards work as a means to an end. The others regard it as tapping intrinsic needs. Surprising gains in

productivity are possible when these needs are aligned with those of the organization.

The empowered organization contrasts sharply with the traditional, patriarchal organization. Work in the latter tends to be directed toward gaining the approval of one's superiors (the patriarchs), which leads to undue concern about promotion, avoidance of risk, and control of one's work environment. Attention is directed upward (What does the boss think?) and risk is diversified by name-dropping and diffusing responsibility. Management style is often manipulative and calculating. In the empowered organization, however, work means contributing to important shared goals, mastering important skills, finding meaning in thought and action, acting out one's sense of integrity, and having a positive impact on people.

Table 6 depicts what is generally expected from an organization. Responsiveness to mission and adaptability to environmental change is at the top of the triangle. Productivity is at the four-o'clock position—how well the mission is accomplished will determine the organization's long-run health. The pressure to do more with less is nearly always present. Quality of work life is at eight o'clock—doing the job well over the long haul depends on employee commitment and morale.

How are these things accomplished? The traditional answer has been found within the patriarchal strategy. The best answer, however, is *empowerment*.

Table 5 Results of the Stanford Finance Service Training Sessions

Good service reinforced as a priority
- Support from top management was made visible in the sessions.
- Importance of good service to clients was recognized.

Clients identified and client relations enhanced through client interviews.

Services clarified and defined
- Unnecessary services were eliminated.
- Value services were acknowledged.
- Service strengths and issues were identified.

Service skills reviewed
- Characteristics of good and bad service were discussed (accessibility follow-through, courtesy).
- Effects of Stanford culture on service was examined.

Team building among group members was significantly enhanced (this was the first exposure to team building for some groups).

Self-image of work groups was improved through understanding their contribution to Stanford.

Communications examined
- Work group members in the sessions improved their communications.
- Departmental communications were improved by means of interviews.
- Managers attended sessions and were interviewed.
- Ongoing direct client feedback was initiated.

Many specific service improvements were put in place.

Improvement suggestions identified
- Service improvement plans were developed by every group.
- Management team committed to following up on issues presented by the work groups.

The patriarchal strategy concentrates responsibility and leadership at the top and stresses belief in consistency, control, and predictability. The organization tells the employee "Do as I say and I will take care of you." The implicit patriarchal contract is to submit to authority, to deny self-expression, and to sacrifice now for often unstated promises—all in return for being "taken care of." Employees are instruments, tools to be controlled and prevented from diverting resources. The limits of the patriarchal strategy are that it alienates the doing of work from the managing of work, values internal stability for its own sake, encourages narrow functional thinking, limits ownership of plans and ideas, and breeds caution and resistance to change. Over time, employees feel betrayed if rewards are not forthcoming at the level they have grown to expect. The patriarchal strategy tends to produce victims who become envious of victors to the detriment of teamwork and productivity. The balance of forces tends to favor the status quo and to actively inhibit behavior that deviates from it—even if that behavior stands a good chance of furthering the vision.

The empowerment strategy, on the other hand, strives for commitment and leadership at every level and stresses diversity, innovation, and personal responsibility. The organization tells the employee, "We will support autonomy and choice." The empowerment contract is to accept your own authority and accountability, encourage straight communication, and make commitments based on their meaning—not how they may look to the boss. Setbacks are taken at face value rather than as an excuse for feeling like a victim. The value of empowerment is that people will think of the whole organization rather than think in narrow functional or personal terms. The empowered organization values change, so things don't have to be "broke" before they can be improved. (Remember, though, that the improvements should be in implementation quality and not necessarily design quality.) Empowerment allows unique responses as situations demand, with no need to wait for multiple levels of approval or instructions from higher authority. Finally, empowerment integrates the doing of work and the management of work with substantial dividends for productivity.

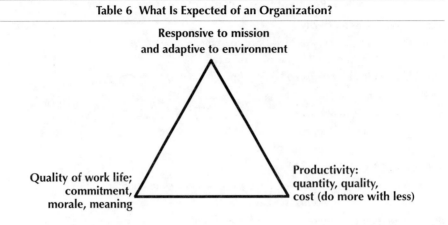

Table 6 What Is Expected of an Organization?

Responsive to mission
and adaptive to environment

Quality of work life;
commitment,
morale, meaning

Productivity:
quantity, quality,
cost (do more with less)

Employees must empower themselves, though the organization plays a critical role in removing barriers and providing encouragement. In the final analysis, the empowered employee will be strong enough and free enough to decide whether to accept a setback with continued commitment or decline to participate further. The decision to exit may take the form of changing employment or simply hunkering down and riding out the storm—in effect returning to the patriarchal model. This option is always present, and it provides leaders with the continuing challenge of keeping the environment for empowerment green.

Empowerment is not designed solely or even mainly to make people happy. The empowered organization is not "easy," but it does tend to have good morale. The tasks may be demanding, and meaning may be achieved only with great difficulty. Integrity means sailing under your own colors and having the strength to say no (not maybe) when you mean no. This can test relations with others, but contrast it with supervision by intimidation. Browbeating employees and ignoring their wants and needs may give the supervisor a sense of personal power, but that style alienates people and destroys productivity. A friend who is CEO of a major corporation says that while trying to have a positive impact on people is intrinsically gratifying and good, a sufficient reason for acting that way is that it works—it furthers the objectives of the organization. To para-

phrase a quote attributed to noted author and former Secretary of the U.S. Department of Health, Education, and Welfare John Gardner, morale is not necessarily happy people and smiling faces. Rather, it is people believing that the organization and its leaders are going in the right direction and doing the right things. For higher education in these times, an important and visible component of the right thing must be to maximize the productivity of administration and support services.

The Action Plan

Imagine that the diagnoses have been completed and that the necessary preconditions for a successful productivity improvement program have been put in place. The momentum of cost-plus pricing has been arrested, and firm resource constraints have been installed. What specific action steps should be undertaken to channel these positive forces toward administration and support-service productivity improvement?

Communications

The first step is to develop a communications strategy. Wide understanding of the reasons why productivity should be high on the institution's agenda is essential for mounting an effective program. Change itself can be painful, and increased productivity requires firm limits on resource outlays in the face of demands for improved performance. Active participation requires that people understand why they are being asked to endure what may well seem like sacrifices.

But communication should be a two-way street. Creating a shared strategic vision requires listening carefully to what people at all levels of the organization are saying even though in the end the vision is heavily conditioned by the outside environment and determined by the leadership. Changes in the outside environment may best be interpreted by people on the firing line, and the overall vision must relate meaningfully to their goals and sense of reality. Genuine two-way communication is much easier in the empowered organization where one does not have to resort to patriarchal games and the adjudication of claims of victimhood. It is possible for a leader to listen carefully and in good faith to employees without abdicating the responsibility to set the organization's agenda. However, a true leader must be willing to explain a final decision but must not feel compelled to *prove* that it will be the right decision. (Such a burden is impossible. Leaders must be empowered to act on their own judgment, provided they are prepared to be held accountable.)

The communication process can take many forms. Management retreats are popular and they can be very effective. "Town meetings" where leaders meet with middle managers and rank-and-file employees can serve the dual purpose of generating a dialogue between top management and these other groups and facilitating communication among them. Management by walking around is another effective way of communicating.

While every situation is different, it is often a good idea to decide on the broad outlines of the vision in a small group setting before taking it on the road. The small group must include senior management, who must ultimately be responsible for vision content, though others who have taken the time to become expert in the issues can also play an important role. The vision is then refined by give-and-take exposure to broader groups. Finally, the basic content of the message is finalized and promulgated as widely as possible.

Video and other technical aids can be helpful in putting out a coherent and consistent message, since the time and energy of the most senior people—who have the greatest source credibility—is limited. However, there is no substitute for personal involvement. One useful format is for the CEO to videotape a message that is then played before a group in his or her presence, after which there is a discussion and questions session. This conserves the CEO's energy, guarantees the consistency of the message from session to session, and makes it possible for the CEO to think about the group during presentation of the core material.

Management Process

The productivity improvement program will not succeed without a well thought-out management process for maintaining its place on the organization's agenda and keeping it on track. Experience suggests that the best method is to charge a high-level management group (a steering committee) with this task and then support it with a small staff that will be responsible for planning and follow-through. Keeping the program on the senior people's agenda despite inevitable distractions is a key responsibility for the staff. So is setting reasonably sized specific tasks, making appropriate delegations (with the support of the program's principals), and tracking the delegations to ensure performance. Since facilitating empowerment is a major goal, the staff must avoid the temptation to perform most of the tasks themselves. That would disempower line managers and ultimately undermine the program. One way to make sure this doesn't happen is for the senior people to keep the support staff very small, which would require it to go out into the organization to get things done. This also helps hold the line on task accretion by the staff group.

The usual way to go out into the organization is to delegate particular tasks to individuals or small groups, usually representative managers or staff with specifically relevant expertise. However, one of the lessons of the quality, service, and productivity (QSP) program my colleagues and I developed for Stanford's business and finance division was that an analog to quality circles can be very effective both in solving particular problems and facilitating empowerment. The variant we used was the quality team (we called them QSP teams), a format developed by the Hewlett-

Packard Corporation. The team roster was constructed as a diagonal section through the organization, from top to bottom and from side to side. (The traditional quality circle is made up of bottom-level people—e.g., those on the factory floor.) The advantage is breadth of experience plus the ability of the few expert and higher-level participants to get information, assess the implementation possibilities of the group's ideas, and help get things done when the time comes. It is important, however, that these higher-level people consider themselves more as facilitators than as managers, lest the insight and energy of the others be stifled through disempowerment.

The steering committee's role in all this is to help conceptualize the process, set priorities for what tasks need to be attended to, and oversee the work of the staff. Another very important role is to provide an audience to which the work product of the task groups will ultimately be presented. In addition to its obvious value, such a role provides the task groups with a focal point for organizing themselves and a sense of recognition or even reward when they have accomplished their charge. Constructively critical questions from senior managers are in fact a powerful kind of recognition—one of the most powerful a motivated professional can achieve. Furthermore, the presentation sessions provide members of the steering committee with an opportunity to interact with employees from levels they would not usually have contact with and to do so in relation to a problem of mutual importance. We found that the QSP teams facilitate two-way communication and provide opportunities for senior managers to send signals about style and what they think is important.

Analysis and Planning

There is, of course, no substitute for having well-conceptualized and well-thought-out strategies and plans. They deal with the what and how of change, and they must be rooted in the objectively real world as well as in peoples' sense of subjective reality. For instance, computer systems that cannot work as envisioned because of technological limitations or because they require too much time or money to develop will not be

helpful no matter how well they fit in with the vision and people's beliefs about what is important. Engineering, financial, market, contractual, legal, and regulatory factors have to be analyzed in depth in order to see possibilities and avoid mistakes. This kind of fact finding and analysis is part of the content of the delegations and charges to teams referred to in the previous section.

For example, an early action in Stanford's QSP program was to charge a team with trying to understand the elements of good service—what it means, how to get it, how to keep it. The team began the task by doing a systematic literature survey and then decided to talk with a number of companies identified as exemplary service providers. Out of this came some general principles: service must be a major organizational commitment (part of the vision, such as productivity must be); people must be trained in how to provide it, empowered to do so, and then held accountable for following through; and client feedback must be collected, as it is essential to understanding how things are going and to making midcourse corrections. Eventually, what was learned by this team was embodied in the service training program discussed in connection with Table 5.

The QSP team on work simplification provides another example. It started by developing a definition and understanding of what is meant by work simplification. This led to the creation of two subteams for doing pilot studies of how Stanford hires and pays people and how Stanford buys things (that is, employment/payroll and procurement/accounts payable). One of their first tasks was to learn about work process flowcharting and then apply it in their own departments. Some of these people discovered they could actually change the way the work was being done. The most spectacular result was in accounts payable, where a change in work flow and procedures reduced the backlog and the use of overtime to virtually nothing while coping with increased transaction volume and maintaining a constant staff—something the finance division had been trying to do for years without success. The final lesson was that much could be accomplished when the people with an intimate knowledge of the process were motivated and empowered to change it and given the tools to do so.

Rewards, Recognition, and Incentives

The "Welcome" section of the Stanford controller's office *RR&I Handbook* begins: "Tom Peters, author of *A Passion for Excellence,* has said that employees come to work equipped with motivation. The manager's job, therefore, is not to motivate, but to capitalize on the resource that is already there by removing minor barriers and constantly recognizing small achievements." The handbook goes on to state: "To be most effective, such recognition must be spontaneous and ongoing. By taking individual responsibility for recognizing our colleagues' daily efforts, we can achieve a culture where recognition is second nature and the incentive to excel accompanies each new task." The *Handbook* presents "simple, straightforward guidelines for recognizing and rewarding day-to-day efforts," some of which are reproduced in Table 7, which appears on the next page. What is particularly impressive is that the guidelines were developed by the line managers themselves rather than by human resource professionals—a tangible example of empowerment.

The more traditional processes of performance evaluations and merit pay should not be overlooked in designing RR&I systems. Written performance evaluations are tremendously important and well worth spending time on. Many organizations, including Stanford, have well-developed processes, including packaged materials and training programs on how to use them. I have found it helpful to ask for a sample of six to twelve of the evaluations written by people who report to me or by those a level lower, who report to them. I do this a month or two after the official performance-evaluation season has ended, partly to look at the performance of the evaluated, partly to see whether the evaluator is doing the job conscientiously, and partly to send a signal that I care about the process. With regard to merit pay, the biggest problem is how to increase the range of variation from a point or two from the guideline to as much as two times it. There is no sure way to do this within traditional merit pay systems, though a process wherein senior managers reject packages with unusually small ranges would certainly be a step in the right direction.

Finally, one might consider a nontraditional program of providing merit salary increments not in the base. The idea is that the half or two-thirds of employees who are doing the best job are given salary increments averaging several percent, but these increments would not be added to the person's base salary for compounding in future years. The increment would keep coming as long as performance held up, but it would not be guaranteed. It would be awarded in addition to the normal compounding increments received by everyone, which in the experiment become simple market adjustments. The program is intended to stretch the range of annual merit variations while avoiding the problem of consistently good or bad performance compounding to greater-than-tolerable disparities. The system would be calibrated so that people who don't get the nonbase increment would be slightly below market while those who got the best increments would be above market.

Measurement

The idea of measurement has permeated much of what I have said about productivity improvement. There are a number of reasons for this. First, no system can function effectively without feedback. The ability to assess the gap between performance and expectations is fundamental to midcourse correction, and no one is smart enough or well-informed enough to create a plan that can work without such corrections. Second, rewards, recognition, and incentives require that someone, somehow, makes an assessment of whether work is good, bad, or indifferent. It works the other way too, of course: accountability requires that an assessment be made of results.

I have already discussed one aspect of measurement in connection with communication. Two-way communication is a form of measurement: What's on your mind and how are we, the management, doing? A friend suggested that the way to approach this kind of measurement is to ask, "If I could sit on a bar stool with everyone in the organization for an hour, what would I suggest we talk about?" One way to do that (other than logging many hours on bar stools) is to hold town meetings and insist on candor in the ensuing discussions. Another is to use impromptu written surveys during town meetings, management retreats, and similar functions. The question-

Table 7 Criteria and Suggestions for Individual and Team Rewards.

Criteria (typical examples of an employee's willingness to go the extra mile)	Rewards (to be used as a menu of rewards and as a catalyst for new ideas)
• Suggested/developed a system or process that improved the quality, service, and/or productivity of work.	• Recognition party or dinner.
• Suggested/developed a system or process for work-simplification.	• Lunch at Stanford Faculty Club.
• Developed a creative solution to meet the needs of a client or department.	• Permission to attend seminars, work-shops, and classes outside of university staff development classes.
• Assumed additional responsibilities during a period of staff shortage.	• Tickets for two to Stanford events such as Lively Arts performances and athletics events.
• Increased job knowledge by voluntarily participating in cross training.	• Attendance at special lectures, presentations, or other university events.
• Exhibited tact and diplomacy in dealing with faculty, staff, or the outside community on a sensitive issue beyond the normal scope of job.	• Behind-the-scenes tour (perhaps with family) of Stanford facilities such as the linear accelerator, the biological preserve, the marine station, or the hospital.
• Made a difficult decision by using sound judgment and reasoning and carefully weighing alternatives.	• A gift from the Stanford bookstore, track house, or art gallery shop.
• Consistently promoting teamwork by help and cooperation outside of requirements.	• Personalized office supplies (pen, etc.).
	• A handwritten thank-you note.

From the *Rewards, Recognition, and Incentives Handbook* produced by the Stanford University controller's office.

naire does not need to be elaborate, though a degree of consistency will permit comparisons to be made across groups and over time. Sometimes the answers can be tabulated and feedback provided to the group at the same meeting. This usually guarantees that the question-and-answer period will be candid and lively.

Constantly taking the pulse of the organization is one of the keys of effective management. The same is true of client feedback. One of the things the QSP team learned about successful service organizations was that they all go out of their way to obtain systematic feedback from clients and then act on it promptly. The process or acquiring and paying attention to feedback is built into the organization's culture. It is part of its vision and part of its performance evaluation criteria. Experience shows that acting on feedback improves results. Measurement of how productivity improvement is being achieved has to be an integral part of any program.

What feedback is likely to be important in a productivity program? First, there needs to be a systematic attempt to chronicle the specific actions being taken to support the program: what decisions, initiatives, investments, resource reallocations, and work simplification

projects are being attempted and what their results are. Sometimes self-assessment is the best or most practical method of evaluation; sometimes it should be done by superiors and sometimes by staff groups, outside consultants, or visiting committees. Whatever the method, the important thing is that there be a description of the action, an a priori statement of the expected outcomes, and an explicit evaluation. The objective is both to learn by doing and to keep score for purposes of RR&I and accountability—the latter being based on the willingness to intelligently act as well as on the efficacy of the final outcome.

The other kind of measure is to keep score on the aggregate performance of operating units with respect to productivity measures. Where the inputs and outputs can be reasonably quantified, the score keeping should be straightforward. Transactions processed per FTE employee is a natural measure in the general accounting department, for instance. Lacking quantification of this sort, it may still be possible to track the number of employees that perform various qualitatively described tasks. It often is possible to measure performance on the basis of budget reallocation that the unit undertakes. Most organizations operate in a dynamic environment, and a long period of organizational stability may well signal a failure to adapt to new requirements or challenges and a stagnation of productivity improvement.

The bottom line is that the organization will tend to pay attention to the things that are posted on the scoreboard—provided, of course, that management makes clear that it is looking at the scoreboard too. The design of a productivity program must include output measures to assess how the program is going. Those measures need to be assessed at the operating unit level where people are close enough to the action to make a difference.

A Postscript on Management Style

There is no magic potion for productivity improvement in colleges and universities. Even when dealing with administrative and support services, the obstacles are large and the gains hard won. No large-scale purchase of capital equipment will make the difference. Even when information technology supplants manual processes, the gains are achieved little by little. Small wins by people newly empowered and eager to make a difference are what add up to the final result. The challenge of leadership is to see that the battles are fought on the right ground and for the right objectives; to recognize, reward, and hold people accountable so that the process continues and gains momentum; and to enable people to achieve these wins.

It is a truism that top managers must wholeheartedly support the program, making it a sine qua non for the organization, if there is to be real success. Their attitude must be positive, and they must be willing to shoulder risks both for the organization and for themselves. There should be a bias toward action, an approach that says "try it, fix it" rather than "study it until we're sure it'll work" or "discuss it until we have consensus."

The members of the management team must learn to work together and, above all, must trust one another. Each must carry the others' proxy—to get things done for the good of the organization, they must recognize transgressions and fix them when they occur rather than play "one up." The management team must "zig and zag together," in the words of

William F. Miller, former provost of Stanford University and president of SRI International, a nonprofit research institute based in Menlo Park, California. Each member of the team must anticipate what the other will do and make maximum use of that knowledge to get the job done. Not only is this a necessary condition for performing the senior group's tasks effectively but it sets an important example for the rest of the organization. And it applies across the boundary between academic and administrative units as well as within the culture of each.

Finally, it may be useful to initially present the productivity-improvement task as removing impediments rather than as instituting an ideal system all at once. All organizations abound with impediments, and this is especially true of many colleges and universities. Creating the right vision and getting back to neutral on productivity by eliminating redundancy; controlling the cost of quality; or progressing toward work simplification, empowerment, and RR&I represent good initial goals. After a few years, the goal should be to make the whole greater than the sum of the parts through better coordination of functions and global optimization of capital and human resource investments. This is an exciting process. When higher education has mastered it, it shall no longer have to be on the defensive with respect to productivity—the public and the political system will recognize higher education's productivity when they see it.

Bibliography

Association of American Universities Ad Hoc Committee on Indirect Costs. *Indirect Costs Associated with Federal Support of Research on University Campuses: Some Suggestions for Change.* Washington: Association of American Universities, 1988.

Allen, Richard, and Paul Brinkman. *Marginal Costing Techniques for Higher Education.* Boulder: National Center for Higher Education Management Systems (NCHEMS), 1983.

Barney, Jay B., and William G. Ouchi. *Organizational Economics.* San Francisco: Jossey-Bass Publishers, 1986.

Baumol, William J., and Sue Anne Batey Blackman. "Electronics, the Cost Disease, and the Operation of Libraries." *Journal of the American Society for Information Sciences,* vol. 34(3): 181–91.

Block, Peter. *The Empowered Manager.* San Francisco: Jossey-Bass Publishers, 1988.

Bowen, William. *The Economics of the Major Private Universities*. New York: Carnegie Commission on Higher Education, 1968.

Davis, Stanley M. *Future Perfect*. Reading, Mass.: Addison-Wesley Publishing Company, 1987.

Finn, Chester E., Jr. "Judgment Time for Higher Education: In the Court of Public Opinion." *Change*. vol. 20:34–39.

Hannaway, Jane. "Supply Creates Demands: An Organizational Process View of Administrative Expansion." *Journal of Policy Analysis and Management*. vol. 7:118–34.

Hauptman, Arthur M. "Why Are College Charges Increasing? Looking Into the Various Explanations." Working draft of a report to the College Board and the American Council of Education, September 1988.

Heskett, James L. "Lessons from the Service Sector." *Harvard Business Review*, (March–April 1987): 118–26.

Hoenack, Stephen A. *Economic Behavior Within Organizations*. New York: Cambridge University Press, 1983.

Maister, David H. "Professional Service Firm Management." Memo no. 20. Boston: Harvard Business School (June 1984).

March, James G. "Emerging Developments in the Study of Organizations." *Review of Higher Education*, vol. 6 (1982): 1–18.

Massy, William F. "Productivity and Cost Increase at Stanford." Discussion paper no. 2. Stanford University Board of Trustees Budget Committee (7 May 1984).

_____. "Financing Higher Education." Tenth annual conference on financing higher education. National Center for Higher Education Management Systems (NCHEMS) (28 November 1984).

_____. "Strategies for Productivity Improvement in College and University Academic Departments." Presented at the Forum for Postsecondary Governance, 30 October 1989, Santa Fe, New Mexico.

Meyer, Marshall W. *Limits to Bureaucratic Growth*. Berlin: Walter de Gruyter, 1985.

Pfeffer, Jeffrey, and Gerald R. Salancik. *The External Control of Organizations: A Recourse Dependence Perspective*. New York: Harper & Row, Publishers, 1978.

The Higher Education Research Program (Sponsored by the Pew Charitable Trusts), "Double Trouble." *Policy Perspectives*, vol. 2, no. 1 (September 1989).

Simon, Herbert A. "The Steam Engine and the Computer: What Makes Technology Revolutionary." *EDUCOM Bulletin*, vol. 22, no. 1 (Spring 1987): 2–5.

Sullivan, Charles Parker. "The Social Construction of Change in Administrative Behavior in Higher Education." Ph.D. diss., Stanford University, 1987.

Weber, Max. "Types of Legitimate Domination." *Economy and Society*, vol. 1. Guenther Roth and Claus Wittick, eds. 212–301. Berkeley: University of California Press, 1978.

Weick, Karl E. "Small Wins: Redefining the Scale of Social Problems." *American Psychologist*, vol. 39, no. 1 (1984): 40–49.

Faculty Participation in Strategic Policy Making

DAVID D. DILL AND KAREN PETERSON HELM

Turning and turning in the widening gyre
The falcon cannot hear the falconer,
Things fall apart; the center cannot hold;
Mere anarchy is loosed upon the world,
The blood-dimmed tide is loosed, and
    everywhere
The ceremony of innocence is drowned;
The best lack all conviction, while the worst
Are full of passionate intensity
William Butler Yeats

A strong case has been made that institutions of higher education in the United States are confronted not simply with increased competition due to declines in enrollment and economic support, but with a fundamental transformation in the nature of their environments (Cameron and Ulrich, 1986).This transformed context will, in turn, require academic decision-makers to think in more fundamental terms about essential programs and processes, emphasizing a strategic perspective sensitive to positioning academic institutions among the shifting sands of opportunities and constraints (Keller, 1983). This entrepreneurial view of academic decision-making—distinctively and characteristically American, one should add— is at odds with the European and more recent American tradition of faculty control and gradual incremental change in academic institutions (Jencks and Riesman, 1977). Thus, the advocates of "strategic management" in academic settings pose unsettling questions about the pace of academic change, about the most efficacious means of governing colleges and universities in turbulent times, and about the internal balance of power within academic institutions. What, for example, is the appropriate faculty role in "strategic" decision-making? Are traditional conceptions of "shared authority" obsolete? What are the effective mechanisms for sustaining faculty involvement? Finally, are traditional conceptions of faculty authority and participation valid in an environment in which capital investment decisions, fund raising, and student recruitment plays such a critical role? Like Yeats's vision of impending revolution, our faith in traditional forms of academic authority is challenged, we are no longer certain as to the appropriateness of existing forms of governance, let alone the new forms to be desired.

Assuming that these transformational conditions and the corresponding demands upon existing governance and decision-making processes are a reality, what has been written about the appropriate form of faculty participation during this new period? Surprisingly, very little. Our review of the major bibliographic indices, leading journals of higher education, and the most recent review of the literature of the field (Floyd, 1985) reveals that the literature on faculty participation per se and on governance, which was such a rich field as recently as 1978 (Millett, 1978; Mortimer and McConnell, 1978), has essentially dried up. Even though there have been some surveys suggesting declines in faculty involvement in decision making (Anderson,1983), there has been little research on

"Faculty Participation in Strategic Policy Making," by David D. Dill and Karen Peterson Helm, reprinted from *Higher Education: Handbook of Theory and Research*, Vol. 8, edited by J. C. Smart, 1988. Agathon Press.

or serious analysis of the issues confronting academic governance during the last ten years.

In this chapter, we will assay the nature of faculty participation in strategic policy-making. First, we will briefly review the history of faculty participation in academic governance in the United States. Second, we will clarify what we mean by strategic policy-making. Third, we will explore the increasing differentiation of the American system of higher education. This differentiation, well established in the research literature, suggests that the ideal of faculty involvement in decision making is a reality for only a small proportion of academic institutions, and that current forces suggest this reality will not change. Fourth, we will review a set of useful guidelines for designing joint participation processes developed from the literature and test these guidelines against six contemporary case studies of faculty participation in strategic policy-making. Finally, we will conclude with an analysis of the current logic for faculty participation in academic governance, and we will compare this view with the insights to be gained from the traditional basis for faculty authority and control.

There is ample theoretical and empirical support for the proposition that as the environmental context of an organization shifts, there is pressure for change within the organization, including the structure of authority and the decision-making process (Aldrich, 1979; Katz and Kahn, 1978; Zammuto, 1986). It is important, however, to stress at the outset that any discussion of the authority structure of an organization cannot be easily and simply separated from the organization's basic values. Satow (1975) has suggested that organizations dominated by professionals, such as academic organizations, are "value-rational" organizations, in which members of the organization have an absolute belief in the values of the enterprise for their own sake, independent of the institution's prospects for success. Satow further suggests that value-rational organizations such as academic institutions are not only identified by their values but bound together by them. As Wolff (1969) similarly argued, reflecting on the student disruptions of the 1960s, the structure of authority in an academic organization is inextricably linked to the types of values and goals the institution pursues. Thus, the nature of the academic enterprise, both its pattern of

authority and its basic techniques of social organization, is dependent upon its core values or culture (Dill, 1982).

Therefore, as this essay will suggest, a study of faculty participation in decision making is not simply an inquiry into the various forms or processes of decision making, but an inquiry into the nature of the academic enterprise itself.

The Three Periods of Faculty Participation

The evolution of American higher education in the twentieth century has been reflected in three different periods of faculty participation in decision making. These three periods will be termed *faculty control, democratic participation,* and *strategic policy-making*.

The history and development of academic governance in the United States has been carefully chronicled by Hofstadter and Metzger (1955). The conception of *faculty control* and authority which informs the 1966 "Statement on Government of Colleges and Universities" is a direct descendant of the medieval university, which operated as a guild of academic men who controlled their own activities. The rituals of the guildlike model are still visible in the direct control of Oxford and Cambridge colleges by English dons, but this romantic image disguises an important conversion in the English and European universities. The evolution of church control into state control over the universities in England and Europe made academics government employees. Thus the state assumed the role of providing the necessary capital and operating funds and delegated to the faculty the control of the institution.

While the founding of Harvard and William and Mary in the seventeenth century followed the English model of faculty control, there were numerous forces which quickly eroded this model: an insufficient number of experienced professors, sectarian control of the institutions, and limited crown, colonial, and, later, state support. These unique American conditions led to the evolution of institutional governing boards composed of laymen, principally sectarian representatives, who provided the legitimating authority for the institution, which in Europe was provided by the state.

The legality of this American model was affirmed in the Dartmouth College case which established that these boards of control were "corporations" independent of the control of the state. Thus the American model of academic governance throughout the eighteenth and most of the nineteenth century was of small colleges (i.e., an average of 10 faculty and 92 students in 1870), with a young teaching staff ruled by a president and a board of trustees. The development of the research universities in the late nineteenth century, with their conception of the faculty member as scholar, changed the nature of the faculty and helped to recover the concept of faculty control and authority. Thus, as Jencks and Riesman (1977) argued, an "academic revolution" occurred throughout the twentieth century, in which the faculty came to possess primary influence over governance, at least in the elite academic institutions. The appearance of the 1966 "Statement on Government of Colleges and Universities," however, suggests that this period was the high-water mark for faculty control and also reveals that even at high tide, there were large numbers and varieties of institutions untouched by the waters.

During the late 1950s, the rapid growth of enrollments, the changing composition of student bodies, and a volatile political climate combined to raise a fundamental question regarding the integrity of the academy (Millett, 1978). During this period, there were intense debates concerning the representativeness of existing governance mechanisms and an interest in experimenting with forms of institutional decision-making which emphasized *democratic participation*. Particularly at the most prestigious colleges and universities where faculty controlled the governance process, the dominant coalition of faculty members and administrators was confronted by demands to democratize the governance process and to include students and other disaffected constituencies in traditional faculty senates (Dill, 1971; Hodgkinson, 1974). Less noted during this period was the growing power exercised by administrators and legislators in new and rapidly growing community colleges, state colleges, and private colleges where faculty control had never flowered (Mortimer and McConnell, 1978). In the late 1960s and the 1970s, this issue came to the fore with the development of collective bar-

gaining. While certain prestigious colleges flirted with or endorsed collective bargaining (cf. Oberlin College and New York University), principally because of a movement toward *too* democratic a process and/or administrative usurpation, the primary location for collective bargaining in higher education was in those community colleges, state colleges, and small private colleges which had never experienced a period of faculty control (Baldridge et al., 1981; Carnegie Council on Policy Studies in Higher Education, 1977). Ironically, collective bargaining extended the concept of democratic participation to the faculties of these institutions, since the process presented in a legal context some of the same issues of influence of a disaffected constituency lacking formal authority, which were addressed by student demands for participation. Also, many collective bargaining contracts democratized the governance process of their institution because nontraditional constituencies such as counselors, librarians, and research personnel were defined as part of the bargaining units which subsequently negotiated policies on the terms and conditions of work. Thus the period of democratic participation included demands for the extension of participation to new groups as well as to those faculties which had never gained faculty control. This period spawned a rich literature on participation and governance (Floyd, 1985).

The period of democratic participation has ended, however. The beginnings of the sea change were detectable in the early 1970s as the strong economic support experienced by higher education since World War II was eroded by inflation and energy costs. Faculty members on all campuses fought for greater influence over decisions on the allocation of financial resources, with particular concern for faculty salaries. By the late 1970s, a series of trends coincided to presage a genuinely new environment for higher education (Mortimer and Tierney, 1979). At the end of the decade, four resource flows critical to institutions of higher education had stabilized or were in actual decline: student enrollments, federal support for research and development, federal support for student financial aid, and real family discretionary income (Leslie, 1980; Zammuto and Cameron, 1985). The effect of this environmental change was to lay bare the underlying market competition among colleges and universities for students, faculty members, revenues, and, ultimately, prestige. This competitive market has existed throughout American history but was rendered practically invisible by the remarkable and continuing growth in market demand for higher education which existed from the founding of Harvard College until the late 1970s. This increasing demand was made possible by the continual growth in the size of the college-age cohort and the proportion of the age cohort attending college, by growth in federal and state allocations, and by a rising standard of living for the population as a whole. These growth conditions in enrollment and economic support have now shifted to an environment of decline (Zammuto, 1986).

The proposed institutional response to this new environment of higher education is *strategic policy-making* designed to help administrators evaluate their institutional strengths and weaknesses in the light of environmental conditions and to allocate resources accordingly (Keller, 1983). These transformational conditions are likely both to continue and to intensify through this century, as colleges and universities confront profit-making, degree-granting agencies with superior new technologies which compete effectively with the traditional functions of teaching, research, and service (Cameron and Ulrich, 1986). Unlike the earlier periods of faculty control and democratic participation, it can now be argued that the *substance* of governance has changed. Institutions will not be faced primarily with maintenance decisions, such as the allocation of incremental budgets, the administration of traditional curricula and programs, and the governing of student behavior. The governance issues of the last ten years and for the foreseeable future will involve policy issues affecting the nature of the enterprise: the types of research, teaching, and service programs to be offered; developing priorities among these programs; and allocating (or reallocating) resources to the highest priority programs (Shirley, 1983).

The tenets, respectively, of faculty control and democratic participation, while different, were articulated during a period of growth and general prosperity for American higher education. The current environment of scarcity and competition is thus strange to both governance perspectives. Therefore, the values and the structural mechanisms of the period of growth are now being applied in a new period of strategic policy-making in which academic decision-makers must confront the most substantive and divisive issues faced by institutions of higher education.

Strategic Policy-making

The concept of strategic policy-making emerges in direct response to the environment of decline now influencing higher education (Zammuto, 1986). Three types of internal institutional strategies have been articulated to deal with decline: (1) *domain offense* involves more effort being put into existing operations to improve effectiveness and to protect market share; (2) *domain consolidation* is a variant of domain offense which involves cutting back in some operations, and reallocating, to improve efficiency; and (3) *domain creation and substitution* require eliminating weak programs and adding new, more "profitable" programs.

There is substantial debate in the literature as to whether all, or even the majority of, institutions will need to address the strategic turnaround strategies of domain creation and substitution (Cameron and Ulrich, 1986) or whether the operating changes of domain offense and consolidation are of principal importance (Chaffee, 1984; Hardy, 1987). We anticipate that the choice of strategy will necessarily vary by type of institution. The types of policy issues in higher education, however, will very likely be the same from institution to institution (Hardy et al., 1983). These policy choices include (1) the elaboration of the basic mission into specific programs and services offered the public; (2) the character of critical inputs such as the type of academic staff, the nature of student enrollments, and the programs for external fund-raising; (3) the academic infrastructure necessary to accomplish the mission, for example, the types of buildings and facilities to construct, the major research equipment to be purchased, and the development of computer systems and libraries; and (4) the structure and forms of academic governance, including the design of the committee system, and the regulations concerning promotion and tenure.

How are faculties to participate in these types of policy choices? The joint AAUP/ACE/AGB "Statement on Government of Colleges and Universities" (1966) has generally served as the standard reference for an *ideal* policy on academic governance. The document assumes three spheres of decision making. The faculty has primary responsibility for curriculum, subject matter and methods of instruction, research, faculty status, and those aspects of student life which relate to the educational process. The governing board and administration have primary responsibility for maintaining the endowment and obtaining the needed capital and operating funds. Shared responsibility and authority exist in areas such as the framing of long-range plans, deciding on buildings and other facilities, allocating financial resources, and determining short- and long-range priorities. A comparison of this document with the strategic decisions outlined by Hardy et al. (1983) suggests that the majority of strategic policy issues fall within the sphere of governance labeled as *shared authority*. From this perspective, the types of decisions confronting colleges and universities in the years ahead should logically require *more* consultation and sharing of authority between administrators and faculty than may have been characteristic of the incremental growth conditions of previous periods of academic governance.

In fact, the research suggests that faculty participation and shared authority is declining during this period of strategic policy-making (Anderson, 1983; Bowen and Glenny, 1980), and that the existing mechanisms and policies seem inadequate to the task (Floyd, 1985). In a study of representative universities, state colleges, liberal arts colleges, and community colleges, Anderson (1983) discovered a constant decline in faculty perceptions of "democratic governance" between 1970 and 1981. Faculty members toward the end of the decade perceived that control, power, and decision making were more closely held by administrators; that "wide faculty involvement" in important decisions about how the institution would be governed was less characteristic; and that the concept of shared authority (faculty and administrators jointly deciding) was not as evident in campus governance. These results are somewhat predictable in that studies in a variety of organizations suggest that as competition, conflict, and demands

for survival increase in an organization, decision making tends to become centralized and less participatory (Zammuto, 1986). Anderson (1983), however, asserts that while administrators of the most "effective" institutions were not shy in exercising authority when needed, particularly in personnel decisions, the most effective institutions were more characterized by shared authority than were the less effective institutions.

The Realities and Possibilities of Shared Authority

While shared authority and joint participation have remained ideal types for the governance of all academic institutions, one of the most consistent discoveries of research on academic institutions is the variation among institutions in the American system on faculty participation and control (Baldridge et al., 1978; Kenen and Kenen, 1978; Mortimer, Gunne, and Leslie, 1976; Ross, 1977). A national survey by Baldridge et al. (1978) presented substantial evidence as to the differentiation between academic institutions in the nature of their environments (e.g., public control versus private flexibility), the nature of the professional task (e.g., the quality of students and the faculty's involvement in research), and institutional size and complexity. On the specific issue of faculty involvement in governance, there were substantial differences between types of institutions. Utilizing a revised version of the typology developed by the Carnegie Commission on Higher Education, Baldridge et al. (1978) suggested that faculty primacy over academic matters and participation in strategic planning and budgeting issues was most likely at research universities and elite liberal arts colleges. The faculty's autonomy and control over their own work, and particularly faculty participation in what we have termed here *strategic policy issues*, declined steadily as one climbed down the pecking order of academic prestige, through public comprehensive colleges, public colleges, and private liberal arts colleges (especially sectarian institutions), and it was least evident in community colleges and private junior colleges. In a comparable analysis of national data collected by T. Parsons and G. Platt, Ross (1977) concluded that faculty's perceptions of their influence on general educational policy and faculty personnel issues were greater in those institutions with higher faculty qualifications as measured by possession of a Ph.D. and scholarly productivity. Similar institutional differences in faculty influence were also identified by Mortimer et al. (1976) and by Kenen and Kenen (1978), who emphasize the primacy of administrators in the governance of community colleges and sectarian colleges. While the concentration of faculty autonomy and shared authority in the research universities and elite liberal arts colleges is clear in each of these studies, the research also consistently reports the obvious control of administration and trustees over financial policy (Finkelstein, 1984).

The most recent study of authority patterns in American higher education confirms the survey reports of Anderson (1983). Faculty control and shared authority, while still in existence, has retreated even further into the ranks of elite research universities and liberal arts colleges; the differentiation between types of institutions is increasing, not decreasing (Clark, 1987). Clark (1987) has suggested the term *authority environments* to describe the general understandings, ground rules, and frames of governance which characterize academic organizations. The research university is characterized by collegial control of major academic decision-making, faculty criteria for key administrative appointments, and a process of department-based, bottom-up governance. At the other end of the spectrum, the community college authority environment is characterized by a more bureaucratic decision-making process on faculty hiring and curriculum, by more centralized procedures bearing the imprint of school administration, and by contractual obligations detailed in collective bargaining agreements:

> Interviews in institutions situated between the extremes of research universities and community colleges demonstrated that as one moves up the status hierarchy, one encounters more professional control, and as one moves down, one observes more administrative dominance and even autocracy. (Clark, 1987, p. 268)

There are gray areas in such a hierarchy. For example, Baldridge et al. (1978) argued that many liberal arts colleges may closely approximate the collegial ideal of shared authority on

institution-wide decisions, because of a weak departmental structure and small size. Similarly, Finkelstein and Pfinister (1984), in a study of liberal arts colleges drawn from Carnegie Classifications I and II, discovered an increase in faculty participation in collegewide decision-making, budgetary planning, and promotion and tenure based upon data through 1978. These authors attributed these changes to an increase in faculty expertise and sophistication in these settings brought about by the increased market supply of Ph.D.'s.

Research on collective bargaining confirms the argument for a differentiated system of higher education. The majority of bargaining units have been formed in that stratum of higher education which already possessed little faculty autonomy or participation (Baldridge et al., 1981). Further, the focus of collective bargaining has been limited to the terms and conditions of contracts (Begin, 1978). To the extent that the relationship between collective bargaining and strategic policy-making has been subject to research, it suggests that collective negotiation has led to greater administrative centralization on strategic issues outside of the terms and conditions of employment (Floyd, 1985).

This consistent pattern of research suggests that while the concept of shared authority and faculty participation in decision making is an "ideal type" for all academic institutions, it has consistently occurred only within a limited stratum of American higher education (Baldridge, 1982). Furthermore, as recent research indicates, the "authority environments" conducive to faculty participation are becoming more rare, being eroded by state and federal legislation, and by entrepreneurial or autocratic executive decision-making. The tradition of faculty authority and control is increasingly restricted to a certain class of institutions: elite research universities and liberal arts colleges.

The Process Approach to Faculty Participation

The limited contemporary research on governance suggests that neither the traditional forms of faculty control (e.g., departmental autonomy and faculty senates) nor the structures of democratic participation (e.g., unicameral senates and collective bargaining) appear to be useful models for faculty participation during the evolving period of strategic policy-making (Powers and Powers, 1984). Instead, a focus on process, on consultative decision-making and the means of involving and utilizing faculty experience and expertise, is advocated as likely to be a more fruitful and more generalizable approach (Hardy et al., 1983; Mortimer and McConnell, 1978; Powers and Powers, 1983). Although the models vary, six general stages of consultation can be detected.

1. *Early consultation.* It is critical that the individuals or groups to be involved in decision making have the opportunity to consider the phrasing of issues as well as the formulation of alternatives well before choices are made. We do not judge as consultation informing faculty groups of decisions after they are made and asking for assistance in implementation. Early consultation also involves the effective use of experience and expertise. The forming of committees based upon political representation without regard to the professional experience or expertise of the members lessens the potential for creative and strategically valuable contributions (Bradford and Bradford, 1981). Finally, early consultation does not stifle but encourages managerial initiative in the phrasing of issues and alternatives. A good example of this technique was the leadership of Clark Kerr, who as chancellor at Berkeley regularly would draft a report for the discussion of a major issue, discuss it at length with a faculty committee, and then revise it in light of their comments (McConnell and Mortimer, 1971). Similarly, Powers and Powers (1983) advocate initiating consultation processes through the circulation of a "white paper."

2. *Joint formulation of procedures.* A characteristic of a successful strategic policy-making process is *a priori* joint consultation over the procedures to be followed in the consultation process itself. This, of course, is a characteristic of the collective bargaining process, but as Hardy et al. (1983) indicate, the design of the processes to be utilized for decision making is itself one of the critical strategic policy issues to be considered.

3. *Time to formulate responses.* Timing is often used by administrators as a device for avoiding participation, for example, scheduling key student-related decisions over the summer months. Involvement of faculty expertise and perspective requires adequate time for consid-

eration and response. However, some administrators err by not setting explicit timetables for consultation and adhering to them.

4. *Availability of information.* Within obvious limits, such as confidential personnel files, faculty engaged in consultation should have access to the information they need. One characteristic of successful faculty committee work is that the committee is often assigned a staff member from a related administrative office (e.g., finance or institutional research) to help provide data and the interpretation of data.

5. *Adequate feedback.* Following the rendering of advice, those participating in the consultation deserve an adequate response. While there is an obvious reluctance to provide written responses on critical personnel issues, the provision of a basis for the modification or the rejection of a committee report is critical to preventing the type of alienation which often exists between faculty and administrators (Austin and Gamson, 1983).

6. *Communication of decision.* How a decision is to be implemented or communicated is a fair issue for discussion during the consultation process. Implementation is a stage where many decisions founder precisely because inadequate time has been given to examining the acceptability and adoption of the decision (Vroom, 1984). Given the unique organization of colleges and universities, in which "professional judgment" controls so many of the operating procedures of the institution, implementation is a much more critical step than in the "top-down" hierarchy of corporate settings.

While these six processes appear unexceptional, there has been little research or study of the application of this model in the new period of strategic policy-making. What type of process works in the critical areas of program review and evaluation, priority setting, and budgetary allocation or reallocation? How is faculty expertise utilized in this process? What is the appropriate balance and relationship between *ad hoc* advisory groups and ongoing structures? How is "shared authority" achieved'? In the section, which follows, we will analyze several case studies to gain some insight into the utility of this model of consultative strategic policy-making. We will then review the implications of these cases for our understanding of the process and bases of faculty participation in policy making and turn to implications for research.

Modes of Faculty Participation in Strategic Decision-Making

A review of leading research journals, popular administrative journals, monographs available from the National Center for Higher Education Management Systems, and a small sample of conference presentations and institutional documents produced only a handful of case studies describing a strategic decision-policy process in which the pattern of faculty involvement could be clearly identified (see Table 1). In this section, we will examine some of the patterns observed among these case studies in an effort to highlight the more common modes of faculty participation. Then, we will look more closely at six of the cases which best illustrate these modes and evaluate them according to the six stages of consultation described in the model above.

Faculty are involved in strategic policy-making in a variety of functional areas, which are well described by Zammuto's (1986) three categories. Among the processes normally re-

sulting in domain offense strategies are program review, curriculum reform, reorganization, and revision of promotion and tenure policies. Among the processes normally resulting in domain consolidation strategies are planning and budgeting. Among the processes resulting in domain creation and substitution strategies are retrenchment and related policies governing the declaration of fiscal exigency and releasing tenured faculty.

Strategic policy-making processes differ not only according to functional area, but also according to two characteristics describing the modes of faculty participation: duration of involvement and degree of integration with administrative decision-making. First, in some cases, faculty is involved permanently in ongoing processes through representation on *standing committees*, such as faculty senate committees or budget and planning committees. In others, faculty are consulted temporarily on episodic issues through *ad hoc committees* charged, for example, with retrenchment planning, reorganization, or mission review. Second, faculty in some cases serve on *joint committees* as equal voting partners with administrators, for

Table 1   Strategic Domains and Modes of Participation by Institutional Type[a]

Type (see below)	Number	Strategic domains			Modes of participation			
		Domain offense	Domain consolidation	Domain substitution/ creation	Ad hoc coms.	Standing coms.	Joint coms.	Separate coms.
R/Us	10	1	5	4	6	4	4	6
D/Gs	4	2	1	1	3	1	2	2
C/Us	5	2	3	0	2	3	4	1
L/As	5	3	2	0	2	3	3	2
C/Cs	1	0	1	0	0	1	0	1
Total:	25	8	12	5	13	12	13	12

R/Us (Research Universities): Berkeley (Trow, 1983); Duke (Franklin, 1982; Peterson, 1985); Emory (Teel, 1981); Michigan State (Crawley, 1981); NCSU (Peterson and Moazed, 1986); Princeton (Herring et al., 1979); Stanford (Chaffee, 1983); SUNY–Albany (Caruthers and Lott, 1981); West Virginia (Kieft, 1978; Poulton, 1980); Univ. of Minnesota (Heydinger, 1982).

D/Gs (Doctoral Granting Universities): Bowling Green Univ. (Moore, 1978); Ohio Univ. (Armijo et al., 1980); Old Dominion (Darby et al., 1979); Univ. of Vermont (Tashman, Carlson and Parke, 1984).

C/Us (Comprehensive Universities): King's College (Farmer, 1983); Mt. St. Mary's (Campbell, 1983); Univ. of Richmond (Vulgamore, 1981); Univ. of Toledo (Reid, 1982); Western Washington Univ. (Kieft, 1978).

L/As (Liberal Arts Colleges): Birmingham–Southern (Bette and O'Neil, 1980); Curry College (Hill, 1985); Lewis and Clark (Arch and Kirschner, 1984); Villa Maria (Kieft, 1978); Willamette Univ. (Armijo et al., 1980).

C/Cs (Community Colleges): Lorain County Community College (Armijo et al., 1980).

[a]Based upon *The Carnegie Classification of Higher Education* (Carnegie Foundation, 1987).

example, in recommending priorities among budget requests. In other cases, the administration seeks faculty opinion by consulting a *separate committee*, as a distinct stage in the decision-making process.

Among the case studies in our small, certainly unscientific sample, the mode of faculty participation as described by these two characteristics did not vary according to class of institutions. Research universities, comprehensive universities, and liberal arts colleges seem to involve faculty in similar ways. Instead, the mode of faculty participation varied according to functional area (Table 2).

In processes involving domain offense (for example, program review, curriculum review, and reorganization), the mode of faculty participation is generally through separate *ad hoc* committees. Policies in these particular areas need be established only on a periodic basis and are quite dependent on the faculty's disciplinary expertise. Frequently, such processes involve faculty from a given set of disciplines or fields, rather than representatives from the institution as a whole.

In processes involving domain consolidation (for example, planning and budgeting), the mode of faculty participation is generally through joint standing committees. In contrast to program evaluation efforts, these decisions require institutionwide processes and are not discipline-specific. Here, faculty represent the general interests of critical stakeholders, much as trustees.

In processes involving domain creation and substitution (for example, retrenchment and fiscal exigency policies), the mode of faculty participation is through separate *ad hoc* committees. The reason for such committees to have only a temporary life is obvious; however, the rationale for separating faculty from administrative deliberations on such pivotal decisions deserves closer scrutiny, and we will return to this issue later.

Now we will examine in greater detail six case studies which provided sufficient information on faculty participation to permit analysis of the process of faculty involvement. Not surprisingly, these six institutions reflect our earlier point regarding the limited group of institutions whose authority environments can be characterized as *shared authority*. Four of the cases describe strategic policy-making in Research I universities, one case a Research II university, and one case a Liberal Arts I college (Carnegie Foundation for the Advancement of Teaching, 1987). We conclude with the latter case, a negative instance, because it summarizes a number of the themes we wish to explore in the final sections.

The University of California at Berkeley

The extensive review and reorganization of the biological sciences undertaken by the University of California at Berkeley in the late 1970s and early 1980s (Trow, 1983) is an example of a domain offense strategy employing, initially, a separate *ad hoc* faculty committee. The committee's deliberations resulted in a strategic policy to secure and invest new resources in redefined program emphases in an effort to protect the university's high national rankings in those fields.

At Berkeley, as elsewhere, the biological disciplines and hence the academic departments were originally defined according to categories of living things, for example, zoology, botany, bacteriology, and entomology. As a consequence of developments in molecular theory, biochemistry, and advanced research technologies, biologists have in this century turned to the study of underlying similarities in the composition of all living organisms. Molecular genetics, cell biology, and other new disciplines emerged, each overlapping the

Table 2 Strategic Domains by Modes of Faculty Participation

	Ad hoc com.	Standing com.	Joint com.	Separate com.
I. Domain offense	7	1	2	6
II. Domain consolidation	1	11	10	2
III. Domain substitution	5	–	1	4
Total (N = 25)	13	12	13	12

more traditional disciplines and crossing departmental lines. At Berkeley, the result was nineteen or twenty different departments in the biological sciences located in five schools, most of which had developed a full complement of faculty representing the same range of "new" disciplines.

Administrators' awareness of the need to reorganize the biological sciences was precipitated by the poor condition and the growing obsolescence of the university's research and teaching laboratories. Departments began having difficulty competing successfully for the best young faculty, and a national assessment of graduate programs showed Berkeley's rank falling in several fields at once. An external review committee reported that graduate programs had not developed fully in spite of outstanding individual faculty members; the lack of an effective means for coordination and interchange in the newer, interdisciplinary subject areas limited development in several emerging fields.

There was widespread agreement that a new building and vast improvements in laboratory facilities were necessary to attract desirable faculty and to regain Berkeley's standing. In order to evaluate exactly what kinds of faculties were needed, the administration conducted an inventory of all biological research on campus and organized the information according to areas of research rather than by department. As expected, the inventory highlighted the expected organizational issues. In response, the administration appointed an *ad hoc* faculty Internal Biological Sciences Review Committee to evaluate all programs and to analyze space needs. Four subcommittees were organized around the four interdepartmental research areas that had emerged during the inventory stage.

The committee's final report outlined the rationale for recommended changes based on the evolution of the biological sciences; recommended specific research areas deserving of special attention; assessed the space needs for all biological fields, regardless of department; recommended the establishment of interdepartmental "affinity groups"; and recommended that laboratory facilities in the new building be organized in a way that would permit researchers from different departments to focus on similar problems in a common work environment. The committee considered but declined a recommendation to reorganize all biological departments into a single college with internal divisions more closely allied with emerging research areas than with traditional disciplines. Instead, the committee recommended the establishment of a new standing committee, an Advisory Council on Biology, which would advise the deans and the chancellor on strengthening the biological sciences and on the distribution of faculty positions and the composition of faculty search committees.

The report and each of its recommendations were approved by the chancellor, who has been successful in obtaining support for the new building from the system administration, the legislature, and private donors. Until the time when major reorganization becomes appropriate, the Advisory Committee will function as a means of tapping faculty expertise regarding the development of resources in areas where Berkeley can make the most significant contributions to the fields of biology.

West Virginia University

West Virginia University (WVU) is the state's land-grant and major research university with an enrollment of approximately 21,000. Since the late 1960s, WVU has developed an integrated, comprehensive planning process that translates academic goals into the annual operating budget and influences facilities management (Poulton, 1980; Kieft, 1978). This domain consolidation strategy utilizes a standing committee comprised jointly of faculty members, administrators, and students.

The rationale for faculty participation in the annual planning and budgeting process is based on the belief that an academic plan ought to provide the cornerstone for planning in other functional areas, including the budget, and that faculty ought to play a key role in describing the future of academic programs, within situational constraints and parameters. Participation is effected at two levels. At the institutional level, a University Council on Planning advises the president on the formulation of planning assumptions and reviews the plans and budget proposals submitted by group activity centers (i.e., academic departments, divisions, and centers). Its membership includes 9 faculty members, 3 students, and 3 *ex officio* administrators, including the provost for planning, who sits in the chair.

At the program level, faculty participate in the development of local planning assumptions and of annual plans. By 1977–1978, 30 of 45 group activity centers had appointed planning councils whose membership and responsibilities are similar to the University Council on Planning.

The annual planning and budgeting process at WVU includes the following steps. The University Council on Planning develops a set of institutional planning assumptions for a given period of time, which are then used by group activity centers to develop planning assumptions for their own units, according to local planning processes. The group activity centers then prepare plans according to a common outline, which requires that all proposals for new programs be ranked in priority order, be justified according to local and university planning assumptions, and detail budget requirements.

The first level of review by the president's office includes oral presentations by the dean or director of each group activity center. Then, the university's annual plan and operating budget request is prepared using the planning assumptions prepared by the University Council on Planning as criteria for evaluating program proposals and identifying priorities among competing claims for resources.

A few months after the university's annual plan and budget request are submitted to the Board of Regents, each group activity center has the opportunity to alter its priorities and to suggest new proposals based on information and needs that may have come to light since the process was initiated. Again, each change is justified and evaluated on the basis of stated objectives and the decision criteria identified earlier. Once funds are allocated by the Board of Regents, the preliminary plan and budget requests are translated into operating plans for the coming year.

Throughout the year, group activity centers may submit to the president's office requests to alter their plans and to shift resources accordingly. All requests are reviewed against the same decision criteria used throughout the planning process.

At West Virginia University, this planning and budgeting process is the means of coordinating and prioritizing the allocation of resources according to an academic plan that outlines programmatic goals and objectives. The budget is, in a sense, program goals translated into dollars (Kieft, 1978). Faculty plays a critical advisory role through standing committees that develop planning assumptions and that review program proposals at both the local and the institutional levels.

Princeton University

A mature university, with an enrollment of around 6,000 and a high degree of shared values and interests, Princeton University has employed a standing joint faculty, student, and administrative committee to advise the president on the allocation of resources for more than fifteen years (Herring et. al., 1979). As at West Virginia University, this planning and budgeting process illustrates a domain consolidation strategy.

The charge to the Priorities Committee is to make recommendations on matters affecting the annual budget for the following year, including both income projections and broad priorities among possible expenditures, and to make recommendations on matters affecting longer range plans for resource allocation. The committee's membership includes six faculty members, including one from each of the four main divisions of the university; four undergraduates; two graduate students; and three *ex officio* administrators: the provost (the chairman), the dean of the faculty, and the financial vice-president and treasurer.

The Priorities Committee concentrates its work in about three months, from mid-October to mid-January. For six to eight weeks, it reviews budget requests from academic and administrative units and reports on major budgetary concerns, such as salaries and auxiliary income. The administrative head of each unit also makes an oral presentation to the committee, at which time questions may be asked about the rationale or the impact of a budget reduction or a modification of priorities.

After listening to all requests, the committee reviews all income and expenditure items not under the university's direct control, such as endowment earnings. Then, based on the committee's overall income projections and the total of all budget requests, the controller's office assembles a budget showing, of course, a large deficit. The committee then sets about reducing that deficit by increasing income or reducing expenditures.

Before the holidays, the committee produces a tentative budget package, which is reported to the larger university community. During the holidays, the staff draft a final report, which summarizes the proposed budget and analyzes its implications for future budgets. The committee makes whatever changes it wishes and reports to the president in early January. After consultation with the committee and members of the larger university, the president forwards a budget to the Board of Trustees.

Throughout the committee's deliberations, regular reports are made to the university community through the campus newspapers, and all budget requests are made available to anyone who wishes to review them. Although working sessions are closed, the committee holds a public hearing wherein faculty, staff, and students may express their views with respect to the university's financial situation and future priorities. In the mid-1970s, a ground swell rose among students to argue against increases in tuition and fees and reduction in certain services, and general interest in the budgeting process has increased over time. Although increased interest may threaten the process by reducing rationality and politicizing the process, it has also improved the committee's understanding of the views of its public and vice versa.

That the priorities committee has played a critical role in the development of Princeton's budget for many years, and that its membership and charge have remained essentially unchanged demonstrate its effectiveness as a means of universitywide review of institutional goals as they are translated into the budget. During some periods, such as the energy crisis of 1974, the committee has been challenged to reduce expenditures in order to eliminate a sizable deficit. In other periods, the committee has selectively recommended increases and new initiatives.

Duke University

During the 1970s, Duke University faculty and administrators shared the belief that the university had considerable potential for significantly improving its national reputation as a research university. A growing endowment and an application pool increasing in size and quality contributed to rising expectations for the university, whose enrollment was approaching 10,000 and whose eight schools included a large medical center. However, the challenges shared by higher education during this period—increasing costs and competition for students—began to threaten the financial base on which the community could build to compete successfully with institutions in the top rung of American universities. Duke's attempts to address this environment illustrate aspects of a domain creation and substitution strategy, utilizing a separate *ad hoc* faculty committee.

The chancellor believed that the regular budgeting process, which normally provided incremental increases, would not result in strategic reallocations to the programs with the greatest potential for reaching or maintaining a high ranking nationally (Peterson, 1985; Franklin, 1982). In 1977, he assembled an *ad hoc* Long Range Planning Committee (LRPC), consisting of ten faculty, eight of whom were nominated by the primary faculty representative body (the Academic Council) and, in fact, were the current leaders of that body. After consulting with this group privately for eighteen months, the chancellor recommended to the board of trustees that the university undertake a planning process that would reduce the scope of its activities and concentrate its resources on fewer programs. His report, which he drafted on the basis of his conversations with the LRPC, provided a rationale for retrenchment, the criteria for discontinuance, and a planning calendar recommending at least eighteen months for consideration by the entire university community. No programs were identified as potential targets; the report recommended only the details of a planning process. The Board of Trustees approved the report in December 1978.

No actions were taken by the administration for eight months, while the university community mulled over the retrenchment process. After minimal debate about whether the faculty, not the Board of Trustees, had the authority to eliminate degree programs, the Academic Council recommended that the LRPC continue to represent the faculty, that its membership be expanded to include two additional council members, and that the LRPC be permitted to advise the administration directly, without requiring full review first by the council as a whole. The chancellor stated that if the LRPC did not agree with his final recommendations, the committee would be invited to address the board of trustees.

In August 1979, the chancellor issued a second report, in which he identified six programs to be considered for discontinuance and proposed a process for reviewing each of these programs according to the criteria identified in the earlier report. The LRPC was divided into six subcommittees, each of which was supplemented with another member of the general faculty and was responsible for reviewing one of the six programs. Based on its own analysis of institutional data, consultation with the affected program administrators, and the reports of external reviewers, each subcommittee made a recommendation for retrenchment, reorganization, or continuance to the full committee, which made its final recommendations to the chancellor in June 1980.

In September, the chancellor submitted the committee's recommendations, unaltered, to the Board of Trustees *for its information*. It was at this stage that the larger university community had the opportunity to react to the recommendations. The Academic Council listened to testimony from each of the affected units during the following three months and endorsed the recommendations in December. The Board of Trustees gave its approval immediately thereafter. One school and one degree program was discontinued; one school and one research laboratory were continued, contingent on further review; one department was reorganized; and one department remained intact.

Yale University

In the late 1960s, Yale like many universities was deeply engaged in debates about the nature of the relationship between the university and the external society. A particular issue at

Yale was university investments and relationships to corporations in which the university held securities. In 1969, President Kingman Brewster asked a group of faculty members to organize an interdisciplinary seminar to explore investor responsibility issues. One result of the seminar was a book, *The Ethical Investor: Universities and Corporate Responsibility* (Simon, Powers, and Gunnemann, 1972), which examined universities' ethical responsibilities in managing investments and outlined "Guidelines for the Consideration of Factors Other Than Maximum Return in the Management of the University's Investments." These guidelines, in reality a sample policy designed for adoption by colleges and universities, established criteria and procedures by which a university could respond to requests from members of its community that the university take into account values in addition to economic return when making investment decisions and when exercising its rights as a shareholder. In 1972, the Yale Corporation adopted a version of these guidelines as a formal policy, and the guidelines subsequently served as a blueprint for ethical investment policies adopted by other universities.

While Yale's ethical investment policy does not fit neatly into any of the strategic categories we have discussed thus far, we have included it as an example of faculty participation in a domain creation and substitution strategy for several specific reasons. First, the policy "repositions" Yale with regard to several key external constituencies, including donors, alumni, and corporations in which Yale invests. The university no longer takes a value-neutral position on investments, nor does it invest solely on the basis of maximum economic return. Rather, it has formally adopted a policy, which includes the criterion of minimizing social injury from the activities of companies in which Yale holds securities. Thus the ethical investment policy significantly altered Yale's relationship with its environment, particularly in 1972, when a policy of this type was unique. Therefore the policy represents a strategic action of no minor consequence to a private university heavily dependent upon private funds. Second, the policy involves sharing authority over financially related issues that have traditionally fallen under the exclusive control of administration and trustees.

The Yale policy involved the creation of two standing committees, the Corporation Committee on Investor Responsibility (CCIR) and the Advisory Committee on Investor Responsibility (ACIR). The CCIR is composed exclusively of members of the corporation (Yale's trustees) and retains control over investment policy and all investment decisions. In discharging its responsibility, the CCIR is assisted by the ACIR, composed of two students, two alumni, two faculty, and two staff members, all of whom are appointed by the president of Yale. The ACIR performs the practical work of policy implementation for the CCIR. Two of its principal tasks are to advise on the voting of corporate proxies dealing with ethical issues and to communicate with companies regarding compliance with Yale policy.

The dynamics of this policy and process have varied over the last fifteen years. During the first six years, several hundred issues were raised and resolved through this mechanism. More recently, the major issue under study has been divestment from South Africa. The establishment of the policy and process has not necessarily led to preemptory action; as of the spring of 1988, Yale had not totally divested its holdings in companies doing business with South Africa. The existence of the dual committees, particularly the ACIR, has been perceived to be of value in providing a campus-based forum to focus discussion and analysis of ethical investment issues before submission to the corporation.

There are several interesting elements of this example of shared authority on strategic policy. First, a draft policy and supporting philosophy were developed by a group of faculty and students with relevant expertise (i.e., law, philosophy, ethics, economics, and religious studies) who worked together over the course of a year and sought broad-ranging criticism. Second, the policy as implemented by the corporation retains trustee control over the policy and over final decisions on investments. This not only maintains the tradition of administrative (trustee) primacy on financial issues but also places the locus of decision making in the hands of individuals formally separated from the academic community, thus helping to limit the politicization of the academic community itself. Third, the creation of the ACIR puts into place a group of individuals from the academic

community who can provide advice and analysis to the corporation committee. While this is not an unusual device, the Yale policy explicitly calls for individuals to be named to the ACIR who have knowledge of the subject-matter areas in which investment questions are likely to occur and/or who have training in one of the various disciplines pertinent to the resolution of the questions which are likely to arise. This concern with "expertise," as opposed to representation of plural interests, is a usual aspect of the Yale policy. The concept was explicitly outlined by Simon et al. (1972), who made a strong case that certain professional, scientific, and analytical skills on policy questions of this type exist within the academic community and should be brought to bear on strategic policy issues. The stress on expertise extended to the provision of financial staff to the ACIR as a means of assisting in the assessment of corporate issues. To provide more thorough and efficient research and analysis of ethical investment issues, Yale joined with other universities and foundations in establishing the Investor Responsibility Research Center (IRRC) in 1972. An independent, not-for-profit clearinghouse, the IRRC conducts research and publishes impartial reports on contemporary social and public policy issues and the impact of those issues on major corporations and institutional investors.

While the Yale ethical investment policy does not deal exclusively with faculty participation (other constituencies are also involved), it provides an interesting example of a process and a structure for faculty participation in strategic policy issues.

Antioch College

Following World War II, Antioch College held a reputation as one of the most distinctive liberal arts colleges of quality in the United States (Clark, 1970). The college was particularly well known for its collegial form of governance and, in the 1960s, helped to articulate an early position statement on shared governance (Keeton, 1971). Since that time, Antioch has gone through a marked decline, culminating in the suspension of pay to all employees in 1979. While Antioch continues as a viable institution, its rapid decline serves as a negative case of strategic policy-making in the context of a liberal arts college (Wilson, 1985).

Indeed, the case of Antioch College serves as a microcosm for many of the points made in this essay. During the last twenty years, the college was confronting a changing environment of opportunities and threats as represented by differing cohorts of new faculty, students, and administrators; the emergence of active social movements with strong attractions to Antioch; changes in federal student funding with substantial impact upon a campus fully committed to a work-study program; and the changing agendas of prominent foundations. Liberal arts colleges, particularly those with innovative traditions such as Antioch, have boundaries,which are quite permeable to changing social and cultural intrusions. Therefore a critical function of strategic policy-making is to identify those intrusions that promote the institution's purpose and those which do not, and to devise mechanisms to capitalize on the former and to minimize the latter.

In the case of Antioch, several strategic policies were chosen which led to its decline. The first was the development of a laissez-faire first-year program with credit automatically awarded, partially funded by grants from the Danforth and Exxon Foundations. The second was the active recruitment in 1968–1973 of urban ghetto black students, unfamiliar and uncomfortable with the academic traditions of a liberal arts college. This program was supported by the Rockefeller Foundation. The third, and most significant, policy was the creation of the Network, a program of satellite campuses designed to empower through education Vietnam veterans, prisoners, urban ethnic groups, and the rural poor of Appalachia. The programs of these satellite campuses were heterogeneous and the sites widely scattered; the rapid growth of the network was supported by funds from the Ford Foundation. Ultimately, the president's office was relocated from the traditional Yellow Springs campus, and Antioch was renamed a university, with the attendant problems of loss of control over faculty recruitment, admissions, quality control, and financial resources by the Yellow Springs faculty, as well as increasing demands for local autonomy by the satellite campuses.

While much of this change was fostered by a single president, it is reasonable to ask why faculty authority and governance were not influential in altering those strategic policies which threatened the institution's integrity and led to its decline. Wilson (1985) suggests several currents of the external culture which had a profound impact at Antioch. First, the value of equality which was influential on many institutions during the governance period of democratic participation made a substantial impact upon the governance process at Antioch, possibly because of a strong Quaker tradition of community rather than collegial government. Distinctions between staff members, even the appropriateness of differentiating the role and unique skill of faculty members, came to be seen as invidious. Individual faculty selection came to be based upon a rough equality of potential, and work was judged by universal criteria. Teachers, administrators, and persons involved in job placement were equally faculty: at one point, the longtime headwaiter at the Tea Room was made an honorary faculty member. Once the classification *faculty* was diluted, it had a profound effect on governance, since the title of faculty member conferred an equal vote in shaping organization policy and practice. Furthermore, the commitment to equality, at least in this setting, led to an antagonism to evaluation. Hence, there was little incentive to assess the relative effectiveness of various products, procedures, or "processors."

A second valued characteristic of the larger society was pluralism, interpreted as a celebration of diversity, tolerance, and the open marketplace of ideas. Wilson suggests that pluralism can also lead to an indifference to the public costs of private aggrandizement. In the absence of shared beliefs, groups will rationally act in their own self-interest, because investment in the community's welfare provides an insufficient return to the individual or group. The assumption that the welfare of the larger academic community will be maintained by an "invisible hand" through the competing interests of rival groups therefore proved false in the Antioch case. The demands of interest groups, constituencies internal to the traditional campus or the new satellite campuses themselves, had no limits and tended to outrun the potential resources. Lacking the common value commitment of faculty members to the maintenance of an academic enterprise, the centrifugal forces of the interest groups caused the continuing organization to fly apart.

The net effect of these collective forces appears to be one of devolving the governance process at Antioch from a collegial structure, involving the formal agencies of administration and the tenured faculty with a long-term commitment, to informal pressure groups of students and others with a transient interest in the community. Consequently, the changes in the institution's environment, moderated by adaptations in the institution's governance process, were influential in the college's decline.

Effectiveness of Consultation Strategies

The six stages of consultation listed earlier provide a useful basis for the analysis of these six case studies. A major point of variation is the nature of the consultation, whether faculty participation is through an *ad hoc* process to study a particular strategic issue, or through a standing committee with oversight responsibility. The cases reported here represent the practice as illustrated in the larger literature. Standing committees are most typically employed in the domain consolidation strategy of ongoing planning and budgeting processes, as at Princeton and West Virginia. *Ad hoc* committees are most typically employed in domain offense or domain creation and substitution strategies, such as program review and retrenchment, as at Berkeley and Duke.

The distinction between *ad hoc* and standing committees is useful for examining the process of *early consultation*. As a step in a consultative process, early consultation is most critical for *ad hoc* committees and task forces, since by definition they often represent initial attempts to grapple with a problem or issue. In the two cases of Berkeley and Duke, consultation with *ad hoc* committees seemed to play a very important role in defining the issue. Before naming the Internal Biological Sciences Review Committee, the responsible vice-chancellor at Berkeley had numerous discussions with faculty and administrators and had commissioned a study of the situation, which was widely circulated before the committee was named. At Duke University, the chancellor spent eight full months discussing the situation and considering alternative approaches with the Long Range Planning Committee (which

represented the faculty leadership) before proposing a possible planning process for the university community's consideration. In both situations, the faculty's opportunity to shape the agenda was largely through informal discussions rather than through formal negotiations. As Reid (1982) suggested in an analysis of administrative evaluation at the University of Toledo, if *ad hoc* faculty participation is to be effective it must occur early, at the point of the development of general policy, such as evaluation criteria and procedures.

In the case of ongoing standing committees, early consultation is common but is structured in a different manner. For example, as at Yale, where a faculty seminar was the basis for the initial thinking on a possible policy for ethical investment, standing committees are often themselves the products of initial *ad hoc* committees or task forces which develop a recommendation for the president and/or the trustees. Thus the alternative forms and procedures for ongoing strategic policy-making in these institutions are often set in place through early consultation with faculty-dominated committees. Even with well-established standing committees on planning and budgeting, such as those at Princeton and West Virginia, faculty input in the annual cycle is emphasized *early*, usually at the stage of generating planning assumptions and budgetary criteria, rather than attempting to involve faculty members in the frequently frantic last moments of budgetary allocations.

As illustrated in these cases, the *joint formulation of procedures* occurs, but usually not in a joint committee structure. As at Berkeley, Duke, and Yale, the administration anticipates an area of strategic action such as retrenchment or ethical investment and then turns first to *ad hoc* faculty groups to outline the policies, procedures, and criteria by which these strategic policies should be implemented. Based upon our review of the literature, *ad hoc* committees in program review and retrenchment are frequently composed exclusively of faculty members, as at Berkeley and Duke, for the purpose of maintaining the integrity of faculty primacy in academic programs and procedure. The joint formulations of procedures for strategic policy-making usually begin with the administration's setting the agenda by charging an *ad hoc* task force, and by circulating background papers. A period of bargaining then follows in which administrators negotiate with faculty committees over subsequent recommendations. What is distinctive about the Antioch College case is the apparent bypassing of the faculty for a community wide constituency for defining and deciding strategic policy questions.

In contrast to these largely *ad hoc* processes of joint formulation, the more familiar "joint committee" procedure is visible in the planning and budgeting committees at Princeton and West Virginia. In those cases, standing committees are composed of senior members of the faculty, the chief academic and financial officers of the institution, and other members of the academic community. In the case of Yale, the use of hierarchically related committees (the CCIR, with ultimate responsibility for policy decisions, and the campus-based ACIR, which carries out the function of issue identification and analysis) provides a joint process of decision making. While standing committee structures emphasize joint deliberation, their effectiveness is greatest when the values and processes by which they work are firmly established by earlier consultation, by previous iterations of the same committee, or by well-understood institutional traditions.

Sufficient *time to formulate responses* is always relative, but critical is the care and seriousness with which responses are sought. Berkeley, for example, set in motion an extended process involving an internal committee, an external visiting committee, and several studies prior to the implementation of programmatic decisions. Yale's establishment of a standing advisory committee on ethical investment with analytical support and opportunity for submissions by members of the academic community suggests a commitment to seeking responses. The Duke University case provides an excellent example of how a decision-making process can be designed to give both the committee and all constituencies at large the opportunity and time to consider questions of process and to generate alternative recommendations. It is not clear to what degree the Long-Range Planning Committee supported the determination that retrenchment was necessary, and certain avenues of participation were not offered by the administration. However, once the Board of Trustees had approved the general concept of retrenchment, the faculty had sev-

eral months to consider how the process should be undertaken and what the roles of the committee and the Academic Council should be. Before any potential targets were named, there was widespread support for the criteria and procedures that would be used to make the decision. In addition, after the administration made its recommendations to the trustees, three months were allotted for widespread consideration of the recommendations before final action was taken.

In all five positive cases, the administration provided healthy staff support and made relevant *information available* to assist the committees in making their recommendations. Special studies were made, and presentations or hearings were organized at all five institutions. The reports of external reviewers were employed at Berkeley and Duke. The two standing committees at West Virginia and Princeton utilized budgetary data and planning submissions, which have become standard in their deliberations.

Yale's use of a faculty seminar involving expertise from law, ethics, and economics was a unique and academically appropriate means of developing alternatives and criteria in an extremely contentious area. The university also committed financial staff to analyzing corporate practices and eventually joined with other nonprofit entities to found the Investor Responsibility Research Center, which now provides analytical investment services to many organizations. In this context, it is appropriate to note Wilson's (1985) observation that a critical weakness of the Antioch community was an opposition to the evaluation of different procedures and processes. Critical to the wise selection of strategic opportunities and to the evidence of inappropriate ones, Wilson argues, is effective organizational intelligence, or research and development, on the dynamic connection between organizational procedures and product.

The best context for *adequate feedback* and the *communication of decisions* is one in which it is very clear before the consultation process is initiated exactly how the results will be used. In five of the six cases, the planning assumptions, budget priorities, retrenchment recommendations, and ethical criteria fit neatly into a larger decision-making process to which the administration was fully committed and which *required* the results of faculty deliberation in order to move forward. Because the faculty's recommendation had a critical role to play, information was freely provided, and feedback came in the satisfying form of subsequent, even immediate, action. For example, in the Berkeley case, Trow (1983) reports that the vice-chancellor began implementing some of the recommendations even before the committee had completed its work. In the other four positive-case instances, committee recommendations were carried to the next level of decision making almost immediately, which requires that one assume adequate informal consultation between committee and administration throughout the process.

This ongoing informal consultation was characteristic of several processes. Informal discussions were held between the Duke chancellor and the Program Review Committee. Hearings were used in the Duke, Princeton, and West Virginia instances because they promote both the opportunities for in-person representation and immediate feedback. Princeton's budget and planning committee regularly distributed reports of its activities through the campus newspaper to inform the larger community. Also, by virtue of their joint composition and involvement in the budgeting cycle, the faculty and student members of the Princeton and West Virginia committees are continually apprised of administrative reactions to their proposals. Within the parallel structure at Yale University, the ACIR formulates and presents recommendations to the CCIR directly and thereby is assured of immediate feedback.

In contrast to these various feedback mechanisms, the communication of decisions *appears* straightforward. Decisions are made, the academic community is thus notified. The size, complexity, and variety of constituencies within colleges and universities give the lie to this simple assumption. At Princeton and West Virginia, the implementation of the budget clearly signals the decisions made, but at Duke and Berkeley, the administration was cognizant of the importance of communicating not only the decisions made about academic programs but also the values behind the decisions and the processes used. Given the structure of academic communities, strategic policies offer an important opportunity to communicate the basic culture and values of an institution, particularly those that represent strategic shifts from previous traditions (Feldman and March, 1981). For

this reason, extensive written analyses are often a hallmark of communicating decisions. The leadership at Yale, for example, felt it necessary to distribute to all members of the community a detailed broadsheet, "Yale University Investments in South Africa" (1986), explaining the institution's position on South African investments and its relationship to the existing ethical investment policy. Perhaps the best known and most effective use of communicating strategic policies in a way that builds and maintains community values is Stanford's annual report on its operating budget (Chaffee, 1983). Distributed annually to all members of the academic community, this document articulates the issues confronting Stanford, the priorities to be implemented through the upcoming budget, and the allocation of the operating budget to achieve the stated ends. Thus, the members of the academic community are not required to seek out what decisions have been made, or to try to interpret the purpose of decisions; rather, the logic of decisions and their relationship to the community's values and norms are presented to each participant, each year.

Expertise: The Missing Element of Faculty Participation

The six cases just reviewed also suggest some dimensions of faculty participation in strategic decision-making, which are not emphasized in recent writings on the subject (Floyd, 1985; Mortimer and McConnell, 1978; Powers and Powers, 1983). The most notable is the dimension of faculty experience and expertise. For example, in the Berkeley case, an internal team of respected scholars evaluated the quality of faculty research in the multiple departments of the biological sciences on the campus. Partially as a result of their findings, the various departments were placed in a form of receivership, and all future personnel decisions of each department were to be screened by a campus committee of distinguished biologists. Similarly, in the Yale case, a strong argument was made that members of the Advisory Committee on Investor Responsibility should be selected not simply to represent various constituencies of the academic community, but at least partly by the criteria of expertise, that is, with regard to their professional knowledge of relevant policy issues (e.g., environmental pollution) and/or basic fields of knowledge (e.g., economics or ethics). In their analysis of the concept of ethical investment, Simon et al. (1972) explicitly argue that the university community possesses professional, scientific, and analytical skills which should be brought to bear on the policy issues confronting universities. In both cases, there appears to be recognition that certain strategic questions posed to contemporary colleges and universities require not representative opinion, but expert academic opinion.

This represents an apparent shift in the bases for authority and participation, from those commonly articulated during the period of democratic participation. During that period, the templates of "representative democracies" (McConnell and Mortimer, 1971) and of "oligarchies" (Eckert and Hanson, 1973) were laid against the prevailing models of faculty senates, and the senates were found wanting in the first instance and predictably flawed in the second. Even as late as 1978, Mortimer and McConnell criticized the composition of the Committee on Budget and Interdepartmental Relations at Berkeley, which appraises qualifications for merit salary increases and for appointment, tenure, and promotion. Mortimer and McConnell report that "only senior scholars with records of superior research productivity were appointed to the Budget Committee. *The definition of superior research productivity was so restrictive as to exclude all but a small number of Berkeley's faculty members*" (p. 39; italics added). It is ironic to examine this criticism of the distribution of faculty authority at Berkeley in 1978, in the light of the current effort to reorganize the biological sciences at the campus.

The attention to experience and expertise also represents a different perspective from the current organizational involvement model (Austin and Gamson, 1983, Floyd, 1985). In this perspective, the contemporary arguments of organizational theory and Japanese management are introduced as a rationale for faculty (and staff) participation in increasingly centralized strategic decisions (Lawler, 1986). The lack of participation, particularly among highly educated professionals, is assumed to promote faculty alienation, dissatisfaction, and lowered

commitment to the organization. A sense of individual satisfaction and involvement requires building a "corporate" vision or culture, which can be achieved only through participative mechanisms and joint decision-making.

These studies provide useful insights into the possible causes for low morale, low satisfaction, and faculty turnover. But similar to the arguments for democratic participation, they diminish academic organizations to the category of organizations committed to political or economic purposes. While the proponents of democratic participation adopt a political perspective which leads to equal representation in decision making (Wilson, 1985), the proponents of "involvement" adopt a therapeutic perspective which similarly leads to a need to involve all parties. Neither model is attentive to the changing *content* of academic decision-making. The net effect is to lessen the centrality of faculty expertise and authority in the determination of the core processes and procedures of academic organizations.

Both the proponents of democratic participation and the contemporary proponents of faculty and staff involvement ignore the traditional argument for faculty participation: the notion of a self-governing guild or community of scholars, who controlled the judgments necessary for maintaining the community because they *possessed the knowledge and expertise necessary for the decisions* (Clark, 1963). Furthermore, research on organizations in changing environments suggests that it is precisely in these conditions that professional experience and expertise become critical, because of the need to make strategic policy choices concerning core programs, technologies, and processes (Cameron and Ulrich, 1986; Katz, 1974; Wilson, 1985). Academic organizations reverse the hierarchy of business organizations in that faculty members possess the "line" expertise necessary to evaluate the feasibility of strategic proposals brought forward by administrative staff relating to academic programs, research, and the supporting infrastructure (Etzioni, 1964). But under the pressure of transformational environments, college and university administrators may usurp strategic policy-making because the emerging policy issues transcend the traditional departmental locus of faculty authority (e.g., policies on universitywide computer systems), and/or because the collegial norms and controls which support shared authority have eroded (Clark, 1983). We would argue, therefore, that the philosophical basis for faculty participation in strategic policy-making ironically rests in a renewed appreciation of traditional forms of faculty authority and control.

The Guild Model and Strategic Policy-Making

Clark (1983) has argued that "guild authority," characteristic of traditional academic organizations, is composed of personal authority, which is grounded in functionally based expertise, and collegial authority, which is collective control by a body of peers through norms congenial to the expression of expert judgment. The concept of a guild is conventionally seen as archaic, if not oppressive, perhaps because guild systems of masters can act to retard or repress creativity or innovation among "journeymen" (cf. the view that tenure and promotion decisions in academia act to promote conventional ideologies). Marx (1965) argued that guild systems would disappear in a capitalist society as the patriarchal relationship between master and journeyman came to be replaced by the monetary relationship between capitalist and worker. This replacement has largely occurred in modern society and is part of the reason for the current orientation toward participation and involvement as a means of diminishing the alienation which has supposedly ensued (Lawler, 1986). The guild model has persisted, however, particularly in elite research universities and liberal arts colleges, where collegial forms of governance dominated by senior academics selected on merit still exist.

The fundamental conflict between the traditional guild model and democratic participation was articulated by Wolff (1969). He suggested, similarly to Wilson (1985), that the portrayal of a university as a "multiversity" (Kerr, 1963), composed of equal but competing subcommunities, leads to the adoption of the American model of democratic pluralism as a model for internal governance (see, e.g., Baldridge, 1971). Wolff (1969) argues that reliance on the pressure-group politics of pluralistic democracy leaves the institution unable to distinguish between good and bad pressures, or between legitimate and illegitimate policy choices (cf. the Antioch College case). Second, pluralism provides no collegial standards for decisions regarding the allocation of scarce resources; hence the resort to internal competitive markets, or "every tub on its own bottom," as a basis for the allocation of goods (Zemsky, Porter, and Oedel, 1978). Finally, Wolff questions whether the art of compromise characteristic of a pluralistic democracy, which makes sense when "interests" conflict, still makes sense when principals or central values conflict (e.g., in the Yale investment policy).

Instead, because of his view of the purpose of the university as educational excellence, Wolff (1969) called for a distribution of authority based upon demonstrated competence. Thus (1) standards of competence should be set by members of the profession who have demonstrated their own competence; (2) the relative superiority of competence should be acknowledged within the profession; (3) final authority should rest in the hands of the masters of each field, whose proven competence equips them to pass judgment; (4) the preponderance of authority belongs by right to the ablest members of the profession (regardless of age!); and (5) the administration ought to be a servant of the faculty, for as administration it *lacks the knowledge to define or enforce professional standards in a university.*

Viewed simply as a rhetorical device, Wolff's argument is helpful in highlighting the distinctions between the respective models of faculty control and democratic participation. But it can also be viewed as a contemporary rearticulation of the guild model of governance, in which masters, by virtue of individual authority vested in their academic expertise, act collegially to set the fundamental conditions for the practice of the profession.

From this perspective, the observed behaviors in our six case studies can be reviewed. First, faculty participation in strategic policy-making appears most effective when faculty "masters" articulate the collegial norms whereby subsequent decisions are to be made and interpreted. In this manner, the collegial norms which help to sustain the guild and to control the behavior of overly entrepreneurial or independent administrators can be maintained. These collegial norms, or policies, include, for example, the criteria and process for closing programs at Duke, *not* the programs to be closed; and the priorities and criteria for university investment decisions at West Virginia and Princeton, *not* the budgetary allocations themselves. Second, on academically strategic or policy initiating issues, the faculty masters should initially act independently in order to maintain and sustain the reality of faculty authority (e.g., as at Duke, Berkeley, and Yale and, as a negative example, Antioch). Third, in establishing faculty committees, *competence* should take precedence over interest group representation. The primacy of competence in the case of the Berkeley review is remarkable, and it illustrates in part the reaction against the model of democratic participation and pluralism in the current transformational environment. However, in many strategic decisions (for example, the type of computer infrastructure in which the university should invest), the *nature* of the appropriate competence is not always obvious. Here Yale's argument for expertise in policy-related areas (e.g., a faculty member with acknowledged experience with large-scale computerized data bases) or for knowledge in a substantively related field (e.g., an electrical engineer) may be relevant to committee composition. In this sense, as strategic policies become increasingly technical and related to fundamental academic processes, such as the design of research facilities, the maintenance of the democratic participation governance model can become destructive to the effectiveness of the institution.

In sum, we would argue that the effective employment of faculty participation in strategic policy-making can be interpreted as the reassertion of a guild tradition of faculty authority over the recent models of democratic participation and pluralism. Fundamental to this development is attention to the primacy of academic expertise in the establishment of collegial norms to govern strategic decisions.

Conclusion

The contemporary environmental pressures for strategic policy-making can lead to an alteration in the structure of authority within academic institutions. In its most dysfunctional form, this change in structure can result in ad-

ministrative centralization or autocracy. But in the cases of faculty participation reviewed here, the response to strategic change appears in the most effective instances to have led to a reassertion of academic meritocracy over pluralism and democratic participation.

We have argued that the critical importance of expertise in strategic policy-making provides some guidance to the issue of the distribution of authority and the role of faculty participation. Hardy et al. (1983) have suggested that the strategic decisions of institutions of higher education introduced previously can be partitioned into those of administrative fiat (comparable to administrative primacy), professional judgment (comparable to faculty primacy), and collective judgment (comparable to shared authority). Administrators possess the expertise to make strategic decisions regarding financial investments, buying and selling property, embarking on fund-raising campaigns, and a number of support services clearly under administrative control, such as alumni and public relations, athletics and archives, accounting and payroll, printing, and building services and physical plant. In all of these areas, the professional expertise for making decisions of domain creation and substitution, domain offense, or consolidation is most likely to rest in administrative hands. Professional judgment, by contrast, clearly controls what matters to research and teaching. But because of the potential for the research activity or teaching interests of a single faculty member to evolve into a unique new program, Hardy et al. (1983) rightly note that the exercise of professional judgment by individual faculty members can often produce strategic consequences such as a whole new product or activity for an institution. In contrast, overt strategic policies need to be articulated by a process of collective choice utilizing a variety of interactive processes involving faculty members and administrators. These policies include (1) the definition, creation, design, and discontinuation of programs, departments, and research centers; (2) promotion, tenure and hiring decisions; (3) budgeting priorities; and (4) the design of critical academic support services, such as libraries and computers. Thus both the traditional "Statement on Government of Colleges and Universities" (1966) and the analysis of organizational theorists (Hardy et al., 1983) reach similar conclusions about the types of decisions which need to be arrived at through shared authority or collective choice.

Our review of the contemporary literature on strategic decision-making suggests a number of different mechanisms of participation whereby faculty knowledge and expertise are brought to bear on strategic policy issues. In addition, we have raised a number of related questions, which might help to guide and reinvigorate research on academic governance.

1. Research on academic governance must be more attentive to the variance in authority environments among institutions of higher education which exists and appears to be increasing. More systematic analyses of the dynamics of collective bargaining in community and junior colleges, of the process of collegial decision-making in liberal arts colleges, and of mechanisms for the collective exercise of faculty expertise in research universities are needed to increase our understanding. In each of these instances, an attention to the *process* of decision making is critical. In contrast, models or analyses of faculty governance which sample institutions without sensitivity to existing variations within institutions are of little value.

2. Mechanisms to promote what Wilson (1985) has termed *centripetal forces*—and what we would term *collegial norms*—are of critical importance to academic institutions, given their inevitable tendency toward differentiation and specialization. In this sense, the communication of decisions is an understudied and potentially critical component of the maintenance of collegial forms of governance. As Feldman and March (1981) have suggested, academic decision-making is itself a symbolic representation of the academic community's belief in the pursuit of truth. Therefore, the process for reaching those decisions and communicating them offers a critical opportunity for maintaining an institution's core culture. The communication and implementation stage of academic decision-making has received very little attention, possibly because of a bias toward political models of participation.

3. The relationship between academic governance and the quality and nature of information available for decision making is an interesting and growing area of importance. As Wilson (1985) suggests, traditional models of academic

authority are difficult to sustain, particularly in times of change, without careful "research and development" on the relationships between processes and products. It might even be asserted, that in the absence of some concrete institutional "screening mechanism" to identify the characteristics of a college or university's products, it is spurious to argue that any common institutional goals exist (Dill, 1988). In this sense, the current concern with measuring "academic outcomes" (see Ewell, this volume) represents another example of the fundamental change occurring in the nature of the policy choices confronting contemporary colleges and universities. The relationship between institutional efforts toward serious research and development (e.g., background research and professional staffing of faculty committees, or investment in outcomes assessment) and the maintenance of faculty authority and control is a topic of significant importance for the decades ahead.

4. We have suggested that the environmental factors affecting colleges and universities are changing and that market forces will lead to increasing differentiation among types of institutions of higher education. One model which could be usefully applied in understanding the dynamics of this process and its implications for the distribution of authority within academic institutions is the ecological model of organizations (Aldrich, 1979; Birnbaum, 1983).

At the outset, we argued that because academic organizations are "value-rational" organizations, an inquiry into the bases of authority of these institutions constitutes an inquiry into their core values as well. The application of "political models" to academic institutions (Baldridge, 1971; Kerr, 1963) can thereby be seen as not simply a descriptive exercise, but a normative one as well, with profound implications for our conceptions of academic institutions. The significance of this shift in orientation and tone is only now being examined (Wilson, 1985), although the larger debate between pluralism and community is now active in our society (Bellah et al., 1985; Bloom, 1987; MacIntyre, 1981). Perhaps the most fundamental and needed scholarship is that which examines the changing models and underlying values which inform our study of academic governance.

References

Aldrich, H. E. (1979). *Organizations and Environments.* Englewood Cliffs, NJ: Prentice-Hall.

Anderson. R. E. (1983). *Finance and Effectiveness: A Study of College Environments.* Princeton, NJ: Educational Testing Service.

Arch, E., and Kirschner, S. (1984). Lewis and Clark College: gender balancing as a catalyst for institutional change. *Educational Record* 65: 48–52.

Armijo, F., Hall, R. S., Lenning, O. T., Jonas, S., Cherin, E., and Harrington, C. (1980). *Comprehensive Institutional Planning: Studies in Implementation.* Boulder, CO: National Center for Higher Education Management Systems.

Austin, A. E., and Gamson, Z. F. (1983). *Academic Workplace: New Demands, Heightened Tensions.* (ASHE-ERIC/Higher Education Research Report No. 10.) Washington, DC: Association for the Study of Higher Education.

Baldridge, J. V. (1971). *Power and Conflict in the University: Research in the Sociology of Complex Organizations.* New York: Wiley.

Baldridge, J. V. (1982). Shared governance: a fable about the lost magic kingdom. *Academe* 68: 12–15.

Baldridge, J. V., Curtis, D. V., Ecker, G., and Riley, G. L. (1978). *Policy Making and Effective Leadership.* San Francisco: Jossey-Bass.

Baldridge, J. V., Kemerer, F. R., and associates. (1981). *Assessing the Impact of Faculty Collective Bargaining.* (AAHE-ERIC/Higher Education Research Report No. 8.) Washington, DC: American Association for Higher Education.

Begin, J. P. (1978). Statutory definitions of the scope of negotiations: the implications for traditional faculty governance. *Journal of Higher Education* 49: 247–260.

Bellah, R. N., Madsen, R., Sullivan, W. M., Swidler, A., and Tipton, S. M. (1985). *Habits of the Heart: Individualism and Commitment in American Life.* Berkeley: University of California Press.

Berte, N. R., and O'Neil, E. H. (1980). Managing the liberal arts institution: a case study. *Educational Record* 61: 25–33.

Birnbaum, R. (1983). *Maintaining Diversity in Higher Education.* San Francisco: Jossey-Bass.

Bloom, A. (1987). *The Closing of the American Mind.* New York: Simon & Schuster.

Bowen, F. M., and Glenny, L. A. (1980). *Uncertainty in Public Higher Education: Responses to Stress at Ten California Colleges and Universities.* Sacramento: California Postsecondary Education Commission.

Bradford, D. L., and Bradford, L. P. (1981). Temporary committees as ad hoc groups. In R. Payne and C. Cooper (eds.), *Groups at Work.* London: Wiley.

Cameron, K. S., and Ulrich, D. O. (1986). Transformational leadership in colleges and universities. In J. C. Smart (ed.), *Higher Education: Handbook of Theory and Research,* Vol. 2. New York: Agathon Press.

Campbell, J. W. (1983). Mount St. Mary's College: how one small liberal arts college involved the faculty in core curriculum revision. *Educational Record* 64: 57–60.

Carnegie Council on Policy Studies in Higher Education. (1977). *Faculty Bargaining in Public Higher Education.* San Francisco: Jossey-Bass.

Carnegie Foundation for the Advancement of Teaching. (1987). *The Carnegie Classification of Higher Education.* Princeton, NJ: Princeton University Press.

Caruthers, J. K., and Lott, G. B. (1981). *Mission Review: Foundation for Strategic Planning.* Boulder, CO: National Center for Higher Education Management Systems.

Chaffee, E. E. (1983). The role of rationality in university budgeting. *Research in Higher Education* 19: 387–406.

Chaffee, E. E. (1984). Successful strategic management in small private colleges. *Journal of Higher Education* 55: 212–241.

Clark, B. R. (1963). Faculty organization and authority. In T. F. Lunsford (ed.), *The Study of Academic Administration.* Boulder, CO: Western Interstate Commission for Higher Education.

Clark. B. R. (1970). *The Distinctive College: Antioch, Reed, and Swarthmore.* Chicago: Aldine Press.

Clark, B. R. (1983). *The Higher Education System.* Berkeley: The University of California Press.

Clark, B. R. (1987). *The Academic Life: Small Worlds, Different Worlds.* Princeton: Carnegie Foundation for the Advancement of Teaching.

Crawley, N. (1981). A tight budget forces Michigan State to make hard decisions. *Change* 13: 44–45.

Darby, D. A., Robinson, J. E., and Lick, D. W. (1979). A faculty-managed approach to instructional development. *Educational Record* 60: 87–92.

Dill, D. D. (1971). *Case Studies in University Governance.* Washington, DC: National Association of State Universities and Land-Grant Colleges.

Dill, D. D. (1982). The management of academic culture: notes on the management of meaning and social integration. *Higher Education* 11: 303–320.

Dill, D. D. (1988). Toward a system of educational quality control: national achievement tests and the "theory of screening." In R. Haskins and D. MacRae, Jr. (eds.), *Policies for America's Public Schools.* Norwood, NJ: Ablex.

Eckert, R. E., and Hanson, M. S. (1973). *The University Senate and Its Committees: An Analysis and Critique.* Minneapolis: College of Education, University of Minnesota.

Etzioni, A. (1964). *Modern Organizations.* Englewood Cliffs, NJ: Prentice-Hall.

Farmer, D. W. (1983). Developing a collegial approach to integrated planning at a small college: communication, understanding, and cooperation. *Planning for Higher Education* 11: 18–24.

Feldman, M., and March, J. G. (1981). Information in organizations as signal and symbol. *Administrative Science Quarterly* 16: 171–186.

Finkelstein, M. J. (1984). *The American Academic Profession: A Synthesis of Social Scientific Inquiry since World War II.* Columbus: Ohio State University Press.

Finkelstein, M., and Pfinister, A. O. (1984). The diminishing role of faculty in institutional governance: liberal arts colleges as the negative case. Paper presented at the annual meeting of the Association for the Study of Higher Education, Chicago, IL.

Floyd, C. E. (1985). *Faculty Participation in Decision-Making.* (ASHE-ERIC Higher Education Report No. 8.) Washington, DC: Association for the Study of Higher Education.

Franklin, P. (1982). Duke University: retrenchment can be accomplished without alienating the university community from its administration. *Educational Record* 63: 34–38.

Hardy, C. (1987). Turnaround strategies in universities. *Planning for Higher Education* 16: 9–23.

Hardy, C., Langley, A., Mintzberg, H., and Rose, J. (1983). Strategy formation in the university setting. *Review of Higher Education* 6: 407–433.

Herring, C. P., Lemonick, A., McCrudden, C., Schafer, C., and Spies, R. R. (1979). *Budgeting and Resource Allocation at Princeton University: Report of a Demonstration Project Supported by the Ford Foundation,* Vol. 2. Princeton, NJ: Princeton University Press.

Heydinger, R. B. (1982). *Using Program Priorities to Make Retrenchment Decisions: The Case of the University of Minnesota.* Atlanta: South Regional Education Board.

Hill, J. E. (1985). On a roll: term contracts at Curry College. *Educational Record* 66: 52–56.

Hodgkinson, H. L. (1974). *The Campus Senate: Experiment in Campus Democracy.* Berkeley: Center for Research and Development in Higher Education, University of California.

Hofstadter, R., and Metzger, W. P. (1955). *The development of academic freedom in the United States.* New York: Columbia University Press.

Jencks, C., and Riesman, D. (1977). *The Academic Revolution.* Chicago: University of Chicago Press.

Katz, D., and Kahn, R. L. (1978). *The Social Psychology of Organizations* (2nd ed.). New York: Wiley.

Katz, R. L. (1974). Skills of an effective administrator,. *Harvard Business Review.* (September–October): 90–102.

Keeton, M. (197 1). *Shared Authority on Campus.* Washington, DC: American Association for Higher Education.

Keller, G. (1983). *Academic Strategy: The Management Revolution in American Higher Education.* Baltimore: Johns Hopkins.

Kenen, P. B., and Kenen, R. H. (1978). Who thinks who's in charge here: faculty perceptions of influence and power in the university. *Sociology of Education* 51: 113–23.

Kerr, C. (1963). *The Uses of the University.* New York: Harper & Row.

Kieft, R. N. (1978). *Academic Planning: Four Institutional Case Studies.* Boulder, CO: National Center for Higher Education Management Systems.

Lawler, E. E., III (1986). *High-Involvement Management.* San Francisco: Jossey-Bass.

Leslie, L. L. (1980). The financial prospects for higher education in the 1980's. *Journal of Education* 51: 1–17.

MacIntyre, A. (1981). *After Virtue: A Study in Moral Theory.* Notre Dame: University of Notre Dame Press.

Marx, K. (1965). *Pre-Capitalist Economic Formations.* New York: International Publishers.

McConnell, T. R., and Mortimer, K. P. (1971). *The Faculty in University Governance.* Berkeley: Center for Research and Development in Higher Education, University of California.

Millett, J. C. (1978). *New Structures of Campus Power: Success and Failures of Emerging Forms of Institutional Governance.* San Francisco: Jossey-Bass.

Moore, M. A. (1978). On launching into exigency planning. *Journal of Higher Education* 49: 620–638.

Mortimer, K. P., Gunne, M. G., and Leslie, D. W. (1976). Perceived legitimacy of decision making and academic governance patterns in higher education: a comparative analysis. *Research in Higher Education* 4: 273–90.

Mortimer, K. P., and McConnell, T. R. (1978). *Sharing Authority Effectively.* San Francisco: Jossey-Bass.

Mortimer, K. P., and Tierney, M. L. (1979). *The Three "R's" of the Eighties: Reduction, Reallocation, and Retrenchment.* (AAHE-ERIC/Higher Education Research Report No. 4.) Washington, DC: American Association for Higher Education.

Peterson, K. R. (1985). Constraints on faculty participation in university governance: politics of retrenchment. Unpublished paper, North Carolina State University.

Peterson, K. R., and Moazed, K. L. (1986). Effective faculty participation in planning and decision-making. Paper presented at the annual meeting of the Society for College and University Planning, San Diego.

Poulton, N. L. (1980). Strategies of large universities. In P. Jedamus and M. W. Peterson (eds.), *Improving Academic Management.* San Francisco: Jossey-Bass.

Powers, D. R., and Powers, M. F. (1983). *Making Participatory Management Work.* San Francisco: Jossey-Bass.

Powers, D. R., and Powers, M. F. (1984). How to orchestrate participatory strategic planning without sacrificing momentum. *Educational Record* 65: 48–52.

Reid, J. Y. (1982). Politics and quality in administrator evaluation. *Research in Higher Education* 16: 27–39.

Ross, R. D. (1977). Faculty qualifications and collegiality: the role of influence in university decision making. *Research in Higher Education* 6: 201–214.

Satow, R. L. (1975). Value-rational authority and professional organizations: Weber's missing type. *Administrative Science Quarterly* 20: 526–531.

Shirley, R. C. (1983). Identifying the levels of strategy for a college or university. *Long Range Planning* 16: 10–15.

Simon, J. G., Powers, C. W., and Gunneman, J. P. (1972). *The Ethical Investor: Universities and Corporate Responsibility*. New Haven: Yale University Press.

Statement on government of colleges and universities. (1966). (Statement of the AAUP, ACE, and AGB). *AAUP Bulletin* 52: 375–379.

Tashman, L. J., Carlson, R., and Parke, E. L. (1984). A management lesson in curricular development. *Educational Record* 65: 54–56.

Teel, L. R. (1981). A coke and a smile: Emory University decides how to allot. *Change* 13: 12–21.

Trow, M. A. (1983). Organizing the biological sciences at Berkeley. *Change* 15: 28–53.

Vroom, V. H. (1984). Leaders and leadership in academe. In J. L. Bess (ed.), *College and University Organization: Insights from the Behavioral Sciences*. New York: New York University Press.

Vulgamore, M. L. (1981). Planning: the University of Richmond experience. *Educational Record* 62: 55–57.

Wilson, E. K. (1985). What counts in the death or transformation of an organization. *Social Forces* 64: 259–280.

Wolff, R. P. (1969). *The Ideal of the University*. Boston: The Beacon Press.

Yale University investments and South Africa. (1986). Office of the Vice President for Finance and Treasurer, Yale University.

Zammuto, R. F. (1986). Managing decline in American higher education. In J. C. Small (ed.), *Higher Education: Handbook of Theory and Research*, Vol. 2. New York: Agathon Press.

Zammuto, R. F., and Cameron, K. S. (1985). Environmental decline and organizational response. *Research in Organizational Behavior* 7: 223–262.

Zemsky, R., Porter, R., and Oedel, L. P. (1978). Decentralized planning: to share responsibility. *Educational Record* 59: 229–53.

Expanding Information and Decision-Support Systems

Dennis P. Jones

As noted in the introductory chapter to this volume, the context within which the planning function is being performed in higher education is becoming more complex and less predictable. For most institutions, both the size and nature of student demand are becoming more variable. Performance expectations—as expressed by all external clients—are rising and being stated in more explicit, and frequently more narrowly defined, ways. The explosion in educational technology and telecommunications creates enormous opportunities for innovation and change in teaching and learning activities, and in how that information can be stored and used in support of planning and management functions. However, this same technology has created conditions under which many more providers—both inside and outside the established academy—can offer instruction to students in any given location. Coupled with the actions of the western governors to create a "virtual university" that would award credentials as well as promote delivery of instruction through use of technology, this heightened capacity promises to significantly change the higher education landscape in the coming decades. And while the external environment is becoming more chaotic, there is less and less margin for error in institutional decision making; years of tight budgets and more precise budgeting practices have long since removed the cushion in most institutions.

The unforgiving nature of the decision-making environment creates an understandable demand from college administrators for information that can reduce some of the uncertainty. Interestingly, the same set of environmental forces creates a demand for more, and different, information on the part of external constituents as well. There is behavioral evidence that more state governments are seeking to define their relationships with higher education institutions through market mechanisms rather than solely through control and regulatory devices. (Witness, for example, the rising popularity of incentive and performance funding schemes.) State and federal agencies are also assuming a responsibility in the marketplace on behalf of students, recognizing that the free-market system works only to the extent that consumers are fully informed about the existence, and consequences, of available choices. With this in mind, it may well be that a feature of future decision-support systems is the extent to which they not only are *about* the external environment but represent the interests of the external environment as well.

The impact of technology must be noted again at this juncture. It is not only a major factor that must be considered in institutional planning; advances in computing and other technologies provide those responsible for the planning function with much more powerful tools than were previously available. This technology allows analysts the luxury of creating and effectively using much larger databases than were feasible just a few years ago. They can build databases with more records; more importantly, they can accommodate more data elements per record. As a result, fewer data are

"Expanding Information and Decision-Support Systems," by Dennis P. Jones, reprinted from *Planning and Management for a Changing Environment*, edited by M. W. Peterson, D.D. Dill and L. A. Mets, 1997. Jossey-Bass Publishers, Inc.

lost between the point of original collection and the creation of the analytical database. This capacity has a downside in that it largely removes the need for discipline in the creation of databases; everything can get entered, without prior judgment about use and utility.

Technology is also becoming less and less expensive, allowing more and more capacity to be widely distributed within the institution. The tools that go with this capacity are also becoming cheaper and much more powerful. Available tools allow users to retrieve data in almost any conceivable combination and to display the results in whatever formats best suit the needs of the user, all without the requirement of considerable technical expertise.

Finally, technology has opened the door to almost limitless supplies of data and information that originate and reside at sites external to the campus. Data about demographics, employment, the economy, and many other factors that must be considered in the planning process are now available on CD-ROM and, increasingly, on the Internet. The latest research findings and ideas about the use of these data are available electronically as well. And when all else fails, electronic bulletin boards allow planners and analysts to ask questions of, and seek help from, colleagues around the globe.

The changes mentioned here are combining to overwhelm most institutions, which are not planning for the significant reforms that will allow them to align comfortably with emerging realities. Rather, they are seeking ways to continue business as usual—within the reality of increased demands and constrained resources. In addition, few are harnessing the power of the available technology to help themselves in meeting these challenges. Most institutions are awash in data but have very limited capacity to convert those data to information that supports planning. It is true that off-the-shelf tools allow users to shift the focus from the technology of building databases and retrieving data to use of data, that is, to analysis, interpretation, and the search for meaning. But most institutions have not made that leap. Although the technology also allows decentralization of data use and analysis, large numbers of institutions are still stuck in a mindset that funnels access to data through offices of institutional research or planning. In those places where the capacity to access data has been

widely dispersed, the operational failure to enforce a standard data architecture and to ensure that users have access to the same data has often created more problems than the technical capacity has resolved.

This brief overview paints a bleak picture of the increasingly chaotic environment in which higher education institutions are functioning, and of the institutions' capacity to support a planning function attuned to the forces within that environment. Creating and using the decision-support systems (DSS, or DS systems) that are most helpful in this evolving environment require a considerable change in the state of the art at most institutions. This chapter describes the ways in which decision-support systems have to change in order to help decision makers function effectively in the future. It starts with a description of the different perspectives—the needs of those different kinds of decision makers—that must be reflected in the design of DSS. Then the chapter describes the changes in current capacity and thinking that are required to serve the needs of internal and external decision makers, respectively. Throughout, the emphasis is on the contents and conceptual structures of the DSS rather than the technology or technologies through which decision-support systems are implemented. This focus reflects the author's observations that these are the areas in greatest need of attention.

The Matter of Perspective

At the most basic level, a decision-support system can be viewed as the capacity to compile and store appropriate pieces of data and to retrieve and organize these data (to transform data into information) in such a way that they (1) help a particular user or type of user (2) address a particular problem or issue. Thus, in thinking about the design and development of a decision-support system, the central question is "for whom?" Once this question is answered, subsequent questions about the kinds of problems or issues to which the system must be responsive become more readily apparent.

Because this chapter deals with decision support for planning (as opposed to operating) decisions, the answer to the central question is "for those individuals—presidents, vice presidents, board members, and administrators and faculty serving on institutionwide committees—who are engaged in making the strategic decisions about the future of the institution." Decision makers at this level deal with issues that are broad in scope, are often poorly defined, and do not recur on a regular basis. These characteristics have major implications for the design of DSS. Specifically, the systems must contain a broad array of data that can be accessed and used very flexibly. (Excluded are almost all applications of "expert systems," which have the most to offer in applying decision rules based on experts' judgments to operating decisions that must be made on a frequently recurring basis.)

By focusing on only these internal audiences, however, the developers of DSS run the risk of perpetuating a solely provider-driven perspective on critical issues and possible responses to them. Thus, they serve to reinforce the status quo. If there is any merit to the argument that changing demands and constrained resources force institutions to change in significant ways in order to be successful, then decision-support systems that congeal thinking around business as usual do a real disservice.

As an antidote to such hardening of the conceptual arteries, it is suggested that DSS be designed with a set of external users in mind, *regardless of whether or not these external users actually have access to it.* The design issue is not one of access; rather, access is one of the perspectives reflected in the design. It has often been said that there has been no significant change in higher education absent an impetus

from external forces. Given that market mechanisms are one of the means through which these external forces are most likely to bear upon colleges and universities, it is increasingly important that institutions understand their current (and potential future) position in that marketplace. There is perhaps no better way to accomplish this particular objective than by creating conditions under which institutional planners and decision makers can see the institution through the lenses of external clients of (that is to say, investors in) the enterprise. Consider the simple diagram presented in Figure 1.

From the perspective of someone situated within the institution (at point A), the view is of currently enrolled students (at point B), the competitors for potential students (other providers), and the existing set of relationships with state government and other external constituents. The student sees not only the institution at point A but the whole array of potential service providers, and a quite different set of relationships with state government. Decision makers at the state level necessarily see the demand expressed by all students as well as the full array of providers available to respond to that demand. This diagram also calls attention to the fact that the relationships among the entities, not just the characteristics of the entities themselves, are the important considerations in the planning process.

If institutional decision makers could put themselves in the shoes of critical external constituents—students, the state, employers, graduate/transfer institutions—and create the ca-

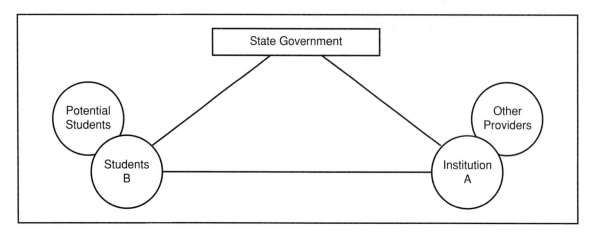

Figure 1 Perspectives on the Higher Education System.

pacity to inform the kinds of judgments these constituents routinely make, they would be in a much stronger position to make sound judgments within their own sphere of responsibility. From this point of departure, it is possible to deal more systematically with the kinds of information that will be required to support the planning function in colleges and universities in the difficult years ahead.

Planning as a Change Process

Planning is essentially a change process. As such, it requires explicit attention to:

- The "reality check": an honest appraisal of current conditions within the institution and in the external environment

- A determination of the desirable (or most likely) future conditions, along with an assessment of the extent to which external forces allow (or, indeed, require) the institution to move in these directions

- The kinds of steps necessary to move from the current position to the desired future condition

These generic steps apply as well to students selecting a college; to employers investing in workplace training or applied research; and to state governments concerned with improving K–12 education, with accommodating enrollment growth, or with other objectives involving higher education.

While the set of considerations is, on the surface, the same for a wide range of decision makers both inside and outside the enterprise, real differences appear when the specific interests of these different kinds of decision makers are addressed. As the old saying goes, the devil is in the details. As a consequence, it is instructive to address the prototypical questions faced by these different groups of decision makers and to explore the implications for the decision-support systems germane to such issues. Through this exercise, the changing requirements for the *contents* of a DSS can be brought into sharper focus.

Intra-Institutional Planning Decisions

In the final analysis, strategic planning within a college or university typically revolves around decisions about:

- Clientele: the different student bodies and other groups (types of employers and so on) that are the intended audiences and beneficiaries of the institution's programs and services

- Program: the array of programs and services to be offered

- Comparative advantage: characteristics of the institution and the ways it does business that are particularly attractive to clients and that distinguish it from competitors

- Asset structure: the creation and ongoing maintenance of the assets needed in order for the institution to fulfill its mission (including attention to human and programmatic assets as well as physical assets such as buildings, equipment, and library books)

- Mission: the statement of institutional purpose and uniqueness that encapsulates consideration of clientele, programs, and comparative advantage

These are the decision areas given most consideration in existing decision-support systems. A more in-depth review of these systems, however, usually reveals some serious gaps and design flaws. Among the major problems are:

- Missing data, more often than not occasioned by adopting a singular, internal perspective on any given issue.

- Failure to focus on the relationships. Either the necessary data to examine relationships are missing (for example, data about competitors or about underlying populations from which students are drawn) or the variables that allow the links to be made easily are absent.

- Failure to allow for appropriate disaggregations. Most analyses proceed from a general observation to more detailed investigations conducted in order to seek explanations for an observed phenomenon. Ewell (1995) labels the process "thinking in layers." Again, what is required is to include variables that allow the necessary disaggregations to be made.

- Inability to flag discrepancies. As noted previously, technology allows the user to "warehouse" almost limitless supplies of data. Often, the more data that are available, the more difficult it is to find meaning within them. Thus, DS systems have to be designed (using comparative statistics, trend data, and so on) to draw attention to conditions needing further analytic attention. Too frequently, information systems contain only cross-sectional, descriptive data that are insufficient for the task of flagging key changes or discrepancies.

Some of the typical problem areas, organized under the headings of the key strategic planning decisions. are noted in the following paragraphs.

Clientele

Data about clientele are rapidly becoming one of the stronger elements of the decision-support capacity at most institutions. Most institutions have a long-standing ability to provide descriptive, cross-sectional data about applicants and enrolled students. Spurred by student right-to-know legislation and by actions of state agencies and accrediting bodies, the capacity to conduct longitudinal, cohort-based student tracking studies has expanded rapidly in recent years. Even so, important gaps remain. To some extent, these gaps arise from a failure to capture the necessary data elements about current students. Ewell, Parker, and Jones (1988) indicate the array of data about existing clientele required to support the planning function:

- Demographic: student characteristics as well as data about the underlying populations from which they are drawn
- Educational background
- Enrollment status
- Student goals and objectives (included as part of enrollment status in the document cited)

- Term-by-term tracking data, including academic activity, academic performance, and remediation status
- Follow-up data that indicate students' involvement with other institutions of higher education and employers

Within this array, the data most frequently missing deal with outcomes, particularly those arising from sources outside the institution—from alumni and employers, for example. In addition, the data about prior academic history are likely to undergo substantial change in the next decade. Typically, these data reflect students' experiences at traditional educational institutions: high schools, colleges, and universities. Increasingly, however, students are receiving formal education in the workplace and having their learning recognized in the form of certifications that are widely accepted and utilized by employers. The Certified Network Engineer (CNE) and related certifications bestowed by Novell, Inc., are prime examples. Acceptance of such experiences and the competencies attained as legitimate components of prior academic history is likely to be increasingly important to clients of higher education and therefore to higher education institutions as well.

Missing in most institutional data systems are data about student goals and expectations. Historically, it has been assumed that students enroll in an institution to obtain a degree or certificate at that institution. A recent study (Adelman, 1996) found, however, that more than 60 percent of the students who began their studies in 1982 and received bachelor's degrees by 1995 attended two or more institutions; this proportion was up from about one-third a decade earlier (Adelman, 1996). In addition, many students who "drop out" before receiving a degree do so because they have fulfilled their objectives. In an increasingly market-driven environment with very mobile participants, most institutions will find it necessary to acquire and utilize data about student goals. Further, the fact that goals change means that these data have to be updated at least annually.

A larger gap, however, is failure to systematically acquire data on clients other than current students. Absence of data about employers is particularly notable. It is rare that data gathered through continuing education activities undertaken for employers or data found in business offices as a result of corporate tuition assistance programs find their way into planning databases. Even more rare is conscientious compilation of data about place of employment for current students. At a time when most students work and when workplace-based learning is increasingly important, failure to compile data that would allow an institution to identify the existing, student-created networks is especially problematic.

Another weak spot is failure to compile data about *potential* students. Most institutions do a reasonably good job of compiling data about recent high school graduates. Missing in most, however, is systematic attention to demographic data that would allow projection of part-time student enrollments—for example, Bureau of the Census data about numbers of twenty-five to forty-four-year-olds in the service area who have educational attainment levels that would qualify them for the institution's programs or employment data (from the State Occupational Information Coordinating Committee—SOICC—or other local sources) that would provide information on markets for continuing professional education. This weak spot reflects less an absence of available data than a failure to tap the rich array of data regularly collected by state and federal agencies. To make these data more readily available, agencies such as the Bureau of the Census and the Bureau of Labor Statistics are making basic data available on their Web sites.

Interestingly, some of the more important gaps arise out of analytic rather than database shortcomings; the data are there, but they are not utilized to full advantage. It is not uncommon, for example, to find situations in which longitudinal data are used in calculating retention or attrition rates, but the more extensive analyses are not being performed that would indicate characteristics of students who are not being successful at the institution. More common are circumstances in which data about important student activities or experiences—often experiences such as counseling or tutoring explicitly designed to help ensure academic success—are either not gathered at all or are gathered but not integrated into the longitudinal database. It is typical to find situations in which data about students' involvement with various support services are captured somewhere in the institution but never used in the analyses that explore the absence (or presence) of student success. Equally common are instances in which investment of student aid funds is not investigated for its impact on student retention and success. This is one of the rare instances in which data and the technology to use it are widely available but use of that capacity falls far short of its potential. Perhaps this is because analyses of longitudinal student data arise in response to external pressures; analysts develop a compliance mentality early on. In that environment, it is typical that analysts devise "hard wired" responses—COBOL programs that generate the required annual data report as a production run in the computer center—rather than flexible tools that allow successive disaggregation of data for use internally in the institution. Perhaps this is because the techniques have not been widely used for a sufficient period of time to yield a body of conventional wisdom about productive avenues for investigation. Whatever the reason, efforts that could ensure that the power of this capacity is brought to bear on key academic policy issues—the structure of the curricula, admissions policies, the availability of academic support services, and so on—are a requirement of decision-support terms designed to meet the needs of the coming decade.

Programs

Data about programs and services offered also are often incomplete because of the singular, provider perspective from which they have traditionally been developed. This provider perspective has led to the ready availability of certain kinds of data at most institutions, including those about:

- Levels of activity: student credit hours produced in instructional programs, revenues from research and contract training programs, and numbers of clients served in the various student service programs.

- Resources consumed: expenditures in various budget categories and, much less frequently, the full-time equivalents (FTEs) of various kinds of personnel utilized in the program.

- Outputs: numbers of degrees granted in instructional programs; numbers of books, journal articles, or creative works produced under the aegis of research and scholarly works programs; and reports and other products as a consequence of service program activities. With regard to the outputs of research and service programs, it is typical that the basic data are collected in individual personnel files but not entered into a planning database that would make the data available to decision makers in aggregate, trend form.

Most of these data are simply descriptive of a single dimension of the program.

Missing in this program-specific catalog of data are those simple data of program *counts* that would provide managerial insight into program proliferation and the changing mix of programs and services. This applies not only to instructional programs but to research, public service, and student service activities as well. It is instructive, for example, to compile trend data on such measures as the number of organizational units engaged in direct provision of student support services or on the number of programs in which degrees were granted relative to the size of the student body. These data are even more useful when placed in a comparative context. Data about numbers of fields in which degrees are granted are available through the Integrated Postsecondary Education Data System (IPEDS) maintained by the National Center for Education Statistics (NCES). Data about numbers of service programs require special studies or involvement in consortial programs such as the American Association of Universities' (AAU's) Data Exchange. It is likewise instructive to compile data that reveal trends in the distribution of personnel effort across the primary academic functions of instruction, research, and service. As with program outputs, this is an area in which data are typically available on an individual basis (usually in personnel folders) but where the analyses and aggregations that shed light on departmental, collegewide, or institutional trends are seldom performed.

To be truly effective, the DSS of the future has to contain not only data about costs and productivity of programs but about the clients for these programs (reflecting the fact that institutions serve numerous client groups and student subgroups) and the extent to which client needs have been satisfied. That is, there has to be an emphasis on the relationships between clients and programs, not just on program descriptors. From this perspective, it is important that a DSS be capable of providing information about:

- The characteristics of students who are attracted to each of the institution's programs. Recognizing that almost all institutions serve multiple student bodies (described in terms of such characteristics as age, academic preparation, academic objectives, full-timeness of study, and so on), it is critical that data be readily available indicating the characteristics of the clientele for the various academic programs and support services. This need extends to employers and other clients beyond the student (for example, understanding the characteristics of clients for research and service activities of various units within the institution).

- The nature of the interactions of students with the program: the order in which they experience the curriculum, presence of work experiences (internships, co-ops, and so on), the degree to which they experience "good practice" and utilization of support services.

- The consequences of this involvement, the outcomes associated with participation. Information about employment and subsequent postsecondary education activities is high in importance; however, other data should also be considered. Among the candidates are data that reflect student satisfaction with their academic experience and those that reflect students' self-assessments of things they learned well along with areas in which their education was deficient.

In short, it is important that the DSS of the future be at least as focused on the primary clients of higher education—the students, employers, and others served by the enterprise—as on the ways in which institutions go about providing those services.

Comparative Advantage

In an environment in which almost all institutions must compete actively for students, it is not enough to simply understand the characteristics of enrolled students; it is also important to understand insofar as is possible *why* students enroll and why other clients are attracted to the institution. Some of this can be determined by analyses of data about:

- Characteristics of students who enroll vis-à-vis those of students who are accepted but don't enroll

- Characteristics of competitors to which institutions lose significant numbers of accepted students

- Characteristics of competing institutions to (and from) which students transfer

- Students' stated reasons for selecting the institution

The results of such analyses frequently yield answers indicating that key factors are location, price, and program availability. Often, however, the results of such analyses are inconclusive. In such instances, it is necessary to dig deeper, into issues of institutional culture and image. This almost always means collecting data through means of surveys. Among the possibilities of off-the-shelf surveys are:

- The Institutional Goals Inventory (IGI) of the ETS, which asks internal stakeholders questions about institutional goals in an "is/should be" format.

- The National Center for Higher Education Management Systems' (NCHEMS) Institutional Performance Survey (IPS), which asks these same internal stakeholders a wide variety of questions about institutional functioning and culture.

- The Cooperative Institutional Research Program (CIRP) survey, which collects data about prior experiences, priorities, and values from incoming freshmen. Since this survey is nationally normed, it provides a basis for understanding those dimensions along which a particular institution's incoming class is significantly different from the norm.

- The College Student Experiences Questionnaire (CSEQ), which collects data on student activities and the levels of time and effort they are investing in their own education.

Using locally designed surveys, it is possible to gather "image" data about the institution and its primary competitors, for example by asking respondents to provide (or select from) a list of adjectives they would use to describe each institution.

These data reflect the importance of "market research" in a market-driven world. In such an environment, having data that help delineate a market niche and understand areas in which the institution is strongly attuned to (or in conflict with) client preferences is critically important. It is a type of data that, increasingly, institutions ignore at their peril.

Assets

Finally, from an intra-institutional perspective, the DDS designed with future decisions in mind has to be much more capable of supporting decisions about institutional assets and their creation, maintenance, and utilization. In this context, the concept of *assets* is used in the broadest sense, to include human (faculty, staff, and student body) and programmatic (investment in curricula) assets as well as buildings and equipment. In each case there is a need for data, as follows.

General Descriptive Data. Central to data about assets are those items that serve to characterize the amount and nature of the various assets available to an institution: square feet of facilities of various room use classifications; FTE of employees of various classifications, gender, age, ethnicity, and educational attainment; number of volumes of books and other materials in the library; and so on. These are commonly collected data, and it is unlikely that the DSS of the future will require substantially different kinds or amounts of data than would be suggested by current good practice. The one likely exception is educational technology, where future requirements will certainly demand more thorough attention to the kinds and amounts of technology in place within the institution.

Acquisition Costs. With regard to buildings and equipment, these costs are relatively easy to establish and the data are usually readily available. The notion of an "acquisition cost" for human assets, however, is a foreign concept. As a result, the appropriate data are seldom developed—and if they are, they are seldom compiled in a way that makes them useful for management purposes. For clarity, the acquisition cost of a faculty member would include not only base compensation but the costs of any inducements offered to attract the individual to the campus. For a superstar researcher, such inducements may be numerous, including equipping a laboratory, providing graduate students, guaranteeing summer salary, and a reduced teaching load. At the other end of the spectrum, such costs may include nothing more than partial reimbursement for moving expenses and a personal computer. The acquisition costs of a student body are the costs of student financial aid (or the amounts of forgone income arising from price discounts) required to recruit a student body of the required size and characteristics. Similarly, the acquisition (development) costs of curricula are seldom calculated. Occasionally, special projects are created for the purpose of revising some portion of the curriculum. At best, such projects reflect but a fraction of the total investment in curricula. The major part of the investment is in faculty time devoted to curricular improvement, the costs of which are seldom if ever calculated. Historically, this failure has not been critical. However, as more and more courses or course modules are developed elsewhere and made available through licensing and other arrangements, information about these development costs takes on increasing importance. In the absence of such information, there is no comparative data upon which to base the make-or-buy decision.

Maintenance Costs. While inclusion of acquisition cost information in DSS design is currently spotty, data about the costs of maintaining institutions' assets are almost uniformly absent from such systems. This deficiency must be overcome in DS systems designed to serve the emerging needs of higher education executives. In some cases the requirements are obvious; annual depreciation costs of buildings and equipment along with expenditures on building renewal and renovation and equipment re-

placement are key components. Equally important, but almost never included, are data about annual expenditures on faculty and staff development and on improvements to curricula. The former is particularly important. Faculty and staff are the key assets of almost all colleges and universities. Yet almost no overt and conscious attention is given to the ongoing maintenance of those assets. This substantial hole must be plugged in the DSS of the future.

Utilization of Assets. Again, most current DS systems have adequate data about utilization of some institutional assets; data about room assignments and classroom utilization are generally available as are data about program majors and course enrollments (the equivalent of program utilization data). Again, the major deficiency utilization of data is in dealing with the utilization of human assets. Most DS systems make no provision for centrally capturing data about assignment of personnel to different institutional functions (instruction, research, student services, administration) or for the aggregation of these data in ways that allow decision makers to ascertain trends in allocation of human resources to various functions. An additional need is now emerging: the need for data about allocation of faculty effort to various activities within the instruction function. As technology becomes an increasingly important component of the teaching/learning environment, the role of faculty inevitably changes, with more emphasis being placed on development of curricular materials and on helping students interact with that material, and less on transmittal of information. As this transformation occurs, it becomes increasingly important that institutional administrators be able to track the amount of effort—and therefore money—being devoted to key instructional activities: curricular planning and design, development (and maintenance) of materials, transmittal of information, mediating students' interactions with these materials and information, and evaluating learning outcomes. These needs create requirements for entirely new elements of a DSS.

Further Guidelines. For more details about facilities asset data, readers are referred to National Center for Education Statistics (1994); for human asset data to National Center for Education Statistics (forthcoming). There are no similar guides for data about equipment and programmatic assets.

Mission

An institution's mission is reflected in the clients it serves, the services it offers, and the values and characteristics (the elements of comparative advantage) that it cultivates. Therefore, if a DSS contains data appropriate to these other domains, data necessary for review of institutional mission are included as well.

Information Defined by External Perspectives

In addition to those items of information defined by internal decision-making requirements, the DSS of the future is likely have to include information that reflects the needs of important external constituents—data not only *about* these constituents, but *for* them. To some extent this information is determined by the decision-making requirements of these external audiences, and to some extent by the accountability requirements imposed by these audiences. In the end, however, this information is required by an institutional obligation to understand the perspectives of these key constituents, to monitor how well the institution is performing in the eyes of these constituents, and to take steps to improve that performance. Focus groups conducted with representatives of these external constituents reveal that they have substantially different needs and expectations (see Education Commission of the States, 1995; and Ewell and Jones, 1994). The design of the DSS of the future should be informed by an explicit understanding of these different perspectives.

Students

Students represent a key constituency for all institutions of higher education. From an institutional perspective, these individuals make one overriding decision: whether to attend a particular college or university. In making that decision, the prospective student seeks answers to some very basic questions (Education Commission of the States, 1995; Ewell and Jones, 1994; and Ewell and Jones, 1996):

- Will I have access to the academic programs and courses I want and the resources and support services I need if I attend this institution?

- What's the likelihood of success for a student like me—similar in socioeconomic status, academic preparation, and so on—at this particular institution?

- What happens to students who are successful in the programs in which I am especially interested? What kinds of jobs do they get? What kinds of graduate programs are they accepted into?

- With what aspects of their collegiate experience have students like me been most satisfied? Least satisfied?

Developing answers to these questions requires data from four different sources, all of which are necessary to provide information needed by institutional decision makers. The key difference is the way the data are organized and presented for use by student decision makers. First, there is a need for data selected from the internal record systems of the institution, information about access to core courses (were students closed out in the registration process?), majors (how many were admitted, how many denied admission?), small classes (what proportion of freshmen have at least two classes small enough for effective, active learning?), senior faculty (what proportion of lower-division student credit hours are taught by full-time faculty?), and support services (what proportion of applicants for child care services are denied, and what level of academic support services will be encountered?). Second, there are data gleaned from institutional records and organized in a longitudinal fashion. For this purpose, the required data are those demographic and academic history variables that allow characterization of "students like me," along with data about academic experiences (courses taken, performance in those courses, and support services utilized). The bottom line is the measures of student persistence, retention, and attrition. Third, there are data that can be gathered most easily through use of course evaluation forms, data about the incidence of written assignments and group work, hours per week of study time required in the core courses, and so on. Fourth and finally, there are data gathered through use of alumni surveys, data about job placement, subsequent educational activities, and areas of particular satisfaction and dissatisfaction.

These data, gathered to address the key questions of prospective students, are of enormous importance to institutional planners and academic administrators. For an institution to be successful in the long run, a part of the planning process almost necessarily must focus on efforts to see the institution through the eyes of prospective clients and to rectify shortcomings identified through the use of these data. At this juncture, it is interesting to note that student right-to-know, the impetus for most institutions' enhancing their ability to conduct longitudinal analyses of student data, led many institutions to violate good practice in using the methodology in support of internal decision making. The law encourages a focus on a single retention number, rather than separate numbers of each student subpopulation; it did not encourage inclusion of explanatory variables; and it ignored consideration of follow-up data.

An intriguing, related question is whether and how these data are made available to those prospective students on whose behalf they were ostensibly derived. Feasibility is no longer at issue. Technology allows these data to be made available to such potential users. In at least one state, discussions are progressing on using the Internet and the World Wide Web as a vehicle for interactively soliciting student profile information and then delivering institutional performance information for the group of previously enrolled students meeting that profile. This would be a substantial step in the provision of consumer information—and an enormous threat to at least some institutions.

Employers

In the main, employers view institutional accountability along a single dimension: are students who graduate from the institution prepared to enter the workforce as fully functioning, effective members? In some regards, their expectations may be impossibly high; almost all employers require their employees to have specialized knowledge and skills that can be learned only on the job. For the most part, however, they ask reasonable questions:

- Have graduates had experiences that acquaint them with the realities of the world of work: internships, co-ops, and so on?

- Do they possess high levels of important skills? Can they communicate well? Are they good problem solvers? Do they function effectively as members of a team?

- Have they learned the basic content of their major field of study?

The first of these questions can be addressed by easily acquired descriptive information. The last can be answered by references to the kinds of data normally compiled on student transcripts. It is on the second question that higher education institutions almost uniformly stub their toes. They have neither clear statements of expectation nor relevant measures of performance, whether devised as internal assessments or designed to systematically reflect employer (or subsequent college) judgments as to level of preparation on an array of critical skills. While there are numerous avenues available for acquisition of such data, credibility of the data (and of the institution) is enhanced when follow-up data are collected from employers or institutions to which students transfer and the judgments of outsiders are made an important part of assessment.

It can be anticipated that the data developed to serve the needs of employers, data about levels of competence in various knowledge and skill areas acquired by college graduates, represent one of the largest departures from current practice in design of a DSS. Their preferences, if colleges and universities accommodate them, change the coin of the realm from credit hours to levels of competence. This is another area in which data gathered in response to the needs of an external client can be an invaluable planning and decision-making tool for academics.

State Policy Makers

In many respects, state political leaders have the same set of interests as potential students and employers. After all, these institutional clients are the policy makers' political constituents. Failure to serve these constituents is, more often than not, duly noted. In addition to interests that are congruent with those of major constituents, however, state policy makers have agendas that are uniquely theirs. Each state, implicitly or explicitly, has a "public agenda," a set of issues that has captured the imagination and attention of these policy makers. These issues vary greatly from state to state but frequently include such items as reform of the K–12 system of education, diversification of the state's economic base, protection or improvement of the environment and the state's quality of life, and changing the way the state is dealing with a variety of social problems. The question for the state's system of higher education is "What are you doing that contributes to the solution of these priority statewide issues?" Successful planning requires not only that institutional administrators have a clear understanding of this agenda but that information be available that helps them monitor their institution's contribution to the attainment of that agenda.

Additional External Data

The kinds of data suggested so far as being central to support planning in the coming decades are largely under the control of institutions; they are derived from institutional record systems or can be compiled by institutions by asking questions of their primary constituents. There is, however, another set of data that may well prove essential to the planning process and that is much more difficult to compile: data about the extent to which competition is arising from noninstitutional providers of postsecondary instruction.

Technology, and people's access to it, has evolved to the point where it now promises to provide the primary method of access to certain kinds of education for an increasingly large number of individuals. Technologically delivered education is particularly attractive to individuals whom colleges and universities have typically labeled as their nontraditional students. To some extent, technology (particularly computer-based technology) will expand the market for postsecondary education. It is particularly effective at delivering "just in time" education, assistance in learning a narrowly defined skill or acquiring a particular piece of knowledge that has particular import to the learner at a given point in time. In this format, technology expands access to large numbers of individuals who would not enroll in a semester-long college course to acquire this information. In other instances, however, technology provides direct competition for clients

and services that have historically been within the purview of institutions of higher education. Employers are becoming less and less dependent on local colleges and universities to deliver specialized instruction at the workplace. Much instruction of this sort can now come as easily from across the globe as across town. Similarly, more and more instruction is available through the Internet on terms that meet the requirements of individual learners.

This emerging capacity suggests the critical importance of institutions' monitoring the changing size and nature of their nontraditional and corporate client base. In addition, it is increasingly important to ask questions of these clients that have heretofore gone unasked. Specifically, institutions need to begin systematic gathering of "intelligence" about the other providers of instruction being tapped by their clients. As time goes on, it may be important to commission special studies (conducted by telephone polling firms or other such entities) that will help decision makers better understand the extent and nature of the competition being provided through alternative providers.

Summary

The decision support systems that support planning for the twenty-first century have many features in common with those currently in place. However, even the best of the current DS systems have to be expanded to include new or additional data on a variety of topics. Among these are:

- The costs of acquiring/developing and maintaining the key assets of the institution. The need for expansion is particularly acute with regard to human assets and curricula.

- The utilization of these assets. Again, the new elements focus on human assets and the allocation of effort to both functions and instructional activities.

- Performance of the institution as measured in terms that reflect the needs and priorities of key external constituents: prospective students, employers, and state policy makers among others. The major refinements in this arena are information about competencies achieved by students and more systematic information about students' educational, employment, and civic activities after leaving college (along with external judgments concerning their level of preparation for these activities).

- The nature and extent of competition arising from noninstitutional sources of instructional programming.

None of these represents an insurmountable problem. The skill with which these data are compiled and presented to institutional decision makers, however, undoubtedly affects the quality of future planning exercises—and the ability of many institutions to meet the challenges of the coming decades.

Further Reading

The literature on decision support systems is extensive. Some of the better conceptual articles have been written by Gorry and Scott Morton (see, for example, Morton and Morton, 1989). Because this field is changing so rapidly, however, the literature on the applications of these ideas quickly becomes outdated. Some of the best information is found on World Wide Web sites and through Internet discussion lists that deal with decision support systems or, increasingly, under the nomenclature *executive support systems* (ESS).

References

Adelman, C. "Nothing Ever Stays the Same—Or Does It? Curriculum, Grading, and Attendance Patterns, 1972–1993." Paper presented at the AAHE Conference on Assessment and Quality, Washington, D.C., June 1996.

Education Commission of the States. *Making Quality Count in Undergraduate Education.* Denver: Education Commission of the States, 1995.

Ewell, P. T. (ed.). *Student Tracking: New Techniques, New Demands.* New Directions for Institutional Research, no. 87. San Francisco: Jossey-Bass, 1995.

Ewell, P. T., and Jones, D. P. "Pointing the Way: indicators as Policy Tools in Higher Education." In S. Ruppert (ed.), *Charting Higher Education Accountability: A Sourcebook on State-Level Performance Indicators.* Denver: Education Commission of the States, 1994.

Ewell, P. T., and Jones, D. P. *Indicators of "Good Practice" in Undergraduate Education: A Handbook for Development and Implementation.* Boulder, Colo.: National Center for Higher Education Management Systems, 1996.

Ewell, P. T., Parker, R., and Jones, D. P. *Establishing a Longitudinal Student Tracking System: An Implementation Handbook.* Boulder, Colo.: National Center for Higher Education Management Systems, 1988.

Morton, G., and Morton, S. "A Framework for Management Information Systems." *Sloan Management Review,* Spring 1989.

National Center for Education Statistics. *Handbook on Human Resources: Recordkeeping and Analysis.* Washington, D.C.: U.S. Department of Education, forthcoming.

National Center for Education Statistics. *Postsecondary Education Facilities Inventory and Classification Manual (Revised and Reprinted 1994).* Washington, D.C.: U.S. Department of Education, 1994.

Productivity in Postsecondary Education: A New Approach

WILLIAM F. MASSY AND ANDREA K. WILGER

The purpose of this article is to develop a conceptual structure for examining college and university productivity and to propose an explanation for why productivity—as seen by those who pay for higher education—has declined. The authors examine public criticism of higher education and the accompanying loss of public trust. They argue that much of the problem results from the shift of faculty effort toward research and professional activity and away from undergraduate teaching—a phenomenon dubbed the academic ratchet.

Between 1980 and 1990, the price of attending college in the United States rose significantly. Tuition and fees increased by an average of 9.5% annually, nearly twice the rate of inflation. The price increase in higher education was much greater than increases in other areas such as health care and the price of a new house (Hauptman, 1990). The pattern of spiraling prices evident in the 1980s stands in sharp contrast to the previous decade when tuition and fees grew less than inflation.

The trend in tuition was most pronounced at America's prestigious institutions. Between 1980 and 1988, the median price of an undergraduate education at elite private colleges and universities grew almost 6 points faster than the consumer price index. Likewise, the increase at prestigious public institutions was 5 points faster than the consumer price index. These figures contrast with per capita personal disposable income, which grew by less than 2 points over inflation in the same period. Tuition has become very expensive in absolute as well as relative terms. In 1989–1990, the aver-

age price (for tuition, room, and board) of a private, 4-year college was $15,318. The average price of a public, 4-year college was $6,991.

There is little doubt that cost rise has been the primary driver of tuition. The increases in real unit costs are well documented. Between 1975 and 1986, real expenditure per fulltime-equivalent student at private colleges and universities rose anywhere from 2.5% (at lower-priced institutions) to 3.5% (at research institutions). Real expenditures per student at public institutions rose only slightly less (Hauptmann, 1990).

While few commentators dispute higher education's claim that the cost rise has been driven by real increases in salaries and the prices of other inputs, increased government regulation, micromanagement, and cost shifting, they ask why these forces cannot be mitigated by productivity improvements. Arguments that colleges and universities gain productivity by improving quality, and that they cannot be expected to achieve quantitative productivity gains, are falling on deaf ears. Increasingly, higher education's friends and critics alike are asking hard questions about institutional productivity, the possible causes for its malaise, and what can be done to improve the situation.

The purpose of this article is to develop a conceptual structure for examining college and university productivity and to propose an explanation for why productivity—as seen by those who pay for education—has not increased and may have declined. The work has

"Productivity in Postsecondary Education: A New Approach," by William F. Massy and Andrea K. Wilger, reprinted from *Educational Evaluation and Policy Analysis*, Vol. 14, No. 4, Winter 1992. American Educational Research Association.

been informed by the Pew Higher Education Research Program, directed by Professor Robert Zemsky of the University of Pennsylvania—to whom we are extremely grateful—and by the higher education productivity project conducted by the first author for the National Center for Postsecondary Governance and Finance (Massy, 1989a, 1989b, 1990). It is part of our current study of higher education productivity, in which the concepts presented herein will be evaluated empirically as outlined at the end of the paper. First, however, we will review the public criticism of higher education's cost rise in more detail.

Public Criticism of Higher Education

The spiraling price of attending a college or university has received significant attention from higher education's key constituents. Students and parents fear that a college education, especially at a private institution, is beyond their financial grasp. The scope of tuition increases is most dramatically demonstrated in comparison with the growth in family income. Data compiled by the College Board show that average tuition at a 4-year private institution rose from 16.5% of median family income in 1976–1977 to 22.1% of median family income in 1987–1988. The average tuition at a 4-year public institution rose from 4.1% to 4.8% of median family income over the same period (DeLoughry, 1990).

Students and their parents increasingly question whether a college education is worth the price. The president of the College Board, Donald M. Steward, echoes their anxiety, claiming that the large increases in tuition have left many confused and panicked about the cost of going to college (Evangelauf, 1991). He is not alone in voicing concerns. Former Secretary of Education Lauro F. Cavazos urged college presidents to hold down tuition costs in order to ensure that higher education was affordable to all qualified students (U.S. Department of Education, 1990).

Rising costs have been of great interest to other public officials. Beginning in the mid-1980s then–Education Secretary William J. Bennett began an assault on higher education, especially the sharp increase in tuition. He blamed institutional officials for lack of efficiency and

even greed, claiming that he had never witnessed anybody with a greater interest in money. Bennett encouraged state and local officials as well as students and their parents to ask tough questions about whether they were getting their money's worth from colleges and universities (Williams, 1985).

Although William Bennett has since turned his attention to other issues, his ideas are now voiced by others whose criticism has put institutions on the defensive with regard to tuition increases. At the national and state levels, accountability has become a buzzword for legislatures when dealing with higher education. Lawmakers are curious as to why tuition increases continually outpace inflation (DeLoughry, 1991).

Criticism of higher education has not been limited to an outcry against rising tuition rates. The concerns about increasing prices have been coupled with other criticisms of higher education and important environmental factors to produce a deep skepticism and loss of confidence in American postsecondary education. The long-standing goodwill enjoyed by colleges and universities has been seriously eroded.

At the state level, shrinking revenues have forced lawmakers to reexamine allocations to higher education. In 1991, 30 states cut their higher education budgets an average of 3.9%. In eight of those states, cuts reached double digits, forcing institutions to cope with serious budget reductions (Cage, 1991). In 1992, midyear budget cuts were reported in 22 states while 10 other states expected appropriations to be slashed before the end of the fiscal year (Cage, 1992). Cuts in appropriations have led public institutions to raise tuition in order to recoup lost revenues. This, however, further aggravates the public perceptions about the spiraling price of attending college.

In response to shrinking revenues, state lawmakers are probing other aspects of higher education; many have begun to link rising prices and institutional costs to quality. Continuing where Bennett left off, state officials believe that many colleges and universities, particularly research institutions, have lost sight of their essential mission—the teaching of undergraduate students—as faculty members spend more time away from the classroom engaged in research and other professional activities. In effect, they argue that institutions are charging students more at the same time they are delivering less. To combat this trend, several states have launched investigations into how much time faculty spend working with undergraduates. Surveys of faculty workload have been administered in Mississippi, New York, and Virginia. Arizona and North Carolina have similar studies under way. State officials believe that work-load studies have the potential to produce both cost savings and better undergraduate education.

Linking tuition increases and rises in institutional costs to the quality of undergraduate education is not the exclusive province of state lawmakers. Several prominent critics of higher education have espoused similar themes. Lynne Cheney, chair of the National Endowment for the Humanities (NEH), has chastised colleges and universities for relying on a reward system that values research over teaching. According to Cheney, faculty spend more time researching and writing for publication than teaching. Institutions are then forced to hire more faculty to teach. This system results in higher tuition rates for students (Watkins, 1990). Charles Sykes (1988), in his famous work *Profscam*, touches upon the same theme, depicting the American professoriate as underworked and overpaid. Other well-known critics of higher education include Alan Bloom and Dinish D'Sousa.

Even friends of the academy have become critical of rising prices and associated institutional practices. Page Smith, in *Killing the Spirit* (1990), outlines many of the problems plaguing colleges and universities. Among the most troubling for Smith are: (a) reduced faculty teaching loads resulting from the imbalance between teaching and research and the associated reliance on part-time instructional staff and graduate teaching assistants; (b) overreliance on external funding and the erosion of faculty loyalty to the institution; (c) the increasing demand by all institutions for faculty research, regardless of its value, and the associated attempt by many colleges to achieve university status, duplicating the role of research institutions; and (d) excessive specialization in academic disciplines. The results of these problems include greatly increased institutional costs, which are then passed on to students in the form of higher tuition. Even more important to Smith is the apparent neglect of the pri-

mary task of colleges and universities: the teaching of undergraduates.

The increased importance of research and other professional activity at the expense of undergraduate teaching also has been highlighted by Bowen and Schuster (1986) in their work on American professors and by Henry Rosovsky (1991), who linked this phenomenon to the unusual degree of control faculty exert over their time. Many of the same themes have been elaborated by the Pew Higher Education Research Program (1989, 1990) in *Policy Perspectives*. Some of the issues set forth by the Pew Program include the problem of increased tuition and institutional costs, the loss of focus and mission definition, and the decline of public confidence and trust in higher education.

The current malaise afflicting colleges and universities was addressed by Robert M. Rosenzweig (1986), president of the Association of American Universities, who reflected upon the tarnished image of higher education in an essay entitled "Seeing Ourselves as Others See Us." Noting the increased cynicism about higher education among policymakers, Rosenzweig reminds the reader that public confidence and goodwill are crucial to the long-term strength of higher education. The tendency among colleges and universities to become large, complex organizations resembling businesses rather than educational institutions negatively impacts public perceptions. He encourages institutions to reflect upon their real purposes and alter their behavior if necessary.

The message from all of these sources is clear; higher education is in turmoil, stung by criticism from both within and outside the academy. An enterprise once treasured by Americans now seems to have lost its way.

Productivity Definitions

Before developing our conceptual structure for cost rise and productivity erosion, we must develop a working definition of the productivity concept itself. Economists define productivity as "the ratio of output to input in an organization" (Corrallo, Gilmore, & To, 1988, p. 12; Price & Mueller, 1986, p. 26). Productivity can be determined once the outputs of goods and services are known and linked to the inputs used to produce them. Because costs often are attached to inputs, the study of productivity tries to answer the question "Are you getting what you pay for?" (Corrallo et al., 1988, p. 12). Other, less precise definitions of productivity can be found throughout the literature. Sadlak (1978, p. 216) defines productivity as "the ratio between performance and costs," while Wallhaus (1975, p. 1) uses "the value of outputs relative to the value of inputs." Both of these definitions stress the importance of quality. This is reinforced by Corrallo et al. (1988, p. 212), who write, "a gain in the number of outputs per unit of input would not represent an increase in productivity if, at the same time, the quality of the outputs decreased." However, quality is difficult to define because it consists of intangible factors (Hopkins & Massy, 1981) and means different things to different audiences (Birnbaum, 1989; Meisinger, Purves, & Schmidtlein, 1975; Mingle, 1989). These factors help to explain why scholars disagree about the conceptualization and definition of quality (Shenhav & Haberfeld, 1988).

Defining productivity for higher education illustrates many of the problems referred to above. Reaching consensus about exact definitions for quality is virtually impossible, and it is best to avoid having to do so. Baumol, Blackman, and Wolff (1989, p. 235) offer just such a mechanism. They define *gross productivity* as "the number of units of output produced per unit of input, *with no attempt to adjust for any accompanying changes in product quality.*" They demonstrate the importance of gross productivity "in explaining the behavior over time of relative prices of different goods and services, in budgetary planning for various public sector activities [including public and private higher education], and in planning to meet future manpower requirements." The rise in unit costs of higher education cited by critics as evidence of malaise is, in fact, a gross productivity indicator (Massy, 1990).

Higher education officials and policymakers should accept gross productivity as a meaningful measure, examine the evidence, and evaluate the causes of changes. In so doing, they also should ask the question "Have changes in quality been sufficient to compensate for the observed changes in unit costs?" Many commentators are concluding that the answer is "no," which suggests that "produc-tivity" as well as "gross productivity" may have declined (Massy, 1990, p. 2).

The Causes of Cost Escalation

Although many theories have been postulated to explain tuition increases and cost escalation, the general public and many policymakers tend to blame cost rise on so-called "organizational slack." They conjure up images of waste and abuse by confusing faculty contact hours with total faculty work load. Popular books such as *Profscam* charge that the American professoriate is "overpaid, grotesquely underworked, and the architects of academia's vast empires of waste" (Sykes, 1988, p. 5).

Yet, to internal observers, there is little doubt that most faculty work very hard. Similarly, there is little evidence of overt waste, despite the flexibility in time utilization enjoyed by many professors. When organizational slack exists, it can represent poor use of resources, or the existence of the wherewithal for developing innovative ideas, which may be useful to the institution at some time in the future (Cyert & March, 1963). The problem is that in professional organizations it is difficult to differentiate between legitimate investments in the future and the diversion of resources to personal ends. We believe that the public view is oversimplified, and therefore we must look elsewhere for factors that explain higher education's cost escalation.

The most significant causes of cost escalation can be divided into five categories: (a) regulation, micromanagement, and cost shifting; (b) the cost disease; (c) the growth force; (d) the administrative lattice; and (e) the academic ratchet. Each of the five causes has contributed to higher education's cost rise and productivity malaise, but whereas the first two are beyond the control of college and university authorities, the last three arise from institutional choice—that is to say, they are "the problem," not an explanation or excuse for the problem.

Taken together, the last three explanations for cost rise can be viewed as a special case of collective-action theory. The theory, originally postulated by Mancur Olson (1965), holds that organizations become less efficient when not constrained by market forces. In colleges and universities, the theory implies that a lack of pricing discipline has allowed growth forces to proliferate and administrative and support costs to expand beyond the point of diminishing returns.

Furthermore, we will argue that a lack of quality discipline in undergraduate education has encouraged faculty effort to shift toward research and professional activity—the phenomenon we have dubbed the academic ratchet. The ratchet mechanism is reinforced by institutions' quest for prestige and the research-funding structure, which relies heavily upon external grants and contracts; the resulting competition in the sponsored research "markets" attracts faculty effort away from the more permissive undergraduate education sector. We believe that the academic ratchet is the core issue for higher education productivity, and it is the central focus of this article. First, however, we will describe the other causes of cost rise.

Regulation, Micromanagement, and Cost Shifting

Regulation and micromanagement are familiar grievances in higher education. Increased reporting responsibilities combined with the bulk and complexity of data required by both state and federal governments as well as governing boards and trustees have forced institutions to expand administrative staffs in order to comply.

Declines in federal and state aid to higher education have negatively impacted costs by shifting the funding responsibility from government to students and institutions. Under Ronald Reagan, the amount of federal aid available for college students declined dramatically. Between 1980 and 1987, federal student-aid grants lost one half the level of their purchasing power (Frances, 1990). This has forced students to rely on loans rather than grants or to seek assistance directly from their institution.

In a different arena, the nation's research universities have been confronted with cost shifting of massive proportions as the federal government recalculates the amount of money it will reimburse institutions for the indirect costs of research. Furthermore, institutions are being forced to spend large sums to protect themselves from aggressive auditors who push detailed regulation and micromanagement beyond the point of social cost effectiveness.

The Cost Disease

Colleges and universities are paying more for the goods and services they purchase. This is particularly true for salaries, which account for the lion's share of cost. As measured by the Higher Education Price Index (HEPI), faculty and staff salaries grew at an annual rate of 7%—two percentage points above general inflation—from 1980 to 1987. This translates to unusually large real compensation increases for employees and is generally attributed to a reversal of the subinflation increases awarded during the 1970s (Hauptman, 1990).

These real compensation increases, coupled with higher education's labor intensity, represent a phenomenon known as the "cost disease." To understand the cost disease, assume that technology is fixed and the student-faculty ratio does not increase over time. Then it follows that real teaching costs will rise by an amount approaching the productivity improvement rate for the economy as a whole. This mechanism is well illustrated by the example of the string quartet. It is impossible to play a half-hour piece in less than 2 musician-hours without a decline in quality. Other industries, however, do generate productivity growth, which produces rising real wages. Musicians' salaries must have these increases in order for the "industry" to remain competitive, which forces up the quartet's costs. This example is provided by Baumol and Blackman (1983), who coined the term "cost disease" to describe the phenomenon. It is important to remember, however, that it assumes technology to be fixed. The possibility that the quartet can increase its effective productivity by selling compact disks to subsidize the live performances is not considered.

With no internal efficiency improvement in higher education, annual cost escalations per student would be higher than inflation even on the basis of the cost disease alone. There is irony here—because colleges and universities contribute to the economy-wide productivity through research; the better we do our jobs, the more cost pressure we experience.

The Growth Force

The growth force provides another explanation for rising tuition costs. In essence, the idea is that "quality" costs and that institutions should continually labor to improve quality. This concept, originally articulated by Bowen (1980), can be seen in the unending production of new knowledge at research institutions. New knowledge leads to the need for greater technology, new classes, and even new disciplines. Yet old knowledge remains relevant. The effect is a constant layering of new ideas and methods on top of old ones, and this results in an unending pressure to add courses, faculty, technology, and facilities to keep pace with expanding knowledge.

Enrollment stabilization has amplified the growth force's effect on cost. Although the bleak demographic projections first forecast in the 1970s did not materialize, enrollments have grown on average by only about 1% per year since the mid-1970s. This represents a sharp contrast to the rapid growth of the 1960s and early 1970s and results in greater costs spread over a largely stagnant population, hence larger per capita costs (Hauptman, 1990). It is relatively easy to accommodate the growth force when enrollments are increasing, but in a period of enrollment stability, the growth force can outpace even the most abundant income sources. The pressure for constant growth prompted Stanford President Donald Kennedy (1986) to ask, "How can we look so rich, yet feel so poor?"

Higher education leaders cite regulation, micromanagement and cost shifting, the cost disease, and the growth force as the reasons costs are increasing. This is true as far as it goes, but the explanations no longer seem satisfying. Critics of higher education doubt that regulation and micromanagement, the cost disease, and the necessary consequences of the growth force could possibly account for the observed cost escalation. In addition, they claim that some of these "causes" of cost rise are little more than excuses developed by institutions to avoid tough questions about priorities and budgets. The antidote to the growth force is to focus the institution more precisely, setting priorities and making choices about what is essential for the school's mission. Colleges and universities do not have to be "all things to all people," and it is up to institutional leaders to maintain the needed focus. Likewise, the responsibility for relieving the administrative lattice and the academic ratchet lies squarely in the hands of the institution—not with some external authority or unassailable causality.

The Administrative Lattice

In 1990, Karen Grassmuck charted the growth of administrative and academic support staffs at colleges and universities. Using data obtained from the U.S. Equal Employment Opportunity Commission, she demonstrated the alarming increase in administrative personnel. She found that administrative staffs had grown an average of 60% between 1975 and 1985. By contrast, faculty increased by less than 6% on average for the same time period. Significant increases in administrative staffs occurred at all types of institutions, not just large research universities. The result of the increases in administrative and academic support services has been "an extension of the scale and scope of an administrative lattice that has grown, much like a crystalline structure, to incorporate ever more elaborate and intricate linkages within itself"(Pew Higher Education Research Program, 1990, p. 3).

We believe that the administrative lattice arises from administrative entrepreneurism, consensus management, and risk aversion, which interact unfavorably with the external regulation and micromanagement we cited earlier (Massy & Warner, 1991).

Consensus management, which first arose out of the turmoil of the late 1960s and early 1970s, has become the norm for conducting business throughout higher education. Administrative and academic support staff are widely consulted on a variety of issues. Agreements are hammered out before decisions are made. Although this process has the merit of being broadly participatory, it has many drawbacks. It is time consuming to solicit input from a significant number of people. Reaching a consensus may be a difficult process requiring keen negotiating skills on the part of managers. Also, accountability is difficult to assign if every decision is the product of several people. Consensus management has proven to be very costly (Pew Higher Education Research Program, 1990, p. 3). It reinforces the natural bureaucratic tendency toward risk aversion. No one is willing to stand apart from the group—to make the tough decision. The result is often a layering of responses to external threats, which adds costs that are disproportionate to the benefits achieved.

The pervasiveness of an administrative entrepreneurism has also increased institutional costs. As administrative staffs have increased in size, they have tended to become more professional. One consequence of employing more highly trained individuals has been better management. Institutions have become more technologically sophisticated and better able to serve their clientele. An unintended consequence has been that academic and administrative support staffs have come to "own" their jobs in much the same way that faculty do. They have created their own set of goals and priorities for the institution. Inevitably, one of their goals is to expand their own area (Pew Higher Education Research Program, 1990, p. 3).

Output Creep— The Academic Ratchet

Although the increase in regulation and micromanagement, the cost disease, the growth force, and the administrative lattice help explain higher education's cost escalation, an even more potent force—output creep—is at work as well. By output creep we mean the slow change in product mix observed at many colleges and universities. The American professoriate has undergone an evolution since World War II. No longer do faculty members devote the majority of their time to teaching and related activities such as academic advising and mentoring. Rather, the primary focus of faculty effort increasingly is research, scholarship, and other professional activity. The process is gradual, which is why we have labeled it output "creep."

Not all institutions suffer from output creep to the same extent. The phenomenon occurs most dramatically at elite research institutions, where competition for admission allows institutions to dictate the "output mix" that students buy. Higher education is still dominated by colleges and universities whose faculty devote most of their time to teaching or whose institutions, constantly concerned with enrollment and financial matters, are more likely to emphasize the role of professor as teacher. However, the prestigious research institutions receive most of the publicity, and to the extent that other institutions emulate their behavior, output creep affects much of higher education.

While quantitative data to demonstrate the ratchet are sparse, the discretionary time model developed by Massy and Zemsky (1992a, 1992b) shows that faculty do behave in ways that are consistent with the concept. Furthermore, the feeling that professors spend less time in the classroom than their predecessors has been noted by several critics of higher education. For example, NEH Chair Lynne Cheney has observed that professors devote far too much time to research and too little to teaching (Watkins, 1990). A similar claim is made by Burton Clark, who focuses his critique on the overabundance of rewards for research and the dearth of those for teaching (1987, pp. 98–101).

Faculty can spend more time in self-selected activities (generally research and scholarship) than they did 20 or more years ago because of increases in support staff, augmented in some cases by increases in faculty-student ratios. While external research funding pays for some of this, much of the responsibility for paying for the extra staff falls to the institution. The result is a shift in the output mix paid for by those who provide general institutional funds. Unfortunately, those payers—for example, students, their parents, and state and federal policymakers—are taking exception to this new mix. To the extent they do, they perceive institutions as being less cost effective.

The behavioral drivers of output creep are based mainly in the academic department. The department is considered the fundamental unit of organization in an institution of higher education, regardless of its size or mission. Departments are the gateways to an institution's faculty; any successful efforts to bring about change in the academic culture must work through departmental channels. The academic department is also the key regulator of faculty behavior. As the primary unit through which rewards and incentives are distributed, the department is the natural center of accountability for the action of its members. It is regarded, quite properly, as the primary agent for maintaining and improving the quality and productivity of undergraduate education. Any attempt to contain costs while simultaneously maintaining or improving the quality of teaching and learning should begin with an understanding of the dynamics of the academic department.

Although so far we have focused on what the faculty no longer do, several functions have become more prevalent as a result of the output-creep process. Examining the gainers and losers of output creep will aid our understanding of why costs are rising.

Gainers

The primary gainers from output creep are (a) research, publication, and professional service and (b) curriculum scope and specialization.

Research, Publication, and Professional Service

These activities compete with teaching for faculty time. From an institutional standpoint, research is desirable as it does not represent a diversion of resources. Research and professional activities are also integral components of the mission of elite institutions. Publication and professional service complement research, permitting faculty to share the results of their work and learn from the work of others.

At the individual level, research, publication, and professional service are highly valued. They satisfy creative desires instilled by doctoral programs. They build reputations outside the institution and increase faculty members' market power. They enrich the lives of faculty members by providing diversion from the classroom routine. The importance of scholarship and professional activity to faculty members has been explored in several works (Fulton & Trow, 1974; Needham, 1982; Shaw, 1983; Zemsky & Massy, 1990).

Curriculum Scope and Specialization

Curriculum scope refers to the coverage of an academic discipline in terms of both breadth and depth. A deep curriculum includes specialized courses that allow students to study intensively in a few areas. In contrast, a broad curriculum attempts to provide ample coverage of all subjects in a given area. The emphasis is on fundamentals and general concepts. Adding courses usually expands scope and specialization. When enrollment is constant, adding courses also reduces average class size.

This hypothesis about curriculum scope and specialization is supported by the work of several scholars. In 1976, the Carnegie Council on Policy Studies in Higher Education pub-

lished the results of a comprehensive examination of changes in college and university curricula from 1967 to 1974. The Council concluded that undergraduate course-taking patterns had changed considerably. Students at all types of institutions were spending much less time in "breadth" courses and much more time in "depth" courses. General education and distribution requirements had declined significantly and were replaced by electives. The Council found that the majority of students chose depth electives over breadth electives (Blackburn, Armstrong, Conrad, Didham, & McKune, 1976, p. 29). A clear pattern of increased enrollment in specialized courses was identified.

Similar findings were reported by the Association of American Colleges (1985). The group reflects upon the decay of the college curriculum and concludes that "electives are being used to fatten majors and diminish breadth" (p. 3).

Losers

We believe that the primary losers from output creep include (a) curriculum structure; (b) teaching quality; and (c) advising, mentoring, and tutoring.

Curriculum structure

Curriculum structure is the degree to which courses in an academic department are interrelated. A curriculum where courses are relatively independent of each other is said to have low structure; a curriculum where courses are heavily dependent upon previous courses in the same department has greater structure. Before output creep, departments tended to have greater structure. Students were led through introductory, mid-level, and advanced courses in the major. Each course built upon the knowledge and methods developed in previous courses.

As noted above, the destructuring of the curriculum has been cited in several studies. The 1985 Association of American Colleges' report states that colleges and universities lack a clear mission. This has led to a collapse of curricular structure and to a "marketplace philosophy: it is a supermarket where students are shoppers and professors are merchants of learning." The report places much of the blame for curricular degradation on faculty in academic departments who have become "protectors and advocates of their own interests, at the expense of institutional responsibilities and curricular coherence" (Association of American Colleges, 1985, pp. 2, 4).

Derek Bok also recognizes that college curricula became fragmented in the 1960s and 1970s as institutions relaxed requirements (Bok, 1986, p. 41). Even popular books such as *Profscam* belittle the current curricula for lack of structure and coherence (Sykes, 1988, pp. 79–82).

Teaching Quality

While many factors affect the quality of classroom teaching, time spent developing classroom material and presentation methods, grading exams and papers, and meeting to discuss work with students is important. These are all time-consuming activities, especially when done well, and compete with the demands of research and professional activities.

Advising, Mentoring, and Tutoring

These out-of-class teaching functions are vital to the success of undergraduate teaching programs. They are especially critical for at-risk students. Once an integral component of the faculty role, these activities have been pushed aside in favor of research.

Albert Hood and Catherine Arceneaux, writing about the development of student services, claim that the field really began to emerge in the late 1940s mostly by default, taking over responsibilities and tasks that were abandoned by faculty and other administrators (1990, p. 17). They further make the case by stating that "student services developed because faculty involvement in the development of the whole student declined as emphasis on the research and knowledge-transmitting functions increased" (1990, pp. 17–18).

Robert Fenske describes a similar process, claiming that professional student service workers took over necessary and often unpopular tasks abandoned by faculty and administrators. Faculty involvement in what are now defined as student service functions "changed from total involvement to detachment" (1980, p. 12). Page Smith (1990) reinforces this notion in his most recent work.

These gainers and losers offer preliminary evidence that processes exist within academic departments that have resulted in the shift we refer to as output creep and the process that drives it, the academic ratchet. Understanding the underlying organizational processes that have led to output creep is the first step in redressing the balance between teaching and other faculty activities, improving what is generally considered as productivity in higher education.

The Dynamics of the Ratchet

We believe that output creep results from the interaction of several departmental processes, which we collectively characterize as the academic ratchet. The processes are (a) pursuit of faculty lines, (b) leveraging faculty time, (c) destructuring the curriculum, and (d) "enactment" of group norms and internalization of perceived property rights. A clear understanding of the dynamics of these processes is crucial to cost containment efforts.

Pursuit of Faculty Lines

Most department chairs list the hiring of new faculty as a top priority. This is true even if enrollments are level. Likewise, most faculty want additional colleagues. Both faculty and chairs view the addition of new faculty as a way to serve students more effectively, increase the amount and visibility of research emanating from the department, and bring lively, interesting individuals into the faculty fold. The push to hire more faculty is strong whether they are wanted for their ability to enhance department prestige, teach introductory courses, or just increase the intellectual climate of the department.

Leveraging Faculty Time

Productivity increases in labor-intensive industries such as higher education are difficult to achieve (see above discussion of the cost disease). The primary way in which productivity is improved is by substituting individuals with lower levels of training and expertise for those with higher levels of expertise. In academic departments, this means hiring graduate teaching and research assistants, administrative assistants and secretaries, and technicians to take over certain faculty functions. Utilizing less costly individuals frees up faculty time for research and other professional activities. In many cases, colleges and universities spend considerable sums of money on additional personnel whose primary purpose is to leverage faculty time (see above discussion of advising, mentoring and tutoring, and the administrative lattice). In addition to adding personnel, departments have increased their use of computers and other technological advancements to further leverage faculty time. Leveraging faculty time is a complex issue in higher education, one that has many possible outcomes, as Table 1 demonstrates.

It is clear that in most cases, leveraging faculty time drives up the costs of education. Whether this expense is justified depends largely upon the audience. While faculty might argue that increased time for research ultimately improves their classroom performance, students paying high tuition for classes taught by graduate students, classes on narrowly defined topics, and limited out-of-class contact with faculty might believe otherwise.

Destructuring the Curriculum

Beginning in the 1960s, students demanded an increased involvement in the structure and content of the curriculum. They wanted to be free to choose from a large menu of courses, unconstrained by traditional sequence requirements. They wanted to work closely with faculty in designing individual courses of study.

To a large extent, many of their desires have been realized—the curriculum is less

structured than it used to be. Unfortunately, curriculum destructuring has been accompanied by several unintended consequences. Less overall structure places additional burdens on faculty and departmental staff who must coordinate individual courses. This requires time and effort, which in some cases may be significant. So rather than allowing students to interact more closely with faculty to make curricular decisions, destructuring has made yet another demand on faculty time. (It is important to note that destructuring has not occurred equally across disciplines. In general, high-paradigm natural science and mathematics departments have been less affected by the trend than lower-paradigm humanities and social science departments.)

Table 2 demonstrates how destructuring the curriculum can potentially decrease costs. In this case, the more likely outcome is increased leverage of faculty time.

The processes outlined above describe the tension between faculty desire for the increased leverage of their time and the financial realities of the department. Figure 1 demonstrates diagrammatically how faculty leverage, faculty lines, and curriculum structure affect the output mix of academic departments.

Enactment of Group Norms and Propagation of Perceived Property Rights

Yet another process is at work in the academic department which reinforces output creep—the enactment of group norms and propagation of perceived property rights. This final, and perhaps most powerful, dynamic solidi-

Table 1 Alternative Effects of Leveraging Faculty Time

Outcome	Quality of education	Research, publication, professional service	Cost of education
More time spent in other educational tasks (e.g., contact hours, curriculum development, advising and mentoring)	Up	Same	Up
More time spent in research	Same	Up	Up
More time spent in personal pursuits (e.g., private consulting, moonlighting, leisure)	Same	Same	Up
Same time mix; fewer faculty	Same	Same	Down

Table 2 Alternative Effects of Curriculum Destructuring

Outcome	Quality of education	Research, publication, professional service	Cost of education
More time spent in other educational tasks (e.g., contact hours, curriculum development, advising and mentoring)	Up	Same	Same
More time spent in research	Same	Up	Same
More time spent in personal pursuits (e.g., private consulting, moonlighting, leisure)	Same	Same	Same
Same time mix; fewer faculty	Same	Same	Down

fies and even magnifies the three processes described above.

Faculty members in all academic departments possess "enacted norms," which are strongly held, shared beliefs about their relationship to their environment. On the basis of these norms, they develop certain "property rights" that they believe are inherent in the faculty position and that they use to govern their activities. The concept of enacted norms is derived from organization theories, particularly resource-dependence theory (e.g., Pfeffer &

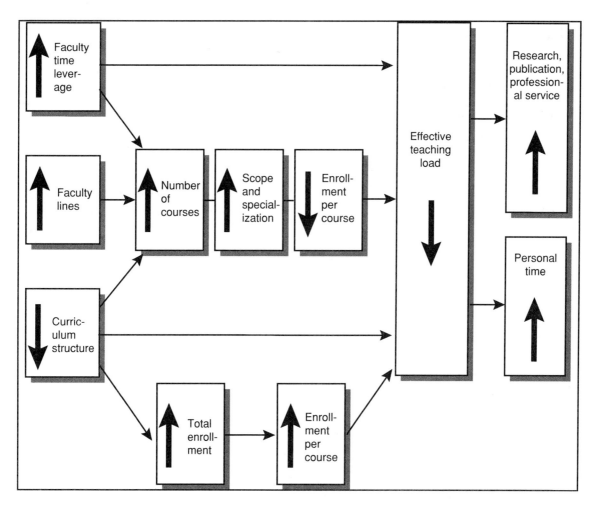

Figure 1 Effect of Faculty, Faculty Lines, and Curriculum Structure on the Departmental Activity Mix

Salancik, 1978) and institutional theory (e.g., Meyer & Rowan, 1977). In essence, enactment occurs because individuals must interpret the multiple organizational, professional, and cultural environments in which they exist. Whether their interpretations are correct or not matters little, for individuals will act upon their perceptions of the environment.

In the case of large organizations, members sometimes collectively come to an understanding of their environments. Specific mappings between resources and desirable outcomes are enacted into shared understandings or norms. Norms are subject to simple rules of appropriateness (Steinbruner, 1974). A norm has an acceptable range or variation based on past experience and in comparison with the norms of similar organizations or their units. Norms become embedded in the routines of the organization and, most of the time, are taken for granted by individuals (March, 1981).

In the context of higher education, many norms stem from enactments of local environments both in departments and in colleges, and from larger professional and multi-institutional environments. The process of enactment includes accepting as reality certain behavioral and technological formulations such as student-teacher ratios, number of courses taught per term, the division of teaching between upper and lower division courses, and ideal class sizes. Norms are strongly rooted in disciplinary professions (e.g., introductory science is best taught in large lecture courses; academic programs should exist as long as reasonable levels of quality are maintained, regardless of how well they relate to the goals and mission of the institution). They also involve comparisons with peer institutions or national leaders in higher education (e.g., "at Harvard, faculty teach only two courses per term").

The enactment of norms within a group often leads to its exercise of a set of perceived property rights. The economic theory of property rights refers to the ability of some organizational participants to use resources in their own interest in ways that might differ from those of other stakeholders or the organization's clients (Levin, 1991). In the case of higher education, desirable circumstances and working conditions are seen as entitlements or rights once they are achieved. For example, certain teaching load levels, student-faculty ratios,

department support for research, and so on are expected to continue.

Ratchet Phases

Planning and budgeting gets intertwined with property rights at many institutions, resulting in the creation of a ratchet mechanism that reinforces desirable activities at the expense of less desirable activities. In effect, this shifts the output mix of departments in the direction of research and away from teaching. Figure 2 demonstrates how we believe the "academic ratchet" process works.

In phase 1, enrollment rises for reasons not connected to output creep; the number of faculty is fixed in the short run so faculty are forced to teach more. This causes the departmental research to fall below the level generally considered to be normal.

In phase 2, lower departmental research represents a violation of perceived property rights, which triggers a demand for more faculty. When this is acceded to, which usually happens if the problem lasts long enough, teaching loads and departmental research return to their normal levels.

In phase 3, enrollment drops back to its original level (again for reasons unrelated to output creep), and a combination of perceived property rights and faculty employment contracts (e.g., tenure) prevents immediate downsizing; faculty members teach less, so departmental research rises above its normal level.

In phase 4, the stickiness in faculty size persist long enough for the new departmental

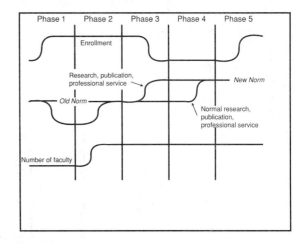

Figure 2 The "Rachet"

research level to become embedded in the department's sense of social reality, that is, to become a perceived property right.

In phase 5, there is a new enrollment surge; the process starts over again, but now from a higher base. The "ratchet" has operated.

The academic ratchet is shaped by several factors that may exist more strongly in some institutions than in others. These include (a) strongly held beliefs about the intrinsic worth of teaching and research programs, (b) a collegial approach to decision making which places consensus at the center and allows little room for alternative points of view, (c) powerful beliefs about academic freedom which are sometimes interpreted as forbidding interference in faculty activities, and (d) the influence of students and alumni who do not want to see the reputation of their program or department negatively impacted.

It is difficult to underestimate the force of enactment and faculty property rights. Their power comes from the ultimate threat of losing unhappy faculty to competing institutions. The academic ratchet is reinforced both internally, by faculty members who prefer research to teaching and administrators who see the benefits of sponsored research, and externally, by students, alumni, and donors who want their programs and departments to be of the highest caliber.

To reiterate, the interaction between perceived rights to "normal" departmental research and the downward-stickiness of faculty size, coupled with exogenous variations in enrollments and other environmental factors, produces a slow shift upward in the normal and actual levels of departmental research. Significant cuts in funding can break the ratchet temporarily, resetting the process to the lower base, but unless the fundamental system dynamics are altered, the upward shift will begin again when the crisis has passed.

Future Research

Having outlined our ideas, we next need to test the accuracy of our framework in the field. Our work will unfold in three stages.

In stage 1, existing data bases (for example IPEDS, CASPAR) will be examined for information that may inform our project. This would include any data that help suggest the existence of the academic ratchet as well as information that will help in selecting institutions for site visits. Final institutional selection will be made in consultation with the project's expert panel.

In stage 2, data from departmental and institutional archives will be collected from participating institutions. Analysis of the documents will include attempts to uncover evidence of a ratchet mechanism (e.g., changes in teaching loads, arguments put forward to support such changes, changes in number of days per semester, increases in faculty publication rates, and changes in staffing patterns of departmental administrative staff and teaching assistants).

In stage 3, on-campus interviews will be conducted with faculty, department chairs, and administrators. Interviews will probe for information about current values, norms, and incentives. We also will conduct oral history interviews with senior faculty about shifts in values and norms. Campus interviews will be a key source of information.

We are confident that this program of fieldwork will provide the insights needed to assess our conceptual structure. Among other things, we will learn how faculty themselves understand and describe the phenomena, and we will be able to point to specific examples that tend to support or refute the theory. Finally, we hope to develop policy recommendations for addressing higher education's cost rise and productivity problems—while at the same time safeguarding the strengths that have made America's colleges and universities the envy of the world.

Note

This article was presented at the Association for Public Policy Analysis and Management's annual research conference. The work was supported by the Finance Center of the Consortium for Policy Research in Education, sponsored by the U.S. Department of Education's Office of Educational Research and Improvement (OERI). The authors acknowledge the collaboration of Professor Robert Zemsky of the University of Pennsylvania and the assistance of participants in the Higher Education

Research Program sponsored by the Pew Charitable Trusts. The responsibility for errors and omissions is, of course, our own.

References

Association of American Colleges. (1985). *Integrity in the college curriculum: A report to the academic community*. Washington, DC: Author.

Baumol, W. J., & Blackman, S. B. (1983). Electronics, the cost disease, and the operation of libraries. *Journal of the American Society for Information Sciences, 34*(3), 181–191.

Baumol, W. J., Blackman. S. B., & Wolff., E. N. (1989). *Productivity and American leadership*. Cambridge, MA: The M.I.T. Press.

Birnbaum, R. (1989, October). Why productivity doesn't improve: The view from the campus. Unpublished manuscript (draft). Presented at the Symposium on Productivity in Higher Education, sponsored by the Forum for College Financing, Annapolis, MD.

Blackburn, R., Armstrong, E., Conrad, C., Didham, J., & McKune, T. (1976). *Changing practices in undergraduate education: A report for the Carnegie Council on Policy Studies in Higher Education*. Berkeley, CA: The Carnegie Council on Policy Studies in Higher Education.

Bok, D. (1986). *Higher learning*. Cambridge, MA: Harvard University Press.

Bowen, H. (1980). *The cost of higher education: How much do colleges and universities spend per student and how much should they spend?* San Francisco: Jossey-Bass.

Bowen, H., & Schuster, J. (1986). *American professors: A national resource imperiled*. New York: Oxford University Press.

Cage, M. C. (1991). 30 states cut higher education budgets by an average of 3.9% in fiscal 1990–91. *The Chronicle of Higher Education, 37*(41), A1, A17.

Cage, M. C. (1992). Mid-year budget cuts reported by public colleges in 22 states. *The Chronicle of Higher Education, 38*(23), A30.

Clark, B. (1987). *The academic life*. Princeton, NJ: Carnegie Foundation for the Advancement of Teaching.

Corrallo, S., Gilmore, J. L., & To, D. (1988). The productivity of American higher education: Issues, problems, and approaches to the problem. Washington, DC: U.S. Department of Education, Office of Educational Research and Improvement.

Cyert, R., & March, J. (1963). *A behavioral theory of the firm*. Englewood Cliffs, NJ: Prentice Hall.

DeLoughry, T. (1990). Education secretary calls on colleges to hold down costs. *The Chronicle of Higher Education, 37*(14), A1, A26.

DeLoughry, T. (1991). New Congress plans to ask colleges tough questions. *The Chronicle of Higher Education, 37*(18), A1, A27.

Evangelauf, J. (1991). Fees rise more slowly this year, but surpass inflation rate again. *The Chronicle of Higher Education, 37*(5), A1, A36.

Fenske, R. (1980). Historical foundations. In U. Delworth and G. Hanson (Eds.), *Student services: A handbook for the profession*. San Francisco: Jossey-Bass.

Frances, C. (1990). *What factors affect college tuition?* Washington, DC: American Association of State Colleges and Universities.

Fulton, O., & Trow, M. (1974). Research activity in American higher education. *Sociology of Education, 47*, 29–73.

Grassmuck, K. (1990). Colleges feel effects of economic downturn in student aid, endowments, job hunting. *The Chronicle of Higher Education, 37*(14), A1, A27.

Hauptman, A. M. (1990). *The college tuition spiral*. Washington, DC: American Council on Education and the College Board.

Hood, A. B., & Arceneaux, C. (1990). *Key resources on student services: A guide to the field and its literature*. San Francisco: Jossey-Bass.

Hopkins, D. S. P., & Massy, W. F. (1981). *Planning models for colleges and universities*. Stanford, CA: Stanford University Press.

Kennedy, D. (1986, March). *How can we look so rich, yet feel so poor?* Paper presented at the Stanford University Los Angeles Alumni Conference, Los Angeles.

Levin, H. M. (1991). Raising productivity in higher education. Prepared for the Higher Education Research Program of the University of Pennsylvania and the Pew Memorial Trust.

March, J. G. (1981). Footnotes to organizational change. *Administrative Science Quarterly, 26*, 663–677.

Massy, W. F. (1989a). Improvement strategies for administration and support services. In R. E. Anderson & J. W. Myerson (Eds.), *Productivity and higher education* (pp. 49–83). Princeton, NJ: Peterson's Guides.

Massy, W. F. (1989b). A strategy for productivity improvement in college and university academic departments. Stanford, CA: Stanford Institute for Higher Education Research.

Massy, W. F. (1990). Productivity in higher education: Results of a preliminary study. Stanford, CA: Stanford Institute for Higher Education Research.

Massy, W. F., & Warner, T. R. (1991). Causes and cures of cost escalation in college and university administrative and support services. *National symposium on strategic higher education, finance and management issues: Proceedings* (pp. 179–199). Washington, DC: National Association of College and University Business Officers.

Massy, W. F., & Zemsky, R. (1992a). Faculty discretionary time: Departments and the academic ratchet. Stanford, CA: Stanford Institute for Higher Education Research.

Massy, W. F., & Zemsky, R. (1992b). A utility model for teaching load decisions in academic departments. Stanford, CA: Stanford Institute for Higher Education Research.

Meisinger, R. J., Purves, R. A., & Schmidtlein, F. A. (1975). Productivity from an interorganizational perspective. *New Directions for Institutional Research, 8,* 91–115.

Meyer, J. W., & Rowan, B. (1977). Institutionalized organizations: Formal structure as myth and ceremony. *American Journal of Sociology, 83,* 340–363.

Mingle, J. R. (1989, March). The political meaning of quality. Paper presented at the National Center for Postsecondary Governance and Finance National Advisory Panel Meeting, Baltimore, MD.

Needham, D. (1982). Improving faculty evaluation and reward systems. *Journal of Economic Education, 13*(1), 6–18.

Olson, M. (1965). The logic of collective action: Public goods and the theory of groups. New York: Schocken.

Pew Higher Education Research Program. (1989). The business of the business. *Policy Perspectives, 1*(4).

Pew Higher Education Research Program. (1990). The lattice and the ratchet. *Policy Perspectives, 2*(4).

Pfeffer, J., & Salancik, J. R. (1978). *The external control of organizations: A resource dependence perspective.* San Francisco: Harper & Row.

Price, J. L., & Mueller, C. W. (1986). *Handbook of organizational measurement.* Marshfield, MA: Pitman.

Rosenzweig, R. M. (1986). Seeing ourselves as others see us. *The Chronicle of Higher Education, 33*(10), A49.

Rosovsky, H. (1991). *Annual report of the dean of the faculty of arts and sciences, 1990–91* (Presentation to faculty of arts and sciences). Cambridge, MA: Harvard University.

Sadlak, J. (1978). Efficiency in higher education: Concepts and problems. *Higher Education, 7,* 213–220.

Shaw, B. M. (1983). Motivation research versus the art of faculty management. *Review of Higher Education, 6,* 301–322.

Shenhav, Y. A., & Haberfeld, Y. (1988). The various faces of scientific productivity: A contingency analysis. *Quality and Quantity, 22,* 365–380.

Smith, P. (1990). *Killing the spirit.* New York: Viking.

Steinbruner, J. D. (1974). *The cybernetic theory of decision.* Princeton, NJ: Princeton University Press.

Sykes, C. J. (1988). *Profscam: Professors and the demise of higher education.* New York: St. Martin's Press.

U.S. Department of Education. (1990). *Tough choices: A guide to administrative cost management in colleges and universities.* Washington, DC: Author.

Wallhaus, R. A. (1975). The many dimensions of productivity. *New Directions for Institutional Research, 8,* 1–16.

Watkins, B. (1990). Practices gone wrong, pervade education, humanities fund chief says. *The Chronicle of Higher Education, 37*(11), A1, A22.

Williams, D. A. (1985, April 29). Is college worth it? *Newsweek,* pp. 66–67.

Zemsky, R., & Massy, W. F. (1990). Cost containment: Committing to a new economic reality. *Change, 22,* 16–22.

PART IV

INSTITUTIONAL RESEARCH TOPICS AND ISSUES

CHAPTER IV

INSTITUTIONAL RESEARCH TOPICS AND ISSUES

Institutional research and analytic activities designed to understand one's institution or inform planning and decision making can be focused on many different topics in college or university life, dynamics, and functioning. Similarly, the issues encountered in attempting to conduct institutional research are extensive. Some are generic issues of research and analysis, and others reflect those encountered in conducting these activities in an applied institutional context. Clearly, the multitude of diverse topics, methods and issues related to institutional research cannot be covered in this section. The items selected cover important current topics and methodological distinctions and issues confronting the field of institutional research. Again, those interested in specific topics, methods or issues may wish to consult chapters in the Related Higher Education Reference Books (Section V-A), *New Directions for Institutional Research*, and the *AIR Professional File* series. The volumes of NDIR are designed to cover current topics and general issues confronting the field of institutional research. The *AIR Professional File* series focuses primarily on specific research methods and techniques used in the practice of conducting institutional research.

Two references in this section focus on identifying or gathering data on institutional performance. Cameron and Whetten, in "Organizational Effectiveness and Quality: The Second Generation," provide an excellent overview of various ways of conceptualizing effectiveness and the newer perspectives on quality that are emerging in higher education. A recent perspective on quality and effectiveness is captured in Dolence and Norris's "Using Key Performance Indicators to Drive Strategic Decision Making."

The increased attention of institutional research on the core academic functions in the latter 1980's and 1990's has raised several institutional research topics or issues reflected by the next three pieces. Ewell provides us with significant assistance in "Identifying Indicators of Curricular Quality" and in the area of "Outcomes, Assessment, and Academic Improvement: In Search of Usable Knowledge." On a more perennial issue, Layzell reviews "Faculty Workload and Productivity: Recurrent Issues with New Imperatives."

Two final selections address serious data collection and information system issues. McLaughlin, Howard, Balkan and Blythe lay out a systematic description of the nature of "Information and Organization" in an institution of higher education and address how institutional research can relate to the information infrastructure of an institution in "Something New: Management Information." Finally, in "Environmental Scanning," Morrison provides a discussion of what to scan for and how environmental scanning can be approached.

Organizational Effectiveness and Quality: The Second Generation[1]

Kim S. Cameron and David A. Whetten

A fundamental shift has occurred recently in the literature of higher education. This shift has been more gradual and less dramatic than it has been in the broader organizational studies literature, but it has been significant nevertheless. It is a shift away from considerations of the construct of effectiveness to describe organizational performance in institutions of higher education and toward considerations of the construct of quality. Quality has begun to replace effectiveness as the central organization-level variable in higher education. With a few notable exceptions, effectiveness has largely been abandoned and quality has become the preeminent construct.

In this paper we discuss the advantages and disadvantages of such a shift—what is given up, what is gained, and what can be learned from both literatures that can inform future research on organizational performance and, especially, the performance of higher education institutions. We first document the nature of the shift away from effectiveness both in organizational studies and in higher education. Then, by taking a historical approach, we review the lessons learned in more than two decades of research on organizational effectiveness in higher education. We discuss the historical development and the emergent approaches in organizational effectiveness from the perspective of the organizational studies literature. It is this literature that served as the original source for higher education applications of effectiveness. We also summarize the main methodological issues associated with effectiveness and the guidelines developed over

more than two decades that have steered effectiveness research. Then, in the second part of the chapter, we describe the "new effectiveness movement" in which the construct of quality is examined in light of its role in supplanting organizational effectiveness as the fashionable organizational performance variable of choice. A comparison is made between traditional effectiveness research and this new quality approach, and we examine the advantages of sticking with the construct of effectiveness versus shifting to a new construct. This discussion highlights lessons learned from past effectiveness literature as well as the utility of quality as a replacement construct that may help guide future research on organizational performance. We conclude the chapter with suggestions of the attributes that should characterize any newly emerging research stream relating to organizational effectiveness or quality in higher education.

Historical Overview of Effectiveness Models

More than a decade ago, we organized a symposium at the annual Academy of Management meetings in which several well-known scholars discussed the current state of organizational effectiveness. That symposium highlighted the disarray and conceptual confusion that surrounded this construct. From that discussion emerged several conclusions: (1) Multiple models of organizational effectiveness are products of multiple, often arbitrary

"Organizational Effectiveness and Quality: The Second Generation," by Kim S. Cameron and David A. Whetten, reprinted from *Higher Education: Handbook of Theory and Research*, Vol. 11, 1996. Agathon Press.

models of organization. No model of organization can be argued to be better than any other, so no model of effectiveness has an advantage over any other. (2) The conceptual boundaries of effectiveness are unknown. It is not clear what criteria are indicators of effectiveness, what criteria are predictors of effectiveness, and what criteria are outcomes of effectiveness. (3) The best criteria for assessing organizational effectiveness are unknown and unknowable. Because individuals often cannot identify their own preferences and expectations, because preferences and expectations change over time, and because contradictory preferences and expectations are held by different constituency groups, a stable set of effectiveness criteria simply are not available for organizations (See Cameron and Whetten, 1983).

That symposium occurred in the midst of ongoing debates in the scholarly literature about which models of organizational effectiveness were the best ones. Seven books were produced on the topic in the late 1970s and early 1980s, and a flurry of articles was published, each arguing for a particular effectiveness model. Bluedorn (1980), for example, argued that the goal model was best, i.e., organizations are effective to the extent to which they accomplish their goals. Seashore

and Yuchtman (1967) and Pfeffer and Salancik (1978) argued for a resource dependence model, i.e., organizations are effective to the extent to which they acquire needed resources. Nadler and Tushman (1980) proposed an internal congruence model, i.e., organizations are effective to the extent to which their internal functioning is consistent and without strain. Connolly, Conlon, and Deutsch (1980) and Tsui (1990) maintained that a strategic constituency model was best, i.e., organizations are effective to the extent to which they satisfy strategic constituencies. Many other models were proposed as well, and Table 1 summarizes the most popular models of organizational effectiveness available during the 1980s.

None of these models of effectiveness emerged as the model of choice, and some writers became so frustrated by the confusion that they recommended a "moratorium on all studies of organizational effectiveness, books on organizational effectiveness, and chapters on organizational effectiveness" (Goodman, 1979, p. 4; also, Hannan and Freeman, 1977).

In 1983, we responded to this recommendation by arguing that "despite its chaotic conceptual condition, organizational effectiveness is not likely to go away" (Cameron and Whetten, 1983, p. 1). We recounted three main rea-

Table 1 Common Models of Organizational Effectiveness

MODEL	DEFINITION	WHEN USEFUL
	An organization is effective if . . .	The model is preferred when . . .
Goal	It accomplishes its stated goals.	Goals are clear, timebound, consensual, and measurable.
System resource	It acquires needed resources	Inputs and outputs are clearly connected.
Internal processes	It has smooth functioning and no strain.	Processes and performance are clearly connected.
Strategic constituencies	All constituencies are minimally satisfied.	Constituencies have power over/in the organization.
Competing values	Trade-offs are balanced.	Paradoxical pressures are encountered.
Legitimacy	It survives by engaging in legitimate activity.	Survival or demise is of interest.
Fault-driven	It has an absence of ineffectiveness indicators.	Mistakes are fatal.

Source: K.S. Cameron (1984)

sons why effectiveness was here to stay. First, organizational effectiveness lies at the center of all models and theories of organization. That is, all conceptualizations of organization have embedded in them some notion of the difference between effective and ineffective functioning. Second, we argued that effectiveness was the ultimate dependent variable in organizational research. Evidence of effective performance is required in most research on organizations. Third, individuals are constantly faced with the need to make judgments about the effectiveness of organizations. Pragmatic choices are continually made about effectiveness—which public school will close, which institution will get a contract, in which organization an investment will be made, and so on.

Despite our prediction, however, scholarly research largely ceased on the topic of organizational effectiveness. From a total of more than 20 articles appearing on the topic of organizational effectiveness in the Academy of Management journals (*Journal, Review, Executive*) and *Administrative Science Quarterly* from 1975 to 1985, (and several hundred more before that time [see Cameron, 1982 for a review]), only one single article in *ASQ* (Tsui, 1990) and no books appeared on effectiveness during the next eight years.

This trend was also noticeable in the higher education literature. After a special issue of *The Review of Higher Education* on institutional effectiveness in 1985 (Vol. 9, No. 1), no articles on that topic have appeared in *RHE* since, and only one has appeared in *The Journal of Higher Education* (Cameron and Tschirhart, 1992). Similarly, one chapter appeared in *Higher Education: Handbook of Theory and Research* in 1989 on the effectiveness of state systems (Chaffee, 1989), but no other chapters have addressed higher education effectiveness in *The Handbook* since then. John Smart has almost singlehandedly kept the effectiveness construct alive by continuing to publish analyses from studies of two-year colleges and from Cameron's NCHEMS data base on effectiveness (e.g., Smart, 1989; Smart and Hamm, 1993a, b; Fjortoft and Smart, 1994), but most other researchers have abandoned the topic. Two studies of institutional productivity (a frequent proxy for effectiveness) appeared in *JHE*

(McGuire, Richman, Daly, and Jorjani, 1988; Levin, 1991), but in neither case was productivity treated as a proxy for effectiveness. The conclusion reached by most scholars seems to have been similar to that drawn by us in 1983: ". . . multiple viewpoints all may be equally legitimate but under different circumstances and with different types of organizations" (Cameron and Whetten, 1983, p. 274). The trouble was, by concluding that everyone in the previous years' effectiveness debates could be right, the bloom was taken off the effectiveness rose. Researchers lost interest.

However, it was only the construct of organizational effectiveness that faded away, not the need to assess organizational performance and to make judgments about excellent practices. With the publication of popular books such as Peters and Waterman's *In Search of Excellence* (1982), Deming's *Out of the Crisis* (1986), Imai's *Kaizen* (1988), Pascale's *Managing on the Edge* (1990), Tichy and Sherman's *Control Your Destiny or Somebody Else Will* (1993), the emphasis changed from organizational effectiveness to excellence, quality, continuous improvement, transformation, revitalization, and so on. In addition, scholars began to investigate organizational phenomena that had been largely ignored prior to the mid-1980s—namely, high reliability systems, hyper-turbulent environments, one-of-a-kind disasters, and unusually high levels of performance (Weick and Roberts, 1992; Perrow, 1984). Both sets of events—the mushrooming popular interest in best practices, and the investigation of non-normal organizational dynamics—helped fuel the emergence of a new kind of research related to organizational effectiveness.

To understand the advantages and disadvantages of this new direction away from traditional effectiveness research, we review briefly the historical development of organizational effectiveness approaches. That discussion highlights the hard-won lessons associated with the theoretical and empirical writing that was central to the literature for many years. Whereas the construct of effectiveness may have seen its day, we argue that these lessons should not be abandoned so quickly.

The Development of Organizational Effectiveness Approaches

Ideal Types

The earliest models of organizational effectiveness emphasized "ideal types," that is, forms of organization which maximized certain attributes. Weber's characterization of bureaucracies is the most obvious and well-known example (1947). This "rational-legal" form of organization was characterized by decisions based on rules, equal treatment for all employees, separation of the position from its occupant, staffing and promotions based on skills and expertise, specific work standards, and documented work performance. These characteristics were operationalized as dimensions of bureaucracy, including: formalization of procedures, specialization of work, centralization of decision making (Hall, 1963).

Early applications of the bureaucratic model to the topic of effectiveness argued that efficiency was the appropriate measure of organizational performance. Given this performance criteria, the more nearly an organization approached the "ideal" bureaucratic characteristics, the more effective (i.e., efficient) it was. Specifically, the more specialized, formalized, and centralized, the better. In defense of this perspective, Perrow argued that most of the criticisms of the "sins" of bureaucracy are actually the result of bureaucratic principles not being implemented fully. "Where all organizations strive toward efficiency as defined by the owners, the rational-legal form of bureaucracy is the most efficient form of administration known in industrial societies" (1986, p. 4).

Subsequent models of organizing began to challenge these assumptions, however, suggesting that effective organizations were non-bureaucratic. Chester Barnard's influential book, *The Functions of the Executive* (1938) argued that organizations are at their core cooperative systems. Furthermore, he argued that it was the role of leaders to channel and direct those cooperative processes to accomplish productive outcomes. An effective organization, therefore, needed to satisfy the needs of its members through providing adequate inducements to sustain their required contributions. It

must ensure that the actions of members are bridled by institutionalized goals and decision making processes. In addition, it needed to legitimate its role in society by shrouding its activities in broad social values.

Perrow (1986, p. 63) argued: "'This enormously influential and remarkable book contains within it the seeds of three distinct trends of organizational theory that were to dominate the field for the next three decades. One was the institutional school as represented by Philip Selznick (1948); another was the decision-making school as represented by Herbert Simon (1956); the third was the human relations school (Roethlisberger and Dickson, 1947)." In one sense, each of these schools of thought became a competing ideal type. It was logical for devotees to argue that effectiveness should be measured by the standard of their "ideal" organization. They disagreed over the criteria for assessing effectiveness; they agreed that effectiveness should be measured against the standard of an ideal type.

Over the years, the ideal types proliferated. Early researchers used as their ideal organizational goal accomplishment (Bluedorn, 1980). Then advocates of the "natural systems" view of organizations (Scott, 1992) argued that goal accomplishment ultimately depends on controlling critical resources, e.g., human and financial capital (Yuchtman and Seashore, 1967; Pfeffer and Salancik, 1978). This challenge to the rational model opened the flood gates of alternative standards, including the quality of an organization's communication and "interpretive" processes (Weick and Daft, 1983), the satisfaction of members (Schneider, 1983), and the extent to which organizational policies and practices complied with the norms of social equality (Keeley, 1978). In the higher education literature the collegial model (Baldridge, 1971), the professional bureaucratic model (Mintzberg, 1979), and the loosely coupled systems model (Weick, 1978) all captured additional advocates. The common ingredient during this era was a passion for finding the Holy Grail of organizational theory: the definitive, universalistic definition of organizational effectiveness.

Contingency Approaches

Challenges to the soundness of Weber's reasoning, coupled with mounting frustration over the truth claims of competing models, gave rise to "contingency theory." This perspective argued that effectiveness was not a function of the extent to which an organization reflected the qualities of an ideal profile, but instead, it depended on the match between an organization's profile and environmental conditions. The challenge for researchers became identifying the relevant environmental and organizational dimensions and building theories of "fit."

Burns and Stalker's (1961) classic treatise on organic versus mechanistic types represents an early bridge from ideal type to contingency theory thinking. They argued that mechanistic organizations (those high on Weber's bureaucratic dimensions) were best suited for highly stable and relatively simple environments. In contrast, organic organizations (those high on Barnard's characteristics) were better suited for rapidly changing, highly complex situations. This kernel of an idea bore fruit in several large scale studies of congruence between organizational and environmental dimensions during the late 1960s and 1970s. These included Lawrence and Lorsch's (1967) study of multiple industries, the Aston studies in England (Pugh, Hickson, and Hinings, 1969) and Van de Ven and Ferry's (1980) development of the "Organizational Assessment Survey" (OAS).

The critical difference between ideal type and contingency theory thinking was that the former assumed that "one size fits all." That is, effective organizations were distinguished by their fit with a universal set of characteristics, an ideal type. An effective organization emphasized X, Y, or Z, depending on the theoretical bias. In contrast, contingency theory argued that effective organizations matched their profiles with prevailing environmental conditions. If the organization was in an X type environment, then it should emphasize X design features. What these two views shared in common was an emphasis on organizational dimensions. While the referent for judging effectiveness differed, the way it was measured, or assessed, was the same. Organizational dimensions like standardization, centralization, satisfaction, and size, and environmental dimensions like simple, dynamic, and patterned were common to both ideal type and contingency theory perspectives.

In the higher education literature, contingency approaches were exemplified by Cameron's (1981) studies of "domains" of organizational effectiveness in which different types of colleges displayed different patterns of effectiveness depending on their institutional types and characteristics. Smart (1989) found different effectiveness patterns among institutions in decline and with different organizational cultures. Effectiveness patterns in colleges, as reported in all of these contingency studies, differed depending on their environments.

Multiple Constituencies

A third approach to organizational effectiveness began to emerge when authors focused less on the assessment criteria of abstract dimensions and more on the concrete expressions of stake holders' expectations (Connolly, Conlon, and Deutsch, 1980; Zammuto, 1984). Effective organizations were viewed as those which had accurate information about the expectations of strategically critical constituents and adapted internal organizational activities, goals, and values to match those expectations. Proponents of the stake holders' perspective view organizations as highly elastic entities operating in a dynamic force field which literally pulls the organization's shape and form in different directions—molding the organization to the demands of powerful interest groups, including stockholders, unions, government regulators, competitors, customers, and so forth. Effectiveness is, therefore, a function of organizational qualities like learning, responsiveness, and influence management.

The "multiple constituencies" model spawned a large number of research studies (Whetten, 1978; Cameron, 1978; Mahoney, 1967; Osborn and Hunt, 1974; Tsui, 1990). Researchers using this approach encountered four difficult methodological challenges (Cameron and Whetten, 1983, p. 12). (1) When asked, individual stake holders have difficulty explicating their personal expectations for an organization. (2) A stake holder's expectations change, sometimes dramatically, over time. (3) A variety of contradictory expectations are almost always pursued simultaneously in an organization. (4) The expectations of strategic constituencies frequently are unrelated, or negatively related, to their overall judgments of an organization's effectiveness (see Cameron and Whetten, 1983).

The multiple constituencies model is aptly portrayed in Zammuto's (1984) discussion of ways to deal with the dilemmas of unclear, contradictory, unrelated expectations held by an organization's multiple stake holders. He suggested four alternatives: (1) strive to provide as much as possible to each stake holder without harming any one stake holder, (2) strive to satisfy the expectations of the most powerful or dominant stake holders first, (3) favor the least advantaged stake holders who are most likely to be harmed, and (4) develop the capacity to be flexible and adaptable so as to be able to respond to the changing set of stake holder expectations. In higher education, discussions of value-added education, faculty reputation, student outcomes, and so forth (e.g., Astin, 1985; Bowen, 1977), while not representative of organizational effectiveness studies, nevertheless exemplify the orientation toward accounting for multiple stake holder perspectives.

Paradox Model

The recognition that organizations are simultaneously pulled in opposite directions by the expectations of multiple constituencies led Quinn and his associates (Quinn and Cameron, 1982; Quinn and Rohrbaugh, 1981; Faehrman and Quinn, 1985) to introduce the Competing Values Model of organizational effectiveness. This model recognizes the inherently paradoxical nature of organizational functioning. Administrators must not only make tradeoffs between day-to-day competing demands on the organization's resources, but, more importantly, they must balance competing expectations regarding the core identity of the organization as an institution. From this point of view, effective organizations are both short and long-term focused, flexible and rigid, centralized and decentralized, goal and resource control oriented, concerned about the needs of members and the demands of customers.

The "paradoxical model" of organizational effectiveness represents the natural, logical extension of earlier eras of thought. It borrows from contingency theory the emphasis on matching external and internal attributes. Like strategic constituencies it uses expectations (rather than dimensions) as the criteria for measuring effectiveness. In a sense, the para-

doxical model can be viewed as a more complex form of its predecessors—it allows for the likelihood of organizations operating simultaneously in different environmental domains, with each domain conveying different expectations. Whereas contingency theory assumed a single domain for sake of matching organizational and environmental characteristics, the paradoxical extension allows for multiple domains requiring multiple, simultaneous, and contradictory matches.

The role of paradoxical logic in the higher education literature is illustrated, for example, by Cameron's (1986) review of several empirical studies of effectiveness in colleges and universities. He found the presence of paradox to be synonymous with the presence of effectiveness in organizations faced with turbulence, change, and complexity. In a study of 14 declining colleges, 7 of which eventually reversed their declining trends, for example, the major difference between institutions that recovered and those that continued to decline was the presence of paradox: entrepreneurship and conservatism, enacting the environment and buffering against the environment, defensiveness and aggressiveness, reinforcing and destroying traditions. In another study of 334 colleges (see Cameron, 1986b), a similar conclusion was reached: "These general findings help illustrate the presence of simultaneous opposites in organizations that are highly effective, or that improve in their effectiveness, particularly under turbulent conditions (p. 547)." The review of several empirical studies led to the conclusion that, "It is not just the presence of mutually exclusive opposites that makes for effectiveness, but it is the creative leaps, the flexibility, and the unity made possible by them that leads to excellence . . . the presence of creative tension arising from paradoxical attributes helps foster organizational effectiveness" (Cameron, 1986, p. 549).

In the organizational studies literature, Peters and Waterman (1982) found that effective firms possess a variety of paradoxical characteristics such as simultaneous loose and tight coupling, productivity through participation along with a bias for action (nonparticipation), entrepreneurship along with sticking-to-the-knitting, and so forth. They asserted, "The excellent companies have learned how to manage paradox" (p. 100). Eisenhart and Wescott (1988)

Table 2 Evolution of Approaches to Organizational Effectiveness

	Examples of Authors	Basic Approach	Common Models
Ideal Types	Weber; Barnard; Price	Matching the organization's profile and the ideal type	Goal models Internal process models
Contingency Theory	Burns & Stalker; Aston studies; Van de Ven and Ferry; Seashore and Yuchtman	Matching the organization's profile and the environmental conditions	System resource
Multiple Constituencies	Pfeffer and Salancik; Tsui; Connolly et al.	Matching the organization's activities and the constituencies' expectations	Strategic constituency models
Paradox Approach	Quinn and Cameron	Combining contradictory elements and managing inconsistent expectations	Competing values model

also found paradox to be inherent in successful just-in-time manufacturing. Their investigation of quality control, production planning, inventory control, and capital investments in manufacturing firms emphasized that "manufacturers who adopt the paradox philosophy which produced these [just-in-time] practices probably have greater and more continuous success" (p. 192).

Proponents of paradoxical thinking (e.g., Quinn and Cameron, 1988) use these conclusions to argue that effective organizations are not those that simply match an ideal profile, or personify a universalistic model, nor are they characterized by hyper-responsiveness in juggling competing constituencies' demands. Instead, they are best characterized as hybrid forms consisting of uncomplimentary elements. They are both large and small, both growing and downsizing, both tightly coupled and flexible, both consistent and inconsistent.

Summary of Current Conceptual Thinking

Looking back over the past three decades, there have been at least three major evolutionary shifts in the prevailing views of organizational effectiveness. They are summarized in Table 2. This intellectual odyssey has yielded progressively more complex views of organizations as behavioral systems. As a natural consequence, the theories of organizational effectiveness have also in-

creased in complexity. In particular, they reflect more complex and dynamic views of organizational goals, outcomes, and constituencies.

Assessment Issues

In addition to the evolutionary conceptual development of organizational effectiveness, issues relating to empirical assessment also have progressed. The bulk of empirical assessments in the 1960s, 1970s, and 1980s used generalized summary ratings of overall effectiveness (Webster, 1985; McGuire, et al., 1988). A single rating of overall performance was the norm in empirical investigations. In the higher education literature this was generally reflected as reputational ratings or prestige rankings. Relatively little sophistication characterized most of these assessments. Sometimes multiple outcomes were included (e.g., selectivity, productivity, student achievement), but few identified empirically the relationships among the dimensions or their predictors, and paltry attention was given to their association with objective performance criteria. Several efficiency formulas comparing input measures to output measures were introduced as substitutes for effectiveness (e.g., Lewin and Minton, 1986), but the reliable and accurate evaluation effectiveness in the organizational studies literature continued to be almost universally identified as a conundrum. It became clear that an informed assessment of organizational effectiveness must address several critical design parameters, and we proposed the following seven questions as guidelines (Cameron and Whetten, 1983, pp. 269–274):

1. *What time frame is being employed?* Short-term effects may differ from long-term effects, and different stages in an organization's life cycle may produce different levels of performance.

2. *What level of analysis is being used?* Effectiveness at different levels of analysis in an organization (e.g., subunit activities versus organizational adaptation) may be incompatible.

3. *From whose perspective is effectiveness being judged?* The criteria used by different constituencies to define effectiveness often differ markedly and often follow from unique constituency interests.

4. *On what domain of activity is the judgment focused?* Achieving high levels of effectiveness in one domain of activity in an organization may mitigate against effectiveness in another domain.

5. *What is the purpose for judging effectiveness?* Changing the purposes of an evaluation may change the consequences and the criteria being evaluated.

6. *What type of data are being used for judgments of effectiveness?* Official documents, perceptions of members, participant observations, and symbolic or cultural artifacts all may produce a different conclusion about the effectiveness of an organization.

7. *What is the referent against which effectiveness is judged?* No universal standard exists against which to evaluate performance, and different standards will produce different conclusions about effectiveness.

To illustrate the richness of issues associated with each of these seven questions, we explain the first three in slightly more detail below. For an elaboration of all seven issues, see Cameron and Whetten (1983). Our purpose in elaborating this discussion here is to highlight some of the important considerations that have emerged from the effectiveness literature that may not have received as much attention in the recent literature. We discuss issues related to time frame, level of analysis, and constituencies.

Time Frame

The adage, "Timing is everything," has a special significance for research on organizational effectiveness. The "when" of an assessment will effect the outcome of the assessment in two ways. First, short-term and long-term measures of effectiveness often produced strikingly different results. For example, in a study of the U.S. tobacco industry, Miles and Cameron (1982) found that one company was the least effective of the six firms when short-term criteria were applied, but it jumped to second most effective when long-term criteria were used. Another firm was the most effective firm in the short term, but it dropped to fifth in the long term. Differences in long-term and short-term assessments may vary either because the organization is deliberately sacrificing performance in one time frame in hopes of increasing it in the other, or because the effects of organizational performance are not detected because the wrong time frame is being utilized.

The second reason why timing may effect the outcome of an organizational assessment is related to the life cycle of organizations. The application of the biological metaphor to patterns of organizational change (e.g., Spencer, 1897; Parsons, 1964; Miller; 1978, Katz and Kahn, 1978; McKelvey, 1982), the generalization of small group stage models to organizational development (Cameron and Whetten, 1983b), and the application of product life cycle models to organizational strategy (BCG, 1970) has led most organizational scholars to conclude that organizations develop through certain identifiable life cycle stages over time. Cameron and Whetten (1981) found, for example, that the criteria of effectiveness held by participants in simulated organizations changed as the organizations progressed through different stages of the organization life cycle. They concluded that ". . . significant variation existed in the ratings of effectiveness of individual, department, and organization levels, depending on the organization's stage of development" (p. 537). Similarly, Quinn and Cameron's (1983) study of the formulation and maturing of a state government agency found that a different model of effectiveness predominated in each of four different stages of development. In the first stage (labelled entrepreneurial stage) the open systems model was most important. In stage 2 (the collectivity stage), the human relations and open systems models took precedence. Stage 3 (the formalization stage) was dominated by rational goal and internal process criteria, and in stage 4 (the elaboration of structure stage) the open systems and rational goal models were relied on to make judgments of effectiveness.

Level of Analysis

It follows from our understanding of organizations as complex social systems that the unit, or level of analysis in assessing organizational effectiveness matters a great deal. Judgments of "organizational" effectiveness can be made at the individual level (e.g., Is the human dignity of organizational members being preserved?), at the unit level (e.g., Is the work group cohesive?), at the organization level (e.g., Does the organization acquire needed resources?), at the population or system level (e.g., Does the organization's performance enhance the legitimacy of the entire system?), or at the societal level (e.g., What is the effect of the organization's outputs on society?). It is generally the case that assessments of effectiveness at one level do not match assessments made at another level. Indeed, Freeman (1980) argued that selecting the appropriate level of analysis is critical because data on effectiveness at one level are often nonsensical when viewed from another level.

This awareness is critical as knowledge is accumulated about organizational effectiveness at different levels of analysis. For example, Tsui studied effectiveness at the individual (1984) and unit level (1990), Cameron (1984) focused on the organizational level, and Ehreth (1988) concentrated on the societal level. The well-known, but often overlooked, problems of making comparisons across levels of analysis include lack of construct isomorphism, cross-level effects, and emergent properties (Rousseau, 1985).

These concerns are reflected in what a recent task force of the National Academy of Sciences' Division on Human Factors referred to as the "productivity paradox" (Harris, Goodman and Sink, 1993). That is, when all the dollars that

an organization invests in increasing the productivity of its various operations (everything from word processing to manufacturing) are added up and then compared with widely accepted measures of organizational-level productivity, a negligible correlation exists.

In the process of analyzing this problem, the task force concluded that the existing models of organizational effectiveness, personal performance, and group productivity are ill-equipped to guide investigations of the causes of this paradox. The core deficiency with all these models is that they focus on a single level of analysis (either the person, the group, or the organization). Therefore, they are appropriate for answering the question, "How can we increase the productivity (or effectiveness) of X (where X is a person, group, or organization)," but they shed little light on the question, "Given an increase in the productivity (or effectiveness) of X (person, group, or organization), under what conditions are we likely to see an increase in the productivity of Y (a different level in the organization)." In other words, we recognized that we knew almost nothing about cross-level processes or their effects.

Constituencies

The homily, "Where you stand affects what you see," captures the essence of the current writing on the differences in constituencies' perspectives. Studies by Whetten (1978) and Friedlander and Pickle (1968), for example, found low and even negative correlations among the ratings of effectiveness by different stake holder groups. Scott (1992), explained this phenomenon by predicting that different constituencies can be expected to espouse different criteria for measuring organizational performance. These preferences reflect the stake holder's interests in the organization or the organizational unit. For example, he identified four kinds of effectiveness criteria that differ among stake holders: (1) *Strategic focus*, or direction, has to do with whether the organization is doing the "right things." That is, are resources being deployed to solve the right problems or pursue the right objectives? (2) *Outcomes*, or effects, focus on the quality of the organization's services or products. This criteria examines whether the organization is doing "things right." (3) *Processes* focuses on the quantity or quality of the activities used by the organization to produce its outcomes. Whereas outcomes relate to effect, processes relate to effort. It is an assessment of an organization's "throughput." (4) *Structural capabilities* address the organization's capacity for effective performance. These might include the quality and quantity of a manufacturer's equipment and the technical training of equipment operators. These factors are typically treated as "inputs" in econometric models of performance.

Scott (1992) argued that different stake holders focus on unique elements of the total effectiveness model and treat that particular element as a surrogate for the whole. Administrators, for example, focus primarily on capabilities, whereas employees (e.g., faculty and staff) focus on processes, clients, students, or customers focus on outcomes, and regulators or accreditors (and to some extent stock holders) emphasize strategic focus. Hence, different stake holders may rate effectiveness very differently from one another.

Summary of Empirical Issues

Again, the purpose of discussing in somewhat more detail three of these questions is to illustrate the complexity that has accompanied systematic empirical assessment of effectiveness over the past three decades. Measuring effectiveness has not been an easy task. A transition has occurred from single, universalistic evaluations of effectiveness to the identification and assessment of multiple, even paradoxical, effectiveness dimensions. Our seven guidelines for research have given evaluators of effectiveness research, at a minimum, an apparatus with which to assess the thoroughness, precision, and applicability of the effectiveness criteria being employed. Moreover, they help create a boundary for the conceptual definition of effectiveness in particular studies. Effectiveness in higher education, for example, that is measured from the standpoint of administrators, relying on long-term data, using financial performance, and being compared to peer institutions, would produce a different definition of effectiveness than if the construct was assessed using a different set of constraints. These assessment guidelines, then, link with the conceptual issues surrounding effectiveness by affecting definitions and approaches.

Foundations of a New Effectiveness Movement

This discussion of the evolutionary development of conceptual and empirical issues surrounding organizational effectiveness, and the three transitions that comprise that development, help provide a foundation with which to examine the new trends in research on organizational performance. Because current work seems to be leading toward another transition in effectiveness approaches, away from the effectiveness construct as a focus of research, the second part of this chapter highlights the rudiments of this "new organizational effectiveness movement." This movement currently occupies center stage in discussions about organizational performance. It presents a challenge to the predominance of the construct of organizational effectiveness in the organizational sciences and, in turn, in the higher education literature. Of course, this new movement may merely be a temporary intellectual fad, that is, an overly popular but underdeveloped trend which grabs a great deal of attention for a short time but adds little to our fundamental understanding of organizations. On the other hand, it appears that the challenge to traditional effectiveness research is nontrivial. Consequently, our comparison of the contributions of this new focus on quality with the contributions emerging from past learning about effectiveness helps fashion our recommendations for future research needs.

Precursors to Abandoning Effectiveness in Research

Recently, at least two additional modifications have occurred in conceptualizations of effectiveness that have dramatically affected its use (or lack thereof) in the organizational studies literature. Because these modifications have had the effect of halting empirical and theoretical writing on the construct of effectiveness per se, and of substituting another construct for it, a discussion of these modifications, the development of the replacement construct, and the applicability of the lessons learned from the effectiveness literature to this new movement should be informative. Knowing how approaches to effectiveness evolved in the past provide insight into the issues to be faced in the coming decade with a construct that, while capturing the attention of the organizational scholars, is still in its infancy in organizational research. Without scrutiny, it is not clear whether the new movement will cause effectiveness work to advance or to retrogress.

The first modification has been a dramatically intensified emphasis on pragmatics in organizational studies in the 1990s. With the escalating cry for relevance in schools, the attacks on scholarly research as lagging practice, the loss of competitiveness and high failure rate in U.S. businesses, (e.g., Whetten and Cameron, 1991, pp. 1–11), and the continued erosion of confidence in higher education, the approach to effectiveness took a decided pivot. As discussed above, whereas the 1960s through the 1980s were marked by debates about which definition, which criteria, or which framework of effectiveness were most appropriate, the 1990s are marked by little debate at all. Instead of arguing with colleagues about conceptual issues, scholars are now more often focusing on identifying "best practices" in organizations, or describing the changes, improvements, or blunders that organizations are experiencing. Less attention is being given to conceptual dimensions and definitions and more is given to identifying appropriate organizational practices and means for accomplishing desirable outcomes. Hence, a perceptible shift has occurred from discussions of effectiveness that were criticized by practitioners as too ethereal and theoretical to discussions of effectiveness that are now criticized by scholars as too pragmatic, thin, and over-simplified (e.g., Scott, 1992). This is represented by a significant trend toward identifying managerial implications in effectiveness research. Emphasis on definitional debates has given way to an emphasis on finding appropriate guidelines for management practice—a shift from ends to means.

The second significant modification is related to fundamental changes in the assumptions being made about the nature of effective organizations. These changes were at least partially motivated by the examination in recent research of new types of organizational performance and unusual occurrences, as well as by the influence of other academic disciplines in studying organizational phenomena. Specifically, at the beginning of the 1980s, a perusal of

organizational effectiveness literature led to the conclusion that (1) bigger organizations indicate better organizations (e.g., Greiner, 1967), (2) unending growth is a natural and desirable process in organizational life cycle development (e.g., Cameron and Whetten, 1981), (3) slack resources, loose coupling, and redundancy are associated with organizational adaptability and flexibility (Weick, 1976), and (4) consistency and congruence are hallmarks of effective organizations (Nadler and Tushman, 1980).

By the beginning of the 1990s, however, a dramatic change had occurred in these fundamental assumptions underlying organizational performance. Each of these assumptions had been challenged, not because new theories were developed, but because of the changing dynamics observed and investigated in organizations. Researchers who had previously been guided by the four assumptions above were motivated to revise their perspectives on the basis of what they observed in highly effective organizations. The replacement assumptions were representative of the paradoxical approach to effectiveness in that they were opposite the original assumptions as well as being supplemental, namely: (1) smaller (as well as larger) organizations also indicate better organizations (Peters, 1993); (2) downsizing and decline (as well as growth) are also natural and desirable parts of the life cycle process (Cameron, Freeman, and Michra, 1993); (3) tight coupling and nonredundancy (as well as slack resources and loose coupling) are also associated with adaptability and flexibility (Weick and Roberts, 1992); and (4) conflict and inconsistency (as well as congruence and consistency) are also indicative of organizational effectiveness (Cameron, 1986). While these revised assumptions partly represent an integration of the concept of paradox into organizational assumptions, they, along with the new pragmatic focus, led work on organizational effectiveness (now called by a variety of different names in the literature, hardly ever by effectiveness) to begin moving in a decidedly different direction. The most frequent substitute for effectiveness, and the construct most responsible for the dramatic shifts in effectiveness research over the past half decade or so, is **quality**.

Clarifying the Meaning of Quality

In the scholarly literature prior to the late 1980s, quality was treated as a predictor of effectiveness (Campbell, 1977; Conrad and Blackburn, 1985). Quality referred to the rate of errors or defects in goods-producing organizations (Crosby, 1979), to institutional reputation in higher education organizations (Webster, 1981), to ambiance and talent in arts organizations (Tschirhart, 1993), to recovery in health care organizations (Scott, Flood, Ewy, and Forrest, 1978), and so on. In every case, quality was **one** of the desired attributes of the outcomes produced by organizations, and it was always used as a qualifier in describing some product or service, i.e., high quality products, high quality education, high quality art, high quality health care. It was merely an attribute of what organizations were interested in accomplishing.

However, motivated by the unmistakable and highly visible decline in U.S. competitiveness relative to the Japanese (in particular) because of poor quality products, the loss of consumer confidence in U.S. products and services (including education) as a result of perceptions of poor quality, the introduction of the prestigious Malcolm Baldrige National Quality Award (MBNQA) by the U.S. Commerce Department, and the increase in attention to "best practices" in the popular press, the use of and focus on quality changed. More and more, quality began to take on the appearance of the *summum bonum* relative to organizational performance. Managers and organization members became converted to the pursuit of quality as the single most important organizational objective (Deming, 1986), and scholars scrambled to catch up by substituting quality as the dependent variable of choice. In 1993, for example, quality was the most frequently appearing topic in research papers at the Academy of Management, as well as in the various professional meetings associated with the field of higher education (e.g., ASHE, AAHE, SCUP). Whereas effectiveness had largely disappeared from the organizational studies and higher education literatures, articles and books published since 1985 on quality now number in the hundreds (see Peterson and Cameron, 1994, for an annotated bibliography on quality in higher education). This indicates, simply, that quality has begun to be elevated to a conceptual level formerly afforded only to effectiveness, that is, as a construct designated as the central objective of organizational action. It is beginning to encompass multiple outcomes, effects, and processes.

For example, a distinction was invented differentiating a "big Q" approach to quality from a "little q" approach (Juran, 1993). The former refers to quality as an overall, encompassing culture of the organization, and the latter refers to specific tools, techniques, activities, or product and service attributes within an organization. Little 'q' is associated with quality as an attribute of a product or a process. Big 'Q' is associated with the strategy and overall functioning of the organization in addition to the ultimate outcome produced by its products and services. The phrase "total quality management" (TQM) is generally substituted for big 'Q' quality (Sashkin and Kiser, 1993).

Quality only recently has taken on the TQM or big 'Q' connotation. Traditionally, quality was treated as a reliability engineering or statistical control issue and appeared mainly in engineering, operations management, and applied statistics literatures. It was limited in its application to products or processes, not to overall organizational performance. For example, Garvin (1988) identified four "quality eras" in the United States: (1) *an inspection era*, in which quality was associated with mistakes and errors detected in products or services after they were produced; (2) *a statistical control era*, in which defects were reduced by statistical sampling and testing and by controlling variability in the processes that produced products; (3) *a quality assurance era*, in which quality techniques and philosophies were expanded beyond the production of outputs to "total quality control" where top management took responsibility for ensuring quality in all parts of the organization; and (4) *a strategic quality management era*, in which quality was defined from the customer's point of view and the organization's strategy became centered on quality. This shift from the first era to the fourth era was largely a shift from little 'q' to big 'Q' quality. It is this big 'Q' or TQM use of quality that has begun to appear in the organizational studies and higher education literatures and has begun to rival effectiveness as the key organizational-level dependent variable.

Interestingly, Garvin's quality eras also

parallel quite closely the evolutionary shifts in effectiveness definitions. For example, the first two quality eras, inspection and statistical control, best characterized by Shewhart's (1931) classic *Economic Control of Quality of Manufactured Product,* represent an ideal type approach. Similar to the ideal type models of organizational effectiveness, Shewhart outlined universalistic techniques of quality control as well as a philosophy that emphasized one correct way to define and achieve quality. The next quality era—quality assurance—is similar to the contingency view of effectiveness. Juran (1951) and Fiegenbaum (1961), for example, motivated the shift to a new quality era by identifying different approaches to and different meanings of quality depending on which part of an organization was being considered. Quality definitions could differ among functions (e.g., manufacturing, purchasing, sales) as well as among activities (e.g., new product design, inventory control, assembly) (Fiegenbaum, 1961). The fourth era—strategic quality management— parallels the multiple constituency approach to effectiveness in emphasizing the key role of the organization's stake holders (i.e., customers, suppliers, beneficiaries). Quality in this era is defined from the customer's point of view, and the organization's strategy, processes, measurements, and activities are focused on satisfying the customer (Garvin, 1988).

The similarities in these stages of development are immaterial except that, as a proposed replacement for effectiveness, the level of quality's theoretical development takes on added importance. In fact, in order to discuss the future of organizational-level quality research as a replacement for effectiveness, it is important to be more precise about the current definitions of quality so that an adequate examination of its merit can be made.

One difficulty with studying quality, as with effectiveness, is that its definition is neither precise nor consensual. As is clear from our previous discussion, both effectiveness and quality are *constructs,* not *concepts,* and no objective referents exist. Their definitions are *constructed* in the minds of definers (Cameron 1981), so no one definition is ever completely correct. Table 1, for example, provided several of the most frequently appearing definitions of effectiveness in the literature. Table 3 identifies several current definitions of (or approaches to) quality as well.

A common theme in the top five definitions is they focus on quality as an attribute of products and services (little 'q'). The bottom two definitions focus on quality from a more comprehensive, organization-level perspective (big 'Q' or TQM). This latter perspective is typical of the approach to quality that rivals the construct of effectiveness. These definitions of quality are generally described as incorporating a variety of attributes or characteristics. That is, when explaining big 'Q' quality or TQM, the following characteristics are an inherent part of that construct (see, for example, MBNQA, 1992; Deming, 1986; Juran, 1992):

Continuous improvement in all activities and people

Customer satisfaction for internal and external customers

Efficient deployment of resources

Employee, supplier, and customer development

Environmental well-being

Exemplary, visionary, and aggressive leadership

Fast response time

Full participation of employees, suppliers, and customers

Life-long relationships with customers

Long-range perspectives

Partnerships upstream, downstream, and across functions

Prevention of error by designing in quality

Process mapping and process improvement

Providing customer value

Quantitative measurement and management-by-fact

Root cause analysis

Shared values, vision. and culture

Standard quality tools (such as SPC, QFD, DOE, etc.)

Waste reduction and cost containment

These key attributes, while not comprehensive, are important in understanding why the construct of quality has begun to supplant effectiveness in organizational research. Without explaining each of these key attributes (which is impossible here because of space limitations), they introduce some of the advantages of quality over effectiveness. In particular, because the

Table 3 Major Definitions of Quality

Approach	Definition	Example
Transcendent	"Quality is neither mind nor matter, but a third entity independent of the two . . . even though Quality cannot be defined, you know what it is" (Pirsig, 1974).	Innate excellence Timeless beauty Universal appeal
Product-based	"Quality refers to the amounts of the unpriced attributes contained in each unit of the priced attribute" (Leffler, 1982).	Durability Extra desired attributes Wanted features
User-based	"Quality is fitness for use" (Juran, 1974). "Quality consists of the capacity to satisfy wants" (Edwards, 1968).	Satisfies customers Meets needs Fulfills expectations
Manufacturing-based	"Quality means conformance to requirements" (Crosby, 1979).	Reliability Adherence to specifications Variation within tolerance limits
Value-based	"Quality means best for certain conditions . . . (a) the actual use and (b) Value for the selling price" (Fiegenbaum, 1961).	Performance at an acceptable price Value for the money spent Affordable excellence
System-based	"[Quality is] a system of means to economically produce goods or services which satisfy customers' requirements" (Japanese Industrial Standard Z8101, 1981).	Utilizing accepted quality procedures Quality processes Integrated approach
Philosophical	"[Quality] means that the organization's culture is defined by and supports the constant attainment of customer satisfaction through an integrated system of tools, techniques, and training" (Sashkin and Kiser, 1993).	Management philosophy Life style Mind-set

attributes include inputs, processes, outcomes, constituency preferences, and even paradox, they appear to provide some integration of the models usually separated in the traditional effectiveness approaches. In the next section we identify three attributes of quality that seem to provide an advantage over current approaches to effectiveness. We then identify some problems with the construct of quality and discuss attributes of effectiveness that provide advantages over quality. We conclude with a summary comparison of quality and effectiveness and a suggestion regarding the future of research on organizational effectiveness.

Advantages of Quality Over Effectiveness

Several issues have continued to impede progress in effectiveness research that seem to be addressed by switching to quality. They include (1) discord among different models or approaches to effectiveness, (2) a lack of integration between processes and outcomes, and (3) a lack of comprehensiveness by ignoring organizational culture. Each of these issues is addressed in the big 'Q' or TQM definition of quality.

Integration. One advantage associated with quality that differentiates it from effectiveness is that current approaches to quality help to harmonize several models of effectiveness that have been treated as competing in the past literature. For example, consider the models listed in Table 2 as illustrations of the four developmental approaches to effectiveness—the goal model, the internal processes model, the system resource model, the strategic constituencies model, and the competing values model. The debates in the literature regarding which of these approaches to effectiveness is most appropriate have been intense and, sometimes, heated (Seashore and Yuchtman, 1977; Bluedorn, 1980; Steers, 1978; Connolly, Conlon, and Deutsch, 1980; Price, 1982; Quinn and Rohrbaugh, 1981). The current big 'Q' or TQM approach to quality, however, appears to encompass each of these effectiveness models. That is, the key attributes of quality include such things as the production of perfect, defect-free outputs and services and the continuous improvement of goals (goal model), the adoption of processes and practices that ensure smooth, efficient organizational functioning (internal processes model), the integration of suppliers and resource providers into the planning, design, and budgeting of products and services (system resource model), the satisfaction of customers (multiple constituencies model), and the simultaneous pursuit of innovation and creativity with stable, controlled efficiency (competing values model). The construct of quality assumes that each of these attributes is inherently necessary and interdependent in achieving high levels of performance. No tension is present concerning which model of effectiveness is best, therefore, since the substitution of quality for effectiveness reveals that all these models may be a part of a larger construct. Whereas the traditional debates surrounding effectiveness models were aimed at highlighting differences among the models and the superiority of one perspective over another, a focus on quality has emphasized the integration of these perspectives under one broad approach.

A specific example of this point is illustrated by comparing these five effectiveness models with the framework used by the U.S. Commerce Department to organize the seven MBNQA categories. These seven categories are clusters of criteria defined as the core attributes of a quality organization. Quality is defined by these categories, and the categories are assumed to be comprehensive. Figure 1, for example, illustrates how the five models of effec-

tiveness relate to the seven quality categories. This figure, taken from the 1992 MBNQA Application Guidelines, symbolizes the fact that each model—organizational goals, internal processes, system resource, constituency satisfaction, competing values—is represented in this comprehensive model of quality. They are not in competition with one another as in the traditional effectiveness literature, but are integrated into a framework of total quality for the organization.

Processes and outcomes. A second apparent advantage of quality over effectiveness is that it integrates methods and tools for accomplishing quality along with desired organizational outcomes. An inherent part of the construct itself, in other words, is the assumption that particular processes and procedures are in operation in quality organizations in addition to the achievement of desired outputs. Greene (1993), for example, identified 24 "approaches to total quality" which describe the processes that comprise a quality organization. Whereas he indicated that no single organization may be characterized by all 24 processes (inasmuch as the processes he described are not all named and discussed in the U.S. literature nor are all named and discussed in the Japanese literature), they are, nevertheless, requisite to what constitutes a quality organization. Table 4 lists these 24 processes. This list, although not comprehensive or exclusive, illustrates that, unlike effectiveness, current approaches to quality almost always subsume methods, practices, and systems along with organizational outcomes and effects. In other words, quality appears to be more encompassing of both means and ends, how-to's as well as what-to's, than is effectiveness.

Some authors have been critical of the construct of quality precisely because of what they view as an overemphasis on processes and practices to the exclusion of outcomes and effects (e.g., Bowles, 1992; Crosby, 1992; Hammond, 1992; Crawford-Mason, 1992; McKeown, 1992). They argue, among other things, that quality is a narrower construct than effectiveness because, in its common usage, it overemphasizes internal processes instead of accomplishments. Much criticism has been leveled at the MBNQA criteria, in particular. To investigate the extent to which common quality processes and commonly desired outcomes are as-

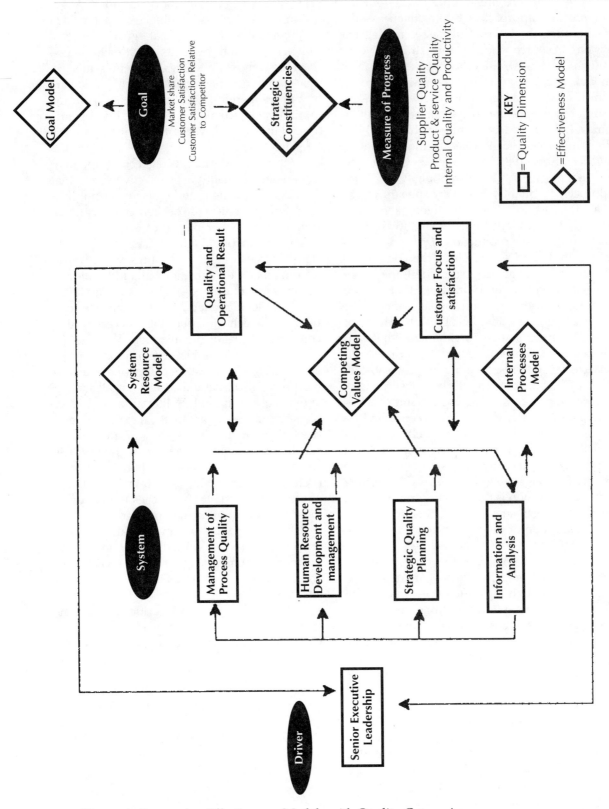

Figure. 1: Comparing Effectiveness Models with Quality Categories

sociated with one another, the U.S. General Accounting Office conducted a study of organizations which had implemented quality processes to a high degree. The 20 firms being investigated all were finalists in the MBNQA competition in 1988 and 1989. Table 5 summarizes the annual percent improvement in four categories of commonly desired outcomes associated with prescribed quality processes. The major conclusion of the study was that, not only does a high degree of positive correlation exist between

Table 4 Greene's Twenty Four Total Quality Processes

MAJOR APPROACH   Specific Process

Debuffering Approaches
    Inventory Buffers: Just-in-Time
    Tolerance Buffers: Statistical Process Control
    Authority Buffers: Quality Circles
    Functional Department Buffers: Total Quality Control

Scientific Styling
    Scientific Prevention: Total Preventive Maintenance
    Scientific Design: Taguchi Methods
    Scientific Cognition: 14 Statistical and Management Tools
    Scientific Application: High Technology Circles

Workforce Deployment
    Automation Deployment: Buy Time
    New Technology Deployment: Buys Customer Satisfaction
    Quality Function Deployment: Buys Customer Understanding
    Policy Deployment: Anticipates Customer Needs

Process Engineering
    Process Architecting
    Process Improving
    Process Deployment
    Process Execution Automation

Organizational Transparency
    System Inclusion of Customers: Customer Aided Design
    Product Inclusion of Customers: Customer Managed Corporation
    Feeling Inclusion of Customers: Kansei Engineering
    Generation Inclusion: Middle-Up-Down Management

Cognitive Competitiveness
    Learning Organizations: Cognitive Quality of Life
    Learning Self-Management: Meta-Cognitive Organization
    University Workgroups: Social Democratic Quality
    Learning Invention: Democratic Scientific Management

quality processes and quality outcomes, a causal relationship is likely to be present as well. In other words, organizations that implement the processes commonly associated with a quality organization are highly likely to produce desirable outcomes as well. Hence, the emphasis on integrating processes and outcomes, which was seldom the case in the effectiveness literature, has helped quality begin to take priority over effectiveness as a descriptor of desirable organizational performance.

Comprehensiveness and quality culture. A third advantage, which is related to the two points above, is that quality may have a comprehensiveness advantage over effectiveness. Quality has begun to be treated as an "organizational culture," that is, as a paradigm, a set of values, a way of approaching work and people. In the big 'Q' or TQM sense, it represents a peculiar organizational mind-set in addition to being a set of processes and outcomes. It may, therefore, represent a broader construct than the one typical of the effectiveness literature. This cultural aspect of quality is illustrated by an assertion of George Bush (1992):

Table 5 Results of a General Accounting Office Study of the Relationships Between Quality Processes and Desired Outcomes

Outcome Category Improvement	*Reported Annual Percent*
Employee Related Indicators	
Employee Satisfaction	1.4%
Attendance	1.0%
Turnover (decrease)	6.0%
Safety and Health	1.8%
Suggestions	16.6%
Operating Indicators	
Reliability	11.3%
On-time Delivery	4.7%
Order-processing Time	12.0%
Errors or Defects	10.3%
Product Lead Time	5.8%
Inventory Turnover	7.2%
Costs of Quality	9.0%
Customer Satisfaction Indicators	
Overall Customer Satisfaction	2.5%
Customer Complaints (decrease)	11.6%
Customer Retention	1.0%
Financial Performance Indicators	
Market Share	13.7%
Sales Per Employee	8.6%
Return on Assets	1.3%
Return of Sales	.4%

Source. Government Accounting Office (1991)

Table 6 A Model of Quality Cultures:
Three Stages

Error Detection

Regarding Products
Avoid mistakes
Reduce waste, rework, repair
Detect problems
Focus on outputs

Regarding Customers
Avoid annoying customers
Respond to complaints efficiently and accurately
Assess satisfaction after-the-fact
Focus on needs and requirements

Error Prevention

Regarding Products
Expect zero defects
Prevent errors and mistakes
Hold everyone accountable
Focus on processes and root causes

Regarding Customers
Satisfy customers and exceed expectations
Eliminate problems in advance
Involve customers in design
Focus on preferences or "nice-to-have" attributes

Perpetual Creative Quality

Regarding Products
Constant improvement and escalating standards
Concentrate on things-gone-right
Emphasize breakthroughs
Focus on improvement in suppliers, customers, and processes

Regarding Customers
Expect lifelong loyalty
Surprise and delight customers
Anticipate expectations
Create new preferences

Source: Cameron (1992)

> Quality management is not just a strategy. It must be a new style of working, even a new style of thinking. A dedication to quality and excellence is more than good business. It is a way of life, giving something back to society, offering your best to others.

Whereas we argued above that different models of organizational effectiveness arise from different conceptualizations of organizations, and that the conceptualizations may represent organizational paradigms, the effectiveness models that have emerged from these paradigms are all more restrictive than quality. Organizational effectiveness models have never been so broad as to include notions of organizational culture.

A "culture of organizational quality" has only begun to be investigated in the scholarly literature, and only rudimentary conceptual development has occurred. Cameron (1991), for example, formulated a model of quality culture in which three different mind-sets or generalized orientations toward quality were described. These approaches were measured as cultural approaches to quality through interviews and surveys. Different profiles indicating various degrees of emphasis across these quality cultures were found to exist in a more than 100 manufacturing and service organizations. Table 6 summarizes the attributes of each of the three types of cultures. No organization was characterized by a single quality culture, but almost all had a dominant type of quality culture.

In explaining differences among the cultures, Cameron claimed that different quality cultures have emerged developmentally over the last few decades in for-profit organizations. Through the 1970s, for example, most U.S. organizations were characterized by a quality culture centered on *error detection*. Organizations emphasized inspecting and detecting errors, avoiding mistakes, reducing waste, and finding and fixing errors. Quality control auditors inspected products and services after they were produced. A major focus was to avoid irritating internal and external customers in service delivery. Systems were developed that responded to customer requirements and specifications accurately and on time.

In higher education this culture might be reflected by an emphasis on outcomes and final results, a reliance on audits, tests, and final exams to assess individual and institutional performance, and a focus on the essential needs of those being served and minimum standards in the education process. What might be most observable is the attention paid to auditing and accreditation, examination scores, assessments of student outcomes, or faculty publication counts as evidence of quality. Individual and institutional improvement opportunities are provided on the basis of specified need or requirement.

The 1980s saw the transition to *an error prevention* culture, or avoiding making mistakes instead of correcting them after-the-fact. The goal was to achieve zero defects (perfection) by doing work right the first time, and by emphasizing root (common) causes of problems, process controls, and holding all workers accountable for quality, not just end-of-the-line inspectors. A major focus was on pleasing and satisfying constituents (not just avoiding annoying them), and providing service that creates customer loyalty through exceeding expectations. Obtaining customer preferences in advance and monitoring customer satisfaction after service delivery were crucial aspects of this new approach.

In higher education this culture might be reflected by a greater emphasis on excellence in processes and methods for producing individual and institutional outcomes than the achievement of outcomes. The pursuit of quality and excellence in all activities becomes a way of life for each staff member and faculty. Emphasis is placed on designing processes and systems, both in the classroom and in support functions so that the possibility of mistakes and aberrations for excellence are not allowed to occur. What might be most observable is the development of learning partnerships among students and faculty, assessments of the process of development, ongoing mechanisms for feedback and feedforward, and a customer orientation as indicators of institutional quality. Individual and institutional improvement opportunities are provided even before a specified need arises.

A third quality culture emerged during the late 1980s and 1990s centered on *creative quality and continuous improvement*. This culture, typical of only a few notable organizations, couples continuous improvement (small, incremental changes) with innovation (large, breakthrough changes), so that current *standards* of performance are always changing and improving. The focus shifts to designing and producing "things-gone-right" as well as avoiding "things-gone-wrong." Helping to improve suppliers' and customers' quality become equally important to improving the firm's own work processes and employees. Creating new expectations and surprising and delighting customers occur as a result of solving customer problems no one expected to be solved.

In higher education this culture might be reflected by a focus on producing peak experiences and defining events for both those being served (e.g., students) and those delivering the service (e.g., support staff or faculty). Improvement, in addition to achieving excellence, be-

comes a way of life and is associated with every activity pursued by the institution. Innovation and creativity characterize the work of all faculty and staff members in that those being served are regularly surprised and delighted with the processes and outcomes of the institution. What might be most observable is the frequency of defining moments available to institution members, assessments of continuous improvement, evidence of constant organizational learning, and indicators of breakthrough thinking as criteria for institutional quality. Individual and institutional improvement is continuous and focused on future developmental opportunities.

Cameron's (1992) research on these three culture types among more than 200 manufacturing and service organizations revealed that organizations in a status quo condition (paying little attention to quality) or that were dominated by an *error detection* culture were significantly lower performers on every process and outcome measure than were organizations which were dominated by *error prevention* and *creative quality* cultures. Organizations dominated by a *creative quality* culture scored highest on all process and outcome measures. The *error prevention* firms scored second highest. (The processes and outcomes used in the study included defect levels, financial performance over five years, ratings of organizational effectiveness, effective leadership, effective information gathering and analysis, appropriate structure, effective information use, effective planning, effective human resource utilization, customer satisfaction, use of quality tools, downsizing, and amount of past improvement.)

What is most relevant about these findings for purposes of this paper is that, whereas a variety of process and outcome variables discriminated significantly among the different quality cultures, measures of organizational effectiveness did not discriminate. That is, measures and patterns of quality and of effectiveness were not synonymous in these organizations, and the quality culture of the firms was more predictive of desirable outcomes and processes than were measures of effectiveness. The construct of quality, therefore, seemed to provide an advantage over effectiveness in understanding the performance of these organizations.

Advantages of Effectiveness Over Quality

Of course, we are not arguing that the organizational sciences and higher education are to a point where we should throw out the construct of organizational effectiveness. Quite the contrary, a review of effectiveness research highlights some important reasons why the construct has endured and is useful in investigations of organizational performance. Organizational studies research on quality as an indicator of organizational performance, on the other hand, is still in its infancy. Whereas much publication has been done, little empirical work has appeared, and most writing has yet to tackle several important issues that have dominated the effectiveness literature for more than two decades. That is, organizational effectiveness still appears to have several advantages over quality as a construct of choice in the organizational studies and higher education. They relate to: (1) the prescriptive and normative nature of quality, (2) problems with customer preferences and customer satisfaction, and (3) a lack of conceptual bounding of quality.

Normative nature. As discussed above, the earliest models of organizational effectiveness were prescriptive in nature and were based on ideal type assumptions. The pursuit of scholars, and the debates among authors, focused on identifying the single best model of effectiveness. A similar tendency toward one ideal approach exists in the current literature on quality. Whereas multiple definitions of quality exist (e.g., Table 3), by and large they are not in conflict with one another since they are treated as aspects of a more encompassing construct. (Exceptions exist, for example, in discussions about which "quality guru" is correct, Crosby, Deming, Juran, Taguchi, Ishikawa, and so on.) In the big 'Q' or TQM sense, however, organizational quality includes the definitions in Table 3 related to value, customers, product attributes, culture, and so on.

What was missing from the effectiveness literature in the ideal type era, however, was the realization that under different environmental conditions, different dimensions of effectiveness, even completely different models, became relevant. The uncovering of dimensions of effectiveness helped provide alternatives that could be matched with different environmental dimensions. Thus far, little work has been done on dimensions of quality (Garvin [1988] and the MBNQA are exceptions), and acknowledgment that different approaches to quality may be appropriate under different environmental conditions is absent from the literature. The assumption that quality is inherently worthwhile under all circumstances and in all organizations still permeates most writing. Authors have discussed quality as it applies to different settings such as universities, hospitals, manufacturing firms, and so on (e.g., Seymour, 1992), but that discussion does not include an examination of contingencies that may alter quality's definition or dimensions.

An introduction to the rudiments of contingency thinking has occurred with the recent reemphasis on the concept of "value" (e.g. Sherman, 1992), but it is yet to be examined empirically in the organizational sciences. Value, simply defined, means that the organization produces exactly what the customer is willing to acquire and nothing more. That is, resources are not expended on product attributes, services, or other organizational processes and outcomes that do not have value to some constituency and for which they are not willing to spend resources. The basic assumption is that value may be defined uniquely by different constituency groups, and that different organizations may provide different types of value. In the effectiveness literature, that is a basic assumption; in the quality literature, it is as yet unacknowledged.

This introduction of value for customers raises a second issue that illustrates the advantage of effectiveness over quality. It relates to customer preferences.

Customer preferences. The growing trend in the quality literature is to treat customer satisfaction as the single most important indicator of quality (Heskett, Sasser, and Hart, 1990). In fact, some writers have equated quality and customer satisfaction as completely interchangeable constructs. The trouble is, as we have argued before, at least four important issues surround customer satisfaction: (1) customers often cannot identify their own preferences or expectations; (2) expectations change, sometimes very quickly, and sometimes as a result of having old preferences satisfied; (3) contradictory preferences are present among different customers; and (4) preferences are often unrelated to organizational performance

(Cameron and Whetten, 1983, pp. 12–19). In cases where satisfying customer preferences is associated with a single product or service (little 'q' quality), it is simple to measure customer satisfaction with that product or service (for example, percent of customers satisfied with an automobile). But when quality refers to an organization's culture or the sum of its processes and outcomes (big 'Q' or TQM quality), assessing customer satisfaction becomes more complex. Little acknowledgment has been provided in organizational-level quality studies of such complexity.

The finding that different models of organizational effectiveness are associated with different life cycle stages (e.g., Cameron and Whetten, 1981) also has no counterpart in the quality literature. It is unclear if customer preferences change, if different customer groups represent different levels of priority to the organization itself, if different quality processes are associated with different outcomes in different stages, if the concept of "value" changes over time, and so on. Moreover, distinctions in the effectiveness literature between, for example, doing *good* versus doing *well* (Miles and Cameron, 1982), *desired* results versus *desirable* results (Zammuto, 1984), and doing *things right* versus doing *the right things* (Kanter and Brinkerhoff, 1981), highlight the subtleties that have emerged as empirical research on effectiveness progressed over time. No similar refinements have emerged from the stream of research on quality.

In addition, among the most controversial issues surrounding the application of quality to institutions of higher education is the concept of customer. The question is, who is a customer? Are students customers, suppliers, partners, or part of the production process? Are faculty customers? Of whom? What role do state government, benefactors, parents, and sponsors play? To what extent are they to be treated as customers? In the effectiveness literature, each of these groups is treated as a constituency with legitimate claims on the organization. In the quality literature, it is unclear if a customer satisfaction perspective can legitimately apply.

Conceptual boundaries. In the effectiveness literature, seven guidelines were proposed (as discussed earlier) that helped established boundaries for the definition and empirical assessment of organizational effectiveness. No similar boundary specification has occurred with the construct of quality. Whereas quality is treated as a comprehensive organizational performance construct that encompasses multiple processes and outcomes, what is inside and what is outside the construct has not yet been precisely established. For example, is satisfaction a predictor, an indicator, or an outcome of quality? Is efficiency a predictor, indicator, or outcome of quality? One might argue that satisfied customers *lead to* an evaluation of a quality organization, that satisfied customers are the most important *indicator* of quality, or that quality *produces* the result of satisfied customers. The same logic applies to efficiency. At present, writing on quality is not so precise as to address such issues, and writers largely base their construct boundaries on their own idiosyncratic preferences.

Another manifestation of the conceptual boundary issue is the development of different effectiveness models resulting from different paradigms of organizations. When organizations are conceived of differently—as networks (Tichy and Fombrun, 1979), information processing units (Galbraith, 1977), garbage cans (March and Olsen, 1976), social contracts (Keeley, 1980), rational goal achievers (Perrow, 1970), and so on—different phenomena are highlighted and different criteria become relevant for organizational performance. The quality literature, thus far, has not addressed the variety in criteria that may emerge from different organizational metaphors. The point, simply, is that more than two decades of theoretical and empirical work on effectiveness has produced a more well-developed and more precisely defined construct than is typical of the current work on TQM or big 'Q' quality.

Summary Comparisons Between Quality and Effectiveness

What we are pointing out with these examples of the advantages of one construct over the other is that an increased understanding of organizational performance—whether labelled effectiveness or quality—may occur best if the strengths of each construct are used to inform future investigations. It may be less important which construct predominates than that future research be informed by the lessons of both.

The comprehensiveness and integration associated with quality, especially the intermingling of means and ends, for example, can help expand conceptualizations of effectiveness and highlight compatibilities among models. Quality's tendency toward pragmatics and useful guidelines for organizational practitioners may be especially important in an era where research on improved organizational performance is badly needed by the practitioner community. The conceptual complexities uncovered by effectiveness scholars, on the other hand—such as underlying dimensions and multiple models—as well as the proposed guidelines for more precise empirical research on these kinds of amorphous constructs, can help inform empirical investigations of quality that are not now considered.

Whereas the current trend in scholarly writing in organizational studies and higher education is clear—quality is prevailing and effectiveness is increasingly ignored—it is not clear that future research will continue to follow this drift and that our understanding of organizational performance will be enhanced if effectiveness is forgotten. In fact, although quality seems to be the construct of the 1990s in relation to organizational performance, the field will retrogress if the advantages of decades of work on effectiveness are ignored. On the other hand, while it may be premature to completely abandon effectiveness as a central construct in organizational studies and higher education, to doggedly hang on to an outmoded construct is equally grievous. As a way to highlight the contributions and differences of each, several of the characteristics of effectiveness and quality are compared in Table 7 This table helps highlight the trade-offs that will be made as researchers use one construct as opposed to the other in future investigations.

With regard to definitions, for example, effectiveness has usually been defined from the standpoint of managers or administrators, and different constituencies have generally used different definitions. Effectiveness for students, for instance, is not the same as effectiveness for faculty or administrators (Cameron, 1986b). Effectiveness is traditionally contrasted with efficiency in focusing on "doing the right things" (i.e., effectiveness) as opposed to "doing things right" (i.e., efficiency). A consensual set of val-

ues has never been associated with effectiveness definitions. On the other hand, TQM or big 'Q' quality is usually defined from the standpoint of the customer, but no differences in definition occur when considering different types of customers (i.e., administrators and students can both be customers). Both efficiency and effectiveness perspectives are combined in defining quality, i.e., both "doing things right" and "doing the right things," and a relatively consistent set of values are associated with the definition of quality (e.g., improvement, empowerment, perfection, satisfaction).

The effectiveness literature has its roots in organizational behavior and sociology and, over time, more specific, but unique, models have emerged. Different conceptualizations of organizations led to different effectiveness definitions (see Table 2). The quality literature, on the other hand, has its roots in engineering, manufacturing, operations management, and statistics. Time has led to a more and more consensual, overall model of quality rather than several differentiated ones, regardless of the organizational conceptualization adopted. For example, definitions of quality in the TQM sense have converged more and more on the latter two definitions in Table 3, whether higher education or, say, manufacturing organizations are considered.

Assessments of effectiveness have often been carelessly conducted in research and have frequently relied on one overall, summary rating. No necessary and sufficient set of criteria can be identified for effectiveness, although the seven critical questions discussed above have placed measurement issues at the center of the effectiveness literature (Cameron and Whetten, 1983). In the quality literature, on the other hand, virtually no empirical measures have appeared on organization-level quality. Yet, precise, quantitative measurement is a hallmark of the quality movement, and general agreement exists regarding key indicators of quality. The seven critical questions have not been applied to assessments of quality, however, and assessment issues do not play a major role in the quality literature.

In the effectiveness literature, quality is viewed as either a predictor variable or as a singular dimension subsumed by effectiveness. Effectiveness is viewed as the ultimate organization-level dependent variable, while quality applies only to qualifiers of products or services. In the quality literature, on the other hand, quality applies to everything that happens in the organization, including processes and practices, and effectiveness is viewed as narrowly focused on outputs. Quality is the ultimate dependent variable and transcends effectiveness from a TQM point of view.

Organizational effectiveness has sometimes been called a *divergent* problem (Zammuto, 1982) in that its definition is its central problem. A major challenge relating to this construct is identifying appropriate criteria and reliable dimensionality. Quality, on the other hand, is a *convergent* problem (Schumacher, 1977) in that its definition is not its most central issue. Instead, the major challenge associated with quality is identifying appropriate implementation procedures. Far more emphasis is placed on *how* to achieve quality than on *what* quality is.

The major criticisms of effectiveness relate to its being too imprecise and conceptual for practitioners, and of overemphasizing outcomes at the expense of internal processes. Quality, on the other hand, is accused of being underdeveloped conceptually and theoretically, and overemphasizing processes and systems applications at the expense of outcomes. A common question, for example, is, "So what if you achieved high quality. Did you make money . . . or produce better students . . . or beat the competition?" The latter are all consistent with uses of effectiveness.

Summary and Proposals for Future Research

We began this chapter by suggesting that a review of the evolutionary development of organizational effectiveness would help guide future research on this construct in general, and in higher education organizations in particular. We described the conceptual sophistication that emerged during the formulation of new organizational effectiveness models and the increasing precision provided by the guidelines for empirical measurements. At the same time, we described the cessation of the appearance of effectiveness in the organizational literature after the mid-1980s and the ascendance of TQM or big 'Q' quality as a performance vari-

able of choice. This increased emphasis on the construct of quality in the literature provided an opportunity to compare and contrast it with organizational effectiveness and to highlight strengths of each construct that can guide future research on organization-level performance. In particular, we highlighted the integrative function associated with the quality construct and the emphasis on practical process criteria linked to outcomes and effects. We discussed advantages that quality has over effectiveness and that effectiveness has over quality, and we suggested that lessons learned from quality, coupled with the past effectiveness literature, can improve future investigations of organizational performance. Without any attempt to provide the last word on the future of effectiveness research or the most important future directions to be addressed, we offer two propositions that describe attributes we believe should characterize future research on organizational effectiveness in institutions of higher education.

First, research on organizational effectiveness in higher education should integrate processes, outcomes, and effects. Imai (1988) asserted that the most significant difference between Japanese models of organizational performance and American models is the prominent emphasis on process criteria in Japan and its absence from U.S. models. Process criteria relate to how work is done or how performance is accomplished as opposed to results criteria which relate to what is produced or what is accomplished. Imai argued that this omission accounts for the competitive success of Japanese organizations over U.S. organizations in the past as well as the likely triumph of Japanese organizations in the future. He included educational as well as goods-producing organizations in his prediction.

While we may disagree with Imai's conclusion and prediction, we do agree that much more emphasis is needed on the integration of processes, outcomes, and effects in future organizational effectiveness research. Instead of focusing exclusively on outcomes, as has been traditional, effectiveness research should give equal attention to process criteria and to the linkages among processes, outcomes, and effects (i.e., *how* outcomes are produced as well as *what* is produced and their *consequences*). In higher education institutions this means in-

Table 7 A Comparison of Organizational Effectiveness and Quality

Organizational Effectiveness	*Organizational Quality*
1) The construct is usually defined from the standpoint of managers; different definitions are used by different constituencies.	1) The construct is usually defined from the standpoint of customers; similar definitions are ordinarily used by different constituencies.
2) Defined as "doing the right things" (contrasted to efficiency, "doing things right").	2) Defined as "doing the right things right" (a combination of effectiveness and efficiency).
3) Major puzzles have focused on identifying dimensionality.	3) Major puzzles have focused on identifying successful implementation techniques.
4) Over time, more specificity has developed; identifiable models of effectiveness have emerged.	4) Over time less specificity has emerged, with more and more concepts being subsumed under the rubric of quality (e.g., empowerment, teamwork, continuous improvement, customer focus, process control).
5) Literature accused of overemphasizing outcomes, especially goal accomplishment, at the expense of internal processes.	5) Literature accused of overemphasizing internal processes and systems at the expense of outcomes.
6) Quality was treated either as a predictor variable in effectiveness research or as a singular dimension of effectiveness.	6) Quality is treated as a dependent variable and transcends organizational effectiveness.
7) Assessments of effectiveness have often been carelessly done (mainly, using one overall subjective rating of effectiveness), but measurement issues occupy a dominant place in the literature.	7) Assessments of quality are mainly empirical and precise, but conceptual measurement issues are not yet central in the literature.
8) Effectiveness is applied to organizational attributes or outcomes, not to specific products or services.	8) Quality is applied mainly to products and services (e.g., actions, things) rather than to organizations.
9) The major effectiveness challenges relate to criteria, i.e., identifying the appropriate criteria.	9) The major quality challenges relate to application, i.e., identifying appropriate processes or tools.
10) Different conceptualizations of the organization have produced different approaches to and definitions of effectiveness.	10) Different conceptualizations of organizations have produced largely consensual approaches to quality.
11) No necessary and/or sufficient set of criteria of effectiveness can be identified.	11) General consensus exists regarding core indicators of quality.
12) Approaches to research on effectiveness are idiosyncratic, depending on answers to the seven "critical questions."	12) Answers to the seven critical research questions have not been addressed in the literature discussing quality.
13) Effectiveness is a "divergent problem" (Schumacher, 1977) in that its definition *is* the problem.	13) Quality is a "convergent problem" (Schumacher, 1977) in that a solution and definition can be specified.
14) Effectiveness literature does not espouse or perpetuate a consensual set of values.	14) Quality has espoused and focused attention on some "inherent" human values—improvement, empowerment, caring, perfection.
15) The effectiveness literature was accused of being too conceptual for practitioners (i.e., focused on imprecise constructs).	15) The quality literature is accused of being too underdeveloped conceptually (i.e., focused on measurement and problem solving tools and techniques).
16) The effectiveness literature developed mainly in organizational behavior and organizational sociology.	16) The quality literature spans several disciplines including engineering, manufacturing, operations management, statistics, accounting, organizational behavior, and psychology.

cluding the processes of educational delivery, their consequences, and the outcomes produced by the organization. Linkages among these factors also should lead to a reemphasis on integrating the various models of effectiveness. When quality is used in place of effectiveness, goal attainment, resource acquisition, efficiency, constituent satisfaction, and the pursuit of paradoxical criteria (c.f., Table 2) all can be conceived as compatible. A similar transition could occur in the effectiveness literature, not because one grand definition or model triumphs, but because integration is often inhibited by the debates about which model is best. Rather than producing a better comprehension of or description for high/low performing organizations, traditional effectiveness writing has become mired too often in conceptual bantering typified by exclusivity. One lesson learned from our review of evolutionary shifts in effectiveness approaches, in fact, is that increased understanding can actually result from increased complexity of constructs. That is, integrating quality's emphasis on process with effectiveness' emphasis on dimensionality can help address questions such as: What specific processes are associated with what specific outcomes and effects in what specific environments? Under what circumstances are desirable processes not linked to desirable outcomes? How are effectiveness-producing paradoxes managed and resolved? How do organizations reach a high reliability (zero-defects) state?

Our second proposal is, *research on organizational effectiveness in higher education should become both more comprehensive and more precise.* The seven guidelines for empirical assessment, the four issues related to constituency preferences, and the identification of paradoxical tensions in organizations were discussed above and are embedded in the traditional effectiveness literature. Each of these three sets of factors has the potential to make effectiveness research more precise and more accurate in definition and approach. Unfortunately, because the effectiveness literature waned before much empirical research was published in higher education using these factors, and because the quality literature has not yet considered these guidelines, issues, and tensions at all, very little research is available to address questions such as: Under what circumstances

are specific answers to the seven guidelines more appropriate than others? Are certain choices relative to the seven guidelines more internally compatible than others? Can organizations supersede changing or contradictory constituency preferences by producing surprises and delights? Must paradoxes in organizations be resolved to produce effectiveness? How much paradoxical tension is compatible with effectiveness?

In addition to being more precise by means of the seven guidelines, effectiveness research also should become more comprehensive. For instance, with the increasing realization that high quality organizations are characterized by a special culture as well as by the ability to acquire resources, by efficient processes, by capacity, by appropriate structures, or by output production (e.g., Scott, 1992), research on effectiveness should begin taking into account more comprehensive criteria such as the nature of culture as well. The integration of culture into the construct of quality, for example, raises the possibility that a unique way of thinking, lifestyle, mind-set, or set of values may be inherently connected to high organizational-level performance. To date, meager attention has been paid to the integration of effectiveness and culture except as predictors of one another (e.g., Dennison, 1990). Yet, research questions such as the following remain unaddressed, based on findings from the quality literature: What are the dimensions of a highly effective organizational culture? Do cultural models match effectiveness models? What is the relationship between an advanced quality culture and organizational effectiveness? What contingencies affect the development of an effective culture?

In sum, the study of organizational-level performance in higher education seems to be on something of a cusp at the present time. The old approach focusing on the construct of effectiveness may be on the verge of a demise and a replacement construct may be on the verge of ascendance. On the other hand, higher education has a tradition of being caught up in intellectual fads with little resulting long-term contribution. Whether quality is a fad or a substitute for effectiveness is, in our opinions, less important than that we learn from the contributions of both constructs in future work.

Note

1. The first part of this chapter is based on a longer review of the literature on organizational effectiveness by the authors entitled "Organizational Effectiveness: Old Models and New Constructs" in Jerald Greenberg (ed.), *Organizational Behavior: The State of the Science*. Hillsdale, NJ: Lawrence Erlbaum Associates, 1994.

References

Astin, A. W. (1985). *Achieving Academic Excellence*. San Francisco: Jossey-Bass.

Baldridge, V., (1971). *Power and Conflict in the University*. New York: Wiley.

Barnard, C. I. (1938). *The Functions of the Executive*. Cambridge, MA: Harvard University Press.

Bluedorn, A. C. (1980). Cutting the gordian knot: A critique of the effectiveness tradition in organization research. *Sociology and Social Research* 64: 477–496.

Bowen, H. R. (1977). *Investment in Learning*. San Francisco: Jossey-Bass.

Boston Consulting Group (1970). *The Product Portfolio*. Boston: BCG.

Bowles, J. (1992) Does the Baldrige Award really work? *Harvard Business Review* 70:127.

Burns, T., and Stalker, G. M. (1961). *The management of innovation*. New York: Barnes and Noble.

Bush, G. P. (1992). Quotation in the Malcolm Baldrige National Quality Award Application Guidelines. (p. 1) Washington, D.C.: U.S. Department of Commerce.

Business Week (1991). *The Quality Imperative*. Special Issue, October 25.

Cameron, K. S. (1978). Measuring organizational effectiveness in institutions of higher education. *Administrative Science Quarterly* 23: 604–632.

Cameron, K. S. (1981). "Construct and subjectivity problems in organizational effectiveness." *Public Productivity Review* 7: 105–121.

Cameron, K. S. (1982). Organizational effectiveness: A bibliography through 1981. Boulder, CO: National Center for Higher Education Management Systems.

Cameron, K. S. (1984). "The effectiveness of ineffectiveness." In B. M. Staw and L. L. Cummings (Eds.) *Research in Organizational Behavior*, Vol. 6. Greenwich, CT: JAI Press.

Cameron, K. S. (1984b). An empirical investigation of the multiple constituency model of organizational effectiveness. Working paper, School of Business Administration, University of Michigan.

Cameron, K. S. (1986). "Effectiveness as paradox: Consensus and conflict in conceptions of organizational effectiveness." *Management Science* 32: 539–553.

Cameron, K. S. (1986b). "A study of organizational effectiveness and its predictors." *Management Science* 32: 87–112.

Cameron, K. S. (1991). The quality and continuous improvement movement: A second generation organizational effectiveness approach. Paper delivered at the Academy of Management Meetings, Miami, Florida.

Cameron, K. S. (1992). In what ways do organizations implement total quality? Paper delivered at the Academy of Management Meetings, Las Vegas, Nevada.

Cameron, K. S. Freeman, S., and Michra, A. (1993). Organizational downsizing and redesign. In G. Huber and W. Glick (eds.). *Organizational downsizing and redesign*. New York: Oxford University Press.

Cameron, K. S., and Tschirhart, M. (1992). Postindustrial environments and organizational effectiveness in colleges and universities. *Journal of Higher Education* 63:87–108.

Cameron, K. S., and Whetten. D. A. (1981). Perceptions of organizational effectiveness over organizational life cycles. *Administrative Science Quarterly* 26: 525–544.

Cameron, K., and Whetten, D. A. (1983). *Organizational effectiveness: A comparison of multiple models*. New York: Academic Press.

Cameron, K. S. and Whetten D. A. (1983b). "Models of the organizational life cycle: Applications to higher education." *Review of Higher Education* 6:269–299.

Campbell, J. P. (1977). On the nature of organizational effectiveness. In Goodman, P. S. and Pennings, J. M. (eds.), *New Perspectives of Organizational Effectiveness*. San Francisco: Jossey-Bass.

Chaffee, E. E. (1989) Strategy and effectiveness in systems of higher education. In J. C. Smart (ed.), *Higher Education: Handbook of Theory and Research*. New York: Agathon.

Connolly, T., Conlon, E .J., and Deutsch, S. J. (1980). Organizational effectiveness: A multiple-constituency approach. *Academy of Management Review* 5:211–217.

Conrad, C. F., and Blackburn, R. T. (1985). Program quality in higher education. In J. C. Smart (ed.), *Higher Education: Handbook of Theory and Research*. New York: Agathon.

Crawford-Mason, C. (1992). Does the Baldrige Award really work? *Harvard Business Review* 70: 134–136.

Crosby, P. B. (1992). Does the Baldrige Award really work? *Harvard Business Review* 70: 127–128.

Deming, W. E. (1982). *Quality, Productivity, and Competitive Position*. Cambridge, MA: MIT Press.

Deming, W. E. (1986). *Out of the Crisis*. Cambridge, MA: MIT Press.

Denison, D. (1990). *Corporate Culture and Organizational Effectiveness*. New York: Wiley.

Edwards, C. D. (1968). The meaning of quality. *Quality Progress*. October: p. 37.

Ehreth, J. (1988). A competitive constituency model of organizational effectiveness and its application in the health industry. Paper presented at the Academy of Management Annual Meeting. Anaheim, CA.

Eisenhart, K. M. and Wescott, B. J. (1988). Paradoxical demands and the creation of excellence: The case of just-in-time manufacturing. In R. E. Quinn and K. S. Cameron (eds.). *Paradox and Transformation*. Cambridge, MA: Ballinger.

Faerman, S. R., and Quinn, R. E. (1985). Effectiveness: The perspective from organizational theory. *Review of Higher Education* 9: 83–100.

Fiegenbaum, A. V. (1961). *Total Quality Control*. New York: McGraw-Hill.

Fjortoft, N., and Smart, J. C. (in press). Enhancing organizational effectiveness: The importance of culture type and mission agreement. *Higher Education*.

Freeman, J. (1980). The unit problem in organizational research. In W. Evan (ed.). *Frontiers in organization and management*. New York: Praeger.

Friedlander, E. and Pickle. H. (1968). Components of effectiveness in small organizations. *Administrative Science Quarterly* 13:289–304.

Galbraith, J. (1977). *Organizational Design: An Information Processing View*. Reading, MA: Addison-Wesley.

Garvin, D. A. (1988). *Managing Quality: The Strategic and Competitive Edge*. New York: Free Press.

Goodman, P. S., and Pennings, J. M. (eds.). (1977). *New perspectives in organizational effectiveness*. San Francisco: Jossey-Bass.

Goodman, P. S., Atkin, R. S., Schoorman, D. F. (1983). On the demise of organizational effectiveness studies. In K. S. Cameron and D. A. Whetten (eds.), *Organizational Effectiveness: A Comparison of Multiple Models*. New York: Academic Press.

Government Accounting Office (1991). *Management Practices: U.S. Companies Improve Performance Through Quality Efforts*. Washington, DC: U.S. Government Accounting Office.

Greene, R. T. (1993). *Beyond Japan in Quality*. Methuen, MA: GOAL/QPC Press.

Greiner, L. (1972). Evolution and revolution as organizations grow. *Harvard Business Review* 49: 37–46.

Hall, R. H. (1987). *Organizations: Structure and Process*. Englewood Cliffs, NJ: Prentice-Hall.

Hall, R. H. (1963). The concept of bureaucracy: An empirical assessment. *American Journal of Sociology* 69: 32–40.

Hammond, J. (1992). Does the Baldrige Award really work? *Harvard Business Review* 70: 132.

Hannan, M. T, and Freeman, J. H., (1977). Obstacles to the comparative study of organizational effectiveness. In P. S. Goodman and J. M. Pennings (Eds.) *New Perspectives on Organizational Effectiveness*. San Francisco: Jossey-Bass.

Harris, D. H., Goodman, P. S., and Sink, D. S (eds.). (1993). *Organizational linkages: Understanding the productivity paradox*. Washington. DC: National Academy Press.

Heskett, J. L., Sasser, W. E., and Hart, C. W. L. (1990). *Service Breakthroughs*. New York: Free Press.

Huber, G. P., Glick, W., and Associates (1993). *Organizational Change and Redesign*. New York: Oxford University Press.

Imai, M. (1988). *Kaizen*. New York: Random House.

Juran, J. M. (1951). *The Quality Control Handbook*. New York: McGraw-Hill.

Juran, J. M. (1974). *The Quality Control Handbook*. New York: McGraw-Hill.

Juran, J. M. (1992). *Juran on Quality by Design*. New York: Free Press.

Kanter, R. M., and Brinkerhoff, D. (1981). Organizational performance: Recent developments in measurement. *Annual Review of Sociology* 7: 321–349.

Katz, D., and Kahn, R. L. (1978). *The Social Psychology of Organizations*. New York: Wiley.

Keeley, M. (1978). A social justice approach to organizational evaluation. *Administrative Science Quarterly*, 22, 272–292.

Lawrence, P., and Lorsch, J. (1967). *Organization and environment*. Cambridge, Mass: Harvard University Press.

Leffler, K. B. (1982). Ambiguous changes in product quality. *American Economic Review*. December p. 956.

Levin, H. M. (1991). Raising productivity in higher education. *Journal of Higher Education* 62: 241–262.

Lewin, A. Y., and Minton, J. W. (1986). Determining organizational effectiveness: Another look, and an agenda for research. *Management Science* 32: 514–538.

Mahoney, T. A. (1967). Managerial perceptions of organizational effectiveness. *Administrative Science Quarterly* 14: 357–365.

March, J. G., and Olsen, J. P. (1976). *Ambiguity and Choice in Organizations*. Oslo, Norway: Universitetforlaget.

McGuire, J. W., Richman. M. L., Daly, R. F., and Jodani, S. (1988). The efficient production of reputation by prestige research universities in the United States. *Journal of Higher Education* 59: 365–389.

McKelvey, B. (1982). *Organizational Systematics: Taxonomy, Evolution, Classification*. Berkeley, CA: University of California Press.

McKeown, K. (1992). Does the Baldrige Award really work? *Harvard Business Review* 70: 140.

Meyer, M. W., and Zucker, L. G. (1989). *Permanently failing organizations*. Newbury Park, CA.: Sage Publications.

Miles, R. H., and Cameron, K. C. (1982). *Coffin nails and corporate strategies.* Englewood Cliffs. NJ: Prentice-Hall.

Miller, J. G. (1978). *Living Systems.* New York: McGraw-Hill.

Mintzberg. H. (1979). *The Structuring of Organizations.* Englewood Cliffs. NJ: Prentice-Hall.

Nadler, D. A., and Tushman, M. L. (1980). A congruence model for organizational assessment. In E. E. Lawler, D. A. Nadler, and C. Cammann, C. (eds.), *Organizational assessment.* New York: Wiley.

Osborn, R. N., and Hunt, J. C. (1974). Environment and organizational effectiveness. *Administrative Science Quarterly* 19: 231–246.

Parsons, T. (1964). Evolutionary universals in society. *American Sociological Review* 29: 339–357.

Pascale, R. T. (1990). *Managing on the Edge.* New York: Simon and Schuster.

Perrow, C. (1984). *Normal Accidents.* New York: Basic Books.

Perrow, C. (1986). *Complex organizations: A critical essay* (3rd ed.). New York: Random House.

Peters, T. (1987). *Thriving on Chaos.* New York: Alfred Knopf.

Peters, T. and Waterman R. H. (1982). *In Search of Excellence.* New York: Harper and Row.

Peterson, M., and Cameron, K. (1994). *An Annotated Bibliography of Quality in Higher Education.* Center for the Student of Higher and Postsecondary Education, University of Michigan.

Pfeffer, J., and Salancik, G. R. (1978). *The External Control of Organizations.* New York: Harper and Row.

Pirsig, R. (1974). *Zen and the Art of Motorcycle Maintenance.* New York: Bantam.

Price, J. L. (1968). *Organizational Effectiveness: An Inventory of Propositions.* Homewood, IL: Irwin.

Price, J. L. (1982). The study of organizational effectiveness. *Sociological Quarterly* 13: 3–15.

Pugh, D. S., Hickson, D. J., and Hinings, C. R. (1969). An empirical taxonomy of structures in work organizations. *Administrative Science Quarterly* 14: 115–26.

Quinn, R. E., and Cameron, K. S. (1982). Life cycles and shifting criteria of effectiveness: Some preliminary evidence. *Management Science* 27: 450–460.

Quinn, R. E., and Rohrbaugh, J. (1981). A competing values approach to organizational effectiveness. *Public Productivity Review* 5: 122–140.

Quinn, R. E., and Cameron, K. S. (1988). *Paradox and Transformation: Towards a Theory of Change in Organizations.* Cambridge, MA: Ballinger.

Roethlisberger, F. J., and Dickson, W. J. (1947). *Management and the Worker.* Cambridge, Mass: Harvard University Press.

Rousseau, D. M. (1985). Issues of level in organizational research: Multi-level and cross-level perspectives. In B. M. Staw and L. L. Cummings (eds.), *Research in organizational behavior* (pp. 1–37). Greenwich, CT: JAI Press.

Sashkin, M., and Kiser, K. J. (1993). *Putting Total Quality Management to Work.* San Francisco: Barrett-Koehler.

Schneider, B. (1983). An interactionist perspective on organizational effectiveness. In Cameron, K. C., and Whetten, D. A. (eds.), *Organizational effectiveness: A comparison of multiple models* (pp. 27–54). New York: Academic Press.

Scott, W. R., Flood, A. B., Ewy, W., and Forrest, W. H. (1978). "Organizational effectiveness and the quality of surgical care in hospitals." In M. Meyer (ed.), *Environments and Organizations.* San Francisco: Jossey-Bass.

Scott, W. R. (1992). *Organizations: Rational, Natural, and Open Systems* (3rd ed.). Englewood Cliffs, NJ.: Prentice Hall.

Seashore, S. E., and Yuchtman, E. (1967). Factorial analysis of organizational performance. *Administrative Science Quarterly* 12: 377–395

Selznick, P. (1948). Foundations of a theory of organizations. *American Sociological Review* 13: 25–35.

Seymour, D. T. (1992). *On Q.* New York: ACE/Macmillan.

Sherman, S. (1992). How to prosper in the value decade. *Fortune* 126: 90–103.

Shewhart, W. A. (1931). *The Economic Control of Quality of Manufactured Product.* New York: Van Nostrand.

Simon, H. (1956). *Models of man.* New York: John Wiley and Sons.

Smart, J. C. (1989). Organizational decline and effectiveness in private higher education. *Research in Higher Education* 30: 387–401.

Smart, J. C., and Hamm, R. E. (1993a). Organizational culture and effectiveness in two-year colleges. *Research in Higher Education* 34: 95–106.

Smart, J. C., and Hamm, R. E. (1993b). Organizational effectiveness and mission orientations of two-year colleges. *Research in Higher Education* 34: 489–502.

Spencer, H. (1897). *The Principles of Sociology.* New York: Appleton, Century, Crofts.

Steers, R. (1978). Problems in the measurement of organizational effectiveness. *Administrative Science Quarterly* 20:546–558.

Tichy, N., and Fombrun, C. (1979). Network analysis in social settings. *Human Relations* 32: 923–965.

Tschirhart, M. (1993). The management of problems with stakeholders. Unpublished doctoral dissertation, University of Michigan.

Tsui, A. S. (1984). A role set analysis of managerial reputation. *Organizational Behavior and Human Performance* 34: 64–94.

Tsui, A. S. (1990). A multiple-constituency model of effectiveness: An empirical examination at the human resource subunit level. *Administrative Science Quarterly* 35: 458–483.

Van de Ven, A. H., and Ferry, D. L. (1980). *Measuring and Assessing Organizations*. New York: John Wiley, Wiley-Interscience.

Weber, M. (1967). *The Theory of Social and Economic Organization*. Translated and edited by A. M. Henderson and T. Parsons. New York: Oxford University Press.

Webster, D. S. (1981). Methods of assessing quality. *Change* (October): 20–24.

Webster, D. S. (1985). Institutional effectiveness using scholarly peer assessments as the major criteria. *Review of Higher Education* 9: 67–82.

Weick, K. E., and Daft, R. L. (1983). The effectiveness of interpretation systems. In K. C. Cameron and D. A. Whetten (eds.), *Organizational Effectiveness: A Comparison of Multiple Models*. New York: Academic Press.

Weick, K. E. (1976). Education organizations as loosely coupled systems. *Administrative Science Quarterly* 21: 1–19.

Weick, K. E., and Roberts, K. H. (1992). Organizational theories of high reliability. Working paper, School of Business Administration, University of Michigan.

Whetten, D. A. (1978). Coping with incompatible expectations: An integrated view of role conflict. *Administrative Science Quarterly* 23: 254–271.

Whetten, D. A. (1978). Coping with incompatible expectations: An undergraduate view of role conflict. *Administrative Science Quarterly* 23: 254–271.

Whetten, D. A., and Cameron, K. S. (1991). *Developing Management Skills*. New York: Harper-Collins.

Yuchtman, E., and Seashore, S. E. (1967). A system resource approach to organizational effectiveness. *American Sociological Review* 32: 891–903.

Zammuto, R. F. (1984). A comparison of multiple constituency models of organizational effectiveness. *Academy of Management Review* 9: 606–616.

Using Key Performance Indicators to Drive Strategic Decision Making

Michael G. Dolence and Donald M. Norris

Strategic planning isn't strategic thinking. One is analysis, the other is synthesis.
Henry Mintzberg, *Harvard Business Review*, Jan.–Feb. 1994

What Makes a Decision Strategic?

Strategic decisions are those that align an organization with its changing environment. To be effective, a strategic decision must influence action at all appropriate levels within the organization. To influence action at all levels, the decision must be understood throughout the organization, which requires access to information that defines the issue or problem, familiarity with the context and impact of the problem for the organization, and the willingness to recognize and act on an issue or problem once it is identified.

Strategic decisions occur at almost all levels within an organization. One challenge is to make sure individuals recognize when they are making a strategic decision so that they can align their decision with agreed-upon organizational strategy. A second challenge is to ensure that the strategy is the one that has the highest probability of positioning the organization for success. A third challenge is to furnish decision makers with information that reveals whether the strategy is working, and if it is not, provides insight into the nature of the problem and its potential solution. Decision makers in college and universities and in other organizations serving postsecondary education can use key performance indicators to help meet these challenges.

Using Key Performance Indicators to Drive Strategic Decisions

Key performance indicators (KPIs) are measures that are monitored in order to determine the health, effectiveness, and efficiency of an organization. They are not broad general categorical metrics, such as quality, resources, satisfaction, efficiency, or effectiveness. They are specific quantitative measures that tell stakeholders, managers, and other staff whether the college or university is accomplishing its goals using an acceptable level of resources. KPIs are precise numbers that have one and only one definition throughout the organization.

When strategic decisions are linked with KPIs, they can be especially effective in aligning a college or university within its environment, prioritizing resource allocations and program initiatives, focusing attention, and setting a course of action for the organization as a whole. KPIs allow concrete specification of the milestones and indicators that mark institutional progress. In short, they guide the organization, ensuring that it becomes more effective and more competitive.

This chapter will describe a methodology for linking strategic decision making with key performance indicators. The strategic decision

"Using Key Performance Indicators to Drive Strategic Decision Making," by Michael G. Dolence and Donald M. Norris, reprinted from *New Directions for Institutional Research*, No. 82. edited by V. M. H. Borden and T. W. Banta, Summer 1994. Jossey-Bass Publishers, Inc.

engine (SDE) is a nine-step cyclic method that helps complex organizations make strategic decisions at all levels. It is based on the development and use of key performance indicators. The SDE is a simple methodology to follow. At the same time, it is effective at keeping diverse groups of decision makers focused on the most important elements of the organization's success. After describing the SDE methodology, we will present examples of its application at two higher education institutions.

The Strategic Decision Engine

The SDE model is graphically illustrated in Figure 1. The nine steps of the model are as follows:

1. Gather, rank, and cull KPIs.

2. Perform an external assessment.

3. Perform an internal assessment.

4. Conduct a cross-impact analysis to determine the impact of environmental strengths, weaknesses, opportunities, and threats (SWOT) on the organization's ability to achieve its KPIs.

5. Generate ideas that make strengths stronger and weaknesses weaker, take advantages of opportunities, and neutralize threats.

6. Conduct a cross-impact analysis to determine the impact of the proposed ideas on the organization's ability to achieve its KPIs.

7. Formulate strategy, mission, goals, and objectives.

8. Conduct a cross-impact analysis to determine the impact of the proposed strategies, goals, and objectives on the organization's ability to achieve its KPIs.

9. Finalize and implement strategies, goals, and objectives.

Development of Key Performance Indicators (Step 1). The foundation of the strategic decision engine is a series of key performance indicators. The first step in the SDE is to gather, rank, and cull organizational KPIs. Gathering is done in a brainstorming session by a strategic planning steering group. The primary question for this brainstorming session is, What are

the measures that our stakeholders and managers should look at to determine whether we are being successful? For example, a bank's KPIs might include number of depositors, average account balance, number of loans, average loan amount, loan default rates, net profits, and net assets. A manufacturer's list might include number of sales, number of prospects, mean time to product failure, and number of widgets produced per employee. A college's list might include number of students enrolled, tuition rate, and graduation rate.

KPIs can be aggregated and disaggregated throughout the organization. A primary KPI for a university may be total number of enrolled students, which is the sum of students enrolled in component programs. Therefore, the business school would have an enrollment KPI that contributes to the institution's overall KPI and the departments of accounting, finance, marketing, and the MBA program have enrollment KPIs that contribute to the school's KPI. KPIs thus form a pyramid, with the organization-wide KPIs sitting at the top, division KPIs sitting one layer underneath, and major unit and department level KPIs forming the foundation.

The group charged with formulating KPIs may at first adamantly refuse to get specific in developing them. They may instead formulate broad general categories such as quality, resources, satisfaction, efficiency, or effectiveness. These categories can be used to help the group construct more specific KPIs within each general category. For example, quality may be measured by mean time to response, number of complaints, or scores on a monthly service evaluation survey. Initially, KPIs should use available data but it is likely that the group will identify measures requiring data that are not readily available.

External Assessment (Step 2). Once the initial set of KPIs is articulated, the planning group is ready to turn its attention to the external environment. The SDE characterizes the external environment in three domains: political, economic, sociological, and technological events and trends; collaborators; and competitors.

PEST Trends Analysis (Step 2A). The first domain is defined by a PEST analysis, which evaluates political, economic, sociological, and technological trends and events. The acronym also reflects how many groups feel about the

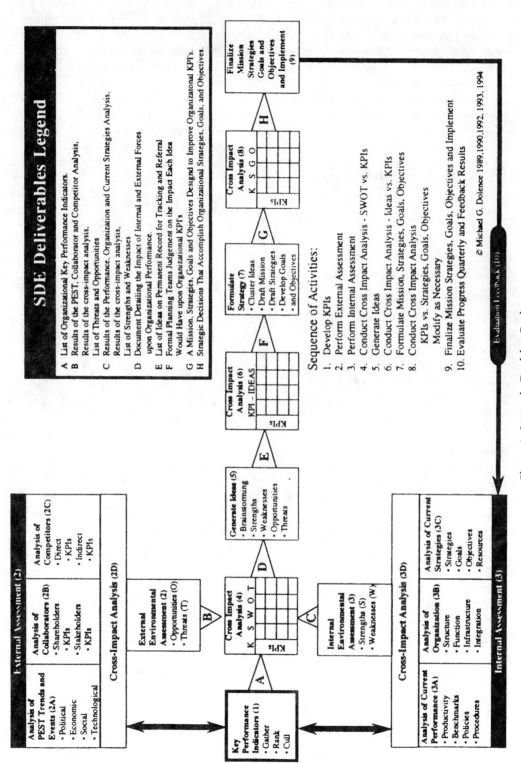

Figure 1 Strategic Decision Engine

process. The purpose of the PEST analysis is threefold. First, it illuminates trends and events that may have a positive or negative impact on the organization's health. Second, it furnishes the planning group with an in-depth understanding of these factors and their effects. Third, and most important, the PEST analysis determines the degree to which the organization is properly aligned with the full range of significant factors in its environment. By focusing on changes in the environment, the analysis highlights where these changes can create misalignments unless the college or university takes action in anticipation of the changes.

The PEST analysis helps the planning group avoid three frequent pitfalls of the planning process. First, the analysis recognizes weak environmental signals whose presence is not widely felt or understood by the organization but that may have significant negative impact. Most organizations usually avoid this category of environmental factor. Second, the PEST analysis also recognizes that the importance and impact of each trend and event is different. This allows the group to focus attention on the more important ones and minimize time and effort devoted to less influential external forces. Finally, this form of PEST analysis avoids "paralysis by analysis" by focusing attention on only the trends and events that impact the KPIs. By viewing the environment through the lens of the KPIs, the PEST analysis is much more focused than traditional environmental scanning analyses. The focus comes from the process of centering discussion and analysis on the impact of specific environmental trends and events on specific aspects of organizational performance.

During the PEST analysis, the planning group is likely to discover that it has omitted an important KPI that should be monitored. The KPI is added and the analysis continues. Once the most important PEST trends and events are identified, their potential impact on the organizational KPIs is assessed. This impact assessment is accomplished using a cross-impact analysis, explained in a later section.

Analysis of Collaborators (Step 2B). The second domain of the external analysis is an analytical look at the organization's collaborators, or stakeholders. These stakeholders are individuals and organizations who have a vested interest in the institution's success. Examples include employers, parents, students, suppliers, lenders, employee unions, special interest groups, government agencies, and professional associations. For public institutions, the state legislature and the executive branch of state government are especially important stakeholders.

The analysis first requires identification by name of these stakeholders, followed by an articulation of the KPIs that they use to measure their own success and the KPIs by which they would measure the success of the institution with which they collaborate. A cross-impact analysis of these stakeholder KPIs with the institution's own KPIs allows the planning group to identify win-win scenarios, pinpoint potential collaborations, and recognize possible opportunities and threats to the institution.

Analysis of Competitors (Step 2C). The third domain of the external analysis is an analytical look at the organization's competitors. Competitors are organizations that have a "negative interest" in the institution. They seek attention and resources from the same customers, suppliers, and providers. In the postsecondary education context, competitors include other institutions. For state institutions, competitors also include other entities vying for state funding—K–12 education, law enforcement, prisons, health care, and economic development, to name a few. Again, identification of these competitors is the first step in the analytic process, followed by specification of their KPIs. These activities can take the form of competitive market and peer group analyses. In addition to identifying important competitors, this analysis helps to illuminate their strategies and tactics and to understand how they affect the organization's own success as expressed through the KPIs identified in Step 1. The competitor KPIs are included in the culminating cross-impact analysis stage of Step 2.

Cross-Impact Analysis (Step 2D). The cross-impact analysis (CIA) is a Delphi technique that gives the planning group a clear vision of how a set of factors affects the achievement of the organization's KPIs. The method will be illustrated as implemented at the culmination of the external environment analysis—Step 2D in Figure 1. The CIA is a technique for harvesting the collective judgment of the group and focusing group discussion and supporting analysis. It is conducted using a two-dimensional matrix where the organization's KPIs are arrayed down the rows; the factors to be considered for their impact on KPIs are arrayed across the columns. The factors whose effects on the institution's KPIs are to be evaluated could include PEST trends and events, stakeholders' KPIs, and competitors' KPIs. Table 1 illustrates a portion of the matrix for Step 2D. Each member of the group assesses the impact that each trend and event would have on each KPI using the scale in Table 1.

Table 2 shows an example of one group member's assessments of the impact of four environmental trends and events on a state university's KPIs. Examining the scores in each cell provokes questions regarding what reasoning was applied to arrive at the assigned values. Why, for example, did the individual believe that the election of a new governor with a platform of low taxes, low tuition, and a commitment to reduce the state budget by cutting all agencies would result in a strong positive influence on the institution's five-year graduation rate?

Open discussion of the perceived impact of trends and events on organizational KPIs is the first step in preparing the planning group for effective decision making. Compiling group aggregate scores is a useful tool toward this end. Table 3 reports the means and standard deviations for each cell. The mean provides the group response and the standard deviation indicates the degree of consensus. The higher the standard deviation, the more widely spread the group members' individual judgments. High standard deviations reveal that more discussion may be needed to reach consensus. The CIA group scores can also be derived by public group discussion with a facilitator seeking verbal consensus. This approach may not work well in groups composed of members of unequal status. In such cases, a variety of techniques can be used to eliminate status barriers, such as the use of a computer-based decision room or electronic voting pads that mask the identity of the individual and count everyone's vote equally.

The CIA is used to evaluate the impact of all PEST trends and events as well as the collaborator and competitor KPIs.

Internal Assessment (Step 3). The purpose of the internal assessment is to evaluate the influence that organizational form, function, resources, strategies, goals, and objectives have on achieving the KPIs. Organizational units tend to use this type of review to make the case for more resources. This tendency should be avoided during this stage of the planning process. The analysis should be taken as an opportunity to describe the current state of the institution as a baseline for change. It includes assessments of three interrelated components; organizational performance, organizational strategies, and organizational form.

Analysis of Current Performance (Step 3A). The analysis of current performance begins by establishing benchmarks. These can be the average performance metrics of like institutions, performance levels of the closest competitors, or a compilation of the "best practices in the industry." Benchmarks help anchor the internal analysis in performance standards.

Productivity is a second essential element of organizational performance that can be measured in a number of different ways. It can be evaluated based on performance per work hour or number of FTE staff; it can be expressed in ratios of personnel to workload, or

Table 1 Cross-Impact Matrix for PEST Analysis

	Political Trend or Event	Economic Trend or Event	Social Trend or Event	Technological Trend or Event
KPI 1	Cell 1	Cell 6	Cell 11	Cell 16
KPI 2	Cell 2	Cell 7	Cell 12	Cell 17
KPI 3	Cell 3	Cell 8	Cell 13	Cell 18
KPI 4	Cell 4	Cell 9	Cell 14	Cell 19
KPI 5	Cell 5	Cell 10	Cell 15	Cell 20

Scale for rating impact in each cell:
6 = strong positive influence   5 = moderate positive influence
4 = weak positive influence   3 = weak negative influence
2 = moderate negative influence   1 = strong negative influence
0 = neutral, don't know, no impact, not applicable

Table 2 Sample Individual Scores for PEST Cross-Impact Analysis

	New governor platform: low tuition, low taxes, cut state agency budgets	High inflation rate and unemployment, new jobs require a college education	Population increase in the region; birth rate increase; immigration increase	Using technology to personalize instruction = 20% increase in grades
FTE enrollment	1	6	6	5
Tuition rate	1	3	0	3
Graduation rate	6	2	0	5
State appropriations	1	3	3	0
Financial aid	0	2	4	0

workload to cost. Both benchmarks and productivity measures are interrelated indicators that help institutions monitor the organization's performance. They may include some of the KPIs established in Step 1, but may also include other, less strategic elements. Table 4 displays samples of benchmark and productivity measures.

Progress on KPIs can be achieved only if organizational policies and procedures facilitate their realization. Ultimately every organizational policy and procedure should be passed through a cross-impact analysis. In this way, the planning group can assess the impact of each policy on KPIs, benchmarks, and productivity measures. During the analysis of organizational performance, the planning group should at least review major policies and procedures in this way.

Analysis of Organizational Form (Step 3B). Four components of organizational form are evaluated, including structure, function, infrastructure, and integration. The purpose of this analysis is to gain insights into the impact of organizational form on organizational KPIs. Structure is defined as the authority, governance, and reporting relationships that establish rules of operation within an organization. It is often diagrammed in organizational charts that can be classified into organizational typologies such as hierarchical, flat, or star. When structure is combined with division, unit, and individual functions and analyzed against organizational KPIs, some interesting insights begin to emerge. For example, it could be found that hierarchical, function-based organizational structures retard the achievement of institutional KPI targets for enrollment and

Table 3 Sample Group Scores for PEST Cross-Impact Analysis

	New governor platform: low tuition, low taxes, cut state agency budgets	High inflation rate and unemployment, new jobs require a college education	Population increase in the region; birth rate increase; immigration increase	Using technology to personalize instruction = 20% increase in grades
FTE enrollment	Mean 1.3 STD .34	Mean 5.5 STD .01	Mean 5.9 STD .01	Mean 5.8 STD .01
Tuition rate	Mean 1.2 STD .46	Mean 3.2 STD .01	Mean 4.2 STD .01	Mean 2.3 STD .01
Graduation rate	Mean 0.9 STD 3.11	Mean 2.1 STD 1.01	Mean 2.6 STD 2.01	Mean 5.1 STD 1.51
State appropriations	Mean 1.4 STD .02	Mean 1.8 STD .01	Mean 3.7 STD 2.84	Mean 2.8 STD .26
Financial aid	Mean 2.1 STD .01	Mean 2.1 STD .01	Mean 3.3 STD 4.72	Mean 3.4 STD .32

retention of students. Analysis of organization infrastructure should include a consideration of the physical plant, telecommunications networks, administrative and academic information systems, and classroom equipment. The final dimension of organizational form is how well the different divisions, units, and even individuals integrate their activity and efforts. The analysis should include judgments on the level of cross-unit integration and communication within the organization.

Analysis of Current Strategies (Step 3C). The planning group should next articulate the organization's present strategies, goals, objectives, tactics, and resources. This activity should be done through the lens of both the KPIs and the benchmark and productivity measures. Strategies are initiatives that align, realign, or maintain alignment between the organization and the environment. They are, or should be, long-term in nature, although they may have significant short-term impact on the organization, its collaborators, and its competitors. Goals are milestones achieved, usually over more than one year, and objectives are more immediate, time-bound, and measurable desired outcomes. Tactics are activities that move the orga-

nization closer to achieving its goals and objectives. Resources are the fiscal, human, technological, and organizational inputs to the organization's operations.

Internal Assessment CIA (Step 3D). After performing all three components of the internal assessment, the planning group engages in a cross-impact analysis to analyze the impact of the identified strengths and weaknesses on the KPIs. Again, the CIA is used to focus on the more consequential factors and to achieve consensus on the impact of these factors on institutional progress.

KPI–SWOT CIA (Step 4). As a result of the internal and external analyses, the planning group will have uncovered many of the organization's strengths, weaknesses, opportunities, and threats. In the fourth step of the SDE, these planning factors are evaluated against the organization's KPIs using the cross-impact analysis method described earlier. The purpose of this step is to measure the impact each strength, weakness, opportunity, and threat has on the KPIs. The KSWOT should be a blind vote with each participant receiving a single vote. This method mitigates the potential of having opinion leaders disproportionately in-

Table 4 Sample Benchmark and Productivity Measures

Instruction	Finance	Enrollment	Technology
Student-faculty ratio measured for full- and part-time faculty	Instructional cost per FTE student	Cost of recruiting a new student	Number of open access personal computers
Graduation rate measure for 4, 5, 6+ year intervals	Preventive maintenance expenditures per gross square foot	Ratio of institutional financial aid to total tuition revenue	Percentage of courses requiring technology access
Percentage of lower-division courses taught by full-time faculty	Faculty salary schedule	Fall-to-fall retention rates for different subcategories of students	Percentage of faculty with personal computers
Percentage of faculty with terminal degree	Annual or per credit hour tuition rate	Average course unit load per student	Percentage of faculty connected to Internet
Percentage of faculty with tenure	Student fees	Percentage of inquiries who apply	Ratio of personal computers to students
Average high school GPA of incoming students	Room charges	Percentage of applicants who are accepted	Number of campus network users
Diversity of faculty	Board charges	Percentage of accepted students who enroll	Software availability
Faculty salary equity	Annual fund giving	Ratio of students transferring in to students transferring out	Inventory of desktop functions

fluencing the vote. The result of this step is a ranked scoring of the external and internal factors that affect an organization's KPIs.

Idea Generation (Step 5). With a common and focused frame of reference provided by the results of the preceding steps, the planning group is ready to generate ideas. An open brainstorming session is used to solicit ideas on ways to improve the organization's performance as indicated by the KPIs. That is, the planning group members must think of ways to reduce the impacts of threats and weaknesses and to enhance the benefits of opportunities and strengths. Ideas can be contributed blindly and then listed without attribution or simply gathered in an open meeting. One important rule applies: participants must be free to say what they wish without negative comment by anyone. Negative comments can seriously reduce the quality of the ideas. If such comments are observed, the group should move to a blind contribution process.

KPI–Idea CIA (Step 6). Once the ideas are generated, discussed, and clarified, they are evaluated against the KPIs by a cross-impact analysis. This helps to refine the ideas generated in the brainstorming session as well as to cluster them into meaningful groups and determine their impact on the KPIs. Ideas without form or specificity must be discussed and refined so that the group members can assign values from the CIA scale. Ideas of little or negative impact begin to fall out of serious consideration in this analysis.

Strategy Formulation (Step 7). The process of formulating the organization's mission, strategies, goals, and objectives is the culmination of the preceding six steps. It can now occur with a common understanding of the purpose of actions to be outlined and a group expectation as to the impact of these actions on organizational performance. A review of prior step results prepares the group to cluster ideas into strategies, develop tactics, and assign organizational goals, objectives, and responsibilities.

Strategy, Goal, and Objectives CIA (Step 8). Once again, the CIA technique is used to evaluate how the strategies, goals, and objectives will affect the organization's KPIs. As with all previous CIA implementations, the group members vote anonymously and their tallies are aggregated into a composite matrix. Cells with large standard deviations are dis-

cussed further to see whether consensus can be reached. Even if consensus cannot be reached the strategies, goals, and objectives should be clarified to reach at least a uniform understanding of their definition.

Finalize Strategies, Goals, and Objectives for Implementation (Step 9). With the final analysis as a guide, the group fine-tunes its decisions and assigns them to managers, units, and individual work plans for implementation. As part of this implementation, responsibility must be given to units to maintain the information required to monitor progress according to the KPIs. Although these responsibilities may be spread throughout the organization, it is recommended that a centralized support unit, such as an institutional research office, be given both a facilitative and coordinating role in assembling KPI results in a systematic fashion.

In practice, the application of the SDE is tailored to each specific setting. The nature of the college or university, its particular set of opportunities and challenges, the history of planning on the campus, and the quality of campus leadership all affect the customization of the SDE. This tailoring affects the composition of the planning group; the balance between different parts of the SDE; and the nature of the KPIs, strategies, and goals that result. The following two examples illustrate the differences in the KPIs that were developed by two different educational institutions.

University of Northern Colorado

The University of Northern Colorado, located in Greeley, approximately fifty miles north of Denver, was founded in 1889 as the State Normal School. UNC is classified as a Doctoral-Granting I university within the Carnegie Classification system. One of twelve institutions in Colorado offering four-year degree programs and one of six providing doctoral education, the university is organized into seven colleges: Education, Arts and Sciences, Performing and Visual Arts, Business, Health and Human Services, the Graduate School, and Continuing Education. UNC operates within an annual budget of $89.8 million (1993–1994), including $30.7 million from state general fund appropriations, $25.1 million from tuition authorizations, $3.1 million from sponsored programs, and $31.1 million from auxiliary service activities such as housing and food services.

UNC enrolls approximately 8,300 undergraduate and 1,450 graduate FTE students. The average entering student has a high school GPA of 3.10 on a four-point scale and either a 907 combined SAT score or a 21.7 composite ACT score. A majority of students live on campus or in Greeley. They are largely from Colorado (about 90 percent), just over 10 percent are minority students, and 58 percent are female. In 1992–1993, UNC awarded 1,613 baccalaureate, 656 master's, and 55 doctoral degrees. The 462 full-time faculty are 39 percent female, 59 percent tenured. Sixty-eight percent of the full-time faculty hold terminal degrees and 8 percent are minorities.

A number of the political and economic factors currently affecting UNC stem from state legislative actions. The Colorado legislature recently passed House Bill 1187, mandating a lead role for UNC in statewide teacher education. Senate Bill 136 shifts more of the cost of education from general fund dollars to tuition and sets a limit on the percentage of out-of-state students allowed in Colorado public colleges and universities. The legislature also recently enacted Amendment I, imposing strict fiscal constraints on all state agencies and institutions. Finally, Senate Bill 136 establishes a new system for setting appropriation levels. Socially, the state of Colorado is becoming more culturally diverse and is experiencing population growth through in-migration and increasing birth rates. On the technological front, UNC must prepare its students to succeed in the emerging information-based economy and global society.

To deal effectively with these and a host of other factors, the university initiated the KPI-based strategic planning system described in this chapter. The process was designed and facilitated by one of the authors in collaboration with campus leadership. The process included more than 300 campus representatives who were brought together through the use of a decision-support facility housed in the UNC College of Business. Electronic brainstorming conducted by the numerous representatives resulted in almost 100 candidate key performance indicators, which were sifted and prioritized into the 20 primary institutional KPIs found in Table 5. The cross-impact of factors

from the external and internal analyses on the KPIs resulted in a sharp focus in four strategic areas: enrollment management, academic program development, information technology, and university resources and services.

A formal strategic enrollment management (SEM) program was launched by assembling a team to build an implementation plan based on a combination of financial, quality, and enrollment factors. The group's decision-making activities were sharply focused by the effects enrollment changes have on finances, retention, academic quality, and strategic position, which were identified in the analysis processes of the SDE methodology. The insights generated through the application of the SDE and the SEM program enabled the group to set reasonable targets for 1993–1994 enrollment that were met precisely.

Academic program strategies recognized significant increases in competition for quality students. Competitive strategies are being assembled within the academic context of UNC. Competition for resources was identified as another significant factor to be considered. Priorities for action emerged in the areas of making the faculty salary schedule at UNC more competitive with peer institutions and reallocating scarce development dollars toward realigning academic expertise and programs with constituent needs and expectations. Academic strategic planning continues to develop at UNC at the college and department levels.

Unanimous agreement was reached that the current technological infrastructure was inadequate to position UNC students in the forefront of graduates in competition for scarce employment opportunities. A number of initiatives are underway including the completion of a new fiber optic backbone, the acquisition and implementation of a completely integrated administrative information system, and the redesign of the academic technology infrastructure to support global scholarship and alternative learning styles.

Availability of resources is key to implementing strategy. Strategies that emerged included tightening the model used to manage enrollments, ensuring that UNC met the strategic intent of recent legislation, refining services and increasing productivity per unit, developing new revenue sources, enhancing development activities, and monitoring service performance.

Table 5 Summary of KPIs for University of Northern Colorado

KPI	Current Value	Five-Year Goal	Ten-Year Goal	Metric
1. Undergraduate FTE enrollment	8,271	9,250	10,000	Number units attempted divided by 15
2. Graduate FTE enrollment	1,435	1,600	2,000	Number units attempted divided by 12
3. Off-campus cash funded enrollment	834.8	1,150	1,500	Number units attempted divided by 15
4. Academic quality of entering freshmen	97.7	100	103	CCHE index combining SAT, ACT, and GPA
5. In-state resident students	89%	85%	79%	Percentage of students who are Colorado residents
6. Minority share of UNC graduates	7.9%	15%	20%	Percentage of minority bachelor's degree recipients
7. Six-year graduation rate	41.2%	50%	60%	Percentage of full-time first-year students who graduate within six years
8. Undergraduate fall-to-fall retention rate	77.2%	80%	85%	Percentage of students who enroll the following fall
9. Doctoral degrees awarded	55	75	100	Number of doctoral degrees awarded annually
10. Alumni attitude audit	85%	85%	85%	Percentage of alumni rating UNC Good or Very Good
11. Faculty quality	To be determined by faculty evaluation task force			
12. Faculty teaching contribution	63%	TBD	TBD	Percentage of lower-division courses taught by full-time faculty
13. Teacher certification ratio	23.1%	25%	25%	UNC students as a percentage of all students recommended for teaching certification
14. Placement of graduates	93.8%	93.8%	93.8%	Percent of graduates employed or in advanced study one year after graduation
15. Instructional cost	$2,840	TBD	TBD	State general fund for instruction divided by student FTE
16. Funds generated by research corporation	$6.4 million	$10.3 million	$15 million	Total dollars generated by sponsored programs
17. Funds generated by UNC foundation	$1.8 million	$2.7 million	$4 million	Total dollars generated by annual giving
18. Institutional grant and scholarship aid per FTE	22.5%	25%	30%	Percentage of institutional aid of total aid
19. On-campus student support services cost	$683	TBD	TBD	Expenditures for student services divided by student FTE
20. Meeting authorized state appropriation	$30.7 million	TBD	TBD	Annual appropriated dollars from all sources

Illinois Benedictine College

Illinois Benedictine College (IBC) is a denominational college affiliated with St. Procopius Abbey and located in the western suburbs of Chicago, Illinois. Its undergraduate programs enroll 1,650 students, of whom about 600 live on campus. The pipeline for new undergraduate students is about equally divided between first-time and transfer students. The college serves many adult learners. Its major claim to undergraduate program distinction is its science programs, which have an excellent reputation for preparing students for medical school. Several years ago, IBC acquired the graduate programs of the failing George Williams College, and today its master's programs in business administration, counseling psychology, exercise physiology, management information systems, organizational behavior, and public health enroll 950 students. The college is located on a 100-acre campus in a pleasant, safe suburban setting.

The college engaged in a four-month strategic planning process orchestrated by one of the authors, using a variation of the SDE. The strategic planning team consisted of administrators, faculty, and students. One variation from the model was that the college also asked the consultant to develop a five-year financial model that would focus the impact of strategies on resource allocation and the overall financial health of the institution.

The planning team found that the college had significant strengths and weaknesses. Its location in the Chicago suburbs presented many advantages and opportunities. While IBC had experienced modest enrollment growth, it was experiencing ballooning student aid requirements and difficulties in maintaining the student profile it desired. Moreover, IBC was not in robust financial condition. Lacking a significant endowment, it had annually balanced its budgets, but at the expense of a large accumulated deferred maintenance balance. It lacked any real campus master plan, and had no vision for campus facilities and programs that might capture the imagination of faculty, students, donors, and the community. The campus also needed to find ways to unify around a shared purpose the various factions of the campus community. Strong leadership was required at all levels.

To achieve these ends, the planning team proceeded to develop a statement of strategic intent and mission; conduct an analysis of strengths, weaknesses, opportunities, and threats; and develop a set of KPIs. It then proceeded to craft strategies that were driven by the KPIs. The strategies fell into five groupings: leadership, physical facilities and infrastructure, financial resources, strategic enrollment management, and academic programs. To achieve these strategies, the planning team developed specific actions and objectives indicators by which they could measure the completion of the actions. They set annual targets for the KPIs out to five years from the baseline period.

Table 6 portrays the KPIs developed by Illinois Benedictine College to drive its strategies and decisions. The table presents the baseline values and the annual targets that were established. These KPIs include both quantitative and qualitative targets. The index column expresses the final year's (1998–1999) values as a proportion of the baseline year (1993–1994).

IBC chose a set of KPI drivers in eight categories: enrollment, student progress, quality of students, quality of programs, faculty, financial conditions, facilities, and campus and community life. The combination of these KPIs enabled the college to focus on different drivers for its undergraduate and graduate programs, develop a financial model for the health of the institution, and understand the interconnection between the different KPIs. This approach has led not only to the adoption of the strategies, actions, and indicators, but to the use of a financial resources model that enables members of the campus community to understand better the contributing factors to the programmatic and financial health of the campus.

Conclusion: KPIs Can Drive Strategic Decision Making

We have found that KPIs can drive strategic decision making in colleges and universities. To this end, we have successfully applied two levels of KPIs in the strategic planning process.

First, we have developed institutional-level KPIs that are the important, campus-wide measures of student quality and progress, institutional size, resources, and desired institu-

Table 6 Summary of KPIs for Illinois Benedictine College

KPI	1993–1994	1994–1995	1995–1996	1996–1997	1997–1998	1998–1999	Index
Enrollment							
FTE students	269	269	265	277	279	277	1.030
New transfers	241	241	242	235	242	234	0.971
Residential students	595	595	595	595	595	595	1.000
Undergraduate headcount	1,650	1,650	1,642	1,646	1,662	1,647	0.995
Undergraduate FTE	1,320	1,320	1,320	1,310	1,300	1,300	0.985
Minority student body (%)	10	11	12	13	14	15	1.500
Total graduate headcount	951	951	977	1,004	1,030	1,058	1.110
Graduate SCH	18,000	18,000	18,500	19,000	19,500	20,000	1.111
Graduate FTE	443.8	443.8	456.1	468.5	480.8	493.1	1.111
Student Progress							
Undergraduate fall-to-fall retention	85	85	86	86	87	87	1.024
Undergraduate five-year graduation rate	52	53	55	58	60	60	1.154
Graduate retention rate	TBD	TBD	TBD	TBD	TBD	TBD	TBD
Graduate graduation rate	TBD	TBD	TBD	TBD	TBD	TBD	TBD
Quality of Students							
Top high school quartile %	48	49	50	51	52	53	1.104
Average ACT score	22.7	22.8	22.9	23.0	23.1	23.2	1.022
Percent < minimum ACT	23	21	19	17	15	13	0.565
Percent over 28 ACT	9.7	10.0	10.5	11.0	11.5	12.0	1.237
Quality of Programs							
Program quality standards	TBD	TBD	TBD	TBD	TBD	TBD	TBD
Faculty							
Percent minority	4	4	5	6	7	8	2.000
Student–faculty ratio	14	14	14	14	14	14	1.000
% Undergraduate SCH by PT faculty	22	22	22	20	20	20	0.909
Average graduate class size	18.5	19.0	19.5	20.0	20.0	20.0	1.081
Financial Conditions							
Annual philanthropic contributions (millions)	2.0	2.4	2.8	3.2	3.6	4.0	2.000
Value of endowment (millions)	7.437	TBD	TBD	TBD	TBD	TBD	TBD
True endowment (millions)	5.000	TBD	TBD	TBD	TBD	TBD	TBD
Funds balance (millions)	0.849	TBD	TBD	TBD	TBD	TBD	TBD
Contribution from academic programs (millions)	4.441	4.776	4.194	5.624	6.246	6.884	1.550
Tuition as % of revenue	74.8	74.8	74.8	74.7	74.6	74.5	0.996
Tuition discounting (%)	30	27	27	27	27	27	0.900
Deferred maintenance (millions)	20.0	20.0	19.5	18.5	17.5	16.5	0.825
Facilities							
Facilities quality index	TBD	TBD	TBD	TBD	TBD	TBD	TBD
Campus/Community Life							
Campus life quality index	TBD	TBD	TBD	TBD	TBD	TBD	TBD

tional outcomes. Most institutions develop twenty to thirty such KPIs. Strategies and initiatives are given higher priorities if they are judged to make more substantial contributions to achieving the targets established for the institution-level KPIs.

Second, there are program-level KPIs that deal with issues of program outcomes and quality. For some programs, this means customer service and meeting stakeholder needs. In these cases, the program must develop the capacity to answer a three-part question: What are the needs and wants of my customers or stakeholders? How successfully are we meeting those needs and wants? and What are the areas for improvement? The development of these measures typically is left to the individual programs, in collaboration with campus leadership. However, the program's leadership must be held accountable for achieving clearly identified targets for quality and satisfaction.

The SDE easily accommodates reengineering, continuous quality improvement (CQI), and other tools of transformation, either as independent strategies or as integral parts of other strategies. KPIs are an integral component of reengineering and CQI initiatives. As colleges and universities confront the need to realign themselves to dramatically changing environments and stakeholder expectations, they will come to appreciate the utility of KPIs as drivers of decision making and an essential element of transformation.

MICHAEL G. DOLENCE is strategic planning administrator at California State University, Los Angeles, and a management consultant who has served as a principal on a variety of projects for Strategic Initiatives, Inc.

DONALD M. NORRIS is president of Strategic Initiatives, Inc., a management consulting firm located in Herndon, Virginia.

Identifying Indicators
of Curricular Quality

Peter T. Ewell

In the atmosphere of fiscal uncertainty and intellectual restlessness faced by most of those charged with managing curricula in the 1990s, a principal imperative is simply to know what is going on. The explosion of knowledge itself, together with multiple and insistent challenges to traditional canons of content and delivery, has led to accelerating curricular diversity both within and across institutions. The resulting size and complexity of today's curricula make them less and less easy to administer by touch and feel. At the same time, the need to stretch increasingly scarce resources across this growing territory has led to equally pressing demands for curricular consolidation and coherence to achieve greater efficiencies. Here as well, the managerial need is for more and better information about how things are working, and how they might be made to work better. If this were not enough, pressures for the public disclosure of such information are escalating as funders and accreditors focus increasingly on outcomes and effectiveness. Given these forces, growing interest in the topic of quality indicators both as tools for academic management and as key ingredients of the new accountability should come as no surprise.

Definitions and Purposes

The term *indicator* has been used for many years in social and economic policy circles to describe a relevant, easily calculable statistic that reflects the overall condition of an enterprise, or the progress of a particular set of events (Burstein, Oakes, and Guiton, 1992). Among the most prominent national examples are the Department of Labor's unemployment rate and the Department of Commerce's report on gross domestic product, both of which are used to assess the nation's overall economic health. More recently, statistical indicators have been used in industry to monitor processes of manufacturing and service delivery and to provide a reliable base for tracking and improving quality (Gitlow and Gitlow, 1987). Examples here are varied, but include such things as component failure rates for manufactured products, cycle times for responding to customer requests, and the like. Many similar indicators are beginning to be used in such areas as student registration or business operations in college and university settings (Seymour, 1991; Sherr and Teeter, 1991).

To be useful as an indicator, a particular piece of data must communicate something important about what is happening in a complex domain. It is not necessary for the statistic to be causally related to the phenomenon of interest. The infant mortality rate, for instance, is commonly used as an indicator of the overall health of a nation or culture, but it would not be appropriate to concentrate all resources on delivering prenatal health care in an attempt to improve the overall situation. Indicator statistics are thus often labeled proxies or indirect measures of condition or attainment, and cautions on their use are advised. For similar reasons, indicators are best used in combination. In higher education, as in any field, the

"Identifying Indicators of Curricular Quality," by Peter T. Ewell, reprinted from *Handbook of the Undergraduate Curriculum: A Comprehensive Guide to Purposes, Structures, Practices, and Change*, edited by J. G. Gaff, J. L. Ratcliff, & Associates, 1996. Jossey-Bass Publishers, Inc.

best indicator systems are carefully constructed to provide mutually reinforcing measures that together provide an appropriate picture of what is occurring (Ewell and Jones, 1994).

What lies behind the growing prominence of performance indicators of this kind in national discussions of academic efficiency and effectiveness? A first stimulus comes from state and federal authorities—as well as institutional accrediting bodies—who in the last decade have become far more specific in their demands for information. In the early to mid-1980s, such demands centered largely on the unexplored and controversial territory of academic outcomes, and helped spark the kinds of institutional assessment approaches described in previous chapters. More recently, such demands have become more focused—centered prominently on the need to allocate scarce public resources and to inform individual consumer choices among colleges or universities (Ewell, 1994). Two things have happened as a result. First, the external market for performance information has gradually expanded from an exclusive concern with outcomes to address core questions of instructional organization and delivery. Second, the particular form in which information of all types has been requested by external actors has become increasingly terse and truncated, placing a premium on quantitative, easily compared measures of condition and performance (Ruppert, 1994). Combined, these two phenomena have yielded a growing number of statistical report cards prepared by sources ranging from state governments to *USA Today*.

A second stimulus for the use of performance indicators is internal. Faced with growing fiscal pressures and unabated student demand, many colleges and universities are beginning to adopt new management approaches based on Total Quality Management (TQM). Initially confined to administrative support functions, TQM concepts (though with many caveats) are gradually finding their way into academic functions as well (Seymour, 1991). In contrast to assessment's apparent emphasis on inspection at the end, such approaches emphasize continuously gathering data about how core processes are actually working, and focus especially on the ways apparently different functions are supposed to fit together to achieve common ends (Ewell,

1993). This particular emphasis is quite consistent with curricular reform themes of the last decade, which stress coherence and integration. But it also demands concrete information to monitor such connections, and to determine where appropriate improvements can be made.

Consistent with both stimuli, quality indicators are effective for some things and not for others. In general, indicators of quality or performance are particularly useful for three purposes in higher education settings: to quickly compare relative performance across units, institutions, or settings; to monitor what is happening within a particular unit, institution, or setting over time; and to explicitly examine the effects of intervention or policy change—either across settings or over time.

In all three applications, moreover, important caveats apply. First, indicators should not be used singly or in isolation. As noted, the most effective systems consist of multiple indicators designed to be mutually reinforcing. At the same time, the information contained in a given indicator always lies in comparison of values for it—across different settings, at different points in time, or before and after intervention. Basing any conclusion on a single observation can be dangerous. Second, the specific settings across which indicators are compared must be sufficiently similar to allow meaningful conclusions to be drawn. It makes little sense, for instance, to directly compare the student retention rates of a community college and a selective liberal arts college; these two types of institutions have substantial differences in mission and student clientele. At the very least, additional indicators should be constructed that reflect these differences, so that they may be taken directly into account in interpreting performance (in the example noted, for instance, an additional indicator of entering student ability might be constructed). Third, indicators are at their best when used to raise questions or identify potential problems; they are not very good at rendering summative judgments about adequacy or performance. As a result, quality measures of the kind described in this chapter should always be used in conjunction with the in-depth assessments described in other chapters. Nonetheless, the increasing use of indicators in academic settings testifies to their growing utility to academic managers when used for appropriate purposes.

Indicators of Curricular Quality: Some General Issues

Until recently, the idea of managing the curriculum was rare. Since the mid-1980s, however, a number of forces have coalesced that render explicit attention to curricular management issues imperative. One is a growing concern about curricular coherence and integration, especially in the realm of general education. Here such documents as *Integrity in the College Curriculum* (Association of American Colleges, 1985) and *Involvement in Learning* (National Institute of Education, 1984) marked a major resurgence of interest in designing curricula to achieve common, cross-cutting learning objectives, and helped to stimulate strong interest in assessment. Increasingly, however, attention has shifted from exclusive concern with curricular design and outcomes to include the mechanics of curriculum delivery. In part, this shift has been due to growing recognition that what goes on inside the classroom is at least as important in achieving coherence as the way curricula are designed. And in part it is due to a new awareness, based on experience, that simply implementing new curricula does not ensure that the courses and sequences they contain are deployed as designed.

Assessment, of course, represents another visible stimulus to the development of curricular quality indicators. As institutional assessment approaches became more sophisticated, institutions began collecting data about student experiences and inputs to explore the dynamics of outcomes (Ewell, 1991). Most discovered that it made little sense, beyond accountability, to collect detailed outcomes data without simultaneously knowing something about the stimulus conditions that might be responsible for such outcomes, and that might be susceptible to change. Astin's (1991) Input-Environment-Outcomes (I-E-O) schema for assessment both summarized and stimulated such trends, and has proven especially helpful in guiding more comprehensive approaches to curriculum evaluation at the institutional level. Because they are covered in Chapters Twenty-Eight and Twenty-Nine, this chapter will intentionally exclude topics related to the direct assessment of learning outcomes—probably the best bottom line for assessing quality. But following Astin's (1991) admonition, readers should be cautioned that in-

formation drawn both from assessment (on outcomes) and from curriculum monitoring (on processes) is needed to inform improvement.

New demands for efficiency constitute a final impetus for developing indicators of curricular shape and structure. Since the late 1990s, most institutions have been under substantial financial pressure and have begun actively searching for ways to deliver equivalent instructional content at lower unit cost. Naturally, attention has turned to methods for streamlining curricula—delivering in three years what was formerly taught in four, reducing or cutting underenrolled classes, or eliminating duplicative or overlapping course offerings (for example, see Zemsky, Massy, and Oedel, 1993; or Massy and Zemsky, 1992). While early attention to curricular modifications of this kind was unsophisticated, consisting largely of pruning the curriculum, more recent efforts have turned to more far-reaching and complex forms of restructuring (State Council on Higher Education in Virginia, 1994). Prominent here have been attempts to rethink curricular delivery in terms of common outcomes and efforts to carefully monitor student course-taking patterns to determine specific student markets for particular course sequences and to discover where modifications might be made to accelerate student progress.

It is curious that the new demand for efficiency has caused modifications in curriculum often surprisingly consistent with earlier and more academic concerns about coherence. Both require clear objectives, careful monitoring of delivery, and mapping actual patterns of course content and student flow to determine if course sequences are working as intended. Indicators of curricular quality and delivery, of course, can play a major role in this process.

Another important conceptual issue affecting the development of indicators in this domain is exactly what is meant by *curriculum*. As Stark and others (Stark and Lowther, 1986) have pointed out, institutions may have multiple curricula in place—designed, taught, and experienced by students—that have little to do with one another in content, coverage, or effectiveness. For purposes of indicators development, therefore, it is useful to operate with at least four distinct conceptions of curriculum, each of which might independently be assessed across a number of domains:

- The *designed* curriculum, consisting of catalogue and syllabus descriptions. This curriculum tends to dominate faculty attention, regardless of whether it has reality in practice. While increasingly recognizing explicit learning outcomes as part of the design, the bulk of attention here remains focused on content and course sequence, as defined by institutional or departmental policy.

- The *expectational* curriculum, consisting of the specific assignments and levels of performance expected of students and the manner in which student performance is assessed. This reflects what is more often the student's view of a given curriculum—based not on course content but rather on the requirements that must be met and the levels of performance needed to meet them. Though an aspect of design, examining expectations can also be revealing for curriculum assessment. For instance, a stated objective of the general education curriculum may be to develop students' oral communications proficiency. An examination of required performances across general education courses reveals that students are rarely asked to demonstrate this proficiency in class and are never evaluated on it.

- The *delivered* curriculum, consisting of what faculty actually teach and the consistency with which they do so. In contrast to design, this curriculum is behavioral, and may vary significantly across classrooms and from original design specifications. For any established curriculum—especially in general education—the phenomenon of course drift occurs: as new faculty teaching assignments to a given course are made, both content and teaching methods may vary increasingly from the vision embodied in the original design. Similarly, significant unintended variation may occur from section to section in a multisection course. Typically, institutions know very little about the extent and impact of such variations beyond simply acknowledging that they occur.

- The *experienced* curriculum, consisting of what students actually do. This curriculum is also behavioral and can usefully be separated into two quite different components. One concerns student course-taking patterns—especially when these occur within a distributional or elective design. Formal structure may prescribe particular arrays of courses that meet specific requirements, but how do different types of students in fact act out these requirements in the actual course choices that they make? A second aspect of the experienced curriculum is student learning behavior. Regardless of what a syllabus analysis might indicate, for instance, how much writing do students typically engage in to meet their class assignments? What kinds of writing do they really need to employ? How much actual exercise of oral communications skills do they report as having occurred in the classes that they take? Again, institutions typically know very little about such matters—though they often devote meticulous up-front attention to them in the design process.

All four aspects of curriculum are important in assessing quality, and appropriate indicator systems should be designed to reflect them all. Indeed, the best such systems are especially configured to detect discontinuities among these four aspects—examining, for instance, the ways in which particular elements of design are not being effectively translated into teaching practice and student experience.

Indicators can in principle be developed for virtually any dimension of curricular structure or performance, but they are especially suited to particular domains. From the outset, moreover, a distinction must be made between indicators designed to compare performance across institutions and intended primarily for accountability, and those focused on internal curricular functioning and intended primarily for local monitoring and improvement.

Comparing Curricula Across Institutions

Curricula differ in many ways from institution to institution, and the choice of which aspects to compare depends upon one's purposes. For purposes of accountability, attention has centered primarily on standards and student experiences. Concerned about what they perceive as declining quality and eroding levels of customer service to students, public policy makers are interested in such topics as what is expected of students and whether students are obtaining real access to faculty or getting the courses they need to graduate in a timely manner. Another typical perspective for comparison is that of an individual institution seeking peer-based information about curricular structure and delivery for purposes of accreditation or internal review. Principal dimensions of interest here typically center on coverage and content, or the overall shape of the curriculum with respect to numbers of electives and required courses.

Regardless of perspective, a fairly limited number of aspects of any curriculum are suitable for the development of comparative indicators. Indicators in each of these domains can also be monitored over time within a given institution to uncover long-term trends in instructional delivery, or to examine the impact of particular curricular policies.

- *Content and coverage.* What in particular is covered, and at what level of detail, constitutes probably the most commonly discussed and compared aspect of any curriculum. Detailed specifications of coverage with explicit standards, as embodied in the traditional *trivium* and *quadrivium,* are as old as the academy itself. Their more modern incarnations are present in the highly detailed course coverage and sequence specifications often used by professional accreditation bodies. More recently, coverage concerns have partially shifted away from disciplinary content toward the development of specified skills that cut across courses. Occurring principally in the realm of general education (and in part stimulated by assessment's demand that curricular outcomes be identified explicitly), the most common crosscutting skills embrace areas such as writing and critical thinking (see Chapter Eighteen). The process of developing indicators development in this domain is conceptually straightforward, though operationally challenging. In essence, it addresses a single question: How much of what is taught where?

- *Sequence and structure.* Another classic basis on which to compare curricula is their degree of structural elaboration. Some, especially in the sciences and in technical fields, are highly specified with respect to sequence and structure—the familiar lock-step design. Others allow considerable flexibility and choice as the student progresses. Attempts to capture such notions empirically, however, have been rare. Among the most useful are those based on concepts of breadth and depth (for example, Zemsky, 1989)—in essence the proportion of total coursework in a given curriculum (either on paper or as recorded empirically through an analysis of transcripts) that is delivered within or outside of a particular discipline or academic area. In the realm of general education, where breadth is usually intended by definition, the more common question is one of coherence: to what degree does curricular structure embody courses intended to fit together or to induce students to make connections across disparate disciplines? Behind both approaches are several specific components of curricular design suitable for the development of indicators. One is concentration—in essence, the degree to which a single field or discipline is dominant. Another is choice, or the degree to which specific courses are mandated or students are free to elect them. A final dimension is linearity, or the degree to which specified prerequisite sequences or requirements are present.

- *Exposure versus application.* This domain reflects somewhat newer concerns about the balance between the traditional concept of delivery of disciplinary content and a more recent emphasis on the ongoing application or practice of learned skills. The most visible curricular features related to application include internships, practica, or capstone experiences—settings in which students are expected to actively deploy and demonstrate what they have learned. Quite naturally, such applied curricular features have been especially emphasized in professional programs. Increasingly, however, hands-on experiences and exercises are being emphasized as a part of active learning in all fields—whether they are formally included as a discrete curricular component or are built into existing coursework in the form of assignments or applications exercises. Indicators development in this domain concentrates principally on the presence or absence of such curricular features. Naturally, these are easier to detect when they are present as formal catalogue requirements that can be counted. But based on syllabus review or student self-reports, useful indicators can also be developed that reflect the degree to which the general delivery of coursework stresses opportunities for practical application.

• *Incidence of good practice.* As attention to articulating common curricular outcomes increased throughout the 1980s, so did concerns about effective instructional practices. Partly this was due to contemporary reforms in pedagogy that went beyond teaching to emphasize active, collaborative approaches to learning. Partly it was a natural extension of wider assessment-for-improvement initiatives, which quickly recognized that information about instructional processes and student experience would be critical in making sense of any data about outcomes (Astin, 1991). The specifics of instructional good practice were given a powerful vehicle for dissemination in "Seven Principles for Good Practice in Undergraduate Education" (Chickering and Gamson, 1987), which not only succinctly codified the majority of these practices but also provided concrete inventories for assessing the degree to which they are actually engaged in (Gamson and Poulsen, 1989). Growing interest in Classroom Research (Angelo and Cross, 1993) has given further impetus to these developments, as well as providing an additional set of good practices to count. Building good indicators within this domain, however, can be complex as it generally entails digging deeper than the visible aspects of curricular design. As a result, most work in this area has relied on faculty and student reports of their own behavior.

Indicators in all four of these domains have in some fashion been developed for purposes of peer comparison or public reporting. Probably the most visible are those contained in state performance indicators reports for public institutions now in place in some fifteen states (Ruppert, 1994). While the majority of these provide basic statistics on institutional activity—for instance, graduation rates or time-to-degree—many include measures of curricular delivery as well. South Carolina, for instance, requires institutions to report on levels of undergraduate student apprenticeship in faculty research activities, while Florida monitors the amount of writing required in a student's first year. Proposals currently being finalized in Virginia (and already in place in the Minnesota State University System's "Q-7" program, a seven-step quality improvement initiative) include measures that reflect the proportion of students engaging in capstone integrative experiences (State Council on Higher Education in Virginia, 1994). At the same time, a range of curricular good practice indicators have been proposed for postsecondary education at the national level (National Center for Higher Education Management Systems, 1994).

Beyond accountability, the use of indicators for peer comparison centers largely in the areas of structure and good practice. Projects of such organizations as the Association of American Colleges and Universities in general education, for instance, incorporate measures of overall breadth and depth (Zemsky, 1989), while new scales are currently being developed for the widely used "College Student Experiences Questionnaire" (Pace, 1984) to better reflect student-faculty contact and active learning experiences.

Monitoring Internal Curricular Design and Delivery

Indicators in the above domains, of course, can be equally useful at the institutional level for monitoring trends in the curriculum. Particularly prominent here have been attempts to develop local indicators of good practice (for example, Winona State University, 1990; Ewell and Jones, 1996). But a far more frequent application of the indicators concept for internal planning and evaluation has been in connection with assessment. As institutions increasingly develop comprehensive outcomes assessment models to inform improvement, their needs have increased for information related to instructional experiences and delivery. Not surprisingly, one of the first findings is that the curriculum is not being delivered or received as intended (National Center for Higher Education Management Systems, 1991). Consistent with this experience, two particularly useful additional domains for the development of institution-level indicators arise:

- *Conformity with objectives.* A key question for any institution or department is the degree to which the curriculum as designed, delivered, or received is in fact aligned with the learning objectives it is intended to develop. So long as the principal concern in curricular design was content coverage, answers to this question were straightforward. Courses themselves tended to be organized in neat content packages that could easily be monitored. From the typical faculty standpoint, moreover, the question of content coverage was both legitimate and immediately intelligible. Curricular discussions about conformity with objectives, therefore, tended to be informal and routine. As such discussions throughout the 1980s increasingly centered on the development of identifiable common outcomes or the provision of specific learning experiences, however, the question became more complicated. In general education courses, for instance, faculty might be called upon not only to teach their discipline but to foster critical thinking or provide collaborative learning experiences as well. Often such additional, apparently noncontroversial, objectives were adopted quickly without much thought about what they might mean operationally. As assessment proceeded, however, it became reasonable to ask whether, where, and in what manner such objectives were being addressed in the classroom.

- *Internal articulation.* A parallel question is the degree to which the curriculum is actually working as intended—particularly with regard to the connections intended among its individual courses. In even the most loosely designed curricular structure,

students are expected to be able to effectively apply knowledge and skills learned in the context of one course to that of another. The most visible aspect of this expectation is a structure of prerequisites, but many less formal such connections may be expected as students progress. To what degree are such connections actually operating as intended? At least two dimensions of this question can be used to guide the development of indicators. First, are designed prerequisite structures and curricular sequences actually manifested in patterns of student course-taking behavior, and what are the consequences if they are not? This is on one hand a question of longitudinal curricular flow involving identification of the overall degree of variation from expected paths that might be occurring. On the other hand, it is a question of the impact of such patterns if identified: do they lead to lower student performance or do such violations of sequence appear to not really matter very much? If the latter is the case—that is, if students fail to follow intended paths and it does not affect their ultimate success—it may be legitimate to ask why such requirements should be maintained.

A second dimension of internal articulation concerns the fit between important pairs of courses. Partly this is a more specific question of content and coverage: for instance, how much and what particular aspects of what is taught in a calculus sequence delivered by the math department, or a freshman composition course delivered by the English department, are really required for effective performance in, say, a third-year engineering course or a second-year sociology course for which these two lower-level courses serve as prerequisites? Identifying these specific areas of common ownership may be critical to fostering cross-departmental conversations about relative teaching priorities. At the same time, articulation of this kind involves a question of performance: can students work effectively in subsequent courses, and what types of errors do they make? Here, appropriately designed indicators can help point to the particular prerequisite sequences that need attention, and can help identify some of the specific deficiencies to be corrected.

The development of indicators for domains such as these, as might be expected, is generally part of a larger approach to curriculum improvement or redesign. Often this approach itself is explicitly guided by a continuous quality improvement philosophy that aims at achieving better outcomes and greater efficiencies simultaneously by eliminating unneeded curricular paths, and by cutting down on the need to repeat particular topics or skills that were not learned appropriately the first time (Baugher, 1992; Harris and Baggett, 1992). In other cases—especially in two-year college settings—curriculum improvement indicators are consistent with wider efforts aimed at improving student retention and success rates (O'Banion and Associates, 1994).

Sample Indicators and Their Construction

Indicators of curricular quality can be derived from many specific data sources, and the best approaches draw information from a range of methods. As might be expected, moreover, some of these approaches are more suited to providing data for some domains than they are for others. While a complete catalogue of the many specific indicators that can or have been used to assess curricula is well beyond the scope of this chapter, it is feasible to present concrete illustrations of some of the major types.

For a variety of reasons, this task is best undertaken by a data source. Not only does this allow a more systematic treatment of the many different methodologies available, but it also helps highlight the ways that information drawn from different sources can be mutually reinforcing.

• *Indicators based on catalogue or syllabus review.* Probably the most straightforward method for developing useful indicators of content and coverage or conformity with objectives in the designed curriculum is based on published descriptions of courses. At the broadest level, this approach allows the construction of indicators for the overall structure and coverage of the curriculum. For example, the following simple ratios and percentages can generally be constructed using available catalogue material:

Proportions of total general education credits or courses allocated to particular areas of study, or to the development of specific prerequisite skills (writing, math, oral communication, and so on)—a measure of curricular *coverage.*

The number of courses available among which students may choose to fulfill a given curricular requirement, divided by the number of courses needed to meet the requirement—a measure of *choice.*

The proportion (or absolute number) of total credits needed to complete a given major program of study that must be completed in the major discipline—a measure of *disciplinary concentration.*

The proportion of courses needed to complete a given major program of study broken down by the total number of prerequisite and implied prerequisite courses associated with each (that is, the percentage for which no prerequisites are required, the percentage for which at least one is required, two, and so on—taking into account the entire chain of implied prerequisites for each required course)—a measure of *sequence* and *structure.*

Tapping the rich array of individual syllabus material available on most campuses can yield data on the ways in which the curriculum is actually being delivered. Additional calculations such as the following become possible:

The average amount of writing required to complete a given program of study, based on an analysis of assignments—a measure of *expectations* and of *skills coverage.*

For each identified outcome or goal of general education, the number of courses that identify this intended outcome explicitly as a course goal, the number addressing the goal implicitly in what is covered (or how it is covered), or the number explicitly assessing students on achievement with respect to this outcome—a measure of *conformity to objectives* (often presented in matrix form, as in Ewell and Lisensky, 1988, Chapter Two).

At the highest level of detail, it is possible to match syllabus material to explicitly identified levels of competency on core outcomes in order to physically map the specific places in a curricular sequence at which these levels are developed, required, and tested. An excellent illustration of this process is provided by the "competence growth plans" prepared by individual departments at King's College (Farmer, 1988).

• *Indicators based on transcripts or student records.* Transcript records provide what is probably the most comprehensive basis on which to determine the shape of the behavioral curriculum. Unfortunately, they are also one of the most intractable sources of information available, as student records systems at most institutions are not designed to aggregate or otherwise analyze student course-taking patterns. Fortunately, some progress has been made in two arenas. First, useful national standards for coding samples of transcripts have been developed that allow comparisons across quite different institutions and settings (Adelman, 1990). Second, some general course-taking measures have been developed that allow reduction of extremely complex transcript records into a few broad behavioral patterns (Zemsky, 1989). Using approaches such as these, even a simple coding of longitudinal course enrollments can yield indicators such as the following:

Percentage of students graduating (by field) never having enrolled for a course in a foreign language—a measure of specific *disciplinary or skills exposure.*

The proportion of courses in a given discipline for which at least three-quarters of enrollments were generated by students in the same academic year of study (Zemsky, 1989)—a measure of *temporal focus.*

Percentage of enrollments (by course or discipline) violating current placement policies or prerequisite sequences—a measure of the *implementation of curricular policy.*

The average length of time (by course or discipline) occurring between particular course enrollments and the prior completion of any established prerequisite course requirement—a measure of the actual *realization* of a given sequential curriculum design.

The two latter measures, of course, are useful not only as indicators in themselves, but as factors to be associated with student performance. Transcript files can also allow some measurement of performance in the form of grades earned or subsequent courses passed. If individual assessment results are also included in the institution's records system (or can be

matched to individual student records via an identifier), more powerful indicators of curricular performance can be constructed:

The average GPAs (or alternatively, the proportion passed with a grade of C or better) of students taking a given set of upper-level courses under varying prerequisite conditions (such as having met or not met such prerequisites, the amount of time elapsed since completing prerequisite courses, or the actual prior performance in prerequisite courses)—a measure of the *adequacy of prior curricular preparation.*

Specific types or clusters of courses taken by students that are associated with gains in achievement on external assessment measures such as standardized tests, certification or licensure passage, and so on—a measure reflecting the different *contributions of particular curricular components* with respect to outcomes (see Ratcliff, 1993).

Detailed methods for conducting analyses using combinations of student transcript record and assessment data are available from several sources. One example is the "differential coursework methodology" developed by the National Center on Postsecondary Teaching, Learning, and Assessment at Penn State (Ratcliff and Associates, 1988). Another is the approach used by Astin (1992) in the Exxon Study of General Education to identify specific curricular experiences linked to student gains in self-reported achievement.

• *Indicators based on reports from faculty and students.* What faculty say they do and value, and what students say is delivered or experienced, constitute the most straightforward methods available to get at the behavioral aspects of curriculum. Indicators of curriculum quality based on student self-reports, for instance, are ideally suited to assess good practice. While syllabi and transcript records can record levels of expectations and patterns of attendance far more accurately and completely than student recollections, students themselves are probably in the best position to report on such matters as their own levels of effort, whether or not they spoke in class and how frequently, and the degree of group work they might have engaged in.

Currently, of course, most institutions already use such methods to evaluate individual classes through the familiar mechanism of student ratings of instruction. But such instruments are generally aimed at a single purpose: evaluating instructor behavior for purposes of promotion and tenure. Increasingly, however, such questionnaires are being reconfigured to capture students' own behavior or perceived learning as well (Ewell, 1991). This trend has been given a powerful impetus by the Classroom Research movement (Angelo and Cross, 1993) described in Chapter Twenty-Eight, but is different in the sense that the results of Classroom Research are not intended to be codified or shared widely across the institution. An important caution involved in using information from such sources for indicators development, therefore, is to ensure a proper level of aggregation in reporting the resulting information. It is generally inappropriate, for instance, to report student testimony on such matters on a class-by-class or instructor-by-instructor basis.

Some of the specific indicators that have been developed using this approach are:

The average number of out-of-class hours per week spent studying reported by students in different types of classes—a measure of *student quality of effort.*

The percentage of students reporting high levels of discussion with peers on topics related to the course, or the percentage reporting at least three face-to-face conversations with faculty on topics related to course material outside of class—measures of *engagement* and *active learning.*

The number and types of self-reported connections made by students between material or ideas presented in a general education course and some other course they are taking at the same time—a measure of *connected learning.*

The percentage of students reporting that they almost always receive graded assignments back from instructors within a week—a measure of *frequent feedback.*

While all these examples are suitable for (and have been used in) end-of-course questionnaires, similar items on self-reported behaviors are equally appropriate for inclusion in broader questionnaires administered periodically to larger samples of students. The most prominent national examples of such instruments are the Cooperative Institutional Research Follow-Up Survey (Astin and Associ-

ates, 1992), administered to nationally normed samples of students for research purposes, and the College Student Experiences Questionnaire (Pace, 1984), now available through Indiana University. Most institutions, however, design and administer their own such instruments and, where present, these provide an excellent vehicle for collecting information about reported curricular experiences.

Reports from faculty constitute a similar but less well-tapped source of information about the delivered curriculum. Some such surveys have been designed to document common instructional practices—for instance, the model instruments designed to assess use of the "Seven Principles of Effectiveness in Undergraduate Education" (Gamson and Poulsen, 1989). Others are more oriented toward determining broader underlying instructional values or attitudes toward teaching (for example, Astin, 1992). Among the specific indicators that can be developed using such sources are:

Percent of faculty time per week allocated to teaching, advising, and other instructional support tasks—a measure of *teaching investment.*

Percent of faculty reporting that support and encouragement for teaching innovations are strongly present in or strongly supported by their departments—a measure of *instructional climate.*

Percent of faculty reporting that they frequently engage in a set of identified classroom practices in their teaching, such as group work, active learning techniques, or classroom research—a measure of *classroom behavior.*

With self-reports of any kind, of course, questions about validity often arise. These are generally of two kinds. One is the credibility of self-reports themselves. Faculty, for instance, are more likely to serve as credible witnesses of the general value placed on teaching in their departments than they are about their own behaviors. Similarly, students are usually better judges of what they have done (that is, how they spent their time) than they are of how much they have learned. A second difficulty with self-reported data—especially relevant to the construction of indicators—is that data based on surveys rarely yield usable point estimates of performance. The fact that 58 percent of students majoring in biology said they were extremely satisfied with instruction in their major, for instance, is far less useful in itself than knowing that this value was 76 percent for last year's graduating class, or that a difference of 15 percent separates the men from the women. As a result, the best uses of such data rely strongly on analyses of trends over time or of the differing experiences of particular student subpopulations. (For an excellent example of how survey analysis of this kind can paint a compelling picture of the curriculum as experienced, see College of William and Mary, 1994.)

• *Indicators based on direct assessment.* Direct assessment of cognitive or affective development, of course, provides the most convincing evidence of curricular effectiveness, and such methods are discussed in Chapters Twenty-Eight and Twenty-Nine. Quite properly, direct assessment indicators are focused on the two extremes of the teaching and learning continuum—determining overall patterns of institutional goal-attainment and guiding the process of learning within individual classrooms. But most treatments of this topic ignore two additional roles of direct assessment that can be used to examine curricular functioning.

One is the often considerable amount of information that can be gained about real curricular content using assessment techniques. Long-time observers of assessment in action have particularly emphasized the indirect benefits of the process in clarifying goals (Banta and Schneider, 1988; Banta and Associates, 1993). Others have noted how assessment evidence often has as much to say about curriculum structure as it does about outcomes—or more (Ewell, 1991). A common example is the increasingly popular portfolio approach to assessment, in which student work samples are systematically compiled to determine the degree to which cross-cutting curricular outcomes like writing or critical thinking are being accomplished. In more than a few cases, institutions have found these exercises more valuable in determining what faculty are really assigning, and the alignment of these assignments with curricular goals, than in directly documenting student attainment (for example, Northeast Missouri State University, 1994; College of William and Mary, cited in Ewell, 1991).

Among the specific indicators of curricular functioning that might arise as by-products of direct assessment are the following:

> Numbers of written assignments in general education courses compiled from student

portfolios that contain multiple or cross-disciplinary references—a measure of *integration in the delivered curriculum.*

Proportion of written assignments in all disciplines compiled as part of a portfolio process that require students to display such analytical skills as comparing or contrasting different situations or determining flaws in an argument—a measure of *coverage in the delivered curriculum.*

A second underattended application of direct assessment in examining curricular functioning is to determine more precisely whether intended connections among courses designed into a given sequence are in fact occurring. Much evidence on this topic, as noted earlier, can be compiled through transcripts and student enrollment records. But more direct methods are available for determining the degree to which previously learned content and skills are being effectively deployed in new contexts. One such approach is to embed pretests and posttests directly into specific course sequences, designed especially to determine if prerequisite skills present at the end of one course are in fact present in the next (for example, see Farmer, 1988). Another is the use of common assignments in paired courses—taken simultaneously by students—explicitly designed to assess multicontextual skills. Specific indicators of curricular functioning consistent with these approaches might include:

> Numbers and types of errors in applying previously learned statistical techniques occurring on pretests (or in portfolios of subsequent assignments) in a given set of social science courses for which statistics is a prerequisite—a measure of *curricular integration.*
>
> Relative performance on pretests of prerequisite skills administered in a given set of courses between students who actually took required prerequisite courses and those who placed out of such requirements by other means—a measure of current *academic policy.*

In closing, it is important to reemphasize that the most powerful approaches to assessing curricular quality make use of both outcomes and process measures. In developing appropriate indicator systems for purposes of either external accountability or internal curricular improvement, institutions are well advised to pay equal attention to both.

Future Prospects

Evidence strongly suggests that incentives for paying more systematic attention to documenting and monitoring curricular functioning are here to stay. On one hand, demands for greater accountability show no signs of diminishing. Indeed, they are markedly shifting in character from the predominant concern with outcomes evident in the late 1980s to a growing interest in instructional processes and student experiences (Ewell, 1994). At the same time, growing fiscal pressures and the consequent inability of colleges and universities to do everything for everybody are inducing more and more institutions to contemplate serious curricular restructuring—often guided by approaches drawn from continuous quality improvement. In both arenas, increasingly, the coin of the realm is statistical. Performance indicator approaches have permanent appeal to public officials because of their succinct and comparative nature. At the same time, they are seen as an appropriate response to growing pressures for information to inform consumer choice. In parallel, serious restructuring demands concrete information about the functioning of key processes to keep it on course—and this information must be regularly collected and easily understandable at all levels of the organization. Both trends suggest that indicators of curricular quality will be with us for the long haul.

Recognition that indicators are not a fad, however, does not imply that they are a panacea. As in the early days of assessment, the tyranny of numbers can easily overwhelm reasoned analysis of complex bodies of evidence. Because of their apparent concreteness, indicators systems in any field are particularly susceptible to such perversion. While recognizing their power to inform action, therefore, academic leaders should be constantly vigilant to ensure that any indicators of curriculum are multiple, mutually reinforcing, and appropriate. Above all, they should ensure that at every level, such data are used to raise questions and not to provide final answers.

References

Adelman, C. *A College Course Map: Taxonomy and Transcript Data.* Washington, D.C.: Office of Educational Research and Improvement (OERI), U.S. Department of Education, 1990.

Angelo, T. A., and Cross, K. P. *Classroom Assessment Techniques: A Handbook for College Teachers.* (2nd ed.) San Francisco: Jossey-Bass, 1993.

Astin, A. W. *Assessment for Excellence: The Philosophy and Practice of Assessment and Evaluation in Higher Education.* New York: ACE/Macmillan, 1991.

Astin, A. W. *What Matters in College? Four Critical Years Revisited.* San Francisco: Jossey-Bass, 1992.

Astin, A. W. and Associates. *Cooperative Institutional Research Program (CIRP).* Los Angeles: Higher Education Research Institute (OERI), University of California, Los Angeles, 1992.

Banta, T. W. and Schneider, J. A. "Using Faculty-Developed Exit Examinations to Evaluate Academic Programs." *Journal of Higher Education,* 1988, *59,* 69–83.

Banta, T. W., and Associates. *Making a Difference: Outcomes of a Decade of Assessment in Higher Education.* San Francisco: Jossey-Bass, 1993.

Baugher, K. *Learn: Student Quality Team Manual.* Birmingham, Ala.: Samford University, 1992.

Burstein, L., Oakes J., and Guiton, G. "Education Indicators." In M. Alkin (ed.), *Encyclopedia of Educational Research.* (6th ed.) Old Tappan, N.J.: Macmillan, 1992.

Chickering, A. W., and Gamson, Z. F. "Seven Principles for Good Practice in Undergraduate Education." *AAHE Bulletin,* 1987, *39*(7), 3–7.

College of William and Mary. *Assessment of Undergraduate Liberal Education.* Interim summary to the State Council on Higher Education in Virginia. Williamsburg, Va.: College of William and Mary, 1994.

Ewell, P. T. "To Capture the Ineffable: New Forms of Assessment in Higher Education." In G. Grant (ed.), *Review of Research in Education.* Washington, D.C.: American Educational Research Association, 1991.

Ewell, P. T. "Total Quality and Academic Practice: The Idea We've Been Waiting For?" *Change,* 1993, *25*(3), 49–55.

Ewell, P. T. "Developing Statewide Performance Indicators for Higher Education: Policy Themes and Variations." In S. S. Ruppert (ed.), *Charting Higher Education Accountability: A Sourcebook on State-Level Performance Indicators.* Denver: Education Commission of the States, 1994.

Ewell, P. T., and Jones, D. P. "Pointing the Way: Indicators as Policy Tools in Higher Education." In S. Ruppert (ed.), *Charting Higher Education Ac-*

countability: A Sourcebook on State-Level Performance Indicators. Denver: Education Commission of the States, 1994.

Ewell, P. T., and Jones, D. P. Developing Indicators of "Good Practice" in Undergraduate Education: A Guide to Implementation. Boulder, Colo.: National Center for Higher Education Management Systems, 1996.

Ewell, P. T., and Lisensky, R. P. Assessing Institutional Effectiveness: Redirecting the Self-Study Process. Washington, D.C.: Consortium for the Advancement of Private Higher Education, 1988.

Farmer, D. W. Enhancing Student Learning: Emphasizing Essential Competencies in Academic Programs. Wilkes-Barre, Pa.: King's College, 1988.

Gamson, Z. F. and Poulsen, S. J. "Inventories of Good Practice: The Next Step for the Seven Principles for Good Practice in Undergraduate Education." AAHE Bulletin, 1989, 42, 7–8.

Gitlow, H. S., and Gitlow, S. J. The Deming Guide to Quality and Competitive Position. Englewood Cliffs, N.J.: Prentice Hall, 1987.

Harris, J. W., and Baggett, J. M. Quality Quest in the Academic Process. Birmingham, Ala.: Samford University, 1992.

Massy, W. F. and Zemsky, R. "Faculty Discretionary Time: Departments and the Academic Ratchet." Pew Policy Perspectives. Philadelphia: Pew Charitable Trusts, 1992.

National Center for Higher Education Management Systems. "Enrollment Analysis and Student Tracking: What We Have Been Learning." NCHEMS Newsletter, Summer 1991, pp. 2–3.

National Center for Higher Education Management Systems. "A Preliminary Study of the Feasibility and Utility for National Policy of Instructional 'Good Practice' Indicators in Undergraduate Education." Washington, D.C.: Office of Educational Research and Improvement (OERI), U.S. Department of Education, 1994.

National Institute of Education. Involvement in Learning: Realizing the Potential of American Higher Education. Report of the Study Group on the Conditions of Excellence in American Higher Education. Washington, D.C.: U.S. Government Printing Office, 1984.

Northeast Missouri State University. Report of the Committee on the Liberal Arts and Sciences Core. Kirksville: Northeast Missouri State University, 1994.

O'Banion, T., and Associates. Teaching and Learning in the Community College. Washington, D.C.: Community College Press, American Association of Community Colleges, 1994.

Pace, C. R. Measuring the Quality of Student Experiences: An Account of the Development and Use of the College Student Experiences Questionnaire. Los Angeles: Higher Education Research Institute, University of California, 1984.

Ratcliff, J. L. (ed.). Assessment and Curricular Reform. University Park: National Center on Postsecondary Teaching, Learning, and Assessment, Pennsylvania State University, 1993.

Ratcliff, J. L., and Associates. Development and Testing of a Cluster-Analytic Model for Identifying Coursework Patterns Associated with General Learned Abilities of Students (Progress Report #6). Ames: College of Education, Iowa State University, 1988.

Ruppert, S. S. Charting Higher Education Accountability: A Sourcebook on State-Level Performance Indicators. Denver: Education Commission of the States, 1994.

Seymour, D. T. On Q: Causing Quality in Higher Education. Washington, D.C.: ACE, 1991.

Sherr, L. A., and Teeter, D. J. (eds.). Total Quality Management in Higher Education. New Directions for Institutional Research, no. 71. San Francisco: Jossey-Bass, 1991.

Stark, J. S., and Lowther, M. A. Designing the Learning Plan: A Review of Research and Theory Related to College Curricula. Ann Arbor: National Center for Research on Postsecondary Teaching and Learning, University of Michigan, 1986. (ED 287 439)

State Council on Higher Education in Virginia. Summary of Restructuring Processes in Virginia Public Universities. Working Document. Richmond: State Council on Higher Education in Virginia, 1994.

Winona State University. Indicators for Improving Undergraduate Instructional Quality. Winona, Minn.: Winona State University, 1990.

Zemsky, R. Structure and Coherence: Measuring the Undergraduate Curriculum. Washington, D.C.: Association of American Colleges, 1989.

Zemsky, R., Massy, W. F., and Oedel, P, "On Reversing the Ratchet." Change, May/June 1993, pp. 56–62.

Outcomes, Assessment, and Academic Improvement: In Search of Usable Knowledge

PETER T. EWELL

Assessing and improving the outcomes of undergraduate instruction have recently taken on a new urgency in public dialogue. National reports such as *Involvement in Learning* (NIE, 1984), *Integrity in the College Curriculum* (AAC, 1985), and *To Reclaim a Legacy* (Bennett, 1984) have not only directed attention toward the effectiveness of undergraduate instruction but have also raised many questions about how "effectiveness" is to be defined and attained.

Such attention, of course, is not new. Indeed, it is one of the features of American higher education to periodically raise and wrestle with such questions. But a key aspect of the current discussion is its claim to be empirically rather than normatively grounded. First, most recommendations are advanced and justified on the basis of a considerable body of findings about the impact of college on students. Recommendations for heavy investment of instructional resources in the first two years of college and for learning technologies that increase the amount of direct contact between students and faculty, for example, are advanced on grounds of past research on retention and student involvement (NIE, 1984; Astin, 1985). But a second "empirical" element is equally apparent in recent calls for reform. In addition to identifying problems and remedies, research on student learning and development is seen as part of the solution itself. Ongoing "assessment" of both students and institutions is proposed as a permanent mechanism to attain and maintain quality.

Both claims raise thorny questions about the adequacy of our existing knowledge base with respect to student outcomes. While a great deal has indeed been written about college impact, how much of the knowledge that has been gained is "usable knowledge" in the sense of informing academic policy? And given the knowledge to correctly determine policy, what is in fact known about our ability to effectively implement it—particularly in the area of assessing student learning and development at the campus level? The tenor of reports from outside the academy (for example, National Governors' Association, 1986), and an emerging pattern of state initiatives on undergraduate assessment (Boyer et al., 1987) suggest that action will likely not wait until these questions are fully answered.

The purpose of this chapter is therefore dual. One requirement is to reexamine the research literature on college impact from the perspective of academic policy. Of necessity, this will be a selective exercise. Excellent summaries of this literature in its own right already exist (Pascarella, 1985a; Pace, 1979; Bowen, 1977a; Feldman and Newcomb, 1969), and need little amplification beyond sharpening their policy focus. But a focused review may help administrators to begin to determine which of a myriad of distinct findings provides sufficient "leverage" on improvement to be worth pursuing in practice. A second requirement is more complex. If information on student outcomes is to be used to inform practice, research on the utilization of evaluation results and emerging institutional experience with assessment suggest that it must be of a particular kind and character. By examining the much more fragmentary literature on recent information-based change efforts, lessons can be drawn

"Outcomes, Assessment, and Academic Improvement: In Search of Usable Knowledge," by Peter T. Ewell, reprinted from *Higher Education: Handbook of Theory and Research*, Vol. 4, edited by J. C. Smart, 1988. Agathon Press.

not only about the most fruitful lines of inquiry for future research, but also about the forms, methods, and types of studies that will probably yield the greatest policy dividends.

It is important to stress that much past work on the impact of college was originally intended as action research. Pace (1979) documents the establishment of numerous offices at major universities in the mid-thirties charged with local educational research. Their activities included, among others, evaluating alternative curricular forms, assessing student development and achievement, and comparing teaching methods. Among these offices were the "Bureau of Institutional Research" at the University of Minnesota and the "Division of Educational Reference" at Purdue. Resnick and Goulden (1987) argue that this surge of applied educational research emerged out of a need to reevaluate basic curricular questions in a period of enrollment consolidation. In the great expansion of higher education in the postwar period, Pace contends, this original conception of "institutional research" was lost, and the function of such offices shifted toward questions of cost, efficiency, and internal management. The history of college impact research that Pascarella (1985a) recounts, beginning with the "Jacobs Report" in the mid-fifties, is therefore largely a history of scholarly, rather than of policy-oriented work.

Changes in the notion of "institutional research," however, did not mean abandonment of the notion of investigating impact from the point of view of action. Indeed, it is in the mid-sixties that the term "student outcomes" becomes explicitly visible in discussions of higher education management. Documenting "outcomes" was an integral part (though admittedly the most difficult part) of implementing increasingly fashionable new systems of "Planning, Management, and Evaluation" imported from other public sectors. A prime example of this line of inquiry was a multiyear, federally-funded effort at the National Center for Higher Education Management Systems (NCHEMS) in the mid-seventies (Lenning et al., 1977). Though never fully carried out, the major intent of this project was to "standardize" discussions of postsecondary effectiveness through construction of a common taxonomy and suggested procedures for gathering information on higher education outcomes. The promise of these activities seemed considerable in a period yet to experience the limits of "scientific management." But large-scale implementation of such concepts foundered on questions of operationalization and utility, and was generally dropped as higher education suffered increasing retrenchment.

Current reemergence of the outcomes issue in the guise of "assessment" partakes of both these earlier action research traditions. First, assessment aims at recreating the kinds of campus-based applied research offices that were typical five decades ago. It is no coincidence that a surviving office of this type, the Learning Research Center at the University of Tennessee, Knoxville, played a significant role in shaping the state of Tennessee's experiment in outcomes-based "performance funding" (Branscomb et al., 1977) in the late seventies, or that this office currently is considered a leader in campus-based assessment for purposes of local program improvement. Secondly, consistent with the tenets of "scientific management," there has been an increasing tendency to formally incorporate information on student outcomes into decision making. For example, Ewell (1985b) notes rising utilization in two areas—budget making and program review—at the institutional level. Similar trends have been observed in statewide program review (Shapiro, 1986; Barak, 1982), and in institutional and program accreditation (Thrash, 1984).

What is needed to sustain these developments? If their central intent is to inform actions designed to improve the undergraduate product, three kinds of questions need to be posed. First, what in fact *is* the "product?" Recent confusions about use of the term "assessment" (e.g., Edgerton, 1987) only echo myriad earlier definitions of the term "outcome. " Reviewing some of these many definitions and understanding their commonalities and differences is thus a critical prerequisite for both effective action and for directed research. Second, given an adequate description of the "product," is it possible to specify the "production function" that produced it? This is a much more difficult question, and answers will necessarily be incomplete. At the very least, however, a review of past research can suggest some fruitful lines of action and can point out some critical gaps in our knowledge. Finally, can we in fact intervene in the "production function" in ways that have the potential to actually change outcomes? Critical questions here are both the manipulability and range of variation of some available management levers, and particularly the degree to which assessment-based improvements can actually be implemented in complex institutional settings. Again, a review of emerging experience, though fragmentary, can both suggest immediate direction and can note places where more systematic inquiry is needed.

Structuring Inquiry: Outcomes Taxonomies as a Point Of Departure

A major challenge in reviewing the outcomes literature is to determine exactly what is meant by an "outcome." Surveying the literature on outcomes taxonomies a decade ago, Lenning identified and described 89 distinct classifications (Lenning, 1977). Since that review, several dozen additional examples have emerged—mostly for purposes of curriculum planning at individual institutions. In examining this considerable array, four rough categories emerge. Some classifications, like Astin's fourfold typology of college outcomes, were developed to support particular research efforts (Astin, Panos, and Creager, 1967). Others, like Harshman's taxonomy of student outcomes (1979), Bloom's taxonomy of cognitive objectives (1956), and Chickering's "vectors of identity" (1969), were primarily constructed to summarize and structure the result of past research in a particular area of impact. Still others, like Lenning's own "Outcomes Structures for Postsecondary Education" (Lenning et al., 1977), or Ewell's "Classification of Outcomes Dimensions" (1984), result from attempts to build a common language for policy making, institutional comparison, or data exchange. Finally, a substantial number of taxonomies, for example, the classic Harvard List of General Educational Behavioral Goals, the Clapp Commission Classification of College Outcomes, or the Association of American College's "Nine Criteria Defining Undergraduate Learning" (AAC, 1985), were primarily intended to establish goals for curriculum planning.

The characteristics of each of these major types reflects its intended purpose. Therefore

each possesses important limitations when applied outside its original conceptual environment. In examining the literature on outcomes taxonomies, therefore, two approaches are useful. First, it is important to briefly discuss a few of the most commonly used and broadly representative outcomes classification schemes. Intended for different purposes, each constructs the universe of inquiry in a somewhat different way. Collectively, however, they raise a series of definitional and operational issues that are applicable to all such efforts. More importantly, discussion of these common taxonomic issues provides an excellent point of departure for reviewing findings of the outcomes literature itself.

Probably the most widely used taxonomy of educational outcomes is Bloom's (1956). Originally designed to inform curriculum building and evaluation at the elementary and secondary level, the taxonomy has also been widely used as a basis for discussion and evaluation of higher education outcomes. The Bloom taxonomy is confined to the cognitive domain, and consists of six types of learning arranged in a hierarchical order—knowledge, comprehension, application, analysis, synthesis, and evaluation. The presumed cognitive progression implied by this hierarchy is of two types: from simple to complex mental operations, and from concrete to abstract applications. In its distinction among types of cognitive process and in its hierarchical organization, the Bloom taxonomy resembles other more recent schemes for describing outcomes. For example, Perry's (1970) widely discussed framework for student development is also hierarchical. Students progress through nine "positions" in this hierarchy ranging from "dualistic" judgments of right and wrong, through "relativistic" positions in which many analytic frames of reference are recognized, to "commitment" in which a personal affirmation or choice of perspective is accomplished. "Staging" of cognitive processes is also recognized in such operational documents as a recent proposal to evaluate "general intellectual skills" in New Jersey (COEP, 1987). Here, three independent cognitive operations are identified—getting information, manipulating information, and presenting information. Each of these operations is intended to define a distinct focus for collecting statewide performance information at the freshman, sophomore, and senior years.

The most heavily cited classification of student outcomes in higher education is probably the fourfold conceptual scheme developed by Astin and his associates at UCLA (Astin et al., 1967). Originally designed to organize and report findings of the Cooperative Institutional Research Program (CIRP) in the mid-sixties, this typology classifies outcomes on two dimensions. The first, "type of outcome," distinguishes cognitive from noncognitive outcomes. The second, "type of data," distinguishes outcomes that are observable in overt student behaviors from those that must be detected and measured psychometrically. The resulting four cells—psychological/cognitive, psychological/affective, behavioral/cognitive, and behavioral/affective—have been used both to summarize research results and to identify broad classes of inquiry. For example, Pascarella (1985a) chooses Astin's psychological/cognitive cell to delimit his review of college impact. In later formulations, Astin adds a time dimension (for example, 1975, 1977) that is treated as a continuous variable. Using these three dimensions, Ewell (1985a) identifies three methodologically distinct "clusters" of research activity that have dominated recent assessment efforts: (1) cognitive/psychological/within-college based largely on cognitive testing, (2) affective/psychological/within- and after-college based largely on survey methods, and (3) behavioral/within-college based on student tracking and "trace data" methods.

In his comprehensive review of the benefits of higher education, Bowen (1977a) uses a somewhat similar classification of individual outcomes. His "goals for individual students" include three major headings: cognitive learning, emotional and moral development, and "practical competence" (the last including such traits as "need for achievement, adaptability, citizenship, and consumer efficiency"). Three additional types of outcomes—personal self-discovery, career choice and placement, and satisfaction/enjoyment—are identified as "by-products" of the educational experience. In a more recent formulation, Astin recognizes this latter category by referring to such outcomes as "fringe" and "existential" benefits (1985). Moreover, Bowen's classification involves a further distinction between "disposi-

tions" and "behaviors" quite similar to Astin's psychological/behavioral dimension, but not quite so tied to data collection. Speaking as an economist, Bowen asserts that behaviors are the ultimate goal of instruction, and that each individual outcome of experience can be described in terms of both a disposition to act and an actual behavioral manifestation. More importantly, Bowen's classification moves beyond the individual to include an explicit catalogue of "societal" outcomes ranging from the satisfactions and enjoyments of an educated population to enhanced economic efficiency and growth due to increases in trained manpower. Several of these categories have spawned highly specialized research literatures of their own, for example, the "rate of return" on economic investments in higher education (Douglass, 1977; Leslie and Brinkman, 1986).

Probably the most comprehensive single classification of outcomes is that of Lenning and his associates at NCHEMS (Lenning et al., 1977). Reflecting Bowen's shift of perspective from the individual to society, early formulations of this scheme noted three types of outcome: individual student benefits, "private" (or in economic terms "separable") postgraduate benefits, and "societal" (or nonseparable) benefits (Lenning, 1974). The complete taxonomy, intended to classify all forms of postsecondary outcomes as a basis for common data collection, is organized around three major dimensions. A "Type of Outcome" dimension identifies the particular "entity" that is intended to be changed or maintained through higher education. Examples included economic outcomes; human characteristic outcomes such as aspirations, satisfactions, and competence in particular skill areas; knowledge, technology and art form outcomes; and resource and service provision outcomes. An "Audience" dimension identifies particular types of beneficiaries that receive or are affected by a particular outcome. These range from individuals, through various types of defined "communities" to society at large. Finally, a "Time" dimension identifies the particular point at which specified benefits are realized by a particular beneficiary.

These four examples suffice to raise most of the issues involved in building and using an outcomes taxonomy, and are representative of the wider classification literature. What are their real commonalities and differences? Two observations are appropriate to begin this discussion. First, it is apparent that most architects of outcomes taxonomies are viewing the same landscape. Most recognize core phenomena of cognitive and affective development during instruction; most define and describe these core phenomena in roughly similar ways. On the other hand, considerable diversity occurs when additional conceptual dimensions are added to amplify or constrain descriptions of these core phenomena. In some cases, additional dimensions are intended to further break down distinct elements within the cognitive or affective arena. Bloom's framework consists of such an attempt within the cognitive realm that is representative of a wide body of taxonomic work (e.g., Gagne, 1977; Guilford, 1967). Such formulations as Chickering (1969) and Perry (1970) extend discussion to the affective area, though many of the categories used in these classifications represent combinations of cognitive and affective traits. In most cases, however, additional conceptual dimensions are constructed in order to describe ways in which core phenomena are located, constrained, or observed. These include the temporal occurrence and duration of the phenomenon, the unit of analysis or entity experiencing it, the manner in which the outcome is made manifest, and the kinds of observations or measurements necessary to detect it.

A primary difficulty with most of these formulations, however, is that modifying dimensions of this kind are not clearly distinguished from those that describe core phenomena. More importantly, different value perspectives on the conceptual or empirical importance of such ancillary dimensions often lead to subtle but substantial disagreements. Bowen's (1977a) and Astin's (1985) treatment of personal development and satisfaction outcomes as "externalities" is thus strongly at variance with the tradition of Chickering (1969) and Heath (1968) who see such results as primary intended outcomes of the college experience. Such differences are of relatively little importance so long as each tradition pursues an independent line of inquiry. But they become important when the issue is one of informed intervention. Here a somewhat different approach to conceptualization is needed. Figure 1 represents one attempt to address this need. Like all such schemes, it emanates from a particular phenomenal and value perspective—that of the administrator or manager concerned with understanding the system with a view toward manipulating it. Rather than constructing an additional taxonomy, however, the intent is to advance a series of analytical and operational questions that are driven by the salient features of past classification schemes, and that can be posed of any particular set of higher education outcomes. This, in itself, can be a valid and valuable planning exercise. At the same time, these analytical questions serve as a useful frame for organizing a discussion of relevant findings from the college impact literature.

The heart of this scheme is a definition of "outcome" consisting of three distinct components. Each component frames a series of questions that in turn uncover a set of concrete research and measurement issues. First, an "outcome" is a *result*. It is of primary interest less as a phenomenon than as a product—one that action and intervention can at least hope to influence. Moreover, it is a *specifiable* result. It is (or ideally can be made to be) concrete enough to determine its direction and degree, and it may be of many particular kinds. Primary analytical questions raised at this point are questions of identification and assessment. To what degree can we in fact specify the result with respect to magnitude, location, and particularity? Secondly, an "outcome" is the result of an *experience*. Like the result itself, the experience must be specifiable. If it cannot be minimally specified, there is little hope of influencing the result. More importantly, the experience is "constructed." That is, it takes place in a particular setting (Sarason, 1972) or environment whose elements are not only organized, but are *intentional*. Here the primary analytical questions are those of attribution: To what extent can particular aspects of the experience be isolated and linked to particular attributes of the result? Finally, because it is intentional, an "outcome" is never value-neutral. The same result may be viewed by different constituencies in quite different ways, depending on their goals and levels of investment in the process (Ewell, 1984). Thus a final set of analytical questions, though beyond the scope of the outcomes literature, has to do with valuation. Once a demonstrated link between result and experience is established, how critical is the need for action, and what will be its

"An *outcome* is . . .
• A specifiable *result*
 	
**Identification
and
Assessment**
	Analytical Questions
	• Of What Kind?
	• In What Direction and
	   Magnitude?
	→ • For Whom?
	• Manifested in What
	   Manner?
	• At What Time?
		Particular Research issues
		Classification/Taxonomy
		"Value-Added" Assessment
		Subgroup Disaggregation
		Behavioral/Psychometric
		   Evidence
		Timing/Sequencing of
		   Observation

• . . . of a constructed
experience
 	
     Attribution
	• Of What Kinds?
	• At What Level of
	   Aggregation?
	→ • Involving What Particular
	   Activities or Settings?
	• Requiring Investments
	   on Whose Part?
		Documenting Environment
		Unit of Analysis
		Observation/Experimental
		   Design
		Incentives/"Quality of Effort"

• . . . viewed from
a particular *goal
perspective.*"
 	
   Valuation
	• Whose Perspective?
	• With What Values?
	• With What Stake in the
	   Result?
		Intentions Analysis
		Views of "Effectiveness"
		Cost-Benefit/Rate of Return

Figure 1 Analytical questions for constructing or evaluating statements of higher education outcomes.

likely payoff given current goals and investments? Each of these areas frames a wide field for discussion of prior research.

More importantly, each frames a distinct arena for management action. In specifying intended results through formal planning and goal-setting, management action both articulates and constrains institutional activity. Moreover, in its consistency and its explicit reference to established goals, management action helps to determine the degree to which such goals are internalized throughout the institution or remain artificial or vestigal. In allocating and manipulating the flow of resources, management action provides and shapes the institutional environment within which instructional experiences are "constructed." While the actual construction is done by others, their actions are directly conditioned by both the current content of management action and its past accumulation. Finally, a crucial role of management—formal or informal—is evaluation, to review accomplished results from the perspective of intended goals and of broader organizational interests. Prominent among the latter may be the satisfaction of key external constituencies critical to the institution's future survival.

Defining the Product: Outcomes as Goal Specifications

In response to the impetus of such reports as *Involvement in Learning* and *Integrity in the College Curriculum,* many institutions are currently engaged in the process more concretely describing the goals of their undergraduate curricula. In doing so, they pose questions of identifying and assessing educational results that have been raised and discussed in the outcomes literature many times before. Such questions generally involve, as a prerequisite for actual investigation or for effective planning, further specification of the nature of impact, of the types of students involved, and of the ways in which evidence of attainment is exhibited and assembled. Following the logic of Figure 1, these may be discussed in terms of a set of explicit questions about "result."

Outcomes of What Kind?

A first issue is that of explicitly specifying the intended core phenomenon, and this generally involves making a number of typological distinctions. Virtually all outcomes taxonomies recognize a distinction between cognitive and affective outcomes, a distinction rooted firmly in psychology, which constitutes the grounding discipline of most outcomes work. In general, more research has been directed toward affective than toward cognitive outcomes, partly because they appear somewhat easier to define and detect (Bowen, 1977a). Apparent ease of definition, however, also leads to a profusion of operational measures. Feldman and Newcomb (1969), for example, report freshman-to-senior gains on such diverse attributes as "open-mindedness" and "independence," "decreased conservatism," and "sensitivity to aesthetic and inner experiences," based on studies that operationalize these traits in vastly different ways. Astin's (1977) research notes broad changes in all types of students at all types of institutions in such attributes as "social and intellectual competence," "increased liberalism," decreased "religiosity," and "need for status." Most of these trends, however, obscure considerable variations among particular student subgroups and among different institutional environments.

Cognitive outcomes are more difficult to definitively detect, but again a wide range of gains have been reported. Bowen's (1977a) review of this literature notes typical gains in the range of half to a full standard deviation between the freshman and senior years on most measures of verbal and quantitative skill, and of two-thirds to a full standard deviation on substantive knowledge measures. Studies based on student self-reports of cognitive gain (for example, Spaeth and Greely, 1970) tend to confirm these findings. One significant exception to general gain, however, appears to be in quantitative skill areas, where regressions have been widely reported (Robertshaw and Wolfle, 1982; Lenning, Munday, and Maxey, 1969). As with affective development, however, general population findings obscure considerable differences among particular subpopulations and environments. More importantly, many fewer cognitive than affective studies are able to credibly link changes in outcome measures with particular aspects of the institutional environment (Pascarella, 1985a), or with such "exogenous" policy variables as selectivity (Astin, 1968) or resources per student invested (Bowen 1980, 1981).

Major difficulties with the cognitive/affective distinction only occur in such areas as intellectual persistence, aesthetic awareness and enjoyment, and value neutrality when applied to inquiry. For example, McKeachie and his colleagues (1986) include in their "taxonomy of learning strategies" a set of attributes labelled "resource management strategies." Together with skills like scheduling and goal-setting, this category includes such partially attitudinal elements as attribution of result to effort, mood, and self-reinforcement. At the same time, a prominent element of the literature on critical thinking emphasizes "relativism" or value neutrality with respect to content as part of the process of cognitive development (e.g., Perry, 1970). Similarly, Bowen (1977a) lists "intellectual tolerance" as a "cognitive" goal of higher education. Findings at Alverno College on such traits as "self-sustaining learning" or "attributions about the value of experience in learning" are equally difficult to fully classify in terms of the cognitive/affective distinction (Mentkowski and Doherty, 1984). For most observers most of the time, however, this distinction remains solid, and provides a reasonable guide for specification.

Typical outcomes taxonomies further differentiate "knowledge" from "skills" within the cognitive domain, a distinction based upon perceived differences between raw cognitive content and the ability to perform explicit tasks. While this distinction appears to work well for so-called "basic skills" (reading, writing, and computation) that have a considerable history of independent assessment, there remains considerable controversy about the degree to which such "higher-order" skills as critical thinking and problem-solving are separable from a particular knowledge base (e.g., Campione and Armbruster, 1985). Proponents of "metacognition" argue that such attributes as the general awareness of and control of individual cognition on the part of individual learners can be taught, and many current assessment models (see, e.g., Alverno College Faculty, 1979) are founded upon the generalizability of higher-order skills. On the other hand, there is some experimental evidence that these distinctions are not as clear in practice as they might be. For example, based on a series of experiments involving textual learning, Marton (1979) argued that most "skills" are acquired, processed, and manipulated in the same ways as more traditional content elements.

The actual specification of such higher-order skills as critical thinking also remains a problem. In reviewing 27 studies on determinants of critical thinking ability in college, McMillan (1987) found little pattern of impact for particular instructional methods or approaches; he did, however, indicate a general positive trend as a result of college attendance. Part of the explanation was felt to be the lack of a good definition of critical thinking with appropriate instrumentation to support it. Bowen (1977a) and Pascarella (1985a) also report generally positive results between critical thinking and college attendance, but both note that the magnitude of change in such higher-order skills attributes is considerably less than for basic skills or substantive knowledge outcomes.

A final definitional difficulty is specifying the nature of the experience itself. Some outcomes models (among them the popular "value-added" construct) rest on what might be termed a "mechanistic" view of instruction. Under this view, student characteristics are seen largely as input conditions to a process supplied and managed by the institution. Quite different are conceptions that conceive of the learning process as "organic"—involving equally important actions and investments on the part of the learner. In choosing the word "impact" to circumscribe their comprehensive review of learner outcomes, Feldman and Newcomb (1969) wished particularly to call attention to the interactive aspect of the experience. Going somewhat farther, Pace throughout his work uses the term "impress" rather than "impact" to describe the influence of educational environments; his explicit object is to suggest the importance of "content-provision" rather than "production" aspects of a given educational environment (Pace, 1974, 1979). Probably the most vivid example of this distinction is Marton's portrayal of two kinds of learning from the student's perspective: learning is "something that you do" as opposed to "something that happens to you" (Marton, 1979).

In What Direction and Magnitude?

A more compelling definitional question is that of the direction and magnitude of change. Here there has been considerable debate in the outcomes literature on the appropriateness and technological difficulty of assessing growth. Much of the former has revolved around the terms "value-added" or "talent development" made current by Astin (1974, 1977, 1985). The essence of this position is that institutional quality or effectiveness is best assessed in terms of the changes in student outcomes that can be observed from entry to exit, and that can be attributed to institutional action.

Clearly, there is little real disagreement in the research literature about the importance of assessing development. As Pascarella points out, the entire "value-added" controversy can be readily subsumed under the traditional researcher's question: To what degree can observed developmental outcomes be ascribed to the college experience? (See Pascarella, 1987.) From a policy perspective, however, the issue can be real and concrete: Are institutions and programs to be judged primarily in terms of the degree to which they "develop talent" or in terms of the degree to which their ultimate products meet accepted standards? This issue is more than theoretical, as documented by recent debates about the use of assessment evidence in state policy in Tennessee and New Jersey. Ewell (1984) notes that while these are different questions, both answers are important for policy.

Moreover, from a planning perspective, it may be important for an institution to explicitly determine those particular dimensions on which it expects to induce considerable change from those where the instructional objective is to maintain skills at an acceptable level (Ewell, 1983). Determinations of this kind may appropriately vary from program to program depending on the particular content and value perspectives of each. In the absence of such distinctions, use of a "value-added" model may be actively misleading because it fails to distinguish arenas where gains are not intended from those where producing gain is critical for meeting established instructional goals. Furthermore, value-added models may fail to detect situations, again consistent with instructional objectives, where instruction has been effective in maintaining skills that would otherwise have eroded (Pascarella, 1987).

Far more difficult than determining the appropriateness of such concepts are the technical issues involved in documenting change in the first place. Most large-scale operational uses of the "value-added" construct rely on a pre-test/post-test design using a single instrument (see, for example, McClain, 1984; Dumont and Troelstrup, 1981; Banta, 1986). As discussed by Hanson, however, such designs are vulnerable to a range of measurement and attribution problems including sample attrition, regression effects, and compound measurement error (Hanson, 1982).

Outcomes for Whom?

A third major analytical question involves specifying the entity experiencing the outcome. Operationally, this is a question of both determining appropriate levels of aggregation, and of selecting appropriate variables to be used in differentiating among particular subpopulations. As Pascarella points out, there is powerful evidence that different kinds of students experience college in different ways (Pascarella, 1985a); many problems in interpreting findings in the impact literature are therefore due to the fact that a high level of aggregation may obscure quite real subgroup differences. Bowen (1977b) makes a similar point in observing that research on outcomes is based upon analytical groups, and that a finding of "no effect" may be the joint product of many individuals experiencing significant positive and negative impacts. Both these observations call for considerable care in disaggregating student study populations, both when specifying intended outcomes and when assessing effects.

A first set of differences among student subpopulations concerns aptitude and learning style. Though most examinations of such differences have been in elementary and secondary education, there appear to be substantial grounds for generalizing findings to postsecondary classrooms and environments (McKeachie et al., 1986). In a major review of the literature on individual learning styles, Messick (1976) summarizes the effects on learning styles of such factors as sex and cultural background, and concludes that different types of students learn best using idiosyncratic styles, modes, and strategies. Examining the literature on individual learner differences some ten years later, Corno and Snow (1986) concluded that major differences involved (1) intellectual abilities—"enabling cognitive abilities and skills"; (2) personality characteristics—

"motivational and affective traits"; and (3) cognitive styles—"predispositions for processing information."

Viewing such differences from a broader frame of reference, Feldman and Newcomb (1969) suggest that overall college impact is mediated by the relative degrees of "openness" with which students approach the experience of college. Moreover, they view differences on "openness" on two independent dimensions—openness to new experiences and stimuli, and openness to the influence of others (peers and faculty). A major research question, however, is the degree to which such differences have a direct effect on outcomes, or are mediated by different types of experiences and instruction. Cronbach and Snow (1977) provide many examples of the way important interactions among student characteristics and particular classroom learning situations can condition cognitive outcomes. Pascarella (1985a) further cites a range of postsecondary studies that document differential effects of this kind, including such factors as race, career aspiration, and mode of instruction.

A major difficulty with this line of inquiry in higher education, however, is the fact that the "learning environment" often goes far beyond the individual classroom. One of the most fruitful types of analytical disaggregation, therefore, involves distinguishing among student subcultures. For example, Clark and Trow's classic typology of student subcultures specified four types (academic, nonconformist, collegiate, and vocational) based on the intersection of two orientation dimensions, amount of involvement with ideas, and amount of identification with the institution (Clark and Trow, 1966). Although largely dated, research experience with the Clark/Trow typology has indicated substantial differences among student goals for students subscribing to each type (Kees, 1974). A more recent attempt at classification was attempted by Katchadourian and Boli at Stanford (1985). Also using a two-dimensional classification scheme (constructed on scales of "intellectualism" and "careerism"), they distinguished four student types: careerist, intellectual, striver, and unconnected. Based on longitudinal interviews over a five year period, a major finding was the distinctiveness of self-intended outcomes among these populations. Indeed, students in each category tended to ascribe to the institution as a whole their own distinctive outcomes goals. Differences were also noted in such important in-college behaviors as amount and initiation of out-of-class contact with faculty members.

Differences in the environmental perceptions of different types of students may also substantially influence patterns of outcomes and experience. In an early study involving both public and private institutions, Pace and Baird (1966) attempted to relate student-reported institutional outcomes with identified characteristics of the college environment as assessed by the College Characteristics Index, and with individual personality characteristics. They found both significant, though student perceptions of the environment appeared more powerful. Pace (1963) makes a similar point in reviewing development of the College and University Environment Scales (CUES) instrument: pilot research revealed many instances where the same physical and social environment was viewed differently by students in different programs, at different levels, and who exhibited different amounts of involvement with the campus. Examining student perceptions of institutional "effectiveness domains" at three state universities, Kleemann and Richardson (1985) report significant differences in perceived outcomes for different types of students. Moreover, they observed that perceived outcomes were considerably more positive for students whose own goals appeared congruent with those of the institution.

Among other conclusions, these studies suggest the importance of ascertaining differences in student goals and motivations as a prerequisite to specifying or explaining outcomes. This conclusion is particularly salient when applied to "nontraditional" students, or in multiclientele settings such as urban public universities or community colleges. In a three-year statewide longitudinal study of 6,550 community college students in California, for example, Sheldon (1981) distinguished among eighteen distinct student subpopulations, based upon expressed goals and revealed enrollment behavior. These groups showed markedly different patterns of persistence and success. Walleri and Japely (1986), studying a different population of community college students, found significant differences in persistence and outcomes based on initial intent. Ex-

amining patterns of academic integration among commuting students in a four-year institution, Iverson and associates (Iverson, Pascarella, and Terenzini, 1984) found markedly different patterns of faculty/student interactions than those typical of resident students. A most important finding was the salience of motivation; students with high aspirations initiated contacts with faculty and experienced levels of academic integration on a par with resident students. Similar evidence on motivation is suggested by a study by Erwin (1986). Using such outcome measures as the Scale of Intellectual Development, Erwin's findings indicated that students who financed at least 75% of their own postsecondary education showed higher gains than their peers in such areas as sense of personal direction and the ability to express thoughts and values.

In What Manner Are Outcomes Manifested?

A fourth and analytical question concerns the ways in which a given core outcome is exhibited. Consistent with Bowen's notion of "disposition" and Astin's "psychological/behavioral" distinction, a particular cognitive or affective state may manifest itself in action, or it may remain latent. The importance of this distinction in practice depends largely upon an institution's or program's identification of particular behaviors as explicit instructional goals. For example, job and graduate school placements are both commonly used as indicators of undergraduate major program effectiveness. It makes a considerable difference, however, whether the basic reason for the program's existence—as in a community college occupational program—is to *produce* placements, or whether placements are interpreted as manifestations of the attainment of more basic instructional goals.

To what degree does research evidence indicate that psychological and behavioral outcomes are really different manifestations of the same core result? Concrete evidence is scarce because most studies of behavioral outcomes have tended to be postcollege, while those involving direct assessment of cognition and affect have been within-college. Nevertheless, some suggestive parallels can be drawn. Astin's findings (1977) that postgraduate income and professional success is related to undergraduate performance, and that early and continuous exposure to the major field results in more consistent attainment of career objectives, resonate well with Pace's (1979) summary of cognitive impact that indicates the greatest growth in areas of greatest exposure. Results reported by Bowen (1977a) under the heading of "practical competence" indicate roughly similar parallels between dispositions and actions. While hardly startling, these parallels point toward some consistency between the correlates of psychological and behavioral outcomes. More compelling are the results of attempts to use theories of college attrition to also explain changes in cognition and affect. For example, a series of recent studies using Tinto's (1975) concepts of academic and social integration as mediating variables has convincingly demonstrated the efficacy of employing these concepts in explanations of such outcomes as self-reported personal growth (Terenzini and Wright, 1987), goal development in "liberal education" (Theophilides, Terenzini, and Lorang, 1984), grade performance and academic growth (Terenzini, Pascarella, and Lorang, 1982), satisfaction with college (Pascarella, 1984), and intellectual self-concept and educational aspiration (Pascarella, 1985b).

The Timing of Outcomes

The timing and sequencing of particular outcomes raise similar questions of specification. Indeed, it is possible to maintain that the time dimension represents a special case of "manifestation" discussed above. Just as Bowen argues that an individual may have learned a "disposition" to act without actually having done so, certain outcomes of college may be consistently present, but latent. Part of this may be due to the individual's inability to recognize their presence and thus offer them to researchers in the form of self-reports (Ewell, 1983).

Virtually all major outcomes taxonomies recognize the importance of time, though they model it differently. As noted by Lenning and associates (1977), time may be important in a number of ways. First, certain bodies of content or particular learning experiences may have little effect until they are "triggered" by a need or opportunity for use. Other outcomes will differ

in how long they persist. Most long-term research on postcollege cognitive results, for example, notes considerable atrophy in such skills as computation and quantitative reasoning that are rarely practiced (Pace, 1979).

Staged learning models such as Perry (1970) or those employed at Alverno College (Alverno College Faculty, 1979), as well as developmental models such as those of Chickering (1969) or Heath (1968), are time-dependent in a different sense. Here the importance of time is ordinal: to array expected and achieved outcomes in terms of a stepwise or prerequisite pattern. Research focusing on student development from year to year raises similar issues of sequencing. Summarizing a considerable body of early work on student development, Feldman and Newcomb (1969) report considerable differences in the perceptions of entering and continuing students at different stages of progress. In their study of Stanford students, Katchadourian and Boli (1985) characterize each year of a four-year undergraduate sequence as a somewhat different arena of experience. At the same time, Terenzini and Wright (1987) found identifiable differences in the factors responsible for self-reported outcomes among freshmen and sophomores, based upon changes in the mediating effects of academic and social integration. Confirming findings reported by Feldman and Newcomb (1969) that entering freshmen tended to overestimate the "academic" aspects of the college experience, Terenzini and Wright noted that academic integration was considerably more important for freshmen than for sophomores in explaining self-assessments of personal development. Year-to-year variations of this kind are also consistent with findings on the differences in retention correlates between freshmen and later years (Lenning, Beal, and Sauer, 1980).

Finally, from a policy or action perspective the time categories of particular interest to different types of decision makers may themselves be different. As noted by Lenning (1977) and Pace (1985), those focusing on the effects of a particular course or sequence will appropriately use a quite different time frame from those whose interest is campuswide. It may also be extremely difficult in practice to link long-term outcomes to actual changes that might be made in institutional policy or practice, both because of difficulties in attribution and because during the time elapsed between a graduate's report and his actual experience, many shifts in institutional practices, environment, and clientele may have occurred.

Linking Outcomes and Experience: Attribution as Potential Action

Questions of identification and assessment raise numerous issues for the design and conduct of "action research" on student outcomes. But far more complex are questions having to do with attribution—the degree to which a specifiable result can credibly be linked to identifiable elements of "constructed experience."

Many methodological difficulties are associated with studies of this kind. First, lack of appropriate control groups means that it is extremely difficult to unambiguously attribute observed changes to actual college attendance (Astin 1970a,b). Furthermore, if multi-institutional samples are used, there are substantial differences in aptitude, motivation, and background among student populations at different institutions due to self-selection (Astin 1970a, 1977). The same observation can generally be applied to studies that attempt to document the differential effects of different departments and instructional experiences. Finally, few true longitudinal studies exist, and those that do are subject to such difficulties as panel attrition and regression effects (Astin, 1977; Pascarella, 1987).

Methodological challenges of these kinds have made it difficult for past research to unambiguously establish cause. Reviewing the literature on cognitive impact, Pascarella (1985a) cites considerable disappointing early evidence of links between institutional characteristics and achievement, once entering student attributes were statistically controlled (for example, Astin and Panos, 1969; Nichols, 1964). Though somewhat better evidence of differential effect was reported when the institution rather than the student was used as the unit of analysis (for example, Centra and Rock, 1971), findings remain inconclusive. Pascarella attributes these results to four possible difficulties, including (1) lack of sufficient variation in the types of institutions studied, (2) insufficient specification and definition of differences in institutional characteristics,

(3) too high a level of aggregation in analysis that obscures real effects among subpopulations, and (4) insufficient specificity and precision in the way cognitive outcomes are measured. He then proposes a number of methodological remedies to counter these conditions, among them greater attention to causal modeling and multilevel analysis. Evidence of progress in this regard is provided by Kuh and associates (1986). Based on a review of 1,189 studies of college students appearing in eleven selected journals since 1969, they found a decrease in the absolute number of impact studies, but an increase in their methodological sophistication as indicated by such features as the use of true longitudinal designs and multivariate statistical techniques. Reflecting the difficulty of definitionally specifying and operationalizing outcomes measures, however, they also found an increasing trend toward nonstandardization and institution-specific measures.

Despite methodological difficulties, considerable weight of evidence about particular impacts exists. One useful way of assembling such evidence is to structure discussion around a further set of analytical questions noted in Figure 1, this time dealing with specific aspects of "constructed experience."

What Particular Kinds of Experience?

As a guide to action, answers to the researcher's question "Does college make a difference?" are clearly insufficient. It is also necessary to provide evidence of reliable linkages between desired outcomes and particular, manipulable aspects of the "constructed experience" provided at each institution. The question of specifying experience first calls attention to a need to thoroughly *describe* particular patterns of student behavior. For example, Shapiro (1986) notes that concern in higher education evaluation is currently as much focused on specifying "stimuli" as in cataloging results. The use of carefully constructed cross-sectional studies applied to carefully selected student subpopulations as advocated by Pascarella (1985a, 1987), or "trace-data" approaches such as transcript analyses or documentation of aggregate student course-taking patterns to determine the "behavioral curriculum" (Terenzini, 1987; Grose, 1976) represent proven methods for beginning to meet this need. But the use of such approaches remains uncommon. Based on the extant literature, what are some of the dimensions of experience that seem most fruitful for further exploration as foci for intervention?

One appears to be the sheer magnitude of exposure. Studies of cognitive development dating back to the thirties indicate the importance of "time-on-task" to the gain achieved (e.g., Learned and Wood, 1938). In general, the greater a given student's exposure to a body of material, as indicated by the number of courses taken or the student's choice of major field, the higher the established gains (Pace, 1979). Moreover, there are suggestions that performance in class may not be as important in the long term as simple exposure to and interaction with a particular body of material. In a study using the CLEP battery on freshmen and sophomore students, Harris (1970) found that students' course-grade performance did not generally affect their level of subsequent knowledge; students failing the course achieved scores not markedly different from those who did well, while both scored significantly above those who were not exposed to the material.

A second body of findings involves the impact of specific aspects of the institutional environment. Despite problems of attribution due to self-selection, numerous studies have documented differences in affective and in certain behavioral outcomes by institutional type. Particularly prominent have been findings linking institutional characteristics such as size and type (liberal arts curriculum, private control, or religious affiliation), with a range of noncognitive outcomes including authoritarianism (Trent and Medsker, 1968), liberalism and personal adjustment (Clark et al., 1972), aesthetic and religious orientation (Pace, 1972, 1974; Astin, 1977), and altruism/interpersonal self-esteem (Astin, 1977). The distinctive environments provided by single-sex institutions has also been linked to particular outcomes, for example, increased ambition and success among women in entering male-dominated fields (Bressler and Wendell, 1980). Moreover, findings summarized by Feldman and Newcomb (1969) indicate that initial noncognitive differences among students in different institutions tend to be amplified rather than decreased, and that students appear to internalize learning goals consistent with those that the institution

publicly espouses (Winter, McClelland, and Stewart, 1981). These results suggest that careful attention to maintaining distinctiveness in both instructional goals and in ensuring provision of an institutional environment consistent with these goals may be a policy consideration with considerable payoff.

Such findings have not been without exception. For example, in a study of twelve small liberal arts colleges, Chickering (1970) documented considerable similarities among patterns of student development, despite what he saw as substantial differences in institutional characteristics. A partial explanation of this result is the consistent emergence in most multi-institutional studies of the small liberal arts college as a distinctive environment in its own right. For example, Astin's work with the CIRP (1968, 1977; Astin and Lee, 1972) yields few differences in noncognitive or "existential" benefits due to selectivity, but it does show significant differences associated with private control and small size. Moreover, in a summary of CUES results on 247 institutions, Pace notes a particular environmental emphasis on the "community" dimension at private liberal arts colleges, regardless of level of selectivity (Pace, 1979). Small private liberal arts institutions also achieve the highest ratings on ten of fourteen scales on involvement and "quality of student effort" in research using Pace's more recent College Student Experiences Questionnaire (Pace, 1984; Friedlander, 1980).

Findings on exposure and distinctiveness provide important clues about the particular elements of "constructed experience" that appear linked to desirable outcomes. Many of these can be conveniently summarized in terms of Astin's concept of "involvement." Originally developed to synthesize results of research on student persistence (Astin, 1975), the theory of involvement is considerably elaborated in Astin's later work on the differential effects of institutional characteristics on affective and behavioral outcomes (1977). In discussing the positive impact of such characteristics as small size, student residence on campus, on-campus employment, and time spent in academic, research, and athletic pursuits, Astin noted that all these factors tended to increase students' "involvement" with the campus. Moreover, such factors appeared to be much more powerful in explaining outcomes than either student or institutional characteristics. Moving the discussion to a policy perspective, Astin has recently advocated a number of actions intended to promote involvement (Astin, 1979, 1985). Among these are better monitoring of student time and on-campus activities, greater attention to promoting faculty/student interaction in the first two years of enrollment, and the establishment of "learning communities" within larger institutions.

Somewhat similar are the concepts of "academic and social integration" proposed by Tinto (1975). Also developed originally to summarize research on student retention, Tinto's construct has fruitfully been applied in broader work on student outcomes. Unlike Astin's more general concept of involvement, academic and social integration are held to be reasonably independent, and indeed, most work that has operationalized these constructs as scaled sets of questionnaire items has established their empirical distinctiveness (e.g., Terenzini and Pascarella, 1977). Specifically, Tinto's definition of integration follows Durkheim's classic investigation of suicide behavior. As such, the concept involves specific psychological elements relating to identification with and positive affect toward the institution's academic and social environment, and a range of behaviors that both sustain and reveal these traits. Following this logic, academic integration is generally operationalized using questionnaire items that deal with such areas as faculty/student interaction, time spent in academic pursuits, and faculty concern for student development and teaching. Social integration is similarly operationalized by means of such items as the number of hours per week spent in organized extracurricular activities, extent and quality of peer interaction, and quality of nonacademic contacts with faculty.

Though already cited as aspects of both involvement and academic integration, student/faculty interaction is also worth noting as a salient aspect of environment in its own right. Both in and out of the classroom, contact with faculty emerges in a wide range of studies as a factor significantly associated with a wide range of outcomes. Investigating the impact of various institutional characteristics on GRE scores at 27 liberal arts colleges, for example, Centra and Rock (1971) determined that student perceptions of faculty/student interac-

tions were clearly associated with gains in the humanities and natural sciences. Gaff (1973) found involvement with faculty an important predictive variable in all eight institutions studied, using perceived cognitive gain as a dependent variable.

Similarly, in a single-institution study of freshmen, Terenzini et al. (1982) established important relationships between the frequency and quality of faculty contact, and dependent variables such as grade performance and perceptions of academic and personal growth. Factors also identified as important in this study included student perceptions of their level of involvement in the classroom and their own goal commitments. Parallel studies have noted strong relationships between the extent and quality of student/faculty contact and such outcomes as student perceptions of "liberal education" goal development (Theophilides et al., 1984), student retention (Pascarella and Terenzini, 1980), and a range of personal development goals (Terenzini and Wright, 1987). Finally, in his ongoing analysis of the CIRP database, Astin has repeatedly identified faculty/student interaction as the strongest single variable associated with overall student satisfaction with the college experience (Astin, 1977, 1979, 1985).

Concepts such as involvement and integration are helpful both in summarizing a wide range of effects and in emphasizing that the impact of such institutional factors as size, instructional emphasis, instructional delivery, or residence arrangements, may be indirect. As emphasized in the discussions that follow, the indirect nature of these relationships has profound implications for management intervention.

At What Level of Aggregation?

Pascarella (1985a) indicates that one reason why the results of many attempts to specify linkages between environmental factors and cognitive outcomes are disappointing is because analysis takes place at too great a level of aggregation. Baird (1976) echoes this concern from an action perspective by noting that changes in curriculum or policy may have no observable effect on outcomes because "everyday life" in the classroom or residence hall remains the same. Most institutions are sufficiently large that they themselves do not constitute an "environment"; rather they represent collections of quite distinctive but overlapping microenvironments, each of which may operate differently. Addressing this condition requires much more finely focused research approaches and models of college impact (Korn, 1986). A related issue involves the need to carefully match particular outcomes measures with the level of analysis at which they may legitimately be expected to emerge. Many popular institutional outcomes measures—for example, the ACT College Outcomes Measures Project (COMP)—have proven ambiguous in their ability to isolate particular curricular effects (Banta et al., 1987). As Pace puts it, "if you choose to think big about the scope and significance of outcomes, then you must also think big about the magnitude of college experiences when you seek explanations" (Pace, 1985, p. 17).

One of the most comprehensive treatments of disaggregated educational environments is that of Moos (1979). Reporting on a range of studies and experiments conducted in university residence hall settings and in elementary/ secondary classrooms, Moos concludes that many aspects of these quite different environments operate in similar ways. A critical factor, however, is to isolate and observe student experiences in particular "microsettings" where peer interactions take place. Furthermore, once identified, Moos argues that such microsettings must be treated holistically. To investigate the effects of student living arrangements, for example, Moos used the University Residential Environment Scales to build a typology of residence environments. Included were living groups characterized as relationship oriented, traditionally socially oriented, supportive achievement oriented, competition oriented, independence oriented, and intellectually oriented. Using his own instrument to assess student activity and involvement, he then investigated the effects of microsettings in several different institutions. Results were summarized in three ways. First, microsettings exerted notable impact on students' development of such characteristics as autonomy and identity, and on their patterns of social relationships. Secondly, most of the differences in such settings were attributable to the differing characteristics of the students who inhabited them. Finally, reflecting earlier work re-

ported by Feldman and Newcomb (1969), there was a "press to conformity" in most microsettings; not only did students "select themselves" into different environments, but the environments appeared to act back on them, accentuating many of the characteristics that initially distinguished the students who chose them.

One prime candidate for analysis as a microsetting is the academic department. Not only do departments provide an increasing source of identification for students as they progress, but they also structure patterns of peer and faculty interaction. Considerable work on departmental culture confirms (though it does not completely specify) marked differences in values and perceptions (e.g., Biglan, 1973), and in several dimensions of personality (e.g., Smart, 1982) on the part of faculty in different disciplines. Similarly, students of different backgrounds and abilities tend to select themselves into different undergraduate fields of study (Astin, 1977). Feldman and Newcomb (1969) summarize a range of early studies documenting both differences in student attributes across major fields and differences in the interactive and values environments provided by different departments. Although considerable shifts in student demand for particular major programs over two decades render the particulars of these results problematic, evidence that the same phenomenon may be currently occurring is provided by the Stanford students studied by Katchadourian and Boli (1985). Not only did different student types tend to major in different fields, but they also tended to ascribe to the entire institution the kinds of instructional goals and intellectual values characteristic of their chosen fields.

Probably of more enduring validity are studies on departmental environments reported by Feldman and Newcomb (1969), using variants of the College and University Environment Scales and the College Characteristics Index. Not only did the majority of these studies show that environments among departments differed, but that like residence groupings their diversity tended to accentuate initial student differences on a range of intellectual values. It remains unclear from the results of these studies whether established differences were due to distinct curricula or simply to continuing exposure to a particular body of peers. Also unclear is whether it is possible to generalize any detected "discipline cultures" across institutions, as hoped by early researchers (e.g., Pace, 1963). The latter point is amplified in the cognitive domain by Hartnett and Centra (1977). Using results of the UAP Field examinations as a measure of cognitive attainment, Hartnett and Centra found significantly greater variance in impact when departments rather than institutions were used as the unit of analysis.

In What Particular Institutional Activities and Settings?

Certainly the most relevant and potentially manipulable "microsettings" in colleges and universities are provided by individual classrooms. Less, however, is known about the impact of instructional mode and curricular design in higher education settings than in elementary and secondary classrooms. Recent reviews of college curriculum (Stark and Lowther, 1986) and of postsecondary teaching and learning (McKeachie et al., 1986) both turn frequently to comparable K–12 literature in making important points. While it is beyond the purposes of this chapter to provide an in-depth review of this topic, a number of consistent findings from the instructional literature are of considerable relevance.

One set of findings concerns the relative effectiveness of different instructional modes. Reviewing the literature on classroom process, Schalock (1976) found few consistent differences in mode on students' ability to recall content. Indeed, many of the studies cited by McKeachie and associates report lecture modes slightly superior to discussions or student-centered strategies for producing factual recall. Discussion appears better for fostering higher-order skills and for enhancing student motivation. Evidence of the impact of class size within instructional mode is mixed. Size appears to have more effect within discussion-oriented classrooms than in lectures, but of much more importance than size is the quality of interaction or engagement taking place (McKeachie et al.) Strategies attempting to maximize such interaction, for example, peer-tutoring, learning "cells," and "student-centered teaching," show few consistent cognitive effects across studies, beyond clear increases in student motivation. Partly this is because these strategies appear to

be experienced differently by different kinds of students.

McKeachie and associates conclude that student-centered approaches appear better for developing higher-order skills than do other methods, and that such methods are at least as good as traditional approaches in developing knowledge of content and basic skills. Moreover, they argue that student-centered methods also teach important social functioning skills, including leadership and appropriate group membership behavior. More extensive claims are made for individualized but often highly structured instructional modes, such as mastery learning. Studies cited in Schalock (1976) and Astin (1985) show significant gains in effectiveness for these methods over more traditional approaches, particularly in building such higher-order skills as critical thinking.

A second issue has to do with structure and level of difficulty. Citing a range of impact studies, Feldman and Newcomb argue that students learn best when they experience "a continuing series of not-too-threatening discontinuities" (1969, p. 295). The policy implication is to promote experiences that highlight discontinuity while maintaining a careful balance between novelty and familiarity. Classroom research indicates that creating structure may be important in managing discontinuity, particularly when the object is to communicate content. Examining literature on interactions between student aptitudes and instructional modes, for example, McKeachie et al. (1986) report that logical, externally imposed structures appear superior to "learner-controlled" sequencing of instruction for students without prior knowledge of course material at all aptitude levels. Similarly, they make the salient observation that all aspects of structure within the environment must remain consistent. This is particularly important with respect to testing, as students will quite rightly focus their energy on learning strategies most appropriate to good test performance.

A final set of findings concerns the nature of interaction within the classroom. Prominent among these is the importance of frequent and consistent feedback on student performance. Citing numerous studies of cognitive gain in elementary and secondary classrooms, Gagne (1977) stresses the importance of "'knowledge of results" as a causal factor. Similarly, Wilson and associates (1975) reported results of two multi-institutional studies focused on identifying and specifying the attributes of "effective" instructors. They found that the most effective faculty members were those who regarded students as partners in a common learning enterprise, as manifested by high levels of interaction both in and outside the classroom, and by attempts to relate class material to other situations.

Summarizing much of the research in this tradition, Cross (1976) stresses the importance of differences among students and the consequent need to "individualize" the curriculum. The "design criteria" that she proposes for instruction serve as an excellent summary of the issues raised above. They include (1) active rather than passive modes of instruction, (2) clear and explicitly presented goals for instruction, (3) small lesson units each organized around a single concept, (4) frequent feedback and evaluation, and (5) self-pacing to reflect different learning styles. These criteria serve as a useful template in terms of which to review extant curricula and classroom practices.

Requiring Investments on Whose Part?

Constructing "microsettings" that meet the kinds of criteria noted by Cross in both the classroom and in the wider institutional environment requires "investments" of many kinds. Most important, however, are those required of faculty and of students. Given the repeated finding that the extent and quality of peer and faculty interaction is associated with valued outcomes, a fundamental focus of institutional policy becomes the manner in which explicit structures and incentives can be designed to encourage and maintain such investments.

Certainly for faculty, a primary factor is willingness to devote scarce time and attention to instruction. Strongly conditioning this decision, of course, is the existence of competing interests such as research and scholarship that in most institutional settings (and perhaps more importantly, in most disciplinary cultures) remain highly rewarded. Astin (1985) and Gamson et al. (1984) thus see a major challenge to improving outcomes in providing institutional structures that promote faculty/ student interaction and visible incentives that reward teaching innovation and sheer time-on-task.

A much deeper issue is one of relative values. In a discussion that remains compelling, Feldman and Newcomb (1969) described the challenge as one of bridging "two cultures"— one associated with faculty and one with students. Summarizing a number of studies comparing faculty and student views about the relative importance of instrumental, aesthetic, and intellectual values, they noted that these perceptions often differed. Moreover, faculty themselves may differ considerably in these values, both by discipline and by type. Smart (1982), for example, used the Holland personality classification scheme in a study of undergraduate teaching goals to demonstrate that particular personalities are both drawn to particular disciplines and teach them in particular ways. Similarly, a range of studies cited by Feldman and Newcomb (1969) demonstrate that students seem to desire different qualities of instructors in different disciplines. Most marked in this respect were the natural sciences, where qualities of organization and clarity were generally ranked higher than involvement and dynamism.

As noted by Wilson and associates (1975), those faculty identified as being good teachers also engage in certain recognizable activities such as out-of-class contact with students and making frequent connections between their disciplines and broader issues and concerns. Certainly these findings suggest important areas to pursue in faculty development and recognition. But it is important not to view any of these results as mechanistic or uniform. In the realm of student/faculty contact, for example, evidence is strong that students are less interested in and benefit less from sheer personal interaction with individual faculty members, than they do from encounters with clear intellectual or professional content (Baird, 1976).

Equally important, though often neglected, are the investments made by students. As noted by Astin (1979, 1985) and Bloom (1974), probably the most relevant disposable resource for students is time. As a result, how student time is spent, how it is organized, and how its disposal might be profitably channeled become important elements of what Astin terms "student-oriented management." A considerable body of learning research highlights these observations. Thomas and Rohwer (1986), for example, note that internalization of time-management strategies on the part of students is a critical factor in cognitive development. Other identified "resource management strategies" for learning (McKeachie et al., 1986) include constructing and managing a congenial study environment, managing the support of others, and managing students' own motivations and attitudes toward learning. Combinations of such strategies are often deemed of greater importance than any one of them. Sternberg (1985), for example, subsumes such elements under the notion of "practical intelligence," and stresses particularly the ability of students to know where and from whom they can seek assistance upon encountering difficulty. Similarly, Corno and Rohrkemper (1985) use the term "self-regulating learners" to describe students who practice effective combinations of resource management and cognitive learning strategies.

One of the most powerful constructs describing student resource investment is Pace's notion of "quality of student effort." Using the College Student Experiences Questionnaire (CSEQ), an instrument designed to assess student involvement with various aspects of the institutional environment based on self-reported behavior, Pace and his associates have examined both the impact of quality of effort on achievement and the levels of involvement characteristic of different types of institutions. For example, in studies involving more than 10,000 students at over 40 institutions, quality of effort has been demonstrated to make independent and large contributions toward explaining student achievement using both self-reports of cognitive gain and actual grades received (Pace, 1984). At the same time, particular types of institutions—notably small private liberal arts colleges—appear particularly to be characterized by high "quality of effort" as assessed by the CSEQ (Porter, 1982). Because it focuses on actual student behavior, the notion of "quality of effort" combines elements of resource management and motivation. By focusing on the actual content rather than simply the extent of student investment, however, this line of inquiry avoids many pitfalls. Based on CSEQ results from thirty institutions, for example, Friedlander (1980) demonstrated that simple time-on-task is powerfully mediated by quality of effort. Students who spend a great deal of time at below average levels of effort

make considerably less progress than those investing less time at higher levels of effort.

Specifying the "Production Function"

The above review highlights two important characteristics of the literature on outcomes correlates. First, causality is complex and is difficult to firmly establish. Associations between particular outcomes and a bewildering array of structural and process characteristics have been demonstrated, but there is often no clear evidence of the degree to which particular elements of environment are substitutable or act in concert. Second, the effects that have been identified often vary considerably across different types of students and different types of settings. There appear to be very few mechanisms that work for all students or that apply to all types of institutional environments. Together, these two characteristics constitute a major challenge to improvement. Though generalizations can assuredly be made, they must be advanced with appropriate caution and with due regard for variations in local conditions and clienteles. More importantly, these findings suggest that a critical policy need is for appropriate local studies to establish the manner in which the kinds of relationships noted in the research literature operate in practice on each campus.

One attempt to systematize these generalizations is presented in Figure 2. The purpose of this conceptual scheme is twofold. First, it attempts to array the primary factors that appear associated with positive outcomes in the research literature in rough order of conceptual priority. Though not a "causal model" in the formal sense, the intent is to organize findings so that their conceptual flow is intelligible. This leads to a second purpose: to identify some explicit points in this body of findings that appear able to be influenced through administrative action. While it is beyond the scope of this discussion to treat each potential point of intervention in detail, the presentation should be sufficient both to note connections with other bodies of research that shed light on the potential efficacy of such action, and to suggest fruitful areas for additional inquiry.

The scheme proposed is roughly based on similar models advanced by Bowen (1977a),

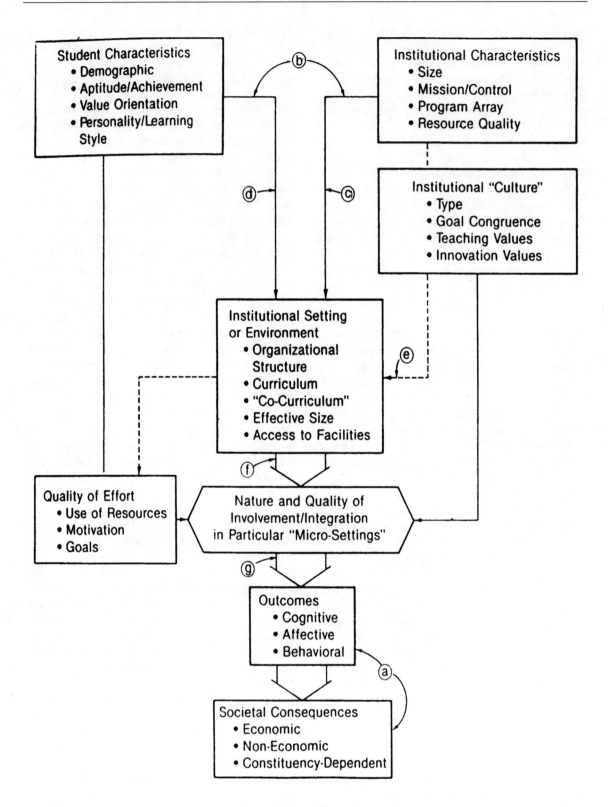

Figure 2 Conceptual scheme for identifying types of intervention in the process of producing outcomes.

Key. Intervention points for managerial action: (a) planning/goal-setting; (b) selectivity/enrollment management; (c) curriculum/academic policy; (d) person/environment fit; (e) academic leadership; (f) instructional/faculty development; (g) assessment/evaluation.

Pace (1979), Peterson et al. (1986), and Pascarella (1985a). Given a particular focus on administrative and academic policy, several of its features are worth noting. First, its heart is the nature and quality of involvement/integration in particular "microsettings" such as the classroom, residence hall, student organization, or informal peer group. This is the factor ascribed primarily responsible for the "production" of outcomes, with all prior elements modifying its operation. Critical for policy is to recognize that this central factor, and not the outcomes themselves, constitutes the primary dependent variable for action. Second, with the addition of Bowen's concern with societal impacts, the focus of attention is not exclusively intrainstitutional. Policy must also specify and take account of the ways in which outcomes are consistent with and influence a range of wider societal purposes—particularly as they are embodied in the perceptions and values of critical constituencies.

Finally, the impact of such concrete factors as student characteristics and institutional structure is relatively far removed from the outcomes themselves. Both operate indirectly through such intermediate mechanisms as student quality of effort and institutional culture (which also may have their own unique impacts), and the particular institutional setting or environment. While well-designed research on the causal linkage between institutional or student characteristics and outcomes remains rare (Pascarella, 1985a), those few studies that do employ and estimate causal models strongly suggest that the impact of institutional and student characteristics on both cognitive and affective outcomes is indirect, mediated by such factors as student involvement, motivation, and integration (e.g., Pascarella, 1984, 1985b; Pascarella, Terenzini, and Wolfle, 1986; Lacy, 1978).

Relationships described by this scheme suggest a number of points of attack for institutional policy.

Planning and Goal Setting

One important point of leverage for institutional action is the specification and definition of outcomes themselves. Though most extant planning processes begin with goal setting, goals are rarely of sufficient specificity to adequately encompass expected educational out-

comes. Outcomes-oriented planning, however, has considerable potential for focusing and redirecting institutional discussions about mission. First, particularly when planning discussions are curricular or programmatic, an outcomes focus has the benefit of rendering such discussions concrete enough that concerted action is possible (Banta and Fisher, 1984). Second, an outcomes focus in strategic planning raises important questions both about the kinds of external constituency needs that are most salient to the institution, and about the areas in which the institution is distinctive enough to possess a strategic advantage (e.g., Caruthers and Lott, 1981). Both processes are often able to mobilize and manipulate scarce channels of institutional attention.

Enrollment Management

Most discussions of enrollment management tend to focus relatively narrowly on recruitment (Hossler, 1984, 1986). An important aspect of the concept, however, emphasizes achievement of a careful match between student characteristics and institutional environments in order to ensure later retention and student success. By treating student attributes and attainments as a critical institutional resource, those in charge of enrollment management policies should first recognize that their primary goal is to help *create* specific kinds of environments that are consistent with institutional goals and values. Even if an institution is nonselective, it can nevertheless in certain areas be distinctive, and can therefore devote attention to obtaining and retaining students whose values and aspirations are consistent with its educational vision. And in so far as the institution serves many constituencies, it should be minimally aware of the characteristics and experiences of each of its various student bodies, and the fact that each may experience the institutional environment in a different way.

Curricular and Academic Policy

As emphasized by Stark and Lowther (1986), from a policy perspective the curriculum is an "academic plan." As such, it is subject to the canons of good planning including the need to carefully specify both outcomes and the means to achieve them. Conrad and Pratt (1986) note that there is very little systematic research that provides evidence of clear linkages between curricular structure and particular outcomes, though a large body of emerging case material strongly suggests that such linkages may eventually be established for alternative curricular forms (e.g., Gamson et al., 1984, Mentkowski and Doherty, 1984). Moreover, the notion of "academic policy" goes beyond curriculum design to include planning additional concrete aspects of the institutional environment. Among these are organizational issues encompassing the existence and influence of units responsible for undergraduate instruction or for instructional development, policies governing a range of "cocurricular" activities including cultural programming and student activities, policies directly affecting the way institutional environments are configured such as learning/residence groupings or thematic learning communities, and policies affecting student access to campus resources such as the library, laboratory facilities, and cultural facilities. Rarely, however, are the myriad factors shaping academic policy in this sense treated in a coherent fashion. A strong implication of the research literature, in contrast, is that institutions should view such environments as students see them—in a holistic and relatively undifferentiated fashion.

Person/Environment Fit

While enrollment management highlights the need for policy intended to carefully match potential students and institutions, an additional fruitful arena for intervention is to develop programs that carefully match existing students with particular elements of environment. In the area of curriculum and classroom practice, notions of individualized or "tailored" instruction advocated by Cross (1976) and Astin (1985) are of particular relevance. Learning/residence communities that attempt to foster interaction among students and faculty around particular ongoing topics or interests represent a similar approach at a different level of aggregation (e.g., Gamson et al., 1984). For other aspects of the environment, suggestive experiments have been undertaken using a range of assessment instruments to help determine residence groupings or to similarly establish parameters for peer interaction (Moos, 1979). As in curriculum design, little systematic work as yet exists documenting the effectiveness of such practices on

particular outcomes. Given evidence of considerable diversity among institutions, however, a primary requirement is again the need for each to determine through local research the kinds of "subject/treatment interactions" experienced on its own campus.

Academic Leadership

If the research literature on linkages between outcomes and such factors as curricular structure and person/environment fit is limited, that establishing linkages between outcomes and institutional culture is almost nonexistent (Peterson et al., 1986). Partially this is due to lack of agreement on what institutional culture really means. In an attempt to meet this difficulty, the conceptual scheme in Figure 2 restricts the term to (1) perceived patterns of action, communication, and decision making as embodied in such classifications as Cameron's (1978) typology of institutional cultures—clan, hierarchy, market, and emergent; (2) goal congruence as embodied in both the content and degree of internalization of commonly held institutional goals; and (3) specific values about the importance of teaching and receptivity to innovation.

With this more restricted definition, some evidence of the importance of "culture" can be cited. Most important is probably work by Pace and Baird (1966) with the College and University Environment Scales (CUES), suggesting that agreement about the importance of teaching as a value is an important element in accounting for outcomes. Examining institutional culture more directly, Ewell (1985b) used results from the Assessment of the Performance of Colleges and Universities (ACPU) survey administered to faculty and staff at 320 four-year institutions; findings indicated that linkages between institutional characteristics and perceived outcomes were strongly mediated by variables such as mission direction and specification, reward for recognition and achievement, and a "clanlike" institutional culture.

Managing this "mediation" seems clearly a task for academic leadership. As March (1984) points out, managerial action can always be viewed on two planes—active and interpretative—and the latter may well be the more decisive. By articulating centrally held values, and by ensuring their visibility through a range of symbolic actions intended to "manage meaning" (Dill, 1982), an important role of leadership is to monitor and challenge the consistency between articulated values and the structure of the institutional environment. Where such values are academic, symbolic action of this sort involves both explicit references to tradition and concrete structures for providing recognition and nonmaterial rewards for exemplary faculty, students, and support personnel.

Instructional/Faculty Development

The specific ways in which aspects of the institution's environment are made manifest in particular "microsettings" is largely a function of how faculty, staff, and students behave, and of the ways in which classroom and other immediate experiences are structured. The effects of administrative action will therefore necessarily be indirect. Nevertheless, such actions may facilitate other more direct processes. Examples include support and encouragement for faculty development aimed at fostering a range of classroom and assessment skills, or for instructional development efforts intended to improve or supplement classroom practices. The linkages between environment and behavior in particular "microsettings" may also be positively influenced by a number of changes in institutional incentives. These include increased attention to teaching in promotion and tenure decisions, visible recognition and reward for effective changes in classroom practice, and the use of discretionary funds for unit-level experiments or pilot programs. Again, the nonmaterial dimension of such incentives should not be overlooked; as Dill (1982) puts it, incentives of this sort might emphasize the "selection, canonization, and celebration of faculty exemplars."

Assessment and Evaluation

Considerable emerging evidence indicates that the presence and use of explicit information on instructional performance is among the most powerful administrative levers for inducing institutional action along any of the above lines. Some evidence of this kind will be examined in the following section. At this point it is sufficient to emphasize that powerful though it appears to be, assessment represents an approach to change that is indirect in a compound manner. First, its role is to support, direct, and induce other kinds of administrative actions. Administrative actions themselves then operate indirectly to influence the actual practice of teaching and learning. Current claims for the assessment movement now popular in higher education should be tempered by this observation. More importantly, the potential value of assessment and evaluation in improving outcomes should not be obscured by research that fails to properly specify the indirect nature of these activities with respect to the production of observable outcomes.

Getting There: Using Outcomes Information as a Change Agent

While assessment and evaluation represents but one of many potential management levers to improve outcomes, the emerging literature on its potential is worth further exploration for at least three reasons. First, the issue of assessment is prominent in public discussion, and constitutes a major focus of current policy concern. Second, many of the issues of implementation and use raised by discussions of assessment are equally applicable to any type of management intervention. Finally, because of the strong "action research" tradition in the outcomes literature, discussions of implementation form an integral part of any comprehensive review.

Some Evidence from the Field

Knowledge about the utilization of outcomes information is currently based largely on participant observation in particular field settings. A great deal of this has taken place in multi-institutional demonstration projects exploring the impact of outcomes information on curriculum and management practice (e.g., Astin, 1976; Baldridge and Tierney, 1979; Kemerer, Baldridge, and Green, 1982; Ewell, 1984; Kinnick, 1985; AASCU, 1986). Additional observations have been generated by attempts to design and implement local assessment programs on the part of individual institutions (e.g., Mentkowski and Doherty, 1984; Mentkowski and Loacker, 1985; McClain, 1984; McClain and Krueger, 1985; Banta, 1985, 1986; Banta and Fisher, 1984; Dumont and Troelstrup, 1980; Palola, 1981; Palola and Lehman, 1976). Useful lessons also arise from related efforts to use information to affect academic decision making through such areas as program evaluation and review, teacher evaluation, and student retention or enrollment management programs.

One of the first multi-institutional attempts to systematically incorporate outcomes information in decision making was Astin's ACE/CIRP Dissemination Project (Astin, 1976). Using a sample of 20 institutions in the early 1970s, the structure of the project involved providing institutions with data packages containing summary comparative information based on CIRP surveys. Each campus was expected to convene a local committee on data utilization charged with examining the data, drawing conclusions, and making recommendations on program change. Regression-based methods were used to compute "expected" results profiles based on institutional characteristics (Astin, 1977). These profiles were then compared to actual results in order to stimulate discussion.

The impact of the project was mixed at best, as a total of eight of the twenty original participants failed to complete the task. (Similarly disappointing results were reported by Baird in 1976 for a project attempting to "feed back" results of a multi-institutional survey of student and college characteristics.) Indeed, Astin's report on the ACE/CIRP project (Astin, 1976) is much more useful for its perceptive analysis of the functioning of faculty committees, and for its "theory of institutional conservatism" than for its positive evidence of the effectiveness of information-based improvement. Nevertheless, important lessons emerged, including the need to involve faculty thoroughly in planning and implementation, the need for clear (but not constant) top administrative support, and the need for flexibility in the ways information is packaged and communicated.

A related effort, though not confined to student outcomes, was the Exxon/ RAMP project on management training (Baldridge and Tierney, 1979). Involving a total of 49 institutions in a set of local projects directed toward database development and implementation of MBO-based planning approaches, this project too met with mixed success. Baldridge and Tierney provide an estimate of 50% success based on actual changes made, but it is interesting to note that participants themselves

rated the impact of the project much higher. Lessons learned parallel Astin's and include the need for top administrative support, for consistent involvement, and for clear links between information and the institution's regular incentive structure. The Exxon/RAMP project also reiterated the need to communicate policy information in different formats for different audiences, and Baldridge and Tierney noted such now familiar phenomena as "information glut" and "the tyranny of numbers" as typical of participating institutions.

A somewhat later large scale multi-institutional effort was the NCHEMS/Kellogg Student Outcomes Project (Ewell, 1984, 1985a; Kinnick, 1985). Eventually involving 22 public and private institutions, the intent of the project was to demonstrate the use of existing information on student outcomes in institutional planning and decision making. Rather than using a common approach, each participating institution undertook a local project intended to address a particular problem on campus. Like the ACE/CIRP project, substantial responsibility was placed on local committees for implementation, but perceived success rates were higher largely because these committees were able to deal with strictly local problems of high salience. Results of the project strongly confirmed earlier lessons about top management support, the need for broad-based involvement and participation, and the need to carefully tailor data-based communications to local needs. In addition, the project demonstrated the existence of substantial bodies of underutilized information on most campuses, highlighted the need for considerable disaggregation in data analysis and interpretation, and emphasized a need to decentralize implementation to the departmental and unit level.

Other recent multi-institutional projects provide additional evidence in support of these basic lessons. For example, the AASCU Academic Program Evaluation Project (APEP) involved 10 institutions in a multiyear project to identify and assess "generic intellectual skills" associated with a baccalaureate degree (AASCU, 1986). Among the skills agreed upon were communication, quantification, analysis, synthesis, and valuing. Each participating institution undertook a locally defined and implemented project to further specify and assess these skills, though by the end of the project most had not yet used the resulting information in decision making. Nevertheless, many institutions reported that reviewing curricula from an outcomes perspective and carefully thinking about sources of evidence in themselves helped to induce needed curricular improvements. This last observation echoes a range of emerging institutional experience. Reporting on the design of a comprehensive assessment program at the University of Tennessee, Knoxville, Banta (1985, 1986) notes that a significant impact of efforts to design major field examinations was that it forced faculty to rethink the structure and intended outcomes of their curricula. As a result, changes in curriculum occurred even before outcomes data were collected and disseminated.

Institutional experience also highlights the importance of multiple methods and broad participation in assessing outcomes. For example, guided by a Master Question—"What kinds of students working with what kinds of faculty in what kinds of learning programs change in what ways at what cost?"—the Program Effectiveness and Related Costs (PERC) model at Empire State College employs such methods as goal inventories, standardized tests, evaluation of student portfolios, and interviews to build a comprehensive picture of student experience (Palola and Lehman, 1976). Assessment programs at the University of Tennessee, Knoxville (Banta, 1985, 1986), Northeast Missouri State University (McClain and Krueger, 1985), and other institutions currently experimenting with assessment (Ewell, 1985c) generally involve at least three distinct kinds of instruments: standardized national examinations, locally designed examinations, and assessments (generally in the major field), and student surveys. One of the most comprehensive evaluation efforts of this kind is at Alverno College, where the Office of Research and Evaluation regularly conducts research on student development using quantitative and qualitative measures, and employing both nationally recognized and locally developed instruments (Mentkowski and Doherty, 1984). Among the latter are the Kolb Learning Styles Inventory, McBer's Behavioral Event Interview, the Watson-Glaser Critical Thinking Appraisal, and a range of measures of moral, ego, and intellectual development as described by Kohlberg, Loevinger, Piaget, and Perry.

Another important attribute of these programs is their stress on communicating the results of outcomes information in a manner designed to stimulate a "dialogue" about implications. Describing the PERC project at Empire State, Palola (1981) noted that participation was increased when individual departments were given a chance to generate their own information to "correct" centrally provided statistics. Similar results are reported by Kinnick (1985) in describing data communications formats designed to induce local responses on the part of faculty and unit-level administrators. In the NCHEMS/Kellogg Project, information-based "dialogue" of this kind was considerably enhanced when the kinds of results communicated centered visibly on an institutional problem of clear salience to most parties (Ewell, 1984). A risk in this situation, however, is that once the identified problem was successfully addressed, many of informal mechanisms supporting information-based improvement tended to atrophy if not intentionally institutionalized.

Emerging institutional experience also emphasizes that "utilization of information" with respect to outcomes should not be constructed too narrowly. Reviewing the literature on the utilization of evaluation results in higher education generally, Shapiro (1986) notes that a major line of recent inquiry centers around changes in the notion of "use." While a few studies show that evaluation information has a direct impact on the content of particular decisions, evaluation results can nevertheless influence policy through such mechanisms as "conceptual use" where information is used to help set context and formulate problems, and "symbolic use," where it is used to justify or legitimize action.

Such alternative uses of information emerge strongly in the literature on developing and implementing outcomes programs. Forrest (1981), for example, reports that a major feature of early utilization of the ACT-COMP was to "sell" nontraditional programs to external constituencies who doubted their effectiveness. Similarly, in examining a range of cases where institutions attempted to use information on effectiveness for improvement, Ewell and Chaffee (1984) identified four different types of information utilization beyond the "rational decision making" paradigm. These included the use of information to (1) identify the existence of problems or decision alternatives, (2) set context for informing broad classes of decisions, (3) induce action and end discussion, and (4) legitimize action previously decided on other grounds. Kinnick (1985) reports similar results on the basis of the NCHEMS/Kellogg Project, and notes that patterns of utilization may differ depending upon whether intended audiences are internal or external.

A Clarification of Issues and Lessons

Based on experiences such as these, most observers exhibit a consistent view of both the major obstacles and issues surrounding successful use of assessment as an agent of change, and the primary lessons that ought to guide such an effort. Figure 3 represents one attempt to identify these commonalities in general terms. Appendix A provides a detailed presentation of selected comments on assessment by source.

Philosophical issues generally begin with reservations about assessing the "ineffable" consequences of a complex educational experience. Although most such difficulties can ultimately be reduced to a series of more concrete concerns, many faculty objections to assessment-based improvement are initially voiced in philosophical language (Ewell, 1986b). One set of issues has to do with anticipated consequences of allowing concrete evaluation pro-

cesses—possibly designed and implemented by those outside the academy—to provide evidence of the effectiveness of higher education (e.g., Smith, 1986). Another manifestation of this point of view is that assessment violates tenets of individual academic freedom. As Adelman (1986) points out, assessment may symbolically raise the question of whether or not we trust our faculty. A second set of issues has to do with anticipated effects on curriculum and classroom practice. "Teaching to the test" and narrowed curricula covering only those areas to be assessed are topics commonly raised in this regard (e.g., Smith, 1986). A third set of issues revolves around the difficulties of defining broad qualitative outcomes. Not a measurement objection, this position concentrates on the difficulty of even specifying outcomes in such a way that they are not rendered mechanical and meaningless (e.g., Hanson, 1982; Warren, 1984). Related topics center around defining outcomes in ways that go beyond traditional litanies of basic skills and minimal behaviors (e.g., Hartle, 1986; Adelman, 1986b; Nettles, 1987). A final set of concerns addresses possible negative impacts on student access, particularly for minority students who may be victims of assessment approaches that are culturally biased, or that attempt to control access through setting minimum qualifications (Hartle, 1986; Nettles, 1987).

	Issues/Concerns	Themes of Successful Efforts
Philosophical	Threats to institutional autonomy/academic freedom	
	Narrowing curriculum/ "teaching to the test"	Curriculum specificity
	Problems in defining "quality"	Link to goals/priorities
	Impact on minority access	
Organizational	Lack of commitment/incentives	Visibility link to incentives
	Fragmented responsibilities	Create forum for discussion/ center for coordination
	Fear of abuse	Maximize involvement/ participation
Practical	Excessive cost	Build on strength
	Few channels of communication	Create an information "dialogue"
	Lack of action focus	Focus on recognized problems
Technical	Imprecision/measurement error	Multiple methods/ "triangulation"
	Credibility/" face validity"	Keep it simple
	Interpretation/dissemination	Tailored reporting around audiences/issues

Figure 3 Issues and themes of outcomes-based improvement projects.

Noted characteristics of successful change efforts that partially address these concerns include ensuring that all assessment is tailored to the curriculum as taught at each institution, and ensuring that the goals to be assessed are truly important goals for the institution (Bowen, 1977b; Hartle, 1986; Nettles, 1987). An important ingredient of success, therefore, is likely to be disaggregation. Bess (1979), for example, lists six distinct institutional decision areas, each of which requires a different "tailored" approach to information-gathering and utilization. Like philosophical issues, many of the ingredients of these two admonitions are contained in other, more concrete, observations. Particularly relevant, however, is Bowen's observation that "whole persons" should be the primary focus of all assessment (1977b).

Organizational issues raised by outcomes assessment programs are particularly generalizable to other attempts at management-initiated instructional improvement. A first set of issues centers around incentives and commitment. As Baldridge and Tierney (1979) observe from the Exxon/RAMP project, little change can be expected unless information is directly tied to unit or individual reward. Most attempts at curriculum change, moreover, are merely that (Stark and Lowther, 1986); they do not involve changes in the priority given undergraduate instruction at the institution or the reward structure that surrounds it. As a result, many of the attributes of successful change efforts involve changes in incentives. For example, a number of observers note the importance of pilot programs and department-specific initiatives that make discretionary funds available for units to experiment with assessment or improvement efforts (e.g., Banta, 1985; Banta and Fisher, 1984; Ewell, 1984). Attempts at "performance funding" as practiced by Tennessee also fall within this category (e.g., Bogue and Brown, 1982). An observation shared by most observers, however, is that reform approaches that concentrate on modifying incentive structures are at their best when they are marginal; entire reconstructions of familiar reward systems are simply too threatening to have a long-term impact (Levy, 1986; Ewell, 1986b).

A second set of organizational issues focuses on the fact that undergraduate education is rarely centrally coordinated—particularly in

the arena of general education. Attributes of successful efforts generally cited in response to this condition involve the creation of central offices responsible for assessment and improvement activities—generally reporting to a high administrative level. Such offices generally span many functions, but three appear critical. First, they serve as visible embodiments of the institution's commitment to change (Ewell, 1987). Second, they are proactive in assisting faculty in individual departments to undertake their own assessment efforts (Banta, 1986; Mentkowski and Doherty, 1984; Palola and Lehman, 1976). Finally, they are changed with coordinating, maintaining, and enhancing, and helping to interpret information about student learning and development (Astin, 1985; Baldridge and Tierney, 1979; Gamson, 1984). Each of these functions can also to a lesser extent be played by institution-wide committees (e.g., Ewell, 1984; Banta, 1985). Here a chief function is to create a legitimate forum for discussing implications and new ideas.

Fear of abuse also constitutes a formidable organizational issue mentioned by most observers. In many cases the locus of concern is the anticipated use of outcomes information by state authorities and others outside the academy (e.g., Smith, 1986). Within institutions, the locus of concern is most likely to be anticipated use in faculty evaluation (Ewell, 1987). In both cases, substantial involvement of interested parties throughout the development process is seen as an attribute of success (e.g., Palola, 1981; Braskamp, 1982). Moreover, it is important to recognize that achieving broad-based involvement is likely to take considerable time, and that successful assessment-based change efforts have evolved over many years (Ewell, 1984, 1985a).

Practical issues cover a range of topics, but the most frequently mentioned is probably cost. Even the most ardent proponents of assessment recognize that substantial investments are likely to be involved, so most discussions of this issue attempt to frame the issue in "cost/benefit" terms (e.g., Ewell, 1986b; Nettles, 1987; Bowen, 1977b). Nevertheless, observers of successful change efforts note that they are founded on considerable existing information, and consequently involve sustained activities that build on data-gathering mechanisms already in place (e.g., McClain and Krueger, 1985; Palola, 1981; AASCU, 1986; Ewell, 1985a). Astin (1979, 1985) observes, for example, that most institutions invest substantially in "assessment" data collection, but that these data are rarely integrated and used for program improvement. Incremental costs of information-based programs are thus likely to be less than initially anticipated (Ewell and Jones, 1986). Other practical issues include the fact that outcomes information is rarely "decision-specific" information (e.g., Kinnick, 1985), and that few opportunities exist to discuss its implications with those who are affected.

Observations focused on overcoming these difficulties include the benefits of focusing investigation and discussion on recognized problems at the unit level, or that command sufficient attention that institutionwide committees can legitimately address them. Also prominent are observations stressing the need for constant dialogue about the possible implications of assessment findings. Enthoven's (1970) early observation that a good way to induce change using information about results is to engage in "analysis to stimulate 'counteranalysis'" is particularly appropriate in this context. The results of field experience as reported by Palola (1981), Lindquist (1981b), and Kinnick (1985) emphasize the importance of communicating information in formats that encourage or provoke active responses of this kind.

Technical issues cover both questions of the adequacy of particular measurement approaches and techniques, and of the unique challenges associated with communicating complex information to a diverse audience of users and affected parties. Most measurement issues are identical to those raised earlier by the research community. They include problems of validity and reliability associated with particular instruments or techniques (e.g., Banta et al., 1987), observations about the difficulties of adequately assessing change (e.g., Hanson, 1982; Pascarella, 1987), and problems of attribution and control. Observers of successful programs for the most part concede that considerable methodological difficulties are apparent, but that the use of multiple methods and such techniques as sensitivity analysis in

particular decision contexts allows them to be in practice overcome (e.g., Mentkowski and Loacker, 1985; Ewell, 1985a).

A final set of practical issues concerns the communication of assessment results in such a way that they will be used to effect change. As such observers in Guba (1969), Shapiro (1986), and Newman, Brown, and Braskamp (1980) point out, this is an old problem in educational evaluation. A particular challenge in using outcomes results, however, is that the kinds of research designs necessary to establish reliable findings are complex; communicating them simply therefore constitutes a considerable challenge (e.g., Ewell, 1983). Techniques reported by Kinnick (1985) or Palola (1981) involving heavy use of graphics and tailored reports for identified audiences, or the use of innovative qualitative techniques to supplement more traditional measurement (e.g., Lindquist, 1981b; Mentkowski and Doherty, 1984) constitute excellent examples of attempts to overcome such difficulties.

Toward an Agenda for Action Research

Emerging lessons from assessment-based improvement projects serve as a reminder that research intended to inform administrative action is constrained in multiple ways. First, it must be conceptually sound and methodologically well-founded. Second, it must focus on arenas where management action can actually expect to influence outcomes. Finally, it must be credible, accessible, and usable in an often political and value-laden operational context. Each of these constraints helps determine the shape and content of needed research. Furthermore, inquiry useful for policy direction has always appropriately proceeded on two planes. Large-scale, methodologically rigorous, and primarily "discipline-based" studies are needed to establish generalizable findings. But at least as important are multiple local research efforts intended to specify and describe how these general mechanisms operate for particular students in particular environments on particular campuses.

Some Implications for the Study of College Impact

Without doubt, informed action requires further developments in scholarly research on college impact. But the major emphasis of such studies should increasingly be focused upon establishing specific causal sequences among the many factors that have in the past been bilaterally associated with particular outcomes. Research on student learning and development that allows patterns of causality to be meaningfully identified remains distressingly infrequent, and certainly the technical requirements for executing such studies are daunting. But balancing this observation is the fact that powerful methods and appropriate multi-institutional datasets to ground research of this kind are increasingly available.

Most of the requisites for improving such research are familiar and echo the concerns of prior observers (e.g., Pascarella, 1985a). First, more and better longitudinal studies are needed. While a great deal can be learned from well-designed cross-sectional studies of selected student populations (Pace, 1979), longitudinal studies are still required to unambiguously specify the nature and sequence of different types of college impact. Secondly, more and better multi-institutional studies are needed. Available databases based on student self-reports such as the CIRP are increasingly being supplemented by newer multi-institutional counterparts such as the CSEQ. At the same time, the rising salience of assessment as an issue has meant heavy institutional use of such cognitive instruments as the ACT-COMP, CLEP, and a range of standardized basic skills examinations. Though institutional representation in such databases is uneven due to self-selection, they constitute a rich potential resource for undertaking multi-institutional studies. Finally, more studies are needed that are driven by clear theoretical frameworks and that employ appropriate statistical procedures to estimate causal priorities and isolate indirect effects. LISREL, path analysis and causal modelling, and a range of other multiple regression-based techniques are becoming widely available through statistical packages. Furthermore, the upgraded file handling capabilities of such packages as SPSS-X and SAS mean that it is now a manageable procedure to assemble for use in a common analysis variables of quite different sources and types.

Given these methodological imperatives, what particular topics might such studies address? A first requirement is to more fully document student behavior. In most choice-based curricula, for example, there is little likelihood that students in the same program will have taken the same pattern and sequence of courses. And there is even less likelihood that their patterns of interaction outside the curriculum are standard. Without further specification, then, studies attempting to isolate the effects of students in different curricula are extremely problematic. Approaches to documenting behavior based on self-reports such as the CSEQ represent one way to approach this problem. But equally important may be the use of "trace data" drawn from student records or other unobtrusive methods (e.g., Terenzini, 1987). A second requirement is to more fully describe "environment." Specifications of the "nonmaterial" aspects of environment such as institutional culture or perceived patterns of institutional values and reward are in their infancy. Proven instruments such as the CUES need to be updated to reflect a heavily nontraditional student population. More importantly, instruments that examine a wider arena of faculty and staff perceptions of institutional culture and values might be beneficially included in research investigating instructional outcomes.

Finally, past studies of student impact have been disappointingly noncumulative. Primarily this has been because studies operationalize outcomes concepts in quite different ways. This condition limits attempts to meaningfully generalize findings across studies. Techniques such as metaanalysis that have proven useful for summarizing knowledge in other fields are largely inapplicable for this reason. But as syntheses such as those of Bowen (1977a) and Pascarella (1985a) illustrate, it is possible to use "effect sizes" to support generalization, provided that the studies included supply requisite baseline information about the type and range of variation of the measures employed. It is also helpful for generalization if information on study contexts (for example, important characteristics of the student clientele and institutional environment) and on the conceptual framework employed is also clearly presented. Consequently, an important directive to individual researchers is to report all results with more general uses of this kind explicitly in mind.

A Call for Local Action Research

At least as important as scholarly work is a need to undertake more locally based action research on student outcomes. In contrast to basic research on impact, however, the proper emphasis of local studies is diversity. Guided by more general findings concerning causal sequence and priority, the prime focus of work of this kind should be to investigate linkages between particular observed patterns of student experience and locally valued outcomes. Following this logic, effective studies will disaggregate student experience in at least two ways. One involves using units of analysis that correspond to the actual levels at which such experiences take place: programs and curricula, classrooms, living units, and other identifiable "microsettings." A good example is a recent proposal by Cross (1987) that faculty themselves engage in informal research on student learning and development in their own classrooms. Another form of disaggregation involves carefully specifying student subpopulations in terms of their characteristics, their aptitudes and values, and their actual behavior. It is important to recognize here that the particular kinds of analytical disaggregations needed will appropriately vary across institutions. Indeed, a critical task for the local researcher is to carefully select variables to guide disaggregation that are appropriate to both the distinctive structure of the institutional environment and the developmental goals that the institution purports to achieve.

A second important point is that local action research of this kind need be no less rigorous than its more scholarly counterpart. Indeed, most of the admonitions on method noted above are equally applicable to both types of studies. But local research also involves considerable opportunities for methodological innovation. For example, the need to isolate experiences in "microsettings" raises excellent opportunities for qualitative or ethnographic investigation. Though published as part of the wider literature, for example, Katchadourian and Boli's (1985) in-depth study of Stanford students began as a local evaluation effort. Similar longitudinal efforts involving participant observation and in-depth interviewing are often of particular value in isolating promising avenues for action and in-

tervention (Lindquist, 1981b). Even such "quick and dirty" methods as transcript studies and teaching evaluations can be rendered rigorous if part of a more general, mutually reinforcing local research program. Finally, it is important to recognize that studies intended primarily to inform local policy can also make significant contributions to wider knowledge if they are approached in the light of a common guiding policy framework or research question. Palola's work at Empire State (1981); Banta's at the University of Tennessee, Knoxville (Banta, 1985, 1986); and Mentkowski's at Alverno College (Mentkowski and Doherty, 1984) are all instructive in this regard.

An Emerging Need for Implementation Research

A final important research question goes beyond the immediate scope of outcomes investigation. As greater numbers of institutions initiate activities intended to improve instruction, a significant knowledge gap is emerging about the factors responsible for the successful implementation of such efforts. Emerging institutional assessment programs represent only one of many possible objects of inquiry within this arena. Nevertheless, they present an excellent available research opportunity. In several states (for example, Virginia, Missouri, and Colorado) all public institutions are being required to undertake identifiable assessment programs, and most are in the earliest stages of development. Such states constitute a universe of "natural experiments" for investigating the impact of a specified innovation across a range of institutional settings. Second, assessment programs usually fuse a variety of mechanisms for change, and their implementation raises a number of issues that are typical of any intervention. Among these are organizational and political issues such as the location of responsibility, the nature and extent of faculty involvement, and the consequences of action. Such programs also raise issues of institutional culture including the symbolic value of information and the degree of agreement on and internalization of goals. Most importantly, they involve direct examination of goals themselves, and consequently have the potential to raise latent conflicts about appropriate values. Finally, assessment programs are usually directly linked to a range of additional types of intervention, among them new structures for curricula, of incentives, and of faculty and staff development. Because of these linkages, research focused on the organizational implementation of such programs constitutes an excellent point of departure for more focused investigations of the fielding and impact of additional undergraduate reforms.

Certainly, considerably greater knowledge is needed about such interventions in themselves. As Conrad and Pratt (1986) and Stark and Lowther (1986) point out, very little is known about the consequences or about the factors associated with successful implementation of various approaches to curriculum design. McKeachie and associates (1986) identify parallel needs to further specify the outcomes consequences of particular types of teaching modality and classroom activity. Investigations of the precise forms of incentives capable of inducing different kinds of faculty to alter classroom practices constitutes yet another promising line of inquiry. As Blackburn and associates (1986) note, very little research has been able to link extrinsic reward structures with effective teaching, and very few have explicitly explored the nature and impact of intrinsic reward. Pointing out such needs, however, comes perilously close to posing a classic academic dilemma: the requirement to know everything before attempting anything. The most important demand, therefore, remains the resolution to act on what has already been determined. Posed as a challenge to outcomes research almost two decades ago, Enthoven's observation remains germane: "Because there is no agreement on purposes or on relative values, there is no 'optimum' program for the university. There are only better and worse programs. Avoiding bad programs is a sufficiently ambitious goal to keep us all occupied for many years" (1970, p. 53).

References

Adelman, Clifford, ed. (1986a). *Assessment in American Higher Education: Issues and Contexts.* Washington, DC: OERI, Department of Education.

Adelman, C. (1986b). To imagine an adverb. In Adelman, *Assessment in American Higher Education,* pp. 73–82.

Alverno College Faculty (1979). *Assessments at Alverno College.* Milwaukee: Alverno Publications.

American Association of State Colleges and Universities (1986). *Defining and Assessing Baccalaureate Skills.* Washington, DC.

Association of American Colleges (1985). *Integrity in the College Curriculum: A Report to the Academic Community.* Washington, DC: Association of American Colleges.

Astin, A. W. (1985). *Achieving Educational Excellence.* San Francisco: Jossey-Bass.

Astin, A. W. (1979). Student-oriented management: a proposal for change. In *Evaluating Educational Quality: A Conference Summary.* Washington, DC: Council on Postsecondary Accreditation (COPA).

Astin, A. W. (1977). *Four Critical Years: Effects of College on Beliefs, Values, and Knowledge.* San Francisco: Jossey-Bass.

Astin, A. W. (1976). *Academic Gamesmanship: Student-Oriented Change in Higher Education.* New York: Praeger.

Astin, A. W. (1975). *Preventing Students from Dropping Out.* San Francisco: Jossey-Bass.

Astin, A. W. (1974). Measuring the outcomes of higher education. In H. W. Bowen (ed.), *Evaluating Institutions for Accountability,* New Directions for Institutional Research. San Francisco: Jossey-Bass.

Astin, A. W. (1970a). The methodology of research on college impact (I). *Sociology of Education* 43: 223–254.

Astin, A. W. (1970b). The methodology of research on college impact (II). *Sociology of Education* 43: 437–450.

Astin, A. W. (1968). Undergraduate achievement and institutional excellence. *Science* 161:661–668.

Astin, A. W. and Lee, C. B. T. (1972). *The Invisible Colleges.* New York: McGraw-Hill.

Astin, A. W. and Panos, R. (1969). *The Educational and Vocational Development of College Students.* Washington, DC: ACE, 1969.

Astin, A. W., Panos, R. J., and Creager, J. A. (1967). *National Norms for Entering College Freshmen—Fall 1966.* Washington, DC: AE.

Baird, L. (1976). Structuring the environment to improve outcomes. In O. T. Lenning (ed.), *Improving Educational Outcomes.* New Directions for Higher Education, No. 16, pp. 1–23.

Baird, L. (1974). The practical utility of measures of college environments. *Review of Educational Research* 44: 307–329.

Baldridge, J. V., and Tierney, M. L. (1979). *New Approaches to Management: Creative, Practical Systems of Management Information and Management by Objective.* San Francisco: Jossey-Bass.

Banta, T. W. (1986). *Performance Funding in Higher Education: A Critical Analysis of Tennessee's Experience.* Boulder, CO: National Center for Higher Education Management Systems [NCHEMS].

Banta, T. W. (1985). Use of outcomes information at the University of Tennessee, Knoxville. In Ewell, *Assessing Educational Outcomes,* pp. 19–32.

Banta, T. W., and Fisher, H. S. (1984). Performance funding: Tennessee's experiment. In J. Folger (ed.), *Financial Incentives for Academic Quality*. New Directions for Higher Education, No. 48, pp. 29–41. San Francisco: Jossey-Bass.

Banta, T. W., Lambert, E. W., Pike, G. R., Schmidhammer, J. L., and Schneider, J. A. (1987). Estimated score gain on the ACT COMP exam: valid tool for institutional assessment? Paper presented at the annual meeting of the American Educational Research Association, Washington, D.C., April.

Barak, R. (1982). *Program Review in Higher Education: Within and Without*. Boulder, CO:NCHEMS.

Bennett, W. J. (1984). *To Reclaim a Legacy: A Report on the Humanities in Higher Education*. Washington, DC: National Endowment for the Humanities.

Bess, J. L. (1979). Classroom and management decisions using student data. *Journal of Higher Education* 5: 256–279.

Biglan, A. (1973). Relationships between subject matter characteristics and the structure and output of university departments. *Journal of Applied Psychology* 57: 204–213.

Blackburn, R. T., Lawrence, J. H., Ross, S., Okoloko, V. P., Meiland, R., Bieber, J., and Street, T. (1986). *Faculty as a Key Resource: A Review of the Research Literature*. Ann Arbor: NCRIPTAL, University of Michigan.

Bloom, B. S. (1974). Time and learning. *American Psychologist*, 1974, 683–688.

Bloom, B. S., ed. (1956). *Taxonomy of Educational Objectives, Handbook 1: Cognitive Domain*. New York: David McKay.

Bogue, E. G., and Brown, W. (1982). Performance incentives for state colleges. *Harvard Business Review*, Nov./Dec., 123–128.

Bowen, H. R. (1981). Cost differences: the amazing disparity among institutions of higher education in educational costs per student. *Change*, Jan./Feb., 21–27.

Bowen, H. R. (1980). *The Costs of Higher Education: How Much Do Colleges and Universities Spend per Student and How Much Should They Spend?* San Francisco: Jossey-Bass.

Bowen, H. R. (1978). Outcomes planning: solution or dream? In *Planning, Managing and Financing in the 1980s: Proceedings of the NCHEMS 1977 National Assembly*, pp. 41–51. Boulder, CO: NCHEMS.

Bowen, H. R. (1977a). *Investment in Learning*. San Francisco: Jossey-Bass.

Bowen, H. R. (1977b). Outcome data and educational decisionmaking. In Carl R. Adams (ed.), *Appraising Information Needs of Decisionmakers*. New Directions for Institutional Research, No. 15. San Francisco: Jossey-Bass.

Boyer, C. M., Ewell, P. T., Finney, J. E., and Mingle, J. R. (1987). Assessment and outcomes measurement: a view from the states. *AAHE Bulletin*, March, pp. 8–12.

Branscomb, H., Milton, O., Richardson, J., and Spivey, H. (1977). *The Competent College Student: An Essay on the Objectives and Quality of Higher Education*. Nashville: Tennessee Higher Education Commission.

Braskamp, L. A. (1982). Evaluation systems are more than information systems. In R. Wilson (ed.), *Designing Academic Program Reviews*. New Directions for Higher Education, No. 37, pp. 55–66. San Francisco: Jossey-Bass.

Bressler, M., and Wendell, P. (1980). The sex composition of selective colleges and gender differences in career aspirations. *Journal of Higher Education* 51: 651–663.

Cameron, K. S. (1978). Measuring organizational effectiveness in institutions of higher education. *Administrative Science Quarterly* 23: 604–632.

Campione, J. C., and Armbruster, B. B. (1985). Acquiring information from texts: an analysis of four approaches. In J. W. Segal, S. F. Chipman, and R. Glaser (eds.), *Thinking and Learning Skills VI*, pp. 317–362. Hillsdale, NJ: Lawrence Erlbaum Associates.

Caruthers, J. K., and Lott, G. B. (1981). *Mission Review: Foundation for Strategic Planning*. Boulder, CO: NCHEMS.

Centra, J., and Rock, D. (1971). College environments and student academic achievement. *American Educational Research Journal* 8: 623–634.

Chickering, A. W. (1970). College experience and student development. Paper delivered at Annual Meeting of the American Association for the Advancement of Science, December.

Chickering, A. W. (1969). *Education and Identity*. San Francisco: Jossey-Bass.

Clark, B., Heist, P., McConnell, T., Trow, M., and Yonge, G. (1972). *Students and Colleges: Interaction and Change*. Berkeley: Center for Research and Development in Higher Education, University of California-Berkeley.

Clark, B. R., and Trow, M. (1966). The organizational context. In T. M. Newcomb and E. K. Wilson (eds.), *College Peer Groups: Problems and Prospects for Research*, pp. 17–70. Chicago: Aldine.

College Outcomes Evaluation Program (COEP), State of New Jersey Department of Higher Education (1987). *Fifth Progress Report of the Student Learning Outcomes Subcommittee*. Trenton: Department of Higher Education.

Conrad, C. F., and Pratt, A. M. (1986). Research on academic programs: an inquiry into an emerging field. In J. C. Smart (ed.), *Higher Education: Handbook of Theory and Research*, Vol. II, pp. 235–273. New York: Agathon Press.

Corno, L., and Rohrkemper, M. M. (1985). The intrinsic motivation to learn in classrooms. In C. Ames and R. Ames (eds.), *Research on Motivation in Education*. New York: Academic Press.

Corno, L., and Snow, R. E. (1986). Adapting teaching to individual differences among learnings. In

M. Wittrack (ed.), *Handbook of Research on Teaching*. New York: Macmillan.

Cronbach, L., and Snow, R. (1977). *Aptitudes and Instructional Methods: A Handbook for Research on Interactions*. New York: Irvington.

Cross, K. P. (1987). Teaching for learning. *AAHE Bulletin* 39 (April): 3–7.

Cross, K. P. (1976). *Accent on Learning: Improving Instruction and Reshaping the Curriculum*. San Francisco: Jossey-Bass.

Dill, D. D. (1982). The management of academic culture: notes on the management of meaning and social integration. *Higher Education* 11: 303–320.

Douglass, G. K. (1977). Economic returns on investments in higher education. In Bowen, *Investment in Learning*, pp. 359–387.

Dumont, R. G., and Troelstrup, R. L. (1981). Measures and predictors of educational growth with four years of college. *Research in Higher Education* 14: 31–47.

Dumont, R. G., and Troelstrup, R. L. (1980). Exploring relationships between objective and subjective measures of instructional outcomes. *Research in Higher Education* 12: 37–51.

Edgerton, R. (1987). An assessment of assessment. In ETS, *Assessing the Outcomes of Higher Education*, pp. 93 -110.

Educational Testing Service (1987). *Assessing the Outcomes of Higher Education*. Proceedings of the 1986 ETS Invitational Conference, Princeton, NJ.

Enthoven, A. C. (1970). Measures of the outputs of higher education: some practical suggestions for their development and use. In G. B. Lawrence, G. Weathersby, and V. W. Patterson (eds.), *Outputs of Higher Education: Their Identification, Measurement, and Evaluation*, pp. 51–58. Boulder, CO: WICHE.

Erwin, T. D. (1986). Students' contributions to their college costs and intellectual development. *Research in Higher Education* 25: 194–203.

Ewell, P. T. (1987). Establishing a campus-based assessment program: a framework for choice. In D. Halpern (ed.), *Student Outcomes Assessment: A Tool for Improving Teaching and Learning*. New Directions in Higher Education. San Francisco: Jossey-Bass.

Ewell, P. T. (1986a). Transformational leadership for improving student outcomes. In M. D. Waggoner, R. L. Alfred, M. C. Francis, M. W. Peterson (eds.), *Academic Effectiveness: Transforming Colleges and Universities for the 1990s*, pp. 25–30. Ann Arbor: University of Michigan.

Ewell, P. T. (1986b). The state role in assessing college outcomes: policy choices and probable impacts. In *Time for Results: The Governors' 1991 Report on Education—Task Force on College Quality: Supporting Works*, pp. 43–73. Washington, DC: National Governors Association.

Ewell, P. T., ed. (1985a). *Assessing Educational Outcomes*. New Directions for Institutional Research, No. 47. San Francisco: Jossey-Bass.

Ewell, P. T. (1985b). Linking outcomes and institutional characteristics: the importance of looking deeper. Boulder, CO: NCHEMS.

Ewell, P. T. (1985c). Assessment: what's it all about? *Change*, Nov./Dec., 32–36.

Ewell, P. T. (1984). *The Self-Regarding Institution: Information for Excellence*. Boulder, CO:NCHEMS.

Ewell, P. T. (1983). *Information on Student Outcomes: How to Get It and How to Use It*. Boulder, CO: NCHEMS.

Ewell, P. T., and Chaffee, E. E. (1984). Promoting the effective use of information in decisionmaking. Boulder, CO: NCHEMS.

Ewell, P. T., and Jones, D. P. (1986). The costs of assessment. In Adelman, *Assessment in American Higher Education*, pp. 33–46.

Feldman, K. A., and Newcomb, T. M. (1969). *The Impact of College on Students*. San Francisco: Jossey-Bass.

Forrest, A. W. (1981). Outcome evaluation for revitalizing general education. In Lindquist, *Increasing the Use of Institutional Research*, pp. 59–71.

Friedlander, J. H. (1980). The importance of quality of effort in predicting college student attainment. Ph.D. dissertation, Graduate School of Education, University of California at Los Angeles.

Gaff, J. G. (1973). Making a difference: the impacts of faculty. *Journal of Higher Education*, Nov., 605–622.

Gagne, R. M. (1977). *The Conditions of Learning*, 3rd ed. New York: Holt, Rinehart, & Winston.

Gamson, Z. F. and associates (1984). *Liberating Education*. San Francisco: Jossey-Bass (Cited in the text as Gamson.)

Grose, R. F. (1976). The use of academic histories in decisionmaking. Paper presented at the Third Annual Meeting of the Northeast Association of Institutional Research.

Guba, E. G. (1969). The failure of educational evaluation. *Educational Technology* 9: 29–38.

Guilford, J. P. (1967). *The Nature of Human Intelligence*. New York: McGraw-Hill.

Hanson, G. R. (1982). Critical issues in the assessment of student development. In G. R. Hanson (ed.), *Measuring Student Development*. New Directions for Student Services, No. 20. San Francisco: Jossey-Bass.

Harris, J. (1986). Assessing outcomes in higher education. In Adelman, *Assessment in American Higher Education*, pp. 13-31.

Harris, J. (1970). Gain scores on the CLEP general examination and an overview of research. Paper presented at the annual meeting of AERA, Minneapolis.

Harshman, C. L. (1979). *A Model for Assessing the Quality of Non-Traditional Programs in Higher Education*. St. Louis: Metropolitan College, St. Louis University.

Hartle, T. W. (1986). The growing interest in measuring the educational achievement of students. In Adelman, *Assessment in American Higher Education*, pp. 1–11.

Hartnett, R., and Centra, J. (1977). The effects of academic departments on student learning. *Journal of Higher Education* 48: 491–507.

Heath, D. (1968). *Growing Up in College*. San Francisco: Jossey-Bass.

Hossler, D. (1986). *Creating Effective Enrollment Management Systems*. New York: College Entrance Examination Board.

Hossler, D. (1984). *Enrollment Management: An Integrated Approach*. New York: College Entrance Examination Board.

Iverson, B. K., Pascarella, E. T., and Terenzini, P. T. (1984). Informal faculty-student contact and commuter college freshmen. *Research in Higher Education* 21: 123–136.

Katchadourian, H. A., and Boli, J. (1985). *Careerism and Intellectualism Among College Students*. San Francisco: Jossey-Bass.

Kees, D. J. (1974). The Clark-Trow typology revisited. *Journal of College Student Personnel* 15: 140–144.

Kemerer, F. R., Baldridge, J. V., and Green, K. C. (1982). *Strategies for Effective Enrollment Management*. Washington, DC: AASCU.

Kinnick, M. K. (1985). Increasing the use of student outcomes information. In Ewell, *Assessing Educational Outcomes*, pp. 93–110.

Kleemann, G. L., and Richardson, R. C., Jr. (1985). Student characteristics and perceptions of university effectiveness. *Review of Higher Education* 9: 5–20.

Korn, H. A. (1986). Psychological models explaining the impact of college on students. Ann Arbor: NCRIPTAL at University of Michigan.

Kuh, G. D., Bean, J. P., Bradley, R. K., Coomes, M. D., and Hunter, D. E. (1986). Changes in research on college students published in selected journals between 1969 and 1983. *Review of Higher Education* 9: 177–192.

Lacy, W. (1978). Interpersonal relationships as mediators of structural effects: college student socialization in a traditional and an experimental university environment. *Sociology of Education* 51: 201–211.

Learned, W. S., and Wood, B. D. (1938). *The Student and His Knowledge: A Report to the Carnegie Foundation on the Results of the High School and College Examinations of 1928, 1930, and 1932*. New York: Carnegie Foundation for the Advancement of Teaching.

Lenning, O. T. (1977). *Previous Attempts to Structure Educational Outcomes and Outcome-Related Concepts: A Compilation and Review of the Literature*. Boulder, CO: NCHEMS.

Lenning, O. T. (1974). *The Benefits Crisis in Higher Education*. Washington, DC: American Association of Higher Education.

Lenning, O. T., Beal, P. E., and Sauer, K. (1980). *Retention and Attrition: Evidence for Action and Research*. Boulder, CO: NCHEMS.

Lenning, O. T., Lee, Y. S., Micek, S. S., and Service, A. L. (1977). *A Structure for the Outcomes and Outcome-Related Concepts: A Compilation and Review of the Literature*. Boulder, CO: NCHEMS.

Lenning, O., Munday, L., and Maxey, J. (1969). Student educational growth during the first two years of college. *College and University* 44: 145–153.

Leslie, L. L., and Brinkman, P. T. (1986). Rates of return to higher education: an intensive examination. In J. C. Smart (ed.), *Higher Education: Handbook of Theory and Research*, Vol. II, pp. 207–234. New York: Agathon Press.

Levy, R. A. (1986). Development of performance funding criteria by the Tennessee Higher Education Commission: a chronology and evaluation. In Banta, *Performance Funding in Higher Education*, pp. 13–26.

Lindquist, J., ed. (1981a). *Increasing the Use of Institutional Research*. New Directions for Institutional Research, No. 32. San Francisco: Jossey-Bass.

Lindquist, J. (1981b). Quick, dirty, and useful. In J. Lindquist (ed.), *Increasing the Use of Institutional Research*. New Directions for Institutional Research, No. 32, pp. 87–97. San Francisco: Jossey-Bass.

March, J. G. (1984). How we talk and how we act: administrative theory and administrative life. In T. J. Sergiovanni and J. E. Corbally (eds.), *Leadership and Organizational Culture*. Urbana, IL: University of Illinois Press.

Marton, F. (1979). Skill as an aspect of knowledge. *Journal of Higher Education* 50 (Sept./Oct.): 602–614.

McClain, C. J. (1984). *In Pursuit of Degrees with Integrity: A Value-Added Approach to Undergraduate Assessment*. Washington, DC: AASCU.

McClain, C. J., and Krueger, D. W. (1985). Using outcomes assessment: a case study in institutional change. In Ewell, *Assessing Educational Outcomes*, pp. 33–46.

McKeachie, W. J., Pintrich, P. R., Lin, Y., and Smith, D. A. F. (1986). *Teaching and Learning in the College Classroom: A Review of the Research Literature*. Ann Arbor: NCRIPTAL at University of Michigan, 1986.

McMillan, J. H. (1987). Enhancing college students' critical thinking: a review of studies. *Research in Higher Education* 26: 3–29.

Mentkowski, M., and Doherty, A. (1984). *Careering After College: Establishing the Validity of Abilities*

Learned in College for Later Careering and Performance. Milwaukee: Alverno Productions.

Mentkowski, M., and Loacker, G. (1985). Assessing and validating the outcomes of college. In Ewell, *Assessing Educational Outcomes*, pp. 47–64.

Messick, S., and associates (1976). *Individuality in Learning*. San Francisco: Jossey-Bass.

Moos, R. H. (1979). *Evaluating Educational Environments*. San Francisco: Jossey-Bass.

National Governors' Association (1986). *Time for Results: The Governors' 1991 Report on Education*. Washington, DC: NGA.

National Institute of Education, Study Group on the Conditions of Excellence in American Higher Education (1984). *Involvement in Learning: Realizing the Potential of American Higher Education*. Washington, DC: U.S. Government Printing Office.

Nettles, M. T. (1987). The emergence of college outcome assessments: prospects for enhancing state colleges and universities. Trenton: New Jersey State College Governing Boards Association.

Newman, D. L., Brown, R. D., and Braskamp, L. A. (1980). Communication theory and the utilization of evaluation. In L. Braskamp and R. D. Brown (eds.), *Utilization of Evaluative Information*. New Directions for Program Evaluation, No. 5, pp. 29–35. San Francisco: Jossey-Bass.

Nichols, R. (1964). Effects of various college characteristics on student aptitude test scores. *Journal of Educational Psychology* 55: 45–54.

Pace, C. R. Perspectives and problems in student outcomes research. In Ewell, *Assessing Educational Outcomes*, pp. 7–18.

Pace, C. R. (1984). *Measuring the Quality of College Student Experiences*. Los Angeles: Higher Education Research Institute at the University of California, Los Angeles.

Pace, C. R. (1979). *Measuring the Outcomes of College*. San Francisco: Jossey-Bass.

Pace, C. R. (1974). *The Demise of Diversity: A Comparative Profile of Eight Types of Institutions*. Berkeley: The Carnegie Commission on Higher Education.

Pace, C. R. (1972). *Education and Evangelism*. New York: McGraw-Hill.

Pace, C. R. (1963). *Preliminary Technical Manual: College and University Environment Scales*. Princeton, NJ: Educational Testing Service.

Pace, C. R., and Baird, L. (1966). Attainment parameters in the environmental press of college subcultures. In T. Newcomb and E. Wilson (eds.), *College Peer Groups*. Chicago: Aldine.

Palola, E. G. (1981). Multiple perspectives, multiple channels. In Lindquist, *Increasing the Use of Institutional Research*, pp. 45–58.

Palola, E. G., and Lehmann, T. (1976). Improving student outcomes and institutional decisionmaking with PERC. In O. T. Lenning (ed.), *Improving Educational Outcomes*, New Directions for Higher Education, No. 16, pp. 73–92.

Pascarella, E. T. (1987). Are value-added analyses valuable? In ETS, *Assessing the Outcomes of Higher Education*, pp. 71–91.

Pascarella, E. T. (1985a). College environmental influences on learning and cognitive development: a critical review and synthesis. In J. C. Smart (ed.), *Higher Education: Handbook of Theory and Research*, Vol. I, pp. 1–61. New York: Agathon Press.

Pascarella, E. T. (1985b). Students' affective development within the college environment. *Journal of Higher Education* 56 (Nov./Dec.): 640–663.

Pascarella, E. T. (1984). Reassessing the effects of living on-campus versus commuting to college: a causal modelling approach. *Review of Higher Education* 7: 247–260.

Pascarella, E. T., and Terenzini, P. T. (1980). Predicting freshman persistence and voluntary dropout decisions from a theoretical model. *Journal of Higher Education* 51 (Jan./Feb.): 60–75.

Pascarella, E. T., Terenzini, P. T., and Wolfle, L. M. (1986). Orientation to college and freshman year persistence/withdrawal decisions. *Journal of Higher Education* 57 (Mar./Apr.).

Perry, W. J., Jr. (1970). *Forms of Intellectual and Ethical Development in the College Years: A Schema*. New York: Holt, Rinehart, & Winston.

Peterson, M. W., Cameron, K. S., Mets, L. A., Jones, P., and Ettington, D. (1986). *The Organizational Context for Teaching and Learning: A Review of the Research Literature*. Ann Arbor: NCRIPTAL, University of Michigan.

Porter, O. (1982). The role of quality of effort in defining institutional environments: An attempt to understand college uniqueness. Ph.D. dissertation, Graduate School of Education, University of California at Los Angeles.

Resnick, D., and Goulden, M. (1987). Assessment, curriculum and expansion in American higher education: a historical perspective. In Diane Halpern (ed.), *Student Assessment: A Tool for Improving Teaching and Learning*. San Francisco: Jossey-Bass.

Robertshaw, D., and Wolfle, L. (1982). The cognitive value of two-year colleges for whites and blacks. *Integrated Education* 19: 68–71.

Romney, L. C., Bogen, G., and Micek, S. S. (1979). Assessing institutional performance: the importance of being *careful*. *International Journal of Institutional Management in Higher Education* 3 (May): 79–89.

Sarason, S. B. (1972). *The Creation of Settings and the Future Societies*. San Francisco: Jossey-Bass.

Schalock, H. D. (1976). Structuring process to improve student outcomes. In O. T. Lenning (ed.), *Improving Educational Outcomes*. New Directions for Higher Education, No. 16. San Francisco: Jossey-Bass.

Shapiro, J. Z. (1986). Evaluation research and educational decisionmaking. In J. C. Smart (ed.), *Higher Education: Handbook of Theory and Research*, Vol. II, pp. 163–206. New York; Agathon Press.

Sheldon, M. S. (1981). *Statewide Longitudinal Study: 1978–81 Final Report.* Los Angeles, Los Angeles Pierce College.

Smart, J. C. (1982). Faculty teaching goals: a test of Holland's theory. *Journal of Educational Psychology* 74: 180–188.

Smith, H. L. (1986). Testimony for the National Governors' Association task force on college quality on behalf of the American Association of State Colleges and Universities. Washington, D.C.

Spaeth, J., and Greely, A. (1970). *Recent Alumni and Higher Education: A Survey of College Graduates.* New York: McGraw-Hill.

Stark, J. S., and Lowther, M. (1986). *Designing the Learning Plan: A Review of Research and Theory Related to College Curricula.* Ann Arbor: NCRIPTAL at University of Michigan.

Sternberg, R. J. (1985). *Beyond IQ: A Triarchic Theory of Human Intelligence.* Cambridge: Cambridge University Press.

Terenzini, P. T. The case for unobtrusive measures. In ETS, *Assessing the Outcomes of Higher Education,* pp. 47–61.

Terenzini, P. T., and Pascarella, E. T. (1977). Voluntary freshman attrition and patterns of social and academic integration in a university: a test of a conceptual model. *Research in Higher Education* 6: 25–43.

Terenzini, P. T., Pascarella, E. T., and Lorang, W. (1982). An assessment of the academic and social influences on freshman year educational outcomes. *Review of Higher Education* 5: 86–109.

Terenzini, P. T., and Wright, T. M. (1987). Students' personal growth during the first two years of college. Paper presented at the annual meeting of the Association for the Study of Higher Education, San Diego.

Theophilides, C., Terenzini, P. T., and Lorang, W. (1984). Relation between freshman year experience and perceived importance of four major educational goals. *Research in Higher Education* 20: 235–252.

Thomas, J. W., and Rohwer, W. D., Jr. (1986). Academic studying: the role of learning strategies. *Educational Psychologist* 21: 19–41.

Thrash, P. R. (1984). Accreditation and the evaluation of educational outcomes. Paper presented at a professional development session sponsored by the Council of Specialized Accrediting Agencies (CSAA) and the Council on Postsecondary Accreditation (COPA).

Tinto, V. (1975). Dropout from higher education: a theoretical synthesis of recent research. *Review of Educational Research* 45 (Winter): 89–125.

Trent, J. W., and Medsker, L. (1968). *Beyond High School: A Psychosociological Study of 10,000 High School Graduates.* San Francisco: Jossey-Bass.

Walleri, R. D., and Japely, S. M. (1986). Student intent, persistence, and outcomes. Paper delivered at the 26th Annual Forum of the Association for Institutional Research, Orlando, Fla.

Warren, J. (1984). The blind alley of value-added. *AAHE Bulletin,* Sept., pp. 10–13.

Wilson, R. C., Gaff, J. G., Dienst, E. R., Wood, L., and Barry, J. L. (1975). *College Professors and Their Impact on Students.* New York: Wiley.

Winter, D. G., McClelland, D. C., and Stewart, A. J. (1981). *A New Case for the Liberal Arts.* San Francisco: Jossey-Bass.

Faculty Workload and Productivity: Recurrent Issues with New Imperatives

Daniel T. Layzell

Introduction

One of the more highly charged and controversial topics pertaining to public higher education today is that of faculty workload and productivity. Powerful external constituencies—governors, legislators, business people, journalists, and the general public—see productivity as the key to evaluating higher education's claim on scarce resources. As such, the primary focus of this paper is on public higher education and is shaped by external views of the issue of faculty workload and productivity. Faculty productivity is clearly a complex and multidimensional issue; consequently, this paper reviews the literature on faculty workload and productivity from a broad perspective. The article covers the following topical areas:

- Issues in defining and measuring faculty workload and productivity
- Research on faculty workload and productivity
- Legislation, policies, and recent external actions relating to faculty workload and productivity
- Explanations for "declining" faculty workload and productivity

The literature included in this review represents a sampling of the most recent and representative pieces covering these topical areas. The paper ends with an assessment of where we are with this issue and some strategies for the future.

Why the Current Concern?

There are two primary reasons why faculty work and faculty productivity are currently in the spotlight. The first is that state funding for higher education—the major source of funding for public institution operating expenses—has waned in recent years. In some states it has even declined. Chief among the contributing factors have been struggling state budgets and increasing competition for limited state budget dollars from other state-funded services. The second reason is an increased interest in "accountability" for higher education at state and national levels. Accountability itself has become an umbrella for a variety of issues such as the quality of and access to undergraduate education, affordability, and administrative costs. While the laundry list of issues varies from state to state, the common thread running throughout is an increased emphasis on quality, outcomes, and product, primarily in undergraduate instruction.

Together, these factors have resulted in a resurgent interest in what faculty do, how much they work, and what they accomplish. Faculty salaries constitute a large portion of institutional budgets, and faculty therefore figure heavily in institutional economies. Concerns about the outcomes of higher education and accountability initiatives have, at their core, uncertainty and perhaps even skepticism about the entirety of faculty work. Most policymakers realize that faculty provide instruction to students. However, the other activities that fac-

"Faculty Workload and Productivity: Recurrent Issues with New Imperatives," by Daniel T. Layzell, reprinted from *Review of Higher Education*, Vol. 19, No. 3, Spring 1996. Association for the Study of Higher Education.

ulty engage in, such as research and service, are seen as at best tangential to the "true" mission of colleges and universities and at worst as not even remotely understood. A sharp reminder of this fact came recently in an interview with a Virginia legislator who, when asked about public interest in faculty research, said, "The vast majority of people aren't aware that research goes on" (in Pratt 1993, 16).

Some within public colleges and universities might find it tempting to ignore external concerns and wait for better fiscal days to come around again. Certainly, those with a sense of "institutional memory" will recognize the waxing and waning of these issues with changes in fiscal condition. Faculty workload and productivity are hardly new issues: they have surfaced at various times during the twentieth century, usually in times of fiscal downturn. However, it is not altogether certain that better fiscal days will return anytime soon, or that higher education will be anywhere near the head of the line when state budgets do improve. The results of the 1994 elections indicated that governmental reform, crime, public safety, and welfare reform are foremost on people's minds. To be fair, some researchers have argued that higher education is a "stagnant industry" due to its labor-intensive nature and that it is largely unable to implement significant productivity improvements through technology or other means (Levin 1991). However, the current signals from our external stakeholders are far too loud and clear to ignore. Denial and/or resignation to the roadblocks are not viable options. In short, there is a need to critically examine what is known and not known about faculty productivity.

Issues in Defining and Measuring Faculty Productivity

At the broadest level, *productivity* refers to the way in which a firm transforms inputs (e.g., labor and capital) into outputs (Hopkins 1990). In industrial settings, productivity is relatively easy to define and measure. One need only take a selected output for a firm and divide by the input of choice (e.g., per worker). Colleges and universities, however, are not steel mills or auto plants. While some inputs are quantifiable

(e.g., number of students, faculty time), "outcomes are diffuse, and difficult to measure" in higher education (Mingle and Lenth 1989, 13).

There are various reasons why the definition and measurement of productivity in higher education is so vexing.[1] One reason is related to the types of inputs and outputs in higher education. David Hopkins (1990) points out that for institutions of higher education there are both tangible and intangible inputs and outputs. Tangible inputs include such things as the number of new students, faculty time and effort, library holdings, and equipment. Intangible inputs include the quality of new students, the quality of the faculty, and so on. Tangible outputs include student enrollment in courses, the number of degrees awarded, and the number of scholarly works produced by the faculty. Intangible outputs include the quality of instruction provided in courses, the knowledge gained by students over their college careers, and the quality of faculty scholarship. Because of these "intangible" aspects of academic productivity, Hopkins notes that "all efforts to date at specifying and estimating the higher education production function have provided only partial results" (1990, 13). Thus, while we may be able to identify certain inputs and outputs in higher education (i.e., the "tangible"), capturing productivity in its entirety as some joint result of the tangible and intangible is unlikely at this point. While it can be said that firms in the private sector also must deal with the qualitative aspects of production, I would argue that it is much less of a measurement issue for the private firm, given its primary focus on such quantifiable aspects as unit cost and profit maximization.

The problem of being able to measure only "tangible" activities is further complicated by the fact that the primary activities of most institutions of higher education (instruction, research, and service) are often jointly produced by faculty. Thus, evaluating one specific aspect of production (e.g., contact hours in undergraduate courses) without controlling for the other activities that the faculty engages in provides an incomplete picture of faculty productivity. Further, increasing the production of one of these activities may come at the expense of the other. Hopkins (1990) also notes that for institutions of higher education, the joint production of undergraduate instruction and research/graduate instruction are subject to both the effects of complementarity and substitutability. Complementary effect means that, given any level of faculty resources, there is a small region on the production possibility curve in which an institution engaged almost exclusively in either undergraduate instruction or research/graduate instruction can produce more of each with no additional resources. Most institutions operate in the region of substitutability, however, meaning that increased production of undergraduate instruction results in less research/graduate instruction, and vice versa. In short, assuming no increase in faculty resources, increasing faculty productivity in undergraduate education may result in decreased productivity in graduate education and research activities. In fact, a recent study found a tradeoff between teaching productivity and research productivity (Gilmore and To 1992).[2]

Research on Faculty Workload and Productivity

Concerns about the hazards and shortfalls of defining and measuring productivity notwithstanding, there have been three broad categories of empirical studies aiming at a better understanding of faculty work and its products: faculty activity studies, instructional workload analyses, and noninstructional productivity.

Faculty Activity Studies

Analyses of faculty work activities are not new. Harold Yuker (1984) notes that the first study of faculty workloads occurred in 1919. Subsequent studies of this issue have shown a fairly consistent pattern of total hours worked and a fairly consistent distribution of faculty activity within the traditional tripartite workload model (instruction, research, and public service). While there are variations among different types of institutions, disciplines, and instructional staff types, faculty generally report working fifty to sixty hours per week, with approximately half of the time devoted to teaching and other instructional activities (Yuker 1984).

The 1988 National Survey of Postsecondary Faculty (NSOPF-1988) results were consistent with those of past studies. Full-time faculty at all institutions (public and private) reported working fifty-three hours per week in the fall of 1987 (Russell et al. 1991). Among the various types of public institutions, this average ranged from fifty-seven hours per week at research universities to forty-seven hours per week at two-year institutions. Data from this survey on the allocation of faculty time among the different workload categories indicate that for all institutions, faculty spend an average of 56 percent of their time in teaching activities, 16 percent in research, 13 percent in administration, and the remainder in community service and other activities. This distribution varied predictably among the various types of public institutions with faculty at research universities spending more time than average in research and faculty at comprehensive and two-year institutions spending more time than average in instructional activities.

Instructional Workload Studies

Another type of faculty productivity analysis focuses on the instructional workload of faculty. Typically such studies focus on average course loads, contact hours, and credit loads. Yuker (1984) reported that course loads in the United States tend to vary from six to fifteen credits per semester. His analysis of the literature also found the following variances:

- Type of institution: Faculty at research universities tend to have lighter teaching loads than faculty at comprehensive institutions and community colleges.

- Discipline: Faculty in the "soft" disciplines (e.g., humanities) tend to devote more time to instruction than faculty in the "hard" disciplines (e.g., sciences).

- Faculty rank: Studies have found an inverse relationship between rank and teaching load. Full professors tend to have the lightest teaching load while assistant professors and instructors tend to have the heaviest teaching loads.

NSOPF-88 examined two measures of instructional productivity: classroom contact hours and student contact hours.[3] In fall 1987, faculty at all institutions reported an average of 9.8 classroom contact hours and an average of 302 student contact hours for fall 1987 semester. Among public institutions, average classroom contact hours ranged from 6.6 at research universities to 15.2 at two-year institutions. Average student contact hours ranged from 259 at research universities to 427 at two-year institutions. Given that NSOPF-88 was essentially baseline data, evidence on trends in instructional productivity remain largely at the institutional level.[4] For example, Michael Middaugh and David Hollowell (1992) found in their study of instructional productivity at the University of Delaware between 1985 and 1991 that average faculty course loads, classroom contact hours, and student/faculty ratios all declined.

Productivity in Noninstructional Activities

Much of what is known about faculty productivity in noninstructional activities is descriptive and is confined to research activities. For example, NSOPF-88 found that faculty in research and doctoral institutions produced greater than average numbers of journal articles, books/book chapters and monographs than did faculty in comprehensive and two-year institutions. Variance across discipline areas was attributable somewhat to differences in modes of publication among disciplines. For example, faculty in the health sciences and natural sciences had above average numbers of journal articles while faculty in agriculture/home economics and engineering produced above average numbers of technical reports and nonrefereed articles.

Weaknesses of Current Workload and Productivity Analyses

The traditional ways of analyzing faculty workload and productivity examined here have a number of drawbacks. First, as noted previously, there is the problem of capturing the "intangible" inputs and outputs. Measuring the hours spent in a classroom or the number of journal articles produced tells us little about the quality of instruction provided or the quality of the scholarship. Unfortunately, while many have attempted to develop theoretical frame-

works incorporating these "intangible" aspects of academic productivity (e.g., Hopkins 1990), there have been no empirical studies to test their explanatory usefulness (Gilmore and To 1992). It is interesting to note here the observations of John W. Hicks commenting on faculty workload in a 1960 study: "To the best knowledge of the author, no objective study has ever been made of the relationship between quality of faculty performance and faculty workload. It is not at all certain that such a study could be made" (1960, 4). A generation later, we're no further along on this particular issue.

Another weakness related specifically to measures of instructional workload is the fact that such measures as average classroom contact hours do not account for the time spent by faculty in preparing for that class, time spent with students outside of the classroom, or other instruction-related activities. No algorithm is available to provide a reliable estimate of how faculty allocate these elements of their time, nor to estimate the outcomes associated with them.

A final weakness relating to faculty activity studies is in their reliance on self-reported data. While some researchers have argued that the consistency in the findings of faculty activity studies over time lend validity to such data (Jordan 1994), critics of such data note that it may result in inflated estimates of how much time faculty actually do spend at work or in the distribution of time among their various activities (Jordan 1994; Miller 1994). Critics outside the academy tend to give low weight to the validity of self-reported data. For example, in its 1993 evaluation of instructional workload in the University of Wisconsin System, the Wisconsin Legislative Audit Bureau (LAB) called such data "unreliable" (1993, 20).

Legislation, Policies, and Recent Activities

Much of the current flurry of activity involving the workload/productivity issue in public higher education has been driven by external interest, primarily from state legislators and other state policymakers. In May 1992, the State Higher Education Executive Officers (SHEEO) organization surveyed SHEEO agencies (typically coordinating boards) and multi-institutional system governing boards (including state community college boards) on faculty workload issues and other related concerns. All fifty states were included in the survey and SHEEO received responses from seventy-one coordinating boards and/or governing boards representing forty-five.

Existing or Pending Legislation

The SHEEO study found that seven states had existing legislation related to faculty teaching load or workload and an additional seven states were considering such legislation. Alene B. Russell's (1992) report of the SHEEO survey points out, however, that the intent of such legislation varies from state to state. Some states (e.g., Minnesota) simply require the reporting of faculty workloads to the legislature. Other states (e.g., Kentucky and Florida) require the reporting of workload information as part of a broader accountability initiative for higher education. Still others (e.g., Nevada) have legislation that recommends or sets standards for faculty workload.

Current Workload Policies and Standards

Of the seventy-one coordinating and multi-institution governing boards responding to the SHEEO survey, 28 (39.4 percent) had existing faculty teaching load/workload policies or standards and 18 (25.4 percent) were considering policies or standards. These forty-six boards represented thirty-four states. The responses generally did not provide much detail on existing policies and standards in the other states.

The data suggest that governing boards are much more likely to have existing faculty teaching load and workload policies than coordinating boards. Of the twenty-eight boards indicating existing policies and standards, twenty-five were governing boards or community college boards. However, even among governing boards, there were comments that the actual setting of teaching loads/workloads was at the campus level or lower, indicating a very decentralized process. Seven governing boards indicated that teaching loads were set through collective bargaining with faculty unions.

The responses also suggest, however, that there may be a move toward more centralized

activity. Of the twenty-seven state coordinating board respondents, nine reported that they were considering establishing policies or standards relating to faculty teaching load/workload, possibly indicating a trend toward more state-level involvement in this issue. In Texas the state coordinating board requires that campuses set their own policies and standards and then report back to the coordinating board on the level of compliance with these policies and standards. In Missouri, a task force established by the state coordinating board has recommended minimum average teaching loads for all tenured and tenure-track faculty by institutional type (nine contact hours at highly selective, selective, and research institutions and twelve hours at all other public four-year institutions).

Recent State-Level Activities

According to the *Chronicle for Higher Education*, twenty-four states conducted faculty workload studies in 1993–94 (Almanac, 12). Of particular interest, of course, is the amount of time that faculty spend in the classroom. A report in the January 1993 SHEEO/NCES Communication *Network News* highlighted four states currently addressing faculty workload and productivity: Arizona, Mississippi, Oregon, and Virginia. Case studies from these four states reveal patterns indicative of the external pressures that have made faculty workload and productivity a major issue nationally: state resource constraints; enrollment pressures/access concerns; and quality concerns ("Focus" 1993). Again, the activities of these four states suggest a more active role at the state level in addressing this issue, either through a state-level higher education board or in conjunction with the governor or legislature.

A recent study released by the Maryland Higher Education Commission (MHEC) went directly to the heart of the workload and productivity issue as seen by state policymakers: the potential budget savings resulting from increased faculty teaching loads (MHEC 1994). The MHEC analysis was based on a standard course load of eight courses per year at comprehensive institutions and five courses per year at research institutions, a figure derived from the American Association of University Professors' recommended standard. The analysis found potential budget savings of $34 mil-

592 ASHE Reader on Planning and Institutional Research

lion if core faculty in the University of Maryland System were teaching at the relevant standard. While somewhat simplistic, this analysis provides a powerful illustration of how state policymakers view this issue.

"Declining" Academic Productivity: Some Explanations

The research has not indicated that faculty are working any less now than before; however, there is some evidence of less time being spent overall in instructional activities, specifically at the undergraduate level (Jordan 1994). William Massy, a researcher at Stanford University, posits "the Ratchet" as the reason why faculty instructional productivity may be declining. "The Ratchet" works as follows for any given academic department (assuming constant or declining enrollments):

- Increases in the number of faculty in a department or in the leveraging of faculty time with lower cost teaching assistants or part-time instructional staff lead to a broader and more specialized curricular array for the department. They also lead to smaller classes because existing enrollments are spread out over a larger number of course offerings.

- This leads to a lower average teaching load for the faculty.

- The lowered average faculty teaching load leads to increased time spent in other activities, namely research and scholarship (Massy 1990, 13).

Massy and Robert Zemsky recently tested this concept using data collected from four liberal arts colleges and two research universities. They concluded that "research university departments prefer smaller teaching loads more fervently than do departments in the liberal arts colleges" (1994, 20). While this finding is hardly surprising, it does reinforce the popular perception that faculty at research institutions seek to maximize their discretionary time available for research and scholarship through lowered teaching loads.

As in any organization, colleges and universities have reward structures, incentives, and disincentives to develop certain behaviors.

Increasingly, we hear anecdotally that research and publications, not teaching, drive reward structures. As noted by James Mingle, Executive Director of the State Higher Education Executive Officers, "teaching credentials aren't very portable, while research credentials can carry one from institution to institution" (1993, 5). Among the evidence that the rewards go to researchers is a recent study by the National Center on Postsecondary Teaching, Learning, and Assessment, which found that for full-time tenure track faculty, generally:

- The more time spent on teaching and instruction, the lower the salary.

- The more time spent in the classroom, the lower the salary.

- The more time spent doing research, the higher the salary.

- The more publications one had, the higher the salary (Fairweather 1993).

These findings suggest that the rational faculty member would want to spend more time conducting research and less time in instructional activities. Again, there is evidence that this is the case. The 1988 National Survey of Postsecondary Faculty (NSOPF-88) posed the question, "If you changed jobs, would you want to do less, the same, or more teaching and research?" For all institutions, 50 percent of full-time faculty responding to that question chose more research while only 11 percent wanted more teaching. On the other hand, only 8 percent would want to do less research while 30 percent would want to do less teaching (Russell et al. 1991, 11). At a broader level, this trend speaks to the issue of faculty work within the context of institutional mission. Stephen Jordan (1994) notes that many institutions experienced "mission drift" recently—or a systematic movement away from the stated mission of an institution, typically from a focus on undergraduate instruction to an increased focus on research and graduate education. This, of course, fuels "the Ratchet" and pushes policymakers closer to the model of mandated workloads. In the words of one California legislator, "For years, universities faced with decreasing budgets would rather get rid of students than increase faculty workload. They all want to be like Harvard and lessen the teaching load. That can't continue" ("Higher Education" 1992, 20).

Conclusions and Future Strategies

This review yields three major conclusions:

- Traditional means of assessing faculty workload and productivity have yielded consistent results over time. However, these methods have numerous drawbacks, namely, the inability to account for such intangible aspects of productivity as the quality of output. They also fail to separate the results of joint production among several faculty activities.

- External interest in this issue is primarily driven by concerns over the cost of higher education and the quality and availability of undergraduate education.

- The focus still rests on the input side, not the output side, of the productivity function.

Clearly, we haven't come very far in how we look at this issue. So where do we go from here? The cynical and easy view would be to resign ourselves to the "fact" that faculty are convenient scapegoats for state budget-cutters in a period of fiscal stringency, and that it really doesn't matter what is done to improve productivity, because colleges and universities will still be criticized. This is not a particularly uplifting or satisfying solution, nor is it an accurate perception.

Alternatively we could be more proactive in "explaining" the many roles of faculty to the public. While we should be less obtuse and defensive about what faculty do and how they do it, improved public relations is no lasting solution to this issue. Knowing more about the research and service activities of faculty, while interesting and important, does little to meet this fundamental need nor does it assuage external concerns about accountability, access, or quality. We *know* that the incentives to do research are greater than those for instruction and we have a sense how this happens. What we haven't addressed is the means for satisfying the public's concerns about quality and outcomes.

So where do we go from here? I see a combined strategy of addressing both the process and measurement of faculty workload and productivity as being necessary. The process aspect of the strategy encompasses the issues of inputs and outputs; it works on maximizing

faculty talents within the role and mission of the institution. Bruce Johnstone argues that increasing faculty teaching loads in response to productivity concerns is simply a short-run fix that, in the end, actually results in declines in productivity. Instead, he argues that the focus should be on learning productivity: "Learning productivity relates the input of faculty and staff not to enrollments or to courses taught or to credit or classroom hours assigned, but to learning—i.e., the demonstrated mastery of a defined body of knowledge or skills" (1993, 2). This approach shifts the attention from the amount of time faculty spend in the classroom to the learning gained by students in the classroom within a given period of time. He feels that, with the right incentives and structuring of the curriculum, students could learn more in shorter periods of time, resulting in increased productivity. Johnstone notes, "Learning is more productive when it masters a given body of skills in less time and/or with less costly inputs" (p. 3). In short, this viewpoint changes the focus on productivity from the input side to the output side. Such an approach requires a clear sense of focus and timing in the curriculum as well as clear expectations for faculty.

I agree with Johnstone's model. Viewing the issue in terms of increased undergraduate *learning* productivity that is framed by clear expectations and outcomes for both teacher *and* student begins to get to the heart of these concerns. In the end, outcomes are the heart of the productivity issue. This is not to say that we should or even can lose track of the traditional inputs to the process. As stewards of public funds, public colleges and universities must remain mindful of their resources. However, inputs don't have to be the main focus. Improving the quality and quantity of student learning (with the same inputs) in a faster period of time would be a *real* productivity improvement that could place the focus where it matters most—student outcomes.

Further, such an approach does not diminish the role or importance of graduate education and research or service. It also does not mean that the emphasis on or content of undergraduate education would be the same at every institution. However, it does mean that there needs to be a clear, articulated vision of what undergraduate education is about and the expected role of the faculty therein at every institution.

Another major component of productivity improvement is in the maximization of faculty talents within the role and mission of the institution. One potential model is the Tenured Faculty Review and Development Policy currently being implemented by the University of Wisconsin System at all of its campuses (two doctoral campuses, eleven comprehensive campuses, thirteen freshman-sophomore centers). This policy, adopted by the UW Board of Regents in 1992, "aims to promote continuing growth and development in faculty professional skills and to encourage faculty to explore new ways to promote academic excellence. It also seeks to provide assurances of accountability to the public" (Portch, Kaufman, and Ross 1993, 17). The policy is being implemented through each campus's academic governance structure. Through this policy, the performance and activities of each tenured faculty member in the UW System are reviewed every five years in accordance with the mission of the faculty member's institution.

Two key aspects of the Wisconsin policy are the review criteria employed and the linkage of the review to the institutional reward structure. Henry Levin (1991) notes that one key to improved productivity in higher education is to develop a clear set of goals for the institution that are directly linked to the institution's mission and to back them up with incentives. By doing so, academic departments get signals about the overall priorities of the institution and can act accordingly.

The second aspect of this strategy addresses the measurement of faculty workload and productivity. For good or ill, policymakers and the public need measures of faculty work and productivity. Certainly there will be internal needs for improved measures to evaluate our own efforts, both from the input and output sides of the productivity issue. As previously described, a number of weaknesses hamper current methods of measuring faculty workload and productivity. However, "if members of the higher education community do not develop credible and sophisticated alternatives, the public and its representatives will apply their common sense definitions and categories to the academy, and the fit is often a bad one" (Miller 1994, 12). Measures will have to cover inputs and outputs, both tangible and intangible, and should not only be objective and

methodologically rigorous but also accessible to our external stakeholders. In short, "these analyses must combine hard data with explanatory narrative that is comprehensible to the college educated nonacademic" (Miller 1994, 13).

In conclusion, the measures I propose here are but one strategy for beginning to address the faculty workload and productivity conundrum. There are, no doubt, other viable strategies. Lurking behind these high-minded ideals, however, is a very real and practical imperative. Both the SHEEO survey and the Maryland study spell out that if higher education does not begin to fashion creative solutions to the *real* concerns of the public, potentially less desirable solutions will be fashioned to "fix" the situation.

Daniel T. Layzell *is Director of the Office of Policy Analysis and Research at the University of Wisconsin System. The genesis of this review essay is a commissioned paper the author cowrote in January 1994 with* Dr. Cheryl D. Lovell, *then of the National Center for Higher Education Management Systems (NCHEMS) and now at State Higher Education Executive Officers (SHEEO), and with Dr. Judith Gill, then of the Western Interstate Commission for Higher Education and now at the Massachusetts Higher Education Council. However, he is solely responsible for the contents of this essay.*

Notes

1. The term "productivity" in this essay refers to academic productivity only (i.e., what faculty produce).
2. Some economists have hypothesized that if the production of one service supports another, then the joint production of each may be more efficient than producing each one separately—"economies of scope" (Halstead 1991). Paul Brinkman (1990) notes that there have been few studies of this issue, although there is some evidence that economies of scope do exist for instruction and research.
3. "Classroom contact hours" are the number of hours spent teaching group instruction courses. "Student contact hours" are the number of hours spent teaching group instruction courses multiplied by the numbers of students in those courses.
4. A follow-up study to NSOPF-88, the 1993 National Survey of Postsecondary Faculty (NSOPF-93), has been completed. A series of analytical reports on the results of NSOPF-93, including comparisons with NSOPF-88, will

be released by the National Center for Education Statistics in the spring or summer of 1995.

Bibliography

Almanac Issue. *Chronicle of Higher Education*, 1 September 1994.

Brinkman, Paul. "Higher Education Cost Functions." In *The Economics of American Universities*, edited by Stephen Hoenack and Eileen Collins, 107–28. Albany, N.Y.: SUNY Press, 1990.

Fairweather, James. *Teaching, Research, and Faculty Rewards: A Summary of the Research Findings of the Faculty Profile Project.* University Park, Pa.: National Center on Postsecondary Teaching, Learning, and Assessment, 1993.

"Focus on Faculty Data: Workload, Productivity, and Other Issues." *SHEEO/NCES Network News*, 12, no. 1 (January 1993): whole issue.

Gilmore, Jeffrey, and Duc To. "Evaluating Academic Productivity and Quality." In *Containing Costs and Improving Productivity in Higher Education*, edited by Carol Hollins, 35–47. New Directions for Institutional Research, No. 75. San Francisco: Jossey-Bass, 1992.

Halstead, Kent. *Higher Education Revenues and Expenditures: A Study of Institutional Costs.* Washington, D.C.: Research Associates of Washington, 1991.

Hicks, John W. "Faculty Workload—An Overview." In *Faculty Workload: A Conference Report*, edited by Kevin Bunnell, 3–11. Washington, D.C.: American Council on Education, 1960.

"Higher Education Strategy," *State Policy Reports* 10, no. 5 (March 1992): 17–20.

Hopkins, David. "The Higher Education Production Function: Theoretical Foundations and Empirical Findings." In *The Economics of American Universities*, edited by Stephen Hoenack and Eileen Collins, 11–32. Albany, N.Y.: SUNY Press, 1990.

Johnstone, D. Bruce. "Learning Productivity: A New Imperative for American Higher Education." *SUNY Studies in Public Higher Education*, No. 3. Albany, N.Y.: State University of New York, April 1993.

Jordan, Stephen M. "What We Have Learned About Faculty Workload: The Best Evidence." In *Analyzing Faculty Workload*, edited by Jon F. Wergin, 15–24. New Directions for Institutional Research, No. 83. San Francisco: Jossey-Bass, 1994.

Levin, Henry. "Raising Productivity in Higher Education." *Journal of Higher Education* 61, no. 5 (1991): 241–62.

Maryland Higher Education Commission. "Core Faculty Teaching and the Enhancement of Campus Budget Flexibility." *Currents* 1 (March 1994): whole issue.

Massy, William. "The Dynamics of Academic Productivity." In *The Dynamics of Academic Productivity: Proceedings from a SHEEO Seminar*, 1–27. Denver, Colo.: State Higher Education Executive Officers, March 1990.

Massy, William F., and Robert Zemsky. "Faculty Discretionary Time: Departments and the 'Academic Ratchet.'" *Journal of Higher Education* 65, no. 1 (January/February 1994): 1–22.

Middaugh, Michael, and David Hollowell. "Examining Academic and Administrative Productivity Measures." In *Containing Costs and Improving Productivity in Higher Education*, edited by Carol Hollins, 61–76. New Directions for Institutional Research, No. 75. San Francisco: Jossey-Bass, 1992.

Miller, Margaret A. "Pressures to Measure Faculty Work." In *Analyzing Faculty Workload*, edited by Jon F. Wergin, 5–14. New Directions for Institutional Research, No. 83. San Francisco: Jossey-Bass, 1994.

Mingle, James. "Faculty Work and the Costs/Quality/Access Collision." *AAHE Bulletin* 45, no. 7 (March 1993): 3–6, 13.

Mingle, James, and Charles Lenth. "A New Approach to Accountability and Productivity in Higher Education." Denver, Colo.: State Higher Education Executive Officers, 1989.

Portch, Stephen R., Nancy J. Kaufman, and Jacqueline R. Ross. "From Frog to Prince: From Posttenure Review to Faculty Development and Roles." *Change* 25, no. 4 (July/August 1993): 17.

Pratt, Anne. "Public Perceptions, Public Policy" *AAHE Bulletin* 46, no. 3, 15–17, November 1993.

Russell, Alene B. *Faculty Workload: State and System Perspectives.* Denver, Colo.: State Higher Education Executive Officers, November 1992.

Russell, Susan H., Robert S. Cox, Cynthia Williamson, James Boismier, Harold Javitz, James Fairweather. *Profiles of Faculty in Higher Education Institutions, 1988* (Contractor report on 1988 National Survey of Postsecondary Faculty-NSOPF 88), NCES 91–389. Washington, D.C.: U.S. Department of Education, Office of Educational Research and Improvement, 1991.

Wisconsin Legislative Audit Bureau. *An Evaluation of Instructional Workload in The University of Wisconsin System, Report 93–15.* Madison: Wisconsin Legislative Audit Bureau, June 1993.

Yuker, Harold. *Faculty Workload: Research, Theory, and Interpretation.* ASHE-ERIC Higher Education Research Report, No. 10. Washington, D.C.: Association for the Study of Higher Education, 1984.

People, Processes, and Managing Data

G. W. McLaughlin, R. A. Howard, L. A. Balkan, and E. W. Blythe

Chapter 1: Information and the Organization

The second requirement of knowledge-based innovation is a clear focus on the strategic position. It cannot be introduced tentatively. The fact that the introduction of the innovation creates excitement, and attracts a host of others, means that the innovator has to be right the first time. He is unlikely to get a second chance. (Drucker, p. 117)

In all sectors of our society and economy, information is used to reduce the level of uncertainty in decision making. It is both an intuitive and methodical process by which more knowledge about the environment is accumulated. Our educational institutions are no exception. Higher education is facing serious management challenges as institutions cope with rapidly changing technology, a fluctuating economy, and increasing demands to produce more with less. These challenges change the way decisions are made, what data are useful, and what data are necessary. All organizations are challenged to create an environment where relevant and usable information can be accessed when needed by both employees and management.

Making Data Usable

The effectiveness of institutional research in supporting an institution's decision making depends heavily on the availability of usable data. Usable implies that the data are sufficiently accurate, timely, and collected systematically. The institutional research function is often called upon to provide data or create usable information to depict history, describe the current status, and anticipate the future. There are natural barriers which limit the value of data and information.

Data problems are mentioned most often as the major barrier limiting the effectiveness of institutional research and, as such, planning and decision making. Unfortunately, there is often a lack of understanding about the way that the data should be used, skepticism about the validity of the data, distrust because of obvious data defects or errors, lack of access to the data, and often only lukewarm management support for remedying these problems.

The most common factors which limit data quality and which have been identified over the years at professional gatherings of people who do institutional research include:

Consistency of data definitions. Limiting factors here include no agreement on definitions; incorrect interpretations; data collected in varying forms across campus; and, lack of adequate comprehensive measures.

Technology. Obstacles here are unsophisticated computer programs; lack of tools to maintain, transfer and analyze data; poor data collection processes; lack of data management tools; and, lack of ability to support distributed decision making.

Data Access. Problems in data access include the inability to access data, and limited

Ch. 1: "Information and the Organization," Ch. 2: "Something New: Management Information," reprinted from *People, Processes, and Managing Data* by G. W. McLaughlin, R. A. Howard, L. A. Balkan, and E.W. Blythe, 1998. Association for Institutional Research.

user knowledge about what data exist and where those data can be obtained.

The improvement of data is critical to the success of the institutional research function's ability to add value to our institutions planning and decision making, and is closely associated with many of our traditional functions. Years of experience tell us that there is no single best way to deal with the need to improve data quality. There are, however, some strategies which are more likely to be successful. In total, they amount to creating a data management culture across the organization.

While the data do not need to be perfect, they do need to be good enough to meet the needs of the institution. To achieve appropriate data quality, an organization first needs to understand itself. The discussion of managing data needs to start with an understanding of common problems that plague our organizations. All organizations are unique, but they do have some common characteristics. The stage for using data must be set in terms of the organization's ability to learn. As noted earlier, the use of data is a learning process. The ability to manage the information infrastructure is a learned process, and institutional research is a process of assimilating information to support institutional learning. And, as stated earlier, increased knowledge and understanding reduces uncertainty in decision making.

Disabilities in Learning to Improve

Peter Senge, in his book *The Fifth Discipline,* provides two views of organizations. One view examines the learning disabilities, which can exist in an organization. The second view presents the organization as a learning organization, which uses the knowledge it acquires to continually improve. Senge's organizational learning disabilities (discussed below) are extremely appropriate when applied to the challenges we face when trying to use data to support decision making.

I am my position. People in the institution focus only on their tasks and have little concern for how this affects other people. Data flows across numerous desks and functional lines in the organization. The registrar who only works to clean data for registrar functions will never be a source of usable student data for other needs. The vice president who only wants

clean summaries will never be the source of high quality detail data. The department head, who needs restructured data based at the program level, has little reason to input better data into a faculty timetable system.

The enemy is out there. Each of us has a tendency to blame people outside our immediate unit or department for organizational problems. Since data must flow across organizational lines, blaming others for data problems is natural. If systems are put in place that allow and expect blame, then data will always be a strong candidate for fault. Since perfect data only exist as a fantasy, the means, motive, and opportunity exist for blaming others for faults in the data, and for abdicating responsibility.

The illusion of taking charge. Many of our reward systems require that the leader get in front and do something. This is particularly expected when an obvious problem exists. Every so often, there will be a glaring problem with the data resulting in situations such as people who are deceased being invited to the president's reception, some receiving several invitations, or alumni, who have graduated, being contacted and asked why they are no longer enrolled. "Take-charge" leadership to quickly resolve such problems can be disastrous when the take-charge person does not understand complex technical processes. While symptoms are addressed, the underlying problems remain, with opportunities for real improvement displaced by hostilities directed at short-sighted, reactionary solutions.

The fixation on events. As a continuation of the take-charge process, the leader is prone to focus on events rather than results. *Data management is a process* that tends to focus on improving ineffective structures and events. As such, it is very difficult to maintain the support of a sponsor or senior manager while continuously focusing on errors. The presence of good information is difficult to demonstrate as an event because it is simply assumed or expected. Furthermore, data improvement does not lend itself to being an exciting key performance indicator.

The parable of the boiled frog. If you throw a frog into boiling water, it will jump out. This, of course, makes some assumptions about the frog, the water, and the pot. If, however, the frog is placed in warm water, as the water is slowly brought to boiling, the frog will not hop out (at least this is what the book says). The availability of detailed data has gradually attracted the increased interest and awareness of senior executives to the point where data access is sometimes an ego trip rather than the means for better decisions. Substituting "detail" for "intelligence" often occurs gradually until the data manager is confronted with the "awash in a sea of data" accusation by those who suddenly realize that they do not "know" any more than they did in the years before the arrival of executive information systems (EIS).

The delusion of learning from experiences. "We learn best from experience but we never directly experience the consequences of many of our most important decisions" (Senge, p. 23). Some critical decisions are the hardware and software purchases made by the institution. The choice of a particular technology impacts many people other than those making the decisions, often several years after the decisions are made. While we learn from these experiences, sometimes painfully, we usually fail to apply this knowledge to the decision process. The decision process is often isolated from the experience.

The myth of the management team. Teams in organizations often tend to spend all their time fighting for turf, avoiding the hard decisions and avoiding things that make them look bad, all the while pretending to work as a cohesive team. This is strikingly similar to what has been referred to as the collegial process. For example, how many true team efforts exist between senior faculty and administrators? Yet data management requires the team effort of administrators and faculty. How many true team efforts occur between academics, facilities management, and financial administrators in a college or university? Yet these groups must combine management activities to capture, store, restructure, and deliver valid and reliable data. As we create credible data, the way decisions are made and the outcome of the decisions will change. This will ultimately shift the balance of power. Improved data is, therefore, a threat to some of the more powerful individuals at our institutions. This learning disability is the most regrettable, as it is the cumulative mechanism which allows and perhaps fosters the existence of the other disabilities.

A learning organization will not evolve naturally, but requires significant effort at all levels of the organization. The institutional research function is positioned to be an effective force in this evolution. Enhancing the value of data to create knowledge is traditionally an expectation of institutional research offices, growing out of a history of institutional research as a user, a producer, and sometimes the source of data for key institutional decisions. The institutional research function at most institutions has the relevant experience and expertise to meet the challenge of providing or facilitating effective data management to support the learning organization.

The Learning Disciplines

With the backdrop of the organizational learning disabilities as they relate to data management, consider Senge's alternative for creating a learning organization that would provide the foundation for meeting the data management challenges. The following are antidotes and vaccines for the learning disabilities. They provide a way to either eliminate the learning disabilities, or reduce their impact on the organization. The examples provided with each discipline demonstrate sound data management as an integral part of the foundation for organizational change.

Personal Mastery. Personal mastery is founded on personal competence and skills, and extends to an awareness of the opportunities to evolve one's life as a creative work. Mastery requires applying an understanding of current reality to the shaping of one's future. The strategy used in writing this monograph was to focus on the mastery of skills in areas most appropriate to individuals working with institutional data. We hope this will help to identify and guide in the development of skills necessary to provide data and information as one component of a credible and stable decision-making infrastructure.

Those who would help or lead others are advised by Senge: "The core leadership strategy is simple: be a model. Commit yourself to your own personal mastery. Talking about personal mastery may open people's minds somewhat, but actions always speak louder than words. There's nothing more powerful you can do to encourage others in their quest for personal mastery than to be serious in your own quest" (Senge, p. 173).

Mental Models. ". . . the discipline of managing mental models—surfacing, testing, and improving our internal pictures of how the world works—promises to be a major breakthrough for building learning organizations" (Senge, p. 174). This monograph supports the development and use of mental models by presenting the process of managing data as a conceptual model having five functions, three roles, and two properties. We develop the five functions in Chapter 3 and the three roles in Chapters 4, 5, and 6. Finally, in Chapter 7, the two properties of the model are discussed.

We feel that the development of a mental model is itself one of the integral parts of successful data management. The refinement of this model comes after the use of data to influence a situation, frequently by a decision being made. It is when a decision is made that we see the value of structuring data to create information which is finally transformed into organizational intelligence. However, because our model is circular, the process is iterative. It is always necessary to review the process of creating the information and the usefulness of the information to the decision maker. Our model supports the learning organization precisely because it represents a process of continuous reduction of uncertainty and improvement.

Shared Vision. Shared vision occurs when multiple individuals have a deep commitment to a commonly held purpose. Individuals are bound together by shared aspirations. The best shared visions reflect, and extend, the visions of individuals. As described in Chapter 2, our vision for data management is simple: *Quality in our organizations must be supported by quality in our data.* This vision, as represented by our circular model, is quality through knowledge and knowledge from learning. The best management is a process by which adjustments and key decisions are supported in an intelligence-rich environment in which the focus is on continued learning. For a vision to be accepted, it must become a shared vision. Shared vision is only possible if it is understood to be constantly evolving.

Team Learning. Team learning occurs when there is an alignment of the individual team members in the process of working together toward the next higher level of awareness. There are three critical dimensions. First, there is a need to think insightfully about complex is-

sues. Second, learning is supported by innovative coordinated actions. Third, there is a need to identify and use multiple tools for data access and retrieval. The roles described in Chapters 4, 5, and 6 are intended to support the development of teams, which function across these three dimensions. We suggest processes and activities by which teams can work to fulfill the necessary roles. Additionally, in Chapter 5, we identify and discuss various groups that can be formed to learn collaboratively and work cooperatively toward data management goals. In Chapter 7, a discussion of lessons learned and issues related to the change process, provides a background of shared experiences so that others can more quickly develop innovative coordinated actions.

Systems Thinking. The fundamental "information problem faced by managers is not too little information, but too much information. What we most need are ways to know what is important and what is not important, what variables to focus on and which to pay less attention to . . . and we need ways to do this which can help groups or teams develop shared understanding" (Senge, p. 129). Systems thinking involves seeing fewer parts and looking at the whole. By building on a circular model with the interlocking roles, we present a very complex process as a system. By identifying problems and symptoms, we provide a structured way of thinking about this system and thereby simplify it. There can be no quality in the management of data unless all the parts work together and recognize their interdependence. This interdependence implies willingness to adapt and to change, as does the Information Support Circle, continually improving and evolving data to intelligence. In the final chapter, we discuss change as a systematic process.

Institutional Research and a Strategy for Change

The institutional research function can be an effective change agent in a cultural evolution, leading institutions toward becoming true learning organizations. This monograph provides a basic strategy from which institutional researchers can influence the major stakeholders in this evolution through a process of continually improving data quality, extending and expanding the use of management information across our institutions of higher learning.

The management of data and the ability of an organization to learn are intrinsically linked. The improvement of decision making comes from the increase of organizational intelligence. The symbiotic relationship between reduced uncertainty and organizational intelligence evidences the need for a close linkage between the learning organization and the improved management of data. The management of data, as we think of it, fits the paradigm for discussing the learning organization. Unfortunately, the learning disabilities discussed above also fit.

Institutional research has an interest in the proper performance of key activities in functions which are responsible for creating planning and decision support information. It has an interest in the effective performance of the roles in a learning culture. Above all, it has an ongoing responsibility to affect change and learning by adding value to institutional data and information in our colleges and universities.

In the next chapter, we focus on describing the basis for our own learning that led to the creation of a conceptual model for achieving effective data management and information support. Chapter 2 begins with a basic view of the organization and the organizational roles that relate to information.

Chapter 2 Something New: Management Information

The critical issue is not one of tools and systems but involvement in the quality efforts of the business units. (Radding, p. 100)

The impact of technology on our organizations is changing the way we do business. Just as the automobile changed from a luxury to a necessity, information technology is now integrated into the way we manage our institutions. An IBM advertising campaign once called for "new ideas for new challenges." This concept has three key elements relevant to those who work with information. First, there is a strong theme of change. New is the norm and change is the standard. A second theme is survival in

the face of challenges. The way we do everything is subject to question because our world is changing at an ever increasing rate. This theme acknowledges the ever-present threat that, if we fail to adjust, we will become obsolete. A third theme is less apparent, but provides the key to open new doors as we close the old. This third theme uses the word "ideas" to show that thinking is the source of influence and change.

There is the belief that change will come from creating vision and from new ideas generated at all levels of our organizations. We ask the people at the pulse of every activity to interact and generate innovative ideas. The necessity of acquiring new skills and knowledge is accepted. The ability to learn new skills is critical. Ideas are molded into plans. Resources are reallocated to support training on the new and improved practices and products. Learning from others comes by generalizing from their experiences and avoids the unwarranted expense of everyone learning everything anew in an organizational culture of "fail and trail" and "discover and recover."

A key organizational challenge is to make better decisions and provide better support for stakeholders. Information support must enable managers and decision makers to:

1. understand a situation and recognize the need to take action;

2. identify and rank alternatives considering resources, causality, and desirability of outcomes;

3. select an alternative, act upon it; and,

4. validate and defend the action.

The successful use of information for decision support depends on an information support structure that assures the quality and availability of relevant data that can be restructured for use by the decision makers. The old ways of providing information support do not adequately support new ways of doing business. The disappearance of middle management, the development of intelligent devices, and the refinement of strategic management, are all components of the new challenge. To meet this challenge, we need new ideas about providing information support for our organizations.

Organizational Changes

There have been rapid changes in the technology that we employ to manage data. Complementary changes are now occurring in our organizations and in our concepts about information systems. We are experiencing a simultaneous push by technology and pull by management to deliver useful information. We have traditionally only focused on maintaining data in operational, or legacy systems which were organized by staff function: finance, student, personnel, etc. It is naive to assume that all required management information resides in these historical legacy systems, and that the challenge is simply to implement new technology that will deliver data on demand to an ever expanding clientele. Management's requirements are driven by new needs to perform analyses related to both long-term and short-term decisions. The operational systems that perform day-to-day transactions have not been designed to support management decision making, and probably do not contain sufficiently standardized or normalized data for the integrated, recombined, and longitudinal views required for analysis.

In response to the increasing pressures on legacy systems, existing internal and external reporting functions often use informal procedures to obtain data and interpret the variables. Often, there is not a predominance of historical files, census files, or standardized data maintained by the operating functions. In addition, there is often no formal assignment of responsibility for data management. The result is often a lack of policies to govern the processes by which those who manage operational systems capture, store, define, secure, or provide data and reports to institutional management.

Typically, when management requests for information fan out to different operational areas, each area responds by providing data from the perspective of its functional activity. The result is that: (1) the executive drowns in data with no options to analyze and transform the data to useful information; (2) the executive receives multiple, biased, and conflicting information; (3) the information is based on incomplete assumptions about the desired analysis and on data that are not integrated; and, (4) the failure to properly obtain the information produces organizational overhead, requiring the expenditure of extra resources.

Nevertheless, there are several organizational trends at many of our colleges and universities which offset the rather gloomy picture painted above and set the stage for creating a data management culture that can effectively respond to management information requirements.

The first trend is toward greater efficiency and competitiveness. With this comes a willingness to consider a variety of strategic alternatives. These strategies include changes in support structures, processes, and responsibilities. They also often produce an analysis of data needs. The second trend is the migration to new operational systems, and increasingly distributed modes of operation. New development tools, as well as off-the-shelf software, include structured methodology for building an enterprise's data architecture, data definitions, and standard code usage. Since these methodologies provide the foundation for any executive information system, the migration presents the opportunity to analyze management's information requirements. The third trend is recognition that there is a need for more participative management. (Harper, p. 10–11)

The use of participative management extends the number and also the skill-set of managers who need to access and use data from across the organization. It also changes the focus and organization of the data needed.

Decision makers often need an integrated view of multiple operational systems. This includes peripheral systems that are often not prime candidates for migration to integrated operational systems. This leads to the realization that there are ongoing data management activities that must be maintained to assure the availability of high quality information from all operational systems to support proactive decision making.

Trade magazines and journals have labeled these trends as "reengineering," "right-sizing," and "total quality management." Each term points toward improvement of the information support functions and spurs an interest in what can be done to accelerate progress. However, the lack of a structured process for coordinating various data management activities and relationships across the organization limits and jeopardizes potential momentum toward progress. Still, there remains a multitude of potential opportunities within the existing culture to leverage traditional relationships and friendships and to develop prototypes that push management's "hot buttons," thereby creating support for ongoing, quality data management work. Because organizational culture is dynamic, it is often accompanied by pressure to produce quick results that benefit the current culture. Producing relevant prototypes that address current needs increases the likelihood that quality data management projects will be included as part of other evolving organizational changes.

We can start with an understanding of the information support process, which focuses on the decision maker's needs (Table 1).

Table 1 Decision Maker's Needs

Needs...	Instead of...
• Tactics, techniques, and procedures	• Long-range plans
• Incremental changes	• Major decisions
• Majority of time spent on defining the problems, and developing possible solutions	• Majority of time spent on making a decision

We also need to define the authority and responsibilities of those who deal directly with operations and train those individuals to respond to opportunities and challenges based on the purpose of the organization, various alternative actions, and the authority inherent in the situation. Critical in this process are the acceptance and understanding of a conceptual model which includes operation functions, the process of decision support, and the use of technology which enables information flow. Equally important is the awareness that real progress depends on small incremental steps rather than large leaps.

Basic Concepts of Information Support

When our organizations were more static, information flowed on a consistent and traditional path. Management by evolution was perfected by incremental trial and error. Change was not anticipated and tended to evolve slowly, allowing the management culture to adapt slowly and comfortably. Today's dynamic organization needs a managed data resource whereby information flow can be adapted daily to meet current needs. We no longer have the luxury of evolving our information management any more than we have the luxury of evolving our organization. The future needs of the organization must be anticipated. Concurrently with the anticipation of new organizational structures and functions, there need to be new decision-support infrastructures. By understanding the steps in providing information and data, we can provide the required facts where the organi-

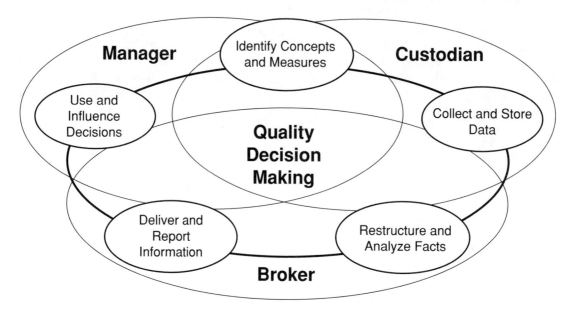

Figure 1 Information Support Circle

zation needs them, when the organization needs them. *The old ways of changing the information support structure after the organization is changed will result in the data never catching up to a decision maker's needs.*

We think the Information Support Circle (Figure 1) is a useful conceptual model for creating a relevant and sufficient awareness of these issues. As a model, it admittedly is a simplification of reality. However, it provides a basis for discussion of the process of creating decision support information.

The Information Support Circle has five basic functions, three key roles, and two major properties. The five functions provide a basic framework for the tasks associated with helping people make informed decisions. The roles provide a structure in which specific tasks can be organized and assigned to individuals in the organization. The properties guide us in improving the quality of information provided to the decision process.

The Five Functions

The five functions provide a framework within the Information Support Circle for describing specific steps and activities (Figure 2). Each function has two sequential activities and a standard of quality. A short description of each function follows. Specific activities and quality standards are discussed in detail in Chapter 3.

1. *Identify Concepts and Measures.* Develop a conceptual model of the situation. Describe its major components. Include measurements which explain the feasibility of alternatives, desirability of outcomes, and availability of resources. Identify the key individuals and groups of individuals who have a stake in the process. Define the essential elements required to make the decision.

2. *Collect and Store Data.* Obtain data from various relevant sources. Include qualitative as well as quantitative facts. Store data so that they are secure and accessible to authorized users. Use technology where appropriate. Standardize the codes used and develop a collection of definitions and documentation. Edit and audit for correctness. Document the procedure, the situation, and the process of data capture and storage.

3. *Restructure and Analyze Facts.* Bring the data together from the various sources. Integrate using standard merging variables. Link to qualitative facts. Analyze with appropriate statistical and deterministic procedures. Summarize and focus the data on the situation. Compare with peer groups, look at trends, and describe limitations in the methodology.

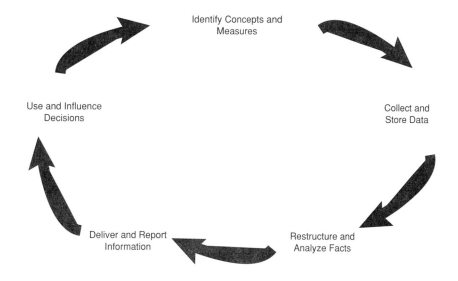

Figure 2 Information Support Circle
Five Functions

4. *Deliver and Report Information.* Apply the information to the situation. This includes using appropriate delivery technology to make the restructured facts available for further restructuring. Interpret instances where there may be differences or gaps between the collection of the data and the current need to make decisions. Identify systemic sources of bias. Focus reporting on the specific alternatives and support interpretations of causality and desirability of outcomes.

5. *Use and Influence Decisions.* Use facts to clarify the situation, to make a decision, or to advocate a belief or value. Identify the way the new knowledge expands the previous understanding. Determine the changes in the environment and what is assumed about the situation. Consider the importance of new information relative to the issues incorporated in the previous conceptual model.

Three Key Roles

The roles explain the way the functions, described above, are related to institutional management. These roles may be thought of as clusters of tasks and activities that can be assigned. The roles bridge the separate tasks of the functions into sets of authorities, responsibilities, and abilities (Figure 3). The following are brief descriptions of the three roles in the paradigm. More complete descriptions are provided in Chapters 4, 5, and 6.

1. *Custodian.* The custodian focuses on the integrity of the data and helps select appropriate data for the analysis. The custodian adds value by contributing operational knowledge. The custodian needs skills in the management and administration of data. The custodian also influences the selection of the methodology and the development of the essential questions which identify the information need.

2. *Broker.* The broker works to transform the data into information. This involves integrating data from various sources, restructuring data to focus on the areas of concern, and analyzing the data to look for causality, desirability of outcomes, and parsimony of elements. The broker participates and consults in the selection of the methodology and the development of the essential questions for decision making.

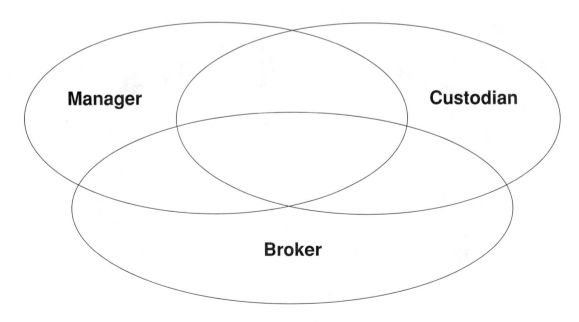

Figure 3 Information Support Circle
Three Roles

3. *Manager.* The manager takes the information and applies it to the situation. In this manner, the information becomes part of the intelligence of the situation and reduces the uncertainty of the situation. The manager is often the decision maker but may also be someone responsible for supporting the decision process. Some of the decisions are external, such as identifying what product to buy. Other decisions are intermediate and internal, such as evaluating business processes. The manager has a primary responsibility to identify the important elements of the problem, and also the unknowns.

Two Major Properties

Two properties provide a mechanism for evaluating the functions and the roles. They are the core values of the model, governing the essential actions: *DO THIS* and *GET THAT.* We have found it useful to conceptualize two properties although they are not mutually exclusive. Dependency is the property which deals with the influence each function has on the others. Cooperation is the property which deals with the relationships between the three roles. These properties are briefly described below and further developed in Chapter 7.

1. *Dependency.* The five functions form a circle (Figure 2). The value, which can be added for each function, is dependent on the quality of the preceding function. No function can produce quality or add value beyond the quality of the preceding function. For example, if the reliability of the data from the capture and storage step is poor, then no sophistication in methodology or increase in the amount of resources for analysis will overcome the low reliability. If the conceptual model is weak and erroneous content is selected for measurement, the resulting information will be seriously compromised regardless of the resources employed. The quality of the information produced is only as good as the quality of the weakest link in the circle of functions.

2. *Cooperation.* The ability to provide quality management comes from mutual investment and interaction of the three roles (Figure 3). If the individual filling any one of the roles decides to act in their own best interest, the integrity of the information support process is negatively impacted. In this scenario, the data custodian may change the definition of a variable to support a new operational need and inadvertently compromise the intended use in another area. The broker may propose an analysis requiring data that does not exist. The manager may start looking at new problems without notifying either the broker or the custodian.

Cooperative interaction among the three roles permits identification of opportunities to solve specific problems while positioning the data structure to support future needs. It allows the use of analytical procedures (1) to be focused on identified needs and (2) which are sufficient for the integrity of operational data. This synchronization provides the highest quality information to support the best organizational outcomes given the constraints of time and resources.

Changing Users

As institutions manage change, one likely outcome is downsizing. During downsizing, individuals typically leave organizations based on their readiness to leave, rather than the needs of the organization. Downsizing and rightsizing typically occur in the middle of the organization, the domain of staff specialists and middle managers. Further, reorganizing and restructuring often result in nontraditional management structures such as matrix reporting, task forces, or cross-functional teams. All of this requires individuals to develop a broader skill set. "Empowered" individuals need to be able to solve problems and recognize when they need to involve others in the problem solving.

The manager of tomorrow needs a broader and more flexible range of skills. This monograph helps meet this need in two key ways. First, a set of categories in which skills may be necessary are identified. Second, it shows related areas and types of activities that require cooperative work.

Each data management role encompasses a set of skills and expertise that can be brought to bear on any situation. The custodian supports the functional area. This requires traditional business skills such as accounting, personnel, and finance. The broker role requires experience with methodologies including management science, statistics, decision science, and computer science. These are the methodologies which facilitate the translation of data from the functional areas into information to be provided to those who apply the information to a specific situation. The integrator role requires an understanding of decision science, organizational behavior, and knowledge of specific characteristics of the industry. A manager in any of these areas needs to understand and appreciate the contribution of the others.

When institutional change becomes an identified need, reactions are often much the same as outlined by Kubler-Ross (1974) in an individual's acceptance of death and dying. The first reaction is denial that the change is required. The second reaction is hostility that results from uncertainty and anxiety as individuals admit the rules are changing. This is when cooperative work between units across the organization is most essential to both organizational and individual well-being. At the same time however, cooperation may also be extremely difficult to achieve due to individuals' insecurities. In this situation, quality information can be leveraged to bring the fearful together and create a frame of reference for ongoing cooperative work.

Changing Data Support Structures

The data support for the new organization will depend on the development of effective management data. This requires focusing on the decision process and on the uses of the data. Decision makers need an integrated set of data from both internal and external sources, including both current data and point-in-time historical longitudinal data. Since users operate in a variety of technological environments, the support structure must adapt with new software tools, expanded skill sets and training, and a new appreciation for the final product—management information.

In order to create a viable data support structure, the following will have to be developed and/or implemented at the institution:

Data Requirements

- Standard and integrated current data: selected data, defined and restructured to reflect the business needs as viewed by decision makers
- Standard and integrated historical data: selected data, defined and restructured to reflect changes, which are comparable with other institutions and usable in trend analysis

Software Tool Requirements

- Inter-connectivity tools: software to access and integrate the separate databases, which support multiple types of networks and is easy to use
- Relational and analysis tools: software which creates data structures and supports statistical analysis of the data, tabular and graphical displays, and "what if" analyses
- Security tools that are designed for a networked environment: software that limits access to sets of measures and groups of people

Skills and Training Requirements

- Skills: to analyze and restructure the data with the knowledge of the appropriate tools to use and when to use them
- Training and support: in technology and methodology (including statistical sophistication and awareness of the latest developments for data access)
- Knowledge: of complex analytical procedures
- Ability: to verify data validity and reliability

The Changing Institutional Research Function

Technical tools are necessary, but not sufficient to provide quality information support. The mission of institutional research is to enhance institutional effectiveness by providing information which supports and strengthens operations management, decision making, and the planning processes of administration. The institutional research function is most closely aligned to the information broker role and relates to data in three ways:

User. Institutional research is a user of all the critical and key administrative data elements. As such, it has many of the needs of managers.

Producer. Institutional research is a producer, dealing with data quality issues and data integration challenges in order to provide internally and externally standardized extracts of time variant data. This can be thought of as populating a data warehouse.

Supplier. Institutional research has an obligation to both its internal and external customers to supply current levels of information and analysis support while creating more effective delivery strategies to address requirements of various users of institutional data.

It is clear the successful institutional researcher is dependent on positive relationships with data suppliers and on the quality of their data. Simply put, institutional research is the basic process of adding value to the information and data available to a manager. Recent workshops conducted on effective institutional research highlighted four goals for effective institutional research related to data. These included providing accurate and timely data, developing a system of data collection, creating usable data, and providing trend data. Not surprisingly, participants identified data problems as the major barrier to their effectiveness in meeting these goals. Specific data problems include:

Data Definitions. Disagreement on definitions; incorrect interpretations; data collected in different forms; and, lack of adequate comprehensive measures.

Technology. Lack of hardware and software resources to maintain, transfer and analyze data; poor data collection tools; lack of data management tools; and, lack of decision support tools.

Data Access. Inaccessible data at both the local and state level and lack of data about the data (where the data are located, how the user obtains access, etc.).

To increase effectiveness, institutional research must support efforts to improve the quality of data. There are several reasons for this. As a comprehensive user and customer, institutional research has extensive data-use methodology skills. Further, those in institutional research can teach these skills. These skills include

using statistical, comparative, projective, and qualitative methodologies. Also, as an office which often coordinates reporting with external agencies, institutional research is heavily involved in negotiating definitions and supporting the institutional reporting and information requirements. Standardization can enhance the value of state and national databases. When offering support to various internal offices, institutional research can often assist custodian efforts to improve standardization of data and definition of codes. This is also the opportunity to bring the manager together with the data custodian so both can better understand the need to obtain and properly use data.

A View for Adding Value

We have discussed the new management challenge facing our institutions, a sea change which forces changes in the way decisions are made. This impacts how decision makers are supported and increases management's demand for useful data. The institutional research function is positioned to be an effective force in the improvement of the integrity and value of the data and, therefore, is at the root of our institutions' response to change.

There is no best way to improve the management of data. There are, however, some strategies which are likely to be successful. The ideas and thoughts in this monograph are presented to help focus on some of these strategies. The ideas are organized to work through a sequence of looking at the need for improving data management, to describe some of the steps which we and our colleagues can take to overcome the problems in our data, and, finally, to look at what can be done to make things better.

These discussions challenge all of us to deal with three questions, which lead the way to knowledge:

- What do we know?
- What does it mean?
- So what?

In the next chapter, we discuss the five functions of the Information Support Circle and the problems, or "diseases," which are often associated with each.

Environmental Scanning

JAMES L. MORRISON

Issues

Successful management of colleges and universities depends upon the ability of the senior leaders to adapt to rapidly changing external environment. Unfortunately, the lead time once enjoyed by decisionmakers to analyze and respond to these and other changes is decreasing. Traditional long-range planning models, with their inward focus and reliance on historical data, do not encourage decisionmakers to anticipate environmental changes and assess their impact on the organization (Cope, 1981). The underlying assumption of such models is that any future change is a continuation of the direction and rate of present trends among a limited number of social, technological, economic, and political variables. Thus, the future for the institution is assumed to reflect the past and present or, in essence, to be "surprise-free." However, we know that this is not true, and the further we plan into the future, the less it will be true.

What is needed is a method that enables decisionmakers both to understand the external environment and the interconnections of its various sectors and to translate this understanding into the institution's planning and decisionmaking processes. *Environmental scanning* is a method of accomplishing this.

Brown and Weiner (1985) define environmental scanning as "a kind of radar to scan the world systematically and signal the new, the unexpected, the major and the minor" (p. ix). Aguilar (1967), in his study of the information-gathering practices of managers, defined scanning as the systematic collection of external information in order to (1) lessen the randomness of information flowing into the organization and (2) provide early warnings for managers of changing external conditions. More specifically, Coates (1985) identified the following objectives of an environmental scanning system:

- detecting scientific, technical, economic, social, and political trends and events important to the institution,

- defining the potential threats, opportunities, or changes for the institution implied by those trends and events,

- promoting a future orientation in the thinking of management and staff, and

- alerting management and staff to trends that are converging, diverging, speeding up, slowing down, or interacting.

Fahey and Narayanan (1986) suggest that an effective environmental scanning program should enable decisionmakers to understand current and potential changes taking place in their institutions' external environments. Scanning provides strategic intelligence useful in determining organizational strategies. The consequences of this activity include fostering an understanding of the effects of change on organizations, aiding in forecasting, and bringing expectations of change to bear on decisionmaking.

A number of writers on educational planning encourage college and university decisionmakers to use environmental scanning as

"Environmental Scanning," by James L. Morrison, reprinted from *The Primer for Institutional Research*, Revised Edition, edited by M. A. Whiteley, J. D. Porter and R. H. Fenske, 1992. Association for Institutional Research.

part of their strategic planning models. This chapter reviews several environmental scanning models and discusses how environmental scanning is used in higher education. Also included are suggestions on establishing an environmental scanning process at your institution and a listing of useful scanning resources.

Background

Environmental scanning is one of four activities comprising external analysis. As illustrated in Figure 1, **external analysis** is the broader activity of understanding the changing external environment that may impact the organization. In describing external analysis, Fahey and Narayanan (1986) suggest that organizations *scan* the environment to identify changing trends and patterns, *monitor* specific trends and patterns, *forecast* the future direction of these changes and patterns, and *assess* their organizational impact. Merged with **internal analysis** of the organization's vision, mission, strengths, and weaknesses, external analysis assists decisionmakers in formulating strategic directions and strategic plans.

The goal of environmental scanning is to alert decisionmakers to potentially significant external changes before they crystallize so that decisionmakers have sufficient lead time to react to the change. Consequently, the scope of environmental scanning is broad.

Defining Environment

When we scan, it is useful to view the environment in a manner that organizes our scanning efforts. Fahey and Narayanan (1986) help by identifying three levels of environment for scanning. The **task environment** is the institution's set of customers. In higher education, this may include students and potential students, parents of students and of potential students, political leaders, and employers and potential employers of students. The task environment relates to a particular institution. Although the task environments of a community college and a research university within 20 miles of each other may overlap, they also differ.

The **industry environment** comprises all enterprises associated with an organization in society. For higher education, factors such as public confidence in higher education or student aid legislation are industry factors affecting all institutions.

At the broadest level is the **macroenvironment**, where changes in the social, technological, economic, environmental, and political (**STEEP**) sectors affect organizations directly and indirectly. For example, a national or global recession increases the probability of budget cuts in state government and, consequently, budget reductions in publicly supported colleges and universities.

Defining Scanning

There are a number of ways to conceptualize scanning. Aguilar (1967) identified four types

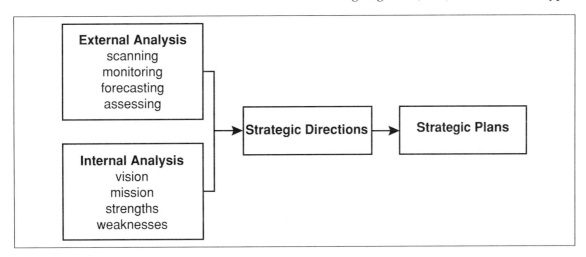

Figure 1 The Role of External Analysis in Strategic Planning

of scanning. **Undirected viewing** consists of reading a variety of publications for no specific purpose other than to be informed. **Conditioned** viewing consists of responding to this information in terms of assessing its relevance to the organization. **Informal searching** consists of actively seeking specific information but doing it in a relatively unstructured way. These activities are in contrast to **formal searching**, a proactive mode of scanning entailing formal methodologies for obtaining information for specific purposes.

Morrison, Renfro, and Boucher (1984) simplified Aguilar's four scanning types as either passive or active scanning. **Passive scanning** is what most of us do when we read journals and newspapers. We tend to read the same kinds of materials—our local newspaper, perhaps a national newspaper like *The New York Times* or *The Wall Street Journal*, or an industry newspaper like *The Chronicle of Higher Education*. However, the organizational consequences of passive scanning are that we do not systematically use the information as strategic information for planning, and we miss many ideas that signal changes in the environment.

Active scanning focuses attention on information resources that span the task and industry environments as well as the macroenvironment. In active scanning, it is important to include information resources that represent different views of each STEEP sector.

Another way of looking at scanning was described by Fahey, King, and Narayanan (1981). Their typology views scanning as irregular, periodic, and continuous. **Irregular** systems are used on an ad hoc basis and tend to be crisis-initiated. These systems are used when an organization needs information for planning assumptions and conducts a scan for that purpose only. **Periodic** systems are used when the planners periodically update a scan, perhaps in preparation for a new planning cycle. **Continuous** systems use the active scanning mode of data collection to systematically inform the strategic planning function of the organization. The rationale undergirding active scanning is that potentially relevant "data" are limited only by your conception of the environment. These data are inherently scattered, vague, and imprecise and come from a host of sources. Since early signals often show up in unexpected places, your scanning must be on-

going, fully integrated within your institution, and sufficiently comprehensive to cover the environments important to your decisionmakers.

Scanning in Higher Education

Many colleges and universities incorporate environmental scanning in strategic planning. Friedel, Coker, and Blong (1991) surveyed 991 two-year colleges in spring 1991 to identify those institutions that currently conduct environmental scans. Based upon a 60 percent response rate, they found that 40 percent of the responding institutions conduct some form of environmental scanning. Of these institutions, 20 percent use an irregular system, 40 percent use a periodic system, and 32 percent use a continuous system. Meixell (1990), in a survey of 134 public research and doctorate-granting institutions, found environmental scanning activities in the planning processes at half of the institutions surveyed.

The best discussion of how postsecondary institutions implement environmental scanning is found in Pritchett (1990). Pritchett discusses how three institutions, a public doctoral-granting university, a comprehensive university, and a two-year college, use environmental scanning in the planning process. Two institutions use an ad hoc environmental analysis committee appointed by the president. At the other institution, the committee is directed by the planning and budget office and consists of experts and community representatives.

Pritchett found common patterns in how the environmental scanning activity developed in these institutions. New presidential leadership and active governing boards were critical in two institutions; reductions in state appropriations and enrollment declines were influential at all three. In all institutions, presidential recognition and support for the formal scanning process were essential elements of the planning process.

Getting Started

The first step in establishing environmental scanning is to decide which level of scanning commitment is best for your institution at this time: irregular, periodic, or continuous. Most colleges and universities operate an irregular or periodic system, focusing on the task environment. These levels require less resource commitment from the institution, but they only address the immediate needs for information about the external environment. You may satisfy the requirements of these levels through several means. A quick way of getting started is to interview major decisionmakers regarding their view of the most critical trends and developments that could affect the institution. Use the interviews and conversations with your colleagues (including those at other institutions) to identify critical trends and potential developments. Also examine past program reviews, the last institutional self-study, and the most current master plan.

Establishing a continuous scanning system requires more effort and resources. First, secure a resource commitment from the senior official responsible for planning. At a minimum, a continuous scanning system requires a professional and a support person to devote half of their time to the enterprise. Further, a continuous scanning program requires a number of scanners who agree to rigorously and systematically review specific information resources. Assuming that you secure the resources, your next step is to recruit and train volunteers to perform active scanning.

Training

One approach to recruiting scanners is to offer a half- to full-day environmental scanning workshop. Invite faculty members from all disciplines as well as key administrators from all functional areas. Be sure to include members of the institution's planning committee as well as senior executives and members of the board of trustees and/or board of visitors, if appropriate. Heterogeneity of backgrounds, experiences, and perspectives guards against parochial viewpoints and will help you see into the future with less hindrance from the "blinders" of the past.

The invitation should convey the idea that environmental scanning information is essential for the institution and its academic departments. Also stress that the information obtained in the environmental scanning process will inform the ongoing strategic planning process. Participants are scanning for information that impacts the future of the institution and its programs.

After explaining how environmental scanning fits into external analysis and how external analysis is merged with internal analysis to formulate strategic plans (see Figure 1), initiate a series of exercises where participants identify and prioritize critical trends and emerging issues. These exercises allow participants to bring their individual knowledge of the external environment to the discussion and to develop an event and trend set to guide monitoring. Instruct participants to:

- *Seek signs of change.* Review the STEEP sectors, looking for signs of change. This requires examining sources for movement in relevant variables. For example, changes in the average SAT score of entering college freshmen or percentage of Black males applying for college could be significant to your institution.

- *Look for signals of potential events on the horizon.* For example, research on Alzheimer's disease may produce a drug with side effects to enhance memory capabilities. New research on solar or wind energy may portend significant savings in energy costs. An increasing number of interactive videodiscs and CD Roms may signal a major change in how information is presented to students. All of these trends could have significant impact on higher education, with implications for faculty development programs.

- *Look for forecasts of experts.* Some experts maintain we are moving toward a sustainable world in which attention will focus on energy efficiency, recycling, protection of biological and environmental bases, and the feeding and stabilization of the world population. Ask participants to consider the implications of the experts' forecasts for your institution.

- *Look for indirect effects.* It is important to remember that many trends or events that do not have direct implications for your institution may have second- or third-order effects.

- *Be aware that there are few guidelines on how to do scanning.* There are no hard and fast rules that lead to "correct" interpretations. The data do not speak for themselves. Scanners' skills, abilities, experiences, and judgments are critical to interpreting the data.

- *Write abstracts.* Abstracts are excellent vehicles to crystallize thoughts and communicate what is known about changing trends and patterns. When preparing abstracts, write the lead sentence in response to these questions: "If I had only a few minutes to describe this trend to a friend, what would I say? What is the most important idea or event that indicates change?" The responses to these questions should be contained in a one-paragraph explanation. Whenever possible, include statistical data. Limit the summary to no more than one-half page of single-spaced, typewritten copy. Depending upon your institution's culture, you may want to include a statement of the implications of the article for the institution.

Monitoring Taxonomy

The trends and events identified in the initial workshop are the beginnings of a scanning/monitoring taxonomy. A scanning/monitoring taxonomy has two objectives: (1) to provide a comprehensive set of categories to organize information and (2) to provide a numbering method for storing information. The STEEP sectors are an elementary taxonomy. Each category is usually subdivided. For example, the social sector may be divided into education, values, and demographics. With an electronic bibliographic database program, it is easy to build your taxonomy "as you go," using keywords to denote the categories. Be aware that developing, storing, and maintaining an environmental scanning database requires a good deal of time and effort.

Scanning Structure

The structure of the scanning system does not need to be elaborate. The chair of the scanning committee is responsible for assigning information sources to each scanner and for collecting and filing copies of articles and scanning abstracts. Assigning scanners specific materials for regular monitoring provides a measure of confidence that most "blips" on the radar screen will be spotted. In making this assignment, ascertain first what sources are reviewed regularly by the scanners. This list should be

compared to the list of important information resources identified by the scanning committee. Assign scanners material they already regularly review. Also ask for volunteers to review material not regularly read by committee members. If there is an abundance of scanners, build in redundancy by having two or more scanners review the same information resource.

Periodically the planning committee should meet to sort, sift, and evaluate the significance of the abstracts the scanners write. At the conclusion, the planners should summarize by sector (i.e., social, technological, economic, environmental, and political) all abstracts for use in the institution's strategic planning process.

Resources

There is no lack of resources available for environmental scanning. The 1988–89 *Future Survey Annual* lists 454 futures-relevant periodicals. Marien (1991) reports there are 46 publications in international economics and development, 45 in environment/resources/energy, and 31 in health and human services that frequently have futures-relevant information.

In addition, there are a number of general newspapers and magazines that each provide discussion on a broad spectrum of issues. Newspapers you should systematically scan include *The New York Times, The Washington Post, The Wall Street Journal, The Miami Herald, The Chicago Tribune, The Los Angeles Times, The Christian Science Monitor,* and *The Times* of London. Magazines include *Vital Speeches of the Day, Across the Board, Time, Newsweek, U.S. News and World Report, Futures, The Forum for Applied Research and Public Policy, World Monitor, Atlantic, The Nation, Ms.,* and *The Futurist.*

The most important criterion for literature selection is diversity. To ensure that you adequately scan the task environment, industry environment, and macroenvironment, identify information resources in each of the STEEP sectors. If your institution does not have the human resources to implement a continuous scanning system, you may wish to employ a scanning service. Both Weiner, Erich and Brown, Inc. and the Wilkinson Group offer such services.

The Macroenvironment

In conjunction with its Program in Educational Leadership, the University of North Carolina at Chapel Hill publishes *On the Horizon,* the environmental scanning newsletter for higher education. A comprehensive list of information resources by STEEP sector in the macroenvironment includes the following:

- *Social/demographic/values/lifestyles.* Data from periodic publications or statistics from the Census Bureau and other federal, state, and local governmental agencies provide the basics on population trends and characteristics. The Department of Labor and the Department of Commerce's National Technical and Information Services make available specific types of demographic analyses. The National Center for Health Statistics provides data on trends in areas such as fertility and life expectancy. The U.S. League of Savings Associations studies changes in homebuyer demographics, and the American Council of Life Insurance's Social Research Services conducts demographic studies. The United Nations and the Organization for Economic Cooperation and Development publish periodic reports detailing international developments in this area.

- *Technology literature.* Discussion of technological advances and future possibilities can be found in a variety of periodic sources, including *Technology Review, Datamation, BYTE, Computer World, Discover, Infoworld, Science, Scientific American, The Whole Earth Review,* and *Proceedings of the National Academy of Sciences.*

- *Economic literature.* There are a number of periodicals focusing on economic trends and forecasts, including *Business Week, The Economist, Fortune, The Monthly Labor Review,* and *Money, Inc.* You can obtain monthly reports from the Department of Commerce's Bureau of Economic Analysis as well as reports from the Departments of Commerce, Labor, Energy, and Treasury. State and local governmental agencies provide regional economic data.

- *Environmental literature.* Recommended periodicals on the environment are *Ecodecision* and *Environment.* Several organiza-

tions publish futures-oriented reports on the environment (e.g., Global Tomorrow Coalition, Worldwatch Institute, and Island Press). The Audubon Society and Sierra Club also publish periodic reports in this area.

- *Political literature.* What is happening in the political/legislative arena is covered by *New Republic, The National Review, The National Journal, In These Times, Mother Jones, Federal Register,* and *Congressional Quarterly Weekly Report.* Other sources include public opinion leaders, social critics, futures-oriented research institutes (e.g., the Hudson Institute and the Institute for the Future), public policy research centers (e.g., the Brookings Institute and the American Enterprise Institute for Public Policy Research), governmental documents, proposed bills to the legislature, and statements or opinions by social critics, experts, and activists. Finally, consult *State Legislatures* for a periodic summary of pertinent legislation being considered in state legislatures throughout the country.

- *Electronic databases.* There are a number of electronic databases containing up-to-date descriptions of articles (by title and, many times, by abstract) available on a subscription basis. ABI Inform, ERIC, and PAIS are a few examples. Two database services, Dialog and BRS, contain hundreds more databases specializing in all areas. Undoubtedly, your library already subscribes to these databases and database services. These resources are amenable to monitoring (i.e., to retrieving information about critical trends and potential events that you identified in your scanning). In addition, you can use electronic bibliographic databases to file and store information. Such programs facilitate review, referral, and updating. It is also possible to develop consortium relationships with other institutions by using an electronic filing system.

The Industry Environment

Key sources on the higher education industry environment include *The Chronicle of Higher Education, Education Week,* and *Higher Education Daily.* A number of newsletters serving the industry environment are available as well. In addition, many individuals and colleges/universities put their environmental scans on ERIC.

Perhaps the most useful resource is your own network of friends and colleagues within the profession. Frequently you can phone a colleague at another institution and get information quickly. Or you can post your question in the Association for Institutional Research's or the Society for College and University Planning's electronic newsletters.

The Task Environment

Information resources for scanning the task environment include local, state, and regional newspapers, local and state government reports, and experts in demography, sociology, and political science departments in your institution.

Communication

A scanning newsletter brings important trends and events to the attention of all members of your institution and, at the same time, provides recognition for the efforts of the scanners. Make the newsletter a "stand alone" document and distribute it widely. You may want to consider a logo, present the newsletter on distinctive paper, and have special boxes labeled "Wild Speculations," "Left Field," or "Wild Cards." The important point is that the newsletter only contain items that have implications for the institution. Solicit comments and contributions from all who read the newsletter, and make the format easy to read in form and content. An excellent vehicle for communicating the results of the scanning/monitoring committee's work is to distribute selected abstracts, drawing attention to the implications of a particular trend or potential event or series of interrelated trends and events.

Remember

We all do informal environmental scanning. However, continuous scanning is required if decisionmakers are to understand, anticipate, and respond to the threats and opportunities posed by changes in the external environment. It is important that campus decisionmakers participate in this process. Through participation, they develop a shared understanding of high priority issues and a view of the dynamics of the changing environment.

Remember that environmental scanning is something of an art form; guidelines on how to scan are necessarily few. There are no hard and fast rules to lead to a "correct" interpretation of information. Be careful to structure your scanning process to minimize the possibility of being "blind-sided" by a change in the environment that you should have seen coming.

Finally, remember that environmental scanning is only one component of external analysis. It is the starting point, however, from which you and your colleagues can identify trends and events in the environment worthy of monitoring. More importantly, it provides a basis for discerning the strategic direction of your institution from which you may plan far more effectively.

Editor's Note:

The Readers' Guide to Periodical Literature, published by the H. W. Wilson Company, is an index to English language periodicals of general interest available in most libraries. We consider a periodical to be readily accessible if it is indexed in the *Readers' Guide*. For those periodicals not included in the *Readers' Guide*, we provide the address and, in most cases, the phone number to guide you in your scanning.

The Encyclopedia of Associations, published by Gale Research, Inc., is a guide to over 22,000 national and international organizations. Information about how to contact the organizations mentioned in this chapter is from the 1992 edition of *The Encyclopedia of Associations* and is available in most libraries.

Publications of U.S. government agencies are indexed in the *Monthly Catalog of United States Government Publications*. Most publications included in the *Monthly Catalog* are available from The Superintendent of Documents, U.S. Government Printing Office, 732 N. Capitol St., NW, Washington, DC 20401. Information: 202/275–3648, orders and inquiries: 202/783–3238.

For overviews of environmental scanning, see:

Aguilar, F. (1967). *Scanning the business environment.* New York: Macmillan.

Cope, R. G. (1981). Environmental assessments for strategic planning. In N.L. Poulton (Ed.), Evaluation of management and planning systems. *New Directions for Institutional Research, 31,* 5–15. San Francisco: Jossey-Bass.

Fahey, L., King, W. R., & Narayanan, V. K. (1981). Environmental scanning and forecasting in strategic planning: The state of the art. *Long Range Planning, 14*(1), 32–39.

Brown, A., & Weiner, E. (1985). *Supermanaging: How to harness change for personal and organizational success.* New York: Mentor.

Coates, J. F., Inc. (1985). *Issues identification and management: The state of the art of methods and techniques* (Research Project 2345-28). Electric Power Research Institute, 3412 Hillview Ave., Palo Alto, CA 94304. Phone: 415/855-2000.

Fahey, L., & Narayanan, V. K. (1986). *Macroenvironmental analysis for strategic management.* St. Paul, MN: West.

For a discussion on environmental scanning in higher education planning, see:

Keller, G. (1983). *Academic strategy: The management revolution in American higher education.* Baltimore, MD: Johns Hopkins University Press.

Morrison, J. L., Renfro, W.L., & Boucher, W. I. (1984). *Futures research and the strategic planning process: Implications for higher education* (ASHE-ERIC Higher Education Research Report No. 9). Washington, DC: Association for the Study of Higher Education. (ERIC Document Reproduction Service No. ED 259 692)

Callan, P. M. (Ed.). (1986). Environmental scanning for strategic leadership. *New Directions in Institutional Research, 52.* San Francisco: Jossey-Bass.

Morrison, J. L. (1986–1987). Establishing an environmental scanning system to augment college and university planning. *Planning for Higher Education, 15*(1), 7–22.

Morrison, J. L., & Mecca, T. V. (1989). Managing uncertainty. In J. C. Smart (Ed.), *Handbook of theory and research in higher education: Vol. 5* (pp. 351–382). New York: Agathon.

For reports on scanning activity in colleges and universities, see:

Pritchett, M. S. (1990). *Environmental scanning in support of planning and decisionmaking. Case studies at selected institutions of higher education.* Paper presented at the annual forum of the Association for Institutional Research, Louisville, KY. (ERIC Document Reproduction Service No. ED 321 693)

Friedel, J. N., Coker, D. R., & Blong, J. T. (1991). *A survey of environmental scanning in U.S. technical and community colleges.* Paper presented at the annual forum of the Association for Institutional Research, San Francisco. (ERIC Document Reproduction Service No. ED 333 923)

Meixell, J. M. (1990) *Environmental scanning activities at public research and doctorate-granting universities.* Paper presented at the annual meeting of the Society for College and University Planning. (ERIC Document Reproduction Service No. ED 323 857)

Scanning Resources

Overviews

Future Survey Annual and *Future Survey.* World Future Society, 4916 St. Elmo Ave., Bethesda, MD 20814. Phone: 301/656–8274.

John Naisbitt's Trend Letter. Global Network, 1101 30th St., NW, Ste. 301, Washington, DC 20007. Phone: 202/337-5960.

Marien, M. (1991). Scanning: An imperfect activity in an era of fragmentation and uncertainty. *Futures Research Quarterly, 7*(3),82–90.

What Lies Ahead. United Way of America, 701 N. Fairfax St., Alexandria, VA 22314. Phone: 703/836–7100.

What's Happening. Wilkinson Group, 8128 Pine Lake Ct., Alexandria, VA 22309. Phone: 703/780–6170.

General Periodicals

Newspapers

The New York Times, 229 W. 43rd St., New York, NY 10036. Phone: 1-800-631-2500.

The Washington Post, 1150 15th St., NW, Washington, DC 20071. Phone: 1-800-477-4679.

The Wall Street Journal, 200 Liberty St., New York, NY 10281. Phone: 1-800-841-8000, ext. 472.

The Miami Herald, 1 Herald Plaza, Miami FL 33132–1693. Phone: 1-800-825-MAIL.

Chicago Tribune, Tribune Tower, 435 N. Michigan Ave., Chicago, IL 60611. Phone: 1-800-TRIBUNE.

The Los Angeles Times, The Times Mirror Company, Times Mirror Square, Los Angeles, CA 90053. Phone: 1-800-LATIMES.

The Christian Science Monitor, The Christian Science Publishing Society, One Norway St., Boston, MA 02115. Phone: 1-800-456-2220.

The Times (of London), 1 Pennington St., London E19XN, England. Phone: 071-782-5000.

Magazines

Vital Speeches of the Day. See *Readers' Guide*.

Across the Board, Conference Board, Inc., 845 Third Ave., New York, NY 10022. Phone: 212/759-0900.

Time. See *Readers' Guide*.

Newsweek. See *Readers' Guide*.

U.S. News and World Report. See *Readers' Guide*.

Futures, Butterworth-Heinemann Ltd., P.O. Box 63, Westbury House, Bury St., Guilford, Surrey GU25BH, England. Phone: 048-330-0966.

Forum for Applied Research and Public Policy, University of Tennessee, Energy, Environment, and Resources Center, Knoxville, TN 37966–0710. FAX: 615/974-1838.

Atlantic. See *Readers' Guide*.

The Nation. See *Readers' Guide*.

Ms. See *Readers' Guide*.

The Futurist. See *Readers' Guide*.

Social/Demographic

Periodicals

American Demographics, Box 68, Ithaca, NY 14851-0068. Phone: 607/273-6343.

Public Opinion Quarterly. American Association for Public Opinion Research, University of Chicago Press, Journals Division, 5720 S. Woodlawn Ave., Chicago, IL 60637. Phone: 312/753-3347.

U.S. Government Agencies

U.S. Department of Commerce, National Technical and Information Services. See *GPO Monthly Catalog*.

U.S. Department of Labor. See *GPO Monthly Catalog*.

U.S. Department of Health and Human Services, National Center for Health Statistics. See *GPO Monthly Catalog*.

Associations

United States League of Savings Institutions, 1709 New York Ave., NW, Ste. 801, Washington, DC 20006. Phone: 202/637-8900.

American Council of Life Insurance, Social Research Services, 1001 Pennsylvania Ave., NW, Washington, DC 20004-2599. Phone: 202/624-2000.

International

United Nations, First Ave. & 46th St., New York, NY 10017. Phone: 212/963-1234.

Organization for Economic Cooperation and Development, 2, rue Andre Pascal, 75775, Paris Cedex 16, France. Phone: 1-45-24-8200.

The UNESCO Future Scan: A Bibliographic Bulletin of Future-Oriented Literature. United Nations Educational, Scientific, and Cultural Organization, Place de Fontenoy, 75700 Paris, France. Phone: 1-45-68-1000.

Technological

Periodicals

Technology Review, Building W59, Massachusetts Institute of Technology, Cambridge, MA 02139. Phone: 617/253-8250.

Datamation. Cahners Publishing Company, Division of Reed Publishing Inc., 275 Washington St., Newton, MA 02158-1630. Phone: 617/964-3030.

Byte. See *Readers' Guide*.

Computer World. See *Readers' Guide*.

Discover. See *Readers' Guide*.

Infoworld. Infoworld Publishing, 1060 Marsh Road, Menlo Park, CA 94025. Phone: 415/328-4602.

Science. See *Readers' Guide*.

Scientific American. See *Reader's Guide*.

The Whole Earth Review. Point Foundation, 27 Gate Five Rd., Sausalito, CA 94965. Phone: 415/332-1716.

Associations

Proceedings of the National Academy of Sciences. National Academy of Sciences, Office of News and Public Information, 2102 Constitution Ave., NW, Washington, DC 20418. Phone: 202/334-2138.

Economic

Periodicals

Business Week. See *Readers' Guide*.

The Economist. Economist Newspaper, 10 Rockefeller Plaza, 10th Floor, New York, NY 10020. Phone: 212/541-5930.

Fortune. See *Readers' Guide*.

Money, Inc. See *Readers' Guide*.

The Monthly Labor Review. See *Readers' Guide*.

U.S. Government Agencies

U.S. Department of Commerce, Bureau of Economic Analysis. See *GPO Monthly Catalog*.

U.S. Department of Labor. See *GPO Monthly Catalog*.

U.S. Department of Energy. See *GPO Monthly Catalog*.

U.S. Department of the Treasury. See *GPO Monthly Catalog*.

Environmental

Periodicals

Ecodecision. Royal Society of Canada, 276 Rue Saint-Jacque, Oest, Bureau 924, Montreal H241N3 Canada.

Environment. Heldres Publications, 4000 Albemarle St., NW, Washington, DC 20016. Phone: 202/362-6445.

Associations

Global Tomorrow Coalition, 1325 6 St., NW, Ste. 915, Washington, DC 20005-3140. Phone: 202/628-4016.

Worldwatch Institute, 1776 Massachusetts Ave., NW, Washington, DC 20036. Phone: 202/452-1999.

Island Press, 1718 Connecticut Ave., NW, Ste. 300, Washington, DC 20009. Phone: 202/232-7933.

Audubon Society, 950 Third Ave., New York, NY 10022. Phone: 212/832-3200.

Sierra Club, 730 Polk St., San Francisco, CA 94109. Phone: 415/776-2211.

Political

Periodicals

New Republic. See Readers' Guide.

The National Review. See *Readers' Guide.*

The National Journal, 1730 M St. NW, Ste. 1100, Washington, DC. Phone: 202/857-1400.

In These Times. Institute for Public Affairs, 2040 N. Milwaukee Ave., 2nd Fl., Chicago, IL 60647-4002. Phone: 312/472-5700.

Kiplinger Washington Letter. Kiplinger Washington Editors, Inc., 1729 H St. NW, Washington, DC 20006. Phone: 202/887-6400.

Mother Jones. See *Readers' Guide.*

Federal Register. U.S. Office of the Federal Register, National Archives and Records Administration, Washington, DC 20408. Phone: 202/523-5240.

Congressional Quarterly Weekly Report. Congressional Quarterly, Inc., 1414 22nd St., NW, Washington, DC 20037. Phone: 800-432-2250.

Institutes

Hudson Institute, Herman Kahn Center, 5395 Emerson Way, P.O. Box 26919, Indianapolis, IN 46226. Phone: 317/545-1000.

Institute for the Future, 2740 Sand Hill Rd., Menlo Park, CA 94025. Phone: 415/854-6322.

Brookings Institute, 1775 Massachusetts Ave., NW, Washington, DC 20036 Phone: 202/797-6000.

American Enterprise Institute for Public Policy Research, 1150 17th St., NW, Washington, DC 20036. Phone: 202/862-5800.

Associations

State Legislatures. National Conference of State Legislatures, Marketing Department, 1560 Broadway, Ste. 700, Denver, CO 80202. Phone: 303/623-7800.

For scanning resources on higher education, see:

Periodicals

The Chronicle of Higher Education, 1255 23rd St., NW, Ste. 700, Washington, DC 20037. Phone: 202/466-1000.

Education Week. Editorial Projects in Education, Inc., 4301 Connecticut Ave., NW, Ste. 250, Washington, DC 20008. Phone: 202/364-4114.

Higher Education Daily. Capitol Publishers, Inc., 1101 King St., Ste. 444, Alexandria, VA 22314. Phone: 703/683-4100.

Newsletters

On the Horizon. Program in Educational Leadership, School of Education, University of North Carolina, CB3500 Peabody Hall, Chapel Hill, NC 27599. Phone: 919/966-1354.

Higher Education and National Affairs. American Council on Education, Publications Division, One DuPont Circle, Washington, DC 20036. Phone: 202/939-9450

Communication Network News. State Higher Education Executive Officers/National Center for Education Statistics, 707 17th St., Ste. 32700, Denver, CO 80202-3427. Phone: 303/399-3685.

Memo to the President. American Association of State Colleges and Universities, One DuPont Circle, Washington, DC 20036. Phone: 202/293-7070.

E-Mail

E-Mail News, Society for College and University Planning, Joanne Cate (Ed.), BUDLAO@UCCVMA.BITNET. Phone: 510/987-0963.

The Electronic AIR, Association for Institutional Research, Larry Nelson (Ed.), NELSON_ L @PLU.BITNET.

College/University Scans

Cantonsville (Maryland) Community College. (1989). *External scan and forecast, 1989.* (ERIC Document Reproduction Service No. ED 309 817)

Osborn, F. (1989, May). *Environmental scan: A strategic planning document.* Rochester, NY: Monroe Community College. (ERIC Document Reproduction Service No. ED 307009)

Friedel, J. (1989, September). *2020 perfect vision for the next century: An environmental scan.* Bettendorf, IA: Eastern Iowa Community College District. (ERIC Document Reproduction Service No. ED 319 451)

Scanning Services

Weiner, Erich & Brown, Inc., 200 E. 33rd St., Ste. 9–I, New York, NY 10016. Phone: 212/889-7007.

Wilkinson Group, 8128 Pine Lake Court, Alexandria, VA 22309. Phone: 703/780-6170.

The following newsletter editors agree to respond to your questions if you are thinking of developing a newsletter for your campus:

Donna McGinty, Center for Continuing Education, University of Georgia, Athens, GA 30602. Phone: 404/542-3451.

Lowell Lueck, Director of Institutional Research and Planning, Western Illinois University, 312 Sherman Hall, Macomb, IL 61455. Phone: 309/298-1185.

Robert Wilkinson, Director of Institutional Research, 212 Russ Hall, Pittsburgh State University, Pittsburgh, KS. Phone: 316/231–7000.

PART V

OTHER RESOURCES

V. Other Resources

A. Related Higher Education Reference Books

1. Recommended Texts

Books listed in this section provide comprehensive coverage of planning and institutional research in postsecondary education, are recently published, and were frequently mentioned by our Higher Education Faculty Resource Group as useful texts for their courses.

Bryson, J. M. (1995). *Strategic planning for public and nonprofit organizations: A guide to strengthening and sustaining organizational achievement* (Rev. ed.). San Francisco: Jossey-Bass.

Middaugh, M. F., Trusheim, D. W., & Bauer, K. W. (1994). *Strategies for the practice of institutional research: Concepts, resources, & applications*. Tallahassee, FL: Association for Institutional Research.

Peterson, M. W., Dill, D. D., Mets, L. A., & Associates (Eds.). (1997). *Planning and management for a changing environment: A handbook on redesigning postsecondary institutions*. San Francisco: Jossey-Bass.

2. Useful Higher Education Reference Texts

Some books in this section either address institutional research and planning comprehensively but are dated, or have a very practitioner oriented approach. Others are more specialized and focus on a specific area of institutional research and planning or address management functions to which IR and planning relate or institutional issues they address. These were also mentioned by our Higher Education Resource Faculty group but as specialized references.

Balderston, F. E. (1995). *Managing today's university: Strategies for viability, change and excellence* (2nd ed.). San Francisco: Jossey-Bass.

Banta, T. W., Lund, J. P., Black, K. E., & Oblander, F. W. (1996). *Assessment in practice: Putting principles to work on college campuses*. San Francisco: Jossey-Bass.

Bogue, E. G., & Saunders, R. L. (1992). *The evidence for quality: Strengthening the tests of academic and administrative effectiveness*. San Francisco: Jossey-Bass.

Clagett, C. A., & Huntington, R. B. (1990). *The institutional research practitioner: A guidebook to effective performance*. Silver Spring, MD: Red.

Clark, B. R. (1998). *Creating entrepreneurial universities: Organizational pathways of transformation*. New York: Pergamon.

Cohen, A. R., & Brawer, F. B. (Eds.). (1994). *Managing community colleges: A handbook for effective practice*. San Francisco: Jossey-Bass.

Coughlin, M. A., & Pagano, M. (1997). *Case study applications of statistics in institutional research*. Tallahassee, FL: Association for Institutional Research.

Dober, R. P. (1996). *Campus architecture: Building in the groves of academe*. New York: McGraw-Hill.

Dober, R. P. (1996). (Reissued). *Campus planning*. Ann Arbor, MI: Society for College and University Planning.

Dolence, M. G., Lujan, H. D., & Rowley, D. J. (1997). *Strategic change in colleges and universities: Planning to survive and prosper*. San Francisco: Jossey-Bass.

Dolence, M. G., & Norris, D. M. (1995). *Transforming higher education: A vision for learning in the 21st century*. Ann Arbor, MI: Society for College and University Planning.

Dressel, P. L. (1976). *Handbook of academic evaluation: Assessing institutional effectiveness, student progress, and professional performance for decision making in higher education*. San Francisco: Jossey-Bass.

Dressel, P. L., & Associates. (1972). *Institutional research in the university: A handbook*. San Francisco: Jossey-Bass.

621

Dunn, J. A., Jr. (1989). *Financial planning guidelines for facility renewal and adaptation.* Ann Arbor, MI: Society for College and University Planning.

Erwin, T. D. (1991). *Assessing student learning and development: A guide to the principles, goals, and methods of determining college outcomes.* San Francisco: Jossey-Bass.

Fendley, W. R., & Seeloff, L. T. (Eds.). (1993). *Reference sources: An annotated bibliography for institutional research.* Tallahassee, FL: Association for Institutional Research.

Hossler, D., Bean, J. P., & Associates (1990). *The strategic management of college enrollments.* San Francisco: Jossey-Bass.

Jedamus, P., & Peterson, M. W. (Eds.). (1980). *Improving academic management: A handbook of planning and institutional research.* San Francisco: Jossey-Bass.

Keller, G. (1983). *Academic strategy: The management revolution in higher education.* Baltimore: Johns Hopkins University.

Keller, G. (Ed.). (1997). *The best of planning for higher education.* Ann Arbor, MI: Society for College and University Planning.

Kells, H. R. (1994). *Self-study processes: A guide to self-evaluation in higher education* (4th ed.). Phoenix: Oryx.

Martin, J., Samels, J. E., & Associates (1994). *Merging colleges for mutual growth: A new strategy for academic managers.* Baltimore: Johns Hopkins University.

Massy, W. F. (Ed.). (1996). *Resource allocation in higher education.* Ann Arbor, MI: University of Michigan.

Massy, W. F., & Meyerson, V. W. (1994). *Measuring institutional performance in higher education.* Princeton, NJ: Peterson's Guides.

McLaughlin, G. W., Howard, R., Balkan, L., & Blythe, E. (1998). *People, processes, and managing data.* Tallahassee, FL: Association for Institutional Research.

Mintzberg, H. (1994). *The rise and fall of strategic planning: Reconceiving roles for planning, plans, planners.* New York: Free Press.

Nedwek, B. P. (1996). *Doing academic planning: Effective tools for decision making.* Ann Arbor, MI: Society for College and University Planning.

Norris, D. M. (1997). *Revolutionary strategy for the knowledge age.* Ann Arbor, MI: Society for College and University Planning.

Norris, D. M., & Malloch, T. R. (1998). *Unleashing the power of perpetual learning.* Ann Arbor, MI: Society for College and University Planning.

Norris, D. M., & Poulton, N. L. (1991). *A guide for new planners.* Ann Arbor, MI: Society for College and University Planning.

Peterson, M. W., Chaffee, E. E., & White, T. H. (Eds.). (1991). *ASHE Reader on Organization and governance in higher education* (4th ed.). Needham Heights, MA: Ginn. [Available from Simon & Schuster.]

Peterson, M. W., & Mets, L. A. (1987). *Key resources on higher education governance, management, and leadership.* San Francisco: Jossey-Bass.

Rourke, F. E., & Brooks, G. E. (1966). *The managerial revolution in higher education.* Baltimore: Johns Hopkins University.

Rowley, D. J., Lujan, H. D., & Dolence, M. G. (1997). *Strategic change in colleges and universities: Planning to survive and prosper.* San Francisco: Jossey-Bass.

Russell, A. B., & Christal, M. E. (1996). *Compendium of national data sources on higher education.* Denver, CO: State Higher Education Executive Officers.

Stark, J. S., & Lattuca, L. R. (1997). *Shaping the college curriculum: Academic plans in action.* Boston: Allyn and Bacon.

Stark, J. S., & Thomas, A. (1994). *Assessment and program evaluation.* Needham Heights, MA: Simon & Schuster.

Suskie, L. A. (1997). *Questionnaire survey research: What works* (2nd ed.). Resources for Institutional Research, Number Six. Tallahassee, FL: Association for Institutional Research.

Taylor, B., & Massy, W. (1996). *Strategic indicators for higher education, 1996* (2nd ed.). Princeton, NJ: Peterson's Guides.

Tierney, W. G. (Ed.). (1998). *The responsive university: Restructuring for high performance.* Baltimore: Johns Hopkins University.

Whiteley, M. A., Porter, J. D., & Fenske, R. H. (1992). *The primer for institutional research* (Rev. ed.). Tallahassee, FL: Association for Institutional Research.

B. Related Publications

The following regular publications are useful resources for professionals in institutional research and planning. Students in the field will want to become familiar with them.

1. Monograph Series

ASHE/ERIC Higher Education Reports. Washington, DC: The George Washington University.

Higher Education: Handbook of Theory and Research. Smart, J. (Ed.). New York: Agathon.

New Directions for Community Colleges. San Francisco: Jossey-Bass.

New Directions for Higher Education. San Francisco: Jossey-Bass.

New Directions for Institutional Research. San Francisco: Jossey-Bass.

2. Journals

Cause and Effect Magazine. Boulder, CO: EDUCAUSE.

Change: The Magazine of Higher Learning. Washington, DC: Heldref.

Community College Journal. Washington, DC: American Association of Community Colleges.

EDUCOM Review. Washington, DC: EDUCAUSE.

Higher Education. Amsterdam: Elsevier.

The Journal of Higher Education. Columbus: Ohio State University.

Planning for Higher Education. Ann Arbor, MI: Society for College and University Planning.

Research in Higher Education. New York: Human Services.

Review of Higher Education. Baltimore: Johns Hopkins University.

3. Periodicals

AGB Occasional Paper Series. Washington, DC: Association of Governing Boards of Universities and Colleges.

AIR Professional File. Tallahassee, FL: Association for Institutional Research.

Assessment Update: Progress, Trends, and Practices in Higher Education. Banta, T. W. (Ed.). San Francisco: Jossey-Bass.

The Chronicle of Higher Education. Washington, DC.

Executive Strategies. Washington, DC: NACUBO.

On the Horizon: The Environmental Scanning Publication for Educational Leaders. Morrison, J. L. (Ed.). San Francisco: Jossey-Bass.

Research Briefs. Washington, DC: American Council on Education.

C. Data Base Resources, Services, and Surveys

1. American College Testing Services

Freshman Class Profile Service—Provides a comprehensive description of a college's entering freshmen and a parallel description of students who sent their ACT assessment scores to the institution but did not enroll.

Prediction Research Service—Describes the academic achievements and potentials of currently enrolled freshmen and develops the prediction equations used in forecasting the overall performance of future students.

Enrollment Information Service—Provides information to help enrollment planners address various marketing concerns by geographical/customized market segments. In-

cludes almost the entire population of ACT-tested students who graduated in a given year and represents the traditional ACT-tested college bound student market.

The Yield Analysis Service—Supports the enrollment management process by reporting actual enrollment/yield figures for an institution. Also allows for an analysis of collegiate competition in terms of market penetration and includes a table showing the highest-yielding high schools in a particular segment and a table showing the greatest number of ACT-tested students.

ACT Course Placement Service—Provides information that can be used to judge the effectiveness of test scores or other placement variables (such as high school grades) for identifying underprepared students. The report also provides information that can be used to select cutoff scores for placing students in appropriate courses.

ASSET and COMPASS Research Services—ASSET is a paper and pencil placement testing and advising program for two-year institutions. COMPASS is a computerized course placement and diagnostic assessment system for two- and four-year institutions. Reports available with these systems include:

Entering Student Descriptive Report

Returning Student Retention Report

Course Placement Report

Underprepared Student Follow-up Report

College Outcomes Survey Report

College Program Improvement Report

Surveys

Adult Learner Needs Assessment Survey

Alumni Survey

Alumni Survey (2-Year College Form)

Alumni Outcomes Survey

College Outcomes Survey

College Student Needs Assessment Survey

Entering Student Survey

Financial Aid Student Services Survey

Student Opinion Survey

Student Opinion Survey (2-Year College Form)

Survey of Academic Advising

Survey of Current Activities and Plans (Surveys candidates who were accepted for admission but chose not to enroll)

Survey of Postsecondary Plans (Evaluates the educational plans and preferences of prospective students while they are still enrolled in secondary school)

Withdrawing/Nonreturning Student Survey

Withdrawing/Nonreturning Student Survey (Short Form)

For further information contact:

American College Testing
Research Services (64)
Box 168
2255 N. Dubuque Rd.
Iowa City, IA 52243
ph 319-337-1111
fax 319-337-1551

2. The College Board

Annual Survey of Colleges—A national database which provides data regarding institutional characteristics, admissions policies and requirements, student profiles, foreign student information, enrollment, academic offerings and policies, and annual expenses and financial aid. Various types of reports, including custom reports, are available. License fees are based upon data use.

For further information contact:
The College Board
Guidance Publishing Information Services
45 Columbus Avenue
New York, New York 10023-6992
ph 212-713-8000

3. Higher Education Research Institute

The American College Teacher. A faculty survey on national norms, including professional goals, instructional methods, sources of stress, and student/faculty interaction. Surveys were conducted in 1989, 1992, 1995, and 1998. For the most recent report about the data see:

The American college teacher: National norms for the 1995-96 HERI faculty survey. (1996). Sax, L. J., Astin, A. W., Arredondo, M., & Korn, W. S. Higher Education Research Institute, University of California, Los Angeles.

The Cooperative Institutional Research Program's (CIRP) Longitudinal Study on the American College Student. Designed to examine the impact of different types of college environments on student development, this survey has been conducted at various times throughout the 1980s and 1990s.

Numerous publications are available including:

The American freshman: National norms. (Annual Publication). Los Angeles: Higher Education Research Institute, UCLA.

The American freshman: Thirty year trends. (1996). Astin, A. W., Parrott, S. A., Korn, W. S., & Sax, L. J. Los Angeles: Higher Education Research Institute, UCLA.

Degree attainment in American colleges and universities: Effects of race, gender, and institutional type. (1996). Astin, A. W., Tsui, L. & Avalos, J. Los Angeles: Higher Education Research Institute, UCLA.

What matters in college? Four critical years revisited. (1993). Astin, A. W. Los Angeles: Higher Education Research Institute, UCLA.

For information regarding requirements for obtaining data collected by the Higher Education Research Institute, please contact:

Director
Higher Education Research Institute
The University of California, Los Angeles
Graduate School of Education
and Information Studies
3005 Moore Hall
Box 951521
Los Angeles, CA 90095-1521
ph 310-825-1925
fax 310-206-2228

4. Inter-University Consortium for Political and Social Research

Monitoring the Future: A Continuing Study of the Lifestyles and Values of Youth. Explores changes in important values, behaviors, and lifestyle orientations of contemporary American youth. Subjects include attitudes toward government, social institutions, race relations, changing roles for women, educational aspirations, occupational aims, and marital and family plans.

For further information regarding requirements for obtaining data collected by the Inter-University Consortium for Political and Social Research, please contact:

User Support
Inter-University Consortium for Political and
Social Research
The University of Michigan
4269 Institute for Social Research
426 Thompson
Ann Arbor, MI 48109-1248
ph 734-763-5010
fax 734-764-8041

5. National Association of Student Financial Aid Administrators

Survey of Undergraduate Financial Aid Practices and Policies—Provides data regarding individual colleges' financial aid practices and awards, including number of awards, average size, and packaging make-up. Researchers are encouraged to work through the financial aid office on their campus to obtain access to these data.

6. National Center for Education Statistics

There are two types of data available from the National Center for Education Statistics (NCES)–restricted-use data and public-use data. Numerous reports, related to virtually all of the databases described below, have been published. For a list of these publications, visit the NCES homepage at http://nces.ed.gov/. Also, the Office of Educational Research and Improvement (OERI) produces a quarterly bulletin listing the release of data reports and other materials produced by NCES and OERI. To be added to the *OERI Bulletin* mailing list free of charge, send your name and address to:

OERI Bulletin
Outreach and Customer Service Division
Office of Educational Research and
Improvement
U.S. Department of Education
555 New Jersey Avenue, NW
Washington, DC 20202-5725

Restricted-Use Data Bases

To apply for a license to obtain restricted-use data, you can call or write NCES/OERI and request a copy of the *Restricted-Use Data Procedures Manual*. Four documents must be submitted to NCES, including a formal letter of request, a license document, affidavits of nondisclosure, and a security plan. The Data Security Officer can be contacted at (202) 219-1920 or (202) 219-2199. Mail can be addressed to:

NCES Data Security Officer
Statistical Standards and Methodology
Division (SSMD)
NCES/OERI—Room 408
U. S. Department of Education
555 New Jersey Avenue, NW
Washington, D. C. 20208-5654

Baccalaureate and Beyond Longitudinal Study—Provides information concerning education and work experiences of individuals who have completed the bachelor's degree. This survey will follow up on participants in the National Postsecondary Student Aid Study (NPSAS) for a 12-year period. First conducted in 1994, this study replaces the Recent College Graduates Study.

Beginning Postsecondary Students Longitudinal Survey—Designed to complement the high school cohort longitudinal studies and to improve data on participants in postsecondary education. Issues addressed include "traditional" and "non-traditional" student persistence, progress, and attainment from the initial time of entry into postsecondary education through leaving and entering the work force. This survey, begun in 1992, will follow first-time beginning students at 2–3 year intervals.

High School and Beyond—Includes both high school sophomore and senior cohorts and addresses such topics as how, when, and why students enroll in postsecondary education institutions, whether individuals who attend college earn more than those who do not attend college, and the effect of student financial aid. Data were collected in 1980, 1982, 1984, 1986, and 1992.

National Educational Longitudinal Survey of 1988—Intended to produce a general purpose data set for the development and examination of education policy. It is designed to examine the changes over time in the operation of the educational system, and the effects various elements of the system have on the lives of the individuals who go through it. This study continues and expands upon the efforts of the two prior major longitudinal studies sponsored by NCES–the National Longitudinal Study of 1972 and High School and Beyond–and includes the 1988 Base Year, First Follow-up (1990), Second Follow-up (1992), and Third Follow-up (1994). The next follow-up is tentatively scheduled for 2000.

National Postsecondary Student Aid Survey—The most comprehensive nationwide study of financial assistance to students attending postsecondary institutions. Conducted in 1987, 1990, 1993, and 1996, this study examines how students and their families pay for postsecondary education. The next NPSAS is planned for 1999.

National Survey of Postsecondary Faculty—Provides information on a variety of topics including faculty backgrounds, workloads, salaries and benefits, faculty composition and turnover, and attitudes of full-time and part-time faculty in their institutions. Components include an Institutional Survey, Department Chairperson Survey (1988 only), and a Faculty Survey. Conducted in 1987-1988 and 1992-1993, the next survey is scheduled for 1999-2000.

Recent College Graduates Study—Collected data on post-degree employment and educational experience of individuals who obtained bachelor's or master's degrees. The emphasis was on estimating the potential supply of newly qualified teachers. Conducted periodically between 1976 to 1991, this survey was replaced by the Baccalaureate and Beyond survey in 1993.

Public-Use Data Bases

These data are available electronically using either ftp with anonymous logon:

ftp://ftp.ed.gov/ncesgopher/data/postsec/ipeds/publications/postsec/ipeds/>.

or the World Wide Web:

http://nces.ed.gov/

For further information regarding electronic access, contact:

Carl M. Schmitt
National Center for Education Statistics
555 New Jersey Avenue, NW
Rm 331D, Capitol Place
Washington, DC 20208-5661
ph 202-219-1642
fax 202-219-1679
E-mail: carl_schmitt@ed.gov

Integrated Post-Secondary Education Data System—Completions Survey/*Degrees Conferred and Other Awards Conferred by Institutions of Higher Education*. Collects information about degrees conferred by postsecondary institutions. It is categorized by programs/fields of study, degrees/awards granted, completions by level, and completions by sex and race/ethnicity.

Integrated Post-Secondary Education Data System—Fall Enrollment Survey. Collects enrollment data by institution for numerous student characteristics including sex, year and level of study, race/ethnicity, selected major field of study, age, and residence status.

Integrated Post-Secondary Education Data System—Fall Staff Survey. Collects data on all persons employed by postsecondary institutions in the United States (the focus is on race/ethnicity and sex). Information about the types of services institutions seek from outside individuals or firms is also collected.

Integrated Post-Secondary Education Data System—Finance Survey. Collects data on the financial condition of postsecondary education in this country and monitors changes in postsecondary finance.

Integrated Post-Secondary Education Data System—Salaries, Tenure, and Fringe Benefits of Full-Time Instructional Faculty Survey. Collects data on salaries, tenure, and fringe benefits, and analyzes national faculty data in conjunction with enrollment and degrees granted as an indicator of manpower demand.

Specialized Analyses

The National Education Data Resource Center (NEDRC) provides access to much of the data that NCES maintains. Users can request specific statistical analyses on a data set and NDRC will provide tables and reports using the SAS programming language. There is no charge for this service, and the normal turnaround time is five to ten working days. By request, NDRC will provide institutional listings and mailing labels also.

Currently the available databases include all IPEDS surveys, Schools and Staffing Survey, National Survey of Postsecondary Faculty, High School and Beyond, Recent College Graduate Study, Common Core of Data, Beginning Postsecondary Students, National Postsecondary Student Aid Study, the 1988 National Education Longitudinal Study, and the National Household Education Survey. For more information on the National Data Resource Center contact:

Carl Schmitt
Elementary and Secondary Education
Statistics Division
National Center for Education Statistics
555 New Jersey Avenue NW
Rm 331D, Capitol Place
Washington, DC 20208-5661
ph 202-219-1642
fax 202-219-1679
E-mail: carl_schmitt@ed.gov

7. National Science Foundation

The National Science Foundation maintains data regarding federal support to universities and colleges, as well as academic expenditures. Data on enrollment, personnel issues, and research and development indicators are also maintained. Information regarding the survey data sets and reports which highlight the findings are available on the World Wide Web at:

http://www.nsf.gov/sbe/srs/stats.htm.

CASPAR—NSF maintains an integrated data system which provides web access to a wide range of educational data sets, including IPEDS (see No. 6 above). This is especially useful for researchers interested in longitudinal data analysis. The data can be accessed at:

http://caspar.nsf.gov/

National Survey of College Graduates. Biennial survey designed to provide data on the number and characteristics of individuals with training and/or employment in science and engineering in the United States. Data include citizenship, race/ethnicity, level of degree, labor force status, and years of professional experience.

National Survey of Recent College Graduates. Collects information biennially about individuals who recently obtained bachelor's or master's degrees in a science or engineering field. Data collected include citizenship, educational history, occupation, salary, and sector of employment.

Survey of Earned Doctorates. Collects information annually about individuals who earned a doctorate from a U.S. institution.

Survey of Federal Support to Universities, Colleges, and Nonprofit Institutions. Collects data annually about the status and trends in federal support for science and engineering research and development including total federal obligations for operations and

capital construction, locations of research, and type of support.

Survey of Graduate Students and Postdoctorates in Science and Engineering. Collects data annually about students' citizenship, academic institution, enrollment status (full-time, part-time), field of study, and primary source of financial support.

You can contact the National Science Foundation's Division of Science Resources Studies by:

e-mail: info@nsf.gov
ph 703-306-1780
fax: 703-306-0510
mail: Division of Science Resources Studies
4201 Wilson Boulevard
Suite 965
Arlington, VA 22230

8. U.S. Bureau of Labor Statistics

The Current Population Survey—Monthly survey which includes a sample of 60,000 households. Data are available regarding respondents' college attainment, earnings, age, sex, race, marital status, and geographic location. The data can be accessed at:

http://www.bls.gov/

9. U.S. Census Bureau

The Census Bureau's website offers researchers a wide array of information regarding this country's population, including their educational attainment, field of training, economic status, income, age, race, sex, and geographic location. Data can be accessed at:

http://www.census.gov/

10. Washington State Higher Education Coordinating Board

This Coordinating Board collects longitudinal data regarding tuition rates for various types of public institutions in each state. To inquire about obtaining these data, contact:

Washington State Higher Education
Coordinating Board
917 Lakeridge Way
P.O. Box 43430
Olympia, WA 98504-3430
ph 360-753-7800

D. Periodic Data Reports and Summaries

1. *Administrative compensation survey.* Washington, DC: College and University Personnel Association.

    An annual survey of senior administrators' level of compensation in the nation's public and private colleges and universities.

2. *Annual report on the economic status of the profession.* Published in Academe, (March-April Issue). Washington, DC: American Association of University Professors.

    An annual report of faculty salaries. For a recent issue see:

    Doing better: The annual report on the economic status of the profession, 1997–1998. Academe, 84(2). (March-April 1998).

3. *Annual survey of graduate enrollment.* Washington, DC: Council of Graduate Schools.

    A survey, conducted jointly by the Council of Graduate Schools and the Graduate Record Examinations Board, which provides data on fall graduate enrollments and on graduate degrees awarded over the previous academic year. The annual report is published each August.

4. *APPA comparative costs and staffing report for college and university facilities.* (Biennial Publication). Alexandria, VA: APPA Publications.

    A report on the maintenance, operations, and staffing of higher education facilities.

5. *The Almanac of Higher Education* (Annual Publication). Chicago: University of Chicago Press.

    National and state-by-state summary data compiled by the Chronicle of Higher Education. General topics include students, faculty and staff, resources, and institutions. For the latest publication, see:

    The Almanac of Higher Education (1998). Chicago: University of Chicago Press.

6. *College costs and financial aid handbook.* (Annual Publication). New York: The College Board.

    A guide for students and parents about the expected costs of college.

7. *The college handbook.* (Annual Publication). New York: The College Board.

    A compilation of information on undergraduate institutions. This is a resource for those selecting and applying to college.

8. *Compendium of national data sources on higher education.*

    A description of numerous data sources and how to access them. For the latest publication see:

    Russell, A. B., & Christal, M. E. (Eds.) (1996). *Compendium of national data sources on higher education.* Denver, CO: State Higher Education Executive Officers.

9. *The decision to go to college: A College Board/Gallup survey of high school seniors.* Washington, DC: The College Board.

    A survey of factors which may influence students' decisions to attend a four-year college. Two reports have been published:

    The decision to go to college: Practices, attitudes, and experiences associated with college attendance among low-income students (1996). Washington, DC: The College Board. (Intended for college admissions and financial aid professionals.)

    Improving the odds: Factors that increase the likelihood of college attendance among high school seniors. (1996). Washington, DC: The College Board. (Part of the College Board Research Report series, this publication is designed for policy makers and researchers.)

10. Fact book on higher education. Phoenix, AZ: Oryx Press.

    A sourcebook published periodically by the American Council on Education. It includes extensive national information in seven subject areas: demographic and economic data, enrollment, institutional characteristics, faculty and staff, students, earned degrees, and student aid. For the latest publication see:

    Anderson, C. (1998). *Fact book on higher education.* Phoenix, AZ: Oryx Press

11. *The Grapevine.* Normal: Illinois State University, Center for Higher Education.

    A monthly report on total state appropriations for higher education, including tax appropriations for universities, colleges, community colleges, and state higher education agencies. Hard-copy versions of The Grapevine are published annually by the State Higher Education Executive Officers (SHEEO) in *State Higher Education Appropriations* (see listing in this section). Up-to-date information is available at the web site:

http://www.ilstu.edu/depts/coe/grpvine.htm

12. *Higher education abstracts.* Claremont, CA: The Claremont Graduate School.

Contains abstracts of materials pertaining to current research and theory about the participants in higher education, their functions, and their environment. A quarterly publication.

13. *Minorities in higher education, annual status report.* Washington, DC: American Council on Education.

A report on the progress of African Americans, Hispanics, Asian Americans, and American Indians in postsecondary education.

14. National Center for Education Statistics *Basic student charges at postsecondary institutions.* (Annual Publication). Washington, DC: National Center for Education Statistics.

A report based on the Integrated Postsecondary Education Data System Institutional Characteristics Survey. It contains institutional data on basic student charges for resident and nonresident students at postsecondary institutions. The report is available in written form through the Education Publications Center at:

http://www.ed.gov/edpubs.html and in electronic form at:

http://www.ed.gov/NCES

The condition of education. (Annual Publication). Washington, DC: National Center for Education Statistics.

A report with indicators of the condition of education in the United States. These indicators are divided into six areas: 1) access, participation, and progress; 2) achievement, attainment, and curriculum; 3) economic and other outcomes of education; 4) size and growth of educational institutions; 5) climate, classrooms, and diversity; and 6) human and financial resources of educational institutions. This re-

port is available from NCES and is on the World Wide Web at the address listed above.

Digest of education statistics. (Annual Publication). Washington, DC: National Center for Education Statistics.

A digest of statistical information on all levels of education. The report is available through NCES and on the World Wide Web. A pocket-sized abstract called the *Mini Digest of Education Statistics* is also available.

Federal support for education. (Annual Publication). Washington, DC: National Center for Education Statistics.

A report providing a comprehensive picture of total federal financial support for education since 1980. Additional tables have data for fiscal years 1965, 1970, and 1975. This report is available from NCES and is on the World Wide Web.

Historically black colleges and universities. Washington, DC: National Center for Education Statistics.

A periodic report offering a statistical overview of the 103 historically black colleges and universities (HBCUs) in the United States. Included are summary data on all HBCUs, institutionally-specific data, and comparisons to higher education institutions in general. This report is available from NCES and is on the World Wide Web. For the latest report see:

Historically black colleges and universities, 1976–94. (1996). Washington, DC: National Center for Education Statistics.

Projections of education statistics to 2006. (Annual Publication). Washington, DC: National Center for Education Statistics.

A report with projections for enrollment, graduates, instructional staff, and expenditures for all levels of education. It is available from NCES and over the World Wide Web. A summary of the report, called *Pocket Projections,* is also available.

15. *National faculty salary survey by discipline and rank.* Washington, DC: College and University Personnel Association.

Presents data from the annual survey of faculty salaries by discipline and rank in the nation's colleges and universities. For the latest reports, see:

National faculty salary survey by discipline and rank in private four-year colleges and universities, 1997–1998. Washington, DC: College and University Personnel Association.

National faculty salary survey by discipline and rank in public four-year colleges and universities, 1997–1998. Washington, DC: College and University Personnel Association.

16. Research Associates of Washington

Higher education report card: Comparisons of state public higher education systems and national trends. Washington, DC: Research Associates of Washington.

A periodic study which synthesizes the major findings of the organization's reports. For the latest report see:

Higher education report card, 1995: Comparisons of state public higher education systems and national trends. Washington, DC: Research Associates of Washington.

Higher education revenues and expenditures: A study of institutional costs. Washington, DC: Research Associates of Washington.

Helps readers conduct comparative cost analyses by providing a grounding in the nature of cost comparisons, reviewing the basic factors determining cost variance, and describing the education cost environment and necessary adjustment factors. For the latest report see:

Higher education revenues and expenditures: A study of institutional costs. (1991). Washington, DC: Research Associates of Washington.

Higher education revenues and expenditures: Institutional data volume. (Annual Publication). Washington, DC: Research Associates of Washington.

Data collected by the National Center for Education Statistics. Includes current funds revenues by source per FTE student and current funds expenditures by function. Data are also available on diskette.

Higher education tuition. Washington, DC: Research Associates of Washington.

A periodic report with information on both public and private tuition policies. Topics include how tuition, room and board, and other expenses vary by type and control of institution, how inflation affects tuition, and why tuition is rising.

Inflation measures for schools, colleges, and libraries. (Annual Publication). Washington, DC: Research Associates of Washington.

A study that reports longitudinally the Higher Education Price Index (HEPI), the School Price Index (SPI), the Research and Development Price Index (R&DPI), the University Library Price Index (ULPI), the Public Library Price Index (PLPI), the Tuition Price Index (TPI), the Boeckh Construction Index and, for comparison purposes, the Consumer Price Index (CPI). This is available as a report or data can be purchased on diskette.

State profiles: Financing public higher education. (Annual Publication). Washington, DC: Research Associates of Washington.

A report which presents state-level appropriations, tuition, enrollment, and supporting data for public higher education financing. Data are normalized by indices of relative system costs and geographical price differences to aid in inter-state comparability. Trend data from 1978 to present are also available on diskette.

Wages, amenities, and cost of living: Theory and measurement of geographical differentials. (1992). Washington, DC: Research Associates of Washington.

Presents the theory and procedures for measuring geographical differentials in prevailing wages for service-type workers, location-specific quality of life amenities, family cost of living, and cost of government services.

17. *State higher education appropriations.* Denver, CO: State Higher Education Executive Officers Association.

An annual compilation of state higher education appropriations summarized and placed in a historical context with analysis of short-term and long-term trends. The data are first reported monthly in *The Grapevine,* a publication of the Center for Higher Education at Illinois State University. For the latest report, see:

Hines, E. R. (1997–98). *State higher education appropriations.* Denver, CO: State Higher Education Executive Officers Association.

18. *SREB fact book on higher education.* (Biennial Publication). Atlanta, GA: Southern Regional Education Board.

A book of comparative national and regional data highlighting significant trends affecting colleges and universities in each of the 15 Southern Regional Education Board (SREB) states. For the latest publication, see:

Marks, J. L. (Ed.). (1996–1997). *SREB fact book on higher education*. Atlanta, GA: Southern Regional Education Board.

19. *State postsecondary education structures handbook*. Denver, CO: Education Commission of the States.

A basic reference document for those interested in the historical background, current status, and emerging patterns of state higher education structures. For the latest publication, see:

McGuinness, A. C. Jr., Epper, R. M., & Arredondo, S. (1994). *State postsecondary education structures handbook, 1994. State coordinating and governing boards: Profiles, roles and responsibilities, membership, staffing*. Denver, CO: Education Commission of the States.

20. *Summary statistics*. (Annual Publication). New York: The College Board.

A compilation of 60 tables of aggregate data which are based on data gathered from the College Board's Annual Survey of Colleges.

21. *Women, minorities, and persons with disabilities in science and engineering*. (Biennial Publication). Arlington, VA: National Science Foundation.

A summary of information on the demographic composition of this population from elementary school through workforce participation. Factors are highlighted that appear to cause or influence the under-representation of women, minorities, and persons with disabilities in science and engineering.

E. Related Professional Associations

1. **Association for Institutional Research**—Offers a variety of professional programs and publications to institutional research professionals. Publications include the *AIR Professional File* series; the *Resources for Institutional Research* book series; the *Research in* *Higher Education* journal; the bi-weekly Electronic AIR newsletter; *AIR Currents*, the quarterly newsletter; and *AIR Alerts*, monthly briefings on data policy issues. The *New Directions for Institutional Research* monograph series is sponsored by AIR (published by Jossey-Bass) and the annual book, *Higher Education: Handbook of Theory and Research*, is co-sponsored by AIR and ASHE. A forum is held each May and summer institutes are offered to provide beginning and advanced training in institutional research.

To obtain membership information, contact:

The Association for Institutional Research
114 Stone Building
Florida State University
Tallahassee, FL 32306-3038
ph 904-644-4470
fax 904-644-8824
E-mail: air@mailer.fsu.edu

There are also other international organizations for institutional research including the European Higher Education Association (EAIR), the Australasian Association for Institutional Research (AAIR), and the Southern African Association for Institutional Research (SAAIR). For further information about these organizations contact the AIR office.

2. **Association for the Study of Higher Education**—A society of scholars, researchers, practitioners, and graduate students dedicated to higher education as a field of study. Publications include *The Review of Higher Education*, the *ASHE-ERIC Higher Education Report Series*, the *ASHE Reader Series*, and the quarterly ASHE Newsletter. The annual book, *Higher Education: Handbook of Theory and Research*, is co-sponsored by ASHE and AIR. An annual conference is also held.

To obtain membership information, contact:

Association for the Study of Higher Education
University of Missouri-Columbia
College of Education
Department of Educational Leadership
and Policy Analysis
211 Hill Hall
Columbia, MO 65211
ph 573-882-9645
fax 573-884-2197
E-mail: ashe@tiger.coe.missouri.edu

3. **Society for College and University Planning**—An association focusing on the pro-

motion, advancement, and application of effective planning in higher education. Publications include the journal *Planning for Higher Education*; *SCUP News*, a weekly online newsletter; *Plan Ahead*, an online magazine; as well as various book and monographs. Seminars, workshops, and an annual conference are all offered at the national level. Eight regional organizations also offer conferences and seminars.

To obtain membership information, contact:
Society for College and University Planning
311 Maynard Street
Ann Arbor, MI 48104-2211
ph 734-998-7832
fax 734-998-6532
E-mail: scup@umich.edu

4. Other Related Associations

The following administrative associations represent groups whose interests often overlap with planning and institutional research. We have not included the institutionally-based membership organizations which represent higher education interests on an institution-wide basis.

American Association for Higher Education

American Association of Collegiate Registrars and Admissions Officers

American Association of University Administrators

American Educational Research Association, Division J—Postsecondary Education

APPA: The Association of Higher Education Facilities Officers

College and University Personnel Association

Council for Advancement and Support of Education

Council on Governmental Relations

EDUCAUSE

National Association of College and University Business Officers

National Association of Student Financial Aid Administrators

National Association of Student Personnel Administrators

National Council of University Research Administrators

For further information about these associations, consult :

Rodenhouse, M. P. (Ed.). *Higher Education Directory*. (Annual Publication). Falls Church, VA: Higher Education Publications.

F. Using the Internet as a Resource for IR and Planning

John H. Milam, Jr.
George Mason University

It is important when introducing people to the World Wide Web to provide a perspective on just how much information is available and how easy it is to get access to it. The web is so vast and the number and types of resources are growing and changing at such a rate that all assumptions about what is possible need to be questioned as obsolete and simplistic. The development of new search engine capabilities, web browsers, e-mail clients, web servers, helper applications, plug-in software, rapid application development software, and other revolutionary tools such as Java from Sun and ActiveX from Microsoft makes the Internet of today an entirely different world than the Gopher menus designed just a few years ago.

This document reviews the basic types of World Wide Web resources which are available, outlines the current state of Internet sites useful to institutional research and planning, discusses the concept of the Intranet in higher education, and provides a link to case studies of how to use the Internet for work.

We need to appreciate that this change in how information is presented and disseminated electronically is taking place at the paradigm level—representing a fundamental shift in the nature of how knowledge is produced and consumed. The information infrastructure of higher education is being revolutionized because of the web and we need to be active participants in envisioning how to make use of it. In this age of decreased state funding, continued legislative scrutiny, downsizing, and privatization, the future success of institutional research, planning, and higher education lies in our ability to serve as complex information brokers using the cutting edge of available tools.

Types of Web Resources

Many campus-wide information systems for the Internet began with the introduction of Gopher software. These online menu systems required users to follow a linear, hierarchical subject tree of menu choices to locate an Internet resource. The Veronica and Archie search tools have been replaced with sophisticated search engines, robots, and intelligent agents. Hundreds of online search engines are available, among them Yahoo, started by two Stanford students and now seen as the leader in helping users navigate the web; Excite, which links keywords to concepts and ideas; and AltaVista's LiveTopics, which builds tables of terms related to the user's search criteria. Free online services and shareware software such as SavvySearch, Metasearch, and WebFerret allow users to search multiple databases simultaneously. Other search engines offer individualized maps, access to newsgroup postings, e-mail addresses, specialized business Yellow Pages, and the entire U.S. phone book.

Many Internet subject catalogs such as the Argus Clearinghouse have evolved out of the efforts of librarians to make sense of the web. Numerous online tutorials offer schemas for understanding the different kinds of resources. It has become unnecessary to keep more than a few bookmarks or favorite links because the search engines, subject guides, and clearinghouses have become so easy to use. There are a number of rating services which rank web sites according to their organization and design, though many of the annotated reviews do not provide an evaluation of a homepage's unique content.

In the homepage "Types of Internet Resources" (*http://apollo.gmu.edu/~jmilam/types .html*), I categorize 12 basic ways in which to think about web resources for institutional research and planning. These include using: listservs, newsgroups, and e-mail discussion groups; links to federal, state, and local government; electronic publications; library access catalogs/literature searches; peer comparisons; admissions guides; fact books, management information systems, and Intranets; policy studies; environmental scanning; professional development/associations; higher education research; and online surveys/questionnaire research.

A few definitions: Listservs send e-mail to a list of people interested in a topic. Online discussion groups or forums are a feature of web sites, giving users a chance to post ideas and comments directly on a homepage that is broken into threads of different subject topics. Newsgroups are provided through news servers maintained by Internet Service Providers (ISPs) and local web servers. Over 15,000 newsgroups are available worldwide. Readers can follow these groups by topic, sorted by thread, date, or the person who posted a message. Search engines are available to find posts in newsgroups. Many online discussion groups/forums provide a search utility on their homepage. Listservs usually maintain an archive of postings which is available either online or by ftp.

Many people fail to realize how much listservs have to offer because these lists evolve and flow with member contributions. A good listserv provides archives of postings and you should temporarily subscribe to a listserv and review its archives if you want to understand current discussion on a topic. (To subscribe to any of the discussion lists described below, use the web subscription form if available or send an e-mail to the listserv e-mail address with a message that reads "subscribe yourname nameoflistserv").

There is no single listserv or newsgroup meeting the complex needs of IR and planning. A list of over 400 higher education listservs and newsgroups in 20 broad categories is maintained at the URL *http://apollo.gmu.edu/~ jmilam/air95/listserv.html*. Darell Glenn of West Virginia's State College and University Systems Central Office produces a feature in *The Electronic AIR* called ListWatch which explores and monitors the utility of listservs for IR. *The Electronic AIR* (*http://www.fsu.edu/~air/airform .htm*) and SCUP E-Mail News (*http://www-personal.umich.edu/ ~scup/SENsub.html*) are not really discussion groups, but edited, electronic publications. SCUP's E-Mail News is now more brief and provides links to articles and features in the Society's new online magazine called "Plan Ahead."

Listservs such as AIR-PAL (policy discussions; AIR-PAL@lists.nau.edu) have great promise but have not had as much electronic dialogue as one would expect. Several listservs are maintained by regional IR associations, including:
- NEAIR-L (New England AIR; listserv@acfcluster.nyu.edu),
- TAIR-L (Texas AIR; *http://www.dcccd.edu/ecc/tair/docs/tairlist.html*),
- KAIR (Kentucky AIR; *http://www.uky.edu/~lexcamp/kair/listserv.htm 632l*)
- GAIRPAQ (Georgia AIR; *http://www.oiri.mcg.edu/gairpaq/howctoc.htm*)

- CAIRNet (California AIR; *http://www.cair.org/cairnet/*)
- SAIRMAIL (Southern AIR—a good source of job vacancy information and SAIR news; send e-mail for information to SAIR@uga.cc.uga.edu).

Listservs offered by Bates College include: JCAR-L (Joint Commission on Accountability Reporting; majordomo@abacus.bates.edu), Rank-L (college rankings; majordomo@abacus.bates.edu), IPEDS-L (IPEDS surveys; majordomo@abacus.bates.edu), SRK-L (Student Right to Know issues; majordomo@abacus.bates.edu), and Recert-L (recertification issues; majordomo@abacus.bates.edu). These are exciting opportunities, if institutional researchers use them. The CDS-COLLEGEBOARD listserv (majordomo@aspin.asu.edu) is designed to review potential survey questions and requirements of the publisher's group in creating a common data set for admissions guides. NDIRCOOP (listserv@mitvma. mit.edu) was started to foster dialogue between the authors and readers of a *New Directions for Institutional Research* volume about data exchanges.

Other listservs useful to institutional researchers and planners include AERA-J (American Educational Research Association Division J—post-secondary; listserv@asu.edu), ASHE-L (Association for the Study of Higher Education; ASHE-L@american.edu), ASHPOL-L (ASHE listserv about campus, state, and national policy; ASHPOL-L@psuvm.psu.edu), COMMCOLL (community college issues; listserv @lsv.uky.edu), EDINFO (U.S. Department of Education list; listproc@inet.ed.gov), ETHICS-L (ethics in institutional research; majordomo @abacus.bates.edu), GOVREL-L (government relations of AACRAO; listserv@asuvm.inre. asu.edu), NCCRP (National Community College Research and Planning list; listserv@centralia. ctc.edu), NDIRGRAD (assessing graduate and professional programs; listserv@mitvma.mit. edu), and REGIST-L (registrar issues; listproc @listproc.gsu.edu).

Some institutions participate in special e-mail discussion groups (examples include SUG and AAU). Postings are sent to a central e-mail address, then routed to other institutions, allowing for the careful screening of requests and content. Participating offices respond quickly to requests as part of a tacit agreement with peers, sharing data and quick surveys about policy issues.

The 100,000+ newsgroups which are available depending on your Internet service provider (ISP) offer an infinite world for discussion. Many institutions have their own newsgroups for students, researchers, and the university community and these provide an interesting glimpse into college life. Whether it is an arcane discussion of problems with a software package or learning to use HTML forms, you will find one or more newsgroups dedicated to the discussion. In contrast to some listservs, newsgroups move very quickly and can have very invested participants. Examples of higher education-related newsgroups include alt.college.food, soc.college.admissions, and rec.sport.basketball.college.

Two additional groupware or team-based tools which are not used much for IR and planning, but should be, are online conferences and chat rooms. Online conferences, also known as forums or bulletin boards, allow readers to post and reply to messages which are threaded (grouped) by topic. Forums can be seen everywhere from the *New York Times* to software support homepages such as the Allaire Developer Conference for users of Cold Fusion. These combine the best features of Lotus Notes and Collabra Share models for team use of electronic documents, although without some of the features of work flow processing and complicated transaction processing associated with Notes. Discussion groups are being incorporated into the new web sites for AIR and SAIR.

Chat rooms permit users to post comments and read replies in the "real time" of a live discussion. It is possible to host a virtual meeting of IR professionals all clicked in to the same chat room discussing a hot topic or holding an association board meeting. A chat room for IR is available at the URL: *http://apollo.gmu.edu/ ~jmilam/cgi/chat/chat.cgi*. Other untapped possibilities include electronic whiteboards; live, Internet phone calls; and two-way, color, video teleconferencing, all available at very low cost. The bandwidth issues involved in downloading video with software such as RealMedia or QuickTime VR preclude some of this technology except for use on campus. The evolution of products such as web TV, ISDN, ASDN, cable modems, satellite Internet links such as DirectPC, and web-based Telnet software suggest that bandwidth may not be an issue for very long. With initiatives for the Next Generation

Internet (NGI) and Internet2, higher education is at the forefront of high speed backbone technology.

Many publications are available electronically, including almost 100 higher education-related journals, magazines (e-zines), and newsletters, ranging from the *Educom Review* to *Nacubo Business Officer*. Historical issues are available as part of electronic journal storage efforts such as JSTOR. Full text back issues of the *Journal of Higher Education* from 1930 to 1992 are available for free online use. Campus newspapers, national and statewide newspapers, and internal employee publications are online. The *Chronicle of Higher Education* (*http://chronicle.com*) is in a category by itself, just for its searchable index of job listings. With a print subscription, you have access to the web site "Academe Today," which offers full text searching, articles, and cited documents such as Supreme Court rulings and federal budgets. The annual *Almanac of Higher Education* and various databases such as campus crime statistics, NCAA graduation rates, and tuition and fees charges are available by institution. A daily e-mail service with news-breaking headlines is offered. There are lists of and features about web resources and a searchable index to the full text of eight years of back issues.

The combination of sophisticated search engines, web queries to library catalogs such as the Library of Congress site, and the unprecedented access to proprietary datasets formerly available only on CD-Rom makes the web a librarian's paradise. No longer is one bound by geographic location and cumbersome library software systems, as forms are available to automatically translate your search criteria into many libraries' public access catalogs.

The web offers all levels of information and data for peer comparisons, from policy studies to data collection. Finally there is some payoff to the hours spent completing college guide questionnaires. Vendors such as Peterson's and U.S. News have their own homepages, where you can view the results of your submission and obtain data on peer institutions.

If you spend much time on the web, you will encounter a reader survey. The forms capability of web browsers offers an inexpensive assessment research tool. The next time you want to conduct a survey, whether of students, faculty, or colleagues at peer institutions, try doing it on the web. Software tools such as WebForms allow survey forms to be quickly generated and collected via e-mail, doing away with the need for complicated CGI scripts.

When the tools for environmental scanning meant paying attention to newspaper clippings and everything else listed in *Megatrends*, it was very difficult and time consuming to get a handle on this process. With the advent of the World Wide Web, Jim Morrison's work on environmental scanning comes to life with his "On the Horizon" homepage (*http:// sunsite.unc.edu/horizon/*). Services such as CRAYON and PointCast, along with features in the newer versions of Netscape and Microsoft Explorer, offer users the chance to create their own personalized homepage of favorite links, complete with music and graphics. Netscape's InBox Direct service automatically sends electronic publications such as the Wall Street Journal Interactive and Web Review to you via e-mail. New broadcast technologies let webmasters "push" or send news and specialized programs onto end-users' client computers. The bottom line on scanning—the world is now wide open because of the Internet, with little if any cost to higher education.

Current Sites Useful to IR and Planning

By January 1998, at least 250 institutional research offices; 250 higher education associations (not including the many discipline-specific organizations with a web presence); 60 State Higher Education Executive Offices (SHEEOs), system offices, and private consortia; over 100 student affairs offices in 17 functional areas; and 70 higher education research centers, sites, and graduate programs have homepages on the web. While many of these simply offer an online version of printed text, tables, and graphics, others are experimenting with special features such as searchable databases, sound files, digital photography, animated graphics, and making word processing and spreadsheet files available in different formats such as Adobe PDF for readers to print on demand. The homepage "A Field Guide to IR Homepages" (*http://apollo.gmu.edu/~jmilam/fieldguide.html*) documents some of the efforts of institutional research and planning offices around the world.

There are literally millions of sites to explore and thousands of these impact higher education. In the homepage "Internet Resources for Institutional Research" (*http://apollo.gmu. edu/~jmilam/air95.html*), I list approximately 2,000 links in 11 broad categories and 57 topics. Some of the topics include links to: accrediting agencies, admissions guides, affirmative action, census data, conferences and professional development, facilities, finance, financial aid, grants/sponsored research, higher education publications in electronic format, jobs, K-12 partnerships, law/legal issues, legislation, sports, state government, statistics/research methods, technology issues, testing, and virtual universities. The Student Affairs Virtual Compass   (*http://www.studentaffairs.com/main.html*) does the same thing for the student affairs field, with links to web sites and listservs in different functional areas.

The sites which have been developed by the U.S. Department of Education and the National Science Foundation are phenomenal in what they offer planners, administrators, and researchers. Federal and state agencies are finding that it is necessary for them to publicize and make their data available over the Internet in order to justify their existence. They have learned that the web is the best and cheapest way to disseminate complex documents and data. The ERIC Clearinghouse on Higher Education   (*http://www.gwu.edu/~eriche/*)   and   the ERIC Clearinghouse on Community Colleges (*http://www.gse.ucla.edu/ERIC/eric.html*)   have emerged as premier sites for finding web and print resources.

The Computer-Aided Science Policy Analysis and Research (CASPAR) database system is available free on the web from NSF (*http://caspar.nsf.gov/*). WebCASPAR offers user-friendly access to historical data in many national datasets, among them IPEDS, NRC Doctoral   Recipient,   and   NSF   Science   and Engineering survey data. Historical survey data are also available at the school level in NSF's Institutional Profile series (*http://www. nsf.gov/sbe/srs/profiles/start.htm*). NSF's Scientists and Engineers Statistical Data System (SE-STAT) is also online with data from the National Survey of College Graduates (NSCG), the National Survey of Recent College Graduates, and the Survey of Doctorate Recipients (*http://srsstats.sbe.nsf.gov/*).

IPEDS and other survey data such as the National Study of Postsecondary Faculty (NSOPF) and the National Postsecondary Stu-

dent Aid Study (NPSAS) are available on CD-Rom and at the NCES web site (*http:// nces.ed.gov/surveys/datasurv.html#postsecondary*). The National Center for Education Statistics (*http://www.ed.gov/NCES/*)   is   experimenting with providing more complicated query access to all survey data. Interactive county and city, economic, election, and census data are available in useful query and report formats. An example of these kinds of sites is the "Interactive Data Resources" site at the University of Virginia Social Sciences Data Center (*http:// www.lib.virginia.edu/socsci/interactives.html*).

Gene Glass at the University of Arizona has made current American Association of University Professors (AAUP) data on faculty salaries and IPEDS student enrollment data by ethnicity available by institution on the web (*http:// 129.219.88.111/ipeds.html*).

The NCES, NSF, Glass, and *Chronicle* web sites are possible because of five evolving technologies: (1) web server software which serves documents and data to users/clients across platforms, including PC, Mac, and UNIX environments; (2) HTML forms, which allow users to complete a form or survey that submits or requests data; (3) Structured Query Language (SQL), providing a common programming method for extracting, aggregating, and presenting data; (4) Open Database Connectivity (ODBC) drivers, which permit SQL queries to access many types of data formats, including DBase, Access, Excel, SAS, and AASCII datasets (new Java database connectivity tools have arrived too); and (5) programming scripts in C++, Perl, Cold Fusion, LiveScript, Active-X, and other software tools which help web servers use HTML forms to process queries against ODBC-compliant databases.

In the past, NCES, NSF, and other agencies made a significant investment in creating special software to generate tables of report data so that researchers do not have to manipulate the raw data with SAS or SPSS. The advent of web database applications provides unprecedented access to data with complex report design features. Almost every federal, state, county, and city government agency with a local area network and access to an ISP now has a web presence and staying in touch with their homepages is essential. Contact names, phone numbers, online versions of print forms, newsletters, publications, and grant award information are disseminated more quickly and more accurately on the web. County offices are using geographic information systems and sharing these data on the web. SHEEOs, purchasing agencies, human resources offices, and state legislatures also have a growing presence. Almost every level of government that institutions interact with, whether in compliance reporting or public affairs, offers current reports and data on the web.

Associations in higher education, such as the Association for Institutional Research (*http://airweb.org/*) and the Society for College and University Planning (*http://www.scup.org/*), have found the web invaluable for serving members; doing advertising; keeping print costs low; and offering professional development resources and information about membership, upcoming conference programs, and subscriptions to publications. AIR, SCUP, ASHE, EDUCAUSE, and AAHE make their conference programs available online. Most associations offer links to useful Internet resources and some offer special databases of data or monographs. While one can read association journals such as *Planning for Higher Education* without being a member of SCUP, in the past you couldn't get to know an association without attending its conferences and joining its membership. Using their homepages is the next best thing, if not better.

The Concept of the Intranet

When considering the future of the web for IR and planning, the concept of the Intranet may have the most potential. Both Netscape and Microsoft have prepared white papers and resource collections about what Intranets offer organizations. Bernard (1996) in *Building the Corporate Intranet* documents how Intranets offer visionary, web-based applications for management information systems, executive information systems, groupware with collaborative workgroups and interdepartmental communication, online reference materials, interactive communication, database query/update capabilities, training, and customer support. The web offers immediate, low cost distribution and secure control of external and internal data with a surprisingly low level of programming requirements.

The vision of client server architecture for distributed information systems which was hailed in the early 1990s as the future of computing will only be fully realized in the context of the graphical user interface (GUI) capabilities of the World Wide Web. The dream of creating a data warehouse with historical, census, and operational files of student, human resources, and financial data with customized reports and 3D graphics is now possible with rapid web database development applications such as Cold Fusion. Java applets are available to automatically generate bar, pie, and line charts.

With Microsoft's Office 97, Active Desktop, and Internet Explorer 4.0, the concepts of web browser and desktop computing get blurred. It no longer matters whether the document you want to access is on your hard disk, your LAN, or across the world. The integration of documents across the web is becoming seamless. Electronic document distribution and imaging and work flow processes are being revolutionized with the competing visions of Netscape, Microsoft, IBM, Apple, Sun, and other companies.

Case Studies of Using the Internet for IR

In order to visualize how these many Internet resources may be used for institutional research and planning, I have developed the homepage "Case Studies: Using the Internet for Institutional Research" (*http://apollo.gmu. edu/~jmilam/cases.html*). Whether comparing NSF research expenditures, projecting the potential for a new degree program, setting targets for admission yield rates and SAT scores, or analyzing in-state versus out-of-state enrollment trends, there is a virtual IR office full of data out there on the web just waiting for you to click. As you explore the web and create your own HTML documents, I invite you to contribute your own case study of how you use the Internet.

Suggested Readings/Resources:

Andreessen, Marc, and The Netscape Product Team. "The Networked Enterprise: Netscape Enterprise Vision and Product Roadmap." 1998.

<http://www.netscape.com/comprod/at_work/white_ paper/vision/intro.html>. (20 January 1998).

"Beginner Guides." Yahoo. *<http://www.yahoo.com/Computers_and_Internet/I nternet/Information_and_Documentation/Beginner s_Guides/>* (20 January 1998).

Bernard, Ryan. "Building a Corporate Intranet: An Online Education Site for Intranet Builders." *<http://webcom.com/wordmark/sem1.html>*. (20 January 1998).

Center for Technology in Government. "The World Wide Web as a Universal Interface to Government Services." December 1996. *<http://www.ctg.albany.edu/resources/htmlrpt/ittfnl rp.html>*. (20 January 1998).

Kotlas, Carolyn. "Intranets: Readings and Resources." July 31, 1997. *<http://www.iat.unc.edu/guides/irg-34.html>*. (20 January 1998).

Microsoft. Intranet Solutions Center. 1998. *<http://www.microsoft.com/intranet/default.asp>*. (20 January 1998).

Milam, John. "Internet Resources for Institutional Research." January 18, 1998. *<http://apollo.gmu.edu/~jmilam/air95.html>*. (20 January 1998).

Milam, John. "Case Studies: Internet Applications for Institutional Research." May 8th, 1996. *<http://apollo.gmu.edu/~jmilam/cases.html>*. (20 January 1998).

Milam, John. "A Field Guide to IR Homepages." *<http://apollo.gmu.edu/~jmilam/fieldguide.html>*. (20 January 1998).

Netscape. "Education Solutions—Case Studies." 1998. *<http://home.netscape.com/comprod/business_solu tions/education/stories/index.html>*. (20 January 1998).

Niles, Robert. "Finding Data on the Internet." *<http://nilesonline.com/data/>*. (20 January 1998).

Pincince, Thomas J., Goodtree, David, and Barth, Carolyn. "The Full Service Intranet." The Forrester Report 10(4). March 1, 1996. *<http://www.forrester.com/hp_mar96nsr.htm>*. (20 January 1998).

"Robin Williams on Hypertext and the Inside of His Head." January 15, 1997. *<http://www5.zdnet.com/yil/content/mag/9702/robin /rw970115.html>*.

Scientific American. "The Internet: Bringing Order from Chaos." March 1997. *<http://www.sciam.com/0397issue/0397intro.html>*. (20 January 1998).

Ulanoff, Lance N. "Build Your Own Web Site." PC Magazine Online. *<http://www.pcmag.com/IU/fea tures/1515/intro/intro.htm>*. (20 January 1998).

"Understanding and Using the Internet." PBS Online. *<http://www.pbs.org/uti/>*. (20 January 1998).